Encyclopedia of Educational Research

Encyclopedia of Educational Research

FIFTH EDITION

Sponsored by the American Educational Research Association

Editor in Chief
Harold E. Mitzel

Associate Editors
John Hardin Best and William Rabinowitz

Volume 3

THE FREE PRESS, *A Division of Macmillan Publishing Co., Inc.*, NEW YORK
Collier Macmillan Publishers, LONDON

THE FREE PRESS
A Division of Macmillan Publishing Co., Inc.
866 Third Avenue, New York, NY 10022

Collier Macmillan Canada, Inc.

Library of Congress Catalog Card Number: 82–2332

Printed in the United States of America

printing number

1 2 3 4 5 6 7 8 9 10

Library of Congress Cataloging in Publication Data
Main entry under title:

Encyclopedia of educational research.

 Includes bibliographies and index.
  1. Educational research—United States—Directories.
2. Education—Bibliography. 3. Universities and colleges
—United States—Directories. 4. Education—Dictionaries.
I. Mitzel, Harold E. II. Best, John Hardin. III. Rabinowitz, William. IV. American Educational Research Association.
L901.E57 1982   370′.7′8073   82–2332
ISBN 0–02–900450–0 (set)   AACR2

Contributors' acknowledgments, some of which are relevant
to the copyright status of certain articles, appear in a
special section at the back of volume 4.

L

(CONTINUED)

LEARNING DISABILITIES

The term "learning disabled" is applied to a heterogeneous group of children who experience difficulty in maintaining normal progress in school but who are not mentally retarded, emotionally disturbed, or physically handicapped. Usually, there is a significant discrepancy between what is expected of the child based on mental and chronological age norms and the child's performance on school tasks or standardized tests. Learning-disabled children also frequently show very different levels of attainment within different areas of school performance or in different basic mental skills.

This article discusses the following aspects of learning disability: (1) definitions, (2) incidence, (3) history, (4) assessment, (5) research, (6) theories and etiology, (7) educational programs, (8) drug treatment, and (9) sources of information.

Definitions. Two commonly cited definitions of learning disability highlight some important issues in the field. The following is from a report by the National Advisory Committee on Handicapped Children (1968):

Children with special learning disabilities exhibit a disorder in one or more of the basic psychological processes involved in understanding or in using spoken or written language. These may be manifested in disorders of listening, thinking, talking, reading, spelling, or arithmetic. They include conditions which have been referred to as perceptual handicaps, brain injury, minimal brain dysfunction, dyslexia, developmental aphasia, etc. They do not include learning problems which are due primarily to visual, hearing, or motor handicaps, to mental retardation, emotional disturbance, or to environmental disadvantage.

Here is a more recent definition by Kirk and Gallagher (1979):

A specific learning disability is a psychological or neurological impediment to spoken or written language or perceptual, cognitive, or motor behavior. The impediment (1) is manifested by discrepancies among specific behaviors and achievements or between evidenced ability and academic achievement, (2) is of such nature and extent that the child does not learn by the instructional methods and materials appropriate for the majority of children and requires specialized procedures for development, and (3) is not primarily due to severe mental retardation, sensory handicaps, emotional problems, or lack of opportunity to learn. (p. 285)

Note that although Kirk and Gallagher broaden the definition to include almost any behavioral disability, these definitions emphasize language disabilities. As a consequence, the area of reading disorders is significant within the general category of learning disability. The definitions apply only to children whose disability in one area is incongruent with their performance in other areas. They do not meet expectations based on their age and general mental ability, and the discrepancy cannot be explained in terms of obvious environmental of genetic factors.

The first definition mentions certain conditions, such as brain injury and dyslexia, that are important in the historical development of the concept of learning disability. The conditions that overlap most often with learning disability are reading disorders, minimal brain dysfunctions, hyperactivity, and hyperkinetic syndrome. Most people with one or more of these conditions would be classified as learning disabled, but some learning-disabled children have none of them.

Governmental influence on the definition of learning disability in both research and practice is substantial. During the 1960s, there was much debate over the appropriate terminology and how to define the conditions that have now been subsumed under the broad rubric "learning disability." The Learning Disability Act of 1969 adopted the 1968 definition of the National Advisory Committee on Handicapped Children. This definition has also been used in the Education for All Handicapped Children Act of 1975 (Public Law 94-142) and is at the time of this writing part of the statutory basis for using the concept of learning disability. Given that public moneys are assigned to children based on their ability to qualify as learning disabled under the regulations pursuant to the definition (*Federal Register*, 1977, p. 65083), the definition is more than an intellectual construction. Since all states now recognize learning disability as a handicapping condition (though terminology varies), the statutory role played by the federal government has ramifications both for service and for research.

The ramifications of a statutory definition are most apparent in the arena of public education, where special services are afforded children who meet certain requirements. These additional services are specifically mandated on the basis of rather broad criteria. The limiting factors in service are program availability, personnel expertise, and fiscal resources. Often these three factors reduce essentially to the fiscal ability of a given school entity to provide personnel, equipment, and space. The federal definition has been adopted by most states, though small variations provide for a myriad of different interpretations. For example, some states, in an effort to control the number of people defined as "learning disabled" adopted operational definitions of a psychometric nature (Mercer, Forgnone, & Wolking, 1976). This tactic, similar to that proposed by the federal government (*Federal Register*, 1976), aims at assessing the difference between intelligence and measured performance. This difference is the most widely accepted sign of learning disability. Other states also wishing to limit the number of people categorized as learning disabled, and hence eligible for fiscal assistance, have adopted other methods. For example, one state requires evidence of neurological impairment in order for the child to be classified as learning disabled. The major point here is that the looseness of the federal definition compels the states to adopt procedures to limit the number of children served. The operational definitions seldom capture the richness of the conceptual definition (Senf, 1978).

Research is also affected by governmental influence on definitions, and on the procedures used to select children for learning-disability programs. Naming a concept has a tendency to reify it, and researchers have accepted as learning disabled those children who have been so designated by school systems. Consequently, research deals with samples of learning-disabled subjects who may not have very much in common from one research site to the next. The question immediately arises of whether discrepant research results may be due as much to differences in the samples studied as to experimental manipulations (Senf, 1976, 1977). Thus, research results cannot be interpreted with confidence. Comparability of study to study across time and space requires that researchers agree on a definition of the term "learning disability" and select subjects accordingly (Senf, 1977).

Incidence. The federal government, on the basis of expert testimony, concluded that 1 to 3 percent of the children aged 3 to 21 have a significant learning disability. This percentage is arbitrary, however, because the term "learning disability" was not first defined and because no empirical assessment was ever made. Rather, the figure 1 to 3 percent was simply accepted, and assessment procedures were then designed in such a way that no more than 3 percent of those assessed have been categorized as learning disabled (*Second Annual Report to Congress*, 1980). Naturally, the incidence of learning disability is not the same in all school districts or in all states; the incidence varies widely as a function of such variables as available services, affluence, the history of special education programs, and so on. Estimates of incidence pertain to elementary-age children in most cases, but there has been an increasing emphasis on identifying learning disabilities at the secondary level, in college, and among adults who are not students (Barbaro, 1981).

It is crucial to recognize the extreme heterogeneity of the learning-disabled population. This stems from a number of different causes, including broad conceptual definitions, a lack of standardized operational definitions, and the strong influence of political, social, and fiscal factors on the labeling process. Underachievement and failure to respond satisfactorily to the regular classroom environment are central to the identification of learning disability. Dealing with the failure of a child to adapt to an educational environment involves understanding the characteristics of both the child and the educational environment. Fiscal considerations also have a strong influence on the labeling process; labeling a child "learning disabled" creates an obligation to provide special services, which are more expensive than the regular instructional program. In summary, since there is no standard procedure for diagnosing learning disabilities, incidence statistics depend primarily on how the discrepancy between potential and performance is defined and measured, on the school's definition of nonadaptive behavior, and on the availability of funds to serve learning-disabled children.

History. The concept of learning disability is relatively new in comparison with other major concepts in special education—for example, mental retardation, emotional disturbance, and physical handicap. The concept, introduced by Kirk in 1962, overlapped such earlier concepts as reading disorders, perceptual handicaps, and minimal brain dysfunction, and was more descriptive of the behavioral deficit without being limited to any etiological explanation.

The history of the study of learning disability goes back to earlier studies of brain-injured and otherwise neurologically impaired children. The link between the two fields of study is in the overlap of symptoms. Many children with no known history of brain injury display, in a mild form, many of the behaviors that characterize children known to have brain injury.

Orton (1937) argued that delays or dysfunctions in the development of cerebral dominance were responsible for many of the language disabilities observed in children. According to Orton, normal development of language skills requires that one cerebral hemisphere control the production and processing of linguistic stimuli, and if such normal cerebral specialization does not develop, the child experiences difficulties in language and symbol processing. Werner and Strauss (1941) studied children with language- and perceptual-processing disabilities and introduced the idea of exogenous symptoms (resulting from brain injury) and endogenous symptoms (genetically determined anomalies).

The behaviorist orientation of the early 1960s emphasized descriptions of behavior rather than research on the etiology of behavior. This was also the period during which language and mathematical abilities were analyzed into many specific components on the basis of information-processing models. This led to the practice of defining learning disabilities in terms of behavioral disabilities in such specific tasks as visual discrimination, auditory-visual integration, auditory-sequential memory, and visual-motor integration. The earlier emphasis on neurological explanations of learning disabilities was diminished by the behavioral, environmental emphases in the late 1960s and early 1970s.

More recently there has been a growth of interest in neuropsychological explanations of learning disabilities (Gaddes, 1980), primarily as a result of discoveries in the neurosciences. Most current perspectives on learning disability call both for descriptions of specific behaviors and for an awareness of the complex interactions among genetic, environmental, and neurological factors. Senf (1973) and Wiederhold (1974) provide more extensive historical reviews of the study of learning disability.

Assessment.   The procedures used to identify learning-disabled children follow from the definition used of "learning disability." The sequence of events leading to the assessment of a child as learning disabled usually includes the following. (1) The child fails to perform at an expected level in one or more school-related tasks. (2) The academic problem persists and does not lessen in response to regular classroom activities. (3) Possible causes of the academic problem are checked out and eliminated—for example, motivational problems, emotional problems, or physical disability; mental retardation; sensory impairment; or economic or cultural disadvantage. (4) Diagnostic testing using standardized measures of general mental ability and specific cognitive abilities identifies patterns of abilities and disabilities. (5) The child is classified as learning disabled, and a remediation plan is prescribed.

The classroom teacher is usually the first to take note of anomalous patterns of behavior. In a few school districts, screening for early identification of specific learning disabilities takes place at a prekindergarten or kindergarten level (Keogh, 1977; Wedell, 1980), but usually the first step in the identification process is a teacher referral. It has been claimed that this largely results in the referral of hyperactive children, with problems in maintaining attention and in inhibiting their physical activity, because these children are disruptive and demanding of attention (Ross, 1976). Hypoactive or withdrawn children with similar patterns of academic performance are less likely to be referred.

When a child's performance does not reach desired levels within the classroom setting, the child is referred to a diagnostic specialist, such as a school psychologist or a learning-disability specialist, who does diagnostic testing and tries to determine the cause of the problem. Such a procedure would most likely include classroom observation, screening for auditory and visual acuity, parent interviews, and administration of a test of general mental ability, such as the Stanford-Binet Intelligence Test or the Wechsler Intelligence Scale for Children (WISC). If the child achieves an IQ score below 80, the poor classroom performance might be attributed to general mental retardation. Identification as learning disabled usually requires an IQ in the normal range (but see Ames, 1977, for further discussion of this issue).

The WISC is one of the most commonly used diagnostic instruments because it measures twelve different areas of performance. Six of the tests measure verbal abilities, and six measure other areas of nonverbal performance. A common pattern on the WISC among learning-disabled children is a low score on the Verbal scale in comparison to the score on the Performance scale. However, children who perform at the "gifted" level on the verbal scale may be identified as learning disabled because of low scores on the Performance scale (Schiff, Kaufman, & Kaufman, 1981). The Verbal scale includes subtests in areas directly related to reading and language problems (Vocabulary, General Information, and Similarities), as well as in arithmetic. Since referral by the teacher is often made because of below-average performance in reading or arithmetic, one would expect such children to perform poorly on tests that measure related skills.

Further diagnostic testing is usually done in specific academic skill areas in order to ascertain the nature of the problem. Diagnostic reading tests such as the Gates-McKillop Reading Diagnostic Test (Gates & McKillop, 1962) and the Spache Diagnostic Reading Scales (Spache, 1963) break down the reading process into components. Arithmetic skills can be assessed using such a test as the Stanford Diagnostic Arithmetic Test (Beatty, Madden, & Gardner, 1966) and underlying language processes with the Illinois Test of Psycholinguistic Abilities (Kirk, McCarthy, & Kirk, 1968). Perceptual abilities are assessed under the assumption that perceptual disabilities can explain certain anomalous patterns of behavior. Visual perception, visual-motor integration, and auditory-visual integration are perceptual areas often explored through diagnostic testing.

Neuropsychological assessment is also frequently done, especially in medically oriented settings. Although many of the tests in this area were originally validated on persons known to have brain damage, the tests have been adapted so that neuropsychological models can be used to describe a specific pattern of performance (Gaddes, 1980). Among the most commonly used neuropsychological batteries are the Spreen-Benton Comprehensive Examination for Aphasia (1977) and the Halstead-Reitan Neuropsychological Test Battery.

This, generally, is the assessment process, but the specific procedures used vary widely. To a great extent, assessment depends on the particular setting and on the training and theoretical orientation of the diagnostician. Just as there has been considerable controversy over the definition of the term "learning disability," so there is a wide range of assessment procedures and decision rules used to identify a learning-disabled child.

Research. Most of the research on learning disabilities has compared groups of children identified as learning disabled with groups of "regular" classroom children (Senf, 1976). Hundreds of different characteristics have been studied in such research (Weener, 1981). Some studies have focused on achievement and on performance on measures of mental ability similar to those used in the selection process, while other studies are designed to test particular hypotheses about specific deficiencies in learning-disabled children.

A common finding of these studies is that the average score of the learning-disabled group is significantly below the average score of the regular classroom group. Both groups show a very wide range of scores on all variables that have been studied, and the range of scores within the learning-disabled group is as great as the range of scores within the regular classroom group. In a typical comparative study 23 percent of the learning-disabled group scored higher than the average of the regular classroom group (Weener, 1981). The picture is of consistent and significant group differences, but also of considerable overlap between the two groups. Weener estimates that in the typical study the average difference between the scores of the learning-disabled and regular classroom groups was about one-sixth of the range within either group.

Learning-disabled and regular classroom groups consistently differ to a great extent with respect to some variables, whereas other variables show relatively small and inconsistent differences. A study of these differences can provide an understanding of how learning disabilities are identified. The most consistent difference is in reading comprehension, but groups of learning-disabled children consistently score lower in mathematics as well. The Wechsler Intelligence Scale for Children (WISC) provides interesting comparisons because it consists of subscales measuring different cognitive processes.

The subscales on the WISC on which groups of learning-disabled children show the greatest deficits are Information, Arithmetic, Similarities, Digit Span, Vocabulary, and Coding. Subscales on which the learning-disabled groups show no consistent deficit are Picture Completion, Picture Arrangement, Object Assembly, and Mazes. Bannatyne (1968) suggests grouping the subscales into three categories—conceptual, spatial, and sequential—according to the cognitive skill tested. When Rugel (1974) reviewed

twenty-five studies that had reported WISC scores of learning-disabled readers, he found (in line with Bannatyne's suggestion) that in twenty-two of the twenty-five studies the subscales measuring spatial abilities yielded the highest scores and that in every study, performance on the spatial subscales was better than performance on the sequential subscales. It is not uncommon to find that children identified as learning disabled or reading disabled score higher than control groups on tasks requiring holistic visual processing, such as the Mazes or Picture Completion subtests of the WISC. The August-September 1981 issue of the *Journal of Learning Disabilities* reviews this line of research and presents a series of original papers on the topic.

Many studies of learning-disabled children have been designed to test specific hypotheses about the nature of their deficits. Most of these "deficit hypothesis" studies focus on some aspect of information processing, although a small number look at such social and personality variables as empathy (Bachara, 1976), self-esteem (Larsen, Parker, & Jorjorian, 1973), and ego and superego strength (Stawar & Lamp, 1974).

Attention and memory are the two most commonly measured variables showing consistent deficits for the learning-disabled group. Various aspects of attention have also been studied, including vigilance (Doyle, Anderson, & Halcomb, 1976), motor impulsivity (Dykman et al., 1971), auditory distractability (Lasky & Tobin, 1973), and selective attention (Tarver et al., 1976). Others have studied heart rate as a physiological index of attending behavior (Porges et al., 1975; Sroufe et al., 1973). Disruptive behavior in the classroom is one of the first factors noted in identifying learning-disabled children; therefore, it is not surprising that studies show that deficits in the area of attention are both great and consistently observed.

Studies of memory have also shown consistent deficits among the learning disabled. The deficits are present for both language and nonlanguage stimuli presented either aurally or visually (Swanson, 1978; Torgesen, Murphy, & Ivey, 1979; Bauer, 1977; Guthrie & Tyler, 1976). Usually, the performance of a learning-disabled group is like that of a regular classroom group two years younger, but Torgesen & Hall (1981) have found small groups of learning-disabled children with memory deficits of four grade levels and more. One of the most common explanations of memory deficit is that certain children do not develop normal rehearsal strategies. Research on central and incidental memory indicates that learning-disabled children use memory techniques similar to those used by younger children (Hagen & Barclay, 1981). Control of attention is also important in memory; it may be that the two processes are not separate, but are alternative ways of looking at one phenomenon.

Etiology. The only well-developed theories of the causes of learning disability involve neurological factors, including brain damage, genetically determined brain anomalies, or neurochemical deficiencies. The definition of learning disabilities effectively excludes competing etiological explanations, by excluding behavioral anomalies which are caused by mental retardation, emotional problems, physical disability, or environmental deprivation. The interesting aspect of this etiological bind is that the term was well received largely because it replaced the more stigmatizing label "brain damaged." In the early 1960s the term "minimal brain damage" was discarded in favor of a behavioral description of disability. At that time, etiology was seen as irrelevant to the issue of remediation.

The efficacy of neurological explanations of learning disabilities is a function of what is known in the field of neurology and the subfield of developmental neuropsychology. One should, of course, beware of the fallacious argument that all behavior is controlled by the brain and therefore a person with behavior problems must have something wrong with his or her brain. However, recent developments in the brain sciences have served as the basis for potentially more differentiated explanations of learning disability. Research on split-brain patients and on patients known to have brain injury has led to the formulation of theories of functional specialization in the brain. In particular, the role of the right hemisphere in spatial, holistic processes and of the left hemisphere in linear, analytic processes has been extended to apply to many educational issues. The primary application of these ideas in the area of learning disability is in the hypothesis that some learning-disabled children fail to develop normal hemispheric specialization. Letter reversal and a general inability to relate visual forms to auditory representations are seen as symptomatic of a lack of functional separation of the right and left hemispheres. This idea has a long history, going back to Orton (1937), who asserted that reading problems resulted from the failure of one hemisphere to become the dominant processor of linguistic stimuli. More recently, Witelson (1976) hypothesized that spatial perception abilities, which are usually localized in the right hemisphere, may be represented in the left hemisphere also in disabled readers, producing decoding and comprehension problems. Although such notions have intrigued many theoreticians, there has been scant empirical support for the idea that functional specialization develops differently in normal children from the way it develops in learning-disabled children (Kinsbourne, 1980; Canning, Orr, & Rourke, 1980).

To a great extent, neuropsychological theories of learning disability are based on knowledge of brain functioning, much of which was obtained from studies of patients known to have brain injuries. Studies of the behavior of people known to have brain injuries or surgical excisions have revealed some of the relationships between location and function in the brain. When it was noticed that some children without brain injury display some of the same behavior as people with certain brain lesions, it was inferred that such children suffered from a dysfunction or developmental lag in the same part of the brain. However, there is not a neat one-to-one relationship between

behavior and particular locations in the brain; therefore, inferences from behavioral disabilities to brain dysfunctions are tenuous. Gaddes (1980) characterizes a variety of learning disabilities in terms of brain functioning.

Neuropsychological theories treat cognitive abilities as functions of different parts of the cortex; attention and alertness are described as functions of the reticular activation system, which includes spinal-cortical connections and the mid-brain, in particular the hypothalamus, which plays a key role in integrating sensory information with physical responses. The rather high incidence of abnormal electroencephalographic (EEG) patterns among learning-disabled children is also used as evidence for neurological explanations of attentional disorders (Gross & Wilson, 1974). The similarities of the EEG anomalies in learning-disabled children to the EEG anomalies associated with cerebral palsy and epilepsy are used to support the hypothesis that the underlying problem in learning-disabled children is neurological.

Biochemical theories of learning disability are, in a sense, neurological theories, because explanations are in terms of the neurochemistry of the brain. The biochemical theory set forth by Wender (1977) accounts for the behavior of children with hyperkinetic behavior syndrome. This theory asserts that many problems of attention and learning can be explained by a "functional underactivity of one or more of the monoaminergic systems" (p. 18). These monoamines are hypothesized to play a key role in increasing and decreasing the amount of neurotransmitters at neuronal junctions. The neurotransmitters determine both the appropriateness and the rapidity of a response to a situation. There is some direct evidence for monoamine deficiencies in some learning-disabled children, but for the most part, the theory rests on inferences and analogies from studies of diseases and from animal studies.

Another biochemical hypothesis concerns the effects of food additives on attention and learning. Feingold (1975) suggests that hyperactivity in some children is the result of a nonallergic reaction to food dyes and artificial flavors. Furthermore, Feingold suggests, there may be a genetic explanation of why some children react to these chemicals while others do not. The dyes and flavors are presumed to effect neurotransmitters in a manner similar to that described by Wender (1977). Conners (1980) reports the results of a series of studies that discount some of the strong claims made by the proponents of the theory, but also presents evidence for a strong effect in some learning-disabled children. Conners attributes much of the positive effect of treatment to changes in parent and child expectations and to the restructuring of family relationships that results from initiating a new diet.

Neurological explanations leave unanswered the question of the origin of neurological conditions. Genetic factors are investigated by studying the incidence of behavioral anomalies in ancestors and siblings. Environmental factors are studied by trying to determine whether particular incidents or living conditions play a role. There are no genetic explanations that can be applied to all types of learning disability, but some investigators advocate a genetic explanation of certain reading disorders. The fact that the incidence of learning disability is five times as great among boys as among girls is cited as evidence that certain differences in brain function may be sex-linked.

Environmental and neurological explanations tend to focus on prenatal events and on events during birth. A relatively high percentage of learning-disabled children are involved in some type of prenatal or birth trauma (Rudel, 1978).

Ideas about the etiology of learning disability will continue to change as long as new relationships between human behavior and the external milieu are found. Simplistic theories will always have their appeal, but most current theories acknowledge the complex relationships among behavioral stimuli, people's expectations, and genetic factors. Learning disabilities are many in number, and there will probably never be a single theory which explains the causes of all learning disabilities. Rather, different theories will be developed as progress is made in separating the symptoms associated with specific learning disabilities into more homogeneous subgroups.

Educational Programs. Prior to the enactment of the Education for All Handicapped Children Act of 1975 (P.L. 94-142), there was a tendency for learning-disabled children to be served in separate facilities. Often, these facilities were connected with universities or were private facilities designed to serve both psychological and educational needs. With the Education for All Handicapped Children Act (and through services provided prior to the act to those categorized as "crippled and other health impaired"), the federal government and state governments encouraged local education agencies to provide programs for learning-disabled children. In the last half of the 1960s, these programs were primarily based on a model appropriate for the very severely handicapped. Children were in special settings for a majority, if not the entirety, of the school day. Often, learning-disabled children were segregated for their entire educational program, sometimes to the extent of being placed in a so-called special school.

This trend gave way to the resource room model, which called for regular class placement but with a significant amount of time spent in a special classroom for instruction in areas in which the children were substantially deficient. A resource room was staffed by a specialist, had a small student-teacher ratio, and had instructional materials, teaching devices, and other professional support services that lent themselves to individualized instruction.

The resource room would often be a child's primary classroom, though increasingly it was a place to go for remediation in one or two curriculum areas. Pressures for fiscal restraint and the belief that children do better when with their peers led to less widespread use of resource rooms and special segregated classes and to the serving of learning-disabled children through the regular educational program. This reintegration was formalized in Public Law 94-142, which requires that handicapped children be educated in the "least restrictive environment." Much argument subsequently ensued over what was meant by that phrase, with some maintaining, quite correctly, that the regular classroom greatly restricted learning-disabled children—it was, after all, the environment in which such children had initially failed (Cruickshank, 1977b). However, it became widely accepted that "least restricted environment" referred to the regular classroom; thus, mainstreaming—the serving of learning-disabled children in the regular classroom—was mandated without evidence of its effectiveness. It is obvious that fiscal and political considerations dictated this circumstance.

Educational programming considerations gave rise to a new professional role, that of the itinerant, or consulting, teacher. This person, often a specialist in learning disability, assists the regular classroom teacher in developing special lessons for learning-disabled youngsters in the regular classroom. Often, children still spend some portion of their time in a resource room, while the learning-disability specialist helps ease their transition into the regular classroom. While such a procedure is certainly cost-effective and may possibly reduce the stigma of being labeled "learning disabled," questions remain as to whether the services provided the child are as effective as those provided in more segregated settings (Ito, 1980). Given that the placements are so heavily determined by funding and, hence, political considerations, the change in practices over time has been so rapid as to prohibit sufficient empirical analysis of the benefits and deficiencies of the various placement arrangements.

Educational programs for learning-disabled children can aim directly at particular deficiencies in cognitive skills or achievement (e.g., word recognition or sound-symbol associations), or programs can focus on attentional and motivational issues. One of the dominant approaches to treating deficits in achievement or cognitive skills is the diagnostic-prescriptive procedure. This begins with a broad analysis of achievement in specific areas and of the cognitive skills that are presumed to underlie academic achievement. On the basis of performance on diagnostic tests, areas are selected for remedial activity. The teacher or specialist then develops or selects (from available resources) activities intended to help the child reduce the deficit. Such remedial activity could involve specific skills in reading or arithmetic or specific cognitive functions, such as short-term memory, auditory-visual association, or visual-motor coordination. For each of the commonly used diagnostic tests, there are published aids and materials for strengthening specific deficit areas.

It should be recognized that remedial programs are based on assumptions and values held about education. Implicit in the diagnostic-prescriptive procedure are ideas about the value of the well-rounded individual and the importance of basic language and mathematical abilities. A model of education that values the development of unique, idiosyncratic abilities would not give as much emphasis to the remediation of specific deficits, but would provide opportunities for the expression of individual strengths and propensities.

Programs have been developed to deal with issues of attentional control. Douglas (1972) designed a series of cues and written messages to reorient the child to relevant tasks and reduce the time spent attending to irrelevant stimuli. Meichenbaum (1976) designed procedures to teach children self-control. This method, referred to as "cognitive behavior modification," involves a series of steps combining adult modeling, verbal reinforcement, and self-instruction. Cruickshank (1977a) strongly advocates that the environment of the child with attentional problems be controlled so that all stimuli unrelated to the learning task are eliminated. Such a classroom would include learning carrels with blank walls and a classroom which is stripped bare of all but the essential elements. In such a classroom, Cruickshank argues, the intensity of the learning material is increased because the background against which the material is presented is so bare and uninteresting.

Other educational programs are based on hypotheses about underlying developmental deficits in perceptual or perceptual-motor systems. Auditory-visual integration processes related to reading (Birch & Belmont, 1964) and certain aspects of perceptual-motor development (Frostig & Maslow, 1973; Kephart, 1971) are presumed to underlie academic achievement. Remedial exercises involving such perceptual systems have been developed for classroom purposes, but methodologically sound studies of the efficacy of these exercises are lacking (Myers & Hammill, 1976).

Drug Treatment. Three types of drugs have been used in the treatment of children with learning disabilities: (1) central nervous system stimulants, (2) antianxiety and antipsychotic agents, and (3) antihistaminic and anticonvulsant drugs. Central nervous system stimulants are the drugs of choice because of the high percentage of positive responses and the relatively low percentage of negative side effects (Millichap, 1977b). The most commonly used drugs of this class are methylphenidate (Ritalin) and dextroamphetamine (Dexedrine). Common dosages for Ritalin are 10–20 mg per day, and for Dexedrine are 5–10 mg per day. These are relatively short-acting drugs that act on the peripheral nervous system in such a way as to produce an effect similar to that produced by the stimulation of the sympathetic branch of the autonomic nervous system. The physiological effects of amphetamines include dilation of pupils, rise of blood pressure, increase of heart rate, constriction of blood vessels, variability of cardiac output, and relaxation of intestinal muscles (Kornetsky, 1975).

These drugs reduce the amount of negative behavior associated with hyperactivity. Some children show a prompt and dramatic improvement; a majority show some or considerable improvement; and some do not respond or become worse (Omenn, 1973). Millichap (1977b) re-

ported that of 367 children treated with Ritalin, 84 percent showed improvement, and that of 610 children treated with Dexedrine, 69 percent showed improvement. The positive behavioral effects include an increase in attention span and a decrease in restlessness, in inappropriate behavior, and in impulsiveness (Van Duyne, 1976). Negative side effects of the amphetamines include anorexia (food aversion), weight loss, insomnia, depressive reaction, headache, increased restlessness, and skin rash. Anorexia occurs in approximately 50 percent of children taking Ritalin, but the weight loss stabilizes after four weeks in most cases (Millichap, 1977b). Long-term suppression of growth in height and weight was reported in a study by Safer, Allen, and Barr (1972), but Millichap (1977a) reported no evidence of growth suppression.

The amphetamine drugs are presumed to have their positive effects through their influence on arousal, orienting, and attention. Although positive effects on school achievement, on performance on intelligence tests, and on social behavior are often reported, these effects are considered secondary to the primary effects on selection attention. Use of these drugs is considered when learning disabilities can be linked to hyperkinetic behavior. It is unlikely that the drugs would have a positive effect on children who have deficits in cognitive functions underlying basic reading skills, such as discrimination or auditory-visual integration, or in memory or rote learning.

Considerable concern has been expressed over the use of drugs to alter behavior in young children. It has been claimed that such use of drugs is a method by which those in power (parents, teachers, and doctors) define what is acceptable behavior and, through drugs, control the behavior of the powerless (children) to fit this definition of acceptability. Other concerns have been expressed over the long-term effects of drug dependence and drug susceptibility in later years, although at the present time there is no evidence on these matters. Controversy also surrounds the issue of deciding when and to whom drug treatment is administered. Medically trained personnel are more likely to advocate the use of the drugs for hyperkinetic behavior. Wender (1971) argues for "a trial of stimulant (amphetamine or methylphenidate) therapy in all children in whom the diagnosis of MBD (minimal brain dysfunction) is suspected" (p. 130). For the most part, educators and psychologists believe that medication should be used only as a last resort, after or in conjunction with remedial education or behavior therapy. Ross (1976) argues: "The changes in hyperactivity, attention, and motor control which can sometimes be brought about by drugs can also be produced without the use of drugs by the application of psychological principals in classroom management" (p. 101).

In summary, stimulant drugs produce a wide variety of changes in behavior and in cognitive and perceptual-motor functions. Although the precise mechanism of action of these drugs in children is not known, it is presumed that the positive effects result from improvements in selective attention resulting from active inhibition or voluntary control (Connors, 1976). The question of what are the proper roles of behavioral and drug treatment of learning disabilities remains controversial.

Sources of Information. In its two-decade history, the study of learning disability has generated a number of central information sources. The oldest monthly source specifically geared to researchers and practitioners in the multidisciplinary field of learning disability is the *Journal of Learning Disabilities.* Another journal is the *Learning Disability Quarterly,* a publication of the Division for Children with Learning Disabilities of the Council for Exceptional Children. A journal that carries practical information regarding children having school problems not limited to learning disability is *Academic Therapy.* The interested reader should be sure to examine journals in related fields, such as reading, speech and hearing, abnormal psychology, school psychology, pediatrics, neurology, neuropsychology, optometry, psychiatry, social work, occupational therapy, and psycholinguistics, to name only the most important.

A number of organizations are heavily involved in serving the learning disabled, as well as in forming professional groups concerned with personnel preparation and research, for example, the Division for Children with Learning Disabilities of the Council for Exceptional Children. The Association for Children with Learning Disabilities (ACLD) has a network of chapters nationwide that provide information and services to parents, professionals, and children. The ACLD also publishes a newsletter, *ACLD Newsbriefs,* which contains an occasional article and current information on issues in the field. The Orton Society publishes a yearly bulletin; it is a most important resource for those who study language disorders.

The most comprehensive source of information on contact persons in the field is the *Directory of Learning Disability Resources.* This directory lists the names and addresses of persons involved in federal and state government, journals and other written materials, the location of personnel preparation programs, and other information.

Information on a given state's programs can be obtained by writing to the Coordinator of Learning Disability Programs, Division of Special Education, Department of Education in the state capital. This address should suffice, and your letter should reach the appropriate person.

Paul D. Weener
Gerald M. Senf

See also Handicapped Individuals; Individual Differences; Mental Retardation; Psychological Services; Neurosciences; Rehabilitation Services; Special Education.

REFERENCES

Ames, L. B. Learning disabilities: Time to check our roadmaps. *Journal of Learning Disabilities,* 1977, *10,* 328–330.

Bachara, G. H. Empathy in learning disabled children. *Perceptual and Motor Skills,* 1976, *43,* 541–542.

Bannatyne, A. Diagnosing learning disabilities and writing remedial prescriptions. *Journal of Learning Disabilities,* 1968, *1,* 28–35.

Barbaro, F. The learning-disabled college student: Some considerations in setting objectives. *Journal of Learning Disabilities,* 1981, *14.*

Bauer, R. H. Memory processes in children with learning disabilities: Evidence for deficient rehearsal. *Journal of Experimental Child Psychology,* 1977, *24,* 415–530.

Beatty, L.; Madden, R.; & Gardner, E. *Stanford Diagnostic Arithmetic Test.* New York: Harcourt Brace & World, 1966.

Birch, H. G., & Belmont, L. Auditory-visual integration in normal and retarded readers. *American Journal of Orthopsychiatry,* 1964, *34,* 852–861.

Canning, P. M.; Orr, R. R.; & Rourke, B. P. Sex differences in perceptual, visual motor, linguistic, and concept-formation abilities of retarded readers? *Journal of Learning Disabilities,* 1980, *13,* 563–567.

Conners, C. K. Learning disabilities and stimulant drugs in children: Theoretical implications. In R. M. Knights & D. J. Bakker (Eds.), *The Neuropsychology of Learning Disorders: Theoretical Approaches.* Baltimore: University Park Press, 1976.

Conners, C. K. *Food Additives and Hyperactive Children.* New York: Plenum Press, 1980.

Cruickshank, W. M. *Learning Disabilities in Home, School, and Community.* Syracuse, N.Y.: Syracuse University Press, 1977. (a)

Cruickshank, W. M. Least restrictive placement: Administrative wishful thinking. *Journal of Learning Disabilities,* 1977, *10,* 193–194. (b)

Douglas, V. I. Stop, look, and listen: The problem of sustained attention and impulse control in hyperactive and normal children. *Canadian Journal of Behavior Science,* 1972, *4,* 259–281.

Doyle, R. B.; Anderson, R. P.; & Halcomb, C. G. Attention deficit and the effects of visual distraction. *Journal of Learning Disabilities,* 1976, *9,* 48–54.

Dykman, R. A.; Ackerman, P. T.; Clements, S. D.; & Peters, J. E. Specific learning disabilities: An attentional deficit syndrome. In H. R. Myklebust (Ed.), *Progress in Learning Disabilities* (Vol. 2). New York: Grune & Stratton, 1971.

Federal Register. November 26, 1976.

Federal Register. November 29, 1977.

Feingold, B. F. *Why Your Child Is Hyperactive.* New York: Random House, 1975.

Frostig, M., & Maslow, P. *Learning Problems in the Classroom: Prevention and Remediation.* New York: Grune & Stratton, 1973.

Gaddes, W. H. *Learning Disabilities and Brain Function.* New York: Springer-Verlag, 1980.

Gates-McKillop Reading Diagnostic Test. New York: Teachers College, Bureau of Publications, 1962.

Gross, M. O., & Wilson, W. C. *Minimal Brain Dysfunction.* New York: Brunner/Mazel, 1974.

Guthrie, J. T., & Tyler, S. J. Psycholinguistic processing in reading and listening among good and poor readers. *Journal of Reading Behavior,* 1976, *8,* 415–426.

Hagen, J., & Barclay, C. *The Development of Memory Skills in Children.* Paper presented at the meeting of the International Conference of the Association for Children and Adults with Learning Disabilities, Atlanta, 1981.

Ito, R. H. Long-term effects of resource room programs on learning-disabled children's reading. *Journal of Learning Disabilities*, 1980, *13*, 322–326.

Keogh, B. Current issues in educational methods. In J. G. Millichap (Ed.), *Learning Disabilities and Related Disorders: Facts and Current Issues*. Chicago: Year Book Medical Publishers, 1977.

Kephart, N. C. *The Slow Learner in the Classroom*. Columbus, Ohio: Merrill, 1971.

Kinsbourne, M. Cognition and the brain. In M. C. Wittrock (Ed.), *The Brain and Psychology*. New York: Academic Press, 1980.

Kirk, S. A., & Gallagher, J. J. *Educating Exceptional Children* (3rd ed.). Boston: Houghton Mifflin, 1979.

Kirk, S. A.; McCarthy, J. J.; & Kirk, W. D. *Illinois Test of Psycholinguistic Abilities* (Rev. ed.). Urbana: University of Illinois Press, 1968.

Kornetsky, C. Minimal brain dysfunction and drugs. In W. P. Cruickshank & D. P. Hallahan (Eds.), *Perceptual and Learning Disabilities in Children* (Vol. 2). Syracuse, N.Y.: Syracuse University Press, 1975.

Larsen, S. C.; Parker, R.; & Jorjorian, S. Differences in self-concept of normal and learning-disabled children. *Perceptual and Motor Skills*, 1973, *37*, 510.

Lasky, E., & Tobin, H. Linguistic and nonlinguistic competing message effects. *Journal of Learning Disabilities*, 1973, *6*, 243–250.

Meichenbaum, D. Cognitive-functional approach to cognitive factors as determinants of learning disabilities. In R. M. Knights & D. J. Bakker (Eds.), *The Neuropsychology of Learning Disorders: Theoretical Approaches*. Baltimore: University Park Press, 1976.

Mercer, C. D.; Forgnone, C.; & Wolking, W. O. Definition of learning disabilities used in the United States. *Journal of Learning Disabilities*, 1976, *9*, 376–386.

Millichap, J. G. Growth of hyperactive children treated with methylphenidate: A possible growth stimulation effect. In J. G. Millichap (Ed.), *Learning Disabilities and Related Disorders: Facts and Current Issues*. Chicago: Year Book Medical Publishers, 1977. (a)

Millichap, J. G. Medications as aids to education. In J. G. Millichap (Ed.), *Learning Disabilities and Related Disorders: Facts and Current Issues*. Chicago: Year Book Medical Publishers, 1977. (b)

Myers, P. I., & Hammill, D. D. *Methods for Learning Disorders*. New York: Wiley, 1976.

National Advisory Committee, Special Education for Handicapped Children. *The First Annual Report of the National Advisory Committee on Handicapped Children*. Washington, D.C.: U.S. Department of Health, Education, and Welfare, Office of Education, 1968.

Omenn, G. S. genetic issues in the syndrome of minimal brain dysfunction. In S. Walzer & P. H. Wolff (Eds.), *Minimal Cerebral Dysfunction in Children*. New York: Grune & Stratton, 1973.

Orton, S. *Reading, Writing, and Speech Problems in Children*. New York: Norton, 1937.

Porges, S. W.; Walter, G. F.; Korb, R. J.; & Sprague, R. L. The influence of methylphenidate on heart rate and behavioral measures of attention in hyperactive children. *Child Development*, 1975, *46*, 727–733.

Ross, A. O. *Psychological Aspects of Learning Disabilities and Reading Disorders*. New York: McGraw-Hill, 1976.

Rudel, R. G. Neuroplasticity: Implications for development and

education. In J. S. Chall & A. F. Mirsky (Eds.), *Education and the Brain*. Chicago: National Society for the Study of Education, 1978.

Rugel, R. P. WISC subtest scores of disabled readers: A review with respect to Bannatyne's recategorization. *Journal of Learning Disabilities*, 1974, *7*, 57–64.

Safer, D. J.; Allen, R. P.; & Barr, E. Depression of growth in hyperactive children on stimulant drugs. *New England Journal of Medicine*, 1972, *287*, 217–219.

Schiff, M. M.; Kaufman, A. S.; & Kaufman, N. L. Scatter analyses of WISC-R profiles for learning disabled children with superior intelligence. *Journal of Learning Disabilities*, 1981, *14*, 400–404.

Second Annual Report to Congress on the Implementation of Public Law 94-142. Washington, D.C.: U.S. Office of Education, and U.S. Government Printing Office, 1980.

Senf, G. M. Learning disabilities. In H. J. Grossman (Ed.), *Pediatric Clinics of North America*, 1973, *20*, 607–640.

Senf, G. M. Some methodological considerations in the study of abnormal conditions. In R. M. Walsh & W. T. Greenough (Eds.), *Environments as Therapy for Brain Dysfunction*. New York: Plenum Press, 1976.

Senf, G. M. A perspective on the definition of LD. *Journal of Learning Disabilities*, 1977, *10*, 8–10.

Senf, G. M. Implications of the final procedures for evaluating specific learning disabilities. *Journal of Learning Disabilities*, 1978, *11*, 124–126.

Spache, G. D. *Diagnostic Reading Scales*. Monterey, Calif.: California Test Bureau, 1963.

Spreen, O., & Benton, A. L. *Neurosensory Center Comprehensive Examination for Aphasia*. Victoria, B.C: University of Victoria, Department of Psychology, 1968 and 1977 (Rev. ed.).

Sroufe, L. A.; Sonies, B. C.; West, W. D.; & Wright, F. S. Anticipatory heart-rate deceleration and reaction time in children with and without referral for learning disability. *Child Development*, 1973, *44*, 267–273.

Stawar, T. L., & Lamp, R. E. IES test performance by learning-disabled boys. *Perceptual and Motor Skills*, 1974, *38*, 695–699.

Swanson, L. Comparison of normal and disabled children on a non-verbal short-term memory serial position task. *Journal of Genetic Psychology*, 1978, *133*, 119–127.

Tarver, S. G.; Hallahan, D. P.; Kauffman, J. M.; & Ball, D. W. Verbal rehearsal and selective attention in children with learning disabilities: A developmental lag. *Journal of Experimental Child Psychology*, 1976, *22*, 375–385.

Torgesen, J., & Hall, J. *Memory Skills in Special Sub-groups of LD Children*. Paper presented at the meeting of the International Conference of the Association for Children and Adults with Learning Disabilities, Atlanta, 1981.

Torgesen, J. K.; Murphy, H. A.; & Ivey, C. The influence of an orienting task on the memory performance of children with reading problems. *Journal of Learning Disabilities*, 1979, *12*, 43–48.

Van Duyne, H. J. Effects of stimulant drug therapy on learning behavior in hyperactive/MBO children. In R. M. Knights & D. J. Bakker (Eds.), *The Neuropsychology of Learning Disorders*. Baltimore: University Park Press, 1976.

Wedell, K. Early identification and compensatory interaction. In R. M. Knights & D. J. Bakker (Eds.), *Treatment of Hyperactive and Learning-disordered Children*. Baltimore: University Park Press, 1980.

Weener, P. On comparing learning-disabled and regular classroom children. *Journal of Learning Disabilities*, 1981, *14*, 227–232.

Wender, P. H. *Minimal Brain Dysfunction in Children*. New York: Wiley Interscience, 1971.

Wender, P. H. Speculations concerning a possible biochemical basis of MBD. In J. G. Millichap (Ed.), *Learning Disabilities and Related Disorders: Facts and Current Issues*. Chicago: Year Book Medical Publishers, 1977.

Werner, H., & Strauss, A. A. Pathology of figure-background relation in the child. *Journal of Abnormal and Social Psychology*, 1941, *36*, 236–248.

Wiederhold, J. L. Historical perspectives on the education of the learning disabled. In L. Mann & D. Sabatino (Eds.), *The Second Review of Special Education*. Philadelphia: JSE Press, 1974.

Witelson, S. F. Abnormal right-hemisphere specialization in developmental dyslexia. In R. M. Knights & D. J. Bakker (Eds.), *The Neuropsychology of Learning Disorders: Theoretical Approaches*. Baltimore: University Park Press, 1976.

LEGAL EDUCATION

See Licensing and Certification; Professions Education.

LEGISLATION

Throughout most of American history, the states and local districts have carried the primary responsibility for public education. The relatively passive federal role was limited to a few areas of clear national concern or responsibility. This began to change during the early 1960s, as an era of federal social activism developed that would endure through the 1970s. Early in this era the civil rights movement and associated court decisions helped lead to the enactment of laws intended to end racial discrimination and segregation in the nation's schools and colleges. Concurrently, the Johnson administration enlisted education in its War on Poverty. Later, as standardized achievement test scores test scores fell and public dissatisfaction rose, Congress and the states tried to legislate improved educational quality.

This article focuses on federal and state education legislation of the past twenty years. It is organized into three major sections. The first section discusses civil rights legislation. The second and third sections consider strictly educational legislation, looking first at the elementary and secondary education and then at higher education.

Civil Rights

During the 1960s and 1970s Congress enacted civil rights legislation to clarify and extend the guarantees of the Fourteenth Amendment. Most crucial to understand from the educational point of view are the Civil Rights Act of 1964, Title IX of the Education Amendments of 1972, Section 504 of the Rehabilitation Act of 1973, and the 1978 amendment to the Age Discrimination in Employment Act of 1967.

Civil Rights Act of 1964. The U.S. Supreme Court handed down its famous decisions in *Brown* v. *Board of Education* in 1954 and 1955, outlawing the South's ubiquitous *de jure* dual public school systems. Southern legislatures responded to *Brown* by enacting obstructionist legislation, the most effective known as "pupil assignment laws," which resisted desegregation by making transfer cumbersome and time-consuming and by placing the burden of forcing compliance on black children and their parents. This strategy was successful; ten years after *Brown*, fewer than 10 out of every 100 southern black children were attending school with whites.

Meanwhile, the civil rights movement grew apace. Congress responded by enacting the Civil Rights Act of 1964. Titles IV and VI applied significantly to public education. Title IV, Desegregation of Public Education, designated three duties for federal officials. First, the commissioner of education was instructed to survey "the lack of availability of equal educational opportunities for individuals . . . in public educational institutions" and to report his findings within two years. The resulting report, entitled *Equality of Educational Opportunity* (Coleman et al., 1966) and known as the "Coleman report," was popularly interpreted as offering support to desegregation policies and raised an enduring controversy. Second, the commissioner was authorized to render technical assistance to local districts to prepare and implement desegregation plans. This authorization grew into a $40 million program by the late 1970s. Finally, the attorney general of the United States, after receiving and reviewing a complaint alleging an equal protection or access violation, was authorized to institute a civil action for relief. Title IX of the Civil Rights Act supplemented this provision by empowering the attorney general to intervene in any suit alleging denial of equal protection rights that he believes is of general public importance.

Title VI, Nondiscrimination in Federally Assisted Programs, asserted in Section 601: "No person in the United States shall, on the ground of race, color, or national origin, be excluded from participation in, be denied the benefits of, or be subjected to discrimination under any program or activity receiving Federal financial assistance." All federal departments and agencies, including the Department of Health, Education, and Welfare (HEW), that made aid payments were directed to issue guidelines to enforce Section 601. Failure by aid recipients to comply could result in the termination of federal assistance. This provision and the Title IV funding incentives gave the federal government important alternatives to litigation.

Ironically, the Civil Rights Act has been least effective in helping to eradicate school desegregation throughout the North, the region of the country that provided the political support needed for enactment in 1964. Southern school desegregation was generally complete by 1971, following a set of tough Supreme Court rulings late in 1968 and in 1969, which mandated immediate and comprehensive action and which elevated the HEW Title VI compliance guidelines to the status of standards. The Supreme Court then turned its attention to the North, first, in *Swann* v. *Charlotte-Mecklenburg County Board of Education* (1971), by declaring busing an acceptable means of school desegregation and second, in *Keyes* v. *School District No. 1, Denver Colorado* (1972), by asserting that northern segregation was of a *de jure* nature and by requiring districtwide remedies. With the specter of forced districtwide busing a reality, northern public opinion reversed, manifesting itself in congressional "busing amendments" that set strict limits on the use of federal funds to pay for busing. Title VIII of the Education Amendments of 1972 and the Equal Educational Opportunity Act of 1974 are early examples of this sort of congressional action. Unfortunately, these laws succeeded merely in placing heavier desegregation expenses on the states and local districts and in delaying passage of important funding legislation. Meanwhile, court-ordered busing mandates remained in effect. As the nation enters the 1980s, new desegregation activity has slowed considerably.

Title VI has also served as the basis for federal guidelines for bilingual education in school districts educating significant numbers of students with limited proficiency in English because they have been brought up speaking another language. Known as the "*Lau* remedies," the guidelines stemmed directly from the U.S. Supreme Court, which held in its 1957 decision in *Lau* v. *Nichols* that Title VI required affirmative steps by the schools to meet the needs of such students. The remedies outline acceptable pedagogical approaches and designate requirements for districts as they develop and submit program plans to the Office of Civil Rights (OCR). Since 1975, OCR has negotiated agreements with several hundred districts, including those enrolling students who in the majority speak limited English. Although the *Lau* remedies remain in effect, they have undergone harsh attacks in Congress and by education groups.

Finally, litigation involving Title VI and institutions of higher education has demonstrated the law's inescapable ambiguity. In 1973, for example, a U.S. court of appeals decided in *Adams* v. *Richardson* first, that dual state systems of higher education must be eliminated, and second, that the traditional black colleges, which have served as important sources of community and racial pride while preparing many of the nation's black professionals, should be strengthened. The 1978 U.S. Supreme Court decision in *Bakke* v. *The Regents of the University of California* was another important ruling. The five-to-four majority declared that the university had unlawfully discriminated against Bakke, a Caucasian, on the basis of race in denying him admission to the medical school at Davis. But while the Court accepted Bakke's claim of "reverse discrimination," it also voted five to four that admissions decisions may appropriately take race and ethnic origin into account.

Title IX. Congress extended civil rights protections to women through Title IX, Prohibition of Sex Discrimination, of the Education Amendments of 1972 as follows: "No person in the United States shall, on the basis of sex, be excluded from participation in, be denied the benefits of, or be subjected to discrimination under any education program or activity receiving Federal financial assistance." In 1979, Shirley Chisholm, Democratic congresswoman from New York, evaluated the significance of Title IX by stating: "Women have always occupied a secondary status in the United States. And, in the same way that it was necessary for Blacks to get recognition by virtue of the Voting Rights Act and the Civil Rights Act—Title IX is of the same import to women ("An Interview," 1979, p. 504).

Controversy has surrounded Title IX, which, unlike Title VI of the Civil Rights Act, applied only to education. University presidents and football coaches flocked to Washington to express their concerns and fears. Regulations were issued in 1975. Since their adoption, many compliance agreements have been negotiated, especially in areas such as vocational education, physical education, and elementary school extracurricular activities. Opponents, however, have generally been successful, by recourse to the courts, in avoiding compliance enforcement in employment areas. Perhaps the most successful congressional opposition tactic has been to attach limiting amendments to budget authorization bills. The fact remains, however, that discrimination on the basis of sex in education is now against the law of the land. Although complaints have been loud and widespread and compliance is far from universal, genuine progress has been made by women through Title IX.

Section 504. Section 504 of the Rehabilitation Act of 1973, resulting partially from two federal district court decisions in 1971 and 1972, has been called the "civil rights act for the handicapped." It states: "No otherwise qualified handicapped individual in the United States . . . shall, solely by reason of his handicap, be excluded from the participation in, be denied the benefits of, or be subjected to discrimination under any program or activity receiving Federal financial assistance." Congress applied this mandate to public schooling with passage of Public Law 94-142, the Education for All Handicapped Children Act of 1975, requiring that all handicapped children be provided a free and appropriate education program. By 1980 all states had mounted comprehensive programs and were making substantial progress toward guaranteeing the educational rights of their handicapped youth. Section 504 has also significantly affected institutions of higher education, especially after 1977 when HEW regulations were issued, that frequently resulted in expensive building and grounds alterations to provide better physical accessibility for handicapped students.

Age Discrimination in Employment Act. Congress passed the Age Discrimination in Employment Act (ADEA) in 1967, forbidding discrimination in employment on the basis of age for people between 40 and 65 and generally setting the minimum mandatory retirement age at 65. In 1978 Congress amended ADEA. Prior debate had centered on the upper age limit for mandatory retirement, which had been accepted in 1967 with almost no discussion. Some argued that no upper age should be set, that age alone is a poor indicator of ability to work productively, and that forced retirement for many is equivalent to forced unemployment and hardship; others asserted that room must be made for younger, frequently disadvantaged, job applicants who deserve access to the work force and that younger employees would do better work. Congress responded with a compromise, raising the minimum mandatory retirement age to 70, except for tenured college and university faculty members, whose minimum mandatory retirement age remained at 65 until July 1, 1982, when their protections were extended to age 70. From the institutional point of view, some maintain, the 1978 ADEA amendments will exacerbate the already serious problem of too many faculty members with tenure, which restricts entry of young scholars and thereby significantly diminishes the quality of research and teaching. However, these assertions are debatable.

Elementary and Secondary Education

The Johnson administration's War on Poverty got under way with passage of the Economic Opportunity Act of 1964, which included the Job Corps, Community Action, and Head Start. The following year, concerted federal activism in education exploded upon the scene with congressional enactment of the Elementary and Secondary Education Act (ESEA). ESEA contained a major title to provide compensatory education services for economically disadvantaged students, three titles to improve the general quality of elementary and secondary schooling, and a fifth title to strengthen the traditionally weak state education agencies. Congress subsequently expanded the purviews of ESEA over the following fifteen years. Through all of this, federal action tended to stimulate complementary state legislation.

Three important areas of elementary and secondary education legislation concerned equality of educational opportunity in school funding and programming, quality of schooling, and collective bargaining rights for public school employees.

Equality of Educational Opportunity. Equality of educational opportunity entered public policy debates during the mid-1960s. Evolving out of the larger civil rights movement and federal antipoverty activity, equality of educational opportunity had to do with both the goal of desegregation in the nation's schools and the idea of using public elementary and secondary schools to compensate poor and minority children for disadvantageous home backgrounds. The schools, in other words, were expected to give special help to the educationally needy so that by the time of high school graduation they would be prepared to com-

pete with children from middle-class families for success in America. In practice, this led to efforts to provide schools in disadvantaged areas with resources at least equal to those received by schools enrolling more advantaged students. This section treats equality of educational opportunity legislation as it relates to school funding and programming.

Funding. For years people believed that a major cause of different educational outcomes among schools was different levels of expenditure among the schools. Although this view has been discredited by a variety of studies, beginning with the Coleman Report (Coleman et al., 1966), the agreement that there should not be great disparity in funding among school districts has had persistent legal and social acceptance. Both federal and state legislation has addressed this issue.

Since 1965, overall spending on public elementary and secondary education has risen markedly, but after an initial increase in 1965 the federal share has remained relatively small and confined to targeted populations, such as the poor or those who speak limited English. Federal money has made up roughly 8 to 9 percent of total revenues annually for the past fifteen years. Through ESEA and subsequent legislation, the federal share has had only a small influence on the equalizing of school expenditures among and within states. Brown and Ginsburg (1978) argued that at the interdistrict level "federal aid does little to reduce . . . local property wealth-based advantages, . . . partly because the federal share of total revenues is small and partly because federal programs tend to be directed toward low-income areas rather than areas of low property wealth" (pp. 121–122). Finally, beginning in 1971, after promulgation of the Office of Education's "comparability regulations," whereby equal distribution of local and state resources throughout district must be guaranteed before Title I money can be used, some intradistrict funding disparities in large urban areas have been alleviated.

Court decisions throughout the 1970s have encouraged finance reform and limited that reform primarily to the state level. *Serrano* v. *Priest,* a set of California Supreme Court decisions between 1971 and 1976, adopted the position first argued by Coons, Clune, and Sugarman (1970) that local district property wealth per pupil should not determine the distribution of educational resources. This standard of fiscal neutrality, based on the equal protection clause of the California state constitution, forced the legislature to develop an acceptable alternative. Meanwhile, in 1973 the U.S. Supreme Court ruling on a Texas Supreme Court decision, *Rodriguez* v. *San Antonio,* decided that education does not fall under the equal protection clause of the U.S. Constitution. This decision raised national concern that the nascent financial reform movement begun by *Serrano* was dead. Five weeks later, however, the New Jersey Supreme Court ruled on *Robinson* v. *Cahill,* deciding that the New Jersey structure violated the education clause of the state constitution and allaying the fears raised by *Rodriguez*. Since *Robinson*, state-level finance litigation has virtually been continuous. Legislators have had to respond to the courts.

About one-half the states have produced school finance reform laws in the largely unsuccessful effort to equalize expenditures. This legislation may be divided into three categories: (1) foundation programs that require a certain minimum expenditure per pupil in all districts; (2) equalizing programs that generally determine per-pupil expenditures by reference to the district property-tax rate, regardless of the wealth of that district; and (3) programs that combine a foundation requirement with rewards to less wealthy districts that exert extra effort through a high property-tax rate. At best these programs have allowed some states to make slight progress in reducing per-pupil expenditure differences at a time when states without reform laws have tended to lose ground because of demographic shifts and associated conditions.

In recent years difficult economic times and general public displeasure with the quality of public schooling have led to discussion of and some movement toward more drastic changes in the financing of education. Tax or spending limitations have now been incorporated by legislation or referenda into the funding structures of almost two-thirds of the states. Two important by-products of these efforts have been increases in the state proportions of spending on public schooling and movement toward equalization of expenditures within states. Ironically, the tax-limitation movement, opposed by many who favor reform in educational finance, may inadvertently be accomplishing what the reformers failed to do.

At the federal level, spurred on by high inflation and the so-called mandate to curtail government involvement with elementary and secondary education, the Reagan administration has succeeded in orchestrating congressional passage of deep budget cuts and of the Education Consolidation and Improvement Act of 1981 (ECIA). These steps will affect school finance in two important ways. First, the deep reductions in federal expenditures that began to take effect in the fall of 1981 will, by the 1982/83 school years, have reduced the federal share of the nation's school budget to its smallest portion since 1965, approximately 5 percent.

Second, ECIA increases the power of states and localities to control the distribution of federal education funds. The administration initially proposed block grant legislation that would have combined the large ESEA Title I compensatory education program and the Education for All Handicapped Children Act provisions into one title, leaving the states free to parcel out and administer a huge bulk of funds as they might choose. A second title would have combined about forty small federal programs, giving the money to the states for general discretionary purposes. Civil rights groups and others concerned about maintaining services and protections guaranteed only by federal categorical aids legislation consistently opposed the first title. Its defeat was assured when school boards, school administrators, and state superintendents organizations (groups that favored consolidation in principle) came out strongly in opposition, primarily because they did not want to make the extremely difficult decisions about the allocation of resources between the poor and the handicapped and also because they began to perceive the proposed bill as possibly representing the beginning of the end of federal support for education. Bowing to this widespread and intense opposition, the administration dropped its plan to consolidate the large programs. The administration settled, instead, on a bill that simplified Title I by reducing certain reporting requirements (Chapter I) and which consolidates over 30 small programs into a single block grant to the state and local agencies (Chapter II).

Voucher and tax credit programs are also under serious discussion. Both types of programs would provide government money to students to attend nonpublic schools. Vouchers usually are considered at the local and state levels. No proposed legislation has been adopted, although attempts have been made in several states to place proposals on the ballot. Vouchers would function as admission tickets to any school meeting specified minimum standards. Tuition tax credits, operated through the income tax system, would be allowed to offset expenses associated with sending one's child to a private elementary or secondary school. Several states, including Pennsylvania, Rhode Island, and New Jersey, have adopted forms of tax credit legislation, although most of the laws have been struck down by the courts as unconstitutional on church-state grounds. In 1978 the House of Representatives passed and the Senate narrowly defeated a federal tuition tax credit bill. At the time of this writing, senators Moynihan and Packwood have reintroduced tax credit legislation, with the strong backing of President Reagan and in line with the 1980 Republican platform.

Education service programs. Efforts to achieve equality of educational opportunity in programming at the federal and state levels have been under way since the mid-1960s. Four of the most significant areas of effort are discussed here: compensatory education, school desegregation, bilingual education, and education of the handicapped.

Congress led the way in compensatory education programming by passing Title I of ESEA in 1965. Section 101 of this landmark art declared,

> In recognition of the special educational needs of children of low-income families and the impact that concentrations of low-income families have on the ability of local educational agencies to support adequate educational programs, the Congress hereby declares it to be the policy of the United States to provide financial assistance . . . to local educational agencies serving areas with concentrations of children from low-income families to expand and improve their educational programs by various means (including preschool programs) which contribute particularly to meeting the special educational needs of educationally deprived children.

In addition to providing aid to local districts for special programs, Title I assists state programs for migrant children, the handicapped, and neglected and delinquent youth. Initially funded at over $1 billion in 1965, during 1980 Title I distributed over $3.2 billion in categorical aids to all the states and most of the nation's public school districts, maintaining support for programs that serve about one-half of an estimated ten million eligible children.

Since 1974 Congress has debated whether Title I programs should continue to be funded on the basis of poverty or in terms of scholastic achievement. Studies and compromises have essentially left the original approach in place. In 1978, the Carter administration urged and the Congress enacted the Special Incentive Grants provision, which has designed to encourage and reward higher state spending on compensatory education programs by providing one federal dollar for every two appropriated by the state. Congress has not, however, funded this provision.

Title I effectiveness has been evaluated in terms of program implementation and student achievement. Studies of program implementation indicated numerous problems and weaknesses (cf. McLaughlin, 1974), and the Washington Research Project and the NAACP Legal Defense Fund (1969) produced evidence that Title I funds were frequently being used improperly as general aid. This led to a tightening of administrative reins and the introduction of clear fiscal controls (for example, comparability). More recent evaluations indicate that although problems remain, the basic program principles and purposes have been widely accepted and that a viable fiscal accountability system is now in operation. Estimates of Title I effectiveness in raising student achievement levels are less sanguine. Although a variety of studies have demonstrated that children in the program obtain short-term (one-year) improvement in achievement there is no evidence that these gains are sustained over a longer period of time.

Levels of program implementation and effectiveness notwithstanding, by 1980 sixteen states had enacted categorical compensatory education laws intended to augment Title I funding that would probably meet requirements for incentive grants. Six additional states, which do not qualify for incentive grants, provide funding for compensatory education services by including weighted elements in their general aid formulas.

In 1970 the Nixon administration prompted congressional action in response to Supreme Court efforts to accomplish immediate school desegregation. Funded at $75 million annually for two years, the Emergency School Assistance Program (ESAP) was supposed to help public schools overcome desegregation-related program difficulties. According to critics, however, ESAP functioned primarily as a payoff to districts that had resisted complete desegregation or as a mechanism to distribute funds for general aid use.

In 1972 Congress replaced ESAP with Emergency School Aid Act (ESAA), which was designed to provide programming support to end racial isolation and discrimination and to ameliorate their effects. ESAA distributes money on the basis of minority enrollment levels and through national competitions, which identify districts that will benefit from supplemental funds to address the immediate effects of school desegregation. By 1980 ESAA had developed into a $290-million-per-year program.

In 1967 Congress added a component on bilingual education, Title VII, to ESEA to fund programs for an estimated 2 to 3.5 million children with limited proficiency in the English language. Appropriations have grown from $7.5 million in 1969 to $167 million in 1980. Allocation has been on the basis of competition for grants. Title VII funds have occasionally been used to implement the *Lau* remedies, and during the last few years attempts have been made to coordinate these two programs. Following the federal lead, the states have taken a substantial role in legislating bilingual education. In all, twenty-two states, including those with the largest numbers of Spanish-surnamed students, have sponsored bilingual programs.

The states took the lead in providing access to public education for the handicapped. During the 1960s, Massachusetts and New Jersey passed laws that provided model standards for classification, testing, individual programs, special services, and so on. All fifty states have now enacted special education legislation. Meanwhile, Congress, following passage of Section 504 of the Rehabilitation Act of 1973, debated a comprehensive bill that it enacted two years later. Public Law 94-142, the Education for All Handicapped Children Act of 1975, mandates that all handicapped children be provided with an opportunity to receive a free appropriate public education, no matter how severe their handicap. At the present time the federal government through Public Law 94-142 provides roughly 12 percent of the cost of the special services required for handicapped students.

Public Law 94-142 contains three important mandates. First, the school must provide the least restrictive educational environment for each handicapped child. This requirement has led to "mainstreaming," or the integrating of many handicapped children into regular classrooms. Second, the school must provide each handicapped child with an Individualized Education Program (IEP), developed in consultation with the child's parents. Progress must be assessed periodically in terms of the IEP, and the IEP itself must be reviewed from time to time to keep it in line with the child's progress. Finally, parents or guardians of handicapped children are guaranteed due process rights concerning access to student records, proposed IEP changes, and related matters. At the time of this writing, most state legislatures have brought their statutes into general conformity with federal law, although there is growing interest in reducing certain requirements. Local and state educators argue, for example, that strict federal requirements, such as those involving IEPs, are unwarranted in light of the small share of total funding for the handicapped provided by the national government.

As the 1970s ended, the Carter administration proposed

the Youth Act of 1980, a categorical grant program to address the problems of youth unemployment and the reform of junior and senior high schools in high-poverty areas. The proposed legislation passed the House with overwhelming bipartisan support, but failed in the Senate after reaching the floor late in the summer session of 1980, when it appeared that President Carter was opposed by a majority of the electorate.

The proposed Youth Act may be the last major categorical education program to have had a chance to pass the Congress for quite some time. Congress has passed ECIA Chapter I which removes many of the fiscal and administrative protections for the poor that are built into the categorical legislation. In place of these requirements is a far greater dependence on the good faith and judgment of local school administrators to use federal funds in the most effective ways to educate students needing special help. Chapter II of ECIA consolidates the Emergency School Assistance Act along with over 30 other small programs essentially into a block grant to the states. The other major categorical programs promoting equal opportunity are untouched to date.

Many legislators continue to support the ultimate consolidation of the major education programs. To some observers consolidation is overdue. Federal legislative and regulatory requirements, they complain, have created a maze of procedures for local school people. In schools with particularly high percentages of poor and otherwise needy students, the rules frequently create situations that can only obstruct effective education programming. Programs using bilingual-education and Title I funds, for example, are required to track the use of the funds within schools. This frequently leads to segregation of students for long parts of the day, primarily to ease record keeping requirements. In contrast, the Education for All Handicapped Children Act, encourages the integration of students of all kinds in the regular classroom. These conflicting approaches serve to complicate an already difficult task.

Also, as we have indicated, federal programs for the underserved have been emulated by many states. A strong argument can be made that the federal effort to stimulate states and local agencies to take far greater responsibility for these children has been successful.

To others, however, the consolidation initiative is simply another indication that the federal government is turning its back on the needy. They point to discrimination and favoritism throughout the nation, and some feel compelled to advocate ever stronger federal controls. For those moderating this debate, the task will be to grant local school authorities the responsibility of developing effective educational programs and at the same time to offer protections for the needy to insure that they receive necessary and appropriate services. As the Reagan administration's failure to enact its first consolidation proposal for the largest programs demonstrates, the civil rights and professional education communities remain unconvinced that an equitable solution to these problems has been developed.

Quality of Schooling. Federal and state legislators have attempted to improve the general quality of public elementary and secondary education. Legislation has usually taken the form either of accountability requirements or of funding for new programs.

Accountability. The federal approach to accountability since 1965 has emphasized program evaluation, including activity mandated at the local and state levels. By the mid-1970s, for example, the total federal, state, and local expenditures for Title I evaluation activities exceeded $30 million per year. The law provides for local evaluation in every district receiving Title I funds, for national evaluations, and for the establishment of centers nationwide to give local evaluators technical assistance. Throughout the late 1960s and early 1970s, extensive evaluation requirements were included in many federal education service program laws, such as the Vocational Education Act, ESAA, the Bilingual Education Act, and Public Law 94-142.

A second major approach to accountability at the federal level has involved testing to evaluate the quality of general education. During the debates over the 1978 amendments to ESEA, with prodding from President Carter, HEW considered developing legislation that would authorise a national testing program. In the ensuing debate, support for the idea rose from the frustration some felt over the apparent decline in the quality of schools in spite of fifteen years of federal effort. Opposition came from most of the education groups, testing experts, and civil rights advocates—all of whom pointed to methodological and administrative problems and to the possibility that a federal test might well discriminate against minorities and women and lead to situations where a federal curriculum could overthrow traditional systems of local and state control. In the end the Carter administration did not propose special legislation and the Congress also decided against it. The Education Amendments of 1978 did contain provisions authorizing financial support for state competency-based testing programs and for remedial activities for students failing the tests. To date no funds have been appropriated for this program.

Between 1976 and 1980 the interest in testing found enthusiastic expression in such states as California, Florida, and Texas, with traditions of strong centralized control over public schooling. Statewide minimum competency testing programs, largely in response to grassroots pressures, were mandated in thirty-eight states. The earliest programs emphasized testing to qualify for high school graduation, while the later ones were more concerned with identifying children who require remedial help. This mandating activity slowed considerably after 1978, as legislators and others began to clarify expectations and tighten procedural controls. Although controversies abound over particular issues, such as the definition of minimum standards and teacher competency, the testing laws are securely in place and may be expected to provide the major force behind the state-level accountability action in the foreseeable future.

Research and development. Passage of the National Defense Education Act in 1958 and funding of the development of new mathematics and science curricula by the National Science Foundation (NSF) were the first major federal steps into education research and development (R & D). Over the last fifteen years the NSF has provided considerable funding for R & D in science education and in social science areas related to education. In the late 1960s the momentum for these expenditures was halted by an important controversy over a social studies curriculum funded by NSF. The curriculum, *Man, A Course of Study,* was viewed by critics as espousing anti-Christian and anti-American values. Funds for projects of this sort were cut off by Congress, and the overall NSF effort in education-related R & D was reduced. By the late 1970s, however, it had built back up into a significant enterprise. Ironically, as the Republican administration took charge in 1981 many of the same critics and much of the same criticism of NSF curriculum and social science programs reemerged.

Partly because of the goodwill remaining from early NSF efforts, there was little argument about whether the financing of R & D is a legitimate federal role when ESEA passed in 1965. Title IV of ESEA expanded a project grants program for R & D administered by the U.S. Office of Education and authorized a network of institutional R & D centers based at major universities. Supplemental legislation in 1966 established a number of regional laboratories intended to provide technical assistance and to disseminate materials and information to state and local education agencies.

During the 1970s, the core responsibility for federal R & D programs was transferred to the National Institute of Education (NIE), which was established by the Education Amendments of 1972. Over the years, the purposes of NIE have been debated vigorously. Some see it as a basic research agency; others, as having a more practical role as a development and dissemination unit. NIE funding reached a high of roughly $120 million during its second year and has since declined. There has been a concomitant reduction in the number of R & D centers and regional laboratories, from the original thirty-four to the present seventeen.

Other legislated and federally funded R & D work has included the Follow Through program, which was authorized in 1967 as part of the Economic Opportunity Act of 1964, provisions in the Education for All Handicapped Children Act, and the Programs of National Significance in the Vocational Education Act. The Follow Through program was the most ambitious of the federally sponsored efforts to experiment with different approaches to educational programming. This applied research, costing over $50 million per year for over ten years, was an effort to determine whether there were significant differences in the effects of some fifteen different early elementary school curricula. Few major differences were found, although the evidence indicated that highly structured cur-

ricula are particularly effective in the teaching of reading and arithmetic. Work for the handicapped is administered by the Office of the Handicapped; the development of prosthetic devices to assist the physically handicapped has provided dramatic evidence of the importance of R & D. The states have given very little attention to educational R & D legislation.

Teacher Training. Teacher training became a topic of major concern during the late 1960s, when educators began to anticipate a teacher shortage. In 1965, as part of the Higher Education Act, Congress passed legislation establishing the Teacher Corps to train new teachers to work in inner cities. Over the years the Teacher Corps grew to a $37.5 million program, and by the mid-1970s it had changed its emphasis to in-service training. In 1967 Congress passed the Education Professions Development Act (EPDA), a comprehensive approach to preservice and in-service training programs involving local and state agencies and colleges of education. As federal planners gained the information that the anticipated teacher shortage would become an actual surplus in the near future, Congress abandoned most of the EPDA programs before they were ever funded.

Federal attention to special programs for teachers lapsed until 1976, when Teacher Center legislation was passed. Advocated by teacher organizations, Teacher Centers were intended to provide in-service programming under the guidance of teachers themselves. Although authorization for this program exceeded $50 million, the appropriations by 1980 had not exceeded $15 million in any year. Programs tied to specific categorical purposes fared better during the late 1960s and the 1970s. For example, enabling legislation for upgrading teacher training in specific areas was included in the large categorical programs, such as the Vocational Education Act, the Education for All Handicapped Children Act, and the Bilingual Education Act.

Special programs to improve schools. During the past fifteen years, the federal government has directly administered a large number of special programs to improve the quality of elementary and secondary education. In the Education Amendments of 1978, for example, Congress either reauthorized or passed new categorical legislation for about twenty federally administered programs in such areas as metric education, the arts in education, consumer education, corrections education, and population education. In almost every instance these programs provide grant or contract funds for demonstration projects and materials development and for technical assistance to local agencies by states, institutions of higher education, and other agencies and organizations. Although their mandate is broad, the annual funding for any one of these programs has rarely exceeded $5 million. The 1978 amendments also included a new ESEA Title II, replacing the old Right-to-Read program with the Basic Skills Improvement program.

One view of these small programs, which are intended

to meet problems of national scope, is that they have been too poorly funded to accomplish much and that the problems they address can better be dealt with by publishers in the private sector or by other institutions without federal funding. A second view is that their existence in federal legislation has attracted national attention and that the few dollars spent on the programs have served as a catalyst for other public and private sector activity in important areas. A third view is that if the designated areas deserve attention, it is better for states to deal with them as they arise.

The federal government has also supported extensive development and improvement efforts administered by state governments. Title II of the original ESEA contained funding authorization for school library materials and other materials—a program that has now provided well over $1 billion to purchase school materials. Title III of ESEA was originally a small project grant program for demonstration and development administered by regional offices of the U.S. Office of Education. By the late 1970s this program (now Title IV-C of ESEA) had grown to an annual appropriation level of over $190 million and had been transferred to the states for administrative purposes.

As the 1970s ended, there was considerable concern over federal and state sponsorship of isolated curricular or topical reform and innovation strategies. Research throughout the decade concerning the mechanisms of school change and project implementation generally indicated that top-down and fragmented strategies, such as improving a new mathematics curriculum, are ineffective without strong local control by the school staff over the nature of the curriculum and its implementation. These findings have made skeptics of many former advocates for federally sponsored change, as the difference has become apparent between what is appropriate locally and what is a matter of federal or even statewide policies.

In July 1981, therefore, the skeptics were pleased by congressional passage of ECIA Title II. This title replaces some thirty small programs (including ESEA Titles II–VI, VIII, and IX, the Teacher Corps, and Teacher Center programs) with a single block grant to the states. Total funding for Title II is expected to be in the $500–$600 million range for fiscal year 1982. Eighty percent of a state's funds are to be passed on directly to local education agencies, with 20 percent retained by states for their use. The effect of ECIA Title II will be to remove the federal government from all school improvement activity except that conducted as part of NIE's research and development work. It remains to be seen what the states and local agencies will do with their new resources.

Before passage of ECIA some states were already heading in an apparently productive direction by providing for comprehensive, rather than fragmented, programs to improve schools. California and Florida are leaders. The California School Improvement Program (SIP), adopted by the legislature in 1977, is a governance strategy whereby school site councils, consisting of parents, school staff, and community members, plan and control a unified school program, ideally focusing all core, categorical, and other aids upon children's educational needs. Evaluation takes the form of program review, which includes complex rating procedures and technical assistance. Although the state conducts program review at the moment, counties are developing the capacity to take over this function. In 1979 the Florida legislature established the Primary Education Program (PREP), which mandates readiness and skill tests, curriculum groupings, program coordinators, promotion standards, staff development and teacher training standards, and other elements. Although critics of testing dispute the point, PREP supporters believe they have established a program that can identify and remediate learning problems as they occur, before they become unmanageable.

Collective Bargaining. The granting of collective bargaining rights for public school teachers has been a state-level legislative phenomenon. As of September 1980, thirty states and the District of Columbia had granted some form of collective bargaining rights to public school teachers. This legislation, mostly enacted between 1965 and 1975, was part of a larger movement to grant collective bargaining rights to public employees generally. Early legislation responded primarily to strikes intended to force the granting of bargaining rights. Subsequently, the frequency of strikes has paralleled the extension of bargaining rights, leading some observers to conclude that legislation has actually encouraged labor strife. In any case, no state legislature has rescinded bargaining rights, and most continue to refine the laws.

Higher Education

During the two decades following 1944, Congress started on the path that would end in a federal policy of making postsecondary education opportunities available to all qualified applicants. The GI Bill provided direct financial assistance to veterans who chose to continue their education. The National Defense Education Act of 1958 (NDEA), responding to the unprecedented technological accomplishment of the successful launching of *Sputnik* by the Soviet Union in 1957, set up a need-based low-interest college loan program administered by institutions and made research and development money available. Finally, the Higher Education Facilities Act of 1963, in anticipation of large enrollment increases, helped pay for needed physical plant additions.

Full-scale federal involvement with postsecondary education began with the enactment of the Higher Education Act of 1965 (HEA), which had provisions to fund libraries, sponsor community educational services, strengthen developing institutions, and expand student financial assistance. Periodically amended, HEA programs significantly expanded opportunities for poor and minority high school graduates to attend college. For example, the percentages of black and white high school graduates who go on to postsecondary education, greatly unequal in 1967, were roughly equal by 1976, though a far higher percentage of white students continued to attend four-year or other higher-status institutions. This section describes federal and state legislative activity since 1965 that dealt with financial assistance for individual students, aid to institutions for particular programmatic purposes, and other federal legislative mandates that influence higher education.

Financial Assistance to Students. Student financial assistance legislation between 1965 and 1981 was enacted roughly in four phases. The first phase was the passage of HEA, which established the need-based Educational Opportunity Grants program and the Guaranteed Student Loan program (GSL), which gave incentives to banks to offer low-interest loans to needy students. By 1968, the College Work-Study program, authorized independently in the Economic Opportunities Act of 1964, had been added to HEA.

The second phase took place within the context of a general debate over the most appropriate means of providing federal support for higher education. Observers could find no coherent or coordinating federal policy to hold the existing hodgepodge of higher education aids programs together. Concern over this situation led to a debate over whether federal support should take the form primarily of direct aid to students or to institutions.

Congress finally resolved this debate with enactment of the Education Amendments of 1972 by placing the major emphasis on direct aid to students. The heart of this approach is the Basic Educational Opportunity Grants (BEOG), now known as Pell Grants (after Senator Pell of Rhode Island), which provide funds to students on the basis of family income and college attendance costs. In order to help appease advocates of institutional assistance, Congress also authorized a set of supplementary aid programs that channel funds to colleges for disbursement to individual students. These programs included (1) the Supplemental Equal Opportunity Grants (SEOG) program, a revision of the old Equal Opportunity Grant provision; (2) the College Work-Study program; and (3) the National Direct Student Loan program, descended from NDEA. Finally, Congress authorized the State Student Incentive Grants (SSIG) program, which was designed to encourage states to provide supplemental grant aid to needy students. These programs, along with the GSL program, which was expanded in 1976 to involve the states heavily as lending agencies, offered comprehensive choices to students seeking assistance to pay college expenses. In 1978 over $4 billion in student assistance was disbursed through these programs, with the largest share (over $2 billion) coming through the BEOG program.

The third phase of activity culminated with the enactment of the Middle Income Student Assistance Act of 1978 (MISAA). Crafted in the heat of a legislative battle over tuition tax credits, MISAA was designated to provide more federal help to students from middle-income families. MISAA's major provisions amended the GSL and BEOG programs, making persons of any income eligible for loans that require no interest payments while schooling continues and increasing the maximum income eligibility limits for BEOGs from approximately $20,000 to $25,000.

The fourth phase is now in process. MISAA has fueled an explosive budgetary situation, through the GSL program, by obligating the federal government to pay interest and subsidies on greatly increased numbers of loans made by state and private agencies. With inflation as an aggravating condition, GSL program costs skyrocketed from less than $300 million in 1977 to over $1.8 billion projected for 1981. The rising expenditures, which have gone primarily to the upper-income public, banks, and state agencies, have been made at the expense of elementary, secondary, and higher education programs that serve the poor, the handicapped, and the otherwise needy.

By late 1979 the gravity of the budget situation and the fact that the distribution of student assistance funds was rapidly shifting away from the needy had become clear to the Carter administration. Administration proposals for the reauthorization of HEA in 1980 included attempts to extend heavily subsidized loans only to the needy, to curb the profits of the banks and other lenders, and to require students to contribute to their college payments through work. These proposals were uniformly beaten back by a coalition of higher education interest groups that encouraged Congress to pass a package of amendments that further increased benefits to the middle-income and upper-income students and to institutions of all sorts.

By July 1981, however, a dramatic shift in direction had occurred. The lack of restraint shown by interest groups and Congress in 1980 fueled a conservative coalition. The Reagan budget included proposals that would return the BEOG and GSL programs to their pre-1978, need-based status. These measures, passed by Congress, will result in an overall reduction in student assistance, bringing the programs closer to their original purpose of supplying aid to especially needy students. At the same time, however, the new administration is supporting the establishment of a tuition tax-credit program that would be as uncontrollable and regressive as the GSL program is now.

Institutional Aid. Although student financial assistance has by far the highest fiscal priority among federal programs focused on colleges and universities, the Congress has not been reluctant to authorize programs in other areas. HEA, for example, included provisions to provide general aid for developing institutions (Title III) and two-year community colleges (Title X). Congress enacted Title III primarily to assist the approximately 100 public and private predominantly black colleges. In order to generate sufficient votes to pass the measure the eligibility was expanded to include all institutions "struggling for survival." By the late 1970s Title III appropriations had grown to $120 million, serving over 500 institutions, including community colleges. Meanwhile, Title X, although periodically reauthorized by the Congress, has never been funded.

Colleges and universities may also receive grants under HEA legislation to provide targeted services for certain groups of students. The Trio Programs in Title IV, for example, are designed to assist institutions in their efforts to attract and maintain promising low-income and minority students. The largest of these programs is Upward Bound, which provides assistance for counseling, tutoring, and otherwise preparing needy high school students for entrance into college. Recent evaluations of this program clearly indicate that it makes it more likely that participating youngsters will attend and complete college. The second largest of these programs, Special Services, provides funds for institutions to assist poor and minority students once they are enrolled. Taken together these programs serve to support the equal opportunity emphasis of student aid programs such as BEOG.

HEA also authorized grants to institutions for expansion of facilities, improvement of college libraries, and development of programs to provide opportunities for older students. Also, in a provision similar in intent to Title V of ESEA, HEA provided assistance to states to develop and maintain higher education planning commissions. Over the years, HEA has expanded as Congress has found it easier to add than to delete authorizations. In 1972, for instance, Congress established the Fund for the Improvement of Postsecondary Education, a popular and effective program, which provided seed money to support a broad range of innovations in programs and operations. By 1980 the amendments to HEA contained 137 pages of legislation, thirteen titles and around fifty separate authorizations, including such legislation as the Urban Grant Universities program and the Navajo Community College Assistance program.

Mandates. Legislative and regulatory mandates have affected many areas of postsecondary education. Examples in the area of civil rights are mentioned above. Four other examples are discussed briefly here to indicate the breadth of application of these mandates. First, many statutes require that only institutions that have received accreditation from a nationally recognized accrediting agency or association may receive federal aid. While the congressional intention clearly is to establish safeguards of program quality and organizational substance, an attendant result has been to strengthen and greatly extend the power of the accrediting organizations vis-à-vis institutions of higher education. Second, with passage of the Occupational Safety and Health Act of 1970 (OSHA), Congress mandated that private postsecondary institutions provide working conditions free of "recognized hazards that are causing or are likely to cause death or serious physical harm." Although public institutions are exempt from OSHA, they generally must conform to parallel state regulations. Third, the Family Educational Rights and Privacy Act of 1974, known as the "Buckley Amendment," greatly extended students' rights regarding access to and control of their educational records. The Buckley Amendment, through regulations issued in 1976, has forced significant changes in record keeping policies and procedures at virtually all institutions of postsecondary education. Finally, the 1976 General Revision of the Copyright Law, which went into effect on January 1, 1978, was partially intended to clarify the scholarly and teaching use of copyrighted materials. Strict enforcement of this law has been hampered, however, by the revision's ambiguous language. Taken separately, the requirements imposed on colleges and universities by the various provisions generally seem sensible. The cumulative effect, however, of these and other requirements has been to foster an increasing dissatisfaction with federal involvement in higher education.

Conclusions

Serious federal government activism in education began during the mid-1960s with passage of the Civil Rights Act and the Economic Opportunity Act in 1964 and of the Elementary and Secondary Education Act and the Higher Education Act in 1965. By the late 1970s the federal presence was felt in almost every school and every institution of higher education in the country. Federal law and regulation provide guidelines for the education of children who are handicapped or who have limited proficiency in English and for the ways in which state and local funds are distributed among schools. At the university level the federal hand is felt in admissions, in hiring and firing policies, in the ways in which athletic departments expend funds, and in the manner in which research is conducted.

This extraordinary effort in social engineering has created great benefits. Students are no longer excluded from school because of their handicaps; low-achieving youngsters in schools in high-poverty areas are provided with special assistance to catch up with more advanced students, and women and girls have new opportunities for participation in sports. Perhaps most important, there has been an extraordinary increase in the enrollment of minority and poor students in college during the past fifteen years, an increase substantially attributable to the availability of student financial assistance.

By 1980 this era had culminated in three events—the passage of omnibus legislation in elementary and secondary education and in higher education and the legislative establishment of the cabinet-level Department of Education. Resulting partially from intense lobbying by the National Education Association, this legislation marks a pinnacle of federal interest and involvement in education. For the first time the top federal official in education reported directly to the president.

Yet, to many, the price for the success of the federal presence has been high. In a country where decentralized control over education is an article of faith, the provisions that have led the nation closer to equality of opportunity are seen as federal intrusion into the business of responsible local and state officials. Less than a year after the formation of the new department the nation elected a president who promised far less regulation and greatly reduced support for and control of such programs as bilingual education, special education, and compensatory education and the quick elimination of the Department of Education. By September 1981 President Reagan had been extraordinarily effective. Congress agreed to his request for a dramatically reduced budget; Title I of ESEA (now Chapter I of ECIA) has been greatly simplified; and over thirty small education programs have been consolidated (into Chapter II of ECIA) with control fully vested in state and local governments, and the uncontrolled BEOG and GSL programs have been contained. The next few years will see substantial controversy as this president attempts to carry out his remaining promises.

Marshall S. Smith
John W. Jenkins

See also Federal Influence on Education; Governance of Schools; Handicapped Individuals; Judicial Decisions; State Influences on Education; U.S. Department of Education.

REFERENCES

Brown, L. L., III, & Ginsburg, A. L. A Federal Role in the General Program of School Finance. In M. Timpane (Ed.), *The Federal Interest in Financing Schooling* (Rand Educational Policy Study). Cambridge, Mass.: Ballinger, 1978, 119–172.

Coleman, J. S.; Cambell, E. Q.; Hobson, C. J.; McPartland, J.; Mood, A. M.; Weinfeld, F. D.; & York, R. L. *Equality of Educational Opportunity.* Washington, D.C.: U.S. Government Printing Office, 1966.

Compensatory Education Study: Final Report to Congress from the National Institute of Education. Washington, D.C.: U.S. Department of Health, Education, and Welfare, 1978. (ERIC Document Reproduction Service No. ED 161 996)

Coons, J. E.; Clune, W. H., III; & Sugarman, S. D. *Private Wealth and Public Education.* Cambridge, Mass.: Harvard University Press, Belknap Press, 1970.

Elementary and Secondary Education Act of 1965, Section 101 (Public Law 89-10). In *A Compilation of Federal Education Laws: Volume 2—Elementary and Secondary Education and Related Programs as Amended through December 31, 1980.* Prepared for the use of the Committee on Education and Labor, House of Representatives. Washington, D.C.: U.S. Government Printing Office, 1981.

An interview on Title IX with Shirley Chisholm, Holly Knox, Leslie R. Wolfe, Cynthia G. Brown, and Mary Kaaren Jolly. *Harvard Educational Review,* 1979, *49,* 504.

McLaughlin, M. W. *Evaluation and Reform: the Elementary and Secondary Education Act of 1965, Title I* (R-1292-RC). Santa Monica, Calif.: Rand Corporation, January 1974.

Washington Research Project and NAACP Legal Defense and Education fund. *Title I of ESEA; Is It Helping Poor Children?* Washington, D.C.: Washington Research Report of the Southern Center for Studies in Public Policy and the NAACP Legal Defense and Educational Fund, 1969.

LIBRARIES

Throughout the development of civilization, up to the modern era, libraries and books played an integral part of cultural, political, and social development. Libraries tended to serve an archival function. The role of the library and the librarian was to store and provide access to materials, mostly books. Those responsibilities are the same today. However, the sheer volume of published materials has created strains on the archival function of the library. Although the output of books in the United States appears to have stabilized in the past decade, a large number are still produced. For example, in 1950 a total of 11,022 items were published, versus a fairly stable annual output of 30,000 to 35,000 during the 1970s (*Bowker Annual,* 1967, 1977, 1978). There is also an increase in variety and output by type of publication, such as periodicals, serials, media, and microforms. The total volume of materials added to U.S. libraries is staggering. For example, in 1976–1977 over 22 million bound volumes, 76 million government documents, 172 million microfilm physical units, and 88 million other items, such as audiovisuals, were added to academic libraries alone. Large numbers of volumes in libraries necessarily create space problems and a resulting difficulty in access. Added to the problem created by the large number of materials is the cost, which has grown dramatically in the past years. For example, the average price of a hardbound book increased from $12.20 in 1973 to $20.10 in 1978, and a serial for the same year went from $109.31 to $153.95 (*Bowker Annual,* 1979). Periodical subscriptions in particular have increased in price, more than doubling from an average of $16.20 in 1973 to an average of $34.54 in 1980 (*Library Journal,* 1980b).

The common view of libraries is that they are storehouses of the knowledge of civilization. However, the modern library, although still serving the archival function, also has an active, assertive role in providing information to users. The demands made on libraries to fulfill the needs of a wide variety of users are great. This is particularly true when one considers the size of the population, its changing age pattern and demographics, and the variability in information needs of users as diverse as the elementary school child and the research scientist.

Types of Libraries. Traditionally, libraries are viewed and categorized as institutional entities that serve a variety of user categories. These entities typically include the following: the 71,037 school libraries, which serve the needs of the learner from preschool through high school and the supporting professional staff; the 14,418 public libraries, which serve a wide range of clientele including children, young adults, people from local businesses and professions, readers of current best-sellers, shut-ins, researchers, and people from local government; 4,129 academic libraries, which serve the educational needs of students, faculty, and researchers in community colleges, undergraduate colleges, and universities; and 29,897 special libraries, which serve the specific information needs of people in such diverse areas as law, medicine, religion, business, and technology (*Bowker Annual,* 1979). In addition, technological advances have made possible the storage and retrieval of information outside the library institution or building; this includes the operations of information brokers, who, for a fee, provide on-line computer searching and document retrieval and reproduction.

Academic. Academic libraries include a range of institutions, from large research libraries such as that of Harvard University, with holdings of approximately 10 million volumes and an operating budget of more than $14 million in 1977 (Beazley, 1980), to small, private institutions with barely adequate resources and funding. Even though these libraries differ in size, they face similar problems. These include a decline in overall support and in student enrollments (DeGennaro, 1979). Additionally, inflation has created dramatic increases in book prices, postal rates, and salaries and wages. But even though these problems exist, attempts are being made to continue to satisfy the information needs of faculty and students. One of the major thrusts in the use of bibliographic utilities is the sharing and coproduction of catalog copy through organizations such as OCLC, Inc., and Research Libraries Information Network (RLIN); this reduces or holds constant the rise in processing costs. These utilities provide additional services as by-products, such as computerized interlibrary loan services. OCLC is by far the larger utility, with approximately 2,000 users and a data base of more than 6 million bibliographic records (*American Libraries,* 1980). However, RLIN, an outgrowth of the BALLOTS system developed at Stanford University, is utilized by a number of prestigious academic research libraries, such as Yale and New York University, and by research-oriented special libraries. Services provided by these utilities will expand into other processing areas of the library, such as acquisition and serials.

In order to make users aware of their services and to educate them in the complexities of library use, academic libraries have been active in developing bibliographic instruction programs. This interest has led to the development of a wide variety of instructional media for use in library orientation and bibliographic instruction programs and to the evaluation of such programs (Lubans, 1974). To assist the academic library in developing instructional programs, the Association of College and Research Libraries (ACRL) has formulated a standard set of behavioral objectives for library instruction purposes (*College and Research Libraries News,* 1975).

Three projects that stand out in the history of orientation and bibliographic instruction are those at Monteith College, Earlham College, and Sangamon State University. The Monteith College experiment was a tightly structured program that had as its goal the incorporation of library instruction into the core curriculum of the college. The legacy of the Monteith experiment is a body of tested library instruction materials. It was the first program to provide a means for testing, quantifying, and therefore scientifically evaluating a bibliographic instruction pro-

gram (Knapp, 1966). A similar project was the Earlham College program, which undertook a plan of integrated library instruction in 1965. The integrated library instruction program offered in the English and biology departments comes closest to the ideal course envisioned by the Earlham librarians (Kennedy, Kirk, & Weaver, 1971)

Another approach to solving the problem of library instruction is the teaching library, which has been successfully utilized at Sangamon State University in Springfield, Illinois. In addition to producing guides to library resources and teaching workshops in library research, Sangamon's librarians acted as liaisons between the library and the faculty. The librarians taught those portions of courses that would ultimately require the students to use the library in preparation of class projects. Students who evaluated the program reported that their skills in using the library had improved. Some faculty members suggested that their teaching methods had improved after their exposure to innovations demonstrated or suggested by the librarians (Dillon, 1975).

One of the most significant accomplishments of the Sangamon program for librarianship was the development of a job description for the instructional services librarian. This new position has great importance for the future of library instruction and for the future of reference services in academic libraries. The existence of these job descriptions indicates that academic libraries and librarians are beginning to acknowledge that much of the current problem in library instruction centers on the coordination of existing bibliographic instruction activities. The methods and techniques for solving the problem exist and many of these are already in use in academic libraries. The problem currently being faced by librarians is how to organize these techniques into a program that will produce desired objectives. Today a trend is emerging to use an instructional services librarian to unify and coordinate techniques and programs into one program with concrete goals and objectives. Librarians feel that with proper planning such a program is assured of success.

Management issues have been a major concern of academic librarians. These include such diverse issues as library evaluation and personnel classification. To assist in evaluation, the ACRL has developed a set of qualitative standards that can be used to measure the strengths and weaknesses of a university library. The widely discussed Pittsburgh Study analyzed the use of library materials and the cost of such use. The findings, such as the high percentage of books that never circulate (39.8 percent of 1969–1975 acquisitions) and the high unit total cost for in-house science journal use ($4.12 for physics journals and $10.07 for mathematics journals), raised more issues than they resolved. Additionally, the investigators were open to attack on the basis of their research methodology and statistics from both the library profession and the faculty library committee at the university (*Use of Library Materials,* 1979). However, this type of study is crucial since it is imperative that such issues be addressed.

The issue of whether or not librarians are considered teaching faculty is critical for many librarians, faculty members, and administrators. This issue relates not only to status but also to salary and benefits. In some institutions, librarians are equal in all respects to the teaching faculty; in other instances they are considered academic or administrative employees with a different salary and benefit schedule. Many academic librarians who have faculty rank now must be evaluated by the same criteria as teaching faculty, which can include the publishing requirement. Other academic librarians face the issues of unionization, certification, and participatory management. Personnel and other management issues are complex in academic libraries when the size of the budget, type of personnel, and complex user demands are considered. The Association of Research Libraries (ARL) Office of Management Studies is assisting academic librarians by developing self-study programs and management skills training (*American Library Association Yearbook*, 1980). Additionally, the Council on Library Resources (CLR) has funded the Academic Library Management Intern Program to provide midcareer librarians the opportunity to work with the administrative staff of outstanding major academic libraries (*Bowker Annual*, 1979).

Public. During the past several decades, public libraries experienced growth and fairly stable local financial support. But the changing economic climate has created a wide variety of problems. Perhaps California's Proposition 13 and similar tax relief measures in other states have been the most visible of the financial issues facing public libraries. For the most part, these measures reduced the overall amount of money available to public libraries. Additionally, they now have to compete more earnestly with other city and county agencies for operating support. But many public libraries faced these budget-cutting issues squarely and looked for means to continue providing service. These efforts included the merger of city and county systems, use of volunteers and CETA employees, and intertype library cooperation. Like school libraries, public libraries have utilized cooperative networks and systems for sharing resources, services, processing, and machine-readable bibliographic information. Besides OCLC and RLIN, these network services and systems include the Washington Library Network (WLN) and the California Library Authority for Systems and Services (CLASS). Additionally, some local, state, federal, and foundation support, in the form of sources for materials, and cultural and educational programs, has come to the aid of public libraries.

But even while public libraries are facing financial issues, they are in the process of building new services and programs in addition to the more traditional ones, such as story hours for children, film lending, and reading clubs. Some of these new services include services to minority groups, such as bilingual programs for Hispanics, and innovative programs such as microcomputers for patron use. There is a continuing discussion among public library tra-

ditionalists and social activists as to the role the library should play in providing these types of programs and services. The issue is further aggravated by the present state of public funding.

In addition to the financial issues, public libraries are currently experiencing a number of changes in patterns of governance. The first of these is the trend away from lay-board governance toward management by professional administrators. The second change is the increasing development of jurisdictional and contractual ties between libraries and local jurisdictional units. Increasingly, libraries are coming under the payroll, finance, and operating procedures established by their local city or county government. A third change is the increased prominence and power of the city or county manager as the chief administrative agent, with broad authority over the budgets and affairs of all local agencies, including libraries. These changes are due to new state and local legislation (Molz, 1979).

School. Like academic libraries, school libraries face problems of declining support and declining student enrollments. Like public libraries, they face the financial problems created by a depressed economy and requirements imposed by legislation, such as Public Law 94-142, the Education for All Handicapped Children Act. As a result, there is retrenchment and change in school library print and media services and programs.

Like the educational enterprise in general, school libraries have had to address the issue of accountability. They have been forced to prove that they are necessary to the overall educational program. As a result, there is greater interest in research to document the impact of school library and library media programs. Positive attempts are being made to help reduce costs and to justify programs. These include networks and computerization, association with groups of allied interest, and leadership from a professionally active association, the American Association of School Librarians (AASL) (*American Library Association Yearbook*, 1980).

Special. The wide array of libraries that are found in private business and industrial organizations and governmental agencies, as well as in large universities or public library settings, are more dissimilar than alike. But they share a common denominator: they exist to serve the user needs of a specific organization, which typically has a subject-matter orientation. Thus the organization, management, resources, and services of these libraries vary considerably, depending on those needs. Of all types of libraries, special libraries probably house the widest range of types of materials. These include books, documents, reports, reprints, microforms, magnetic computer records and files on tape and disk, all types of internally generated records and data, and the widest range of media and realia. These materials create a level of processing and access complexity unknown in types of libraries that deal primarily with books.

Certain common trends are evident in special libraries.

In general, the number of such libraries has increased; and membership in the Special Libraries Association (SLA), one of the main professional organizations, has increased 30 percent, to 11,000 professional members, in the past five years (*American Library Association Yearbook*, 1980). The utilization of online searching is common in many types of special libraries, such as medical libraries (MEDLINE), science and technology libraries (NASA/RECON and data bases available through ORBIT, DIALOG, and BRS), and law libraries (LEXIS and WESTLAW) (Williams, 1979). A more recent development is the utilization of nonbibliographic data bases that provide the actual data rather than a citation to the data. Examples of these data bases include Chase Econometrics, Predicasts, Annual Time Series, and Manlabs (*Directory of Online Databases*, 1979). The utilization of the computer is not limited to reference and search services, for special libraries have been leaders in the development of in-house computerized library processing systems.

Special libraries face many of the same problems confronting academic, public, and school libraries. These include the critical issues of finance and changing patterns of use. But all these types of libraries, to a certain degree, have additional issues in common.

Copyright. On January 1, 1978, the new copyright law became effective. Major aspects of the law relating to libraries include the following:

1. It is the opinion of legal scholars that authorship suggests automatic copyright; thus there is no need to publish or register the copyright. But those desiring full protection should register.
2. Copyright protection is guaranteed regardless of form. The copy need not necessarily be in human-readable form.
3. The fair-use requirement is outlined in more detail; for example, copying should not be for commercial use.
4. A notice of copyright must be included in reproduced copy.
5. Libraries can make a copy of a periodical article or small portion of another work with no copyright infringement if the copyright statement from the Register of Copyright is displayed.
6. Entire works can be photocopied if another copy is not available at fair prices and if the copy is for personal use.
7. Photocopying is allowed for interlibrary loan purposes. However, interlibrary loans should not be considered a substitute for purchase or subscription (Keplinger, 1980).

Although the law is complex and there are problems of interpretation, it seems to be working well. Areas that still need to be analyzed include the overall effects of the law and the impact on access to and flow of information. Still left unresolved is the major issue of off-the-air taping for educational use.

Part of the requirement of the law is a report to Congress in five-year intervals by the Register of Copyrights. Meetings have already occurred regarding the law's photocopying aspect. Some areas of examination for this review include an analysis of library data on interlibrary loan photocopying, a determination of corporate library compliance to the law, an analysis of the relationship between libraries and publishers' permission departments, and a review of the payment practices by reprint and document fulfillment agencies (*Bowker Annual*, 1979)

Intellectual Freedom. A related legal issue is censorship in libraries. The basic tenet of intellectual freedom for libraries is the defense of the principle of free access to any book, film, or other material in their collections so as to allow analysis of all points of view. The Library Bill of Rights, an official American Library Association (ALA) statement on intellectual freedom, and the ALA Committee on Intellectual Freedom provide the basic policy and professional support to safeguard intellectual freedom for library users.

The basic tenet of intellectual freedom has been under attack many times in libraries, and instances of censorship continue to be reported and acted upon. Even the library profession itself is not immune to its own intellectual freedom issue. The ALA produced a film, *The Speaker*, on the issue of intellectual freedom and the First Amendment. A group of librarians created a furor when they requested the removal of the film from circulation because of its purportedly racist viewpoint. However, acting under great negative pressure, the ALA council (the governing board of the association) upheld the basic tenet of freedom of access (Berninghausen, 1979).

User Fees. Traditionally, modern publicly funded library services have been free. Citizens pay taxes that are allocated to agencies, such as the library, which in turn provide services to users. Although there have been instances where fees have been assessed, it was not until the advent of computer searching in libraries, new information demands, the growth of the information industry, and the changing economic climate that the issue became of interest. The debate centers on various arguments: for example, that fees discriminate against users who do not have resources to pay for services and reduce public backing for tax-supported information services. On the other side of the argument, fees can provide a source of alternate funding in an era of destabilized tax support. The current practice in libraries varies, with some libraries adamantly opposed to fees and others offering selected services on a fee basis (Waldhart & Bellardo, 1980).

Cataloging Rules. A major topic of recent concern in many libraries is the Anglo-American Cataloging Rules, second edition (AACR2), which requires librarians to learn new rules and to inaugurate various new procedures. For example, AACR2 requires new subject headings and changes in the body of the cataloging record. The decision by the Library of Congress to introduce AACR2 impacts on libraries throughout the United States that rely heavily on Library of Congress catalog copy. Along with the adoption of AACR2, the Library of Congress decided to close its catalog and inaugurate an on-line catalog with a temporary backup new card catalog. This approach is logical, since linking old and new records in a large catalog would be an expensive operation and probably create more difficulties for the user than closing the old catalog and beginning a new one. Other libraries are considering following the same or a similar pattern. If a library decides not to close its catalog, the new rules could require the change of a portion of its headings or the provision of a large number of "see also" references. The percentage of changes and cost of such linking between old and new is still being debated by the profession, but it may be a major cost to libraries. There are many questions still unanswered in this area, such as the impact of AACR2 on reference services, library processing routine, and various users. Results from experience will be available after 1981, when the Library of Congress inaugurates its plan (Gaspen & Juergens, 1980).

Physical Environment.   Libraries face numerous issues associated with their operating physical environment. Construction has continued in all types of libraries, but overall the number of new facilities has been reduced. For example, the number of new public library buildings is down, from a high of 187 new facilities in 1976 to 90 in 1980 (*Library Journal*, 1980c). The number of remodeled facilities, however, appears to be fairly stable over the past ten years. Of particular concern to libraries has been the emphasis on energy conservation and providing access for the handicapped.

Preservation of materials is of vital concern, with libraries microfilming certain materials and attempting to stop deterioration of older materials through deacidification efforts. Unfortunately, there is no existing technique for mass deacidification. Temperature and humidity contribute to material decay, and recently a new freeze-drying process developed by the National Aeronautics and Space Administration and used by Stanford University in 1979 has been effective in restoring water-damaged books (Buchanan, 1979).

Besides preserving materials, libraries need to secure them from theft. Theft of library materials has increased, and the problem of replacing them is compounded by their high cost, assuming replacements can be located. Many libraries (approximately 6,500 by 1979) have installed security systems. It has been estimated that such security systems pay for themselves in three years (*American Library Association Yearbook*, 1980).

Developments.   Today libraries face many challenges, but they have utilized a number of measures and innovations to fulfill their mission. Some of these include the use of technology, the application of management science and operations research methodologies, and the beginnings of the development of a national library and information plan.

Technology.   The use of technology in the form of computers and micrographics has become increasingly more common in libraries in order to reduce costs, increase services, ease storage problems, and facilitate access. The computer has been used in libraries since the early 1960s to automate various library subsystems or departments, such as acquisitions and serials. Other uses include the development of integrated library systems based on processing the library's primary file, the catalog (Hayes & Becker, 1974). Today there are a number of trends evident in computer applications to libraries. These include the development of computer mainframe-based bibliographic networks and utilities, such as OCLC, RLIN, and WLN, and the on-line data bases available from data-base vendors such as Lockheed, System Development Corporation, and BRS. Other developments include the trend toward the procurement of turn-key systems, or total systems available from vendors. These systems tend to be minicomputer-based and are primarily directed to providing circulation control. Examples of minicomputer-based circulation systems include CLSI, GEAC, and Dataphase (Grosch, 1979). Because these circulation systems require some bibliographic data in storage, a current data-processing issue relates to the interface of bibliographic utilities to these minicomputer-based circulation systems (Boss, 1979). Additionally, libraries are beginning to use microcomputers for text-processing and word-processing functions, for the preparation of local bibliographies, and as a method for improving on-line data-base searching (Pratt, 1980).

Microforms are a common means of storing information in libraries. Initially, this included storage on microfilm of the back files of periodicals and newspapers. In addition, entire document collections, such as *ERIC* and *NASA*, became available on microfiche. These collections are particularly useful in supporting requests for materials emanating from on-line searching. Recently, libraries have begun to use computer-output microfilm (COM) as a replacement for card files or computer printouts. Numerous libraries now have their catalog on computer-generated microfilm. Additionally, COM is being used as a publishing mechanism. For example, the Library of Congress subject headings are available on computer-generated microfiche (Saffady, 1978).

Both systems analysis and community needs analysis have been used in libraries: systems analysis primarily as a prelude to computerization, and community needs analysis as a prelude to development of new services. One of the most promising, although complex, methodologies is operations research (OR). Using OR, a manager can conceptualize library operations by means of mathematical models. The correct utilization of OR methodologies can lead to valid management decisions. Many OR techniques applied to libraries have been borrowed from the military, business, and industry (Bookstein & Kochen, 1979). These techniques include queuing theory, a method of analyzing waiting lines. This technique has direct applicability to library circulation lines (Hindle, Buckland, & Brophy, 1976). Other OR methods, referred to as bibliometric techniques, are specifically related to the nature of literature and information. Examples include Lotka's law, which deals with information productivity; Zipf's law, which deals with regularity in the number of times words appear in a text; and Bradford's law of scattering, which indicates that citations appear over all the journal literature of a discipline but a core set of journals exists that has a high percentage of the citations. These findings have implications for libraries in that the core set of journals in a discipline could be the titles that are selected for purchase. Bibliometric studies have become easier to perform owing to the development of computer-citation indexing, specifically through processing computer files available from the Institute for Scientific Information, such as *Science Citation Index* (Garfield, 1979).

Library and information planning. Information and libraries are considered a national resource. As a resource they need planning and coordination. The National Commission on Libraries and Information Science (NCLIS), a permanent, independent federal agency, is responsible for coordinating national library and information efforts. One of its main activities was the planning and conducting of the White House Conference on Library and Information Services, held November 15–19, 1979, in Washington, D.C. In order to obtain the largest amount of input for the conference, NCLIS coordinated a series of fifty-seven preconferences held in each state and territory and other jurisdictions. In addition, a number of theme conferences and planning sessions were held before the conference. Numerous national professional library associations assisted NCLIS in developing the conference. These included the American Association of Law Librarians (AALL), the American Association of Library Schools (AALS), the American Library Association (ALA), the American Society for Information Science (ASIS), and the Special Libraries Association (SLA). Other related information associations, such as the Information Industry Association (IIA), were also involved. The conference itself went smoothly and provided a vehicle for citizens and librarians to express their concerns for libraries in the 1980s. The conference reaffirmed the concept of intellectual freedom, requested that citizens not be restricted from access to information by the imposition of fees, endorsed a national library act, and recommended the development of a comprehensive, multitype library network with coordination performed by a library authority housed within the Department of Education (*Library Journal*, 1980a). The development of these networks interrelates closely with advances in technology, but the development of nationwide library networks is a complex undertaking, with numerous bibliographic, technical, and governance issues to be resolved in addition to a determination of the economic viability of such a system (Avram, 1978).

Library schools. The complexity of all these issues has a direct bearing on educational programs for librarians. Today library schools are facing challenges to which they must respond if the institutions are to continue to survive

as strong components of the library and information science profession. From one side, the schools face challenges brought about by their very nature, such as costs for operation due to inflation and steadily increasing fixed costs. From another side, a challenge arises from pressures brought by the schools' constituency, the profession, and the professionals. At this moment, for example, there is a basic attack on the validity of the Master of Library Science as a entry credential for the profession. Certification programs have been developed in response to attempts to satisfy affirmative action needs. Certain groups have not had an opportunity to become librarians because of various kinds of discrimination, and through certification they can now have access to these positions. Another challenge comes from the massive changes occurring in society. The impact of technological change has resulted in a need for new courses and approaches to information and library science. User needs are vastly more complex and there is a variety of sophisticated technological options for accessing a wide variety of information.

Library schools today are struggling to adapt themselves to the pressures and problems of providing high-quality, effective library education. Some schools have recently implemented changes in their programs. The University of North Carolina, the University of Southern California, the University of Toronto, and the University of California at Los Angeles are examples. Each school has made specific adaptations in its educational program, but emphasis is on theory, curriculum revision, development of two-year programs, establishment of interdisciplinary efforts, research activities, and development of information and media technologies laboratories (Darling & Belanger, 1980). Changed curricula and related activities for the formal degree are not the only methods by which library schools are meeting current instructional challenges. In order to extend their activities and their perceived education responsibilities, library schools have instituted career and professional development programs of continuing education.

These developments indicate that library schools are adapting to current challenges. The changes being made are means by which the demands of traditional librarianship, as well as those of the new information professions, can be met in a single unified program.

Edward Kazlauskas

See also Archives and Records Management; Information Management and Computing; Media Use in Education; Museums; New Technologies in Education.

REFERENCES

American Libraries, 1980, *11*, 262–279.
American Library Association Yearbook: A Review of Library Events, 1979. Chicago: The Association, 1980.
Avram, D. Towards a nationwide library network. *Journal of Library Automation*, 1978, *11*, 285–298.
Beazley, M. *Library Statistics of Colleges and Universities: 1977*

Institutional Data. Washington, D.C.: U.S. Department of Education, 1980.

Berninghausen, K. Intellectual freedom in librarianship: Advances and retreats. *Advances in Librarianship,* 1979, *9,* 1–29.

Bookstein, A., & Kochen, M. Operations research in libraries. *Advances in Librarianship,* 1979, *9,* 143–184.

Boss, R. W. General trends in implementation of automated circulation systems. *Journal of Library Automation,* 1979, *12,* 198–202.

Bowker Annual of Library and Book Trade Information. New York: Bowker, 1967, 1977, 1978, 1979.

Buchanan, S. The Stanford Library Flood Restoration Project. *College and Research Libraries,* 1979, *40,* 539–548.

College and Research Libraries News, 1975, *36,* 137–139, 169–171.

Darling, L. R., & Belanger, T. *Extended Library Education Program* (Proceedings of a Conference Held at the School of Library Service, Columbia University, March 1980). New York: Columbia University, 1980.

DeGennaro, R. Research libraries enter the information age. *Library Journal,* 1979, *104,* 2405–2410.

Dillon, H. W. Organizing the academic library for instruction. *Journal of Academic Librarianship,* 1975, *1*(4), 4–7.

Directory of Online Databases. Santa Monica, Calif.: Cuadra Associates, Inc., 1979.

Garfield, E. *Citation Indexing: Its Theory and Application in Science, Technology, and Humanities.* New York: Wiley, 1979.

Gaspen, D. K., & Juergens, B. (Eds.). *Closing the Catalog* (Proceedings of the 1978 and 1979 Library and Information Technology Association Institutes). Phoenix: Oryx Press, 1980.

Grosch, N. *Minicomputers in Libraries, 1979–1980.* White Plains, N.Y.: Knowledge Industry Publications, 1979.

Hayes, R. M., & Becker, J. *Handbook of Data Processing for Libraries.* New York: Wiley, 1974.

Hindle, A.; Buckland, M. K.; & Brophy, T. The techniques of operations research. *Reader in Operations Research for Libraries.* Englewood, Colo.: Information Handling Service, 1976, pp. 3–28.

Kennedy, J. R.; Kirk, T. G.; & Weaver, G. A. Course-related library institution: A case study of the English and biology departments at Earlham College. *Drexel Library Quarterly,* 1971, *1,* 282–291.

Keplinger, M. S. Copyright and information technology. *Annual Review of Information Science and Technology,* 1980, *15,* 3–33.

Knapp, P. *The Monteith College Library Experiment.* Metuchen, N.J.: Scarecrow Press, 1966.

Library Journal, 1980, *105,* 149–166. (a)

Library Journal, 1980, *105,* 1486–1491. (b)

Library Journal, 1980, *105,* 2469–2477. (c)

Lubans, J., Jr. (Ed.). *Educating the Library User.* New York: Bowker, 1974.

Molz, K. Issues of goverance and their implication for libraries. *Library Trends,* 1979, *27,* 299–313.

Pratt, A. D. The use of microcomputers in libraries. *Journal of Library Automation,* 1980, *13,* 7–17.

Saffady, W. *Computer-Output Microfilm: Its Library Application.* Chicago: American Library Association, 1978.

Use of Library Materials: The University of Pittsburgh Study. New York: Dekker, 1979.

Waldhart, T. J., & Bellardo, T. User fees in publicly funded libraries. *Advances in Librarianship,* 1980, *9,* 31–61.

Williams, M. E. *Computer-readable Data Bases: A Directory and Data Source Book.* Washington, D.C.: American Society for Information Science, 1979.

LICENSING AND CERTIFICATION

There are over eight hundred occupations in the United States that can be practiced only after one has received permission to do so from a government agency (Greene & Gay, forthcoming). There are hundreds of other occupations in which use of a designated occupational title is restricted. The former group of occupations are "licensed"; the latter are "certified."

Definition. "Licensing" is defined "as a process by which an agency or government grants permission to an individual to engage in a given occupation upon finding that the applicant has attained the minimal degree of competency required to ensure that the public health, safety, and welfare will be reasonably well protected" (U.S. Department of Health, Education, and Welfare, 1977, p. 1).

Licensing laws are sometimes referred to as "practice acts" because they usually contain "scope of practice" statements, which define what a licensed practitioner may do. It is illegal for anyone not licensed to engage in any of the activities defined by the scope of practice. Typical examples of licensed occupations are architects, barbers, certified public accountants, cosmetologists, dentists, electricians, engineers, funeral directors, nurses, pharmacists, physicians, and veterinarians.

"Certification" is a process by which a governmental or nongovernmental agency grants recognition to an individual who has met certain predetermined qualifications set by the credentialing agency. Certification is sometimes referred to as a form of "title control." It is a way of identifying individuals who have met some standard. Unlike licensure, a certification law does not prohibit uncertified individuals from practicing their occupations. However, only those who have met the standards and have been credentialed are permitted to use a designated title. A wide range of occupational and professional groups conduct voluntary certification programs, including auto mechanics, travel agents, medical technologists, and dental assistants.

In certain professions, especially in the health area, licensing and certification are part of a two-tiered system. For example, physicians must be licensed by a state in order to practice. However, they may voluntarily seek to be certified by one of the twenty-three nongovernmental medical specialty boards. Boards certify physicians in such fields as internal medicine, surgery, psychiatry, and general practice. Physicians seeking certification voluntarily agree to submit their credentials and to take examinations to demonstrate a higher level of competence than that required for licensing. Certification usually carries with it considerable prestige and is often a determining factor in hospital appointments.

Development. Licensing in the United States evolved out of social necessity. Prior to the enactment of state licensure laws in the late 1800s, anyone could practice medicine, dentistry, pharmacy, or other professions, regardless of whether he or she had received appropriate training. Quacks and charlatans abounded. Some of the professions attempted to cope with the problem by forming societies that would admit to membership only those practitioners who could meet minimum training and experience requirements and who were willing to subscribe to the societies' codes of ethics. Whereas unqualified practitioners could not gain admission to the society, they could nevertheless continue to practice because there was no legal prohibition against it.

Frustrated by their inability to prevent unqualified individuals from practicing, leaders of several health-related professional societies asked their state legislatures to invoke the police power of the state to prevent practice by individuals who might do harm to the public health, safety, or welfare. State legislatures responded by passing licensing laws setting forth general qualifications for licensure and establishing licensing boards made up of practitioners from the licensed occupations to implement the laws. These boards were given broad authority to set specific training and experience requirements, to examine applicants regarding their fitness to practice, to set standards of practice and conduct, and to discipline licensees who failed to adhere to the boards' standards. Boards were also granted a high degree of autonomy in carrying out their licensing responsibilities. For example, they had the power to promulgate rules and regulations, which had the force of law, as long as they were acting within the framework established by the enabling legislation.

Since the purpose of licensing is to protect the public health, safety, and welfare, licensing boards are supposed to be concerned with establishing minimum standards, which are intended to exclude only those who lack sufficient competence to provide services in a safe and effective manner. Certification agencies, by contrast, usually set considerably higher standards. Certification is supposed to signify that the individual is well-qualified, not merely "minimally qualified," as in licensure.

Requirements. Except for the fact that standards may differ as to level of competence required, licensing and certification agencies tend to follow similar procedures in awarding credentials. Meeting specified training and experience requirements is usually a prerequisite to taking a competency examination. Each of these qualifying hurdles will be examined separately.

Training. Most licensing and certification agencies require that training be received in an accredited institution or in a school or program that has been approved by the agency. Thus, access to certain types of training experience can determine whether or not an individual will be eligible for licensure. If accrediting agencies withdraw accreditation from training institutions or deny accreditation to new institutions, the supply of licensed practitioners can be limited, since the output of training institutions (on which eligibility depends) will be restricted.

In the skilled trades, access to apprenticeship programs can also limit the number of individuals who will be licensed. For example, an electrician's licensing board may decree that only those who complete an approved electrical trades apprenticeship program will be eligible for licensure. Graduates of secondary or postsecondary vocational training programs would not be allowed to take the licensing examination even though they might have received training of high quality and be fully competent to perform entry-level functions. In certain fields, such as cosmetology, traditional training programs usually specify that students must complete a specified number of hours of training before they are allowed to take the licensing examination. In Oregon, the Board of Barbers and Hairdressers has approved a competency-based curriculum that enables students to proceed through the program at their own rates and to be examined when they have completed course units covering all the required skills. They are not required to complete a fixed number of hours of training. A study by Chilson (1980), a psychologist-educator who owns a cosmetology school in Hillsboro, Oregon, found that in the opinion of employers surveyed, graduates of his competency-based program are just as competent as those trained in traditional programs. Moreover, the earnings of graduates of the competency-based program are equal to or better than those of graduates of traditional programs.

Experience. In a number of fields such as nursing or physical therapy, clinical experience is part of the curriculum. In many of the skilled trades, experience is gained through apprenticeship. In many other fields, however, the training itself may be highly theoretical, and trainees are expected to gain experience after they have completed their formal training. Such experience is supposed to provide assurance that the licensed or certified individual will be able to function independently in a safe and effective manner.

Legislatures that have incorporated experience requirements into licensing laws seem to have done so on a case-by-case basis without regard to similarities among occupations. In California, a dispensing optician who fits and sells eye glasses only upon prescription of an optometrist or an opthalmologist must have five years of experience before becoming eligible for licensure. Yet a hearing aid dispenser who diagnoses hearing disorders and fits and sells hearing aids is not required to have any experience.

In an effort to determine the reasonableness of prior experience as a requirement for licensure, Cathcart and Graff (1978) evaluated each of fifty-eight licensed occupations in California in terms of three factors: (1) seriousness of impact on consumers; (2) need for discretion on the part of the licensee; and (3) need for additional practical training beyond formal coursework. Their analysis showed wide discrepancies in the experience requirement among occupations with similar scores on the three rating factors. Despite the confusion and contradictions inherent in their findings, Cathcart and Graff do not propose the abolition of the experience requirement. Rather, they suggest that more refined procedures are needed to determine the appropriateness and length of experience as a requirement.

Examinations and other procedures. Those who meet the training and experience prerequisites are usually required to demonstrate on an examination that they possess the knowledge, skills, and other abilities needed for the level of performance attested to by the credential.

In order to ascertain what should be measured by the examination, most licensing and certification agencies conduct some type of occupational analysis. In its simplest form, such an analysis may represent little more than the judgments of practitioners associated with the board or agency. In some situations, the agency may call on experts from the field to pool their judgments on what represents a minimum (or higher) level of competence. Increasingly, licensing and certification agencies are having formal job analyses performed by their testing consultants to identify not only the abilities required, but also the extent to which each ability is critical and whether it can be learned on the job or must be acquired prior to job entry. On the basis of such analyses, test specifications are developed and suitable examinations are devised to assess the most critical job dimensions that are measurable in a fair and reliable way. Because of difficulties in measurement, potential for abuse, and limited financial resources, most boards measure only the cognitive aspects of the job, using written multiple choice tests, and to a lesser extent, essay and oral tests. Performance tests are used in a number of fields, including dentistry, cosmetology, and opthalmic dispensing. However, because of the high cost of administering and scoring such tests, most licensing boards tend to rely on accredited training institutions to attest to the performance skills of their graduates.

A survey of assessment practices of forty-two health certifying agencies revealed that thirty-seven were using multiple-choice tests. However, many supplemented these with other types of tests. Sixteen agencies used essay tests, fifteen used practical (performance) tests, six used oral examinations, and two used paper and pencil simulation exercises, often referred to in the medical field as "patient management problems" (National Commission for Health Certifying Agencies, 1980, p. 26).

If tests are to be useful for making licensure or certification decisions, it is essential that they be reliable (consistent) and valid. "Validity" refers to the correctness of the inferences that are drawn from a particular set of test scores. When planning a validation study one should have a clear idea of the purpose for which the test will be used. In an employment situation one usually uses scores to predict which applicants will turn out to be most successful on the job. For this purpose, "criterion-related validity"

is an appropriate validation strategy. In the licensing or certification situation, the purpose of the test is to identify those applicants who must meet a specific competence standard. For this purpose, "content validity" is an appropriate validation strategy.

In order to demonstrate the content validity of a test, one must be able to show that the test questions and problems are representative of a specified job-content domain, of which the test is a sample. The content domain is usually defined by conducting some type of job analysis to identify important behaviors required for safe and effective performance. Crucial questions to be answered are: (1) Do the test questions and problems assess the performance or the knowledge, skills, and abilities that the scores are intended to represent? (2) Are the different tasks, skills, and areas of knowledge represented at the levels of complexity and in the proportions indicated by the intended interpretation of the scores?

On a licensing test, the scores are intended to represent a level of knowledge and skill that will provide reasonable assurance that the public health, safety, and welfare will be protected. On a certification test, intended to signify a higher level of competence, one would expect to find tasks of suitable complexity represented in proportion to their importance in the work situation.

Some measurement experts such as Hecht (1979) and Hogan (1979) believe that licensing and certification examinations should be validated against job-related performance criteria in the same manner as are employment tests. However, in order to carry out a criterion-related validity study, one needs suitable criteria by which to judge the performance of those in the job. Such criterion measures are more likely to be available in the employment situation than in the licensing or certification situation. When job applicants are tested and later hired for job openings, they usually work for the same employer, perform similar tasks, and are expected to adhere to common performance standards. It is thus possible to relate scores on the selection test to a performance criterion (productivity, sales, supervisory ratings). If those who rank high on the selection test also rank high on the performance criterion, the test is likely to be useful for selecting new employees because it *predicts* future performance.

In the licensing/certification situation, the agency that administers the test and grants the credential is not an employer. Once individuals have been licensed or certified, it is up to them to find suitable employment. Unlike the job applicants who were tested and then placed in similar jobs with a single employer, those who are licensed or certified are likely to work for many different employers at many different jobs and in many different settings. For example, newly licensed physicians may go into private practice, work in a clinic, engage in public health activities, or take administrative positions in a hospital. Although all will be legally authorized to practice medicine, what they actually do on the job and the standards by which their work will be evaluated will vary from situation to situation. Finding or developing suitable performance criteria by which to evaluate licensing or certification tests for physicians would be a difficult task. For these reasons, carrying out criterion-related validity studies of specific licensing or certification tests may not be technically feasible.

Legal Considerations. As tests and other assessment procedures have come to play an increasingly important role in the lives of people seeking employment, advancement, or some type of credential, they have come under increased legal scrutiny. Beginning with the landmark U.S. Supreme Court decision, *Griggs* v. *Duke Power Company* (1971), most judicial inquiry to date has been into the "job-relatedness" of selection and promotion examinations. Standards for validating tests and other procedures used for selection and promotion are discussed in considerable detail in the *Uniform Guidelines on Employee Selection Procedures* (U.S. Government, 1978) as well as in the *Principles for the Validation and Use of Personnel Selection Procedures* issued by the Division of Industrial Organizational Psychology of the American Psychological Association (1980). The *Guidelines* are a set of technical standards for the validation of those selection procedures used in employment that have an "adverse impact" (disproportionate exclusionary effect) on members of classes protected by Title VII of the Civil Rights Act of 1964 (minorities and women). Although not constituting regulations having the force of law, the *Guidelines* have been considered in a number of employment discrimination cases since 1978, together with other recognized sets of validation standards. See, for example, *Guardian's Association* v. *Civil Service Commission* (1980).

The question of whether or not the *Uniform Guidelines* apply to tests used for licensing and certification purposes has not been resolved. Whereas Title VII of the Civil Rights Act of 1964, as amended, speaks of employers, labor unions, and employment agencies as groups to which the *Guidelines* apply, the drafters of the *Guidelines* assert that they may also have jurisdiction over licensing and certification agencies. For example, in the definition of test "user" (*Guidelines*, p. 383080), one finds that "whenever an employer, labor organization, or employment agency is required by law to restrict recruitment for any occupation to those applicants who have met licensing or certification requirements, the licensing or certifying agency, to the extent it may be covered by Federal equal employment law, will be considered the user with respect to those licensing and certification requirements." Although the U.S. Supreme Court has not ruled on the question, decisions of at least two federal circuit courts that have considered the issue (*Tyler* v. *Vickery*, 1975; *Richardson* v. *McFadden*, 1976) suggest that Title VII does not apply to the licensing activities of state agencies.

The question of whether or not the *Guidelines* apply to employers who use certification credentials in making employment decisions (regardless of whether the credential is required by law or is obtained voluntarily by practi-

tioners) must also ultimately be resolved by the courts. The Equal Employment Opportunity Commission and other executive agencies that prepared a preface to the *Guidelines* (U.S. Government, 1978) argue that "if an employer relies upon such certification in making employment decisions, the employer is the user and must be prepared to justify, under Federal Law, that reliance as it would any other selection procedure" (p. 38294). It should be noted that generally the *Guidelines* would apply to a particular part of a selection procedure (such as a certification credential) only if the selection procedure as a whole had adverse impact.

Social and Policy Questions. In addition to technical and legal questions, there are a number of broad social and policy questions that occupy the attention of legislators, leaders in the professions, consumers, and others who are concerned with the impact of licensure and certification. These include such issues as (1) assuring continued competence of practitioners; (2) reducing the proliferation of unnecessary licensing and certification; (3) removing restrictions on the optimal use of skilled manpower; (4) strengthening the role of "public members" of regulatory boards; (5) centralizing licensure functions; and (6) reforming licensing practices through "sunset" and other regulatory review procedures. Following are brief discussions of these six topics. For a more detailed discussion of these and related topics, see Shimberg (1980).

Assuring continued competence. Although licensing and certification agencies have shown considerable zeal in seeking to make sure that applicants are initially competent to practice, they have been much less zealous in monitoring the continued competence of licensees and certificate holders after they have been initially credentialed. In the United States, there is a tradition that once individuals have been licensed or certified they may retain their credentials for life. Most licensing laws provide that a license may be suspended or revoked only after the licensee has been accorded a formal hearing and been found to be seriously incompetent, negligent, or otherwise unfit to practice.

Increased consumer concern about continued competence has given rise to demands that steps be taken to assure that practitioners have kept up to date and have maintained their skills. The response of many professional groups to such demands has been to suggest the imposition of some minimum number of hours of approved continuing education as a condition of license or certificate renewal. New Mexico was the first state to impose mandatory continuing education as a condition of license renewal. Since then, nearly all other states have passed laws that either authorize boards to establish continuing education requirements or actually impose such requirements in law. According to Phillips (1980), optometrists, nursing home administrators, certified public accountants, physicians, pharmacists, and veterinarians are among the professions most frequently subject to continuing education requirements.

There is considerable difference of opinion as to the efficacy of continuing education as a method of assuring the continued competence of professionals. In a literature search for all studies of medical continuing education published in English between 1960 and 1977, Bertram and Brooks-Bertram (1977) found 65 published articles reporting on a total of 113 studies. Of these, only 29 studies used true or quasi-experimental designs and only 13 used statistical techniques to compare groups that had or had not been exposed to continuing education. Limiting themselves to studies that demonstrated what they considered to be good experimental design, the Bertrams found positive effects attributable to continuing education in only 6 of the 113 studies. And in only 3 of the studies were the positive effects still present at or beyond six weeks after the conclusion of the program. The Bertrams concluded that "at the present time . . . a consistent and significant documentation of benefits is absent." However, they urge continued research with regard to the effectiveness of continuing medical education because "it may prove to be the weakest link in the profession's attempt at improving the quality of its own performance" (pp. 344–345).

A contrary conclusion is rendered by Stein (1981), who reported on eight continuing medical education studies published during the 1970s. He states that "when physician learning activities are organized on the basis of sound educational principles, continuing medical education (CME) can result in changed physician performance (and, presumably improved patient care)." He concludes that "a crucial factor in each study is that learners recognized the need for improved performance and participated fully in needs identification, planning the educational intervention and the evaluation of outcomes" (p. 109).

Several medical specialty certification boards have introduced reexamination programs, and all twenty-three such boards are committed to some form of reassessment programs in the future. However, under guidelines adopted by the American Board of Medical Specialties (ABMS), no board may rescind an initial certificate (no matter how long ago it was issued) unless a date of expiration was a condition of original certification. In accordance with this policy, those boards that have introduced reexamination procedures have made them available on a voluntary basis. However, at least one board, the National Board of Family Practice (NBFP) has made reexamination mandatory. Certificates issued by NBFP are valid for only six years; certificate holders must meet certain continuing education requirements and complete the reassessment process if they wish to remain certified.

Both the voluntary and mandatory reexamination programs supplement written multiple-choice tests with other procedures, including hospital chart audits and peer reviews. A common feature of the reassessment process is the use of simulations, also known as patient management problems. McGuire, Solomon, and Forman (1976) have described the development and scoring of written simulations in considerable detail. Senior (1976) has reported on efforts to devise a computer-based system for assessing physician competence.

Thus far, no state has instituted a mandatory reassessment program. However, Michigan may have taken a step in this direction when the legislature adopted a new public health code (Public Act 368). Article 15 of the code mandates that licensing boards establish pilot programs for assessing the continuing competence of licensees. During a six-year period, boards are encouraged to experiment with a variety of approaches, including reexamination, continuing education, peer reviews, and practice audits. At the end of the six-year period, boards will be expected to establish, by rule, some system of continuing competence assurance to be met by licensees at least every four years as a condition of license renewal.

Reducing licensing proliferation. The rapid growth in the number of licensed occupations has troubled some legislators, regulatory officials, and consumer leaders. Following a study of credentialing in the health field, the secretary of the U.S. Department of Health, Education, and Welfare (1971) called for a two-year moratorium on new licensure of health occupations. It was his belief that further proliferation would not only lead to the undesirable fragmentation of services but would also result in increased health care costs.

In the late 1960s and early 1970s, consumer groups began to develop doubts about licensure as a consumer-protection mechanism. The Federal Trade Commission (FTC) was especially active in pointing out that licensing boards sometimes used their powers to restrict competition, thereby raising the cost of such products as prescription drugs, eyeglasses, and funerals. Studies by Shimberg, Kruger, and Esser (1972) provided documentation regarding the ways in which some boards restrict entry into occupations and limit the interstate mobility of skilled workers and professionals. The impact of such restrictions was discussed in detail in the proceedings of a conference on occupational licensure sponsored by the American Enterprise Institute (Rottenberg, 1980).

Even as federal agencies and consumer groups were stressing the negative aspects of licensure (and frequently suggesting certification as an alternative), new groups, such as social workers, were clamoring to become licensed. They insisted that licensure was needed to protect the public, but they also indicated that licensure was necessary to enhance the group's image, to increase professionalization, and possibly to make the profession eligible for reimbursement under various health insurance plans.

A good example of the conflicting pressures within and among professions may be seen in the area of psychotherapy, where physicians, psychologists, social workers, marriage and family counselors, and others are seeking to fashion regulatory systems that will safeguard their own interests as well as those of the public. Hogan (1979) has examined the philosophy and practice of professional regulation, reviewed malpractice suits involving psychotherapists, and provided a compendium of state laws and a resource bibliography in a four-volume work, *The Regulation of Psychotherapists*. Hogan concludes "that traditional modes of professional regulations have not done a particularly good job of protecting the public. Licensing boards, the courts, and professional associations are not likely to provide the forum in which effective regulation will take place, at least as traditionally conceived. The difficulties in adequately defining the nature and limits of psychotherapy, the lack of standards and criteria for determining what practices are harmful, and the lack of valid and reliable methods of selection exacerbate all the problems associated with traditional forms of professional regulation" (p. 350).

Legislators are also recognizing that regulation of occupations may entail hidden social costs that can sometimes outweigh the benefits. After having said yes to so many requests for regulation in the past, legislators are now finding it difficult to say no. Two states—Minnesota and Virginia—have attempted to deal with the problem of proliferation of unnecessary licensure by creating mechanisms designed to assist public officials in arriving at more rational decisions about granting licensure. Virginia has established a Board of Commerce that carefully reviews all applications for licensure from new groups and recommends action to the legislature. The Minnesota system involves the use of a broad-based commission, also outside of the formal legislative framework, to review applications from groups seeking to be regulated and to assemble as much data as possible regarding the need for regulation and alternative modes of doing so. The commission may conclude that no regulation is needed, that some lesser type of regulation (such as certification) will suffice, or that licensure is indeed warranted. When licensure is recommended, formal action by the legislature is necessary to implement the recommendation. Since 1976, the commission has considered fifteen applications from groups seeking regulation. In not a single instance has licensure been granted.

A booklet, *Occupational Licensing: Questions a Legislator Should Ask*, by Shimberg and Roederer (1978) has been published by the Council of State Governments. It provides legislators and other state officials with background information about a number of licensure issues, raises eighteen questions that legislators should ask groups that are seeking licensure, and describes efforts by several states to deal with regulatory problems.

Removing restrictions on manpower use. When most of the early licensing laws were passed, the occupational groups seeking licensure usually sought to define broadly their "scopes of practice." As technology has advanced and as new occupational groups have emerged, conflicts over "scope of practice" have arisen with increased frequency. Members of emerging groups found that they could not engage in the activities they had been trained to perform because such activities often encroached on the scope of practice of an already licensed group. For

example, licensed psychologists frequently accused unlicensed counselors of practicing psychology when they undertook to help a client with a personal, social, or emotional problem. In order to gain the right to practice their profession, counselors have sought licensed status in many states. Dental technicians, who make dentures from impressions taken by dentists, have sought the right to take the impressions themselves, and then make, fit, and sell dentures directly to the public, as is the case in Canada and many European countries. Dentists have resisted these efforts as illegal trespass on their territory. Thus far the dental technicians, who call themselves "denturists," have been successful in gaining licensed status in only one state, Oregon.

There have also been conflicts when licensed groups have sought to expand their scopes of practice. At legislative hearings on such requests, experts from the already established groups have usually cautioned legislators against acceding to requests from paraprofessionals for expanded functions, citing lack of adequate training, possible complications, and other dangers to the public. The legislators, understandably, have tended to follow the counsel of these respected experts, although in many instances, witnesses were probably expressing their personal opinions without necessarily having had any actual experience with the proposed innovations.

In 1973 the California legislature passed the Health Manpower Pilot Projects (HMPP) Act, which authorized the Office of Statewide Health Planning and Development, situated within the state Department of Health, to approve projects that would train, utilize, and evaluate new or expanded roles of health workers. The act makes possible expanding the scopes of practice of existing categories of workers beyond current legal definitions. In effect, practitioners participating in HMPP projects are exempted from certain healing arts licensing laws in order to permit collection of objective data with respect to the safety of care providers as well as the impact that these new regulations are likely to have upon the quality and availability of health workers.

Each institutional group seeking approval under the HMPP law must specify the tasks trainees will perform, training facilities, institutional resources, faculty, and how the institution plans to evaluate its trainees. All trainees are held to the same standards of care in performing the expanded functions as persons currently licensed to perform such functions. According to a recent report of the Office of Statewide Health Planning and Development (1979), twenty-six projects were under way at that time; these provided expanded roles for registered nurses, physician's assistants, emergency medical technicians, pharmacists, dental assistants, and dentists.

Strengthening the role of public members. When self-regulatory boards were initially created, neither professionals nor legislators saw any role for lay persons. After all, what did layment know about entry qualifications, practice standards, or professional ethics? In recent years, however, consumers have come to recognize that what boards do can affect the cost, quality, and availability of services; they have insisted upon a voice in the decision-making process. The idea has gained a high degree of acceptance, and public members are now found on one or more licensing boards in nearly every state. Public members constitute a minority of boards in all states except California, where they are a majority, with the exception of the accountancy board and the various health-related boards. The need for training public board members has been documented by Stellman (1977) and by Hinshaw and Clemons (1979). Training materials for public members have been developed by Clark and Savage (1979) and by Arkansas Consumer Research (1980). An orientation program designed to familiarize all board members with their duties and responsibilities has been developed by the New Jersey Department of Consumer Affairs (1981). To date there have been few studies of what public members contribute to the work of the boards on which they serve. One such study, conducted by Chesney (1981) for the Michigan Health Occupations Council and the Michigan Department of Licensing and Regulation, found that public members give themselves generally low evaluations on effectiveness in most areas of board functions. They receive similarly low ratings from their professional colleagues or boards. Schutz, Musolf, and Shepard (1980) suggest ways to assess the impact of public board members in future studies.

Centralizing licensure. In most states, when licensing boards were initially created, they were given a high degree of autonomy. They were not attached to any department of government. Each board hired its own staff, promulgated rules and regulations, prepared and administered examinations, collected fees, investigated complaints, and took disciplinary action where indicated. As the number of autonomous boards increased, some states established centralized "umbrella" agencies in the interest of greater efficiency and to increase accountability. Five such centralized agencies existed prior to 1930, in New York, Illinois, Washington, Pennsylvania, and California. A study by the Council of State Governments (1969) identified sixteen states that had central agencies performing some occupational and professional licensing functions. A survey by Roederer and Shimberg (1980) found thirty-one states in which a central licensing agency is the predominant model with varying degrees of responsibility control. The latter study showed that

- Seven states had autonomous boards within a central agency that provides mainly housekeeping services, but plays no role in policy formulation.
- In eighteen states, the central agency's task goes beyond the routine activities of the housekeeping role. While boards play a dominant role in such areas as reviewing qualifications, setting standards, and dealing with disciplinary matters, the central agency exerts a degree of

influence through its control of budgets, personnel, and other administrative functions.
- In four states, certain decisions of boards are subject to review by the central agency.
- In two states, boards do not have final decision-making power. They are essentially advisory to the central licensure agency.

In the course of their survey, Roederer and Shimberg (1980) asked respondents (board officials, agency administrators, and legislative staff personnel) to cite reasons for favoring or opposing the centralization of licensure functions. The following were the principal arguments in favor of retaining autonomous boards:

1. Professional expertise is needed to assure adequate review of professional practice standards, to develop examinations, and to make judgments in disciplinary cases.
2. A centralized agency adds additional layers of bureaucracy, increases costs, and usually results in poorer service to consumers.
3. Autonomous boards made up of dedicated professionals are better insulated against political pressure than a politically appointed agency administration.
4. Autonomous boards are more accountable because they must operate under a system of checks and balances. Centralization might result in a significant loss of control by the legislature.

Proponents of centralization advanced the following arguments:

1. There would be increased administrative efficiency through better use of staff and facilities.
2. A central agency can coordinate activities of individual boards and resolve jurisdictional disputes. The central agency, rather than individual boards, would interact with the legislature and executive branches. By working through a central agency an executive can enunciate and implement a consistent regulatory policy.
3. The central agency provides an oversight mechanism. Actions by individual boards—including rule making, setting of standards, and disciplinary decisions—may be reviewed by the agency to ensure equity.
4. The central agency may become the focal point for accountability to citizens. The agency director usually serves at the pleasure of the executive and may be removed for acting in an arbitrary fashion or exceeding his or her statutory authority.

"Sunset" legislation. Passage by the Colorado legislature of the nation's first "sunset" law in 1976 provided a stimulus to the regulatory reform movement that had been gathering strength during the late 1960s and early 1970s. The concept underlying sunset was that many existing agencies and programs in state government had outlived their usefulness, whereas others, although still needed,

might not be accomplishing their intended objectives. Sunset legislation established a schedule of dates when specified agencies and programs would automatically go out of existence unless the legislature acted affirmatively to continue them. Colorado and many other states decided to initiate the sunset process with a review of licensing boards and certain other regulatory agencies because these tended to be smaller and more manageable than the "superagencies." Typically, sunset review staffs conduct investigations of each agency on the sunset schedule and recommend to the appropriate legislative committee whether to continue, terminate, or make changes in the agency. Hearings are then held, during which a committee hears witnesses from the agency, the occupational group, and the public. A recommendation is then transmitted to the legislature for action.

As of April 1981, thirty-four states had adopted sunset legislation. Experience has demonstrated that sunset is no panacea. In many states, the investigative agency has lacked the personnel and resources needed to probe deeply into an agency's way of performing its functions. Frequently, the investigators were dependent upon board members and agency staffs for evaluative information and had no way of verifying such information from independent sources. Proponents of sunset who expected that there would be wholesale abolition of government agencies and programs have been disappointed. Relatively few agencies have been abolished; a number were consolidated, such as barber and cosmetology boards. There is evidence that the threat of sunset may have motivated some boards to put their houses in better order. In at least one state (Florida), sunset appears to have provided the stimulus for a major reorganization of the licensing system. However, in most states there has been only modest reform. Common Cause (1978) has summarized the results of the first two years of experience with sunset.

Some states have initiated regulatory reform activites without a formal sunset process. In California, for example, the Department of Consumer Affairs established a professionally staffed Regulatory Review Task Force that conducted examinations of seventeen regulatory boards within the department. The report of the task force (Summerfield, 1979) provides many examples of the California boards shortcomings and suggests ways to strengthen the regulatory system in that state.

Strengthening Health-certifying Agencies. A weakness of voluntary certification as a credentialing device is the absence of standards. Any group wishing to establish its own certification agency is free to do so. It can issue credentials that represent a high level of attainment or it can issue credentials that involve no demonstration of competency whatsoever. Since there has been no governmental regulation of voluntary certification agencies and no system of nongovernmental accreditation, the public had no way of knowing how much credence to place in

a certification credential without also knowing about the certification agency and its standards.

In an effort to establish standards and bring some stability and order to the health credential field, the Department of Health, Education, and Welfare (HEW; now the Department of Health and Human Services) proposed the creation of a nongovernmental entity that would, in effect, accredit health-certifying agencies. "The effort was remarkable" states a National Commission for Health Certifying Agencies (NCHCA) publication (1980) "reflecting the conviction of HEW . . . that the awarding of credentials to members of health occupations is too complicated, sensitive, and de-centralized a function to be performed effectively by the federal bureaucracy, and could best be done by marshalling the talents and dedication of people in the private sector" (p. 5). NCHCA is an organization of organizations. It evaluates certification agencies and admits to membership those that meet the rigorous criteria that have been adopted. For example, certifying bodies closely linked to professional associations are required to sever such relationships. They must demonstrate not only their fiscal independence from the association but also that the association has no control over the appointment of board members or board policies. In the three years since its founding, only six certifying agencies have satisfied the criteria and been granted full membership. Nine other agencies have been accorded "conditional membership," which signifies that the group has met most, but not all, of the basic requirements.

Future Prospects. The ferment that presently exists within the licensing and certification domain makes it hazardous to attempt to predict the future. A wide variety of proposals for drastic reform have been advanced. Hogan (1979), for example, would abolish licensing altogether except for those involved in dispensing drugs or performing surgery. For other occupations, he favors allowing anyone to practice provided that they first register with the state and disclose (to the state and to their clients) "their intended field of practice, relevant experience, and academic training, the methods they intend to use, the goals of treatment, and a statement of ethical beliefs" (p. 361).

Harris Cohen (1980), a senior policy analyst in the Department of Health and Human Services, advocates retaining the existing system of boards where necessary, but would transfer decision-making power from members of the regulated occupation to financially disinterested lay persons. He believes that "members of boards . . . would be selected for their expertise in such areas as education, health, economics, health care administration, manpower or consumer advocacy" and that "this would provide some safeguard against the capture by the 'experts' since board members would be expected to have important expertise of their own" (p. 304).

A different approach is advocated by Andrew Dolan (1981), director of the Center for Health Services Research at the University of Washington. Dolan supports the idea of institutional licensure advanced by Hershey (1969) more than a decade ago. Dolan would like to abolish all peer control over occupational licensing and permit no formal input from professionals except when necessary to devise exams or write scopes of practice. His philosophy may be summed up as "experts on tap, not on top" (p. 5).

Dolan seems to suggest that these or similar proposals are not likely to gain sufficient support from the public in the foreseeable future to bring about significant changes in the regulatory system. It is more likely in this author's opinion that gradual change will continue in response to the pressures discussed previously. More radical change might come about if escalating health care costs prompt a comprehensive examination of all the factors in our society that contribute to these costs. Such a study is likely to look at factors that limit the supply and distribution of health service workers, impede the introduction of cost-saving innovations, and prevent new methods of delivering health services from emerging. If licensing or certification is found to be a significant factor in determining the cost and availability of services, as seems likely, there may be a critical reassessment of the social costs and benefits of licensure, which has not occurred previously. Such a reassessment could pave the way for a search for alternatives, out of which might emerge a new system with few occupations licensed, a greater reliance upon less restrictive modes of regulation (such as certification), greater involvement of the public, and a decreased role for professionals in the regulatory process.

Benjamin Shimberg

See also Professions Education; State Influences on Education; Teacher Certification.

REFERENCES

American Psychological Association, Division of Industrial-Organizational Psychology. *Principles for the Validation and Use of Personnel Selection Procedures* (2nd ed.). Berkeley, Calif.: The Association, 1980.

Arkansas Consumer Research. *Manual for Members of State Boards and Commissions.* Little Rock: Arkansas Consumer Research, 1980.

Bertram, D. A., & Brooks-Bertram, P. A. The evaluation of continuing medical education: A literature review. *Health Education Monographs,* 1977, *5,* 330–362.

Cathcart, J. A., & Graff, G. Occupational licensing: Factoring it out. *Pacific Law Journal,* 1978, *9,* 147–163.

Chesney, J. F. *Report on the Role and Effectiveness of Public Members on Licensing Boards.* Lansing, Mich.: Health Occupations Council, 1981.

Chilson, J. *Competency-training Research Project.* Unpublished manuscript, 1980. (Available from author, Hillsboro School of Beauty, Hillsboro, Oreg.).

Clark, B., & Savage, H. *Effective Consumer Representation: An Orientation Manual for Board Members.* Baltimore: Maryland Citizens Consumer Foundation and Consumer Council, Office of the Attorney General, 1979.

Cohen, H. Professional power and conflict of interest. *Journal of Health, Politics, Policy, and Law,* Summer 1980.

Common Cause. *Making Government Work: A Common Cause Report on State Sunset Activity.* Washington, D.C.: Issue Development Office, 1978.

Council of State Governments. *Central Service Agencies for Occupational Licensing Boards* (Report RM 428). Lexington, Ky.: Council of State Governments, March 1969.

Dolan, A. Regulating the professions: Is there an ideal way? Cited in *Pro Forum* (Center for the Study of the Professions), *3,* 1981.

Greene, K., & Gay, R. *Occupational Regulation in the United States.* Washington, D.C.: U.S. Department of Labor, Employment and Training Administration, forthcoming.

Griggs v. *Duke Power Company,* 401 U.S. 424 (1971).

Guardian's Association of New York Police Department, Inc. v. *Civil Service Commission of City of New York,* 23 FEP cases 909 (2d Cir. 1980).

Hecht, K. A. Current status and methodological problems of validating professional licensing and certification examinations. In M. A. Budra & J. F. Sanders (Eds.), *Practices and Problems in Competency-based Education.* Washington, D.C.: National Council on Measurement Education, 1979, pp. 16–27.

Hershey, N. An alternative to licensing of health professionals. *Hospital Progress,* March 1969.

Hinshaw, C., & Clemons, S. *Public Members and Accountability: Arkansas Boards and Commissions.* Little Rock: Arkansas Consumer Research, October 1979.

Hogan, D. B. *The Regulation of Psychotherapists* (4 vols.). Cambridge, Mass.: Ballinger, 1979.

McGuire, C.; Solomon, L. M.; & Forman, P. M. *Clinical Simulations: Selected Problems in Patient Management.* New York: Appleton-Century-Crofts, 1976.

National Commission for Health Certifying Agencies. *Perspectives on Health Occupational Credentialing.* Washington, D.C.: The Commission, 1979.

National Commission for Health Certifying Agencies. *General Information Booklet.* Washington, D.C.: The Commission, 1980.

New Jersey Department of Consumer Affairs. *Manual for Members of Professional and Occupational Licensing Boards of the State of New Jersey.* Newark, N.J.: Department of Law and Public Safety, 1981.

Office of Statewide Health Planning and Development, Division of Health Professions Development. *Annual Report to the Legislature, State of California, and to the Healing Arts Licensing Boards.* Sacramento: The Office, 1979.

Phillips, L. E. *Status of Mandatory Continuing Education for Selected Professions.* Greenville, S.C.: Furman University, 1980. Table available from author.

Richardson v. *McFadden,* 540 F. 2d 744 (4th Cir. 1976).

Roederer, D., & Shimberg, B. *Occupational Licensing: Centralization of State Licensure Functions.* Lexington, Ky.: Council of State Governments, 1980.

Rottenberg, S. (Ed.) *Occupational Licensure and Regulation.* Washington, D.C.: American Enterprise Institute for Public Policy Research, 1980.

Schutz, H. G.; Musolf, L. D.; & Shepard, L. *Regulating Occupations in California: The Role of Public Members on State Boards* (California Policy Seminars Monograph No. 7). Berkeley, Calif.: Institute of Governmental Studies, University of California, 1980.

Senior, J. R. *Toward the Measurement of Competence in Medicine* (Report of Computer-based Examination Project Sponsored by the National Board of Medical Examiners and the American

Board of Internal Medicine). Philadelphia: Privately published, 1976. Available from National Board of Medical Examiners, Philadelphia.

Shimberg, B. *Occupational Licensing: A Public Perspective.* Princeton, N.J.: Educational Testing Service, 1980.

Shimberg, B.; Kruger, D.; & Esser, B. *Occupational Licensing: Practices and Policies.* Washington, D.C.: Public Affairs Press, 1972.

Shimberg, B., & Roederer, D. *Occupational Licensing: Questions a Legislator Should Ask.* Lexington, Ky.: Council of State Governments, 1978.

Stein, L. S. The effectiveness of continuing medical education: Eight research reports. *Journal of Medical Education,* 1981, *56,* 103–110.

Stellman, C. *Consumer Representatives, Department of Licensing and Regulation.* Baltimore: Office of the Attorney General, Consumer Council, 1977.

Summerfield, H. *Regulation of Occupations: Report of the Regulatory Review Task Force.* Sacramento: Department of Consumer Affairs, 1979.

Tyler v. *Vickery,* 517 F. 2d 1089 (5th Cir. 1975), *cert. denied.* 96 S. Ct. 2660 (1975).

U.S. Department of Health, Education, and Welfare, *Report on Licensure and Related Health Personnel Credentialing* (DHEW Publication No. (HSM) 72-11). Washington, D.C.: U.S. Government Printing Office, 1971. (ERIC Document Reproduction Service No. ED 061 420)

U.S. Department of Health, Education, and Welfare, Public Health Service. *Credentialing Health Manpower* (DHEW Publication No. (05) 77-50057). Washington, D.C.: U.S. Government Printing Office, July 1977.

U.S. Government. *Uniform Guidelines on Employee Selection Procedures.* Printed in *Federal Register,* 1978, *43,* 38290–38309.

LIFE-SPAN DEVELOPMENT

During the past two decades, increasing attention has been given to a life-span orientation within both the fields of developmental psychology and education. Although never a dominant approach, the life-span perspective has had its proponents throughout the history of both disciplines (Baltes, 1979; Riegel, 1977). It may be of particular interest to educators that Sidney Pressey, known for his pioneering work on teaching machines, coauthored one of the earliest life-span texts in American psychology (Pressey, Janney, & Kuhlen, 1939). Even earlier there was E. L. Thorndike's major work on adult learning (Thorndike et al., 1928).

The recent revival of interest in a life-span approach can be linked to a number of contemporaneous events. First, there is the growing shift in the age structure of Western industrialized societies, including the United States. As the average life expectancy has increased in this century, the number of persons over age 65 in the United States has doubled from 1950 to 1980. In contrast, there has been a decline in the proportion of the population in childhood and adolescence. The age shift is pro-

jected to accelerate into the next century. Given the traditional emphasis on youth within both disciplines, such demographic trends have important implications and consequences. One of the most evident changes has been the increasing focus upon the adult years within developmental psychology and education. Although a life-span perspective should not be equated with the study of adult development and aging, greater attention to this relatively neglected age period (in contrast to the early years) is useful in the development of an integrative life-span orientation. Some of the most recent proponents of the life-span movement have been prominent in the gerontological literature (Baltes & Willis, 1979; Neugarten & Havighurst, 1976; Riegel & Meacham, 1975; Riley, 1979; Schaie, 1979). Particularly important in developmental psychology have been a number of longitudinal studies focusing upon adult development. These longitudinal studies included both research specifically on development across the adult years (Neugarten, 1968; Palmore, 1974; Schaie, 1979) and also follow-up studies on aging participants from several child growth studies (Bayley, 1968; Eichorn, 1973; Honzik & Macfarlane, 1973). As longer portions of the life span have begun to be examined, a number of methodological procedures and issues have gained increasing attention. It appears likely that these matters, currently associated with a life-span approach, will become more important for future developmental and educational research. Thus, both sociocultural trends, with related implications for educational and social policy, and a more comprehensive knowledge base with respect to human development have contributed to the renewed interest in a life-span approach.

This article will begin by discussing several critical features of a life-span perspective that differentiate it from more traditional youth-oriented approaches to developmental psychology. Second, three methodological issues evolving primarily from a life-span orientation to development will be examined. Finally, implications of a life-span perspective for educational research and practice will be considered.

The Life-span Orientation. Life-span developmental psychology is best characterized as a perspective or an approach to the study of development rather than as a specific theory or model of development. The life-span perspective is not linked to a specific area of development (such as cognition) or age period (such as adulthood), nor is it necessarily aligned with one particular theoretical persuasion (cognitive developmental or behavioral). Rather, it seeks to understand the developing individual across the entire life course within a changing sociocultural context. One could, for example, study parent-child (intergenerational) relationships across the life course from a social learning, cognitive developmental, or behavioral orientation. Within a life-span approach, consideration would also be given to the impact of cultural change on the developing parent-child relationship. In this section, several features of a life-span orientation will be discussed that distinguish it from more traditional perspectives of developmental psychology.

Age-segmented versus life-span focus. A historical review of developmental psychology suggests that the field has evolved largely as a set of distinct, age-segmented specialties: infancy, child development, adolescence, adulthood, and aging. These life-stage specialties have developed their own unique theoretical and empirical knowledge bases with relatively little communication or linkage across developmental periods. The age-specific orientation is reflected, for example, in the psychometric approach to intellectual functioning and assessment. Global intelligence measures, such as the Wechsler and Stanford-Binet, have focused upon age-graded tests and have assessed knowledge and skills specific to a particular age period rather than the individual's changing understanding of the same concept across the life course (Baltes & Willis, 1979; Labouvie-Vief, 1977). Such an approach may be useful for the description of interindividual differences at a given age period, but is less appropriate for understanding the course of cognitive development and change across the life span.

In contrast to an age-segmented approach, a life-span perspective seeks to define patterns or sequences of developmental change across the life course, to examine the interrelationships among developmental periods, and to identify antecedents and processes associated with change. Whereas chronological age is a very prominent index variable within an age-segmented approach, the focus of a life-span approach is on the pattern of developmental change, which may not be highly correlated with chronological age. Particularly in adulthood, chronological age may not be the most useful index of developmental change for psychological processes, such as intellectual functioning. For example, verbal ability throughout much of adulthood appears to be more closely associated with educational level or sociocultural experience than with chronological age per se.

Continuing developmental change. A life-span perspective assumes that significant developmental change occurs across the total life course and seeks to examine the nature and sequence of this change (Baltes & Willis, 1979; Brim & Kagan, 1980). This position is in contrast to a view that the most important developmental changes occur primarily during childhood and adolescence, and that adulthood, for the most part, is characterized by stability in the early and middle years, with sharp and pervasive decline in old age. Such a traditional view assumes that adult development is largely defined and constrained by events occurring in childhood. For example, within the Piagetian theory of cognitive development, the final stage occurs in adolescence or young adulthood. Similarly, the psychoanalytic approach focuses upon stages in childhood and their impact on the rest of the life course. A life-span approach, by broadening the definition of what is considered developmental change, argues that important change can and does occur across the total life course. Early life

experiences can interact with and may be transformed by events in adulthood. Also, some behavioral events occurring at early life stages (particularly in infancy) may simply be required to permit the individual to survive until a subsequent life stage is reached, and may have no predictive import in themselves for later behaviors (Kagan, 1980).

In the study of life-span development, it is important to consider both quantitative change (in level, rate, degree) and qualitative change (in nature or type). For example, change in adult intellectual functioning may involve not only quantitative change in the adult's level of performance but also qualitatively different forms of intelligence unique to adulthood (for example, wisdom). Intellectual functioning in adulthood may involve primarily knowledge synthesis, integration, and evaluation rather than the knowledge acquisition more characteristic of childhood (Labouvie-Vief, 1977; Schaie, 1977–1978).

Developmental change across the life course is also multidirectional. In childhood and adolescence, the dominant pattern is unidirectional and incremental. That is, children increase in height, motor complexity, and abstractness of thought processes. In adulthood, however, multidirectional developmental patterns may be observed for different areas of development. Speed of responding may decrease; size of vocabulary may increase; and certain personality dimensions, such as extroversion, may remain stable.

An important consequence of a focus upon continuing change is the recognition that behavioral plasticity continues across the life span. Thus, the potential exists for modifying personal characteristics across the life span. Positive growth and change usually have been expected and encouraged in childhood and adolescence. As a society, we have expended considerable resources for intervention programs to modify and facilitate development in childhood. Through these efforts, knowledge has been gained about the range of developmental plasticity in physical, cognitive, or social development during the early years. In contrast to the emphasis on positive change in childhood, the study of change in adulthood has focused frequently upon decrement, particularly physical and mental decline. This emphasis on negative change in adulthood has often led to assumptions regarding the irreversibility of behavioral decrement. A life-span focus on developmental change requires that the range of plasticity or modifiability of functioning be examined in adulthood as well as in childhood.

Increasing individual differences. A life-span perspective emphasizes the importance of examining both intraindividual change and individual differences across the life course. Study of a number of developmental phenomena (such as intellectual functioning or sensory acuity) indicates that the range of individual differences increases across the life span. That is, the range of variability or differences between individuals of the same chronological age increases from childhood to adulthood.

Whereas most normal children achieve developmental milestones, such as walking or entering school, within a relatively restricted age range, adults vary considerably in the chronological age associated with developmental milestones such as marriage, birth of first child, graying of hair, or menopause. It is likely that the more narrow age band within which individual differences occur in childhood is associated with the greater isomorphy between biological and behavioral development in the early years. The rate and sequence of physiological development impose a timetable on many aspects of behavioral development in childhood. In addition, age-graded cultural institutions and norms associated with youth (age guidelines for schooling, driver's license) may promote a close alignment between chronological age and certain developmental events (Riley, 1976). In contrast, the adult has reached biological maturity, and behavioral development is less closely linked to biologically determined maturational processes until, perhaps, very old age. Nor are there as many culturally imposed, age-related restrictions on adult behavior. As age-related biological and cultural moderators diminish in importance in the adult years, environmental and experiential factors come to play a far more pervasive role in adult development. Such environmental factors become not only more influential but also more diverse in adulthood. This diversity of experiences, in turn, contributes to the increasing individual differences in adulthood. Environmental influences may range from specific experiences unique to a given individual (for example, great wealth) to broad-scale, historically significant events, such as war or depression, affecting an entire generation. Given the importance of differential experiences in adulthood, some authors have questioned whether there are truly universal, normative events or stages in adulthood comparable to those in childhood (Flavell, 1970; Hultsch & Plemons, 1979). The greater variability in both developmental patterns and in the environmental factors affecting life-course change has important implications for designing educational efforts in the adult years, to be discussed in a later section. The focus upon environmental influences leads, then, to consideration of a fourth critical feature.

Sociocultural change and development. Over the past few decades, the child development literature has shown increasing sensitivity to the importance of environmental influences (Bronfenbrenner, 1977). However, less consideration has been given to sociocultural change as it effects development. An exception is Roche's recent monograph (1979) on secular trends in physical development. For the most part, recent discussions of development as a function of person-environment interactions have involved a static conception of the cultural context. However, it is well documented that current generations are experiencing dramatic cultural change across the life span and that this change is affecting development. Whereas the cumulative impact of cultural change becomes most evident in adulthood, it may affect development at any period in the life span. For example, changing

medical trends in the use of anesthesia during childbirth have been shown to affect basic forms of learning in the newborn (Porges, 1975).

Since generations will differ in the nature and rate of cultural change experienced over their life spans, it becomes important within developmental psychology to examine between-cohort (generational) differences in individual development. It is necessary to study a developmental phenomenon over the same chronological age range in several cohorts to differentiate cohort-specific from more universal patterns of development. In much of developmental research, the study of developmental (or educational) change has been confounded with possible generational effects. A striking example of the impact of generational change is found in the literature on adult intelligence. Typically, changes in intellectual functioning during adulthood have been studied by comparing the performance of persons of differing ages (20, 30, 40 . . .); and lower levels of performance in the older years have been reported for abilities such as spatial orientation or abstract reasoning. However, Schaie's longitudinal study (1979) of several cohorts over the same chronological age period suggests that prior findings of lower performance associated with age are partially a function of generational confounds. That is, earlier cohorts performed at a lower level on intellectual tests than did later cohorts when assessed at the same chronological age. Thus, lower performance levels in the aged are more a function of generational effects than drastic age-related decline. Methodological procedures for differentiating change associated with generational (cohort) versus developmental effects will be considered in the second section.

Influences on developmental change. Within a traditional child-oriented approach, explanatory models of development have focused upon maturational-biological and environmental (physical and social) factors and their interaction. A life-span perspective suggests a somewhat different conceptualization of these sources or antecedents of developmental change. Three major systems of influence have been proposed by Baltes (1979): age-graded, history-graded, and non-normative. "Age-graded" influences have been examined most extensively within traditional child-oriented developmental approaches. These include both biological/maturational and environmental (socialization) determinants that are highly correlated with chronological age. Age-graded biological-based influences include both neurophysiological processes moderating development in the early years and possible physical decline factors affecting behavior in very old age. Age-related environmental factors include the age-graded tasks and socialization experiences defined by a particular culture. For example, schooling in the first part of the life span has been a major age-graded socialization experience, with not only instruction itself age-graded but also age-segmented consequences moderating the timing of youth's entry into the labor force and assumption of responsibilities and privileges associated with adulthood.

A life-span perspective suggests that human development occurs within a changing sociocultural context and that particularly in adulthood, unique non-normative life events may be important sources of change. "History-graded" influences reflect such sociocultural change and are highly correlated with historical time rather than chronological age. For example, history-graded influences such as inflation (or depression) and changing perception of women's roles interact with age-graded events such as child rearing to produce cohort effects. Likewise, politically motivated events such as the social programs associated with the War on Poverty can produce cohort effects with regard to early education. Such history-graded effects apply to most individuals within a given culture during a particular historical period.

A third source of influence, "non-normative" life events, involves those incidents that are not universal and that do not occur for most individuals. Non-normative events specific to the individual may include serious illness, death of a significant other, or particular opportunities. The occurrence of such events may be particularly stressful because they are not associated with a normative developmental pattern. The individual, of course, has received little or no socialization for non-normative events and may, therefore, require special educational efforts or interventions to cope with them. At the same time, what are considered non-normative events in one particular historical period may become increasingly more common (quasi-normative) events in succeeding time periods. For example, postsecondary education (college or vocational) has become an increasingly normative event during the past few decades.

The above sources of influence, of course, interact in producing developmental change across the life course. Whereas all three sources of influence may occur at any period of development, age-graded influences have been associated most frequently with childhood, and the likelihood of non-normative events becomes cumulative in adulthood. Such categories of developmental influences may have important useful implications for conceptions of lifelong learning and education.

Methodological Issues. The study of developmental processes across the life span is fraught with all the methodological problems faced by developmental scientists working with any particular stage of life. However, what may be minor confounds and caveats raised by perfectionist researchers at a single life stage become major threats to the validity of inferences when long periods of time or age spans are covered. In this section, we will consider three major methodological issues: (1) the problems caused by the indiscriminate inference of age changes from data based upon age differences; (2) the question of construct equivalence across the life span; and (3) the role of descriptive and experimental approaches in research on life span development.

Age and sociocultural change. Although this article cannot cover in detail the problems involved in the correct interpretation of developmental data obtained from cross-sectional, longitudinal, or sequential methods, the assumptions required for use of the more commonly encountered research designs should be recognized (for more detailed technical discussions, see Baltes, Reese, & Nesselroade, 1977; Nesselroade & Baltes, 1979; Schaie, 1973, 1977; Schaie & Hertzog, 1982).

Many studies of age effects, comparing the behavior of persons at widely differing ages, employ the "cross-sectional method." In this approach, individuals from two or more age groups are compared at one point in time. By definition, members of different groups must belong to different birth cohorts that may have had different prior experience. For example, if we compare a 20-year-old and a 70-year-old group, we cannot assume that the oldsters had experiences during their first twenty years of life similar to those of the current 20-year-olds. Cross-sectional data, therefore, will always confound ontogenetic (individual) change with generational differences. When widely different age groups are compared, generational differences may well be far greater than the magnitude of change within the same individual. Although information on age differences may be useful for concurrent policy decisions (for example, cohort differences in life expectancy), they are inappropriate for predicting age changes within a given individual, and they tell us nothing about individual patterns of aging.

To investigate ontogenetic or "true" age change, it is necessary to conduct "longitudinal studies" in which the same individuals are followed over the course of their development and are measured at two or more points in time. However, longitudinal studies have methodological hazards as well, because change within individuals may be confounded with the effects of sociocultural change occurring during the particular historical period of the longitudinal study. Generational differences and sociocultural change are likely to affect many behavioral variables. For example, sociocultural change in educational practices may influence certain aspects of intellectual functioning, career patterns, cross-racial relations, among others. It is therefore unlikely that findings of cross-sectional age differences can agree with those obtained from the study of longitudinal age changes. Nevertheless, it is the longitudinal study that permits assessment of patterns of age changes, their interrelation over time, and the explication of individual age functions.

A third approach has often been employed by investigators who wish to compare the behaviors of different cohorts at one specific age. For example, one might like to know whether a certain level of reading skill remains characteristic for several generations of sixth-graders. The comparison of different cohorts of individuals at the same age is called the "time-lag method." Its users must recognize that comparisons of two groups (cohorts) by the time-lag method will confound generational differences with specific sociocultural events occurring at a particular assessment point. The issues associated with time-lag methodology are relevant to recent concerns over performance decline in college entrance exams and in the application of achievement norms established for one cohort to succeeding generations.

A number of alternate strategies, known as "sequential methods," have been suggested to deal with problems of cross-sectional, longitudinal, and time-lag designs. Researchers interested in age-related, ontogenetic change across the life course must show that such change does not simply describe the impact of quite specific historical events (such as the great Depression) upon a single birth cohort. To deal with this problem, a research design is needed that involves the longitudinal study of two or more successive cohorts (for example, born in 1950 and 1960) over the same age range (ages 6 to 12). This is known as a "cohort-sequential design." To the extent that similar longitudinal changes are observed over several cohorts, it is then possible to speak of ontogenetic change as distinct from change that may be cohort-specific. For example, to examine the ontogenetic nature of Piagetian stages, it is important to examine their development in several cohorts.

A second type of sequential methodology is of importance to researchers who are concerned with the question of whether age differences in the young and old at one point in time are a function of generational differences. In this case, it is necessary to determine whether such generational differences are replicable across several young-old cohort pairs or are an artifact of the selection of particular age-cohort samples experiencing a specific form of sociocultural change. This involves a "time-sequential design" in which several independent samples of young and old are examined over the same age range but, of necessity, at different points in time. For example, it would be of interest to examine generational differences in attitudes toward higher education expressed by middle-aged parents and young adult children in 1960 versus 1970.

However, for most of the adult years (from maturity to early old age), there are few ontogenetic changes. Researchers interested in midlife issues therefore may want to use the "cross-sequential design." Two or more successive cohorts are examined over the same two or more measurement points. This design permits separate estimation of effects attributable to generational differences and those due to time-specific sociocultural change. For example, consider two cohorts of women born in 1930 and 1940 and assessed in 1970 (ages 30 and 40), and 1980 (ages 40 and 50) with respect to their attitudes toward female career aspirations. Generational differences in attitudes of middle-aged women can be assessed in 1970 and 1980. These differences can be compared with similarity of the two cohorts' attitudes at each measurement point as a function of time-specific cultural change. In some instances, the cross-sequential design is also useful for the simultaneous collection of data on age changes and age differences.

It should be stressed, however, that choice of any of the above strategies requires certain prior assumptions about the nature of the variables to be investigated. Thus, use of the longitudinal or cohort-sequential designs makes sense only if the investigator is willing to postulate trivial time-specific sociocultural change affecting the dependent variables over the age range to be studied. Similarly, the cross-sectional and time-sequential designs imply the assumption of trivial cohort-specific effects (if they are to be used to estimate age effects), and the cross-sequential design postulates trivial ontogenetic change over the age range investigated.

Equivalence of life-span constructs. It was noted earlier that development from one life stage to another may involve both quantitative and qualitative change. For example, an individual's score on the Binet intelligence test may change quantitatively. In addition, there are qualitative changes as reflected by different types of items to measure general intelligence at different age levels. Factor analytic studies of tests such as the Wechsler Adult Intelligence Scale (WAIS) have shown that the same measures may assess qualitatively different constructs across the adult age span (arithmetic tests becoming memory tests). Psychologists distinguish between directly observable behaviors ("phenotypes" or surface traits) and constructs ("genotypes" or latent traits). The former would be represented by a specific item on an intelligence test or personality questionnaire, the latter by ability factors such as "inductive reasoning," "recognition memory," or "introversion," requiring several measures of the construct. It is critical to examine changes across the life span in the relation of genotypic observable behaviors to a given construct they are assumed to represent.

The specific technique traditionally used to obtain quantifiable estimates of the phenotype-genotype relationship is factor analysis. Use of comparative factor analysis has become of major importance for students of life-span development in examining quantitative and qualitative developmental change. Its application permits specific inferences regarding developmental differences between groups at different life stages or of changes within groups at different ages. Although there may be age-related shifts in specific observable behaviors, true quantitative change of a developmental nature can be substantiated only if there is a mean difference between factor scores estimated for the construct.

Qualitative change at different ages or qualitative differences between age-cohort groups can be said to occur if there are significant changes or differences in factor structure. Given comparable sets of observable behavior, changes in factor structure can take the form of a lesser or a greater number of factors (that is, the observables no longer measure a construct, or a new construct is now measured by the observables); a change in the correlation (factor loadings) of the observables with the construct (that is, a given observable becomes a more or less efficient measure of the construct); or the factor angles (correlation among constructs) change (that is, shifts occur in the interaction of different constructs).

In the realm of intellectual abilities, for example, the following quantitative and qualitative changes have been noted: (1) factor scores increase through middle adulthood and decrease in advanced age, suggesting quantitative change; (2) the number of factors required for an adequate description of intelligence increases from early childhood to adulthood, suggesting a qualitatively greater differentiation of intellectual abilities; (3) factor loadings on the same factors change across much of the adult age range, suggesting changes in the relation of observables to the construct represented; (4) in old age, factor intercorrelations increase, suggesting a progressive reintegration of intellectual abilities (Reinert, 1970; Schaie, 1982).

Furthermore, because of age-related and generation-related differences among subjects in life-span studies, attention must be given to the appropriateness of the test format. That is, personality questionnaires for children require different language levels than those for adults. Social stereotypes and slang terms are quite different for adults born several decades apart. In addition, age-specific respondent characteristics must be considered, such as the incompletely developed motor coordination of young children or the typically mild visual impairment of the elderly. All of these variables may pose threats to the construct validity of measures used with subjects at widely varying ages in the life span.

Descriptive versus experimental approaches to research. When long-term predictions are to be made regarding future developmental trends, or when the later life consequences or developmental antecedents are to be identified, developmental scientists are somewhat handicapped by the fact that they cannot conduct true experiments. That is, the age variable or any other index of developmental status cannot be assigned at random. It is not possible to assign subjects to a specific age or, in some nice symmetric fashion, measure some persons in a longitudinal study at an older age *before* assessing them at a younger age. Developmental studies must therefore always be quasi experiments and subject to all of the validity threats characteristic of that class of investigation (Campbell & Stanley, 1963; Cook & Campbell, 1975; Schaie, 1977). Nevertheless, we can readily distinguish between two types of developmental studies—descriptive studies in which maturation or life experiences are the only treatment; and those experimental studies in which a treatment is used to examine a variable thought to account for the initial developmental or performance differences between two groups.

Descriptive developmental studies are typically of a pretest-treatment-posttest design, with maturation as the only treatment. Such studies are plagued with the possibility of erroneously inferring effects due to maturation that can be attributed more parsimoniously to other design confounds. The confounds of most serious concern to the life-span developmentalist involve history, testing effects,

experimental mortality, statistical regression, and selection.

"History" refers to the problem that, in a longitudinal study extending over a lengthy period of time, environmental impacts may occur that are specific to the historical period during which a sample is being followed and that may not be found during a subsequent period. Replication of the study would be a suitable control for this problem. "Testing effects" refer to practice effects accruing when there are multiple assessment periods. Use of additional control samples from the same cohort at each succeeding measurement point to assess for testing effects is one procedure for examining this confound. Ideally, these additional controls should be randomly drawn at the beginning of the study. "Experimental mortality" is the dropping out of some subjects due to death, disappearance, loss of interest, or experimenter ineptness. Unfortunately, dropout is rarely random with respect to the variables under investigation. It is necessary, therefore, to study differences in performance at the first assessment point between study survivors and dropouts to estimate the extent to which the attrited sample is still representative of the population originally sampled. "Statistical regression" occurs because extreme scores observed on one test occasion are likely to err in the extreme direction and, consequently, they will tend to regress toward the population mean in subsequent measurements. This effect could spuriously suggest developmental changes and is more serious the less reliable the measure used. Control here is maintained by attending to measurement reliability issues and investigating developmental trends for subsamples at different levels of the range of talent for the variable studied. Finally, "selection" refers to the problem that a developmental phenomenon may be of low incidence or may be exaggerated in a particular sample, particularly if the sample is either quite homogeneous or heterogeneous in characteristics related to the phenomenon of interest. Although these confounds have been studied primarily in descriptive studies, problems such as testing effects and experimental mortality also apply to control groups in experimental studies. Typically, such control groups receive only pretest and posttest assessments, with maturation as the only treatment.

Although it has been argued that descriptive studies can merely suggest the presence of relationships but make no contribution to scientific explanation, this conclusion is not entirely warranted for developmental data. The reason for this statement is that the flow of time in developmental studies will furnish a formidable causal measure. That is, in longitudinal studies, antecedents and consequents can be demarcated clearly by time. It is possible, therefore, to use powerful techniques such a cross-lagged correlations (in the univariate case) or path analysis and linear structural analysis (in the multivariate case) to engage in causal modeling and to test competing deductions from theory by means of descriptive data. The interested reader is referred to more detailed discussions of recently developed methodological advances by Jöreskog (1979), Rogosa (1979), and by Schaie and Hertzog (1982).

Two different approaches to experimental developmental studies are found in the literature. The first is a between-age-groups design, in which it is sought to determine whether an experimentally controlled variable would explain behavioral differences between two or more different age groups. The second design is usually employed within a single-age group to assess the degree of plasticity or modifiability for a given variable.

In the first type of study, two samples of differing age are selected that show performance differences on some variable, say problem-solving ability. A training paradigm is then employed, and the hypothesis is tested that the lower performing (younger age) group benefits more from training than does the initially higher-performing older group. What is of major concern here is the interaction and not the main effects. A significant interaction would support the hypothesis that the training paradigm indeed models the maturational process. A prominent example of this approach is provided by the Piagetian training studies that attempt to accelerate the attainment of more advanced states with younger children. It should be noted that a possibly even more powerful paradigm, rarely found in the literature, would be to show that a given skill could be advanced for younger but reduced in older subjects.

In the second type of study, individuals in a single-age group are divided randomly into experimental and control groups, the experimental group being trained on a skill which should be demonstrated at that age. For example, compensatory educational studies with disadvantaged children have been used to examine the range of remediation (behavioral plasticity) with training. Such single-age training studies in later adulthood are aimed at examining the range of improvement relative to normative patterns of performance at this age. Adult studies of this type, ideally, ought to be done with persons with known developmental histories. That is, we need to know whether a given individual has actually experienced a loss on the variable to be trained or whether we are trying to build a new skill not previously exercised by our trainee.

Experimental investigations of the first type are important obviously for the development of life-span developmental theory. The latter are crucial both to our understanding of the range of modifiability of behavior at different ages and to the generation of an applied developmental psychology that seeks to provide techniques and knowledge for the remediation of developmental defects and optimization of developmental attainments.

Implications for Lifelong Learning. Just as a life-span perspective suggests a qualitatively different approach to developmental psychology, lifelong learning entails a unique approach to education (Dave, 1976; Schaie & Willis, 1978). In this section, some of the critical features of a life-span perspective as they may apply to lifelong learning will be examined.

Critical features. Foremost is the implication that focus upon continuing development and change across the life span calls for a redistribution of educational efforts across the total life course. This perspective is significantly different than that taken by traditional approaches to development and education. Such traditional views assume that most of the critical life events (initial job entry, first marriage, child rearing) occur early in development and are largely age-related; thus, the greatest educational "need" occurs during the first quarter of the life span. Implicit in such a perspective is the assumption that development in later life stages is primarily rooted in early developmental periods, and thus educational efforts during the early years can "prepare" the individual for later life events. However, a life-span perspective suggests that critical life events occur at all life stages and require educational efforts appropriate to that developmental event and period. In addition, the impact of sociocultural change on development and the increasing occurrence and prominence of non-normative life events in the adult years argues for the need for continuing educational intervention across the life span. Thus, a lifelong learning perspective requires the reallocation of educational resources across the life span, paralleling continuing developmental change at all life stages.

Secondly, an integrative rather than age-segmented approach to life-span education is critical. That is, lifelong learning does not necessarily imply a succession of unrelated, age-segmented educational efforts across the life course. More is implied than the addition of adult education to the currently existing educational efforts at earlier ages. Just as a life-span perspective of development emphasizes the linkages and relationships among developmental periods and events, an integrative approach to lifelong learning would focus upon the sequence and relationships among educational efforts across various life stages. For example, whereas early education may focus on knowledge and skill acquisition, later educational efforts may focus on knowledge and skill synthesis, application, and evaluation. In addition, it would be important to provide remedial educational opportunities at various points in the life course to offset prior educational deficiencies as well as potential obsolescence associated with rapid technological change. Specification of the interrelationships among educational efforts at various developmental periods will be a critical task in designing comprehensive lifelong learning models.

Third, the increase in the range of interindividual differences for various developmental phenomena across the life span has important implications for lifelong learning. There has been increasing recognition of individual differences as a critical factor in educational programming in the early years. This is reflected in recent consideration of issues such as cultural pluralism and individualized instruction. Individual differences will become an even more salient issue within a lifelong learning perspective. In order to accommodate the lifelong learner, educational efforts will need to become increasingly adaptive and differentiated. Such educational adaptiveness and differentiation is represented in issues such as formal/informal education, full-time/part-time learning, and direct/distance instruction.

Fourth, consideration of multiple, interacting sources of developmental change should be of relevance within a life-span approach (Baltes, Reese, & Lipsitt, 1980). Traditional educational efforts have focused primarily upon what has been defined in this article as age-graded, biological, and environmental influences on development. Education has been concerned with the child's acquisition of knowledge and skills considered age-appropriate within our culture. In this vein, education has served as a powerful age-graded socialization agent in development (Parelius, 1975). However, as a life-span approach to education is considered, the importance of history-graded and non-normative life events as foci and moderators of educational efforts becomes increasingly salient. Education has, of necessity, been somewhat responsive to sociocultural change or history-graded factors. In periods of rapid and pervasive change, it becomes even more critical that both preventive and remedial educational efforts be systematically implemented to facilitate human development within a changing world. History-graded influences have important implications both for early life education and for educational efforts in the adult years focusing upon "updating" and obsolescence remediation. In addition, educational intervention associated within non-normative life events will be important. Because such events are unique and thus not part of normative socialization experiences, special educational programs to enable the individual to adapt and profit from these events will be particularly useful.

Expanding the educational context. As the role of education broadens conceptually and lengthens temporally, the context for education must also expand. With lifelong learning, only a small portion of the individual's education would actually be acquired within a classroom. Except for the years of formal schooling, most of the individual's education is experiential and active, rather than receptive, and occurs in the context of daily living. Thus, the home, work place, and public facilities are all contexts for education (Cross, 1981). Education can extend geographically across the individual's total life space as well as temporally across the life span.

Moreover, lifelong learning suggests changes in the teacher-learner role. The role of the teacher across the life span appears to change from director of learning to that of a facilitator or resource person. Whereas society and the educator direct the education of the young, the content and method of learning in adulthood are largely determined by the learner. Developmental changes in the learner across the life span suggest the need for qualitatively different types of teacher training for educators working with different age groups. The techniques of the high school or even college instructor may be inappropriate in teaching middle-aged or older persons. Teacher-

training institutions must be involved in translating the information concerning adult learning into a delineation of skills required of the adult educator. Much has been said about changing characteristics as the learner ages, but we should not forget that career teachers age as well. Thus, principles that apply to the adult learner may apply equally to the teacher's own continued updating and learning endeavors.

Summary. In this article, some of the conceptual and methodological issues associated with a life-span perspective of human development have been discussed. It has been suggested that a life-span approach involves more than chronicling the major developmental events associated with each age and life stage. Critical to a life-span approach is the identification of developmental patterns, processes, and relationships defining the total life course. Four such features of a life-span perspective were discussed. First, there is continuing development and change across the life span. Critical developmental changes and life events occur in adulthood as well as in childhood. Such developmental events in later life cannot be totally predicted or dealt with in terms of earlier life stages. This focus upon continuing developmental change suggests considerable plasticity in functioning across the life course, with the potential and need for educational intervention at all life stages.

Second, it is suggested that chronological age may not be the most salient index of many types of developmental change. The isomorphy between biological and behavioral change characteristics of early life stages becomes less evident across much of adulthood. Developmental change, particularly in adulthood, is often not directly age-related. Thus, an age-graded approach to development is not particularly useful in describing or intervening in many developmental phenomena.

Third, many developmental events are characterized by increasing interindividual variability across the life course. Such increased variability is associated with the greater impact of environmental sources of influence during the adult years. As the diversity of environmental influences increases, the range of individual differences expands.

Fourth, life-span development involves multiple, interacting change influences. These include age-graded, history-graded, and non-normative life events.

As longer spans of the life course are examined, several methodological issues become increasingly salient. First, there is the need to differentiate behavioral change associated with ontogenetic development, cohort differences, and time-specific cultural events. A series of sequential methodological strategies are available to differentiate such effects. Second, equivalence of developmental constructs and instruments used to assess such constructs becomes important in assessing life span change. Both quantitative and qualitative change associated with such constructs must be examined, and appropriate methodological procedures considered. Third, there is the issue of descriptive versus experimental approaches to the study of developmental change.

Finally, several critical features of a life span approach are applicable to lifelong learning. It is suggested that a life-span focus would involve a qualitatively different perspective of the educational enterprise, requiring the reallocation of educational efforts and resources across the total life span.

K. Warner Schaie
Sherry L. Willis

See also Adolescent Development; Adult Development; Adult Education; Aging; Early Childhood Development; Infant Development; Middle Years Development; Preadolescent Development; Women's Education.

REFERENCES

Baltes, P. B. Life-span developmental psychology: Observations on history and theory. In P. B. Baltes & O. G. Brim, Jr. (Eds.), *Life-span Development and Behavior* (Vol. 2). New York: Academic Press, 1979.

Baltes, P. B.; Reese, H. W.; & Lipsitt, L. P. Life-span developmental psychology. *Annual Review of Psychology*, 1980, *31*, 65–110.

Baltes, P. B.; Reese, H. W.; & Nesselroade, J. R. *Life-span Developmental Psychology: Introduction to Research Methods*. Monterey, Calif.: Brooks/Cole, 1977.

Baltes, P. B., & Willis, S. L. Life-span developmental psychology, cognitive functioning, and social policy. In M. W. Riley (Ed.), *Aging from Birth to Death*. Boulder, Colo.: Westview Press, 1979.

Bayley, N. Behavioral correlates of mental growth: Birth to thirty-six years. *American Psychologist*, 1968, *23*, 1–17.

Brim, O. G., Jr., & Kagan, J. (Eds.). *Constancy and Change in Human Development*. Cambridge, Mass.: Harvard University Press, 1980.

Bronfenbrenner, U. Toward an experimental ecology of human development. *American Psychologist*, 1977, *32*, 513–531.

Campbell, D. T., & Stanley, J. C. *Experimental and Quasi-experimental Designs for Research*. Chicago: Rand McNally, 1963.

Cook, T. D., & Campbell, D. T. The design and conduct of quasi-experiments and true experiments in field settings. In M. D. Dunnette (Ed.), *Handbook of Industrial and Organizational Research*. Chicago: Rand McNally, 1975.

Cross, K. P. *Adults as Learners*. San Francisco: Jossey-Bass, 1981.

Dave, R. H. (Ed.). *Foundations of Lifelong Education*. Oxford: Pergamon Press, 1976.

Eichorn, D. H. The Institute of Human Development Studies, Berkeley and Oakland. In L. F. Jarvik, C. Eisdorfer, & J. E. Blum (Eds.), *Intellectual Functioning in Adults*. New York: Springer-Verlag, 1973.

Flavell, J. Cognitive changes in adulthood. In L. R. Goulet & P. B. Baltes (Eds.), *Life-span Developmental Psychology: Research and Theory*. New York: Academic Press, 1970.

Honzik, M., & Macfarlane, J. Personality development and intellectual functioning from twenty-one months to forty years. In L. F. Jarvik, C. Eisdorfer, & J. E. Blum (Eds.), *Intellectual Functioning in Adults*. New York: Springer-Verlag, 1973.

Hultsch, D. F., & Plemons, J. K. Life events and life-span development. In P. B. Baltes & O. G. Brim, Jr. (Eds.), *Life-span Devel-*

opment and Behavior (Vol. 2). New York: Academic Press, 1979.

Jöreskog, K. G. Statistical estimation of structural models in longitudinal-developmental investigations. In J. R. Nesselroade & P. B. Baltes (Eds.), *Longitudinal Research in the Study of Behavior and Development*. New York: Academic Press, 1979.

Kagan, J. Perspectives on continuity. In O. G. Brim, Jr., & J. Kagan (Eds.), *Constancy and Change in Human Development*. Cambridge, Mass.: Harvard University Press, 1980.

Labouvie-Vief, G. Adult cognitive development: In search of alternative interpretations. *Merrill-Palmer Quarterly*, 1977, *23*, 227–263.

Nesselroade, J. R., & Baltes, P. B. (Eds.). *Longitudinal Research in the Study of Behavior and Development*. New York: Academic Press, 1979.

Neugarten, B. L. *Middle Age and Aging*. Chicago: University of Chicago Press, 1968.

Neugarten, B. L., & Havighurst, R. J. (Eds.). *Social Policy, Social Ethics, and the Aging Society*. University of Chicago: Committee on Human Development, 1976.

Palmore, E. (Ed.). *Normative Aging II: Reports from the Duke Longitudinal Studies, 1970–1973*. Durham, N.C.: Duke University Press, 1974.

Parelius, A. P. Lifelong education and age stratification. *American Behavioral Scientist*, 1975, *19*, 206–223.

Porges, S. W. Cohort effects and apparent secular trends in infant research. In K. F. Riegel & J. A. Meacham (Eds.), *Social and Environmental Issues*. Vol. 2 of *The Developing Individual in a Changing World*. The Hague: Mouton, 1975.

Pressey, S. L.; Janney, J. E.; & Kuhlen, J. E. *Life: A Psychological Survey*. New York: Harper & Brothers, 1939.

Reinert, G. Comparative factor analytic studies of intelligence throughout the human life span. In L. Goulet & P. Baltes (Eds.), *Life-span Developmental Psychology: Theory and Research*. New York: Academic Press, 1970.

Riegel, K. F. History of psychological gerontology. In J. E. Birren & K. W. Schaie (Eds.), *Handbook of the Psychology of Aging*. New York: Van Nostrand Reinhold, 1977.

Riegel, K. F., & Meacham, J. (Eds.). Social and Environmental Issues. Vol. 2 of *The Developing Individual in a Changing World*. The Hague: Mouton, 1975.

Riley, M. W. Age strata in social systems. In E. Shanas & R. Binstock (Eds.), *Handbook of Aging and the Social Sciences*. New York: Van Nostrand Reinhold, 1976.

Riley, M. W. *Aging from Birth to Death: Interdisciplinary Perspectives*. Boulder, Colo.: Westview Press, 1979.

Roche, A. F. (Ed.). Secular trends in human growth, maturation, and development. *Monographs of the Society for Research in Child Development*, 1979, *44*, 3–4.

Rogosa, D. Causal models in longitudinal research: Rationale, formulation, and interpretation. In J. R. Nesselroade & P. B. Baltes (Eds.), *Longitudinal Research in the Study of Behavior and Development*. New York: Academic Press, 1979.

Schaie, K. W. Methodological problems in descriptive developmental research on adulthood and aging. In J. R. Nesselroade & H. W. Reese (Eds.), *Life-span Developmental Psychology: Methodological Issues*. New York: Academic Press, 1973.

Schaie, K. W. Quasi-experimental research designs in the psychology of aging. In J. E. Birren & K. W. Schaie (Eds.), *Handbook of the Psychology of Aging*. New York: Van Nostrand Reinhold, 1977.

Schaie, K. W. Toward a stage theory of adult cognitive development. *Journal of Aging and Human Development,* 1977–1978, 8, 129–138.

Schaie, K. W. The primary mental abilities in adulthood: An exploration in the development of psychometric intelligence. In P. B. Baltes & O. G. Brim, Jr. (Eds.), *Life-span Development and Behavior* (Vol. 2). New York: Academic Press, 1979.

Schaie, K. W. The Seattle Longitudinal Study: A twenty-one year investigation of psychometric intelligence. In K. W. Schaie (Ed.), *Longitudinal Studies of Adult Psychological Development.* New York: Gulford Press, 1982.

Schaie, K. W., & Hertzog, C. Longitudinal methods. In B. B. Wollman (Ed.), *Handbook of Developmental Psychology.* Englewood Cliffs, N.J.: Prentice-Hall, 1982.

Schaie, K. W., & Willis, S. L. Life-span development: Implications for education. In L. Shulman (Ed.), *Review of Research in Education* (Vol. 6). Itasca, Ill.: F. E. Peacock, 1978.

Thorndike, E. L.; Bregman, E. O.; Tilton, J. W.; & Woodyard, E. *Adult Learning.* New York: Macmillan, 1928.

LINGUISTICS

See English Language Education; Language Development; Reading; Second Language Acquisition.

LISTENING

Listening is "the process by which spoken language is converted to meaning in the mind" (Lundsteen, 1979, p. 1). This process is, however, still only imperfectly understood. And because it is only imperfectly understood, neither researchers nor educators have as yet achieved a common vocabulary or standard set of definitions that permits easy comparison of either theoretical viewpoints or research results. Nevertheless, since serious study of listening behavior began (generally dating from Rankin's 1926 doctoral study measuring ability to understand spoken language and his observation that people generally spend 42 percent of their communicating time in listening), enough information has accumulated to provide the basis for designing efficient instructional programs in listening and to document the benefit of such programs in improving general communication competence (Devine, 1978). This article summarizes the definition of listening, attributes of listening, and more recent attempts to develop and refine hierarchical listings of listening skills and behavior to provide the basis for more sophisticated research on instructional programs. The relationship of listening to the other language arts and to sociocultural and psychological factors is briefly described. This description is followed by a survey of school programs, curricula, teaching methodology, and measurement instruments. The article concludes with a brief description of needed research in the area.

Although there is no current definition of listening that is generally accepted by researchers and educators, the process of listening has been broken down into three stages. Those who study physical and psychological aspects of the auditory process have identified three stages by which oral language is "heard." The first is "hearing," during which sounds are received and modified by the ear. The second, specifically called "listening," involves the identification of component sounds and sound sequences so that words are recognizable within the sounds. Finally comes "auditing," translating the continuous flow of words into meaning (Taylor, 1964).

Lundsteen (1979) has done the most careful analysis of all available data about listening to date. She lists some of the critical attributes of listening; compares listening attributes with those of speaking, reading, and writing; and enumerates the operations of a proficient listener. A person's ability to listen effectively is based on the previous knowledge that the individual has, the listening material itself, the physiological activities (hearing, sensation, perception) that occur, attention or concentration, and the productive thought that permits the message to be integrated at the time of listening and extended beyond the time of listening (Lundsteen, 1979). Generally, the last three components can be broken into ten steps: "(1) hear, (2) hold in memory, (3) attend, (4) form images, (5) search the past store of ideas, (6) compare, (7) test the cues, (8) recode, (9) get meaning, and (10) intellectualize beyond the listening moment" (Lundsteen, 1979, p. 18). "The 'best' listener in any group . . . is a person who most consistently, in the least time and in the greatest variety of circumstances, most closely comprehends the speaker's meaning in the widest variety of spoken material" (Lundsteen, 1979, p. 74).

Weaver and Rutherford (1974) have developed a hierarchy of listening skills for normal and visually handicapped children, based on theories of development of auditory abilities described in the literature. They emphasized, at the time of their report, that no research had actually indicated a specific sequence. To date, there is still no published research defining a developmental sequence of listening skills as there is, for example, for the articulation of sounds. Weaver and Rutherford's hierarchy is divided into three sections. The "environmental section" includes skills spanning the prenatal period (i.e., fetal movement in response to sound) to a 9-to-11-year-old's identification of sounds in the environment at certain times of the day and a child's evaluation of them in terms of direction and type of sound. This latter skill is especially important at this age for the visually handicapped. The "discrimination section" includes skills ranging from an infant's responding differentially to sounds to a 6-to-8-year-old's discrimination of temporal order of sounds within words. The comprehension section includes skills ranging from an infant's responding to his or her name to a 9-to-10-year-old's comparing or contrasting, then evaluating statements.

Further work on the development of a hierarchy of listening skills for instructional purposes has been provided by Lundsteen (1979). Her taxonomic listing of listening skills resulted in a hierarchy of listening skills objectives, both for general listening and for critical listening. These objectives incorporate both cognitive and affective domains and include the social, interpersonal skills of role taking and listener empathy. Lundsteen's inclusion of these skills (role taking and empathy) highlights the interactive aspects of the communication process.

Lundsteen also points to the differences in sophistication levels of egocentric and nonegocentric communicators. Her work is particularly important because it provides a rationale for educators, psychologists, and other interested professionals to use as a guide to understanding listening behavior and listener needs. The egocentric speaker sends the listener a message about events that reflects the speaker's own meaning codes and does not change them to suit the attributes of the listener. The nonegocentric speaker, however, recodes events as a message he or she thinks is appropriate for the listener's needs (Lundsteen, 1979; Menyuk, 1977). Thus the egocentric speaker is likely to say, "I'm responsible only for what I said, not what you heard." The nonegocentric speaker evidences a much greater understanding of the audience (listener) who is receiving the message. Studies to support this work are primarily related to messages that deal with information; they tend to neglect self-expressive, literary, or persuasive messages (Lundsteen, 1979).

Factors that may affect both the speaker and the listener even more than the egocentric-nonegocentric dichotomy include a lack of a sufficiently developed repertoire of language, difficulties in searching the language possibilities (a retrieval problem), and an insufficient organization of the contextual variables (Menyuk, 1977).

Interrelationships among Language Skills. A number of researchers have examined the relationships of listening, reading, speaking, writing, and intelligence to one another (Lundsteen, 1979; Devine, 1978; Marten, 1978). Most early research assumed that since reading and listening are receptive skills, they are highly interdependent. More recent work does not completely support this contention (Devine, 1967).

Hildyard (1978), for example, compared third-grade and fifth-grade readers' and listeners' comprehension of a narrative text and found that listeners paid more attention to what was "meant," and readers paid more attention to what was "said." She concluded that readers and listeners do adopt different strategies when comprehending narrative texts.

Schallert, Kleiman, and Rubin (1977) argue that there are differences between oral and written English that entail differences in the skills and knowledge necessary to comprehend them. They point to differences in the physical nature, use, and characteristics of the two modes. Written language is generally more complex. The reader sets his own pace; the writer cannot tailor the message to a specific audience as a speaker often can. Listeners have more cues—voice, gestures, facial expression—than do readers, who must depend upon syntactic and semantic

cues. Listeners can ask for clarification. These researchers also note that most prior work "neglected to distinguish orally-presented written text from natural oral language, and spoken material written down from natural written language" (Schallert, Kleiman, & Rubin, 1977, p. 18).

Sociocultural and Psychological Considerations. Anthropologists, linguists, psychologists, and sociologists have done a good deal of research on interpreting communication from different sociocultural perspectives (Cazden, John, & Hymes, 1972). These researchers have used linguistic and ethnographic approaches both inside and outside the classroom to demonstrate that children and adults do have different communication patterns for both listening and speaking that affect their opportunities to learn. For example, it has been shown that some American Indian children do not interact verbally in classrooms because the social conditions in the classroom differ dramatically from those in the community (Philips, 1972). Studies of Black dialect speakers, Spanish speakers, and others have described the differences between norms of the school and the community in language use, language environment, and communication context where, for example, differences in norms for eye contact or the use of familiar cues for gaining and giving attention such as a pointed finger can seriously interfere with comprehension and response (Cazden, John, & Hymes, 1972). Even the cultural effects of communication "in space" (the physical positioning of speaker and listener) differ by culture and age and are hypothesized to create a barrier to effective communication (Wood, 1976).

There is only limited evidence in currently available listening research that modifying the learning environment in order to improve the acquisition and effectiveness of listening and speaking skills does, in fact, improve these skills. Nor has there been much research that attempts to ascertain whether, by providing teachers with more linguistic and cultural information, children's language acquisition and development is improved, in spite of the 1979 federal court ruling mandating such training for inservice teachers of Black English speakers in Michigan (Center for Applied Linguistics, 1979).

Listening Programs and Curricula. Although there is evidence that a number of excellent school programs for listening have been developed (Marten, 1978), listening is still not generally a part of the standard curriculum in schools (Devine, 1978). Both theory and research on listening suggest that it needs to be taught. Devine (1978), in his analysis of recent listening research, concludes that teachers and curriculum designers should be aware "that children and adults spend more time listening than they do reading, speaking or writing," and hence "writers who point to the peculiar power of listening to influence opinions and behaviors" should be heeded (p. 299). Additional research has also demonstrated that adults may be worse listeners than children (Rossiter, 1970).

Research spanning thirty years clearly supports the notion that listening can be taught (Devine, 1978), although specific teaching methods have had to be inferred from the research reports (Marten, 1978). Several research-based reports provide specific and detailed information on teacher roles, instructional strategies, listening materials, and instructional objectives for teaching general listening, critical listening, and problem solving at all levels. Friedman (1978) has examined the listening research pertinent to providing an adequate listening environment in the classroom, focusing on the components of attentiveness, selection, and organization, and evaluation of three types of messages: those that emphasize content or information; those that affect feelings or intensity of involvement; and those that are meant to have an aesthetic impact. His report describes those factors that inhibit listening and those that enhance it.

Enhancing factors include such items as relevance of the message to the listener's current life interests; background, or setting in which the message is delivered; intensity, extensity (size), and concreteness of the stimulus; redundancy features of the message; involvement level required of the listener; listener's familiarity with the topics covered; and identification of the speakers with the listener. Inhibiting factors include physical needs, such as hunger and fatigue, as well as psychological factors, such as "cost" of listening to a message that is evaluative of the listener or relates to a topic that arouses negative or fearful reactions (for example, death, divorce, war).

Wolvin and Coakley (1979) have examined research to support the development of listening programs at the high school and college levels. Their analysis, although similar to Friedman's, focuses on why people listen rather than on the message itself. They identify five goals for listening: appreciation, discrimination, comprehension, therapy, and critical analysis. They have constructed exercises designed to develop listening awareness and to build effective listening skills.

Instructional objectives, teaching strategies, instructional materials, and listening programs, based on basic and applied research, as well as practice, are described and analyzed by Lundsteen (1979).

Listening can be measured (Devine, 1978), but there is no one comprehensive diagnostic listening test (Marten, 1978). A small number of published tests of listening skills are available. Subtests of the Illinois Test of Psycholinguistic Abilities (designed for ages $2\frac{1}{2}$ to 9 years) measure auditory decoding, auditory-vocal association, auditory-vocal automatic ability, and auditory-vocal sequencing. The Wepman Auditory Discrimination Test (ages 5 to 9) measures children's abilities to discriminate between sounds in words. The Sequential Tests of Educational Progress Listening Tests (ages 9 through adult) measure listening comprehension. The Brown-Carlson Listening Comprehension Test (ages 14 through adult) also measures comprehension. The validity, reliability, and usefulness of all of these instruments have been questioned (Lundsteen, 1979; Devine, 1978, 1967; Marten, 1978).

Compressed Speech. Numerous studies have examined compressed speech as a method for improving comprehension. Since people normally talk at a rate of 120 words per minute and since most spoken language can be comprehended equally well at rates twice that (Friedman, 1978), varying the speed at which messages are delivered might substantially improve comprehension for selected listeners. Research results are conflicting (Marten, 1978), and listening programs have not generally been developed to test the utility of this technologically assisted tool for improving comprehension of recorded material ordinarily used in school programs. At least one researcher (Carver, 1973) has argued that compressed speech presentations may interfere with comprehension since they may exceed what many listeners can tolerate.

Conversely, research studies have supported slower rates of presentation for young children, the auditorially disabled, and the verbally disadvantaged (McCroskey & Thompson, 1973; Berry & Erickson, 1973).

Recent Trends and Future Research. In 1964, the Association for Childhood Education International, the Association for Supervision and Curriculum Development, the International Reading Association, and the National Council of Teachers of English issued an unprecedented joint statement calling for a reexamination of the school's role in teaching speaking and listening. The writing team representing each of these organizations stated unequivocally that speaking and listening deserved as much time as reading and writing in the curriculum at all levels (Mackintosh, 1964).

In the ensuing years, a number of events and social changes have occurred that necessitate more research on children's listening skills and the effects of school programs designed to sharpen these skills. There has been political pressure for more basic education stressing oral language as well as reading and writing. Research agencies have indicated a willingness to fund research as well as demonstration projects in these areas.

The growth and importance of mass media in our lives make it necessary to examine the effects of listening on attitudes, skills, behavior patterns, and understanding. The pervasiveness of the mass media, as well as the continued changes in our personal communication patterns, argues for using research methodology more sensitive to the personal requirements of children and the needs of educational programming.

Although the research reviewed here has provided a basis for the design of instructional programs, it is remarkably undeveloped in relation to what has been developed in the other receptive-skill areas of reading and viewing of nonprint media. Studies are particularly needed on how the listener uses language skill and knowledge to develop critical, therapeutic, and appreciative listening skills. Coupled with such basic research on processes, more sophisticated study of effective teaching methodologies and instructional materials needs to be done. To date, most studies have been quantitative and of brief duration. Longitudinal study using both quantitative and qualitative methodologies should be undertaken. The research into biological, psychological, and social and cultural factors that enhance or inhibit communication has been promising, but has not yet produced results that can guide instructional practice.

John M. Kean

See also Hearing Impairment; Language Development; Speech Communication.

REFERENCES

Berry, M. D., & Erickson, R. L. Speaking rate: Effects on children's comprehension of normal speech. *Journal of Speech and Hearing Research*, 1973, *16*, 367–374.

Carver, R. P. Effect of increasing the rate of speech presentation upon comprehension. *Journal of Educational Psychology*, 1973, *65*, 118–126.

Cazden, C. B.; John, V. P.; & Hymes, D. (Eds.). *Functions of Language in the Classroom*. New York: Teachers College Press, 1972.

Center for Applied Linguistics. *The Ann Arbor Decision: Memorandum Opinion and Order and the Educational Plan*. Arlington, Va.: The Center, 1979.

Devine, T. G. Listening. *Review of Educational Research*, 1967, *37*(2), 152–158.

Devine, T. G. Listening: What do we know after fifty years of research and theorizing? *Journal of Reading*, 1978, *21*(4), 296–304.

Friedman, P. G. *Listening Processes: Attention, Understanding, Evaluation (What Research Says to the Teacher)*. Washington, D.C.: National Education Association, 1978. (ERIC Document Reproduction Service No. ED 176 283)

Hildyard, A. *On the Bias of Oral and Written Language in the Drawing of Inferences on Text*. Ontario: Ontario Institute for Studies in Education, 1978. (ERIC Document Reproduction Service No. ED 154 358)

Lundsteen, S. W. *Listening: Its Impact on Reading and the Other Language Arts* (2nd ed.). Urbana, Ill.: National Council of Teachers of English, 1979. (ERIC Document Reproduction Service No. ED 169 537)

Mackintosh, H. K. (Ed.). *Children and Oral Language*. Washington, D.C.: Association for Childhood Education and Association for Supervision and Curriculum Development; Newark, Del.: International Reading Association; Champaign, Ill.: National Council of Teachers of English, 1964.

Marten, M. Listening in review. In H. G. Shane & J. Walden (Eds.), *Classroom-relevant Research in the Language Arts*. Washington, D.C.: Association for Supervision and Curriculum Development, 1978. (ERIC Document Reproduction Service No. ED 158 333)

McCroskey, R. L., & Thompson, H. W. Comprehension of rate-controlled speech by children with special learning disabilities. *Journal of Learning Disabilities*, 1973, *6*, 621–627.

Menyuk, P. *Language and Maturation*. Cambridge, Mass.: MIT Press, 1977.

Philips, S. U. Participant structures and communicative competence: Warm Springs children in community and classroom. In C. B. Cazden, V. P. John, & D. Hymes (Eds.), *Functions of Language in the Classroom*. New York: Teachers College Press, 1972.

Rankin, P. T. *Measurement of the Ability to Understand Spoken Language*. Unpublished doctoral dissertation, University of Michigan, 1926.

Rossiter, C. M., Jr. Chronological age and listening of adult students. *Adult Education*, 1970, *21*, 40–43.

Schallert, D. L.; Kleiman, G. M.; & Rubin, A. D. *Analysis of Differences between Written and Oral Language* (Technical Report No. 29). Urbana-Champaign: Center for the Study of Reading, University of Illinois, 1977. (ERIC Document Reproduction Service No. ED 144 038)

Taylor, S. E. *Listening (What Research Says to the Teacher)*. Washington, D.C.: National Education Association, 1964. (ERIC Document Reproduction Service No. ED 026 120)

Weaver, S. W., & Rutherford, W. L. A hierarchy of listening skills. *Elementary English*, 1974, *51*, 1146–1150.

Wolvin, A. D., & Coakley, C. G. *Listening Instruction*. Urbana, Ill.: ERIC Clearinghouse on Reading and Communication Skills, 1979. (ERIC Document Reproduction Service No. ED 170 827)

Wood, B. S. *Children and Communication: Verbal and Nonverbal Language Development*. Englewood Cliffs, N.J.: Prentice-Hall, 1976.

LITERATURE

During the nineteenth century, a loosely related series of instructional activities came together as a single curriculum area called the teaching of English. Rhetoric, oratory, spelling, grammar, literary history, and reading all had their place in the curriculum, often competing with one another for attention. Many of these activities are clearly functional, and as such, have helped justify a central role for English in the curriculum at all levels, from elementary school through college. Other aspects of English teaching, in particular the teaching of literature, are less clearly functional, drawing their impetus from the importance of a "cultural heritage" or from their presumed importance in developing "values" and "ethics." Although English teachers have usually been forced to cite the more functional aspects of their subject area when justifying its central place in school programs, they have usually placed literature at the center of the curricula they have planned. Hard pressed to formulate the importance of literary instruction in any but the most general terms, they have repeatedly turned to scholarly studies about literature as a source of material for instruction. Research in instructional procedures, as well as in comprehension of literary texts, has been hampered by the difficulty of clearly specifying the value of literature to the individual student or to society at large.

Research during the last decade has clarified our understanding of the historical background of literature as a school subject and has provided new tools for studying the nature of literary response. This article begins with an examination of the historical role of literature in the curriculum, drawing on a number of recent syntheses (in particular, Applebee, 1974; Hook, 1979; Judy & England, 1979; Piche, 1977). It then summarizes what we have learned from empirical studies of literature and literature instruction, under the general headings of status surveys, reading interests, responses to literature, and instructional techniques. A final section looks briefly at promising new directions for empirical and conceptual analysis.

History of Literature in the Curriculum

The study of vernacular literature became an established part of the American school curriculum during the nineteenth century, in the course of the struggle between the "ancient" and the "modern" curriculum. Although "belles lettres" was esteemed and literary societies flourished as extracurricular activities (Rudolph, 1962; Witt, 1968), two obstacles prevented literary studies from being incorporated into the formal curriculum. One was the lack of established methods of literary study to guarantee the rigorous "mental discipline" that provided the rationale for all academic study. The other was a mistrust generated by the reliance on "emotion" rather than "reason" in literary texts. Both obstacles were overcome by 1900.

Eighteenth and Nineteenth Centuries. Because it lacked a methodology of its own, literature initially entered the curriculum as part of other studies. During the eighteenth century, Hugh Blair (1783) and other Scottish rhetoricians had begun to use texts from the vernacular literature as material for grammatical parsing and rhetorical analysis, all in the service of writing skills. By the middle of the nineteenth century, these approaches were well established in American schools, and such Latinate texts as *Paradise Lost* and *An Essay on Man* were relatively widely used as exercise material for analysis. Literary history offered an alternative source of mental discipline, with details of authors' lives and works to be memorized. Thomas Budge Shaw's *Outlines of English Literature* (1848) became the first important school text and generated many successors during the remainder of the century (Applebee, 1974).

Although rhetoric and history brought literature into the curriculum, the development of techniques of philological analysis made the study of literary texts academically respectable. Philology involved the scientific study of language, in an effort to trace the linguistic and historical roots of a culture. Its goals—to develop a biography of a nation—were lofty; however, in the hands of all but the greatest scholars, philology degenerated into pedantic textual criticism. Between 1850 and 1900, philological studies legitimized the study of literature in American universities, spreading from there to the schools.

During this same period, literature was earning a new reputation as a reservoir of cultural values, a bulwark against the dehumanization caused by industrialization. Through the work of the Romantic poets and critics, the suspicion of "emotion" was replaced by a conception of culture that lifted literary study to a special place within society at large. Matthew Arnold in *Culture and Anarchy* (1867), provided a widely read interpretation of culture as a source of a new principle of authority to replace the eroding bonds of class and religion (Wilson, 1932). Although Arnold explicitly argued the value of the classical tradition over all that came later, his arguments mainly benefited the emerging studies of vernacular literature.

Philology provided a respectable method for the study of literature; the Romantic interpretation of culture provided a reason. It remained for the pressures of an examination system to ensure a rapid institutionalization of literature in the school curriculum. The first college entrance requirement involving literary texts was set by Harvard University for students entering in 1874, as part of a test of writing ability. Other colleges followed with their own lists of required titles, gradually shifting the emphasis from writing ability to the study of the literary texts themselves. By 1894, the conflicting lists of required titles were causing enough of a problem that a National Conference on Uniform Entrance Requirements in English was established to bring some consistency and order to the syllabus. The pronouncements of this national conference succeeded those of Harvard in shaping the teaching of literature.

By 1900, the teaching of English in general and of literature in particular was well established in American schools and colleges, although it was still a new and uncertain enterprise. Annotated texts, based on the lists for the college entrance examinations, coexisted with literary histories, selections for grammatical analysis, and collections of excerpts for elementary reading instruction. A high school literary canon was well established, a mixture, on the one hand, of Shakespearean texts, Milton, and the Augustans from the early studies of grammar and rhetoric, and, on the other, of the then-contemporary works of the English Romantics and of American authors, such as Washington Irving, Nathaniel Hawthorne, and James Fenimore Cooper. Data on secondary programs gathered by the U.S. commissioner of education (1902) showed considerable variability in the proportion of high school students who were enrolled in literature courses; proportions ranged from 22 percent in Idaho to 84 percent in California. Even at this late date, more students were studying Latin than were studying English.

Broadening the Curriculum: 1900–1917. During the first decade of the twentieth century, the texts required for the small proportion of students applying to college determined the curriculum for all students. High school teachers quickly came to resent this situation; their discontent culminated in 1911, with the establishment of the National Council of Teachers of English (NCTE) as a specific means to focus and direct their protests. Although NCTE went on to many other missions, its efforts led to the development of an alternate "comprehensive" examination by 1916. By 1931, the restricted examination (and with it, the National Conference on Uniform Entrance Requirements in English) disappeared altogether.

If the required texts were to be abolished, other approaches needed to be developed to take their place. Teachers experimented enthusiastically with a wide variety of alternatives, including courses organized by genres or types, emphases on "content" and "values" rather than on close textual study, contemporary selections (including newspapers and magazines) familiar to students, drama and oral interpretation, and a wide variety of aids designed to promote interest in literature (maps, slides, records, silent films, pictures, lists of books for home reading, and school libraries).

These diverse experiments culminated in *Reorganization of English in Secondary Schools* (Hosic, 1917), the first comprehensive curriculum statement in the field. This reorganization report stated firmly that the emphasis on college preparation had led to a "monotonous and unintelligent uniformity" (p. 7); instead, English classes should be "social in content and social in methods of acquirement." Although the emphasis shifted from formal discipline to "social value" (p. 27), the classic texts were viewed as having the greatest social value and dominated the suggestions for grade-by-grade curriculum. This curriculum was planned around principles of child development articulated earlier by Hall (1904); many of its vestiges continue in current curricular sequencing of literary works. The *Iliad*, the *Odyssey*, and similar adventures were placed in eighth and ninth grades. *The Merchant of Venice* and *Julius Caesar*, taught in the tenth grade, would raise "serious questions of right and wrong." *The Idylls of the King* and *Silas Marner*, taught in the eleventh grade, would deal with "the relations of men and women." For the twelfth grade, the report suggested a chronologically organized survey of British and American literature (pp. 69–70). The report singled out texts for class study from a much broader list for individual reading, justifying a rapid expansion of literary studies and contributing to the eventual abandonment of required examination texts.

Progressive Principles. The concern with broadening the curriculum evident in *Reorganization of English in Secondary Schools* (Hosic, 1917) was part of the first stages of the progressive era in education. Progressive principles emphasizing child-centered approaches, the importance of learning through doing, and the value of scientific study of education, influenced the teaching of literature in two stages. During the first stage, culminating in the late 1930s, literary studies were defined around the metaphors of "experience" and "exploration"; during the second phase, culminating in the middle 1950s, the boundaries of the curriculum were narrowed around more pragmatic goals of "communication" and "life adjustment."

In the 1920s, English teachers built upon the methodological suggestions of progressives such as Kilpatrick (1925) to justify the teaching of literature as a "broadening" of experience. Leonard (1922) provided the fullest early statement of this view in *Essential Principles of Teaching Reading and Literature*. Experiments with ways to stimulate interest continued, and new overall structures for the literature curriculum were sought, using the project method and syllabi organized around "themes" or "topics." As teachers' emphases changed, publishers began to provide anthologies offering wider selections of literary works. The more conservative anthologies were little more than collections of the required examination texts, bound under one cover; but many sought to provide the breadth and variety implied by an "experience" approach to literature. The most successful collection was Scott, Foresman's Literature and Life Series (1922–1924), which managed a synthesis of the two points of view. It included the required college entrance texts but supplemented them with many contemporary selections.

The reorganization report of 1917 was largely a declaration of independence from the colleges; by the 1930s, there was a need for both (1) a theoretical synthesis of the implications of the metaphor of experience, and (2) a detailed formulation of a model curriculum. NCTE, working through a Curriculum Commission, provided the pattern curriculum in *An Experience Curriculum in English* (Hatfield, 1935). Rosenblatt (1938) provided the comprehensive theoretical statement in *Literature as Exploration*. Together, the two books illustrated both the strengths and weaknesses of the experience approach. Rosenblatt drew on an extensive background in sociology, anthropology, and psychology to detail the transaction that takes place between a particular reader and a particular text, and placed the heart of literary study in examining the nature of this transaction. Her scholarship was extensive, even intimidating; the suggestions for classroom techniques were few and abstract. Faced with implementing a similar philosophy, the Curriculum Commission settled on "experience strands" that were a traditional blend of popular approaches (among others, "Exploring the Social World," "Solving Puzzles," and "Enjoying Photoplays"). The objectives led students to such knowledge as "the effects of widening trade horizons on our daily lives" (p. 49) rather than to an understanding of what literature contributes to that knowledge.

For many teachers, the metaphor of experience was simply too broad to serve as an organizing principle for their work. During the 1940s and 1950s, they narrowed the focus of their literary studies around such concepts as "general education," "communication skills," "life adjustment," and "adolescent needs." Whereas earlier approaches had stressed literature as a broadening, liberating study, the narrower view saw it as a way to solve immediate problems and prepare students for the adult world. Matching selections to specific problems of pupils was especially important in this approach and took several forms. One approach was simply a reinterpretation of the values of the classic texts. *Silas Marner*, for example, was taught as a "storehouse of information necessary for understanding friends, family, and one's self" (Applebee, 1974, p.

152). Another approach was to provide extensive book lists keyed to student problems. Lenrow's *Reader's Guide to Prose Fiction* (1940), prepared under the auspices of the Committee on the Function of English in General Education, was the earliest and most extensive; Taba's *Reading Ladders for Human Relations* (1947) had considerably greater influence and continues in print to the present day (Tway, 1981). The third approach involved the cultivation of an extensive body of literature dealing with specific developmental problems. Although teachers had long been concerned with good books suitable for children, the 1940s and 1950s saw the development of a new literary genre with its own authors and highly specialized audiences of adolescent readers. Although some important books came into the curriculum in this way, including *The Diary of Anne Frank* (1950) and *The Catcher in the Rye* (1951), many popular adolescent novels were shallow and formulaic.

The most elaborate synthesis of the new concerns was again provided by an NCTE Commission on the English Curriculum. Organized in 1945, the commission produced a series of reports beginning in 1952. As summarized in the third volume of the series (NCTE, 1956), literary studies had two dimensions: meeting youth's needs through literature and developing competence in reading. Organized around units even more diverse than those in *An Experience Curriculum in English,* the series as a whole suffered from a lack of clear structuring principles. Instead, the commission relied upon a metaphor of "growth" that justified virtually any kind of activity, allowing the program in literature to be dominated by peripheral activities often having little to do with "literary values."

An Academic Model. Even as the NCTE Commission on the English Curriculum was publishing its volumes, the Progressive movement as a whole was under serious attack for its trivialization of the curriculum, lack of standards of intellectual discipline, and narrow focus on "life adjustment." Although the search for new approaches began much earlier, the launching of *Sputnik* in 1957 seemed to symbolize all that was wrong with American education, prompting English teachers and their leaders in the professional associations to search for a new basis for the curriculum. Rather than continuing with the metaphor of experience or the literature of child development, teachers turned toward recent scholarship in their field for a new set of structuring principles.

In literary studies, these principles were exemplified in Brooks and Warren's *Understanding Poetry,* published in 1938 but having little impact on the schools before 1960. This anthology presented not only texts for study but also lengthy discussions that modeled a radically new emphasis on close reading of text and sought criteria of literary value in formal properties rather than in "values" or "needs." Although the New Criticism, as this approach came to be called, dominated scholarly work by the 1950s, its major proponents were not cited at all in the work of the Curriculum Commission.

The first attempt to define a new, academic model for English grew out of a 1958 conference cosponsored by NCTE, the Modern Language Association, the American Studies Association, and the College English Association. The widely distributed conference report, *The Basic Issues in the Teaching of English* (NCTE, 1959), asserted that English is a "fundamental liberal discipline," with a body of specific knowledge to be preserved and transmitted. By identifying this subject matter as the core of English, issues such as the importance of specific works, the role of technical vocabulary, and the relationships among authors and works were opened to professional debate. The basic issues conference was followed, in 1965, by a more comprehensive curriculum statement sponsored by the Commission on English of the College Entrance Examination Board. The commission stressed the importance of English teachers as professionals, able to select appropriate works out of the depth and rigor of their academic training. Once works were selected, however, the techniques of study were to be those of the New Critics, emphasizing close, analytic reading of the text.

The mid-1960s were a time of great excitement in English studies, with renewed involvement of college professors in issues of curriculum and instruction, and new funds for program development and teacher training through an expansion of the National Defense Education Act. Over two dozen curriculum study centers were eventually funded, bringing together teachers and scholars to restructure the English curriculum. Most relied on established conceptions of literary studies, however and did not undertake fundamentally new work. Bruner's spiral curriculum (1960) and Frye's "pregeneric modes" (1957) were used to structure the literature curriculum at most of the centers (Hart, 1979). Although a few of the centers produced materials or reports that were widely used (e.g., Fader & Shaevitz, 1966), they mainly influenced the individuals directly involved in the process of curriculum development.

Social Issues. The focus on an academic model of English was relatively short-lived. By the late 1960s, attention shifted toward more socially relevant programs. The shift had many causes, including the general social upheaval generated by the civil rights movement and the Vietnam protests, as well as new views of the nature of schooling. In the teaching of literature, major changes were brought about by exposure to child-centered models of teaching that had developed in British schools, where the emphasis was on personal and linguistic "growth through English" rather than on academic knowledge. The Dartmouth Conference, an international gathering of educators from Australia, Canada, the United Kingdom, and the United States, was particularly influential, both through its effect upon the participants, many of whom had been leaders in the development of the academic model, and through its widely distributed conference reports (Dixon, 1967; Muller, 1967). These reports emphasized a version of literary studies in which the development of response was more important than critical techniques, and in which contemporary works took their place beside, or even replaced, classic texts of more enduring value.

In developing programs that were more relevant, one of the most significant innovations was the large-scale adoption of elective programs in English. Taking many different forms, these programs effectively destroyed any three-year or four-year sequence of literary studies, replacing it with a potpourri of courses, some traditional and some innovative. Defended as a response to student interests, elective programs in literature became in many schools a reflection of teachers' favorite themes and authors (Hillocks, 1972).

By the mid-1970s, the excesses of the student-centered curricula were in turn generating a call for more "basic" studies. The effects of this shift on the teaching of literature are still unclear, although generally there has been a return to more traditional curriculum models, and some retreat from contemporary works toward the classical canon of texts. The relatively rapid shift of curriculum models during the 1960s and 1970s has left teachers without a powerful central metaphor to guide their teaching of literature, with the result that eclecticism predominates. This is particularly evident in a recent curriculum statement prepared by the Curriculum Commission of NCTE. Unlike its predecessors, the new report (Mandell, 1980) offers no model of the teaching of English in general or of literature in particular. Instead, it describes three competing models, one based on cultural heritage, one based on personal growth, and one based on the development of specific competencies. Teachers are left to make their own choices among the conflicting assumptions of these models or to create their own idiosyncratic syntheses.

Empirical Studies

Empirical studies related to the teaching of literature will be discussed in four sections: status surveys, studies of reading interests, responses to literature, and instructional techniques.

Status Surveys. During the past fifty years, several large-scale surveys have examined either teaching practices or student achievement in literature; these serve as benchmarks for the place of literature in school programs.

As part of the search for alternatives to lists of required texts as a basis for the literature curriculum, an early committee of NCTE examined national practices in the teaching of English. Expecting to find a variety of approaches, they discovered instead that the curriculum in literature was with few exceptions based on a list of required texts; there were no differing organizational approaches to investigate (NCTE, 1913).

Two decades later, Smith took a more comprehensive look at the English curriculum, both nationally (1933) and in New York State (1941). The findings from both studies were similar and indicated that although conditions had changed considerably since the 1913 study, a large gap

remained between discussions in the professional journals and classroom practice. Specifically, she found that although long philological analysis of single texts was no longer common, too much time continued to be devoted to reading single works, and too little to extensive reading. Anthologies organized by types or genres were widely used, although teacher-led recitations involving the whole class predominated over any sort of individualized instruction.

In the early 1960s, Squire and Applebee (1968, 1969) undertook an extensive study of English programs in both American and British schools. Although they initially focused on "outstanding" programs nominated by a variety of experts, their report ended up providing a more general portrait of the academic model for literature instruction. It also foreshadowed trends that reshaped programs during the late 1960s and early 1970s.

In their American schools, Squire and Applebee found exciting and well-developed programs for higher-achieving students, and a nationwide neglect of the lower tracks. Literary studies accounted for some 52 percent of class time. Similarly, writing topics usually focused on analyses of or responses to literary works. As in Smith's earlier studies, recitation dominated most classrooms, with little group work and little in the way of innovative approaches to organizing the curriculum. Close study of individual texts was lauded when it was found, but was used extensively by only about one-quarter of the teachers. The best programs, however, were built around careful study and close reading of individual texts, supported by a broadly based program of guided individual reading.

When Squire and Applebee (1969) extended their study to British schools, the patterns they observed and the interpretations they drew were very different. Literary studies occupied only 39 percent of class time, and teaching was generally more student-centered. Drama activities impressed the observers, as did small-group and project work that had rarely been seen in American classrooms. Distressed by the lack of sequence and structure in some British programs and by the willingness of some teachers to abandon the literary tradition completely in favor of contemporary works, the observers nonetheless concluded that some British practices would prove useful in American programs. The most important of these involved the need for more emphasis on the development of personal response to literature, even at the expense of rigorous formal studies.

During the 1970s, two large-scale assessments focused on student achievement in literature rather than on teaching practices. The largest was the ten-country study sponsored by the International Association for the Evaluation of Educational Achievement (IEA) (Purves, 1973). In each country, two populations were sampled: 14-year-olds and students in their preuniversity year. In addition to measures of interest and comprehension, response-preference measures were developed that reflected issues of importance to students. Achievement results suggested that home and school environments had a greater effect on achievement than particular curricula. Between-country achievement differences depended largely upon socioeconomic levels and cultural resources available to the majority of students. However, curriculum did have an effect on students' preferred responses to literary works. Significant between-country effects on these measures were interpreted as reflecting different teaching emphases and critical traditions within the countries studied. Thus, curriculum variations led to different kinds of achievement rather than to different levels of achievement.

During the 1970s, the National Assessment of Educational Progress (NAEP) began to study the educational achievement of Americans aged 9, 13, 17, and 23. NAEP tests are designed to measure objectives specified by committees formed for each of the subject areas assessed. The first round of testing in literature occurred during the 1970/71 school year; the second round was combined with an assessment of reading achievement during the 1979/80 school year. First-round results were organized around four themes: (1) recognizing literary works and characters (NAEP, 1973a), (2) understanding imaginative language (NAEP, 1973b), (3) responding to literature (NAEP, 1973c), and (4) a survey of reading habits (NAEP, 1973d). As in all subject areas tested, first-round results in literature were most interesting as baseline data for comparison with subsequent rounds of assessments, although the objectives were revised substantially in preparation for the second round (NAEP, 1980). The results suggested that achievement increased with age, and they highlighted achievement deficits in urban areas and among minority populations. Regional and sex differences were also reported for many of the exercises. Second-round results, released in 1981, showed little change in achievement of 9-year-olds across the decade of the seventies, but some decline in the achievement of 17-year-olds. At all ages assessed, students were relatively successful at multiple-choice and short-answer tasks. They had marked difficulty, however, when asked to explain or defend their judgments and interpretations (NAEP, 1981).

Studies of Reading Interests. Studies of reading interests represent one of the oldest traditions of research in literature, dating back at least to G. S. Hall's editorship of *Pedagogical Seminary* in the 1890s. For the most part, the goals of these studies have been pragmatic, seeking either to help teachers and librarians suggest books to children or to evaluate books for possible inclusion in the literature curriculum. For a variety of reasons, neither goal has been successfully achieved, although investigators have described broad patterns of interest that have remained remarkably stable across time.

Mott (1970) provides a summary of reading-interest studies between 1919 and 1969, drawing extensively on unpublished research in master's degree and doctoral theses as well as on published sources. Generalizations that emerge from fifty years of work include the following six. (1) Recreational reading peaks during the junior high school years, with amount of reading declining after seventh or eighth grade. (2) Boys and girls differ significantly in their reading interests. In general, boys prefer books about adventure, sports, science fiction, war, and outdoor life. Girls prefer books about romance, home and school life, adventure (mild), and mystery stories. Girls' tastes are more catholic, however; they also read "boys' books," whereas boys rarely read "girls' books." (3) Intelligence influences the amount, quality, and range of works enjoyed but does not appear to influence the areas of selection. (4) Reading interests are highly influenced by the availability and accessibility of reading materials, as well as by recommendations from within the peer group. (5) In general, students dislike poetry, subtle humor, long passages of description, complicated syntax, wordiness, and slow-moving sections. (6) By age 15, reading interests differ little from those of adults.

More recent studies have tended to confirm the patterns of earlier investigations (Fisher, 1979; Terry, 1974; Whitehead et al., 1977; Yarlott & Harpin, 1971). Whereas these patterns have proven to be remarkably stable across a range of populations and over time, this line of research has been unsuccessful in its goals for instructional planning. Interests of individual students, as well as the developmental patterns that these interests assume over time, are highly variable and idiosyncratic. The research base, although extensive, offers little to help a teacher plan a curriculum or to suggest further reading to individual students.

Research problems. One of the reasons that reading-interest studies have been relatively unproductive has been their focus on diffuse categories of books. Animal stories, for example, is a traditional category in these studies, but they comprise stories as diverse as *Wind in the Willows*, *White Fang*, and *Watership Down*. In order to move beyond these limits, some investigators have traced more specific processes influencing reading interest, including such factors as identification (Barrett & Barrett, 1966); nature of the conflict (Peller, 1959; Bloomer, 1968); verbal complexity (Kammann, 1966); and congruence of cultural setting (Johns, 1975; Ross, 1978). Favat (1977) reconceptualized one area of reading-interest data by relating changing patterns of interest in fairy tales to developmental patterns in children's thought. His report is one of the most thorough attempts to explain rather than simply to describe interest in one type of literature.

A second problem in the majority of studies of reading interests has been their failure to recognize the variety of purposes for which people read. Kammann (1966), studying undergraduates' preferences for poetry, found differences in response when the choices involved discussion by a professor, memorization for future reference, debate with a peer holding a different view, and discussion with a friend. Applebee (1973), using repertory-grid techniques with high school students, found some separation between personal liking for a poem and judgments by the same students based on literary criteria. In a related study, a variety of selections chosen as individual favorites reflected a spectrum from serious, difficult works to light, escapist entertainment (Applebee, 1976).

The most interesting future work in this area is likely to focus on explaining (rather than describing) reading interests in the context of specific reading purposes.

Responses to Literature. Reading interest is, in effect, an outcome of an individual's cumulative experiences in reading specific works; a second line of research has focused directly on the processes involved in this reading. The classic study in this tradition is Richards's *Practical Criticism* (1929), in which he described the difficulties even superior college-level readers had in interpreting poetry. His classification of common problems has continued to shape later work: (1) failure to understand plain, overt meaning; (2) difficulties of sensuous apprehension, that is, in responding to the natural movement and rhythm of words; (3) difficulties in ability to "visualize," including problems with imagery; (4) mnemonic irrelevancies based on personal memories; (5) stock responses; (6) sentimentality; (7) inhibition; (8) doctrinal adhesions; (9) technical presuppositions; and (10) general critical preconceptions. Richards used extensive citations from response protocols to document the difficulties he found, blaming errors in interpretation on bad training and avoidable mistakes.

Methods of analysis. Richards's techniques of analysis were those of a literary critic rather than those of an empiricist; although widely cited, his work generated little research until Squire (1964) used content-analytic techniques to examine the responses of adolescents to short stories. Segmenting the reading selections in order to describe development of response over the course of a reading, Squire focused his analysis on six general categories of response: literary judgment, interpretational responses, narrational responses, associational responses, self-involvement, and prescriptive judgment. Squire was able to describe characteristic shifts in the nature of the response at different points in time, as well as associations between responses of different types. He found, for example, that readers who become highly involved in a story are also more likely to evaluate its literary qualities, and that the quality of individual interpretations is generally unrelated to intelligence or reading ability. When Squire examined sources of difficulty in literary interpretation, his findings generally confirmed Richards's earlier work. The major difficulties stem from failure to grasp obvious meanings; reliance on stock responses; happiness-binding; critical predispositions; irrelevant associations; and need for certainty in interpretation and unwillingness to suspend judgment.

Squire's report opened up a whole series of questions for later research, and some investigators have adopted his analytic procedures quite directly (Fanselow, 1971; Sanders, 1970; Shablak, 1973; Wilson, 1966). Most, however, have adopted the more extensive system of content analysis developed by Purves and Rippere (1968). The elements that they analyze range from such literary devices as "allusion" and "irony" to general statements of "thematic importance" or "identification"—139 elements in all, combined into 24 subcategories and 5 major categories. The specificity of the elements has made them applicable to a wide range of research questions, and they have proven flexible enough to be applied to media as diverse as film, novel, short story, fairy tale, and poem and to response modes as diverse as structured and unstructured written and oral responses, tape recordings of whole class and group discussions, and multiple-choice questionnaires. In a review of studies published in the eight-year period following publication of the elements, Applebee (1977) found thirty different investigations incorporating the Purves and Rippere system.

Factors affecting responses. Although many of the response-to-literature studies have been small-scale and improperly analyzed, taken together they allow a number of generalizations about factors influencing response processes. Age effects have been clearly demonstrated in a number of investigations. Responses of preadolescent children focus primarily on the "content" or "action," shifting during adolescence toward explanations of the behavior of characters or of the structure of the work (Applebee, 1978; Mason, 1974; NAEP, 1973c). These changes can be related to other studies of comprehension and production, which show characteristic differences in the kinds of inferences children make about literary episodes at different developmental stages (Applebee, 1978; Billow, 1975; Gardner, 1973; Gardner et al., 1975; McGhee, 1971). Sex differences in patterns of response have been minimal, although girls seem somewhat more willing to comment on their direct engagement with literary materials (Purves, 1973; NAEP, 1973c). Later work has also confirmed Squire's finding that ability and achievement differences have little effect on the nature of expressed response, except as by-products of difficulty in comprehending a work (Angelotti, 1972; Auerbach, 1974; Faggiani, 1971; Pollock, 1972; Somers, 1972). When a student does have difficulty in comprehension, there is a decrease in interpretation and increased attention to the "content," or literal meaning. Overall, there is somewhat more preference for interpretive or formal-analytic responses among the more able students, just as there is among older and more mature students in contrast with younger ones (Bennett, 1978; Cooper, 1969; NAEP, 1973c; Purves, 1973). Although a few studies have sought links between measures of personality and characteristics of response, few consistent results have emerged from the empirical studies (Cornaby, 1974; Kuehn, 1973; Faggiani, 1971).

Although Squire's seminal study portrayed the development of response over time, most of the work that has followed has treated "response" as something static, occurring in a fixed and measurable form after exposure to a literary work. Those studies that have moved beyond this conceptualization have found that reaction to a literary work involves a complex unfolding of meaning and interpretation. Britton (1954), studying the responses of advanced students, asked students to rate a group of poems, some of which were "true poems" and some of which were "false poems" constructed specifically for the study. He found that although the false poems were valued in the initial readings, at a retest six months later responses converged toward the true poems. In a related study, Harding (1968) had undergraduates sort thirty poems into four categories: too difficult but promising; attractive and understood; attractive but easy; and unappealing and likely to grow more so. Across four readings in two sessions, an increasing proportion of the poems were rated "attractive but easy," and a decreasing proportion as "too difficult but promising."

Over shorter time periods, Beach (1972) studied college students in the process of formulating their responses to poetry in a variety of response formats. Across modes of response, students demonstrated a need to establish the facts of the poem and engage in personal digressions before moving on toward engagement (in oral response modes) or interpretation (in written responses).

A number of studies have sought to demonstrate direct links between the study of literature and changes in student's attitudes or beliefs. Although it is relatively easy to gather reports from readers providing anecdotal evidence that reading has at some point "influenced" them (e.g., Shirley, 1968), it is much harder to find convincing empirical support for such claims. Purves and Beach (1972) point out that a number of experimental studies indicate that attitudes toward a topic change after reading a selection of works on the topic, but also that a larger and better-designed group of studies indicate that such change is at best short-lived.

Research problems. Studies of response to literature pose a number of difficult problems for the investigator. The most critical is that response is ultimately a personal and private process: studies of response rely on readers' reports of what they have been thinking and feeling rather than on direct measures. In recent years, techniques for analyzing and synthesizing these expressed responses have become more sophisticated, including not only systems for content analysis, such as those proposed by Squire (1964) and by Purves and Rippere (1968), but also a variety of semantic-differential and repertory-grid formats for studying complex patterns of reaction to specific works (Applebee, 1976; Brewbaker, 1972; Forehand, 1966; Hansson, 1973; Harpin, 1966; Wilson, 1975). However, very few studies have sought more direct measures of response, such as the physiological changes tapped by early investigators of reactions to films and radio drama (DeBoer, 1938; Dysinger & Ruckmick, 1933). Similarly, very few have compared response across a variety of media, which young children in particular can use to express their literary reactions (Cappa, 1958; Hickman, 1980).

A second problem of response studies stems from the variety of factors producing changes in the expressed response. Rather than general patterns that can be attributed to individuals or groups, response varies from work to work and genre to genre. It is also affected by minor variations in the wording of the stimulus questions and by change from oral to written response modes. Thus, general conclusions about response can only be drawn from patterns that can be traced across a variety of tasks and circumstances.

A third problem of most response research derives from the cumulative, evolutionary nature of the process. Responses differ during different phases in the reading of a work and show characteristic patterns of development as readers reflect back upon previous reading experiences. Because most studies of response have simply tried to describe response, we have no good formal models to untangle the processes involved in comprehending, interpreting, and "appreciating" works of literature.

The fourth problem is related to the third. Partly because we have no good models of the process of response to literature (and of how response to literature differs from response to expository discourse), research on the effects of reading literature has remained anecdotal and unconvincing. Except for case studies of bibliotherapy (Shrodes, 1950), in which the reading situation is exceptional rather than typical, we have little empirical evidence of the effects of literary studies on individual attitudes, beliefs, or activities. Like the work in reading interests, studies of the effects of reading are unlikely to be productive until they combine a clearer sense of the variety of purposes for which we read with a stronger conceptual framework for explaining the response process.

Instructional Techniques. The third major area of research in literature has focused on the effects, and the effectiveness, of various instructional approaches. The first important empirical study of methods in the teaching of literature was Coryell's doctoral project (1927). Coryell contrasted rapid reading of a comparatively large number of literary works with detailed analytic study of a smaller number of works drawn from the same corpus. Measures included a fairly extensive battery of standardized tests and a final examination constructed to cover only the books studied by both groups. Finding that at the end of the year the two groups had progressed equally, Coryell concluded that the extensive readers, having done five times as much reading, had probably learned five times as much as the intensive readers.

Later studies comparing "extensive," "free," or "individualized" reading programs with more intensive study of fewer books have tended to confirm and amplify Coryell's results (Ciampoli, 1977; LaBrant, 1961; LaBrant & Heller, 1939; Lennox, Small, & Keeling, 1978; Millsop, 1977; Norvell, 1941). In general, the reading of more books leads to more favorable attitudes toward reading, without hindering growth in reading skills.

Effects. Studies of other aspects of instruction have successfully demonstrated that what a teacher does in the classroom influences how students respond to literature. However, disagreements about goals of literary study prevent unambiguous identification of successful approaches. Hoetker's study (1971) of tenth-grade students is one of the most carefully designed and analyzed, but, like other studies of teaching methods, the results are generally disappointing. The experiment evaluated differing instructional procedures in preparing students for professional theater production. The instructional variables included timing of classroom instruction (before or after viewing the professional performance of the play), content of the lesson (study of the specific play or a related play), brief versus intensive study of background, and brief versus intensive study of the text. Although thirteen outcome measures involving 1,300 students in the classes of 52 teachers were used, few significant differences emerged. Those that did reflected earlier predictions by teachers (who valued cognitive understanding) and by actors (who valued appreciation) about the direction of instructional effects, although both groups overestimated the size of these effects. Which approaches were "better" thus depended upon assumptions about desired outcomes.

Studies of instructional approaches have been summarized by Squire (1969), Purves and Beach (1972), and Applebee (1977). Weiss (1968) used the Purves-Rippere elements of response to compare programmed instruction with inductive teaching, finding that the inductive approach led to an increase in "perception" and "interpretation." Grindstaff (1968), Grimme (1970), and Karre (reported by Porter, 1976) found that structural analysis, such as that advocated by the New Critics, led to narrational and interpretive responses, whereas experiential approaches led to interpretation coupled with more engagement and personal response. Green (1977) found that a response-centered approach also led to a better attitude toward poetry.

Other instructional studies have looked at a wide range of techniques, including questioning skills (Lucking, 1975); study methods involving film, tape recordings, or discussion (Casey, 1977; Cowgill, 1975; Powers, 1977; Staples, 1979); guided silent reading (Aulls & Gelbert, 1980); training in synthesis-level conceptualization (Oliver, 1978); training in how to interpret literature (Sanders, 1970); reading aloud by the teacher (Weidner, 1976); use of adolescent novels (Blount, 1965); and effect of poet-teachers on comprehension of metaphoric language (Folta, 1979). Although many of these studies found larger treatment effects that Hoetker (1971) was able to demonstrate, the best overall interpretation of the results is that students learn to respond to literature in the ways they are taught to respond. What is lacking in almost all of the studies is a well-defended separation of the "better" responses from those that are simply "different." (Recall the cross-national differences in learned patterns of response in the IEA studies.)

Research problems. The failure of instructional research to provide clear guidelines for teaching literature, is sometimes blamed on difficulties in measuring "achievement" in studying literature. Efforts to quantify achievement in this field date back at least to Abbott and Trabue's measure of ability to judge poetry and have become increasingly sophisticated since that work was published (Abbott & Trabue, 1921). Most of the measures described previously, including both content-analytic and rating-scale techniques, can be used as measures of instructional outcomes. Some can also be adapted for computerized scoring (Madden, 1979) or reformulated as multiple-choice items (Choppin, 1969; Choppin & Purves, 1969). By drawing on item formats from the NAEP, the IEA, and other measurement efforts, reasonably coherent assessment materials can be constructed (Cooper, 1971; Cooper & Purves, 1973; Purves, 1979). Rather than lacking measures of outcomes in teaching literature, research has lacked a well-developed conceptual framework for relating those outcomes to longer-term instructional goals. Until we have better models of the processes involved in comprehending and interpreting literature, of the ways in which those processes develop over time, and of how they vary in response to such factors as purposes for reading, instructional research is unlikely to provide clear guidelines for teachers or curriculum developers.

Future Directions

Research in literary response and the teaching of literature enjoyed a resurgence of interest during the late 1960s and early 1970s, partly as a function of the general concern with student-centered studies in the educational community as a whole. By the end of the decade, however, studies focusing on literature seemed to have reached a plateau. This effect occurred partly because the educational community shifted its interest toward more clearly functional issues, and partly because the largely descriptive, nontheoretical orientations guiding previous work had largely exhausted their possibilities. The most promising studies of literature and the teaching of literature are increasingly placing their data within more powerful theoretical frameworks. Some of these frameworks have been developed within the field of English, while others originate in related disciplines.

Literary Perspectives. Within the field of English studies, the most influential perspectives have been those developed by Rosenblatt (1938, 1978) and Britton (1970; Britton et al., 1975). Focusing directly on the nature of experience in reading literary texts, Rosenblatt draws a distinction between "efferent reading" (for information from expository prose) and "aesthetic reading" (for experience from literary texts). In an important and well-developed theoretical statement, she argues that a literary event exists only in the transaction between an individual reader and an individual text; in spite of commonalities brought about by culturally conditioned or conventional responses to certain aspects of text, each literary experience is fundamentally unique and individual. Studies of both the pedagogical implications of, and the model of comprehension in, her work should prove very fruitful (e.g., Culp, 1977).

Rosenblatt's efferent and aesthetic modes of reading are paralleled in Britton's analyses by participant and spectator roles of language use (Britton, 1976; Britton et al., 1975). Although Britton's and Rosenblatt's models are derived from quite different disciplinary bases, they are fundamentally similar in the distinctions that are made. Britton's roles of language use differentiate two types of relationship between the language user and the language experience. In the "participant role," language is being used toward an overt end, whether to inform, persuade, argue, make a request, or build a theoretical framework. In the "spectator role," language is used to share an experience through a structured "verbal artifact" or literary work. Britton's terminology unifies the anecdote and the great novel, the storytelling of the child and that of the accomplished poet or artist. He manages this by basing the distinction between participant and spectator on the role that language plays in the life of the language user rather than on formal characteristics of the text itself. As with Rosenblatt's work, Britton's theories have both conceptual and pedagogical implications (Applebee, 1978; Martin et al., 1976).

Cognitive Perspectives. Outside the field of English, interesting and related work is being carried out in the fields of psychology and linguistics. Cognitive psychologists, for example, have been using story comprehension tasks as a tool for exploring the nature of language comprehension, particularly as part of the reading process. Recent work has detailed highly formal "grammars" that underlie simple story structures (Mandler & Johnson, 1977; Stein & Glenn, 1979; Thorndyke, 1977); the many different levels of background knowledge that are brought to bear on understanding stories (Adams and Bruce, forthcoming; Green et al., 1980; Pichert & Anderson, 1976; Rumelhart, 1975); the ways in which relevant knowledge is organized into hierarchically related schemata governing both comprehension and production (Anderson, 1977; Neisser, 1976; Rumelhart & Ortony, 1977; Schank & Abelson, 1977); and the integrative processes at work in the organization of information based on linguistic components of text (Halliday & Hasan, 1976; Kintsch & Kozminsky, 1977). This work has been important in providing formal, explanatory models of complex comprehension processes and in shifting the focus in empirical studies from "text" to the creation of meaning through a reader-text interaction (e.g., Langer & Smith-Burke, 1982).

The initial work from a cognitive perspective has had two shortcomings, both of which may be overcome as the field matures. One has been a tendency to treat schemata as static, whereas for educators, change and development in schemata are of the greatest importance. The second has been to minimize the differences among different types of literary and nonliterary contexts. Although exposition and "stories" have sometimes been separately examined, definitions of "story" have been superficial. To the extent that, as Britton and Rosenblatt claim, we bring differing frames of reference and standards of judgment to our comprehension of literary text, cognitive studies have been neglecting an important aspect of language compre-

hension; they have used literary texts without analyzing the factors that make them "literary" in the first place. As such issues are recognized and addressed, we may see important advances in literature as a field of empirical research.

Psychoanalytic Perspectives. Another group of recent studies has evolved out of the psychoanalytic tradition, applying Freudian or neo-Freudian frameworks to the process of response. Holland (1968, 1975) has been particularly important in demonstrating the extent to which the meaning that a reader derives from a literary work is a highly personal construction, built up out of past experience and a need to confirm the individual's "identity theme" or orientation toward the world. Stemming from a totally different perspective than the work of Rosenblatt, Britton, or the cognitive psychologists, Holland nevertheless emphasizes the importance of many of the same features, including the central role of the reader's contribution to a literary experience. Other researchers in the psychoanalytic tradition have sought to derive pedagogical principles (Bleich, 1975); to integrate Freudian frameworks into a developmental perspective (Petrosky, 1977); to explain the power of fairy tales (Bettelheim, 1976); and to explain the themes children deal with in their own storytelling (Ames, 1966; Pitcher & Prelinger, 1963).

Children's Use of Literature. Other recent studies have approached literary awareness through detailed observation of the uses of language in children's lives, usually in the context of evolving skills with written language (Ferreiro, 1978; Harste, Burke, & Woodward, 1982; Heath, forthcoming). These studies differ in two very important ways from earlier research in literature. First, they begin by looking at the way literary events function in the lives of individual children—at the uses of literature (and other language episodes), rather than at responses to them. Because of this methodology, these studies address such very basic issues as the role of literature in cultural and individual development. Second, these studies recognize the fundamental unity and complex interrelationships among written and oral experiences. Thus it becomes possible to trace "sense of story," for example, through the stories children hear, the stories they tell, the stories they read, and the stories they write (Applebee, 1978). Viewed in this way, literary experience becomes a part of the individual's developing competence in an increasingly differentiated set of language functions (Halliday, 1977) and can be explained within the conceptual and analytic frameworks appropriate for language study.

Many fundamental questions are yet to be answered by research in literature, questions made all the more urgent in a political context that stresses efficiency, economy, and basic skills and that may treat literary experiences as unnecessary frills. Questions yet to be answered fall into four groups. (1) What exactly are the functions of literature in individual and cultural development? What do we gain from literature, and what do we lose without it? (2) What is the nature of a "cultural heritage," and how can that heritage be nurtured through literary texts? Is there a way of conceptualizing this heritage that is appropriate in a diverse, multicultural society? (3) What do we learn from literary experiences? How does this learning differ from what we learn from expository texts or personal experience? (4) What cognitive and affective skills are involved in comprehension of literary texts? What is the developmental course of these skills? What factors in the text, the reader, and the context for reading advance or impede comprehension?

Until we have a firm basis for answering these questions, our attempts to specify goals for literary study, to compare methods of instruction, to assess achievement, and to formulate guidelines for individual reading will remain fragmentary, unsystematic, and deficient in explanatory power or theoretical interest.

Arthur N. Applebee

See also English Language Education; Racism and Sexism in Children's Literature; Reading; Textbooks.

REFERENCES

Abbott, A., & Trabue, M. R. A measure of ability to judge poetry. *Teachers College Record*, 1921, *22*, 101–126.

Adams, M. J., & Bruce, B. C. Background knowledge and reading comprehension. In J. Langer & M. Smith-Burke (Eds.), *Reader Meets Author—Bridging the Gap: A Psycholinguistic and Sociolinguistic Perspective*. Newark, Del.: International Reading Association, forthcoming.

Ames, L. B. Children's stories. *Genetic Psychology Monographs*, 1966, *73*, 337–396.

Anderson, R. C. The notion of schemata and the educational enterprise. In R. C. Anderson; R. J. Spiro; & W. E. Montague (Eds.), *Schooling and the Acquisition of Knowledge*. Hillsdale, N.J.: Lawrence Erlbaum Associates, 1977.

Angelotti, M. L. *A Comparison of Elements in the Written Free Responses of Eighth Graders to a Junior Novel and an Adult Novel*. Unpublished doctoral dissertation, Florida State University, 1972.

Applebee, A. N. *The Spectator Role: Theoretical and Developmental Studies of Ideas about the Responses to Literature, with Special Reference to Four Age Levels*. Unpublished doctoral dissertation, University of London, 1973.

Applebee, A. N. *Tradition and Reform in the Teaching of English: A History*. Urbana, Ill.: National Council of Teachers of English, 1974. (ERIC Document Reproduction Service No. ED 097 703)

Applebee, A. N. Children's construal of stories and related genres as measured with repertory grid techniques. *Research in the Teaching of English*, 1976, *10*, 226–238.

Applebee, A. N. The elements of response to a literary work: What we have learned. *Research in the Teaching of English*, 1977, *11*, 255–271.

Applebee, A. N. *The Child's Concept of Story: Ages Two to Seventeen*. Chicago: University of Chicago Press, 1978.

Auerbach, L. *The Interaction between Social Attitude and Response to Three Short Stories*. Unpublished doctoral dissertation, New York University, 1974.

Aulls, M., & Gelbert, F. Effects of method of instruction and ability on literal comprehension of short stories. *Research in the Teaching of English*, 1980, *14*, 51–59.

Ball, E. R. *An Investigation into the Effects of a Specifically Designed Introductory Poetry Unit on the Cognitive Gains and Affective Responses of Ninth-grade Students*. Unpublished doctoral dissertation, University of North Carolina, 1979.

Barrett, C. P., & Barrett, G. V. Enjoyment of stories in terms of role identification. *Perceptual and Motor Skills*, 1966, *23*, 1164.

Beach, R. W. *The Literary Response Process of College Students While Reading and Discussing Three Poems*. Unpublished doctoral dissertation, University of Illinois, 1972.

Bennett, S. *The Relationship between Adolescents' Levels of Moral Development and Their Responses to Short Stories*. Unpublished doctoral dissertation, University of California, Berkeley, 1978.

Bettelheim, B. *The Uses of Enchantment*. New York: Knopf, 1976.

Billow, R. M. A cognitive developmental study of metaphor comprehension. *Developmental Psychology*, 1975, *11*, 415–423.

Blair, H. *Lectures in Rhetoric and Belles Lettres*. Dublin, 1783.

Bleich, D. *Readings and Feelings*. Urbana, Ill.: National Council of Teachers of English, 1975. (ERIC Document Reproduction Service No. ED 103 832)

Bloomer, R. H. Characteristics of portrayal and conflict and children's attraction to books. *Psychological Reports*, 1968, *23*, 99–106.

Blount, N. S. The effect of selected junior novels and selected adult novels on students' attitudes toward the "ideal novel." *Journal of Educational Research*, 1965, *59*, 179–182.

Brewbaker, J. M. *The Relationship between the Race of Characters in a Literary Selection and the Literary Responses of Negro and White Adolescent Readers*. Unpublished doctoral dissertation, University of Virginia, 1972.

Britton, J. N. Evidence of improvement in poetic judgment. *British Journal of Psychology*, 1954, *45*, 196–208.

Britton, J. N. *Language and Learning*. London: Allen Lane, The Penguin Press, 1970.

Britton, J. N.; Burgess, T.; Martin, N.; McLeod, A.; & Rosen, H. *The Development of Writing Abilities (11–18)*. London: Macmillan, 1975.

Brooks, C., & Warren, R. P. *Understanding Poetry*. New York: Holt, 1938.

Bruner, J. S. *The Process of Education*. Cambridge, Mass.: Harvard University Press, 1960.

Cappa, D. Kindergarten children's spontaneous responses to storybooks read by teachers. *Journal of Educational Research*, 1958, *52*, 75.

Casey, J. P. *The Affective Responses of Adolescents to a Poem Read in Three Different Classroom Situations of Reading: Teacher-directed Class Discussion, Self-directed Small Group Discussion, and Private Reading*. Unpublished doctoral dissertation, Rutgers University, 1977.

Choppin, B. H. Can literary appreciation be measured objectively? *International Review of Education*, 1969, *15*, 241–247.

Choppin, B. H., & Purves, A. A comparision of open-ended and multiple-choice items dealing with literary understanding. *Research in the Teaching of English*, 1969, *3*, 15–29.

Ciampoli, A. R. *A Comparison of an Individualized Reading Approach to Literature with a Directed Reading Activity Approach with Eighth-grade Inner-city Pupils on Selected Reading-related Factors*. Unpublished doctoral dissertation, Temple University, 1977.

Commission on English. *Freedom and Discipline in English*. New York: College Entrance Examination Board, 1965.

Cooper, C. R. *Preferred Modes of Literary Response: The Characteristics of High School Juniors in Relation to the Consistency of their Reactions to Three Dissimilar Short Stories*. Unpublished doctoral dissertation, University of California at Berkeley, 1969.

Cooper, C. R. Measuring appreciation of literature: A review of attempts. *Research in the Teaching of English*, 1971, *5*, 5–23.

Cooper, C. R., & Purves, A. C. *A Guide to Evaluation*. Lexington, Mass.: Ginn, 1973.

Cornaby, B. J. B. *A Study of the Influence of Form on Responses of Twelfth-grade Students in College-preparatory Classes to Dissimilar Novels, a Short Story, and a Poem*. Unpublished doctoral dissertation, University of Washington, 1974.

Coryell, N. G. *An Evaluation of Extensive and Intensive Teaching of Literature: A Year's Experiment in the Eleventh Grade*. New York: Columbia University, Teachers College, 1927.

Cowgill, G. A. *A Study of the Differential Effects of Short Films, Audiotapes, and Class Discussions on the Unstructured Written Response of Senior Students to Poetry*. Unpublished doctoral dissertation, University of Pittsburgh, 1975.

Culp, M. B. Case studies of the influence of literature on the attitudes, values, and behavior of adolescents. *Research in the Teaching of English*, 1977, *11*, 245–253.

DeBoer, J. J. *The Emotional Responses of Children to Radio Drama*. Unpublished doctoral dissertation, University of Chicago, 1938.

Dixon, J. *Growth through English*. Reading, England: National Association for the Teaching of English, 1967. (ERIC Document Reproduction Service, No. ED 001 024)

Dysinger, W. S., & Ruckmick, C. A. *The Emotional Responses of Children to the Motion Picture Situation*. New York: Macmillan, 1933.

Fader, D. N., & Shaevitz, M. H. *Hooked on Books*. New York: Berkeley, 1966.

Faggiani, L. A. *The Relationship of Attitude to Response in the Reading of a Poem by Ninth-grade Students*. Unpublished doctoral dissertation, New York University, 1971.

Fanselow, J. F. *The Responses of Ninth-grade Bilingual Adolescents to Four Short Stories*. Unpublished doctoral dissertation, Columbia University, 1971.

Favat, F. A. *Child and Tale: The Origins of Interest* (Research Report No. 19). Urbana, Ill.: National Council of Teachers of English, 1977. (ERIC Document Reproduction Service No. ED 137 830)

Ferreiro, E. What is written in a written sentence?: A developmental answer. *Journal of Education*, 1978, *160*, 28–41.

Fisher, C. J., & Natarella, M. A. *Poetry Preferences of Primary Graders* (Studies in Language Education, Report No. 35). Athens: University of Georgia, 1979. (ERIC Document Reproduction Service No. ED 172 261)

Folta, B. D. *Effects of Three Approaches to Teaching Poetry to Sixth-grade Students*. Unpublished doctoral dissertation, Purdue University, 1979.

Forehand, G. A. Problems of measuring response to literature. *Clearinghouse*, 1966, *40*, 369–375.

Frye, N. *Anatomy of Criticism*. Princeton, N.J.: Princeton University Press, 1957.

Gardner, H. *The Arts and Human Development: A Psychological Study of the Artistic Process*. New York: Wiley, 1973.

Gardner, H.; Kircher, M.; Winner, E.; & Perkins, D. Children's metaphoric productions and preferences. *Journal of Child Language*, 1975, *2*, 125–141.

Green, G. M.; Kantor, R. N.; Morgan, J. L.; Stein, N. L.; Hermon, G.; Salzillo, R.; Sellner, M. B.; Bruce, B. C.; Gentner, D.; & Webber, B. L. *Problems and Techniques of Text Analysis* (Center for the Study of Reading, Technical Report No. 168). Urbana, Ill.: Center for the Study of Reading, 1980. (ERIC Document Reproduction Service No. ED 185 513)

Green, M. *An Investigation of an Objective Approach and a Response-centered Approach to Teaching Renaissance Poetry in a Survey Course*. Unpublished doctoral dissertation, Ohio State University, 1977.

Grimme, D. A. *The Responses of College Freshmen to Lyric Poetry*. Unpublished doctoral dissertation, University of Northern Colorado, 1970.

Grindstaff, F. L. *The Responses of Tenth-grade Students to Four Novels*. Unpublished doctoral dissertation, Colorado State College, 1968.

Hall, G. S. *Adolescence: Its Psychology and Its Relation to Physiology, Anthropology, Sociology, Sex, Crime, Religion, and Education*. New York: D. Appleton, 1904.

Halliday, M. A. K. *Learning How to Mean*. New York: Elsevier, 1977.

Halliday, M. A. K., & Hasan, R. *Cohesion in English*. London: Longman, 1976.

Hansson, G. Some types of research on response to literature. *Research in the Teaching of English*, 1973, *7*, 260–284.

Harding, D. W. Practice at liking: A study in experimental aesthetics. *Bulletin of British Psychological Society*, 1968, *21*, 3–10.

Harpin, W. S. The appreciation of prose: Measurement and evaluation with especial reference to the novel, using the semantic differential. *Educational Review*, 1966, *19*, 13–22.

Harste, J. C.; Burke, C. L.; & Woodward, V. Children's language and world: Initial encounters with print. In J. Langer & M. Smith-Burke (Eds.), *Reader Meets Author—Bridging the Gap: A Psycholinguistic and Sociolinguistic Perspective*. Newark, Del.: International Reading Association, 1982.

Hart, B. T., Jr. *A Content Analysis of Secondary English Instructional Materials in Literature Produced by Project English Centers*. Unpublished doctoral dissertation, University of Rochester, 1979.

Hatfield, W. W. *An Experience Curriculum in English*. New York: D. Appleton-Century, 1935.

Heath, S. B. Protean shapes in literacy events. In P. Tanner (Ed.), *Spoken and Written Language*. Norwood, N.J.: Ablex, forthcoming.

Hickman, J. Children's response to literature: What happens in the classroom. *Language Arts*, 1980, *57*, 524–529.

Hillocks, G., Jr. *Alternatives in English*. Urbana, Ill.: National Council of Teachers of English, 1972. (ERIC Document Reproduction Service No. ED 068 951)

Hoetker, J. *Students as Audiences: An Experimental Study of the Relationships between Classroom Study of Drama and Attendance at the Theatre* (National Council of Teachers of English Research Report No. 11). Urbana, Ill.: National Council of Teachers of English, 1971. (ERIC Document Reproduction Service No. ED 070 084)

Holland, N. *The Dynamics of Literary Response*. New York: Oxford University Press, 1968.

Holland, N. *Five Readers Reading*. New Haven: Yale University Press, 1975.

Hook, J. N. *A Long Way Together: A Personal View of the National*

Council of Teachers of English's First Sixty-seven Years. Urbana, Ill.: National Council of Teachers of English, 1979. (ERIC Document Reproduction Service No. ED 178 912)

Hosic, J. F. *Reorganization of English in Secondary Schools* (Bureau of Education Bulletin No. 2). Washington, D.C.: U.S. Government Printing Office, 1917. (ERIC Document Reproduction Service No. ED 090 533)

Johns, J. L. Reading preferences of urban students in grades four through six. *Journal of Educational Research,* 1975, *68,* 306–309.

Judy, S. N., & England, D. A. (Eds.). An historical primer in the teaching of English. *English Journal,* 1979, *64.*

Kammann, R. Verbal complexity and preferences in poetry. *Journal of Verbal Learning and Verbal Behavior,* 1966, *5,* 536–540.

Kilpatrick, W. H. *Foundations of Method.* New York: Macmillan, 1925.

Kintsch, W., & Kosminsky, E. Summarizing stories after reading and listening. *Journal of Educational Psychology,* 1977, *69,* 491–499.

Kuehn, W. L. *Self-actualization and Engagement-Involvement Response to Literature among Adolescents.* Unpublished doctoral dissertation, University of Minnesota, 1973.

LaBrant, L. L. The use of communication media. In M. Willis (Ed.), *The Guinea Pigs after Twenty Years.* Columbus: Ohio State University, 1961, pp. 127–164.

LaBrant, L. L., & Heller, F. M. *An Evaluation of Free Reading in Grades Seven to Twelve Inclusive* (Contributions in Education, No. 4). Columbus: Ohio State University Press, 1939.

Langer, J. A., & Smith-Burke, M. *Reader Meets Author—Bridging the Gap: A Psycholinguistic and Sociolinguistic Perspective.* Newark, Del.: International Reading Association, 1982.

Lennox, W. N.; Small, J. J.; & Keeling, B. An experiment in teaching poetry to high school boys. *Research in the Teaching of English,* 1978, *12,* 307–320.

Lenrow, Elbert. *Reader's Guide to Prose Fiction.* New York: D. Appleton-Century, 1940.

Leonard, S. A. *Essential Principles of Teaching Reading and Literature in the Intermediate Grades and the High School.* Philadelphia: Lippincott, 1922.

Lucking, R. *A Study of the Effects of a Hierarchically Ordered Questioning Technique on Adolescents' Responses to Short Stories.* Unpublished doctoral dissertation, University of Nebraska at Lincoln, 1975.

Madden, F. F. *Computerized Content Analysis of Literary Response: A Feasibility Study.* Unpublished doctoral dissertation, New York University, 1979.

Mandell, B. J. *Three Language Arts Curriculum Models: Prekindergarten through College.* Urbana, Ill.: National Council of Teachers of English, 1980. (ERIC Document Reproduction Service No. ED 193 643)

Mandler, J. M., & Johnson, N. S. Remembrance of things parsed: Story structure and recall. *Cognitive Psychology,* 1977, *9,* 111–151.

Martin, N.; D'Arcy, P.; Newton, B.; Parker, R. *Writing and Learning across the Curriculum, Eleven to Sixteen.* London: Ward Lock Educational, 1976.

Mason, J. S. Adolescent judgement as evidenced in response to poetry. *Educational Review,* 1974, *26,* 124–139.

McGhee, P. E. The role of operational thinking in children's comprehension and appreciation of humor. *Child Development,* 1971, *42,* 733–744.

Millsop, L. A. *The Amount of Free Reading Done by Junior High School Students after Exposure to Free Reading Time in School.* Unpublished doctoral dissertation, Indiana University, 1977.

Mott, J. H. *Reading Interests of Adolescents: A Critical Study of Fifty Years of Research.* Unpublished doctoral dissertation, University of Northern Colorado, 1970.

Muller, H. J. *The Uses of English.* New York: Holt, Rinehart & Winston, 1967.

National Assessment of Educational Progress. *Recognizing Literary Works and Characters.* Washington, D.C.: U.S. Government Printing Office for the Education Commission of the States, 1973. (a) (ERIC Document Reproduction Service No. ED 078 425)

National Assessment of Educational Progress. *Understanding Imaginative Language.* Washington, D.C.: U.S. Government Printing Office for the Education Commission of the States, 1973. (b) (ERIC Document Reproduction Service No. ED 077 002)

National Assessment of Educational Progress. *Responding to Literature.* Washington, D.C.: U.S. Government Printing Office for the Education Commission of the States, 1973. (c) (ERIC Document Reproduction Service No. ED 077 020)

National Assessment of Educational Progress. *A Survey of Reading Habits.* Washington, D.C.: U.S. Government Printing Office for the Education Commission of the States, 1973. (d) (ERIC Document Reproduction Service No. ED 078 366)

National Assessment of Educational Progress. *Reading and Literature Objectives.* Denver: Education Commission of the States, 1980. (ERIC Document Reproduction Service No. ED 185 503)

National Assessment of Educational Progress. *Reading, Thinking, and Writing: Results from the 1979/80 National Assessment of Reading/Literature.* Denver: Education Commission of the States, 1981.

National Council of Teachers of English, Committee on the High School Course in English. Types of organization of high school English. *English Journal,* 1913, *2,* 575–596.

National Council of Teachers of English, Commission on the English Curriculum. *The English Language Arts in the Secondary School.* New York: Appleton, 1956.

National Council of Teachers of English. *The Basic Issues in the Teaching of English.* Champaign, Ill.: National Council of Teachers of English, 1959. (ERIC Document Reproduction Service No. ED 016 640)

Neisser, U. *Cognition and Reality.* San Francisco: Freeman, 1976.

Norvell, G. W. Wide individual reading compared with the traditional plan of studying literature. *School Review,* 1941, *49,* 603–613.

Oliver, J. E. *The Effects of Training in Synthesis-level Conceptualization upon Low-achieving First and Fifth Graders Involved in a Literature-based Cross-age Tutoring Program.* Unpublished doctoral dissertation, University of Georgia, 1978.

Peller, L. Daydreams and children's favorite books: Psychoanalytic comments. *Psychoanalytic Study of the Child,* 1959, *14,* 114–133.

Petrosky, A. R. Genetic epistemology and psychoanalytic ego psychology: Clinical support for the study of response to literature. *Research in the Teaching of English,* 1977, *11,* 28–38.

Piche, G. L. Class and culture in the development of the high school English curriculum, 1880–1900. *Research in the Teaching of English,* 1977, *11,* 17–27.

Pichert, J. W., & Anderson, R. C. *Taking Different Perspectives on a Story* (Center for the Study of Reading, Technical Report

No. 14). Urbana, Ill.: Center for the Study of Reading, 1976. (ERIC Document Reproduction Service No. ED 134 936)

Pitcher, E. G., & Prelinger, E. *Children Tell Stories: An Analysis of Fantasy.* New York: International Universities Press, 1963.

Pollock, J. C. *A Study of Responses to Short Stories by Selected Groups of Ninth Graders, Eleventh Graders, and College Freshmen.* Unpublished doctoral dissertation, University of Colorado, 1972.

Porter, J. Research report. *Language Arts,* 1976, *53,* 341–346.

Powers, R. L. *A Study of Three Methods of Presenting Short Stories.* Unpublished doctoral dissertation, Louisiana State University, 1977.

Purves, A. C. *Literature Education in Ten Countries.* Stockholm: Almqvist & Winksell, 1973.

Purves, A. C. Evaluation of learning in literature. *Evaluation in Education,* 1979, *3,* 93–172.

Purves, A. C., & Beach, R. *Literature and the Reader: Research in Response to Literature, Reading Interests, and the Teaching of Literature.* Urbana, Ill.: National Council of Teachers of English, 1972. (ERIC Document Reproduction Service No. ED 068 973)

Purves, A. C., & Rippere, V. *Elements of Writing about a Literary Work: A Study of Response to Literature.* Urbana, Ill.: National Council of Teachers of English, 1968. (ERIC Document Reproduction Service No. ED 018 431)

Richards, I. A. *Practical Criticism: A Study of Literary Judgment.* London: Kegan Paul, Trench, Trubner & Co., 1929.

Rosenblatt, L. *Literature as Exploration.* New York: Appleton-Century, 1938.

Rosenblatt, L. *The Reader, the Text, the Poem.* Carbondale, Ill.: University Press, 1978.

Ross, C. A comparative study of the responses made by grade eleven Vancouver students to Canadian and New Zealand poems. *Research in the Teaching of English,* 1978, *12,* 297–306.

Rudolph, F. *The American College and University: A History.* New York: Random House, Vintage Books, 1962.

Rumelhart, D. E. Notes on a schema for stories. In D. G. Bobrow & A. M. Collins (Eds.), *Representation and Understanding: Studies in Cognitive Science.* New York: Academic Press, 1975.

Rumelhart, D. E., & Ortony, A. The representation of knowledge in memory. In R. C. Anderson; R. J. Spiro; & W. E. Montague (Eds.), *Schooling and the Acquisition of Knowledge.* Hillsdale, N. J.: Lawrence Erlbaum Associates, 1977.

Sanders, P. L. *An Investigation of the Effects of Instruction in the Interpretation of Literature on the Responses of Adolescents to Selected Short Stories.* Unpublished doctoral dissertation, Syracuse University, 1970.

Schank, R. C., & Abelson, R. P. *Scripts, Plans, Goals, and Understanding.* Hillsdale, N.J.: Lawrence Erlbaum Associates, 1977.

Shablak, S. L. *The Effects of Different Types of Guide Materials and Manner of Presentation on Ninth-graders' Curiosity toward and Response to Selected Short Stories.* Unpublished doctoral dissertation, Syracuse University, 1973.

Shirley, F. L. The influence of reading on concepts, attitudes, and behavior. *Journal of the Reading Specialist,* 1968, *8,* 50–57.

Shrodes, C. *Bibliotherapy: A Theoretical and Clinical Experimental Study.* Unpublished doctoral dissertation, University of California, 1950.

Smith, D. V. *Instruction in English* (Bureau of Education Bulletin,

No. 17). Washington, D.C.: U.S. Government Printing Office, 1933.

Smith, D. V. *Evaluating Instruction in Secondary School English.* Urbana, Ill.: National Council of Teachers of English, 1941.

Somers, A. B. *Responses of Advanced and Average Readers in Grades Seven, Nine, and Eleven to Two Dissimilar Short Stories.* Unpublished doctoral dissertation, Florida State University, 1972.

Squire, J. R. *The Responses of Adolescents While Reading Four Short Stories* (Research Report No. 2). Champaign, Ill.: National Council of Teachers of English, 1964. (ERIC Document Reproduction Service No. ED 022 756)

Squire, J. R. English literature. In R. L. Ebel (Ed.), *Encyclopedia of Educational Research* (4th ed.). New York: Macmillan, 1969.

Squire, J. R., & Applebee, R. K. *High School English Instruction Today.* New York: Appleton-Century-Crofts, 1968.

Squire, J. R., & Applebee, R. K. *Teaching English in the United Kingdom.* Urbana, Ill.: National Council of Teachers of English, 1969.

Staples, E. S. *Cognitive and Affective Results of Three Methods of Presenting Stories to Third-grade Students.* Unpublished doctoral dissertation, Louisiana State University, 1979.

Stein, N. L., & Glenn, C. G. An analysis of story comprehension in elementary school children. In R. O. Freedle (Ed.), *New Directions in Discourse Processing Volume II.* Norwood, N. J.: Ablex, 1979.

Taba, H. *Reading Ladders for Human Relations.* Washington, D.C.: American Council on Education, 1947.

Terry, A. *Children's Poetry Preferences: A National Survey of Upper Elementary Grades* (Research Report No. 16). Urbana, Ill.: National Council of Teachers of English, 1974. (ERIC Document Reproduction Service No. ED 092 983)

Thorndyke, P. W. Cognitive structures in comprehension and memory of narrative discourse. *Cognitive Psychology,* 1977, *9,* 77–110.

Tway, E. *Reading Ladders for Human Relations* (6th ed.). Washington, D.C.: American Council on Education, 1981.

U.S. Commissioner of Education. *Report for the Year 1900–1901.* Washington, D.C.: U.S. Government Printing Office, 1902.

Weidner, M. J. *A Study of the Effects of Teacher Oral Reading of Children's Literature on the Listening and Reading Achievement of Grade Four Students.* Unpublished doctoral dissertation, Boston University, 1976.

Weiss, J. D. *The Relative Effects upon High School Students of Inductive and Programmed Instruction in the Close Reading of Poetry.* Unpublished doctoral dissertation, New York University, 1968.

Whitehead, F.; Capey, A. C.; Maddren, W.; & Wellings, A. *Children and Their Books.* London: Macmillan, 1977.

Wilson, J. D. (Ed.). *Matthew Arnold, Culture, and Anarchy.* Cambridge, England: Cambridge University Press, 1932.

Wilson, J. R. *Responses of College Freshman to Three Novels.* Unpublished doctoral dissertation, University of California, 1966.

Wilson, R. R., Jr. *In-depth Book Discussions of Selected Sixth-graders: Response to Literature.* Unpublished doctoral dissertation, Ohio State University, 1975.

Witt, P. D. *The Beginnings of the Teaching of Vernacular Literature in the Secondary Schools of Massachusetts.* Unpublished doctoral dissertation, Harvard University, 1968.

Yarlott, G., & Harpin, W. S. 1000 responses to English literature (2). *Educational Research,* 1971, *13,* 87–97.

LOCAL INFLUENCES ON EDUCATION

Perhaps the first question to ask about local influences on education is "Are there any?" As strange as it may sound, much of the recent research relevant to this topic (Guthrie, 1974; Guthrie & Thomason, 1975; Kirst & Garms, 1980; van Geel, 1976; Zeigler & Jennings, 1974) concludes that local citizen control and influence over public schools in the United States has been almost totally lost to the ever-increasing power of professional educators (school administrators and unionized teachers) and external forces (e.g., state and national agencies). Yet, the United States is still far from following the highly centralized European "ministry of education" model. With some 15,000 local public school districts still in existence, each one with a locally elected governing board to act as a conduit for the expression of local preferences and influences, it appears, to paraphrase Mark Twain, that rumors of the demise of local control and influence are greatly exaggerated. But suppose, as some observers contend, that local school boards have been reduced to little more than debating societies, symbolic of a lost tradition of grass roots control of local governmental affairs. What then? Are there any local influences on public education of any real importance left? And, if so, what are they; under what circumstances do they exist; and what are their consequences?

Approaches to Study of Power. Unquestionably, the latitude for local control and local influences to be felt in public schools has been reduced drastically by a variety of legal and governmental developments over the past two decades (van Geel, 1976). Nevertheless, contrary to the view that local influences now count for naught in the face of ever mounting external and professional forces, there is evidence of continuing, but diminished, local influence of significance for public schools (Boyd, 1976; Lutz & Iannaccone, 1978). To understand the present situation, and to answer the questions posed above, it is first necessary to address two subsidiary questions: (1) What constitutes "influence," and how is it exercised? (2) And, to what extent have external forces actually limited (or eliminated) opportunities for local influences?

It has been said that we all know what we mean by "power" and "influence" until we are asked to define these terms. As political scientists have learned to their sorrow, both terms contain large and apparently inescapable elements of ambiguity, which have marred and blurred research that uses them as central concepts (Bell, Edwards & Wagner, 1969; Hawley & Wirt, 1974; Lukes, 1974; March, 1966). For scientific reasons, therefore, it might be desirable to banish the terms from our vocabulary. But, as a practical matter, discussions of power and influence, and related concepts, such as authority and control, are inescapable. This article is written in that light, with an attempt to make as clear as possible a subject that is certain to retain some murky aspects.

Following Dahl (1961), for the purposes of this discussion power and influence are treated as synonyms and defined as follows: "A has power over B to the extent that he can get B to do something that B would not otherwise do" (Dahl, 1969, p. 80). Perhaps the best way of illuminating the power or influence relationship is in terms of a bargaining model that contrasts the cost of agreeing with the costs of disagreeing with another party (Cartter & Fray, 1972, pp. 290–298). Thus, it is the imposition of costs and changing costs that get actors to do what they otherwise would not do (cf. Dahl, 1961, pp. 309–310).

The scientific detection of the presence and effects of power or influence has turned out to be extraordinarily problematic, mainly because of the ambiguity surrounding the terms. Without going into the remarkable complexities of the matter—reflected in a vast and controversial scholarly literature (Bell, Edwards, & Wagner, 1969; Hawley & Wirt, 1974; Lukes, 1974)—a brief sketch of the main approaches to the study of power will help set the stage for the remainder of the discussion. To begin with, what can be called a "positional" approach to power assumes that power resides with those who hold key official positions in government. The difficulty with this "civics book" approach is that the key officials sometimes seem to be heavily influenced or even controlled (i.e., as puppets) by persons or groups outside of government or, on occasion, by persons in less obvious positions within government. (For examples of this in school politics, see Vidich & Bensman, 1958.) This possibility is taken into account in what is called the "reputational" approach to power. Using this approach, a researcher develops a ranking of persons thought to be most influential in the community by combining rankings of this type obtained from informed actors within the community. Typically, this approach, pioneered by Hunter (1953), who popularized the notion of a "community power structure," will tend to find that the persons thought to be most influential are not elected officials; instead, they are likely to be wealthy business and industrial leaders (cf. Kimbrough, 1964).

By calling attention to the significance of a reputation for power, Hunter identified what has come to be one of the most troublesome aspects of the study of power, namely, the difference between potential and actual use of power or influence. Because some groups and individuals, as a result of the resources they command, have an unusually high potential for power because of the costs that they could impose on those who displease them, elected officials and others may try to anticipate the reactions of such groups and individuals in planning their own behavior. In addition to the reactions of "powerful" individuals, elected officials may also enter into their calculations the probable reactions of blocs of voters and of others active in political affairs, giving them what Dahl (1961) calls "indirect influence." Thus, a reputation, or potential for power, may influence the behavior of others, but without any action being taken by those reputed or potentially powerful. The question thus arises, "Is this an exercise of power and influence and, in any event, how can one research it since those reputed or potentially powerful did nothing observable?"

Just because one has a reputation, or potential for power, does not necessarily mean that one will exercise this power in every instance. Other matters may divert one's attention, or one may not care as much about the issue at hand as some may have thought. Consequently, political scientists, such as Dahl (1961), have favored the "decisional" approach to power since it focuses, not on the potential for influence, but on actual behavior with reference to concrete decisions. An actor is said to have shown power if he can initiate and gain acceptance for a policy proposal or, alternatively, if he can successfully veto a policy proposal. By studying the actual participation of actors in these terms in a set of "key" issues in a variety of policy areas (e.g., urban renewal, public education, and political party nominations in Dahl's (1961) classic study of New Haven), the researcher hopes to document who actually exercised power.

Unfortunately, the decisional approach does not solve the problems of researching power. In a well-known article, Bachrach and Baratz (1962) argue that there are two faces of power—one manifest in participation in actual political disputes and their resolution, and the other expressed covertly through the ability of powerful interests to control the agenda of decision making, and to prevent the discussion of issues "unsafe" or "undesirable" from their point of view. The suppression of potential issues or policy alternatives—what Bachrach and Baratz call "nondecision making"—can result from them being vetoed in nonpublic deliberations; or, even more effectively, by the creation by powerful interests (past and present) of a "mobilization of bias" in terms of widespread and pervasive values and beliefs (throughout an organization, community, region or society), which delimits what it is "safe" to do and what "should not" be done. Actors, in the context of a mobilization of bias, will anticipate the reactions of powerful interests and ordinarily act in accordance, fearing the costs they otherwise will sustain. Alternatively, the mobilization of bias may be so pervasive that certain potential issues and grievances will not even be recognized by the aggrieved parties (Lukes, 1974).

By keeping some potential issues and policy alternatives from being discussed or, in some cases, even recognized, nondecision making and the mobilization of bias are formidable barriers to change. It is precisely because of the strength of local, regional, and ethnocultural mobilizations of bias that reformers often have to work so hard at "consciousness raising" to get their reform proposals taken seriously. For example, as Tyler (1974) notes in reviewing the educational issues attacked by the federal government during the 1960s, such as racial segregation and the problems of the disadvantaged, "in most cases, they were not even recognized as problems on the local level until the Congressional debates and the availability of federal funds brought them to local attention" (p. 185). And, of course,

in matters such as the segregation issue, it took years of effort to get the initial federal action started.

A profound difficulty with the nondecision-making approach is that, since it involves indirect and covert forms of influence, it is difficult (to impossible) to study or document non–decision making in strict behavioral terms. A person can assert that something failed to happen or failed to be raised as an issue because of the potential influence of certain powerful parties. But if something did not happen, and the accused powerful parties did nothing observable, then the researcher is left trying to document two nonevents. Although some ingenious attempts have been made to deal with these problems (Crenson, 1971; Lukes, 1974), some researchers take the view that one does not have to see the behaviors or decisions that led to certain outcomes. Instead, as Bowles and Gintis (1976) contend, one can look at the outcomes typically produced by governments and argue back from them, saying, as they do, that "it is no accident" that public schooling in America is structured and performs the way it does (i.e., in their view as an important mechanism perpetuating the inegalitarian social class stratification of the capitalist system).

In summary, influence can be direct and observable, as in the decisional approach, or indirect and covert, as in the reputational and nondecisional approaches. Although direct influence requires actual participation in the decision-making process, it should be noted that under the right circumstances (e.g., when their votes and support are deemed important by school officials) citizens can have indirect influence without extensive participation, which is a costly matter in terms of foregone opportunities. Because the latitude for direct action and control over local public schooling has been shrinking rapidly, due to nationalizing forces (Campbell, 1959) and contractual constraints as a result of collective bargaining with teachers unions, a large part of the local influence that remains is of the indirect variety. Still, there are important matters yet in the hands of local authorities, as shown at the conclusion of the following discussion of the structure for public school governance.

Governance Structure. Since the Constitution of the United States makes no mention of education, the states, by law, have plenary power over this function. Thus, public education is a state function, locally administered. But the operation of local school districts proceeds under a tradition, and governmental structure, of supervision by elected school boards composed of local citizens, who typically think of themselves as more accountable to the local community than to the state. In theory, then, the cherished tradition of local control enables citizens, through their representatives on the school board, to determine the purposes and character of education in their schools; thus, permitting them to maintain a type of schooling that is consonant with, and responsive to, local community values. According to this view, the educators who are hired by the local school district simply carry out the wishes of the public, supplying the needed expertise and means to attain the goals set by the school board.

In practice, however, a number of substantial problems have developed that impede the realization of local control. In the first place, as Goldhammer (1964) has noted, "with the passing of the small village school, there also passed much of the direct control of the local board of education" (p. 35). This loss of direct control was due to the fact that as school districts became larger, and the process and organization of schooling became more complex, school boards had to turn the actual administration of the schools over to trained educators. Moreover, school boards composed of laymen serving on a part-time basis found themselves increasingly dependent on their full-time professional school administrators for advice, recommendations, and information about the schools and education in general. Thus, as Goldhammer put it, "the professional's skills, experience, and insight gave him a considerable amount of [informal] authority and power over the board" (p. 35). Indeed, Goldhammer's observation is readily recognizable today as one of the central themes in the literature on American school politics: namely, the view that, as a result of their expertise and other strategic advantages, school superintendents and their supporting administrative staff typically dominate their school boards and the educational policy-making process and frequently turn their boards into little more than "rubber stamps" for the legitimation of their preferred policies (Kerr, 1964; Zeigler & Jennings, 1974; but see Boyd, 1976).

The increasing complexity and professionalization of school administration, and the ensuing tension between local and professional control, can be seen as part of a larger development in modern societies involving what Warren (1963) has called the growth of the "vertical axis" of community organization. Warren noted that although organizations relate horizontally to one another in the local community, their more important linkages increasingly are vertically upward, out of the local community, to their corporate and professional counterparts at higher levels. In other words, interaction among people and organizations performing certain functions, regardless of where they live or are located, has become more important in many respects than interaction within the local community (cf. Hays, 1974). Recognition of this development dispels the myth of the "autonomous community" by calling attention to external influences and dependencies that greatly affect both the character of the community power structure and what passes for "local" decision making (Walton, 1968; Wirt, 1974). A problem with this line of analysis, however, is that it sometimes moves in the direction of creating a new myth of the "powerless community," since it is inclined to ignore the ways in which communities still exercise a margin of control over their destinies through differences in policies on such matters as taxing,

spending, zoning, education, and community development (but see Peterson, 1981).

Another way of viewing the growing importance of the vertical axis, and the increasing tension between local and professional control of education, is in terms of the difference between community leaders with "local" and "cosmopolitan" orientations (Merton, 1957). Those leaders with a local orientation derive their influence mainly from local connections and from "who they know," whereas those leaders with a cosmopolitan orientation enjoy influence more because of "what they know" (i.e., their professional expertise and external networks for professional information). Since knowledge, or expertise, becomes ever more important as a power or political resource as society becomes more complex, bureaucratized, and technological, such knowledge enhances the potential influence of persons with cosmopolitan orientations.

External influences on public schools increased rapidly during the past two decades. Prior to that time, the federal government's role in education was a minor and supportive one. But in the wake of the civil rights movement, all three branches of the federal government took a more activist stance, using the "general welfare" and "due process" provisions of the Constitution as justifications for intervention in public education. The great difficulty, of course, is that from the national perspective the strength of local control is also its weakness. By allowing local school districts to maintain a type of schooling that is consonant with, and responsive to, local community values and biases, certain national interests, including the protection of minorities, may not be well served. As a result, state and federal authorities have increasingly intervened to change practices in local school districts in the interest of greater equality and efficiency.

The civil rights movement not only led to efforts to end racial discrimination and segregation in schools, but it also led to the discovery of whole new classes of disadvantaged students and forms of discrimination (e.g., non–English-speaking students, handicapped students, and sex discrimination). Further, in a number of states, lawsuits successfully challenged inequities in per-pupil spending between school districts as being impermissible under the states' constitutions. Finally, a number of developments, including particularly the prohibition against prayer in the public schools, have led to a more "secular" curriculum, in conflict with traditional "sacred" community values (van Geel, 1976).

A wide variety of categorically funded programs, guidelines, mandates, laws, court orders, judicial decisions, and lawsuits have been used in a "carrot and stick" fashion to bring about change in practices in local school districts. Meeting the requirements and paperwork generated by such initiatives has taken an increasing amount of the time of local authorities. As long ago as the mid-1960s, Scribner (1966) concluded, from an in-depth analysis of a single school board's activities over a school year, that rather than making policy the board more often was engaged in a quasi-judicial role, mediating the terms for applying externally determined policy to local circumstances. The requirements and complexities of implementing federal guidelines, court orders, and the like have tended to make school boards more dependent than ever upon the expertise of their professional administrative staff. Indeed, the politics of expertise loom ever larger in the changing structure of public school governance. For school board members, not to mention citizens in general, to have influence on policy making, they increasingly must be able to enlist expertise on their side, especially legal expertise; and they must be able to reach outside their community to higher levels of government via skilled professionals, lobbyists, and politicians (cf. Budoff, 1975).

The far-reaching changes in the structure of authority over the public schools in recent years have been well documented by van Geel (1976). The educational policy-making system is now more complex, legalized, centralized, and bureaucratized and includes more actors and more veto points. The big losers in this restructuring of authority, van Geel concludes, are local school boards and parents. This is so because the trends toward centralization, legalization, and bureaucratization of authority not only move control substantially away from the local community (further professionalizing the policy-making process), but they enhance the already large influence of professional educators and teachers unions by concomitantly increasing the importance of expertise as a political resource; by increasing the costs of obtaining relevant information about the more complex policy-making system; and by generally complicating and reducing the opportunities for meaningful citizen participation in policy making.

Although local school authorities are now significantly constrained in terms of what they must do and what they may not do, large areas of the structure of schooling and of the curriculum still are not mandated by state or federal requirements. We do not yet have a national curriculum, and many states still leave local school districts some substantial areas of discretion concerning the character of schooling and the curriculum (Wirt, 1977). Moreover, significant per-pupil spending differences remain between school districts in many states where arrangements for school finance have yet to be reformed. Such latitude permits local communities the freedom to spend in accordance with local tastes and resources, but, of course, it perpetuates inequities based on wealth. Finally, the heavy emphasis on the value of equality and, to a lesser extent, on efficiency, aggressively pursued by activist governmental agencies at the federal and state levels, has contributed to a reaction against big government and in favor of greater liberty, or choice, at the opening of the 1980s (cf. Garms, Guthrie, & Pierce, 1978). One policy alternative now being considered that would substantially increase local control and influence is the replacement of many categorically funded programs with unrestricted block grants, which could be spent according to local preferences. Proposals for tuition tax credits and educational voucher plans also would increase local influences since they would decentralize a sensitive phase of educational decision making to the family unit.

The discussion thus far should convey a sense of the external constraints upon local control and influence over public schools. At this point, therefore, the focus shifts toward conclusions about what affects the remaining degree of local influence.

Local Influence. The overall argument of this article is that the degree of local influence on public schools is contingent upon three factors: (1) the institutional rules shaping the political economy of public schools within our federal system (e.g., the structure of authority, accountability, and financial arrangements for public schools); (2) the type of local community involved; and (3) the type of issue or policy question faced. An examination of the first of these, the institutional rules, reveals in greater detail the factors that favor the influence of professional educators over local citizens.

Changes in the institutional rules shaping the political economy of public schools can increase or depress local citizen participation—and, consequently, the influence of local citizens—by reducing or increasing the costs and benefits of action by individual citizens or interest groups; and by facilitating or inhibiting the formation and maintenance of interest groups. Clearly, the institutional rules, which have been changing in such a way as to diminish local influence, could be structured so as to virtually eliminate all local control and influence. For instance, the financing of public schools in our federal system is typically shared by all three levels of government (i.e., local, state, and federal). The local share is raised by locally controlled property taxes, and research has shown that much of the citizen participation that does occur in local school government is related to fiscal concerns (O'Shea, 1971). In the interest of reducing inequalities in the amount spent per pupil in local school districts with varying fiscal capacities and inclinations to spend, school finance reform measures have tended to increase the state's share of the funding, diminishing the local contribution. The trouble with this is that as the fiscal incentive for participation weakens, the volume, frequency, and intensity of the remaining local citizen participation may be inadequate for keeping the residual degree of local lay control alive. School officials, for example, will have less reason to fear being threatened by citizen participation and will be less inclined to anticipate community reactions in formulating educational policies. Thus, an important component of community control may be lost.

With the exception of the school superintendent, the institutional rules structuring the political economy of public schools do not provide strong lines of accountability between educators and citizens. Indeed, an analysis using the concepts of political economy provides another approach to understanding who is likely to have influence relevant to public schools. This is so because, by revealing the structure of incentives, costs, and benefits facing educators and citizens, such an analysis shows who generally will face the lowest costs in attempting to advance their interests.

To begin with, public schools are insensitive to the mechanisms of the marketplace. They are quasi-monopolistic, nonprofit organizations whose financial support comes through a political process in the form of a tax-supplied budget rather than directly from satisfied clients. As Michaelsen (1977) argues, this means that the crucial linkage that insures consumer sovereignty is broken because of the assurance of a budget independent of the degree to which individual consumers are satisfied. Moreover, since there are no profits in public schools to motivate and reward managers (and teacher's salaries are based on seniority rather than performance), educators, as rational, self-interested persons seeking to maximize their own welfare, will be inclined to maximize their nonpecuniary benefits (Chambers, 1975; Michaelson, 1977). Thus, in place of profits (which would be dependent on satisfied consumers), public educators will seek to maximize such things as the scope of their activities, the ease of their work, and their power and prestige. On the other hand, they will try to minimize their psychic costs by avoiding risks and conflict insofar as possible.

The trouble with these perfectly human responses to the structure of incentives they face is that they tend to lead to perverse results from the point of view of the public interest. Administrators, according to this line of analysis, will be inclined to maximize the size of budgets rather than student achievement and client satisfaction, and teachers will tend to put their needs and comfort ahead of students' needs. In a word, the personal goals of employees in public schools often will take precedence over the official goals of the schools because the costs of inefficient behavior, in terms of the official goals, are low (Chambers, 1975).

Although this kind of economic analysis seems unpleasantly accurate (Boyd & Crowson, 1981; Griffiths, 1979; Perrow, 1978), it probably overstates the case. Inefficient behavior may be more costly for school decision makers than Chambers (1975) believes: because Chambers's analysis neglects the career and reputational benefits at stake for the decision makers and underestimates the survival pressures felt by key actors, the school superintendents (cf. Lutz & Iannaccone, 1978; Wirt, 1976). Thus, although most school board members may serve out of a sense of civic duty rather than political ambition, and hence may be insensitive to the survival mechanism of future elections (Zeigler & Jennings, 1974), they do have their reputations to protect. More important, school superintendents clearly have a career interest at stake, and they rise or fall according to their performance. Further, both superintendents and board members are sensitive to the continuation of fiscal support for the school system and also generally wish to avoid opposition and conflict, if possible. These

concerns, which touch both survival and psychic costs, tend to produce responsiveness to the public. But the degree of responsiveness depends upon the degree to which school officials and the school system are dependent upon the support of the local electorate. In turn, as noted above regarding arrangements for school finance, this varies with the institutional rules or statutory provisions structuring school governance in our federal system.

If school superintendents are accountable to the public, the same does not appear to be true of teachers. Not only are they tenured civil servants, but, as both citizens (i.e., voters) and members of unions engaging in public-sector collective bargaining, through political action they may be able to elect (and indeed have done so on occasion) both sides of the bargaining table. In other words, collective bargaining in the public sector is qualitatively different than in the private sector and may give teachers (and other public employees) a degree of influence that is contrary to the public interest (Mitchell et al., 1981; Wellington & Winter, 1971).

In a similar vein, drawing on Downs's "economic theory of democracy" (Downs, 1957), West (1967) and Michaelsen (1977) show how public employees, as compared with the lay public, stand to gain greater benefits and face lower costs (e.g., lower information, opportunity, and political mobilization costs) in pursuing personal benefits from the organization than does the public in seeking to insure the adequate achievement of the official goals or benefits of public schools. Downs (1957) and Niskanen (1971) also show the vulnerability of legislatures (e.g., school boards) to manipulation and lobbying by public employees and executives. Finally, the exclusivity of the personal benefits for employees and the nonexclusivity of the official benefits create substantial difficulties (especially the "free rider" problem) in mobilizing collective action (i.e., in forming and maintaining interest groups) for the public that are not faced by employees or others interested in personal benefits from school organizations (Olson, 1965; Peterson, 1974).

The political economy of public schooling interacts with local community factors to produce a context in which the main effects of local influences tend to be conservative. Many of these local influences are connected to various forms of nondecision making (Boyd, 1978). For instance, a vivid example of the problems associated with the mobilization of bias—in terms of the Waspish myth of the culturally homogeneous, unitary community and its educational corollary that all students should be treated alike—is found in the frequent "invisibility" of culturally different students (Waserstein, 1975). As with various classes of students with special physical, emotional, or learning problems, the needs of culturally different students tend to be ignored or unrecognized until extraordinary political or legal pressures are brought to bear in their behalf (Budoff, 1975).

Another example of the impact of nondecision making at the local level is found in the inclination of local authorities, in some settings, to hire only local people as teachers. This practice, which seems especially prevalent in rural communities (Peshkin, 1977; Vidich & Bensman, 1958) reinforces and protects local values and customs. On the other hand, as a result of their professional training and socialization, teachers and school administrators tend to reflect and represent a special set of professional and universalistic values which introduces a nonlocal influence into the community. Some scholars, who believe that there is a middle class bias built into the value structure of professional educators, argue that this bias produces far-reaching (nonlocal) effects in terms of social class discrimination (Karabel & Halsey, 1977).

Within the boundaries set by the mobilization of bias in a given community, and the predominant community values and expectations concerning the public schools, there exists a "zone of tolerance" within which local educators are free to exercise professional leadership (Charters, 1953; McGivney & Moynihan, 1972). However, when educators exceed the boundaries of the zone of tolerance (which may be broad or narrow, and clearly or poorly defined), they come into conflict with values dear to the particular community and face the likelihood of controversy and opposition. For a number of reasons, educators are strongly inclined to avoid conflict and, hence, are cautious about testing the boundaries of the zone of tolerance (Boyd, 1976). Thus, this cautiousness inhibits educational innovation.

Conflict avoidance tends to be a salient orientation in the minds of school administrators because it is a leading theme in the ideology of their profession; because it is reinforced through the nature of the typical recruitment and socialization process they undergo; and because of their frequently keen sense of political vulnerability (Callahan, 1962). This sense of vulnerability, along with the paucity of incentives for risk taking within the political economy of public schools, tends to make school administrators and teachers reluctant to incur the psychic costs and risks of innovation and possible controversy.

Teachers have long recognized that educators can get into a great deal of trouble by teaching about controversial matters. But even when educators have substantial public support and are willing to take the "heat" that may be generated by venturing into sensitive areas, those who are offended, even if only a small minority, sometimes can exploit the situation to gain their ends through a "politics of controversy." As Block and van Geel (1975) have observed,

[T]o stop a program it often is unnecessary to show its lack of merit in any objective way—if one can merely make the program "controversial" there is a good chance both politicians and bureaucrats will back off from it. Besides the energy they save by avoiding rather than resolving the problem, the officials satisfy those parents who, without involving themselves in the details of curriculum debates, feel better if what their children are being taught is not "controversial." (p. 78)

The politics of controversy not only discourages innovation in the school districts in which it occurs and, by example, in other school districts as well, but has perhaps its greatest impact on education by causing textbook publishers to go to great lengths to try to avoid inclusion of potentially controversial material in their publications. With very large investments at stake in the production of new textbooks, most publishers feel that they cannot take the risks of controversy (Broudy, 1975). The effects of overt censorship and prior censorship, or "nonpublication," on the curriculum might not be quite so bad if teachers and school systems commonly produced their own basic or supplementary curriculum materials. However, the vast majority of teachers and systems are almost entirely dependent upon the available published materials. The consequence of such dependency is that although most curriculum decisions ultimately are made at the local school district level, the choices usually are restricted to the available alternatives prepared, and generally precensored in anticipation of parochial local objections, by external groups.

Research indicates that the zone of tolerance, or the "latitude or area of maneuverability granted (or yielded) to the leadership of the schools by the local community" (McGivney & Moynihan, 1972, p. 221), varies primarily according to the type of community and, even within communities, according to the type of issue or policy question that is faced (Boyd, 1976). As the size, social heterogeneity, and degree of urbanism of school district populations increase, the responsiveness of school administrators and the public's ability to hold them accountable tend to decrease. Studies, such as that by Zeigler and Jennings (1974), suggest that smaller, less urban communities use informal networks to communicate political information and as a result, the school board, resting on powerful, informal networks, can dominate its superintendent when it needs to. By contrast, larger, more urban communities require formal channels for demand articulation, and so forth, and in this context the superintendent, who has expertise and privileged information that can be exploited in a formalistic setting, can more effectively thwart board control and public influences.

Beyond the effects of powerful informal networks of influence, local influences are also enhanced in suburbs, small towns, and rural communities because they tend to be not only smaller, but more homogeneous than cities. And, as Lyke (1968, 1970) has argued, drawing upon his research in urban and suburban school districts, community homogeneity promotes the likelihood that school officials will try to anticipate the demands of community groups when formulating educational policy. In heterogeneous communities, by contrast, it is difficult for school officials to anticipate and satisfy community demands because these demands are diverse and often in competition. Because of the problems and pressures this competition among demands introduces into school policy making,

Lyke (1970) contends that the school authorities in heterogeneous communities are inclined to encapsulate themselves and become unresponsive to public demands in general.

Although the size and heterogeneity of school districts are usually positively associated, size alone has independent effects on the responsiveness of school officials. As the size of the school system increases, the visibility of lay opposition groups tends to decrease, and school system bureaucracy, the social distance to the school authorities, and the ability of the system to maintain "business as usual" in the face of lay opposition tend to increase.

Although the heterogeneity of population, which tends to go along with the size of city school districts, usually produces a pluralism of ideologies and preferences about education, the (usually) *de facto* segregation of people according to social class and, sometimes, religion, which is common in many suburban districts, tends to result in distinctive expectations and influences that affect the curriculum. For example, comparison of working-class and upper-middle-class suburban school districts reveals significant variations not only in expectations for educational services and the ability to pay for them, but also in the amount of deference to the professional expertise of educators and the degree of congruence between community and professional educators' values (Minar, 1966). These differences produce differences in school policy that go beyond those that arise simply from varying community fiscal ability. Thus, all-white working-class suburban districts may not only reject cosmopolitan educational innovations (e.g., the "open" classroom, sex education) but, out of devotion to their neighborhood (K–8) schools, may even successfully resist the introduction of the junior high organizational scheme, which is scarcely a new concept (Boyd, 1973). Moreover, even when community social class and fiscal ability are held constant, important differences may emerge. For instance, heavily Catholic and conservative middle-class suburban districts may resist participation in federally funded programs and emphasize "basic education" and operational economy, whereas neighboring middle-class suburban districts possessing numerous Jewish and liberal constituents will demand the latest educational innovations and will pass numerous tax and bond referenda to support them (Boyd, 1973).

The management skills and associated attitudes, and the "good government" political culture of the populaces of higher-status communities often combine to provide an ideal setting for the harmonious workings of professional administrative expertise. Because community interests are so often being anticipated or reflected by their school authorities, middle-class and upper-middle-class communities are frequently content to delegate most of the tasks of governance to these authorities, who then seem to act with great autonomy—a state of affairs that appears undemocratic. Yet, why should the community oppose, and the school board not "rubber stamp," the proposals of educators as long as the community is getting what it wants? (Cf. Hawley & Wirt, 1974, pp. 6–7.)

Some political scientists (e.g., Zeigler & Jennings, 1974), however, are quite committed to the idea that democracy requires more or less continuous opposition and, applying this standard to school districts, are quite disappointed by what they find. Contrary to the implication that unopposed educators may be unresponsive to community wishes, the fact is, as documented in Salisbury's study of six St. Louis suburban districts of varied socioeconomic status, that most of what citizen participation occurs is supportive of existing school practices and programs (Salisbury, 1980). Indeed, Zeigler's latest study (Tucker & Zeigler, 1980), like the earlier one (Zeigler & Jennings, 1974), presents a good deal of data inconsistent with his interpretation that professional educators tend to dominate policy making in a way that is unresponsive to the public's wishes (Boyd, 1976; Cibulka, 1980; Firestone, 1981).

One of the most important points ignored by those committed to the "continuous opposition theory of democracy" is that a substantial body of research on school governance has documented the significant consequences of periodic or episodic crises. Supporting what they have called the "dissatisfaction" theory of democracy (Lutz & Iannaccone, 1978), Iannaccone and Lutz (1970) have shown that when, from time to time, discontent does build up in school districts, a predictable pattern of events will tend to occur. First, incumbent school board members seeking reelection will be defeated; then a new majority on the board will form; and finally, the incumbent school superintendent will be replaced by one who is responsive to the changed policy preferences of the new majority on the board. By this series of developments, communities reassert their control of school policy-making structures that have failed to respond adequately to changing preferences in the community.

Apart from episodic crises, the fact remains that ongoing citizen participation in school governance tends to be minimal, perfunctory, and reactive (Schaffarzick, 1975; Tucker & Zeigler, 1980; Zeigler & Jennings, 1974). To the extent that citizens get what they desire in the public schools, this usually occurs because local educators anticipate, or happen to agree with, their desires. But, as shown earlier, the latitude within which educators can shape educational programs in accordance with local preferences has been reduced substantially by recent developments external to the local school district. And, to the extent that state and federal authorities take issues and options out of the hands of local authorities, such actions also tend to depress, or remove reasons for, local citizen participation.

Yet, as Schaffarzick (1975) has documented, citizens can be influential when they become activated. In his comparative case study of 112 instances of curriculum change consideration in 34 San Francisco Bay Area school districts, Schaffarzick found that although 62 percent of the change-consideration cases involved no lay participation, and the bulk of the cases involved no identifiable political interaction—in the sense of conflict, bargaining, and compromise, but rather were characterized by apathy and indifference—the change cases were not always insulated from the political process and dominated by professional educators. Indeed, in the 19 cases involving distinguishable, significant conflicts, lay groups nearly always prevailed. So, the question of the circumstances under which citizens become activated remains an important one. Apart from the notion of excursions beyond a community's "zone of tolerance" precipitating citizen participation, perhaps the best answer revolves around the type of issue or policy question that is under consideration.

As discussed in detail elsewhere (Boyd, 1976), the public's influence varies not only according to community type, but also according to the type of issue or policy question faced. This consideration helps to explain why and when the citizens in school districts of all types are relatively active or passive in relation to local educators. Several helpful distinctions can be made among types of issues and policies. First, one can distinguish between "routine" and "strategic" decisions in the life of an organization or polity. In line with Zald's (1969) analysis of the significance of different phases of organizational development and activity for the power of governing boards, a good deal of evidence shows that both community and school board power will be mobilized when major phase problems or strategic decision points are encountered. These include, according to Zald, three types of broad-phased problems: (1) life-cycle problems (i.e., "organization genesis," "character crisis and transformation," and "identity crisis"); (2) the problem of choosing a chief executive successor; and (3) fund-raising and facilities-expansion problems. The ebb and flow of influence between communities and their school boards and superintendents with the different phases of the life of school districts is best documented by the Iannaccone and Lutz studies (1970).

The mobilization of community and school board power is also significantly affected by the allocative characteristics of policy questions. Following Lowi (1964), one can distinguish between "distributive" and "redistributive" policies. The former involve the dispensing of values and resources, which can be parceled out in such a way that "the indulged and the deprived, the loser and the recipient, need never come into direct confrontation" (Lowi, 1964, p. 690). Redistributive policies, on the other hand, produce clear winners and losers since they involve, in crude terms, taking from the rich to give to the poor. Redistributive issues are thus likely to produce widespread and acrimonious conflict, which may tend to immobilize public officials. Significantly, as Weeres (1971a) has noted, the heterogeneity and cleavages of large city school systems tend to generate redistributive policy issues, whereas homogeneous school districts (e.g., the "typical" suburb) often have been able to confine policy making primarily to distributive issues.

Another useful distinction is between "internal" and "external" policy issues. Internal issues involve decisions on such matters as the school curriculum and personnel policy, the consequences of which are generally perceived to be largely confined to the school system itself, at least in the short run. Internal issues also involve the kinds of matters for which the expertise of professional educators is thought most relevant in decision making. External issues, on the other hand, involve matters such as decisions on school construction and facilities and school finance, which have immediate visible and tangible effects on the ecology of the community as well as on the school system itself. Here, the opinion of the public tends to carry as much, and often more, weight than the expertise of the professionals. In fact, most studies (e.g., Zeigler & Jennings, 1974, pp. 125–128) of school politics provide abundant evidence that external, rather than internal, issues most often excite citizen concern and activity in school affairs. Indeed, Weeres (1971b) even found that the citizens groups active and influential in school affairs in thirty-three neighborhood areas in Chicago usually were not educational groups at all but organizations, such as businessmen's associations and property and homeowners' associations, whose main purposes were noneducational. These groups provided tangible, selective benefits for their members (e.g., zoning changes, street repairs, licenses) and their interests in education were restricted to the effects of school policies on the ecology of the community. As a result, issues involving curriculum and teaching problems rarely were raised.

Weeres's finding brings us to a final important distinction that can be made between policy questions that lie on different ends of the continuum between (pure) "separable" or "selective" goods and (pure) "collective" goods. Briefly, Olson (1965) called attention to the fact that when certain kinds of goods or benefits are provided to one member of a community, they simultaneously are provided to all members of that community. Such collective benefits as clean air cannot be provided to one person in a given area without being simultaneously available to all other persons in the area. Thus, this characteristic of collective benefits causes rational, self-interested persons to realize that it is not to their advantage to contribute to the cost of providing collective goods since they can take a "free ride" and enjoy the benefits at no cost. Of course, in the case of the schools, parents with children in public schools benefit more than those without children in public schools. Even among parents using public schools, however, the great majority are content to enjoy the benefits produced by education-oriented groups, such as the Parent-Teacher Association (PTA), without contributing to the provision of these benefits. Thus, such groups usually have difficulty maintaining themselves. By contrast, the exclusivity of the personal or selective benefits available from the school organziation for employees gives them a keen incentive for maintaining their own mutual benefit organizations (i.e., unions), although even these organizations prefer mandatory membership requirements to avoid "free riders."

Another reason why lay educational groups have difficulty organizing and maintaining themselves is that school authorities tend to follow policies and practices based on bureaucratic norms of equal treatment (Weeres, 1971b). The benefits that an educational group may obtain rarely can be restricted to its members, thus inhibiting its ability to attract and retain members. But, despite the emphasis on equal treatment, or universalism, certain accepted educational programs do have some of the properties of selective goods; that is, they benefit certain groups more than they do others (e.g., music, vocational, special, and physical education programs). Such selective benefits explain the active special interest groups that develop to support these programs. In other words, because the parents of retarded children, for instance, have a disproportionate interest in special education programs, they are willing to incur substantial costs in supporting these programs.

Perhaps of equal importance in overall school politics is the fact that the teacher and professional groups associated with the provision of special programs are inclined to become potent lobbies to protect and enhance their programs. Indeed, as illustrated in the effort to reform special education in Massachusetts (Budoff, 1975), professional groups may provide—and in fact may be one of the few sources for—most of the expertise and organizational resources needed for successful campaigns to change educational practices. And, of course, as compared with the usually transient interests of parents in schooling, educators in general—not just those associated with special programs—have an ongoing, important stake in the enterprise and support substantial, ongoing organizations to protect and advance their interests.

The difficulties that lay educational organizations face in trying to secure the resources, or selective benefits, for members needed to maintain themselves make them vulnerable to manipulation by the professionals in school systems and other agencies upon whom they may depend, to a greater or lesser extent, for such resources (Peterson, 1974). These problems are well documented in a recent study of sixteen community organizations in three cities: Boston, Atlanta, and Los Angeles (Gittell et al., 1980). Gittell and her associates found that recent federal policy thrusts, in terms of the mandating of parental involvement (e.g., parent advisory councils for Title I of the Elementary and Secondary Education Act, 1965—ESEA), and of the funding of community organizations to engage in service delivery, seem to have profoundly influenced the character and behavior of community organizations in poor, minority areas. Not only were they surprised to find "no school-issue-oriented, self-initiated, lower-income organization in any of the three cities" (p. 7), but they also found that the dependency of the organizations that they studied on external or school system sources precluded the use

of advocacy strategies in pursuit of educational reform. In effect, these organizations appeared to be "toothless tigers." Gittell and her colleagues conclude that, although more affluent populations have the resources to support independent community organizations (which thus can pursue advocacy strategies when needed), lower-income populations lack this ability. Consequently, the prospects for effective citizen participation by lower-income populations appear dim.

Summary. The extent of local influences on public education depends upon the institutional rules shaping the political economy of the public schools within our federal system, the type of local community involved, and the type of issue, or policy question, faced. Although educators usually dominate local educational policy making, they operate within constraints imposed by the local community and school board—not to mention those imposed by state and national forces. The local constraints (or, put another way, the influence of the community and the board) are likely to vary primarily with the type of community and with the type of policy issue that is faced. The influence of the local citizenry and the board will be more pronounced in external, redistributive, and strategic policy decisions, and in smaller and more homogeneous communities where the professionals tend to anticipate or reflect (especially in middle-class and upper-middle-class communities) community demands. The professionals, on the other hand, will tend to have more influence in internal and routine policy decisions, and in larger and more heterogeneous communities. The extent to which a given policy question involves selective or collective benefits will profoundly affect who participates, and which organizations and interests will be heard or will remain inchoate. The combination of all these factors indicates that the bleakest situation for local, public influence is found in large city school systems.

Within the changing institutional rules or structure of authority over public schooling, and the consequently much diminished latitude for local control and influence, it is not very clear how much real responsiveness by educators to local desires and influences remains. On one hand, an economic analysis of the structure for public school governance indicates that schools and educators are substantially insulated from the mechanisms of both the marketplace and the ballot box. On the other hand, the standard economic analysis probably overstates the case. There is evidence that some responsiveness occurs, particularly as a result of the effects of conflict-avoidance and the anticipation of public demands by educators, responses that in fact are consistent with the economic model. The consequences of these effects, overall, are that most local influences that remain tend to have a conservative impact on the character of the curriculum and schooling. Finally, and most important, local influences ultimately are highly dependent upon the institutional structure for governance, which has been changing rapidly in such a way as to remove opportunities for local influences to be felt.

William Lowe Boyd

See also Financing Schools; Governance of Schools; Home-School Relationships; School Boards.

REFERENCES

Bachrach, P., & Baratz, M. Two faces of power. *American Political Science Review*, 1962, *56*, 947–952.

Bell, R.; Edwards, D. V.; & Wagner, R. H. (Eds.). *Political Power: A Reader in Theory and Research*. New York: Free Press, 1969.

Block, A., & van Geel, T. State of Arizona curriculum law. In T. van Geel, with assistance of A. Block, *Authority to Control the School Curriculum: An Assessment of Rights in Conflict*. A study completed under a grant from the National Institute of Education, 1975. (ERIC Document Reproduction Service No. ED 125 070)

Bowles, S., & Gintis, H. *Schooling in Capitalist America: Educational Reform and the Contradictions of Economic Life*. New York: Basic Books, 1976.

Boyd, W. L. *Community Status, Citizen Participation, and Conflict in Suburban School Politics*. Unpublished doctoral dissertation, University of Chicago, 1973.

Boyd, W. L. The public, the professionals, and educational policy-making: Who governs? *Teachers College Record*, 1976, *77*, 539–577.

Boyd, W. L. The changing politics of curriculum policy-making for American schools. *Review of Educational Research*, 1978, *48*, 577–628.

Boyd, W. L., & Crowson, R. L. The changing conception and practice of public school administration. In D. C. Berliner (Ed.), *Review of Research in Education, 9*, 1981.

Broudy, E. The trouble with textbooks. *Teachers College Record*, 1975, *77*, 13–34.

Budoff, M. Engendering change in special education practices. *Harvard Educational Review*, 1975, *45*, 507–526.

Callahan, R. *Education and the Cult of Efficiency*. Chicago: University of Chicago Press, 1962.

Campbell, R. F. The folklore of local school control. *School Review*, 1959, *67*, 1–16.

Cartter, A. M., & Fray, M. *Labor Economics* (Rev. ed.). Homewood, Ill.: Irwin, 1972.

Chambers, J. G. *An Economic Analysis of Decision-making in Public School Districts*. Unpublished manuscript, University of Rochester, 1975.

Charters, W. W., Jr. Social class analysis and the control of public education. *Harvard Educational Review*, 1953, *24*, 268–283.

Cibulka, J. G. Review of *Professionals versus the Public* by H. J. Tucker and L. H. Zeigler. *Educational Evaluation and Policy Analysis*, 1980, *2*,(6), 85–90.

Crenson, M. A. *The Un-politics of Air Pollution: A Study of Non-decisionmaking in the Cities*. Baltimore: Johns Hopkins Press, 1971.

Dahl, R. A. *Who Governs? Democracy and Power in an American City*. New Haven, Conn.: Yale University Press, 1961.

Dahl, R. A. The concept of power. In R. Bell, D. V. Edwards, & R. H. Wagner (Eds.), *Political Power: A Reader in Theory and Research*. New York: Free Press, 1969.

Downs, A. *An Economic Theory of Democracy*. New York: Harper & Brothers, 1957.

Firestone, W. A. Is "who governs?" the right question? *American Journal of Education*, 1981, *89*, 212–222.

Garms, W. I.; Guthrie, J. W.; & Pierce, L. C. *School Finance: The Economics and Politics of Public Education*. Englewood Cliffs, N.J.: Prentice-Hall, 1978.

Gittell, M., with Hoffacker, B.; Rollins, E.; & Foster, S. *Citizen Organizations: Citizen Participation in Educational Decision-making* (Executive summary). Report prepared by the Institute for Responsive Education pursuant to Contract No. 400-76-0115 with the National Institute of Education, May 1980. (ERIC Document Reproduction Service No. ED 181 090)

Goldhammer, K. *The School Board*. New York: Center for Applied Research in Education, 1964.

Griffiths, D. E. Intellectual turmoil in educational administration. *Educational Administration Quarterly*, 1979, *15*, 43–65.

Guthrie, J. W. Public control of schools: Can we get it back? *Public Affairs Report* (Bulletin of the Institute of Governmental Studies, University of California, Berkeley), 1974, *15*(3).

Guthrie, J. W., & Thomason, D. K. The erosion of lay control. In National Committee for Citizens in Education, *Public Testimony on Public Schools*. Berkeley, Calif.: McCutchan, 1975, pp. 76–121.

Hawley, W. D., & Wirt, F. M. (Eds.). *The Search for Community Power* (2nd ed.). Englewood Cliffs, N.J.: Prentice-Hall, 1974.

Hays, S. P. The changing political structure of the city in industrial America. *Journal of Urban History*, 1974, *1*, 6–38.

Hunter, F. *Community Power Structure*. Chapel Hill: University of North Carolina Press, 1953.

Iannaccone, L., & Lutz, F. W. *Politics, Power, and Policy: The Governing of Local School Districts*. Columbus, Ohio: Merrill, 1970.

Karabel, J., & Halsey, A. H. Educational research: A review and an interpretation. In J. Karabel & A. H. Halsey (Eds.), *Power and Ideology in Education*. New York: Oxford University Press, 1977.

Kerr, N. D. The school board as an agency of legitimation. *Sociology of Education*, 1964, *38*, 34–59.

Kimbrough, R. *Political Power and Educational Decision-making*. Chicago: Rand McNally, 1964.

Kirst, M. W., & Garms, W. I. The political environment of school finance policy in the 1980s. In J. W. Guthrie (Ed.), *School Finance Policies and Practices—The 1980s: A Decade of Conflict*. Cambridge, Mass.: Ballinger, 1980.

Lowi, T. J. American business, public policy, case studies, and political theory. *World Politics*, 1964, *16*, 677–715.

Lukes, S. *Power: A Radical View*. London: Macmillan, 1974.

Lutz, F. W., & Iannaccone, L. (Eds.). *Public Participation in Local School Districts*. Lexington, Mass.: Heath, 1978.

Lyke, R. F. *Suburban School Politics*. Unpublished doctoral dissertation, Yale University, 1968.

Lyke, R. F. Representation and urban school boards. In H. M. Levin (Ed.), *Community Control of Schools*. Washington, D.C.: Brookings Institution, 1970, pp. 138–168.

March, J. G. The power of power. In D. Easton (Ed.), *Varieties of Political Theories*. Englewood Cliffs, N.J.: Prentice-Hall, 1966.

McGivney, J. H., & Moynihan, W. School and community. *Teachers College Record*, 1972, *74*, 317–356.

Merton, R. K. *Social Theory and Social Structure*. (Rev. ed.) New York: Free Press, 1957.

Michaelsen, J. B. Revision, bureaucracy, and school reform. *School Review*, 1977, *85*, 229–246.

Minar, D. W. The community basis of conflict in school system politics. *American Sociological Review*, 1966, *31*, 822–834.

Mitchell, D. E.; Kerchner, C. T.; Erck, W.; & Pryor, G. The impact of collective bargaining on school management and policy. *American Journal of Education*, 1981, *89*, 147–188.

Niskanen, W. A. *Bureaucracy and Representative Government*. Hawthorne, N.Y.: Aldine, 1971.

Olson, M., Jr. *The Logic of Collective Action*. Cambridge, Mass.: Harvard University Press, 1965.

O'Shea, D. W. *School Board-Community Relations and Local Resource Utilization*. Unpublished doctoral dissertation. Chicago: University of Chicago, 1971.

Perrow, C. Demystifying organizations. In R. C. Sarri & Y. Hasenfeld (Eds.), *The Management of Human Services*. New York: Columbia University Press, 1978.

Peshkin, A. Whom shall the schools serve? Some dilemmas of local control in a rural school district. *Curriculum Inquiry*, 1977, *6*, 181–204.

Peterson, P. E. Community representation and the "free rider." *Administrator's Notebook*, 1974, *22*(8).

Peterson, P. E. *City Limits*. Chicago: University of Chicago Press, 1981.

Salisbury, R. H. *Citizen Participation in the Public Schools*. Lexington, Mass.: Heath, 1980.

Schaffarzick, J. *The Consideration of Curriculum Change at the Local Level*. Unpublished doctoral dissertation, Stanford University, 1975.

Scribner, J. D. A functional-systems framework for analyzing school board action. *Educational Administration Quarterly*, 1966, *2*(3), 204–215.

Tucker, H. J., & Zeigler, L. H. *Professionals versus the Public: Attitudes, Communication, and Response in School Districts*. New York: Longmans, 1980.

Tyler, R. W. The federal role in education. *Public Interest*, Winter 1974, *34*, 164–187.

van Geel, T. *Authority to Control the School Program*. Lexington, Mass.: Heath, 1976.

Vidich, A. J., & Bensman, J. *Small Town in Mass Society*. Princeton, N.J.: Princeton University Press, 1958.

Walton, J. The vertical axis of community organization and the structure of power. *Social Science Quarterly* (Southwestern), 1968, *48*, 353–368.

Warren, R. *The Community in America*. Chicago: Rand McNally, 1963.

Waserstein, A. Organizing for bilingual education: One community's experience. *Inequality in Education*, February 1975, *19*, 23–30.

Weeres, J. G. School-community conflict in a large urban school system. *Administrator's Notebook*, 1971, *19*(9). (a)

Weeres, J. G. *School Politics in Thirty-three of the Local Community Areas with the City of Chicago*. Unpublished doctoral dissertation, University of Chicago, 1971. (b)

Wellington, H. H., & Winter, R. K., Jr. *The Unions and the Cities*. Washington, D.C.: Brookings Institution, 1971.

West, E. G. The political economy of American public school legislation. *Journal of Law and Economics*, 1967, *10*, 101–128.

Wirt, F. M. *Power in the City*. Berkeley: University of California Press, 1974.

Wirt, F. M. Contemporary school turbulence and administrative authority. In R. Lineberry & L. Masotti (Eds.), *The New Urban Politics*. Cambridge, Mass.: Ballinger, 1976.

Wirt, F. M. School policy culture and state decentralization. In J. Scribner (Ed.), *The Politics of Education: Yearbook of the National Society for the Study of Education*. Chicago: University of Chicago Press, 1977.

Zald, M. N. The power and functions of boards of directors. *American Journal of Sociology*, 1969, *75*, 97–111.

Zeigler, L. H., & Jennings, M. K. *Governing American Schools*. North Scituate, Mass.: Duxbury Press, 1974.

LOG-LINEAR ANALYSIS

Log-linear analysis is a relatively new generalized approach to the statistical analysis of qualitative/categorical data, data consisting of cross-tabulations within the context of contingency tables. Although log-linear methodology is of recent vintage, its use is well established in sociology and is rapidly gaining momentum in other areas of behavioral inquiry. So trenchant has been the impact of this methodology during the past decade that, in the words of Knoke and Burke (1980), "a revolution in contingency table analysis has swept through the social sciences, casting aside most of the older forms for determining relationships among variables measured at discrete levels" (p. 7). This article serves as a brief introduction to log-linear analysis.

A Brief Perspective.   Prior to log-linear analysis the statistical theory and computational techniques for the analysis of contingency table data were limited, for the most part, to a consideration of two-dimensional tables. For such tables the use of Pearson's classic nonparametric chi square was the established procedure for testing either the symmetrical hypothesis of variable independence or the asymmetrical hypothesis of homogeneity of proportional response (cf. Hays, 1973, p. 721). But often researchers possessed information on more than two categorical variables. And whereas traditional chi-square procedures were and are adequate for two-variable situations, the simultaneous analysis of three or more categorical variables presented serious problems that were only partially ameliorated by the much misunderstood partitioning method proposed by Lancaster (1951).

The nascency of the "revolution in contingency table analysis" can be traced to a series of journal articles appearing in the 1960s and early years of the 1970s in the statistics, behavioral science, and biological science literature; for example, Birch (1963), Mosteller (1968), Bishop (1969), Fienberg (1970), Goodman (1970), and Grizzle and Williams (1972). Concurrent with the continued refinement of the log-linear method, serious efforts also were made to synthesize this emerging body of work, characterized by diversity in notation and terminology, underlying methods of parameter estimation (i.e., least squares versus maximum likelihood), and points of view. Recondite texts written primarily for the statistically sophisticated and reflecting the respective approaches of their authors were offered by Haberman (1974), Plackett (1974), and Bishop,

Fienberg, and Holland, (1975). In addition, several of the important journal writings of Goodman were compiled into book form (Goodman, 1978).

These texts, however, failed to address the needs of practicing researchers in either the social sciences or education. These needs have now been met to some degree by commendable papers directed particularly to psychologists by Shaffer (1973) and to educators by Marks (1975). Moreover, textbooks with a purported applied emphasis have been published recently by Fienberg (1977) and Haberman (1978), and texts written decidedly for nonstatisticians have also appeared (Everitt, 1977; Upton, 1978). Most recent, has been the welcome monograph by Knoke and Burke (1980), which presents elementary concepts with considerable lucidity, drawing heavily on the approach advanced by Goodman, and which contains numerous examples, though mostly from political sociology. Thus, given the current availability of computer programs (e.g., ECTA and BMDP-3F) and an increasing body of didactic publications for nonstatisticians, the 1980s should see the revolution in contingency table analysis take firm hold in education.

Requisite Conditions and Major Operations. A log-linear analysis is appropriate only when all variables of interest are categorical. Variables may be ordered (e.g., grade level) or unordered (e.g., ethnic background). Concurrently, variables may be dichotomies (e.g., sex) or polytomies (e.g., political affiliation consisting of Democrats, Independents, Republicans, etc.). The number of categorical variables in a single analysis may be as few as two. However, major benefits are realized with three to six variables, that is, $2 \leq k \leq 6$.

Subsequent to variable identification and definition, members of a research sample of size n are cross-classified on the basis of selected variables, producing a k-dimensional contingency table. Relative to statistical inference, exact discrete sampling distributions under specified null hypotheses can be determined. Recall that for a symmetrical analysis (inquiry in pursuit of relationships between or among variables) exact sampling distributions are given by the multinomial law. For an asymmetrical analysis (inquiry in which at least one variable is viewed as a dependent or response variable) exact distributions are governed by the product-multinomial law. In either case calculations involved in generating an exact sampling distribution under these laws tend to be tedious. Fortunately this tedium can be circumvented, for it is well known that the discrete multinomial distribution approaches the exact continuous chi-square distribution as n's become sufficiently large (see Hays, 1973, pp. 305–309). It is also known that resultant distributions of Pearson's familiar nonparametric chi-square statistic and Fisher's (1924) less familiar likelihood-ratio chi-square statistic, L^2 both serve as adequate approximations to the exact chi square. Hence both the Pearsonian and Fisherian goodness-of-fit statistics are appropriate for use in log-linear work. But to comply with the parent multinomial law and to satisfy the system of approxima-

tions briefly described, the following conditions should be met.

1. *Independence of response.* Members of the sample should be randomly and independently drawn from the background population. Although in practice it is possible to relax the requirement of strict random selection, the requirement that the responses of subjects not be correlated is less tractable. Consequently the use of "repeated measurements," common to many ANOVA designs, is precluded in a conventional log-linear analysis.

2. *Mutual exclusivity and exhaustiveness.* To comply with the former each categorical variable should be structured such that sample members are assigned to one and only one category. The latter implies that each variable possesses sufficient categories to accommodate all members of the defined population.

3. *Sufficiency of sample size.* Because chi-square goodness-of-fit tests constitute a major component of a log-linear analysis, for each log-linear model it is desirable that the n be large enough to ensure that most elementary cells of the k-dimensional table contain at least five *expected* frequencies (F's). However, since goodness of fit does not constitute the entire analysis, mild violations of this condition are permitted. But major violations, especially in the presence of very small proportions (e.g., $p = .05$), not only can be expected to affect the goodness-of-fit component adversely, but they have been shown to bias positively log-linear estimates of parameter effects (i.e., lambdas). For a discussion of a related problem, that of observed zero entries (f's) in contingency tables, see Fienberg (1977, chap. 8).

An additional consideration affecting sampling is the nature of the inquiry. If the inquiry is symmetrical, only the size of the total sample is fixed prior to obtaining the sample, preferably at random. Simple random sampling under a fixed n assures that resultant marginal proportions constitute maximum-likelihood estimators of corresponding population proportions. On the other hand, if the inquiry is asymmetrical, restricted use of random selection will suffice. For example, if the intent is to determine whether males and females (the explanatory variable) hold different views on an issue such as abortion (the response variable), maximum statistical efficiency is achieved by fixing the number of males and females in advance so that they are equally represented in the sample.

Finally, subsequent to structuring two or more categorical variables, establishing the nature of inquiry, executing a sampling plan, and cross-classifying members of the sample, the ensuing operations are implemented in a typical log-linear analysis:

1. A series of "ANOVA-like" log-linear models are generated, usually in hierarchical fashion, and each model is used to produce a different set of expected elementary cell frequencies.
2. Goodness-of-fit comparisons are made between the expected frequencies given by each model (F's) and ob-

served sample frequencies (f's), and intramodel comparisons are made using component chi-square procedures.

3. From among competing models, one deemed most acceptable is selected for interpretation.
4. The acceptable model is interpreted in terms of either omnibus symmetrical concepts (e.g., mutual association, partial association) or asymmetrical concepts (e.g., main effects, interaction).
5. If needed, follow-up procedures are used either to estimate the strength of relations or to determine the specific nature of group effects.

A Concrete Example. The results of an experiment reported by Holton and Nott (1980) will be used to illustrate major log-linear operations. Two features of this research are of particular interest. The first is the way in which a pre-posttest variable was handled as two separate variables so as to avoid a violation of the assumption concerning independence of response. The second is that the analysis is asymmetrical, termed a logit-model analysis (Goodman, 1972). Given the nature of most research in education, the logit-model approach appears to possess great utility, and yet it has received little attention in current expository writings.

Subjects ($n = 101$) were preservice teachers who either were exposed to reflective teaching, a relatively new form of on-campus laboratory teaching experience, or served as controls. One hypothesis was that exposure to reflective teaching will enhance the ability of subjects to express themselves in a more analytical manner on matters concerning learning. Raw data were the written responses of subjects to the stimulus "What I think about learning," gathered prior to and following the experiment. Pretest responses were subjected to a grammatical structural analysis that ultimately led to subjects being placed in one of four categories on the basis of predominant mode of response. Pretest categories were (1) analytical, (2) evidential, (3) declarative, and (4) indeterminate, with the last containing subjects who could not be classified into one of the other three categories. Posttest responses to the stimulus were categorized by identical methods. There were, therefore, three categorical variables of interest: pretest responses (variable A), treatment group (variable B), and posttest response (the logit or response variable, variable C). Consequently subjects were assigned to one of 16 cells in a $4 \times 2 \times 4$ contingency table and the independence assumption was satisfied with respect to variables A and C.

Generating models and expected cell frequencies. For an asymmetrical analysis logit models must contain all terms representing irrelevant effects among fixed categories. Thus the null logit model for the Holton–Nott study, and all subsequent models, must incorporate terms representing the main marginal effects of the three variables plus the first-order interaction term associated with the fixed 2×4 {AB} configuration. Hence the null model is

$$\ln F_{ijk} = \lambda + \lambda_i^a + \lambda_j^b + \lambda_k^c + \lambda_{ij}^{ab}, \qquad (1)$$

where the natural logarithms of expected elementary cell frequencies produced by this model are the sums of λ (lambda), the natural log of the geometric mean of F_{ijk}'s, plus respective effects. The latter constitute differences between logs that are directly parallel to effects in the ANOVA. For example, the first-order interaction term may be defined as

$$\lambda_{ij}^{ab} = \ln f_{ij}^{ab} - \lambda - \lambda_i^a - \lambda_j^b.$$

Additional logit models, presented hierarchically, are

$$\ln F_{ijk} = \lambda + \lambda_i^a + \lambda_j^b + \lambda_k^c + \lambda_{ij}^{ab} + \lambda_{ik}^{ac} \qquad (2)$$

$$\ln F_{ijk} = \lambda + \lambda_i^a + \lambda_j^b + \lambda_k^c + \lambda_{ij}^{ab} + \lambda_{ik}^{ac} + \lambda_{jk}^{bc} \qquad (3)$$

$$\ln F_{ijk} = \lambda + \lambda_i^a + \lambda_j^b + \lambda_k^c + \lambda_{ij}^{ab} + \lambda_{ik}^{ac} + \lambda_{jk}^{bc} + \lambda_{ijk}^{abc} \qquad (4)$$

Looking ahead to the fourth operation, each model above is linked to a different omnibus interpretation. For example, should model (2) be accepted, then, because of the need to fit λ_{ik}^{ac}, responses of members in the four pretest groups are *not* independently distributed over categories of the posttest variable. In short, adoption of this model would indicate the presence of main effects for pretest groupings. Adoption of model (3) is suggestive of main effects between the experimental and control conditions, independent of pretest main effects. Finally, acceptance of model (4), termed the saturated model, would indicate interaction between variables A and B with respect to posttest response.

Returning to the first operation, the F_{ijk}'s for relatively complicated models, such as model (3), cannot be obtained directly; rather, they are obtained through iterative procedures. The least complicated algorithm to iteratively fit F_{ijk}'s for hierarchical models was developed by Deming and Stephan (1940), described by Fienberg (1970) and Goodman (1970), translated into Fortran by Haberman (1972), and has been most clearly illustrated by Fienberg (1977, pp. 33–36). Essentially it is the Deming–Stephan algorithm that is used in ECTA and BMDP-3F, currently the two most popular computer programs.

Comparing models. Typically it is the likelihood-ratio chi square (L^2) that is used to compare the F_{ijk}'s given by each model with observed f_{ijk}'s for goodness of fit. Because of its additive properties, this statistic also permits a partitioning of chi-square values into components (i.e., differences between goodness of fit L^2) associated with particular terms in log-linear models. Hence component L^2 values can be used to identify specific terms that contribute markedly to goodness of fit. These two versions of L^2 for the Holton–Nott study are shown in Table 1.

Selecting the most acceptable model. As Fienberg (1977) has stated, "Unfortunately, there is no all-purpose, best method of model selection" (p. 47). Nevertheless, a broad principle and two supporting statistical criteria are generally used in the absence of strong *a priori* theory. The principle is that of parsimony. The most acceptable

TABLE 1. *Goodness-of-fit and component chi-square values for logit models reported by Holton and Nott*[1]

Model/Source	Goodness of fit			Component		
	L^2	df	p	L^2	df	p
(1) Null/total	29.32	21	.10			
(2) Result of pretest	18.40	12	.10	10.92	9	.28
(3) Result of treatment	8.09	9	.53	10.31	3	.02
(4) Result of interaction	0.00	0	1.00	8.09	9	.53

[1] This analysis (Holton & Nott, 1980) partitions the variation of the logit variable about the fixed {AB} configuration (given by $L^2 = 29.32$) into three additive components: that attributable to pretest effects; that attributable to treatment effects subsequent to adjustments for pretest effects; and that attributable to interaction between pretests and treatment.

SOURCE: Derived from Holton & Nott, 1980.

model is the model with fewest terms that still fits observed data reasonably well. Hence goodness-of-fit L^2's are used initially to eliminate simple models that obviously do not provide adequate fit. Examination of Table 1 reveals that none of the models can be initially eliminated by this criterion since all failed to produce a significant result at the previously established .05 level. The application of the second criterion, however, does point to an acceptable model. Specifically, an examination of component L^2's, beginning with the saturated model and proceeding in "stepdown" fashion, reveals that model (3) could be chosen over model (4) without experiencing a significant loss of fit, L^2 (9) = 8.09, $p < .53$, but model (2) should not be chosen over model (3) because its selection would result in a significant loss of fit, L^2 (3) = 10.31, $p < .02$. In sum, Holton and Nott adopted model (3) as the most acceptable explanation of observed data.

Interpreting the selected model. As noted, there is a different overall conclusion linked with each model. Since the last term in the model selected by Holton and Nott was λ_{jk}^{bc}, indicating that interaction effects between variables B and C should be present to achieve a reasonable fit, the conclusion advanced is that members of the experi-

mental and control groups do not exhibit the same pattern of proportional response over categories of the posttest variable irrespective of pretest main effects, which, incidentally, do not appear to be prominent in their data.

Following up omnibus findings. Understandably, *post hoc* methodology has not yet been fully developed. Graphical procedures for following up complex interactions, patterned after *post hoc* ANOVA procedures, have been illustrated by Marks (1975). For main effects, however, a straightforward study of relevant lambda parameters in the selected model appears adequate. Holton and Nott, for example, subjected their relevant λ_{jk}^{bc} parameters to normal deviate test (z tests) using standard errors proposed by Lee (1977). And as shown in Table 2, one significant difference was documented: a difference between treatment groups with respect to analytical response, $z = \pm 2.61$, $p < .005$. Therefore, the hypothesis that subjects experiencing reflective teaching would produce more analytical statements at the end of the experiment was supported.

John J. Kennedy

See also Statistical Methods.

TABLE 2. *Observed {BC} frequencies, lambda parameters, and normal deviate tests of lambdas for Holton–Nott data*

Posttest Variable	Treatment variable					
	Experimental group			Control group		
	Frequency	Lambda	z test	Frequency	Lambda	z test
Indeterminant	14	−.026	−0.15	12	.026	0.15
Analytical	23	.527	2.61*	5	−.527	−2.61*
Evidential	12	−.280	−1.33	20	.280	1.33
Declarative	6	−.221	−1.04	9	.221	1.04

* $p < .005$

SOURCE: Derived from Holton & Nott, 1980.

REFERENCES

Birch, M. W. Maximum likelihood in three-way contingency tables. *Journal of the Royal Statistical Society*, 1963, *B25*, 220–233.

Bishop, Y. M. M. Full contingency tables, logits, and split contingency tables. *Biometrics*, 1969, *25*, 383–400.

Bishop, Y. M. M.; Fienberg, S. E.; & Holland, P. W. *Discrete Multivariate Analysis: Theory and Practice*. Cambridge, Mass.: MIT Press, 1975.

Cook, G. W. Estimation of contrasts of log-frequencies. *Biometrics*, 1977, *33*, 548–552.

Deming, W. E., & Stephan, F. F. On a least squares adjustment of a sampled frequency table when the expected marginal totals are known. *Annals of Mathematical Statistics*, 1940, *11*, 427–444.

Everitt, B. S. *The Analysis of Contingency Tables*. New York: Wiley, 1977.

Fienberg, S. E. The analysis of multidimensional contingency tables. *Ecology*, 1970, *51*, 419–433.

Fienberg, S. E. *The Analysis of Cross-classified Categorical Data*. Cambridge, Mass.: MIT Press, 1977.

Fisher, R. A. The conditions under which χ^2 measures the discrepancy between observations and hypothesis. *Journal of the Royal Statistical Society*, 1924, *87*, 442–450.

Goodman, L. A. The multivariate analysis of qualitative data: Interactions among multiple classifications. *Journal of the American Statistical Association*, 1970, *65*, 226–256.

Goodman, L. A. A modified multiple regression approach to the analysis of dichotomous variables. *American Sociological Review*, 1972, *37*, 28–46.

Goodman, L. A. *Analyzing Qualitative/Categorical Data*. Cambridge, Mass.: Abt Books, 1978.

Grizzle, J. E., & Williams, O. D. Log-linear models and tests of independence for contingency tables. *Biometrics*, 1972, *28*, 137–156.

Haberman, S. J. Log-linear fit for contingency tables (Algorithm AS 51). *Applied Statistics*, 1972, *21*, 218–225.

Haberman, S. J. *The Analysis of Frequency Data*. Chicago: University of Chicago Press, 1974.

Haberman, S. J. *Analysis of Qualitative Data* (Vol. 1). New York: Academic Press, 1978.

Hays, W. L. *Statistics for the Social Sciences* (2nd ed.). New York: Holt, Rinehart & Winston, 1973.

Holton, J., & Nott, D. L. *The Experimental Effects of Reflective Teaching upon Preservice Teachers' Ability to Think and Talk Critically about Teaching*. Paper presented at the meeting of the American Educational Research Association, Boston, April 1980.

Knoke, D., & Burke, P. J. *Log-linear Models* (Sage University Paper Series on Quantitative Applications in the Social Sciences, Series No. 07-020). Beverly Hills, Calif.: Sage, 1980.

Lancaster, H. O. Complex contingency tables treated by the partition of chi-square. *Journal of the Royal Statistical Society*, 1951, *B13*, 242–249.

Lee, S. K. On the asymptotic variances of $\hat{\mu}$ terms in log-linear models of multidimensional contingency tables. *Journal of the American Statistical Association*, 1977, *72*, 412–419.

Marks, E. Methods for analyzing multidimensional contingency tables. *Research in Higher Education*, 1975, *3*, 217–231.

Mosteller, F. Association and estimation in contingency tables. *Journal of the American Statistical Association*, 1968, *63*, 1–28.

Plackett, R. L. *The Analysis of Categorical Data*. London: Griffin, 1974.

Shaffer, J. P. Defining and testing hypotheses in multidimensional contingency tables. *Psychological Bulletin*, 1973, *79*, 127–141.

Upton, G. J. G. *The Analysis of Cross-tabulated Data*. New York: Wiley, 1978.

MAINSTREAMING

See Deinstitutionalization of the Handicapped; Handicapped Individuals; Legislation; Special Education.

MANAGEMENT EDUCATION

See Adult Education; Professions Education.

MARKETING AND DISTRIBUTIVE EDUCATION

"Marketing and distributive education" (MDE) is a generic term used to identify vocational instruction programs in public education designed to meet the needs of persons who have entered or are preparing to enter marketing occupations or occupations requiring competence in one or more of the marketing functions (adapted from Crawford, 1975). This entry will define marketing occupations and explore the mission of MDE with respect to marketing. The premises upon which this mission is based will be listed, and the goals adopted by the profession will be summarized. Then, in order to further describe MDE, the following topics will be addressed: philosophy, instructional programs, curricula, methods, clientele, evaluation, and research.

Marketing Occupations. Marketing occupations are concerned with functions and tasks directed toward and incident to the flow of industrial and consumer goods in channels of trade or the provision of services from producers to consumers or users, including ownership and management of enterprises engaged in marketing. Individuals are prepared to perform functions such as selling, buying,

pricing, promoting, financing, transporting, storing, marketing research, and marketing management (Nelson, 1979).

A major segment of the labor force is employed in marketing occupations. According to data from the *Occupational Outlook Handbook* (U.S. Department of Labor, 1980), it is anticipated that industries and businesses primarily involved with the marketing of goods and services will enjoy relatively large employment growth between 1978 and 1990. It has been estimated that "upwards to 30% of the labor force can be judged to be in an occupation requiring marketing skills" (Nelson, 1979).

Mission, Premises, Goals. Evidence supports the integrity and maturity of the field of MDE. For example, the directions that the profession should follow have been identified and studied. These directions have been provided by the identification and affirmation of a mission statement for the program, premises upon which this mission is based, and goals that the MDE profession will pursue during the 1980s. Furthermore, the mission, premises, and goals may serve as basic concepts in the formation of policies affecting MDE throughout the 1980s and probably beyond.

The following mission statement was developed by Samson (1980), based upon previous writings in the field, and was affirmed by the 270 participants attending a national conference for MDE: "The mission of Marketing and Distributive Education is to develop competent workers in and for the major occupational areas within marketing and distribution, assist in the improvement of marketing techniques, and build understandings of the wide range of social and economic responsibilities which accompany the right to engage in marketing businesses in a free enterprise system" (p. 27).

In addition to the mission statement, Samson (1980) presented the following fundamental premises essential to the implementation of the mission:

1. The discipline of marketing is the content base for all instruction.
2. Instruction will be offered to any personnel and in whatever settings necessary to meet community needs.
3. Programs will deliver a range of instruction covering functional skills, career competency development, operational management, and entrepreneurial development.
4. Instruction will stress application to and direct involvement with marketing businesses and be carried out by a variety of methods.
5. Professional personnel in the field of marketing and distributive education will have training in marketing, in marketing education, and possess business experience in marketing.
6. Where offered, marketing and distributive education will be considered an integral part of the institution's educational program, with direction and counsel coming largely from a business community advisory group. (Samson, 1980)

A national study is currently ascertaining the level of agreement within five selected groups with the mission statement and premises for MDE. These populations include secondary school MDE teachers, school administrators, business people, state supervisors, and teacher educators (Jacobsen, 1981).

Also, twelve goals for the MDE profession to pursue during the 1980s were initially presented by Samson (1980) and subsequently revised at the national conference. These goals included target dates for the development of a comprehensive national plan and promotional plan for MDE, the establishment of short-term and long-term goals by each state and territory, the evaluation of each local MDE and teacher education program, the implementation of a professional development experience for every MDE professional regarding such topics as the history, goals, and objectives of MDE, the updating and upgrading of all MDE teachers in marketing, the creation of models demonstrating the utilization and involvement of business personnel in state and local MDE activites, the assurance that all MDE program graduates will have an understanding of the free enterprise system, the pursuit of increased enrollment in adult MDE, the execution of a national conference for MDE leaders for the purpose of following up the 1980 conference, and the establishment of a national office for MDE. These goals were supported by the respondents to a survey of 1980 national conference participants. Then, a set of strategies for reaching the goals was developed at the conference.

At the time of this writing, the mission statement, premises, goals, and strategies were to be used as input to the development of a national plan for MDE in the 1980s and beyond. This plan should serve as a major source of information for future decision makers establishing policies affecting MDE.

Philosophy. In the area of philosophy, Crawford (1967a, 1967b, 1975) completed landmark studies that found a common philosophy to exist among MDE state supervisors, teacher educators, and teacher coordinators. In this study, 114 basic beliefs were identified and categorized within the elements of goals, definitions, guidance, coordination, curriculum, administration, and teacher education. The Crawford studies have been used as the basis for many subsequent research endeavors throughout the country in areas such as curriculum, instruction, teacher education, and evaluation.

Instructional Programs, Curricula, and Methods. MDE is responsible for developing instructional programs that are representative of the principal environments in which marketing occupations are found in substantial numbers in the labor force (Ely, 1978). Examples of these environments include fashion merchandising, advertising, real estate, industrial sales, entrepreneurship, floristry, banking, insurance, supermarket marketing, hotel and motel management, tourism, international marketing, wholesaling, and service station retailing. A significant development in recent years has been the implementation of specialized programs in which instruction is provided to a class (or classes) of students with a common occupational interest, such as fashion merchandising or supermarket marketing. Marketing classes in which students have a variety of occupational interests continue to be widespread, especially at the high school level; their success in meeting the needs of students with numerous career interests in marketing appears to be due to the use of various plans for individualizing instruction.

The curriculum in MDE grows out of a conceptual framework with three major dimensions: (1) the seventy-three marketing instructional programs indentified by the federal Department of Education, (2) five broad competency areas, and (3) four levels of marketing employment. The seventy-three marketing instructional programs have been incorporated into the *Classification of Instructional Programs,* a publication of the National Center for Educational Statistics. The five broad competency areas are marketing skills, product and service technology skills, applied basic skills, applied social skills, and economic concepts of private enterprise. The four levels of marketing employment are threshold entry, career sustaining, specialized, and entrepreneurial.

Curriculum research and development were predominant activities within MDE throughout the 1970s. Berns, Burrow, and Wallace (1980) cited curriculum as an area of research within marketing and distributive education in which there has been a consistent focus and design since the 1967 Crawford studies. Competencies needed by marketing employees have been identified by surveying workers and supervisors, observing workers, and interviewing business persons. These competencies have served as the research base for the development of compentency-based instructional materials for use in

MDE programs (e.g., Crawford, 1967a; Lynch & Kohns, 1977; Jacobs, 1978; Williams, Berns, & Heath-Sipos, 1979).

Before 1963 the cooperative method served as the only vehicle for training in distributive education programs, because federal legislation mandated that all students be employed in marketing occupations. The cooperative method is a means by which an organized sequence of on-the-job learning experiences to develop competencies related to each student's marketing occupational interest is correlated with classroom instruction (Crawford, 1975). Thus, each student enrolled in a distributive education program prior to 1963 was employed in a marketing job. With the passage of the federal Vocational Education Act of 1963, distributive education began to provide instruction designed to prepare individuals for future employment in marketing. The method by which preparatory training occurs is the project (or simulation) method. Thus, since 1963, the primary means for vocational application of instruction have been the cooperative and project methods, although variations of these methods have been developed and implemented.

An important component of MDE programs and curriculums is an organization for students enrolled in MDE programs, the Distributive Education Clubs of America (DECA). This organization provides and encourages activities designed to supplement and enhance instruction provided in MDE programs. Research studies by Corbin (1976) and Callahan (1979) identified goals and objectives for DECA's high school and junior collegiate divisions, respectively. These goals and objectives are congruent with the philosophy of MDE (Crawford, 1967a,b, 1975) and support the belief that DECA, as a cocurricular activity, should be an integral part of the curriculum and should provide opportunities to develop further competencies in marketing, including leadership and social skills. Research designed to determine the impact of DECA participation on students enrolled in MDE has provided evidence supporting the importance of DECA in MDE programs (Berns, Burrow, & Wallace, 1980).

Clientele. Professionals in MDE indicate that instructional programs should serve people of diverse talents, abilities, interests, and backgrounds who want and can benefit from instruction in marketing (Crawford, 1975). This belief is congruent with recent federal vocational education legislation designed to provide comprehensive programs so that persons of all ages in all communities will have ready access to vocational training or retraining suited to their needs, interests, and abilities. In keeping with this philosophy and congressional mandate, vocational programs in marketing and distributive education have been established for students at the following levels: middle school (primarily marketing exploration courses), high school, postsecondary, and adult. Furthermore, disadvantaged and handicapped learners have been either mainstreamed (when factors have permitted) or enrolled in separate classes designed specifically for their particular situation.

Enrollments in MDE programs have not approached the need for trained workers in marketing occupations. The best available information suggests that the total enrollment in MDE nearly doubled during the 1970s, from approximately 529,000 in 1969/70 to 942,000 in 1978/79, and significant increases were apparent at each level of instruction. However, keeping in mind that up to 30 percent of the labor force may be engaged in marketing occupations, the data on enrollments in marketing and distributive education clearly suggest that the states and localities have not planned vocational instructional programs in marketing and distributive education "in light of manpower needs and composition of the labor force" (Nelson, 1979).

Evaluation. Research efforts involving evaluation have examined questions pertaining to the validity, effectiveness, or efficiency of MDE programs as indicated by student achievement and by the judgments of people who are considered to be "expert" and qualified to judge. Investigations using student attainment of specified objectives as the dependent variable have been rather rare. Instead, follow-up studies often request opinions of samples of MDE students, teacher coordinators, school principals, and MDE employers about specific components of the program in an attempt to assess quality (Berns, Burrow, & Wallace, 1980).

Both program and product evaluation efforts have been undertaken. Standards used for program evaluation are typically based upon the philosophy of MDE. A set of program characteristics for use in the evaluation of MDE secondary school programs appears in *Evaluative Criteria,* published by the National Study of School Evaluation (1978). Harris and Manlove (1979) identified 288 evidence statements to aid in determining the degree to which program characteristics are met. Fifty-seven of these statements were rated as highly important by secondary MDE teachers in thirteen centrally located states (Wubbena, 1980). Guemple (1979) validated a set of standards and criteria for the evaluation of postsecondary MDE programs in Minnesota.

One method of evaluating the outcomes of a program is to develop rating scales and ask employers to rate their own employees, including MDE students and non-MDE students. Wilkinson (1974), Murphy (1975), and Wilkinson and Miles (1977) conducted such studies. They found that the MDE graduates secured employment faster, exhibited more job stability, obtained higher beginning wages, and received more salary increases during the first fifteen months of employment. Also, Wilkinson and Miles reported that the employers evaluated the MDE students as having better attitudes than non-MDE student employees. Furthermore, MDE students were rated much higher than non-MDE students on such factors as dependability, loyalty, and ability to accept criticism.

Other measures of the success of MDE programs are the degree to which past students remain in the field of marketing and the factors associated with student retention in the field. Such research is typically conducted locally and through state departments of education and not reported nationally. However, results of these studies are often available directly from the state education departments.

Evaluation of teacher education programs has been of interest to several researchers. Strydesky (1977) used a six-round Delphi procedure to identify 50 standards and 189 criteria by which to evaluate marketing and distributive teacher education programs and, subsequently, validated them by a national, geographically stratified random sample of teacher educators. These standards and criteria may be used for self-evaluation by teacher education programs, for accreditation in conjunction with state or national guidelines, and for other efforts at evaluating marketing and distributive teacher education.

Research. The number of research studies in MDE is growing yearly (Berns, Burrow, & Wallace, 1980). Furthermore, an increase is evident not only in the quantity of doctoral dissertations but also in the number of research endeavors completed other than in graduate programs. These investigations are often sponsored by agencies such as the U.S. Department of Education, state departments of education, universities, and private corporations.

A strength among MDE research studies continues to be the clear purposes specified and the applicability of the results. This practicality of research, the increasing number of studies being conducted, and the increasing willingness of various agencies to sponsor research in MDE are indicators of the growing importance being placed upon research as a basis for making decisions that affect marketing and distributive education.

Summary. Marketing and distributive education may be understood by studying its mission, the premises upon which the mission is based, the common philosophy of MDE professionals, the curricula of the instructional programs, the methodology used in the programs, the clientele served by the programs, and the needs of the marketing community that the programs seek to meet.

Recent research and development activities within the MDE profession have provided the seeds for growth and development of programs throughout the 1980s and beyond. Furthermore, the need for increased numbers of workers in marketing should give impetus to this trend. "The scope of programs in a given area is limited only by the imagination and expertise of program planners at the state and local levels" (Trapnell, 1979, p. 12). The development and implementation of new and creative programs should meet the needs of increasing numbers of persons of diverse talents, abilities, interests, cultural backgrounds, and ages. In addition, the needs of the marketing community will be further served, and as these needs are met, the mission of MDE will be continually accomplished.

Robert G. Berns

See also Business Education; Secondary Education; Vocational Education.

REFERENCES

Berns, R.; Burrow, J.; & Wallace, H. *Marketing and Distributive Education: Review and Synthesis of the Research.* Columbus: National Center for Research in Vocational Education, Ohio State University, 1980. (ERIC Document Reproduction Service No. ED 193 533)

Callahan, R. *The Identification of Goals for the Junior Collegiate Division of the Distributive Education Clubs of America.* Unpublished doctoral dissertation, Auburn University, 1979.

Corbin, S. *Formulation of Goals and Objectives for the High School Division of Distributive Education Clubs of America.* Unpublished doctoral dissertation, Virginia Polytechnic Institute and State University, 1976.

Crawford, L. *A Competency Pattern Approach to Curriculum Construction in Distributive Teacher Education.* Blacksburg: Virginia Polytechnic Institute and State University, 1967. (a) (ERIC Document Reproduction Service No. ED 032 383-386)

Crawford, L. *A Philosophy of Distributive Education: A Report of the First Step in the Research Project to Identify a Competency Pattern Approach to Curriculum Construction in Distributive Teacher Education.* Blacksburg: Virginia Polytechnic Institute and State University, 1967. (b) (ERIC Document Reproduction Service No. ED 019 412)

Crawford, L. *A Philosophy of Distributive Education.* Blacksburg: Virginia Polytechnic Institute and State University, 1975.

Ely, V. *Distributive Education Programs: A Program Information Publication.* Washington, D.C.: U.S. Department of Health, Education, and Welfare, Office of Education, 1978. (ERIC Document Reproduction Service No. ED 160 827)

Guemple, G. *Design and Feasibility Test of Evaluation Standards and Criteria for Postsecondary Distributive Education Programs.* Unpublished doctoral dissertation, University of Minnesota, 1979.

Harris, E., & Manlove, D. *Distributive Education Program Evaluation: An Aid for Use with Section 4-4, "Evaluative Criteria"* (5th ed.). Columbus: Ohio State University, Distributive Education Materials Lab, 1979.

Jacobs, B. *A Study to Identify a Competency Pattern for the Manufacturer's Salesperson.* Unpublished doctoral dissertation, University of Minnesota, 1978.

Jacobsen, W. *A National Study to Ascertain the Level of Unanimity within Five Selected Groups of the Mission Statement and Six Premises Statements for Marketing and Distributive Education.* Madison: University of Wisconsin, 1981.

Lynch, R., & Kohns, D. *Broad Content Outlines in Marketing and Distribution.* Blacksburg: Virginia Polytechnic Institute and State University, 1977.

Murphy, D. *Determination of the Extent to Which Distributive Education Trained Work Experience Students Utilize Accepted Retail Sales Techniques in Comparison with Non-distributive Education Trained Retail Salespeople.* Unpublished doctoral dissertation, Temple University, 1975.

National Study of School Evaluation. *Evaluative Criteria* (5th ed.). Washington, D.C.: American Council on Education, 1978.

Nelson, E. *Commissioner's Report, FY 78: Distributive Education.* Washington, D.C.: U.S. Department of Education, 1979.

Samson, H. *Distributive Education: Identity and Image.* Paper presented at the National Conference on Marketing and Distributive Education, Vail, Colo., 1980.

Strydesky, R. *The Validation of Evaluative Standards and Criteria for Distributive Teacher Education through Use of the Delphi Technique.* Unpublished doctoral dissertation, University of Maryland, 1977.

Trapnell, G. *Designing Programs for Marketing and Distributive Education.* Arlington, Va.: American Vocational Association, 1979.

U.S. Department of Education, National Center for Education Statistics. *Vocational Education Data System.* Washington, D.C.: U.S. Government Printing Office, 1979.

U.S. Department of Education, National Center for Education Statistics. *A Classification of Instructional Programs.* Washington, D.C.: U.S. Government Printing Office, 1981.

U.S. Department of Health, Education and Welfare, Division of Vocational and Technical Education. *Annual Reports.* Washington, D.C.: U.S. Government Printing Office, 1970–1978.

U.S. Department of Labor. *Occupational Outlook Handbook* (Bulletin No. 2075). Washington, D.C.: U.S. Government Printing Office, 1980.

Wilkinson, D. *A Comparison Study of Cooperative Distributive Education Graduates with Non-cooperative Distributive Education Graduates on Selected Employment Factors in the State of Iowa.* Unpublished doctoral dissertation, University of Wyoming, 1974.

Wilkinson, W., & Miles, E. *A Study of Performance of Cooperative Distributive Education Students as Compared with Regular Part-time High School Students.* Jacksonville: University of North Florida, 1977.

Williams, T.; Berns, R.; & Heath-Sipos, B. *Task Validation of Sixteen General Merchandising Department Store Occupations.* Washington, D.C.: U.S. Department of Education, 1979. (ERIC Document Reproduction Service No. ED 189 272)

Wubbena, D. *Importance and Fulfillment Ratings of Secondary Distributive Education Program Evaluative Criteria.* Unpublished doctoral dissertation, University of Minnesota, 1980.

MARKING SYSTEMS

Marks are summative, numerical or quasi-numerical symbols that both characterize a student's performance in an educational endeavor and become a part of that student's permanent records. Such educational endeavors typically represent either a course or a portion of a course held during a given period of time, often called a marking period. In general, it is the instructor's obligation to assign or provide marks to all the students enrolled in a class, although alternative procedures exist. For example, a department may establish a uniform policy or construct a single examination and indicate that marks must be assigned in accordance with this set procedure. Or an instructor may permit students to assign marks to themselves. Such practices, however, are relatively rare.

The terms "mark" and "grade" are frequently used interchangeably. Marks and grades need to be differentiated from a score that may be assigned a specific test, written report, homework assignment, or the like by the teacher. Marks summarize all the work considered relevant by the instructor over a course or marking period. Traditionally, an instructor alone decides what kinds of information to gather to evaluate pupils (e.g., tests, quizzes, written and oral reports, homework, class participation, attendance), how heavily to weight each of the various sources of information, and which of several frames of reference (described below) to use in assigning the grades. On the other hand, the choice of marking system itself is generally made by the institution or school system. Marking systems are in effect at all levels of the educational enterprise, from elementary school through graduate and professional school. As one might expect, the rationales behind such systems and the needs they fulfill differ according to educational level. That is, elementary school marking systems communicate primarily to parents, and college systems communicate to students and various external organizations.

Marks have a degree of permanence. Although in the elementary grades the prime purpose of grades may be to communicate with a child's parents, other methods of achieving such communication are also present: letters or phone calls from the teacher, parent-teacher conferences, or informal discussions at school and PTA association meetings. These latter methods may provide a source of richer communication but are typically not permanent, whereas marks remain in a child's file.

In a comprehensive review of the history of marking, Smith and Dobbin (1960) characterized the period 1940–1957 as fostering the conviction that marking practices should be consistent with educational objectives. In more recent years as well, especially in light of developments in marking such as grade inflation and developments in education such as the individualization of instruction, schools and colleges are quite concerned that their student evaluation systems serve their educational goals. Thus, the various marking systems are constantly being compared and scrutinized.

Vehement criticisms of marking have been voiced; it has been alleged that grading is unreliable, discriminatory, anxiety-provoking, and poorly communicative and that it generally interrupts the educational process (e.g., Kirschenbaum, Simon, & Napier, 1971). Space does not permit detailed consideration of these criticisms here. However, the marking process should be evaluated in terms of the intents and consequences of grading (Warren, 1975), and these will be discussed below.

Purposes. The use of various marking procedures and the problems involved in grading have often been discussed without first giving adequate consideration to the reasons why marks have been employed in education (e.g., Thorndike, 1969). Rather, grades and grading systems have been often perceived as inevitable to the educational process (Warren, 1971). The chief function of marks is to carry information concisely, without needless detail. This function of grades, to communicate effectively, overrides all other purposes, intended or incidental, and implies that grades must remain both limited in scope and concerned with academic achievement in specific educational endeavors. Marks must be able to communicate to a number of diverse audiences, all of whom employ grades for different purposes. Hills (1976) has listed six major audiences for marks: pupils, parents, school administrators, employers, counselors, and other schools. Each of these audiences employs grades in a somewhat different manner. The two major purposes for grades are to provide information and feedback and to aid in making institutional decisions. Additionally, marks may serve as selection criteria, motivators, research tools, and preparation for life.

Informational. The informational content in marks is intended primarily for pupils themselves, for parents, and for teachers. It is clear that grades are meant to provide feedback to students in regard to their academic performance. Specifically, academic feedback should permit students to judge their performance in detail; lead to modification of their behavior, where appropriate; differentiate strong and weak areas of their performance; and serve as reinforcement for jobs well done. It is unlikely that marks, which in traditional marking systems are singular symbols, can fulfill these purposes effectively. However, students receive a great deal of feedback (e.g., test scores, scores and written comments on tests and papers, and oral comments from teachers and other students), and the fact that overall grades add little to this feedback is probably not a major problem. On the other hand, report cards sent to parents may well provide them with useful information about their child's performance. In addition to learning about their child's performance across different curricular and skill areas, to assess relative strengths and weaknesses, parents may be able to formulate questions to ask their child's teacher.

Teachers, too, may benefit from a careful inspection of the marks they have assigned. In reviewing marks teachers may formulate new approaches to presenting material, consider new ways to instruct specific children, or change a course in the future.

Institutional. Marks are employed for a variety of internal administrative purposes by the institution at which they are assigned. These decisions include student promotion, admission to special courses and programs, awarding academic honors, and determination of eligibility for scholarships and extracurricular affairs, including athletic competition. Grades probably serve as valid data upon which to base these decisions in that they indicate a student's status in the educational system. Furthermore, teachers are often aware of these decisions when they assign marks. Thus, marks are targeted for decisions relevant to the student's education.

Sorting and selecting. Grades are often used in choosing individuals for advanced education, employment, fellowships and awards, academic honors, and participation in various professional and institutional activities (Warren, 1971). The nature of these decisions is competitive, and the decision makers are typically from an institution other than the one in which the marks were assigned. Arguments have been presented for and against this selection and sorting function of marks. Jencks and Riesman (1968) contended that the use of grades as a selection device primarily benefits members of high school classes and excludes members of lower classes from consideration. Presenting a counterargument, Glazer (1970) portrayed grades as equitable indexes that serve to improve societal productivity. Regardless of these arguments, grades and grade point averages have been widely used in making selection and placement decisions in education and industry.

Past grades are probably the best predictors of future grades, and the effectiveness of marks as predictors rather than as criteria has dictated their use in making selection and placement decisions. As early as junior high school, grades are used to place students in honors, regular, and remedial classes, and this use continues through high school. High school grades also take on increased importance in that they are employed in making admissions decisions by colleges and universities. Similarly, graduate and professional schools use college grades as indicators of potential for advanced education. The validity of grades as predictors of future academic performance is described below.

Employers sometimes use high school, college, or graduate and professional school grades in making hiring decisions. This use of grades is especially prevalent in some fields; for example, law firms are sometimes quite vehement in stating that only students at the top of their classes will be accepted (Warren, 1971). A discussion of the value of using grades in making employment decisions is also contained in the discussion of validity, later in this entry.

Motivating students. Instructors frequently attempt to use the incentive value of grades to motivate their students to work industriously. Some researchers (e.g., Becker, Geer, & Hughes, 1968) have decried this practice because it presumably promotes single-mindedness of purpose, desire to learn purely to earn an acceptable grade, and negative emotional affect. The finding of Cullen et al. (1975) that high school students were more likely to work to avoid a low grade than to earn a high one indicate this negative effect clearly.

To study the motivational effectiveness of grades, Goldberg (1965) compared the test performance of students accustomed to strict or lenient grading policies. He found no differences between their levels of achievement. His study, however, lacked a control group in which moderate grading standards were employed. Clark (1969) found that the performance of graduate students was significantly higher under conditions in which they competed for grades than under conditions that lacked competition. Other studies typically confound the motivating effect of grading, grading standards, and normal student evaluation procedures such as examinations, and quizzes (see Geisinger, 1980a). Examinations appear to bear more of a motivational influence than course grades; it is possible, however, that examinations derive their incentive value by being associated with grades.

The construct of intrinsic versus extrinsic motivation has some potential for explaining the motivational effects of marks. Intrinsic motivation relates to behavior that is self-perpetuating or performed without external rewards. Students who study predominantly because they want to learn the course material are considered intrinsically motivated. Extrinsic motivation relates to behaviors performed because a student hopes to receive certain rewards or reinforcements. High grades may be generally considered as reinforcers that increase student studying and learning behaviors. Some students are motivated to study primarily to earn high grades or to avoid low ones, whereas other students are motivated to study for intrinsic reasons. Teachers may be afraid that if they do not use the incentive value of marks to their advantage, students may not work hard enough to learn adequately. However, if studying is done purely to obtain the reinforcement of high grades, this behavior will extinguish (or be discontinued) after education is completed. Since educational goals typically stress the development of lifelong habits, this reliance upon grades as motivators may in fact inhibit the achievement of a major educational objective. Furthermore, students may assume that they are "forced" to perform academic behaviors under penalty of earning a low mark and may develop negative attitudes toward academic behavior. Sarafino and DiMattia (1978) have verified that grades and other extrinsic rewards reduce the intrinsic motivation of students. Nonetheless, every instructor in the educational system must decide when and how to use grades as motivators. Most instructors probably conclude that grades should exert some influence upon student behavior. However, one must consider the group being educated in relation to the motivational effect of marks. For example, adult learners in continuing education are rarely influenced by course marks; enrolling in continuing education is probably indicative of their being intrinsically motivated (Eison & Moore, 1980).

Research tools. An often overlooked function of marks is the role they play in educational research—as criteria in admissions studies and as dependent variables in studies either of curriculum reform or of special groups of students. In research on student selection, grades are consistently used as the criterion against which a predictor variable is validated. Marks are readily available and at least partially indicative of the quality of student performance. Nonetheless, marks, which are, after all, ratings, are subject to the problems of all ratings and suffer various psychometric inadequacies (see Willingham, 1974).

Marks are also sometimes used in curriculum research and evaluation. A school may make an instructional or curricular change and wish to assess its value on some index of student performance. However, marks should be used with caution in such endeavors. It is unlikely that marks carry the same meaning both before and after an innovation (see the discussion of instrumentation error in Cook & Campbell, 1979). For example, suppose a high

school has increased its use of laboratory training and experimentation in science classes and compares grades of students before and after this change. Tests designed to assess achievement, before and after the change, are likely to differ accordingly, and grades based on a difference between the two testings are unlikely to be meaningful. Similarly, using either the pretest or the posttest to assign grades on both occasions is likely to yield one set of invalid marks. This lack of comparability before and after reform has occurred is often obscured because the same grading system is employed at both times. It should be further noted that teachers' standards may shift in accordance with the curricular change. If teachers expect higher achievement from students after an instructional change, they may assign marks more stringently. If, on the other hand, they either expect student performance to improve or were aware that grades were to be used as part of an evaluation, standards may decline and grades improve, with no corresponding improvement in educational achievement.

A final research use of marks involves studies of special students. These comparisons are especially appropriate in instances of affirmative action programs. A college that changes its admissions policy will often wish to compare the performance of newly accepted students with more traditional students. For example, the military academies have recently compared the academic performances of male and female students through the use of their grade point averages. A caution in this kind of study involves checking the academic records (course loads, majors, etc.) of the various groups for comparability.

Preparation for life. It is generally assumed that marking students gives them experience that will enable them to adjust to the nonacademic world, primarily the world of work, where people are frequently evaluated. Warren (1971) has argued that marking in most educational settings involves written testing; rarely, if ever, are such procedures employed in job settings. However, successful performance on written tests may be required for an individual to become employed, and other classroom evaluation procedures (e.g., oral class presentations, performance in class discussions, term papers, attendance, instructor assessments of student effort) are probably more relevant to noneducational settings. Furthermore, testing and other marking procedures do prepare students for later educational assessments.

A second aspect of the value of marks in preparing one for life relates to their role as feedback in educational and vocational guidance. By looking at a student's entire record, the student and a counselor may determine strengths, weaknesses, and interests and use this information to face important life choices about future education and career. While research studies of the effectiveness of marks in this function have not been performed, it would appear that they are potentially useful in that they are relatively behavioral in nature and oriented to performance rather than self-report.

Marking Systems. Because marks are symbolic in nature, there are numerous systems of symbols that can be used to denote and evaluate student performance. The following discussion summarizes the two most common grading systems, percentage and letter-grade marking, and describes a number of other models (pass-fail, nonpunitive grading, contract grading, self-assessment, and descriptive evaluation systems). These latter models are typically used as modifications of the two common systems but sometimes constitute the entire marking system of an educational institution.

Percentage grading. Smith and Dobbin (1960) and Cureton (1971) reported that percentage grading was the most popular system during the latter half of the nineteenth century and early part of the twentieth. In this system, a teacher assigns each student a number between 0 and 100; often this number is supposed to correspond to the percentage of the material that the student has learned. This procedure implies an analogy between educational and physical measurements that is more apparent than real. Perhaps a more serious problem was the finding of Starch (1913) that teachers were generally unable to make distinctions of less than 4 to 7 points out of the total 100. Therefore, they suggested that only scores that are multiples of five be used. Furthermore, the entire scale in percentage grading is rarely used, because scores below 50 are infrequently given. Equipped with the above information, most educational institutions switched from numerical to letter grades during the 1930s and 1940s, and most recently only about 16 percent of American high schools use percentage grading (Hills, 1976).

Letter grades. Letter grades have become by far the most commonly used grading system—certainly more than percentage grading, for the reasons cited above. Additionally, it is relatively easy to translate from letter grading to percentage grading and back. Although there are many such conversions from percentage to letter grades, one common method assigns letter grades based upon the following percentages:

Letter Grade	Percentage Grade
A	93–100
B	85–92
C	75–84
D	60–74
F	Below 60

Different teachers, institutions, and school systems have adapted their own rules of thumb in converting percentage ranges to letter grades. These conversion tables are often a convenience, because a teacher is able to record all student information on a numerical basis, to weight and average this information, and to assign letter grades accordingly.

The grading system presented above employs five marks, with A being the highest and F the lowest. The letter F typically represents failing performance, and D may connote special meaning, such as a passing performance that does not permit the student to continue to take courses in the discipline or to count the course toward the student's major.

Terwilliger (1966) found that the letter-grade system was used by 68 percent of American high schools. The five letter symbols, or some of them, may also be modified by being coupled with the symbols + or −. At some institutions only a few letters are modified with plusses or minuses; B+ and C+ are frequently used, while A+ and D− are not. Thus, although the system has basically five levels, it may be increased to a maximum of 15, or to a more typical 12 or 13 scale points quite easily. Furthermore, with the wide use of the letter-grade system, the grades generally communicate quite adequately. Another advantage of this system is that letter grades can be easily averaged to form a summary index called a grade point average (GPA). To calculate a GPA, letter grades need to be transformed first to numerical values. For example, a typical system would translate A to 4.00, B to 3.00, C to 2.00, D to 1.00, and F to 0.00; use of a plus or minus typically adds or subtracts a fraction, respectively. For each course, the numerical value is then multiplied by the number of credit hours assigned to that course, these products are then summed over all courses taken, and this sum is divided by the total number of credit hours.

Together, letter grading and percentage grading constitute the vast majority of grading systems in the United States (National Educational Association, 1967; Pinchak & Breland, 1974). However, some schools have adopted other systems. In some cases, these systems parallel letter grades closely; one system, for example, assigns the numerals 4, 3, 2, 1, and 0.

Pass-fail grading. Many colleges and some high schools have permitted students to take courses on a Pass-Fail (P-F) basis rather than for traditional A-to-F letter grades. (These courses are also sometimes graded as Satisfactory-Unsatisfactory, or S-U.) Typically, schools limit the number of courses students may take on a P-F basis, and schools may prohibit P-F grades for required course work (Chansky, 1973). Schools may also limit eligibility to take P-F courses to upper-class students or students who have surpassed some minimal GPA. There are, however, a few schools that use only P-F grades.

The rationale for P-F grading is that students taking courses on a P-F basis can concentrate on learning the material for their own purposes rather than on earning high marks and can take courses in unexplored or threatening subject areas without fear of jeopardizing their GPAs. Furthermore, because of fears that instructors would grade P-F students more rigorously than other, traditionally graded students in the same classes, policies were frequently developed that prohibited a faculty member from knowing which students were, in fact, taking the course on a P-F basis. Thus, a faculty member assigns letter grades to all students in a class. Subsequently, the registrar's office changes the grades of the students who signed up for the course on a P-F basis; in some cases, grades of "D" lead to a "fail" rather than entitling the student to a "pass" grade. At most schools, GPA calculations do not involve P-F courses; at some institutions, fails count but passes do not. However, at almost all institutions, P-F courses taken and passed may be counted toward a student's required number of credit hours for graduation.

Several factors have mitigated P-F marking. Some schools that once used P-F grading entirely later added variations such as "Pass plus," "Pass minus," and "Honors"; in essence, such institutions had returned to a traditional marking system (Trow, 1966). Other studies have documented that student achievement levels decline under P-F systems and in P-F courses (e.g., Gold et al., 1971). A related but yet somewhat less frequently observed phenomenon relates to the differential allocation of student effort across traditionally graded and P-F courses. If students allocate their efforts judiciously, they may earn higher grades than they might have in their traditionally graded classes by reducing study time in their P-F courses. Finally, some graduate and professional schools look with disfavor upon P-F marks when making admissions decisions (Rossman, 1970). In fact, it has even been found that hospitals and universities prefer to select residents who have emerged from medical schools using standard A–F grades rather than P-F grades.

Other nonpunitive grading methods. In general, the other nonpunitive grading methods permit students to perform poorly in a course and not have the course grade entered or remain on the students' permanent records. The argument in support of such grades is that inadequate performance should not serve as punishment for a student; no credit should simply be awarded. For example, at some schools students may register a second time for courses that they have previously failed and may get credit for the second grade. Many schools have also adopted an institutional policy that has been called Pass–No Record grading (Christin, 1970). This is similar to Pass-Fail grading except that no notation is made unless the course is passed. Some schools record a "No Credit" designation in the case of a course failure; others make no mention of the course whatsoever on the student's record. Although some highly selective universities have adopted such practices, these policies predominate at junior colleges and institutions in which a high degree of student heterogeneity prevails.

A final type of nonpunitive grading concerns the option granted to many students, mostly undergraduate and graduate students, to withdraw from courses in which they are not performing as well as they wish (Oliver, 1971). As one might expect, students are able to use this option to the benefit of their GPAs. Geisinger (1979b) has shown that many more students withdrew from classes in which grades assigned were generally low, and Matley (1978) demonstrated that Ws (withdrawns) had essentially replaced Ds and Fs at his institution, because students left courses that they were about to fail.

Descriptive evaluations. Descriptive evaluation systems employ qualitative descriptions of the learning, skills, and abilities that characterize a student's work. The course instructor writes an evaluation of the student's accomplishments in a given course; such a report resembles a letter of recommendation. These evaluations may describe both "process" and "product" (i.e., how a person learns as well as how much) and may involve interaction between student and teacher during their preparation (Bellanca & Kirschenbaum, 1976). Evaluations of this kind may even be stored in computer files so that a student's complete record of evaluations can be compiled in lieu of a traditional transcript.

Descriptive evaluations are not without their disadvantages, of course. If they are used extensively, admissions personnel at all levels would become beleaguered in their attempts to wade through the rather extensive documentation to differentiate among students with noncomparable records. This difficulty has been reduced somewhat by a process practiced by some institutions, which abstract comments made by various instructors throughout a student's academic career and present the compilation of these abstracts as the student's transcript. A second objection leveled against descriptive evaluations concerns their validity; they may well focus on stylistic and personality qualities of the student rather than on the student's potential for success in advanced education. The final objection to descriptive evaluations concerns the labor involved in writing them. Teachers need to be skillful in verbal exposition and to be able to commit large quantities of time to such narratives. An alternative to the verbally composed evaluation is one involving a catalog of statements about students' performances. Such catalogs may be computerized (Burba, 1976). Relatively behavioral statements can be listed by grade level, course, or behavioral domain, and the teacher selects appropriate descriptor statements using a code; the descriptor is then listed permanently on the students' record. To be most effective, the descriptors should be aligned with the behavioral objectives for the course of study. Both this computerized "checklist" approach and the individual narrative method suffer when used with large classes. A teacher with a large class may find it impossible to identify specific skill acquisitions on the part of students unless the teacher is especially talented in test construction. Perhaps if this type of descriptive system were coupled with numerical or letter grades, the communication value to all interested parties—students, parents, the institution, and future schools and employers—would be maximized.

Contract grading. Hassencahl (1979) has reviewed research considering contract grading as an alternative to traditional grading practices. Contract grading differs from the previously discussed methods in that grading is individualized; there is no necessity for all students to be evaluated by the same criteria. The approach is modeled after real-world legal contracts. Contracts specify in writing the work that students stipulate they will perform and how this work will be evaluated in order to achieve a given grade. (Typically, contract grading is used in conjunction with a system of a traditional marking such as letter grading.) Christen (1976) has presented several ways in which contracts may be used. Typically, however, contracts are written by either a teacher or a student and then agreed to by the other party. In the example of the contract constructed by the student and agreed to by the teacher, the contracting procedure might begin in an introductory class meeting in which the instructor describes his or her general expectations concerning student performance for the attainment of certain marks. After this initial statement, students each construct a written document or contract that details what mark they wish to earn, how they plan to reach this goal, and how the attainment of their learning goals will be demonstrated. This draft is brought to the instructor to be negotiated; the instructor may suggest or insist upon modification. If students complete their part of the contract, they receive the grade agreed to. Although this marking system may permit students to individualize their learning and may to some extent eliminate subjectivity from the evaluation process, the quantity of student work is much easier to describe in a contact than the quality, and the quality of work may suffer accordingly (Kirschenbaum, Simon, & Napier, 1971). Furthermore, whereas it has also been reported that student anxiety over being evaluated is reduced under this grading strategy, research has also shown that student reaction to contract grading is mixed (Hassencahl, 1979).

Self-assessment. Two kinds of self-assessment have occasionally been used: self-evaluation and self-grading. In self-evaluation, students formally discuss their progress in a descriptive manner. In self-grading, students determine their own marks. Of course, self-grading cannot be accomplished without a degree of self-evaluation (Kirschenbaum, Simon, & Napier, 1971). The chief advantage of this system is that it forces students to evaluate their performance carefully. However, there are also several disadvantages. First, whereas only one perspective on grading is employed when a teacher assigns marks, all students employ their own perspectives, with a resultant loss of comparability—and reduction in the informational content of the marks. Self-grading also rewards those who overestimate their work and punishes the modest. Furthermore, pressure to earn high grades may couple with self-grading to set up a situation in which dishonesty is actually rewarded. To counter these influences, teachers and students may each assign marks, and an average of the two may be used. However, even this type or grade is subject to the above problems. Self-evaluation and self-grading have not achieved wide use.

Orientations for Assigning Marks. According to some authors (e.g., Terwilliger, 1971), there are four frames of reference for determining what a mark represents: absolute standards, growth or improvement, achievement with respect to ability, and achievement with respect to other students. Other authors (e.g., Hills, 1976) consider a fifth

frame of reference: grading students with respect to the efforts they make. A three-frame model (Thorndike, 1969; Thorndike & Hagen, 1977) is most attractive, because it consolidates Terwilliger's second and third frames with Hills's fifth to form a single orientation. In this model, grades may be assigned in relation to perfection, peers, or potential.

When marking according to perfection, the work of a student is compared with preset standards of competence, usually percentages of material learned. This method is sometimes also referred to as the mastery method, the criterion-referenced method, or the absolute standards method. To some extent, of course, this approach does involve comparisons with other individuals, because standards should be set realistically—that is, they should be based upon previous evidence of student performance. If the standards are set too high, many students will fail; if they are set too low, students will achieve invalidly high marks, and the instructor will earn the wrath of colleagues and school administrators. However, when such preset standards are used, students at least do not compete with one another as they may when peer comparisons are used. Standards also need to be set in close correspondence with the evaluation procedures to be used. If, for example, an institution sets 60 percent as the passing point and inadvertently constructs a very difficult test, many students may fail inappropriately. Travers and Gronlund (1950) found that most college instructors endorsed absolute standards as a method of marking, whereas Terwilliger (1966) found that 22 percent of high school instructors claimed that they employed absolute standards. The approach is clearly most appropriate in subject areas in which the subject matter follows natural units of performance or a hierarchical structure—for example, typing, mathematics, and foreign languages.

Comparing the performances of students with one another constitutes the peer method of grading, sometimes called the comparative or norm-referenced approach. Early advocates of this approach (e.g., Smith, 1953) stressed correspondence between grade distributions and the normal curve. However, even if student performance does follow a normal distribution, which is rare, it is unclear what percentage of a class should be assigned each mark. That is, one instructor may assign 15 percent A's, 25 percent B's, 30 percent C's, and so on, and a second instructor 7 percent A's, 23 percent B's, and 40 percent C's. Both are assigning marks "on the curve." Other faculty members may insist upon looking for natural "breaks"— gaps that fall between clusters of students—and use these gaps as lines of grade demarcation. It is also unclear what normative population should be used to constitute the curve. It can be a single class, a compilation of the performances of previous classes, or even a regional or national sample. Clearly, as one moves to larger samples for norms, one moves toward a combination of peer and perfection marking methods. Terwilliger (1966) found that the peer method was used by between 20 and 30 percent of high school teachers; Geisinger and Rabinowitz (1980) indicated that although most college faculty members said they did not use this method, in practice many did.

Marking students with respect to their potential involves several considerations: their apparent ability levels, their past performances, and the efforts they have made. Under this method, students who perform well relative to their apparent abilities, who improve considerably, or who appear to be making extensive efforts would receive high marks. Thorndike (1969) cited research showing teachers' general inability to grade effectively in this manner. Anastasi (1958) and Anastasi and Geisinger (1980) disagreed with the assumption that ability is unchanging, or "native," and that achievement alone is subject to environmental intervention. This method also suffers from the definitional problems inherent in the overachievement/underachievement research (Thorndike, 1963). Geisinger and Rabinowitz (1979) found that relatively few university faculty members assigned grades in this manner, but Geisinger, Wilson, and Naumann (1980) revealed that considerably more community college faculty members employed this strategy. In contrast, Terwilliger (1966) found that over 50 percent of high school teachers reported using the potential method for assigning marks. Furthermore, Geisinger and Rabinowitz showed that college faculty members who assign marks according to potential are more likely to assess students using term papers, classroom discussion, oral reports, special projects, and subjective impressions and were less likely to use examinations than their criterion- and norm-referenced colleagues.

Psychometric and Statistical Qualities of Marks. Given that it is generally instructors (regardless of their frame of reference) who determine the marks for their classes, few general conclusions may be drawn about the statistical distributions of the marks assigned within a class or institution; individual faculty members simply differ too dramatically from one another. Student grade point averages, on the other hand, have been shown to have a decidedly negative skew (Chansky, 1964) rather than the normal distribution that many might expect. The reliability, factor structure, and validity of grades for various purposes are described below.

Reliability. There are numerous ways to consider the reliability of marks. One may consider either the reliability of grades assigned in individual courses or the reliability of GPAs over some portion of students' careers. In the former, the internal consistency of the observations made and the information gathered by the instructor (primarily tests) for the purpose of assigning grades are of interest. Bendig (1953), for example, conducted one such analysis and found that the reliability of letter grades in various sections of an introductory psychology course ranged from .76 to .84.

Odell (1950) estimated the semester-to-semester reliability of college GPAs to be between .70 and .90. Fricke (1975) also reviewed the research on the internal-consistency reliability of GPAs earned in high school and college.

He concluded, "The grades which students receive from their instructors tend to be rather consistent. This uniformity is remarkable in light of the differences in course areas typically represented, and the variety of testing and grading procedures and standards employed" (p. 24). He concluded that a typical internal consistency coefficient falls in the .80s for the four years of college and suggested that for high school marks these coefficients would probably be higher because of increased variability. Werts, Linn, and Jöreskog (1978) estimated a somewhat lower value, .68, over the four years of college. In any case, however, it must be remembered that it is reliability of marks assigned within an institution that is being estimated; colleges and high schools vary considerably in the average grades that are assigned and one must be cautious comparing grades from more than a single institution.

Factor analyses. Boldt (1970, 1973) analyzed grades from business and law schools and found them to be singular (i.e., composed of single factors) in structure. This finding is consistent with the previously cited research on the apparent reliability of GPAs and implies that using GPA as a criterion in educational prediction studies is reasonable statistically and that therefore a researcher need not break down grades into specific curricular areas to achieve consistency. Schoenfeldt and Brush (1975) factor-analyzed the grades of 1,900 college students at a large university; whereas they generally replicated Boldt's finding of a single main factor indicating academic achievement, they also found a second factor, which they called "grades independent of achievement and aptitude." This second factor apparently represented success in certain applied, rather than purely academic, subjects and was not correlated with scholastic aptitude measures.

Validity in education. Colleges have traditionally used either high school GPA or rank in class (based upon GPA) in screening applicants. Lavin (1965) reported that high school GPA is probably the best predictor of college success (which is also defined as GPA) and cited correlations of .50–.55 as common. Graduate and professional schools have used college GPA similarly (Willingham, 1974). While college GPA is the best predictor of graduate GPA, the levels of prediction are lower than those obtained using high school GPA to predict college GPA, probably because of a restriction in range (mostly high grades are assigned to graduate students) in the criterion. The almost universal use of grades in making educational admissions decisions has been challenged by Humphreys (1968), who has argued that high school GPA only predicts early college grades well; later college performance is predicted significantly less well, because college students' abilities and knowledge bases changed during college. Follow-up studies have yielded mixed results, but in general, the longer the period of time between a predictor and a criterion, the weaker the relationship that has been found.

Validity in industry. A review of forty-six studies concerning college grades and adult success (defined variously in business, teaching, engineering, medicine, scientific research, and miscellaneous other occupations, as well as in nonvocational accomplishments) found that college grades bore little or no relationship to performance in any of these areas (Hoyt, 1965, 1970). This summary paralleled more recent work by the U.S. Office of Personnel Management, which has failed to document relationships between grades and job success (O'Leary, 1980). Apparently, educational success (e.g., high GPAs) is not indicative of job success, and it appears that, in general, scholastic success, defined in terms of marks, should not be used in making employment decisions.

Special Topics. A number of topics related tangentially to marking have received recent attention in educational research, reflecting current concern with the use of qualitative information in evaluation and with accountability problems in educational systems.

Affective components. The question of defining the aspects of student behavior that should be included in a mark takes on special significance in regard to personal characteristics. Some faculty members and researchers argue that marks should be based solely on academic competence, as shown, for example, by performance on tests and assignments. Others believe that school-related, though nonachievement, traits such as motivation, effort, and work habits should also be considered in assigning marks. Still other faculty members suggest the inclusion of characteristics such as dependability, leadership, interpersonal skills, and moral behavior as components in the grading process. Since grades are typically assigned by individual faculty members, every instructor must determine individually whether such characteristics are to be part of a mark, although some institutions have policy statements to guide their faculty. It is unclear how reliably and validly teachers are able to make judgments about the personal qualities of their students, but it is clear that the interpretation of a mark becomes more difficult as the number of varying components teachers use in assessing their students increases. Perhaps the best solution, one frequently used by elementary schools, is to include on the report card ratings or checklists of personal characteristics. Thus, the marks that are assigned can reflect academic competence, and the parents can still receive direct information from the teacher about their child's social skills, work habits, and other personal characteristics.

Grade inflation. American higher education experienced a dramatic and pervasive increase in the grades assigned between the middle 1960s and the early 1970s. GPAs from four-point letter-grade systems (e.g., 0.00 to 4.00) increased on the average about one-half of a letter grade without an apparent corresponding increase in achievement levels. Discussion of grade inflation has included arguments for its beneficial effect (e.g., Kane, 1978), its detrimental effect (e.g., Davidson, 1975; Etzioni, 1975), and the reasons for its occurrence (Birnbaum, 1977; Carney, Isakson, & Ellsworth, 1978; Geisinger & Rabinowitz, 1979). Explanations for the occurrence of grade inflation have considered changes on the part of students, faculty,

institutions of higher education, and society in general. The most probable causes of grade inflation include changes in faculty grading behavior from norm-referenced grading to more individualized, less comparative approaches (Geisinger, 1980b); changes in grading policies, including P-F and withdrawal marks (Geisinger, 1979b), increased use of student ratings of instructors and the desire of instructors to receive high ratings (Longstreth, 1979); influxes of young faculty members (Longstreth & Jones, 1976); and the declining student population and competition for students (Longstreth, 1979). Clearly, no definitive determination of the cause will be forthcoming, and it is probable that numerous influences have combined to bring about the phenomenon.

Perhaps of more current interest are the potential effects of grade inflation. Among these are the declining incentive value of grades to encourage students to work, changes in students' self-assessments of their skills, the increased awarding of academic honors, and the increased difficulty graduate and professional schools encounter in making admissions decisions. In general, Warren (1979) found no basis for these complaints. Evidence has failed to emerge that students have become less motivated. Students who use grades to try to determine whether they have the appropriate abilities and skills for success in various disciplines may not be able to use grades as effectively as previously, but they typically receive other, richer, although less formal, feedback upon which to make career decisions. The incidence of academic honors may be controlled by raising standards—that is, by raising the minimum GPA for awarding such honors. The assertion that graduate and professional school admissions committees have more trouble making decisions was not supported by Singleton and Smith (1978), who found no decrease in the reliability of individual differences in GPA due to grade inflation. However, Geisinger, Grudzina, and Glynn (1981) have shown that adults who apply for admission well after completing college had earned older, uninflated GPAs and hence appear as relatively poorer candidates in contrast to more recent graduates. Women returning for advanced education and older applicants are especially susceptible to this effect.

Student ratings. One frequent complaint in higher education is that student ratings of their instructors are contaminated by the grades students earn or expect to earn. Thus, it is said that some teachers, seeking favorable review for promotion, tenure, or salary purposes, would assign high grades, whereas other faculty members would maintain rigorous standards and would suffer in comparison. This topic has led to numerous research studies, but Centra (1979) concluded that the correlation between ratings and grades is probably low, in the .20 range. Given the sampling distribution of correlations in this range, some studies have found reasonably high correlations, others around zero, and still others negative values. A rare experimental investigation, however, which employed a relatively random assignment of grades to students, documented a convincing, biasing effect of grades upon student ratings of teachers (Vasta & Sarmiento, 1979). In light of this result, further experimental research on this topic is desirable. It should be noted, however, that the relationship between grades and student ratings need not be seen purely as contamination; it may also be perceived as evidence for validity. No one would complain if students learn more from an outstanding instructor, earn high grades, and subsequently rate the instructor higher than they would have graded a less effective instructor.

Differential standards. Numerous studies have demonstrated that individual teachers differ in the kinds of marks they assign and that these differences are stable (Geisinger & Rabinowitz, 1980). These consistent differences appear to be related to the frame of reference teachers choose to employ in assigning marks. Faculty members who use comparative or norm-referenced perspectives assign relatively low marks on the average; faculty members who mark according to potential and growth typically assign higher marks (Geisinger, 1980b).

Furthermore, although extensive differences exist among teachers even within academic departments at colleges and universities, there are large, consistent differences in average marks across departments as well (e.g., Goldman et al., 1974). Explanations for these phenomena have included differences in average levels of student scholastic ability across departments, differences in the nature of content or subject matter in various disciplines, and differential adoption of the grading frames of reference by faculty of different departments. Since it has long been known that high schools and colleges differ widely with respect to the average grades they assign, rank in class has been generally suggested as a better index of student performance. Thus, one must be extremely cautious when comparing grades from two or more instructors, GPAs of individuals who major in different disciplines, or GPAs from different colleges.

Equity. Some social psychologists interested in justice theory have questioned the allocation of merit in social systems, including education. Deutsch (1979) has considered grading from this perspective. His views flow from a comparative approach to grading. He describes grades as artificially scarce rewards, which are allocated on the basis of ability, drive, and character to fill the societal purposes of motivating and socializing children. He argues that comparative grading probably developed to foster a belief in the competitive, meritocratic ideology needed to legitimize socioeconomic inequalities. In contrast, he discusses other value systems through which grades could be awarded and suggests that grades should serve society by helping students gradually make the transition from the family to the world of work. Such relatively data-based, yet philosophical, statements as Deutsch's are likely to spark new research on grading systems and their effects on students.

Conclusions. Marks have long been a part of the education process to the extent that many perceive marking as inevitable. This entry has considered why marks are assigned, what kinds of marking systems are frequently employed, how faculty members assign grades, and what the psychometric properties of marks have been shown to be. It has also highlighted some current and continuing controversies related to marking. As long as marking is perceived as inevitable rather than valuable and as long as its justification is not clear, objections to grading and its consequences will arise.

Kurt F. Geisinger

See also Achievement Testing; Competency Testing; Instruction Processes; Promotion Policy.

REFERENCES

Anastasi, A. *Differential Psychology* (3rd ed.). New York: Macmillan, 1958.

Anastasi, A., & Geisinger, K. F. *Use of Tests with Schoolchildren.* Bronx, N.Y.: Fordham University, 1980. (ERIC Document Reproduction Service No. ED 194 635)

Becker, H. S.; Geer, B.; & Hughes, E. C. *Making the Grade: The Academic Side of College Life.* New York: Wiley, 1968.

Bellanca, J. A., & Kirschenbaum, H. An overview of grading alternatives. In S. B. Simon & J. A. Bellanca (Eds.), *Degrading the Grading Myths: A Primer of Alternatives to Grades and Marks.* Washington, D.C.: Association for Supervision and Curriculum Development, 1976, pp. 51–62.

Bendig, A. W. The reliability of letter grades. *Educational and Psychological Measurement,* 1953, *13,* 311–321.

Birnbaum, R. Factors related to university grade inflation. *Journal of Higher Education,* 1977, *48,* 519–539.

Boldt, R. F. *Factor Analysis of Business School Grades* (ETS-RB-70-49). Princeton, N.J.: Educational Testing Service, 1970.

Boldt, R. F. *Factor Analysis of Law School Grades* (ETS-RB-73-42). Princeton, N.J.: Educational Testing Service, 1973.

Burba, K. V. A computerized alternative to grading. In S. B. Simon and J. A. Bellanca (Eds.), *Degrading the Grading Myths: A Primer of Alternatives to Grades and Marks.* Washington, D.C.: Association for Supervision and Curriculum Development, 1976, pp. 64–69.

Carney, P.; Isakson, R. L.; & Ellsworth, R. An exploration of grade inflation and some related factors in higher education. *College and University,* 1978, *53,* 217–229.

Centra, J. A. *Determining Faculty Effectiveness.* San Francisco: Jossey-Bass, 1979.

Chansky, N. M. A note on the grade-point average in research. *Educational and Psychological Measurement,* 1964, *24,* 95–99.

Chansky, N. M. Resolving the grading problem. *Educational Forum,* 1973, *37,* 189–194.

Christen, W. Contracting for student learning. *Educational Technology,* 1976, *16,* 27.

Christin, R. E. A style for the seventies. *Educational Record,* 1970, *51,* 174–181.

Clark, D. C. Competition for grades and graduate student performance. *Journal of Educational Research,* 1969, *62,* 351–354.

Cook, T. D., & Campbell, D. T. *Quasi-experimentation: Design and Analysis Issues and Field Settings.* Chicago: Rand McNally, 1979.

Cullen, F. T., Jr.; Cullen, J. B.; Hayhow, V. L.; & Plouffe, J. T.

The effects of the use of grades as an incentive. *Journal of Educational Research*, 1975, *68*, 277–279.

Cureton, L. W. The history of grading practices. *National Council on Measurement in Education: Measurement News*, 1971, *2* (Whole No. 4).

Davidson, J. F. Academic interest rates and grade inflation. *Educational Record*, 1975, *56*, 122–125.

Deutsch, M. Educational and distributive justice: Some reflections on grading systems. *American Psychologist*, 1979, *34*, 379–401.

Eison, J., & Moore, J. *Learning Styles and Attitudes of Traditional Age and Adult Students.* Paper presented at the annual meeting of the American Psychological Association, Montreal, September 1980.

Etzioni, A. Grade inflation: Neither freedom nor discipline. *Human Behavior*, 1975, *4*(10), 11–12.

Fricke, B. G. *Report to the Faculty: Grading, Testing, Standards, and All That.* Ann Arbor: University of Michigan, Evaluation and Examination Office, 1975.

Geisinger, K. F. An explanation for grade inflation. Academic and policy-related causes. In K. F. Geisinger (Chair), *University Grade Inflation: Documentation, Causes, and Consequences* Symposium presented at the annual meeting of the American Psychological Association, New York, September 1979. (a)

Geisinger, K. F. A note on grading policies and grade inflation. *Improving College and University Teaching*, 1979, *27*, 113–115. (b)

Geisinger, K. F. Grading, grade inflation, and the psychology of motivation. In M. Preska (Chair), *Sorting, Motivating, Informing: The Functions of Grades.* Symposium presented at the National Conference on Higher Education, Washington, D.C., March 1980. (a)

Geisinger, K. F. Who are giving all those A's? *Journal of Teacher Education*, 1980, *31*(2), 11–15. (b)

Geisinger, K. F.; Grudzina, D. M.; & Glynn, M. A. *Grade Inflation and the Potential for Discrimination in Graduate Admissions.* Paper presented at the annual meeting of the National Council on Measurement in Education, Los Angeles, April 1981.

Geisinger, K. F., & Rabinowitz, W. Grading attitudes and practices among college faculty members. In H. Dahl, A. Lysne, & P. Rand (Eds.), *A Spotlight on Educational Problems.* New York: Columbia University Press, 1979, pp. 145–172.

Geisinger, K. F., & Rabinowitz, W. Individual differences among college faculty in grading. *Journal of Instructional Psychology*, 1980, *1*, 20–27.

Geisinger, K. F.; Wilson, A. N.; & Naumann, J. J. A construct validation of faculty orientations toward grading: Comparative data from three institutions. *Educational and Psychological Measurement*, 1980, *40*, 413–417.

Glazer, N. Are academic standards obsolete? *Change in Higher Education*, 1970, *2*, 38–44.

Gold, R. M.; Reilly, A.; Silberman, R.; & Lehr, R. Academic achievement declines under Pass-Fail grading. *Journal of Experimental Education*, 1971, *39*, 17–21.

Goldberg, L. R. Grades as motivants. *Psychology in the Schools*, 1965, *2*, 17–24.

Goldman, R. D.; Schmidt, D. E.; Hewitt, B. N.; & Fisher, R. E. Grading practices in different major fields. *American Educational Research Journal*, 1974, *11*, 343–357.

Hassencahl, F. Contract grading in the classroom. *Improving College and University Teaching*, 1979, *27*, 30–33.

Hills, J. R. *Measurement and Evaluation in the Classroom.* Columbus, Ohio: Merrill, 1976.

Hoyt, D. P. *The Relationship between College Grades and Adult Achievement: A Review of the Literature* (ACT Research Report No. 7). Iowa City: American College Testing Program, 1965.

Hoyt, D. P. Rationality and the grading process. *Educational Record*, 1970, *41*, 105–109.

Humphreys, L. G. The fleeting nature of the prediction of college academic success. *Journal of Educational Psychology*, 1968, *59*, 375–380.

Jencks, C., & Riesman, D. *The Academic Revolution.* New York: Doubleday, 1968.

Kane, R. J. In defense of grade inflation. *Today's Education*, 1978, *67*(4), 41.

Kirschenbaum, H.; Simon, S. B.; & Napier, R. W. *Wad-ja-get? The Grading Game in American Education.* New York: Hart, 1971.

Lavin, D. E. *The Prediction of Academic Performance:* New York: Wiley, 1965.

Longstreth, L. E. Pressures to reduce academic standards. In K. F. Geisinger (Chair), *University Grade Inflation: Documentation, Causes, and Consequences.* Symposium presented at the annual meeting of the American Psychological Association, New York, September 1979.

Longstreth, L. E., & Jones, D. Some longitudinal data on grading practices at one university. *Teaching of Psychology*, 1976, *3*, 78–81.

Matley, B. G. *Relationship between Grade upon Withdrawal and Time of Withdrawal for Selected Courses.* Unpublished doctoral dissertation, Nova University, 1978. (ERIC Document Reproduction Service No. ED 153 669)

National Educational Association. Reports to parents. *NEA Research Bulletin*, 1967, *45*, 51–53.

Odell, E. W. Marks and marking systems. In W. S. Monroe (Ed.), *Encyclopedia of Educational Research* (2nd ed.). New York: Macmillan, 1950, pp. 711–717.

O'Leary, B. S. *College Grade Point Average as an Indicator of Occupational Success: An Update.* (PRR-80-23). Washington, D.C.: U.S. Office of Personnel Management, Personnel Research and Development Center, 1980.

Oliver, F. E. *The AACRAO Survey of Grading Policies in Member Institutions.* Washington, D.C.: American Association of Collegiate Registrars and Admissions Offices, 1971. (ERIC Document Reproduction Service No. ED 055 546)

Pinchak, B. M., & Breland, H. M. Grading practices in American high schools: National longitudinal study of the high school class of 1972. *Education Digest*, 1974, *39*, 21–23.

Rossman, H. E. Graduate school attitudes to S-U grades. *Educational Record*, 1970, *41*, 310–313.

Sarafino, E. P., & DiMattia, P. A. Does grading undermine intrinsic interest in a college course? *Journal of Educational Psychology*, 1978, *70*, 916–921.

Schoenfeldt, L. F., & Brush, D. H. Patterns of college grads across curricular areas: Some implications for GPA as criterion. *American Educational Research Journal*, 1975, *12*, 313–321.

Singleton, R., Jr., & Smith, E. R. Does grade inflation decrease the reliability of grades? *Journal of Educational Measurement*, 1978, *15*, 37–41.

Smith, A. Z., & Dobbin, J. E. Marks and marking systems. In C. W. Harris (Ed.), *Encyclopedia of Educational Research* (3rd ed.). New York: Macmillan, 1960, pp. 783–791.

Smith, O. The science of grading. *Science Education*, 1953, *37*, 193–205.

Starch, D. Reliability and distribution of grades. *Science*, 1913, *38*, 630–636.

Terwilliger, J. S. Self-reported marking practices and policies in public secondary schools. *National Association of Secondary School Principals Bulletin*, 1966, *50*(3), 5–37.

Terwilliger, J. S. *Assigning Grades to Students*. Glenview, Ill.: Scott, Foresman, 1971.

Thorndike, R. L. *The Concepts of Over- and Underachievement*. New York: Columbia University, Teachers College, Bureau of Publications, 1963.

Thorndike, R. L. Marks and marking systems. In R. L. Ebel (Ed.), *Encyclopedia of Educational Research* (4th ed.). New York: Macmillan, 1969.

Thorndike, R. L., & Hagen, E. P. *Measurement and Evaluation in Psychology and Education* (4th ed.). New York: Wiley, 1977.

Travers, R. M. W., & Gronlund, N. E. The meaning of marks. *Journal of Higher Education*, 1950, *21*, 369–374.

Trow, W. C. On marks, norms, and proficiency scores. *Phi Delta Kappan*, 1966, *48*, 171–173.

Vasta, R., & Sarmiento, R. F. Liberal grading improves evaluations but not performance. *Journal of Educational Psychiatry*, 1979, *71*, 207–221.

Warren, J. R. *College Grading Practices: An Overview* (Report No. 9). Washington, D.C.: ERIC Clearinghouse on Higher Education, 1971. (ERIC Document Reproduction Service No. ED 047 164)

Warren, J. R. *The Continuing Controversy over Grades* (TM Report No. 51). Princeton, N.J.: ERIC Clearinghouse on Tests, Measurement, and Evaluation, 1975. (ERIC Document Reproduction Service No. ED 117 193)

Warren, J. R. The prevalence and consequence of grade inflation. In K. F. Geisinger (Chair), *University Grade Inflation: Documentation, Causes, and Consequences*. Symposium presented at the annual convention of the American Psychological Association, New York, 1979.

Werts, C.; Linn, R. L.; & Jöreskog, K. G. Reliability of college grades from longitudinal data. *Educational and Psychological Measurement*, 1978, *38*, 89–96.

Willingham, W. W. Predicting success in graduate education. *Science*, 1974, *183*, 273–278.

MASS MEDIA

One of the major developments of the twentieth century is the emergence of the mass media as a prominent and influential component of society. Technological innovation has been largely responsible for this development, particularly television, which has eliminated dependence on print for mass communication by combining the accessibility of radio with the compelling attraction of motion pictures. The development of mass media and education interweave in so many ways that a discussion of one is incomplete without reference to the other.

Among the topics of joint relevance are socialization, scholastic achievement, public information, educational policy, industry trends, and mass media careers. Each has been the focus of substantial scholarly and scientific, as well as journalistic and popular, attention.

Although many people construe "mass media" to mean television, daily newspapers, radio, and popular magazines, the concept as used by scholars and analysts of the evolution of the media (Compaine, 1979; Machlup, 1962; McCombs, 1972; McCombs & Eyal, 1980; Sterling & Haight, 1978) also includes movies made for theater distribution, trade book and textbook publishing, cable and pay television, in-home playback software, phonograph records, and all periodicals and newspapers. Obviously, what can be said about the mass media as a whole will only apply in varying degrees to one or another of the media, and what may be true for one will not necessarily hold true for others.

When the mass media are considered broadly over the past century, four trends of social significance become apparent:

1. The penetration of society by the mass media, in terms of the hours spent each day attending to them, has progressively increased (Robinson, 1972; Robinson & Converse, 1972; Szalai, 1972).
2. The knowledge-producing sector of society, which, in addition to the mass media, encompasses education, research, and development, has increased dramatically since 1900 in the proportion of the labor force engaged in it and the proportion of the gross national product devoted to it (Machlup, 1962, 1980).
3. The proportion of the gross national product expended on the mass media has tended to remain roughly stable over the past half century, as if media were a staple.
4. As media compete for the attention and financial support of the public, they transform one another, in the short run as they attempt to hold or enlarge their audience and in the long run as they react to pressure from the medium that has most recently appeared.

The birth of the mass media is conventionally ascribed to Gutenberg, who borrowed movable type from China and cast-metal type from Korea to produce his 42-line Bible in 1456. It is more accurate to specify the century of birth as the seventeenth, when the first newspapers appeared, because the mass media are not simply a technology but a social institution distinguished by three characteristics: (1) calculation and planning in the attempt to devise something to which a large number of people will wish to give attention; (2) an audience as large as possible, given the specific means of dissemination and the genre of the message; and (3) the stepwise regularity by which each newly developed medium has extended the size of the reachable audience until, with television, an event can be conveyed as it happens to eye and ear in almost every household in the country, unhampered even by illiteracy.

Sociologists have specified a number of features that set mass communication apart from other kinds of communication and have identified, with considerable agreement, various functions that the mass media serve in society (Lasswell, 1971; Lazarsfeld & Merton, 1948; Mendelsohn, 1966; Tannenbaum, 1980; Wright, 1975). These features include the size, heterogeneity, and anonymity of the audience, the rapidity of transmission, the transitory nature of the experience, the public availability of the message, and the presence of an organization as the communicator. Functions include the surveillance of the environment, otherwise known as news gathering; interpretation and prescription, or what is often called commentary, opinion, and editorializing; the transfer of culture, a task they share with formal education; the reinforcement of norms and common values, by publicly labeling deviant behavior as such and similarly giving implicit authority to socially sanctioned behavior by the positive ambience with which its dissemination is surrounded; the conferral of status, by the public attention they direct to certain persons and activities; and, of course, the provision of diversion and entertainment.

These features and functions obviously vary in their applicability to any one medium, and a rather clear division of labor has developed among the media (Comstock, 1980; Comstock et al., 1978). Television all over the world is largely an entertainment medium, because its capacity to reach an immense audience can only be fulfilled by the delivery of something that can be enjoyed by a diverse audience that includes those of meager education and scant sophistication. Newspapers function primarily as disseminators of information; the evidence supports the view that, at least in the United States, reliance on them for public affairs coverage is greater among the better-educated and those with higher incomes and that, in fact, they generally play a somewhat larger role in the political process than does television (Clarke & Fredin, 1978; Comstock et al., 1978; Patterson, 1980; Patterson & McClure, 1976; Weaver & Buddenbaum, 1979; Weaver et al., 1981).

Television plays an enormous role in political campaigns in the United States, both through its news coverage and through paid spots and broadcasts. Certainly it is the means by which public attention is focused on election events, and for many it is their principal source of political news. Nevertheless, newspaper reading has been found to be more consistently associated with the recall of information, with establishing the issues that people perceive as important, with the act of voting itself, and with the rational use of information in deciding who and what to vote for. There is a paradox in this, for the public overwhelmingly claims, in survey after survey, that television is the source of most of its news, including political and campaign coverage (Bower, 1973; Mendelsohn & O'Keefe, 1976; Roper Organization, 1979, 1981), and it is partly resolved by the distinction between what the public says and thinks and what it actually does. In fact, newspapers play a much larger role in news delivery than public opinion about the media would suggest, for at least three reasons: (1) Markedly more persons see a newspaper in any given two-week period than watch any part of a regular network evening newscast. (2) The audience for regular network evening news is much smaller and contains a much higher proportion of persons 55 and older than the audience for prime-time entertainment, so that television's impression of mass captivation does not perfectly apply to news. (3) And the average daily newspaper readership of over 100 million and the average weekly readership of about 50 million for the three major newsmagazines (*Newsweek, Time,* and *U.S. News and World Report*) are both significantly greater than the average nightly news audience for the three networks combined of about 35 million (Comstock et al., 1978; Gans, 1979; Robinson, 1971). Unambiguously, however, television is believed by a majority of the public to be the most credible of news media when accounts differ. Such status surely derives from its visual character, which gives the audience access not only to events but to those reporting on them; from the brevity of its reports, which minimizes the possibility of error; and from its ability in continuing crisis coverage—the very coverage that people most vividly identify with television—to correct itself instantly, thus wiping clean a slate that newspapers must maintain until the next edition.

Popular magazines on the whole most closely parallel the emphases of education, although it is naturally the educational emphases of the university adult-extension programs that they most closely mirror. Theater movies, like television, are primarily entertainment, but are considered by most to approximate art. Radio is generally synonymous with recorded music, despite the existence in most major cities of news-only stations. It plays a more central role than either television or newspapers in the rapid dissemination of major news (Mendelsohn, 1964, 1965; Spitzer, 1965), because of its unique accessibility to automobiles, work places, and play places, the frequency of its newscasts, and the low threshold of urgency required to interrupt its regular programming.

Growth and Development. The standard chronology of the media's development (Schramm, 1960) is divided into three stages of growth that include an intermediary "photophonographic" sequence. The print stage included the establishment of the first commercial English press by Caxton (1494), the first English newspaper, *London Gazette* (1665), and the first successful daily newspaper in the United States, *The Pennsylvania Packet and Daily Advertiser,* in Philadelphia (1784). The photophonographic sequence includes the development of a practical means of photography in 1839 by Daguerre, the invention in 1877 of the phonograph by Edison, and the first showing of motion pictures to the public in 1894. The electronic sequence includes the transmission of the first telegraph message in 1844 by Morse, the sending and receiving of wireless messages by Marconi in 1895, the initiation of scheduled broadcasting in 1920 by WWJ in Detroit and KDKA in Pittsburgh, the inauguration of the first radio network, NBC, in 1926, and the expansion of television in the United States when, in 1948, the total number of sets increased from 100,000 to well over 1 million.

What these developments signify for the ecology of contemporary life in the United States is suggested by a few selected statistics (Compaine, 1979; Comstock et al., 1978; Sterling & Haight, 1978). There are about 1,750 daily, 650 Sunday, and 8,500 weekly newspapers, and average daily newspaper circulation exceeds 60 million (a figure naturally smaller than the "readership" cited earlier, since more than one person may look at a single copy). There are about 10,000 periodicals, more than 300 of which are general or farm magazines with a total combined circulation of about 1.5 copies per issue for each adult in the population. About 1,200 different companies publish between 35,000 and 40,000 different book titles each year. Between 9,000 and 10,000 different phonograph records are released annually, and disc and tape sales each year exceed 600 million. There are more than 7,000 commercial AM and FM radio stations, and more than 700 commercial television stations. The proportion of households with television sets exceeds 98 percent, and the average set was turned on more than seven hours a day during the fall and winter at the beginning of the 1980s. As of August, 1980, 22 percent of these television households, over 16 million homes, subscribed to a cable system, and that figure is rapidly accelerating as large communities such as Pittsburgh, Dallas, and Houston introduce cable into their areas. By the summer of 1981, it was expected that over 30 percent of all households with television sets would be connected to cable. Almost all audience research suggests that the progressive absorption of public attention by the media, which owes so much to the photophonographic sequence that made movies and television possible, is likely to continue as choice and diversity are increased by cable and pay television, in-home playback and recording, video discs and cassettes, and satellite transmission.

Socialization. A persistent question has concerned the influence of television on children and the possibility that it is detrimental. The most recent bibliography of works with some claim of pertinence to research on the topic contains 2,676 citations (Murray, 1980), 60 percent of which were published after 1975.

The "classic" investigations of the initial impact of the new medium were conducted at the end of the 1950s by Schramm, Lyle, and Parker (1961) in the United States and by Himmelweit, Oppenheim, and Vince (1958) in England. They are still read and consulted today, for subsequent research has elaborated, confirmed, and extended rather than overturned their conclusions, which were based on data obtained from thousands of young people and hundreds of parents and teachers.

They found that the amount of viewing was substantial, although current A. C. Nielsen averages of thirty-one hours for children 2 to 11 and twenty-four hours for teenagers 12 to 17 during winter weeks represents an approximate increase of 20 percent over the past two decades. Intellectually more capable youngsters viewed less than those of lower abilities, a distinction that may be disappearing with the overall increase in the popularity of television. (Comstock et al., 1978; Lyle, 1972; Lyle & Hoffman, 1972). View-

ing was also greater for those from families of lower socioeconomic status, a distinction that remains because there are more leisure options and more encouragement to use them for children of affluence and education. The skepticism of many educators was confirmed: despite the many hours spent viewing television, its sole contributions to learning were limited to a minor superiority in vocabulary (which disappeared as children advanced in school) and knowledge about the personalities and programming of television. However, it has since become apparent that children may also learn about news events and public controversies from television that would otherwise escape their notice. One general proposition that emerged from these two studies and has received extensive empirical support from subsequent investigations is that television is most likely to influence beliefs or behavior when other sources of information are unavailable, for example, in the portrayal of people from a country a child has not visited. Also, when parents or teachers do not express opinions about the appropriateness or acceptability of something portrayed on television, beliefs are more likely to be influenced.

No single kind of entertainment content has aroused more controversy and been the subject of more research than violence. A series of House and Senate hearings, beginning in 1952, have been devoted to examining the contribution of television violence to aggression, delinquency, and criminal acts on the part of young viewers (United States Congress, House Committee, 1952, 1976, 1977; Senate Committee, 1955a, 1955b, 1963, 1965).

The Himmelweit study (Himmelweit, Oppenheim, & Vince, 1958) found that children generally became accustomed to routinized violence of the sort common in the westerns popular in those days, but were frightened by violence that was unconventional for television, particularly if common household objects were employed or if it was directed at those with whom they identified, such as a dog, a child, or a parent. Studies documenting the effects of violence on aggression can be dated from the early 1960s, when the psychologists Bandura, Berkowitz, and Feshbach published experiments that appeared to demonstrate that young children may imitate the violent acts they see (Bandura, Ross, & Ross, 1963), that college-age viewers may become more punitive after seeing the portrayal of justified punishment (Berkowitz & Rawlings, 1963), and that exposure to a violent portrayal may reduce the display of hostile feelings (Feshbach, 1961). These laboratory experiments were followed by others, by field experiments, by one-time surveys and panel studies (in which the data are collected from the same population at two points in time), by numerous reviews and interpretations, and eventually, by quantitative meta-analyses (Andison, 1977; Hearold, 1979). A central event was the surgeon general's inquiry into television violence at the beginning of the 1970s (Comstock, Rubinstein, & Murray, 1972; Surgeon General's Scientific Advisory Committee on Television and Social Behavior, 1972), an undertaking that paralleled in the sociological and psychological arena the inquiry into the physical effects of smoking.

There are several features to the pattern that has emerged:

1. Young children will learn specific acts of behavior from observing them in a television portrayal, although performance of these acts will depend on a variety of circumstances, including the expected consequences, the degree to which such an act is socially approved, the opportunity to perform it, and the extent to which it is pertinent to the circumstances.

2. Persons of college age may increase in the degree to which they display previously acquired punitive behavior as a consequence of seeing a violent portrayal that alters their inhibitions toward such behavior, such as a portrayal of retribution that is justified, an act of viciousness, or violence aimed at targets that hold cues for real life, such as a portrayal in which the victim resembles someone in the viewers' own environment toward whom they harbor hostility.

3. The decrease in hostility after exposure to a violent portrayal reported by Feshbach is better explained by the inhibition of aggressive impulses as a consequence of exposure to such a stimulus than by the reduction of aggression through vicarious experience, the process popularly referred to as "catharsis."

4. Dozens of laboratory experiments examining the influence of exposure to a violent portrayal on subsequent behavior have been published, and about nine out of ten record an increase in aggressive behavior after such exposure. This majority holds whether the subjects were of nursery school age (when the measure of aggression usually was imitative attacks against a large inflated Bobo doll) or of college age or in between (when the measure usually was the delivery of electric shocks to another person or some other act unlike what was observed in the portrayal).

5. Although there have been more instances overall in which exposure to violent entertainment has had a null association with measured aggression than in the case of laboratory experiments alone, a majority of field experiments conducted under far more naturalistic circumstances and a majority of surveys of regular television viewing and everyday aggressiveness as perceived by peers also have found a positive association between exposure to violent portrayals and aggressiveness.

6. The results of laboratory experiments, which have the virtue of permitting causal inference, roughly concur with those of field experiments and surveys, which do not suffer from the same weaknesses—artificiality of circumstances, immediacy of measurement, absence of the possibility of retaliation, and exclusion of communications distractive from or counter to the violent portrayals—that make generalizing from the laboratory experiments to everyday life problematic. This concurrence gives credence to the notion that violence in entertainment may encourage aggressive behavior in real life.

7. There remains considerable disagreement, and very little in the way of empirical evidence, over the degree to which the documented positive association under some circumstances between exposure to violent portrayals and aggressive behavior crosses the threshold of socially tolerated acts of aggressiveness into seriously hurtful or criminal behavior for children, for adolescents, or even for adults.

The question of whether television violence cultivates negative beliefs has also become the subject of controversy and empirical inquiry (Gerbner, et. al., 1980; Hawkins & Pingree, 1980). The evidence supports the view that there is a positive association between amount of television viewing, a proxy for exposure to violent programming, and two kinds of negative beliefs: (1) fearfulness of falling victim to a crime, and (2) cognitive beliefs of a pessimistic cast, exemplified by a higher estimate of the crime rate or greater skepticism about the performance of public officials. However, there is considerable argument over whether television viewing is causally implicated (Comstock, 1981; Doob & Macdonald, 1979; Hirsch, 1980; 1981; Hughes, 1980). The evidence is slightly stronger for a contribution to pessimistic beliefs than to fearfulness, at least for adults, for whom more data are available.

From the perspective of many psychologists, television has had the effect of entering the mass media into the equation of socialization and thereby reducing somewhat the weight of such agents as parents, communities, and schools. Empirical research supports this view, and the evidence on television violence and aggression is best interpreted as exemplifying broad principles of influence extending into other areas rather than confined to that one type of behavior. The same concerns that have been expressed about television were expressed about media that developed earlier, such as motion pictures and comic books, but television appears to function on a much grander scale in socialization for a number of reasons. These include the presence of television in nearly every household, the absence of restraints imposed by admission fees or literacy, the fact that children are regular viewers long before they become patrons of other media, and the difficulty parents experience in restricting what and how much children view.

Scholastic Achievement. There has been speculation since television receivers began to be widely distributed in American homes over the medium's influence on scholastic achievement. Most of that speculation has been negative, and much of it has focused on reading skill and interest. The early large-scale investigations by Schramm and Himmelweit cited earlier did not find much to support either positive or negative speculation.

In the 1950s television was new and, to some, a threatening medium. Those who were college-educated and could be thought of as having heightened allegiance to a "book culture" or "print culture" were notably more hostile toward the medium than those with less education—a difference that still persists but to a markedly lesser degree (Bower, 1973; Meyersohn, 1965). Average hours

TABLE 1. *California achievement and TV viewing by subject matter, 1979/80*

	Hours watching TV per day						
					4 or more[a]		
	0–1	1–2	2–3	3–4	4–5[b]	5–6[b]	6 or more[b]
Sixth grade (N = 281,907)							
Reading	70.1	69.0	68.3	66.9	62.9	N/A	N/A
Written expression	67.9	66.9	66.1	64.9	60.7	N/A	N/A
Mathematics	61.4	61.3	60.5	59.5	56.0	N/A	N/A
(Percentage of students)	(27%)	(23)	(17)	(11)	(20)	(2% = N/R)	
Twelfth grade (N = 227,549)							
Reading	67.6	64.9	62.3	60.1	58.0	57.4	55.0
Written expression	67.3	64.3	61.4	59.0	57.1	55.7	53.7
Mathematics	72.2	69.4	65.8	62.8	60.3	59.0	57.3
(Percentage of students)	(30%)	(22)	(19)	(12)	(7)	(4)	(6)

[a] Sixth grade only.   [b] Twelfth grade only.

SOURCE: California Assessment Plan, 1980.

of viewing per week by all ages was substantially less then than it is today. Television was in its "golden age" of original, adult drama, which would give way in the next decade to comedy and action-adventure series with greater appeal to younger viewers. Children were being reared by parents and taught by teachers who themselves had not grown up with television. Quantitatively and qualitatively, the medium was neither as prominent nor as accepted a part of children's lives as it would become.

The situation is considerably different today. The two most recent sources of data on the effects of television on achievement are an evaluation of achievement at the sixth and twelfth grades conducted by the California Assessment Program (1980), and a national survey of children 7 to 11 years of age sponsored by the Foundation for Child Development (Zill, 1981; Zill & Peterson, 1981). Both are remarkable for their scope and size, and there is considerable agreement in their results.

The California evaluation obtained data from 99 percent of all students in two grades—280,000 in the sixth grade and 230,000 in the twelfth grade. Achievement was measured in three areas: reading, mathematics, and written expression. The relationship of these measures to self-reported amounts of television viewing was in every instance a negative one (Table 1). On each test and in both grades, scores declined as television viewing increased, although the relationship was more marked for the twelfth than for the sixth grade.

The evaluation produced the usual inverse relationship between amount of television viewing and socioeconomic status of the head of the household. However, when the students were divided into socioeconomic strata on the basis of occupation of head of household—professional, semiprofessional, skilled, and unskilled—the declines associated with increased viewing held for all strata, in both grades and on each of the three tests, except for the lowest

stratum of those in the sixth grade, and were most pronounced for students from households of higher socioeconomic status.

The highest reading scores were obtained by those who watched the least television and read the most, whether for school assignment or for enjoyment. Regardless of the time spent watching television, reading was associated with higher scores; at every level of reading, amount of television viewing and reading ability scores were inversely related. The sole noteworthy departure from the pattern occurred among students of limited English language ability in the sixth grade, whose reading scores rose with increased daily television viewing up to three to four hours per day, after which scores turned downward.

The Foundation for Child Development survey obtained data in 1976 from a probability sample of 2,280 children, their parents, and their teachers. Measures of scholastic competence included a short form of the Peabody vocabulary test and school adjustment scales, one based on parental report, the other on teacher report. Relationships with amount of television viewing, as reported by parents, were, for practical purposes, null. However, this pattern was in contrast with that for reading as an activity, which was related strongly and positively to the measures of scholastic competence.

There were positive relationships between amount of television viewing and various behavioral and affective measures reflecting maladjustment, when those who were said not to view television at all were excluded. Television viewing was associated with greater antisocial behavior, greater misbehavior, greater perceived parental neglect and rejection, greater fear of crime, and lower self-esteem. Whether or not there is any causal or reciprocal involvement of television viewing in these relationships, they make it clear that extensive viewing is part of a syndrome of maladjustment. However, nonviewers had scores similar to those of extensive viewers, suggesting that the total rejection of something so popular and normative as television also reflects maladjustment.

Neither the results for scholastic competence nor those for maladjustment can be ascribed to the influence of demographic characteristics such as sex, age, family size, family income, parent education, community size and type, and geographic region. Many of these variables predict scholastic competence and maladjustment better than amount of viewing, but the relationship with viewing is that which remains after any contribution by these variables has been extracted.

The two studies concur on a major point: television viewing and reading, as activities, have distinctly different relationships with scholastic achievement. The California data are superior in number of measures and extraordinary sample size; the Foundation for Child Development analyses incorporate far more variables simultaneously and thus minimize the possibility that the results are artifactual. Quite possibly, the lack of a perfect parallel is descriptively correct and attributable to the differences in the ages of the two samples, a speculation consistent with the fact that the inverse relationship in the California data was more pronounced among twelfth-graders than among sixth-graders.

The most optimistic interpretation is that television viewing is unproductive scholastically and at comparatively high levels a symptom of maladjustment. The California data encourage the more pessimistic interpretation that greater degrees of viewing are a symptom of lesser scholastic achievement. From the available information, television viewing cannot be identified as cause, consequence, or both. In the context of the continuing nationwide decline among students at all levels of academic progress in widely accepted measures of intellectual achievement, however, the data give renewed vigor to the speculation that television viewing may have a detrimental influence on scholastic achievement.

Industry Trends. Within the broad context of expansion of the audience for the mass media, there have been four trends in the ownership and operation of the media in the United States since World War II that raise questions about their autonomy from one another and from governmental influence; in one of these, education has figured prominently as an institution that is a market for the products of the media:

1. There has been a reduction within major cities of the number of competing daily newspapers, accompanied by the growth of "media empires," in which newspapers are owned by chains and newspaper owners are also the owners of magazines and television and radio stations.
2. Individual ownership of media outlets has shifted to corporate ownership, with consequent increased pres-

sure to return a profit to shareholders comparable to that returned by alternative investments.
3. Corporations and conglomerates have become more prominent as owners of media companies. This has drawn particular attention in book publishing, where there has been an increasing emphasis on serving a mass audience.
4. The federal regulation of radio and television broadcasting, established in 1934 by the Federal Communications Act, became the subject of deregulatory reforms in the 1970s.

The major question raised by the first three of these developments is whether the services provided to the public through information, entertainment, and artistic endeavor are becoming monolithic to the exclusion of diversity. There is no clear answer. Although the potential for monopolistic influence has certainly increased, data suggest that nothing like monopoly has occurred thus far (Compaine, 1979). Newspaper chains and cross-ownership of different media outlets within a market produce products similar in substance to the competition's. Corporate and conglomerate owners generally have let their media properties operate in accord with long-standing ethics and goals, with the proviso that they be profitable. Bookstore chains undeniably emphasize best-sellers, but on the average these outlets stock more titles than the average independent store, and the emphasis by major publishers on titles that have mass appeal has been offset by the steady entry of new companies serving specialized interests. The mass market paperback houses, whose wares are vended in supermarkets, often also maintain steadily selling "backlists" of books of literary and intellectual distinction, and the growth in sales that bookstore chains have encouraged has increased in turn the market for quality paperbacks. There is no clear remedy to the possible excessive growth of corporate or conglomerate control, beyond the enforcement of the antitrust statutes where appropriate and the intervention of the Federal Communications Commission in cross-ownership cases involving broadcast media.

The education market was prominent in the trend toward varied media ownership by larger firms (Whiteside 1980a, 1980b, 1980c, 1981). In the early 1960s, firms such as CBS, Xerox, RCA, and IT & T began to acquire publishing companies, especially those with textbook divisions, in the anticipation of gaining a share of what appeared to be a new and lucrative market involving computer-based instruction, teaching machines, and equipment for the "electronic classroom." Despite robust trading in media firms, the anticipated rewards have never materialized. The siphoning of federal funding away from education and other domestic programs in favor of the Vietnam war, high cost, educator skepticism, teacher resistance, and a narrow range of applications have precluded widespread adoption.

The fourth trend listed above again represents the influence of technology. The rationale for regulation was scarcity of spectrum space, which ostensibly justified federal intervention to preclude overcrowding and to ensure adequate service by those privileged to hold a license to broadcast. The present large number of radio outlets, the increased feasibility of squeezing in new broadcast outlets of modest power, and the diversity of television signals available by satellite, cable television, and pay television have become a strong argument for reducing federal involvement—involvement represented by three-year license renewals, required public affairs coverage, the fairness doctrine (balanced coverage of opposing viewpoints), and the equal-time provision (equal access to candidates for public office).

Career Preparation. The mass media have become employers of many people, and as a result preparation for careers in the media has become a task formally undertaken by educational institutions. Training for the media is offered within a variety of programs, but summary figures have been compiled only for four-year and graduate programs in journalism, broadcasting, and film (Sterling & Haight, 1978).

In 1975 total undergraduate and graduate enrollment in these three areas was 92,314. Enrollments in all three have been increasing, most markedly in broadcasting and film. Journalism courses began to appear in the first decade of the century, with thirty colleges offering them by 1912, and by the 1930s complete programs were commonplace; radio courses began to appear in the 1920s, but it was in the Midwest land grant schools of the 1930s that programs first became plentiful; film programs date from the 1950s, with conspicuous growth in the 1960s and 1970s in response to student interest.

Scholarly Sources. There are a number of bibliographies and statistical compilations that serve as basic guides to the vast scientific literature on the mass media. *Basic Books in the Mass Media,* by Blum (1980), is precisely what the title says, and covers book publishing, broadcasting, editorial journalism, film, magazines, advertising, and general communications. The scrutiny of the media from the perspective of the social and behavioral sciences is covered by Murray with 2,676 citations in *Television and Youth* (1980), by Meringoff with 782 citations in *Children and Advertising* (1980), by Gordon and Verna with 2,704 citations in *Mass Communications Effects and Processes* (1978), and by Comstock and Fisher with 2,392 citations in *Television and Human Behavior: A Guide to the Pertinent Scientific Literature* (1975). None of these five volumes is redundant, because each has a different focus; together, they constitute a desktop reference system.

The best introduction to media statistics is the compilation by Sterling and Haight, *The Mass Media: Aspen Institute Guide to Communication Industry Trends* (1978). It contains 315 tables covering media growth, ownership and control, economics, employment and training, content trends, size and characteristics of media audiences, and

the U.S. media abroad. These and other data are interpreted in terms of concentration of ownership by Compaine (1979) in *Who Owns the Media?*

George Comstock

See also Distance Education; Media Use in Education.

REFERENCES

Andison, F. S. TV violence and viewer aggression: A cumulation of study results, 1956–1976. *Public Opinion Quarterly,* 1977, *41*(3), 314–331.

Bandura, A.; Ross, D.; & Ross, S. A. Imitation of film-mediated aggressive models. *Journal of Abnormal and Social Psychology,* 1963, *66*, 3–11.

Berkowitz, L., & Rawlings, E. Effects of film violence on inhibitions against subsequent aggression. *Journal of Abnormal and Social Psychology,* 1963, *66*, 405–412.

Blum, E. *Basic Books in the Mass Media.* Urbana: University of Illinois Press, 1980.

Bower, R. T. *Television and the Public.* New York: Holt, Rinehart & Winston, 1973.

California Assessment Program. *Student Achievement in California Schools: 1979–80 Annual Report.* Sacramento: State Department of Education, 1980. (Eric Document Reproduction Service No. ED 194 243)

Clarke, P., & Fredin, E. Newspapers, television, and political reasoning. *Public Opinion Quarterly,* 1978, *42*, 143–160.

Compaine, B. M. *Who Owns the Media? Concentration of Ownership in the Mass Media Industry.* New York: Harmony, 1979.

Comstock, G. *Television in America.* Beverly Hills, Calif.: Sage, 1980.

Comstock, G. *Violence in Television Content: An Overview.* Syracuse, N.Y.: Syracuse University, S.I. Newhouse School, 1981.

Comstock, G.; Chaffee, S.; Katzman, N.; McCombs, M.; & Roberts, D. *Television and Human Behavior.* New York: Columbia University Press, 1978.

Comstock, G., & Fisher, M. *Television and Human Behavior: A Guide to the Pertinent Scientific Literature* (Rand R-1746-CF). Santa Monica, Calif.: Rand Corporation, 1975.

Comstock, G. A.; Rubinstein, E. A.; & Murray, J. P. (Eds.). *Television and Social Behavior* (5 vols.). Washington, D.C.: U.S. Government Printing Office, 1972.

Doob, A. N., & Macdonald, G. E. Television viewing and fear of victimization: Is the relationship causal? *Journal of Personality and Social Psychology,* 1979, *37*(2), 170–179.

Feshbach, S. The stimulating versus cathartic effects of a vicarious aggressive activity. *Journal of Abnormal and Social Psychology,* 1961, *63*, 381–385.

Gans, H. *Deciding What's News.* New York: Random House, 1979.

Gerbner, G.; Gross, L.; Morgan, M.; & Signorielli, N. The "mainstreaming" of America: Violence profile no. 11. *Journal of Communication,* Summer 1980, *30*(3), 10–29.

Gordon, T. F., & Verna, M. E. *Mass Communication Effects and Processes: A Comprehensive Bibliography, 1950–1975.* Beverly Hills, Calif.: Sage, 1978.

Hawkins, R. P., & Pingree, S. Some processes in the cultivation effect. *Communication Research,* April 1980, *7*(2), 193–226.

Hearold, S. L. *Meta-analysis of the Effects of Television on Social Behavior.* Unpublished doctoral dissertation, University of Colorado, 1979.

Himmelweit, H. T.; Oppenheim, A. N.; & Vince, P. *Television and the Child*. London: Oxford University Press, 1958. (Reprinted for Oxford University Press by University Microfilms International, 1979.)

Hirsch, P. The "scary world" of the nonviewer and other anomalies: A reanalysis of Gerbner et al.'s findings on cultivation analysis, Part 1. *Communication Research*, October 1980, *7*(4), 403–457.

Hirsch, P. On not learning from one's own mistakes: A reanalysis of Gerbner et al.'s findings on cultivation analysis and a critique of "mainstreaming," Part 2. *Communication Research*, January 1981, *8*(1), 3–37.

Hughes, M. The fruits of cultivation analysis: A re-examination of the effects of television watching on fear of victimization, alienation, and the approval of violence. *Public Opinion Quarterly*, Fall 1980, *44*(3), 287–303.

Lasswell, H. D. The structure and function of communication in society. In W. Schramm & D. F. Roberts (Eds.), *The Process and Effects of Mass Communication* (Rev. ed.). Urbana: University of Illinois Press, 1971.

Lazarsfeld, P. F., & Merton, R. K. Mass communication, popular taste, and organized social action. In L. Bryson (Ed.), *The Communication of Ideas*. New York: Institute for Religious and Social Studies, 1948.

Lyle, J. Television in daily life: Patterns of use overview. In E. A. Rubinstein, G. A. Comstock, & J. P. Murray (Eds.), *Television and Social Behavior* (Vol. 4). Washington, D.C.: U.S. Government Printing Office, 1972.

Lyle, J., & Hoffman, H. R. Children's use of television and other media. In E. A. Rubinstein, G. A. Comstock, & J. P. Murray (Eds.), *Television and Social Behavior* (Vol. 4). Washington, D.C.: U.S. Government Printing Office, 1972.

Machlup, F. *The Production and Distribution of Knowledge in the United States*. Princeton, N.J.: Princeton University Press, 1962.

Machlup, F. *Knowledge: Its Creation, Distribution, and Economic Significance* (Vol. 1). Princeton, N.J.: Princeton University Press, 1980.

McCombs, M. E. Mass media in the marketplace. *Journalism Monographs*, August 1972, No. 24. Lexington, Ky.: Association for Education in Journalism.

McCombs, M. E., & Eyal, C. E. Spending on mass media. *Journal of Communication*, Winter 1980, *30*(1), 153–158.

Mendelsohn, H. A. Broadcasting versus personal sources of information in emergent public crises: The presidential assassination. *Journal of Broadcasting*, 1964, *8*, 147–156.

Mendelsohn, H. A. Comment on Spitzer's " . . . A comparison of six investigations." *Journal of Broadcasting*, 1965, *9*, 51–54.

Mendelsohn, H. A. *Mass Entertainment*. New Haven, Conn.: College and University Press, 1966.

Mendelsohn, H. A., & O'Keefe, G. J. *The People Choose a President*. New York: Praeger, 1976.

Meringoff, L. (Ed.). *Children and Advertising*. New York: Children's Advertising Review Unit, 1980.

Meyersohn, R. B. *Leisure and Television: A Study in Compatibility*. Unpublished doctoral dissertation, Columbia University, 1965.

Murray, J. P. *Television and Youth*. Boys Town, Nebr.: Boys Town Center for the Study of Youth Development, 1980.

Patterson, T. E. *The Mass Media Election: How Americans Choose Their President*. New York: Praeger, 1980.

Patterson, T. E., & McClure, R. D. *The Unseeing Eye*. New York: Putnam, 1976.

Robinson, J. P. The audience for national TV news programs. *Public Opinion Quarterly*, 1971, *35*, 403–405.

Robinson, J. P. Television's impact on everyday life: Some cross-national evidence. In E. A. Rubinstein, G. A. Comstock, & J. P. Murray (Eds.), *Television and Social Behavior* (Vol. 4). Washington, D.C.: U.S. Government Printing Office, 1972.

Robinson, J. P., & Coverse, P. E. The impact of television on mass media usages: A cross-national comparison. In A. Szalai (Ed.), *The Use of Time: Daily Activities of Urban and Suburban Populations in Twelve Countries*. The Hague: Mouton, 1972.

Roper Organization, Inc. *Public Perceptions of Television and Other Mass Media: A Twenty-year Review, 1959–1978*. New York: Television Information Office, 1979.

Roper Organization, Inc. *Evolving Public Attitudes toward Television and Other Mass Media, 1959–1980*. New York: Television Information Office, 1981.

Schramm, W. (Ed.). *Mass Communications: A Book of Readings* (2nd ed.). Urbana: University of Illinois Press, 1960.

Schramm, W.; Lyle, J.; & Parker, E. B. *Television in the Lives of Our Children*. Stanford, Calif.: Stanford University Press, 1961.

Spitzer, S. P. Mass media versus personal sources of information about the presidential assassination: A comparison of six investigations. *Journal of Broadcasting*, 1965, *9*, 45–50.

Sterling, C. H., & Haight, T. R. *The Mass Media: Aspen Institute Guide to Communication Industry Trends*. New York: Praeger, 1978.

Surgeon General's Scientific Advisory Committee on Television and Social Behavior. *Television and Growing Up: The Impact of Televised Violence* (Report to the Surgeon General, U.S. Public Health Service). Washington, D.C.: U.S. Government Printing Office, 1972.

Szalai, A. *The Use of Time: Daily Activities of Urban and Suburban Populations in Twelve Countries*. The Hague: Mouton, 1972.

Tannenbaum, P. H. *The Entertainment Function of Television*. Hillsdale, N.J.: Lawrence Erlbaum Associates, 1980.

United States Congress, House Committee on Interstate and Foreign Commerce (82nd Congress, 2nd session, June 3–December 5, 1952). *Investigation of Radio and Television Programs* (Hearings and report). Washington, D.C.: U.S. Government Printing Office, 1952.

United States Congress, House Committee on Interstate and Foreign Commerce (94th Congress, 2nd session, 1976). *Sex and Violence on TV* (Hearings before the Subcommittee on Communications). Washington, D.C.: U.S. Government Printing Office, 1976.

United States Congress, House Committee on Interstate and Foreign Commerce (95th Congress, 1st session, 1977). *Violence on Television* (Report of the Subcommittee on Communications). Washington, D.C.: U.S. Government Printing Office, 1977.

United States Congress, Senate Committee on the Judiciary (83rd Congress, 2nd session, June 5–October 20, 1954). *Juvenile Delinquency (Television Programs)* (Hearings before the Subcommittee to Investigate Juvenile Delinquency). Washington, D.C.: U.S. Government Printing Office, 1955(a).

United States Congress, Senate Committee on the Judiciary (84th Congress, 1st session, April 6–7, 1955). *Juvenile Delinquency (Television Programs)* (Hearings before the Subcommittee to Investigate Juvenile Delinquency). Washington, D.C.: U.S. Government Printing Office, 1955(b).

United States Congress, Senate Committee on the Judiciary (87th

Congress, 1st and 2nd sessions, June 8, 1961–May 14, 1962). *Juvenile Delinquency (Part 10): Effects on Young People of Violence and Crime Portrayed on Television* (Hearings before the Subcommittee to Investigate Juvenile Delinquency). Washington, D.C.: U.S. Government Printing Office, 1963.

United States Congress, Senate Committee on the Judiciary (88th Congress, 2nd session, July 30, 1964). *Juvenile Delinquency (Part 16): Effects on Young People of Violence and Crime Portrayed on Television* (Hearings before the Subcommittee to Investigate Juvenile Delinquency). Washington, D.C.: U.S. Government Printing Office, 1965.

Weaver, D. H., & Buddenbaum, J. M. Newspapers and television: A review of research on uses and effects. *ANPA News Research Report,* April 20, 1979, No. 19, 1–11.

Weaver, D. H.; Graber, D. A.; McCombs, M. E.; & Eyal, C. E. *Media Agenda-setting in a Presidential Election: Issues, Images, and Interest.* New York: Praeger, 1981.

Whiteside, T. Onward and upward with the arts: The blockbuster complex—I. *New Yorker,* September 29, 1980(a), *56,* 48–101.

Whiteside, T. Onward and upward with the arts: The blockbuster complex—II. *New Yorker,* October 6, 1980(b), *56,* 63–146.

Whiteside, T. Onward and upward with the arts: The blockbuster complex—III. *New Yorker,* October 13, 1980(c), *56,* 52–145.

Whiteside, T. *The Blockbuster Complex.* Middletown, Conn.: Wesleyan University Press, 1981.

Wright, C. R. *Mass Communication: A Sociological Perspective.* New York: Random House, 1975.

Zill, N. *How Are the Children?* New York: Doubleday, 1981.

Zill, N., & Peterson, J. L. Television viewing in the United States and children's intellectual, social, and emotional development. *TV and Children.* Spring 1981, *4*(2), 21–28.

MASTERY LEARNING

See Competency Testing; Individualized Systems of Instruction; Learning; Measurement in Education.

MATHEMATICAL BEHAVIOR OF CHILDREN

The late 1960s saw the emergence of a new approach to the study of mathematics education, characterized by a focus on the "processes" of mathematical thought rather than merely on the "result" or "product" of that thought. It is no exaggeration to speak of this as a major new direction in the study of the teaching and learning of mathematics, with important implications both for school practice and for the continuing development of a theory of mathematical thought. The key ideas are: first, to observe carefully, step-by-step, as a student works on some kind of mathematical task, watching to see what the student does, and how he or she does it; and second, to use these observations as a basis for inferring how the student is thinking about the task, analyzing it, and making choices.

A Process Approach. If one wants to improve a performance, in anything from basketball to mathematics, it is essential to observe carefully how that performance is being achieved and to consider alternative approaches that might work better. With mathematics there is the additional complication that many of the key processes are thought processes, taking place within someone's mind; special methods must therefore be employed in order to study these processes since they are not themselves directly visible.

By far the most common, and probably the most valuable, method is the task-based interview. A student is asked to solve some mathematical problem, writing the work on paper as needed and trying to explain aloud what he or she is doing. Present also are one or more observers and perhaps an interviewer. The entire performance is typically audiotaped or (less frequently) videotaped, so that at the completion of an interview there are several records of what took place: the student's written work is preserved and can be correlated with the audiotape and with written observational notes made by the observers or by the interviewer. Additional notes may be added, from memory, at the end of the student interview. This provides a rich collection of material for analysis. Other methods of data collection are also used, including precise measurements of response times and the analysis of particular patterns of errors.

An early and important result from this process type of study was obtained by Erlwanger (1973, 1974, 1975), who found that fifth-grade and sixth-grade students studying in an individualized school mathematics program, and believed by their teachers to be progressing satisfactorily, had in fact developed serious misconceptions and regularly employed many flagrantly incorrect procedures; these included writing numbers with more than one decimal point in them, as in .3 + 4. = .7. (where the number .7. has two decimal points!) and converting fractions to decimals by the method

$$\frac{5}{12} \to 1.7$$
$$\frac{4}{11} \to 1.5 \, .$$

Five aspects of Erlwanger's results are typical for subsequent research as well.

1. *Discrepant assessment.* Erlwanger's interview studies found unsatisfactory performance in students who, judged by multiple-choice written tests, seemed to be progressing satisfactorily. This phenomenon needs further examination and explanation, but it seems clear that different methods of studying levels of student performance are capable of returning quite different assessments. Can Johnny divide? Your answer may depend on how you let him demonstrate his ability. (See Rosnick & Clement, 1980.) This fact has obvious implications for school testing programs, competency-based education, and so on. Reports of declining scores on standardized tests seem less meaningful when viewed from the perspective of Erlwanger-type interview studies because the test grades seem less useful as indicators of true performance levels. (Additional doubt as to what is measured by standardized tests is presented in Porter, Schwille, Floden, Freeman, Knappen, Kuhs, & Schmidt, 1981; see also Alderman, Swinton, & Braswell, 1979.)

2. *Focus upon knowledge representations.* In typical earlier studies of mathematics learning, it was commonly (though tacitly) assumed that the information taught to students was a reasonably close match to the information learned by students, except for certain kinds of random errors or incompletenesses. In recent decades a different conceptualization of learning has replaced this earlier assumption: the fundamental process of learning is now seen as one of creating knowledge representations within one's own mind (Bobrow & Collins, 1975; Greeno, 1977; Papert, 1980). These knowledge representations have only a modest relationship to the real information from the external world. The reader can see what is meant in part by attempting to draw, from memory, the floor plan of his or her own home. It will immediately be clear that there is much information present in the reality that has not been effectively coded into the mental representation that you retrieved from memory. Of course, the studies we review here primarily compare a student's knowledge with correct knowledge, as demonstrated by adult experts. Consequently, when there is a disagreement between the child learner and the adult expert, there is no immediate way to know how much of the disagreement is due to the child's faulty interpretation of the school curriculum and how much is due to errors that may be present in the school curriculum itself.

3. *The student as builder of knowledge representations.* Piaget focused attention upon the ways in which knowledge representations are built up within a person's mind (for a modern analysis of this aspect of Piaget's work, see Papert, 1980). A teacher has at best a limited ability to reach into a student's mind and participate in the building of knowledge representations; these representations are built by students themselves. Clearly, no one had taught Erlwanger's subjects to write .3 + 4. = .7. (with the symbol .7. containing two decimal points). From interview data, Erlwanger could show that this (incorrect) idea had been worked out independently by the student, from observation of symmetries in the symbols themselves. It is, however, possible for teachers to employ teaching strategies that are intended to maximize accurate modeling in the student's mind; one such strategy is the paradigm teaching strategy (Davis, Jockusch, & McKnight, 1978).

4. *Meaninglessness.* A number of studies (e.g., Davis & McKnight, 1980) indicate clearly that students often possess important, relevant information that they fail to use when thinking about some particular problem. To adults, it is surprising to find students writing

$$2 + \frac{1}{2} = \frac{2}{1} + \frac{1}{2} = \frac{3}{3} = 1,$$

when the students know that 2 is larger than 1, and that adding $\frac{1}{2}$ to 2 should yield a result even larger than 2—hence, surely not equal to 1 (Erlwanger, 1973). But interview studies show clearly that students often proceed by manipulating meaningless symbols, with no attempt to ask what the symbols mean, so that the meaninglessness of .7. is not in fact at all unusual.

5. *The systematic nature of errors.* It is often assumed that student errors are mainly random. Random errors do, in fact, occur, but process studies by Erlwanger (1973), by Brown and Burton (1978), by Matz (1980), and others (e.g., Davis, Jockusch, & McKnight, 1978; Davis, McKnight, Parker, & Elrick, 1979) show clearly that many student errors are entirely systematic. Since the error lies in the procedure that the student is using, the same error appears consistently. Some appearance of randomness does occur as a result of the Matz-Brown law (or the Brown–Van Lehn Law), which states that a student response can be analyzed into major goals and lesser subgoals; if a major goal is threatened because some subgoal cannot be achieved, then some of the constraints on subgoals will be relaxed so that the major goal can be achieved (Matz, 1980; Davis, 1980; Brown & Van Lehn, 1980). It is interesting to note that the regularity of student errors has been independently discovered—and rediscovered—by numerous researchers. An early instance was its clear description by David Page, at least as early as 1958, in unpublished mimeographed notes.

Paradigm Shifts in Science. Kuhn (1970) has pointed out that science does not progress by moving forward in a single, clearly delineated direction. On the contrary, competing groups of scientists, with competing points of view, attempt to head in several different directions, until enough becomes known to reconcile these conflicting views within a new and broader synthesis.

A divergence of this type can be seen today in the study of mathematical behavior. To some extent, at least, mathematics education has divided into one group of researchers who typically emphasize results or answers (for example, answers on multiple choice or standardized tests), and a second group who emphasize observation of the processes by which students solve problems. For process researchers, it is not meaningful to know that a student achieved a certain score on a written test; the process researcher does not feel satisfied until he or she knows how the student thought about the various problems, how the student analyzed or interpreted the various tasks. The division between these groups is expressed forcefully in Krutetskii (1976), discussed in Davis (1967), and illustrated in, for example, Alderman, Swinton, & Braswell (1979). Other perspectives on this question are presented in Ginsburg (1977), Skemp (1979), Houts (1977), Hoffman (1962), and Davis et al. (1980). It seems to be the case that this split is less extreme today than it was in the 1950s and 1960s (Greeno, 1980).

The constructivist approach. In an attempt to define more clearly the new point of view toward mathematics learning, some authors speak of "the constructivist approach," thereby seeking to call attention to the view of the learner as the builder of his or her own ideas. Whereas a more traditional view saw learning as the transfer of knowledge from teacher to student, with the student merely making his own copy of this knowledge, rather like a tape recorder or a photocopy machine, a new view is emerging. Recent work suggests that mathematics learning is a highly personalized construction based upon prior knowledge (and upon rather complex forms of prior knowledge) as well as one's personal belief system consisting of metacognitive abilities and understandings, interests, and attitudes—all of this in addition to obvious forms of prerequisite knowledge of mathematical topics themselves. Furthermore, "retrieval" of knowledge for subsequent use is coming to be seen as a combination of reconstruction (or even new constructions) as well as, or instead of, simple recall.

A good example of the constructivist point of view is provided by Steffe's work in studying a child's early learning about counting and number (Steffe & Thompson, 1979; see also Lawler, 1980). The constructivist approach is demonstrated clearly in Lesh's studies of geometric transformations. Children younger than grade 4 typically have developed the information-processing capability of describing geometric figures in detail but have less complete development of the information-processing capabilities necessary to deal with transformations such as translations, reflections, and rotations; after grade 4, the transformation capability has been developed, so that rotation tasks can now be dealt with by greater use of transformation processing (Lesh, 1977).

Some Important Phenomena. Of course, a major test of any scientific theory is its ability to explain various key phenomena, as Newton's Laws explained the patterns observed by Kepler. Can the process viewpoint explain the observed mathematical behavior of students? In many cases, it can. In this section we consider a few observed phenomena; in later sections we present an outline of the thoery and then show how the theory explains these phenomena.

The Friend phenomenon. It had been known for some years that rectangular addition problems (i.e., those having a rectangular array of addends), such as

$$\begin{array}{r} 1732 \\ 9851 \\ +2386 \end{array}$$

are easier (i.e., students get correct answers more often) than nonrectangular problems, such as

$$\begin{array}{r} 1732 \\ 851 \\ +\ 327 \end{array} \quad \text{or} \quad \begin{array}{r} 21 \\ 136 \\ +\ 95 \end{array}.$$

No one, however, appears to have studied this phenomenon in detail until a report by Jamesine Friend (1979). Friend was able to determine precisely which "nonrec-tangular" problems were the most difficult: namely, those with a single digit in the left-most column, and without any "carry" into that column. Thus, of the three problems

$$\begin{array}{ccc} (A) & (B) & (C) \\ 766 & 786 & 781 \\ +\ 15 & +\ 15 & +232, \end{array}$$

the naive expectation would be that A would be the easiest, since B involves an extra "carry," and C involves an extra addition. Yet, as Friend's careful analysis revealed, in fact problem A is the most difficult!

As we shall see, it is possible to develop a systematic theory of human information processing that predicts the Friend phenomenon and that shows why the naive expectation that problem A is easiest is not in fact correct. Indeed, the theory even predicts the actual wrong answers that are most commonly observed.

The Clement–Kaput phenomenon. In a series of papers (Kaput & Clement, 1979; Clement, Lochhead, & Monk, 1979; Rosnick & Clement, 1980), Clement and his colleagues have reported a very common and very stable error. Given the task of writing a mathematical equation to express the fact that "in a certain college, there are five times as many students as professors," a sizable proportion of students, even among undergraduate engineering students, write the equation

$$5S = P.$$

What is especially important about this phenomenon is that it is remarkably stable. Even when determined tutoring efforts change this to a correct response, the improvement is only temporary. Quite soon the students revert to their earlier, incorrect, version. Both the occurrence of this error and its remarkable persistence require explanation.

The "zero product principle" error. Matz (1980) discusses a very persistent error related to the factoring of quadratic equations. If two numbers, A and B, are multiplied to yield an answer, C, knowledge of C does not in general imply a knowledge of A or of B. There is, however, one exception: if C is zero, then either $A = 0$ or else $B = 0$ (or both). This fact is called the "zero product principle" (Stein & Crabill, 1972) and is used in solving quadratic equations by factoring:

$(x - 2)(x - 3) = 0$
Therefore, either $x - 2 = 0$ (whence $x = 2$)
or else $x - 3 = 0$ (whence $x = 3$).

This principle is regularly misused by students, who apply it in cases where C is not zero, as in:

$(x - 2)(x - 3) = 12$
So, either $x - 2 = 12$ (whence $x = 14$)
or else $x - 3 = 12$ (whence $x = 15$),

which is, of course, incorrect (Davis, Jockusch, & McKnight, 1978). Both the frequency of this error and its persistence in individual students need to be explained.

U-shaped performance growth patterns. Traditional approaches to mathematics education typically assumed that skills and understandings improved as a student advanced through school, both as a result of instruction and as a result of greater maturity. (For example, one assumes that a Grade Level Equivalent [GLE] score of 7 represents better performance than a GLE of 5.)

More recent data show that this assumption is not justified. At certain ages, students' performance shows a temporary dip below earlier levels. Indeed, given recent data on conceptual errors (and their blocking effect) plus the notion that students are busily building up elaborate information-processing structures in their own minds, it is perhaps not surprising that performance should show occasional periods of temporary decline instead of improvement. New and more elaborate information-processing structures, although more effective in the long run, may well produce poorer performance when they are being constructed and first put into use. It is rather like office experience when a new computer is first installed.

This phenomenon of periods of decline in student performance was well-known among curriculum development projects of the 1950s and 1960s and is discussed in unpublished documents from that era. It was generally indicated that, on certain mathematical tasks, fifth-graders would typically outperform seventh-graders or eighth-graders. The first published reports of this phenomenon appear to be Davis (1964) and Murphy (1964). More recently, more thorough studies have been reported by Strauss (1981), Strauss and Stavy (1981), and by Siegler (1978). This phenomenon of temporary dips (which may last as long as several years) has recently been referred to as "U-shaped development."

Examples of creativity and originality. If students build knowledge representations in their own minds, there is clearly a possibility of error, as we have already seen. But, as with any creative production, there is the possibility of unanticipated excellence. This phenomenon also occurs. Barson, Cochran, and Davis (1970) report the invention by a third-grade boy of an original algorithm for subtraction ("Kye's Arithmetic"); original discoveries or inventions by students are frequently reported (Suzuki, 1979; Burkholder, 1979). One such discovery has recently been studied from a different point of view: in adding, it is inferred from precise time measurements that answers are not achieved by "table-look-up" but rather by computation, often a "counting on" strategy, so that $8 + 2$ is computed by "counting on" two beyond the initial 8. To use this procedure makes $2 + 8$ take longer to compute than $8 + 2$ because more counting onward is required. But if many addition problems are presented, a different method will be more efficient: first determine which order will be easier, then use it. Thus, $8 + 2$ would be computed as is, but the problem $2 + 9$ would be replaced by the easier computation $9 + 2$. This "first choose the easier problem" strategy can also be adapted to subtraction. Response-time studies have been reported in Suppes and

Groen (1967), Groen and Parkman (1972), Groen (1973), Woods, Resnick, and Groen (1975), and Resnick (1976). The results show that in the case of subtraction, although the "first choose the easier problem" method is probably not taught in school, by grade 4 all children seem to have discovered it for themselves, and come to make regular use of it.

A Theory of Human Information Processing. Two decades ago the conventional wisdom of educational research commonly ignored human information processing on the grounds that what happens inside a person's mind is unknowable. Today, process studies typically take a quite different point of view, inferring properties of human information processing from observations of mathematical behavior.

The acceptability of this approach has at least four antecedents: Piaget's notions of schemata, assimilation, and accommodation; Soviet process studies; computer science work, including artificial intelligence and computer simulations of human thought processes; and studies of language, including both studies of reading and efforts at computer translation from, say, Russian to English.

All of these studies, in various ways, were ultimately compelled to recognize the inevitability of considering the details of the actual information processing that was taking place, even if this could not be observed directly, but had to be inferred from observations of other phenomena.

Frames. One key concept that has helped make possible a theory of mathematical thought came, in fact, from studies of reading and from studies of the interpretation of visual information. This importation was Minsky's postulation of frames (Minsky, 1975). A "frame," in Minsky's sense, is an integrated information-representation structure, either in a person's mind or in the memory of a computer. Frames have a precise internal structure, involving both an active component (that can be thought of as some kind of typical computer program) and a passive component whereby data are organized systematically, as in a telephone directory or in a dictionary. Similar representation structures have also been postulated by other researchers, under various names: Schank and Abelson (1975) call these organized bits of knowledge "scripts"; Norman, Rumelhart, and the San Diego Group (Norman, Gentner, & Stevens, 1976) speak of "schemata." While there are differences, to a first approximation one could say: a frame or a script or a schema is a representation, within the memory of a human being or within the memory of a computer, for an organized piece of knowledge involving both active and passive capabilities of specific sorts.

Applications of these ideas to the analysis of how students deal with mathematical tasks are presented in Paige and Simon (1966), in Hinsley, Hayes, and Simon (1977), and in Davis and McKnight (1979). In fact, the theory is being developed in several different forms. One of the most important, known under the technical term "production systems," is presented in Newell and Simon (1972); a different form of the general theory is presented in Minsky and Papert (1972) and in Minsky (1980).

How Frame Theory Explains Phenomena. We can now sketch briefly how the theory of "frames" correctly predicts the phenomenon reported by Friend: the algorithm for addition of multiple-digit numbers can be thought of as a procedure, *P*, having the high-level strategic goal of carrying out the addition. In order to do this, procedure *P* must call on assistance from a binary-input "addition facts" frame *F* that provides results for single-digit additions (such as $5 + 2 = 7$). Frame *F* plays a tactical role, with lower-level goals. The Friend phenomenon now results from the fact that frame *F* requires two inputs: one can "add $5 + 2$," but one cannot comply with a request to "add 3."

Each time frame *F* is called upon, it therefore demands two inputs; in every case except Problem *A* (see above), these inputs are forthcoming. However, in the left-most column of Problem *A*, there is the single input "7." Where is the second input? Apparently nowhere! Since the second input cannot be located, frame *F* refuses to perform. Hence the strategic high-level goal of computing the answer is threatened. At this point the Brown–Van Lehn–Matz Law takes over and relaxes some constraints (namely, the column addition specifications of where to seek inputs). Processing can now proceed, and does so, but the procedure now contains a "bug" or "flaw" and leads to an incorrect answer. This not only predicts that Problem *A* will be the most difficult; it even predicts exactly those wrong answers that are observed! (For details, see Davis, 1980.)

In a similar way, the other phenomena discussed above are all capable of being explained in a direct way by the use of frame theory in one or another of its several versions.

Problem Solving. Nowhere is the value of process studies more clearly demonstrated than in research on problem solving. We must first clarify a matter of language: given the Groen, Suppes, Resnick et al. studies, not to mention work of Piaget and Papert, it is clear that all mathematical thought involves "problem solving." Even where an answer is obtained by "table-look-up," there are problems involved in interpreting the input data (or stimulus) correctly, in matching up the input data correctly with cognitive representation structures, in searching through decision trees, in carrying out the correct retrieval from memory, and in assessing the correctness of the final answer. Game show participants, having failed (say) to "name the capital of New York State," are often heard to remark something like: "I know the answer; I just couldn't think of it in time!"

What, then, do we mean when we speak of research into problem solving? This phrase is usually employed to mean studies of mathematical performances where special difficulty lurks in the correct interpretation of the initial statement of the problem, or where especially many decisions must be made in the course of solving the problem, or where relating the problem to relevant knowledge is particularly difficult.

One of the first tasks in studying the problem-solving performances of students is this: how shall we conceptualize the process of problem solving in general? In other words, when we observe a student struggling to solve a mathematics problem, what sort of thing should we be looking for?

A general consensus seems to be emerging that conceives of problem solving somewhat like this:

1. The verbal statement of the problem (or some other presentation of the problem) is an initial input.
2. Typically, not all of these input data are absorbed at once; some *part* of them is accepted.
3. From this partial input, an internal knowledge representation structure is created, through some combination of retrieval and synthesis.
4. Now a process of "extending" takes place; from time to time more data are accepted as input; the representation structure is extended and revised; a dialogue takes place to match retrieved problem-solving procedures with the present problem representation; gaps and mismatches are dealt with. "Understanding" the problem can be characterized, thus, as the building (through synthesis and retrieval) of a sequence of successive understandings, each one an elaboration of an earlier one.

Perhaps the central issues in problem solving are the following five.

1. *Decisions.* Typically, there are several things one could do. Only a few of these will be helpful. The solver has to choose which one (or ones). Examples: After Mary had given Bill six marbles, she had left three more than he had. How many did Mary have originally? [One could add $3 + 6$ to get 9, or one could subtract $6 - 3$ to get 3, or one could multiply 6×3 to get 18, for example. Which, if any, of these will help to solve the problem?]

2. *Tree construction and tree search.* Where a quite large number of alternatives must be considered, or where there are several steps that must be performed in sequence, it is often useful to represent possibilities by a *tree* diagram (Nilsson, 1971) in which every possibility at one step is listed, below which every subsequent choice at the next step is listed (and, in diagrams, a connection is indicated by a line segment). This can be made explicit when written or printed on paper, and a structure of this type can be created within the memory of a computer. It is questionable, however, whether a really complex tree can be built up in one person's mind. But this is by no means the end of the list of difficulties: a large tree cannot usually be searched exhaustively, so some method of "pruning" is usually required in order to eliminate unpromising choices. There is the further difficulty that the solver must create the tree, and he or she will ordinarily omit parts of it "because they didn't come to mind" (Davis, Jockusch, & McKnight, 1978). Still worse, the feedback from a problem will often be misleading (one can seem "to be getting nowhere," or "to be going in the wrong direction"—but this can be misleading; maybe what is required is *more* of the same treatment) (Minsky and Papert, 1972).

3. *Frame retrieval.* Even before one can begin to select possible alternative courses of action, one must make an initial selection of "problem type"; that is to say, the input data must be matched up with some information representation structure retrieved from memory. Students often encounter difficulty at this stage because they misinterpret the kind of problem with which they are dealing, and consequently try to match up the input data with an incorrectly chosen cognitive representation structure.

4. *Planning and control.* In any long problem, one must make plans, try to carry out the plans, and exercise good judgment about when to modify the plan if difficulties are encountered.

5. *Execution.* Of course, after a plan has been thought out, one must carry out the plan by modifying the problem, solving algebraic equations, drawing a diagram, or doing whatever else the plan calls for.

Early milestone work on problem solving was done by Polya (1945). Important work on teaching problem solving has been done by Schoenfeld (1978; 1980). For further studies on problem solving, see Silver (1977, 1979, 1981); Kilpatrick (1967): Kantowski (1974); Kulm and Days (1979); Webb (1975); Heller and Greeno (1981); Greeno (1976; 1977); Michener (1978); Hayes, Waterman, and Robinson (1977); Simon and Hayes (1976); Simon (1978); and Lucas et al. (1979).

Good versus poor problem solvers; heuristics. The recent interest in process studies has made it clear that we know very little about the difference between the behavior of very good problem solvers versus very poor problem solvers. In the last few years, however, some real progress has been made. Schoenfeld (1980), Larkin (1977), and Larkin et al. (1980) report studies that compare the problem-solving behavior of experts with that of novices and indicate a number of specific differences. (See also Simon & Simon, 1978.) Some of the devices used by experts can be explicitly taught to novices, with good results (Schoenfeld, 1978; 1980). These devices often take the form of "heuristics," a kind of vague advice that, interpreted correctly, can often be of very great value in solving difficult problems. Following are examples of heuristics: Can you identify which feature of the problem is making it difficult? Can you modify the problem so as to eliminate this difficulty? Can you think of a somewhat similar problem that you *do* know how to solve? Can you break the problem up into parts, and deal separately with the various parts?

Heuristics are probably not helpful in improving problem-solving performance unless the student also possesses appropriate technical knowledge. "Breaking a problem up into subproblems" is useful only if you are able to solve the subproblems.

A sizable number of studies have dealt with heuristics, but few clear themes seem to have emerged. There does seem to be a difference between specific heuristics (that work for certain types of tasks, but not in general) and general heuristics. Specific heuristics seem to be learned more quickly (Davis, Jockusch, & McKnight, 1978). Effective teaching of heuristics probably takes time, often at least a year (e.g., Schoenfeld, 1980; Davis, Jockusch, & McKnight, 1978). For other research on heuristics, see Ashton (1962), Wilson (1967), Goldberg (1973), Hatfield (1978), Hunt (1978), Lee (1977), Lucas (1972), Post and Brennan (1976), and Schoenfeld (1979).

Matz's extrapolation theory. It is possible to approach problem solving from a different point of view, as Matz (1980) does. She conceptualizes typical mathematical tasks as requiring the creation of a match between a known standard "rule," and a new problem input that does not perfectly match the rule. For example, one standard rule is the distributive law, $A \times (B + C) = (A \times B) + (A \times C)$. Given the task of factoring $(R \times S) + (R \times W) + (R \times T)$, no direct match can be made between the task input and the memorized rule. The gap must be closed, either by extending the standard rule or else by modifying the task input. This is a very general task, occurring in a high percentage of all uses of mathematics. Thus, Matz's theory not only explains much correct performance, but, interestingly, also explains many of the common errors made by students.

Developing New Concepts. All of the preceding studies assume, to a greater or lesser extent, that a student already possesses certain foundation ideas and that further learning builds upon these ideas. But does one never need a truly new idea? And if one does, where can a truly new idea come from? An important series of studies by Carey, Smith, and Wiser deal with the acquisition of new concepts by comparing observations of students (or children) with the history of science and mathematics (Smith, Carey, & Wiser, 1981). This question of the development of new concepts must surely be one of the most important; yet it has received very little attention in recent years.

By a "new concept," we mean an idea that cannot readily be defined in terms of ideas that one already has—rather like the problem of giving the ideas of "blue" and "red" to someone who has been blind since birth. Traditional practice implicitly assumed that no such difficulties lay in the path to mathematical learning; the careful observation of modern process studies has suggested that just such obstacles do exist. Because these obstacles are ignored, they are capable of hampering the advancement of many students.

Computer Simulations. Our understanding of modern mathematical thought has been advanced substantially as a result of computer simulations of human thought processes.

Minsky, Papert, and their colleagues have produced a large outpouring of distinguished work: Evans (1968) presented a computer program that can, in effect, take intelligence tests, at least as far as geometric analogy questions are concerned. A computer program by Winston (1975) can learn structural descriptions if it is shown appropriate examples and nonexamples. Another program can solve word problems from a mathematics textbook—not in the sense of merely doing the calculations, which any calculator could do under direct human control, but rather in this sense: if you type into the computer the statement of a problem just as it appears in the textbook, the computer program will, acting on its own, analyze the problem statement, make up its own plan of solution, and carry out this plan (Bobrow, 1968; Larkin, McDermott, Simon, & Simon, 1980).

For Newell and Simon, a computer program constitutes in itself the most meaningful theory of complex information processing. They typically use computer programs of a certain special type, called "production systems" (Newell & Simon, 1972), within which every command has the same form: "If (some specific thing is true) then do (some specific information-processing action)."

Programs of this type have been created to learn certain portions of ninth-grade algebra on being shown illustrative examples in a certain ninth-grade algebra textbook; or, in another case, to create new portions of mathematics (Lenat, 1976). Klahr has given considerable attention to computer programs that can simulate the learning of young children (Klahr, 1976; Klahr & Wallace, 1976).

With one computer program, ISAAC, it is possible to type in a verbal statement of a textbook problem and to have the computer display a diagram or picture on a television screen. No picture was entered into the computer! The computer *created* the picture by analyzing the statement of the problem.

But there is an important point here; ISAAC does not go directly from the verbal statement to the picture; it inserts an intermediate step of great importance: working from the English-language sentences of the problem statement, ISAAC creates information-representation structures (in the form of node-link "list" representations) in the computer memory, and it is from these representation structures that it creates the pictures on the television screen. In this important sense, ISAAC "understands" certain aspects of the problem *before* it draws the picture. (Of course, after drawing the picture, ISAAC goes on to solve the problem.) If ISAAC is at all similar to human thought, then superficial verbal approaches to problem solving are probably doomed to failure (Novak, 1976; Novak, 1977; Larkin et al., 1980; Larkin, 1977). For related work, see Carry, Lewis, & Bernard (1979) and Anderson et al. (1980).

Perhaps the best-known simulations of mathematical behavior are the computer programs made by John Seely Brown and his colleagues (Brown & Burton, 1978; Brown & Van Lehn, 1980). These computer programs simulate the arithmetic-calculating performances of elementary school children. The computer programs contain variants that include virtually every conceivable systematic error. Since the errors in the computer programs are explicitly known, when a program accurately matches the performance of some student, it can be inferred that the student is making the same error that the computer program is making. From the known computer error, one discovers exactly what error(s) the student is making, after which remediation may be relatively straightforward.

Data Collection Methods. We have emphasized the interpretation of research data because of the very important developments in this area. A balanced view of research activity should, however, also place considerable emphasis on the methods of data collection by very careful observation as children or students work at various mathematical tasks. Perhaps the most meticulous work of all has dealt with children's early number concepts, and especially with the process of counting. See Fuson and Richards (1980) and Fuson and Hall (1981).

Implications. Although process studies, considered together with their theoretical explanations, can seem extremely complex, many of their implications are both clear and important.

First, careful observation shows that many Americans know far less mathematics than one had previously expected. Even many engineering students fail to understand fundamental ideas of mathematics. At every age level, from early school years on, careful observation reveals basic weaknesses in mathematical skills and understandings.

Second, tests that deal only in *products* (i.e., final answers) and neglect the *processes* by which those answers were obtained will not reveal a full picture of understandings and skills.

Third, if computer simulations such as ISAAC point in the correct direction, then superficial verbal approaches to problem solving (which are commonly used in many schools at present) cannot lead to powerful skill in problem solving because they fail to develop the necessary knowledge-representation structures in the student's mind.

Fourth, if Newell and Simon (1972) are correct, schools are paying too much attention to *what* one should do (in solving a mathematical problem) and too little attention to the cues that should tell you *when* to do it (and when not to).

Finally, the important advances made in recent years by process studies suggest that the conventional wisdom of educational research may need to be reexamined: processes may be more important than outcomes, and a theory of human information processing may be not an impossibility but rather an absolute necessity.

Robert B. Davis
Edward A. Silver

See also Arithmetic; Cognitive Development; Comparative Education Achievement; Intelligence; Learning; Mathematics Education.

REFERENCES

Alderman, D. L.; Swinton, S. S.; & Braswell, J. S. Assessing basic arithmetic skills and understanding across curricula: Computer-assisted instruction and compensatory education. *Journal of Children's Mathematical Behavior,* 1979, *2,* 3–28.

Anderson, J. R.; Greeno, J. G.; Kline, P. J.; & Neves, D. M. *Acquisition of Problem-solving Skill* (Technical Report No. 80-5). Pittsburgh: Carnegie-Mellon University, Department of Psychology, 1980.

Ashton, M. R. *Heuristic Methods in Problem Solving in Ninth-grade Algebra.* Unpublished doctoral dissertation, Stanford University, 1962.

Barson, A.; Cochran, B.; & Davis, R. B. Child-created mathematics. *Arithmetic Teacher,* 1970, *17,* 211–215.

Bobrow, D. G. Natural language input for a computer problem-solving system. In M. Minsky (Ed.), *Semantic Information Processing.* Cambridge, Mass.: MIT Press, 1968.

Bobrow, D. G., & Collins, A. *Representation and Understanding: Studies in Cognitive Science.* New York: Academic Press, 1975.

Brown, J. S., & Burton, R. R. Diagnostic models for procedural bugs in basic mathematical skills. *Cognitive Science,* 1978, *2,* 155–192.

Brown, J. S. & Van Lehn, K. *Repair Theory: A Generative Theory of "Bugs."* Palo Alto, Calif.: Xerox Palo Alto Science Center, 1980.

Burkholder, B. Proof of a theorem. *Journal of Children's Mathematical Behavior,* 1979, *2,* 167–169.

Carry, L. R.; Lewis, C.; & Bernard, J. E. *Psychology of Equation Solving: An Information-processing Study.* Austin: University of Texas, Department of Curriculum and Instruction, 1979. (ERIC Document Reproduction Service No. ED 186 243)

Clement, J.; Lochhead, J.; & Monk, G. *Translation Difficulties in Learning Mathematics* (Technical Report, Cognitive Development Project). Amherst: University of Massachusetts, Department of Physics and Astronomy, 1979.

Davis, R. B. The Madison Project's approach to a theory of instruction. *Journal of Research in Science Teaching,* 1964, *2,* 146–162.

Davis, R. B. Mathematics teaching: With special reference to epistemological problems (Monograph No. 1). *Journal of Research and Development in Education.* Athens, Ga.: University of Georgia, College of Education, 1967.

Davis, R. B. The postulation of certain specific, explicit, commonly shared frames. *Journal of Mathematical Behavior,* 1980, *3.*

Davis, R. B.; Jockusch, E.; & McKnight, C. Cognitive processes in learning algebra. *Journal of Children's Mathematical Behavior,* 1978, *2,* 10–320.

Davis, R. B., & McKnight, C. C. Modeling the processes of mathematical thinking. *Journal of Mathematical Behavior,* 1979, *2.*

Davis, R. B., & McKnight, C. C. The influence of semantic content on algorithmic behavior. *Journal of Mathematical Behavior,* 1980, *3.*

Davis, R. B.; McKnight, C. C.; Parker, P.; & Elrick, D. Analysis of student answers to signed-number arithmetic problems. *Journal of Children's Mathematical Behavior,* 1979, *2,* 114–130.

Davis, R. B.; Romberg, T.; Rachlin, S.; & Kantowski, M. G. *An Analysis of Mathematics Education in the Union of Soviet Socialist Republics.* Columbus, Ohio: ERIC Clearinghouse for Science, Mathematics and Environmental Education, 1979. (ERIC Document Reproduction Service No. ED 182 141)

Erlwanger, S. H. Benny's conception of rules and answers in IPI mathematics. *Journal of Children's Mathematical Behavior,* 1973, *1,* 7–26.

Erlwanger, S. H. *Case Studies of Children's Conceptions of Mathematics.* Unpublished doctoral dissertation, University of Illinois at Urbana, 1974.

Erlwanger, S. H. Case studies of children's conceptions of mathematics (Part 1). *Journal of Children's Mathematical Behavior,* 1975, *1,* 157–283.

Evans, T. G. A heuristic program to solve geometric analogy problems. Marvin Minsky (Ed.), *Semantic Information Processing.* Cambridge, Mass.: MIT Press, 1968.

Friend, J. Column addition skills. *Journal of Children's Mathematical Behavior,* 1979, *2,* 29–54.

Fuson, K. C., & Hall, J. W. The acquisition of early-number word meanings. In H. Ginsburg (Ed.), *The Development of Mathematical Thinking.* New York: Academic Press, 1981.

Fuson, K. C., & Richards, J. *Children's Construction of the Counting Numbers: From a Spew to a Bi-directional Chain.* Paper presented at the annual meeting of the American Educational Research Association, 1980.

Ginsburg, H. *Children's Arithmetic: The Learning Process.* New York: Van Nostrand, 1977.

Goldberg, D. J. *The Effects of Training in Heuristic Methods on the Ability to Write Proofs in Number Theory.* Unpublished doctoral dissertation, Columbia University, 1973.

Greeno, J. G. Indefinite goals in well-structured problems. *Psychological Review,* 1976, *83,* 479–491.

Greeno, J. G. Process of understanding in problem solving. In N. J. Castellan, D. B. Pisoni, & G. R. Potts (Eds.), *Cognitive Theory.* Hillsdale, N.J.: Lawrence Erlbaum Associates, 1978.

Greeno, J. G. Psychology of learning, 1960–1980: One participant's observations. *American Psychologist,* 1980, *35,* 713–728.

Groen, G. J. Subtraction and the solution of open-sentence problems. *Journal of Experimental Child Psychology,* 1973, *16,* 292–302.

Groen, G. J., & Parkman, J. M. A chronometric analysis of simple addition. *Psychological Review,* 1972, *79,* 329–343.

Hatfield, L. L. Heuristical emphases in the instruction of mathematical problem solving: Rationales and research. In L. L. Hatfield (Ed.), *Mathematical Problem Solving.* Columbus, Ohio: ERIC Clearinghouse for Science, Mathematics, and Environmental Education, 1978. (ERIC Document Reproduction Service No. ED 156 446)

Hayes, J. R.; Waterman, D. A.; & Robinson, C. S. Identifying the relevant aspects of a problem text. *Cognitive Science,* 1977, *1,* 297–313.

Heller, J. I., & Greeno, J. G. Information-processing analyses of mathematical problem solving. In R. Lesh (Ed.), *Applied Problem Solving.* Columbus, Ohio: ERIC Clearinghouse for Science, Mathematics, and Environmental Education, 1981.

Hinsley, D.; Hayes, J.; & Simon, H. From words to equations: Meaning and representation in algebra word problems. In M. Just & P. Carpenter (Eds.), *Cognitive Processes in Comprehension.* Hillsdale, N.J.: Lawrence Erlbaum Associates, 1977.

Hoffman, B. *The Tyranny of Testing.* New York: Collier Books, 1962.

Houts, P. L. *The Myth of Measurability.* New York: Hart, 1977.

Hunt, M. L. *An Investigation of the Interactions of Student Ability Profiles and Instruction in Heuristic Strategies with Problem-solving Performance and Problem-sorting Schemes.* Unpublished doctoral dissertation, University of New Hampshire, 1978.

Kantowski, E. L. *Processes Involved in Mathematical Problem Solving.* Unpublished doctoral dissertation, University of Georgia, 1974.

Kaput, J. J., & Clement, J. Letter to the editor. *Journal of Children's Mathematical Behavior*, 1979, *2*, 208.

Kilpatrick, J. *Analyzing the Solution of Word Problems in Mathematics: An Exploratory Study*. Unpublished doctoral dissertation, Stanford University, 1967.

Klahr, D. Designing a learner. In D. Klahr (Ed.), *Cognition and Instruction*. Hillsdale, N.J.: Lawrence Erlbaum Associates, 1976, pp. 325–331. (ERIC Document Reproduction Service No. ED 123 584)

Klahr, D., & Wallace, J. G. *Cognitive Development: An Information-processing View*. Hillsdale, N.J.: Lawrence Erlbaum Associates, 1976.

Krutetskii, V. A. *The Psychology of Mathematical Abilities in School Children* (J. Kilpatrick & I. Wirzup, Eds., & J. Teller, Trans.). Chicago: University of Chicago Press, 1976.

Kuhn, T. S. *The Structure of Scientific Revolutions*. Chicago: University of Chicago Press, 1970.

Kulm, G., & Days, H. Information transfer in solving problems. *Journal for Research in Mathematics Education*, 1979, *10*, 94–102.

Larkin, J. H. *Skilled Problem Solving in Experts*. Berkeley: University of California, Group in Science and Mathematics Education, 1977.

Larkin, J. H.; McDermott, J.; Simon, D.; & Simon, H. A. Expert and novice performance in solving physics problems. *Science*, 1980, *208*, 1335–1342.

Lawler, R. W. *Extending a Powerful Idea* (LOGO Memo No. 58). Cambridge, Mass.: MIT Artificial Intelligence Laboratory, July 1980.

Lee, K. *An Exploratory Study of Fourth-grader's Heuristic Problem-solving Behavior*. Unpublished doctoral dissertation, University of Georgia, 1977.

Lenat, D. B. *An Artificial Intelligence Approach to Discovery in Mathematics as Heuristic Search* (Report SAIL AIM-281). Stanford, Calif.: Stanford Artificial Intelligence Laboratory, 1976.

Lesh, R. *Space and Geometry*. Columbus: Ohio State University, ERIC Clearinghouse for Science and Mathematics, 1977.

Lucas, J. F. *An Exploratory Study on the Diagnostic Teaching of Heuristic Problem-solving Strategies in Calculus*. Unpublished doctoral dissertation, University of Wisconsin, 1972.

Lucas, J. F.; Branca, N.; Goldberg, D.; Kantowski, M. G.; Kellogg, H.; & Smith, J. P. A process-sequence coding system for behavioral analysis of mathematical problem solving. In G. A. Goldin & C. E. McClintock (Eds.), *Task Variables in Mathematical Problem-solving*. Columbus, Ohio: ERIC Clearinghouse, 1979. (ERIC Document Reproduction Service No. ED 178 366)

Matz, M. Towards a computational model of algebraic competence. *Journal of Mathematical Behavior*, 1980, *3*.

Michener, E. R. Understanding understanding mathematics. *Cognitive Science*, 1978, *2*, 361–383.

Minsky, M. A framework for representing knowledge. In P. Winston (Ed.), *The Psychology of Computer Vision*. New York: McGraw-Hill, 1975.

Minsky, M. K-lines: A theory of memory. *Cognitive Science*, 1980, *4*, 117–133.

Minsky, M., & Papert, S. *Artificial Intelligence* (LOGO Memo No. 252). Cambridge, Mass.: MIT Artificial Intelligence Laboratory, 1972.

Murphy, J. *Middle Schools*. New York: Ford Foundation, 1964.

Newell, A., & Simon, H. A. *Human Problem Solving*. Englewood Cliffs, N.J.: Prentice-Hall, 1972.

Nilsson, N. J. *Problem-solving Methods in Artificial Intelligence*. New York: McGraw-Hill, 1971.

Norman, D. A.; Gentner, D. R.; & Stevens, A. L. Comments on learning schemata and memory representation. In D. Klahr (Ed.), *Cognition and Instruction*. Hillsdale, N.J.: Lawrence Erlbaum Associates, 1976. (ERIC Document Reproduction Service No. ED 123 584)

Novak, G. S. *Technical Report NL-30*. Austin: University of Texas, Department of Computer Sciences, 1976.

Novak, G. S. *Proceedings of the Fifth International Joint Conference on Artificial Intelligence*. Cambridge, Mass.: 1977.

Paige, J. M., & Simon, H. Cognitive processes in solving algebra word problems. B. Kleinmuntz (Ed.), *Problem Solving: Research, Method, and Theory*. New York: Wiley, 1966.

Papert, S. *Mindstorms: Children, Computers, and Powerful Ideas*. New York: Basic Books, 1980.

Polya, G. *How to Solve It*. Princeton, N.J.: Princeton University Press, 1945.

Porter, A. C.; Schwille, J. R.; Floden, R. E.; Freeman, D. J.; Knappen, L. B.; Kuhs, T. M.; & Schmidt, W. H. Teacher autonomy and the control of content taught. *Journal of Mathematical Behavior*, 1981, *4*.

Post, T. R., & Brennan, M. L. An experimental study of the effectiveness of a formal versus an informal presentation of a general heuristic process on problem solving in tenth-grade geometry. *Journal for Research in Mathematics Education*, 1976, *7*, 59–64.

Resnick, L. B. Task analysis in instructional design: Some cases from mathematics. In D. Klahr (Ed.), *Cognition and Instruction*. Hillsdale, N.J.: Lawrence Erlbaum Associates, 1976. (ERIC Document Reproduction Service No. ED 123 584)

Rosnick, P., & Clement, J. Learning without understanding: The effect of tutoring strategies on algebra misconceptions. *Journal of Mathematical Behavior*, 1980, *3*.

Schank, R., & Abelson, R. *Scripts, Plans, and Knowledge*. Advance papers of the Fourth International Joint Conference on Artificial Intelligence. Tbilisi, Georgia, U.S.S.R., 1975.

Schoenfeld, A. H. Presenting a strategy for indefinite integration. *American Mathematical Monthly*, 1978, *85*, 673–678.

Schoenfeld, A. H. Explicit heuristic training as a variable in problem-solving performance. *Journal for Research in Mathematics Education*, 1979, *10*, 173–187.

Schoenfeld, A. H. Teaching problem-solving skills. *American Mathematical Monthly*, 1980, *87*, 794–805.

Siegler, R. S. The origins of scientific reasoning. In R. S. Siegler (Ed.), *Children's Thinking: What Develops?* Hillsdale, N.J.: Lawrence Erlbaum Associates, 1978, pp. 97–137.

Silver, E. A. *Student Perceptions of Relatedness among Mathematical Verbal Problems*. Unpublished doctoral dissertation, Columbia University, 1977.

Silver, E. A. Student perceptions of relatedness among mathematical verbal problems. *Journal for Research in Mathematics Education*, 1979, *10*, 195–210.

Silver, E. A. Recall of mathematical problem information: Solving related problems. *Journal for Research in Mathematics Education*, 1981, *12*, 54–64.

Simon, D. P., & Simon, H. A. Individual differences in solving physics problems. In R. Siegler (Ed.), *Children's Thinking: What Develops?* Hillsdale, N.J.: Lawrence Erlbaum Associates, 1978.

Simon, H. A. Information-processing theory of human problem solving. In W. K. Estes (Ed.), *Handbook of Learning and Cogni-*

tive Processes. Hillsdale, N.J.: Lawrence Erlbaum Associates, 1978.

Simon, H. A., & Hayes, J. R. The understanding process: Problem isomorphs. *Cognitive Psychology,* 1976, *8,* 165–170.

Skemp, R. R. *Intelligence, Learning, and Action.* New York: Wiley, 1979.

Smith, C.; Carey, S.; & Wiser, M. *Conceptual Change in Children and in Adult Scientists.* Paper presented at Joint National Science Foundation–National Institute of Education Session on Cognitive Processes and the Structure of Knowledge in Science and Mathematics, Washington, D.C., February 1981.

Steffe, L., & Thompson, P. W. *Children's Counting in Arithmetical Problem Solving.* Paper presented at the Wingspread Conference, Racine, Wisconsin, 1979.

Stein, S. K., & Crabill, C. D. *Elementary Algebra: A Guided Inquiry.* Boston: Houghton Mifflin, 1972.

Strauss, S. Appearances, disappearances, nonappearances, and re-appearances of various behaviors: Methodological strategies of experimentation and their implications for models of development. In T. G. Bever (Ed.), *Dips in Learning and Development Curves.* Hillsdale, N.J.: Lawrence Erlbaum Associates, 1981.

Strauss, S., & Stavy, R. U-shaped behavioral growth: Implications for theories of development. In W. W. Hartup (Ed.), *Review of Child Development Research, 6.* Chicago: University of Chicago Press, 1981.

Suppes, P., & Groen, G. Some counting models for first-grade performance data on simple addition facts. In Joseph Michael Scandura (Ed.), *Research in Mathematics Education.* Washington, D.C.: National Council of Teachers of Mathematics, 1967. (ERIC Document Reproduction Service No. ED 035 545)

Suzuki, K. Solutions to problems. *Journal of Children's Mathematical Behavior,* 1979, *2,* 159–173.

Webb, N. *An Exploration of Mathematical Problem-solving Processes.* Unpublished doctoral dissertation, Stanford University, 1975.

Wilson, J. W. *Generality of Heuristics as an Instructional Variable.* Unpublished doctoral dissertation, Stanford University, 1967.

Winston, P. H. Learning structural descriptions from examples. In P. H. Winston (Ed.), *The Psychology of Computer Vision.* New York: McGraw-Hill, 1975.

Woods, S. S.; Resnick, L.; & Groen, G. J. An experimental test of five process models for subtraction. *Journal of Educational Psychology,* 1975, *67,* 17–21.

MATHEMATICS EDUCATION

The teaching and learning of mathematics have always been central concerns in educational research. Since mathematics is a fundamental topic in school curricula, the desire to improve the effectiveness of teaching has stimulated a broad range of studies designed to understand the nature and development of mathematical abilities and the school programs or teaching strategies that produce optimal learning. The highly structured nature of mathematical knowledge has also attracted attention from some psychologists, who have used mathematical learning tasks as vehicles for research that seeks general principles of human learning and ability. Recently, psychologists have proposed the computer, a mathematical-logical machine, as a model for human information processing.

Despite this long and intensive investigation of mathematics teaching and learning, Willoughby (1969) began his *Encyclopedia of Educational Research* article by observing that the results of the research have been disappointing, giving little support for most of the common wisdom in the profession. Any conservative assessment of the situation today leads to the same conclusion. There are no comprehensive, empirically validated theories to guide curriculum development or instruction in mathematics. If one studies any large sample of mathematics classes in action or if one talks to teachers, textbook authors, and teacher educators, one can see that research results play a very limited role in the actual business of mathematics education.

Nevertheless, the work of the past decade has provided a solid basis for progress in research on mathematics education. The National Council of Teachers of Mathematics (NCTM) and a special interest group of the American Educational Research Association (AERA) have stimulated and provided forums for work by a growing group of mathematics educators whose major interest is research. These mathematics educators have begun productive collaboration with leading psychologists and with colleagues around the world. Major studies have produced the first empirical surveys of national patterns in school mathematics curricula, teaching methods, and student achievement. This information has been used as a basis for thoughtful policy analysis and planning. The NCTM Research Advisory Committee produced a professional reference, *Research in Mathematics Education* (Shumway, 1980), that synthesized available knowledge and set research agendas in each problem area of mathematics education. Investigators tackling this research agenda found new sources of financial support that make possible the needed large-scale basic and applied studies. They have applied an increasingly diverse collection of research methods for data collection and analysis, and there are encouraging signs that the new efforts will yield information of value to those who seek improvement of mathematics education.

This article presents an overview of the history, current status, and major problem areas in mathematics education today. The survey is in four sections: (1) evolution of school mathematics; (2) learning and teaching; (3) research on learning and teaching; and (4) methodology and related dimensions. The focus is on the school situation and research in the United States, where, until recently, the vast majority of formal research has been done. However, one of the striking developments of the past decade has been the emergence of important international centers for research in this field. The contributions and influence of such work are indicated at several places.

Each of the four discussions is only a broad introduction to questions that are treated extensively in the research and expository literature of mathematics education. Further references are given in each section.

Evolution of School Mathematics. Mathematics is probably the oldest organized discipline of human knowledge, with a continuous line of development spanning 5,000 years and every major culture. Because mathematics is a body of ideas structured by logical reasoning, the facts, principles, and methods developed in early Mesopotamia, Egypt, and Greece play central roles in the subject as it is learned and used today. The sustaining societal interest in mathematics is based on at least four major themes in its development: (1) the arithmetic of whole numbers and fractions has proved indispensable for recording and ordering commerce and practical affairs; (2) the ideas of algebra, geometry, statistics, and calculus have provided valuable models for describing and predicting behavior in the biological and physical world; (3) the aesthetic qualities of mathematical structures are richly embodied in creative works of every artistic medium; (4) the patterns of logical reasoning used to verify mathematical propositions are prized as fundamental patterns of thought to be used in many other disciplines. Each of these characteristics of mathematics has played a role in shaping school mathematics curricula, and each presents teaching and learning problems that have stimulated research.

Mathematics in U.S. schools has long been presented in two major strands. Arithmetic and its everyday uses have been the core of common elementary mathematics education and the general mathematics of secondary schools. Advanced topics in algebra, geometry, and calculus have been the core of academic programs in secondary schools that prepare students for collegiate study leading to professional, scientific, and technical careers.

Elementary programs. The mathematical content of elementary school arithmetic has always emphasized computation with whole numbers and fractions and the application of those skills to practical problems of money and measurement. However, the pedagogy of this arithmetic curriculum has undergone several transformations, each influenced by the introduction of new theories or research evidence about human learning. DeVault and Weaver (1970) identified four major periods: (1) from the origins of common schools well into the nineteenth century, rote instruction in ciphering dominated practice; (2) as psychological research and knowledge emerged in the late nineteenth and early twentieth centuries, arithmetic instruction was influenced at various times by faculty psychology (valuing mental arithmetic as brain exercise), by connectionism, and by gestalt theories that emphasized meaningful instruction; (3) pedagogical theory in the 1930s and 1940s was dominated by the principles of progressive education philosophy; (4) the "new math" era, from 1955 to 1970, brought interest in broadening the content of elementary mathematics curricula to include rudiments of geometry, algebra, and statistics. But most attention was focused on discovery, laboratory, and individualized approaches to instruction, each with its supporting psycho-logical theory. The most recent trends of the past decade reflect retreat from such enriched curricula and teaching approaches to more traditional content goals and instructional methods.

Secondary programs. In contrast to the situation in elementary schools, secondary mathematics has been influenced more by proposals for change in the content and structure of the curriculum than by psychological or pedagogical theory and research. Osborne and Crosswhite (1970) traced the evolution of mathematics in grades 7–12 through three major periods.

From the beginning of secondary schools until at least 1920, the content and teaching of mathematics were dominated by the goal of preparing students for college entrance. When the National Education Association (NEA) appointed its Committee of Ten (1890) to provide national leadership in standardizing curricula, that action led to a College Entrance Requirements Committee (1895) and, ultimately, to the College Entrance Examination Board (1900). Mathematics was a major concern of each group, and with advice from the American Mathematical Society, guidelines for secondary mathematics programs were first set. This began a pattern of joint school-college collaboration in curriculum planning that has had an enormous influence on the shape of secondary mathematics programs. As algebra and geometry moved from standard college subjects in the nineteenth century to standard prerequisites for college admission, they became the core of the high school program, displacing arithmetic to elementary grades only. Advisory groups have recommended changes in content, emphasis, and teaching style, but the three-year combination of algebra I, geometry, and algebra II remains at the heart of college-preparatory mathematics today.

From 1920 through 1950, access to full secondary school education expanded to include many students with neither interest nor aptitude in high-level college preparatory mathematics. This new situation in secondary schools and the trauma of economic depression put traditional mathematics on the defense against challenges to be of practical value to students heading for vocational careers. Secondary school mathematics programs began to include the general, applied, vocational, and consumer-oriented courses that today enroll over 30 percent of all high school mathematics students. Furthermore, enrollments in the traditional college preparatory courses declined, despite growing total school populations, and mathematics educators faced severe criticism directed at the low functional utility and high failure rates in their courses. The adjustment of mathematics programs to individual ability differences and the sophisticated testing required to assess those differences were begun during this critical period. Today, ability grouping of secondary students into substantially different courses is probably more common in mathematics than in any other school subject, despite research that shows the limited efficacy of this practice (Begle, 1979).

Mathematics education vaulted from its troubled, defensive position into an era of unprecedented challenge and public esteem during World War II. Early in the war it became clear that success in military specialties and related industrial vocations demanded technical expertise not being produced in U.S. schools. After an anxious postwar period of international tension, the national concern about levels of scientific and mathematical competence among school graduates was aroused again by Russia's *Sputnik* launch. Full-scale programs to reconstruct secondary mathematics programs began.

This "new math" era again brought together college mathematicians and schoolteachers to set guidelines for modern mathematics programs. While the space race catalyzed political and financial support, professional concern about school mathematics had been building for several years prior to 1957. Rapid achievement in mathematical research had led to changes in college curricula, making existing high school programs out of date. Some leading private schools had revised their programs, and curriculum developments at the University of Chicago and the University of Illinois were showing the way that new programs might evolve. This background stimulated two major curriculum advisory studies. The 1959 College Board Commission on Mathematics and the 1963 Cambridge Conference on School Mathematics proposed themes and specific agendas for the anticipated curricular revolution. The U.S. Office of Education and the National Science Foundation invested millions of dollars yearly in research, development, and teacher education, allowing major projects, like the School Mathematics Study Group, to set about transforming goals into operational school programs.

The central themes of "new math" projects were use of unifying concepts and processes to restructure school topics in coherent, efficient ways; introduction of new topics shown to be learnable by younger students and of value in emerging applications; and deletion of traditional but outdated topics. The rationale for such change was the increasing mathematization of nearly every scientific and technical area and the consequent need to provide students with an efficient, rapid course to the frontiers of knowledge in those fields. The psychological basis for emphasis on unifying structures and processes was provided by Bruner's eloquent *Process of Education* (1960), reporting a conference of leading science and mathematics educators.

For fifteen years the multifaceted "new math" movement proceeded with substantial, if not universal, public and professional support. In 1969 Willoughby claimed that "all available evidence seems to indicate that programs classified as modern are replacing traditional programs at a very rapid rate—in fact it is hard to find anybody at a meeting of mathematics teachers who does not believe that the program in his school system is at least semi-modern" (p. 768). However, the goals and effectiveness of these new programs did not go unchallenged. Disconcerting signs of declining student achievement and concern for

the mathematical competencies appropriate to all students, not only those headed for technical occupations, made the 1970s a "back-to-basics" decade. Public expectations of secondary school mathematics are now focused on assuring that all students acquire the ability to perform basic computational skills and their applications to practical life situations. The "basics" spirit has also permeated college preparatory courses, where the unifying concepts central to "new math" programs are no longer prominent and innovative topics of the 1960s play a diminished role. The typical college preparatory secondary school mathematics program today includes a year of algebra in grade 9, a year of plane and solid geometry in grade 10, and a year of advanced algebra in grade 11. For those with greatest ability and interest, the algebra might begin in grade 8 and lead eventually to semester courses in trigonometry, analytic geometry, or elementary functions, and then a year of high school calculus. Popular elective courses for such students might include statistics and computer mathematics, the latter a rapidly growing offering.

Prospects. To most leaders in mathematics education, it seems clear that a return to basic skills of several decades past, at the elementary or secondary school level, will be poor preparation for any student facing a working lifetime largely in the twenty-first century. In response to the recent "minimal-competence" mandates from state and local governments, the National Council of Supervisors of Mathematics (NCSM) in 1978 drafted a position paper on basic skills that emphasized (in addition to arithmetic computation) problem solving; applying mathematics in everyday situations; alertness to reasonableness of results; estimation and approximation; geometry; measurement; reading, interpreting, and constructing tables, charts, and graphs; using mathematics to predict; and computer literacy. This broad view of basic skills has gained endorsement by the NCTM and leaders throughout the profession. *An Agenda for Action* (1980), published by the NCTM, in mathematics education, also calls for attention to problem solving, basic skills beyond computational facility, full use of calculators and computers, more required mathematics study for all students, and a more flexible curriculum designed to accommodate the diverse needs of the student population.

The full impact of these recent recommendations remains to be seen. However, of all the impending developments, that which offers the most certain prospect for striking influence on school mathematics is the emergence of microelectronic technology. There are those who predict that in twenty years computers will be able to perform every cognitive function of human beings. Already inexpensive calculators can perform the routine arithmetic that school mathematics programs spend so much time teaching to young people. The challenge to research and development is to determine the knowledge and skill yet important for various individuals to acquire and the best methods of teaching that skill and understanding in a computer-enhanced educational environment.

Learning and Teaching.   In the history of mathematics education the major landmarks are recommendations of prestigious advisory committees or individuals, theories and research findings of outstanding psychologists, and influential social or political events. Trends in the content or teaching of school mathematics are often presumed to follow directly from logically plausible simple causes: the imposition of uniform national college entrance testing seems likely to have caused standardization of curricular offerings; research evidence showing the limited transfer of knowledge from mathematics to other disciplines should have put to rest the idea that mathematics disciplines the mind; and the extension of opportunity for college entrance to disadvantaged students seems a plausible factor in declining SAT scores. In practice, the picture is seldom so clear. For instance, when mathematics test scores showed steady declines during the late 1960s and early 1970s, the obvious culprit was "new math" program innovations of the preceding decade. However, as thoughtful leaders began assessing the proposed cause-and-effect relation, they found gaps in the available information that prevented definitive resolution of the questions (NACOME, 1975).

As recently as 1975, there were very few extensive national surveys of student performance in mathematics, and there was almost no evidence on the extent to which proposed innovative programs became regular classroom practice. However, several major trends in survey research during the past decade offer some promise of solving this critical information problem. In 1982 we have a much better national picture of student attainments in school mathematics at all grade levels and of the content emphases and teaching styles predominant in normal classrooms. The findings of such research are proving invaluable for educational policy formulation and for stimulation of important needed research and development activities.

Achievement and attitudes assessment.   In 1967 Husén reported results of the first international study of achievement in mathematics. Despite serious limitations in the design and reporting of that study, it sparked a major national controversy, largely because U.S. students fared poorly in comparison with their European and Japanese counterparts. That first study by the International Association for Evaluation of Educational Achievement (IEA) was, however, a pioneering effort in the large-scale assessment of student achievement and attitudes in mathematics.

In 1963 the School Mathematics Study Group had begun a five-year National Longitudinal Study of Mathematical Abilities (NLSMA) studying the development of a broad range of mental abilities and attitudes and the relation of numerous teacher, curriculum, and achievement variables to those student abilities. As the NLSMA reports emerged in over thirty volumes during the 1970s, they added another major source of information about components of mathematical ability and the effects of different curricula (Begle, 1973, 1979). The data comparing curricula suggested that at the elementary grade levels, students in "modern" programs fell below those in more traditional programs on computational items but did better on comprehension and problem solving. At the secondary level differences were less consistent or striking, but one of the most clear-cut findings of the entire textbook comparison was the vast difference in performance profiles associated with various texts judged to be modern.

The first U.S. National Assessment of Education Progress (NAEP) in mathematics collected student achievement data in 1973 (Carpenter et al., 1975a, 1975b), and a second NAEP mathematics assessment was conducted in 1978 (Carpenter et al., 1980a, 1980b). People with different expectations have judged those findings differently, but the general appraisal of the 1973 assessment found satisfactory results in whole number and decimal computation and simple problem solving; fractions, percent, measurement, and multistep problem solving were areas of concern. The most notable changes by 1978 were discouraging declines in percent and problem solving—particularly by 17-year-old students. The second assessment also probed student attitudes toward and beliefs about mathematics. The most striking findings were that students seem to enjoy mathematics, believe it to be very important, and want to do well. They see mathematics class as a time to be passive, watching teachers demonstrate rules that they must memorize and practice (Carpenter et al., 1980c, 1980d).

At this writing a second IEA international mathematics study is in progress. Further NAEP mathematics assessments are planned, and data are accumulating from more frequent testing by state and local school systems. The results of national college entrance testing are now widely publicized and studied (Fey & Sonnabend, 1981; Harnischfeger & Wiley, 1975). Taken together, the various national assessments of mathematics performance give an increasingly informative profile of school mathematics program effects. The next, more difficult task is to explain achievement trends by variation in patterns of curriculum, instruction, and student background characteristics.

Status of curriculum and teaching.   In 1974 the Conference Board of the Mathematical Sciences appointed a National Advisory Committee on Mathematics Education (NACOME) to assemble an overview and critical analysis of school mathematics. To construct the description of school programs, the committee collected popular textbooks, published syllabi, content analyses of standardized tests, and reports from mathematics supervisors in every state on "the way things are" in mathematics classrooms. All these secondary sources left the committee very unsure that the resulting collage accurately described life in typical mathematics courses or in day-to-day instruction. So with support from the National Council of Teachers of Mathematics, NACOME conducted an exploratory questionnaire survey of 3,000 elementary school teachers, probing their classroom practices and beliefs about mathematics and its teaching (Price, Kelley, & Kelley, 1977).

The findings gave credence to the increasingly common conjecture that "new math" is an unlikely villain in the test score decline, since it seems to have had such limited implementation, especially at the elementary level.

The questions raised by NACOME, and others concerned about similar issues of curriculum innovation effects in science, led the National Science Foundation to sponsor three major studies on the status of school mathematics, science, and social science instruction across the country. The first study in each area was a comprehensive critical review of the literature on curriculum, instruction, evaluation, and teacher education 1955–1975 (Suydam & Osborne, 1977); the second study was a collection of surveys directed at teachers, parents, administrators, and students in grades K–12 (Weiss, 1978), and the third study was a collection of case reports on individual school systems (Stake & Easley, 1978). The insights of these different approaches to understanding the nature of school mathematics today are another remarkable resource for mathematics education.

The questionnaire data give a broad quantitative picture of school mathematics programs: course offerings and enrollments, requirements for graduation, frequency of various teaching activities, teacher traits like experience and training, teacher and supervisor perceptions of problems in the field, and the extent of implementation by various recent curriculum developments. The case studies provide a deeper, more personal view of life in classrooms: teacher attitudes toward students, mathematics, and the problems of teaching. Both questionnaire and case study reports construct a picture of conventional programs and conservative attitudes at all levels. The standard pattern of instruction in most classes includes correcting homework, briefly introducing new material, and beginning the next day's assignment in class. Most teachers talk of emphasizing very traditional curricular objectives: ability to compute in arithmetic and algebra and the development of the general ability to think logically. As Stake reported, teachers saw themselves in a serious, not very exciting business, wishing that times would change for the better but confident they were doing about as well as could be done (Stake & Easley, 1978).

For many teachers, supervisors, and curriculum developers the picture of school mathematics assembled by the NSF Status Surveys might seem overly critical and pessimistic. The national character of mathematics education is certainly more complex than some average of common practices, and it is easy to conclude that the case studies report teachers in "other schools." However, one of the most striking features of the studies is the sharp disparity between views of professional leaders and views of classroom teachers. The studies have provided a needed, if discouraging, view of classroom reality that those who would change school mathematics must deal with (Fey, 1979a, 1979b). In reflecting on the twenty-year "new math" experience, Suydam and Osborne (1977) made the very telling point that change in mathematics education

is a much more complex phenomenon than the builders of new programs naively imagined.

The lessons from status surveys and reflection on change processes during the past twenty-five years have not been lost on the profession. Looking ahead to an agenda for the next decade, the National Council of Teachers of Mathematics first conducted an extensive survey of the preferences and priorities held by various groups concerned with school mathematics. The Priorities in School Mathematics project (PRISM) (1981) asked elementary, secondary, junior college, and college teachers, supervisors, principals, teacher educators, school board presidents, and PTA presidents their views on projected curricular and instructional changes in mathematics. The aim was to help predict the types of change that might be readily accepted and those that would meet substantial resistance. Among hundreds of findings, the PRISM staff found strong resistance to permitting use of calculators before students have mastered computational skills with paper and pencil algorithms. However, there was broad support for inclusion of computer literacy goals in the mathematics curriculum.

The PRISM Project data, the information from the NSF status surveys, data from National Assessment, and insights from policy analyses like the NACOME report have all begun to provide the important background information on which plans for more effective research, development, and implementation can be based. It remains to be seen whether resources for this kind of background descriptive study will be regularly available.

Research. Research contributions to mathematics education traditionally have come from three main lines of investigation. First, the specialists in mathematics teaching and learning, those who prepare teachers and develop curricula, have taken a practitioner-oriented approach in searching for new and better ways to teach their subject. They have addressed questions like

- Which instructional methods are more effective: Discovery or expository? Inductive or deductive? Laboratory or traditional? Individualized or small group?
- Does training in problem-solving strategies improve student performance on word problems?
- What teacher knowledge and training is necessary for successful teaching of mathematics?
- Which of several competing curricula give best results?

A common type of methods-comparison study is motivated by an investigator's hunch, based on classroom teaching experience, that some alternative to "conventional" instruction will yield better student achievement or attitudes. Until recently, such studies (most done as doctoral dissertations) have suffered from problems of small sample size, lack of control in sample selection or administration of treatments, investigator bias, limited conceptions of appropriate criterion measures, and lack of theoretical basis. Not surprisingly, the results are frequently inconclusive or unconvincing (Fey, 1969); however, as will be shown later, there has been marked improvement in the quality of such research.

The mathematics educators' interest in finding improved classroom teaching, teacher preparation, and curricula has been complemented by generic research on each of those questions. As a major school subject, mathematics has been involved in studies of teaching like the interaction analysis work of Flanders (1970), the studies of teacher characteristics like those of Ryans (1960) or Cooney (1980), or analyses of curriculum development like that of Walker and Schaffarzick (1974). Until recently, this work has not had remarkable payoff or influence in school mathematics. But again, it has led to subsequent lines of research that show promise.

The third major contribution to research in mathematics education has come from psychology. Those psychologists with principal interest in human learning have used mathematical tasks in studies of knowledge acquisition, memory, and transfer. They have proposed theories of development explaining evolution of perceptual and reasoning abilities and special links between mathematics and critical affective variables. The results from many of these investigations have been interpreted for school practice by the psychologists themselves and by mathematics educators who have followed the work closely. Between 1900 and 1930 the teaching of mathematics was noticeably influenced by Thorndike's *The Psychology of Arithmetic* (1922) and *The Psychology of Algebra* (1923); Brownell's studies of meaning in arithmetic (1947) and the structuralism of Piaget (1952) and Bruner (1960) laid important groundwork for "new math" curricular thrusts; and Gagné's neobehaviorism (Gagné et al., 1962) provided psychological rationale for individualized instruction and school accountability initiatives. Psychologists have played a major role in the continuing controversy over discovery learning, and contemporary research on teaching and learning of mathematics is guided by information-processing models generated within psychology. Although there is probably substantial error in each side's understanding of what the other is about, the interaction of psychology and mathematics has been, and promises to continue to be, active and productive.

The business of mathematics education in school is an extremely complex enterprise, influencing by interaction of countless learner, instructional, and content variables. Studies that attempt to isolate individual factors for experimentation are routinely ignored by practitioners who judge them irrelevant amid the complexities of classrooms in action. Having admitted this serious limitation, we may partition the following state-of-the-art review and projection of important research issues into three discussions: (1) learner aptitudes and their development, (2) the teaching and learning of specific types of mathematical content, and (3) curriculum and instruction.

Development of mathematical ability. At the age of 21, Isaac Newton formulated the bases of differential and integral calculus. At 16, C. F. Gauss contributed to the founding of non-Euclidean geometry, and at 19, he gave a complete proof for the important law of quadratic reciprocity in number theory. The works of these two mathematical giants are outstanding examples in a remarkable story of intellectual precocity. In a manner matched only in music, mathematical talent seems to emerge at a very early age (Stanley, Keating, & Fox, 1974), suggesting that the mental abilities required to learn and use the subject are very close to primary, innate aptitudes. For this reason, studies of the nature and development of mathematical abilities have attracted the combined attention of mathematics educators and psychologists.

Although students and laymen commonly look on mathematical ability as a unitary phenomenon ("You've either got it or you haven't; I was never good at mathematics, etc."), research reveals a much more complicated picture. When students are grouped homogeneously for mathematics instruction, the most remarkable feature of the groups is how much the members still vary in the patterns of their mathematical abilities and cognitive style. While some young people seem richly gifted with all the talents that contribute to mathematics learning, there are component abilities that develop at different rates and in different ways for each individual. Fennema and Behr (1980) provide an organizing framework for mathematical abilities that serves as a useful guide in reviewing research progress and prospects for this foundation of mathematics programs.

Starting from the definition of aptitude as a characteristic of an individual that increases (or impairs) the probability of success in learning (Cronbach & Snow, 1977), Fennema and Behr sort aptitudes into two main categories: cognitive and affective. The cognitive aptitudes are further subdivided into abilities and information-processing styles. The learning of mathematics is vitally affected by the natural or instructional development of aptitudes in each category.

A cognitive ability can be viewed as the intellectual power to acquire or produce new information from the facts or structure of a situation. For instance, logical reasoning ability allows a learner to deduce new facts from logically related givens; spatial visualization ability permits comparison of shapes presented in different orientations; ability to perceive abstract similarities in symbolic forms such as $s^2 - t^2 = (s - t)(s + t)$ and $9a^2 - 16b^2 = (3a - 4b)(3a + 4b)$ is critical in algebra; creativity and flexibility help problem solvers generate fresh solution approaches to puzzling problems. These and other cognitive abilities involved in mathematical learning and performance have been studied extensively as part of research that tries to explain their natural maturational development, school practices that induce or inhibit development, and the relation between the abilities and school learning. Despite a long line of such research, there are many important open questions. For instance, special attention has recently been focused on the development and training of spatial abilities, concern sparked by some evidence that male and female students have different abilities in this area (Fennema & Behr, 1980). There is evidence that full logical reasoning ability develops much later than supposed, but the reasons for this pattern of late development are not clear (Sowder, 1980). After a period of limited interest in creativity, the recent concern for problem solving in mathematics seems to have sparked new concern for the nature and nurture of mathematical inventiveness.

The long-standing interest in cognitive abilities and their influence on mathematical productivity has recently extended to cognitive style, the personal preferences for various information-processing modes. Research in psychology and mathematics education has identified several dimensions of processing style that seem related to performance in mathematics. Such processing preferences as visual or verbal imagery, reflective or impulsive problem solving, convergent or divergent thinking, and field dependence or independence have been studied in relation to mathematics learning and teaching. While cognitive abilities are measured from low to high, with high generally advantageous, individual cognitive style dimensions do not have the same low-high connotation: the style that is useful in one type of task might yield to its opposite in another. The contributions of maturation and experience to formation of cognitive style preferences and abilities are just beginning to be understood. The field independence-dependence pair has received most attention in mathematics education research. It seems logical that attention to structure and ability to look at problems from a fresh viewpoint should be related to success in mathematics. There have been consistent positive correlations between field independence and mathematical achievement. However, the availability of an established instrument (Witkin et al., 1977) for measuring the elusive cognitive style has undoubtedly also contributed to interest in field dependence-independence.

The past ten years have seen growth of an equally active and sophisticated interest in affective aptitudes related to mathematics. Despite the plausible connection between enjoyment and success in mathematics, the first instruments to measure attitudes toward mathematics did not appear until very recently (Aiken & Dreger, 1961; Dutton, 1954). Early research revealed a modest correlation between scores on the like-dislike scales and mathematical achievement, but over the past fifteen years several important studies have contributed valuable insight and measurement tools to the field. Swafford (1981) observed that research on affective factors in mathematics learning now considers attitude to be a multidimensional variable. "Subscales include enjoyment, usefulness, confidence, anxiety, motivation, difficulty, perceived nature of mathematics, and attitudes toward success to name a few" (p. 6).

The findings emerging from this more sophisticated approach to attitude assessment (Carpenter et al., 1980c; Kulm, 1980; Swafford, 1981) lead to five conclusions:

1. Attitudes toward mathematics as a school subject peak in early adolescence and decline through high school.
2. Neither the effects of teachers' attitudes on students' attitudes nor the connection between student attitudes and achievement is as easy to confirm as one might expect.
3. There are generally no sex-related differences related to the enjoyment of mathematics. There has been some evidence that males are more self-confident, view mathematics as more useful, and tend to stereotype mathematics as a male domain, but most recent data suggest that there are changing patterns in this view.
4. Positive attitudes toward mathematics and the perceived usefulness of mathematics are highly correlated with mathematics course participation.
5. Students have very different reactions to different facets of mathematics.

The finding on attitudes and course participation is of particular importance for the recent efforts to increase participation of women and minorities in mathematics and its related disciplines.

The theoretical paradigm that has guided much research on mathematical abilities and attitudes is the factor-analytic approach of American psychology that seeks generic description of mental abilities. The past decade has brought active investigation of different models for mathematical ability and the acquisition of mathematical knowledge. For instance, Piaget's work suggested patterns in the evolution of the ability to conserve mathematical properties under mental transformation of situations, but it also proposed a more holistic view of knowledge and mental functioning than the factorial approach.

The work of an active group of Soviet psychologists has also focused on abilities needed in doing mathematical thought. Krutetskii (1976) argues that the information-processing abilities and styles of capable mathematics students can be described in three closely related categories:

1. Obtaining information by grasping the formal structures of a problem;
2. Processing information by logical thought involving quantitative and spatial relationships expressed by symbolic systems; generalization of relations and operations; curtailment of reasoning to key problem elements; flexibility; striving for simplicity, economy, and rationality of solutions; and reversibility of thought;
3. Mathematical memory, characterized by memory of relationships, schemes of argument, and methods of problem solving.

Krutetskii's work has suggested, among other results, that students with mathematical talent commonly forget the particular facts of a situation as soon as they are unneeded, but they retain the structure of a problem and its solution almost indefinitely. Furthermore, the operation of the various forms of reasoning is often so rapid and subconscious among these talented students that they arrive at correct results without recalling the thought processes or arguments used to reach the conclusions. The methods and the findings of Soviet psychomathematics research have stimulated follow-up studies by a number of Western mathematics educators (Silver, 1981).

The identification and measurement of mathematical abilities, information-processing styles, and attitudes contribute stimulating questions and intriguing information to the broader study of human learning. The challenge to determine patterns and mechanisms in development of those aptitudes has had an even greater impact on research in mathematics education and developmental psychology. American mathematics educators discovered Piaget and his work during the 1960s. Sensing that his findings had important implications for teaching mathematical concepts and methods, they quickly initiated tests of the Piagetian theory. Early results from this work confirmed the predicted patterns of performance on conservation of number, area, and volume tasks, and the theory of developmental stages gained wide attention among teacher educators, curriculum developers, and teachers. It appeared that mathematics education had a theory of development that indicated essential stages of progress for every child, gave rough chronological boundaries for those stages, suggested the limitations of what could be taught successfully to students in each stage, and even gave explanation of the mental processes by which these abilities developed. However, as research in mathematics education has probed beyond replication of the basic Piagetian experiments, the situation has become more complex.

One of the most difficult tasks in building a theory of cognitive development is separating the effects of maturation and experiences both in and outside of school. As Carpenter (1980) noted, mathematics educators were quick to challenge the age and sequence patterns suggested by Piaget's theory. Dozens of training studies attempted to accelerate the pace of development ahead of the time schedule which Genevan research had found. A large number of these studies were successful, raising questions about the extent to which cognitive development followed some inflexible internal biological clock. Other research (Brainerd, 1973) challenged Piaget's hypotheses about the sequence in which cognitive abilities and mathematical concepts naturally emerge. Most recently, Hiebert (1981) argued that Piagetian abilities like conservation are apparently not required for learning most mathematical skills.

In response to these challenges of the Piagetian hypotheses, it seems fair to say that Piaget never really claimed to have found a strict linear sequence of development or that development was impervious to influence by experience. In fact, he argued that cognitive structures are built up holistically and that the production mechanisms— assimilation and accommodation—are stimulated in im-

portant ways by the social-cognitive interactions of the learner. If students who are not "conservers" are still able to learn basic measurement skills in mathematics, it might still be true that their knowledge is more shallow and less useful in creative problem solving than that of students who possess the underlying cognitive abilities that appear logically prerequisite for learning measurement in a thorough way.

The early hopes that Piaget's ideas would provide a comprehensive developmental framework for curricular and instructional practice in school mathematics have given way to realization that mathematics educators must look for more complex connections between development and the learning demands of specific mathematical topics. Carpenter (1980) set the agenda as follows: "What is essential is the construction of good measures of children's thinking and the identification of specific relationships between performance on those measures and the learning of particular mathematical concepts. Whether these measures fall into an ordinal scale is not critical. It is important, however, that the measures of children's thinking predict with some accuracy children's ability to learn specific mathematical concepts and skills" (p. 191). There has been active work on this program with basic number concepts and with measurement. However, the critical stage of formal operations, that which underlies so much of secondary school and college mathematics, has been explored only tentatively. The Van Hieles (Hoffer, 1981) have proposed a developmental sequence in learning geometry, and recent information-processing studies of algebra learning (Carry, Lewis, & Bernard, 1980) offer some promise of similar theories for that domain. At the present time, developmental theories offer useful insights into certain specific aspects of mathematics learning (e.g., number and measurement), but they do not offer comprehensive guidelines for the selection, sequence, or instructional presentation of most mathematical ideas.

The Piagetian approach to cognitive development has dominated the attention of recent research in mathematics education (Carpenter, 1980). It clearly addresses concepts seen to be logically fundamental to mathematics, and it explains patterns and mechanisms of development that match the observations of experienced teachers. However, there are critics who argue that this approach is essentially pessimistic, searching for explanations of why children seem unable to learn and offering teachers excuses for not teaching various ideas. The Soviet approach, by contrast, assumes that cognitive development and school learning are linked in fundamental ways. Noting many of the same conceptual misunderstandings the Piagetians find, the Soviets attribute the errors to faulty school experiences and work very hard to find the instructional activities that will clear the way to proper understanding. They distinguish between spontaneous and scientific concepts, the latter being a product of direct instruction from adults, and propose that the interplay between the two types is critical. The formal structure of scientific concepts is seen to be essential in organizing a child's spontaneous concepts. Thus, organized school instruction plays a vital role in the course of development (Carpenter, 1980, pp. 178–180).

The Piagetian and Soviet paradigms for developmental theory are only two competitors in an important and busy research arena. Recent research in neurobiology shows promise of explaining growth of memory ability, and the hemispheric-specialization theories seem related to cognitive processing styles essential in mathematics. At the higher cognitive levels, Perry's scheme (1970) has been conjectured to influence mathematics learning and the decision making of teachers (Davidson, 1978). Whichever approach to cognitive development one finds most promising, there are unanswered questions with important implications for design of effective school mathematics programs.

Organizing concepts. In organizing school mathematics curricula, teachers commonly group topics into fields such as arithmetic, algebra, geometry, and calculus. There has been research focused on the special problems of teaching each of these curriculum topic areas. However, topics in these separate fields often present similar structures as learning tasks. Consider the following list of typical mathematics problems:

- Compute $235 + 461$.
- Construct the midpoint of segment $\overline{AB}$.
- Define "prime number."
- Is $3x + 5 = 7$ a linear equation?
- Does $a(b + c) = ab + a$ hold true for all a, b, c?
- In a right triangle, how are the hypotenuse and the legs related?
- Prove that the base angles of an isosceles triangle are congruent.
- Find the rectangle of maximum area and perimeter 10 meters.

The first two items call for student performance of a routine skill that teachers expect to be available for efficient, accurate use without much thought. The next two items ask students to state or apply conditions for use of a mathematical term, to identify instances of a concept. The third pair of items probe principles relating algebraic operations and properties of geometric shapes: relations between + and × and between length and angle measure, respectively. The last two items call for construction of solutions to nonroutine problems. Since school mathematics, in every content area, involves learning of skills, concepts, principles, and problem solving, there have been major lines of research addressing the special conditions that influence each type of learning (Resnick & Ford, 1980).

Computational skills. Student abilities to add, subtract, multiply, and divide numbers or to manipulate algebraic expressions have long been central goals of school mathematics instruction. Research on teaching and learn-

ing of mathematical skills has been concentrated on the skills of arithmetic, in which the studies can be divided roughly into those that deal with basic facts and those that deal with the computational algorithms by which basic facts are applied to more complex calculations. Suydam and Dessart (1980) have analyzed the research in this area recently and found, despite many studies, more important questions than useful results. On the learning of facts, the basic questions seem to be (1) What are the relative difficulties of various specific facts and operations? (2) What sequence and balance of rote and meaningful instruction lead to best short-term or long-term learning? (3) What practice or drill pattern leads to greatest retention, and what strategies do students naturally use to retain facts? (4) How does the learning of facts for one operation enhance or interfere with that of the other operations? These same issues have been explored with respect to the learning of algorithms, with several important further considerations: (1) What balance of concrete and symbolic experience is optimal in building algorithmic skill, and how is the transition from concrete to abstract formulation best handled? (2) Which of the several available formal algorithms seems most efficient and easiest to teach? (3) What are the implications of hand calculators for arithmetic skill curricula and instruction?

Research on these questions falls into roughly three periods of emphasis. For the first third of this century, theory of arithmetic instruction was dominated by Thorndike's S-R approach to learning and research (Thorndike, 1932). Studies concentrated on determining which basic facts were most difficult and which patterns of drill and practice were most effective in fixing algorithmic behavior. The landmark work of Brownell (1947) shifted the focus of arithmetic research by suggesting that meaning and understanding are essential factors, even in the learning of skills. This view, joined by Piagetian-inspired interest in concrete bases for number learning, set the agenda for research on skills over the past twenty to thirty years. There is still a substantial interest in children's arithmetic errors (Ashlock, 1976) and a recently formed Research Council for Diagnostic and Prescriptive Mathematics. However, those research thrusts look at skills embedded in the full context of mathematical knowledge—not as isolated, rote-trained behaviors. The third major phase in arithmetic skill research lies largely in the future, as electronic calculators become universally available for performance of arithmetic. This new technological environment raises fundamental questions about what skills are still important and how the technology can be used to assist in skill teaching (Esty & Payne, 1977). Early results suggest that free classroom use of calculators need not impair development of computational skills and might enhance the problem-solving strategies of elementary school students (Shumway et al. 1981; Suydam, 1979). Concern about which skills are essential for the curriculum has prompted several groups to study the ways that arithmetic is used in natural settings (Lave, 1981). The research on teaching and learning of arithmetic skills is treated in more detail elsewhere in this volume.

The influence of computing technology has stimulated an equally vital research interest in the learning of algebra skills. Secondary mathematics teachers have long realized that algebra students seem prone, despite the most careful instruction and forceful admonition, to make particular kinds of errors in manipulating expressions. Teachers too often see

$$\frac{x+2}{x+3} = \frac{2}{3}$$

or

$$5(x+y) = 5x + y$$

or

$$(x+y)^2 = x^2 + y^2$$

and a number of other common errors. The prescribed treatment for these mistakes is usually more practice or some clever mnemonic advice. However, recent research is looking more deeply at the underlying information-processing strategies that lead students to successful or flawed performance (Carry, Lewis, & Bernard, 1980; Davis, Jockusch, & McKnight, 1978; Küchemann, 1978). It is too early to determine the potential payoff from this line of research, but it represents the first basic psychological analysis of problems that have previously been approached by alternative curricular or instructional treatments generated from the intuition of teachers.

As an overall summary of research on skill learning in school mathematics, it seems well established that effective skill development cannot be separated from conceptual understanding or its uses in problem solving. There is still a very strong tradition supporting skill development in arithmetic and algebra as central goals of the elementary and secondary curriculum, but the level and type of skilled behavior expected from school graduates of 1990 are likely to be very different from those of today.

Concepts and principles. The conceptual emphasis of new curricula during the 1960s and the concurrent psychological interest in concept learning have stimulated several lines of research in mathematical concept and principle learning. As Sowder (1980) noted, the term "concept" is used by teachers in a wide variety of ways, often with very ambiguous meaning. Psychologists seem to have more clarity and agreement about what is and what is not a concept, and there have been attempts to translate results of their research into guidelines for classroom instruction (Clark, 1971). Unfortunately, the concepts of central importance in mathematics are far more complex than those addressed in the psychological research. While it is possible simply to sort mathematical objects into conceptual categories such as functions-nonfunctions, proofs-nonproofs, equations-nonequations, this simple classification is hardly sufficient evidence to say that a student "knows" a concept in useful ways.

Over the past decade research on concept and principle learning in mathematics has evolved from an approach guided by work in psychology to one equally influenced by the special nature of mathematical subject matter and the classroom settings where those ideas are to be taught and learned. Early work explored attainment of simple concepts in carefully controlled experimental situations. The subjects were given sequences of examples and nonexamples of a concept until they correctly identified the critical criteria (Clark, 1971). The objectives of these studies included understanding the effects of task variables (content, number of attributes, logical structure), subject variables (age, intelligence), and treatment variables (sequence and number of examples, presentation format). Concept research today tackles more complex topics like proportion or function or limit (Taback, 1975; Thomas, 1975). The criterion for attainment of a concept is no longer simply ability to sort objects into example and nonexample classes correctly, but higher levels of understanding such as stating a definition, generating new examples and nonexamples, generalizing to broader classes of similar objects, and using the concept in problem-solving situations. The treatment variables of interest include pragmatic instructional factors like the role of advance organizers or objectives, strategies for introducing names for concepts, review procedures, and sequence or pacing of examples and definitions (Sowder, 1980).

The most useful results of this research in mathematical concepts learning have been findings on the effects of examples and nonexamples. Shumway (1974, 1977) demonstrated the importance of negative examples in teaching mathematical concepts, and several others have indicated the importance of "rational sets" of examples and nonexamples in developing full learning of mathematical ideas. They have shown, for instance, that students who readily recognize perpendicular lines in horizontal-vertical orientation must also see other examples before the concept of perpendicularity is correctly attained (Sowder, 1980). Henderson (1976) and his colleagues have extended this investigation of example presentation to studies of classroom move sequences in concept teaching. They have sought guidelines about the proper mix of example, nonexample, and definition moves in teaching various types of concepts.

Despite the central importance of principle learning in mathematics, there has been very little research seeking guidelines for effective teaching of principles. The past decade has seen notable progress in clarifying terminology, setting criteria for achievement, and organizing the variables likely to be of fundamental influence. However, results of use in teaching are sparse.

Problem solving. In 1969 Kilpatrick summarized the status of problem-solving research: "The preeminence of increased problem-solving ability as a goal of mathematics instruction has long been admitted; but like the weather, problem-solving has been more talked about than predicted, controlled, or understood. . . . Problem solving is not now being investigated systematically by mathematics educators. Few studies build on previous research; few studies have an explicit theoretical rationale" (p. 523). While Kilpatrick's appraisal might have been applied to nearly every area of mathematics education research in 1969, his own subsequent work has had major influence in changing the situation with respect to problem solving.

Despite the obvious importance of problem solving, students find "story problems" and mathematical puzzles very difficult; teachers experience frustration in teaching problem solving, and thus they frequently give it less attention than reason suggests. Before Kilpatrick's review, most research on mathematical problem solving was doctoral theses searching for more effective classroom methods of teaching. The treatments in these studies and much of the accepted wisdom of the profession were based on the intuitions of successful teachers and mathematicians who reflected on their own mental activity in problem solving. The criterion of success was usually problem-solving production: could the experimental group subjects solve more problems than those in a control group?

Kilpatrick's thesis (1968)—and the concurrent emergence of the psychology of artificial intelligence and information-processing—redirected the focus and methodology of research on mathematical problem solving. Polya (1957), a distinguished research mathematician and university teacher, had earlier outlined a general theory of key stages in problem solving, including a variety of specific strategies or heuristics that might be useful in each stage. Kilpatrick started from this framework, but instead of focusing solely on the products of problem solving, he studied the mental processes that students used along the way to solutions or failures. Furthermore, he obtained his data by individual interviews with students who were asked to think out loud. This emphasis on process, rather than product, and on clinical interview research methods, has had enormous influence on problem-solving research over the past decade.

This research has largely abandoned the search for a simple best method of teaching problem solving, in favor of more basic studies of component variables in the complex process. As a consequence, recent work contains small steps of progress, rather than major breakthroughs. Investigation is proceeding on several classes of variables: (1) "task variables" are factors that make problems difficult or easy, such as content, format, context, or logical structure; (2) "subject variables" that affect problem-solving achievement include previous knowledge, cognitive style, and attitudes; (3) "instructional variables" characterize the school experiences that are intended to develop problem-solving skill. An active working group has made progress identifying problem difficulty factors and the ways that problem structural features influence student processes in search of solutions (Goldin & McClintock, 1979). The Soviet research described earlier has also contributed to understanding the cognitive processes of successful problem solvers (Krutetskii, 1976). And a number of coordi-

nated studies have given promise that problem-solving heuristics can be taught successfully (Lester, 1980; Schoenfeld, 1979). Since the National Council of Teachers of Mathematics has made problem solving the top curricular priority of the 1980s, continued research interest in this area seems certain.

Curriculum and instruction. The design of a complete mathematics program for any class, school, or system involves complex planning and decisions regarding content, instructional approach, and evaluation procedures. As a curriculum is developed and implemented, information about learner aptitudes, background knowledge, and educational goals must be balanced with principles of learning and teaching and with the structure of subject matter to be learned. During the 1960s, a golden age for curricular and instructional innovation in mathematics, program development was guided by a pragmatic blend of expert opinion and informal trial-and-error experimentation. Mathematicians gave their opinions on appropriate content for school programs, and gifted teachers sold their ideas through a combination of demonstrations and persuasive argument.

As this first generation of innovative programs met critical resistance, the 1970s brought a greater research emphasis to curricular and instructional design in mathematics. Tradition and the opinions of professional advisory groups still are the dominant factors in choice of content for curricula. However, there are beginnings of efforts to validate those selections empirically. Several projects have analyzed the ways that mathematics is used in other academic disciplines. The functional mathematics programs of many state and local school systems have been accompanied by similar surveys of mathematics in use; some research has given surprising evidence of different school and nonschool modes of mathematical thought (Lave, 1981). The Priorities in School Mathematics project (1981), published by the NCTM, made an effort to assemble comprehensive profiles of curricular priorities held by various interest groups.

Once the topics of a curriculum have been chosen, the major challenge is organizing the topics into an instructional sequence, with some scheme for pacing student progress through the course. The dominant paradigm for structuring content in most "new math" programs was the logical order of mathematics. Bruner (1960) set the agenda for that era by arguing: "We begin with the hypothesis that any subject can be taught effectively in some intellectually honest form to any child at any stage of development. . . . [There is a need to rewrite] the basic subjects and their teaching materials in such a way that the pervading ideas and attitudes relating to them are given a central role" (pp. 33, 18). For no subject in the school curriculum was this emphasis on structure better suited than mathematics. The proposals gained wide support from gifted teachers and mathematicians—as well as from psychologists, who suggested that the sequence of psychological development seemed to follow the axiomatic structure of the subject more closely than the historical development of a field (Bruner, 1960).

The validity of these views about curriculum content and sequence has been hotly debated during the past decade. There is mixed evidence of the effectiveness of programs that tried to follow the theory. Some critics have pointed out that mathematics does not have a single, linear structure; different choices of axioms lead logically to the same facts. Others have argued that mathematical ideas have overlapping, but not identical, logical and psychological structures and that instructional improvement depends on better match of the two (Lesh, 1976).

During the 1970s several major curriculum development and research projects have explored the issues of content and psychological structure. At the Pittsburgh Learning Research and Development Center, the Individually Prescribed Instruction (IPI) program applied the principles of behaviorist learning theory (specific objectives, hierarchies, progress toward mastery) to elementary school mathematics. While evaluators found that students progressed through the objectives at far different rates, there were few overall advantages for this carefully constructed instructional system over more conventional approaches (Fey, 1980). The various tests of individualized systems for delivery of mathematics instruction have not given strong support to this alternative approach (Miller, 1976; Schoen, 1976). The main individualized factor has been the pace of student progress through the curriculum, but the concomitant dependence on student self-study has been challenged severely by studies suggesting that even successful students develop fundamentally flawed ideas about mathematics (Erlwanger, 1973). The collection of discouraging results and traditional resistance to change in schools have led to diminished interest in this way of individualizing mathematics instruction, despite the great promise early in the 1970s.

At the Wisconsin Research and Development Center, a program called Developing Mathematical Processes stressed extensive use of manipulative materials in patient construction of student understanding at the elementary level. In some sense this emphasis was an exploration of implications from Piaget's theory regarding concrete operational thinking of students in the elementary grade years. The Comprehensive School Mathematics Project (CSMP), as yet another regional educational laboratory, produced a third major option in elementary curricula. The CSMP style emphasized structure of mathematical ideas presented through a variety of clever pedagogical techniques, probably closest of the three efforts to Bruner's original proposal. The experiences of these research-and-development activities have not given evidence in favor of any single approach to curriculum structure, but they have enriched the range of options and revealed something of the strengths and weaknesses in each position.

Though ideal instruction has been characterized by a variety of models, from Socratic dialogue to scholar and teacher at either end of a log, the predominant pattern

in classroom teaching of mathematics has always been more pedestrian. While the major development projects experimented with content and global organization of school mathematics, there has been an active interest in alternative approaches in the day-to-day format of classroom instruction. Mathematics educators have explored the potential of discovery teaching versus expository teaching, using advance organizers and postorganizers for instruction, adjusting teaching approaches to capitalize on aptitude-treatment interactions, and various instructional media. The results have seldom been unequivocal or consistent from one study to the next, but several findings stand out, indicating fundamental problems for the field.

For instance, Worthen (1967) explored one facet of the discovery-expository teaching controversy in elementary mathematics, finding that trends favored expository teaching for immediate recall and discovery teaching on retention and transfer. Olander and Robertson (1973) confirmed this pattern but found an interaction between method and student prior knowledge or ability: weaker students seemed to benefit from expository teaching and stronger students from discovery. The special value of these studies is the suggestion that short-term and long-term learning outcomes are influenced by different aspects of instruction and that adequate assessment of instruction requires multiple criteria. The issue is of central concern to those who worry about the impact of accountability-induced trends toward more frequent testing in mathematics. To these critics it seems entirely possible that instructional approaches that are demonstrably effective for short-run gains are far less effective when measured by important long-term goals and that pressure for immediate measurable results distorts curriculum priorities. The recent decline of problem-solving performance has been widely attributed to such overemphasis on expository, show-and-tell and drill, methods and neglect of challenging problem-solving activities.

In another direction, research based in mathematics education has tested Ausubel's (1963) theories about meaningful verbal learning. A number of studies of the advance organizer hypothesis have failed to yield support for such preinstructional aids. Furthermore, Romberg and Wilson (1973) found that presentation of postorganizers might have a negative effect on learners, perhaps conflicting with the conceptualization of knowledge the learners work out for themselves. These results, combined with some work on programmed instruction in which students successfully learned from a program presented in reverse of "logical" order, underscore again the fundamental importance of student internal organization of mathematical ideas. They suggest that the knowledge structures built up by students might be very different from what most teachers imagine they are conveying.

There have been several tests in mathematics of Cronbach and Snow's (1977) ideas about aptitude-treatment interaction (ATI) effects in instruction. The results have not been encouraging, but an optimist could discount this finding as another instance of a promising instructional idea that makes no significant impact in mathematics. The learning of mathematics seems to be driven so strongly by innate mental abilities, the background of previously acquired knowledge, and the internal structure of the ideas themselves that few short-term or moderate alterations in the teaching approach have any noticeable impact on student achievement. Most ATI studies in mathematics have used relatively short treatments, often administered in the artificial environment of programmed instructional materials. Thus, it should probably not be surprising that the treatment variations are overwhelmed by background factors.

The most notable exception to the pattern of no significant differences in instructional research has been recent process-product studies of classroom teaching in mathematics. As comparisons of novel and conventional methods of instruction repeatedly came up empty, research attention refocused on the specific classroom interactions that occur in teaching. The first objective was to characterize and develop procedures for describing moves that teachers and students can or do make (Fey, 1970; Smith & Meux, 1963). Next, research sought patterns of interaction that characterize effective or ineffective classes. Several studies (Evertson, Emmer, & Brophy, 1980; Good and Grouws, 1977) have been able to distinguish such patterns in elementary and junior high school mathematics classes. Good and Grouws have applied those findings in experimental studies that show promising results (Good, 1981). The pattern they found effective in elementary grades was task-focused teaching that included daily review, careful attention to development of meaning and understanding, closely monitored seatwork, and regular homework assignments. While this pattern hardly seems novel, Good and Grouws found that many of their suggestions were not regular practice in elementary school classes. Further, the most encouraging aspect of their work is the fact that very modest training induced the desired instructional treatment behavior. The extension of these findings to secondary school mathematics teaching has just begun. With subject matter specialists in those classes, the chances for simple, dramatic improvement seem less likely, but there is reason to be optimistic.

Prospects.   Taken as a whole, recent research on mathematical abilities, learning, and teaching has produced few broad or strikingly new results suggesting major improvement in effectiveness of school mathematics programs. The complexities of human learning, the mathematical subject matter, and the school-societal settings for instruction seem certain to foil any search for such major breakthroughs (Bauersfeld, 1979). However, having largely abandoned the naive quest for simple best methods of teaching mathematics, we might see in the pattern of recent research the promise of solid progress in a number of more specific problem areas. While it seems unrealistic to expect dramatic progress on any one complex issue,

another decade of work like that of the 1970s should yield notable dividends.

Methodology and Related Dimensions.   The recent increase in sophistication of research questions in mathematics education has been accompanied by equally impressive progress in research methods, support for research work, and dissemination of findings. In 1960 a mathematics educator contemplating research was almost certain to plan a quasi-experimental study that, because of lack of available financial support, would probably face limitations of scale that would vitiate the usefulness of any findings. Once the study was complete, there would be few colleagues actively interested in and critically analyzing the results and limited journal space for publication to even a nontechnical audience of other mathematics educators. In 1981 the situation is remarkably different and better. A researcher today can choose from a variety of accepted research techniques, seek support from several interested funding sources, and report results to several regular professional meetings or in dozens of research journals devoted to mathematics education.

Methodology.   Each recent development in research methodology has been stimulated by key investigators or studies. When the School Mathematics Study Group (SMSG) planned its longitudinal study of mathematical abilities (NLSMA) and the IEA its international study, the complexity of hypotheses and data collection demanded statistical techniques far beyond those typical of earlier research. The models produced by these projects and the graduate students trained by participation in them led to increasing use of complex research designs and the sophisticated multivariate statistical techniques required for data analysis. At the same time, strong interest in Piagetian studies of cognitive development encouraged acceptance of clinical interview research methods, and the Soviet teaching experiments gained respect and application in study of abilities and problem solving. There have been fewer but notable applications of case study, ethnographic, and other field research methods in mathematics education. Each new methodology has been shown to be effective in certain research situations. The clinical study of Erlwanger (1973), the teaching experiment of Kantowski (1977), the case studies of Stake and Easley (1978), and the ethnographic work of Rossi-Becker (1981) each produced useful insights into questions of basic importance in the field.

The special attraction of more qualitative research approaches is their value in hypothesis generation or theory development. However, they also require research resources more likely to be available to doctoral students who cannot muster large samples or sell major treatment intervention to cautious school systems. It is this very attraction of convenience, however, that holds risk for the innovative methods. Where doctoral students once learned complex experimental designs and then sought questions that could be investigated by the designs they had learned, there is now a similar phenomenon involving clinical interview methods. There is risk that the broadened range of acceptable research tools will produce a maze of fuzzy reports that are not sufficiently objective, replicable, or additive to contribute useful information to the field. Further, one can sense an emerging "antistatistical" bias that would be counterproductive as well. Despite these cautions, experiences of the past decade give promise that outweighs the risks, at the moment.

Research using conventional designs and data-collection techniques has also improved during the past ten years. For instance, the work of Good and Grouws (1977) involved traditional experimental-control group comparisons of instructional treatments. Where previous studies of this type made little effort to assure delivery of well-defined treatments, Good and Grouws checked very carefully (by classroom observation) to see that the experimental treatment features were effected. They chose research situations with care to minimize variation due to irrelevant factors; they made special efforts to control for Hawthorne effect; and they considered carefully the appropriateness of their chosen criterion measures—all problems that have been poorly handled in earlier teaching research in mathematics education.

Overall, the increasing range of acceptable research methods and the sophistication with which these methods are being applied are very encouraging trends in mathematics education research. Further, while the majority of studies in the field have always been doctoral theses of people likely to do little more research, there is now a substantial group of mathematics educators regularly involved in research. These researchers have been supported by major federal funding programs, and they share their ideas in new professional research forums.

Support.   Throughout the 1960s the USOE and NSF supported curriculum development and teacher education with tens of millions of dollars invested each year. The 1970s brought noticeable change toward research as the focus of this financial investment in improving school mathematics. When the National Institute of Education (NIE) was formed it was assigned several ongoing Office of Education curriculum projects in mathematics. Those were elementary-level projects located at the R & D centers and laboratories, thus giving a greater research flavor to the projects than had been typical of earlier "new math" curriculum development. NIE also began support of research on basic problems of teaching and learning with major attention to mathematics.

The NSF support for mathematics teacher education, through the popular in-service institutes, has been sharply reduced. However, through the 1970s NSF continued to support varied development projects and began a program for support of basic research in the learning of mathematics.

There have been several similar themes in the R & D priorities of NIE and NSF. In fact, the two agencies have collaborated on two joint programs for mathematics education. The main problem areas targeted for support have been basic skills, participation of women and minorities, cognitive processes and structure of knowledge, and technology and mathematics education.

In addition to these main themes, both NIE and NSF have supported a variety of other basic and applied research projects in mathematics education. These include research on problem solving, applications of mathematics, the national and international assessments of mathematics achievement (NAEP and IEA), and major status surveys and policy analyses (NACOME and PRISM). This support has been of inestimable importance in developing mathematics education research during the past decade.

Dissemination.   There is now a rich network of outlets for presentation of research findings to the mathematics education profession. The *Journal for Research in Mathematics Education* began publication in 1970 and now publishes five times a year, exclusively devoted to research reports and commentaries in mathematics education. *Investigations in Mathematics Education* publishes critical abstracts of mathematics education research appearing elsewhere. The ERIC center for science, mathematics, and environmental education publishes periodic special monographs on specific research topics, and NIE has sponsored a series to publicize *Research within Reach* (Driscoll, 1979). Numerous other American and foreign journals also publish empirical and theoretical research work of interest to the field, notably the *Journal of Children's Mathematical Behavior, For the Learning of Mathematics,* and *Educational Studies in Mathematics,* all begun within the last ten years.

Among these noteworthy developments in research productivity and dissemination, perhaps the most striking is the growth in research work around the world. Each major Western European country now has a center for research and development in mathematics education: In France the Institutes for Research in Mathematics Teaching (IREMs) provide regional centers, in West Germany the Institut for Didaktiks in Mathematics (IDM) is a leader, and in England the Shell Centre produces major studies on teaching of mathematics. The cross-fertilization of information, research styles, and educational systems that results from the shared work of these international centers has been a major stimulus to the field during the past decade and promises to continue that role in the future.

Conclusions.   Research in mathematics education over the past ten years has been a very active field, increasing in sophistication of methodology and questions asked but short on major findings. In looking to prospects for the future, an optimist can see well-founded promise that we will soon know much more about how students learn mathematical ideas and how those ideas can be effectively taught. However, as an area of systematic careful research, mathematics education is a surprisingly young field dealing with very complex phenomena. Practitioners can expect to profit from modest research findings, but perseverance and patience are essential.

James T. Fey

See also Arithmetic; Curriculum Development and Organization; Mathematical Behavior of Children; Metric Education.

REFERENCES

An Agenda for Action: Recommendations for School Mathematics of the 1980s. Reston, Va.: National Council of Teachers of Mathematics, 1980. (ERIC Document Reproduction Service No. ED 186 265)

Aiken, L. R., Jr., & Dreger, R. M. The effects of attitude on performance in mathematics. *Journal of Educational Psychology,* 1961, *52,* 19–24.

Ashlock, R. B. *Error Patterns in Computation* (2nd ed.). Columbus, Ohio: Merrill, 1976.

Ausubel, D. *The Psychology of Meaningful Verbal Learning.* New York: Grune & Stratton, 1963.

Bauersfeld, H. Research related to the mathematical learning process. In B. Christiansen & H. G. Steiner (Eds.), *New Trends in Mathematics Teaching.* Paris: UNESCO, 1979.

Begle, E. G. Some lessons learned by SMSG. *Mathematics Teacher,* 1973, *66,* 207–214.

Begle, E. G. *Critical Variables in Mathematics Education.* Washington, D.C.: Mathematical Association of America, 1979.

Brainerd, C. J. The origins of number concepts. *Scientific American,* 1973, *228,* 101–109.

Brownell, W. A. The place of meaning in the teaching of arithmetic. *Elementary School Journal,* 1947, *47,* 256–265.

Bruner, J. *The Process of Education.* New York: Random House, Vintage Books, 1960.

Carpenter, T. P. Research in cognitive development. In R. J. Shumway (Ed.), *Research in Mathematics Education.* Reston, Va.: National Council of Teachers of Mathematics, 1980. (ERIC Document Reproduction Service No. ED 187 563)

Carpenter, T. P.; Coburn, T. G.; Reys, R. E.; & Wilson, J. W. Results and implications of the NAEP mathematics assessment: Elementary school. *Arithmetic Teacher,* 1975, *22,* 438–450. (a)

Carpenter, T. P.; Coburn, T. G.; Reys, R. E.; & Wilson, J. W. Results and implications of the NAEP mathematics assessment: Secondary school. *Mathematics Teacher,* 1975, *68,* 453–470. (b)

Carpenter, T. P.; Corbitt, M. K.; Kepner, H.; Lindquist, M. M.; & Reys, R. Results and implications of the second NAEP mathematics assessment: Elementary School. *Arithmetic Teacher,* 1980, *27*(8), 10–12. (a)

Carpenter, T. P.; Corbitt, M. K.; Kepner, H.; Lindquist, M. M.; & Reys, R. E. Results and implications of the second NAEP mathematics assessment: Secondary school. *Mathematics Teacher,* 1980, *73,* 329–338. (b)

Carpenter, T. P.; Corbitt, M. K.; Kepner, H.; Lindquist, M. M.; & Reys, R. Students' affective responses to mathematics: NAEP results for elementary school. *Arithmetic Teacher,* 1980, *28*(1), 34–37, 52–53. (c)

Carpenter, T. P.; Corbitt, M. K.; Kepner, H. S.; Lindquist, M. M.; & Reys, R. E. Students' affective responses to mathematics: Secondary school results from national assessment. *Mathematics Teacher,* 1980, *73,* 531–539. (d)

Carry, L. R.; Lewis, C.; & Bernard, J. E. *Psychology of Equation Solving: An Information Processing Study.* Austin: University of Texas, Department of Curriculum and Instruction, 1980. (ERIC Document Reproduction Service No. ED 186 243)

Clark, D. C. Teaching concepts in the classroom: A set of teaching prescriptions derived from experimental research. *Journal of Educational Psychology,* 1971, *62,* 253–278.

Cooney, T. J. Research on teaching and teacher education. In R. J. Shumway (Ed.), *Research in Mathematics Education.* Reston, Va.: National Council of Teachers of Mathematics, 1980. (ERIC Document Reproduction Service No. ED 187 563)

Cronbach, L. J., & Snow, R. E. *Aptitudes and Instructional Methods.* New York: Irvington, 1977.

Davidson, N. A. *Developmental Instruction in Methods of Teaching Secondary Mathematics.* Paper presented at the meeting of the National Council of Teachers of Mathematics, San Diego, April 1978.

Davis, R. B.; Jockusch, E.; & McKnight, C. Cognitive processes in learning algebra. *Journal of Children's Mathematical Behavior,* 1978, *2*(1), 10–32.

DeVault, M. V., & Weaver, J. F. Forces and issues related to curriculum and instruction, K–6. In P. S. Jones (Ed.), *A History of Mathematics Education in the United States and Canada.* Washington, D.C.: National Council of Teachers of Mathematics, 1970.

Driscoll, M. J. *Research within Reach: Elementary School Mathematics.* St. Louis: CEMREL, 1979.

Dutton, W. H. Measuring attitudes toward arithmetic. *Elementary School Journal,* 1954, *55,* 24–31.

Erlwanger, S. Benny's conception of rules and answers in IPI mathematics. *Journal of Children's Mathematical Behavior,* 1973, *1*(2), 7–26.

Esty, E., & Payne, J. (Eds.). *Report of the Conference on Needed Research and Development on Hand-held Calculators in School Mathematics.* Washington, D.C.: National Institute of Education, and National Science Foundation, 1977.

Evertson, C. M.; Emmer, E. T.; & Brophy, J. E. Predictors of effective teaching in junior high mathematics classrooms. *Journal for Research in Mathematics Education,* 1980, *11,* 167–178.

Fennema, E., & Behr, M. J. Individual differences and the learning of mathematics. In R. J. Shumway (Ed.), *Research in Mathematics Education.* Reston, Va.: National Council of Teachers of Mathematics, 1980. (ERIC Document Reproduction Service No. ED 187 563)

Fey, J. T. Classroom teaching of mathematics. *Review of Educational Research,* 1969, *39,* 535–551.

Fey, J. T. *Patterns of Verbal Communication in Mathematics Classes.* New York: Teachers College Press, 1970.

Fey, J. T. Mathematics teaching today: Perspectives from three national surveys. *Arithmetic Teacher,* 1979, *27*(2), 10–14. (a)

Fey, J. T. Mathematics teaching today: Perspectives from three national surveys. *Mathematics Teacher,* 1979, *72,* 490–504. (b)

Fey, J. T. Mathematics education research on curriculum and instruction. In R. J. Shumway (Ed.), *Research in Mathematics Education.* Reston, Va.: National Council of Teachers of Mathematics, 1980. (ERIC Document Reproduction Service No. ED 187 563)

Fey, J. T., & Sonnabend, T. Trends in school mathematics performance. In G. A. Austin & H. J. Garber (Eds.), *The Rise and Fall of Test Scores.* New York: Academic Press, 1981.

Flanders, N. A. *Analyzing Teacher Behavior.* Reading, Mass.: Addison-Wesley, 1970.

Gagné, R. M.; Mayor, J. R.; Garstens, H. L.; & Paradise, N. E.

Factors in acquiring knowledge of a mathematical skill. *Psychological Monographs: General and Applied,* 1962, *76* (Whole No. 526).

Goldin, G. A., & McClintock, C. E. (Eds.). *Task Variables in Mathematical Problem-solving.* Columbus, Ohio: ERIC/SMEAC, 1979. (ERIC Document Reproduction Service No. ED 178 366)

Good, T. L. *Teacher Effectiveness Research: What Implications for the Classroom?* Paper presented at the meeting of the National Council of Teachers of Mathematics, St. Louis, April 1981.

Good, T., & Grouws, D. Teaching effects: A process-product study in fourth-grade mathematics classrooms. *Journal of Teacher Education,* 1977, *28,* 49–54.

Harnischfeger, A., & Wiley, D. E. *Achievement Test Score Decline: Do We Need to Worry?* St. Louis: CEMREL, 1975. (ERIC Document Reproduction Service No. ED 120 263)

Henderson, K. B. Toward the development of pedagogical theory in mathematics. In T. J. Cooney & D. A. Bradbard (Eds.), *Teaching Strategies: Papers from a Research Workshop.* Columbus, Ohio: ERIC/SMEAC, 1976. (ERIC Document Reproduction Service No. ED 123 132)

Hiebert, J. Cognitive development and learning linear measurement. *Journal for Research in Mathematics Education,* 1981, *12,* 197–211.

Hoffer, A. Geometry is more than proof. *Mathematics Teacher,* 1981, *74,* 11–18.

Husén, T. (Ed.). *International Study of Achievement in Mathematics.* New York: Wiley, 1967.

Kantowski, M. G. Processes involved in mathematical problem-solving. *Journal for Research in Mathematics Education,* 1977, *8,* 163–180.

Kilpatrick, J. Analyzing the solution of word problems in mathematics: An exploratory study (Doctoral dissertation, Stanford University, 1967). *Dissertation Abstracts,* 1968, *28,* 4380A.

Kilpatrick, J. Problem solving in mathematics. *Review of Educational Research,* 1969, *39,* 523–534.

Krutetskii, V. A. *The Psychology of Mathematical Abilities in Schoolchildren.* (J. Kilpatrick & I. Wirszup, Eds.). Chicago: University of Chicago Press, 1976.

Küchemann, D. Children's understanding of numerical variables. *Mathematics in School,* 1978, *7*(4), 23–26.

Kulm, G. Research on mathematics attitude. In R. J. Shumway (Ed.), *Research in Mathematics Education.* Reston, Va.: National Council of Teachers of Mathematics, 1980. (ERIC Document Reproduction Service No. ED 187 563)

Lave, J. *The Mature Practice of Arithmetic Problem Solving in the Daily Lives of Americans.* Unpublished manuscript, University of California at Irvine, 1981.

Lesh, R. An interpretation of advanced organizers. *Journal for Research in Mathematics Education,* 1976, *7,* 69–74.

Lester, F. K. Research on mathematical problem solving. In R. J. Shumway (Ed.), *Research in Mathematics Education.* Reston, Va.: National Council of Teachers of Mathematics, 1980. (ERIC Document Reproduction Service No. ED 187 563)

Miller, R. L. Individualized instruction in mathematics: A review of research. *Mathematics Teacher,* 1976, *69,* 345–351.

National Advisory Committee on Mathematics Education. *Overview and Analysis of School Mathematics, K–12.* Washington, D.C.: Conference Board of the Mathematical Sciences, 1975.

National Council of Supervisors of Mathematics. Position statement on basic skills. *Mathematics Teacher,* 1978, *71,* 147–152.

Olander, H. T., & Robertson, H. C. The effectiveness of discovery and expository methods in the teaching of fourth-grade mathematics. *Journal for Research in Mathematics Education,* 1973, *4,* 33–44.

Osborne, A. R., & Crosswhite, F. J. Forces and issues related to curriculum and instruction, 7–12. In P. S. Jones (Ed.), *A History of Mathematics Education in the United States and Canada.* Washington, D.C.: National Council of Teachers of Mathematics, 1970.

Perry, W. G., Jr. *Forms of Intellectual and Ethical Development in the College Years: A Scheme.* New York: Holt, Rinehart, & Winston, 1970.

Piaget, J. *The Child's Conception of Number.* New York: Humanities Press, 1952.

Polya, G. *How to Solve It* (2nd ed.). New York: Doubleday, 1957.

Price, J.; Kelley, J. L.; & Kelley, J. "New math" implementation: A look inside the classroom. *Journal for Research in Mathematics Education,* 1977, *8,* 323–331.

Priorities in School Mathematics: Executive Summary of the PRISM Project. Reston, Va.: National Council of Teachers of Mathematics, 1981.

Resnick, L. B., & Ford, W. W. *The Psychology of Mathematics for Instruction.* Hillsdale, N.J.: Lawrence Erlbaum Associates, 1980.

Romberg, T., & Wilson, J. W. The effect of an advanced organizer, cognitive set, and post-organizer on the learning and retention of written materials. *Journal for Research in Mathematics Education,* 1973, *4,* 68–75.

Rossi-Becker, J. Differential treatment of females and males in mathematics classes. *Journal for Research in Mathematics Education,* 1981, *12,* 40–53.

Ryans, D. G. *Characteristics of Teachers.* Washington, D.C.: American Council on Education, 1960.

Schoen, H. Self-paced mathematics instruction: How effective has it been? *Arithmetic Teacher,* 1976, *23,* 90–96.

Schoenfeld, A. Explicit heuristic training as a variable in problem-solving performance. *Journal for Research in Mathematics Education,* 1979, *10,* 173–187.

Shumway, R. J. Negative instances in mathematical concept acquisition: Transfer effects between the concepts of commutativity and associativity. *Journal for Research in Mathematics Education,* 1974, *5,* 197–211.

Shumway, R. J. Positive versus positive and negative instances and the acquisition of the concepts of distributivity and homomorphism. *Journal of Structural Learning,* 1977, *4,* 331–348.

Shumway, R. J. (Ed.). *Research in Mathematics Education.* Reston, Va.: National Council of Teachers of Mathematics, 1980.

Shumway, R. J.; White, A. L.; Wheatley, G. H.; Reys, R. E.; Coburn, T. G.; & Schoen, H. L. Initial effect of calculators in elementary school mathematics. *Journal for Research in Mathematics Education,* 1981, *12,* 119–141.

Silver, E. A. Recall of mathematical problem information: Solving related problems. *Journal for Research in Mathematics Education,* 1981, *12,* 54–64.

Smith, B. O., & Meux, M. O. *A Study of the Logic of Teaching.* Urbana: University of Illinois, College of Education, Bureau of Educational Research, 1963.

Sowder, L. K. Concept and principle learning. In R. J. Shumway (Ed.), *Research in Mathematics Education.* Reston, Va.: National Council of Teachers of Mathematics, 1980. (ERIC Document Reproduction Service No. ED 187 563)

Stake, R., & Easley, J. *Case Studies in Science Education.* Washington, D.C.: U.S. Government Printing Office, 1978. (ERIC Document Reproduction Service No. ED 166 058-059)

Stanley, J. C.; Keating, D. P.; & Fox, L. (Eds.). *Mathematical Talent: Discovery, Description, and Development.* Baltimore: Johns Hopkins University Press, 1974.

Suydam, M. N. *Calculators: A Categorized Compilation of References.* Columbus, Ohio: ERIC/SMEAC, 1979. (ERIC Document Reproduction Service No. ED 171 572)

Suydam, M. N., & Dessart, D. J. Skill learning. In R. J. Shumway (Ed.), *Research in Mathematics Education.* Reston, Va.: National Council of Teachers of Mathematics, 1980. (ERIC Document Reproduction Service No. ED 187 563)

Suydam, M. N., & Osborne, A. R. *The Status of Pre-college Science, Mathematics, and Social Science Education, 1955–1975: Mathematics Education.* Washington: U.S. Government Printing Office, 1977.

Swafford, J. O. *Student Attitudes and the Learning and Teaching of Mathematics.* Paper presented at the meeting of the National Council of Teachers of Mathematics, St. Louis, April 1981.

Taback, S. The child's concept of limit. In M. F. Rosskopf (Ed.), *Children's Mathematical Concepts: Six Piagetian Studies in Mathematics Education.* New York: Teachers College Press, 1975.

Thomas, H. L. The concept of function. In M. F. Rosskopf (Ed.), *Children's Mathematical Concepts: Six Piagetian Studies in Mathematics Education.* New York: Teachers College Press, 1975.

Thorndike, E. L. *The Psychology of Arithmetic.* New York: Macmillan, 1922.

Thorndike, E. L. *The Psychology of Algebra.* New York: Macmillan, 1923.

Thorndike, E. L. *The Fundamentals of Learning.* New York: Teachers College Press, 1932.

Walker, D., & Schaffarzick, J. Comparing curricula. *Review of Educational Research,* 1974, *44,* 83–111.

Weiss, I. *Report of the 1977 National Survey of Science, Mathematics, and Social Studies Education.* Washington, D.C.: U.S. Government Printing Office, 1978. (ERIC Document Reproduction Service No. ED 152 565)

Willoughby, S. S. Mathematics. In R. L. Ebel (Ed.), *Encyclopedia of Educational Research* (4th ed.). New York: Macmillan, 1969.

Witkin, H. A.; Moore, C. A.; Goodenough, D. R.; & Cox, P. W. Field-dependent and field-independent cognitive styles and their educational implications. *Review of Educational Research,* 1977, *47,* 1–64.

Worthen, B. R. A comparison of discovery and expository sequencing in elementary mathematics instruction. In M. J. Scandura (Ed.), *Research in Mathematics Education.* Washington: National Council of Teachers of Mathematics, 1967. (ERIC Document Reproduction Service No. ED 035 545)

MEASUREMENT IN EDUCATION

The term "measurement" used in an educational context refers to a collection of processes that provide precise and objective appraisal of outcomes and interactions related to a variety of functions of schools. These functions are usually related to the assessment of student learning outcomes, but may also refer to data describing the operation of classroom-teacher units, schools, or school systems that can be applied to a wide variety of problems and decision-making activities.

There are probably as many different definitions of the term "measurement" as there are measurers. Although qualitatively different, all definitions involve the systematic assignment of numerals to objects, individuals, events, or places. Measurement is more than counting and sorting. It is the comparison of something with a unit or standard or quantity of that same thing, in order to represent the magnitude of the variable being measured. A synonym for measurement might be "quantification," specifically the quantification of properties of objects or stimuli, not the objects or stimuli themselves (Churchman & Ratoosh, 1959; Jones, 1971).

Measurement may take many forms, ranging from the application of very elaborate and complex electronic devices, to paper-and-pencil exams, to rating scales or checklists. A test is a particular form of measurement. Implicit in the current usage of the term is the notion of a formal standardized procedure in which the examinee is aware of being tested for a particular purpose at a specified time. A test might be defined as a systematic method of gathering data for the purpose of making intraunit or interunit comparisons, where the unit may be an individual, a class, a school, or a system. A measurement or a test is, however, only a sample on the basis of which inferences and evaluations are made.

Tests might further be characterized as (1) informal (nonnormed) or standardized (normed); (2) oral or written; (3) mastery (of basic knowledge and skills), survey (of general achievement), or diagnostic (of specific disabilities and deficiencies); (4) speed (in responding to items of approximately equal difficulty) or power (in responding to items of increasing difficulty, with speed deemphasized); and (5) verbal, nonverbal, or performance (requiring manipulation of objects). Many other types of classifications are possible, depending upon the needs and philosophy of the developer or user. Research does not support the superiority of one measurement method. The critical questions to be addressed are those related to the match of the measurement with the purpose.

Uses of Measurement Data.　Most educators agree that measurement and evaluation are integral components of the instructional process. Three primary broad use categories of measurement data use can be defined (Payne, 1974): (1) selection, appraisal, and clarification of educational and instructional objectives; (2) determination and reporting of achievement; and (3) planning, directing, and improving of learning experiences. In the first category a differentiation is made between educational and instructional objectives. Instructional objectives are seen as specifically and directly related to the teaching-learning process, whereas educational objectives are generic in nature and broadly concerned with the outcomes of schooling.

The kinds of outcomes considered important in American schools appear to be ever changing. Two different emphases or trends are currently evident. On the one hand, society appears to be pushing the schools to engage exclusively in a basic skill development orientation. The heated rhetoric about reading and mathematics and minimum competencies attests to this public concern. On the other hand, the schools appear to be assuming many of the educational responsibilities that were historically considered the prerogative of parents and other socializing segments of society. Such areas as sex education, human relations (including marriage), and values, morality, and ethics are now addressed in the schools. These affective concerns require evaluation and pose many methodological measurement problems.

It is perhaps in the understanding of the teaching-learning process that measurement has made its greatest contributions to education (Cook, 1951). In particular, measurement data have been found useful in the diagnosis of learning difficulties and the evaluation of their treatments. The use of broad-band survey batteries, particularly of the achievement variety, has gained both historic and contemporary acceptance in the public schools. These tests are seen as useful in directing curriculum emphasis, providing valuable information for a variety of administrative decisions, stimulating and motivating student learning, and aiding in the academic and vocational guidance of students.

On the contemporary education scene, tests continue to be used in traditional ways. Achievement tests are being applied throughout the grade range, and diagnostic tests in the early grades and in special education settings. Selective tests are being used at institutions of higher education for undergraduate, graduate, and professional school students.

An increasing use of tests is found in the area of program and project evaluation. With "accountability" rampant in education and with virtually all funding agencies, especially at the state and federal levels, requiring documentation of program effectiveness, great numbers of educational and psychological measurements are being made.

Historical Overview of Measurement. The forces that have shaped the current stature of testing and measurement in the United States read like a United Nations roster (Thorndike & Hagen, 1977). DuBois (1970), for example, notes that as early as 1115 B.C., during the Chou dynasty in China, candidates for public office were subjected to formal examinations involving an assessment of such basic skills as archery, horsemanship, arithmetic, writing, and music. The process became decentralized to the district level, and eventually a competitive civil service–type system evolved. Out of this experience came an appreciation for objectivity in scoring, uniformity in testing conditions, and the relevance of the test tasks for the nature of the decision to be made. In addition, the liberal use of oral examination techniques, with the advantage of the diag-

nostic possibilities assessing process as well as product, is still prevalent in education today.

German behavioral scientists also contributed directly and indirectly to the measurement movement. The "brass instruments" period of development in the middle and late 1800s focused concern on physiological measurement. This period of development was characterized by concern for measurement precision and the use of the scientific method to identify characteristics that are true of most individuals.

Whereas German psychologists such as Wundt were interested in "universal characteristics," British scientists such as Darwin and Galton were more concerned with describing those characteristics that differentiated individuals. The effect, for example, of Darwin's *Origin of Species* on psychology and education, apart from biology, may never be fully appreciated. This concern for describing individual differences raised some problems with regard to methods useful in analyzing such data. The statistical tools developed by Sir Ronald Fisher, Karl Pearson, and Charles Spearman all contributed significantly to the quantitative development and refinement of psychometric devices.

In France, Alfred Binet and his colleagues constructed procedures to assess intellectual performance. The appearance in the early 1900s of "intelligence scales" both in France and in the United States, in the form of the Stanford-Binet, served as milestones in the assessment of cognitive development. The Stanford-Binet, with the concepts of mental age and intelligence quotient (IQ), thanks to the efforts of Lewis Terman and Maud Merrill (1937), became a standard against which other group and individual intelligence tests are still measured. Although the IQ has at times proved useful, its developer, the German psychologist Wilhelm Stern, himself urged educators to bury the concept. Even the Russians have made some contributions in the areas of operant conditioning and psychophysics.

All of these multicultural influences coalesced into a force that influenced education in the United States. This country was considered a melting pot and experienced psychometric and edumetric simmerings as early as the mid-1800s. The 154-question survey made in the Boston public schools was among the first recorded instances of curriculum evaluation (Caldwell & Courtis, 1971 [1923]). It covered such basic areas as vocabulary, grammar, science, arithmetic, and geography. The results were less than had been hoped for, and reforms were instituted. An even earlier classic illustration of early mass test administration took place in 1895 and is attributed to the efforts of J. M. Rice (1914), who developed and administered a comprehensive spelling test to more than sixteen thousand students in grades four and eight. Rice developed variations on his spelling test, such as spelling in context (sentences), and added measures of basic arithmetic skills.

Interestingly enough, both World Wars I and II contributed to the development of measurement in the United States. The classification problems posed by hundreds of thousands of military personnel required the creation of new and efficient measuring devices, particularly of the so-called general intellectual aptitude variety. Not only were newer tests being developed, but the availability of a large "captive audience" allowed large quantities of very basic psychometric research to be conducted.

Two major instrument development and data collection efforts are currently having a significant effect on educational practice. The first of these, Project TALENT (Flanagan et al., 1962), involved the longitudinal, cross-national testing of high school students with an extensive battery of aptitude and ability measures. In addition, personal experience, life history, and affective data were gathered. The data base generated by Project TALENT is still being examined, and the extensive follow-up studies are among the most ambitious ever undertaken.

The second major effort is embodied in the National Assessment of Educational Progress (Greenbaum, Garet, & Solomon, 1977). NAEP is a cyclical testing program in which tests in ten areas are alternated annually. Tests in the areas of music, reading, writing, art, citizenship, mathematics, science, social studies, literature, and occupational development are administered to carefully selected samples of individuals at four age levels: 9, 13, 17, and from 26 to 35. Results in the form of item data are reported by age, sex, geographic region, race, type of community, and parents' educational status. Many benefits have been derived from NAEP, not the least of which is the refinement of methodologies for implementing large-scale exercise development and data collection activities. It is hoped that the data have influenced school administrators and federal and state legislators to make rational decisions about the allocation of money for educational programs.

Sources of Information. Many organizations and publications exist to assist the student of educational measurement. Among the organizations are the National Council on Measurement in Education, the Division on Evaluation and Measurement of the American Psychological Association, Division D—Measurement and Research Methodology—of the American Educational Research Association, and the Association for Measurement and Evaluation in Guidance of the American Personnel and Guidance Association. In addition, several federally sponsored agencies and organizations disseminate information about tests and testing—including the Center for the Study of Evaluation located at the University of California at Los Angeles; the Educational Resources and Information Center on Tests, Measurement, and Evaluation located at Educational Testing Service in Princeton, New Jersey; and the Buros Institute of Mental Measurements at the University of Nebraska.

Several high-quality professional periodicals devote all or most of their pages to the reporting of research on measurement or the discussion of testing issues. Among the best known are the *Journal of Educational Measurement, Educational and Psychological Measurement, Applied Psychological Measurement,* and *Measurement and*

Evaluation in Guidance. The major emphasis of these journals is on empirical work related to such basic topics as methods for assessing reliability, validity, and the metric properties of items. In addition, space is devoted to description of the development of new measuring devices, refinements of existing instruments, and examinations of hosts of variables that may influence the applicability of tests. Additionally, current measurement-related reports can be found in such newsletters as *Measurement in Education, Measurement News, National Assessment of Educational Progress Newsletter, ERIC-TM Notes* (Clearinghouse on Tests, Measurement, and Evaluation), and *CAP-TRENDS* (Clearinghouse for Applied Performance Testing).

The educational community is fortunate to have available many excellent instructional texts related to the design, construction, refinement, and application of educational measurements. Among these are books by Ebel (1980, 1979), Mehrens and Lehmann (1978), Noll, Scannell, and Craig (1979), Gronlund (1981), Anastasi (1976), Thorndike and Hagen (1977), and Ahmann and Glock (1980). One of the more definitive reference works on educational measurement is the volume edited by Robert L. Thorndike (1971b). It contains twenty chapters written by the measurement fraternity's leading experts on such topics as test objectives and design, validity, item analysis, reliability, test norms, general item writing, test administration and scoring, and essay items and tests. Test theory is also treated in detail in several texts. Building upon the pioneer writings of Gulliksen (1950) and Guilford (1954), several authors have contributed to our understanding and conceptualizations of mental tests, including Nunnally (1978), Lord and Novick (1968), Allen and Yen (1979), and Thorndike (1981).

The *Mental Measurements Yearbooks,* created by the late Oscar K. Buros, constitute one of the most significant bibliographic and evaluative resources in the history of modern measurement. The eighth yearbook (Buros, 1980) lists 1,184 commercially available tests distributed over fifteen categories. It contains 898 original and 140 excerpted reviews of over 700 different tests and 381 book reviews. The final staggering statistic is that the 1980 yearbook contains a total of 17,481 references on the construction, use, reliability, and validity of specific tests. The overall intent of the editor was not only to provide an encyclopedia of critical evaluations of tests, but also to have a positive effect on the quality of tests being produced and their associated documentation, and positively influence how they are being used. An additionally relevant reference work was developed by a joint committee of measurement experts from several professional organizations. The resulting publication, *Standards for Educational and Psychological Tests* (American Psychological Association, 1974), presents criteria and guidelines for both test developers and users. A recent set of commentaries (Brown, 1980) has helped put the *Standards* in perspective relative to recent knowledge, demands, and developments in educational and psychological testing. A book by Lyman (1978) offers additional aids to understanding test uses.

Contemporary Issues. Educational institutions, from the elementary grades through professional school, tend to reflect changes in society. Social forces from a variety of political, legal, religious, or economic origins generally find manifestations in curriculum reform, modified instructional systems, professional training programs, or school assessment practices. Many of these forces are at work in today's schools. Such factors as civil rights, the feminist movement, inflation, and consumer awareness impinge on social practice. Most of the issues to be addressed in the following section are of great concern to educational measurers, as they can be found, in varying degrees, in all our schools (Mehrens, 1975; Tyler & Wolf, 1974).

Assessing affective variables. Both need and controversy surround the teaching and assessing of attitudes, interests, and values in the nation's schools. Many educators feel that the treatment of affective concerns should be pursued not only because they influence learning but also because they influence an individual's ability to participate effectively in a democratic society, are necessary for a healthy life, and interact with occupational and vocational satisfaction. To deal overtly at the instructional level with such topics as ethics, trust, self-concept, citizenship, honesty, and love can lead to confrontation with parents, administrators, or a variety of society's representatives. Many teachers are in fact reluctant to become involved with teaching and evaluating affective objectives because they feel that these kinds of learning outcomes are of only minor importance or that this area is beyond the province of education. Admittedly, affective objectives can prove to be a source of controversy, but the conscious avoidance of dealing with them directly in fact represents an affective stance by teachers. Teachers are also rightly concerned about violating the students' right to privacy. It is becoming increasingly difficult to maintain a value-free posture in contemporary society. Many educators believe that affective outcomes are as important as cognitive ones and therefore deserve equal treatment and time (D. A. Payne, 1980).

Sex bias. The presence of sex bias in instructional materials and tests has been documented. Tittle (1974), for example, reported research that disclosed content bias in the form of the ratio of male and female nouns and pronouns in eight frequently used achievement tests. Sex-role stereotyping was also noted. Harmon (1973) also reported sex bias in interest inventories. Sex-role stereotyping has been noted in the schools and measures developed (B. D. Payne, 1981). Data presented by Moss and Brown (1979), however, revealed no effects for sex of subjects, sex of passage, or sex of items for college students on a reading comprehension task. Again we see how a social influence and force—the women's rights movement—has raised some serious questions in need of educational research. That sex bias and stereotyping exist in society in general and in education in particular is accepted, but it will take the combined and cooperative efforts of test users, developers, and publishers to resolve that part of the issue that relates to measurement. For informative discussions of the general issues surrounding bias in many aspects of educational measurement, see articles by Gardner (1978) and Jaeger (1976).

Minimum competency testing. The minimum competency testing movement is a twentieth-century educational phenomenon. For some it represents the application of a technology to reform education, rectify social ills, and respond to the outcry of society that our public school graduates cannot read, write, spell, count, or calculate. Economic pressures and the need for accountability have helped push educators into a position where they must justify their expenditures and programs. But what is minimum competency?

A minimum competency testing program typically involves the development, modification, or selection of a set of basic skill measures of computational and communication objectives. Such tests are usually criterion-referenced (Popham, 1978; Popham & Lindheim, 1980) and with increasing frequency are tailor-made by the local school system or state education departments. Many programs also include measures of so-called life survival skills, or real life or basic life skills, such as career exploration, consumer evaluation skills, citizenship, and basic physical and mental health maintenance skills. Although minimum competency tests are primarily used as exit exams from high school, some school systems also use them to help make grade-to-grade promotion decisions.

Much controversy (McClung, 1978; Jaeger & Tittle, 1979) and several significant legal battles (Fisher, 1980) have been joined over the installation of minimum competency testing programs. The chief claims for such programs are the establishment of egalitarian and uniform standards. Minimum competencies are perceived as representing realistic goals for educational programs under local control. On the negative side are such factors as long-term start-up and phase-in time, the possibility of the discriminatory use of the tests, the control and setting of standards, overemphasis on minimums with a corresponding deemphasis on maximums, and curricular concerns surrounding what the treatment should be for those who fail, that is, when and how remediation should take place.

Many test development issues present during the design and construction stage of any test are amplified for a minimum competency test. Chief among these is the question whether test items match both curriculum and instructional objectives; in other words, do the test items measure not only the professed educational goals of the system, but also what is actually taught? The demonstration of acceptable types and levels of reliability is also important. It is particularly crucial that the developer of a minimum competency test be able to demonstrate that the test is measuring lasting general characteristics of the examinee.

Test security may also be an issue as many public groups, the board of education, special interest groups, and/or the media may exert political pressure on the local systems or state board of education to release the test items for public perusal. The Freedom of Information Act and "sunshine" laws can also be invoked. The adverse effect on the usefulness of postrelease data is obvious. Needless to say, it would behoove anyone involved in developing or implementing a minimum competency testing program to work closely with an attorney at all times, document all steps used in the development of the instrumentation, and make sure that sound and acceptable practices are used at all stages of instrument development and application.

Testing the disadvantaged. The key phase in test development and application relates to the interpretation of the scores. A basic psychometric question is "Do the scores on this test mean the same thing for all examinees?" A great controversy has arisen within the behavioral sciences about the general applicability of certain kinds of achievement and aptitude tests to minority groups, particularly blacks, Hispanics, and other culturally diverse groups (Samuda, 1975; Wargo & Green, 1978). The controversy rests on the inference that test scores for the disadvantaged may be influenced by factors other than what was intended to be measured. The degree and nature of experience with tests, the motivation to perform well on the test, the appropriateness of the language used in the test and directions, and the perceived and actual relevance of the test for the examinee are only a few of the many potentially significant factors that can militate against the meaningful use of test scores. The effects of these factors can be seen in a number of test characteristics (Deutsch et al., 1964). Test scores for the disadvantaged tend to reflect less score variability than those for other subgroups. The result is less reliability and a corresponding decrease in the ability of the test to discriminate effectively. Because of the effect of various factors such as decreased reliability, it is argued by many testing professionals that separate normative data should be made available for disadvantaged groups when their scores are being interpreted. In addition, both test-related and unrelated factors can adversely affect the validity of score interpretations for the disadvantaged. Contributing to the validity problem is the prediction of complex criteria. Test selection and interpretation remain, however, the key elements in the process. The combination of an inappropriate test and an untrained examiner can lead to disastrous results. Just as a good physician uses a variety of data in making a clinical interpretation, so should a competent test user consider many relevant intratest as well as extratest factors in using the test record to make decisions that may have a lasting effect on the examinee.

Despite the importance of the issues involved in testing the disadvantaged, an insufficient amount of controlled research has been undertaken. That which has been completed sometimes shows surprising results. For example,

in an extensive study of 9,000 students, Jensen (1974) found that race of examiner had no significant effect on test scores. In a study of test content, Schmeiser and Ferguson (1978) did not find any statistically significant results with regard to overall test performance or in test characteristics such as internal consistency or item discrimination indices for tests where test content was systematically varied for culture.

Are there alternatives to the use of standardized or quasi-standardized (teacher-made) tests with the disadvantaged? Some have suggested that grades, prior experience (e.g., biodata forms or the possession of some certificate or diploma), interviews, quotas, lotteries (following the establishment of minimum competency), ratings, or the reliance on recommendation could be used effectively with the disadvantaged. These data sources suffer more than tests from reliability and validity problems and might best be used as supplementary data sources rather than as primary sources (Cleary et al., 1975). What is needed is better instrumentation and training in test interpretation.

Legal issues. Whenever there is an apparent conflict between social policy objectives and sound professional and administrative practices, governmental agencies are found to increase their attacks. Nowhere is this more evident than in several employment-selection discrimination cases that can be traced to Title VII of the 1964 Civil Rights Act, which requires employers to hire individuals without regard to race, religion, national origin, or sex. Such court cases as *Griggs* v. *Duke Power Company* and *United States et al.* v. *Georgia Power Company* involved accusations of discriminatory test use. A resulting Supreme Court decision laid the foundation for the requirement of evidence of empirical test validity (criterion-related) for any test used in making selection decisions.

Because tests are used extensively in diagnosis, guidance, selection, human research, and competency assessment, dangers may arise from the misapplication of tests in a variety of settings. A growing body of literature suggests that this is more likely to occur in particular situations. However, an extensive survey by Kirkpatrick (1968) of test and criterion data on some 1,200 persons—including whites, blacks, and Puerto Ricans—indicates that many of the tests perform equally well in different ethnic groups. In some cases, given tests work best in particular groups.

It is argued by some that it is not the test but the unresponsive society that discriminates. It will be argued by all testing professionals that the use of any test that has no demonstrable job-related validity is inexcusable. There is evidence that certain tests do discriminate between selected groups, particularly in employment situations. If such discrimination can be shown to be a function of the relationship between test content and criterion performance, there are no grounds for objection. Such a test distinguishes between those who have and have not achieved and between those who are and are not likely to be successful. If, on the other hand, a test discriminates on the basis of variables unrelated to validity, it should not be used. Cultural factors can operate to decrease the validity of any test. Some of the issues central to this problem have been highlighted by Cole (1972), Darlington (1971), and Thorndike (1971a).

It is frequently the case, however, that questions of validity are overshadowed and subverted because of perceived adverse test effect on discriminated-against groups. The use of dual standards in making selection decisions is a case in point. The admission criteria for the dominant cultural group are ranked for each criterion, and a decision is made. The same procedure is followed independently for minority group members. The *Bakke* v. *Regents of the University of California* opinion has pointed out the potential legal problems in using a quota system for making educational or training decisions. In addition to the need for guidelines for the use of tests in employment selection and admission decisions, additional measurement issues can be traced to the use of test data to allocate funds for educational programs. The economic implications of the "truth in testing" legislation now in effect in the state of New York with regard to tests used for college admission are staggering. Beyond the obvious economic effect is the influence on the test security of external testing programs and test validity. The spate of well-intentioned state and federal legislation is aimed at curbing abuses of tests. It would probably be best if the testing profession could police its own ranks, but what procedures are available for curbing the misuses of educational and psychological tests? There is, of course, now a legal precedent requiring proof of validity for tests used for selection purposes. Tightening state licensing and certification laws for those who are charged with the responsibility of administering and scoring tests is another avenue for improvement. Voluntary restrictions on the sale and distribution of tests by test publishers is yet another possibility. Perhaps the most powerful pressure for improved testing practices can be exerted within the profession. Preservice and inservice training programs should be expanded and updated. Greater adherence to the recommendations of state and national professional organizations must be secured (American Personnel and Guidance Association, 1972).

Effects of coaching. An additional measurement issue concerns the effect of public, private, and commercial coaching and training programs that have been developed to help students prepare for college admissions tests. It is very difficult to prepare a student for a particular secure test if training involves primarily the examination of old test items. If, however, coaching involves a more elaborate and broadly based educational experience whereby academic skills and knowledge are in fact taught, the likelihood of increasing test scores is improved. Such improvement is, however, very modest. A recent review of the literature by Pike (1978) revealed inconsistent results with respect to the effect of coaching on both verbal and mathematics tests, specifically the *Scholastic Aptitude Test-Verbal* (SAT-V) and *Scholastic Aptitude Test-Math* (SAT-M).

Simply retaking the test in and of itself results in some score gain, so that intentional gains should be judged against these kinds of *practice* change scores. A reasonable estimate of overall math gain resulting from a short-term instructional program (e.g., one to six hours) was found to be around 10 College Entrance Examination Board (CEEB) score units (within the score range of 200–800). For intermediate-term instruction (e.g., fifty hours), gains were found to be between 20 and 25 CEEB units. Comparable results were found for SAT-V coaching programs. Two confounding factors in coaching studies are the ability level of the subjects being coached and the similarity of the coaching materials to the criterion measure. It appears that the greater this similarity and the longer the period of instruction, the greater the positive gain. This coaching effect, numerically, however, is quite small. Confirmatory evidence has been reported by Alderman and Powers (1979). These investigators found a difference of 8 CEEB units between the means of coached versus uncoached groups for the SAT-V. After an average of about thirteen hours of instruction, an average gain of only 8 points was observed. The crucial question here is not whether one can increase the scores but whether the increase (1) is worth the time and financial investment and (2) helps the student perform better in college. The response to both parts of the question is negative. Students might better spend their time being educated rather than coached. In fact, Messick and Jungeblut (1981) have interpreted their extensive review data as suggesting that the student contact time necessary to achieve average score increases much greater than 20 or 30 points rapidly approaches that of full-time schooling. If significant gains had been observed, then a real question of test validity might have been raised. If coaching raised only the scores and did not improve the overall capacity of the student to perform better, then the validity of the test would have been destroyed. Since the score increases are small, the validity question is moot.

Research in Measurement. It is impossible to review adequately the voluminous literature of research in educational measurement that has accumulated since the fourth edition of the *Encyclopedia of Educational Research*. It might be helpful to the reader, however, to highlight several areas in which a "frequency of appearance" criterion suggests the presence of topics of general concern to researchers and apparent trends. No attempt is made here to summarize the many technical studies of reliability and validity, as these are treated elsewhere. Empirical treatments of questions concerning the reliability and validity of existing tests, together with descriptions of the development of new tests, can be found in the journal *Educational and Psychological Measurement*.

Test item formats. As one might expect, the preponderant amount of research within the field of educational measurement during the 1970s focused on ways of asking questions, primarily cognitive ones. Because of their flexibility, adaptability, and efficiency, the so-called objective or short-answer item types enjoy professional acceptance. Not all educators, however, are convinced that a selection-type item can measure what a supply or student-constructed response item can measure. Hogan and Mishler (1980) demonstrated that for samples of third-graders and eighth-graders, moderately strong relationships could be found between objective tests of language skills and performance in a free-writing situation. True/false items continue to be useful procedures despite claims that they are overinfluenced by guessing. Given the same amount of testing time, well-written true/false tests can be shown to have reliabilities equivalent to multiple-choice tests (Ebel, 1975). Multiple-choice items also have their detractors. Although it is known that performances on multiple-choice tests may be influenced by student "testwiseness" and risk taking (Rowley, 1974), it is also known that testwiseness and test anxiety can be experimentally manipulated and "treated" to the advantage of the test taker (Bajtelsmit, 1977). One bit of measurement folklore that may be put to rest is that all multiple-choice items must have four or five alternatives. Based upon some theoretical information-processing work by Tversky (1964), Straton and Catts (1980) have shown that three alternatives per item are as effective as two or four choices, and in some cases superior.

Scoring of essay items.   Educators tend to have favorite measurement approaches. Among the most popular are the essay items and tests. This measurement format has great flexibility in terms of the kinds of learning outcomes that can be assessed. Both cognitive and affective variables are amenable to measurement with this type of test task. Owing either to lack of effort or to the influence of extraneous factors, the essay question does suffer from lower reliability than other types of items. A series of studies by Hales and Tokar (1975) and Hughes, Keeling, and Turk (1980) demonstrated that the quality and grades assigned to preceding essays had significant effect on the evaluation of essay questions that followed. In addition to showing an effect of quality of handwriting, Chase (1979) demonstrated that teacher expectation influenced the essay grade. Greater expectancy for the student yielded a higher essay score. Users of the essay form must be sensitive to the variety of potentially distorting extraneous factors that can lessen objectivity in scoring essay items and tests.

Student evaluations.   The accountability movement in education has caused teachers and instructors to search out data in support of their effectiveness (Centra, 1979). One frequently used data source is student evaluations. Although intrinsically appealing, these measures do suffer from some problems. The research data are equivocal as to whether responses reflect only instruction-related conditions. Freedman, Stumpf, and Aguanno (1979) found that 89 percent of the variance in the ratings of 129 instructors could be explained by variables relevant to the teaching-learning process. On the other hand, such irrelevant variables as student level of achievement, interest, and conve-

nience were together shown by Korth (1979) to be highly related to student evaluations of teaching effectiveness. But assuming that valid measures are used, can the data prove useful? Studies (e.g., Payne & Hobbs, 1979) suggest that feedback of evaluative information to instructors can in fact result in a perceivable change in instructor behavior. Student ratings of instructor effectiveness have high face validity and are readily obtainable, which is reason enough to address and resolve the technical measurement problems.

Changing answers on objective tests.   Part of the folklore of educational measurement revolves around the belief that an examinee's initial response is likely to be his or her most valid one. Research does not confirm this assertion. Students at all educational levels change answers; in fact, frequently 80 percent or more of a class make such changes on selection-type tests. Students who change their answers are more likely to gain as a result (Smith & Moore, 1976). The ratio of gains to losses ranges from about two to one for true-false items to as much as four to one for multiple-choice tests (Mueller & Wasser, 1977; Mueller & Shwedel, 1975). There also appears to be a tendency to change more items measuring high-level cognitive outcomes (Smith, White, & Coop, 1979). It has also been found that, on the average, individual scores are increased by answer-changing behavior, with no significant adverse effect on item discrimination or internal consistency reliability (Crocker & Benson, 1980). All of this research makes logical sense. As an examinee progresses through a test, information is being gained and, it is hoped, better and more rational decisions about questions are based on an increased fund of information.

Guessing on objective tests.   Guessing and the use of guessing strategies and control methods have also been intensively investigated. One of the major problems in attempting to apply corrections for guessing on objective tests is that so often the assumptions underlying the corrections are not met—for example, the assumption that all alternatives for a given multiple-choice item are equally likely. Cross and Frary (1977) report data suggesting that if examinees do *not* guess, they will penalize themselves. If examinees have some information about what is being tested, they can eliminate at least one alternative, and they should guess rather than omit the item. One way to control guessing is to make sure the test and items are of highest quality, clearly phrased, and free from ambiguity, with homogeneous and plausible alternatives. Strang (1977) reports that guessers tend to select longer and nontechnical but familiar options, the inference being that these would be good additional characteristics for multiple-choice item foils. Some experts suggest that an admonition to the examinee against guessing would control test-taking behavior. Research by Wood (1976), however, suggests that the best directions specify that all examinees should try to answer all items. The attempt to control guessing by the use of directions is fraught with problems, as the bold are more likely to take chances than the timid and are therefore more likely to benefit from a guess. This introduces a personality variable into the measurement process and represents unwanted error.

The literature of educational measurement is filled with diversions, data, and dialectic. Perhaps because of the vastness and complexity of individual differences, educators have been unable to identify many universal truths. Solutions to parochial problems, however, have been successfully investigated. Critics of and controversies over educational measurement are numerous (e.g., Houts, 1977; Haney, 1980), but the basic contribution that measurement processes and products have made and will continue to make cannot be denied.

David A. Payne

See also Achievement Testing; Aptitude Measurement; Attitude Measurement; Competency Testing; Intelligence Measurement; Interests Measurement; Marking Systems; Reliability of Measurement; Standards for Tests and Ethical Test Use; Validity of Tests.

REFERENCES

Ahmann, S., & Glock, M. *Evaluating Student Progress: Principles of Tests and Measurement* (6th ed.). Boston: Allyn & Bacon, 1980.

Alderman, D. L., & Powers, D. E. *The Effects of Special Preparation on Scholastic Aptitude Test–Verbal Scores* (Research Report RR-79-1). Princeton, N.J.: College Entrance Examination Board, 1979.

Allen, M. J., & Yen, W. M. *Introduction to Measurement Theory.* Monterey, Calif.: Brooks/Cole, 1979.

American Personnel and Guidance Association. The responsible use of tests. *Measurement and Evaluation in Guidance,* 1972, 5(2), 385–388.

American Psychological Association. *Standards for Educational and Psychological Tests.* Washington, D.C.: American Psychological Association, 1974.

Anastasi, A. *Psychological Testing* (4th ed.). New York: Macmillan, 1976.

Bajtelsmit, J. Test-wiseness and systematic desensitization programs for increasing adult test-taking skills. *Journal of Educational Measurement,* 1977, 14, 335–341.

Brown, F. G. *Guidelines for Test Use.* (Commentary on the Standards for Educational and Psychological Tests). Washington, D.C.: National Council on Measurement in Education, 1980. (ERIC Document Reproduction Service No. ED 193 247)

Buros, O. K. (Ed.) *The Eighth Mental Measurements Yearbook.* Highland Park, N.J.: Gryphon Press, 1980.

Caldwell, O. W., & Courtis, S.A. *Then and Now in Education, 1845–1923.* New York: Arno Press, 1971. (Originally published, 1925)

Centra, J. A. *Determining Faculty Effectiveness.* San Francisco: Jossey-Bass, 1979.

Chase, C. I. The impact of achievement expectations and handwriting quality on scoring essay tests. *Journal of Educational Measurement,* 1979, 16, 39–42.

Churchman, C. W., & Ratoosh, P. (Ed.) *Measurement Definitions and Theories.* New York: Wiley, 1959.

Cleary, T. A.; Humphrey, L. G.; Kendrick, S. A.; & Wesman, A.

Educational uses of tests with disadvantaged students. *American Psychologist,* 1975, 30, 15–41.

Cole, N. *Bias in Selection* (ACT Research Report No. 51). Iowa City: American College Testing Program, Research, and Development Division, May 1972.

Cook, W. W. The functions of measurement in the facilitation of learning. In E. F. Lindquist (Ed.), *Educational Measurement.* Washington, D.C.: American Council on Education, 1951.

Crocker, L., & Benson, J. Does answer-changing affect test quality? *Measurement and Evaluation in Guidance,* 1980, 12, 233–239.

Cross, L., & Frary, R. An empirical test of Lord's theoretical results regarding formula scoring of multiple-choice tests. *Journal of Educational Measurement,* 1977, 14, 313–321.

Darlington, R. B. Another look at "culture fairness." *Journal of Educational Measurement,* 1971, 8, 71–82.

Deutsch, M.; Fishman, J. A.: Kogan, L. S.; North, R. D.; & Whitman, M. Guidelines for testing minority group children. *Journal of Social Issues,* 1964, 20, 129–145.

DuBois, P. H. *History of Psychological Testing.* Boston: Allyn & Bacon, 1970.

Ebel, R. L. Can teachers write good true-false test items? *Journal of Educational Measurement,* 1975, 12, 31–35.

Ebel, R. L. *Essentials of Educational Measurement* (3rd ed.). Englewood Cliffs, N.J.: Prentice-Hall, 1979.

Ebel, R. L. *Practical Problems in Educational Measurement.* Lexington, Mass.: Heath, 1980.

Fisher, T. H. The courts and your minimum competency testing program: A guide to survival. *Measurement in Education,* 1980, 11, 1–12.

Flanagan, J. C.; Dailey, J. T.; Shaycroft, M. F.; Orr, D. B.; & Goldberg, I. *Design for a Study of American Youth.* Boston: Houghton Mifflin, 1962.

Freedman, R. D.; Stumpf, S. A.; & Aguanno, J. C. Validity of the course-faculty instrument (CFI): Intrinsic and extrinsic variables. *Educational and Psychological Measurement,* 1979, 39, 153–158.

Gardner, E. F. Bias. *Measurement in Education,* 1978, 9, 1–5.

Greenbaum, W.; Garet, M. S.; & Solomon, E. R. *Measuring Educational Progress: A Study of the National Assessment.* New York: McGraw-Hill, 1977.

Gronlund, N. E. *Measurement and Evaluation in Teaching* (4th ed.). New York: Macmillan, 1981.

Guilford, J. P. *Psychometric Methods* (2nd ed.) New York: McGraw-Hill, 1954.

Gulliksen, H. *Theory of Mental Tests.* New York: Wiley, 1950.

Hales, L. W., & Tokar, E. The effect of the quality of preceding responses on the grades assigned to subsequent responses to an essay question. *Journal of Educational Measurement,* 1975, 12, 115–117.

Haney, W. Troubles over testing. *Educational Leadership,* 1980, 37(8), 640–650.

Harmon, L. W. Sexual bias in interest measurement. *Measurement and Evaluation in Guidance,* 1973, 5, 496–502.

Hogan, T. P., & Mishler, C. Relationships between essay tests and objective tests of language skills of elementary school students. *Journal of Educational Measurement,* 1980, 17, 219–227.

Houts, P. L. (Ed.). *The Myth of Measurability.* New York: Hart, 1977.

Hughes, D. C.; Keeling, B.; & Turk, B. F. The influence of context position and scoring method on essay scoring. *Journal of Educational Measurement,* 1980, 17, 131–135.

Jaeger, R. M. (Ed.). On bias in selection (Whole Issue). *Journal of Educational Measurement,* 1976, *13,* 1–99.

Jaeger, R. M., & Tittle, C. K. *Minimum Competency Achievement Testing: Motives, Models, Measures, and Consequences.* Washington, D.C.: American Educational Research Association, 1979. (ERIC Document Reproduction Service No. ED 190 633)

Jensen, A. R. The effect of race of examinees on the mental test scores of white and black pupils. *Journal of Educational Measurement,* 1974, *11*(1), 1–14.

Jones, L. V. The nature of measurement. In R. L. Thorndike (Ed.), *Educational Measurement* (2nd ed.). Washington, D.C.: American Council on Education, 1971.

Kirkpatrick, J. *Testing and Fair Employment: Fairness and Validity of Personnel Tests for Different Ethnic Groups.* New York: New York University Press, 1968.

Korth, B. Relationship of extraneous variables to student ratings of instructors. *Journal of Educational Measurement,* 1979, *16,* 27–37.

Lord, F. M., & Novick, M. R. *Statistical Theories of Mental Test Scores.* Menlo Park, Calif.: Addison-Wesley, 1968.

Lyman, H. B. *Test Scores and What They Mean* (3rd ed.). Englewood Cliffs, N.J.: Prentice-Hall, 1978.

McClung, M. S. Are competency testing programs fair? Legal? *Phi Delta Kappan,* 1978, *59,* 397–400.

Mehrens, W. A. *Readings in Measurement and Evaluation in Education and Psychology.* New York: Holt, Rinehart & Winston, 1975.

Mehrens, W. A., & Lehmann, I. J. *Measurement and Evaluation in Education and Psychology.* New York: Holt, Rinehart & Winston, 1978.

Messick, S., & Jungeblut, A. Time and method in coaching for the SAT. *Psychological Bulletin,* 1981, *89,* 191–216.

Moss, J. D., & Brown, F. G. Sex bias and academic performance: An empirical study. *Journal of Educational Measurement,* 1979, *16*(3), 197–201.

Mueller, D. J., & Shwedel, A. Some correlates of net gain resultant from answer changing on objective achievement test items. *Journal of Educational Measurement,* 1975, *12,* 251–254.

Mueller, D. J., & Wasser, V. Implications of changing answers on objective test items. *Journal of Educational Measurement, 1977, 14,* 9–13.

Noll, V. H.; Scannell, D. P.; & Craig, R. C. *Introduction to Educational Measurement* (4th ed.). Boston: Houghton Mifflin, 1979.

Nunnally, J. C. *Psychometric Theory* (2nd ed.). New York: McGraw-Hill, 1978.

Payne, B. D. Sex and age differences in the sex-role stereotyping of third- and fifth-grade children. *Sex Roles,* 1981, *7,* 135–143.

Payne, D. A. *The Assessment of Learning: Cognitive and Affective.* Lexington, Mass.: Heath, 1974.

Payne, D. A. (Ed.). *Recent Developments in Affective Measurement.* San Francisco: Jossey-Bass, 1980.

Payne, D. A., & Hobbs, A. M. The effect of college course evaluation feedback on instructor and student perceptions of instructional climate and effectiveness. *Higher Education,* 1979, *8,* 525–533.

Pike, L. W. *Short-term Instruction, Testwiseness, and the Scholastic Aptitude Test: A Literature Review with Research Recommendations.* (Research Bulletin RB-78-2). Princeton, N.J.: College Entrance Examination Board, 1978.

Popham, W. J. *Criterion-referenced Measurement.* Englewood Cliffs, N.J.: Prentice-Hall, 1978.

Popham, W. J., & Lindheim, E. The practical side of criterion-referenced test development. *Measurement in Education,* 1980, *10,* 1–8.

Rice, J. M. *Scientific Management in Education.* New York: Hinds, Noble & Eldredge, 1914.

Rowley, G. L. Which examinees are most favored by the use of multiple-choice tests? *Journal of Educational Measurement,* 1974, *11,* 15–23.

Samuda, R. J. *Psychological Testing of American Minorities: Issues and Consequences.* New York: Dodd, Mead, 1975.

Schmeiser, C. B., & Ferguson, R. L. Performance of black and white students on test materials containing content based on black and white cultures. *Journal of Educational Measurement,* 1978, *15*(3), 193–200.

Smith, A., & Moore, J. C. The effect of changing answers on scores of non–test-sophisticated examinees. *Measurement and Evaluation in Guidance,* 1976, *8,* 252–254.

Smith, M., III; White, K. P.; & Coop, R. H. The effect of item type on the consequences of changing answers on multiple-choice tests. *Journal of Educational Measurement,* 1979, *16,* 203–208.

Strang, H. R. The effects of technical and unfamiliar options upon guessing on multiple-choice test items. *Journal of Educational Measurement,* 1977, *14,* 253–260.

Straton, R. G., & Catts, R. M. A comparison of two-, three-, and four-choice item tests given a fixed total number of choices. *Educational and Psychological Measurement,* 1980, *40,* 357–365.

Terman, L. M., & Merrill, M. *Measuring Intelligence.* Boston: Houghton Mifflin, 1937.

Thorndike, R. L. Concepts of culture-fairness. *Journal of Educational Measurement,* 1971, *8,* 68–70. (a)

Thorndike, R. L. (Ed.). *Educational Measurement* (2nd ed.). Washington, D.C.: American Council on Education, 1971. (b)

Thorndike, R. L. *Applied Psychometrics.* Boston: Houghton Mifflin, 1981.

Thorndike, R. L., & Hagen, E. P. *Measurement and Evaluation in Psychology and Education* (4th ed.). New York: Wiley, 1977.

Tittle, C. K. Sex bias in educational measurement: Fact or fiction. *Measurement and Evaluation in Guidance,* 1974, *6,* 219–226.

Tversky, A. On the optimal number of alternatives at a choice point. *Journal of Mathematical Psychology,* 1964, *1,* 386–391.

Tyler, R. W., & Wolf, R. M. (Eds.). *Crucial Issues in Testing.* Berkeley, Calif.: McCutchan, 1974.

Wargo, M. J., & Green, D. R. *Achievement Testing of Disadvantaged and Minority Students for Educational Program Evaluation.* Monterey, Calif.: California Test Bureau/McGraw-Hill, 1978.

Wood, R. Inhibiting blind guessing: The effect of instructions. *Journal of Educational Measurement,* 1976, *13,* 297–307.

MEDIA USE IN EDUCATION

Readers should know at the outset approximately what this article is intended to be and what it is not, especially since there are certain constraints and difficulties that it must accommodate. First, although most educators are comfortable enough to use the term "media" and to expect others to understand its meaning, it lacks a commonly accepted definition. Instead, there is a general, somewhat vague understanding that it refers to various audio and/or visual communications technologies which have come to be used by educators. Books and other print materials are, of course, media, too, yet it is usually understood from the context—including the present context—that they are not a part of the topic under consideration.

Also, in this consideration of media, several potentially relevant topics will be largely ignored because they are considered elsewhere in this edition of the *Encyclopedia of Educational Research*. These include computer-assisted instruction, computer-based education, videodisk technology, video cable systems, communications satellites, instructional simulations and games, and the now-widespread uses of Postlethwait's audio-tutorial methods (Postlethwait, Novak, & Murray, 1969). Each of these might have been included here, but to keep duplication of contents to a minimum, they are not.

Another consideration arises from the fact that the evolution or development of media uses in education is less orderly than one might think. Even in the short span of a decade, the demands or circumstances in and around education can change markedly, with the result that the solutions educators seek and the techniques they adopt also change. During the 1960s and even into the early 1970s, schools and colleges were growing; students were actively challenging many things, from the quality of curricula and instruction to society in general; qualified faculty were generally in short supply; and funding, including media-related funding, was relatively easy to secure. But from the early or middle seventies onward, school and college enrollments have stabilized or declined, faculty in some fields have been in surplus, adolescent and older students have sought vocational preparation more than "relevance," and rapid inflation, together with growing disillusionment on several fronts, has added to educators' problems. Unquestionably, the role of media does not stand unaltered by these changes.

Furthermore, the capabilities of communications media or technologies change and develop at least as rapidly as does the educational climate. Consider, for example, that the fourth edition of this encyclopedia, published in 1969, predated by a year or two the availability to educators of videocassette technology, yet these color recording and playback systems are now widely distributed and used in the schools. Moreover, within the last two or three years, two additional videocassette technologies (known as Betamax and VHS) have been introduced into schools as well as homes. It is similarly interesting that, in the report of the President's Commission on Instructional Technology, Parkus (1970) discussed at some length the high cost of implementing computer-assisted instruction (CAI) and voiced a special concern that the available computer systems were already too large, complex, and costly to serve CAI's purposes well, and that the trend toward still larger systems was continuing. A decade later, however, the electronics industry has evolved the ever-smaller hand-held and (now) wrist-worn calculator and, most recently, a bur-

geoning variety of microcomputers, some with ample power and storage to serve CAI purposes, yet selling for prices in the range of a few hundred to a few thousand dollars—that is, even in inflated dollars, selling for about the cost of a basic 1970-vintage computer terminal. The moral is not that technology is bringing CAI within the reach of all, because the development of CAI course materials still proves costly and time-consuming, but that the main premise of Parkus's argument and concern has been so rapidly undermined by technological developments. A recent article in *Science* (Robinson, 1981) reports a further advance: the imminent availability of thirty-two-bit word microcomputers using circuits that contain as many as 100,000 transistors on one silicon chip. The increased power, together with lowered costs of that power, are further signs that forecasting and planning in technologically advanced fields are fraught with risks. There are three other considerations which readers may want to weigh as they interpret the main contents of this article. First, a fair proportion of the media uses in education are intentionally individualistic or innovative, so they are difficult at best to group and characterize. It is, though, a safe assumption that any conceivable modest-scale use of media has been tried by some educator somewhere. Second, although many media uses leave some visible trace or clue, as the borrowing of a film from a lending library or a school's purchase of several audio recorders will, others can remain invisible to almost everyone outside a given classroom. Teachers can and do prepare and use their own sets of instructional slides, they prepare or simply improvise their own transparencies, and they can even assume the roles of author-producer-cameraman-technician—in short, become a one-person television production company—to prepare their own instructional videotape recordings. In any event, the magnitude and variety of these "invisible" uses of media are impossible to judge.

Third and finally, it is worth noting that although current educational media uses may have their principal roots in the post–World War I efforts to introduce visual aids into the schools, such uses are now influenced by certain more recent movements, including those of educational (and commercial) broadcasting, educational research and evaluation, and programmed instruction. Elements from each of these fields are frequently found both in the methods of media materials preparation and in their dissemination and use.

Although this article is not intended to be a sequel to or to parallel Twyford's review entitled "Educational Communications Media" (Twyford, 1969), which appeared in the fourth edition of the *Encyclopedia of Educational Research* (pp. 367–380), some similarities are inevitable. Readers interested in an account of media developments during the 1950s and into the mid-1960s will find Twyford's review useful. It considers a variety of major film and television projects of the period and many of the research and evaluation studies on media use and media variables; it also encompasses work conducted during the period of most active interest in programmed instruction.

This article is organized into three principal and chronologically ordered sections, beginning with the period following World War I, then briefly tracing developments in educational media use into the late 1960s. (In preparing the historical section, Saettler's *History of Instructional Technology* [1968] was especially helpful; we commend the book to those who wish to consider that history further.) Following consideration of that approximate half-century, a principal section considers events of the past decade or, more nearly, the past dozen years. Those events do not reflect a homogeneous time period of mature or stable activity, but a time of changing needs, technologies, and fortunes. The final section considers the future of media use, not as a forecast of the future, since the odds against accurate forecasting are too high, but more as an identification of some issues and tasks which belong to the future.

A Half-century of Development. The early development of media use in education can be traced through three convenient, if not completely distinctive, phases, which might be said to correspond to periods of infancy, childhood, and adolescence. For present purposes, the first phase is considered to be the period between the two world wars, 1918–1941. The next phase extends from 1941 until the late 1950s, the latter date coinciding with the time when major federal legislation such as Public Law 85–864 began to foster the investigation and use of "new educational media" on a relatively large scale. The third phase essentially covers the decade of the 1960s, a period of expanding activity and development beyond which the contemporary media and capabilities can be said to exist and to be establishing themselves as accustomed elements in the educational process.

The early period: 1918–1941. Before 1918, educators had little interest in the nonprint media and their uses, although, as Saettler (1968) indicates, the first educational film catalog had been published in 1910 and Thomas Edison had gone on record in 1913 as saying, "Books will soon be obsolete. Scholars will soon be instructed through the eye. It is possible to teach every branch of human knowledge with the motion picture. Our school system will be completely changed in ten years" (cited in Saettler, p. 98). Edison's forecast might have been among the first of its kind, but it would not be the last to predict more for technology or, specifically, for media, than the near future would deliver. (Almost a half-century later, we find: "A large number of school officials believe that, ten years from now, television will carry some part of the teaching of the great majority of school children in this nation, and it is also expected that television will make available at home to students of whatever age, a large part of the college curriculum" [Stanford University, 1962, p. 3].)

In its infancy, the field of media use saw the first formal credit courses in colleges and universities, the first professional journals, the first visual instruction research, and the beginnings of America's two principal professional associations, the Association for Educational Communications and Technology (AECT) and the National Association of Educational Broadcasters (NAEB). For years, both have been rallying points for educators and other professionals interested in the educational and cultural uses of media. (Note: Late in 1981, just before this article went to press, the NAEB members voted to dissolve the 56-year-old organization; it had become financially nonviable.) Saettler (1968) places all these developments in the period 1918–1924.

Saettler identifies three elements in the theoretical framework underlying the early days of the audiovisual movement, which he refers to as "media and machines, use of particular senses (the eye and the ear), and . . . materials . . . concreteness or abstractness" (p. 121). He further cites a 1910 publication in which a theorized "order of merit" of educational materials is said to range downward in steps from the real object, through models and diagrams, to verbal descriptions. This concern with establishing a theoretical foundation to guide the development of audiovisual materials seems a healthy sign and was a contribution of academics involved in the movement; it helped counteract the views of those early materials producers who believed that entertainment formats would transfer effectively to instructional films with little or no modification. The two central tenets of this early theory—that the combining of auditory and visual channels in a single medium and message, together with the factor of realism in stimulus presentations, would yield improved learning—remain a source of debate to the present.

The dominant form of research during the early or infancy period was one in which gross comparisons were made between the measured learning resulting from instruction with one particular medium and that resulting from conventional instructional methods. In fact, Allen (1971) characterized instructional media research before 1950 as preoccupied with such "evaluative comparisons"; much the same view is expressed by Lumsdaine (1963). There were, however, a few early exceptions to this limited conception of research, and Allen cites Lashley and Watson for conducting "the first respectable study" in the field, a study of film effects in a campaign against venereal disease, whereas Saettler identifies a 1921 study of Weber, which first employed pictorial test items.

Further developments: 1941–1958. After the United States entered the war, late in 1941, both the military and industry were faced with enormous training problems. In responding to these problems, there was a movement away from technology in education and toward the training applications of media (Saettler, 1968).

Allen (1971) refers to this same era, and particularly to the ten-year period immediately following World War II, as "a pivotal one for instructional media research" in which "some of the old values of research were being discarded and new approaches and problems were being investigated" (p. 7). Included were studies, especially at

Pennsylvania State College (now University), which examined the effects of specific film variables by systematically modifying the selected variables in two or more versions of an instructional film (Carpenter & Greenhill, 1956). Three other major programs of research from the same era, all sponsored by the military, deserve mention. Gibson (1947) reported the work which he directed during the latter part of the war, an activity within the U.S. Army Air Force's Aviation Psychology Program. His research group made the first substantial efforts to employ motion pictures as a medium for psychological testing, rather than for training, education, or entertainment. In doing this, he noted that "the characteristics of motion pictures . . . namely motion, sequence, pacing, and realism, presumably have their psychological counterparts. Human behavior, and the capacities latent in it, also involves motion, order, tempo, and the experience of reality. It is reasonable to suppose, therefore, that the motion picture makes available to the test designer not only a special method of measuring known factors of human ability, but also gives him access to new and unnamed functions not accessible to conventional methods of test construction" (p. 20). (Later, some additional studies followed in the tradition Gibson had begun [Carpenter et al., 1954; Seibert & Snow, 1965; Seibert, Reid, & Snow, 1967].)

Shortly after the end of the war, Hovland, Lumsdaine, and Sheffield (1949) documented a series of studies conducted for the U.S. Army, investigating such variables as the effects of audience participation on learning from film and the effects upon attitudes of presenting one or both sides of a controversial issue. The studies of Gibson (1947) and Hovland, Lumsdaine, and Sheffield (1949), were completed during the war and were followed by the Pennsylvania State studies, cited above, under Navy sponsorship and those of Lumsdaine (1961) under Air Force sponsorship.

By the mid-1950s, attention had begun to shift from instructional film to television and to research on its effectiveness. The research group at Pennsylvania State had by then completed its extensive series of film studies and had begun investigations of television, the principal parts of which are described in two reports (Carpenter & Greenhill, 1955, 1958). Other substantial television projects of the period were established at Miami University in Ohio (Miami University, 1956, 1957), Hagerstown, Maryland (see, e.g., Schramm, 1977), Pittsburgh station WQED (see, e.g., Gropper & Lunsdaine, 1961), and several other campuses and schools across the country. The research associated with these projects is summarized by Chu and Schramm (1968) and Reid and MacLennan (1967).

As with much of the earlier film research, the television studies tended to be evaluative or gross comparisons which pitted televised instruction and its effects on learning against conventional or customary instructional methods. The principal finding of the many accumulated studies is simply summarized by Chu and Schramm (1968) as follows: "There can no longer be any real doubt that children

and adults learn a great amount from instructional television" (p. 1).

Approaching maturity: 1958–1968. It may be argued that, although media use had been expanding and growing more varied since early in the century, a technology of instruction did not begin to take shape until about 1958. This date not only marked the passage of important federal legislation, as already indicated, but also the publication of one of B. F. Skinner's most influential articles on education (Skinner, 1958). Morgan (1978) describes the article as a "catalytic force" in effecting "the convergence of three disciplines" and the emergence from them of the new discipline of educational technology (p. 143). Skinner provided a behavioral technology derived from research on learning, management science provided concepts from "the systems approach" to problem solving and planning, and the communications media provided the hardware technologies. The merged procedures and instruments gave the outlines of a method for proceeding from vague educational needs or goals through intermediate and refining steps to the implementation of an instructional design of known effectiveness.

As the methods of instructional systems design have evolved, some features which Skinner advocated have faded, whereas others have remained largely intact. His emphasis on a "teaching machine," which provided continuous, prompt, and "reinforcing" knowledge of results to the learner, has given way to a more varied assortment of communications devices. Also, the implied if not stated emphasis on instruction via the printed word has been modified to encompass any form or medium believed or demonstrated to be appropriate to the instructional task at hand. Third, although individually paced instruction continues to be well regarded and advocated by many practitioners, fixed pace and group methods of instruction are likely now to be judged on their merits.

The instructional technology which has emerged retains an emphasis on the clear definition of the behavior to be learned and on its analysis, where appropriate, into component skills. It also emphasizes the importance of selecting instructional sequences, forms, and media appropriate to the nature of the intended learning. It continues to emphasize the use of procedures whereby an initial or draft version of the instruction is prepared and given an authentic trial with persons like those for whom it is intended. The effects of the draft version are assessed in detail and revisions are made, as needed, to achieve increased effectiveness. Then the trial and revision process is repeated until assessments show satisfactory levels of instructional effectiveness.

The same period that gave birth to instructional technology as a recognizable endeavor also witnessed the publication of several substantial reviews and analyses of the media research literature. Two of these, by Chu and Schramm (1968) and Reid and MacLennan (1967), are mentioned above; the one considers television studies only, and the other considers both film and television. In addition, an early review from the period is by Barrow and Westley (1958), who were concerned that earlier reviews had neither employed nor generated a relevant theoretical structure. They undertook to develop a comprehensive and testable theory of communication, applicable primarily to film and television. Their principal effort was to identify factors deemed essential to maximizing the "relative potency" and "relative comprehensibility" of instructional messages, and their proposed theory, described as "miniature" and "provisional," consisted of a set of fourteen propositions which relate various message design factors and media program quality. An example: *"Hypothesis 4*—Other things equal, potency and comprehensibility will increase as overt audience participation increases" (p. 78).

An extensive review of media research was reported in a volume edited by Travers (1964). He and his associates addressed the problems of developing a model for audiovisual information transmission based on principles from psychological research and of testing the validity of several arguments commonly advanced in support of media effectiveness. Of particular interest were the contentions that audiovisual media have high value for relating the learner to reality and that multichannel communication is generally more effective than single-channel.

The Travers group examined research on such questions as the value of pictorial media in instruction and the relative efficiency of the visual and auditory channels. They concluded that human information processing functions essentially as a single-channel system and that learning is not assisted by information-rich, multichannel presentations. (Carroll [1971] cites an earlier review which arrived at the opposite conclusion.) Travers also stated that "the emphasis on realism that has characterized the audiovisual field emerges as the worship of a false god" (pp. 9, 17).

Another extensive research review is by Lumsdaine (1963), whose concern was with media as "objects of experimental research," with research defined as "empirical inquiry which obtains new behavioral data" that can be formulated into "a science of instruction firmly grounded in experimental findings" (p. 584). The media he considers are those that can present a program of instruction in a predetermined sequence constituting a generally predictable and reproducible presentation; he includes television, motion pictures, audio recordings, and certain self-instructional programs.

Lumsdaine's review focuses on "scientific" studies in which a specified proposition or hypothesis is tested, and he contrasts these with "technological" studies that seek to assess or improve the effectiveness of a single instrument of instruction. Consequently, he considers studies in which specific instructional factors had been manipulated to determine their effects on learning. Most commonly, the factors were variables of stimulus presentation or of learner response to an instructional sequence. The major factors or categories used as organizing themes include active student response, stimulus control factors, content and organization of instruction, and verbal factors in instruction.

Despite the scope and thoroughness of the review, Lumsdaine regards it as "only the beginning in the effort to develop the technology of instructional method which such research can ultimately generate" (p. 669). He also considers the value of the technology to be in its applicability to the "perfection" of instructional instruments, which can then be used repeatedly and reliably to achieve predetermined modifications of behavior, thus making substantial improvements in the "effectiveness and economy of instruction."

A review by Briggs et al. (1967) deserves mention because of the particular problems addressed and the approach employed. The authors focused on the problem of selecting media appropriate to given instructional tasks and on the fact that educators can rarely specify the medium for a given learning sequence, but must choose from those that commercial suppliers make available. Also, the media materials typically are not in their given form for reasons systematically derived from research on learning. In any event, the Briggs review was not in search of a comprehensive "science of instruction" but was a practical attempt to determine what research had to say about the discriminating use of media to serve particular educational purposes. The review is organized on a medium-by-medium basis, rather than on the basis of program design factors, as was Lumsdaine's; it includes television, motion pictures, programmed instruction, filmstrips, radio, and recordings.

In their summation, the authors assert that many studies were of little value for their purposes, the major problem being that "the existing research simply had not asked the right questions" (Campeau, 1967, p. 104). Again, much prior research had only assessed the general effectiveness of a medium in fostering student achievement, without considering the nature of the learning involved in acquiring observed levels of competence. Confronted with this, Briggs et al. call for a "new strategy" for future educational research, one including detailed definitions of the learning tasks to be studied.

The several reviews published during the late 1950s or the sixties were attempts to take stock of instructional media research and of related studies from the preceding twenty years. None of the reviews reflects any doubt that media can function effectively as instruments of instruction, that is, that they demonstrate the capability to achieve serious educational purposes. At the same time, the reviews at least suggest that relatively little of the research has contributed to an improved conception of how media function to achieve their effects or how they might be made more effective instruments of instruction.

Recent Developments. Viewed from a vantage point in 1981, several developments which occurred during the 1970s and the late 1960s help to represent and define that ten-to-twelve-year period. Among these are some signs that certain activities related to media use changed noticeably and also declined during the seventies, yet the meaning of these signs is unclear. Nevertheless, certain statistics derived from the media literature show a striking pattern of change. These statistics were provided by staff of the ERIC clearinghouse at Syracuse University (Laubacher, 1981), and they represent tallies of the number of media-technology-audiovisual reports, articles, or similar items published each year from 1966 through 1980. In conducting the search and preparing the tallies, the ERIC staff counted the number of publications for which any of a variety of audiovisual terms were "major descriptors"; the process was repeated with the same terms as "minor descriptors."

For major descriptors, the annual count of eligible publications increased regularly from 1966—the first publication year represented in the ERIC data base—through 1972. The counts then remain essentially unchanged through 1976; each of these years shows a total of approximately 2,000 publications. Then, in the period 1977–1980, the numbers decline steadily to reach a final level of 640, a reduction of two-thirds. The annual counts based on minor descriptors show essentially the same trends, with a sharp initial rise in the several years after 1966, a peak that is sustained from 1973 through 1976 (at a level of about 4,000 eligible publications), then a decline to the 1980 level of about 1,200 publications; again, a reduction of about two-thirds.

It is more than conceivable that these statistics incorporate some artifacts; for example, the methods of identifying and including items in the ERIC data base may have shifted somewhat with time, or descriptors may have been modified in their meaning and use. However, it is unlikely that the patterns noted are solely attributable to artifacts. What is more likely is that the programs of federal assistance to media use and media research which began in the 1950s had begun to recede in the 1970s, with a resulting decline in related activities.

During the 1970s and the late 1960s, there seem to have been other signs of reduced activity, although these are more difficult to document. The appearance, however, is that the major developments of the period are primarily identified with the first few years of the period, not the later years. These developments, would seem to include the work of the President's Commission on Instructional Technology, which was concluded by 1971; the formation of the Children's Television Workshop (CTW) and Britain's Open University, both officially begun by 1969; and the Carnegie Commission's *Fourth Revolution* report, published in 1972. It is not evident that there were comparable developments associated with the mid-1970s and beyond, with the possible exception of the Annenberg-funded project, which is briefly considered below.

Research on media and the derivation of meaning from that research may indicate a further change is under way. The research reviews considered earlier appear generally similar and traditional. They summarize the methods and results of a group (or groupings) of studies, then discuss the meaning of the results and the effects of the variables which the research has studied. But with media research,

as with some other research fields, the methods of meta-analysis proposed by Glass (1976), demonstrated by him (Smith & Glass, 1977), and applied to media research by Kulik, Kulik, and Cohen (1980) now seem a promising alternative. In addition, there are increasing signs that Cronbach's recommendations for unifying the "two disciplines" of psychology (Cronbach, 1957) are being heeded by media research personnel. These signs appear early in the writings of Snow and Salomon (1968), Clark (1975) and other authors who contributed to a special issue of *AV Communication Review*, and in the major work by Cronbach and Snow (1977) on aptitude-treatment interactions.

President's Commission. During the seventies, possibly the most important media-related publication to appear was the two-volume report of the President's Commission on Instructional Technology (Tickton, 1970, 1971). However, its impact has probably been affected not only by the change in political climate which occurred as the Commission's work progressed, but by the changes in education, society, and technology which continued to occur during the 1970s. The Commission was established under President Johnson, but its work was not completed until after the Nixon administration had taken office, so its impact on government policy was almost certainly lessened. Also, the seventies witnessed important changes in education and in communications technology, no less than in society. As a result, at the close of the decade, educators were attempting to deal with problems and needs different from those of only a few years earlier. These changes have the result of diminishing the relevance of the Commission's efforts. Nevertheless, the summaries, recommendations, appendixes, and requested and submitted papers within the report represent major efforts of many of the most active contributors to the literature of the field.

The Commission's six recommendations are set forth in a twenty-two-page chapter and, although brief, represent the central result of the commission's deliberations. Among the recommendations are a call to establish the National Institutes of Education (NIE) with broad authorization to support "educational research, development, and application." Also recommended is a National Institute of Instructional Technology as a unit within NIE, one function of which would be to encourage the production of instructional materials. Other recommendations emphasize improved distribution of instructional materials, the establishment of selected demonstration projects, improved media-technology training for educators, and the establishment of working relationships between educators and industry to advance the productive use of technology in education.

Children's Television Workshop and Britain's Open University. Two of the most distinctive, venturesome, and (to some) successful uses of media to serve educational ends are represented in a decade and more of activity at both the Children's Television Workshop (CTW) in New York City and the British Open University. While their first appearances may be different, they are in many respects similar. They were begun within a year of each other, at the close of the 1960s; both were prominently concerned with serving an educationally and culturally disadvantaged audience; both approached their tasks through the use of curriculum design-writing-production teams and of research-evaluation evidence to an extent that was uncommon, if not unprecedented; both reflect ambitious goals, intending to achieve full national coverage and impact (and in both cases they achieved an unforeseen but significant level of international impact); and in some respects, television has formed the centerpiece for both, although this is more clearly the case for CTW than for the Open University.

Their similarities are probably best concealed by the fact that CTW was formed to teach a variety of school-related cognitive skills to preschool children, especially to those who were disadvantaged and who had a variety of cognitive deficits (Lesser, 1974), whereas the Open University was formed to provide fully credible, university-level instruction and degrees to adults. These adults were disadvantaged in that the British educational system provided no place for them in universities when they were young. Thus, although it turned out that many of this so-called forgotten million had been trained as teachers or for other technical or professional work, they were not university graduates.

The formation of CTW was officially announced early in 1968, and its purpose then was to develop and arrange for national dissemination of a television series "to promote the intellectual and cultural growth of preschoolers, especially disadvantaged preschoolers" (Cooney, 1968, p. 10). (There has, however, been some confusion concerning the interpretation of this announced purpose [see Lesser, 1974; Francke, 1971].) The series came to be known as "Sesame Street." From the outset, research and evaluation evidence were prominent elements in CTW's planning and programming efforts, and the evidence included many varieties. During the series' early developmental stages, it was particularly important for planners to understand, for example, the nature and variety of children's cognitive skill deficits, the course of cognitive development in preschool children and factors which influenced such development, the television viewing habits of young and of disadvantaged children, and the capabilities and limitations of televised, "purposive" communications. Later, as "Sesame Street" production progressed, formative evaluation evidence came into play (Lesser, 1974; Land, 1971–72) and was an important factor in the development of programs and program segments which not only attracted and held children's attention but effected the intended learning.

Research studies were regularly conducted to determine the size and composition of the audience reached by the series (Lesser, 1974), and, for the most part, the series has done well both in attracting its intended primary audience of disadvantaged preschool children (Land,

1971–72; Lesser, 1974,) and in reaching those middle-class homes which tend to comprise most public television audiences. In the period 1971–1978, "Sesame Street" attracted an audience which ranged between 7 million and 9 million viewers (Children's Television Workshop, 1979). Following the first year of "Sesame Street" broadcasts, its research also included a major summative evaluation study (Ball & Bogatz, 1970) which gave further signs that the series was achieving its purposes well. That study's five principal findings were that children who viewed the most also tended to learn most; that the skills most emphasized by the series were generally the best learned; that learners (viewers) could make good educational progress without formal supervision; that in all studied subgroups, increased viewing was accompanied by increased learning; and that the program *seemed* especially effective for children whose native language was not English.

From the formation of CTW and the beginnings of "Sesame Street," the organization moved on to establish "The Electric Company," a reading series directed principally at children in the early school grades; a health series entitled "Feeling Good," which was less than a success (see Mielke & Swinehart, 1976); and, more recently, a science and technology "literacy" series directed toward young and preadolescent children, entitled "3–2–1 Contact." The international offspring of CTW's early work include "Sesamstraat" a Dutch edition; "Sesamstrasse" in German; "Playa Sesamo" and "Barrio Sesamo," in Spanish; and other versions in Swedish, Italian, Arabic, French, and two in Portuguese. The English-language version continues not only in the United States but in "more than 20 nations and territories" (Children's Television Workshop, 1979, p. 15).

Unquestionably, the success of CTW and, more specifically, of "Sesame Street" is not universally acknowledged, not even by CTW's architects. In his 1974 book, *Children and Television*, Lesser, one of the series' principal architects, not only cites extensively from the works of researchers and writers who express doubts and reservations concerning the impact and value of "Sesame Street," but also discusses CTW's "failure to create a movement toward general improvement in the quality of children's programs" (p. 241).

Great Britain's Open University parallels in several ways the efforts and broad goals of CTW. Initially referred to as a "University of the Air," it was first outlined in 1963 by Harold Wilson, then Leader of the Opposition (The Open University, 1975). By 1964, Wilson had become Prime Minister and took steps to begin planning for the new institution. The planning led to a 1966 White Paper, a 1969 Planning Committee report that confirmed that the University was to provide "a second chance" for adults previously denied entry into higher education, then to a 1969 royal charter as an autonomous institution with degree-granting powers.

In 1966, the name was changed from University of the Air to Open University (Perry, 1977). Thus, even though broadcast programming has represented a continuing element and a major cost in most Open University courses, a variety of factors modified the early and implied emphasis on broadcasting. Among these factors were costs, especially for television production and broadcasting, and the very real limitations on "air time" that the British Broadcasting Corporation (BBC) could make available to the University. (The BBC not only was to serve the University but also had standing commitments to provide school broadcasting and Further [continuing] Education broadcasting services.) In the original agreement between the BBC and the University, thirty hours per week of both radio and television broadcast time were allotted. Later, television time was increased to thirty-six hours (Thomas, 1979). However, with each of the first-level (called "foundation") courses allotted thirty-two television and radio programs of twenty to twenty-five minutes each, with many higher-level courses allotted half of that, with the number of courses expanding regularly, and with the great desirability of repeating broadcasts so that students' personal schedules could be accommodated better, the allocation of broadcasting time among courses has been a continuing challenge.

With the change in name from University of the Air to Open University, there also appears to have been a significant conceptual change. Radio and television remained as elements in the system, but the core of the instructional process became specially prepared correspondence texts and other print materials, supplemented by tutoring and counseling at any of more than 260 study centers throughout Britain; by attendance at brief residential summer sessions; and by experiments, examinations, and assignments (the last including both tutor-graded and computer-graded forms). Although television and radio have continued to serve distinctly instructional functions, they have come to be regarded also as pacing and motivational instruments for students and as public information and University recruitment instruments among other viewers or listeners.

After admitting its first students early in 1971, the University grew from an enrollment of about 20,000 to almost 60,000 in 1978, by which time it also had more than 32,000 graduates and a small graduate studies and research program (Venables, 1979). By March 1981, graduates totaled almost 45,000, with nearly 6,000 of the graduations occurring in the preceding year (On the line, 1981). The 1981 report also indicates that, although teachers comprised 41 percent of the University's most recent graduates, this was a reduction from 86 percent in the first (1972) graduating class. Other analyses show that the University's cost per student has been substantially below that at the conventional British institutions (On the line, 1976), even after allowing for the fact that few Open University students pursue their studies full time, as do most students of the other institutions.

The concept of teaching at a distance, which has become identified with the Open University, is now being adopted and emulated in a growing number of other countries. In the United States, the Open University's materials and courses have been implemented at the University of Maryland, the University of Houston, and at Rutgers University (Mayeske, 1973), and, on a more modest scale, its ideas are evident in the programs of the University of Mid-America, with headquarters in Lincoln, Nebraska. Plans to create similar institutions have been started in other countries, and in some have reached advanced stages. Countries that have undertaken such planning include Israel, the Netherlands, Spain, prerevolutionary Iran, Thailand, Venezuela, Costa Rica, Pakistan, and the People's Republic of China.

By way of final comment on the Children's Television Workshop and the Open University, it might be suggested that they deserve the attention of readers interested in education and its use of media because both represent major undertakings in the field. Both are of such size that they have required that a large and varied group of talents be brought together to achieve their goals, and there was little or no precedent for the involvement of such groups in earlier joint endeavors. Also, while proceeding toward their goals, both have had to devise many of their processes and structures as they went along. They seem, therefore, to have more to teach interested observers than is represented in their instructional plans and programs.

A UNESCO report on media and technology. Dieuzeide (1970), a senior staff member of UNESCO in Paris, prepared an extensive analysis and critique of the uses of educational technology, issuing it as one of twelve UNESCO papers devoted to priority themes of the International Education Year. His paper is noteworthy here for at least two reasons: it considers a variety of technologies and applications, not only in the United States and other industralized nations, but also in less developed or developing countries, and it argues the case for a fundamental rethinking of educational practice (and, to some extent, purpose), including a "transition from technology in education to the technology of education" (1970), p. 11).

In arguing his case, Dieuzeide joins with those who deny that educational technologies are dehumanizing, but believe instead that they free the teacher "from certain purely mechanical tasks of exposition and repetition, thus enabling him to devote himself to the noble and irreplaceable functions of stimulation of interest, diagnosis, motivation, and advice" (p. 13). Furthermore, he questions "whether education must remain the only major human activity in which technology may not increase man's potential" and points to the "paradox whereby education is required to change the world without any concession that it must itself be transformed" (p. 3).

Among his other points, he notes that, in the United States, less than 4 percent of total educational expenditures are invested in educational materials, including textbooks, and that no other country is known to exceed this figure. More than 70 percent of educational budgets is expended on teachers' salaries. In addition, he characterizes many uses of media as too limited in scope, too often based on "the individual initiative of certain teachers," and as "palliatives and stop-gaps," which are "used as a remedy for inherent deficiencies in the [educational] system" (p. 7).

Even though Dieuzeide mentions the special needs and problems of developing countries infrequently, he seems to reflect a special concern that such countries should consider and pursue alternatives to the creation of educational systems which only repeat the process witnessed in currently industrialized countries. For the developing countries and for others, educational technology is presented as an opportunity to rethink educational plans and to devise radically different systems which are efficient and responsive to each country's determined needs and goals. He concludes by acknowledging that, since education is concerned with values and since it has many functions beyond the imparting of knowledge, it cannot be completely rationalized, nor can technological principles and hardware be expected to resolve the "crisis of education." He suggests, though, that the kind of reexamination, the more flexible structures, and the new human relationships represented in the processes and systems discussed would themselves contribute toward fulfillment of education's broader purposes.

The Fourth Revolution. Among the studies and reports prepared by the Carnegie Commission on Higher Education, one, entitled *The Fourth Revolution: Instructional Technology in Higher Education* (1972), considers the past and recommended future roles of instructional technology. Even though the Commission concentrates on higher education, many of its analyses and proposals seem equally relevant to other educational levels. It should be noted, too, that the Commission considered the full range of instructional technologies, rather than the somewhat more limited variety of contemporary media that is considered here.

The Commission's position on instructional technology is signaled by the report's title, the meaning of which is that education has witnessed four revolutions through all of human history, the most recent of which "is portended by developments in electronics, notably those involving the radio, television, tape recorder and computer" (p. 9). These "new media" are thus considered equal in significance to the three earlier educational revolutions: the shifting of educational responsibility from parents and the home to teachers and schools; the adoption of the written word as a tool of education; and the invention of printing, leading to the wide availability of books. The Commission adopted this analysis from one of its members, Sir Eric Ashby, Master of Clare College, Cambridge, England.

Having placed instructional or communications technology so prominently in the history of education and human civilization, the Commission then proceeds to recommend and anticipate major roles for instructional technology in the future. After an overview and introduc-

tion examining the continuing shortages of instructional media materials or "software," a brief review of instructional technology, and a consideration of technology in libraries, the report reviews the spread of technology into higher education. The heart of the report is represented in chapters 6–9, which list and discuss fifteen recommendations for action, and in chapter 10, which sets forth a series of "reasonable goals" for the years 1980–2000.

The Carnegie Commission's recommendations include the following: that the academic disciplines move promptly to correct the "grossly inadequate supply of good quality instructional materials"; that administrative responsibility for technology be placed "at the highest possible level"; that at least seven regional learning-technology centers be established to permit the sharing of costs and facilities among multiple institutions; that federal support for these efforts should rise to a level equaling 1 percent of total higher education costs; that faculty should receive more recognition and rewards for their efforts to advance the use of instructional technology; that colleges which train teachers should prepare them to develop and use instructional materials and technologies; and that the costs and benefits of available technology should be carefully studied and the findings disseminated to decision makers.

The Commission's "reasonable goals" for 1980, 1990, and 2000 are, in several cases, difficult to assess because they are couched in ill-defined terms. For example, by 1980, "*most* colleges and universities will have devised *adequate* administrative and academic authority and procedures for the encouragement and *appropriate* utilization of instructional technology" (p. 90; emphasis added). We know of institutions which have progressed in the last decade toward such a goal, but we can only speculate whether "most" have achieved it. Others of the Commission's 1980 goals refer to the wide acceptance of a broad definition of instructional technology, to a recommended and major federal effort to achieve the development of quality instructional materials, to the creation of at least three cooperative learning-technology centers to serve institutions within their regions, and to the development and operation of a system to identify promising materials and to encourage their development and use. It would appear that, of the Commission's eleven 1980 goals, there has been a decade of some progress toward perhaps seven or eight, but that, on the whole, the rate of progress has been considerably slower than the Commission would have wished. Whether the 1990 and 2000 goals will fare better, time alone can tell.

Television use study. Probably the most detailed of the media use studies from the 1970s is reported by Dirr and Pedone (1979) and was conducted during 1976–1977 under the auspices of the Corporation for Public Broadcasting and the National Center for Educational Statistics. To gauge the in-school use of television, they surveyed carefully drawn samples totaling almost 6,500 superintendents, principals, and teachers of elementary and secondary schools. Their mail survey return rates ranged from 50 percent (teachers) to 61 percent (superintendents), but further telephone follow-ups of subsamples of nonrespondents brought the effective final response rate into the range of 85 to 96 percent.

The calculate that the population of teachers that they address totals about 2.25 million, of whom 72 percent have instructional television (ITV) programming available to them. Of these, 59 percent used ITV to some degree during the year and about 46 percent used at least one series regularly. Elementary school teachers were almost twice as likely as were middle/junior high or high school teachers to use ITV (41 percent versus 24 and 21 percent, respectively). Similarly, whereas 69 percent of the ITV-using elementary teachers mention the direct use of public television broadcasting, only 39 percent of the secondary teachers mentioned this programming source; instead, secondary teachers relied predominantly on videotape for their instructional materials.

It is also worth noting that, as a source of educational materials, commercial station programming was mentioned by about one quarter of all teachers; cable TV was mentioned by 15 percent (a figure which many expect will increase during the 1980s); and Instructional Television Fixed Service (ITFS), a form of limited-distance broadcasting specifically designed for instructional program distribution, is mentioned by only 3 percent.

In addition to the fact that substantial numbers of teachers are using television in their classrooms, there are some other signs which suggest future growth of interest and use. Teachers' attitudes toward ITV were distinctly favorable (e.g., 58 percent of all teachers agreed that "Teachers don't make enough use of ITV," whereas only 8 percent disagreed), as were the attitudes of administrators. In addition, many superintendents reported that new building designs "always" or "usually" included provisions for ITV use, and only a third of those whose schools have ITV programming available to them indicated no plans to expand their ITV capabilities during 1977–1980, whereas the others were planning to add videotape equipment or TV receivers, replace black-and-white receivers with color, or otherwise enhance their schools' ITV capabilities.

Finally, while advocates of media use may find many positive signs in Dirr and Pedone's report, other signs are more sobering. On the average, school districts reported expenditures of only $3.27 per student per year in support of ITV services, whereas the total expenditure per student was on the order of $1,300. Also, in a related and small-scale student survey, only about a third of the respondents reported seeing at least one ITV program during a four-week period. Moreover, not more than a third of the superintendents, teachers, or principals reported that they had had any training in the utilization of ITV. And, although 72 percent of the teachers report that ITV programming is available to them, this leaves more than a quarter of all teachers (and students, presumably) beyond its reach.

We suggest, therefore, that although ITV may have established a foothold in elementary and secondary education, it is not yet in a position to exert major influence on educational practice or results.

Foundation reports on media. Two private foundations that have had substantial interest in promoting the use of educational media and technology have also issued brief reports summarizing recent activities and developments in the field. The more recent of these is from the Sloan Foundation and written by Koerner (1977). The other is a Ford Foundation report by Armsey and Dahl (1973) that, it should be mentioned, was not favorably reviewed in the foremost media research journal (Ofiesh, 1974).

The Koerner report opens with a brief review of the Sloan Foundation's six-year program of support for educational technology projects, then proceeds to a consideration of a variety of computer applications—that is, computers used not only as instructional devices, but also in the development of computer "literacy" and in library operations. In discussing instructional television (specifically in higher education), Koerner, like others (see, e.g., Siepmann, 1970), notes that it has been a disappointment so far and that the reasons are not altogether clear.

Under the heading of "low technology," Koerner discusses audio recordings, radio, slide-tape materials and their variants, and microfiche; he also mentions holography. His consideration of self-paced instruction touches on the so-called Keller Plan and on Postlethwait's audio-tutorial methods, unquestionably the two most widely adopted (and adapted) forms of instructional self-pacing. In considering cost reductions that technology might be expected to provide, he concludes that they remain "distressingly elusive" (p. 28).

The Armsey and Dahl report (1973) begins with a consideration of terms and definitions associated with media or technology (e.g., educational technology is defined in one quotation as "the organized design and implementation of learning systems . . . from modern communications methods, visual aids, classroom organization, and teaching methods"). The report's second chapter considers purposes for which media are commonly used, sources of teacher resistance to media, "software" (instructional materials) problems, media use to individualize instruction, and the role of research and evaluation. Two later chapters consider individual hardware technologies such as television, film, and audio tape recording and present a selective review of several major media application programs and projects (e.g., efforts fostered by the World Bank, Ford Foundation, UNESCO, and the Soviet Union). In their final chapter, the authors examine factors which can influence the success or failure of educational media applications.

Continuing Tasks. No consideration of educational media use would be complete without some examination of the prospects, unresolved questions, and needs of the future. At the same time, in undertaking that examination, we intend not to engage in prophecy or forecasting, both because it would tend to intrude upon matters discussed elsewhere in this encyclopedia and because the accuracy of such prophecies is likely to be poor.

A longstanding and surely a continuing source of problems (as well as some advantages) for educators is the rate at which media equipment or systems emerge and evolve. Often, educators barely learn of one new media design and its acutal or potential uses when another, functionally similar, design appears. Regularly, the new is more versatile than the old, is technically incompatible with the old in one or several respects, and represents new profiles or mixtures of costs and benefits.

The introduction of $\frac{3}{4}$-inch videocassette recorders provides one recent example of the problems that can accompany new technology designs. Consider first that few educators had any access to video recording capability before 1960. Then, in the decade that followed, a variety of capable and low-cost magnetic tape recorders became increasingly available. By about 1970, the $\frac{3}{4}$-inch videocassette systems had appeared and begun to supplant earlier designs, eventually becoming the preferred format of many educators. Now, about one decade later, educators must consider the merits and uses of the newer and less expensive $\frac{1}{2}$-inch videocassette systems (currently available in two mutually incompatible formats or designs), as well as of videodisc equipment (which "plays" prerecorded materials and may give advantages over cassette recorders, but is more expensive and demanding to program and is or will be available in four incompatible formats). Thus, the evaluation by educators of new media designs and formats is potentially a never-ending task and problem, and it is one which requires judgments concerning the future course of events in both education and technology.

The requirements of copyright law remain a source of concern to many educators and are of particular concern to those interested in educational media use. Even though U.S. copyright law was amended to recognize certain "modern" needs, it remained largely intact from 1909 until 1976, when the most recent major revision was enacted. Especially during the latter years of that period, materials copying and dissemination-distribution technologies advanced dramatically and found many uses within education, as elsewhere. Educators' concerns with copyright surely have several bases, including the fact that, as with other law, copyright includes a complex variety of principles and concepts which are difficult for nonspecialists to comprehend. (Miller [1979] even notes that "most scholars find it impossible to write an acceptable definition of fair use," yet fair use is a key concept in—and a contradiction to—the law.) Also, because the law is relatively new, its provisions have not yet been refined by the courts. Further problems can arise from the fact that the newer media or technologies do not always reflect clear parallels to print media, and so principles which may be well established for print can prove difficult to transfer or generalize. And it must also be true that most educators regard the illegal

appropriation of another's intellectual products—that is, copyright violations—as especially troublesome and distasteful.

The educational materials or "courseware" used or presented with media systems still pose a number of problems, part of which may also be related to copyright or to the rapid rate of technological evolution, and these problems can be described from several vantage points. One description of the core problem is that institutions do not yet provide sufficient incentives or rewards to motivate faculty in the adoption and use of media (Tickton, 1970; Carnegie Commission on Higher Education, 1972) and one result is a scarcity of demonstrably effective materials and media programs. Hooper (1969) and Schramm (1977) choose to implicate educators' (or simply people's) natural interest in devices, hardware, or "gadgets," at the expense of the capabilities they represent and the quality of educational programming they can provide to learners. Still others have deplored the "NIH syndrome"; the tendency among educators to avoid or to judge negatively educational materials "not invented here." It is unclear whether such judgments are, for example, more often rooted in basic philosophical differences, ego or professional security threats (see, e.g., Berkman, 1976), tactical considerations, or combinations of these and perhaps other factors. In part, too, such judgments may involve technical system incompatibilities between institutions and copyright or fiscal factors.

For some educators and planners (and of those cited earlier, Dieuzeide provides the best example), the potential of educational media will not be adequately realized until major new initiatives are planned and implemented. In Dieuzeide's case, the call is for future media applications that are systematically planned, thoroughly integrated into the instructional process, and widely implemented; such applications are seen to contrast with the customary and sometimes piecemeal uses of media seen in the past. The Carnegie Commission's *Fourth Revolution* report, as indicated earlier, presents similar recommendations and arguments, although it undertakes to consider only higher education in the United States, not the far broader educational range which Dieuzeide has considered. In any event, both reports describe levels and types of media use which are far from being fully realized, so both represent an agenda which could occupy educators for many years into the future.

During the decade of the eighties, one developing and potentially major application of media will be the recently announced joint project of the Corporation for Public Broadcasting and the Annenberg School of Communications; its purpose is to prepare "college credit courses to be offered through public radio and television and other telecommunications media" (Corporation for Public Broadcasting, 1980). An Annenberg gift of $150 million, spread over fifteen years, is the principal funding for the project, and, if successful, this effort could yield a program of educational offerings similar to that of Britain's Open

University ("Annenberg Grant Comes Through," 1981). Project planning began late in 1980, so the impact of these efforts probably cannot be estimated for several years.

Other tasks and issues likely to appear or reappear on the agenda of the future include continued debate over whether media use is a dehumanizing or depersonalizing influence on education; over the morality of an instructional technology which can or may achieve a degree of control over learner behavior (and the related issues of inculcating passive learning and the adoption of a limited range of "homogenized" goals in a pluralistic system); over the nature and need of educator training in the selection and use of media; over media use as a potential threat to educators' professional roles and job security; and possibly over the appropriateness of visual and pictorial media, which are considered by some to be referred to and processed predominantly by the brain's right hemisphere, to effect and promote propositional, sequential thought, which is similarly considered as the principal work of the left hemisphere—and of education (see, e.g., Cater, 1975; Kiester & Cudhea, 1976; Corballis, 1980).

Warren F. Seibert
Eldon J. Ullmer

See also Computer-Based Education; Mass Media; New Technologies in Education; Systems Design in Instruction; Textbooks.

REFERENCES

Allen, W. H. Instructional media research: Past, present, and future. *AV Communication Review*, 1971, *19*, 5–18.

Annenberg grant comes through. *Current* (National Association of Educational Broadcasters), March 16, 1981, pp. 1, 11.

Armsey, J. W., & Dahl, N. C. *An Inquiry into the Uses of Instructional Technology.* New York: Ford Foundation, 1973.

Ball, S., & Bogatz, G. A. *The First Year of Sesame Street: An Evaluation.* Princeton, N.J.: Educational Testing Service, 1970.

Barrow, L. C., & Westley, B. H. *Television Effects: A Summary of the Literature and Proposed General Theory.* Madison: University of Wisconsin, Television Laboratory, 1958.

Berkman, D. Instructional television: The medium whose future has passed? *Educational Technology*, May 1976, pp. 39–44.

Briggs, L. J.; Campeau, P. L.; Gagné, R. M.; & May, M. A. *Instructional Media: A Procedure for the Design of Multi-media Instruction, a Critical Review of Research, and Suggestions for Future Research.* Pittsburgh: American Institutes for Research, 1967.

Campeau, P. L. Selective review of literature on audiovisual media of instruction. In L. J. Briggs, P. L. Campeau, R. M. Gagné, & M. A. May, *Instructional Media: A Procedure for the Design of Multi-media Instruction, a Critical Review of Research, and Suggestions for Future Research.* Pittsburgh: American Institutes for Research, 1967.

Carnegie Commission on Higher Education. *The Fourth Revolution: Instructional Technology in Higher Education.* Berkeley, Calif.: The Commission, 1972.

Carpenter, C. R., & Greenhill, L. P. *An Investigation of Closed-circuit Television for Teaching University Courses* (Project No. 1). University Park: Pennsylvania State University, 1955.

Carpenter, C. R., & Greenhill, L. P. *Instructional Film Research Reports* (Vol. 2, Technical Report No. SDC 269-7-61). Port Washington, N.Y.: U.S. Naval Training Device Center, 1956.

Carpenter, C. R., & Greenhill, L. P. *An Investigation of Closed-circuit Television for Teaching University Courses* (Report No. 2). University Park: Pennsylvania State University, 1958.

Carpenter, C. R.; Greenhill, L. P.; Hittinger, W. F.; McCoy, E. P.; McIntyre, C. J.; Murnin, J. A.; & Watkins, R. W. The development of a sound motion picture proficiency test. *Personnel Psychology*, 1954, *7*, 509–523.

Carroll, J. B. *Learning from Verbal Discourse in Educational Media: A Review of the Literature* (Final Report, U.S. Office of Education Contract No. 1-707106-4243). Princeton, N.J.: Educational Testing Service, 1971.

Cater, D. The intellectual in videoland. *Saturday Review*, May 31, 1975, pp. 12–16.

Children's Television Workshop. *Sesame Street/Tenth Season* (1979 Corporate Review). New York: The Workshop, 1979.

Chu, G. C., & Schramm, W. *Learning from Television: What the Research Says.* Washington, D.C.: National Association of Educational Broadcasters, 1968. (ERIC Document Reproduction Service No. ED 014 900)

Clark, R. E. Adapting aptitude-treatment interaction methodology to instructional media research. *AV Communication Review*, 1975, *23*, 133–137.

Cooney, J. G. *Excerpts from the Proposal to Create the Children's Television Workshop.* New York: Author, 1968.

Corballis, M. C. Laterality and myth. *American Psychologist*, 1980, *35*, 284–295.

Corporation for Public Broadcasting. Corporation for Public Broadcasting/Annenberg School of Communications announce joint task force. *CPB News Release*, July 21, 1980.

Cronbach, L. J. The two disciplines of scientific psychology. *American Psychologist*, 1957, *12*, 671–684.

Cronbach, L. J., & Snow, R. E. *Aptitudes and Instructional Methods.* New York: Irvington, 1977.

Dieuzeide, H. *Educational Technology and Development of Education.* Paris: UNESCO, International Education Year Special Unit, 1970. (Reprinted in *Educational Broadcasting Review*, 1971, *5*(4), 25–42.)

Dirr, P. J., & Pedone, R. J. *Uses of Television for Instruction: 1976–77.* Washington, D.C.: Corporation of Public Broadcasting, 1979.

Francke, L. The games people play on "Sesame Street." *New York*, April 5, 1971, pp. 26–29.

Gibson, J. J. (Ed.). *Motion-picture Testing and Research* (Army Air Forces Aviation Psychology Program, Report No. 7). Washington, D.C.: U.S. Government Printing Office, 1947.

Glass, G. V. Primary, secondary, and meta-analysis of research. *Educational Researcher*, 1976, *5*, 3–8.

Gropper, G. L., & Lumsdaine, A. A. An experimental comparison of a conventional TV lesson with a programmed TV lesson requiring active student response. In *Studies in Televised Instruction* (Report No. 2, USOE Project No. 336). Pittsburgh: Metropolitan Pittsburgh Education Television Stations WQED-WQEX and American Institutes for Research, 1961.

Hooper, R. A Diagnosis of failure. *AV Communication Review*, 1969, *17*, 245–264.

Hovland, C. I.; Lumsdaine, A. A.; & Sheffield, F. D. *Experiments on Mass Communication.* Princeton, N.J.: Princeton University Press, 1949.

Kiester, E., & Cudhea, D. W. Robert Ornstein: A mind for metaphor. *Human Behavior*, 1976, *5*, 16–23.

Koerner, J. D. *The Present and the Future in Educational Technology.* New York: Alfred P. Sloan Foundation, 1977.

Kulik, C. C.; Kulik, J. A.; & Cohen, P. A. Instructional technology and college teaching. *Teaching of Psychology,* 1980, *7,* 199–205.

Land, H. W. *The Children's Television Workshop: How and Why It Works.* Jericho, N.Y.: Nassau Board of Cooperative Educational Services, 1971–72.

Laubacher, M. R. Personal communication, March 13, 1981.

Lesser, G. S. *Children and Television.* New York: Random House, 1974.

Lumsdaine, A. A. (Ed.). *Student Response in Programmed Instruction.* Washington, D.C.: National Academy of Sciences, National Research Council, 1961.

Lumsdaine, A. A. Instruments and media of instruction. In N. L. Gage (Ed.), *Handbook of Research on Teaching.* Chicago: Rand McNally, 1963.

Mayeske, B. J. Open University experiment: University of Maryland reports on British transplant. *College Board Review,* Summer 1973, pp. 2–5, 24–25.

Miami University. *Experimental Study in Instructional Procedures.* Oxford, Ohio: Author, 1956.

Miami University. *Experimental Study in Instructional Procedures* (Report No. 2). Oxford, Ohio: Author, 1957.

Mielke, K. W., & Swinehart, J. W. *Evaluation of the "Feeling Good" Television Series.* New York: Children's Television Workshop, 1976.

Miller, J. K. *Applying the New Copyright Law: A Guide for Educators and Librarians.* Chicago: American Library Association, 1979.

Morgan, R. M. Educational Technology—Adolescence to adulthood. *Educational Communication and Technology Journal,* 1978, *26,* 142–152.

Ofiesh, G. D. Review of *An Inquiry into the Uses of Instructional Technology* by J. W. Armsey & N. C. Dahl. *AV Communication Review,* 1974, *22,* 108–112.

On the line. *Open Line* (The Open University/BBC International Magazine), November 1976, p. 3.

On the line. *Open Line* (The Open University/BBC International Magazine), March 1981, p. 2.

Open University. *Introduction to the Open University.* Swindon, England: Open University Information Services Department, 1975.

Parkus, L. Computer-assisted instruction in elementary/secondary education: The state of the art. In S. G. Tickton (Ed.), *To Improve Learning: An Evaluation of Instructional Technology* (Vol. 1). New York: Bowker, 1970.

Perry, W. *The Open University.* San Francisco: Jossey-Bass, 1977.

Postlethwait, S. N.; Novak, J.; & Murray, H. T. *The Audio-tutorial Approach to Learning* (2nd ed.). Minneapolis: Burgess, 1969.

Reid, J. C., & MacLennan, D. W. *Research in Instructional Television and Film.* Washington, D.C.: U.S. Office of Education Publication, U.S. Government Printing Office, 1967. (ERIC Document Reproduction Service No. ED 015 673)

Robinson, A. L. Micromainframe is newest computer on a chip. *Science,* 1981, *212,* 572–528, 530–531.

Saettler, P. *A History of Instructional Technology.* New York: McGraw-Hill, 1968.

Schramm, W. *Big Media, Little Media.* Beverly Hills, Calif.: Sage, 1977.

Seibert, W. F.; Reid, J. D.; & Snow, R. E. *Studies in Cine-psychometry II: Continued Factoring of Audio and Visual Cognition and Memory.* Lafayette, Ind.: Purdue University, Audio Visual Center, 1967.

Seibert, W. F., & Snow, R. E. *Studies in Cine-Psychometry I: Preliminary Factor Analysis of Visual Cognition and Memory.* Lafayette, Ind.: Purdue University, Audio Visual Center, 1965.

Siepmann, C. A. The sleeping giant: ITV in higher education. *Educational Television,* May 1970, pp. 13–15, 20.

Skinner, B. F. Teaching machines. *Science,* 1958, *128,* 969–977.

Smith, M. L., & Glass, G. V. Meta-analysis of psychotherapy outcome studies. *American Psychologist,* 1977, *32,* 752–760.

Snow, R. E., & Salomon, G. *Aptitudes and Instructional Media.* Stanford, Calif.: Stanford University, School of Education, 1968.

Stanford University, Institute for Communication Research. *Educational Television: The Next Ten Years.* Stanford, Calif.: Author, 1962.

Thomas, N. Problems of broadcasting. *Open Line* (The Open University/BBC International Magazine), December 1979, pp. 9–10.

Tickton, S. G. (Ed.). *To Improve Learning: An Evaluation of Instructional Technology* (Vol. 1). New York: Bowker, 1970.

Tickton, S. G. (Ed.). *To Improve Learning: An Evaluation of Instructional Technology* (Vol. 2). New York: Bowker, 1971.

Travers, R. M. W. (Ed.). *Research and Theory Related to Audiovisual Information Transmission* (Interim Report, U.S. Office of Education Contract No. 3-20-003). Salt Lake City: University of Utah, Bureau of Educational Research, 1964.

Twyford, L. Educational communications media. In R. L. Ebel (Ed.), *Encyclopedia of Educational Research* (4th ed.). New York: Macmillan, 1969.

Venables, P. A. A brief ten years: Achievement and potential. *Open Line* (The Open University/BBC International Magazine), June 1979, pp. 3–5.

MEDICAL EDUCATION

During the past two centuries, American medical education has evolved from an apprenticeship to a complex, formal process that generally extends throughout the student's professional life. Today, young men and women who aspire to become physicians look forward to four years of undergraduate preprofessional education, four years of medical school, and three to seven years of postgraduate residency (specialty) training. Then, as physicians, they will be expected (by law in some states) to engage in programs of continuing education on an ongoing basis for as long as they practice medicine.

Although the gradual evolution of American medical education can be linked to the tremendous growth in medical knowledge and changing professional and societal expectations, its basic framework was established as a result of a study conducted more than seventy years ago. Shortly after the turn of the century, Abraham Flexner (1910) was commissioned by the Carnegie Foundation to conduct a study of medical education in North America. Flexner visited 155 medical schools and found that most were functioning solely as commercial enterprises. He observed that the admissions "standards" of these schools were established to maintain enrollments rather than to insure adequate preparation. Of the schools studied, for example, only 22 required college preparation; 50 accepted students with a high school diploma; and the remainder had few, if any, academic prerequisites. The instructional programs and resources utilized by these institutions in teaching the basic medical sciences were equally suspect. Teaching facilities generally consisted of a few lecture rooms and outdated laboratories staffed by poorly trained faculty. Clinical instruction was often haphazard and, in many cases, did not allow students direct experience with patients. Flexner's condemnation of these practices resulted in the closing of many institutions and the establishment of standards that continue to serve as the foundation of contemporary medical education. To this day, proposed reforms and innovations in medical education take the Flexner report as their point of departure by indicating how the educational prerequisites or experiences it described are deficient and then explaining how the change will remedy the problem.

Curriculum

Medical studies typically have three phases. The first phase, in the United States and Canada, generally covers the initial two years of medical school and is called "preclinical." It focuses primarily on acquiring knowledge in the disciplines (anatomy, physiology, pharmacology, pathology, etc.) that inform medical practice. The second phase, which covers the rest of medical school and all of postgraduate training (internship, residency, fellowship), involves varying levels of supervised clinical experience. The medical degree is given at the end of two years of this experience, and at that point or shortly thereafter, the new physician is licensed. Formal clinical training (in residencies and fellowships) continues, with steadily increasing responsibilities, but no additional degrees. This long training period is focused on the medical practice itself, with collateral study of the diagnosis, prognosis, and treatment of the diseases and disorders seen in practice. The third phase, which lasts the rest of the physician's lifetime, is one of continuing education. Activities during this phase vary according to the diverse needs and interests of the practicing physician and the requirements of a crowded schedule.

Existing Patterns. The preclinical phase of the curriculum in most medical schools is organized into a series of courses in the relevant disciplines although a significant minority of schools make use of courses organized around major organ systems (cardiovascular, respiratory, gastrointestinal, reproductive, etc.), their function and dysfunction (Association of American Medical Colleges [AAMC], *Curriculum Directory*, 1980). A third form of organization for preclinical studies has been developed recently but is used in only a few of the newer schools. It structures course content around common problems presented by patients (fever, jaundice, children's "failure to thrive," etc.).

A preclinical curriculum that is organized as a series of courses in the biological sciences (with some coursework in the behavioral sciences) has long been familiar in medical education. The curriculum proposed by Flexner (1910) was organized according to discipline, so preclinical study by courses in the separate disciplines is often called "Flexnerian." Flexner, however, advocated extensive use of the teaching laboratory in the sciences to train medical students in scientific thinking. A common emphasis on critical method is one of the major themes connecting the separate courses of Flexner's proposed curriculum. In most contemporary medical schools, the emphasis on lecture material is far greater than that given to laboratory work (AAMC, *Curriculum Directory*, 1980). In this sense, most current curricula are not "Flexnerian."

One of the recurrent problems of the preclinical phase of the curriculum is the student's difficulty in assimilating and integrating a very large body of concepts and information drawn from a widening variety of disciplines. The organization of courses around organ systems was an attempt to develop interdisciplinary teaching that would help the student to make the needed integration (Ham, 1976). This curriculum organization was pioneered at Case Western Reserve University (Williams, 1980) and has since been adopted, in one variant or another, at many other medical schools. The use of common or prototypical patients' problems to organize preclinical studies at Michigan State University and McMaster University was also intended to help students integrate material from their studies in a more meaningful way (Neufeld & Barrows, 1974; Ways, Loftus, & Jones, 1973). Problem-based teaching, usually conducted in small groups, also aims to develop the judgment required for practice (Barrows & Tamblyn, 1980).

The clinical phase of the undergraduate curriculum is organized into placements in a clinical setting (clerkships, rotations, etc.), each placement defined by the profile of cases usually encountered in that setting. The location of placements and the time allotted to each are assigned so that the overall pattern of clinical encounters conforms to the pattern thought appropriate for a given level and specialization of training (McGlynn, Wynn, & Munzenrider, 1978). Some placements are experienced by every physician-in-training (such as basic clerkships in medicine, surgery, pediatrics, psychiatry, and obstetrics and gynecology); others may be experienced only by the few who will pursue a particular type of specialized training (e.g., ophthalmology). There is a major controversy as to how soon specialized placements should dominate the clinical phase of the curriculum. Some groups favor a common course of training through at least the first postgraduate year; others urge that options permitting specialization be given to senior medical students. In general, specialization increases with time.

Continuing medical education (CME) includes both informal and formal study by practicing physicians. Although informal study (such as reading journals) may have the greatest impact, recently there has been increased interest in formal programs of CME (Richards, 1978). These programs are usually short (one hour to one week) and focus on a topic of interest to the practicing community. Continuing medical education has been linked in many areas to relicensure and to recertification, so CME carries some of the burden for quality assurance in medical practice. This linkage has made the choice of topics for CME programs and their relation to the needs of practice increasingly important (Brown & Fleisher, 1971; Williamson, 1971).

Changes in Program. The medical curriculum gives central place to the biological sciences that contribute to an understanding of mechanisms of disease and therapy and to the systematized clinical knowledge related to the diagnosis, prognosis, and treatment of diseases and disorders. Proposals for change in the medical curriculum can be divided into three sets: (1) Some urge that the dominance of the biomedical model be modified to make new areas of instruction as important as the established areas. (2) Some accept the dominance of the biomedical model but ask that the curriculum be modified to reflect new knowledge or changing practice experience. (3) And some accept the existing content of the curriculum but suggest changes in the mix of educational resources and experiences.

Challenges to the biomedical model for medical education are often challenges to existing ideals for the practice of medicine. Some of the more prominent ideals have been those that promote community medicine and preventive care (McKeown, 1979); ambulatory, primary care medicine (Millis, 1966); caring and skillfulness in personal interaction (Cassell, 1976); and medical ethics (Pellegrino, 1979). A variety of instructional strategies have been worked out for each of these areas (e.g., Goldman & Arbuthnot, 1979; Kahn, Cohen, & Jason, 1979; Thomasma, 1979; Werner, Richards, & Fogle, 1978). Their place in the curriculum is likely to be limited and uncertain, however, until the profession resolves its uncertainty about how crucial each area is for the conduct of medicine.

Most curricular modifications involve updating curricular content as adjustments are made for new experience. The need for a revision of the curriculum is often signalled by a comparison of existing curriculum emphases with those indicated by a panel of experts (e.g., Gautreau & Monsen, 1979) or by the demands of current or projected practice (e.g., Hildebrandt & Whitehouse, 1975). Failure to make these adjustments sensibly can lead to a variety of problems in the instructional program (Abrahamson, 1978).

The most significant proposals for change in the arrangements and technology of instruction have been those that attempt to extend the resources for medical education and to increase the output from existing resources. Three examples illustrate the scope of these efforts. Attempts to quicken the pace of medical education by condensing the medical school curriculum into three years became popular in the early 1970s. A second kind of innovation was the use of community resources, both clinical and academic, at some distance from the university medical center. The use of community and Veterans Administration hospitals as a base for the clinical training of medical students has been especially important among medical schools founded after 1960 (Hunt & Weeks, 1979). A third type of innovation employed technologies new to medical education. These innovations typically involved the systematic development and use of sets of learning objectives (e.g., *Curricular Objectives, 1976,* 1976) and sometimes used the computer for managing the instructional system (Folk et al., 1976).

Comparative studies have shown little difference between older and newer instructional schemes in medical education (Cullen et al., 1976; Essex & Sorlie, 1979; Folk et al., 1976; Hallock et al., 1977; Trzebiatowski & Peterson, 1979). However, three-year curricula have almost disappeared along with the federal incentives that supported them (Beran, 1979). Efforts to make more extensive use of community resources continue; and technological innovations in instruction survive where they match the needs and style of the teaching faculty. Use of the newer schemes of instruction appears to depend on how well they mesh with other elements of the system of medical education and medical care.

Trends

Over the past two decades, a number of factors have combined to influence the pattern of American medical education. Perhaps the most significant of these has been a continuing concern for an adequate supply of health personnel in relation to perceived health care requirements. In the early 1960s, fears of impending physician shortages spurred national policy makers to enact legislation designed to increase the supply of personnel, particularly for primary care. The availability of start-up grants and federal subsidies based upon student enrollment resulted in the establishment of new medical schools and increased class sizes in existing institutions.

Many of the new schools established during this period, however, were unable to obtain the resources necessary to construct essential campus-based clinical facilities. As a consequence, they turned to community hospitals as the primary environment for clinical teaching. New and complex administrative arrangements were established to maintain school–community relationships, and educational programs were adapted to compensate for or to reflect the quality of community resources (Hunt & Weeks, 1979). Although conceived as a temporary arrangement, the community-based medical school continues today as an alternative model for medical education.

Over the same period, offices of medical education were founded at most medical schools to identify and bring into use more effective schemes of instruction and evaluation. The organization of these offices and of their associated training activities has been chronicled by one of the pioneers of this development (Miller, 1980).

Concerns about health resources began to shift by the late 1960s. Problems were now perceived in physician distribution across specialties and in selected geographic locations. The expanding knowledge base and the growing technology of medicine had apparently influenced large numbers of graduates to elect careers in limited-practice specialties rather than general medicine. Also, because the technology required to support these specialty practices was usually centralized, the number of physicians entering practice in inner-city, rural, or remote areas declined. Policy makers responded to these problems by providing incentives to develop and expand those educational programs that could strengthen human resources in these areas. As a result of these incentives, residency programs in the new primary care specialty of family medicine (which only recently had evolved from general practice) were established. Medical schools also received support to develop courses and programs to enhance interest in primary care in medically underserved areas. The National Health Service Corps, established in 1974, was another federally sponsored attack on the same problem.

National concerns about the supply of health care providers persist and continue to affect medical education today. The recently published report of the Graduate Medical Education National Advisory Committee (GMENAC Report), which projects a physician oversupply in many areas by 1990 (Tarlov, 1980), is of particular concern to medical educators. Although the full repercussions of this report have not yet been felt, many fear it will result in reduced governmental support and increased external program control.

Another factor that is beginning to influence the structure of medical education is the national concern about increasing health care costs. One response to this problem is the teaching of cost containment to medical students and residents in order to instill cost consciousness in the future practice patterns of these individuals (Aronson, 1979). At another level, however, medical education itself, being intrinsically intertwined with patient care, may be a significant contributor to the cost problem. Because patients are essential to existing models of clinical education, a portion of the cost of their care can reasonably be assigned to the educational process. Although there are reasonable arguments to support this practice, pressures to reduce costs will require an increased understanding and possible revision of the economic relationship between medical education and patient care.

Instruction

The success or failure of any curricular venture is largely related to the effectiveness of the process in which knowledge, skills, and desired behavior are transmitted to students. In medical education, the central and most critical mode of instruction is clinical teaching. Introduced sparingly in the first two years of medical school, clinical teaching serves as the primary means of instruction in clinical clerkships (years three and four) and in residency training. "Clinical teaching" may be broadly defined as an educational encounter between faculty, students, and patients that provides students with opportunities to acquire and apply medically relevant knowledge and skills within the context of patient care. Such teaching normally occurs within a hospital or other health-care facility and may be observed in individualized (one-on-one bedside), small-group (teaching rounds) and large-group (conferences, clinical lectures) settings. The teacher or preceptor is generally an attending or consulting physician although other professionals such as scientists, nurses, and social workers often participate.

Concerns for improving the organization of the curriculum in medical education have been accompanied by a growing recognition that clinical instruction requires equal attention. Critical observers of the process have noted that clinical teaching often emphasizes the acquisition of factual information and neglects problem-solving and other skills relevant to patient care (Yonke, 1979). Bashook (1976), for example, notes that evaluation of student performance focuses on information recall rather than diagnostic and interpersonal skills. As a consequence, students often do not learn the psychological or sociological aspects of patient care (Goroll, Stoeckle, & Lazare, 1974). Direct observation of the process (Reichsman, Browning, & Hinshaw, 1964) confirms that clinical teachers are preoccupied with didactic instruction. In bedside teaching rounds, for example, students are often passive onlookers who are given few opportunities to interact with the patient. When these opportunities do occur, constructive feedback is often not provided. The emphasis on factual information in clinical teaching is apparently reinforced by other faculty who, when rating a colleague's teaching effectiveness, identified "medical knowledge" as the fundamental criterion for a good instructor (Cotsonas & Kaiser, 1963).

Studies of students' perceptions of instructional performance suggest that factors other than medical knowledge may be equally important in effective clinical teaching. Stritter, Hain, & Grimes (1975) identified a number of factors that were viewed by students as important in facilitating their learning. In order of preference these factors are encouragement of active student participation, positive attitude toward teaching on the part of the instructor, emphasis on applied problem solving rather than factual material, student-centered instructional strategies, humanistic orientation, and emphasis on references and research findings. Irby (1978), after analyzing instructional performance ratings, concluded that the best clinical teachers were enthusiastic, clear and well organized, and adept at interacting with students and residents. The importance of teaching methods that actively involve students was confirmed by Byrne & Cohen (1973). They concluded that of ten modes of clerkship instruction observed, three were judged by students as most effective. These were (1) instructed learning (performing procedures and presenting cases under supervision), (2) practice, and (3) team or group problem solving. Lowest ratings were given to didactic and observational methods.

Studies involving the observation of teaching encounters have further defined the components of effective clinical instruction. After observing more than eighty teaching sessions, Reichsman, Browning, & Hinshaw (1964) suggested five criteria for effective clinical teaching: (1) close supervision of students; (2) integration of clinical medicine with didactic instruction; (3) clarity in teaching; (4) effective problem solving; and (5) providing students challenging situations. In another observational study, Adams et al. (1974) concluded that clinical teachers possess individualized models of effective instruction, and that these models are manifested in the instructor's personal teaching style. This study further suggests the importance of instructors becoming aware of their own teaching methods as an initial step in improving instruction.

As a result of these studies, and other research efforts that are beginning to focus on clinical teaching, many medical schools have instituted faculty development training programs to improve the instructional process. However, additional research is needed to define more clearly the components of clinical teaching and to determine their influence on student teaching (Yonke, 1979).

Evaluation

A broad variety of evaluation programs covering all phases of medical education have been developed nationally and locally (Samph & Templeton, 1979). Many of these programs are linked to the testing program or supporting services of the National Board of Medical Examiners (NBME). The NBME prepares tests used to assess readiness for licensure and assists many of the specialty boards to prepare their certification examinations. Perhaps the most influential of NBME tests are the series of three examinations (Parts I, II, and III) offered to students as they complete, in turn, the preclinical curriculum, medical school, and the first postgraduate year. In addition to offering students a route to licensure, scores on these tests are often used as evidence of the effectiveness of medical school curricula. Thus, there has been lively controversy regarding a proposal to eliminate the test that marks the end of the preclinical phase of the curriculum (Part I). This proposal was advanced during a reconsideration of the role of the NBME in licensure and certification (*Evaluation in the Continuum of Medical Education*, 1973).

Assessment Techniques. The two assessment techniques most prevalent in medical education are the objective, multiple-choice question and the performance rating. Multiple-choice testing dominates assessment in the preclinical, knowledge-oriented phase of the curriculum and figures prominently in the tests for licensure and certification. The technology of multiple-choice testing has been

married effectively to the knowledge base of medical education (Hubbard, 1978). Performance ratings are widely used in the clinical phase of medical education. Rating may be the technique best suited to assessment of features crucial to the evaluation of professional clinical performance and related dispositions over an extended period. Studies to appraise and sharpen rating forms and procedures (e.g., Dielman, Hull, & Davis, 1980) have been few, although concern about subjectivity and interrater reliability periodically surfaces.

Various techniques for evaluating clinical performance are available (Barro, 1973). One particular technique has been used so extensively that a supporting technology of test development and production has emerged (McGuire, Solomon, & Bashook, 1976). A simulation of the situation faced by a physician diagnosing and managing a medical problem is generated (McGuire & Solomon, 1971). The examinee works through the simulation, which is known as a Patient Management Problem (PMP), and a record is automatically developed of the choices made in this process. PMPs have been created in several formats (Hubbard, 1978; McGuire, Solomon, & Bashook, 1976) with some interesting scoring variations (Marshall, 1977). Evidence of PMP validity is found in higher scores as academic experience increases, and in positive but low correlations with multiple-choice examinations (McGuire, 1976; Schumacher, 1973). On the other hand, studies (Goran, Williamson, & Gonnella, 1973; Page & Fielding, 1980) have indicated that specific choices made on a PMP are not accurate predictors of the same behavior in real practice environments.

Many other measurement techniques have been developed for assessing ability to solve medical problems or important constituent skills. Some (Voytovich, Rippey, & Copertino, 1980) make use of Weed's problem-oriented system of medical record keeping (Weed, 1971). Others (Friedman, 1973; Helfer & Slater, 1971) have a logic similar to that of PMPs but differ in the way a case is represented and scored. Some (Berner, Bligh, & Guerin, 1977; Painvin et al. 1979; Sprafka, Parmeter, & Elstein, 1979) assess activity at different stages of problem solution. None of these techniques has been used as extensively or tested as thoroughly as PMPs have been.

Other areas of clinical expertise for which evaluation techniques have been developed are physician–patient interaction and clinical examination. Schemes for assessing physician–patient interaction (Grayson, Nugent, & Oken, 1977; Robbins et al., 1979) draw on measurement techniques described in the literature on counseling. Careful development of performance criteria leads to reliable measurement of performance in the clinical examination (Andrew, 1977; Stillman et al., 1980).

The techniques used for the evaluation of instruction in medical education are similar to those used in other areas of higher education (Daggett, Cassie, & Collins, 1979; Rippey, 1981). However, because of its interest to sociologists, medical education has been the beneficiary of a continuing line of studies of professional socialization (e.g., Bosk, 1979; Coombs, 1978) that highlight the internalization of norms of conduct and values. These studies illustrate how the environment shapes the development of the student-physician and offer a very different perspective than traditional program evaluation.

Findings. The problems of evaluating complex and extensive new programs are described graphically in a recent thorough case history of the important curriculum reforms at Case Western Reserve University (Williams, 1980). Changes in educational programs often occur over a period of time, making it difficult to say when a new program was instituted, even as concurrent changes in a school's makeup or reputation make it difficult to isolate the effects of the new program. However, when the program evaluated is more limited, it should be possible to demonstrate its effects. CME programs appear to have these characteristics. Stein (1981) was able to reverse the more pessimistic conclusion of an earlier review by Lloyd and Abrahamson (1979) and point to common features of CME programs that had a demonstrated impact on the practice of their participants. These programs carefully identified the learning needs of their participants, bearing in mind the needs of the participants' patients; involved participants in the process of needs identification; prepared clear objectives; used instructional methods that involved participants and anticipated clinical use; and systematically evaluated program impact.

The most significant studies for medical education may be those that cause reevaluation of the assumptions used in planning educational programs. For example, in working up a case, student-physicians have been urged to undertake thorough and wide-ranging data collection before entertaining serious diagnostic hypotheses. This advice and the value of routinely collecting large amounts of data about a case have been called into question by studies of how experienced physicians solve clinical problems (Barrows et al., 1978; Elstein, Shulman, & Sprafka, 1978). These studies indicate that physicians typically form hypotheses about what is wrong with patients early in the contact using a very limited data base; that much of the data physicians gather is intended to test these rapidly formed hypotheses; and that failure to consider the correct diagnosis is not necessarily remedied by extremely thorough observation of clinical data. These findings suggest new emphases for instruction and evaluation in medical education.

A second example of studies forcing reevaluation of assumptions is again found in studies of physicians' clinical reasoning. According to "conventional wisdom," some physicians were generally acute diagnosticians, whereas others were generally less proficient; this difference was an important part of the distinction between "good" physicians and others. However, studies undertaken as part of the Medical Inquiry Project (Elstein, Shulman, & Sprafka, 1978) failed to confirm this distinction and found instead that there was little correlation between physician perfor-

mance on one case and performance on another. This finding suggests that the assumed consistency of diagnostic performance does not exist and has stimulated consideration of aspects of the clinical situation that may control performance (Bashook, 1976; LaDuca, 1980). This situational analysis may, in turn, alter the ways in which programs of instruction and evaluation are conceived.

A final critical series of studies (Mendenhall, Girard, & Abrahamson, 1978; Girard et al., 1979) describe the patient care provided by physicians in different medical and surgical specialties. These studies have brought into question the assumption that primary care is provided almost exclusively by physicians in "primary care specialties," such as family medicine, general internal medicine, pediatrics, and obstetrics and gynecology. The results indicated that a substantial amount of primary care is provided by physicians in other medical specialties, implying that special attention to graduate training in primary care specialties is not required to assure adequate primary care for the population at large (Aiken et al., 1979). One of the most important spurs to federal intervention in graduate medical education may have been removed by these studies.

Students

Selection. Each year, more than 36,000 students apply for admission to medical schools in the United States. About one third of each annual cohort are repeat applicants. Less than 50 percent are admitted (Gordon, 1979).

Although selection processes vary somewhat from institution to institution, all are designed to identify candidates who will successfully complete a medical education program, will possess or acquire the personal characteristics of professional persons, and, upon completion of training, will perform competently as physicians. In recent years these selection processes have been influenced by regional and national concerns (Cuca, 1976, 1978). National goals for affirmative action, for example, have greatly enhanced opportunities for underrepresented minorities and women. Other factors, such as the residency status of candidates (particularly in state-supported schools) and the need for physicians in particular specialties or in medically underserved areas, have further complicated the admissions procedures of many institutions.

The primary criteria used at most schools in assessing the academic and professional potential of candidates include: past academic achievement as measured by undergraduate grade point average; scores on the standardized Medical College Admissions Test (MCAT); personal interviews; and letters of recommendation from former teachers and premedical advisers. Considering the intense competition and the importance of admissions decisions to both the applicant and the institution, the effectiveness of these criteria as predictors of success remains a central concern of educational research.

It is generally agreed that past academic performance

as measured by premedical grade average is the best single predictor of success in medical school if success is defined by grades and test performance (Gotthiel & Michael, 1957; Gough, Hall, & Harris, 1963; Johnson & Hutchins, 1966; Gough, 1978). The usefulness of the MCAT has been widely debated. The MCAT was originally used to verify grade records by rating applicants with a standardized measure of verbal and quantitative aptitude and of achievement in selected premedical sciences. Over the past two decades, dissatisfaction with the MCAT has become increasingly apparent (Bartlett, 1967; Turner, 1974; Wingard & Williamson, 1973). Critics argued that although the test had been reasonably successful in predicting academic performance in the basic sciences, it did not predict clinical performance in either the last two years of medical school or subsequent practice. They also claim that the test overemphasized recall of specific facts and did not sufficiently emphasize analytic (problem-solving) skills and comprehension of scientific principles.

In response to these criticisms, the Association of American Medical Colleges sponsored the development of a new version of the MCAT that, in addition to providing measures of reading and quantitative comprehension, yields knowledge scores in biology, chemistry, and physics as well as an assessment of problem-solving ability. The new MCAT was first administered in 1977 to students seeking medical school admission in the fall of 1978. In comparing scores from the old and new MCAT, Molidor and Elstein (1979) concluded that although the new test has provided more focused assessments of scientific knowledge and analytical skills, it may have done so at the expense of meaningful measures of verbal ability and of knowledge in the social sciences and humanities. Although preliminary studies of the test as a predictor of medical school performance in the basic sciences are encouraging (Cullen et al., 1980; Friedman & Bakewell, 1980; McGuire, 1980), conclusive evidence of its power to predict total performance, particularly in the clinical domain, is as yet unavailable.

Most medical schools employ a personal interview in addition to grade averages and MCAT scores to screen applicants. Generally, the interview is used to assess interpersonal skills, attitudes, and personal qualities deemed important components of affective professional behavior. The type of interview employed varies from institution to institution. Some schools, for example, interview candidates on a one-to-one basis using trained faculty interviewers; at others, candidates appear before committees. The interview results in a rating that is included in the data for admissions decisions.

The value of the interview as both an information source and a predictor of performance is debatable. Milstein et al. (1981), for example, could not find differences in medical school performance when comparing two groups of applicants: students interviewed and accepted at Yale School of Medicine who chose to attend other medical schools and students who had gone to the same schools but had been rejected by Yale following an interview.

Schofield and Garrard (1975) were also unable to discern differences in performance when comparing a group of students selected solely on the basis of a numerical index (combining grade averages and MCAT scores) with a group selected by conventional committee methods that included interview reports. In a study conducted at the University of Missouri, however, Murden et al. (1978) found a strong relationship between admissions interviewer ratings and subsequent clinical performance. Despite these conflicting findings, the popularity of the interview as a selection device remains high. Inconsistent results across studies are the rule, perhaps because the techniques used and the faculty's skill in interviewing are highly variable.

Debate on the relative effectiveness of the various criteria in the selection process continues. Although most would agree that current measures are reasonable forecasters of conventional academic performance, their predictive value in the more important clinical domain remains suspect.

Of equal concern to many medical educators is the impact on the selection process in limiting admission to a relatively small segment of the population. In the mid-1960s, Rosinski (1965) noted that 50 percent of those entering medical school had upper-class or upper-middle class backgrounds, whereas only 13 percent came from the lower classes. Although some progress has been made in diversifying the types of individuals seeking admission, underrepresentation of applicants from economically disadvantaged backgrounds persists (Gordon & Johnson, 1978). In response to this problem, many schools have adapted admissions requirements to ensure enrollments of underrepresented groups, which in turn, raised concerns about the equity of the process and caused some unsuccessful applicants to appeal admissions decisions in the courts. The much publicized Bakke decision affirmed the appropriateness of considering nonacademic factors (such as race, geographic or economic circumstances, etc.) in the admissions process but ruled that institutions could not set aside numbers of "minority positions" for which nonminorities could not compete (Kaplan, 1980).

The increasing scrutiny of the courts, combined with social pressure to redress perceived inequalities and injustices with respect to groups historically excluded from the medical profession, presents a dilemma to institutions seeking qualified candidates for admission. The resolution of this dilemma may well lie in the development of new admissions procedures that can predict future clinical competence and social utility with the same accuracy as existing procedures predict academic success (Ramsay, 1977).

Retention. Despite continuing concerns about predictive validity, medical school admission processes have been extremely successful in screening out most of those who would be unable to complete the program. In 1980, only 2.14 percent of those attending medical school withdrew or were dismissed. Of these, only 20 percent voluntarily withdrew or were dismissed as a result of poor academic performance; 16 percent withdrew to pursue other advanced study; 11 percent resigned to seek admission at other medical schools; 38 percent were granted special leave for reasons other than study; and 14 percent withdrew for various other personal reasons. The net attrition rate (excluding transfers to other schools and leaves for other advanced study) was higher for women (1.9 percent) than for men (1.3 percent), and the number of withdrawals for financial reasons (0.1 percent) was negligible (AAMC, 1980).

As a group, women and minority students experience the highest attrition from medical school. For women, attrition is generally not caused by academic difficulty but rather by difficulty in coping with a male-dominated institution. Minority attrition appears to be largely the result of inadequate academic preparation commonly associated with disadvantaged socioeconomic conditions. In response to these problems, many medical schools have established special programs for minorities and women to assist them in coping with the stresses of medical education (Beck et al., 1978; Cadbury, 1979; Davidson, 1978; Finseth, 1977; Wellington & Montero, 1978).

In 1981, the costs to individual students of a medical education increased dramatically as interest rates on loans escalated, loans became less available, and schools raised tuition to replace declining federal support. These moves decreased the share of the cost of education borne by the public sector and shifted it to the students. It appears that the impact of these changes will be greatest on working-class and middle-class students who are not eligible for affirmative action support. The effect on the composition of the medical student population and, thus, on the makeup of the profession is not yet known.

Career Choice. Unlike their early predecessors, medical school graduates today may choose from a broad range of career options. Some, for example, may elect to pursue careers in one of the primary care specialties (general internal medicine, family practice, or pediatrics) or in one of the general referral specialties (surgery, psychiatry, or obstetrics and gynecology). Others will choose from among the referral subspecialties (cardiology, endocrinology, neurology, etc.) or the diagnostic support specialties (pathology, radiology, etc.). New physicians also consider the type (solo, group, prepaid, etc.) and geographic location of practice. Although each of these decisions reflects the individual interests and aspirations of the graduate, in total they have a dramatic effect on the availability of health care. Identified shortages of physicians in certain specialties and geographic locations have intensified public interest in the career choices of medical school graduates.

Research focused on identifying the determinants of specialty choice suggests that career decisions are influenced by many factors. One study conducted in the early 1960s suggested that students with low MCAT scores were more likely to enter general practice than were their higher-scoring classmates (Peterson et al., 1963). Another study conducted at the same period found relations be-

tween scores on personality and interest inventories and specialty selection (Schumacher, 1964). More recent work has indicated that career choice may be related to attitudes and values (Plovnick, 1979); to orientations and perceptions of patient care (Kutner, 1978); and to the socioeconomic background of the student's family (Gordon, 1978). Funkenstein (1978), in reviewing data collected between 1958 and 1976 on Harvard medical students and alumni, concluded that career choices were associated more with the social atmosphere of the time than with other factors.

To the disappointment of curriculum developers, medical education programs appear to have little influence on career choice. Using data from the Association of American Medical Colleges' longitudinal study of the class of 1960 and related followup studies, Zuckerman (1978) analyzed the career paths of 2,514 medical students from 28 medical schools to test the hypothesis that career outcomes vary with different patterns of training. No evidence was found to support the hypothesis. Rosenblatt and Alpert (1979) were also unable to discern differences in career patterns when comparing experimental groups that had participated in a family medicine program with nonparticipant control groups. They concluded that external forces have far more effect on career decisions than does curriculum.

Of equal concern to health planners is the geographic locations selected by the new physicians. In a follow-up of 467 graduates, Stefanu, Pate, and Chapman (1979) confirmed the results of earlier studies by stressing the influence of residency location on the selection of a community for practice. The question of whether practice location is, in fact, considered prior to and influences the selection of residency location is as yet unanswered. Other factors that have been described as influencing practice location are specialty choice, socioeconomic background, values, and attitudes toward health care. One study (Skipper & Gliebe, 1977) stresses the importance of the career plans of spouses on the practice location selected by their partners.

Increasing concerns for physician shortages in selected specialties and geographic locations have intensified the need to understand better and possibly to influence the career development processes among medical students.

William S. Abbett
Robert G. Bridgham
Arthur S. Elstein

See also Licensing and Certification; Professions Education.

REFERENCES

Abrahamson, S. Diseases of the curriculum. *Journal of Medical Education*, 1978, *53*, 951–957.

Adams, W. R.; Ham, T. H.; Mawardi, B. H.; Scali, H. A.; & Weisman, R. Research in self-education for clinical teachers. *Journal of Medical Education*, 1974, *49*, 1166–1173.

Aiken, L. H.; Lewis, C. E.; Craig, J.; Mendenhall, R. C.; Blendon, R. J.; & Rogers, D. E. The contribution of specialists to the delivery of primary care. *New England Journal of Medicine,* 1979, *300,* 1363–1370.

Andrew, B. J. The use of behavioral checklists to assess physical examination skills. *Journal of Medical Education,* 1977, *52,* 589–591.

Aronson, S. M. The role of the medical school in cost containment. *Journal of Medical Education,* 1979, *54,* 903.

Association of American Medical Colleges. *Curriculum Directory.* Washington, D.C.: The Association, 1980.

Barro, A. R. Survey and evaluation of approaches to physician performance measurement. *Journal of Medical Education,* 1973, *48,* 1048–1093.

Barrows, H. S.; Feightner, J. W.; Neufeld, V. R.; & Norman, G. R. *Analysis of the Clinical Methods of Medical Students and Physicians* (Final report to Ontario Department of Health for Grant ODH-PR-273 and ODH-DM-226). Hamilton, Ontario: McMaster University, March 1978.

Barrows, H. S., & Tamblyn, R. M. *Problem-based Learning: An Approach to Medical Education.* New York: Springer, 1980.

Bartlett, J. W. Medical school and career performances of medical students with low MCAT scores. *Journal of Medical Education,* 1967, *42,* 231–237.

Bashook, P. G. A conceptual framework for measuring clinical problem-solving. *Journal of Medical Education,* 1976, *51,* 109–114.

Beck, P.; Githens, J. H.; Clinkscales, D.; Yamamoto, D.; Riley, C. M.; & Ward, H. P. Recruitment and retention program for minority and disadvantaged students. *Journal of Medical Education,* 1978, *53,* 651–657.

Beran, R. L. The rise and fall of three-year medical school programs. *Journal of Medical Education,* 1979, *54,* 248–249.

Berner, E. S.; Bligh, T. J.; & Guerin, R. O. An indication for a process dimension in medical problem-solving. *Medical Education,* 1977, *11,* 324–328.

Bosk, C. L. *Forgive and Remember: Managing Medical Failure.* Chicago: University of Chicago Press, 1979.

Brown, C. R., & Fleisher, D. S. The bi-cycle concept: Relating continuing education directly to patient care. In N. S. Stearns, M. E. Getchell, & R. A. Gold (Eds.), *Continuing Medical Education in Community Hospitals: A Manual for Program Development.* Boston: Massachusetts Medical Society, 1971, pp. 88–97.

Byrne, N., & Cohen, R. An observational study of clinical clerkship activities. *Journal of Medical Education,* 1973, *48,* 919–927.

Cadbury, W. E. *Medical Education: Responses to a Challenge.* New York: Futura, 1979.

Cassell, E. J. *The Healer's Art.* Philadelphia: Lippincott, 1976.

Coombs, R. H. *Mastering Medicine: Professional Socialization in Medical Schools.* New York: Free Press, 1978.

Cotsonas, N. J., & Kaiser, H. F. Student evaluation of clinical teaching. *Journal of Medical Education,* 1963, *38,* 742–745.

Cuca, J. *An Analysis of the Admissions Process to U.S. Medical Schools, 1973 and 1976.* Washington, D.C.: Association of American Medical Colleges, 1978.

Cuca, J. *The Medical School Admissions Process: A Review of the Literature, 1955–1976.* Washington, D.C.: Association of American Medical Colleges, 1976.

Cullen, T. J.; Dohner, C. W.; Peckham, P. D.; Samson, W. E.; & Schwarz, M. R. Predicting first quarter test scores from the new Medical College Admissions Test. *Journal of Medical Education,* 1980, *55,* 393–398.

Cullen, T. J.; Dohner, C. W.; Striker, G. E.; & Schwarz, M. R. Evaluating student performance in a decentralized basic sci-

ence program. *Journal of Medical Education,* 1976, *51,* 473–477.

Curricular Objectives, 1976. Springfield: Southern Illinois University School of Medicine, 1976.

Daggett, C. J.; Cassie, J.; & Collins, G. Research on clinical teaching. *Review of Educational Research,* 1979, *49,* 151–169.

Davidson, V. M. Coping styles of women medical students. *Journal of Medical Education,* 1978, *53,* 902–907.

Dielman, T. E.; Hull, A. L.; & Davis, W. K. Psychometric properties of clinical performance ratings. *Evaluation and the Health Professions,* 1980, *3,* 103–117.

Elstein, A. S.; Shulman, L. S.; & Sprafka, S. A. *Medical Problem-solving: An Analysis of Clinical Reasoning.* Cambridge, Mass.: Harvard University Press, 1978.

Essex, D. L., Sorlie, W. E. Effectiveness of instructional computers in teaching basic medical sciences. *Medical Education,* 1979, *13,* 189–193.

Evaluation in the Continuum of Medical Education. Philadelphia: National Board of Medical Examiners, 1973.

Finseth, K. A. Office for women in medicine: A model for social change. *Journal of Medical Education,* 1977, *52,* 928–930.

Flexner, A. S. *Medical Education in the United States and Canada.* New York: Carnegie Foundation, 1910.

Folk, R. L.; Griesen, J. V.; Beran, R. L.; & Camiscioni, J. S. *Individualizing the Study of Medicine: The Ohio State University College of Medicine Independent Study Program.* New York: Westinghouse Learning Corporation, 1976.

Friedman, C. P., & Bakewell, W. E. Incremental validity of the new MCAT. *Journal of Medical Education,* 1980, *55,* 394–404.

Friedman, R. B. A computer program for simulating the patient-physician encounter. *Journal of Medical Education,* 1973, *48,* 92–97.

Funkenstein, P. H. *Medical Students, Medical Schools, and Society during Five Eras: Factors Affecting the Career Choices of Physicians, 1958–1976.* Cambridge, Mass.: Ballinger, 1978.

Gautreau, S., & Monsen, E. R. Priorities of nutritional concepts assigned by health professionals and students. *Journal of Medical Education,* 1979, *54,* 607–612.

Girard, R. A.; Mendenhall, R. C.; Tarlov, A. R.; Radecki, S. E.; & Abrahamson, S. A national study of internal medicine and its specialties: I. An overview of the practice of medicine. *Annals of Internal Medicine,* 1979, *90,* 965–975.

Goldman, S. A., & Arbuthnot, J. Teaching medical ethics: The cognitive developmental approach. *Journal of Medical Ethics,* 1979, *5,* 170–181.

Goran, M. J.; Williamson, J. W.; & Gonnella, J. S. The validity of patient management problems. *Journal of Medical Education,* 1973, *48,* 171–177.

Gordon, T. L. Datagram: 1975 medical student graduates entering family practice. *Journal of Medical Education,* 1978, *53,* 939–942.

Gordon, T. L. Study of U.S. medical school applicants. *Journal of Medical Education,* 1979, *54,* 677–702.

Gordon, T. L., & Johnson, D. G. Study of U.S. medical school applicants, 1976–1977. *Journal of Medical Education,* 1978, *53,* 873–897.

Goroll, A. H.; Stoeckle, J. D.; & Lazare, A. Teaching the clinical interview: An experiment with first year students. *Journal of Medical Education,* 1974, *49,* 957–962.

Gottheil, E., & Michael, C. M. Predictor variables employed in research on the selection of medical students. *Journal of Medical Education,* 1957, *32,* 131–145.

Gough, H. G. Some predictive implications of premedical scientific competence and preferences. *Journal of Medical Education*, 1978, *53*, 291–300.

Gough, H. G.; Hall, W. B.; & Harris, R. E. Admission procedures as forecasters of performance in medical training. *Journal of Medical Education*, 1963, *38*, 983–998.

Grayson, M.; Nugent, C.; & Oken, S. L. A systematic and comprehensive approach to teaching and evaluating interpersonal skills. *Journal of Medical Education*, 1977, *52*, 906–913.

Hallock, J. A.; Christensen, J. A.; Denker, M. W.; Hochberg, C. J.; Trudeau, W. L.; & Williams, J. W. A comparison of the clinical performance of students in three- and four-year curricula. *Journal of Medical Education*, 1977, *52*, 658–663.

Ham, T. H. *The Student as Colleague: Medical Education Experience at Case Western Reserve.* Cleveland: Case Western Reserve University, School of Medicine, Division of Research in Medical Education, 1976.

Helfer, R. E., & Slater, C. H. Measuring the process of solving clinical diagnostic problems. *British Journal of Medical Education*, 1971, *5*, 48–52.

Hildebrandt, H. M., & Whitehouse, F., Jr. Setting educational goals by using diagnosis incidence data. *Proceedings of the Fourteenth Annual Conference on Research in Medical Education*, Washington, D.C., November 1975, pp. 131–136.

Hubbard, J. P. *Measuring Medical Education* (2nd ed.). Philadelphia: Lea & Febiger, 1978.

Hunt, A. D., & Weeks, L. E. (Eds.). *Medical Education since 1960: Marching to a Different Drummer.* East Lansing: Michigan State University Foundation, 1979.

Irby, D. M. Clinical teacher effectiveness in medicine. *Journal of Medical Education*, 1978, *53*, 808–815.

Johnson, F. G., & Hutchins, E. B. Doctor or dropout: A study of medical student attrition. *Journal of Medical Education*, 1966, *41*, 1099–1269.

Kahn, G. S.; Cohen, B., & Jason, H. The teaching of inter-personal skills in U.S. medical schools. *Journal of Medical Education*, 1979, *54*, 29–35.

Kaplan, W. A. *The Law and Higher Education.* San Francisco: Jossey-Bass, 1980.

Kutner, N. G. Medical students' orientation toward the chronically ill. *Journal of Medical Education*, 1978, *53*, 111–118.

LaDuca, A. The structure of competence in health professions. *Evaluation and the Health Professions*, 1980, *3*, 253–288.

Lloyd, J. S., & Abrahamson, S. Effectiveness of continuing medical education: A review of the evidence. *Evaluation and the Health Professions*, 1979, *2*, 251–280.

Marshall, J. Assessment of problem-solving ability. *Medical Education*, 1977, *11*, 329–334.

McGlynn, T. J.; Wynn, J. B.; & Munzenrider, R. F. Resident education in primary care: How residents learn. *Journal of Medical Education*, 1978, *53*, 973–981.

McGuire, C. H. Simulation technique in the teaching and testing of problem-solving skills. *Journal of Research in Science Teaching*, 1976, *13*, 89–100.

McGuire, C. H., & Solomon, L. M. *Clinical Simulations.* New York: Appleton-Century-Crofts, 1971.

McGuire, C. H.; Solomon, L. M.; & Bashook, P. G. *Construction and Use of Written Simulations.* New York: Psychological Corporation, 1976.

McGuire, F. L. The new MCAT and medical student performance. *Journal of Medical Education*, 1980, *55*, 405–408.

McKeown, T. *The Role of Medicine: Dream, Mirage, or Nemesis?* Princeton, N.J.: Princeton University Press, 1979.

Mendenhall, R. C.; Girard, R. A.; & Abrahamson, S. A national study of medical and surgical specialties. I: Background, purpose, and methodology. *Journal of the American Medical Association*, 1978, *240*, 848–852.

Miller, G. E. *Educating Medical Teachers.* Cambridge, Mass.: Harvard University Press, 1980.

Millis, J. S. (Chair). *The Graduate Education of Physicians.* Report of the Citizens' Commission on Graduate Medical Education. Chicago: American Medical Association, 1966.

Milstein, R. M.; Wilkinson, L.; Burrow, G. N.; & Kessen, W. Admissions decisions and performance during medical school. *Journal of Medical Education*, 1981, *56*, 77–82.

Molidor, J. B., & Elstein, A. S. A factor analytic study of the old and new MCAT. *Conference on Research in Medical Education*, 1979, *18*, 139–144.

Murden, R.; Galloway, G. M.; Reid, J. C.; & Colwell, J. M. Academic and personal predictors of clinical success in medical school. *Journal of Medical Education*, 1978, *53*, 711–719.

Neufeld, V. R., & Barrows, H. S. The "McMaster philosophy:" An approach to medical education. *Journal of Medical Education*, 1974, *49*, 1040–1050.

Page, G. G., & Fielding, D. W. Performance on PMPs and performance in practice: Are they related? *Journal of Medical Education*, 1980, *55*, 529–537.

Painvin, C.; Neufeld, V.; Norman, G.; Walker, I.; & Whelan, G. The "triple jump" exercise: A structured measure or problem-solving and self-directed learning. *Proceedings of the Eighteenth Annual Conference on Research in Medical Education*, Washington, D.C., November 1979, pp. 73–77.

Pellegrino, E. D. *Humanism and the Physician.* Knoxville: University of Tennessee Press, 1979.

Peterson, O. L.; Lyden, F. J.; Geiger, H. J.; & Colton, T. Appraisal of medical students' abilities as related to training and careers after graduation. *New England Journal of Medicine*, 1963, *269*, 1174–1182.

Plovnick, N. S. Career orientations in the primary care specialties. *Journal of Medical Education*, 1979, *54*, 655–657.

Ramsay, F. J. The medical school admissions dilemma: Damned if you do, damned if you don't. *Journal of the American Medical Association*, 1977, *237*, 1093–1094.

Reichsman, F.; Browning, F. E.; & Hinshaw, J. R. Observations of undergraduate teaching in action. *Journal of Medical Education*, 1964, *39*, 147–163.

Richards, R. K. *Continuing Medical Education: Perspectives, Problems, Prognosis.* New Haven, Conn.: Yale University Press, 1978.

Rippey, R. M. *The Evaluation of Teaching in Medical Schools.* New York: Springer, 1981.

Robbins, A. S.; Kauss, D. R.; Heinrich, R.; Abrass, I.; Dreyer, J.; & Clyman, B. Interpersonal skills training: Evaluation in an internal medicine residency. *Journal of Medical Education*, 1979, *54*, 885–894.

Rosenblatt, R. A., & Alpert, J. J. The effect of a course in family medicine on future career choice: A long-range follow-up of a controlled experiment in medical education. *Journal of Family Practice*, 1979, *8*, 87–91.

Rosinski, E. F. Social class of medical students. *Journal of the American Medical Association*, 1965, *193*, 95–98.

Samph, T., & Templeton, B. *Evaluation in Medical Education: Past, Present, Future.* Cambridge, Mass.: Ballinger, 1979.

Schofield, W., & Garrard, J. Longitudinal study of medical students selected for admission to medical school by actuarial and committee methods. *British Journal of Medical Education*, 1975, *9*, 86–90.

Schumacher, C. F. Personal characteristics of students choosing different types of medical careers. *Journal of Medical Education*, 1964, *39*, 278–288.

Schumacher, C. F. Validation of the American Board of Internal Medicine written examination. *Annals of Internal Medicine*, 1973, *78*, 131–135.

Skipper, J. K., & Gliebe, W. A. Forgotten person: Physicians' wives and their influence on medical career decisions. *Journal of Medical Education*, 1977, *52*, 764–765.

Sprafka, S. A.; Parmeter, J. T.; & Elstein, A. S. Patient-centered problem-solving evaluation in undergraduate medical education: Development, management, and theoretical perspectives. In A. L. Hunt & L. E. Weeks (Eds.), *Medical Education since 1960: Marching to a Different Drummer*. East Lansing: Michigan State University Foundation, 1979, pp. 108–136.

Stefanu, C.; Pate, M. L.; & Chapman, J. S. Hospitals and medical schools as factors in the selection of location of practice. *Journal of Medical Education*, 1979, *54*, 379–383.

Stein, L. S. The effectiveness of continuing medical education: Eight research reports. *Journal of Medical Education*, 1981, *56*, 103–110.

Stillman, P. S.; Ruggill, J. S.; Rutala, P. J.; Sabers, D. L. Patient instructors as teachers and evaluators. *Journal of Medical Education*, 1980, *55*, 186–193.

Stritter, F. T.; Hain, J. D.; & Grimes, D. A. Clinical teaching re-examined. *Journal of Medical Education*, 1975, *50*, 879–882.

Tarlov, A. R. (Chair). *Report of the Graduate Medical Education National Advisory Committee to the Secretary of the Department of Health and Human Services*. Washington, D.C.: U.S. Department of Health and Human Services, 1980.

Thomasma, D. Medical ethics training: A clinical partnership. *Journal of Medical Education*, 1979, *54*, 897–899.

Trzebiatowski, G. L., & Peterson, S. A study of faculty attitudes toward Ohio State's three-year medical program. *Journal of Medical Education*, 1979, *54*, 205–209.

Turner, E. V. Predictors of clinical performance. *Journal of Medical Education*, 1974, *49*, 338–342.

Voytovich, A. E.; Rippey, R. M.; & Copertino, L. Scorable problem lists as measures of clinical judgment. *Evaluation and the Health Professions*, 1980, *3*, 159–170.

Ways, P.; Loftus, G.; & Jones, J. Focal-problem teaching in medical education. *Journal of Medical Education*, 1973, *48*, 565–571.

Weed, L. L. *Medical Records, Medical Education, and Patient Care*. Chicago: Year Book Medical Publishers, 1971.

Wellington, J. S., & Montero, P. Equal opportunity programs in American medical schools. *Journal of Medical Education*, 1978, *53*, 633–639.

Werner, P. T.; Richards, R. W.; & Fogle, B. Ambulatory family practice experience as the primary and integrating clinical concept: A four-year undergraduate curriculum. *Journal of Family Practice*, 1978, *7*, 325–332.

Williams, G. *Western Reserve's Experiment in Medical Education and Its Outcome*. New York: Oxford University Press, 1980.

Williamson, J. W. Evaluating quality of patient care: A strategy relating outcome and process assessment. *Journal of the American Medical Association*, 1971, *218*, 564–569.

Wingard, J. R., & Williamson, J. W. Grades as predictors of physicians' career performance: An evaluation literature review. *Journal of Medical Education*, 1973, *48*, 311–322.

Yonke, A. M. The art and science of clinical teaching. *Medical Education*, 1979, *13*, 86–90.

Zuckerman, H. S. Structural factors as determinants of career patterns in medicine. *Journal of Medical Education*, 1978, *53*, 453–463.

MEMORY

See Cognition and Memory; Learning.

MENTAL HEALTH

The basic concept of mental health is a controversial notion, based upon the philosophical premise of the separation of mind and body. Out of this questionable dichotomy was born the concept of mental health as analogous to the medical concept of physical health. Even within a medical model this view has distinct limitations. In medicine, health has largely been viewed as the absence of identifiable pathology. An individual is well or healthy when he or she is not sick. The usefulness of such a concept depends largely upon the identification of specific disease entities that have known causes, symptoms and cures. For years psychologists have pointed to the fact that in behavior disorders, or so-called mental illnesses, the simple identification of similar disease entities was the exception rather than the rule. Some psychologists (Eysenck, 1960) have called for the entire notion of disease entities to be banished from the realm of modern psychology.

Another problem with the concept of mental health is the absence of consensual definitions. We have few agreed-upon concepts of what the mentally "healthy" individual looks like or how he or she behaves. Higher levels of human functioning are particularly difficult to describe or even to conceptualize. Some years ago Menninger (1963) wrote about the need to conceptualize a level of human functioning that he called "weller than well." The awkwardness of that phrase demonstrates the limitations inherent in conceptualizing mental health as simply analogous to the traditional medical view of physical health or well-being.

Definition. Jahoda's definition (1950) of some thirty years ago has offered a classic, if somewhat simplistic, view. Briefly, she described the mentally healthy person as one who actively masters his or her environment, demonstrates a considerable unity or consistency of personality, and is able to perceive self and the world realistically. Such a person is also able to function effectively without making undue demands upon others.

Although this description would probably still get considerable support, it has not been without its detractors. For example, the definition has little to say about prosocial functioning. Shoben (1957) went beyond the notion of self-sufficiency to propose that the healthy person is one who extends his or her functioning beyond self-control and personal responsibility into the area of social responsibility and commitment to some set of external values.

Even this expanded view of good mental health is centered totally around the individual. It assumes that the locus of functioning is situated within the individual and is independent of the environment, an assumption probably not even tenable for concepts of physical health. Occupationally related diseases such as the dreaded "black lung" of the coal mining industry are obviously products of interaction between the individual organism and the environment (Hinkle, 1968).

Major criticisms have been raised concerning person-centered concepts of mental health. Caplan and Nelson (1973) contend that person-centered notions of "mental health" and "mental illness" are counterproductive in our society because they focus attention away from the real sources of difficulty in the society, and, instead, foster a "person-blame" philosophy that places responsibility for social problems on the victims of those problems. Writers such as Thomas Szasz (1961), Halleck (1971), and Sharma (1970) have written of mental illness as a myth, and even as an essentially political concept, utilized to stigmatize those who are oppressed or disadvantaged in a society. Whereas the latter view may be extreme, it seems clear, as Brewster Smith has pointed out, that concepts and definitions of mental health and mental illness are inevitably rooted in value judgments about what is good and true and beautiful in human society and in the individual human being (M. B. Smith, 1961). The danger of abuse and misunderstanding arises when such definitions and concepts are understood to be based purely upon scientific analysis and investigation rather than upon social judgments. For these reasons Robert White (1973) has disputed the basic utility of the concept of mental health or the healthy personality. He argues that mental health is merely a metaphor—and a poor one at that—and that the entire concept ought to be abandoned in favor of more precise and meaningful descriptive terms.

A number of such descriptive terms have become current in the psychological literature. These include "self-actualization" (Maslow, 1968), the "mature personality" (Allport, 1963), and the "fully-functioning person" (Rogers, 1962). All of these models of human functioning provide somewhat greater specificity and elaboration than those emerging from the mental health view. They share, however, many of the disadvantages of mental health models; that is, they are rooted in value judgments and tend to view human functioning as "intrapsychic," or totally controlled within the organism.

New approaches. During the past fifteen or twenty years, major changes have occurred in psychological theory and research to alter views of human functioning and human effectiveness. Personality theories that were basically intrapsychic in nature have been supplemented or supplanted by theories that view behavior as the product of interaction between the individual and the environment (Mischel, 1973).

Three major developments have taken the field in this direction. The first is the movement termed "behaviorism," or, more specifically, the experimental analysis of behavior. It focuses upon the interaction between the individual and the reinforcing or nonreinforcing contingencies in the environment. Whereas the genetically endowed capabilities of the organism and its past learning history are not ignored, crucial events are perceived to be the immediate transactions between the individual and the environment. Explanatory constructs about presumed internal structures or traits are not viewed as relevant or useful.

A second influential development in the mental health field is derived from work in experimental social psychology and assumes that behavior is learned in social settings through modeling and the power of social role expectations. Child-rearing patterns, early socialization experiences in the school and home, and expectations of social groups are considered the most powerful determinants of behavior (Bandura, 1978).

A third powerful influence upon psychology has been called the "cognitive revolution" (Dember, 1974). Assuming that the ways in which people process information about environmental events are very important mediators of their behavior, this view emphasizes the basic interdependence of those components of human experience called thinking, feeling, and acting; each aspect affects the others. In this view, concepts such as motivation, self-efficacy, and sense of personal responsibility are products of how people process information about themselves and the world (Klahr & Wallace, 1976).

These three new approaches to mental health share an emphasis upon the interaction between human beings and their environments. Attempts to consider or assess the mental health of an individual in isolation from the person's transactions with the environment are considered fruitless (Ripley & Beuchner, 1967).

Community Mental Health. The most notable development in thinking about mental health that has accompanied these three new approaches has been the community mental health movement, which has signaled a major transformation in the way psychologists think about mental health and psychopathology (Smith & Hobbs, 1966). The community mental health approach differs from traditional approaches based upon personality theories in several major respects. First, it assumes that prevention of pathology is more important to social welfare than is the intensive or in-depth treatment of emotional disturbances (Suinn, 1979). It also focuses upon helping people solve practical problems of everyday living. It views psychopathology not as a result of a maladaptive personality style, or deep-seated psychic conflicts residing inside the individual, but as a series of immediate situational problems demanding practical solution (Lehmann, 1971).

The community mental health model, then, questions the existence of the disease entity concept. This model of mental health seeks to prevent pathology and to find solutions to problems rather than to seek vague cures for dimly understood illnesses. It does not attribute human difficulties solely to processes within the patient (Hersch, 1968). Instead, approaches to treatment are organized to deal with a variety of factors that affect the functioning of an individual and his or her performance. These can include the patient's skills and competencies, family interaction patterns, and environmental variables such as housing, employment, or educational opportunities. Also included among those variables around which treatment may be focused are attitudes and actions of the community or of society toward the identified patient (Iscoe, 1974). The community mental health approach recognizes that mental health problems may be rooted in characteristics of society itself, such as racism, sexism, poverty, unemployment, or restricted educational opportunity (Kelly, 1966; Greenblatt, Emery, & Glueck, 1967).

Empirical support for the community mental health approach stems from evidence that the incidence and severity of mental illness are inversely related to socioeconomic class (Dohrenwend & Dohrenwend, 1969). In other words, mental illness or psychopathology occurs with greater frequency and severity among lower socioeconomic class populations. One view of mental illness derived from these findings is that to some extent, at least, much of what we term mental illness appears to be a reaction to the stresses of living in disorganized and insecure environments (Bradshaw, 1969). Since the community mental health movement grows out of approaches to studying human behavior that stress the importance of interactions between individual and environment, the relationship between social class and mental illness is very significant. There is growing agreement, even among personality theorists, that aspects of the environment must be considered in the study of human personality (Dreger, 1977). From the community mental health perspective, then, the striving for positive mental health is more than a quest for freedom from intrapsychic conflicts or a bid for adjustment or conformity to society. It is, instead, a lifelong engagement between the person and the environment (Leland, 1978).

A logical extension and elaboration of the community mental health perspective and its theoretical antecedents is the "ecological model" of human development (Bronfenbrenner, 1979). This approach tends to view human behavior as understandable primarily within and as part of the natural context within which it occurs. The appropriate unit for analysis of behavior is the ecosystem, that is, the system within which person-environment interaction occurs (Warren, 1977). From this perspective, observation of and treatment for behavior disorders or mental illness is most appropriately accomplished within the natural environments in which the disorders occur.

These changes in thinking about mental health constitute what Suinn (1979) termed a "quiet revolution" in the study of psychopathology. They reflect the decline of the traditional clinical model of mental health practice (Schulberg, 1972) and the emergence of an ecological

model (Kelly, 1966). The role of the schools in mental health practice is very different in the two models.

The Schools and Mental Health. The clinical model was based upon the assumption that psychological abnormality was rooted in the individual. Two distinct processes, diagnosis and treatment, were conceptualized as the appropriate approaches. Treatment was medical, not educational, in orientation. The appropriate locus of treatment was outside the school, in the psychological clinic, or in severe cases, outside the community, in mental hospitals (Levine & Levine, 1970). The role of the school in the clinical model was to identify abnormality. Identification might involve preliminary steps in diagnosis, but teachers and school psychological workers functioned primarily to identify and refer (Meyers, Parsons, & Martin, 1979).

The conceptual change represented by the ecological model is enormous. Dysfunctional behavior is seen as a product of the transactions between the individual and the social system or environment. In many cases psychopathological behavior is seen as learned in social settings, not independent of the attitudes held by other system members toward the identified patient (Brickman, 1970). In this context, the school as a system that labels individuals as abnormal, and that, in a sense, casts them out of the society of normal people, is understood to be part of the problem rather than part of the solution (Hobbs, 1966). From this standpoint the school could be seen as a manufacturer of abnormal behavior. Questions about the nature of the school as a nurturing and socializing environment become relevant. Such questions have turned some of the attention that the clinical model had previously centered upon the child and family back to the school itself. Efforts at prevention of psychopathology and, to a considerable degree, treatment itself are redirected through the school. New roles and expectations for teachers and psychological workers, are emerging from this reorientation (Alderson, 1971; Meyers, Parsons, & Martin, 1979).

In the ecological model of mental health, educators join with other community members, both professional and lay persons, in a comprehensive team effort to prevent mental illness and to enhance the quality of life in community environments. Primary prevention rather than remediation is the highest priority goal in this kind of effort (Caplan, 1974). One example of this kind of inclusive, comprehensive and coordinated approach to community mental health is the Woodlawn program of assessment, early intervention, and evaluation (Kellam et al., 1975). Using a comprehensive model of community mental health, this project directed its efforts toward a black, urban neighborhood community on the South Side of Chicago. Over a six-year period, the project coordinated a systematic program of assessment, intervention, and evaluation directed toward the prevention of mental illness in first-grade children.

The nerve center of this program was a community mental health agency, and the prime vehicles for intervention were the local community schools. The project adopted a twofold concept of mental health that stressed both social adaptation and individual psychological well-being. Teams of professionals representing various disciplines were employed together to utilize the particular combination of resources needed for specific tasks or problems. The total community with all its members and social institutions was seen as the setting for intervention. Targets of intervention included both individuals and the natural constellations of significant others in family, neighborhood, and classroom situations.

The interventions focused not only upon children who were having trouble in school, but came to include all of the children in the first-grade population in the twelve elementary schools of the community. Intervention was aimed at all of the social processes affecting these children. Goals of the program were to strengthen children, improve their social and educational functioning in the classroom, and enhance relevant aspects of the classroom, school, and family environments so that each would more effectively support the adaptation of first-graders in their educational experience.

Three major modes of intervention were employed. Weekly consultations between mental health professionals from the community mental health center and teachers and school administrators were held. Weekly classroom meetings with children, teachers, and mental health professionals were inaugurated. Finally, a variety of sessions with parents were instituted. Some of these included sessions in which teachers and children were also involved.

A major finding of this six-year study was that one of the most important factors in the psychological well-being or mental health of the child is the degree to which the child masters basic educational tasks and earns the approval of the classroom teacher. The implications of this finding clearly seem to be that a primary mental health function of schools is to insure that all children master basic educational and social tasks and are given warm and personal recognition for doing so.

Overall, this study is an example of a contemporary approach to community mental health that involves close cooperation among mental health professionals, educators, and parents, and that focuses upon primary prevention of mental illness or psychopathology. Ideas about the school as a basic learning environment within which students develop intellectually and emotionally have had an impact upon the roles of educators in the United States (Blocher, 1974), Great Britain (Daws, 1968), and France (Louchet, 1967).

Behavioral Dysfunction. Whereas much progress has been made in conceptualizing approaches to mental health services and in focusing upon primary prevention, much more remains to be done. As Ross and Pelham (1981) point out in a comprehensive review of research on child psychopathology, our knowledge of the factors involved in mental illness in children is both sketchy and confused. Research efforts emanating from the traditional medically

defined diagnostic categories has not produced converging and clearly interpretable results about mental and emotional dysfunction.

Diagnostic models. The recent revision of the *Diagnostic and Statistical Manual for Mental Disorders* produced by the American Psychiatric Association (1980) seems to represent a modest, if overdue, attempt to move in the direction of greater precision and specificity in describing behavioral dysfunction. Although still rooted in the medical model, *DSM III*, as this manual is known, attempts to cover a wide range of human concerns including those that are developmental, educational, and vocational. However, criteria for categorizing behaviors as pathological are still largely based upon clinical judgment, and are thus not fully validated in an empirical sense.

The manual defines a mental disorder as a clinically significant behavioral-psychological syndrome or pattern that occurs in an individual and that is typically associated with a painful or distressing symptom or impairment in one or more important areas of functioning. That is, the condition creates a disability.

The system of diagnostic categories by which the manual is organized attempts to distinguish five major axes or bases of dysfunction. These include (1) those not attributable to the mental disorders that are the focus of treatment; (2) personality and developmental disorders; (3) physical disorders or conditions; (4) the overall severity of stressors contributing to the disorder; and (5) the highest previous level of functioning of the individual prior to the onset of the disorder. The diagnostic model is both cumbersome and complex, but it does represent a worthy attempt to move beyond the simple disease-entity concept. It also marks at least a beginning effort to view the individual within an environmental and developmental context. Unfortunately, the manual also attempts to bring educational and vocational functioning under the medical rubric of "mental illness" in what seems to be an obvious political and economic maneuver (Garmezy, 1978). Clearly learning disabilities, for example, are not in themselves psychiatric problems.

The contortions and complexities involved in attempting to bring the full range and context of human behavioral problems and concerns under a mental illness model seem only to highlight the basic limitations and inadequacies of that conceptual approach. It seems doubtful that a full understanding of human effectiveness and especially higher-level functioning will be significantly advanced within a disease-oriented model. Efforts at primary prevention and developmental facilitation seem to demand a totally different paradigm upon which to base research and intervention.

The rudiments of such a useful model for conceptualizing mental health functioning are reported by Prugh (1973). This classification system utilizes a basic four-point scale to provide a unitary measure of level of functioning. The four levels represented on this scale are labeled (1) optimal functioning; (2) functioning but vulnerable; (3) incipient dysfunctioning or moderate dysfunctioning; and (4) severe dysfunction.

A parallel four-point system using the same descriptors is also applied to family functioning so that it is possible to examine the level of functioning of an individual within the context of the overall functioning of an environmental system, the family. Prugh has elaborated the model to describe what he terms "psychosocial functioning" in a system based heavily upon the Erikson (1950) developmental schema and White's concept of competence (1959). This type of classification system, in which the level of functioning of an individual is measured in relation to the functioning of relevant environmental systems such as family, classroom, school, or job, seems to offer the most promise for evaluating programs aimed at goals of primary prevention or growth and development.

The relative lack of progress in both research and intervention efforts in the primary prevention area, despite the existence of considerable evidence demonstrating its utility and feasibility, is one of the most serious social policy problems in our society (Hyman, 1979); the sickness model still prevails in most schools and communities. Despite gaps in our understanding of many mental health problems, existing knowledge could be used more effectively to identify children at risk (Blau, 1979) and to improve the qualities of human environments in schools and families (Kazdin, 1979).

Ethical Concerns. A number of ethical and professional problems in the area of mental health treatment have emerged in recent years. One of these has concerned various aspects of the encounter group movement and related phenomena. It seems clear that, like many other therapeutic processes, encounter groups have the possibility of generating deterioration effects in some members under some conditions (Hartley, Roback, & Abramowitz, 1976). The rapid growth in popularity and proliferation of a wide variety of encounter group activities has caused concern. Such groups may constitute valuable resources for the growth and development of members; it is vitally important, however, that they utilize competently trained leaders and careful screening procedures in selecting members. Group leaders should adhere to the same ethical codes and principles subscribed to by other mental health professionals.

Another area of ethical concern in mental health relates to counseling and psychotherapy with women. The growth of the feminist movement has highlighted concerns about the adequacy and ethical nature of psychotherapy for women. Traditional theoretical approaches to treatment sometimes appear to reflect and intensify values and attitudes about women, their roles, and their needs that are sexist in nature and that help to perpetuate bias and denial of opportunity. Further research on the extent and effects of sex bias in psychotherapy is needed (Stricker, 1977; Whitley, 1979).

Another ethical concern involves the use of aversive therapies, that is, those that use painful or punishing stim-

uli to reduce the frequency of unwanted or maladaptive behaviors. When aversive therapies are used in settings in which doubt exists about the ability or opportunity of patients to give clear consent (as in the case of mentally retarded, psychotic, or incarcerated patients), major ethical questions exist.

This review has focused heavily upon mental health problems and services related to children and adolescence. As Neugarten (1968) has pointed out, many mental health problems are not simple extensions of those that begin in childhood or adolescence. Midlife and old age are life stages that produce their unique problems and concerns. Unfortunately, even less is being done in terms of primary prevention for adult problems than has been attempted with children. The rapid rate of social change in the society over the past two decades has created new mental health problems for adults (Fried, 1964; Goldin, 1970).

Changes in Treatment Methods. One of the most active areas of new research in mental health involves the cognitive treatment of depression (Phillips & Bierman, 1981), which utilizes concepts from both cognitive and behavioral psychology. Results of treatment programs seem most promising at this point. The merger of approaches drawn from both behavioral and cognitive theories that is presently occurring seems to constitute a major move toward convergence in psychotherapeutic thinking, and reverses the direction of the past fifty years. Another encouraging development emerging from the cognitive behavioral approach is the increase in research and development of self-control strategies. Cognitive and behavioral approaches offer great promise in this area because of the relative ease of delivery on a large scale and the wide range of problems to which they can be applied (Kanfer, 1979). A third very active area of research focuses upon training as method of treatment. Social skills training has become a major approach to treating a variety of people experiencing difficulty with practical problems of living (Phillips, 1978). A variety of social behaviors including assertiveness, communication, job seeking, and conflict resolution skills are taught in these programs.

These treatment methods tend to focus upon the practical interactions of troubled people with their environments. The treatments are focused upon behavioral and cognitive functioning rather than deep intrapsychic conflicts. Treatments tend to be structured and relatively short-term. Increasingly, the goals of treatment focus upon the development of social competence. In a very real sense, much of the meaning that has been invested in the concept of mental health has now been translated into the concept of personal and social competence and effectiveness. The acquisition of competence and effectiveness is increasingly seen as the key to prevention of mental health problems (Masters, 1981).

The implication of these trends for education seem rather clear. The major contribution of the schools to mental health lies in their effectiveness in helping students develop the understandings, attitudes, and skills necessary for functioning competently in society. Basic educational, vocational, and social skills are necessary for effective living. Cognitive processes of reasoning, problem solving, decision making, and social and moral judgment are necessary for the achievement of life satisfaction.

Donald H. Blocher

See also Behavior Problems; Counseling; Emotional Development; Personality Assessment; Personality Theory; Psychological Services; Social Development.

REFERENCES

Alderson, J. J. The challenge for change in school social work. *Social Casework,* 1971, *52*(1), 3–10.

Allport, G. W. *Pattern and Growth in Personality.* New York: Holt, Rinehart & Winston, 1963.

American Psychiatric Association. *Diagnostic and Statistical Manual of Mental Disorders* (3rd. ed.). Washington, D.C.: American Psychiatric Association, 1980.

Bandura, A. The self system in reciprocal determinism. *American Psychologist,* 1978, *33*, 344–358.

Blau, T. A. Diagnosis of disturbed children. *American Psychologist,* 1979, *34*, 969–972.

Blocher, D. A. *Developmental Counseling* (2nd. ed.). New York: Ronald Press, 1974.

Bradshaw, C. E. The poverty culture. *Childhood Education,* 1969, *46*(2), 79–84.

Brickman, H. R. Mental health and social change: An ecological perspective. *American Journal of Psychiatry,* 1970, *127*(4), 413–419.

Bronfenbrenner, U. *The Ecology of Human Development.* Cambridge, Mass.: Harvard University Press, 1979.

Caplan, G. *Support Systems and Community Mental Health.* New York: Behavioral Publications, 1974.

Caplan, N., & Nelson, S. D. On being useful: The nature and consequence of research on social problems. *American Psychologist,* 1973, *28*(3), 199–363.

Daws, P. P. The planned development of school guidance services. *Papers in Psychology* (Belfast), 1968, *2*(2), 40–48.

Dember, W. N. Motivation and the cognitive revolution. *American Psychologist,* 1974, *29*, 161–168.

Dohrenwend, B. P., & Dohrenwend, B. S. *Social Status and Psychological Disorder.* New York: Wiley, 1969.

Dreger, R. M. Developmental structural changes in the child's personality. In R. B. Cattell & R. N. Dreger. *Handbook of Modern Personality Theory.* New York: Wiley, 1977, pp. 406–432.

Erikson, E. *Childhood and Society.* New York: Norton, 1950.

Eysenck, H. J. *Behavior Therapy and the Neuroses.* New York: Pergamon Press, 1960.

Fried, M. Effects of social change on mental health. *American Journal of Orthopsychiatry,* 1964, *34*(1), 3–28.

Garmezy, N. DSM III: Never mind the psychologists—Is it good for children? *Clinical Psychologist,* 1978, *31*, 4–6.

Goldin, P. Preparing mental health professionals as race relations consultants. *Professional Psychology,* 1970, *1*(4), 343–350.

Greenblatt, M.; Emery, P. E.; Glueck, B. *Psychiatric Research Report: Poverty and Mental Health* (No. 21). Washington: American Psychiatric Association, 1967.

Halleck, S. L. *Politics of Therapy.* New York: Science House, 1971.

Hartley, D.; Roback, A. B.; & Abramowitz, S. I. Deterioration effects in encounter groups. *American Psychologist,* 1976, *31*, 247–255.

Hersch, C. The discontent explosion in mental health. *American Psychologist,* 1968, *23*(7), 497–506.

Hinkle, L. E., Jr. Relating biochemical, physiological, and psychological disorders to the social environment. *Archives of Environmental Health,* 1968, *16*(1), 77–82.

Hobbs, N. Helping disturbed children: Psychological and ecological strategies. *American Psychologist,* 1966, *21*, 1105–1115.

Hyman, I. A. Psychology, education, and schooling: Social policy implications in the lives of children and youth. *American Psychologist,* 1979, *34*, 1024–1029.

Iscoe, I. Community psychology and the competent community. *American Psychologist,* 1974, *29*(8), 607–613.

Jahoda, M. Toward a social psychology of mental health. In M. J. E. Senn (Ed.), *Symposium on the Healthy Personality.* New York: Josiah Macy, Jr. Foundation, 1950.

Kanfer, F. H. Personal control, social control, and altruism: Can society survive the age of individualism? *American Psychologist,* 1979, *34*, 231–239.

Kazdin, A. E. Advances in child behavior therapy: Applications and implications. *American Psychologist,* 1979, *34*, 981–987.

Kellam, S. G.; Branch, J. D.; Agrawal, N. C.; & Ensminger, M. E. *Mental Health and Going to School.* Chicago: University of Chicago Press, 1975.

Kelly, J. G. Ecological constraints on mental health services. *American Psychologist,* 1966, *21*(6), 535–539.

Klahr, D., & Wallace, J. G. *Cognitive Development: An Information-processing View.* Hillsdale, N.J.: Lawrence Erlbaum Associates, 1976.

Lehmann, S. Community and psychology and community psychology. *American Psychologist,* 1971, *26*(6), 544–560.

Leland, H. W. Theoretical considerations of adaptive behavior. In W. A. Coulter & H. Morrow (Eds.), *Adaptive Behavior.* New York: Grune & Stratton, 1978, pp. 21–44.

Levine, M., & Levine, A. The more things change: A case history of child guidance clinics. *Journal of Social Issues,* 1970, *26*(3), 19–33.

Louchet, P. L'action éducative du conseiller d'O.S.P. en France: Evolution au cours des quinze dernieres années. *Bulletin de Psychologie,* 1967, *20*(10–15), 681–691.

Maslow, A. H. *Toward a Psychology of Being* (2nd. ed.). Princeton, N.J.: Van Nostrand, 1968.

Masters, J. C. Developmental psychology. In *Annual Review of Psychology, 1981.* Palo Alto, Calif.: Annual Reviews, Inc., 1981, pp. 117–151.

Menninger, K. *The Vital Balance.* New York: Viking Press, 1963.

Meyers, J. D.; Parsons, R. D.; & Martin, R. *Mental Health Consultation in the Schools.* San Francisco: Jossey-Bass, 1979.

Mischel, W. Toward a cognitive social learning reconceptualization of personality. *Psychological Review,* 1973, *80*, 252–283.

Neugarten, B. L. The psychology of the life cycle. In B. L. Neugarten (Ed.), *Middle Age and Aging.* Chicago: University of Chicago Press, 1968.

Phillips, E. L. *The Social Skills Basis of Psychopathology: Alternatives to Abnormal Psychology and Psychiatry.* New York: Grune & Stratton, 1978.

Phillips, J. S., & Bierman, K. L. Clinical psychology: Individual methods. *Annual Review of Psychology, 1981.* Palo Alto, Calif.: Annual Reviews, 1981 pp. 405–438.

Prugh, D. G. Psychosocial disorders in childhood and adolescence: Theoretical considerations and an attempt at classification. In Joint Commission on Mental Health of Children, *The Mental*

Health of Children: Services, Research, and Manpower. New York: Harper & Row, 1973, pp. 334–387.

Ripley, S. D., & Beuchner, H. K. Ecosystem science as a point of synthesis. *Daedalus*, 1967, *96*, 1192–1199.

Rogers, C. R. Toward becoming a fully functioning person. In A. W. Combs (Ed.), *Perceiving, Behaving, Becoming.* Washington, D.C.: Association for Supervision and Curriculum Development Yearbook, 1962.

Ross, A. O.; Pelham, W. E. Child psychopathology. *Annual Review of Psychology.* Palo Alto, Calif.: Annual Reviews, Inc., 1981, pp. 243–278.

Schulberg, H. C. Challenge of human service programs for psychologists. *American Psychologist*, 1972, *27*(5), 566–572.

Sharma, S. L. A historical background of the development of nosology in psychiatry and psychology. *American Psychologist*, 1970, *25*, 248–253.

Shoben, E. J. Toward a concept of the normal personality. *American Psychologist*, 1957, *12*, 83–190.

Smith, M. B. "Mental health" reconsidered: A special case of the problem of values in psychology. *American Psychologist*, 1961, *16*, 299–306.

Smith, M. B., & Hobbs, N. The community and the community mental health center. *American Psychologist*, 1966, *21*(6), 499–509.

Stricker, G. Implications of research for psychotherapeutic treatment of women. *American Psychologist*, 1977, *32*, 14–22.

Suinn, R. M. Behavior pathology. In M. E. Meyer (Ed.), *Foundations of Contemporary Psychology.* New York: Oxford Press, 1979, pp. 651–679.

Szasz, T. S. *The Myth of Mental Illness.* New York: Haber, 1961.

Warren, S. F. A useful ecobehavioral perspective for applied behavioral analysis. In A. Rogers-Warren & S. F. Warren (Eds.), *Ecological Perspectives in Behavioral Analysis.* Baltimore: University Park Press, 1977, pp. 173–196.

White, R. Motivation reconsidered: The concept of competence. *Psychological Review*, 1959, *66*, 297–333.

White, R. The concept of healthy personality: What do we really mean? *Counseling Psychologist*, 1973, *4*, 3–12.

Whitley, E. B., Jr. Sex roles and psychotherapy: A current appraisal. *Psychological Bulletin*, 1979, *86*, 1309–1321.

MENTAL RETARDATION

Since 1969 several textbooks have been written that summarize and document much of the accumulated knowledge about mental retardation (Chinn, Drew, & Logan, 1975; Hutt & Gibby, 1979; Ingalls, 1978; Kauffman & Payne, 1975; MacMillan, 1977; Maloney & Ward, 1979; Menolascino, 1977; Neisworth & Smith, 1978; Payne & Patton, 1981; Robinson & Robinson, 1976; Smith, 1971). People interested in conducting research with mentally retarded subjects will find relevant sections of these texts to be of value.

In addition to articles in the standard educational journals, information that is specific to the field of mental retardation can also be located in three journals devoted specifically to this topic. The American Association on Mental Deficiency (AAMD) publishes *Mental Retardation* and the *American Journal of Mental Deficiency*. The Council for Exceptional Children (CEC) publishes *Education and Training of the Mentally Retarded*. CEC also publishes *Exceptional Child Education Resources*, which contains abstracts of articles that have been culled from virtually all of the professional journal literature related to special education.

Because of the vast amount of information available in these publications, this article is, of necessity, restricted to a general overview of the major concepts and issues that are currently of concern to those who work with mentally retarded people. Additional in-depth material can be obtained from the sources cited, and customized computer searches for specific information can be performed at the CEC Information Center in Reston, Virginia, which is part of the Educational Resources Information Center (ERIC) information storage and retrieval system.

New Understandings. Society bases decisions about treatment of the mentally retarded upon its current understanding of the condition. In the past, theories of mental retardation sought to identify, describe, and explain the salient characteristics that differentiate this group from the rest of the populace; the emphasis now has shifted to an appreciation of the ways in which mentally retarded individuals are similar to other handicapped people and to the general population. The evolution of these new understandings can be traced to many factors—advances in research, parent activism, litigation, legislation, and increased public awareness.

During the first half of the twentieth century, public school programs were developed and expanded for children with mild retardation. In 1950, a group of parents banded together to advocate for children with more moderate and severe levels of retardation. This group, now known as the National Association for Retarded Citizens (NARC), had a major effect on both the type and quality of educational services for the retarded.

Numerous studies concerning many aspects of mental retardation were conducted in the 1950s and early 1960s. Several anthologies and reviews of research efforts emerged during this period (e.g., Clarke & Clarke, 1965; Ellis, 1963; Stevens & Heber, 1964). A summary of the characteristics of mentally retarded people can be found in Hunt (1969).

In the late 1960s and 1970s, advocacy for the retarded became the watchword. Exposés describing the squalid conditions that existed in many state-supported residential institutions for the mentally retarded (e.g., Blatt & Kaplan, 1966) received wide circulation. Advocates became more militant in demanding rights for the retarded. Local and state chapters of NARC initiated and supported litigation that resulted in landmark legal decisions confirming that mentally retarded children had been denied their constitutional rights to education (Kindred et al., 1975; Weintraub et al., 1976).

The concept of normalization (Nirje, 1969; Wolfensberger, 1972) has now become the prevailing philosophy for education and treatment of mentally retarded people. Normalization is based upon the belief that handicapped people have the right to as normal an existence as possible. With the advent of this philosophy, the mentally retarded have been accorded increased dignity, value, and visibility as well as important civil and educational rights.

The effects of these social forces culminated in the development of highly significant federal legislation in the early and mid-1970s. Section 504 of the Rehabilitation Act of 1973 (Public Law 93-112) prohibited discrimination on the basis of handicap and the Education for All Handicapped Children Act of 1975 (Public Law 94-142) guaranteed all handicapped children, including the most severely retarded, a free and appropriate public education.

Public Law 94-142 also mandated education in the least restrictive environment. Often mislabeled as "mainstreaming," this practice ensures that handicapped individuals receive services in the educational environment as much like the regular classroom as feasible. For mildly retarded students traditionally segregated from regular class peers by placement in separate special classes, the guarantee of social and instructional integration to the maximum extent appropriate represented an important new direction. Special classes had long been under attack for perpetuating the stigma attached to handicapped students by the labeling process (Hobbs, 1975, 1976), for being no more effective than regular classes in promoting pupil growth (Dunn, 1968), and for containing disproportionate numbers of minority-group students (Mercer, 1973). The decline of the special class was accompanied by the proliferation of part-time resource services for the mildly handicapped of all categories; many mildly retarded students were integrated with normal peers in the regular classroom and with other handicapped students in the special education resource room.

Diagnosis and Definition. The need to accurately identify individuals as mentally retarded in order to provide appropriate services persists despite the problems inherent in labeling. Identification rests upon definition, and the definition proposed by the AAMD is widely accepted. It describes mental retardation as "significantly subaverage general intellectual functioning existing concurrently with deficits in adaptive behavior" (Grossman, 1977, p. 5).

Intellectual functioning is measured by standardized tests of intelligence, commonly labeled "IQ tests." Performance more than two standard deviations below the test mean is considered significantly subaverage and includes (presuming the hypothetical normal distribution) 2.27 percent of the population. Designed in the early 1900s as objective measures of variations in intellect, tests of intelligence have been attacked in recent years as racially and culturally discriminatory. When minority group students were found vastly overrepresented in special classes for the mildly retarded, the use of intelligence tests for educational placement decisions fell under scrutiny. Court cases such as *Diana* (1970) and *Larry P.* (1972) pointed up testing

abuses with Hispanic and black persons; tests of intelligence drew a spate of criticism (Samuda, 1975) and were judged by many as culturally biased and therefore inappropriate for use with minority group students, particularly those with limited English language skills.

One attempt to overcome the limitations of intelligence tests is the inclusion of impaired adaptive behavior as a criterion for mental retardation. Adaptive behavior (or social competence) is defined as "the effectiveness or degree with which an individual meets the standards of personal independence and social responsibility expected for age and cultural group" (Grossman, 1977, p. 11). As noted in *The Six Hour Retarded Child* (President's Committee on Mental Retardation, 1969), students who perform poorly in school and on mental measures may function adequately at home and in the community. If they are able to meet family and social expectations in every arena except the academic classroom, they are not characterized by general intellectual retardation.

Current diagnostic procedures for identification of mental retardation include individually administered intelligence tests such as the Wechsler Intelligence Scale for Children–Revised (Wechsler, 1974) and the Stanford-Binet Intelligence Scale (Terman & Merrill, 1973). Adaptive behavior is evaluated less directly; structured interviews or questionnaires such as the Vineland Social Maturity Scale (Doll, 1965), the AAMD Adaptive Behavior Scale–Public School Version (Lambert et al., 1975), and the Adaptive Behavior Inventory for Children (Mercer & Lewis, 1977) are used to elicit information from parents, teachers, and others familiar with the typical performance of the student.

Today, procedural safeguards lessen the danger of testing abuses. According to Public Law 94-142, students must be evaluated by multidisciplinary teams in all areas related to the suspected disability; and placement may not occur on the basis of only one score (such as an IQ). Measures must also be nondiscriminatory, in the student's native language, validated for the purpose for which they are used, and administered by trained personnel.

Despite these safeguards, many popular instruments lack adequate validation (Salvia & Ysseldyke, 1981), and there is continuing need for development of nonbiased assessment procedures for use with linguistically and culturally different students. With bilingual and non–English-speaking individuals, the dominant language of the student is identified and then assessment continues using measures in that language. The major deterrent to this approach is the scarcity of appropriate measures; for instance, the language, norms, and cultural nuances of tests developed in Mexico City may be inappropriate for Spanish-speaking New Yorkers.

Strategies for overcoming cultural bias include culture-fair tests (which remove factors thought to depress the performance of minority students, such as speed and heavy stress on verbal abilities) and culture-specific measures such as the Black Intelligence Test of Cultural Homogeneity (Williams, 1972). Another approach, exemplified by the System of Multicultural Pluralistic Assessment (SOMPA) (Mercer & Lewis, 1977), is the use of pluralistic or multiple norms. This battery is made up of several instruments, including an individual intelligence test (the WISC–R), the Adaptive Behavior Inventory for Children, and the Sociocultural Scales. WISC–R performance is used as an index of school functioning level rather than IQ; intellectual performance or estimated learning potential is determined by rescoring the WISC–R using the set of norms identified as appropriate by results of the Sociocultural Scales. Mental retardation is considered only when the individual's performance is subaverage in relation to those of the same sociocultural group. None of these approaches, including the SOMPA, has found widespread acceptance; one difficulty has been that such strategies remove many students from consideration for special education services without offering alternative treatment options. The problems of nonbiased assessment remain as yet unsolved (Bailey & Hardin, 1980; Duffey et al., 1981; Oakland, 1980).

Identification of mental retardation in the schools remains a norm-referenced decision; individuals are selected for special services if their performance deviates from that of their peers. As stated in the AAMD definition, this deviation must be global (in that it is manifested in both intellectual performance and adaptive behavior) and it must be of significant magnitude; McLoughlin and Lewis (1981) also include poor school performance as a necessary condition for the provision of special education services. Other conceptualizations of mental retardation, less psychometric in nature, are gaining popularity; according to Bijou (1966), "a retarded individual is one who has a limited repertory of behavior shaped by events that constitute his history" (p. 2). Definitions such as this, although difficult to operationalize for identification purposes, focus attention upon the ultimate goal of treatment.

Etiology and Prevention. The search for various etiologies of mental retardation is significant because in virtually every identified case, a preventive measure has been found (Payne & Patton, 1981). Unfortunately, although more than 250 causes have been identified, these account for only about 10 percent of the cases of mental retardation (Maloney & Ward, 1979).

Following the international system developed by the World Health Organization for the classification of diseases, the AAMD designed a model for etiological classification (Grossman, 1977). Following is an overview of the nine categories into which causes are classified, accompanied by a brief discussion of some of the preventive measures associated with each.

Infections and intoxications can occur either prenatally or postnatally. Congenital rubella, syphilis, and herpes simplex can attack the fetus with drastic effects. Rh-incompatibility between mother and fetus can likewise lead to birth defects. After birth, the child can contract diseases such as meningitis and encephalitis, which can also result in retardation. The effects of the maternal use of drugs and

tobacco are unclear, although most authorities advise against their use during pregnancy. There is increasing evidence that maternal use of alcohol during pregnancy can cause retardation. This condition is known as fetal alcohol syndrome (Smith, Jones, & Hansen, 1976). Preventive measures include abstinence from drugs, alcohol, and other teratogens; prompt and thorough prenatal care; vaccination of Rh-sensitized mothers; close consultation with physicians in the event of childhood diseases; and legislation that bans the use of certain substances that are known to cause retardation (such as lead-based paint).

Trauma or physical agents result in brain damage that can cause mental retardation during the prenatal, perinatal, and postnatal periods. Chief among these are anoxia, due to a twisted umbilical cord, which can result in lack of oxygen to the brain during birth; difficult deliveries; and child abuse. Improved physical care can help to reduce the effects of trauma. Legislation in approximately one-half of the states makes failure to report child abuse a misdemeanor; and legislation in all but one state protects those from prosecution who report suspected child abuse in good faith. These laws should also serve as preventive measures (Kline, 1977).

Metabolic or nutritional factors account for a large number of specified causes of mental retardation. Conditions such as phenylketonuria and galactosemia can be controlled through special diets. Use of thyroxin can lessen the effects of cretinism; and improved nutrition for both children and pregnant mothers can preclude the effects of malnutrition as a factor in the etiology of retardation.

Postnatal gross brain disease includes rather rare genetic disorders such as neurofibromatosis and tuberous sclerosis. Huntington's chorea is a condition that does not appear generally until a person is in the mid-thirties, at which time progressive deterioration of the brain occurs. Preventive measures in such cases rely primarily on genetic counseling or sterilization.

Unknown prenatal influences include all conditions that are present at birth, but for which no specific etiology can be pinpointed. Most frequently, these cases include microcephaly and hydrocephalus. The effects of the latter condition have been dramatically reduced through the use of surgical techniques that involve the implantation of a shunt to drain off the excess cerebrospinal fluid, resulting in a reduction of the cranial pressure that causes brain damage.

Chromosomal anomalies account for a number of different forms of retardation. The most frequent of them is Down's syndrome (formerly referred to as mongolism), which may account for 5 to 6 percent of all retarded people (Payne & Patton, 1981). Chromosomal anomalies can now be detected prior to birth through a surgical technique known as amniocentesis. In this procedure, a sample of the amniotic fluid surrounding the fetus is examined; and, if chromosomal abnormalities are present, it can be determined that the child will be affected. A decision would then need to be made about whether to carry the fetus to full term or to abort the pregnancy. One of the forms of Down's syndrome (Trisomy 21) has been found to be associated with maternal age. Genetic counseling and amniocentesis are important tools in the decisions that older women must make regarding pregnancy.

Gestational disorders primarily result in premature births and low birth weight. The President's Committee on Mental Retardation (1977) identified a number of correlates of prematurity; however, the effects appear to be somewhat unclear. Problems frequently occur with extremely short pregnancies of less than 28 weeks or very low birth weights of less than 1500 grams or $3\frac{1}{2}$ pounds. Situations such as this underscore the need for good prenatal care in an attempt to maximize the probability of carrying pregnancies to full term.

Retardation following psychiatric disorders can occur; however, it is quite difficult to conduct differential diagnoses to unravel the various causes and effects of the two conditions. For example, mental retardation and psychiatric disorders may occur together, they may be the result of some other precipitating factor, or one may serve as an etiological agent for the other. Regardless of the cause, a number of children who have been diagnosed as seriously emotionally disturbed often are functionally mentally retarded (Baker, 1979).

Environmental influences represent, by far, the greatest number of cases for which an etiological classification is given. In this category, the AAMD cites "psychosocial disadvantage" as the primary determinant of mental retardation. The majority of the mildly retarded fall into this category. Although arguments have prevailed over the relative effect of heredity and environment in the etiology of mild retardation, the general position that seems to be most widely accepted is that there is an interaction between heredity and environment. That is, genetics set the theoretical range for a person's potential, and the quality of the environment determines the behavior patterns that the person develops within this range. Thus, a person with average genetic potential may actually function as mentally retarded if reared in an impoverished environment.

The AAMD has developed four criteria that should be adhered to if a person is to be diagnosed as retarded due to psychosocial disadvantages (Grossman, 1977). First, intelligence and adaptive behavior must be at retarded levels of functioning. Second, there must be retarded intellectual functioning in the immediate family and usually within the larger family circle. Third, there must be no clear evidence of brain damage in the child; and, fourth, the home environment is usually impoverished. Prevention, in cases such as this, focuses upon the enrichment of impoverished environments and the provision of high-quality educational and social services.

Alternative Approaches. Within the past decade, the field of special education has undergone a revolution in which resource rooms replaced special classes as the placement of choice for mildly retarded students. Although research on the efficacy of special classes did not conclusively support their abolition (MacMillan, 1977), resource services became increasingly attractive as attacks were leveled on the discriminatory nature of segregated special programs and the pejorative effects of labeling.

Allied is the trend toward noncategorical (or multicategorical) resource services. In this model, students are grouped by educational needs (rather than by handicapping condition), and one special educator provides services to students with several different handicaps. This arrangement is usual for mildly handicapped students identified as mentally retarded, emotionally disturbed (sometimes termed "behavior-disordered"), and learning disabled; Hallahan and Kauffman (1976) maintain that it is not useful to differentiate among these groups in terms of etiology, behavioral characteristics, or teaching methodologies.

Despite the popularity of the resource room, it is recognized that some mentally retarded students require more intensive programs. Public schools must maintain a continuum of alternative placements (such as the cascade of services proposed by Deno, 1973). Typical placements range from the regular class with consultation services for the teacher and/or resource services for the student, to special classes, to special schools and residential facilities for students with severe, comprehensive needs.

With increased opportunities for inclusion of handicapped students in regular classes, special education programs for the mildly retarded have shifted toward emphasis upon the academic skill sequences of the regular curriculum. Direct instruction of academic skills is supported as an effective approach by the growing body of research on teacher behaviors (Stevens & Rosenshine, 1981). With acceptance and utilization of behavioral techniques and technological advances, instruction of retarded students has become more efficient and effective. The texts cited in the first section of this article provide additional information related to specifics of curriculum and instructional approaches. The career education movement (Brolin & Kokaska, 1979; Cegelka, 1981) is gaining impetus as education is conceived as a life span process not only for the handicapped but also for the average citizen.

Severe and Profound Retardation. As a result of the previous neglect of severely and profoundly retarded people, and in response to the federal mandates of Public Law 94-142, the interest of many professional workers in the field of mental retardation was switched to this segment of the retarded population. In fact, a new organization, The Association for the Severely Handicapped (TASH), was founded in the 1970s to serve as a focal point for professionals interested in this area.

Contrary to what many people think, severely and profoundly handicapped children represent a very heterogeneous population. Sontag, Burke, and York (1973) described the array of characteristics that may be found among the severely handicapped. These include "those who are not toilet trained; aggress toward others; do not attend to even the most pronounced social stimuli; self-mutilate; ruminate; self-stimulate; do not walk, speak, hear, or see; manifest durable and intense temper tantrums; are not under even the most rudimentary forms of verbal control; do not imitate; manifest minimally controlled seizures; and/or have extremely brittle medical existences," (p. 21). Although there is yet no universally accepted definition for the severely handicapped, Gast and Berkler (1981) point out that the trend is to consider severe or profound levels of mental retardation as a characteristic common to all people who have been so classified.

The severely and profoundly handicapped present new challenges to public school personnel and other service providers. The movement is to transfer large numbers of severely handicapped people from large residential institutions to smaller, community-based group homes that are located in closer proximity to their parents and families. Thus, living arrangements more closely approximate those of the general population. As part of the normalization movement, this trend is referred to as deinstitutionalization (Menolascino, 1977; Wolfensberger, 1976).

As deinstitutionalization progresses, additional demands are placed upon public school personnel to provide appropriate educational services for the severely handicapped. Heretofore, school officials could exclude such children from schools. Now, however, it is required that educational services be provided for them. Consequently, considerable efforts are being devoted to discover appropriate instructional technologies (e.g., Fredericks et al., 1976; Tawney et al., 1979) and the competencies that are needed by their teachers (e.g., Bricker, 1976; Wilcox, 1977).

Some authorities, such as Haywood (1979) have expressed concern over the recent transfer of interest to the severely and profoundly retarded. Although the change in emphasis has brought significant benefits to this part of the population that has long been denied services, it has had somewhat of a negative effect on research related to the mildly and moderately retarded, who represent approximately 95 percent of those who have been diagnosed a mentally retarded. As Berdine and Blackhurst (1981) pointed out: "The size of the mildly and moderately retarded population alone should dictate that special educators continue to devote attention to this segment of the population. The emphasis of the 1970s on the needs of the severely and profoundly retarded was undoubtedly important in focusing attention on the services provided to them. During the 1980s, however, a more evenly balanced distribution of efforts should be made, without sacrificing any of the benefits acquired during the 1960s and 1970s" (p. 312).

Future Perspectives.   Although great strides have been made in the education of mentally retarded people, much remains to be done. There is a need for additional research relative to more precise ways to identify and evaluate the mentally retarded. More precise measures of adaptive behavior need to be developed. Etiological research needs to continue and efforts related to the prevention of retardation need to be intensified.

For those retarded children in school, studies need to be performed to determine the variables that will predict the most effective placements in the continuum of educational services. At present, educational placements are not always the most appropriate. There is also a need for the study of curriculum for the various levels of mental retardation. Insufficient research has been done in this area.

Technology appears to have great potential in the education of the mentally retarded (Blackhurst & Hofmeister, 1980); yet this potential is far from being realized. Studies need to be initiated relative to technological alternatives and their application. Such studies should focus not only upon media and hardware technology, but also upon instructional technology that uses systematic instructional procedures apart from hardware.

Greater emphasis will be placed on the development of alternative living units for the older retarded and the provision of human services for this portion of the population. Such services will be in greater demand as large residential institutions are closed in favor of smaller, community-based residences for those retarded adults who cannot live at home. Studies need to be performed to determine the best approaches to these problems.

Biomedical advances will be seen in the identification, prevention, and treatment of mental retardation. These advances will lead to more sophisticated genetic counseling services. It is quite likely that efforts will be devoted to genetic engineering in order to attempt to remediate certain genetic defects.

As efforts are expended to solve many of the social problems of society, spin-off benefits should accrue to the mentally retarded. For example, as the problems of poverty and cultural disadvantage are attacked and solved, fewer persons will probably be diagnosed as having retardation due to psychosocial factors.

Finally, efforts need to be intensified to develop more appropriate and accepting attitudes on the part of both the general public and professionals who work with education and other human services. The greatest barrier to the development of improved services is that of negative or inappropriate attitudes. Studies (e.g., Donaldson & Martinson, 1977) have shown that attitudes can be changed in a positive fashion through a variety of media. As attitudes improve, the effect will be improvements in the education and treatment of mentally retarded people.

A. Edward Blackhurst
Rena B. Lewis

See also Cognitive Development; Deinstitutionalization of the Handicapped; Handicapped Individuals; Individual Differences; Intelligence; Intelligence Measurement; Learning Disabilities; Special Education.

REFERENCES

Bailey, D. B., & Hardin, G. L. Nondiscriminatory evaluation. *Exceptional Children*, 1980, *46*, 590–596.

Baker, A. M. Cognitive functioning of psychotic children: A reappraisal. *Exceptional Children*, 1979, *45*, 344–348.

Berdine, W. H., & Blackhurst, A. E. Mental retardation. In A. E. Blackhurst & W. H. Berdine (Eds.), *An Introduction to Special Education*. Boston: Little, Brown, 1981.

Bijou, S. W. A functional analysis of retarded development. In N. R. Ellis (Ed.), *International Review of Research in Mental Retardation* (Vol. 1). New York: Academic Press, 1966, pp. 1–19.

Blackhurst, A. E., & Hofmeister, A. M. Technology in special education. In L. Mann & D. A. Sabatino (Eds.), *The Fourth Review of Special Education*. New York: Grune & Stratton, 1980.

Blatt, B., & Kaplan, F. *Christmas in Purgatory*. Boston: Allyn & Bacon, 1966.

Bricker, D. Educational synthesizer. In M. Thomas (Ed.), *Hey, Don't Forget about Me!* Reston, Va.: Council for Exceptional Children, 1976.

Brolin, D. E., & Kokaska, C. J. *Career Education for Handicapped Children and Youth*. Columbus, Ohio: Merrill, 1979.

Cegelka, P. T. Career education. In J. M. Kauffman & D. P. Hallahan (Eds.), *Handbook of Special Education*. Englewood Cliffs, N.J.: Prentice-Hall, 1981.

Chinn, P. C.; Drew, C. J.; & Logan, D. R. *Mental Retardation: A Life Cycle Approach*. St. Louis: Mosby, 1975.

Clarke, A. M., & Clarke, A. D. B. *Mental Deficiency: The Changing Outlook* (Rev. ed.). New York: Free Press, 1965.

Deno, E. *Instructional Alternatives for Exceptional Children*. Reston, Va.: Council for Exceptional Children, 1973.

Diana v. California State Board of Education. United States District Court, Northern District of California, C-70 37 RFP (1970).

Doll, E. A. *Vineland Social Maturity Scale* (Rev. ed.). Circle Pines, Minn.: American Guidance Service, 1965.

Donaldson, J., & Martinson, M. C. Modifying attitudes toward physically disabled persons. *Exceptional Children*, 1977, *43*, 337–341.

Duffey, J. B.; Salvia, J.; Tucker, J.; & Ysseldyke, J. Nonbiased assessment: A need for operationalism. *Exceptional Children*, 1981, *47*, 427–434.

Dunn, L. M. Special education for the mildly retarded: Is much of it justifiable? *Exceptional Children*, 1968, *35*, 5–22.

Ellis, N. R. (Ed.). *Handbook of Mental Deficiency*. New York: McGraw-Hill, 1963.

Fredericks, H.; Baldwin, V.; Grove, D.; Riggs, C.; Fureg, V.; Moore, W.; Jordan, E.; Gage, M.; Levak, L.; Alrik, G.; & Wadlow, M. *The Teaching Research Curriculum for the Moderately and Severely Handicapped*. Springfield, Ill.: Thomas, 1976.

Gast, D. L., & Berkler, M. Severe and profound handicaps. In A. E. Blackhurst & W. H. Berdine (Eds.), *An Introduction to Special Education*. Boston: Little, Brown, 1981.

Grossman, H. J. (Ed.). *Manual on Terminology and Classification in Mental Retardation* (Rev. ed.). Washington, D.C.: American Association on Mental Deficiency, 1977.

Hallahan, D. P., & Kauffman, J. M. *Introduction to Learning Disabilities*. Englewood Cliffs, N.J.: Prentice-Hall, 1976.

Haywood, H. C. What happened to mild and moderate mental retardation? *American Journal of Mental Deficiency*, 1979, *83*, 427–431.

Hobbs, N. *The Futures of Children*. San Francisco: Jossey-Bass, 1975.

Hobbs, N. *Issues in the Classification of Children* (Vols. 1 and 2). San Francisco: Jossey-Bass, 1976.

Hunt, J. T. Mentally retarded children. In R. Ebel (Ed.), *Encyclopedia of Educational Research* (4th ed.). New York: Macmillan, 1969.

Hutt, M. L., & Gibby, R. G. *The Mentally Retarded Child: Development, Training, and Education* (4th ed.). Boston: Allyn & Bacon, 1979.

Ingalls, R. P. *Mental Retardation: The Changing Outlook*. New York: Wiley, 1978.

Kauffman, J. M., & Payne, J. S. (Eds.) *Mental Retardation: Introduction and Personal Perspectives*. Columbus, Ohio: Merrill, 1975.

Kindred, M.; Cohen, J.; Penrod, J.; & Shaffer, R. *The Mentally Retarded Citizen and the Law*. New York: Free Press, 1975.

Kline, D. F. *Child Abuse and Neglect: A Primer for School Personnel*. Reston, Va.: Council for Exceptional Children, 1977.

Lambert, N.; Windmiller, M.; Cole, L.; & Figueroa, R. *Manual: AAMD Adaptive Behavior Scale, Public School Version* (Rev. ed.). Washington, D.C.: American Association on Mental Deficiency, 1975.

Larry P. et al., Plaintiffs v. *Riles, Superintendent of Public Instruction for the State of California et al.*, United States District Court for the Northern District of California, Before: The Honorable Robert F. Peckham, Chief Judge, No. C–71–2270–RFP (1972).

MacMillan, D. L. *Mental Retardation in School and Society*. Boston: Little, Brown, 1977.

Maloney, M., & Ward, M. P. *Mental Retardation and Modern Society*. New York: Oxford University Press, 1979.

McLoughlin, J. A., & Lewis, R. B. *Assessing Special Students*. Columbus, Ohio: Merrill, 1981.

Menolascino, F. L. *Challenges in Mental Retardation: Progressive Ideology and Sources*. New York: Human Services Press, 1977.

Mercer, J. R. *Labeling the Mentally Retarded*. Berkeley: University of California Press, 1973.

Mercer, J. R., & Lewis, J. F. *System of Multicultural Pluralistic Assessment*. New York: Psychological Corporation, 1977.

Neisworth, J. T., & Smith, R. M. *Retardation: Issues, Assessment, and Intervention*. New York: McGraw-Hill, 1978.

Nirje, B. The normalization principle and its human management implications. In R. B. Kugel & W. Wolfensberger (Eds.), *Changing Patterns in Residential Services for the Mentally Retarded*. Washington, D.C.: U.S. Government Printing Office, 1969, 231–240.

Oakland, T. Nonbiased assessment of minority group children. *Exceptional Education Quarterly*, 1980, *1*(3), 31–46.

Payne, J. S., & Patton, J. R. *Mental Retardation*. Columbus, Ohio: Merrill, 1981.

President's Committee on Mental Retardation. *The Six Hour Retarded Child*. Washington, D.C.: U.S. Department of Health, Education, and Welfare, Bureau of Education for the Handicapped, 1969.

President's Committee on Mental Retardation. *Mental Retardation: The Known and the Unknown*. Washington, D.C.: U.S. Government Printing Office, 1977.

Robinson, N. M., & Robinson, H. B. *The Mentally Retarded Child: A Psychological Approach* (2nd ed.). New York: McGraw-Hill, 1976.

Salvia, J., & Ysseldyke, J. E. *Assessment in Special and Remedial Education* (2nd ed.). Boston: Houghton Mifflin, 1981.

Samuda, R. *Psychological Testing of American Minorities*. New York: Dodd, Mead, 1975.

Smith, D. W.; Jones, K. L.; & Hansen, J. W. Perspectives on the cause and frequency of the fetal alcohol syndrome. *Annals of the New York Academy of Science*, 1976, *23*, 138–139.

Smith, R. M. *An Introduction to Mental Retardation*. New York: McGraw-Hill, 1971.

Sontag, E.; Burke, P.; & York, R. Considerations for serving the severely handicapped. *Education and Training of the Mentally Retarded*, 1973, 8, 20–26.

Stevens, H. A., & Heber, R. *Mental Retardation: A Review of Research*. Chicago: University of Chicago Press, 1964.

Stevens, R., & Rosenshine, B. Advances in research on teaching. *Exceptional Education Quarterly*, 1981, 2(1), 1–9.

Tawney, J.; Knapp, D.; O'Reilly, C.; & Pratt, S. *Programmed Environments Curriculum*. Columbus, Ohio: Merrill, 1979.

Terman, L. M., & Merrill, M. A. *Stanford-Binet Intelligence Scale* (1972 norms ed. Form L-M). Boston: Houghton Mifflin, 1973.

Wechsler, D. *Manual for the Wechsler Intelligence Scale for Children—Revised*. New York: Psychological Corporation, 1974.

Weintraub, F. J.; Abeson, A.; Ballard, J.; & LaVor, M. L. (Eds.). *Public Policy and the Education of Exceptional Children*. Reston, Va.: Council for Exceptional Children, 1976.

Wilcox, B. Competency-based approach to preparing teachers of the severely and profoundly handicapped: Perspective 1. In E. Sontag (Ed.), *Educational Programming for the Severely and Profoundly Handicapped*. Reston, Va.: Council for Exceptional Children, 1977.

Williams, R. L. *The BITCH Test (Black Intelligence Test of Cultural Homogeneity)*. St. Louis: Williams & Associates, 1972.

Wolfensberger, W. *The Principle of Normalization in Human Services*. Toronto: National Institute on Mental Retardation, 1972.

Wolfensberger, W. The origin and nature of our institutional models. In R. B. Kugel & A. Shearer (Eds.), *Changing Patterns in Residential Services for the Mentally Retarded* (Rev. ed.). Washington, D.C.: President's Committee on Mental Retardation, 1976.

META-ANALYSIS

See Research Integration.

METHODS OF RESEARCH

See Curriculum Research; Ethnography; Evaluation of Programs; Experimental Methods; Historiography; Prediction Methods; Research Integration; Statistical Methods; Survey Research Methods; Systematic Observation.

METHODS OF TEACHING

See Instruction Processes; Systems Design in Instruction; Teaching Styles.

METRIC EDUCATION

The signing of the Metric Conversion Act of 1975 (Public Law 94-168) began in the current conversion from the English system of measurement to the International Metric System (SI) of measurement in the United States. History, as summarized by Treat (1971) and DeSimone (1971), shows that the United States finally changed to SI because the surrounding world converted to metrics. By 1974 it became apparent that the United States could no longer afford to continue using a measurement system different from that of other industrial nations. As the last industrial nation to convert, the United States is in a position to benefit from the experience of nations who recently made the metric transition. Chalupsky, Crawford, and Carr (1974) and Chalupsky, Carr, and McDonnell (1975) provided insight into the changeover process. Chalupsky, Carr, and McDonnell (1975) pointed out that government, free enterprise, and public opinion are the pervasive forces that influence the climate in which educators must now work to make the transition to metrics. The Great Britain, Australian, New Zealand, South African, and Canadian experiences show that successful transition is associated with broad-scale involvement during the early planning stage, committed government policy, firm conversion schedules, and communication and coordination among all participants in the changeover process. The experience of the five countries studied by Chalupsky, Carr, and McDonnell (1975) also has direct implications for American education. This study points out the need for a well-planned teacher training strategy, extensive revisions of the schools' curricula, use of teaching procedures that facilitate learning SI, and careful selection of quality instructional materials.

Learning Theory. Learning SI seems to be a psychomotor skill dependent upon cognitive and affective components. Therefore, it is not surprising that Piagetian, Brunerian, and information-processing perspectives have influenced metric education.

Piaget's influence is primarily due to the popularity of his developmental theory with educators and his focus upon concept development through active methods of inquiry. Using Piagetian theory and assessment techniques, metric education activity has pointed to substantial weaknesses in children's and teachers' general measurement skills and quantitative concepts. As a result, some research and curriculum specialists (Sawada & Nelson, 1967; Copeland, 1970) have argued for postponement of formal measurement instruction until conservation of the various concepts such as length and volume occurs. Others (Szabo & Trueblood, 1977) have attempted to incorporate measurement activities into curriculum guides that stimulate development of measurement concepts and skills. The research directly related to metrics is not conclusive. Smith, Trueblood, and Szabo (1981) found no difference between K–2 length conservers and nonconservers using several instructional modes. MacBeth (1971) discovered that preoperational kindergarten children deprived of manipulative experiences did not attain the same level of proficiency with measurement skills as did children provided with such experiences. Until more definitive research is available and disseminated, instructional procedures that match or intentionally mismatch students' stages of development will continue to be used and evaluated.

Bruner (1966) argued that effective learning is accomplished through systematically presenting concepts through enactive (manipulative), iconic (graphic), and symbolic modes of instruction. Few researchers have applied this theory to learning metrics. Smith, Szabo, and Trueblood (1980) found that manipulative instruction in linear metric measurement skills resulted in greater acquisition of these skills than did graphic instruction. Additional studies on metric measurement education are required before a definitive conclusion can be formulated.

Researchers who generally agree that what is learned is largely a function of what has already been learned (Gagné, 1968) have organized and are beginning to test metric content and skill hierarchies. Houser and Trueblood (1975) used computer-assisted instruction to investigate transfer of learning linear metric measurement concepts and skills by preservice teachers. They found that the preservice elementary teachers who mastered metric linear concept skills were able to transfer them to area and volume units.

Research on Metric Education. Those involved in metric education estimate the changeover currently under way will take at least fifty years or longer. Since the metric system is simple and easy to learn, what are the major sources of resistance?

Attitudes toward metrics. Sawada and Sigurdson (1976) and Dubisch (1976) observed that people react negatively to their discomfort with the metric system. The 1973 Gallup poll shows that the majority of persons with a high school education could not identify the metric system by name (Gallup, 1973). The 1980 Gallup poll did not include metrics among the major problems confronting public schools in the 1980s (Gallup, 1980). The general range and intensity of people's negative and positive reactions to the metric system is best observed by reading the pro-metric and anti-metric articles that appear in the mass media and popular press whenever the government has attempted to introduce the metric system through legislative action.

One might expect educators to have a more positive attitude and be less resistant to the metric system than the general public. This is not the case. Shrigley and Trueblood (1979), Szabo and Trueblood (1980), Hess (1978), and Szabo and Kongsasana (1980) found that teachers' attitudes depend upon the extent to which they have used and been exposed to the metric system. These studies also found that mathematics and science teachers are more positive about metrics than teachers who have had little contact with SI. They also found that school administrators tend to be more negative than their teachers. Chalupsky, Carr, and McDonnell (1975) and Szabo and Trueblood (1980) found that pretraining awareness programs decreased anxiety about using metrics and increased the effectiveness of training activities.

What specific factors explain the differences observed among teachers' and administrators' attitudes? Shrigley and Trueblood (1979) found that teachers' attitudes are related to three factors. These include general resistance to change, sociocultural attachment to the customary system, and perception about personal ability to learn to use metrics. Hess (1978), Szabo and Kongsasana (1980), and Szabo and Trueblood (1980) demonstrated that attitudes toward metrics can be significantly improved when teachers are given hands-on activities tailored to meet their needs. Chalupsky, Carr, and McDonnell (1975) found that avoidance of conversion from metric to customary units reduced the anxieties people had about their ability to cope with metrics. Chalupsky, Crawford, and Carr (1974) also found a relationship between people's attitudes towards metrics and explicit changeover deadlines. He cited the attitudes expressed by many Australians when provided with a national mandate. The Australians said, "Now we are stuck with it (the metric system). Let us knuckle down and learn the new system" (Chalupsky, Crawford, & Carr, 1974, p. 95). Based upon the low level of acceptance of metrics among the general public, school administrators, and most teachers in the United States, some deadlines might be required to convince people that the use of metrics should be given a higher priority. This supports Bem's self-perception theory (1972) regarding attitudinal change and development, namely, that people's positive attitudes toward metrics will develop as a result of using the system.

There is evidence (Szabo, Trueblood, & Lamiel-Landy, 1980) suggesting that most adults, including teachers, will learn metrics only when required to do so. This evidence also suggests that adults, particularly teachers, are unsure of their ability to learn metrics. Therefore, instruction for adults should begin by demonstrating that metric measurement is easy to learn and use. In general, adult training should (1) incorporate cooperative rather than competitive learning activities; (2) provide adults with a voice in setting their own instructional objectives; (3) provide a variety of hands-on opportunities that demonstrate to adults their ability to use the metric system; and (4) be consistent and contiguous with job usage requirements.

It is not clear how much instruction adults require to make them proficient in metrics. The figure of fifteen hours appears in the literature on metric training for classroom teachers (Borelli & Morelli, 1979). There is no empirical evidence that this amount of training is adequate for all purposes. Project IMPACT (Trueblood, Szabo, & Smith, 1978) found that at least five days of intensive training is needed to prepare teachers and administrators in both metrics and curriculum development techniques.

Dissemination of metrics. Orlich (1979) cites evidence that, in general, funded innovation waxes as long as external funds and innovative leaders are present and wanes when they both depart. Training for metric awareness or individual proficiency with metrics is one concern. Training change agents how to permanently install an SI curriculum and related instructional strategies is another. The findings of Szabo and Trueblood (1980) and Chalupsky, Carr, and McDonnell (1975) support planning for change at the school district level and then implementing metric changeover at the school building level.

Consistent with the findings of Goodlad (1978) and Cook (1974), Szabo and Trueblood (1978, 1980) found that the most effective leadership for changeover to metrics comes from a building team composed of the principal and competent teachers who have been trained in metrics and organizational and staff development techniques. They also found that school districts that provided this type of training are most likely to sustain metric changeover effort whenever the team is required to develop a metric curriculum and a multiyear changeover plan receiving school board approval.

Quality of curriculum materials. Chalupsky, Crawford, and Carr (1974) and Chalupsky, Carr, and McDonnell (1975) showed that commercial publishers rush in to fill the gap in instructional materials created by metric legislation. These materials are often of poor quality. To help cope with this problem in the United States, the U.S. Metric Association, educational organizations such as the National Council of Teachers of Mathematics, the American Metric Council, and the U.S. Department of Commerce published metric style guides and guidelines to help publishers and users evaluate commercial materials. Szabo and Trueblood (1978) incorporated these recommendations into guidelines and procedures for evaluating published educational materials. These guidelines, which reflect the major concerns of those interested in providing quality instructional materials, are the following: (1) the SI metric system should be the primary measurement system; (2) instructional materials should contain only approved metric names and symbols; (3) a metric program should give a high degree of emphasis to hands-on metric estimation and measurement activity; (4) more than 50 percent of the per-pupil cost should be spent on purchasing quality measuring instruments and written materials that direct hands-on estimation and measuring activity; (5) metrics should be integrated into all subject areas and not limited to science and mathematics; (6) a metric curriculum or program guide should sequence metric content and activities to match students' stages of development.

In addition to commercial materials, most state departments of education developed curriculum guides and related materials for use in teacher training and classrooms (Trueblood, Szabo, & Nippes, 1981). Interestingly, most commercial textbooks continue to include activities to teach both metrics and the customary measurement system. This is based upon their market research data showing that schools are reluctant to purchase textbooks that are solely metric.

Teaching metric. The *U.S. Metric Study Interim Report: Education* (United States Department of Commerce, 1971) states that students should be taught using an active, hands-on approach. In addition, it recommends that the instructional activity of conversion from customary to metric units be avoided. The general opinion of those in-

volved in teaching metrics is that students should be taught to "think metric" and that conversion from English to metric and metric to English units adversely affects students' attitudes while teaching a skill that will not be needed after the changeover to the metric system is completed. "Thinking metric" is defined by the authors to mean the ability to make reasonably accurate estimates using metric units.

Studies have been conducted with a variety of ages of students. The results are inconclusive with respect to whether a "metric-only" approach is most effective in the development of metric skills and knowledge. Marburger (1976) found no significant differences for high-ability students, whereas Brooks (1975) found significant differences favoring metric-only instruction with high-ability students. Love (1977) found differences favoring students who worked with both systems. Stotts (1977) concluded that for the average-ability student taught drafting, the use of metric-only produced significantly better results; differences were not observed for students of lower and higher mental abilities. Brumfield (1977) concluded that for third-grade pupils, metric-only instruction was more effective for retention than was instruction in the metric system and conversion to the customary system. Both were equally effective on achievement and estimation tests given immediately following instruction.

Teacher certification. The largest burden for metric education has fallen upon the U.S. public and private schools. Statewide testing programs currently require students to demonstrate their knowledge of metrics. How have the agencies with responsibility for teacher certification responded to these pressures?

Survey research shows that the content of teacher education programs and state certification standards have not yet been significantly modified. Szabo, Trueblood, and Shockley (1975) found that in 1974 state science and/or mathematics supervisors had been designated by the chief education officers in most states as coordinators of metric changeover. This national survey was repeated in 1977 (Trueblood, Szaba, & Nippes, 1981). It showed that in the two years following the Metric Conversion Act of 1975 only two states out of forty-two responding had published general certification standards pertaining to metrics, and only five states had such standards under consideration. This did not represent a significant change from the 1974 survey. No state in the 1977 survey indicated that it would consider using metric competency statements as the basis for teacher certification.

The state supervisors were also asked to describe how their states' teacher education programs taught metrics to preservice teachers. The procedure reported most often consisted of modules inserted into established methods or mathematics/science content courses. The supervisors also indicated that in-service courses in science and mathematics were the vehicles used to teach metrics to in-service teachers. No certification standard has yet been published that relates to training in-service teachers.

Sponsored Research. The federal government began funding metric education in the early 1970s. Several laws and agencies have been involved including ESEA Titles III, IV, and V and the Metric Education Office Special Projects Act.

Early funding was directed toward the vocational areas. The Bureau of Occupational and Adult Education (DHEW) supported metric education. ESEA Title III produced a community-school changeover effort (Daniel, 1976). The Interstate Consortium on Metric Education, funded from ESEA Title V, made recommendations for preparing children to enter a metric world in the absence of a federal mandate (Tardiff, Hoffmann, & Lorenzen, 1975).

The Special Projects Act of the Educational Amendments of 1974 established categorized program aid for metric education. Appropriations were distributed beginning in fiscal year 1976 to teach 50 million elementary and secondary students plus adults to use the metric system as part of the regular educational program. Approximately 2 million dollars per year were allocated to state education agencies and local education agencies to develop metric education programs for schools. In addition, technical support services were funded for grantees. The funding effort was scattered rather than focused in order to begin as many local "seed" projects as possible. On the other hand, Project IMPACT (Szabo & Trueblood, 1977, 1978, 1980) focused upon training state and regional leadership cadres and supporting their dissemination efforts. This project, along with the Northeast Metric Consortium, focused its activity in the northeastern United States. The results show this to be a viable dissemination procedure.

The National Bureau of Standards, in their role of providing quality assurance for the nation's measurement systems, have promoted SI metrics in many ways, including maintaining a short-lived metric education office, sponsoring an educational conference on the one-hundredth anniversary of the Treaty of the Metre (Odom, 1975), and distributing SI standards (National Bureau of Standards, 1977).

On a much smaller scale, state governments have channeled some federal moneys into metric projects through ESEA Title IV(c). Most have passed metric resolutions for the education sectors, but none has appropriated state funds for metric education *per se* (Trueblood, Szabo, & Nippes, 1981).

Public Policy. National and state metric policies have been established to coordinate the transition to metrics. Congress established the U.S. Metric Board (USMB) as the chief coordinating body in Public Law 94-168, the Metric Conversion Act of 1975. The act's major feature is that it does not provide a legal mandate or deadlines for changing to the metric system. Rather, this act instructs USMB to establish national policy to coordinate the increasing voluntary use of metric measurement. The board initially planned to develop a conversion timetable; USMB has yet to publish such a document. The predictable result is that metric changeover is proceeding by the voluntary acts of the various sectors and segments of society. The major impact of this voluntary activity is that metric transition has not and probably will not be uniform across the nation's business, industrial, and education agencies.

A voluntary national policy has also resulted in each state's issuing separate policy statements. Trueblood, Szabo, and Nippes (1981) found that only five states supported their statements with legislation and only one with appropriation of funds. The states' policies vary from those specifying that all curricula and instructional material should be metric by a specific date (for example, Maryland) to those requiring that both metric and customary systems be taught coequally (for example, Pennsylvania). Given this policy variation and conventional wisdom, educators at the state level are now arguing for a delay in teaching only metrics because they believe that high school graduates will continue to function in a dual measurement society for some unknown length of time. This argument corresponds with what Chalupsky, Carr, & McDonnell (1975) found during the British conversion experience.

At the local school district level, instruction is being conducted in both metrics and the customary system. Most textbook companies still do not provide metric-only textbooks for reasons cited earlier and because no national or state conversion deadline exists.

King (1979) surveyed selected large U.S. firms and industries for the USMB. The results show the status of metric conversion under a voluntary policy. The report (King, 1980) concluded: (1) overall, 32 percent of present sales of the largest U.S. firms are of metric products; (2) only limited planning and coordination activity is evident; (3) the prevailing disposition is a "wait and see" attitude; (4) impediments (whether real or imaginary, legal and nonlegal) continue to hinder both the pace and the degree of metrication; (5) the most frequently mentioned reasons for conversion are customer demands and meeting required international market standards; (6) the median time frame for all the groups surveyed was no more than ten years, but there is evidence that metrication may never be fully implemented over all industries.

Conclusions. The voluntary nature of changeover has had a confusing and detrimental effect upon plans to provide metric education and training in the United States. The study of metric education has uncovered deficiencies in general measurement education and a lack of understanding concerning how to educate and train adults and school-aged youths to use metrics. Conventional wisdom, conflicting state education policies, U.S. industry, and the textbook publishers have created and set the "wait and see" attitude of the public schools toward metric education, one of the most far-reaching curriculum content changes of this century.

Cecil R. Trueblood
Michael Szabo

See also Mathematics Education; Science Education.

REFERENCES

Bem, D. Self-perception theory. In L. Berkowtz (Ed.), *Advances in Experimental Social Psychology* (Vol. 6). New York: Academic Press, 1972.

Borelli, M. L., & Morelli, S. Z. *Implementing Metrics at a District Level: Administrative Guide* (Rev. ed.). Cortland, N.Y.: Cortland-Madison BOCS, 1979. (ERIC Document Reproduction Service No. ED 167 380)

Brooks, H. L. A comparison of instructional approaches in teaching the metric system to seventh-grade students with varying mental abilities. *Dissertation Abstracts International,* July 1975, *36,* 163-A.

Brumfield, R. D. A comparison of the achievement, estimating skills and retention of third-grade students on an introductory unit in linear metric measurement taught independent of and in conjunction with conversion to linear English measurement. *Dissertation Abstracts International,* January 1977, *37,* 4113.

Bruner, J. S. *Toward a Theory of Instruction.* Cambridge, Mass.: Harvard University Press, 1966.

Chalupsky, A. B.; Carr, E. M.; & McDonnell, P. *Metric Inservice Teacher Training: Learning from the English and Australian Experience* (Report No. 48000-3/75 FR.). Palo Alto, Calif.: American Institute for Research, 1975.

Chalupsky, A. B.; Crawford, J. J.; & Carr, E. M. *Going Metric: An Analysis of Experiences in Five Nations and Their Implications for U.S. Educational Planning* (Report No. AIR 41800-2/74 FR.). Palo Alto, Calif.: American Institute for Research, 1974.

Cook, E. J. *Teacher Perceptions of Role Partner Evaluation of Performance and Their Implementation of Science: A Process Approach within Selected Role Sets.* Unpublished doctoral dissertation, State University of New York at Albany, 1974.

Copeland, R. W. *How Children Learn Mathematics: Teaching Implications of Piaget's Research.* New York: Macmillan, 1970.

Daniel, V. *Metrics: The Measure of Your Future.* Chapel Hill, N.C.: Apple Hill Educational Consultants, Inc., 1976.

DeSimone, D. *A Metric America: A Decision Whose Time Has Come* (United States Metric Study). Washington, D.C.: U.S. Government Printing Office, 1971. (ERIC Document Reproduction Service No. ED 055 884)

Dubisch, R. Some comments on teaching the metric system. *Arithmetic Teacher,* 1976, *23,* 106–107.

Gagné, R. M. Learning hierarchies. *Educational Psychologist,* 1968, *6*(1), 3–6.

Gallup, G. H. *The Gallup Poll.* New York: Random House, 1973.

Gallup, G. H. *The Gallup Poll.* New York: Random House, 1980.

Goodlad, J. I. Educational leadership: Toward the third era. *Educational Leadership,* January 1978, *35*(4), 322–331.

Hess, C. *Three Methods of Teaching Metric Measurement and Their Cognitive and Affective Effects on Preservice Elementary Teachers.* Unpublished doctoral dissertation, Pennsylvania State University, 1978.

Houser, L. L., & Trueblood, C. R. Transfer of learning on similar metric learning tasks. *Journal of Educational Research,* 1975.

King, L. *U.S. Metric Board 1979 Survey of Selected Large U.S. Firms and Industries* (USOE No. MB79-581). Rockville, Md.: King Research, Inc., May 1980.

Love, M. L. A comparative study of two methods of teaching metrication to selected seventh-, eight-, and ninth-grade pupils relative to effectiveness on metric measure estimation. *Dissertation Abstracts,* September 1977, *38,* 1344–1345A.

MacBeth, D. R. *The Extent to Which Pupils Manipulate Materials and Attainment of Process Skills in Elementary School Science.* Unpublished doctoral dissertation, Pennsylvania State University, 1971.

Marburger, W. F. The use of the relationship of units between the American and metric systems of measurement as a more effective means of teaching the metric system. *Dissertation Abstracts,* October 1976, *37,* 1963–1964A.

National Bureau of Standards Publication No. 330. Washington, D.C.: U.S. Government Printing Office, 1977.

Odom, J. *Conference on Successful Experiences in Teaching Metrics: Conference Proceedings.* Washington, D.C.: National Bureau of Standards, 1975.

Orlich, D. C. Federal educational policy: The paradox of innovation and centralization. *Educational Researchers,* July–August 1979, *8*(7), 4–9.

Sawada, D., & Nelson, L. D. Conservation of length and teaching of linear measurement: A critique. *Arithmetic Teacher,* 1967, *14,* 345–348.

Sawada, D., & Sigurdson, S. SI and the mathematics curriculum. In *Measurement in School Mathematics: National Council of Teachers of Mathematics Yearbook.* 1976.

Shrigley, R., & Trueblood, C. Designing a likert-type scale to assess attitude toward metrication. *Journal of Research in Science Teaching,* 1979, *16*(1), 73–78.

Smith, S. R.; Szabo, M.; & Trueblood, C. R. Modes of instruction for teaching linear measurement skills. *Journal of Educational Research,* 1980, *73,* 150–154.

Smith, S. R.; Trueblood, C. R.; & Szabo, M. Conservation of length and instruction in linear measurement in young children. *Journal of Research in Science Teaching,* 1981, *18,* 61–68.

Stotts, R. L. A comparison of three methods of teaching metric drafting technology. *Dissertation Abstracts International,* January 1977, *37,* 4183A.

Szabo, M., & Kongsasana, P. *Metric Attitude and Achievement of Preservice Elementary Teachers as a Function of Three Instructional Approaches.* Paper presented at the meeting of the National Association for Research in Science Teaching, Boston, April 1980. (ERIC Document Reproduction Service No. ED 187 539)

Szabo, M., & Trueblood, C. R. *A Survey of the Project Role of Metric Competencies in Teacher Certification in State Departments of Education.* Washington, D.C.: U.S. Office of Education, Metric Education Office, September 1977.

Szabo, M., & Trueblood, C. R. Guidelines for evaluation of published metric materials. *Arithmetic Teacher,* 1978, *25,* 46–50.

Szabo, M., & Trueblood, C. R. *A Change Model for Dissemination of the Metric System through Trained Local Leadership Teams: Project IMPACT* (Proposal to the Joint Dissemination Review Panel). University Park, Pa.: Department of Education, National Diffusion Network, August 1980.

Szabo, M.; Trueblood, C. R.; & Lamiel-Landy, A. *IMPACT III: Instruction in Measurement Processes for Action Classroom Teaching—Final Report* (USOE Grant No. G007902321). University Park, Pa.: U.S. Office of Education, 1980.

Szabo, M.; Trueblood, C. R.; & Shockley. *Metric Education Activities in State and Territorial Department of Education: A Survey.* Columbus, Ohio: ERIC Science Mathematics and Environmental Education Clearinghouse, February 1975.

Tardiff, R.; Hoffmann, J.; & Lorenzen, F. *Interstate Consortium on Metric Education: Final Report.* Sacramento: California State Department of Education, 1975. (ERIC Document Reproduction Service No. ED 103 282)

Treat, C. F. *A History of the Metric System Controversy in the United States* (U.S. Metric Study, Tenth Substudy Report). Washington, D.C.: U.S. Government Printing Office, 1971.

Trueblood, C. R.; Szabo, M.; & Nippes, R. A survey of preparation for metric changeover among supervisors of science and mathematics at the State Department of Education level. *School Science and Mathematics*, 1981, *81*, 9–16.

Trueblood, C. R.; Szabo, M.; & Smith, S. R. *IMPACT II: Instruction in Measurement Processes for Action Classroom Teaching* (USOE Grant No. G007700162). Washington, D.C.: Metric Project Office, 1978, pp. 1–53.

United States Department of Commerce. *U.S. Metric Study Interim Report: Education* (National Bureau of Standards Special Publication 345-6). Washington, D.C.: U.S. Government Printing Office, July 1971. (ERIC Document Reproduction Service No. ED 055 890)

MICROTEACHING

See Games and Simulations; Laboratory Experiences in Teacher Education; Teacher Education Programs.

MIDDLE SCHOOLS

See Junior High and Middle School Education.

MIDDLE YEARS DEVELOPMENT

Middle childhood covers the span from the child's entry into grade school, at approximately age 6, through sixth grade or the transition into junior high, at about age 12. Conceptions of middle childhood and preadolescence overlap, however, and children aged 11 or 12 are usually included in both groups. Such markers as chronological age or grade level are somewhat arbitrary indicators of developmental stage in any event, because they do not convey the wide variation among children. If the period is defined in terms of cognitive, social, or biological criteria, we find that some children move out of early childhood later than others and that the shift toward adolescent attitudes, social patterns, and physical attributes occurs at different points for different children.

In classic Freudian theory, this period has been referred to as "latency," signifying that libidinal, sexually tinged fantasies and urges are dormant, especially in comparison with the turbulent psychosexual characteristics of early childhood and adolescence. Perhaps because of the influence of this theory, there has been a sharp contrast between the almost overwhelming supply of texts dealing with early childhood or adolescent development and the limited availability of sources focused on middle years development (e.g., Minuchin, 1977; Williams & Stith, 1974). Middle childhood, however, is a vigorous period marked by considerable growth, and other developmental theo-

ries, such as those of Piaget and Erikson, have provided specific concepts and material about this stage. Erikson (1950) has seen the psychological issue of this period as the development of a sense of "industry"—a conviction that one can be effective, find out about things, and become competent—in contrast to a sense of inferiority, ineptitude, or defeat. Piaget (1971) has described middle childhood as the period of "concrete operational thinking," in which the child moves from the prelogical thought patterns of early childhood toward more systematic, logical ways of organizing experience and understanding ideas. The relation of both these theories to the child's experience and functioning in school is obvious.

Schooling is crucial, in fact, to middle years development. Children enter first grade with only a rudimentary capacity for organized logical thought, without the basic skills required for functioning in the culture, with little knowledge of history or the physical and social sciences, and with no conception of how they will progress as learners or fare in the school's social system. By the time children are in the upper elementary grades, it is hoped and expected that they will have the fundamental skills, a body of knowledge, a capacity to gather and process information, and a style of functioning effectively in a learning environment. They will also have some concept of the self as a learner and as a person in the classroom peer group and will have developed a set of attitudes about cooperating and competing with others and about expected behavior, fair treatment, and the nature of authority in settings beyond the immediate family. The school has been described as a primary context for intellectual and social development during these years (Minuchin & Shapiro, in press), and decisions concerning educational policy, as well as the child's specific experiences in school, have long-term implications for growth.

This article considers developmental trends in several areas (physical, cognitive, social-interpersonal, and self-concept) and the relation between educational policies or models on the one hand and middle years development on the other.

Developmental Trends

During middle childhood, there are obvious physical, intellectual, and social changes. Children become stronger and more skillful in body control and begin to organize information systematically. This development has implications for a child's sense of competence and for social relations with peers.

Physical Growth. The rate of physical growth is steady during middle childhood until the adolescent spurt, during which sex organs begin to grow and overall changes in body form and proportion increase the evident physical distinction between boys and girls (Tanner, 1970; Williams & Stith, 1974). The middle years are marked by physical flexibility, high energy, and maturation of the nerve and muscle tissue essential for skillful and coordinated physical activity. Although there is a hereditary base for a child's pace and style of growth, the pattern is also affected by general health, nutrition, and exercise.

Middle childhood is a time of lessons, games, and sports. Such activities as bicycle riding, baseball, acrobatics, and playing of musical instruments depend in large part on the capacity for control and intricate body coordination. With growing strength and skill, children are able to work on becoming competent in activities similar to those in the adult world. The trajectory is long, but the beginnings are usually in the middle childhood period. Such activities are also an important coin of social exchange in the peer group. Participation in games and physical activities promotes shared pleasure and a sense of belonging, as well as an opportunity for further physical development. During this period, physical skill has implications for how a child is seen by other children and for acceptance and leadership in the group. Such qualities are generally more important to boys than to girls, and other factors influence peer group status.

Intellectual Development. For many years, the basic approach to understanding intelligence in school children was to assess a child's capacity and learning ability, in comparison with others of the same age, through IQ and achievement tests. Although such concerns are still pertinent for particular purposes, the developmental field is now concerned with broader questions. The focus is on understanding the evolution of thought as children grow older, the characteristics of thinking at different stages, and the mechanisms through which thought patterns are reorganized. From this perspective, the relevant data about a child concern his or her mechanisms of thinking, and the optimal relation between such mechanisms and available learning materials.

Our understanding of middle years thinking is based primarily on the work of Jean Piaget (Piaget, 1971; Piaget & Inhelder, 1969) and the many researchers who have followed in this tradition. According to Piaget, people of all ages try to make sense of the world in some way, but the process of reasoning changes greatly in the course of development, passing through an invariant sequence of stages. The middle years are characterized by transitions at either end of the age span. During the early middle years, children move from what Piaget terms "preoperational intuitive thought," which is essentially egocentric and dominated by perceptual impressions, to concrete operations; and the preadolescent may begin the transition to propositional or formal-operational thought. The period is marked primarily by the growth and establishment of concrete-operational thinking, however. It is concrete in the sense that a child can think logically about the possibilities of real objects and events, and operational in the sense that the child can perform actual or mental operations in a systematic way. These operations are described as (1) "reversibility"—returning mentally to an earlier point in a process and the realizing that it is possible to move back and forth in this way; (2) "combining"—combining

elements, physically or mentally, to create a new group or category covering all the elements; (3) "identity"—applying the same operation to different parts of a system, or applying the converse of a previous system; and (4) "associativity"—following different pathways to arrive at the same end point. Such operations underlie a child's capacity to classify, to order objects in a logical series, and to conserve the essentials of a situation as the elements go through transformations.

Investigators have documented the details of development through a variety of tasks that require a child to make decisions and explain the reasons. For instance, they may present the child with twenty artificial roses and three artificial daffodils and ask, "Are there more flowers or more roses?" (Inhelder & Piaget, 1964). Tasks such as this one test the child's ability to understand hierarchies and the relationships among categories. Or, in a conservation experiment, they may pour an identical amount of water into two glasses, then change the external perceptual correspondence by pouring the water from one glass into a short, wide bowl. The child is then asked if the two containers still hold the same quantity. This experiment assesses the child's ability to reason that nothing has been added or taken away, so the amount must logically be the same; and to understand that a decrease in one dimension (height) is compensated for by an increase in another dimension (width). The capacity to hold two ideas in mind and see their relationship, rather than being led by one dominant perception, marks the movement toward logical and flexible thinking.

The results of such experiments have been clear. An increasing percentage of children demonstrate logical thinking at successive ages through the relevant period, which extends for basic conservation tasks from about age 5 to age 9. There are a number of important associated findings, however, all of which have implications for educators. For one thing, logic is firmly established in relation to some areas before others, depending on the complexity of the material and the child's past experience. For another, children differ widely in the pace and timing of growth. Fogelman (1970) has noted that statements about the average child are potentially misleading, since the attainment of a given concept may vary by several years within a population of normal children. Finally, it is clear that each child goes through transitional stages, in moving from one level of thought to another, and that functioning during this period may be uneven. Previous forms of reasoning may no longer be acceptable to the child, but more systematic mechanisms are not yet well established. Confusion and error may signal a period of intellectual reorganization and growth rather than the lack of attention or effort.

The growth of intellectual mastery involves not only the ability to grasp logical relationships but the capacity to raise questions and search for information. Such capacities also go through developmental change. In a classic study of such strategies, Mosher and Hornsby (1966) worked with children aged 6 to 11, applying the format of Twenty Questions to problem situations. They found a consistent age-related pattern. The 6-year-olds' questions were a series of specific guesses about possible solutions, with no organized plan for gathering useful information. The 8-year-olds' questions were more systematic, but only sporadically and under simple concrete conditions. The 11-year-olds' questions were the most systematic and flexible. They narrowed down the possibilities through their questions, retained their systematic strategies better than younger children when the task became difficult, and followed up more consistently on the information they obtained. In general, the study showed developmental changes both in strategies for gathering information and in the process of sorting and integrating what was known toward the ultimate goal of solution.

Such progress does not happen automatically. Piaget has noted that growth and change occur through the interaction of maturation, physical experience with objects, social experience with people, and the active process of equilibration, which is a self-regulating mental process through which the child integrates experience with internal expectations of "schema." It is generally considered important for the school to maximize these conditions. Learning environments that stress rote learning offer less opportunity for raising questions or gathering and organizing information than classrooms with a discovery or problem-solving orientation, in which the child must take a more active part in the process.

There has been considerable effort to apply Piaget's ideas to the classroom (e.g., Furth, 1970; Gallagher & Reid, 1981; Inhelder, Sinclair, & Bovet, 1974; Schwebel & Raph, 1973; Weybright, Adams, & Voyat, 1976). It has been argued that teachers must understand the nature of cognitive development so that they can assess each child's pattern of thought in approaching the learning material and can structure an environment that fosters growth. Weybright, Adams, and Voyat (1976) point out that children approach reading as they do any other cognitive activity. They are guided and limited by their general capacity to symbolize, decenter, reverse their thought processes, and connect information logically. Teachers can find clues to the child's stage of readiness by listening to the child talk and reason, and by observing the child's play, which contains clues to the relation between concrete and abstract thought. Specific efforts to facilitate the child's movement to more advanced stages have been numerous. Gallagher and Reid (1981) discuss two major approaches, regarding one as more valid and helpful than the other. They believe that "teaching to the task" misses the essential meaning of Piaget's work, since such procedures try to advance performance by training prerequisite skills, rewarding correct responses, and so forth, without concern for the child's methods of organizing information or the limiting effects of developmental level. More useful approaches engage the child in the active construction of theory and in the resolution of intellectual conflict. For instance, if the teacher elicits information on the processes and rules that guide the child's thinking and introduces problems that produce conflict about the adequacy of reasoning, the child may be encouraged toward new adaptations and growth, especially if the teacher designs a program of instruction that fits the particular child. Social interaction between teacher and child, during such a procedure, is also an important stimulant, as is the interaction among children when they work together. In the process of explaining ideas and communicating their reasoning, children produce constructive intellectual conflict for each other. The fact that peer tutoring has been found to benefit the tutors as well as the recipients (e.g., Allen & Feldman, 1973; Murray, 1972) is probably due to the active process of assimilation and accommodation involved in explanation and interchange.

Social and Interpersonal Development. During the middle years, the child's social world expands. The preschool world is essentially bounded by family, but the school-age child comes into contact with new adults who will influence self-image and the concept of authority. The child also becomes part of a peer society, with rules and qualities of its own, and with many important functions in relation to development. In social terms, the period is marked by an expanding capacity to relate reciprocally with other people, by the growth of mechanisms for functioning in the peer group, and by the development of understanding concerning moral issues and social rules.

Relations with people. Children begin to distinguish among people from earliest infancy, relating differentially to family members and strangers. As they grow, however, their perceptions become more complex, reflecting not only experience with people but also new cognitive capacities for organizing impressions and understanding their implications. Research on social development documents an increasing differentiation and objectivity in social perceptions (e.g., Bigner, 1974; Flapan, 1968; Livesley & Bromley, 1973; Peevers & Secord, 1973; Shantz, 1975). Whereas the 6-year-old child describes others in egocentric and specific terms, based on how people look or act and on their particular relationship to the child, older children can describe the qualities of others as independent people and go beyond surface perceptions to inferential ideas about people's thoughts and feelings. An important part of this pattern is that children become increasingly able to see things from another perspective. The capacity to shift viewpoints and to take multiple perspectives was first established by Piaget in relation to the physical universe. Flavell and his coworkers (Flavell et al., 1968) carried this concept to the interpersonal realm through studies of role taking and communication skills in middle childhood. They found that children, as they grow older, are increasingly able to take the perspective of another person and to engage in what is described as socialized communication. Such communication requires awareness and an adaptation to situational and interpersonal requirements. According to this line of research, development of such capacities is most active during the middle years and early adolescence (Feffer, 1970; Flavell et al., 1968; Selman & Byrne, 1974; Shantz, 1975).

The growth of interpersonal sensitivity does not mean that children will necessarily grow more helpful and cooperative in their actual behavior. Studies of prosocial behavior, such as sharing, helping, and nurturance of others, do suggest a significant increase from early childhood to adolescence, because of, as Mussen and Eisenberg-Berg (1977) note, "the enrichment of role-taking and empathic abilities with greater maturity, age-related shifts in moral reasoning, increased skill in helping, or more frequently repeated exposures to inductive (reasoning) child-rearing techniques or parental affection" (p. 66). However, such behavior varies widely among children of any given age, and these differences are a function of many factors. Among the most important are adult behavior, which constitutes a model for children, and adult reinforcement or disapproval, which communicates what is expected and valued. The importance of these factors has been established primarily with family figures, and with adult models in laboratory studies, but the implication is clear for teachers and other school personnel. It has also been suggested that certain school settings and experiences, such as open classrooms, peer tutoring, and cooperative learning structures, may offset the prevailing competitive ethos in American education and encourage prosocial behavior (Horwitz, 1979; Sharan, 1980; Slavin, 1980). In such situations, children work together and use each other as resources, and there is enhanced opportunity for the development of social understanding, communication, and positive relationships.

Peer relationships. The peer group is the social frontier of middle childhood. It constitutes a support for children as they move toward more independence from the family and other adults. It is also a small society, in which children participate in creating rules and norms, and in which they must find acceptance and some place in the social hierarchy. Friendships and peer groups are predominantly composed of children of the same sex, during these years, and conformity to group norms is usually high. Maccoby and Jacklin (1974) note that girls often have a best friend or two, during the early middle years, whereas boys are more often in small groups. In either case, the groupings are apt to change frequently, increasing in stability as children grow older.

The classroom group exists at two levels. At one level, it is a learning community consisting of both children and teachers; at another, it is a network of children, with its own values, activities, subgroups, and hierarchy of popularity. Using a technique called "sociometrics" (Moreno, 1934), investigators have mapped the social structure of classroom groups. They often find a few children who are "stars" or leaders, a few who are "isolates," and a pattern of subgroups and friendships among the others. According to the research, certain qualities are associated with popularity in middle childhood: friendliness, social skills, ease

with other children, intelligence and achievement, and (especially among boys) physical prowess. Quiet children do not necessarily have low status, but anxious, poorly adjusted children tend to be unpopular. In mixed groups, children from minority or less-advantaged backgrounds may have difficulties (Hartup, 1970). Such patterns are not fixed, however. Values differ in different groups, and they change culturally over time. It has also been suggested that adult attitudes and the organizational structure of the school affect the social patterns of the classroom. The bulk of the sociometric research suggests that children who meet the teacher's norms for academic achievement and social behavior in class also have high status with peers (Glidewell et al., 1966). According to Hallinan's analysis and research (1976), however, this pattern has been partly a function of the traditional settings in which sociometric research is usually conducted. In comparative studies, investigators find more diffuse, less hierarchical patterns of friendship in open classrooms with fewer stars and fewer children who are isolates or scapegoats. They also find a higher incidence of friendships among children with dissimilar qualities or levels of ability. In classrooms where interactions are diffuse, rather than centered on a few popular children, Schmuck & Schmuck (1971) report higher group morale, more positive self-feeling among the children, more positive attitudes toward school, and a better utilization of ability. The teacher's role, in relation to the middle years peer group, is complex. It embodies some function as a mediator of conflict and as a catalyst of mutual acceptance among the children. However, it also involves respect for the privacy and autonomy of the group, so that children can explore the issues of social organization and conflict resolution on their own.

Concepts. During the middle years, the understanding of social rules, right and wrong, and issues of fairness go through systematic changes, partly as a function of cognitive growth and partly by virtue of experience in the peer group and with authority. In his studies of moral judgment, Piaget (1948) tapped children's concepts of rules by investigating their understanding of the game of marbles. He found that they progressed from a fragmented, personalized understanding of how the game is played to rigid concepts of the immutable nature of the rules, and, finally, to a more flexible understanding that rules are made by agreement and can be changed. He also investigated concepts of wrongdoing, punishment, fairness, and equality and found a similar pattern, leading him to describe sequential stages of heteronomous, intermediate, and autonomous morality. Young children are geared mostly to adult commands and reactions, and they do not have organized moral conceptions. Middle years children have more internalized conceptions; they understand the need for a system of governing rules and for principles of reciprocity, but they tend to be unbending. Most middle years children, for instance, look for strict equality as a basis for fair treatment. Only with more experience and more complex cognitive structures can they become more relativistic and flexible. For instance, preadolescents may adopt a posture of equity rather than strict equality in relation to justice, and consideration of differential needs and extenuating circumstances in making moral judgments.

The work of Kohlberg (1976) has confirmed and extended these ideas. He has described the development of moral reasoning as a progression from preconventional morality to conventional morality and to principled reasoning. His system has gone through changes, and there is some uncertainty about the relationship between childhood stages and particular levels of moral reasoning. It is reasonably clear, however, that children in the middle years are typically moving beyond the earliest stages, centered on concern for personal consequences, toward middle stages of moral reasoning. These stages involve some grasp of the needs of others as well as oneself, some sense of community, and some understanding of the importance of rules and broad social approval in relation to moral decisions. Turiel (1975) has distinguished concepts of morality from those of social convention; and he has demonstrated that school children understand the difference between moral infractions in the school context, such as hitting another child or stealing, and transgressions that relate to school rules but are not immoral, such as coming late or forgetting one's books.

The development of moral reasoning proceeds more slowly than does logical growth. Research indicates that children do not necessarily progress toward humanistic principles and do not necessarily behave in accordance with their moral understanding. Loyalty, fairness, and concern for human welfare, or the community, depend on what is modeled and on how the child is treated. The general culture is a powerful force in this respect, but families and schools are the primary context for child development. Many years ago, John Dewey (1916) advocated organizing the school so that it would serve as a crucible for participatory democracy. Such ideas are not so prevalent in recent years, but there is still some effort to conceptualize and evaluate the school as a community affecting the moral and social development of children, and to organize the environment toward positive growth (e.g., Kohlberg, 1978; Kohlberg & Turiel, 1971; Lickona, 1977; Minuchin et al, 1969; Power & Reimer, 1978). Specific curricula have also been introduced into the schools, geared to the development of moral reasoning, empathy, values clarification, cooperative behavior, interpersonal skills, and so forth (e.g., Blatt & Kohlberg, 1975; Feshbach, 1979; Lockwood, 1978; Minuchin & Shapiro, in press; Sharan, 1980; Slavin, 1980).

Self-Concept. At least one aspect of self-concept is thought to reflect general growth patterns in cognition. Just as children come to perceive others in more complex ways, during the middle years, they also increase in the complexity of self-concept. They gain in differentiated knowledge of their own qualities, and their self-perceptions become more objective.

Most studies of children's self-concept focus on self-es-

teem. It is generally agreed that positive self-esteem comes from a feeling of psychological security, experiences of success, and positive appraisals from other people. A well-known study (Coopersmith, 1967) investigated the patterns associated with self-esteem among 10-year-old to 12-year-old schoolboys. Boys with high self-esteem were found to be independent, creative and confident, and well-accepted by peers. They were involved in a positive cycle, in which confident expectations, actual success, and appreciation by others confirmed their sense of confidence and encouraged further successful efforts. Boys with low self-esteem were involved in a similar but self-defeating cycle. The antecedents of self-esteem, according to this study, resided in parent attitudes, which included love and acceptance, clear, firm standards, and flexibility. Parents who were themselves confident and self-accepting were helpful identification figures for their sons.

Many educators have been concerned with the connection between self-feeling and the process of learning. Although some stress the importance of a positive self-concept for effective school performance, others stress a cycle of cognitive-affective interaction, in which self-confidence energizes the learning process, and mastery contributes to positive self-feeling. In this viewpoint, both intellectual mastery and a positive, differentiated self-concept are developmental goals that can be fostered by the school (Biber, 1977; Shapiro & Weber, 1981). Approaches to the enhancement of self-knowledge and positive feeling in the school setting have included an emphasis on teacher attitudes and classroom structure, as well as specific affective techniques for the development of self-exploration and knowledge (Allender, 1982). Research on the effects of such techniques and on the relation between different classroom structures and self-esteem has yielded mixed results (Horwitz, 1979). Few educators, however, question the importance of a child's self-confidence and motivation in relation to functioning in school. Efforts to assess personal aspects of the child's adaptation in school have, in fact, become more common and are seen as part of the teacher's understanding of each pupil as an individual. Anderson (1981) and Lidz (1981) have suggested a variety of techniques through which teachers can understand the attitudes, interests, emotional makeup, motivation, and potential of the child, using a broad range of assessment instruments, as well as classroom observation, interviews, play, and drawings.

One other aspect of self-concept is important in the school context: the sense of self as male or female, and the development of gender-associated role expectations. There is extensive literature describing how children learn gender identity and reporting on sex differences among children (e.g., Maccoby & Jacklin, 1974; Mischel, 1970; Weinraub & Brown, in press). The study of sex-role development has become a controversial field, however, as societal attitudes have changed. Earlier articles discuss the learning of "appropriate" sex-role behavior, assuming that clear role distinctions between boys and girls constitute an obvious developmental goal; whereas later articles question this premise and discuss the forces that encourage "stereotyped" rather than "androgynous" behavior.

Certain sex differences in middle childhood are consistently documented (Maccoby & Jacklin, 1974), such as the greater aggressiveness and quantitative, visual-spatial superiority of boys, as compared with the verbal superiority of girls, who also tend to like school better than boys do and to get better grades through the elementary years. Even in these areas, however, the inevitability of the patterns has been questioned, because it is thought that society, families, and the schools shape many aspects of child behavior on the basis of gender. Investigators have focused on the attitudes of teachers, who often confirm conventional stereotypes by differential treatment of boys and girls, on textbooks that convey stereotyped images of males and females, and on organizational aspects of the school that may result in unequal opportunities for boys and girls (Guttentag & Bray, 1976; Pottker & Fishel, 1977; Stockard et al., 1980). Concern for such unequal opportunities has generated federal legislation prohibiting discrimination in schools on the basis of gender.

From this perspective, some hitherto established developmental facts about school-age boys and girls are thought to be a product of the environment and can be expected to change as the environment changes. A few investigators have found evidence for such change by comparing children in conventional school environments to those in open school environments, finding less dichotomized perceptions of male and female roles and more cross-gender contact among children in the latter kind of setting (Berk & Lewis, 1977; Bianchi & Bakeman, 1978; Epstein, 1978; Minuchin, 1965). There are many questions in this area, however, and considerable research can be expected concerning the developmental effects of changing school policies, curriculum materials, and teacher attitudes.

Summary. Some general points about middle years development emerge: (1) Changing capacities for organized, logical thought underlie many aspects of functioning—not only the obvious matters of learning in school but also perceptions of the self and other people, and conceptions of justice, right and wrong, and social organization. (2) The growth of competence is a central aspect of middle years life, involving a variety of skills, as well as the acquisition of knowledge, and including the child's experiences both in and out of school. (3) There is a broadening of the social world to include nonfamily adults and the peer group. In this expansion, new patterns of autonomy and dependence are established with the family, as well as with peers and in the classroom. (4) Normal development during middle childhood includes a period of increasing rigidity in attitudes, values, and behavior before the child becomes more flexible and less conforming. There are also periods of inevitable disorganization for each child as he or she moves through transitional stages of growth. (5) Patterns of development vary as a function of many factors, including the behavior and attitudes of adults impor-

tant to the child, and the nature of family and school environments. Some patterns described as typical may not characterize children growing up in specific circumstances or subcultures, and typical patterns may themselves change as societal values and realities are modified. As an important context for child development, variations among school environments contribute to variations in child growth.

Education and Middle Years Development

The close relationship between middle years development and education has been suggested throughout this review. However, two broad aspects of the educational framework merit specific comment since they determine the details of educational experience: social policy, as it mandates the nature of school composition and opportunity; and educational philosophy, as it shapes the learning and social environment of the school.

Social Policy Decisions. Certain legislative and judicial decisions have had a strong impact on the nature and quality of schooling, and, therefore, on the development of children. Major examples include the Supreme Court decision of 1954 concerning desegregation; Title IX of the Education Amendments of 1972, concerning equal opportunity for girls and boys in school; and the Education for all Handicapped Children Act of 1975, which mandates the mainstreaming of handicapped children, wherever possible, into regular classrooms.

Such equal opportunity decisions are aimed at enhancing learning and improving the self-confidence of all children, including those who have previously had relatively limited opportunities in school. Such decisions also create a more diverse peer group within the classroom (allowing for the possibility of contact, friendship, cooperative learning, and the reduction of stereotypes) among different kinds of children. Optimal implementation of such mandates has not been simple, however, as the history of desegregation efforts indicates; and it has become clear that positive effects depend on what happens within the school and classroom once the children are physically mixed together (Minuchin & Shapiro, in press; Rist, 1979; St. John, 1975; Stephan & Feagin, 1980). In reviewing the research, Slavin (1980) has noted that the improvement of race relations in desegregated schools occurs consistently only under conditions that involve the children in continuing, constructive interaction, such as cooperative learning projects.

Policy decisions at legislative and judicial levels reflect the social ethos of the times and are often evaluated or changed on the basis of political or economic factors that have little to do with the children. It seems evident, however, that if such policies are to be successful they must involve sufficient time for evaluation and informed modification; a continuing concern for children's development as the anchor point for decision making; liaison between schools and communities, so that the children do not bear the burden of local tension; and training and support for teachers, who must provide optimal conditions for mixed groups of children on a daily basis.

Educational Alternatives. American education offers any educator the possibility of choice in establishing an educational setting because it embodies a variety of approaches. Such variations have existed since the early years of the century, as exemplified by Dewey and the progressive education movement; but the reality of alternative models became more vivid in the 1960s and 1970s, when "open education" crossed the Atlantic from England, and planned variation became part of such national programs as Head Start and Follow Through. The various approaches to elementary education cannot be described here but can be found in other publications (e.g., Maccoby & Zellner, 1970; Minuchin, 1977; Stebbins et al., 1977). In general, alternatives range from relatively traditional approaches, which stress basic skills and learning efficiency, to those that stress a problem-solving learning process, broad developmental goals, and the interaction between cognition and affect. The different approaches organize the classroom, the curriculum, and the child's learning experience in different ways. Children in open environments, for instance, are given freedom to move about and work with others, have some choice of learning materials, and are encouraged to raise questions and work autonomously; whereas children in traditional environments are usually expected to work alone on prescribed materials under teacher direction and control.

Comparative research has indicated some differential effects on children, though studies are sometimes contradictory or unclear. Some studies suggest, for instance, that approaches stressing basic skills are more successful than others in training their pupils in those skills (Stebbins et al., 1977), but other studies find no difference in achievement between pupils in open schools and those in traditional schools (Horwitz, 1979; Epstein & McPartland, 1979). Where differences have been found in self-knowledge, autonomy, and cooperative behavior, they have generally been associated with the more open, developmentally oriented school settings—a finding consistent with the educational philosophy (Horwitz, 1979; Minuchin et al., 1969). Despite continuing investigation, it is quite possible that research will not produce definitive answers to the question of comparative effects; educational emphases and value systems may always be a consideration in the choice of educational alternatives. It is important that educators make conscious and informed decisions about the orientation of their classrooms and schools. The middle years are years of intellectual reorganization, expanding relationships with peers, and changing conceptions of self and society. From a developmental point of view, optimal schooling takes account of these several facets of development, adopting an educational approach that is attuned to children's characteristics, and that stretches and supports the child's efforts and growing capacities.

Patricia Minuchin

See also Elementary Education; Life-Span Development.

REFERENCES

Allen, V. L., & Feldman, R. S. Learning through tutoring: Low-achieving children as tutors. *Journal of Experimental Education*, 1973, *42*, 1–5.

Allender, J. Affective education. In H. E. Mitzel (Ed.), *Encyclopedia of Educational Research* (5th ed.). New York: Free Press, 1982.

Anderson, L. W. *Assessing Affective Characteristics in the Schools.* Rockleigh, N.J.: Allyn & Bacon, Longwood Division, 1981.

Berk, L., & Lewis, N. Sex role and social behavior in four school environments. *Elementary School Journal*, 1977, *77*, 205–217.

Bianchi, B., & Bakeman, R. Sex-typed affiliation preferences observed in preschoolers: Traditional and open school differences. *Child Development*, 1978, *49*, 910–912.

Biber, B. A developmental-interaction approach: Bank Street College of Education. In M. C. Day & R. K. Parker (Eds.), *The Preschool in Action.* Boston: Allyn & Bacon, 1977.

Bigner, J. J. A Wernerian developmental analysis of children's descriptions of siblings. *Child Development*, 1974, *45*, 317–323.

Blatt, M., & Kohlberg, L. The effects of classroom moral discussion upon children's level of moral judgment. *Journal of Moral Education*, 1975, *4*, 129–161.

Coopersmith, S. *The Antecedents of Self-esteem.* San Francisco: Freeman, 1967.

Dewey, J. *Democracy and Education: An Introduction to the Philosophy of Education.* New York: Free Press, 1966. (Originally published, 1916)

Epstein, J. *Friends in School: Patterns of Selection and Influence in Secondary Schools* (Report No. 266). Baltimore: Johns Hopkins University Center for Social Organization of Schools, 1978.

Epstein, J., & McPartland, J. Authority structures. In H. J. Walberg (Ed.), *Educational Environments and Effects.* Berkeley, Calif.: McCutchan, 1979.

Erikson, E. *Childhood and Society.* New York: Norton, 1950.

Feffer, M. Developmental analysis of interpersonal behavior. *Psychological Review*, 1970, *77*, 197–214.

Feshbach, N. Empathy training: A field study in affective education. In S. Feshbach & A. Fraczek (Eds.), *Aggression and Behavior Change: Biological and Social Processes.* New York: Praeger, 1979.

Flapan, D. *Children's Understanding of Social Interaction.* New York: Teachers College Press, 1968.

Flavell, J.; Botkin, P.; Fry, C.; Wright, J.; & Jarvis, P. *The Development of Role-taking and Communication Skills in Children.* New York: Wiley, 1968.

Fogelman, K. R. *Piagetian Tests for the Primary School.* London: National Foundation for Educational Research in England and Wales, 1970.

Furth, H. G. *Piaget for Teachers.* Englewood Cliffs, N.J.: Prentice-Hall, 1970.

Gallagher, J., & Reid, D. K. *The Learning Theory of Piaget and Inhelder.* Monterey, Calif.: Brooks/Cole, 1981.

Glidewell, J.; Kantor, M.; Smith, L.; & Stringer, L. Socialization and social structure in the classroom. In M. L. Hoffman and L. W. Hoffman (Eds.), *Review of Research in Child Development* (No 2). New York: Russell Sage, 1966.

Guttentag, M., & Bray, H. *Undoing Sex Stereotypes: Research and Resources for Educators.* New York: McGraw-Hill, 1976.

Hallinan, M. Friendship patterns in open and traditional classrooms. *Sociology of Education,* 1976, *49,* 254–265.

Hartup, W. Peer interaction and social organization. In P. H. Mussen (Ed.), *Carmichael's Manual of Child Psychology* (Vol. 2). New York: Wiley, 1970.

Horwitz, R. Psychological effects of the "open classroom." *Review of Educational Research,* 1979, *49,* 71–86.

Inhelder, B., & Piaget, J. *The Early Growth of Logic in the Child.* London: Routledge & Kegan Paul, 1964.

Inhelder, B.; Sinclair, H.; & Bovet, M. *Learning and the Development of Cognition.* Cambridge, Mass.: Harvard University Press, 1974.

Kohlberg, L. Moral stages and moralization: The cognitive-developmental approach. In T. Lickona (Ed.), *Moral Development and Behavior.* New York: Holt, Rinehart & Winston, 1976.

Kohlberg, L. Revisions in the theory and practice of moral development. In W. Damon (Ed.), *New Directions for Child Development: Moral Development.* San Francisco: Jossey-Bass, 1978.

Kohlberg, L., & Turiel, E. Moral development and moral education. In C. Beck & E. Sullivan (Eds.), *Psychology and Educational Practice.* Glenview, Ill.: Scott, Foresman, 1971.

Lickona, T. Creating the just community with children. *Theory into Practice,* 1977, *16,* 97–104.

Lidz, C. *Improving Assessment of School Children.* San Francisco: Jossey-Bass, 1981.

Livesley, W. J., & Bromley, D. B. *Person Perception in Childhood and Adolescence.* New York: Wiley, 1973.

Lockwood, A. The effects of values clarification and moral development curricula on school-age subjects: A critical review of recent research. *Review of Educational Research,* 1978, *48,* 325–364.

Maccoby, E. E., & Jacklin, C. *The Psychology of Sex Differences.* Stanford, Calif.: Stanford University Press, 1974.

Maccoby, E. E., & Zellner, M. *Experiments in Primary Education: Aspects of Project Follow-Through.* New York: Harcourt Brace Jovanovich, 1970.

Minuchin, P. Sex-role concepts and sex typing in childhood as a function of school and home environments. *Child Development,* 1965, *36,* 1033–1048.

Minuchin, P. *The Middle Years of Childhood.* Monterey, Calif.: Brooks/Cole, 1977.

Minuchin, P.; Biber, B.; Shapiro, E.; & Zimiles, H. *The Psychological Impact of School Experience.* New York: Basic Books, 1969.

Minuchin, P., & Shapiro, E. The school as a context for social development. In P. H. Mussen (Ed.), *Handbook of Child Psychology* (4th ed.; Vol. 3: *Social Development,* E. M. Hetherington, Ed.). New York: Wiley, in press.

Mischel, W. Sex-typing and socialization. In P. H. Mussen (Ed.), *Carmichael's Manual of Child Psychology* (Vol. 2). New York: Wiley, 1970.

Moreno, J. L. *Who Shall Survive?* Washington, D.C.: Nervous and Mental Disease Publishing Co., 1934.

Mosher, F., & Hornsby, J. On asking questions. In J. Bruner, R. Olver, & P. Greenfield (Eds.), *Studies in Cognitive Growth.* New York: Wiley, 1966.

Murray, F. B. Acquisition of conservation through social interaction. *Developmental Psychology,* 1972, *6,* 1–6.

Mussen, P. H., & Eisenberg-Berg, N. *Roots of Caring, Sharing, and Helping: The Development of Prosocial Behavior in Children.* San Francisco: Freeman, 1977.

Peevers, B. H., & Secord, P. F. Developmental changes in attribution of descriptive concepts to persons. *Journal of Personality and Social Psychology,* 1973, *27,* 120–128.

Piaget, J. *The Moral Judgment of the Child* (2nd ed., M. Gabain, Trans.). New York: Free Press, 1948. (Original French Edition, 1932)

Piaget, J. The theory of stages in cognitive development. In D. R. Green, M. P. Ford, & G. B. Flamer (Eds.), *Measurement and Piaget.* New York: McGraw-Hill, 1971.

Piaget, J., & Inhelder, B. *The Psychology of the Child.* New York: Basic Books, 1969.

Pottker, J., & Fishel, A. (Eds.). *Sex Bias in the Schools: The Research Evidence.* Rutherford, N.J.: Associated University Presses, 1977.

Power, C., & Reimer, J. Moral atmosphere: An educational bridge between moral judgment and action. In W. Damon (Ed.), *New Directions for Child Development: Moral Development.* San Francisco: Jossey-Bass, 1978.

Rist, R. *Desegregated Schools: Appraisals of an American Experiment.* New York: Academic Press, 1979.

Schmuck, R., & Schmuck, P. *Group Processes in the Classroom.* Dubuque, Iowa: Brown, 1971.

Schwebel, M., & Raph, J. (Eds.). *Piaget in the Classroom.* New York: Basic Books, 1973.

Selman, R. L., & Byrne, D. F. A structural-developmental analysis of levels of role taking in middle childhood. *Child Development,* 1974, *45,* 803–806.

Shantz, C. The development of social cognition. In E. M. Hetherington (Ed.), *Review of Child Development Research* (Vol. 5). Chicago: University of Chicago Press, 1975.

Shapiro, E. K., & Weber, E. *Cognitive and Affective Growth: Developmental Interaction.* Hillsdale, N.J.: Lawrence Erlbaum Associates, 1981.

Sharan, S. Cooperative learning in small groups: Recent methods and effects on achievement, attitudes, and ethnic relations. *Review of Educational Research,* 1980, *50,* 241–271.

Slavin, R. Cooperative learning. *Review of Educational Research,* 1980, *50,* 315–342.

Stebbins, L.; St. Pierre, R.; Proper, E.; Anderson, R.; & Cerva, T. *An Evaluation of Follow-Through.* Vol. 4A of *Education as Experimentation: A Planned Variation Model.* Cambridge, Mass.: Abt Associates, Inc., 1977.

Stephan, W., & Feagin, J. *School Desegregation: Past, Present, and Future.* New York: Plenum Press, 1980.

St. John, N. *School Desegregation: Outcomes for Children.* New York: Wiley, 1975.

Stockard, J.; Schmuck, P.; Kempner, K.; Williams, P.; Edson, S.; & Smith, M. *Sex Equity in Education.* New York: Academic Press, 1980.

Tanner, J. M. Physical growth. In P. H. Mussen (Ed.), *Carmichael's Manual of Child Psychology.* New York: Wiley, 1970.

Turiel, E. The development of social concepts: Mores, customs, and conventions. In D. J. DePalma & J. M. Foley (Eds.), *Moral Development: Current Theory and Research.* Hillsdale, N.J.: Lawrence Erlbaum Associates, 1975.

Weinraub, M., & Brown, L. M. The development of sex role stereotypes: Crushing realities. In V. Franks & E. Rothblum, *Sex-role Stereotypes and Clinical Issues: Lessons from the Past and Implications for the Future.* New York: Springer, in press.

Weybright, L.; Adams, R.; & Voyat, G. *Piaget and Reading* (Tapes 1 and 2). Fair Lawn, N.J.: JAB Press, 1976.

Williams, J. W., & Stith, M. *Middle Childhood: Behavior and Development.* New York: Macmillan, 1974.

MILITARY EDUCATION

See Vocational Education.

MORAL DEVELOPMENT

Moral development has traditionally been studied under one of three theoretical perspectives: social-learning theory, psychoanalytic theory, and cognitive-developmental theory. The social-learning model, represented by Aronfreed (1961, 1968) and Mischel (1973, 1976), among others, accepts moral learning as a socially learned behavior, transmitted by direct teaching and imitation of appropriate role models. Social-learning theorists believe that environmental influence is of critical importance for the internalization of cultural rules. Research derived from this perspective focuses chiefly on moral behavior as studied through resistance to temptation.

The psychoanalytic model, represented by Hartmann (1960), Sarnoff (1976), and, of course, Sigmund Freud, is tied to a theory of personality development that emphasizes the internalization of standards and values. It focuses on moral feelings as studied through reaction to transgression.

The cognitive-developmental approach, represented by Piaget (1932) and Kohlberg (1964), focuses on the kind of reasoning or moral judgment that people use in making their decisions and on their understanding of justice. Thus, social-learning theory focuses on moral behavior, psychoanalytic theory on moral feelings, and cognitive-developmental theory on moral judgment. Both the psychoanalytic and social-learning models focus on guilt rather than on a concept of justice as the basic motive for morality. Both assume that the child's basic moral system is formed in early childhood and feel that early childrearing practices are critical factors in moral development.

The psychoanalytic model is viewed chiefly as a clinical model and has generated little empirical research. The social-learning model, popular in the 1960s, is less favored in the current era of emphasis on social cognition. Kohlberg and Kramer (1969) feel that the development of social cognition depends not on maturation or learning but on the interaction between the organism and the environment. Shantz (1975) states that "understanding others is . . . organizing what one knows into systems of meaning or belief. What one learns from his experiences with others depends heavily on the structuring of those experiences by the person" (p. 266). Thus, the child's role is seen as an active one rather than the passive one of simply receiving social instruction.

This review will focus chiefly on the cognitive-developmental approach. The reader is referred to Hoffman's chapter on moral development in *Carmichael's Manual of Child Psychology* (1970) for a complete discussion of all three models.

Concern with the topic of moral development, as distinguished from moral education, has surfaced within the last fifty years with the work of Jean Piaget and Lawrence Kohlberg. Piaget's thinking about the development of morality is part of a trend in thinking that includes ideas proposed by J. M. Baldwin (1906), McDougall (1908), Hartshorne and May (1928–1930), J. Dewey and J. H. Tufts (1932), and G. H. Mead (1934). Piaget's writing (1932) stimulated Kohlberg's early work. Kohlberg, in turn, has greatly influenced the work of Turiel (1978), Rest (1979), and Damon (1977), to mention just a few of the current leading researcher-theorists.

Piaget: Understanding Rules. Piaget (1932) reasoned that children's use of rules provided the foundation for their moral development. He observed the ways that children understood and used rules of games they were playing. As a result of his observations, he was able to identify four stages of moral development:

1. *Egocentrism* (infancy to school age). The child is amoral and motivated mainly by his or her own rules, not easily accepting others' wishes before his or her own.
2. *Heteronomy* (early elementary school age). The young child understands that his or her needs and wishes are subject to another's law or authority. The child recognizes that there are rules of behavior and follows them because there is an authority figure to praise or to punish, as the occasion warrants.
3. *Transition* (later elementary school age). The child understands rules and begins to appreciate how rules make things function.
4. *Autonomy* (adolescence). The individual takes control of his or her behavior and acts in accordance with his or her own code of ethics, which has been developed through experiences at earlier stages.

Thus, the individual moves from a morality of heteronomy, or control by others, to one of autonomy, in which the individual takes responsibility for his or her own actions and their consequences.

Piaget believed that an individual moves through stages in a fixed order and as a result of meaningful social experiences coupled with significant cognitive development. Piaget also felt that some of his stages overlap and that an individual can exhibit behavior and thinking across stages.

Piaget's stages, with the interdependence of cognitive and moral development, reflect John Dewey's instrumentalism, in which the thought or idea becomes an instrument for action. Dewey distinguished three levels of human conduct: (1) behavior motivated by nonmoral impulses or needs, (2) action determined by the standards of the group, and (3) actions resulting from individual assessment of the situation. According to Dewey, the process is one through which the individual becomes "more rational, more social, and finally more moral" (McCluskey, 1958, p. 209).

Kohlberg: Social Perspective. Kohlberg's approach to moral development is similar to Piaget's and emphasizes what he calls "social perspective," or the prersonal view of one's relationship to society. Kohlberg, like Piaget, believes that moral development is closely related to the individual's cognitive development and that moral development is an outgrowth of the interaction between cognitive development and social experience. Kohlberg (1964) states: "It seems obvious that moral stages must primarily be the products of the child's interaction with others, rather than the direct unfolding of biological or neurological structure. . . . The fundamental factor causing a structuring of a moral order is social participation and role-taking" (p. 395). Role-taking ability makes it possible for an individual to interpret the thoughts and reactions of others by putting the self in the place of the other. There is no way a young child can explore the viewpoint of others until the child recognizes that a viewpoint differing from his or her own can exist. Therefore, role-taking ability appears only after this perception of the "other" occurs.

Kohlberg identified six stages of moral development, which he divided into three levels: preconventional, conventional, and postconventional.

- Level I. *Preconventional.* Rules and expectations are imposed from outside. Most children under age 9, some adolescents, and many adolescent and adult criminal offenders fall into this level of moral development.
  - Stage 1. *Heteronomous morality.* The obedience-and-punishment orientation.
  - Stage 2. *Individualism, instrumental purpose, and exchange.* The egoistic stage, which aims at considering self first but recognizes the fact that others have rights.
- Level II. *Conventional.* The self accepts the rules and expectations of authorities. Most adolescents and adults fall into this level.
  - Stage 3. *Mutual interpersonal expectations, relationships, and interpersonal conformity.* The Golden Rule morality, in which other's approval is sought by behaving correctly.
  - Stage 4. *Social system and conscience:* Respect for authority and the social-order expectations of others, with a need to support the system.
- Level III. *Postconventional.* Self-selected principles and values. A minority of adults over the age of 20 reach Stages 5 and 6.
  - Stage 5. *Social contract or utility and individual rights.* Legalistic orientation that recognizes the rights of others and majority rule. At this stage, the individual accepts majority rule but also works to change rules that he or she feels are unfair or unjust.
  - Stage 6. *Universal ethical principles.* Conscience or principle orientation, in which the individual follows self-chosen ethical principles in a situation of mutual respect and trust.

Kohlberg's work has generated a great deal of empirical research over the last twenty years that has confirmed the fact that people from a wide sample of cultures on three continents move through the same stages of moral development in a sequentially invariant manner (Carter, 1980). Research also confirms Kohlberg's claim that few people reach the Postconventional level of moral judgment.

There is some evidence that individuals at upper education levels are more likely to reach Stage 5 thinking than individuals with less education. Candee (1978) found that all who reached Stage 5 had some college experience and either grew up in an upper-middle-class family or attained an upper-middle-class occupational status in adulthood. Kohlberg (1981) reports that none of the subjects in a twenty-year longitudinal study begun in 1956 with 72 boys aged 10 to 16 showed Stage 6 thinking even in their thirties. Stage 6 remains more of a theoretical ideal for Kohlberg than an actually occurring stage found in the adolescent or adult population. The area of continuing debate surrounding Kohlberg's work is whether Stage 6 really exists (for a brief time, Kohlberg even proposed a Stage 7), and if it does, whether it is truly the highest stage of moral development or is simply an adult reversion to Stage 2 thinking.

Turiel: Social Convention. Although both Piaget and Kohlberg define stages of moral development, they have employed quite different procedures in their studies. Piaget elicits and accepts children's own reasoning and behavior as clues to their level of moral development. Kohlberg analyzes children's responses to dilemmas that are drawn from adult experiences. Partly because of this adult-centered methodology, Turiel (1978) feels that Kohlberg's stage system fails to deal with much of the child's early knowledge about justice. Nucci (1981) states that "a distinction needs to be made between morality and social convention. Conventions constitute general and shared knowledge or uniformities in social interactions and are determined by the social system in which they are formed. . . . Moral issues are not determined by social regulations or social consensus, but by factors inherent in the social relationship" (p. 489). "Turiel maintains that in contrast with the individual's concepts about convention, which are structured by underlying concepts of social organization, the individual's understandings of morality are based on concepts regarding the welfare and rights of persons, structured by underlying conceptualizations of justice" (pp. 489–490).

In an attempt to get at children's concepts of justice, Nucci and Turiel (1978) and Nucci and Nucci (1979) asked preschool children and children in grades 2, 5, and 7 to differentiate between social convention (rules) and morality (concept of justice). Events that the researchers classified as involving moral transgressions were judged to be wrong by over 80 percent of the children at each grade level regardless of the presence or absence of a school rule pertaining to the act. Events that were classified as involving transgressions of social conventions were judged to be wrong only if a rule pertaining to the act existed in the school.

Whether the focus is children's understanding of rules

of games, social perspective and justice, or social convention, intentionality seems to play a role. In evaluating or judging behavior, both children and adults take intention into account. Darley, Klosson, and Zanna (1978) found that 5-year-old and 6-year-old children were as likely as adults to reduce punishments they assigned to actions that resulted in harm if they discovered reasons excusing that action. Lyons-Ruth (1978) found that children proceeded "from idiosyncratic evaluative judgments at age 2½ to consistent concepts of parentally sanctioned acts at age 4, to a view at age 5 that begins to differentiate motives and outcomes from the act itself" (p. 1205). In their study of first-graders, second-graders, and fifth-graders, Suls, Gutkin, and Kalle (1979) found that the use of "social consequence cues decreased with age, damage cues remained important in all grades tested, and intention cues increased in use" (p. 874). Children also have an understanding of the role of restitution in amending a wrong. They understand that restitution is more important than apology (Irwin & Moore, 1971).

Moral Reasoning and Moral Behavior. The kind of reasoning involved in assessing actions or behaviors based on an individual's intention has been of continuing interest to researchers. A great variety of research has been done in the past twenty years to confirm stages of moral development and to assess the relationship between moral reasoning or judgment and moral behavior. Researchers have also been interested to discover what factors facilitate and reinforce moral development and what factors inhibit or weaken it.

Although a relationship exists between cognitive level and moral reasoning, there does not seem to be a reliable relationship between moral reasoning and moral behavior. The individual may know what is right but does not necessarily do what is right. Frankel (1980), in his review of social science literature and social psychological research studies, finds support for the idea that the level of moral reasoning is associated with an increase in the frequency of moral behavior. However, he also finds quite a discrepancy between what people think they would do in moral-action situations and what they actually do.

People tend to do better when they respond to real-life rather than to hypothetical situations. Rothman (1980) reports on a study (Gerson & Damon, 1975) involving the two kinds of situations. Children tended to use "lower levels of reasoning in response to the concrete situation . . . than in response to the hypothetical dilemma. . . . Only in the practical context were the children directly involved in the outcome of their reasoning. . . . Gerson and Damon, therefore, attributed the discrepancy between the two kinds of reasoning to self-interest" (p. 117).

Better coordination of judgment and behavior seems to exist at higher developmental stages. Piaget contended that it is only among older children that one finds a correspondence between an awareness of the rules and a genuine observation of the rules. Kohlberg and Kramer (1969) state that at the adult level, the trend is "not only toward greater consistency of moral judgment, but toward greater

consistency between moral judgment and moral behavior" (p. 119). Boyce and Jensen (1978) report three conclusions in their review of a variety of studies: "(1) there is a relationship between moral judgments, beliefs, values, and behavior; (2) changes through persuasion or verbal instruction can influence behavior; (3) the stage level of the message is important in determining the amount of the behavioral change that occurs" (p. 119).

Childrearing Practices. A number of studies have identified some of the childrearing practices that can affect moral development. Parental behavior can effect positive growth in moral judgment if the parent is consistent in behavior toward the child and is open to reasoned dialogue with the child on moral behavior issues. Discussion can also develop cognitive conflict, or disequilibrium, which seems to facilitate movement to a higher level of moral reasoning as the individual seeks to resolve that conflict (Kohlberg, 1981).

Hoffman (1970) feels that although the child is more likely to emulate an adult who is warm and nurturant than one who is not, this tends to occur primarily with respect to behaviors requiring little effort of self-denial. Becker (1964) found that internalized reactions to misdeeds in the form of feelings of guilt or acceptance of responsibility for those misdeeds are more likely to occur when the parent is warm and uses the kind of discipline that is based on the love relationship between parent and child. "The use of praise and reasoning appears to have the best effects across studies while love-withdrawing methods seem effective primarily when the parent is high in warmth" (p. 185).

In homes where parents supervise closely and use punishment as a preferred method of discipline, growth in moral development is less impressive. Hoffman and Saltzstein (1967) state that "frequent use of power assertion, especially physical punishment, retards the development of any kind of internal morality. Psychological techniques, especially pointing out the consequences of actions for others, facilitate the development of internal morality" (p. 169). Burton (1976) found that physical punishment can induce so much anxiety that a child is not able to differentiate an unacceptable act from an acceptable one.

In summary, Boyce and Jensen (1978) indicate that the following dimensions of parent-child interaction facilitate moral development: dialogue about moral issues, inductive reasoning, mutual respect and cooperation between parent and child, consistency and trust, and affection and warmth.

Peer Relationships. Relationships with peers can also have a great impact on the development of moral judgment. Piaget felt that although parents have the first role in guiding a child at the early heteronomous stage, it is often peers who cause the child to move to the next higher level of moral development. Interaction with peers leads to a decline of egocentrism and an increase in consideration of others' points of view. Keasey (1971) found that the amount of social participation was related to moral development of fifth-graders and sixth-graders. Kohlberg

(1981) states that in general, the higher an individual child's participation in a social group or institution, the more opportunities he or she has to take the social perspective of others.

Hughes, Tingle, and Sawin (1981) indicate that "Several consistent developmental trends suggest that between 5 and 8 years of age, children become increasingly aware of the other person's perspectives in emotion-eliciting situations and of the personal and psychological characteristics of others (and themselves) that may be involved in emotional experiences" (p. 127). Their findings suggest that children's thinking about their own reactions to emotion in others might improve their understanding of others' internal experiences. They report that Hoffman (1975) found no consistent sex differences in children's assessment of other people's affective or cognitive perspective.

Berkowitz (1981) reports: "In an extensive study of high school moral discussion curricula, Ann Colby and her colleagues (1977) found that development was closely related to the degree of heterogeneity of student moral reasoning in the individual classroom. This was true regardless of the teacher's style and moral sophistication. Therefore, moral education seems to depend on the reasoning of the students more than on the reasoning of the teacher. . . . Peer reasoning is often more seductive, more convincing, and more stimulating" (p. 488).

This does not mean that teachers have no role in the moral development process. In a study involving a sample of preservice teachers, Hurt and Sprinthall (1977) redesigned a course in educational psychology to teach counseling techniques deliberately as a means of stimulating ego and moral development. Over a period of four months, teachers were trained in the application of principles of psychological counseling to their regular classroom interactions with pupils. The researchers were seeking to increase the repertoire of responsiveness to colleagues and to pupils on the part of teachers. The results indicated positive shifts on both the Loevinger test of ego development and the Rest Defining Issues Test (DIT), an objective test based on Kohlberg's stage theory of moral development, with Rest's modifications of the stage characteristics. Hurt and Sprinthall (1977) state that a key element in their results may be a learning experience in the skill of empathy, which Kohlberg has noted is a critical aspect of growth to higher stages.

Other Factors. Lawrence (1980) analyzed fourteen intervention studies using the Defining Issues Test with junior high level students to adults. Several factors emerge that seem to facilitate change. The duration, design, and characteristics of the experimental program seemed most crucial. All the effective studies were of at least one quarter's duration. However, length of intervention alone is not a sufficient condition for change. Lawrence pointed out that few of the experiments provided adequate control groups or control of extraneous variables.

The number of years in school and the individual's age were found to be related to the way subjects judge moral issues as assessed by the DIT (Rest, Davison, Robbins, 1978). "Students moving through high school and into college show the most dramatic change. Adults seem to slow down in moral judgment development in their 20s and to plateau after leaving school" (p. 276). The exception is students in moral philosophy or political science, seminarians, and so on. This group attains much higher scores than the average adult.

If one of the goals in defining the conditions favorable to moral development is to help an individual who is bogged down at an inappropriate level of thinking achieve a breakthrough and continue to grow, there is, according to Lawrence, very little certainty upon which moral educators can base their programming. It would be inappropriate to try to speed up moral development, just as it would be inappropriate to speed physical growth. But if the individual is malnourished or has poor nutrition habits, it is appropriate to intervene to remove those roadblocks that stunt or restrict growth and development. It would seem that one of the more productive techniques would involve the child in discussion about real situations and experiences as these events arise in daily life.

D. Michelle Irwin

See also Cognitive Development; Moral Education; Social Development.

REFERENCES

Aronfreed, J. The nature, variety, and social patterning of moral responses to transgression. *Journal of Abnormal and Social Psychology,* 1961, *63,* 223–240.

Aronfreed, J. *Conduct and Conscience.* New York: Academic Press, 1968.

Baldwin, J. M. *Social and Ethical Interpretations in Mental Development.* New York: Macmillan, 1906.

Becker, W. C. Consequences of different kinds of parental discipline. In M. L. Hoffman & L. W. Hoffman (Eds.), *Review of Child Development Research* (Vol. 1). New York: Russell Sage Foundation, 1964.

Berkowitz, M. W. A critical appraisal of the "plus-one" convention in moral education. *Phi Delta Kappan,* 1981, *62,* 488–489.

Boyce, W. D., & Jensen, L. C. *Moral Reasoning: A Psychological-Philosophical Integration.* Lincoln: University of Nebraska Press, 1978.

Burton, R. Honesty and dishonesty. In T. Lickona (Ed.), *Moral Development and Behavior.* New York: Holt, Rinehart & Winston, 1976. (ERIC Document Reproduction Service No. ED 117 114)

Candee, R. *A Study of Moral Development and Life Outcome.* Cambridge, Mass.: Moral Education Research Foundation, 1978.

Carter, R. E. What is Lawrence Kohlberg doing? *Journal of Moral Education,* 1980, *9,* 88–102.

Colby, A.; Kohlberg, L.; Fenton, E.; Speicher-Dubin, B.; & Leeberman, M. Secondary school moral discussion programs led by social studies teachers. *Journal of Moral Education,* 1977, *7,* pp. 90–111.

Damon, W. *The Social World of the Child.* San Francisco: Jossey-Bass, 1977.

Darley, J. M.; Klosson, E.; & Zanna, M. Intentions and their contexts in the moral judgments of children and adults. *Child Development*, 1978, *49*, 66–74.

Dewey, J., & Tufts, J. H. *Ethics* (Rev. ed.). New York: Holt, 1932.

Frankel, J. *The Relationship between Moral Thought and Moral Action: Implications for Social Studies Education.* 1980. (ERIC Document Reproduction Service No. ED 184 974)

Gerson, R., & Damon, W. Relations between moral behavior in a hypothetical verbal context and in a practical "real life" setting. Paper presented at Eastern Psychological Association, New York City, April 1975.

Hartmann, H. *Psychoanalysis and Moral Values.* New York: International Universities Press, 1960.

Hartshorne, H., & May, M. A. *Studies in the Nature of Character.* New York: Macmillan, 1928–1930.

Hoffman, M. J. Sex differences in moral internalization and values. *Journal of Personality and Social Psychology*, 1975, *32*, 720–729.

Hoffman, M. L. Moral development. In P. H. Mussen (Ed.), *Carmichael's Manual of Child Psychology* (3rd ed.). New York: Wiley, 1970.

Hoffman, M. L., & Saltzstein, H. D. Parent discipline and the child's moral development. *Journal of Personality and Social Psychology*, 1967, *5*, 45–47.

Hughes, R., Jr.; Tingle, B. A.; & Sawin, D. B. Development of empathetic understanding in children. *Child Development*, 1981, *52*, 122–128.

Hurt, B. L., & Sprinthall, N. A. Psychological and moral development for teacher education. *Journal of Moral Education*, 1977, *6*, 112–120.

Irwin, D. M., & Moore, S. The young child's understanding of social justice. *Developmental Psychology*, 1971, *5*, 406–410.

Keasey, C. B. Implicators of cognitive development for moral reasoning. In D. J. DePalma & J. M. Foley (Eds.), *Moral Development: Current Theory and Practice.* Hillsdale, N.J.: Lawrence Erlbaum Associates, 1975.

Kohlberg, L. Development of moral character and moral ideology. In M. L. Hoffman & L. W. Hoffman (Eds.), *Review of Child Development Research* (Vol. 1). New York: Russell Sage Foundation, 1964.

Kohlberg, L. The development of moral judgment and moral character. In L. Kohlberg, R. DeVries, et al. *Developmental Psychology and Early Education.* Unpublished manuscript, 1981.

Kohlberg, L., & Kramer, R. Continuities and discontinuities in childhood and adult development. *Human Development*, 1969, *12*, 93–120.

Lawrence, J. A. Moral judgment intervention studies using the Defining Issues Test. *Journal of Moral Education*, 1980, *9*, 178–191. (ERIC Document Reproduction Service No. ED 160 622)

Lyons-Ruth, K. Moral and personal value judgments of preschool children. *Child Development*, 1978, *49*, 1197–1207.

McCluskey, N. *Public Schools and Moral Education.* New York: Columbia University Press, 1958.

McDougall, W. *An Introduction to Social Psychology.* London: Methuen, 1908.

Mead, G. H. *Mind, Self, and Society.* Chicago: University of Chicago Press, 1934.

Mischel, W. Toward a cognitive social learning reconceptualization of personality. *Psychological Review*, 1973, *80*, 252–283.

Mischel, W., & Mischel, H. N. A cognitive social learning approach to morality and self-regulation. In T. Lickona (Ed.), *Moral Development and Behavior: Theory, Research, and Social Issues.*

New York: Holt, Rinehart & Winston, 1976. (ERIC Document Reproduction Service No. ED 117 114)

Nucci, L. P. The distinction between morality and social convention: Implications for values instruction. *Phi Delta Kappan*, 1981, *62*, 489–493.

Nucci, L. P., & Nucci, M. S. *Social Interactions and the Development of Moral and Societal Concepts.* Paper presented at the meeting of the Society for Research in Child Development, San Francisco, March 1979.

Nucci, L. P., & Turiel, E. Social interactions and the development of social concepts in preschool children. *Child Development*, 1978, *49*, 400–407. (ERIC Document Reproduction Service No. ED 142 299)

Piaget, J. *The Moral Judgment of the Child.* London: Kegan Paul, 1932.

Rest, J. R. New approaches in the assessment of moral judgment. In T. Lickona (Ed.), *Moral Development and Behavior.* New York: Holt, Rinehart & Winston, 1976. (ERIC Document Reproduction Service No. ED 117 114)

Rest, J. R. *Development in Judging Moral Issues.* Minneapolis: University of Minnesota Press, 1979. (ERIC Document Reproduction Service No. ED 144 980)

Rest, J. R.; Davison, M. L.; & Robbins, S. Age trends in judging moral issues: A review of cross-sectional, longitudinal, and sequential studies of the Defining Issues Test. *Child Development*, 1978, *49*, 263–279.

Rest, J. R. *Development in Judging Moral Issues.* Minneapolis: University of Minnesota Press, 1979. (ERIC Document Reproduction Service No. ED 144 980)

Rothman, G. R. The relationship between moral judgment and moral behavior. In M. Windmiller, N. Lambert, & E. Turiel (Eds.), *Moral Development and Socialization.* Boston: Allyn & Bacon, 1980.

Sarnoff, C. *Latency.* New York: Aronson, 1976.

Shantz, C. The development of social cognition. In E. M. Hetherington (Ed.), *Review of Child Development Theory and Research* (Vol. 5). Chicago: University of Chicago Press, 1975.

Suls, J.; Gutkin, D.; & Kalle, R. J. The role of intentions, damage, and social consequences in the moral judgments of children. *Child Development*, 1979, *50*, 874–877.

Turiel, E. The development of concepts of social structure: Social convention. In J. Glick & A. Clarke-Stewart (Eds.), *The Development of Social Understanding.* New York: Gardner Press, 1978.

Windmiller, M.; Lambert, N.; & Turiel, E. (Eds.). *Moral Development and Socialization.* Boston: Allyn & Bacon, 1980.

MORAL EDUCATION

Education and schooling are intrinsically moral enterprises in two respects. First, the content and method constituting any educational regimen represent deliberate selections from a wide variety of possible contents and methods, and those selections must be made and ultimately justified in axiological rather than merely descriptive terms. That is to say, the choice of *this* rather than *that* educational end or means, so long as the determination is considered conscious, free, and rational, rests ultimately on its relation to some outcome regarded as valuable. Second, the educational process invariably includes implicit if not explicit recommendations respecting the choices, judgments, and conduct of its participants, both within the process and outside it. Consequently, some sort of pattern of moral development, as touching both society and the individual, has been fundamental in educational thought and activity at least since Homeric times (Marrou, 1956). With Socrates and Plato, the process of moral development as the fundamental element in education becomes formal and critical. For them, the definition of, and the differentiation between, human beings is adequately to be developed only in moral terms (Jaeger, 1947). The joining of the literary and philosophical educational traditions in the West with the Judeo-Christian theological tradition provided final and overwhelming authority for the essentially morally based "classical education" that then characterized the West virtually unopposed for some two thousand years (Jaeger, 1962; Ulich, 1968). The reciprocal relationship between the good person and the good state, as clearly articulated by Plato in the *Protagoras,* the *Republic,* and the *Laws* (Nettleship, 1935), and as developed by Aristotle in his *Nicomachean Ethics* and *Politics,* and finally as amplified by Jewish and Christian writers, provided the leitmotif of Western educational thought and practice. From that time onward, no significant educational theorist has ever denied the centrality of moral considerations in educational doctrine and practice. John Locke, for example, can still refer to "virtue, then, direct virtue" as "the hard and valuable part to be aimed at in education" (Rusk, 1969, p. 142). Formally similar conceptions of education as a fundamentally social-moral process may also be found in more recent theorists such as Durkheim (1973), Dewey (1897, 1909, 1916), and Mead (1934).

Formal correspondence and substantive unanimity are, however, very different things. With increasing social and cultural complexity, and a corresponding growth of formal schooling deliberately contrived as an instrument of social policy, education becomes increasingly problematical, though obviously no less a moral matter. So long as education and schooling in the West remained principally within the province of family and church, their moral foundations were considered axiomatic and authoritative principles were readily available. With the progressive erosion of philosophical and theological consensus, however, and with the advent of the new, nonsectarian state (and, eventually, of the avowedly pluralistic or secular state), the foundations of educational theory and practice become more problematical still. Finally, with the attempt exhaustively to define and direct education and schooling in strictly empirical terms—that is, with the pursuit of a technically defined "science" of education widely prevalent in American educational circles since the turn of the century, accompanied by the at least tacit notion that such procedures provide the only possible "objective," "value-free" basis for determining educational policy as well as practical pedagogy—the status of education in general and

moral education in particular becomes murky indeed. An explicit, as distinct from an axiomatic, concern for the moral element in education surfaces chiefly during periods of difficulty or confusion either within the educational enterprise or in the larger society and culture whence it derives its meaning. Consequently, the examination of the development and present status of moral education in American schools that follows will focus principally on those periods and problems which have most clearly shaped the enterprise.

The Common Schools. With the gradual fashioning of the American common school ostensibly as an instrument of universal compulsory education, the fundamental issues touching both content and method in moral education come into clear view. Prior to compulsory schooling, the consensus necessary for educational judgment was already present in the various constituencies furnishing the schooling and its participants and personnel. With compulsory schooling, and the gradual development of a pluralistic society and culture, an attempt at fashioning an acceptable body of moral content becomes more obviously urgent. In the nineteenth-century American common school, this necessary activity is chiefly focused on separating moral and religious content. Religion becomes, not the source of moral content, but the private motive and sanction that indirectly serve to justify and authenticate positive moral principles and prescriptions for conduct. These principles are largely seen to be embedded in a "natural" philosophy and to be compatible with a minimal natural theology. Prescriptions for conduct are deducible either from those sources or from appropriate republican social and political principles. Horace Mann devotes extensive attention to this problem in his famous "Reports" as secretary of education for Massachusetts (most notably his ninth, of 1845) and in various other writings, and the pages of early- to mid-nineteenth-century cultural and educational journals are constantly filled with contributions on this question.

The "common" school ideal was, however, an ideal, never a reality. On the one hand, upper-class children continued to be educated and schooled by family-controlled (and frequently ecclesiastically connected) tutors and in private schools, academies, and colleges whose principles and practices were derived from traditional sources. On the other hand, as in the nineteenth century the growingly important cities and other industrial areas were peopled with immigrants, "parochial" schooling increased dramatically. These schools were, practically speaking, exclusively defined by religious purposes and theologically defined moral principles.

In addition to the problem of content, the notion of a universal and compulsory school system embracing the generality of children irrespective of family, culture, or individual motives dictated a radically increased attention to method. With the philosophical shift to epistemology as the controlling question, rather than theology or metaphysics, the problem of knowledge became gradually absorbed by the problem of learning. This was especially evident among the new positivist "empiricists," who came to be closely connected to liberal progressive reform movements such as the movement for schooling. Learning theories, therefore, derived from the increasingly elaborate psychologies that now came to characterize large-scale philosophical systems furnished another element in the increasingly formal attention to moral education. The upshot, beginning in the late eighteenth and early nineteenth centuries, was a new genre of educational theorists, for whom method was as important as the traditional question of content and who could now draw upon radically expanded psychological analyses to develop their practical programs. Examples of such new educational theorists and methodologists are clearly furnished by Rousseau, Pestalozzi, Froebel, and Herbart, whose work provided much of the theoretical underpinning for the American common school, and was not without important influence in more sectarian educational circles as well.

Brief illustration of this important development and some of the conflicts it involved may be had from Rousseau and Herbart. Rousseau's novel *Émile* (1762), subtitled *Traité de l'éducation,* and other provocative educational writings were genuinely revolutionary. At least one principal element in Rousseau's philosophical and pedagogical contribution is its biographical nature. He offers for perhaps the first time a narrative of his "inner" experience while "growing up" and frankly founds his educational recommendations upon it. His rejection of classical formalism rests finally upon his deeply felt antipathy to it—emotional promptings which he took to be revelatory of the deeper reality of "Nature." Implicit in this is his celebrated introduction of crude "stages" of development and a corresponding attribution of peculiar significance to child life, previously subsumed by adult forms. All in all, both his beliefs and his methods threw enormous weight on the side of "Nature," emotion, and the necessity of a primary focus on the individual rather than on society or an abstract culture as the medium of growth. As a consequence, the particular times and conditions for moral development, and the proper methods for achieving it, were consciously addressed and articulated with stages of development rather than by the logic of their content. Religion, once the first study, became the last in point of time, although it would be quite inaccurate to suggest that either morality or religion were not for Rousseau the fundamental background against which education had in general to be plotted. Likewise, in Rousseau we find the first stirrings of opposition to the growing educational dominance of science, technology, and a rather narrow political definition—stirrings which reached full-scale rebellion in the various romantic (and essentially moral) critiques of education and schooling only in the last two decades of our own time.

On the other hand, Herbart (1902), coming out of the Kantian tradition, continued the customary emphasis on the cultural and the social, and developed a very elaborate learning theory and practical regimen which manifested both the logical and the practical centrality of moral development. Herbart's elaborate and careful structuring of the curriculum around its social and moral-religious center recommended itself to late-nineteenth-century school reformers (e.g., DeGarmo, 1896, 1897, 1910), particularly in the context of the rapidly growing high school movement.

Thus, on whatever ground, the nineteenth-century common (and principally "elementary") school—though the latter term is anachronistic—had little doubt about its moral function—a "consensus" protested only by "recalcitrant" Roman Catholics and others who pointedly demonstrated that it tended either to be divorced from religion (and therefore either ineffectual or intolerable) or to be suffused with a sometimes pale, but often robust, evangelical piety which was also unacceptable and divisive. Whether in Webster or Morse or McGuffey, moral instruction (together with dramatic illustrations of the potential effect of moral failure upon both the person and society) was built into the curriculum. As the preface to *McGuffey's Fifth Eclectic Reader* (rev. ed., 1879) remarks, a primary aim of the material included is "to exert a decided and healthful moral influence" (p. iii), and it includes selections on "Respect for the Sabbath Rewarded," "The Righteous Never Forsaken," and "The Hour of Prayer."

Emphasis was also placed on the centrality of moral (and often religious) instruction in German schools. Much later, when the Kaiser attacked his European neighbors, this emphasis became embarrassing, but it was then adroitly reinterpreted as evidence of the futility of direct religious and moral instruction, because by that time the direct method of moral education was out of fashion for other reasons, as we shall see. In the pages of the annual *Proceedings* of the National Education Association (see, e.g., Baldwin, 1892) professional discussion of content and method in moral education at the common school level was a constant though uncontroversial element, as it was in the pages of the professional journals and textbooks which served an egregiously unprepared "teaching force" either in the classrooms of the "normals" or in the reading circles, institutions, and other instrumentalities for what we should today call professional development (White, 1896).

Significant new issues were, however, provided by the rapid rise of the high school as a publicly sponsored institution. In the last three decades of the nineteenth century, public high school attendance increased by nearly 650 percent and graduation by more than 590 percent. Insofar as the high school saw itself in the collegiate tradition (either as preparation for it or as the popularizer and diffuser of it) the content was by convention largely classical: i.e., the traditional studies of language, literature (including history), and mathematics, with a growing scientific and utilitarian component. This classical content had for centuries been regarded as intrinsically moral, productive of both the high moral vision and the will to pursue it. Hence, although colleges had come to incorporate specific courses in moral philosophy (and many academies had followed suit) in an attempt to stem the already apparent tide of moral neutrality or outright secularization, less conscious attention was paid to moral development at the secondary level. One can see this revealed, for example, in the relatively minor role played by any conscious concern with moral education in even so significant a report as that of the prestigious "Committee of Ten" in 1893 (NEA, 1894). By that time, however, and irrespective of the presuppositions of the committee, a new high school was already in the offing. Indeed, a new common school was coming about, defined in the context of a new culture and new ways of viewing the nation and its health and harmony. The implications and problems of this transition for moral education and for educational and school policy were enormous.

Modern Schools. As the nineteenth century gave way to the twentieth, the nature and function of the nation's public school system as a whole appeared to many to be in need of radical reexamination and redefinition. The twin phenomena of industrialization and urbanization, together with the assimilation of a now largely city-bound contingent of immigrants in unprecedented numbers, were widely thought to impose an equally unprecedented burden on the public schools, still seem as the instrumentality of choice for "welding" the nation together and keeping it "moving ahead." At the same time, critics such as Joseph Mayer Rice and a growing body of ostensibly empirical researchers and surveyors were alleging that the schools as then organized and operated were not meeting the demand and that the traditional remedies of more money, more and better personnel (that is, personnel with more schooling themselves), and more time in grade, would not suffice. The requirement was instead a scientifically grounded and technically articulated "system" of instruction which would be more efficient and capable of guaranteeing its result. Furthermore, an enlarged role for government (including the notion of government by expert) paralleling the notion that progress entailed a more complex and technologically oriented socioeconomic system, provided an enormous impetus to the rapidly expanding secondary level of education. In short, whereas the old education had been centered on "imitation" and "virtue," the new was to define itself in terms of functions and utilitarian outcomes.

Upon what could a genuinely new education be built? This was the key question. That is, what could shape the educator's theory and practice in the same way that philosophy, theology, and other humane arts and letters had shaped it for the preceding twenty-four or twenty-five centuries? The possibility of a rigorous science of human nature, and consequently of a science of education and a technically definable notion of schooling, appeared to many to rest squarely on the work of Charles Darwin and the new evolutionary biologists. What Darwin had discovered was not always clear; what Darwin's discoveries

meant was even more problematical. The upshot was a variety of Darwin*isms*. Some hailed Darwin as the "second Newton," who had discovered laws not only of biological but of social and individual development, which paralleled Newton's accomplishments in respect of a new physical mechanics. Educators who followed this line, perhaps most clearly demonstrated in the work of Edward Lee Thorndike, could with little difficulty turn the laws of biological matter into the laws of human development and the techniques of educational change (Thorndike, 1906). For others, however, Darwin raised questions rather than solving them all. Rejecting the crude reductionism of the "psychophysicists" (as the former group had sometimes called themselves), educational theorists such as William James, John Dewey, and James Mark Baldwin (1902) saw evolutionary thought as dissolving all fixities and certainties—*including* those in science as well as those in theology and philosophy—and as offering instead a radically indeterminate reality in the shaping of which human beings were in a crucial sense free to be participants. Obviously, what educational "science" and pedagogical techniques or methods might be would, in the two cases, be radically different. And of course such profound social and cultural issues did not leave moral education untouched. Among the key questions in that domain was the question of the nature and role of reason and emotion, in relation to each other and ultimately in relation to any human action.

The opening decades of the twentieth century were thus marked by severe cultural and social conflict, including political and economic conflict, in the context of which (and, in important respects, in answer to which) a new, public, universal school system of closely defined and articulated grades and levels stretching over a minimum of twelve years was in the making. The ink was scarcely dry on the reports of the Committee of Ten respecting secondary education when a massive new study of the high school was underway, under the leadership of the Commission on the Reorganization of Secondary Education appointed by the National Education Association (NEA, 1918). Its conclusions, summarized in the famous "Cardinal Principles of Secondary Education," gave an important place to moral education. The seventh cardinal principle was defined as "Ethical Character," and it was declared "paramount among the objectives of the secondary school" (p. 15).

The commission's account of the need for a revamping of the secondary school and the need for a central ethical concern was both significant and influential. Pointing to sweeping social and cultural changes seen as radically altering the life of the ordinary citizen, the breakdown of traditional institutions, and the increasing difficulty of balancing the individual and the common good, the commission recommended increased attention to moral elements in both the general curriculum (especially through the medium of literature and the new area now called "social studies") and the social life of the school, as well as "distinct" courses of moral instruction (pp. 1–16). The commission's Special Subcommittee on Moral Values in Secondary Education was chaired by Henry Neumann (1917) and was considerably influenced by his work (1912, 1923, 1926) and that of his colleague at the Ethical Culture Society, Felix Adler (1901, 1918). Neumann's report was a carefully balanced effort, paying respect to current psychological analyses of human behavior and theories of moral development that put a premium upon action and the social setting, but concerned also to "promote a habit of moral thoughtfulness" by means of "careful thinking upon underlying principles" (1917, pp. 8–9).

Spurred on by well-funded private and semipublic agencies—the most notable and interesting examples, perhaps, being those of Milton Fairchild (1916, 1918) and the Moral Education Board—efforts to encourage the public schools to discharge their responsibility for some sort of moral development reached fever pitch from World War I and continued for nearly two decades. By the early twenties some sort of "moral" education program had become mandatory in a majority of states, and few if any school districts ignored the matter entirely. Though there were, and had been, critics (Palmer, 1909; Hart, 1910; McGeough, 1933) it was, as Mark May later reflected, a "heyday"; the whole matter was simply "in the air" everywhere (Chapman, 1977, p. 56; see also NEA, 1926). Nor were institutional support and generously sponsored empirical research lacking. Important centers quickly sprang up at the State University of Iowa, the University of Utah, Teachers College of Columbia University, and (somewhat later) Yale University. There were less ambitious projects at a host of other institutions as well. An outpouring of psychological literature dealing with the nature and development of personality from a variety of perspectives provided material upon which both investigators and practitioners could draw (e.g., Allport, 1921; Roback, 1927b; Little, 1962). Important contributions by philosophers, theologians, and religious educators sprinkled the pages of *Religious Education*, the *International Journal of Ethics*, the *Journal of Education Psychology*, the *Psychological Bulletin*, the *Journal of Philosophy*, and other specialized journals, not to mention the contributions from federal and state bureaus, more general professional journals, and the popular press.

By the late twenties, "the movement" (as it was usually called) took rather precise shape, and "character education" became the term of choice rather than "moral development" or "ethical development." (In fact, "moral" and "ethical" were now treated pejoratively, a stigma from which they cannot be said to have recovered until perhaps the last decade.) Two principal issues of continuing significance for theory and research arose. The more obvious was whether character was an aggregate of traits that could be isolated and taught in specific terms. The second was the relation of reason and emotion to conduct.

W. W. Charters (1927) argued that a trait analysis was not only legitimate but pedagogically necessary in order to rescue teachers from what Charles Judd, his colleague at the University of Chicago, called "vague and abstract" approaches to the problem (Charters, 1927, p. xi). Charters had already distinguished himself by analyzing such other forms of human activity as secretarial and homemaking duties into specific traits, and he would broaden his efforts to apply his approach to teaching competence (Charters & Waples, 1929). Basing his claims on Thorndike's famous list of "original tendencies," Charters (1927, p. 16) defined a "trait" in "the field of character" as a "type of reaction." "The trait of courage," he maintained, "indicates the fact that the individual who possesses this quality is likely to react according to type in a variety of situations." An "Ideal" is "a trait which has become the object of desire" (p. 33).

Among many others, Goodwin Watson (1927c) disagreed vehemently. "Traits" and "virtues" (which had now become almost synonymous) were, he maintained, neither natural units nor persistent entities; they varied with times and situations. "Character traits, virtues and ideals represent moral ruts," he proclaimed, "and as such tend to interfere with creative ethical living" (1927c, p. 288). Watson cited in support of his criticism the landmark research program of the entire movement, Hugh Hartshorne and Mark A. May's "Character Education Inquiry," developed at Teachers College under the direct supervision of Thorndike (see Hartshorne & May, 1927) and aided by important contributions from an influential religious educator, George Albert Coe (1917).

The Character Education Inquiry was an offshoot of John D. Rockefeller's Institute of Social and Religious Research. The inquiry got fully under way in 1925, issuing its major findings in three important volumes under the general title *Studies in the Organization of Character* (Hartshorne & May, 1928–1930). Through a variety of significant smaller pieces as well (e.g., Hartshorne, 1919, 1929, 1930, 1932; May, 1925, 1927, 1928; Hartshorne & May, 1926–1927, 1930), the authors exercised a widespread and seminal influence. Their major work will repay careful study and is still frequently cited. The empirical base for the first volume alone (*Studies in Deceit*, 1928) involved nearly 11,000 public and private school students and more than 170,000 administrations of twenty-one different tests (Book I, pp, 105–109; Book II, pp. 20–21). The approach was stipulated by its authors to be strictly psychological, measuring actual behavior without reference to any absolute moral standards (Book I, pp. 11, 377–378). A number of crucial conclusions were reached, including the following: (1) that no one is (for example) "honest" or "dishonest" by nature (Book I, p. 412); (2) that such "descriptive terms" relate to series of "acts and attitudes" which are "functions" of "situations" (Book I, p. 380); and (3) that "the mere urging of honest behavior by teachers or the discussion of standards and ideals of honesty, no matter how much such general ideas may be 'emotionalized,' has no necessary relation to the control of conduct"—indeed, such a procedure may even be "unwholesome" (Book I, p. 413). The authors' general conclusion was that there was little evidence that effectively organized moral education was taking place. They insisted that the "prevailing ways of inculcating ideals probably do little good and may do some harm" (Hartshorne & May, 1928–1930, Vol. 3, p. 413; see also Hartshorne & May, 1926–1927; 1928–1930, Vol. 1, Book I, pp. 379–390, 412–414; 1928–1930, Vol. 3, pp. 371–379).

The important argument over the specificity of elements and situations in moral character and its development precipitated widespread debate, by Gordon Allport, for example (Chapman, 1969, p. 276). Clearly it also touched on long-argued questions of "transfer" as well as on more general psychological issues. But there were also fundamental philosophical issues connected with the dispute. The most significant perhaps was the relation of reason to conduct, and the implications of that relation for the school's task. Thorndike had long before decreed that the "ideo-motor theory" of human action appeared to be "contrary to fact" (1913–1914, Vol. 1, p. 174; see also pp. 176–185, 289–293). Instead, in the moral realm, if a person "learns to do the right thing [for Thorndike, a social given, it should be noted] in a thousand particular situations, he will, so far as he has the capacity, gain the power to see what act a new situation demands. If he is made to obey a thousand particular 'This is right's' and 'That is right's' he will, so far as he has the capacity, come to connect respect and obedience with the abstractly right and true" (1916, p. 294; see also 1906, pp. 179–197). There was an inclination to label the examination of virtues or moral principles as idle and the inspection of one's own personal conduct as an instance of "priggishness" (Watson, 1927c, p. 287; see also Palmer, 1909). Conclusions such as these mirrored doubt about the role of reason in conduct. As Goodwin Watson (1927c) put it, "modern clinical psychology has demonstrated the deep and devious roots of much human behavior" (p. 288). For example: "Mary may tell lies, not so much because of inadequate training in truthfulness as because of an unrecognized need to escape from some intolerable situation or because of identification with some admired and adept liar or because of satisfactions of phantasy" (p. 289). And Dennis Clayton Troth (1930), reviewing the field, could insist that "a learned psychologist has described the intellect as a mere speck floating in a sea of feelings and emotions. The intellect, though it be educated to the n'th degree, is dominated by the feelings and emotions" (p. 360; see also Chassell, 1935).

In spite of the issues, and the negative conclusions of Hartshorne and May and others, the emphasis on moral education continued unabated into the thirties, not hindered by the widely drawn social and moral implications of the Depression (see, e.g., Heaton, 1933). By now, however, the term "citizenship education" was coming into vogue, and it would soon altogether oust terms like "morality" and ethics" on the grounds that they were too "academic" and "goody-goody" (McKown, 1935, pp. 1–2). The Department of Superintendence of the NEA (1932) devoted its tenth yearbook to publishing the results of another massive study by its Commission on Character Education. The report focused on social and cultural change as the compelling motive for continued effort, attempted to break the persistent link with religious education, and hoped to resolve the problem of relativism that lay under the welter of approaches and programs now current in the schools. The "dilemma" posed by a practical relativism was resolved, however, simply by claiming to offer no particular "pattern" for character other than something called "self-improvement" and deeming "any education worthy of the name" as "character education" (1932, pp. 1–15). The yearbook did, however, offer an important survey of the "several hundred" courses of study, research projects, and discussions of moral education then current. As the period progressed and the problems of definition and "consensus" appeared increasingly ineluctable, attention in both proposals and research tended to be directed more and more on the school's general program and atmosphere and the teacher's personality as the essential factors. To distinguish them as moral education becomes virtually vacuous.

The twenties and thirties were also marked by a number of attempts to resolve the problem of measuring both attitudes in general and more particularly moral character and values. The work of Thurstone (1929) was widely used and acclaimed. May (1925, 1927) reviewed at some length various attempts to construct personality and character tests. (See also Allport & Allport, 1921; Allport, Vernon, & Lindzey, 1931; Briggs, 1920; Roback, 1927a; Rugg, 1921; Symonds, 1924; Hartshorne & May, 1926–1927; Watson, 1927b.) In 1932 the NEA also offered an extensive critical review of tests of personality and character in its *Review of Educational Research* (NEA, 1932).

After the mid-thirties attention to moral education as a conscious problem for the schools diminished markedly, more obvious problems intruding upon the nation and its schools. Soon after the conclusion of World War II, however, a new report from the NEA was forthcoming, the work of its Educational Policies Commission, including Dwight Eisenhower and James Bryant Conant. Issued in 1951 and entitled *Moral and Spiritual Values in the Public Schools* (NEA, 1951), the report continued the trend toward fuzziness and rhetorical vagueness that had set in, and it represented perhaps the last of the old "movement" rather than the beginning of the new emphasis that we are currently witnessing.

As had been obvious, the first half of this century produced an enormous body of material, which can only be hinted at in these pages. Additional contemporary reviews of research, descriptions of actual programs, and bibliographies of the literature produced by the moral or character education movement may be found in Golightly (1926), Troth (1930), and McKown (1935). These will repay study if only to forestall the educator's frequent tendency to proclaim as "innovative" programs of instruction or research that have been tried and exhausted a few decades previously. More recent examinations of the general character of this period of development, including an emphasis on analyzing its social and political characteristics, are available in Chapman (1969, 1977) and Yulish (1980).

Recent Developments. Attributions of cause for the quickly rejuvenated interest in moral education in the public schools are many and varied, but the phenomenon is not only indisputable but worldwide. (In 1950, for example, *Education Index* provided only a handful of references dealing with the question, still catalogued principally under the heading "Character Education." By 1980, there were nearly 200 entries, and they dealt with moral education and judgment, discussing philosophical as well as technical issues.) Recent discussions and proposals clearly indicate a relationship with new social, political, and economic issues, widely debated in strongly moral terms: for example, questions of racial justice, poverty, ecology, peace, and most recently, abortion. In addition, widespread allegations of individual moral failure, "scandals" and "revelations" in government, business, and athletics, and the dramatic rise in violence, including the breakdown of conditions within the schools themselves, have doubtless fostered a new kind of concern for the development of cognitive moral competence and the analysis of personal and social conduct. Again, in traditional American fashion, the remedy for adult social and institutional ills is seen to lie in the process of rearing the nation's children and youth, and the instrumentality is, once again, schooling.

Response to the demand that the educational process take more conscious and critical responsibility for moral development has been facilitated by a number of important contextual factors. As has been suggested, the emphasis on moral education that had run its course in the first half of the twentieth century had dissipated itself in a crushing atmosphere of atomistic learning theory and a parallel subjective relativism, largely psychologically based. The fact that values are individually held and that they have, in common with any human enterprise, an inescapable emotional component led to the unwarranted practical conclusion that their only legitimate definition and justification was therefore private and personal. Educators saw themselves as necessarily reduced to searching for "consensus" among the values children already "had" or "brought with them to school." No such consensus could be found—or, if available, it was produced by definitions of educational aims so broad as to be vacuous: education for "responsible living" or "good citizenship," for example. Furthermore, because of the superficial technical focus demanded by the search for an "efficient" pedagogy, it was generally assumed that schools and educators ought not to posit as instructional goals any outcomes they could not measure and guarantee. The consequence was that moral education was made either so general as to be meaningless or so specific as to be unobtainable.

The new impetus has been marked, in contrast, by a clear demand that education and schooling be positive rather than merely passive and permissive; the question now is whether, and how, an educational institution can fulfill that demand within the limits of its legitimate authority and without violating the rights—the moral rights, in fact—of its members (Butts, Peckinpaugh, & Kirschenbaum, 1977). The crux of the matter is the increased awareness that the social and cultural content of the curriculum in fact presents the teacher and students with moral issues, as indeed does the process of growing up in any social and cultural environment. Rather than searching for "values" or "traits" to be "imposed" or "produced," educators may legitimately direct students' attention to these moral aspects and they may be studied consciously and critically in moral terms—as, of course, they have been for some three thousand years in history and literature and the other arts, not to mention philosophy and theology. They need not be reduced to private emotional matters in deference to some reductivist epistemological doctrine or learning theory (Johnson, 1979, 1980).

This crucial transition has also been aided by two other important developments: a more tolerant and receptive psychology and a more responsive philosophy. The shift in moral education took place in the context of an extensive literature in child development and in "social learning," which had come to pay increasingly serious attention to the matter of moral development (e.g., Ausubel, 1958; Feffer, 1959; Flavell et al., 1968; Mussen, 1970; and Rosen, 1980). In addition, a broadly cognitive learning theory began to make important inroads on the hegemony exercised by the morally debilitating "psychophysics" and the crude practical behaviorism that had largely dominated instructional activity ever since Thorndike (Bruner, 1960). Moral education could once again be conceived of as a problem in thinking, not just feeling.

A revitalization of moral education also required the frank admission that moral choice, and hence moral inquiry and moral development, are philosophical matters and not merely descriptive problems. For there to be any fruitful encounter with education, however, philosophy itself needed to escape from its preoccupation with an equally reductivist positivism, exacerbated by a long fugue into "analysis," which usually rendered moral philosophy uninteresting if not quite meaningless. The required encounter between a broadened and cognitively oriented psychology and an educationally relevant moral-philosophical tradition was certainly preeminently demonstrated by, if not precisely inaugurated by, the contribution of Jean Piaget (1948, 1969). Drawing openly on the previous work of John Dewey and Pierre Bovet, with fresh attention to James Mark Baldwin (1902), and finally bringing to needed prominence the important parallel work of Durkheim, Piaget attempted to do justice to the process of moral development from both philosophical and (structuralist) psychological perspectives, and from both the individual and the social point of view. In so doing, he laid out a basis which, though sometimes disputed, was clearly relevant to education and schooling.

The radically augmented interest in practical moral education that was manifest from the late sixties onward may usefully be examined in three categories: the cognitive-developmental or structural approach (which includes a number of important variants), the values clarification programs, and a residual category comprising a variety of theorists and practitioners who agree that moral education requires cognitive definition but reject any particular developmental scheme or philosophical allegiance as a necessary component in that definition.

No account of contemporary theory or practice in moral education can be adequate without careful consideration of the work of Lawrence Kohlberg, however controversial it has proved to be. Perhaps its most important contribution has been to set the pedagogical issues in fresh terms and thereby precipitate a productive argument. It is important to note that Kohlberg's activity is fully explicable only within the context of radically increased interest in a logically and hierarchically defined conception of intelligence as distinct from those merely quantitatively described notions of learning that had dominated educational thought and practice (and hence research) for so long. As we have seen, this shift had crucial implications for education and schooling in general (Bruner, 1960) and particularly for the school as an active agent in moral development (Kohlberg & Mayer, 1972; Elkind, 1974).

Working from a Kantian perspective and drawing on the psychological and philosophical work of Piaget (1948), Dewey (1909, 1910, 1916), Dewey and Tufts (1932), and Rawls (1971), in a series of provocative papers and articles Kohlberg (1964, 1966, 1969, 1973, 1974, 1976a, 1976b, 1976c; Kohlberg & Kramer, 1969; Kohlberg & DeVries, 1971; Kohlberg & Gilligan, 1971) argued that moral development closely paralleled cognitive development (the latter being the necessary but not sufficient condition of the former); that it was universal, and was structured hierarchically in a series of invariant, irreversible, and sequential stages. From an analysis of this structure a practical moral pedagogy could be constructed that took account both of the psychological and philosophical factors implicit in any adequate program of moral development.

Kohlberg (1976c, p. 33) distinguishes six stages, maintaining that they are best understood through the three "moral levels" under which they are subsumed. The first level, the "preconventional," is characterized by a "concrete individual" social perspective, and is chiefly found in children under age 9, but may also be found in adolescents and adult criminal offenders. The second, or "conventional," level, characterized by a "member-of-society" perspective, is chiefly occupied by the majority of adolescents and adults "in our society and in other societies." The third, or "postconventional or principled," level is achieved by a minority of adults, usually only after age 20. It is characterized by a "prior-to-society" perspective in that the individual "understands and basically accepts society's rules, but acceptance of society's rules is based on formulating and accepting the general moral principles that underlie these rules" (1976c, p. 33).

The stages within each level are two; the second in each case is the "more advanced and organized" form of the basic perspective. The six stages (1976c, pp. 34, 35) are as follows. At Level 1, Stage 1, "heteronomous morality," is an egocentric perspective focusing on the right as defined by power, and "moral" action as based on obedience for the avoidance of punishment. Stage 2, "individualism, instrumental purpose, and exchange," is a "concrete individualistic perspective" in which rules are followed and the rights of others acknowledged only as they relate to and advance one's own interests. At Level II, Stage 3 is defined as "mutual interpersonal expectations, relationships, and interpersonal conformity" and is focused on living up to the expectations of others (especially those closely related), and the maintenance of reputation and accepted roles. There is no systematic perspective. Stage 4, "social system and conscience," entails fulfilling duties and upholding laws in order to maintain the existing social system—sometimes called the "law-and-order" stage. At Level III, Stage 5, "social contract" or "utility and individual rights," involves a sense of mutual contract, reason, and interdependence within the group. Stage 6, "universal ethical principles," is characterized by "following self-chosen ethical principles" that are universal and foundational to any particular laws; by contractual arrangements or social systems; and by the supreme principle of human beings as ends in themselves.

The sixth stage, already perhaps the most controversial, is in some later writings followed by a "speculative" seventh stage, which has also been vigorously debated (Kohlberg, 1973, 1974; Rosen, 1980, pp. 80–88). This ultimate stage is defined in terms not of a social, but a "cosmic," perspective. It approaches, in Kohlberg's view, the crucial question "Why be moral?" According to Kohlberg, this question requires answering on the "religious" or "ontological" level. He insists that the former need have no theistic content, though such content (incapable of proof in the Kantian sense) would not be incompatible.

Kohlberg's straightforward attack on the crude relativism and subjectivism of the prior generation of moral education programs rests upon his definition of morality as fundamentally a problem in judgment and his acceptance of a distinction between the form and the content of those judgments ultimately founded in the Kantian moral tradition. Two important conclusions are presumed to follow. (1) Although the content and conditions of moral judgment may vary from case to case and from culture to culture, the all-important form of moral judgment is universal. (2) The making of moral judgments is essentially a rational, cognitive process and need not—in fact cannot—be defined exclusively in terms of the private, subjective emotional states of persons. Thus, in Kohlberg's view, the dilemmas that had frustrated moral educators since the turn of the century—respecting matters such as consensus, authority, and the relationship of intelligence to conduct—were dissolved. If moral conduct is conceived as principled or rule-determined behavior, the school can then be seen as an appropriate place in which to study and explore that process.

Technically, Kohlberg's notions have advanced in two directions. Practical moral formation can be deliberately fostered by confronting the student with crucial "dilemmas" or moral "issues" and examples of moral reasoning at least one stage higher, formally, in the hierarchy, either as these arise in the customary content of the curriculum or as activities designed to enhance moral development in itself. Kohlberg, and a number of his students and colleagues, have also paid considerable attention to the social milieu of moral development, focusing attention on the construction of morally open and productive communities as the basis for all adequate educational development, including moral development—e.g., the "just community" and the "just school" (Kohlberg, 1976b; 1980; Mosher, 1980).

Kohlberg's work has, from the beginning, received both quick, enthusiastic acceptance and practical application on the one hand (e.g., Fenton, 1967) and close analysis and even vehement criticism on the other—criticism stemming from both psychologists and philosophers. (See Fraenkel, 1976; Kincaid & Cameron, 1979; Kurtines & Greif, 1974; Locke, 1979, 1980; Meyer, 1976; Mischel, 1971; Murphy & Gilligan, 1980; Peters, 1976; Puka, 1976; Purpel & Ryan, 1976; Simpson, 1974; Sullivan, 1975, 1977, 1980; Wilson & Schochet, 1980; Windmiller, Lambert, & Turiel, 1980.) This criticism, and the attempts to meet it through argument and clarification, have also produced appeals to empirical research. Philosophical argument has centered both on the philosophical roots of Kohlbergian theory and on its logical clarity and consistency. In particular, Kohlberg's bold claim (1971) to be able to derive, in some sense, an "ought from an is," and thus to challenge the authority of G. E. Moore's famous "naturalistic fallacy" (Moore, 1959), has drawn a number of philosophers into the debate in a productive fashion, although the debate has too frequently been between philosophers and other philosophers, or between psychologists and practitioners and other psychologists and practitioners rather than on the crucially integrated basis upon which Kohlberg's work is fully defined. Empirical research has addressed not only the demand for "hard data" to substantiate the philosophical claims but also the obvious practical issues entailed— for example, whether the stages can be found universally, justification for the form-content distinction, the exact definition and scope and persistence of the stages, the use of the scheme diagnostically in order to test individuals or prescribe pedagogical strategy, and whether the regimen makes any difference in how individuals actually behave. It is accurate to say that the results of the research have been as ambiguous as the scheme has been problematical, and no magisterial studies—let alone decisive ones—can be pointed to without challenge. However, that is not to say that the research has been either entirely fruitless or uninteresting; and its quality, both methodologically and conceptually, appears to be growing rather than declining. Important studies, or reviews of this research, are numerous (De Palma & Foley, 1975; Educational Testing Service, 1975; Kincaid & Cameron, 1979; Kohlberg, 1964, 1976a; Kohlberg & DeVries, 1971; Kuhmerker, 1980; Lee, 1971; Lickona, 1976; Mosher, 1980; Rest, 1974, 1976, 1979; Simpson, 1974; Superka et al., 1976; Turiel, 1966, 1975; Windmiller, Lambert, & Turiel, 1980).

For all the prominence of Kohlberg and Piaget, however, it is important to note that a number of theorists and researchers, though utilizing the work of one or both, nonetheless either extend it in importantly different directions or utilize it to supplement what they regard as less narrow approaches—that is, approaches which more fully comprehend the complexities of moral development and moral action, especially when viewed in a concrete context. There has been an increasing tendency to adopt the term "structural-developmental," for example, as in the work of Damon (1977, 1980) and Turiel (1980), rather than "cognitive-developmental" to characterize these efforts. Selman (e.g., in Lickona, 1976)—building on the work of Feffer (1959), Flavell et al. (1968), and Hoffman (1963, 1970, 1975)—has focused on role taking or perspective taking and produced a somewhat different structural staging. (See also Selman, 1971; Selman & Damon, 1975.)

On the other hand, at least some "social learning" theorists, although accepting the validity and utility of some of Kohlberg's efforts, may also properly be seen as the descendants of Locke and the earlier American behaviorists, but with a considerable debt to Durkheim, and an interesting methodological parallel to Hartshorne and May (Turiel, 1980). Perhaps most importantly, the social learning moral development theorists see a much less clear and less exhaustive relation between reason and moral actions (see Aronfreed, 1968; Turiel, 1975).

The other approach to moral education which has had enormous practical impact on the schools is the "values clarification" movement, stemming principally from the work of Louis E. Raths, Merrill Harmin, and Sidney B. Simon (Raths, 1962; Raths et al., 1967; Raths, Harmin, & Simon, 1966, 1978). Many others have contributed to the movement, however, perhaps most notably Howard Kirschenbaum (Kirschenbaum, 1973, 1976, 1977; Harmin, Kirschenbaum, & Simon, 1973; Simon & deSherbinin, 1975; Simon, Howe, & Kirschenbaum, 1972; Superka et al., 1976). Although the proponents of values clarification point to roots in Dewey (Raths, Harmin, & Simon, 1978, p. 10), the psychological perspective appears primary and they cite the influence of Gordon Allport (1955), Gardner Murphy, Solomon Asch, and Carl Rogers (Raths, Harmin, & Simon, 1978, p. 11). It is not difficult to view this approach as a continuation of the psychologically based programs of the previous period. More recent work by Rokeach (1968, 1973) and Feather (1975), focused on a generally descriptive approach to values, somewhat in the tradition of Allport (Allport, Vernon, & Lindzey, 1931), is viewed as parallel by some, though far from identical.

Essentially, values clarification views itself as a procedure which, although free of values to be imposed, rests itself upon the value of freedom for children (and others) "to state their own interests, their own purposes and aspirations, their own beliefs and attitudes, and many other possible indicators of values" (Raths, Harmin, & Simon, 1978, p. viii). As a procedure, it offers "assistance" to encourage people to "get clear about their values" who might otherwise "flounder in confusion, apathy, or inconsistency"; this is done by getting such people "to reflect more deliberately and comprehensively about their own values and about the value questions of society as a whole" (Raths, Harmin, & Simon, 1978, p. 4). The authors regard the process of values clarification as synonymous with valuing itself and essentially comprising three subprocesses: choosing, prizing, and acting. One must, however, *choose* "(1) freely (2) from alternatives (3) after thoughtful consideration of the consequences of each alternative"; *prize* in the sense of "(4) cherishing, being happy with the choice (5) enough to be willing to affirm the choice to others"; and one must *act* in the sense of "(6) doing something with the choice" and "(7) repeatedly, in some pattern of life" (Raths, Harmin, & Simon, 1978, p. 29). A wide array of "strategies" have been developed for enabling participants to bring their "values" and value conflicts to the surface and to deal with them. There is also a very large quantity of materials available for this purpose and for the training of teachers in the necessary skills (Raths, Harmin, & Simon, 1978, chaps. 5–9, 15; Harmin, Kirschenbaum, & Simon, 1973; Kirschenbaum, 1977; Simon, Howe, & Kirschenbaum, 1972; Hall, 1973; Superka et al., 1976, chap. 5). Inasmuch as Raths, Harmin, and Simon suggest that values clarification can be fully understood only in practice, a thorough examination of such practical programs is important for students of current moral education (1978, p. 5).

Criticism of the values clarification approach has been widespread, focusing on its alleged practical difficulties and dangers, on its superficiality (that is, that it succeeds in raising value questions but offers no assistance in their resolution at the moral philosophical level), and on its apparent subjectivism and relativism (Lockwood, 1976; Adell, 1976; Stewart, 1976; Bennett & Delattre, 1978). Kirschenbaum (1976) and Simon (1976) have replied to such objections, and the second edition (1978) of Raths, Harmin, and Simon's *Values and Teaching: Working with Values in the Classroom* makes an attempt to meet criticisms of the earlier edition (1966) at various points.

Research support for values clarification approaches has been offered by Raths (1962), by Raths, Harmin, and Simon (1978, chaps. 12, 13), and by Kirschenbaum (1974). Much of the research has, however, been informal rather than rigorous, and the reporting has often been anecdotal. An extensive critical review has been offered by Lockwood (1978), whose analysis also calls for more specific attention to the research design problems peculiar to the field of moral education. John Wilson (1969, 1972, 1973) and Derek Wright (1971) have also focused attention on this important issue, which clearly involves all programs of moral education that claim to demonstrate their effectiveness or substantiate their principles and claims by reference to empirical research. Additional general examinations of the problems furnished by the link between psychological conceptions and experimental data on the one hand and the field of moral education on the other may be found in Trow (1953).

The third category is, as previously noted, largely a residual one, constituted principally of those who hold a generally cognitive view of moral education without single-minded commitment to particular developmental schemes. The works of Barrow (1975); Beck, Crittenden, and Sullivan (1971); Crittenden (1975, 1978); Evans and Applegate (1976); Lipman and the Institute for Philosophy for Children (Lipman, Sharp, & Oscanyan, 1980); Metcalf and his associates (1971); Newman and Oliver (1970); Peters (1967); Scriven (1966, 1976); Shaver and Larkins (1973); and Wilson, Williams, and Sugarman (1968) offer important and influential examples. This approach is frequently focused on the social studies and characteristically highlights issues of public policy rather than being concerned principally with individual moral development. All these writers, however, stress the role of rational analysis, of scientific fact-finding as well as principled argument, and most reject the crudely relativistic and subjective approach characteristic of the more psychologically based approaches.

It should not be assumed, however, that the categories used here for convenience indicate that the field has crystallized. There is considerable ferment within each category. It is perhaps most obvious in the cognitive developmental or structuralist camp, but also notably present in the more general cognitive area as well (Wilson, 1979). New contributions, more mature and rigorous inquiry and research, and a still vigorous critical literature, not only in moral pedagogy but within psychology and philosophy as well, continue to be offered. Some interesting recent contributions are those of Rosen (1980), Blos (1962), Flugel (1945), Gilligan (1976), and Hartmann (1960). Contributions from the psychoanalytical tradition may also be found in Tice (1980) and Mosher (1980), and the standard works on moral development from that perspective will offer an increasingly important practical vantage point if they continue to be examined and applied.

Finally, a word should be said about moral education and higher education. The work of Jacob (1957) tended to dominate considerations of value development in higher education for some time and focus them along largely descriptive lines. However, Perry (1968) has developed a staged schema that is now attracting considerable attention and offers some guidance for practical programs. It is also the case that the question of critical value formation is now discussed with much more seriousness than in the recent past (Collier, Wilson, & Tomlinson, 1974; Bennett, 1980). Furthermore, the philosophical field of applied and professional ethics is rapidly growing and furnishes important direction not only at the level of higher education but in respect to moral education in general and in connection with the development of public policy. The work of the Hastings Center illustrates this interesting new development.

Some Issues. The recent vitality and popularity of the field of moral education may, however, obscure a number of substantial issues that will require attention from serious theorists, program proponents, and researchers if its condition is to remain robust.

Obviously, the question of moral content, broadly defined, upon which consensus was once relatively easy to achieve, but which was called into question for a variety of theoretical and historical reasons, can hardly be said to have been satisfactorily settled (Craig, 1976). The shift to formal or functional definitions of the process of moral development (whether cognitive or affective) scarcely avoids the problem, though it may go some way in providing a more productive framework for dealing with it. It is all well and good to say that it is the question of the formal properties of the moral reasoning process that leads up to judgments about, say, honesty or deceit that is the principal issue, but surely the whole substantive question of honesty and actually being honest also rests upon some more fundamental claim on our behavior that is presumed to exist. Furthermore, while we may legitimately be concerned with the school's "neutrality"—if that is an appropriate term—the culture within which the school operates contains a wide variety of positive moral content that it does not shrink from inculcating through very effective persuasion, perhaps most notably in the popular media (Crittenden, 1978; Johnson, 1980). It is precisely this variety of substantive moral assertions in the society and culture at large that creates the need for individual moral inquiry and judgment and provides a sufficient warrant for the school's responsibility. For reasons such as these, formal adequacy seems at best a necessary but not sufficient condition of a program in moral education.

The problem of teacher competence has also been given grossly inadequate attention (Sprinthall & Bernier, 1977). The notion that being a teacher implies principally a technical competence exercised upon a body of content (simply regarded as a given) will not suffice in the case of moral education. The kind of knowledge a teacher would require for competence in exercising responsibility for moral development has been almost culpably ignored by both theorists and practitioners. Sullivan and his colleagues (1975) have, however, attempted to draw attention to this problem, and for a serious attempt to restore an appropriate moral role to literature and the teacher of literature, the work of Legow (1981) may be cited. Furthermore, if moral development is contingent upon more than the teaching of a formal skill, it appears to have implications for the teacher's *being* rather than his or her mere technical competence of "knowledge base."

The problem that persists through all the historical, the-

oretical, and technical analysis made here is that moral education *is* a philosophical problem—it does not merely raise one. And it *is* also, in itself, a *moral* philosophical problem. The morality of the concepts and the processes in any program for moral education cannot be neatly separated out as questions of technical procedure. Nor can this moral-philosophical problem be resolved by bare description or crude social consensus. In many cases, what we mean by moral action is in fact action at least potentially contrary to the prevailing rules, let alone descriptive norms. Unfortunately, however, in far too many cases both practitioners and researchers are insufficiently acquainted with the three areas that are foundational to the development of any adequate moral education program: the philosophical, the psychological, and the pedagogical, *and* their subtle interrelations with one another (Boyce & Jensen, 1978).

An equally fundamental problem already alluded to is that at present the very notion of what constitutes adequate research in the realm of moral education is puzzling if not ambiguous. The research that has been done in large quantities (though seldom involving large samples) has been largely for the purpose of explicating or vindicating some particular prevailing theoretical proposal. None has attained the practical stature or impact of Hartshorne and May—irrespective of what one may think of their presuppositions or conclusions. And virtually no investigation, experimental or descriptive, has focused at any depth on the more general problems of moral pedagogy: the actual process of teaching as it occurs.

These striking lacunae may indicate that what is needed is more thought—in fact more theoretical research—on research itself. This in turn may have its location in a further problem, perhaps the most fundamental of all: the question of educational research in general.

Professional educators have been fond of thinking that dispassionate inquiry or ostensibly pure empirical research properly *precedes* educational thought and action and provides its one indispensable source and foundation. But that can surely be doubted, if only on the grounds that we investigate what we have a mind to, and that mind is already formed by a delicate interplay of social, cultural, and practical pedagogical factors operating at any given time. (This need not be thought to reduce all research to the level of propaganda, but it should induce an important breadth and tentativeness in our endeavors.) And, surely, a plausible case can be built that for the last several decades—indeed, throughout this century—our research has been shaped by more general educational notions and models, for service to which our particular programs of inquiry were invented. These basic educational concepts and paradigms for pedagogical action, and hence for educational research, may have exhausted themselves and consequently lost any justification they once were thought to possess. It is evident that the traditional patterns of research they have sponsored, a veritable Procrustean bed, do not lend themselves easily to inquiry into moral education. It is in this sense that the fostering of research genuinely adequate to the complex issues and problems raised by moral education may assist the development of more adequate educational thought in general and educational research in particular.

Henry C. Johnson, Jr.

See also Affective Education; Citizenship Education; Moral Development.

REFERENCES

Adell, A. W. Values clarification revised. *Christian Century,* 1976, *93*(16), 436.

Adler, F. *The Moral Instruction of Children.* New York: D. Appleton, 1901.

Adler, F. *An Ethical Philosophy of Life.* New York: D. Appleton, 1918.

Allport, F. H., & Allport, G. W. Personality traits: Their classification and measurement. *Journal of Abnormal Psychology,* 1921, *16,* 6–40.

Allport, G. W. Personality and character. *Psychological Bulletin,* 1921, *18,* 441–445.

Allport, G. W. *Becoming: Basic Considerations for a Psychology of Personality.* New Haven, Conn.: Yale University Press, 1955.

Allport, G. W.; Vernon, P. E.; & Lindzey, G. *A Study of Values.* Boston: Houghton Mifflin, 1931.

Aronfreed, J. *Conduct and Conscience: The Socialization of Internalized Control over Behavior.* New York: Academic Press, 1968.

Ausubel, D. P. *Theory and Problems of Child Development.* New York: Grune & Stratton, 1958.

Baldwin, J. Report of the Committee on Moral Education. *National Education Association Addresses and Proceedings,* 1892, *31,* 759–763.

Baldwin, J. M. *Social and Ethical Interpretations.* New York: Macmillan, 1902.

Barrow, R. *Moral Philosophy for Education.* Hamden, Conn.: Shoe String Press, 1975.

Beck, C.; Crittenden, B. S.; & Sullivan, E. V. (Eds.). *Moral Education: Interdisciplinary Approaches.* New York: Newman Press, 1971.

Bennett, W. J. The teacher, the curriculum, and values education development. *New Directions for Higher Education,* 1980, *8*(3), 27–34.

Bennett, W. J., & Delattre, E. J. Moral education in the schools. *Public Interest,* 1978, *50,* 81–98.

Blos, P. *On Adolescence: A Psychoanalytic Interpretation.* New York: Free Press, 1962.

Boyce, W. O., & Jensen, L. C. *Moral Reasoning: A Psychological-Philosophical Integration.* Lincoln: University of Nebraska Press, 1978.

Briggs, T. H. Can character be taught and measured? *School and Society,* 1920, *12,* 595–601.

Bruner, J. *The Process of Education.* Cambridge, Mass.: Harvard University Press, 1960.

Butts, R. F.; Peckinpaugh, D. H.; & Kirschenbaum, H. *The School's Role as Moral Authority.* Washington, D.C.: Association for Supervision and Curriculum Development, 1977.

Chapman, W. E. *Character Education in the Twenties.* Unpublished doctoral dissertation, Princeton Theological Seminary, 1969.

Chapman, W. E. *Roots of Character Education.* Schenectady, N.Y.: Character Research Press, 1977.

Charters, W. W. *The Teaching of Ideals.* New York: Macmillan, 1927.

Charters, W. W., & Waples, D. *The Commonwealth Teacher-training Study.* Chicago: University of Chicago Press, 1929.

Chassell, C. F. *The Relation between Morality and Intellect.* New York: Teachers College, Columbia University, 1935.

Coe, G. A. *A Social Theory of Religious Education.* New York: Scribner, 1917.

Collier, G.; Wilson, J.; & Tomlinson, P. (Eds.). *Values and Moral Development in Higher Education.* New York: Halsted, 1974.

Craig, R. P. Form, content, and justice in moral reasoning. *Educational Theory,* 1976, *26*(2), 154–157.

Crittenden, B. A comment on cognitive moral education. *Phi Delta Kappan,* 1975, *56*(10), 695–696.

Crittenden, B. *Bearings in Moral Education: A Critical Review of Recent Work.* Hawthorn, Vic.: Australian Council for Educational Research, 1978.

Damon, W. *The Social World of the Child.* San Francisco: Jossey-Bass, 1977.

Damon, W. Structural-developmental theory and the study of moral development. In M. Windmiller, N. Lambert, & E. Turiel (Eds.), *Moral Development and Socialization.* Boston: Allyn & Bacon, 1980, pp. 35–68.

DeGarmo, C. *Herbart and the Herbartians.* New York: Scribner, 1896.

DeGarmo, C. Social aspects of moral education. *National Herbart Society Yearbook,* 1897, *3,* 35–36.

DeGarmo, C. *Principles of Secondary Education: Ethical Training.* New York: Macmillan, 1910.

De Palma, D. J., & Foley, J. M. (Eds.). *Moral Development: Current Theory and Research.* Hillsdale, N.J.: Lawrence Erlbaum Associates, 1975.

Dewey, J. Ethical principles underlying education. *National Herbart Society Yearbook,* 1897, *3,* 7–33.

Dewey, J. *Moral Principles in Education.* Boston: Houghton Mifflin, 1909.

Dewey, J. Intelligence and morals. In *The Influence of Darwin on Philosophy and Other Essays in Contemporary Thought.* New York: Henry Holt, 1910, pp. 46–76.

Dewey, J. *Democracy and Education.* New York: Macmillan, 1916.

Dewey, J., & Tufts, J. H. *Ethics* (Rev. ed.). New York: Henry Holt, 1932.

Durkheim, E. *Moral Education: A Study in the Theory and Application of the Sociology of Education* (E. K. Wilson & H. Schnurer, Trans.). New York: Free Press, 1961.

Educational Testing Service. *Proceedings of Invitational Conference on Moral Development.* Princeton, N.J.: Educational Testing Service, 1975.

Elkind, D. Egocentrism in children and adolescents. In *Children and Adolescents: Interpretive Essays on Jean Piaget* (2nd ed.). New York: Oxford University Press, 1974, pp. 74–95.

Evans, W. K., & Applegate, T. P. Value decisions and the acceptability of value principles. In *Values, Concepts, and Techniques.* Washington, D.C.: National Education Association, 1976, pp. 148–158.

Fairchild, M. The National Morality Codes Competition. *National Education Association Addressses and Proceedings,* 1916, *54,* 1019–1025.

Fairchild, M. Character education. *National Education Association Addresses and Proceedings,* 1918, *56,* 120–122.

Feather, N. T. *Values in Education and Society.* New York: Free Press, 1975.

Feffer, M. H. The cognitive implications of role-taking behavior. *Journal of Personality*, 1959, *27*(2), 152–168.

Fenton, E. *The New Social Studies.* New York: Holt, Rinehart & Winston, 1967.

Flavell, J. H.; Botkin, P.; Fry, C.; Wright, J.; & Jarvis, P. *The Development of Role-taking and Communication Skills in Children.* New York: Wiley, 1968.

Flugel, J. *Man, Morals, and Society: A Psychoanalytical Study.* London: Duckworth, 1945.

Fraenkel, J. R. The Kohlberg bandwagon: Some reservations. In D. Purpel & K. Ryan (Eds.), *Moral Education . . . It Comes with the Territory.* Berkeley, Calif.: McCutchan, 1976.

Gilligan, J. Beyond morality: Psychoanalytic reflections on shame, guilt, and love. In T. Lickona (Ed.), *Moral Development and Behavior: Theory, Research, and Social Issues.* New York: Holt, Rinehart & Winston, 1976, pp. 144–158.

Golightly, T. J. *The Present Status of the Teaching of Morals in the Public High Schools.* (Contributions to Education No. 38). Nashville: George Peabody College for Teachers, 1926.

Hall, B. P. *Value Clarification as Learning Process: A Source Book.* New York: Paulist Press, 1973.

Harmin, M.; Kirschenbaum, H.; & Simon, S. *Clarifying Values through Subject Matter: Applications for the Classroom.* Minneapolis: Winston, 1973.

Hart, J. K. *A Critical Study of Current Theories of Moral Education.* Chicago: University of Chicago Press, 1910.

Hartmann, H. *Psychoanalysis and Moral Values.* New York: International Universities Press, 1960.

Hartshorne, H. *Childhood and Character.* Boston: Pilgrim Press, 1919.

Hartshorne, H. A few principles of character education. *Religious Education*, 1929, *24*, 813–815.

Hartshorne, H. Science and character. *Religious Education*, 1930, *25*(6), 546–554.

Hartshorne, H. *Character in Human Relations.* New York: Scribner, 1932.

Hartshorne, H., & May, M. A. Testing the knowledge of right and wrong. *Religious Education*, 1926–1927, *21–22*: pt. I, *21*, 63–76; pt. II, *21*, 239–252; pt. III, with L. Stidley, *21*, 413–421; pt. IV, with D. E. Sonquist & C. A. Kerr, *21*, 539–554; pt. V, titled "Relation of Standards to Behavior of Individuals," *21*, 621–632; pt. VI, *22*, 523–532.

Hartshorne, H., & May, M. A. The Character Education Inquiry. *Religious Education*, 1927, *22*(9), 958–961.

Hartshorne, H., & May, M. A. *Studies in the Organization of Character* (3 vols.). New York: Macmillan, 1928–1930. Vol. 1, *Studies in Deceit*, 1928. Vol. 2, with J. B. Maller, *Studies in Service and Self-control*, 1929. Vol. 3, with F. Shuttleworth, *Studies in the Nature of Character*, 1930.

Hartshorne, H., & May, M. A. A summary of the work of the Character Education Inquiry. *Religious Education*, 1930, *25*, 607–619, 754–762.

Heaton, K. *The Character Emphasis in Education.* Chicago: University of Chicago Press, 1933.

Herbart, J. F. *Science of Education* (H. M. Felken & E. Felken, Trans.). Boston: Heath, 1902.

Hoffman, M. L. Childrearing practices and moral development: Generalizations from empirical research. *Child Development*, 1963, *34*, 295–318.

Hoffman, M. L. Moral development. In P. H. Mussen (Ed.), *Carmichael's Manual of Child Psychology* (3rd ed., Vol. 2). New York: Wiley, 1970, pp. 261–359.

Hoffman, M. L. The development of altruistic motivation. In D. J. De Palma & J. M. Foley (Eds.), *Moral Development: Current Theory and Research.* Hillsdale, N.J.: Lawrence Erlbaum Associates, 1975, pp. 137–151.

Jacob, P. E. *Changing Values in College: An Exploratory Study of the Impact of College Teaching.* New York: Harper, 1957.

Jaeger, W. *Paideia: The Ideals of Greek Culture* (G. Highet, Trans.). Oxford: Blackwell, 1947.

Jaeger, W. *Early Christianity and Greek Paideia.* Cambridge, Mass.: Harvard University Press, 1962.

Johnson, H. C., Jr. The return to "moral education": Should Dick and Jane tackle the categorical imperative? *Thinking: The Journal of Philosophy for Children*, 1979, *1*(1), 41–48.

Johnson, H. C., Jr. *The Public School and Moral Education.* New York: Pilgrim Press, 1980.

Kincaid, E. B., & Cameron, W. B. A reappraisal of moral development theory. *Journal of Thought*, 1979, *14*(3), 187–193.

Kirschenbaum, H. *Beyond Values Clarification.* Upper Jay, N.Y.: National Humanistic Education Center, 1973.

Kirschenbaum, H. *Recent Research in Values Clarification.* Upper Jay, N.Y.: National Humanistic Education Center, 1974.

Kirschenbaum, H. Clarifying values clarification: Some theoretical issues. In D. Purpel & K. Ryan (Eds.), *Moral Education . . . It Comes with the Territory.* Berkeley, Calif.: McCutchan, 1976, pp. 116–125.

Kirschenbaum, H. *Values Clarification: An Advanced Handbook for Trainers and Teachers.* LaJolla, Calif.: University Associates Press, 1977.

Kohlberg, L. Development of moral character and moral ideology. In M. L. Hoffman & L. W. Hoffman (Eds.), *Review of Child Development Research* (Vol. 1). New York: Russell Sage, 1964, pp. 383–432.

Kohlberg, L. Moral education in the schools: A developmental view. *School Review*, 1966, *74*(1), 1–30.

Kohlberg, L. Stage and sequence: The cognitive-developmental approach to socialization. In D. A. Goslin (Ed.), *Handbook of Socialization Theory and Research.* Chicago: Rand McNally, 1969, pp. 347–480.

Kohlberg, L. From is to ought: How to commit the naturalistic fallacy and get away with it in the study of moral development. In T. Mischel (Ed.), *Cognitive Development and Epistemology.* New York: Academic Press, 1971, pp. 151–235.

Kohlberg, L. Stages and aging in moral development: Some speculations. *Gerontologist*, 1973, *13*, 497–502.

Kohlberg, L. Education, moral development, and faith. *Journal of Moral Education*, 1974, *4*, 5–16.

Kohlberg, L. The cognitive-developmental approach to moral education. In D. Purpel & K. Ryan (Eds.), *Moral Education . . . It Comes with the Territory.* Berkeley, Calif.: McCutchan, 1976, pp. 176–195. (a)

Kohlberg, L. The moral atmosphere of the school. In D. Purpel & K. Ryan (Eds.), *Moral Education . . . It Comes with the Territory.* Berkeley, Calif.: McCutchan, 1976, pp. 196–220. (b)

Kohlberg, L. Moral stages and moralization: The cognitive-developmental approach. In T. Lickona (Ed.), *Moral Development and Behavior: Theory, Research, and Social Issues.* New York: Holt, Rinehart & Winston, 1976, pp. 31–53. (c)

Kohlberg, L. Highschool democracy and educating for a just society. In R. L. Mosher (Ed.), *Moral Education: A First Generation of Research and Development.* New York: Praeger, 1980, pp. 20–57.

Kohlberg, L., & DeVries, R. Relations between Piaget and psychometric assessments of intelligence. In C. Lavatelli (Ed.), *The Natural Curriculum*, Urbana, Ill.: ERIC, 1971.

Kohlberg, L., & Gilligan, C. F. The adolescent as philosopher:

The discovery of the self in a postconventional world. *Daedalus,* 1971, *100,* 1051–1086.

Kohlberg, L., & Kramer, R. Continuities and discontinuities in childhood and adult moral development. *Human Development,* 1969, *12,* 93–120.

Kohlberg, L., & Mayer, R. Development as the aim of education. *Harvard Education Review,* 1972, *42*(4), 449–496.

Kuhmerker, L. (Ed.). *Evaluating Moral Development and Evaluating Educational Programs That Have a Value Dimension.* Schenectady, N.Y.: Character Research Press, 1980.

Kurtines, W., & Greif, E. B. The development of moral thought: Review and evaluation of Kohlberg's approach. *Psychological Bulletin,* 1974, *81*(8), 453–470.

Lee, L. C. The concomitant development of cognitive and moral modes of thought: A test of selected deductions from Piaget's theory. *Genetic Psychology Monographs,* 1971, *83,* 93–146.

Legow, R. G. *The Ethical Dimension: Developing Moral Awareness in High School Literature Classes.* Unpublished doctoral dissertation, Fairleigh Dickinson University, 1981.

Lickona, T. (Ed.). *Moral Development and Behavior: Theory, Research, and Social Issues.* New York: Holt, Rinehart & Winston, 1976.

Lipman, M.; Sharp, A. M.; & Oscanyan, F. S. *Philosophy in the Classroom* (2nd ed.). Philadelphia: Temple University Press, 1980.

Little, L. C. *Researches in Personality, Character, and Religious Education: A Bibliography of American Doctoral Dissertations, 1885–1959.* Pittsburgh, Pa.: University of Pittsburgh Press, 1962.

Locke, D. Cognitive stages or developmental phases? A critique of Kohlberg's stage-structural theory of moral reasoning. *Journal of Moral Education,* 1979, *8*(3), 168–181.

Locke, D. The illusion of stage six. *Journal of Moral Education,* 1980, *9*(2), 103–109.

Lockwood, A. L. A critical view of values clarification. In D. Purpel & K. Ryan (Eds.), *Moral Education . . . It Comes with the Territory.* Berkeley, Calif.: McCutchan, 1976, pp. 152–170.

Lockwood, A. L. The effects of values clarification and moral development curricula on school-age subjects: A critical review of recent research. *Review of Educational Research,* 1978, *48*(3), 325–364.

Marrou, H. I. *A History of Education in Antiquity* (G. Lamb, Trans.). New York: Sheed & Ward, 1956.

May, M. A. Personality and character tests. *Psychological Bulletin,* 1925, *23,* 395–411.

May, M. A. Personality and character tests. *Psychological Bulletin,* 1927, *25,* 418–436.

May, M. A. What science offers on character education. *Religious Education,* 1928, *23,* 566–583.

McGeough, I. *A Critical Evaluation of the Character Education Inquiry, Particularly of the Underlying Philosophy.* Unpublished doctoral dissertation, Fordham University, 1933.

McGuffey's Fifth Eclectic Reader (Rev. ed.). New York: American Book Company, 1879.

McKown, H. C. *Character Education.* New York: McGraw-Hill, 1935.

Mead, G. H. *Mind, Self, and Society.* Chicago: University of Chicago Press, 1934.

Metcalf, L. E. (Ed.). *Values Education: Rationale, Strategies, and Procedures.* Washington, D.C.: National Council for the Social Studies, 1971.

Meyer, J. R. (Ed.). *Reflections on Values Education.* Waterloo, Ont.: Wilfred Laurier University Press, 1976.

Mischel, T. (Ed.). *Cognitive Development and Epistemology.* New York: Academic Press, 1971.

Moore, G. E. *Principia Ethica.* New York: Cambridge University Press, 1959. (Originally published, 1903)

Mosher, R. L. (Ed.). *Moral Education: A First Generation of Research and Development.* New York: Praeger, 1980.

Murphy, J. M., & Gilligan, C. Moral development in late adolescence and adulthood: A critique and reconstruction of Kohlberg's theory. *Human Development,* 1980, *23*(2), 77–104.

Mussen, P. H. (Ed.). *Carmichael's Manual of Child Psychology* (3rd ed., 2 vols.). New York: Wiley, 1970.

National Education Association. *Report of the Committee of Ten.* New York: American Book Company, 1894.

National Education Association. *Cardinal Principles of Secondary Education: A Report of the Commission on the Reorganization of Secondary Education* (Bulletin No. 35). Washington, D.C.: The Association, 1918.

National Education Association. Character education. In *Fourth Yearbook.* Washington, D.C.: The Association, 1926.

National Education Association. Character education. In *Tenth Yearbook.* Washington, D.C.: The Association, 1932. (a)

National Education Association. Tests of personality and character. *Review of Educational Research,* 1932, *2*(4). (b)

National Education Association, Education Policies Commission. *Moral and Spiritual Values in the Public Schools.* Washington, D.C.: The Association, 1951.

Nettleship, R. L. *The Theory of Education in Plato's Republic.* Oxford: Oxford University Press, 1935.

Neumann, H. Misconceptions of moral education. *International Journal of Ethics,* 1912, *22,* 335–347.

Neumann, H. *Moral Values in Secondary Education* (U.S. Bureau of Education Bulletin No. 51). Washington, D.C., 1917.

Neumann, H. *Education for Moral Growth.* New York: D. Appleton, 1923.

Neumann, H. *Moral Values in Secondary Education* (U.S. Bureau of Education Bulletin No. 7). Washington, D.C., 1926.

Newman, F. M., & Oliver, D. W. *Clarifying Public Controversy: An Approach to Teaching Social Studies.* Boston: Little, Brown, 1970.

Palmer, G. H. *Ethical and Moral Instruction in Schools.* Boston: Houghton Mifflin, 1909.

Perry, W. G. *Forms of Intellectual and Ethical Development in the College Years: A Scheme.* New York: Holt, Rinehart & Winston, 1968.

Peters, R. S. *Ethics and Education.* Glenview, Ill.: Scott, Foresman, 1967.

Peters, R. S. Why doesn't Lawrence Kohlberg do his homework? In D. Purpel & K. Ryan (Eds.), *Moral Education . . . It Comes with the Territory.* Berkeley, Calif.: McCutchan, 1976, pp. 233–290.

Piaget, J. *The Moral Judgment of the Child* (2nd ed., M. Gabain, Trans.). New York: Free Press, 1948. (Original French edition, 1932)

Piaget, J., & Inhelder, B. *The Psychology of the Child* (H. Weaver, trans.). New York: Basic Books, 1969.

Puka, B. Moral education and its cure. In J. R. Meyer (Ed.), *Reflections on Values Education.* Waterloo, Ont.: Wilfred Laurier University Press, 1976, pp. 47–87.

Purpel, D., & Ryan, K. (Eds.). *Moral Education . . . It Comes with the Territory.* Berkeley, Calif.: McCutchan, 1976.

Raths, J. Clarifying children's values. *National Elementary Principal,* 1962, *42,* 35–39.

Raths, L.; Harmin, M.; & Simon, S. B. *Values and Teaching.* Columbus, Ohio: Merrill, 1966.

Raths, L.; Harmin, M.; & Simon, S. B. *Values and Teaching* (2nd ed.). Columbus, Ohio: Merrill, 1978.

Raths, L.; Wasserman, S.; Jonas, A.; & Rothstein, A. M. *Teaching for Thinking.* Columbus, Ohio: Merrill, 1967.

Rawls, J. *A Theory of Justice.* Cambridge, Mass.: Harvard University Press, 1971.

Rest, J. R. Developmental psychology as a guide to value education: A review of "Kohlbergian" programs. *Review of Education Research,* 1974, *44,* 241–259.

Rest, J. R. New approaches in the assessment of moral judgment. In T. Lickona (Ed.), *Moral Development and Behavior: Theory, Research, and Social Issues.* New York: Holt, Rinehart & Winston, 1976, pp. 198–218.

Rest, J. R. *Development in Judging Moral Issues.* Minneapolis: University of Minnesota Press, 1979.

Roback, A. A. *A Bibliography of Character and Personality.* Cambridge, Mass.: Sci-Art Publishers, 1927. (a)

Roback, A. A. *The Psychology of Character.* New York: Harcourt Brace, 1927. (b)

Rokeach, M. *Beliefs, Attitudes, and Values.* San Francisco: Jossey-Bass, 1968.

Rokeach, M. *The Nature of Human Values.* New York: Free Press, 1973.

Rosen, H. *The Development of Sociomoral Knowledge: A Cognitive-Structural Approach.* New York: Columbia University Press, 1980.

Rousseau, J. J. *The Minor Educational Writings of Jean Jacques Rousseau* (W. H. Boyd, Ed. and Trans.). New York: Teachers College, Columbia University, 1962.

Rugg, H. Is the rating of human character practicable? *Journal of Educational Psychology,* 1921, *12,* 425–536, 485–501.

Rusk, R. R. *The Doctrines of the Great Educators* (4th ed.). New York: Macmillan, 1969.

Scriven, M. *Primary Philosophy.* New York: McGraw-Hill, 1966.

Scriven, M. Cognitive moral education. In D. Purpel & K. Ryan (Eds.), *Moral Education . . . It Comes with the Territory.* Berkeley, Calif.: McCutchan, 1976, pp. 313–329.

Selman, R. L. The relation of role-taking to the development of moral judgment in children. *Child Development,* 1971, *42,* 79–91.

Selman, R. L. Social-cognitive understanding: A guide to educational and clinical practice. In T. Lickona (Ed.), *Moral Development and Behavior: Theory, Research, and Social Issues.* New York: Holt, Rinehart & Winston, 1976, pp. 299–316.

Selman, R., & Damon, W. The necessity (but insufficiency) of social perspective-taking for conceptions of justice at three early levels. In D. J. De Palma & J. M. Foley (Eds.), *Moral Development: Current Theory and Research.* Hillsdale, N.J.: Lawrence Erlbaum Associates, 1975.

Shaver, J. P., & Larkins, A. G. *Decision-making in a Democracy.* Boston: Houghton Mifflin, 1973.

Simon, S. B. Values clarification vs. indoctrination. In D. Purpel & K. Ryan (Eds.), *Moral Education . . . It Comes with the Territory.* Berkeley, Calif.: McCutchan, 1976, pp. 126–135.

Simon, S. B., & deSherbinin, P. Values clarification: It can start gently and grow deep. *Phi Delta Kappan,* 1975, *56*(10), 679–683.

Simon, S. B.; Howe, L.; & Kirschenbaum, H. *Values Clarification: A Handbook of Practical Strategies for Teachers and Students.* New York: Hart, 1972.

Simpson, E. L. Moral development research: A case study of scientific cultural bias. *Human Development,* 1974, *17,* 81–106.

Sprinthall, N. A., & Bernier, J. E. Moral cognitive development for teachers: A neglected area. In *Programs and Rationale in Value-Moral Education.* Bronx: Fordham University Symposium, 1977.

Stewart, J. S. Problems and contradictions of values clarification. In D. Purpel & K. Ryan (Eds.), *Moral Education . . . It Comes with the Territory.* Berkeley, Calif.: McCutchan, 1976, pp. 136–151.

Sullivan, E. V. *Kohlberg's Structuralism: A Critical Appraisal.* Toronto: Ontario Institute for Studies in Education, 1977.

Sullivan, E. V. Can values be taught? In M. Windmiller, N. Lambert, & E. Turiel (Eds.), *Moral Development and Socialization.* Boston: Allyn & Bacon, 1980, pp. 219–243.

Sullivan, E. V.; Beck, C.; Joy, M.; & Pagliuso, S. *Moral Learning: Some Findings, Issues, and Questions.* Paramus, N.J.: Paulist Press, 1975.

Superka, D. P.; Ahrens, C.; Hedstrom, J. E.; Ford, L. J.; & Johnson, P. L. *Values Education Sourcebook: Conceptual Approaches, Materials Analysis, and an Annotated Bibliography.* Boulder, Colo.: Social Science Education Consortium, 1976.

Symonds, P. The present status of character measurement. *Journal of Educational Psychology,* 1924, *15,* 484–498.

Thorndike, E. L. *Principles of Teaching.* New York: A. G. Seiler, 1906.

Thorndike, E. L. *Educational Psychology* (3 vols.). New York: Teachers College, Columbia University, 1913–1914.

Thorndike, E. L. *The Elements of Psychology* (2nd ed.). New York: A. G. Seiler, 1916.

Thurstone, L. L. *The Measurement of Social Attitudes.* Chicago: University of Chicago Press, 1929.

Tice, T. H. A psychoanalytic perspective. In M. Windmiller, N. Lambert, & E. Turiel (Eds.), *Moral Development and Socialization.* Boston: Allyn & Bacon, 1980, pp. 161–199.

Troth, D. C. *Selected Readings in Character Education.* Boston: Beacon Press, 1930.

Trow, W. C. Value concepts in educational psychology. *Journal of Educational Psychology,* 1953, *46,* 449–462.

Turiel, E. An experimental test of the sequentiality of developmental stages in the child's moral judgments. *Journal of Personality and Social Psychology,* 1966, *3,* 611–618.

Turiel, E. The development of social concepts. In D. J. De Palma & J. M. Foley (Eds.), *Moral Development: Current Theory and Research.* Hillsdale, N.J.: Lawrence Erlbaum Associates, 1975, pp. 7–37.

Turiel, E. The development of social-conventional and moral concepts. In M. Windmiller, N. Lambert, & E. Turiel (Eds.), *Moral Development and Socialization.* Boston: Allyn & Bacon, 1980, pp. 69–106.

Ulich, R. *A History of Religious Education: Documents and Interpretations from the Judeo-Christian Tradition.* New York: New York University Press, 1968.

Watson, G. B. *Experimentation and Measurement in Religious Education.* New York: Association Press, 1927. (a)

Watson, G. B. Character tests. *Religious Education,* 1927, *22,* 500–504. (b)

Watson, G. B. Virtues *versus* virtue. *School and Society,* 1927, *26,* 286–290. (c)

White, E. E. Moral instruction in elementary schools. *National Education Association Addresses and Proceedings,* 1896, *35,* 407–410.

Wilson, J. *Moral Education and the Curriculum: A Guide for*

Teachers and Research Workers. Oxford: Pergamon Press, 1969.

Wilson, J. *Philosophy and Educational Research.* Slough, England: NFER Publishing Co., 1972.

Wilson, J. *The Assessment of Morality.* Windsor, England: NFER Publishing Co., 1973.

Wilson, J. Moral education: Retrospect and prospect. *Journal of Moral Education,* 1979, *9*(1), 3–9.

Wilson, J.; Williams, N.; & Sugarman, B. *Introduction to Moral Education.* London: Penguin Books, 1968.

Wilson, R. W., & Schochet, G. J. *Moral Development and Politics.* New York: Praeger, 1980.

Windmiller, M.; Lambert, N.; & Turiel, E. *Moral Development and Socialization.* Boston: Allyn & Bacon, 1980.

Wright, D. *The Psychology of Moral Behavior.* London: Penguin Books, 1971.

Yulish, S. M. *The Search for a Civic Religion: A History of the Character Education Movement in America, 1890–1935.* Lanham, Md.: University Press of America, 1980.

MOTIVATION

"Motivation" is an umbrella term having a wide variety of connotations and denotations. On the one hand, the classroom teacher sees motivation as the characteristic that makes the "good" student learn; the "lazy" student is said by the teacher to be unmotivated. On the other hand, the psychologist gives motivation a much broader meaning; it refers to the processes involved in the arousing, directing, and sustaining of behavior.

Both conceptions have their usefulness. The teacher has an implicit idea of what a good student is like and tries to develop these qualities in the classroom—tries to motivate the class. The problem is that different teachers have different ideas of what a good (that is, motivated) student is, ranging from a highly active, challenging, and curious student to an obedient, well-mannered, and compliant one. It is difficult to conduct a general discussion of motivation using definitions characterized by idiosyncratic variation. Nonetheless, we shall return to the practical problems of the classroom and the specific needs of the teacher in the concluding sections of this article.

The psychologist's definition will be used for the general discussion because most of the research on motivation has been set within the context of this definition—the arousal, direction, and sustaining of behavior. Five points about motivation need to be emphasized. (1) Motivation is a hypothetical construct that we infer from a person's behavior in a particular environment. We cannot measure motivation directly, given our present state of knowledge. (2) The concept of motivation should not be overused as an explanatory device. What we infer (a person's motivation) does not explain the person's behavior since it was the person's behavior that allowed us to make the inference in the first place. The concept of motivation is nonetheless useful because it does help us to make more accurate pre-

dictions about future behavior of a person or group. (3) Motivation is only one of many constructs presumably affecting a person's behavior. Even if we knew all we possibly could about a person's motivational state, it would not allow us to predict with complete accuracy that person's future behavior. (4) Motivation, as defined here, concerns many processes that are perhaps related. No current theory or research covers and integrates all the concepts that have been proposed under the umbrella term of "motivation." Curiosity (Berlyne, 1963), locus of control (De-Charms, 1976), achievement motivation (Fyans, 1980) anxiety (Tobias, 1979) self-esteem (Coopersmith, 1967), and attribution (Weiner, 1979) are just some of the topics that have received extensive research attention; and although we can attempt a partial coverage and integration, it is impossible to explore all the vast literature or to achieve a full synthesis of motivation-related concepts. (5) Motivation in education necessarily leads us to questions about values. In trying to affect a student's motivation, even if it is merely to increase the degree of motivation already present, the educator is inevitably having an impact upon society. Social motives based upon respect for authority, interpersonal motivation based upon competition and a system of incentives for the best competitors, and intrinsic motives that emphasize personal autonomy and self-reliance are three kinds of classroom motivational environments that potentially can lead to different kinds of wider social structure as well as different kinds of children emerging from the classroom. These five issues have been discussed in greater detail by Ball (1977).

Historical Perspectives. As long as people have speculated about the reasons for their own behavior there have been theories of motivation. In polytheistic societies, the gods were blamed (or praised) for the bad (or good) things that members did. Along with the growth of monotheism the apostrophe was placed before rather than after the "s," and the causal reason for our behavior was given as "God's will." Such supernatural and theistic theories are, of course, still current.

Similarly, but at a different level of explanation, a number of other major theories of motivation have their origins in our early intellectual history, and they too have emerged in modern times in refined versions. Greek philosophers, including Socrates and Plato, argued that right knowing leads to right acting (Windelband, 1957). For example, Plato in *The Republic* believed that if we want citizens to behave properly, we should ensure that they receive care and instruction from only the finest people. The motivational essence of the argument was that the mind causally determines our behavior. Cognitive theories of motivation today represent one of the most dynamic areas of theoretical and research activity.

As a counterpoint to this rational view of motivation is the view of human behavior as caused by forces outside our cognitive control. As Bolles (1967) points out, paraphrasing Freud ([1917] 1959), mankind no longer sees itself as the center of the universe. Copernicus and Darwin foreshadowed Freud by showing that we are not master or mistress of our own house. Copernicus demonstrated that our cosmic sense of centrality was wrong; Darwin showed that we are merely an extension of the infrahuman animal world. And Freud pointed out that unconscious forces sometimes motivated us. From these modern foundations have come many motivational theories, such as instinct theory, theories of unconscious motivation, and behaviorist theories (Cofer & Appley, 1964) built upon the argument that we are subject to the same natural laws of behavior, including laws relating to reinforcement and incentives, as other organisms.

It is impossible in a short space to cover adequately all the historical antecedents of modern motivational theory and research. Nor is it possible to cover all current motivational theory and research. Instead, this article will provide an eclectic selection of some of the more currently active theories and research areas, bearing in mind as a major criterion their significance to educational policy and practice. Those interested in historical antecedents should consult Boring (1950), Graffam (1965), and Cofer and Appley (1964).

Attribution Theory. Perhaps the best statement about attribution theory and research as it applies to education comes from Weiner (1979). Attribution theory assumes that the search for understanding (information seeking) is a mainspring of human motivation. This search for understanding involves asking "why" questions including, of course, those "why" questions dealing with achievement in the kinds of settings (school, interpersonal) in which people find themselves. "Why did I get a lower score than Marita?" or "Why won't Jenny have lunch with me?" lead to attributional responses—attributing causes to success or failure outcomes.

In the school setting, the perceived causes of success or failure have been variously categorized (Elig & Frieze, 1975; Frieze, 1976). Similarly teachers explain student performance using a variety of attributions (Cooper & Burger, 1980). Among the major causes cited are ability, effort, and task difficulty, but the list could be extended indefinitely depending upon the culture, kind of task, and the people involved. In order to systematize these attributed causes, Weiner (1979) offered a three-dimensional table involving locus of control (internal or external), stability (stable or unstable), and level of control (controllable or uncontrollable). As he states it, among the internal causes, ability is stable and uncontrollable, and typical effort is also stable but controllable; task difficulty is seen as external to the learner, stable and uncontrollable from the learner's viewpoint.

Each of the three dimensions (locus of control, stability, and level of control) has a primary function and several secondary functions. Locus of control (Fanelli, 1977) concerns whether people think of themselves as being responsible for their behavior (internal) or whether they attribute their behavior to luck or other circumstances beyond their control (external). If people think their success is caused by ability (internal), then feelings of competence and confidence are experienced. If success is seen as resulting from external factors such as help from others, then gratitude and similar emotions are usually experienced.

To overgeneralize slightly, studies show that students with an internal locus of control tend to have a somewhat higher need for achievement and are more persistent than students with an external locus of control, who are more likely to be characterized by what has been called "learned helplessness." Students with an external locus of control tend to give up in the face of frustration or fatigue (Dweck, 1975). Subsequent work by Dweck et al. (1978) has teased out interesting differences in the ways teachers handle the failures of boys and girls that contribute to sex differences in attributional patterns.

Locus of control seems to be related to other status characteristics. Coleman et al. (1966) found that black children tended to be more external in their locus of control than white children and that "internal" black students performed better in reading than "external" black students. Friend and Neale (1972) seemed to confirm this finding, although there is reason to suspect that educational and social changes may be affecting the locus of control scores of specific groups (Stephens, 1973; Entwisle & Greenberger, 1972). Nonetheless, being disadvantaged does still seem to create a greater degree of externality, as Turney et al. (1978) and Turney, Sinclair, and Cairns (1980) have found with respect to inner-city and geographically isolated rural children.

The second of Weiner's causal dimensions is stability (stable versus unstable). Here it has been found that expectations for future performance are influenced by attributions for previous performance. If a student attributes previous performance to a stable condition, such as ability, then the expectation is made that future performance will have a similar result (Ostrove, 1978; McMahan, 1973). The implications of this perception for the structuring of classroom verbal interactions by the teacher are considered at the end of this article.

The third of Weiner's causal dimensions is controllability. When student failure is seen by the teacher as the result of controllable factors within the failing student, help tends to be withheld; if it is seen as not controllable by the failing student, help is more likely to be forthcoming (Ickes & Kidd, 1976). The implications for teacher education courses are clear. If teachers see student failure as resulting from student laziness, for instance, they are less likely to help that student. If teachers see student failure as resulting from the difficulties of an overcrowded home, however, then more teacher help is likely to be provided. Giving teachers a frame of reference that enables them to see the student as at least partly an object of external pressures is probably a useful thing to do. Curiously, giving students a frame of reference in which they see themselves as controlling their own destinies is also a useful thing to do.

There are some caveats and addenda to this brief discussion of attribution theory. Andrews and Debus (1978) showed that a training program could cause students to make more effort attributions and show more persistence than a control group. Similar kinds of results from previously cited studies (Dweck et al., 1978; DeCharms, 1976) have led Bar-Tal (1978) to argue that "there is a possibility of maximizing achievement behavior by providing students with instructions and feedback that would encourage them to make internal attributions (ability and effort) for success" (p. 267).

One of the purposes in using attribution theory in an educational setting is to make students want to make a greater effort. However, as Covington and Omelich (1979) point out, effort is a "double-edged sword." Despite attempts by teachers through incentives and verbal rewards to encourage student effort, there is, in many schools, a palpable lack of success. Covington and Omelich suggest why this is so by arguing that if a student is to retain high self-esteem with respect to ability, it is wise not to make much effort. If failure follows effort, then one's ability is brought into question. Conversely, failure reflects less on ability, and shame is reduced, if students do little study. In a later study (Covington, Spratt, & Omelich, 1980) the dynamics of this low-effort, low-shame reaction to failure were seen to involve also the need to externalize the reason for low effort. ("It would not have done any good anyway if I had studied because the test was stupid.")

Clearly there is a lot more to be learned about the interplay of attribution and behavior. One other influential factor concerns whether the social setting is cooperative or competitive. The competitive condition seems to cause greater self-punitive reactions to failure and greater ego-enhancing reactions to success (Ames, Ames, & Felker, 1977). In a later and larger study, Ames and Felker (1979) found similar effects. Competitive and individualistic situations, compared to cooperative situations, seemed to emphasize perceived individual differences. They also seemed to emphasize the value placed on successful achievements. There is no simple recipe for educators in all of this. As was pointed out earlier, knowledge of how motivation operates leads us to questions of values. Do we want students to accentuate individual differences and to emphasize success and personal responsibility? Would we rather emphasize group awareness and feelings of collective responsibility?

Achievement Motivation. Closely related to attribution is the body of theory and research known as "achievement motivation." McClelland et al. (1953) initiated research into a motive called "need for achievement" that has blossomed into a complex and sophisticated movement covering a wide variety of issues (Fyans, 1980).

Achievement motivation refers to a pattern of actions and feelings connected to striving to achieve some internalized standard of excellence in performance (Vidler, 1977b). Revelle and Michaels (1976) point out that achievement motivation can be seen as a special case of the inertial tendency postulate, but research has not been carried out to verify this observation.

Atkinson and Feather (1966) and Atkinson and Raynor (1974) provide clear presentations of the expanded theory of achievement motivation. Achievement-oriented behavior is seen to be a function of a number of factors including the motive to succeed, the motive to avoid failure, the perceived probability of success, and the incentive value of success. Of key interest to educators are the practical attempts to increase achievement orientation in students—an early interest of McClelland (1965) and one continued with enthusiasm by his followers (Alschuler, 1973; Alschuler, Tabor, & McIntyre, 1970). The crux of the method is to use a variety of techniques including games, group meetings, and public incentives in order to encourage independence, acceptance of personal responsibility for one's own behavior, and the acceptance of goals that require moderate risk taking for achievement, careful planning, and entrepreneurial activities.

Only moderate success has been found in improving the achievement of students through special motivation courses (McClelland & Alschuler, 1971). However, one reason for this could be that many schools do not allow students to take initiatives and to plan their own academic lives. The skills taught in these courses might have greater impact in less structured environments. Even so, Bridgeman and Shipman (1978) have shown in a longitudinal study of disadvantaged children that achievement motivation scores, as measured by the Gumpgookies test (Adkins, Payne, & Ballif, 1972) in the year prior to entering first grade, contributed significantly to predictions of achievement in third grade. In mathematics, the score accounted for 30 to 35 percent of the variance.

Weiner (1972) has argued that a better understanding of achievement motivation can be obtained by interpreting it through the structures of attribution theory. As he put it, "Causal attributions influence the likelihood of undertaking achievement activities, the intensity of work at these activities, and the degree of persistence in the face of failure" (p. 213). Halperin and Abrams (1978) studied undergraduates and found support for the attribution model of achievement expectations. Previous performance and attributions explained almost all of the variation in the final examination predictions. The question of theoretical interpretation is important; but for most educators there is a problem of greater importance: how well does the McClelland-Atkinson theory of achievement motivation help us to understand and control the dynamics of the classroom? According to Maehr and Sjogren (1971), who looked at such educational practices as ability grouping, programmed instruction, and independent study, achievement motivation suggests "a variety of insights," but it can provide "only limited advice for the practitioner" (p. 157). Limited advice, however, may be all that the practitioner wants from a theory of motivation at this stage of theory development.

Anxiety. The role of anxiety as a motivating force has its roots in Freudian psychoanalytic theory, although Freud ([1925] 1959) himself saw anxiety not as a motivating force but as a signal of unconscious fears.

Sullivan (1948) tried to make clear the distinction between fear and anxiety. Anxiety is a reflection of internal tension, whereas fear is a mechanism for dealing with external and presumably more realistic dangers. As Hansen (1977) points out, anxiety has long been regarded as a less-than-rational, debilitating response to a situation that may or may not be threatening. Considering the origins of the concept, it is perhaps not surprising that it is so negatively regarded, especially by those from clinical and humanistic backgrounds.

Alpert and Haber (1960) argued that anxiety could be facilitating as well as debilitating. Anxiety, at least at mild levels, may serve to arouse what otherwise might be a comatose or at least lethargic student. With respect to test anxiety, as Ball (1982) has pointed out (based in part on the work of French, 1962), "We cannot refute the possibility that test anxiety produces an intensely negative impact for a few students; but, if it does, it probably produces a mildly positive impact for many students. . . ."

High levels of anxiety are debilitating in almost any situation for most people. For example, high levels of anxiety interfere with memory (Sieber, 1969). Deffenbacher (1978) tried to discover the sources of interference that occur with variations of stress in the situation. He studied high-anxious and low-anxious subjects. The high-anxious subjects in the high-stress condition performed most ineffectively and were most distracted from the task by worry, emotionality, and competing wrong responses.

High anxiety levels can be reduced and performance improved in a number of ways (Petty & Harrell, 1977). An excellent treatment of the literature on anxiety-reduction is provided by Tobias (1979). The areas covered by Tobias include desensitization, applied relaxation, self-control training, cognitive coping strategies, and modeling and automated approaches. Evidence for the usefulness of these treatment programs is provided by Allen, Elias, and Zlotlow (1980) and Denney (1980).

The relationship between anxiety and performance is complicated and dependent upon a number of important factors including the complexity of the task and the skill and experience of the person carrying out the task. Very complex tasks are most negatively affected by high levels of anxiety; very experienced and skilled performers are usually less affected by high degrees of stress.

Again, the message to educators cannot be prescriptive if only because values are involved. If freedom from stress is a positive value, then anxiety will be reduced wherever possible—reminiscent of some Eastern religious stances. If, on the other hand, preparation for life is a positive goal (and life is regarded as a competitive struggle) then clearly students have to be presented with stressful situations in order to gradually adapt.

Self-Esteem. It has long been a cliché of educational theory that a student's behavior is a function of the student's self-concept. If a student thinks of himself as a class clown, he will act like a class clown. A resultant implication is that educators and educational programs should seek to "enhance" the self-concept of students. Shavelson, Hub-

ner, and Stanton (1976) cite eight references to support that point.

Self-esteem is seen, then, as being a worthwhile goal in itself as well as being a worthwhile intermediary agent affecting changes in student behavior. The best critical reviews of the literature on self-esteem and self-concept are provided by Shavelson, Hubner, and Stanton (1976), by Shavelson and Bolus (1982), and by Wylie (1979).

Whereas high self-esteem is generally a desirable attribute in a student, a real problem arises when educators fail to recognize the complexity of the construct. Do we want to enhance the self-esteem of all children? Or do we want to make self-esteem more realistic? Is it sensible to raise a child's self-esteem to the point where failure is inevitable? Is it understood that self-esteem varies within each of us depending upon the aspect of self under consideration? After all, I may see myself as a moderately splendid tennis player, but I may also see myself as a miserably inattentive son (Ball, 1963).

Shavelson, Hubner, and Stanton (1976) identify seven features of self-concept that they see as critical to the construct definition—organized, multifaceted, hierarchical, stable, developmental, evaluative, differentiable. Each of these features is a necessary part of the complex construct often glibly referred to as "self-concept." These authors point out that "self-concept studies lack the focus that would result from an agreed-upon definition of self-concept, lack adequate validation of interpretations of self-concept measures, and lack empirical data on the equivalence of the many self-concept measures currently being used" (p. 435).

Correlations between self-esteem and academic achievement usually are positive (about r = .30) (Wylie, 1979). Of course this does not mean that self-esteem necessarily causally affects achievement. Scheirer and Kraut (1979) concluded after reviewing the causal relationship that although self-esteem can be manipulated and academic performance thereby improved, results are at best short-lived and at worst contradictory. The relationship still calls for further investigation.

Unless we take a radical behaviorist position, self-concept has to be an important element in considering motivational theory and educational practice. The problem is that we have taken this axiomatic position too much for granted. Although self-concept is clearly involved in attribution, achievement motivation, and anxiety (as well as the other motivational concepts at our disposal) its very obviousness seems to have caused us to give it insufficient critical study.

Curiosity. This motivational construct is one of the oldest in our repertoire, clearly evolving from the instinct theories of the nineteenth century. If self-esteem has proved to be deceptively obvious, curiosity has proved to be deceptively simple. Vidler (1977a) points to the number of critics who complain at the lack of a clear, acceptable definition.

Fowler (1965) points out that there is no goal object involved when curiosity is the motive. If new stimulation is the goal object, then we have a problem since virtually all behavior to some extent creates a set of new stimuli. Berlyne (1963) differentiates between exploratory and nonexploratory behavior. Curiosity, he argues, motivates exploratory behavior.

Curiosity and exploratory behavior are strongly manifested in early childhood and again, although more narrowly, during adolescence. This is understandable since during these two periods novel stimuli present themselves to the learner. Sinclair (1981) relates curiosity to Hebb's degree-of-arousal figure (1955) demonstrating that, at one end, highly unusual stimuli arouse fear, and, at the other end, very familiar stimuli create boredom. Somewhere in between are mildly novel stimuli that arouse curiosity.

Henderson and Moore (1979) carried out a cross-sectional developmental study of boys and girls. Older children preferred more complex things to explore (the simpler objects presumably being less novel to them), and generally older children tended to explore less. From these findings one can critically consider the complaint that schools "destroy" our children's curiosity. Maybe school routines do have a negative impact on curiosity; but it would be an odd world if most people continued to explore and to manifest curiosity at the same rate and with the same unflagging enthusiasm as preschool-age children. Even the most youthful adults have to become somewhat jaded whether they have gone to school or not.

Curiosity as a motive has had a number of applications in the schools. Allender (1969) showed that independent inquiry (verbal exploratory behavior) is normal among elementary school students when conditions in the classroom allow it to happen. Of course, in highly structured, teacher-dominant classrooms, inquiry behavior was less likely to occur. Learning by discovery, in one or more of its various forms, has become a part of the arsenal of many teachers (Strike, 1975).

Not all students are high in academic curiosity. Fry (1972) found that among bright students, the highly curious learned significantly more under conditions that gave them control over their own learning. On the other hand their relatively noncurious counterparts learned more when students had a low degree of control.

Curiosity would seem to be related to a number of other important educational processes such as divergent thinking and creativity. However, perhaps because of its shaky theoretical underpinnings, curiosity has not been an area of as much active research during the past decade as it had been in the decade before.

Motivational Miscellany. This article cannot be comprehensive in scope any more than it could be comprehensive in depth. However, before proceeding to discuss attempts at theory synthesis, it is useful to consider other motivational factors cited in the educational literature.

Level of aspiration. The motivational aspects of level of aspiration received considerable attention in the 1930s and 1940s in the theoretical writings of Lewin (1935). Lewin's development of a process for assessing level of aspira-

tion also helped stimulate interest. More recently, level of aspiration has tended to be incorporated into the achievement motivation literature under the terms "expectancy" and "risk taking."

Affiliation motivation. Educators seem most interested in motivational constructs that potentially relate to academic achievement. However, there are other areas of concern in an educational setting, with the social domain not the least important. Nonetheless, affiliation motivation has received far less attention than, say, achievement motivation. Clarke (1973) raised the topic in terms of the reliability and validity of the instruments used to measure these motivational constructs. In recent years, the amount of research in affiliation motivation has fallen off sharply.

Biochemical correlates. Reductionism appears on the psychological scene from time to time. Is schizophrenia really reducible to some hormonal deficit? Are moods really chemical processes in the lower brain? Similarly in motivation, linked as it clearly is with affect and emotion, there is apparently a need from time to time to study reductionist ideas. Kasl (1974), for example, inquired about any promising biochemical correlates of achievement motivation. He specifically examined the evidence for serum uric acid (the gout predisposer) and for serum cholesterol. Kasl's review pointed to a number of low correlations. However his conclusion still seems sound. "In short, we need many more studies" (p. 457).

Reinforcement theory. Skinner (1938) gave a great impetus to research in this area. His approach, initially based mainly on research with infrahuman subjects, has led to the field called "behavior modification." In education, behavior modification has been used most prominently in special education. A classic example of this kind of manipulation of the reinforcement environment to remotivate a disturbed child is provided by Harris et al. (1964). Other offshoots of Skinner's work are programmed instruction and teaching machines. Neither of these is as major an area of interest as it was in the 1960s. Skinner's book (1968) on teaching and educational technology is still one of the best available presentations of the reinforcement approach to educational motivation. It emphasizes investigating what reinforces a student's behavior and using it as an incentive under some kind of reinforcement schedule. However, teachers too frequently fail to realize what student behaviors they are reinforcing through the attention they give.

Integrating Theories and Research. There have been a few attempts to achieve some degree of integration of motivational areas during the past decade. Ames (1978) studied the interrelationships of attributions, self-concept, self-reinforcement, and competitive reward structures. It was an empirical investigation mainly, but it had a theoretical basis and implications. She found that self-concept mediated attributions and degree of self-reinforcement. She also found that self-concept mediated the impact of a competitive setting.

Peters (1978) conducted an empirical investigation of the relationship between anxiety and curiosity. Anxiety-heightened situations were found to lower curiosity. Wolk and DuCette (1971) looked at locus of control and achievement motivation. Theoretically, they point out, an overlap is apparent. In practice the obtained correlations were not significant. Measurement problems, the nature of the relationship (linear? quadratic?), and the possibility that the theory is wrong were all suggested as possible explanations. Cooper and Baron (1979) attempted to achieve an integration of expectations, attributions, and the reinforcement behavior of teachers. The integration was incomplete, considering only a small section of the related bodies of literature.

Finally Ball (1977) reports a study by Chiu in which a factor analysis of sixteen separate motivation scales was carried out. Three major motivational factors were noted. One was an intrinsic motivation involving persistence, high level of aspiration, positive self-concept, and past positive reinforcement for schoolwork; a student high on this factor worked because the job was there to do. The second factor involved social competitiveness and recognition. A student high in only this factor would tend to be less motivated if forced to work alone without public recognition of results. The third major factor dealt with anxiety and fear of failure. The argument underlying this study was that a motivational profile of a student based upon a number of motivational factors made better sense than a single score on one motivational scale.

Basically motivation remains an umbrella term covering a wide range of topics. Attempts at integrating this wide range of topics have not been many nor have they aroused much interest.

Practical Implications. Scattered throughout this article are implications for educational practice of the motivational theory and research presented here.

1. Children are differently motivated. What works with one student may not work with another. For example, some need structure, or anxiety overwhelms them; others are turned on by open classrooms that encourage their curiosity and exploratory behavior.

2. Students are more likely to work without extensive supervision if they have an internal locus of control—if they see themselves as responsible for their own behavior.

3. Teachers should lead students to attribute successful performance to ability, or, if relevant, to long-term effort. However, teacher educators should lead teachers to see that external socioeconomic factors are not under the student's control.

4. Competitive learning situations compared to cooperative learning situations increase self-punitive reactions to failure and greater self-esteem after success. Care has to be exercised in dealing with competitive learning situations, especially when involving less able students.

5. Efforts to make children feel that they are the origins of their own behavior and not simply pawns pushed by external forces can be fruitful. This can be done by establishing a classroom climate in which initiative is encouraged, and children are taught to reflect on their feelings when presented with a challenge, to take moderate risks, and to be independent.

6. Getting rid of anxiety in the classroom may make students feel more at ease but is not likely to improve academic performance. Mild anxiety levels may enhance learning, but teachers must be aware that high anxiety is counterproductive. If a student is highly anxious, careful structuring of the environment can help. Let the student know, through joint planning with the teacher, what is required in the short term. Don't emphasize the long term.

7. For humanitarian reasons teachers should try to enhance the way students see themselves. The self-concept, however, is a complex construct and self-concept scores typically have a low correlation with student performance. Teachers probably should concentrate on specifics—such as making students feel confident about their achievements in arithmetic—rather than trying to enhance the vaguely defined "self-concept."

8. Curiosity in the classroom requires the presence of novel stimuli or epistemic bafflement. Teachers who want their students to be curious have to give students the privilege of exploring. Overstructured classrooms inhibit curiosity. Teachers can constructively baffle students by presenting problems, giving a few clues, and then letting student curiosity take over. This process might take longer than a routine teacher lecture, but it certainly adds more positive affect to the classroom experience.

9. Educators should consider the incentive system that operates in their sphere of influence (classroom, department, school). Are the right behaviors being reinforced? Is the noisy child getting too much attention? Is the independent and hardworking child being wrongly ignored? Does the teacher who complains most get the fewest duties? These are the kinds of questions needing consideration. Remember that incentives include social attention and token rewards, but each person has his or her own set of preferred reinforcements.

Hamachek (1973) wrote a monograph for the National Education Association that included a great deal of practical advice on motivation. Many of the suggestions are linked to ways of structuring children's learning. The monograph points out that well-prepared, well-presented lessons, exercises that are within the grasp of the learner but not too easy, variety of experience—in other words, good teaching generally—affect students so that they want to learn. Similarly, the teacher who is warm, friendly, and interested as opposed to cold and sarcastic will also find that students are more likely to be "motivated."

Both theory and scientific research provide the motivational canvas and the motivational oils. It is still up to the teacher to paint the specific classroom picture. The teacher is the artist who must put it together.

Samuel Ball

See also Affective Education; Learning; Personality Theory; Psychology.

REFERENCES

Adkins, D. C.; Payne, F. D.; & Ballif, B. L. Motivation factor scores and response set scores for ten ethnic-cultural groups of preschool children. *American Educational Research Journal,* 1972, *9,* 557–572.

Allen, G. J.; Elias, M. J.; & Zlotlow, S. F. Behavioral interventions for alleviating test anxiety: A methodological overview of current therapeutic practices. In I. G. Sarason (Ed.), *Test Anxiety: Theory, Research and Applications.* Hillsdale, N.J.: Lawrence Erlbaum Associates, 1980.

Allender, J. S. A study of inquiry activity in elementary school children. *American Educational Research Journal,* 1969, *4,* 543–558.

Alpert, R., & Haber, R. N. Anxiety in academic achievement settings. *Journal of Abnormal and Social Psychology,* 1960, *61,* 207–215.

Alschuler, A. S. *Developing Achievement Motivation in Adolescents.* Englewood Cliffs, N.J.: Educational Technology Publications, 1973.

Alschuler, A. S.; Tabor, D.; & McIntyre, J. *Teaching Achievement Motivation.* Middletown, Conn.: Educational Ventures, 1970.

Ames, C. Children's achievement attributions and self-reinforcement: Effects of self-concept and competitive reward structure. *Journal of Educational Psychology,* 1978, *70,* 345–355.

Ames, C.; Ames, R.; & Felker, D. W. Effects of competitive reward structures and valence of outcome on children's achievement attributions. *Journal of Educational Psychology,* 1977, *69,* 1–8.

Ames, C., & Felker, D. W. An examination of children's attributions and achievement-related evaluations in competitive, cooperative, and individualistic reward structures. *Journal of Educational Psychology,* 1979, *71,* 405–412.

Andrews, G. R., & Debus, R. L. Persistence and causal perception of failure: Modifying cognitive attributions. *Journal of Educational Psychology,* 1978, *70,* 154–166.

Atkinson, J. W., & Feather, N. J. *A Theory of Achievement Motivation.* New York: Wiley, 1966.

Atkinson, J. W., & Raynor, J. O. *Motivation and Achievement.* Washington, D.C.: J. H. Winston, 1974.

Ball, S. Self-regard and social acceptability. *Australian Journal of Education,* 1963, *7,* 187–201.

Ball, S. *Motivation in Education.* New York: Academic Press, 1977.

Ball, S. Anxiety and test performance. In C. D. Spielberger & P. R. Vagg (Eds.), *The Measurement and Treatment of Test Anxiety.* New York: McGraw-Hill/Hemisphere, 1982.

Bar-Tal, D. Attribution theory and achievement. *Review of Educational Research,* 1978, *48,* 259–271.

Berlyne, D. E. Motivational problems raised by exploratory and epistemic behavior. In S. Koch (Ed.), *Psychology: A Study of a Science* (Vol. 5). New York: McGraw-Hill, 1963.

Bolles, R. C. *Theory of Motivation,* New York: Harper & Row, 1967.

Boring, E. G. *History of Experimental Psychology* (2nd ed.). New York: Appleton-Century-Crofts, 1950.

Bridgeman, B., & Shipman, V. C. Preschool measures of self-esteem and achievement motivation as predictors of third-grade achievement. *Journal of Educational Psychology,* 1978, *70,* 17–28.

Clarke, D. E. Achievement and affiliation motivation. *Review of Educational Research,* 1973, *43,* 41–51.

Cofer, C. N., & Appley, M. H. *Motivation: Theory and Research.* New York: Wiley, 1964.

Coleman, J.; Campbell, E. Q.; Hobson, C. J.; McPartland, J.; Mood, A. M.; Weinfeld, F. D.; & York, R. L. *Equality of Educational Opportunity.* Washington, D.C.: U.S. Government Printing Office, 1966. (ERIC Document Reproduction Service No. ED 012 275)

Cooper, H. M., & Baron, R. M. Academic expectations, attributed responsibility and teachers' reinforcement behavior: A suggested integration of conflicting literatures. *Journal of Educational Psychology,* 1979, *71,* 274–277.

Cooper, H. M., & Burger, J. M. How teachers explain students' academic performance: A categorization of free response academic attributions. *American Educational Research Journal,* 1980, *17,* 95–109.

Coopersmith, S. *The Antecedents of Self-esteem.* San Francisco: Freeman, 1967.

Covington, M. V., & Omelich, C. L. Effort: The double-edged sword in school achievement. *Journal of Educational Psychology,* 1979, *71,* 169–182.

Covington, M. V.; Spratt, M. F.; & Omelich, C. L. Is effort enough or does diligence count too? Student and teacher reactions to effort stability in failure. *Journal of Educational Psychology,* 1980, *72,* 717–729.

DeCharms, R. *Enhancing Motivation: A Change Project in the Classroom.* New York: Wiley, 1976.

Deffenbacher, J. L. Worry, emotionality, and task-generated interference in test anxiety: An empirical test of attentional theory. *Journal of Educational Psychology,* 1978, *70,* 248–254.

Denney, D. R. Self-control approaches to the treatment of test anxiety. In I. G. Sarason (Ed.), *Test Anxiety: Theory, Research and Applications.* Hillsdale, N.J.: Lawrence Erlbaum Associates, 1980.

Dweck, C. S. The role of expectations and attributions in the alleviation of learned helplessness. *Journal of Personality and Social Psychology,* 1975, *31,* 674–685.

Dweck, C. S.; Davidson, W.; Nelson, S.; & Enna, B. Sex differences in learned helplessness. II: The contingencies of evaluative feedback in the classroom. III: An experimental analysis. *Developmental Psychology,* 1978, *14,* 268–276.

Elig, T. W., & Frieze, I. H. A multidimensional scheme for coding and interpreting perceived causality for success and failure events: The Coding Scheme of Perceived Causality (CSPC) (Ms. No. 1069). *Journal Supplement Abstract Service Catalog of Selected Documents in Psychology,* 1975, *5,* 313.

Entwisle, D. R., & Greenberger, E. Questions about social class, internality, externality, and test anxiety. *Developmental Psychology,* 1972, *7,* 218.

Fanelli, G. C. Locus of control. In S. Ball (Ed.), *Motivation in Education.* New York: Academic Press, 1977.

Fowler, H. *Curiosity and Exploratory Behavior.* New York: Macmillan, 1965.

French, J. W. Effect of anxiety on verbal and mathematical examination scores. *Educational and Psychological Measurement,* 1962, *22,* 553–564.

Freud, S. One of the difficulties of psychoanalysis. In *Collected Papers* (Vol. 4). New York: Basic Books, 1959. (Originally published, 1917)

Freud, S. Inhibitions, symptoms, and anxiety. In *Collected Works* (Vol. 20, J. Strachey, Trans.). London: Hogarth, 1959. (Originally published, 1925.)

Friend, R., & Neale, J. Children's perceptions of success and failure: An attributional analysis of the effects of race and social class. *Developmental Psychology*, 1972, *7*, 124–128.

Frieze, I. H. Causal attributions and information seeking to explain success and failure. *Journal of Research in Personality*, 1976, *10*, 293–305.

Fry, J. P. Interactive relationship between inquisitiveness and student control of instruction. *Journal of Educational Psychology*, 1972, *63*, 459–465.

Fyans, L. J. *Achievement Motivation*. New York: Plenum, 1980.

Graffam, D. T. Brief historical introduction to motivation. In C. L. Stacey & M. F. DeMartino (Eds.), *Understanding Human Motivation*. Cleveland: World Publishing, 1965.

Halperin, M. S., & Abrams, D. L. Sex differences in predicting final examination grades: The influence of past performance attributions, and achievement motivation. *Journal of Educational Psychology*, 1978, *70*, 763–771.

Hamachek, D. E. *Motivation in Teaching and Learning*. Washington, D.C.: National Education Association, 1973.

Hansen, R. A. Anxiety. In S. Ball (Ed.), *Motivation in Education*. New York: Academic Press, 1977.

Harris, F. R.; Johnston, M. K.; Kelly, C. S.; & Wolf, M. M. Effects of positive social reinforcement on regressed crawling of a nursery school child. *Journal of Educational Psychology*, 1964, *55*, 35–41.

Hebb, D. O. Drives and CNS (Conceptual Nervous System). *Psychological Review*, 1955, *62*, 243–254.

Henderson, B., & Moore, S. G. Measuring exploratory behavior in young children: A factor-analytic study. *Developmental Psychology*, 1979, *15*, 113–119.

Ickes, W. J., & Kidd, R. F. An attributional analysis of helping behavior. In J. H. Harvey, W. J. Ickes, & R. F. Kidd (Eds.), *New Directions in Attribution Research* (Vol. 1). Hillsdale, N.J.: Lawrence Erlbaum Associates, 1976.

Kasl, S. V. Are there any promising biochemical correlates of achievement behavior and motivation? The evidence for serum uric acid and serum cholesterol. *Review of Educational Research*, 1974, *44*, 447–462.

Lewin, K. *A Dynamic Theory of Personality: Selected Papers*. (D. K. Adams & K. E. Zener, Trans.). New York: McGraw-Hill, 1935.

Maehr, M. L. & Sjogren, D. D. Atkinson's theory of achievement motivation: First step toward a theory of academic motivation. *Review of Educational Research*, 1971, *41*, 143–161.

McClelland, D. C. Towards a theory of motive acquisition. *American Psychologist*, 1965, *20*, 321–333.

McClelland, D. C., & Alschuler, A. S. The achievement motivation development project. Washington, D.C.: U.S. Office of Education, Bureau of Research, 1971. (ERIC Document Reproduction Service No. ED 062 585)

McClelland, D. C.; Atkinson, J. W.; Clark, R. W.; & Lowell, E. L. *The Achievement Motive*, New York: Appleton-Century-Crofts, 1953.

McMahan, I. D. Relationships between causal attributions and expectancy of success. *Journal of Personality and Social Psychology*, 1973, *28*, 108–114.

Ostrove, N. Expectations for success on effort-determined tasks as a function of incentive and performance feedback. *Journal of Personality and Social Psychology*, 1978, *36*, 909–916.

Peters, R. A. Effects of anxiety, curiosity, and perceived instructor threat on student verbal behavior in the college classroom. *Journal of Educational Psychology*, 1978, *3*, 388–395.

Petty, N. E., & Harrell, E. H. Effect of programmed instruction related to motivation, anxiety, and test wiseness on group IQ

test performance. *Journal of Educational Psychology*, 1977, *5*, 630–635.

Revelle, W., & Michaels, E. J. The theory of achievement motivation revisited: The implications of inertial tendencies. *Psychological Review*, 1976, *83*, 394–404.

Scheirer, M. G., & Kraut, R. E. Increasing educational achievement via self-concept change. *Review of Educational Research*, 1979, *49*, 131–149.

Shavelson, R. J., & Bolus, R. Self-concept: The interplay of theory and methods. *Journal of Educational Psychology*, 1982, *74*(1), 1 ff.

Shavelson, R. J.; Hubner, J. J.; & Stanton, G. C. Self-concept: Validation of construct interpretations. *Review of Educational Research*, 1976, *46*, 407–442.

Sieber, J. E. A paradigm for experimental modification of the effects of test anxiety on cognitive processes. *American Educational Research Journal*, 1969, *6*, 46–61.

Sinclair, K. Knowing the child. In C. Turney (Ed.), *Anatomy of Teaching*. Sydney: Novak, 1981.

Skinner, B. F. *The Behavior of Organisms: An Experimental Approach*. New York: Appleton-Century, 1938.

Skinner, B. F. *The Technology of Teaching*. New York: Appleton-Century-Crofts, 1968.

Stephens, M. W., & Delys, P. External control expectancies among disadvantaged children at pre-school age. *Child Development*, 1973, *44*, 670–674.

Strike, K. A. The logic of learning by discovery. *Review of Educational Research*, 1975, *45*, 461–484.

Sullivan, H. S. *The Meaning of Anxiety in Psychiatry and Life*. Washington, D.C.: William Alanson White Foundation, 1948.

Tobias, S. Anxiety research in educational psychology. *Journal of Educational Psychology*, 1979, *71*, 573–582.

Turney, C.; Inglis, C. B.; Sinclair, K. E.; & Straton, R. G. *Inner-city Schools: Children, Teachers and Parents*. Sydney: Sydney University Press, 1978.

Turney, C.; Sinclair, K. E.; & Cairns, L. G. *Isolated Schools: Teaching, Learning, and Transition to Work*. Sydney: Sydney University Press, 1980.

Vidler, D. C. Achievement motivation. In S. Ball (Ed.), *Motivation in Education*. New York: Academic Press, 1977. (a)

Vidler, D. C. Curiosity. In S. Ball (Ed.), *Motivation in Education*. New York: Academic Press, 1977. (b)

Weiner, B. Attribution theory, achievement motivation, and the educational process. *Review of Educational Research*, 1972, *42*, 203–216.

Weiner, B. A theory of motivation for some classroom experiences. *Journal of Educational Psychology*, 1979, *71*, 3–25.

Windelband, W. *History of Ancient Philosophy*. (H. E. Cushman, trans.). New York: Dover, 1957.

Wolk, S., & DuCette, J. Locus of control and achievement motivation: Theoretical overlap and methodological divergence. *Psychological Reports*, 1971, *29*, 755–758.

Wylie, R. C. *The Self-concept*. Vol. 2 of *Theory and Research on Selected Topics*. Lincoln: University of Nebraska Press, 1979.

MOTOR SKILLS DEVELOPMENT

This article presents an overview of the important components of motor skills development in children. Developmental changes in children are often observed first in the motor domain as manipulatory and ambulatory responses. Motor skills therefore play an extremely important role in the normal development of a child. Because both the appropriateness and efficiency of motor skill expression are rooted in overall cognitive development, quite often a failure to develop age-appropriate motor behaviors is a signal that cognitive development is impaired. In this article, emphasis is placed on three issues: theoretical considerations, old and new; assessment of motor development; and implications for educational programming.

Theoretical Perspectives. Historically, those interested in the study of motor skill behavior have viewed motor learning and motor development as distinct entities. The first group have borrowed heavily from experimental psychology for their theoretical formulations and orientations, while the second have held fast to the traditional stage-dependent theory of a developing child, drawing ideas and orientations from both clinical and differential psychology. The clinical flavor derives from the many observations made on children as they develop their motor abilities, whereas the differential aspects stem from the abundant research energy devoted to the construction of tests to determine the "motor age" of a young child and evaluate whether or not a child is developing at the appropriate rate.

The traditional maturational frameworks used to describe patterns of motor development in children have relied primarily on an endogenous, neurologically based explanation of developing activity. That is, motor development has been assumed to be related to the internal development of the nervous system. The traditional views of Coghill (1929) and McGraw (1945) have more recently been criticized by Schneirla (1966) and Connolly (1970b) for failing to give sufficient theoretical attention to the effects of motor experience on the developing organism. Earlier research by Carmichael (1934), Bridgeman and Carmichael (1935), and Windle (1940) all point to both general and localized responses occurring early in the life of the organism. It is clear that the progressive refinements of a developing child's motor responses come about not only from a process of maturation but also from the effects of experience.

The ten years between 1965 and 1975 saw increased research activity in motor skills development, not only from the point of view of assessing the performance capabilities of children, but also in the sense of asking questions about the specifics of motor skills development. This issue of how skills develop increasingly emphasizes the cognitive aspects of motor development. Researchers discuss the development of motor skills as it relates to a child's ability to process information. The individual is likened to a communication channel (much like a telephone switching center) with an essentially limited capacity to process information. The research findings in this literature (Connolly, 1970a; Wade, 1976) suggest that as processors of information, children are considerably less effi-

cient than adults. For example, when a child is required to perform a motor skill (i.e., solve a motor problem), he or she is faced with a larger and perhaps different array of information, and what appears simple to an adult may prove to be highly complex to a child. Experience tends to rule out a number of hypotheses or strategies for the adult that remain viable to a young child faced with an identical motor problem. All the information a child is required to process is new, and there is no redundancy, or information already processed, in the system; consequently, a child must process more information than an adult in order to solve the identical problem. Although it possesses limitations, the information theory model of skilled behavior allows for the investigation of learning strategies that a developing child uses to evolve appropriate motor skills. Given a limited channel capacity, when a child in some way integrates individual signals, the total level of information in the situation is reduced. Information theory has provided a working model to study the process variables that contribute to the learning and development of skilled motor activity.

Recently a less conventional perspective has been advanced by students of Gibson (1966). Turvey, Shaw and Mace (1978), Fowler and Turvey (1978), Fitch and Turvey (1977), and Kugler, Kelso, and Turvey (1980) all maintain that in order to understand motor skill behavior best, individuals cannot be viewed outside the environmental contexts in which they exist. Fundamental to this interpretation is the notion that our actions and perceptions are body-scaled.

The basic assumption behind body-scaled information is that objects perceived by the organism are defined relative to the organism's capacity for activity. Objects are distinguished not according to geometrical dimensions but according to activity-related dimensions. The use of the term "information" derives from Gibson (1966), and not from Shannon and Weaver (1949). By convention, information reflects the level of uncertainty in the setting, but Gibson's use of the term defines information as the correspondence between environmental properties as they relate to the organism and the energy medium (e.g., light) patterned by those properties. Thus the metrics of activity within the environment are not related to some abstract and animal-independent scale (such as feet, inches, pounds, or feet per second but are environmentally and animal functional. An object passing across the visual field is not perceived as traveling at so many feet per second, at least at the first-order level. Rather questions are posed in such terms as "Can I reach it?" "Can I catch it?" "When will it hit me?" In other words, the organism acting within the environment asks "time-to-contact" questions about the moving object. This perspective is particularly important in performing the wide range of motor activities that require accurate anticipatory or coincident timing behavior (e.g., catching and hitting balls and other moving objects).

Current research on motor skills development focuses

mainly on an examination of information processing in motor skills, with the more controversial ecological perspective seen as a new and emerging focus.

Assessment of Motor Development. In addition to the obvious physiological benefits of muscular activity, a sound program of motor activities for a developing child enhances cognitive as well as physical development. It is the motor domain that first permits children to explore the environment by touching and feeling their surroundings (Piaget, 1952). It is little wonder, therefore, that much of the research activity among those interested in motor skill development has focused upon measuring and recording, across the stages in a child's life, the development of motor behavior. The majority of tests used are intended to provide parents, teachers, and others interested in a child's welfare with information to determine if the child's motor development is proceeding in coordination with the other components of development.

In order to test motor skills development, a distinction is usually drawn between what are termed "gross motor skills" and "fine motor skills." A gross motor skill involves the use and movement of the large joint complexes and is reflected in a child's ability to run, walk, climb, swing, and generally propel or manipulate his or her body by using large muscle actions. Fine motor skills are reflected in activities requiring dexterity, such as manipulations with the fingers, the catching of balls, and the development of various grips in order to manipulate a variety of toys, games, and puzzles.

A survey by Lewko (1974) reported the existence of 256 tests of motor ability, of which 91 were reported in the literature and 165 were, as of then, unpublished. Although a large number of available tests exist, their use is not as widespread as one might imagine. Many of the tests are not suitable for use by practitioners in the field. The tests reflect primarily three main approaches to the evaluation of a child's motor behavior. In the first or traditional approach, which is perhaps best termed "task-oriented" or "descriptive," a group of motor tasks are selected and children are compared individually in their performance with the average performance of children in their age-group. A second but smaller group of tests have been termed "process-oriented" and are used diagnostically. The process-oriented test attempts to determine what a child can do by inferring reasons for the child's performance. The third form of motor testing is reflex testing; the majority of these tests are conducted by personnel in the medical field.

Traditionally, the descriptive approach to testing as used by Bayley (1935), McGraw (1943), and Gesell (1940) determines the sequence of motor development by the careful collection of descriptive data and the charting of progress across chronological age; such tests are clearly the most popular. The milestones of motor development are charted and recorded to provide information regarding the age at which a child can perform different skills; this information can then be used to compare an individu-

als development with the average among age-group peers.

The value of many tests of motor development has been questioned recently because they lack a rationale for their construction. Criticism focuses on the fact that tests tend not to reflect the underlying developmental processes that change over time, but merely reflect the performance capabilities of a child at different stages of development. As might be expected, these stages are certainly neither culture-free nor free from a variety of influences which may impinge upon child's performance at any particular time on any particular test.

Educational Programming. An important consideration in motor development programs for children is recognition of the sensory-perceptual developments that take place in a growing child. Frostig (1970) places great emphasis on this in her approach to the programming of motor activities. From a sensory-perceptual viewpoint, we observe three major changes in a developing child that affect motor behavior. First, there is a shift in dominance in the sensory system. This is reflected in a developmental shift from tactile-kinesthetic (touching) dependence to a primary reliance on the visual system. Second, there is improved intersensory use, shown by a child's capacity to integrate information from several sensory inputs. Third, an improvement occurs in intrasensory discrimination. Again, these developmental changes are perhaps best reflected in the development of the visual system. As Williams (1973) has correctly noted, changes in all three of these basic sensory-perceptual processes play a vital role in a child's motor skill development by both refining and enhancing the precision with which perceptual information is processed.

The basic development in motor behavior from ages 5 through 18 is observed by improvements in five fundamental groups of motor tasks: jumping, running, throwing, balance, and skills involving foot work. Within these fundamental motor activities are a variety of motor skills in which children show improvement. Boys tend to improve up to the age of 18, whereas girls show improvement only up to the age of 14. Keogh (1973) notes that it is "unusual" in senior high school if a girl runs, throws, or jumps better than any but the more poorly performing boys.

Development in fundamental motor tasks is usually directly observable during the preschool and early school years, but as children grow older, a more complex analysis is usually required to detect the subtle changes in the nature and level of performance on these tasks. As children progress into adolescence, variability in their motor performance increases, and they change both socially and biologically at a rate that is different from their chronological development. Thus, chronological age may sometimes be a misleading indicator in the study of changes in motor behavior.

The idea that children pass through specific stages of development has spawned a variety of therapeutic programs designed to accelerate "slow" children to their appropriate level of motor development. Adherents of this motor development therapy (Kephart, 1960; Delacato, 1964; Doman, 1969) regard a child's motor development as proceeding from a bottom-up, unidirectional perspective. In a sense, this is an attempt to backtrack along the sensory-motor developmental trail. Evidence that a child has failed to reach an appropriate stage of motor development requires that the child return to an earlier stage of development in order to relearn the stages up to the point where the motor development went astray. This form of motor remedial work has sparked considerable controversy (Glass, 1967) and should be reviewed by students interested in motor skill development.

Research has demonstrated that programs and activities to develop the motor abilities of children during their formative years are integral to the processes of normal development. Programs of motor activity for young children should begin with emphasis on informality and self-discovery to allow them to appreciate their own movement capabilities. For young children, informal settings with play equipment encouraging a variety of large muscle movements is important. Developing children must appreciate the scope and potential of their motor apparatus before the refinements and constraints of formal skills are placed upon it. As strength, dexterity, endurance, and flexibility develop, children become receptive to the more formal motor skill activities that will become part of their experience. Assessment has its place in planning for motor development activities, but caution should be exercised, for group norms very often fail to reflect an individual's rate of development.

The opportunity to develop motor skills through informal play activity and later in planned physical education and in leisure time is essential to the optimal development of a child. Therefore, planned physical education and leisure are important in the educational curriculum, for they not only develop motor skills useful for both work and play but also play a major role in the socialization process and the development of sound interpersonal relationships.

Michael G. Wade

See also Physical Development; Readiness; Recreation; Rehabilitation Services.

REFERENCES

Bayley, N. The development of motor abilities during the first three years. *Monograph of the Society for Research in Child Development*, 1935, *1*, 1–26.

Bridgeman, C. S., & Carmichael, L. An experimental study of the onset of behavior in the fetal guinea pig. *Journal of General Psychology*, 1935, *47*, 247–267.

Carmichael, L. An experimental study in the prenatal guinea pig of the origin and development of reflexes and patterns of behavior in relation to stimulation of specific receptor areas during the period of active fetal life. *Genetic Psychological Monographs*, 1934, *16*, 337–491.

Coghill, G. E. *Anatomy and the Problem of Behavior*. New York: Cambridge University Press, 1929.

Connolly, K. J. Response speed, temporal sequencing, and information processing in children. In K. J. Connolly (Ed.), *Mechanisms of Motor Skill Development*. New York: Academic Press, 1970. (a)

Connolly, K. J. Skill development: Problems and plans. In K. J. Connolly (Ed.), *Mechanisms of Motor Skill Development*. New York: Academic Press, 1970. (b)

Delacato, C. H. *The Diagnosis and Treatment of Speech and Reading Problems*. Springfield, Ill.: Thomas, 1964.

Doman, R. J. Children with severe brain injuries: Neurological organization in terms of mobility. *Journal of American Medical Association*, 1960, *174*, 257–262.

Fitch, H. L., & Turvey, M. T. On the control of activity: Some remarks from an ecological point of view. In D. M. Landers, & R. W. Christina (Eds.), *Psychology of Motor Behavior and Sport*, Champaign, Ill.: Human Kinetics Press, 1977.

Fowler, C., & Turvey, M. T. Skill acquisition: An event approach with special reference to searching for the optimum of a function of several variables. In G. Stelmach (Ed.), *Information Processing in Motor Control and Learning*. New York: Academic Press, 1978.

Frostig, M. *Movement Education Theory and Practice*. Chicago: Follett, 1970.

Gesell, A. (Ed.). *The First Five Years of Life*. New York: Harper & Brothers, 1940.

Gibson, J. J. *The Senses Considered as Perceptual Systems*. Boston: Houghton Mifflin, 1966.

Glass, G. V. *A Critique of Experiments on the Role of Neurological Organization in Reading Performance*. Champaign: University of Illinois, Center for Instructional Research and Curriculum Evaluation, 1967. (ERIC Document Reproduction Service No. ED 013 523)

Keogh, J. Development in fundamental motor tasks. In C. B. Corbin (Ed.), *A Textbook of Motor Development*. Dubuque, Iowa: Brown, 1973.

Kephart, N. C. *The Slow Learner in the Classroom*. Columbus, Ohio: Merrill, 1960.

Kugler, P. N.; Kelso, J. A. S.; & Turvey, M. T. On the concept of coordinative structures as dissipative structures I: Theoretical lines. In G. E. Stelmach and J. Requin (Eds.), *Tutorials in Motor Behavior*. Amsterdam: North Holland, 1980.

Lewko, J. H. *The Identification of Tests Used in Assessing Motor Impairment*. Paper presented at the Symposium on Physical Education for the Handicapped: Implications for Research, University of Iowa, Iowa City, October 1974.

McGraw, M. G. *The Neuromuscular Maturation of the Human Infant*. New York: Columbia University Press, 1943.

Piaget, J. *The Origins of Intelligence in Children*. New York: International Universities Press, 1952.

Schneirla, T. C. Behavioral development and comparative psychology. *Quarterly Review of Biology*, 1966, *41*, 283–302.

Shannon, C. E., & Weaver, W. *The Mathematical Theory of Communication*. Urbana: University of Illinois Press, 1949.

Turvey, M. T.; Shaw, R. E.; & Mace, W. Issues in the theory of action: Degrees of freedom, coordinative structures, and coalitions. In J. Requin (Ed.), *Attention and Performance VII*. Hillsdale, N.J.: Lawrence Erlbaum Associates, 1978.

Wade, M. G. Developmental motor learning. In J. Keogh, & R. S. Hutton (Eds.), *Exercise and Sport Sciences Reviews* (Vol. 4). Santa Barbara, Calif.: Journal Publishing Affiliates, 1976.

Williams, H. G. Perceptual-motor development in children. In C. B. Corbin (Ed.), *A Textbook of Motor Development*. Dubuque, Iowa: Brown, 1973.

Windle, W. F. *Physiology of the Fetus: Origin and Extent of Function in Prenatal life.* Philadelphia: Saunders, 1940.

MULTICULTURAL AND MINORITY EDUCATION

Multicultural education as an important educational concept in the United States emerged in the 1960s and expanded significantly in the 1970s. A review of the index to the fourth edition of the *Encyclopedia of Educational Research* (1969) reveals only references to "Negroes (and) Minority Groups: politicization of, and textbook bias against" (p. xl). There are no references to multicultural education, bilingual education, Hispanic Americans, Native Americans, Spanish Americans, American Indians, or any of the terms in vogue during the past decade that relate to aspects of multicultural or minority education.

Multicultural awareness and sensitivity can probably be dated to the civil rights movement and the "war on poverty" of the Johnson administration (1964–1968) and the various sit-ins, boycotts, and freedom marches of that decade. During the 1970s an awareness grew of the nature of the different cultures that comprise the United States population; educators began to describe the nation as a salad bowl rather than a melting pot and argued in favor of a formal policy of cultural pluralism (Banks, 1977; Woessner, 1974; Jarolimek, 1979).

The National Council for the Accreditation of Teacher Education (NCATE) adopted a set of standards in 1977, which became effective on January 1, 1979. Standard 2.1.1., entitled Multicultural Education, states, "The institution gives evidence of planning for multicultural education in its teacher education curricula including both the general and professional studies components" (NCATE 1977, p. 4). Mohr (1977) traces the activities of the American Association of Colleges for Teacher Education in its efforts to assist NCATE in modifying its standards for accreditation of teacher education. The justification of standard 2.1.1. also provides the definition that is used throughout this article: multicultural education is preparation for the social, political, and economic realities that individuals experience in culturally diverse and complex human encounters (NCATE, 1977, p. 4).

The formalization of the concept of multicultural education is clearly an American phenomenon. On the international level, the research literature reveals little or no reference to the concept of multicultural education as it is practiced in the United States. The *International Dictionary of Education* (Page and Thomas, 1977) includes no definition for multicultural education but refers the reader to "Cross-cultural education/training," which is defined as "involving a mix of cultures as when a student brought up in one culture receives education at an institution which has the values of another culture" (p. 92). This is clearly an inadequate definition for multicultural education as it has evolved in the United States.

"Multicultural education" is a broader term than "multiethnic" or "bilingual education." In the United States "culture" has been used to include "ethnic heritage," "linguistic background," employment status (as in blue-collar culture), sex, age, race, and condition of handicap, as well as collective experience, such as the "drug culture." Clearly the majority of studies that focused on multicultural phenomena are related to ethnic and linguistic cultures.

This article deals specifically with multicultural education as it relates to teacher preparation and the education of students at the preschool, elementary, and secondary school levels, and with the future of multicultural education as it may affect policy concerning those levels. Multicultural education differs from international education, which traditionally has viewed the world in terms of discrete countries and cultures and more recently has begun to examine the interdependence of such systems as a basis for understanding culture and nation-specific behavior in international relations. Nor does multicultural education address specifically bilingual education, which is an important issue in itself but is specific to the appropriate approach by which instruction should take place for students whose primary language is other than standard English. Clearly certain policy decisions made about bilingual education can have important effects on multiculturalism and multicultural education; however, for purposes of this article discussion will be limited to the broader aspects of multicultural education as it relates to the preparation of teachers and the organization of the school curriculum.

Teacher Preparation. Led by a growing number of educators (Arciniega, 1978; Baker, 1972, 1976, 1977, 1978, 1979; Banks, 1977, 1979, 1980; Gay, 1975, 1979; Glazer, 1981; Sizemore, 1974, 1979; Smith & Otero, 1977) the educational profession realized during the 1970s that four important multicultural needs must be addressed: (1) the need to uphold sound academic standards in the training of teachers (Harris & Valverde, 1976; Mohr, 1977; Rodriguez, 1981); (2) the need to make maximal use of the learner's background and cultural context in the teacher/learner process (Werner, 1979); (3) the need for teachers of culturally diverse backgrounds who can reflect and address the particular concerns of various cultural groups (Chavers, 1979; Lindsay & Harris, 1976); and (4) the need for all teachers to be aware of and sensitive to the cultural differences among learners (Bennett, 1979; Grant, 1979). Not all educators of the 1970s have been enthralled by the term "multicultural" or the specific concept. For example, Grant (1978) argued forcefully that education in a pluralistic society is necessarily multicultural and that using the term "multicultural education" diminishes the importance of the concept.

Curriculum Impact. The authors took a 10 percent sample of the 3,000 titles reviewed for this article and found that nearly 95 percent were hortatory essays of one type or another. Justification for the various proposed instructional approaches was generally not based on research. The influence of cultural differences on curriculum has not been systematically investigated. Jensen (1980) published a comprehensive if controversial summary of cultural and ethnic differences in intelligence. Triandis (1977) proposed a theoretical framework for evaluating the effectiveness of six types of cross-cultural training: general, specific, affective, cognitive, behavioral, and self-inspired. Mitchelmore (1980) and Shar and Geeslin (1980) studying United States, English and Jamaican, and United States and Swiss students, respectively, found significant culture-related differences in how spatial figures are perceived and conceptualized. Wilson and Wilson (1979) found differences between American and Egyptian children related to influences on children's drawings. Feldman and Stone (1978) offered a "culture general" measure of cognitive development.

This article is not the appropriate place to summarize research on cultural or individual differences; however, it is clear that the effectiveness and justification of multicultural approaches to education are not supported by research findings. Moreover those cross-cultural cognitive differences that have been identified through research seldom find their way into discussions of multicultural education. Two recent and well-documented scholarly publications on the subject that point to the need for scholarly research and indicate the direction for future research are *America as a Multicultural Society* (Jones, 1981) and the special issue of the *Journal of Negro Education* on multicultural education in the International Year of the Child (Jones, 1979). Perhaps the sixth edition of the *Encyclopedia of Educational Research* will demonstrate that a research base for a multicultural curriculum has been found.

Alma G. Vasquez
Henry T. Ingle

See also American Indian Education; Asian-American Education; Black Education; Culture and Education Policy; Equity Issues in Education; Hispanic-American Education; Women's Education.

REFERENCES

Arciniega, T. A. *Planning and Organizational Reform Affecting Hispanics in Higher Education.* Paper presented at the Hispanic Education Conference, Alexandria, Va., 1978.

Baker, G. C. *The Effects of Training in Multi-ethnic Education on Preservice Teachers' Perceptions of Ethnic Groups.* Unpublished doctoral dissertation, University of Michigan, 1972.

Baker, G. C. Cultural diversity: Strength of the nation. *Educational Leadership,* 1976, *33,* 257–259.

Baker, G. C. Development of the multicultural program: School of Education, University of Michigan. In *Pluralism and the American Teacher: Issues and Case Studies.* Washington, D.C.: American Association of Colleges for Teacher Education, 1977, pp. 163–169.

Baker, G. C. The role of the school in transmitting the culture of all learners in a free and democratic society. *Educational Leadership,* 1978, *22,* 134–138.

Baker, G. C. Policy issues in multicultural education. *Journal of Negro Education,* 1979, *48*(3), 253–266.

Banks, J. A. *Multiethnic Education: Practices and Promises.* Bloomington, Ind.: Phi Delta Kappa Educational Foundation, 1977.

Banks, J. A. Shaping the future of multicultural education. *Journal of Negro Education,* 1979, *48*(3), 237–252.

Banks, J. A. *Multiethnic Education: Concepts, Issues, and Strategies.* Boston: Allyn & Bacon, 1980.

Bennett, C. T. The preparation of pre-service secondary social studies teachers in multiethnic education. *High School Journal,* 1979, *62*(5), 232–237.

Chavers, D. *The Revolution in Indian Education.* Paper presented at the annual symposium on the American Indian, Northeastern Oklahoma State University, 1979.

Ebel, R. L. (Ed.). *Encyclopedia of Educational Research* (4th ed.). New York: Macmillan, 1969.

Feldman, C. F., & Stone, A. The Colored Blocks Test: A culture-general measure of cognitive development. *Journal of Cross-cultural Psychology,* 1978, *9*(1), 3–22.

Gay, G. Organizing and designing culturally pluralistic curriculum. *Educational Leadership,* 1975, *33,* 176–183.

Gay, G. On behalf of children: A curriculum design for multicultural education in the elementary school. *Journal of Negro Education,* 1979, *48*(3), 324–340.

Glazer, N. Ethnicity and education: Some hard questions. *Phi Delta Kappan,* 1981, *62*(5), 386–389.

Grant, C. A. Education that is multicultural: Isn't that what we mean? *Journal of Teacher Education,* 1978, *29*(5), 45–48.

Grant, C. A. Education that is multicultural as a change agent: Organizing for effectiveness. *Journal of Negro Education,* 1979, *48*(3), 431–446.

Harris, B. M., & Valverde, L. A. Supervisors and educational change. *Theory into Practice,* 1976, *15*(4), 267–273.

Jarolimek, J. Born again ethics: Pluralism in modern America. *Social Education,* 1979, *43*(3), 204–209.

Jensen, A. R. *Bias in Mental Testing.* New York: Free Press, 1980.

Jones, F. C. (Ed.). *Journal of Negro Education,* 1979, *43*(3), special issue on multicultural education in the International Year of the Child.

Jones, G. M. (Ed.). *America as a Multicultural Society.* Annals of the American Academy of Political and Social Science. Philadelphia: Academy of Political and Social Science, 1981. Washington, D.C.: Harvard University Press, 1979.

Lindsay, B., & Harris, J. J., III. Contemporary philosophical directions of black-American higher education. *Urban League Review,* 1976, *2*(1), 10–18.

Mitchelmore, M. C. Three-dimensional geometrical drawing in three cultures. *Educational Studies in Mathematics,* 1980, *11*(2), 205–216.

Mohr, P. Accreditation standards for multicultural education. *Journal of Research and Development in Education,* 1977, *11*(1), 24–32.

National Council for the Accreditation of Teacher Education. *Standards for the Accreditation of Teacher Education.* Washington, D.C.: American Association of Colleges for Teacher Education, 1977.

Page, G. T., & Thomas, J. B. *International Dictionary of Education.* London: Anchor Press, 1977.

Rodriguez, F. *Accreditation and Teacher Education: A Multicultural Perspective.* Lawrence: University of Kansas, 1981.

Shar, A. O., & Geeslin, W. E. Children's spacial-perceptual preferences: A cross-cultural comparison. *Journal of Research In Multicultural Education*, 1980, *11*(2), 156–160.

Sizemore, B. A. Community power and education. In D. Della-Dora & J. E. House (Eds.), *Education for an Open Society*. Alexandria, Va.: Association for Supervision and Curriculum Development, 1974, pp. 109–135.

Sizemore, B. A. The four-M curriculum: A way to shape the future. *Journal of Negro Education*, 1979, *48*(3), 341–356.

Smith, G. R., & Otero, G. C. *Teaching about Cultural Awareness*. Denver: University of Denver, 1977.

Triandis, H. C. Theoretical framework for evaluation of cross-cultural training effectiveness. *International Journal of Intercultural Relations*, 1977, *1*(4), 19–45.

Werner, E. E. Cross-cultural child development: How children influence children. *Children Today*, 1979, *8*(2), 10–15.

Wilson, B., & Wilson, M. Figure structure, figure action, and framing in drawings by American and Egyptian children. *Studies in Art Education*, 1979, *21*(1), 36–43.

Woessner, H. Pluralism as a cultural trap: A clash of positive values in an epoch of operational freedom. *Journal of Instructional Psychology*, 1974, *1*(3), 39–40.

MULTIVARIATE ANALYSIS

Multivariate data arise—and multivariate statistical models may be employed—whenever the outcome of a survey, comparative study, or controlled experiment is best described by two or more conceptually related response measures, that is, whenever several criterion measures together define the response being studied. For example, the evaluation of an instructional unit may yield both a cognitive performance rating and an attitude-toward-the-topic score, or an assessment of an elementary school class may include performance scores in reading, mathematics, social studies, and science, or separate levels of cognitive complexity (e.g., knowledge, comprehension, and application of historical material) also, a word-learning experiment might yield both the number of words correctly memorized, and the time taken and personality-related research may be directed at relating subjects' background characteristics to multiple scales derived from the Rorshach, Minnesota Multiphasic Personality Inventory (MMPI), or other assessment instrument. In each of these examples the multiple response measures will probably have different degrees of nonzero intercorrelation and different variances. Although this is not the primary criterion for treating them as a multivariate set (after all, almost all behavioral measures are intercorrelated), it does suggest that some consideration be given to their different distributions in a statistical analysis.

"Repeated-measures" studies yield data that are inherently multivariate. In repeated-measures investigations each subject is measured on exactly the same scale at more than one time point or under more than one experimental condition. Thus these studies include longitudinal investigations in which the same subjects are measured repeatedly on the same index (e.g., verbal intelligence at 5, 7, 9, 11, and 13 years of age), instructional evaluations in which the same or parallel-form tests are administered before and after an instructional unit is presented (and perhaps later as a follow-up), learning studies with a fixed number of trials to attain mastery, and "within-subjects experiments" (such as asking the same students to produce correct answers to intellectual tasks in both a cooperative and a competitive situation).

The measures described in the examples would usually be considered the dependent variables of an investigation in which they are to be related to some other independent variables, that is, antecedent variables that describe the background of the subjects or the experimental manipulations. In traditional statistical analysis dependent variables are assumed to be random variables (unlike the independent variables that most often are not), and are described in terms of an underlying probability distribution, for example, the binomial or normal distribution. Random variables were dubbed "variates" by Fisher (1925), and thus investigations yielding multiple dependent variables are multivariate.

Are Multivariate Models Important? On the basis that behavior has multiple antecedents and that research outcomes have multiple facets, most behavioral research is multivariate. When a study yields multiple dependent variables, the researcher may consider several ways to approach the data analysis. One approach might be to combine the variates or subtests into a total or weighted total score, for example, a total achievement score formed by summing the knowledge, comprehension, and application subtests, or a factor score formed by weighting and summing all of the scales with a high loading on the first factor. Of course, all variation unique to specific subscales is lost, which perhaps defeats the purpose of collecting multiple measures in the first place. As a second approach, univariate tests of significance may be calculated for each scale separately; this approach often results in long tables of t statistics or F statistics and their significance levels. Since researchers make a number of tests of significance on variables that are correlated with one another, the probability of a Type I or Type II error may be inflated to many times the nominal level at which the investigators think they are working. As a result, many specific, and perhaps contradictory, findings are obtained, and the replicability of the study as a whole is reduced.

Multivarate statistical models yield tests and confidence intervals that apply to the entire set of dependent variables, without forming arbitrary linear combinations of the measures. Multivariate procedures use the intercorrelations among the scales and the variances of the separate measures as an explicit part of the calculations to obtain tests of significance that conform to the researcher-selected Type I (and Type II) error rates. They yield a single decision for each hypothesis pertaining to the data as a whole that has an increased probability of replicating, and provide a number of ways to assess and interpret each effect found significant.

For years the analysis of repeated-measures data has been conducted in a univariate mode, largely as described in the text by Lindquist (1954). More recently, social scientists have become aware that the univariate approach to these studies requires several strong and often unrealistic assumptions about the data. In this case in particular, multivariate models provide a valid set of procedures for a growing class of important behavioral studies.

Specific Multivariate Models. Two sets of procedures for analyzing multivariate data have arisen from different traditions. Factor analysis, and its more recent offspring "covariance structures analysis," require only the variances and covariances, or correlations, among the outcome measures as basic data. These techniques are directed toward the discovery of common human traits, that is, factors or latent variables, that underlie subsets of the observed behaviors. The techniques described here are directed toward analyzing the relationship of the outcome measures with other observed antecedent or independent variables.

When the independent variables comprise discrete categories, the analysis-of-variance (ANOVA) model allows for comparing the mean scores on the dependent measure across the categories. For example, if the independent variable is formed from several distinct experimental conditions, or nonexperimental categorical variables such as sex, school attended, or parents' occupational levels, the ANOVA model provides tests of significance among the experimental conditions or sex groups in mean response on the outcome measure. In addition to statistical tests, the "strength of effect" in ANOVA models is expressed in terms of contrasts among the means of specific groups (e.g., the difference between the mean response of children with professional and with nonprofessional parents). These planned comparisons, together with their standard errors, confidence intervals, and other functions that may be estimated from the mean response levels, provide a concise description of which groups differ from one another, and by how much.

When there is only one categorical independent variable, the model is the one-way or one-factor ANOVA model; when there are two or more categorical independent variables, the model is termed the two-way or two-factor ANOVA model, the three-way model, and so on. The latter are not multivariate models unless there is also more than a single dependent variable.

When the independent variables of an investigation are measures on scales that approach interval properties, the linear model to relate them to a measured outcome is the regression model. The independent variables—which may include test scores, teacher ratings, and amount of time spent on a learning task—are termed "predictor variables." When there is only a single predictor variable, the model is that of simple regression; when there are two or more predictors, the model is that of multiple regression. Multiple regression models also are not multivariate unless there is more than one dependent variable.

Tests of significance in regression analysis consist largely of determining whether the regression coefficients of the dependent variable on the independent variable(s) depart from zero. The predictors may be tested individually for their contribution to criterion variation or in sets. For example, "blockwise" regression provides a test of the simultaneous contribution of two or more conceptually related independent variables (e.g., several aptitude measures) to variation in the dependent measure. Strength of association in regression models is expressed in terms of the simple, partial, and multiple correlations of the predictor variables with the criterion, or else percentages of explainable variation.

When a research study has independent variables that are both categorical and measured (e.g., experimental group and aptitude), the model relating them to the dependent variable is analysis of covariance (ANCOVA). The covariance model allows for examining mean differences (e.g., between experimental groups), eliminating variation due to the "covariate" (aptitude), and for examining the correlation between the covariate and the criterion, eliminating between-group mean differences. Again, ANCOVA models are not multivariate models unless they incorporate more than a single outcome or dependent measure.

Because of the complexity of human behavior, many studies in education and the social sciences yield multiple antecedent measures, of which some are scale scores and others are categorical. A number of methodologically poor practices evolved over the years for dealing with this situation. These include "dummy coding" levels of a categorical independent variable to use it as a predictor in multiple regression analysis, and dichotomizing well-measured scales to include them in a several-factor ANOVA. The availability of general computer programs for ANCOVA that treat each type of variable in its natural metric has made these data-manipulating practices unnecessary.

Multivariate Forms of Models. Multivariate statistical models are written like familiar univariate models, except that each term is a vector with one element corresponding to each dependent variable. As a result, the usual tests of significance are obtained, but they pertain to the multiple outcomes simultaneously. For example, suppose that a random sample of males and females is drawn from a given population, and each individual is randomly assigned to an "experimental" or "traditional" educational program. Suppose, further, that each subject is tested at the end of instruction on three achievement subtests measuring knowledge, comprehension, and the ability to apply the material that was taught. A two-way multivariate ANOVA would be appropriate to compare the mean responses of males and females, and of experimental and nonexperimental instructional groups, for the set of three outcome measures. Such a model could be represented algebraically as

$$y_{ijk} = \mu + \alpha_j + \beta_k + (\alpha\beta)_{jk} + \epsilon_{ijk} . \qquad (1)$$

In model (1) all terms are three-element vectors. For example, y_{ijk} represents the response for observation i in group jk of the 2×2 sampling design. It has three elements, that is, the observed scores for the individual on three achievement subtests. Vectors α_1 and α_2 have three elements representing the effect of being a male or female, respectively, on the means of the three subtests. That is,

$$\alpha_1 = \begin{bmatrix} \alpha_1 \text{ (knowledge)} \\ \alpha_1 \text{ (comprehension)} \\ \alpha_1 \text{ (application)} \end{bmatrix} \qquad (2)$$

$$\text{and} \quad \alpha_2 = \begin{bmatrix} \alpha_2 \text{ (knowledge)} \\ \alpha_2 \text{ (comprehension)} \\ \alpha_2 \text{ (application)} \end{bmatrix} .$$

Statistically, the multivariate ANOVA provides a test of significance of the difference between these vectors. More operationally, this is a test of whether the three means for males are significantly different from the set of three means for females. The null hypothesis is that males and females score equally on the three achievement measures; statistically, this is

$$H_{0_1} : \alpha_1 = \alpha_2 . \qquad (3)$$

Likewise, β_1 contains the effects of being in the experimental group, and β_2 the effects of being in the nonexperimental group, on each of the three subtests. That is,

$$\beta_j = \begin{bmatrix} \beta_j \text{ (knowledge)} \\ \beta_j \text{ (comprehension)} \\ \beta_j \text{ (application)} \end{bmatrix} . \qquad (4)$$

The multivariate ANOVA provides a test of the difference between these vectors. Behaviorally, this is a test of whether there is a significant difference between the mean responses of the experimental and the nonexperimental groups on the set of three outcomes. The null hypothesis is that experimental and nonexperimental groups have the same mean response levels, or

$$H_{0_2} : \beta_1 = \beta_2 . \qquad (5)$$

The interaction terms also are vectors—one for each cell in the sampling design—and the multivariate ANOVA provides a test of whether there is any interaction for one or more of the subtests. The null hypothesis is that there is none, that is,

$$H_{0_3} : \text{All } (\alpha\beta)_{jk} = 0, \qquad (6)$$

where 0 is a vector containing three zeros. It should be apparent that these are the same hypotheses as tested in a two-way univariate ANOVA, except that each test of significance pertains to the set of outcome measures: knowledge, comprehension, and application.

Multivariate regression models also parallel their univariate forms, with vectors representing multiple dependent variables. For example, suppose we wished to study the relationship of mathematical aptitude and interest in mathematics to school performance. Performance, in turn, may be assessed by a three-part test with subtests for computation, concepts, and problem solving. Because there are three dependent variables, a multivariate multiple regression model would be appropriate. This is represented algebraically as

$$y_i = \alpha + x_{i1}\beta_1 + x_{i2}\beta_2 + \epsilon_i . \qquad (7)$$

The model is similar to a two-predictor univariate regression model, except that each of the terms representing the dependent variables is a three-element vector. For example, y_i is a vector with three mathematics subtest scores for subject i; α is a set of three scaling constants, that is, a different constant term for each subtest. If x_{i1} is the score for subject i on aptitude, then β_1 is a vector of three regression weights, reflecting the relationship of aptitude to each of the three outcomes. That is,

$$\beta_1 = \begin{bmatrix} \beta_1 \text{ (computation)} \\ \beta_1 \text{ (concepts)} \\ \beta_1 \text{ (problem solving)} \end{bmatrix} . \qquad (8)$$

Likewise, β_2 may be a three-element vector of weights relating interest in mathematics to each of the response measures.

A researcher with these data would be interested in whether there is a significant relationship between aptitude and some or all of the three learning outcomes, and whether there is a significant relationship between interest and learning. The multivariate model provides a test of significance for each of these questions in the form of a test of whether the respective set of regression weights has one or more nonzero elements. The null hypotheses for aptitude and interest, respectively, are

$$H_{0_1} : \beta_1 = 0 \quad \text{and} \quad H_{0_2} : \beta_2 = 0. \qquad (9)$$

Alternately, the researcher may wish to test whether the two predictors jointly are related to the three outcomes. This question would be more meaningful if the independent variables were several aspects of the same general phenomenon (e.g., x_i = mother's aspirations for the child and x_2 = father's aspirations for the child). As in univariate multiple regression models, a single "blockwise" test of significance is obtained in the multivariate multiple regression model. The null hypothesis may be stated as

$$H_0 : \beta_1 = \beta_2 = 0. \qquad (10)$$

The multivariate extension of the ANCOVA model follows the same pattern. To take a simple example, assume that an experiment was run in which there were two groups of subjects—experimental and control—and an aptitude measure *(x)* was taken before the experiment was begun. If there were also several outcome measures, the multivariate model for relating both experimental conditions and aptitude to the response vector would be

$$y_{ij} = \mu + \alpha_j + x_{ij}\beta + \epsilon_{ij}. \quad (11)$$

Both α_j and β are vectors with as many elements as dependent variables.

In this situation the researcher may wish to determine whether there is a significant difference between the two groups on the dependent variables, eliminating the effect of aptitude, and if aptitude is significantly related to the outcomes within the experimental or control condition or both. Multivariate ANCOVA provides tests for both questions. In algebraic form the tests are of the null hypotheses

$$H_{0_1} : \alpha_1 = \alpha_2 \quad \text{and} \quad H_{0_2} : \beta = 0. \quad (12)$$

How Are Multivariate Tests Obtained?   The principles by which multivariate tests of significance are obtained parallel those for univariate models, but are more complex mathematically. In each of the univariate models a measure of the relationship of each independent variable to the criterion is obtained, and compared with a "baseline" measure that might be obtained if there were no relationship. For example, in analysis of variance a measure of the differences among means (mean square between groups) is calculated, and compared directly with a measure of differences among individuals within the same group (mean square within groups). In regression analysis the proportion of variation attributable to a particular predictor variable or set of predictors is compared directly with the proportion of variation in the criterion not attributable to the predictor(s); these too are often expressed as mean squares—that is, mean-square regression and mean-square residual, respectively.

A similar comparison is made in multivariate analysis, except that each measure of an effect is expressed as a table or matrix. That is, criterion variation is partitioned into multiple "sources" as it would be in univariate ANOVA or regression analysis. However, when there are several dependent variables, variation is expressed as a table containing the variance of each of the separate measures *and* the covariation of each pair of measures. Thus in the two-way ANOVA example the total variation in the three dependent variables would be expressed as a matrix having three rows and three columns. The magnitude of the A main effect would be reflected in a 3×3 matrix, the magnitude of the B main effect in a 3×3 table, and so on. Variation among individuals within groups would be expressed as a 3×3 table of variances and covariances among the three dependent variables, and is termed the "pooled-within-group variance–covariance matrix."

Likewise, multivariate regression analysis yields a partition of variation with each effect represented as an entire matrix, including the residual variation and covariation.

The algebra of these partitions may be found in any standard reference on multivariate procedures and is not repeated here. However, the most important implication is that each test of significance involves comparing an effect represented by an entire matrix of values with another entire matrix representing within-group or residual variation and covariation. As a result, unlike univariate analyses with a single most powerful test procedure (the F ratio), there are several ways to obtain multivariate tests of significance; each is most useful in some situations.

One set of test statistics produces a numerical value that, together with its "degrees of freedom," may be referred to an appropriate distribution to reach a single decision about H_0 for all dependent measures simultaneously. These procedures—including Wilks's likelihood-ratio test, Hotelling's trace statistic, and Pillai's trace statistic—would allow us to maintain or reject each of the three null hypotheses in the two-way analysis of variance example for all three dependent variables jointly. The investigator would then have to determine which of the three measures, or combinations of the measures, are responsible for the mean differences that are found. Similarly, these statistics would provide a single decision for each hypothesis in the regression analysis or ANCOVA models. They allow for exploring a wide range of alternate hypotheses, and seem to be the most commonly used multivariate procedures.

A second type of multivariate test procedure is particularly appropriate when the dependent variables have an inherent order by time or complexity. The step-down tests of Roy and Bargmann (1958) produce as many test statistics for each hypothesis as there are dependent variables; the null hypothesis is rejected if any one step-down test is significant. In comparing means in the two-way ANOVA example, the step-down analysis would test whether there is a significant difference between groups on the first criterion alone (knowledge), a significant difference between groups on the second criterion variable (comprehension) above and beyond differences attributable to knowledge alone, or a significant difference between groups on the third dependent variable (application) that is not attributable just to knowledge and comprehension, and so on. In testing the impact of one or more predictors in regression analysis, the step-down tests reveal whether there is a significant relationship of the predictor(s) to the first dependent variable alone, a significant association with the second dependent variable above and beyond that with the first, and so on. The step-down tests—unlike all of the other test procedures—are specific to the order of the dependent variables and are only likely to be of value when there is an obvious order. For example, there is a logical ordering of the cognitive achievement tests in terms of levels of complexity from knowledge to comprehension to application, but not for mathematical computations, concepts, and problem solving. In the repeated-measures example in a later section, step-down analysis is used to test growth patterns of increasing complexity, that is, linear, quadratic, and cubic trends.

A third set of test statistics is obtained by finding a linear combination of the criterion measures that has maximal association with the independent variables. For example, suppose we are testing sex differences in the hypothetical two-way ANOVA problem with three dependent variables (y_1 = knowledge, y_2 = comprehension, y_3 = application). Then the "discriminant variable" is a new variable formed as a weighted composite of the original three measures, that is,

$$y^* = a_1 y_1 + a_2 y_2 + a_3 y_3 .$$

The weights (a_1, a_2, a_3) are calculated specifically so that the new measure y^* has the maximum possible ratio of "mean square between sex groups" to "mean square within sex groups," that is, the maximum F ratio for sex of any possible combination of the original y's. Given a new measure formed empirically in this manner, the "maximal" F ratio for sex differences may be tested for significance; Roy's largest root criterion, variations on Wilks's likelihood ratio, and Bock's generalized F statistic are appropriate for this purpose. In testing differences among more than two groups, more than a single discriminant variable may be calculated, each with different weights representing differences among group means on additional dimensions; each discriminant variable may be tested for significance separately, providing a picture of the "dimensionality" of between-group differences.

The multivariate multiple regression model (multiple predictors, multiple dependent variables) allows a parallel set of tests. In this case a linear composite of criterion variables is formed that has maximal correlation with a different linear composite of the predictors. The correlation of these two specially formed composites is the "canonical correlation" of the dependent and independent variables, and may be tested for significance in the same manner as the discriminant variables in analysis of variance.

There is some debate among statisticians regarding the most appropriate test statistic for particular situations, especially since computer programs generally print several tests, and one program prints all of them (Finn, 1978). Comparisons have been made of the relative robustness and power of several of the tests in limited situations (Olson, 1976; Stevens, 1979), although experience indicates that in most educational studies they show a high degree of consistency. Statisticians agree that Roy's largest root statistic and Bock's generalized F statistic are more apt to detect group mean differences in a single dimension—that is, when confined to a single composite variable y^*—and that step-down procedures are preferable when the dependent variables have a clear inherent order. Otherwise the simplest or most easily available statistic may be used. All of the multivariate tests of significance reduce to the common univariate F ratio when there is only one dependent variable. Thus univariate models may be viewed as a specialization of the more general multivariate case.

What Assumptions Are Required? The distributional assumptions of multivariate analysis of variance, covariance, or regression parallel those of the common univariate forms. First, observations must be independent of one another; that is, one subject must be responding independently of all others. This may be accomplished by sampling subjects at random and designing the experimental setting so that subjects respond without reference to one another. On the other hand, the multiple dependent variables need not be independent of another, and we would generally expect multiple outcomes to be conceptually and statistically related. Second, the multivariate parallel to the usual homogeneity-of-variance requirement is that the matrix of variances and covariances among the dependent variables must be the same in the populations represented by all groups of a sampling design or, in regression models, the same regardless of the values of the independent variables; that is, there should be "homogeneity of variance–covariance matrices" for multivariate tests. And last, the common forms of multivariate analysis discussed here are based on an assumption of variates that have a multivariate normal distribution. Although this is a complex requirement, it will usually have been met if each separate dependent variable has a normal distribution; this is one of several implications of multivariate normality.

There has been some limited work on the robustness of multivariate procedures with regard to these assumptions. In general, the findings parallel those for univariate models; that is, data may be drawn from relatively nonnormal distributions without affecting the analysis adversely. Also, variance–covariance matrices may differ somewhat, as long as the number of subjects in the different treatment groups is nearly equal. The assumption of independence is the *sine qua non* of assumptions, and cannot easily be circumvented. For further details of this work see Harris (1975).

What Else Can Be Revealed? In multivariate analysis, as in univariate analysis, obtaining tests of significance is only one aspect of explaining effects present in a data set. In addition, the behavioral scientist is interested in identifying particular groups that may differ from others or particular dependent variables that are affected. When the independent variables define discrete categories of subjects (e.g., sex or experimental condition), this is accomplished in multivariate analysis—as in its univariate counterpart—by examining contrasts among the means of particular preselected groups. Once the researcher decides exactly how to compare groups, a multivariate confidence interval may be drawn on mean differences for a set of dependent variables simultaneously, so that the difference for every specific variable has a specified confidence level. Also, a contrast between means for a set of variables may be converted to a single "distance between mean vectors" measure, Mahalanobis's D index; or a multivariate comparison may be expressed in terms of a standardized index, Hotelling's T^2. Thus, from tables of contrasts among pre-specified groups for multiple measures, the researcher may isolate the groups that are most different, and estimate the magnitude of the difference in raw and standardized form.

The discriminant variables offer one way to find the particular variables that discriminate among groups. Some researchers have attempted to use the discriminant weights (a_i) as relative indicators of the importance of each dependent variable. However, the weights depend on the particular set of outcome variables in a given analysis, and on their intercorrelations in particular. Thus the conclusions that are drawn are highly conditional and sometimes misleading. Instead, multivariate analysis allows a direct means for identifying the most affected dependent variable out of a set. Computer programs for multivariate tests of significance also calculate the simple univariate F statistic for each dependent variable separately. Once a null hypothesis is rejected by employing a multivariate test criterion, the univariate statistics are relatively good indicators of which variables have significant between-group differences, and of which are related to the predictor variables and which are not (Hummel & Sligo, 1971). Even if the multivariate test is not significant, the univariate statistics may be compared to provide a direct and simple determination of which variable has the strongest relationship to the independent variables (or largest between-group difference), which is next, and so on.

The strength of association of predictors and criteria in multivariate regression is revealed by the simple and multiple correlations of each criterion measure with the predictors. Also, the canonical correlation analysis may be used to obtain an index of overall association of the two sets of variables. Unfortunately, the canonical correlation weights, like the discriminant weights, may add more complexity to the interpretation of data than their advantages would warrant. Simpler correlation measures and percentages of explained variation usually yield a clearer description of the data.

Uses of Matrix Algebra. Education and social science research has survived for years without resorting to the algebra of matrices. It has not been without cost, however. Even univariate data arise in vectors, and many of the operations we represent with complex double-, triple-, and higher-order summations are more easily carried out in one or two matrix multiplications. Further, multivariate data arise in two-dimensional arrays (matrices); even a set of mean scores requires vector or matrix representation, whereas dispersions must include variances *and* covariances among the dependent variables. It is possible to be a user of multivariate methods without any knowledge of matrix algebra through the use of sophisticated computer programs. It is our view that simple matrix algebra and basic concepts of factoring matrices are necessary to understand multivariate reasoning and, further, are sufficient for all but those who intend to specialize in this methodology.

On the other hand, matrix manipulations are essential

to multivariate computer programs. This requisite has had the effect of opening up a much larger array of possible computations, including those involving the independent variables. For example, an exact least-squares procedure for ANOVA designs with unequal numbers of subjects in the various groups is not possible in scalar algebra for any but the simplest designs. Basic univariate textbooks have adhered to the unrealistic restriction of equal N's, but no multivariate analysis computer program need be so restricted. Thus the multivariate "general linear model" allowing measured predictor variables as well as ANOVA classification factors creating unequal-N designs is a natural outgrowth of applying multivariate techniques. The examples that follow demonstrate these procedures while focusing primarily on the "multivariateness" of the data. Other developments also have been made possible. These include blockwise regression features in which several predictor variables may be tested simultaneously for their contribution to the dependent variable(s) and trend analysis in which the groups are not evenly spaced. For example, a polynomial over time could not traditionally have been fitted to growth data if children were measured at, say, 2, 4, 8, and 24 months of age.

Multivariate Analysis Texts and Computer Programs. There is a growing number of texts on multivariate analysis, some written for the statistician and some for the researcher with less mathematical sophistication. Among the latter, several are particularly lucid and useful. *Multivariate Statistical Methods in Behavioral Research* by Bock (1975) is the most thorough, with much detail and many examples. The monograph by Finn and Mattsson (1978) describes basic multivariate concepts in a very simple non-mathematical fashion, and provides real-data examples run with the MULTIVARIANCE program. Books by Harris (1975), Tatsuoka (1971), and Maxwell (1977) describe multivariate concepts in particularly clear terms, and are excellent reference volumes. Texts by Morrison (1976), Timm (1975), and Finn (1974) present multivariate statistical theory with a stronger mathematical orientation.

Six major computer programs for the multivariate general linear model are capable of performing most or all of the analyses described here: MULTIVARIANCE (Finn, 1978); MANOVA (Cramer, 1974); SAS procedure, GLM (Goodnight, 1976); ACOVSM (Jöreskog, van Thillo, & Gruvaeus, 1971); and SPSS program MANOVA (Cohen & Burns, 1976). Bock and Brandt (1980) reviewed the first five of these; all five perform the identical analysis for testing the same multivariate hypothesis. They differ however in their approach to unequal-N designs, analysis of covariance, and the estimation of effects. MULTIVARIANCE is the only program with automated features for multivariate repeated-measures analysis, and was used in analyzing the data for the examples in the following sections.

Two-way multivariate analysis of variance. The data for this example were obtained from the U.S. Office for Civil Rights by the National Academy of Sciences as part

TABLE 1. *Percentage of minority and white students enrolled in special education classes in the United States, 1978/79 school year*

Program	Minority	White	Log-odds index
Educable mentally retarded (EMR)	2.54	1.06	.89
Trainable mentally retarded (TMR)	.42	.29	.37
Seriously emotionally disturbed (SED)	.33	.19	.55
Specific learning disabilities (SLD)	2.29	2.30	.01
Speech impaired (SI)	1.82	2.02	−.09
None of the above	92.60	94.12	

of an investigation of the disproportionate placement of minorities and males in classes for the mentally retarded. Although the observations were not all chosen at random, they are treated as if they were in order to simplify the example.

It has often been noted that minority students are placed in classes for the educable mentally retarded (EMR) in greater proportions than their nonminority peers. For example, Table 1 gives the national percentage of minority and white students in EMR classes and in four other special education programs during the 1978/79 school year. It is clear that the largest disproportion occurs in EMR placements, the second largest disproportion in seriously emotionally disturbed (SED) placements (although many fewer children are affected), while about equal percentages of whites and minorities are classified as having specific learning disabilities.

To understand the characteristics of districts in which the "overrepresentation" of minorities occurs, data were drawn from the 1978 school survey conducted by the Office for Civil Rights of the U.S. Department of Education. The observations chosen were 433 school districts whose total enrollment is 10,000 students or greater, sampled at random from throughout the country. These districts were classified by geographic region (Northeast, Border, South, Midwest, and West) and the percentage of minority students (0–20, 20–40, 40–60, 60–80, 80–100) enrolled. Cell sizes (N's) in the two-way classification are highly unequal.

The dependent variables provided by each district were five measures of racial disproportion: a scaled index of the difference between the proportion of the district's minority students that are enrolled in EMR classes and the proportion of white students in EMR classes, and four similarly scaled indices of the difference between white and minority percentages in the four other special education programs: trainable mentally retarded, seriously emotionally disturbed, specific learning disability, and speech impaired. The scaled index of the minority-white difference in proportions is the "log-odds ratio," which is positive in districts where minorities are overrepresented in a special classification, relative to whites. It is negative if a smaller proportion of a district's minorities are enrolled in the special program than the proportion of the district's

whites. And it is zero if the proportions for both minorities and whites in a program are equal. For example, the "odds" for minority students in EMR classes is the proportion in EMR relative to the proportion in no special classification. From Table 1 this is 2.54/92.60 = .027; the EMR odds for whites is 1.06/94.12 = .011. The log-odds ratio is the difference of the natural logarithms of the two odds, or ln(.027) − ln(.011) = .89, for EMR placements in the entire country. The distribution of the log-odds ratio is highly normal and homoscedastistic for sampling units of the same general size. (For further detail, see Bishop, Feinberg, & Holland, 1975.) The five disproportion indices were calculated for each of the 433 districts in the sample.

The average disproportion for each special education program in each geographic region is given in Table 2. The correlations among the measures of disproportion and their dispersions are described most succinctly by the pooled within-group correlation matrix and standard deviations (Table 3). The pattern of generally positive correlations indicates a tendency for minorities to be overrepresented in several special education classifications simultaneously. The exception appears to be TMR classes, for which racial differences in placement rates are not highly associated with placement differences in other programs.

The analysis of these data may proceed from the most global tests and findings to the more specific. Table 4 presents the five-variate tests of significance of mean differences among geographic regions (factor A), mean differences across different degrees of minority composition (factor B), and the interaction (i.e., whether the differences among geographic regions are the same regardless of the districts' minority enrollment). Both the likelihood ratio and trace criteria are transformed to approximate F statistics. The conversion sometimes produces fractional degrees of freedom, which may be rounded to the next lower whole number when using the F table, whereas the MULTIVARIANCE program and several others have accurate algorithms for evaluating the F probabilities for the fractional values.

Both test criteria indicate significant differences among regions and among different degrees of minority enrollment in the extent to which there are minority-white spe-

TABLE 2. *Mean log-odds index by region, and by percentage of minority enrollment*

Region	N	Special education classification				
		EMR	TMR	SED	SLD	SI
Northeast	49	.87	−.09	.63	.08	−.01
Border	36	.72	.60	.69	.08	−.20
South	204	1.42	.65	.11	−.02	.13
Midwest	68	.66	.00	.36	.12	.03
West	76	.44	−.01	−.02	.17	.03
Percentage of minority enrollment						
0–20%	197	.90	.43	.51	.15	.07
20–40	123	1.28	.36	.20	.13	.12
40–60	55	1.20	.35	−.01	−.25	.06
60–80	35	.77	.16	−.32	−.04	−.20
80–100	23	.45	−.28	−.60	−.27	−.05

TABLE 3. *Pooled within-group correlations and standard deviations*

Special education classification	Standard deviation	Correlations				
		EMR	TMR	SED	SLD	SI
EMR	.62	1.00				
TMR	.69	.16	1.00			
SED	.79	.17	.05	1.00		
SLD	.60	.38	−.07	.22	1.00	
SI	.60	.26	.02	.04	.24	1.00

cial education disproportions. Further, there is no interaction of these two factors; to the extent that the means of the five dependent variables differ across regions, they differ by the same amount regardless of the districts' percent of minority enrollment.

The discriminant analysis of the same data showed that three different linear combinations of the five dependent variables discriminate significantly among geographic regions; two linear composites, with a third marginally significant at .01, discriminate significantly among levels of minority enrollment. As initially there are only five criterion measures, reduction of the data to three linear combinations of the disproportion measures does not provide a worthwhile simplification.

Having found the main effects significant, a more detailed description of how the subgroups of the design differ is provided by examining (1) mean differences on particular dependent variables, and (2) contrasts among the means of specific groups of districts. As an example of the former, we may reexamine the minority enrollment factor. The effect was found to be significant for all five special education measures jointly. Multivariate computer programs also produce the F ratio among minority enrollment levels for each disproportion measure separately.

The univariate statistics are *not* tests of the multivariate hypothesis, and their significance levels bear no necessary relationship to that of the multivariate tests. For example, the multivariate test statistic may exceed a .05 or .01 critical value, while none, one, a few, or all of the univariate statistics are significant. Conversely, the multivariate test may be nonsignificant, as it is for the interaction, and some of the univariate statistics nevertheless may exceed their respective critical values. These apparent discrepancies emphasize the importance of choosing a multivariate model when the response measures form a meaningful set. The F ratios are useful for identifying the specific variables that are most and least affected. The univariate F ratios for differences by minority enrollment for the five special education categories are $F_{EMR} = 9.59$; $F_{TMR} = 8.44$; $F_{SED} = 17.83$; $F_{SLD} = 6.54$; $F_{SI} = 2.09$. Each has 4 and 408 degrees of freedom, and each exceeds the .01 critical value, except F_{SI} for speech impairment.

From these univariate results we see that racial disproportion in the identification of speech-impaired children is not related to the minority enrollment of a district. However, minority-white differences in programs for the seriously emotionally disturbed are the most strongly related to the percentage of a school district's enrollment that is

TABLE 4. *Multivariate analysis of variance of special education disproportions*

Source of variation	Degrees of freedom	Tests of significance					
		Likelihood ratio	F approximation	Degrees of freedom	Hotelling's trace	F approximation	Degrees of freedom
Grand mean *(M)*	1	—	—		—	—	—
Region *(A)* eliminating *M, B*[a]	4	.52	14.68[b]	20, 1340.9	.81	16.36[b]	20, 881
Percent minority *(B)* eliminating *M, A*[a]	4	.71	7.36[b]	20, 1340.9	.38	7.59[b]	20, 881
Interaction *(AB)* eliminating *M, A, B*[a]	16	.78	1.28	80, 1949.2	.25	1.28	80, 1485

[a] The general least-squares analysis for unequal *N*'s requires ordering the main effects and interactions for a "stepwise" sequence of hypothesis tests.
[b] Significant at $p < .01$.

minority. The mean responses in Table 2 show that minority overrepresentation in SED decreases monotonically as the percent of minorities in the district increases. When minorities make up a small portion of the district's enrollment, greater percentages of minorities than of whites are classified as disturbed; when a district's enrollment is about one-half white and one-half minority, about equal proportions of minorities and whites are classified as emotionally disturbed; and when minorities constitute most of a district's enrollment, greater percentages of whites are assigned to SED programs. (Tests of significance not presented here confirm that there is no deviation from the significant linear effect for the SED placement trend.) These data suggest strongly that the predominant racial/ethnic group in a district defines behavior norms against which other groups may be compared, making it more likely for the latter to be classified as emotionally disturbed.

The second most affected measure is minority-white disproportion in EMR placements. Minorities are overrepresented in EMR classes, on the average, regardless of a district's racial composition. However, the difference in proportions is largest when minorities comprise 20 to 40 percent of a district's enrollment, close to that value for 40 to 60 percent minority enrollment, and smallest in districts where there are few minorities and in those where minorities predominate. (The parabolic relationship of disproportion to minority enrollment may be confirmed through a test of significance for a quadratic trend, which is possible in either the univariate or multivariate model.) It has been hypothesized that educators' concepts of adequate performance are based on the predominant racial/ethnic group in a school or district. These data partially support that hypothesis. In districts with high minority enrollment the overrepresentation of minorities in EMR classes is less. However, alternate explanations of the data are also possible. For example, districts with high minority enrollment may also be recipients of more funds for other special programs (e.g., Title I) that may obviate the need to classify as many students as educable mentally retarded.

A second approach to examining significant multivariate effects in more detail is to focus on contrasts among the means of specific groups, for example, the five geographic regions. Different researchers may choose to examine different contrasts, depending on the major purposes of the investigation; this choice is made in the same way regardless of whether the analysis is univariate or multivariate. For purposes of the example, the mean disproportion in each part of the country is compared with that for the West. The choice may have been made for several reasons. For example, western states have been shown in other studies, as confirmed in this investigation, to have nearly equal proportions of whites and minorities classified as retarded. Further, the western region is dominated by California, which, under recent court mandate to eliminate intelligence tests as a criterion for EMR placement, has reduced dramatically the overall size of its program for the mentally retarded. Thus we shall focus on comparisons:

$$\Psi_1 = \alpha_{\text{Northeast}} - \alpha_{\text{West}}$$
$$\Psi_2 = \alpha_{\text{Border}} - \alpha_{\text{West}}$$
$$\Psi_3 = \alpha_{\text{South}} - \alpha_{\text{West}}$$
$$\Psi_4 = \alpha_{\text{Midwest}} - \alpha_{\text{West}}$$

Each of the α's represents the effect on the means for a particular part of the country, so that each Ψ represents a set of mean differences between two parts of the country. For example, Ψ is a vector containing five numbers, the difference between the average disproportion index for northeastern states, and the average disproportion in the West, in five special education classifications.

The mean differences are presented in Table 5 in both univariate and multivariate form. Each difference was divided by the pooled within-group standard deviation of the specific measure to obtain the number of standard deviations between each region and the West. For example, the racial disproportion in EMR in the Northeast is 1.71 standard deviations higher than that in the West; in the southern states it is 3.46 standard deviations greater than in the West; and so on. It is clear that all sections of the country have greater EMR disproportions than the

TABLE 5. *Contrasts among geographic regions, in standard deviations and as T statistics*

Difference	EMR		TMR		SED		SLD		SI		All		
	SDs	t^a	SDs	t^a	SDs	t^a	SDs	t^a	SDs	t^a	D	T^2	F^b
Northeast–West	1.71	4.15c	−.03	−.06	2.19	5.31c	−.26	−.63	−.02	−.05	2.96	51.39	10.18c
Border–West	1.02	2.24	1.88	4.15c	1.84	4.06c	−.47	−1.04	−.89	−1.95	2.96	42.67	8.45c
South–West	3.46	11.28c	2.40	7.80c	.63	2.04	−.59	−1.92	.41	1.33	4.35	200.37	39.68c
Midwest–West	.74	1.99	.07	.18	.98	2.61c	−.27	−.72	−.05	−.12	1.38	13.62	2.70

[a] Each *t* statistic has 408 degrees of freedom.   [b] Each *F* statistic has 5 and 404 degrees of freedom.   [c] Significant at $p < .01$ (two-tailed test).

western states. Also, the border and southern states exceed the West in TMR disproportion and all regions—especially the northeast—exceed the West in disproportion in emotional disturbance. Finally, the five regions of the country have relatively small racial differences in SLD and SI programs.

Hotelling's D statistic is a multivariate analog of the mean difference in standard deviation units, but pertains to all five disproportion measures. To obtain the D index a new variable is formed that is the linear composite of the five special education measures with maximal between-group variation relative to the variance within groups (this is identically the discriminant function for the particular contrast). Then D is the number of within-group standard deviations separating group means on the new composite variable. From Table 5 it can be seen that for the set of five disproportion measures the northeastern and border states are unlike the West to about the same extent (2.96 standard deviations). The South is most unlike the West in the overall extent of racial disproportion (4.35 standard deviations), and the Midwest is most like the West. Thus D enables the researcher to locate groups that are the most similar or most dissimilar when there are multiple criterion variables.

Either the univariate or multivariate differences can be converted to test-statistic form. For the separate special education measures, these are *t* tests of the specific planned contrasts. For the multivariate difference, the analog of the *t* test is Hotelling's T^2 statistic. Further, T^2 may be transformed into an *F* test so that commonly available tables may be used to test the significance of a particular contrast. From Table 5 it can be seen that all regions of the country except the Midwest differ significantly from the West in their racial disproportions in special education; three of the T^2 statistics, and thus their corresponding *F* statistics, exceed the .01 critical value. The tests for separate special education programs indicate that the disproportion in different programs depends on the region: In the Northeast disproportion is higher than in the West in EMR and SED classes. In the border states disproportion is higher than in the West in TMR and SED. In the South—with the largest discrepancy from the West—disproportion is higher in EMR and TMR programs. These contrasts, in univariate and multivariate form, provide the most con-

cise and yet complete description of effects in fixed-effects ANOVA designs.

Multivariate regression and covariance. Two additional variables are hypothesized to be related to racial/ethnic disproportion in special education assignment. First, districts serving populations with lower socioeconomic standing (SES) may tend to classify relatively more minority students as retarded, whereas districts serving higher SES groups may assign nearly equal numbers of whites and minorities to special classes. The proportion of students paying full price for school meals, as compared with reduced-price of free lunches, provides a rough economic index for a district. Second, it has been noted that southern states, among others, tend to have larger EMR programs in total; it is possible that larger programs allow a greater possibility for racial disproportion to occur in EMR classes, and may also relate to the extent of disproportion in other programs. The percentage of *all* students in a district who are in EMR classes (EMR prevalence) is thus a second additional variable to be tested.

Both SES and EMR prevalence are reasonably well-measured scales. To relate them to the five measures of disproportion, in addition to region and minority enrollment, a multivariate ANCOVA model is appropriate. As part of the analysis, SES and EMR prevalence—the covariates—are related to the criteria through multivariate (five-variate) multiple regression analysis. The two covariates are termed "predictor variables" in their specific use in regression analysis. In addition, differences among regions and minority proportions may be retested, eliminating a portion of the difference attributable to SES and EMR prevalence.

The correlations between the predictors and the five disproportion measures are given in Table 6. These are computed from the pooled within-group variance–covariance matrix so that they represent the degree of association within geographic regions and levels of minority enrollment; that is, the effects of region and minority enrollment have been eliminated. Socioeconomic standing is inversely associated with SED disproportion, and positively with the disproportion in other programs. The size of the EMR program is positively correlated with EMR, TMR, and SED disproportion, and negatively with SLD and SI. However, the two predictors are intercorrelated

TABLE 6. *Pooled within-group correlations between criterion and predictor variables*

| Predictor variable | Special education classification | | | | |
	EMR	TMR	SED	SLD	SI
SES	.03	.01	−.15	.09	.09
EMR prevalence	.07	.10	.23	−.17	−.08

with each other, as are the five criteria, so that multivariate multiple regression tests should be used to decide whether these measures represent real nonzero association of the two sets.

Table 7 presents the multivariate tests obtained from the likelihood-ratio statistic for each predictor and for both jointly. The multivariate F test for SES ($F = 3.52$ with 5 and 403 degrees of freedom) is significant at the .01 level, indicating that SES is related to the set of five disproportion measures; this is a test of H_{0_1} of equation (9). The univariate tests indicate that racial disproportion in programs for the severely emotionally disturbed is most highly associated with SES ($F = 9.02$), even after controlling for geographic region and proportion of minority enrollment in the district. Slightly over 2 percent of the variation in SED disproportion is attributable to SES. Socioeconomic standing is not associated with disproportion in either EMR or TMR programs, above and beyond the two classification factors. In general it is concluded that SES is related to racial disproportion in special education assignments, and in particular to classes for emotionally disturbed children.

Prevalence of EMR is tested for its contribution to criterion variation and covariation beyond the effects of SES. The multivariate test indicates that this predictor also is significantly related to the set of five disproportion measures (multivariate $F = 9.02$ with 5 and 402 degrees of freedom); H_{0_2} of equation (9) is rejected. Prevalence of EMR, like SES, is most highly related to racial disproportion in SED, and is also associated strongly with disproportion in specific learning disability (SLD) classes. The overall

size of a district's EMR program accounts for 3.71 percent of the variation in disproportion in SED classes, and 2.26 percent of the variation in SLD disproportion, beyond the two classification factors and SES. In general it is concluded that the size of a district's EMR program is related to the extent of racial disproportion in special education assignment as represented by five measures. Further, the most noticeable trend is for larger EMR programs to be associated with greater disproportion in SED classes and lower disproportion in SLD classes.

The order of the predictor variables in this analysis was fixed by the investigator in advance of the data analyses. An alternate procedure in univariate multiple regression models is to allow a computer to choose as the first predictor that antecedent variable with the highest simple correlation with the criterion. The second predictor is chosen by finding the variable with the highest partial correlation with the criterion after the first predictor, and so on. Although this procedure has very weak statistical underpinnings and does not allow certain types of analysis (e.g., blockwise regression tests), it is popular because it can be applied to a many-variable data set with a minimum amount of conceptual thinking. The same sort of analysis is not possible in multivariate models because there are many different measures of association and each would yield its own empirical order of predictors.

Blockwise tests and associated interpretive statistics may be made for subsets or all of the predictor variables. Table 7 reports an F statistic of 6.22 with 10 and 804 degrees of freedom, derived from the likelihood-ratio test of all association of the two predictors with the five criterion measures. This is a test of H_0 of equation (10); that is, the ten correlations estimated in Table 6 are all null. The null hypothesis is rejected at $p < .01$. To probe more specifically, the relationship of the two predictors with *each* special education measure may be tested through a univariate F statistic, and the total percentage of variation obtained. For example, the two predictor variables are related especially to SED disproportion ($F = 12.67$) and to SLD disproportion ($F = 6.27$). The prevalence of SES and of EMR together account for 5.87 percent of the varia-

TABLE 7. *Results of regression analysis with five criteria and two predictors*[a]

| Predictor variable | Multivariate F | Degrees of freedom | Special education classification | | | | | | | | | |
| | | | EMR | | TMR | | SED | | SLD | | SI | |
			Percent	F[b]	Percent	F[b]	Percent	F[b]	Percent	F[b]	Percent	F[b]
SES	3.52[c]	5, 403	.09	.35	.01	.02	2.17	9.02[c]	.74	3.02	.87	3.55
EMR prevalence, eliminating SES	9.02[c]	5, 402	.72	2.93	1.31	5.38	3.71	15.99[c]	2.26	9.45[c]	.22	.89
Both	6.22[c]	10, 804	.80	1.64	1.31	2.70	5.87	12.67[c]	3.00	6.27[c]	1.08	2.22

[a] All results are "holding constant" region and proportion minority enrollment.   [b] F statistics for SES have 1 and 407 degrees of freedom; for EMR prevalence, 1 and 406 degrees of freedom; for both, 2 and 406 degrees of freedom.   [c] Significant at $p < .01$.

TABLE 8. *Canonical correlation results for two predictors and five criteria, first correlation only*

Measure	Raw weight	Correlation with composite variate
Criteria:		
EMR	.53	.16
TMR	.19	.26
SED	.98	.67
SLD	−1.20	−.48
SI	−.32	−.24
Predictors:		
SES	−1.59	−.51
EMR prevalence	.99	.98

tion in SED disproportion; this is a hundred times the squared multiple correlation of SED disproportion with the two predictors.

Another way to examine the association of the two predictors with the five criterion variables is through canonical correlation analysis. Both the likelihood-ratio test and Bock's generalized F statistic indicate that all of the significant association between the two sets of variables is "explainable" as the correlation of one linear composite of the predictor variables and one linear composite of the criteria. The weights defining these composites are given in Table 8. In particular, the highest correlation is between variables y^* and x^* where

$$y^* = .53y_1 + .19y_2 + .98y_3 - 1.20y_4 - .32y_5$$

$$x^* = -1.59x_1 + .99x_2,$$

and where the five y's are the special education disproportion measures and the x's are SES and EMR prevalence respectively. Unfortunately, these empirically derived weights do not provide an easy interpretation of the relationship of the two sets of measures. In addition to reflecting the importance of an individual measure to the composite, they reflect the scaling of the measure (i.e., in general, measures with small standard deviations tend to receive large weights) and the intercorrelations among the particular variables in the set. Like regression coefficients, they are conditional on the other variables that have been included, and may change dramatically if a measure is added to or deleted from either set.

These interpretive problems are remedied somewhat by calculating the correlation of each y measure with the composite variable y^* and of each x measure with the composite x^*. The results are given in the second column of Table 8. From the magnitudes and signs of these values we can see that y^*—the variable most highly related to the predictors—is dominated by SED and SLD disproportion, but in opposite directions. x^* is largely a function of the size of a district's EMR program. Thus the association of the disproportion measures with the predictors is

attributable largely to the association of high EMR prevalence with high SED disproportion, and with low disproportion in SLD classes.

This example demonstrates some of the complexities introduced by canonical correlation analysis (which are the same for discriminant function analysis). The major findings are derived from a complex set of interdependent weights that need to be transformed further before a clearer view of the data is possible. In most published examples the interpretation ultimately becomes univariable—that is, how does each individual measure relate to the composite index? Even a quick glance at Table 6 reveals that the same conclusions could have been drawn directly from the simple correlations; EMR prevalence has higher correlations with the dependent variables, and in particular with SED and SLD disproportion. The main interpretive value of canonical correlation or discriminant function analysis is when the simpler univariate results show no clear pattern, in which case the linear-composite approach may be necessary.

To complete the ANCOVA, all of the mean differences were retested after differences attributable to the two covariates were eliminated. None of the multivariate tests of significance became significant or nonsignificant that were not so in the original analysis. Univariate differences across the degrees of minority enrollment (factor B) on TMR disproportion and SLD disproportion dropped to below their critical value. This is attributable largely to the similar patterns of means for the dependent variables and the covariates. For example, the mean TMR disproportion decreases monotonically as the percent of minority enrollment in the districts increases (Table 2); at the same time, the mean SES level decreases monotonically from an average of 74 percent full-priced meals for districts with 0 to 20 percent minority, to an average of 15 percent full-priced meals for those with 80 to 100 percent minority enrollment. In a randomized experiment, groups would not show systematic mean differences on the covariates. However, the covariance model is applicable in comparing means of either experimental or naturally occurring groups.

Multivariate Analysis of Repeated Measures. Repeated-measures designs include pretest-posttest studies, within-subjects experiments in which the same subjects are measured on the same scale under different experimental conditions, and longitudinal studies in which measures are taken on the same scale at two or more points in time. In each case differences among the measurements are of experimental interest, and represent the difference between responses at different time points or under different experimental conditions. This is not usually the case in multivariate data generally, where the multiple measures are qualitatively distinct and on noncomparable scales. In the present example measures of reading skill were obtained for a sample of youngsters in the fifth grade, and on a directly comparable scale when the same children were in grades 7, 9, and 11. The major questions of the investigation concern (1) mean differences in reading skill over the four time points, (2) mean reading differences between male and female students, and (3) the interaction of grade with sex—that is, whether the mean growth curves for the two sex groups are parallel.

Two general statistical models are applicable to repeated-measure data, one univariate and the other multivariate. In the univariate case the measures serve as explicit classification factors in the ANOVA design. These within-subject factors are crossed with individual subjects. Thus the statement "each subject serves as his/her own control" is sometimes used in this context. Subjects are treated as random effects nested within mutually exclusive experimental or naturally occurring groups (Lindquist, 1954; Winer, 1971). The univariate design for the reading study would involve a 2 × 4 (sex × grade) fixed-effects portion, and a large random dimension of subjects within sex groups, crossed with grade.

In contrast, in the multivariate approach, measures at different times are treated as multiple intercorrelated dependent variables. The design is a simple one-way two-groups (males and females) setup, with subjects being multiple observations within each group. Each subject has four measures—the reading scores at four grade levels.

Before conducting a repeated-measures analysis, the researcher should consider which of the two models is appropriate for the particular data set. Because subjects are treated as a dimension of classification in the univariate analysis, unusually stringent distributional assumptions must be met for the resulting F ratios to be valid. First, as with other univariate ANOVA procedures, the response variable is assumed to be distributed normally. Second, the usual equality-of-variance condition implies that the responses under each treatment or at each point in time have equal variances. This is rarely the case in within-subjects experiments because different experimental treatments produce greater or less response variability; it is true even less often in longitudinal studies, as individual differences on most characteristics increase with age. Third, the usual assumption of independence of observations is necessarily violated for repeated measures taken from the same subjects. It was shown in early statistical work, however, that a substitute condition may be met instead. Specifically, the F statistics will still be valid if, in addition to equal variances, the measures under different conditions or at different time points all have the same constant covariance (or correlation) with one another. The joint requirement of equal variance of the measures and equal covariances of all pairs of measures is termed "compound symmetry"; this pattern is rarely found in behavioral data.

More recent statistical work has shown that compound symmetry of variances and covariances is only one pattern of dispersions that satisfies the conditions of the univariate analysis of repeated-measures data; the larger class of variance–covariance matrices are termed "reducible" ma-

trices. Unfortunately, reducible variance–covariance matrices cannot be identified easily by inspection. However, a test of significance to determine whether the variance–covariance matrix among measures is reducible is given in Bock (1975, p. 459). If there is significant deviation from this pattern in the data, the univariate model should not be employed.

In the multivariate approach the repeated measurements are considered multiple criterion variables. Thus they may have unequal variances and any pattern of covariances and correlations. Because of this the multivariate approach not only is less restrictive but also more realistic. The multivariate analysis of repeated-measures data is described in greater depth in Bock (1975, chap. 7) and Finn and Mattsson (1978), and the univariate and multivariate approaches and their corresponding assumptions are compared in Davidson (1972), McCall and Applebaum (1973), and Poor (1973).

Data for the present example were selected from a 10-year longitudinal study of academic growth (Hilton, Beaton, & Bower, 1971). As part of the study the Sequential Tests of Educational Progress were given to children in grade 5, and again to the same youngsters in grades 7, 9, and 11 in a representative sample of 18 school systems. The data reported here, from a longitudinal study executed by the Educational Testing Service under a grant from the National Institute of Education, are scores on the reading subtest for 418 white male and 474 white female students. Mean scores for both sex groups at each grade level are given in Table 9. The tests have been vertically scaled so that scores at each time point are directly comparable and display a monotonically increasing trend for both sex groups, with the largest increase between grades 5 and 7. The correlations and standard deviations of the reading scale are given in Table 10. In spite of the apparent homogeneity of the standard deviations, and also of the intercorrelations, the test of whether the variance–covariance matrix is reducible is statistically significant; these data do not fit the necessary conditions for a valid univariate repeated-measures analysis.

For the multivariate analysis the design is considered a one-way two-group setup (males and females) with four response measures per subject. Tests of the sex and grade effects and the interaction of grade with sex depend on transforming the original four variables into contrasts among the measures, chosen by the investigator. For example, the overall sex effect is tested by creating a new score that is the sum of the four measures for each student. Let the original four measures be represented by y_1 through y_4, where

$$y_1 = \text{grade 5 reading score},$$
$$y_2 = \text{grade 7 reading score},$$
$$y_3 = \text{grade 9 reading score, and}$$
$$y_4 = \text{grade 11 reading score}.$$

TABLE 9. *Mean reading scores, by sex and grade*

Sex group	N	\multicolumn{4}{c}{Grade}
		5	7	9	11
Male	418	258.21	272.15	283.91	294.22
Female	474	262.05	276.28	287.69	297.94
All	892	260.25	274.34	285.92	296.20

TABLE 10. *Pooled within-sex correlations and standard deviations*

Grade	Standard deviation	\multicolumn{4}{c}{Correlations}
		5	7	9	11
5	15.11	1.00			
7	16.62	.74	1.00		
9	14.97	.67	.77	1.00	
11	16.19	.67	.71	.76	1.00

Then we may create a new score, y_1^*, by

$$y_1^* = y_1 + y_2 + y_3 + y_4. \tag{13}$$

Once each subject has been provided this total score, the test of the difference between sex groups is done through a simple t or F test of the difference of two means.

For the analysis of growth across the grade levels, we may choose to examine any of a number of differences—for example, each grade compared with the next higher grade, or each grade compared with the average of all lower grades. Alternately, we might examine the pattern of growth rather than specific differences. There may be linearity of growth across the four grade levels, with either increasing or decreasing means. Or there may be quadratic growth across grade levels with means first increasing rapidly and then decelerating. A third possibility is cubic growth, with an S-shaped pattern of means across time.

To test these patterns of growth, particular linear combinations of the four grade-level means are formed by weighting the original four scales and summing. The weights for linear, quadratic, and cubic trends over time are the orthogonal polynomial weights given in many texts

TABLE 11. *Orthogonal polynomial weights for four-time-point factor*

Trend	\multicolumn{4}{c}{Variable}
	y_1	y_2	y_3	y_4
Linear	−3	−1	1	3
Quadratic	1	−1	−1	1
Cubic	−1	3	−3	1

(e.g., Bock, 1975, app. B), or they may be generated internally by computer programs. The weights for a factor having four levels (i.e., grades) are given in Table 11. The three rows of the matrix are the respective weights for linear, quadratic, and cubic trends across grade levels.

Thus three new dependent variables are created, y_2^*, y_3^*, and y_4^*, where

$$y_2^* = -3y_1 - y_2 + y_3 + 3y_4, \tag{14}$$

$$y_3^* = y_1 - y_2 - y_3 + y_4, \tag{15}$$

$$y_4^* = -y_1 + 3y_2 - 3y_3 + y_4. \tag{16}$$

If there is a linear trend across grade levels, then the mean of all the subjects on y_2^* will be significantly different from zero. If there is a quadratic (one-bend) trend, then the mean of all the subjects on y_3^* will be significantly different from zero. If there is a cubic (two-bend) trend across grade levels, then the mean of all subjects on y_3^* will be significantly different from zero. Since y_2^*, y_3^*, and y_4^* are intercorrelated, multivariate tests should be employed.

The first major hypothesis, that the means for the two sex groups are equal over all time points, can be represented in terms of y_1^*, the total of all the time measures. Statistically, the null hypothesis is

$$H_{0_1} : [\mu_1^*]_{\text{male}} = [\mu_1^*]_{\text{female}}. \tag{17}$$

To test this hypothesis, the mean square for the sex difference on y_1^* is divided by the mean square within groups on y_1^*. In the example the result is an F ratio for sex of 17.04, with 1 and 890 degrees of freedom (see Table 12). This exceeds the .01 critical value; overall, females in this age range have higher reading scores than males.

To test for significant grade differences, y_2^*, y_3^*, and y_4^* are treated as simultaneous criterion measures. The null hypothesis is that the means for all subjects (the "grand mean") on these three difference measures are simultaneously zero. This can be represented as

$$H_{0_2} : \begin{bmatrix} \mu_2^* \\ \mu_3^* \\ \mu_4^* \end{bmatrix} = \begin{bmatrix} 0 \\ 0 \\ 0 \end{bmatrix}. \tag{18}$$

Because the three measures are intercorrelated, overall differences among grade levels can be tested only with multivariate procedures. In particular, the step-down analysis provides a test of the linear effect of the quadratic effect eliminating the linear effect, and of the cubic effect beyond both linear and quadratic trends. Table 12 shows a highly significant linear trend, $F(1,890) = 7,241.35$, $p < .01$. In addition, the quadratic effect exceeds the .02 critical value, $F(1,889) = 5.57$. Presumably the deceleration of growth in reading would be expected over grades 5 through 11 so that, even at $\alpha = .01$, the significant one-tail value would substantiate the hypothesized trend.

The final major hypothesis is that of interaction between sex and grade. The null form is represented as

TABLE 12. *Tests of significance of longitudinal reading study*

Source of variation	Degrees of freedom	Total	Step-down tests		
			Linear	Quadratic, eliminating linear	Cubic, eliminating linear and quadratic
Grand mean	1	—	7,241.35[a]	5.57[b]	3.03
Sex, eliminating grand mean	1	17.04[a]	.06	.11	.15
			Univariate mean squares		
Within groups	890	780.51	87.82	68.48	54.05
Total	892				

[a] $p < .01$.   [b] $p < .02$.

$$H_{0_3}: \begin{bmatrix} \mu_2^* \\ \mu_3^* \\ \mu_4^* \end{bmatrix}_{male} = \begin{bmatrix} \mu_2^* \\ \mu_3^* \\ \mu_4^* \end{bmatrix}_{female}. \qquad (19)$$

A multivariate test procedure (the step-down tests) is employed to test equality of the three grade differences for the two sex groups. As shown in Table 12, none of the step-down tests for the differences between sex groups is significant. Thus, the same decelerating growth curve describes reading trends for both males and females. The only difference between them is that the average reading score for females is higher than that for males.

Conclusions. In past years one of the recommendations that accompanied much of the published empirical investigations in the social sciences was "more research taking a multivariate approach to the problem is needed." The authors probably intended to recommend multivariate conceptual models, theories, and frames of reference, having realized that both the antecedents and outcomes they were investigating were more complex than they originally thought. Multivariate statistical techniques cannot substitute for the development of complex conceptual frameworks involving many variables. However, in many instances these methods are the most appropriate for data from an empirical investigation in which many variables are studied. They are also the most realistic for complex behavioral data, in that they correspond to a global view of a phenomenon with many aspects that may be measured.

In basic research studies the results of multivariate statistical tests are likely to be more replicable than for single aspects of the response; the need for increased replicability seems to be particularly important to behavioral researchers. In policy-related research a multivariate viewpoint may prevent decisions from being based on partial information. For example, the well-known "Equality of Educational Opportunity" survey (Coleman et al., 1966) concluded that school differences account for little variation in student's performance, beyond the child's home background. This conclusion—which had an enormous impact on U.S. educational decision making—was based largely on a single outcome measure of verbal ability. Other school performance measures (e.g., mathematics), however, have been shown to be more highly related to in-school factors (cf. Bock, 1975, p. 253). A multivariate set of performance measures thus would have provided the basis for a much more rational view of U.S. schools.

A tally of articles published in the *American Educational Research Journal (AERJ)*, the *Journal of Educational Psychology (JEP)*, and the *Journal of Counseling Psychology (JCP)* from 1971 through 1980 shows us that indeed the vast majority of empirical investigations yield multiple dependent variables. However, only about 17 percent of the *AERJ* articles, 9 percent of the *JEP* articles, and 8 percent of the *JCP* articles employed multivariate statistical models. Two of the journals, *JEP* and *JCP*, show a distinct increase from 1971–1975 to 1975–1980 in the number of articles using multivariate analysis of variance. It is likely that as researchers become more familiar with multivariate methods, and editors more receptive, statistical models that fit the basic multivariate nature of human behavior will become predominant.

Jeremy D. Finn
Peter J. D. Carnevale

See also Analysis of Variance and Covariance; Factor Analysis; Regression Analysis; Statistical Methods.

REFERENCES

Bishop, Y. M. M.; Feinberg, S. E.; & Holland, P. W. *Discrete Multivariate Analysis: Theory and Practice.* Cambridge, Mass.: MIT Press, 1975.

Bock, R. D. *Multivariate Statistical Methods in Behavioral Research.* New York: McGraw-Hill, 1975.

Bock, R. D., & Brandt, D. Comparison of some computer programs for univariate and multivariate analysis of variance. In P. R. Krishnaiah (Ed.), *Handbook of Statistics* (Vol. 1). Amsterdam: North Holland, 1980.

Cohen, E., & Burns, P. *SPSS-MANOVA: Multivariate Analysis of Variance and Covariance.* Chicago: SPSS, Inc., 1976.

Coleman, J. S.; Campbell, E. Q.; Hobson, C. J.; McPartland, J.;

Mood, A. M.; Weinfeld, F. D.; & York, R. L. *Equality of Educational Opportunity.* (OE-3800). Washington, D.C.: U.S. Government Printing Office, 1966.

Cramer, E. M. *Revised MANOVA Program.* Chapel Hill: University of North Carolina, Thurstone Psychometric Laboratory, 1974.

Davidson, M. L. Univariate versus multivariate tests in repeated measures experiments. *Psychological Bulletin,* 1972, 77, 446–452.

Finn, J. D. *A General Model for Multivariate Analysis.* New York: Holt, Rinehart & Winston, 1974.

Finn, J. D. *MULTIVARIANCE: Univariate and Multivariate Analysis of Variance, Covariance, Regression, and Repeated Measures.* Version VI. Chicago: National Educational Resources, Inc., 1978.

Finn, J. D., & Mattsson, I. *Multivariate Analysis in Educational Research: Applications of the MULTIVARIANCE Program.* Chicago: National Educational Resources, 1978.

Fisher, R. A. *Statistical Methods for Research Workers.* London: Oliver & Boyd, 1925.

Goodnight, J. H. *SAS Procedure GLM.* Raleigh, N.C.: SAS Institute, Inc., 1976.

Harris, R. J. *A Primer of Multivariate Statistics.* New York: McGraw-Hill, 1975.

Hilton, T. L.; Beaton, A. E.; & Bower, C. P. *Stability and Instability in Academic Growth: A Compilation of Longitudinal Data* (Final Report, Research No. 0-0140). Washington, D.C.: U.S. Office of Education, August 1971. (ERIC Document Reproduction Service No. ED 072 075)

Hummel, T. J., & Sligo, J. R. Empirical comparison of univariate and multivariate analysis of variance procedures. *Psychological Bulletin,* 1971, 76, 49–57.

Jöreskog, K. G.; van Thillo, M.; & Gruvaeus, G. T. *ACOVSM: A General Computer Program for Analysis of Covariance Structures Including Generalized MANOVA* (Research Bulletin 71-01). Princeton, N.J.: Educational Testing Service, 1971.

Lindquist, E. F. *Design and Analysis of Experiments in Psychology and Education.* Boston: Houghton Mifflin, 1954.

Maxwell, A. E. *Multivariate Analysis in Behavioral Research.* London: Chapman & Hall, 1977.

McCall, R. B., & Applebaum, M. L. Bias in the analysis of repeated-measures design: Some alternative approaches. *Child Development,* 1973, 44, 401–415.

Morrison, D. F. *Multivariate Analysis* (2nd ed.). New York: McGraw-Hill, 1976.

Olson, C. L. On choosing a test statistic in multivariate analysis of variance. *Psychological Bulletin,* 1976, 83, 579–586.

Poor, D. D. S. Analysis of variance for repeated measures designs: Two approaches. *Psychological Bulletin,* 1973, 80, 204–209.

Roy, S. N., & Bargmann, R. E. Tests of multiple independence and the associated confidence bounds. *Annals of Mathematical Statistics,* 1958, 29, 491–503.

Stevens, J. Comment on Olson: Choosing a test statistic in multivariate analysis of variance. *Psychological Bulletin,* 1979, 86, 355–360.

Tatsuoka, M. M. *Multivariate Analysis.* New York: Wiley, 1971.

Timm, N. *Multivariate Analysis with Applications in Education and Psychology.* Monterey, Calif.: Brooks/Cole, 1975.

Winer, B. J. *Statistical Principles in Experimental Design* (2nd ed.). New York: McGraw-Hill, 1971.

MUSEUMS

Museums as educational institutions in the United States are presently in existence in some form or another in almost every community. American museums that house permanent collections open to the public number 4,609 (Glaser, 1980a). No two of these museums are exactly alike; however, 93 percent of American museums conduct educational programs involving such activities as museum tours, outreach programs, visits to schools, circulating exhibitions, mobile units, internships, and studio or study classes (Newson, 1975).

Museum Functions. Education in American museums is conducted by museum educators who are assigned to sizable educational departments in major museums. Education may also be conducted by professionals in small museums who also hold responsibility for many functions other than education. Basically, however, the curator in a museum is the highly specialized professional with responsibility for collecting, preserving, designing, and displaying the museum's collection. The educator in a museum is the specialized professional with responsibility for conducting the educational services of the museum (Proctor, 1973). These services are often supplemented by the docent, who is normally a museum volunteer conducting tours and receiving visitors (Jones, 1977).

The traditional function of museums in the United States has been the acquisition, preservation, and exhibition of significant artifacts and objects. Education, sometimes called communication or interpretation, has only recently assumed an equal position with traditional museum functions, even though early American museums were organized to promote learning. The explosion in museum attendance, with approximately 353 million people visiting museums each year, as well as the explosion in museum building programs (2,156 museums existed in the United States in 1970; 4,609 museums now exist) indicate the emphasis that Americans are placing on museums. Furthermore, Public Law 93-380 has stipulated that museums be resources for schools, and as such, they are considered educational institutions, their costs being frequently borne by educational institutions and agencies benefiting from the educational functions of museums (Breun, 1975).

Thousands of museums in the United States are attended by masses of people each year. American museums are categorized into the following thirteen types: are museums; children's and junior museums; college and university museums; company museums; exhibit areas in communities; general knowledge museums; history museums; libraries with collections other than books; national and state agencies, councils, and commissions with collections and their own museums; nature centers and zoos; park museums and visitor centers; science museums; and specialized subject matter museums.

An institution is accredited as a museum by the American Association of Museums, which defines it as an organized and permanent nonprofit institution, essentially educational or aesthetic in purpose, with professional staff, that owns and utilizes tangible objects, cares for them, and exhibits them to the public on some regular schedule. American museums have the additional function of education in the museum. Some museums claim that they are institutions of culture that have aesthetic rather than didactic purposes. Thus a diversification of objectives exists in museums, with the result that meaningful didactic programs need to relate to the total goals of the museum. Education in museums consequently has developed services to schools as well as to the public long after formal education is completed.

Museums and Schools. As the vast majority of the American population reaches adulthood in the future, more emphasis will be devoted to adult education in museums. Presently, school-age students continue to compose a major segment of the audience in museums. Cooperation between museums and schools continues to exist as museum educators and classroom teachers strive to work effectively toward meaningful museum learning experiences. In some cases, school districts, such as those of Cleveland, Philadelphia, and New York City, assign teachers to permanent positions in museums to assist with museum school programs.

Museum education for schools is devoting itself to the study of objects from the past, the uses of museum objects for the understanding and enrichment of contemporary life, and the transmission or study of cultural values for the future. Through museum education, young scholars may explore the past, the present, and the future in a tangible form. Museum education provides opportunities for students to discover, inquire, conceptualize, and create, by using all their human resources in relation to objects in museum collections. The collections in museums provide source materials for learners that reflect the highest achievements and genius of mankind. With such sources of knowledge and with effective museum learning methods, museum education permits students to transcend the command of facts with understanding and creative or innovative activity (Perrot, 1980).

An international network of exchange assists museums in the practice of museum education. Serving museums and education are the American Association for State and Local History, the National Art Education Association, the Committee on Education and Cultural Action of the International Council of Museums, and the Education Committee of the American Association of Museums. In addition, active educational committees having hundreds of members are included within the Northeast Museums Conference, the Southwest Museums Conference, the New England Museums Conference, the Midwest Museums Conference and the Western Museums Conference (Ott, 1980). These professional organizations provide a forum through literature and study committees that serve to develop museum education in the United States.

Museum Systems. Museums teach in their galleries and in their communities. Self-operative concept-oriented exhibitions within many museums perpetuate participatory learning and are designed as a basis for perception, inquiry, and response. Museums reach out into communities by taking their exhibitions and programs beyond the four walls of their institutions with the help of vans, converted buses, trains, and art cart projects. Outreach museum programs take place in neighborhood centers organized in shopping centers, abandoned elementary school buildings, and in downtown storefront facilities. Thematic workshops, holiday and weekend programs, related and integrated subject study sessions, workbook and game catalogs, discovery rooms, and teacher-education institutes are undertaken to assist schools in cooperative education for students. Experimentation, research, and innovation between schools and museums serve to develop museum education as a vital link in the educational process.

Special museum programs reflecting current educational processes for students are found in junior museums, children's museums, and hands-on museums.

Junior museums. Junior museums are usually housed in a wing or a permanent area within a museum. The rationale for the existence of junior museums is similar to the concept of children's reading rooms in libraries. The material in a junior museum or in a children's library is selected to relate to the interests and needs of the young participant. Junior museums continuously provide objects in the museum's collections that relate directly to school-age children; they are formative learning centers within the larger museums. Several participatory educational exhibitions usually exist within the junior museum structure, supplemented by classrooms, lunchrooms, rest rooms, coat rooms, media centers, and libraries—all providing a self-contained schoollike environment within the museum.

Junior museum educational programs, however, are not necessarily confined to a designated area within the museum. The junior museum of the Metropolitan Museum of Art is an example of a system that uses the entire museum for its educational program. The technique of a "treasure hunt" at the Metropolitan permits effective use of the galleries in the museum by organizing the discovery and perceptions of young scholars toward an understanding of form observed in objects on display, such as chairs, sarcophagi, and paintings by Vermeer, Seurat, and Albers. Children are introduced to the how of creating a work of art, and armed with this background knowledge, they become comfortable in adult exhibitions and galleries. Junior museums, such as that at the Metropolitan, vividly present techniques and tools used in the arts from ancient to modern times. School groups explore self-contained junior museum exhibitions, view films, and are then conducted through galleries carefully selected and related to their study programs at the Metropolitan (Condit, 1973). By confronting students with artifacts of history or culture, such as a sculpted image of a pharaoh or an ancient tomb, the junior museum brings much of what is remote in the classroom alive.

Children's museums. Children's museums, uniquely American contributions to the field, are self-contained environments, usually in a separate museum building. Children's museums contain their own collections but usually do not limit themselves to concepts illuminated by the objects in their collections alone. Education in children's museums is approached through self-expression and self-discovery and is usually process-oriented. Learning is often the result of a progressive, multisensory approach to understanding concepts in subject matter. The Children's Museum of New Haven, Connecticut, is an example of a museum combining art and science into real experiences for children. As a museum, it is designed to provide for play exploration and is organized for interpreting play experiences cognitively in order to demonstrate relationships in the subject matter. Most children's museums provide differing activity centers that revolve around life situations of children and teach concepts and skills. Exhibitions, activities, and learning centers may evolve from the supermarket, signs and vehicles of the city, literature, the cultural heritage of various groups in the community, work roles of people, the function of the human body, or an understanding of animals and their lives.

Hands-on museums. Hands-on museums, exemplifying a contemporary category of museums, are devoted to school-age children. "Hands-on" is a popular term that often describes the participatory, discovery-based learning that takes place in children's museums, youth museums, junior museums, and nature museums. Hands-on museums are experience-oriented rather than object-oriented and perpetuate the basic philosophy that the student learns best through experience as an active participant. Participation takes the form of touching artifacts or live animals, trying out an experiment, measuring one's own pulse rate, going on a fossil dig, or playing a game with a computer. Hands-on is meant to be a total involvement approach in museum education rather than merely a viewing approach. Many hands-on museums were founded by teachers and parents to provide learning experiences about the real world that books and filmstrips could not provide.

The Boston Children's Museum is an example of a hands-on museum. Originally founded by the Science Teachers Bureau of Boston as an educational center for the exchange of ideas and materials relevant to teaching, the Boston Children's Museum is a model of a museum emphasizing participatory learning. The museum's workshop areas, exhibit centers, auditoriums, and recycle shops are organized for active and total involvement by both students and teachers.

The Brooklyn Children's Museum was the first children's museum in the world, established in 1899 and devoted to a total teaching environment. Its current, innovative museum building, almost entirely underground, houses educational exhibitions that explore content ranging from that of primitive culture through the elements of fire and light to the phenomena of the circus. At Brooklyn, most displays are meant to be used by students. Examples of such participatory displays are the two giant, clear-plastic models of a protein molecule and a diamond crystal, both magnified 8 billion times to resemble foam-bubble bridges and both mounted into the lobby of the museum, beckoning children to climb around inside their labyrinthine surfaces (Newsom, 1978).

The Exploratorium in San Francisco, California, also exemplifies the hands-on museum. Opening in 1968, the Exploratorium was founded by the San Francisco Department of Recreation and is housed in the 1915 Panama-Pacific Exposition Hall near the Golden Gate Bridge. The Exploratorium is known for its numerous participatory exhibitions that students can visit at their own pace within the enormous open space of the Exposition Hall. Exhibitions at the Exploratorium are based upon some aspect of perception and convey the essence and understanding of basic principles of knowledge. Light, sound, color, the physiological mechanism of the eye, and the brain's response to perceptual stimuli are typical subjects explored by students at the Exploratorium (Kohn, 1978).

The range of hands-on museums in the United States is constantly growing. Other examples of museums of this type are located at the Fort Worth Museum of Science and History in Fort Worth, Texas; the Museum of Science and Natural History in Little Rock, Arkansas; the Jacksonville Children's Museum in Jacksonville, Florida; the Museum for Children in Denver, Colorado; the Children's Museum in Indianapolis, Indiana; the Walker Art Center in Minneapolis, Minnesota; and the Capitol Children's Museum in Washington, D.C. (Educational Facilities Laboratory, 1975).

Museum Teachers. In the past, a museum educator was a teacher holding a graduate degree in a traditional academic subject. Museum methodology was usually learned on the job, with little or no knowledge of the child's learning development and little consideration of the needs of school curricula. Interest in training in these areas began in England in 1932, but museum training in the United States did not require these kinds of knowledge until considerably later.

The foundations of current programs in teacher education for museums began at at the Fogg Art Museum of Harvard University. Today, professional museum education for teachers offers numerous graduate-level museum studies programs at universities and museums throughout the United States (Glaser, 1980b). General specifications for teacher-education programs for museums stipulate that programs are to be on the graduate level, are to be taught on a cooperative basis by an accredited university and one or more accredited museums, are to include courses in relevant academic disciplines, are to contain aspects of theoretical museum work, and are to include internship experiences in at least one accredited museum for a minimum period of two months.

Formal professional preparation for the museum educator provides teachers in museums with an essential knowledge of their subject matter, museum theory, knowledge of the literature of the museum profession, and practical knowledge acquired from acceptable educational methodology. Museums continue to be staffed by educators who possess an understanding of the ideal, as well as the real world, of museums and schools. Museum educators are professionals committed to the development of their profession within the total educational community.

Robert W. Ott

See also Aesthetic Education; Art Education.

REFERENCES

Breun, R. L. Academic credit for museum education. *Museum News*, 1975, 54(2), 38.

Condit, L. Children and art. In D. V. Proctor, *Museums, Imagination, and Education.* Paris: UNESCO, 1973, p. 61.

Educational Facilities Laboratories. *Hands-on Museums: Partners in Learning.* New York: Educational Facilities Laboratories, 1975. (ERIC Document Reproduction Service No. ED 113 832)

Glaser, J. R. Museum studies: Suggested qualifications for museum positions. *Museum News,* 1980, 59(2), 26–31. (a)

Glaser, J. R. Questions students should ask about graduate programs in museum studies. *Museum News*, 1980, 59(2), 32. (b)

Jones, L. S. Volunteer guides and classroom teachers in school visitation programs in European and North American museums. *Studies in Art Education*, 1977, *3*, 31–40.

Kohn, S. D. It's OK to touch at the new-style hands-on exhibits. *Smithsonian*, 1978, 9(6), 78.

Newson, B. Y. On understanding art museums. *Studies in Art Education*, 1975, *16*(2), 47.

Newson, B. Y., & Silvers, A. Z. (Eds.). *The Art Museum as Educator.* Berkeley: Council on Museum and Education in the Visual Arts, University of California Press, 1978.

Ott, R. W. Museums and schools as universal partners in art education. *Art Education*, 1980, 33(1), 8.

Perrot, P. N. Children, museums, and changing societies. *Roundtable Reports* (Museum Education Roundtable), 1980, *5*(2), 9.

Proctor, D. V. Museum: Teachers, students, children. In *Museums, Imagination, and Education.* Paris: UNESCO, 1973, p. 23.

Robbins, M. W. (Ed.). *America's Museums: The Belmont Report.* Washington, D.C.: Federal Council on the Arts and the Humanities, American Association of Museums, 1968.

MUSIC EDUCATION

Research in music education has its roots in Carl Seashore's psychology of music research at the University of Iowa during the first third of the twentieth century (Leonhard & Colwell, 1976). Research in music psychology and music education often is directed toward the same end, and there is no clear demarcation between the two. A broad generalization, however, is that music psychology research focuses more on developing an understanding of music behavior and cognition, whereas music education research examines instructional and pedagogical behavior.

Specific areas and methodologies of research in music education are diverse and often not clearly demarcated. Generally, the trend of research in the 1970s has been toward more quantification of data than in previous decades, perhaps reflecting the increased accessibility of calculators and computers that facilitate sophisticated data analysis. For the purposes of the present discussion, research in music education is examined under three broad categories: perceptual abilities, teaching and learning, and curricular movements.

Perceptual Abilities

Perceptual abilities underlie the human listener's interactions with music. Response to musical tone as tone includes judgments of pitch, duration, loudness, and timbre, which are related, but not perfectly, to the physical variables of frequency, time, intensity, and waveform. In general, relationships between the psychological variables (pitch, duration, loudness, and timbre) and the physical variables are confounded by interactions. Also, musical tones, which are complex tones as opposed to pure tones, depend on central pitch processing (cortical level) for eliciting particular pitch sensations (Houtsma & Goldstein, 1972).

The perception of loudness has been examined most thoroughly by Stevens (1975) and his students. Loudness grows lawfully as a function of increasing sound pressure or intensity, but in general, loudness grows more rapidly for lower frequencies. Also, a wind instrument "played louder" not only sounds louder but has a different timbre than it does for softer tones; the relative prominence of higher frequency components is greater (Benade, 1973; Hall, 1980).

Although absolute judgments of the apparent duration of a musical tone are rarely important, a minimum of about .015 seconds is necessary for a sound to build to maximal loudness (Roederer, 1975). The onset portion of a tone is particularly important for identifying timbres, as evidenced by studies in which removal of the opening portion of a tone makes tone source recognition far more difficult (Elliott, 1975).

Melody, Harmony, and Rhythm.   Whereas pitch, duration, loudness, and timbre are basic tonal characteristics, melody, harmony, and rhythm result from patterns of tone. Perceiving them requires tonal memory and organization.

Research on melodic perception indicates, not surprisingly, that tonal melodies are easier to recall than atonal ones (Long, 1975). The amount of time required before recalling a tone, the tone's position in a sequence, and length of the sequence affect the ability to sing a tone heard in a prior sequence (Williams, 1975). Of particular interest to music educators is the evidence that recognition and recall of melodies may not require exact pitch information. Dowling and Fujitani (1971) demonstrated that distortion of interval sizes caused fewer melodic recognition problems than distortion of melodic contour. Melody results from the overall pattern rather than from particular pitches.

Melodic perception expands as a function of human development. Kresteff (1963) and Bentley (1966b) have described young children's increasing degree of tonal awareness and intervalic accuracy. Sergeant and Roche (1973) documented a perceptual shift: between ages three and six, individual pitches lose and melodic pattern attributes (contour, interval size, tonality) gain in salience. Melodic recognition skills may continue to improve into adulthood (Funk, 1977).

Harmonic perception involves a sensation of tonality and detection of changes in sequential vertical structures. Tonality evidently is a learned phenomenon, tied to music expectancy (Farnsworth, 1969; J. Taylor, 1976), and Thackray (1973) has demonstrated that harmonic perception is teachable. Wassum (1980) noted the importance of training in the singing of songs and scales in the development of tonality.

Just as melodic perception does not require note-by-note processing, so too does harmonic perception not require exact knowledge of each vertical structure in a harmonic progression. The patterns formed by return to key tones, falling inflection of horizontal lines, and interval size are important (Farnsworth, 1969).

Rhythmic perception requires organizing patterns of sound and silence across time. Foot tapping and clapping clearly aid perceptual organization as demonstrated through performance (Boyle, 1968); patterns of relatively regular accents are easier to organize than irregular patterns (Sturges & Martin, 1974).

As with perception of pitch and harmony, rhythm perception generally improves as a function of child development. Moog (1976) noted increasing coordination of movement with rhythm in very young children from 4 to 18 months of age. Movements of individual body parts gradually are added to whole body movements. S. Taylor (1973) described rhythmic development in children and reported significant increases in rhythmic behaviors between ages 7 and 8 but not between ages 10 and 11. Madsen's research (1979) suggests that people are more alert at detecting tempo decreases than increases, but they prefer faster tempos. Rhythm perception probably is facilitated by movement and exemplars contrasting sound and silence, but research suggests no one optimum way.

Measures of Musical Ability. The measurement of musical ability is a time-honored topic in the psychology of music. Lehman's observation (1968) of a general lack of agreement regarding what constitutes musical aptitude or ability remains true. Currently available tests in which at least one section measures perceptual aspects of musical ability include those of Seashore, Lewis, and Saetveit (1960), Wing (1961), Gaston (1957), Drake (1957), Bentley (1966a), and Gordon (1965, 1979). Thackray's (1968) measures of rhythmic perception probably should be explored further.

Achievement measures are not, strictly speaking, measures of perceptual ability; but the ability to organize melodic, harmonic, and rhythmic structures certainly will influence performance on the measures of Simons (1974), Colwell (1968), and Gordon (1971a).

Musical ability is best measured by an assessment of realistic musical skills, intellectual ability, academic achievement, environmental stimulation, and, where necessary, physical attributes (Radocy & Boyle, 1979). No research-based instrument appears available at present to measure adequately that combination. Blacking's description (1973) of the Venda musical culture, in which no person is considered unmusical, is nettlesome for anyone who would use musical ability, perceptual or otherwise, as a hurdle for music education.

Teaching and Learning

No one theory accounts completely for music learning, and no one definitive research study conclusively supports one theoretical view of learning over another. Music education has seen little attempt to test applications of the learning theories so elegantly discussed by Bower and Hilgard (1981). Some music education research is theoretically based; however, other research is more atheoretical, with particular approaches to a pedagogical problem compared in one instructional setting.

Theoretical Bases. In one example, Marchand (1975) demonstrated that in learning expressive performance, musically experienced college nonmusic majors learned better from a teacher-oriented expository approach, whereas inexperienced students learned better from a student-oriented discovery approach.

Conservation is of continuing interest to music educators. In one representative study, Foley (1975) trained second-graders in conservation of tonal and rhythmic patterns. An experimental approach stressing varied musical experiences and contexts was superior to a non–conservation-oriented approach in developing conservation of tonal patterns (while rhythm patterns were deformed) and rhythm patterns (while tonal patterns were deformed). In a study describing conservation of metric time, Perney (1976) presented five musical tasks to second-graders and third-graders. The tasks essentially involved ordering notes, recognizing tempo independently of the amount of notes, and recognizing independence of metronomic speed and clock time. Findings included no difference between children who played instruments and those who did not; superiority (in conservation) of girls over boys; a positive correlation between task ability and verbal ability; and the lack of an invariant difficulty sequence.

In another study based upon Piaget's theory, Jones (1976), working with 5-to-12-year-olds, ascertained a general difficulty order for eleven tasks related to development of the time concept. Almost all children, even the youngest, could do simple seriation; only 38 percent of the 12-year-olds could conserve meter. Although the particular task difficulty order is not invariant, Jones's study did support Piaget's idea of time concept developing across three stages.

A continuing quest for normative data regarding musical development, regardless of the theoretical base, inspires studies such as that of Hufstader (1977), who administered a test of aural perception to 596 children in grades 1, 3, 5, and 7 and found a learning sequence of timbre, rhythm, melodic pitch patterns, and harmony.

Instructional Technology. Record and tape players, projectors, and electronic tuning aids are routine in many classrooms today. The 1970s saw growth in computerized instruction and the use of videotape.

Videotape's increasing availability has stimulated numerous applications. For example, Gonzo and Forsythe (1976) developed tapes to demonstrate choral rehearsal techniques, at junior and senior high school and college levels, for music education undergraduates. Students using the tape developed superior rehearsal observation techniques and a better attitude than did students not using the tapes. Brand (1977) showed that music education majors who viewed videotapes of simulated encounters with behavior management problems performed at a superior level in an actual classroom teaching situation with respect to students who studied behavior management by means of a lecture-discussion method. Stuart (1979) used videotape successfully to teach skills in detection of errors in string performance.

Computer applications to music education are common. Two studies by Hofstetter (1978, 1980) provide recent examples. In one study (1978), freshman music theory students practiced harmonic dictation as administered through the Graded Units for Interactive Dictation Operative (GUIDO) system, in which the computer directs performance from a digital synthesizer, displays notation on a graphics terminal, and records student responses. In addition to the drill aspects, the GUIDO system was valuable in identifying particular confusions in chord perception. In another study, Hofstetter (1980) investigated instruction via GUIDO in chord quality recognition, including interval structure (major, minor, augmented, diminished), inversion, and position (closed or open). Students improved their ability to hear chord qualities, skills were transferred between positions, and confusion patterns were identified.

Shrader (1970), using a stereotape teaching machine, developed a program for teaching rhythm reading. The program, known as the TAP (Temporal Acuity Products) System, provides feedback regarding the number of correct responses on a given exercise. Subsequent research by Swope (1977), Utley (1978), and Parker (1979) has shown the system to be effective in facilitating music reading.

Future research efforts may use the computer's capabili-

ties for rapid individualization of stimulus presentations in accordance with student input to compare alternative theoretical approaches to instruction. The increasing availability of microcomputers and associated software mitigates the cost problem, which until recently has limited the feasibility of computer-based instructional technology.

Music Reading. Although music reading is of great practical importance in the learning and performing of music, Sloboda (1978) maintains that the psychological study of music reading is a neglected area of research. Perhaps this neglect is due partially to the nature of the task, which does not allow convenient isolation of reading variables from other musical skills, since by traditional definition music reading involves music performance. Even studies of aural-visual perceptual skills are confounded by separate tonal and rhythmic variables. Pitch and rhythm sight reading involve different conceptual bases. Further, reading music vocally and instrumentally involve quite different tasks, although it has been argued (Radocy & Boyle, 1979) that even vocal reading is best facilitated through instrumental experience.

Other variables also have been investigated. Feedback provided by a teaching machine regarding accuracy of rhythmic performance has been effective in improving rhythm-reading skills (Shrader, 1970; Swope, 1977; Utley, 1978; Parker, 1979). Bobbitt (1970) found that a step-by-step program based on Skinnerian principles was effective in improving fifth-graders' music-reading skills. Notational variables also have been investigated, although Gregory's study (1972) of the effects of four types of notation on the sight-reading ability of seventh-grade instrumentalists revealed no significant differences in sight-reading performance.

It has been demonstrated that first-grade children can learn to read music. Klemish (1968) examined the effects of "pseudo-notation" in developing a vocabulary of tonal patterns, and Woskowiak (1973) applied certain principles of Orff, Kodaly, and Dalcroze in developing music-reading games. Stephens (1974) compared the effects of Richards's *Threshold to Music,* which is based on the work of Kodaly, and a traditional drill approach on fifth-graders' and sixth-graders' music-reading ability. Both methods resulted in significant improvement, but there were no differences in the two methods' effectiveness. Palmer (1976) compared the Richards' approach with Edwin Gordon's approach, and the results were similar to the Stephens' study. Both approaches resulted in significant improvements, but no clear-cut differences were shown between the two.

Arguments continue about the relative merits of "movable do" and "fixed do" as methods for teaching sight singing. Gordon (1971b) concludes that "movable do" is best in developing a relative pitch reading; Multer (1978) also recognizes the merits of "movable do," but argues that in the long run, musicians need to be able to use "fixed do."

Studies involving foot tapping as an aid in sight reading instrumental music (Skornicka, 1958; Boyle, 1968) report better sight-reading scores on the Watkins-Farnum Performance Scale for young instrumentalists using foot tapping than for those not using foot tapping. MacKnight (1975) reports that introducing new pitches in series of tonal patterns also improves sight-reading skills of beginning instrumentalists.

It is apparent that a variety of approaches are effective in improving music-reading skills, whether instrumental or vocal, but there appears to be little conclusive evidence demonstrating differences in the effects of different methods. It is clear, however, that a systematic method for teaching music reading, whatever it is, is more effective than no systematic method.

Vocal Performance.   Research related to vocal performance is both limited and fragmented. Gonzo (1973) groups it under four categories: (1) history of public school choral performance, (2) physiological aspects of choral singing, (3) choral rehearsal techniques, and (4) pitch, rhythmic, and harmonic detection ability of choral students and directors. Kramme (1976) discusses it under three categories: (1) vocal production, (2) the adolescent voice, and (3) the teaching-learning process. Welch's (1979a) review focuses upon poor pitch singing. The present review, also necessarily selective, discusses the literature under two headings: (1) pitch singing and (2) vocal range of children and adolescents.

Pitch singing.   A basic concern in research on poor pitch singing is terminology. Bentley (1968) used the term "monotones" in his extensive study of the status of the problem. His data suggest that the problem decreased with age, but that even in the 12-year-old to 14-year-old range, 7 to 8 percent of girls were still monotones. Bentley uses the term "monotones" to include children who cannot match tones. Other terms for essentially the same problem are "poor pitch singer" and "imperfect pitch singer" (Davies & Roberts, 1975; Roberts & Davies, 1975, 1976) and "uncertain singer" (McNitt, 1971; Yank, 1975). Strictly speaking, a monotone is able to produce only one tone, regardless of the stimulus. Such people are extremely rare; the other terms are preferable for people who sing with restricted ranges or have difficulty matching pitches.

Klemish (1974) reported that tape-recorded feedback was effective in improving the singing skills of uncertain singers in the first grade and second grade. Other types of remedial programs at a variety of age levels ranging from first grade through college level also have been effective in improving accuracy of pitch singing (Joyner, 1969; McNitt, 1971; Richner, 1976; Roberts & Davies, 1975, 1976). Cobes (1969) and Porter (1977) both found that pitch-matching responses of uncertain singers could be "shaped" through reinforcement techniques. Greer, Randall, and Timberlake (1971) also found that music listening could be an effective contingency in improving vocal pitch acuity. Heller (1969) reports that a combination of visual and auditory feedback was more effective than aural feedback alone in improving pitch-matching skills.

In summary, it is apparent that pitch-matching behaviors of uncertain singers can be improved through training. Reinforcement strategies appear to be particularly effective.

Vocal Range of Children and Adolescents.   Following Jersild and Bienstock's classic study (1934) of children's ability to sing, little research was directed toward the assessment of children's vocal range until the 1960s. Vocal ranges reported by Jersild and Bienstock tended to be somewhat greater than those reported in more recent studies, leading Welch (1979b) to suggest that the evaluative criteria might have been different. Kirkpatrick (1962) observed that the vocal ranges of preschool children tend to be about a diminished fifth lower than the ranges of songs in a kindergarten music book. Welch (1979b) provides an excellent review of these studies and several others of this type that were conducted in Great Britain.

Studies of older children (puberty and early adolescence) (Adcock, 1970; Joseph, 1966) reveal that vocal pitch range changes with maturation and appears to correlate with the development of certain physical characteristics. A comparison of voice change patterns in 1939 and 1971 (Friesen, 1972) reveals that voice change in adolescent males tends to occur earlier than in former years. Boys tend to have a much more limited range than girls. Adcock noted that a majority of songs in music series texts for this age level were actually unsingable with respect to range.

The prevailing theme of research on vocal range is that music educators need to be much more careful in selecting music that is in an appropriate range for children's and adolescents' singing ranges.

Instrumental Performance.   Research on instrumental performance also is limited and reflects a variety of interests. Duerksen (1972) reviewed research on various aspects of school instrumental programs, instrumental methods, and outcomes of instruction; Rainbow's review (1973) focused on instructional problems for which objective data could be obtained, such as electromyographical analysis of facial muscles during embouchure placement and the use of fluoroscopic and x-ray techniques in examining tongue placement. D. S. Ramsey (1976) examined research on beginning band programs. The present discussion examines selected research related to four particular concerns: (1) effects of chamber music experience, (2) technology in instrumental music instruction, (3) developing musical understanding through instrumental music, and (4) predicting success in instrumental music.

Chamber music experience.   Many music educators espouse the values of chamber music in a school music program, although a recent survey revealed that chamber music programs are not nearly so prevalent as most advocates would desire (Houpt, 1980). Research suggests that chamber music experiences are more effective than large ensembles in improving students' achievement, as measured by the Watkins-Farnum Performance Scale and several subtests of Colwell's Music Achievement Tests, but that they had no similar positive effect on attitudes (Olson,

1975). Zorn (1973), comparing ensemble experience and sectional rehearsal experience for ninth-graders, reported no differences in performance achievement, but did find that ensemble experiences resulted in more positive attitudes.

Computers in instrumental instruction. Computers appear to be useful in instrumental music instruction. Deihl and Radocy (1969) developed a computer-assisted instructional (CAI) program to facilitate development of aural and aural-visual concepts related to instrumental music. A follow-up CAI study (Deihl & Zeigler, 1973) was effective in teaching articulation, phrasing, and rhythm to intermediate level students. Peters (1974), using an interface device with the PLATO III system, developed a procedure for computer analysis of trumpet performances. More recently, Higgins (1981) demonstrated that a microcomputer was an effective tool in teaching beginning clarinet classes. The potentials of computers and microcomputers are great, but both Peters and Higgins caution that some students report negative attitudes toward their experiences with computers.

Understanding through instrumental music. Teaching musical knowledge and understanding through instrumental performance groups is strongly supported by many music educators. Rouintree (1975) developed a theoretical model of sequential concept learning through band programs. Other researchers have developed and evaluated various types of instructional programs' effects on musical understanding. Mitchell (1974) developed an instructional packet to foster understanding of musical structure in a specially composed piece for band. Culbert (1974) used a portion of rehearsal time to develop students' descriptive skills. Croft (1970) developed a related arts program to be taught as part of a school band program. Garofalo and Whaley (1979) found that a "unit study composition" approach was effective in developing students' conceptual knowledge, aural skills, and performance proficiency, whereas Grashel (1979) reported that concepts of musical form could be taught effectively in seventh-grade and eighth-grade instrumental classes. Clearly, research has demonstrated that music understanding can be developed through performance classes.

Predicting success. Rainbow's classic study (1965) of musical aptitude revealed that a number of nonmusical variables are useful predictors of musical ability. Although not negating the value of musical aptitude tests as predictors of musical success, three other studies suggest that intelligence and/or academic achievement also are useful predictors. Boyle (1968) noted that intelligence was a better predictor of rhythm-reading success than a rhythm aptitude measure. Webber (1974) found that the Iowa Test of Basic Skills was a better predictor of music-reading skills than was a measure of musicality. Hufstader (1974), using a discriminant function analysis of seven variables for predicting success in instrumental music, reported that the three best predictors were intelligence, musicality, and academic achievement.

Music Listening. Music listening involves perceptual and analytic responses to aurally presented musical stimuli. It includes a diversity of skills ranging from tasks such as general thematic recognition to recognition and discrimination of and among various aspects of the structural components of music.

Areas of research on music listening are not conveniently demarcated. Prince (1972) argues that little definitive research has been done in the area. Hedden (1980) recognizes three overlapping areas of research concerned with the development of listening skills through instruction: (1) notated and other visual aids to listening, (2) guided listening, and (3) methods and techniques. In another review (Hedden, 1981), he examines listening skills in terms of developmental levels and music listening preferences in response to various instructional variables. J. H. Ramsey's review (1976) examined the effects of various approaches and techniques for developing elementary children's listening skills. A particular problem in research on music listening programs is the criterion of success: should it be cognitive (recognition, discrimination, analysis) or affective (appreciation, preference)?

Research on the topic includes the development of a model listening program reflecting structural and cyclic theories of Piaget, Bruner, and Ausubel (Hagan, 1971). A major portion of the research on music listening, however, examines the effects of various strategies and methods for developing listening skills. Thompson (1972) found no differences in the effectiveness of line drawings, descriptive words, and a combination of both on fifth-graders' and sixth-graders' ability to perceive melodic direction, rhythmic shape, beat, meter, and tempo. Smith (1973) reports that specific procedures for tracking musical form were effective in promoting seventh-graders' and eighth-graders' understanding of musical form. Davies and Yelland (1977) reported that silent rehearsal of recently heard tonal patterns was an effective procedure for facilitating the drawing of melodic contours of the patterns. Tan (1979) observed that tonality cues were an effective strategy for some musicians in detecting specific pairs of tones in melodies.

Other researchers have examined listening skills in relation to affective criteria. Zumbrunn (1972) reported that a guided listening program had no effect on junior high school students' aesthetic judgment. Prince (1974), also studying the effects of a guided listening program, noted that analytic commentary does not lead junior high school students to have an increased liking for Baroque and twentieth-century music. Bartlett (1973) observed that preference for classical music did not increase significantly as a result of increased discrimination skills.

On the basis of a Test of Aural Perception Skills administered to first-graders, third-graders, fifth-graders, and seventh graders, Hufstader (1977) reported a learning sequence for listening skills: timbre, rhythm, melodic pitch patterns, and harmony. Research on variables influencing the development of listening skills reveals that socioeconomic level (McDonald, 1974), instrumental experience (May & Elliott, 1980), complexity of pattern (McMullen, 1974), and conformity to peer judgment (Radocy, 1975) may influence listening responses.

From this cursory examination it is apparent that a need exists for more systematic and coordinated research on music listening. Prince's paradigm (1972) for research on music listening warrants serious consideration. He identified four areas in which research is needed: (1) defining and developing measures of listening ability; (2) studies of the relationships among variables influencing music listening; (3) studies of the effects of subject characteristics on response variables; and (4) studies of the effects of teaching and learning on particular response variables. Particular emphasis should be given to examination of relationships among cognitive listening skills and affective response.

Other Instruction. The dynamics of teacher-student interactions in classroom and rehearsal settings constitute another important variable in the teaching and learning of music. Dorman (1978) reviewed seven major studies concerned with interactions of students and teachers in music (Verrastro, 1970; Whitehill, 1970; Erbes, 1972; Reynolds, 1974; Froehlich, 1976; Hedrick, 1976; Hicks, 1976). Although most of these studies were concerned with interactions in classroom situations, Erbes (1972) developed an observational system for a choral rehearsal, and Reynolds (1974) modified a system for use in small performance groups. Gipson (1978) further adapted the Reynolds system for use in analyzing interactions in private wind instrument instruction at the college level.

Observational techniques also have been employed to study attending behavior, that is, concentration on or participation in a particular activity (Forsythe, 1977). Forsythe noted that attending behavior is partly a function of the nature of the activity in which students participate.

Madsen, Greer, and Madsen (1975) and their students have been leaders in applying behavioral techniques in music. Two distinct types of research are being conducted: (1) research in which music is used as a reinforcer and (2) studies of the effects of reinforcement techniques on music behavior. By and large reinforcement techniques have proven effective both in modifying nonmusical behavior and in modifying musical behaviors through application of reinforcement techniques.

Wolff (1978) and Hanshumaker (1980) provide excellent reviews of research in which music is a means for arriving at nonmusical learning. Besides the use of music as a reinforcer, other uses of music to attain nonmusical educational goals involve facilitation of general and specific learning transfer with background music. A variety of studies have been conducted, and music's effects have been examined with respect to language development, reading readiness, mathematics, creativity, attitudes toward learning, self-concept, socialization, personality, and certain physical activities. Generally, music has no deleterious effects on learning or development with respect to these variables, and a surprisingly large number of studies suggest that music has positive effects. Wolff, however, cautions that inadequacies in experimental designs partially account for these positive results and that definitive evidence of the effects of music on most nonmusical behaviors is yet to be provided.

The "accountability movement" has inspired a certain amount of research on evaluation in music education. Whybrew (1974) provides an overview of the traditional areas of evaluation in music: aptitude measurement, achievement testing, evaluation of performance, measurement of music appreciation, and test development. Abeles (1973) and Kidd (1975) developed performance scales for clarinet and trombone respectively, and Cooksey (1977) developed a rating scale for choral performance. Hylton (1980) evaluated the meaning of the high school performance experience. Hoffer and Long (Hoffer, 1977) developed a test of musicianship for high school bandsmen. The competency-based education movement discussed below is an outgrowth of the accountability movement.

Curricular Movements

Although a number of curricular movements have received some acceptance in the field, the movements generally are not products of extensive evaluative research. Leonhard (1980) refers to these popular curricular movements as cults and separatist movements because they seem to offer simplistic solutions to the problems of music education. Research related to most movements is sparse, suggesting that serious evaluative efforts should be directed toward them during the 1980s. A major concern in evaluating the various movements is determining if the criteria for success should be cognitive, psychomotor, or affective, or some combination thereof?

Early Music Efforts. Interest in early childhood music has increased greatly in the past two decades, reflecting general recognition of the importance of learning and development during early childhood on later learning and development. Simons (1978) compiled a bibliography of research conducted between 1960 and 1975. He synthesized the findings and found evidence for the effects of infant and early childhood music experiences on musical development. There has not been sufficient research to provide a solid knowledge base for the improvement of teaching and learning, however.

In another review of research in early childhood music, Greenberg (1976) noted that a vacuum exists in music education curriculum development research for preschool children. He maintains that priority must be given to the formulation of some theoretical basis and structure for the development of preschool music curricula.

Klemish's review (1973) of research on elementary school music suggests that much research involves merely descriptive and subjective accounts of innovative curricular practices. She notes the dearth of longitudinal studies, particularly those examining relationships between responsiveness to musical elements and teaching methods and materials.

Three curricular movements that have received much attention in elementary school music are the Kodaly method, the Orff approach, and the Manhattanville Music Curriculum Program. These movements are promoted primarily through workshops and descriptive accounts of successful practices. Very little research has been conducted to substantiate the effects of the respective movements.

Woskowiak (1973) incorporated Orff, Kodaly, and Dalcroze principles into a series of music-reading games for first-graders, and Stephens (1974) compared the effects of Richards' adaptation of the Kodaly method with a traditional approach to music reading. McDaniel (1974) also examined the effects of Richards's adaptation on children's scores on Colwell's Music Achievement Tests and concluded that there were no differences between its effects and those of a traditional approach.

The role of research in the development of elementary school music curricula is negligible, and it appears that curriculum development in elementary school music has been almost totally relegated to the writers of basal music textbook series rather than to researchers. Given the need for accountability in music education, curricular research in elementary school music should become a high priority in the 1980s.

Secondary School Music. General music in the secondary schools is an area in which the need for curricular reform is perhaps the greatest. Often it is a required course in grades 7 and 8, but few schools have a general music program beyond the eighth grade. Whereas a number of curricular development projects were undertaken in the late 1950s and during the 1960s, there has been comparatively little broad curricular research on secondary general music in the 1970s. Glenn (1972) and E. Schneider (1969) reviewed some of the earlier research.

Two studies conducted in the 1970s, however, are of particular importance. Lawrence (1973) compared the effects of three recognized methods of instruction: (1) Bennett Reimer's Aesthetic Education Curriculum, (2) George Kyme's Composition Curriculum, and (3) a traditional curriculum. The curricula were taught at three ability levels, and evaluative criteria included tests of music perception, music achievement, and aesthetic judgment. He concluded that the aesthetic education curriculum was best for students at all ability levels and that the composition curriculum was least effective for low-ability students.

W. P. Smith (1972) analyzed the characteristics of five junior high school general music programs that had been identified as outstanding. He reported that successful programs could be developed through several different approaches, generally depending on the teacher's background and interests. Two important similarities were noted among the five programs. (1) Their major objectives included aesthetic awareness, perceptive listening, and

discriminative evaluation of musical performance; and (2) affective objectives seemed to receive more emphasis than cognitive or psychomotor objectives.

Two other studies reflect music educators' increased interest in music of different ethnic groups. Nyberg (1975) developed and evaluated a course in music of the American Indian and the East Indian. Criterion-referenced evaluation was employed, and the curriculum was found to be successful in terms of enabling students to attain both listening and values objectives.

Gamble (1978) used the music of Java and Bali to develop a model spiral curriculum based upon the concepts of Mursell and Bruner. The curriculum extends from kindergarten through grade 8 and provides behavioral objectives and activities for conceptual development over the nine-year span.

The philosophy and goals of junior high school general music need to be reexamined in light of the values and needs of contemporary students. Status research regarding the scope and content of secondary general music and the extent to which various aspects of the program are judged successful, both from educators' and students' viewpoints, is necessary. Curricular priorities need to be established, and efficient and motivating instructional programs need to be developed and evaluated.

Comprehensive Musicianship. Comprehensive musicianship is a curricular movement that examines music as a unitary experience. Music instruction should develop analysis, creation, and performance skills simultaneously. Excessive concentration on any one skill area or any one musical style is discouraged in comprehensive musicianship programs.

The Symposium on the Evaluation of Comprehensive Musicianship (SECM) coordinated thirteen teachers who were identified as strong advocates of comprehensive musicianship. Each teacher formulated behavioral objectives for his or her programs. Objective attainment was assessed by criterion-referenced testing specifically designed for each teacher. Site visits monitored the application of comprehensive musicianship principles. For almost all teachers, there were significant pretest-posttest improvements. SECM showed that comprehensive musicianship could be evaluated in behavioral terms (Boyle & Radocy, 1973).

Composition is an important part of comprehensive musicianship. Dodson (1980) compared a creative-comprehensive approach to teaching music fundamentals with a performance approach. Differences in skill attainment between the groups were nonsignificant, but the creative-comprehensive group developed considerably greater self-confidence in dealing with music, which is critical for non-music majors.

Although comprehensive musicianship may be somewhat difficult to define, there is ample evidence that an approach to music instruction integrating composition, analysis, and performance is feasible. Research is needed to demonstrate the philosophy's efficacy in many instructional situations.

Aesthetic Education. The aesthetic education movement has grown considerably during the 1970s, receiving much of its impetus from three programs: (1) the United States Office of Education (USOE)-sponsored Arts IMPACT Project (Interdisciplinary Model Program in the Arts for Children and Teachers), (2) the Central Midwestern Regional Educational Laboratory (CEMREL) Aesthetic Education Program, and (3) the John D. Rockefeller III Fund's Arts in Education Program. Essentially, aesthetic education programs are multiarts programs designed to foster aesthetic growth and responsiveness to the arts for the general student.

The Arts IMPACT Project sought to raise the level of arts programs in schools primarily through in-service programs for teachers. The project was implemented in five school districts, and a common evaluation model was applied to all sites (Lathrop & Boyle, 1972). The project was effective in increasing participation in and positive attitudes toward the arts.

The John D. Rockefeller III Fund's Arts in Education Programs supported a number of programs in the arts during the 1960s and 1970s. Included among them were the Arts in General Education Project in the school district of University City, Missouri (Madeja, 1969) and the Pennsylvania Arts in Basic Education Project, which was administered by the Fine Arts Program of the Pennsylvania Department of Education (1964). Both projects involved multiarts experiences for the general student.

Perhaps the greatest impetus for aesthetic education has been through programs of the Central Midwestern Regional Educational Laboratory (CEMREL) (Madeja, 1975). The early emphasis of the laboratory was on the development of curricular materials. The materials were field tested in a number of school districts in twenty-one states. The evaluation model for the program primarily involved formative evaluation (Hall & Thuernau, 1975). More recently, CEMREL has entered the field of teacher education, establishing a number of Aesthetic Education Learning Centers (Arts, Education, and Americans Panel, 1977).

Partially due to stimulation through the above programs and various federal programs, a number of local arts projects have been developed throughout the country. The projects of the Alternatives in Education Program of the California Arts Council are examples of such programs (Piper, Greer, & Zwissler, 1979). Most have involved teacher in-service and/or artists-in-schools programs. The residual effects of these programs when the outside support is no longer available are yet to be studied to any extent and represent a major area of needed research. Also, music education researchers need to examine objectively the relative merits of multiarts programs and music programs.

Competency-based Curricula. Competency-based education (CBE) stresses mastery of well-defined observable objectives at a level beyond traditional course requirements. It may require more intensive, extensive, and individualized instruction and study than a less explicit approach. Focus upon doing rather than "only" knowing is characteristic; competency-based programs in teacher education stress field-based experiences in teaching.

A statement of competencies, admittedly somewhat arbitrary, is essential for a CBE program in music education. Stegall, Blackburn, and Coop (1978) obtained ratings from 232 officials at schools accredited by the National Association of Schools of Music on ninety-nine statements for a competency-based undergraduate music education program. Eighty-three statements met the authors' criterion of a 3.5 mean rating on a five-point scale: eighteen basic musicianship competencies, seven competencies related to the principal instrument or voice, six basic learning competencies, seventeen competencies for teaching elementary general music, twelve competencies for teaching performing groups, and thirteen and ten competencies specific to teaching instrumental and choral performing groups respectively.

Teaching via a competency-based approach is exemplified by Hofstetter (1979), who contrasted a competency-based and a more traditional approach to teaching aural internal identification. The essential aspect of the CBE approach was that students had to meet a criterion of 90 percent accuracy, within a response time of four seconds, in each of eight units. The CBE group learned significantly more and spent a greater proportion of learning time on the more difficult materials.

Holding a group to a task until a criterion is attained is reminiscent of Bloom's "mastery learning" (Bloom, Hastings, & Madaus, 1971). Future research efforts probably will address the questions of reconciling time needed for mastery with time available for instruction, obtaining agreement among music educators as to what desirable competencies are, and using instructional technology to facilitate individual competency attainment.

Performance Orientation. One continuing curricular issue, at least at the level of discussion if not of serious research, is the academic stress that performing groups should receive. As an aural art, music must be performed, but do school music groups' performances represent aesthetic education, entertainment, or exploitation, and in what combinations? Is rehearsal time the most important aspect of a music curriculum? Does performance build favorable attitudes toward music?

Maddox (1973) assessed what he called the "relevance perception" of 218 graduates of fourteen North Carolina high school band programs. Students were classified in terms of whether bands were "superior" (had earned a first division contest rating for each of the past three years) or "category II" (had received no more than one second division rating, with all other ratings lower for the past three years). The perceived relevance of high school band experience was only slightly greater for the superior bands' alumni; the bands' correlation between contest ratings and mean relevance ranks was nonsignificant. Individual graduates with high perceptions of the band experiences tended to play their instruments more frequently, attend more concerts, and own more classical recordings, regardless of their band's contest history.

Marciniak (1974) contrasted students from three "superior" and three "not superior" Illinois bands. He found that music perception (perceiving details of musical elements and expression) was related significantly to musical aptitude, academic achievement, amount of ensemble experience, and amount of instruction in music theory and history. There was no significant relationship between music perception and literature quality, directors' backgrounds, or band performance level. Again, a superior group performance environment does not necessarily build what elusively could be called "musicality."

A performance orientation will not build superior musical attitudes or awareness by virtue of performance alone; but, as some of the comprehensive musicianship research shows, one does not have to "sacrifice" performance for the sake of musicality. If one directs instruction toward mechanical performances, that is what will result. If one also teaches for musical awareness, that may result in addition.

Research Needs

Research needs in music education are great. Music curricula should be based upon perceptual and learning principles appropriate for the developmental levels of the learners. They should be concerned with affective as well as cognitive and psychomotor development. Such curricula are not likely to be developed through the fragmented research efforts of graduate students. Leonhard and Colwell's conditions (1976) for major long-term commitments to particular research programs must be realized if music education research is to have a significant effect on school music curricula.

J. David Boyle
Rudolf E. Radocy

See also Aesthetic Education; Creativity.

REFERENCES

Abeles, H. F. Development and validation of a clarinet performance adjudication scale. *Journal of Research in Music Education*, 1973, *21*, 246–255.

Adcock, E. J. A comparative analysis of vocal range in the middle school general music curriculum (Doctoral dissertation, Florida State University, 1970). *Dissertation Abstracts International*, 1971, *31*, 4811A. (University Microfilms No. 71-6952)

Arts, Education, and Americans Panel (D. Rockefeller, Chairman). *Coming to Our Senses: The Significance of the Arts in American Education*. New York: McGraw-Hill, 1977.

Bartlett, D. L. Effect of repeated listenings on structural discrimination and affective response. *Journal of Research in Music Education*, 1973, *21*, 302–317.

Benade, A. H. The physics of brasses. *Scientific American*, 1973, *229*(1), 24–35.

Bentley, A. *Measure of Musical Abilities*. New York: October House, 1966. (a)

Bentley, A. *Musical Ability in Children and Its Measurement*. New York: October House, 1966. (b)

Bentley, A. *Monotones* (Music Education Research Paper No. 1). London: Novello, 1968.

Blacking, J. *How Musical Is Man?* Seattle: University of Washington Press, 1973.

Bloom, B. S.; Hastings, J. T.; & Madaus, G. F. *Handbook on Formative and Summative Evaluation of Student Learning*. New York: McGraw-Hill, 1971.

Bobbitt, R. The development of music reading skills. *Journal of Research in Music Education*, 1970, *18*, 143–156.

Bower, G. H., & Hilgard, E. R. *Theories of Learning* (5th ed.). Englewood Cliffs, N.J.: Prentice-Hall, 1981.

Boyle, J. D. The effects of prescribed rhythmical movements on the ability to sight-read music (Doctoral dissertation, University of Kansas, 1968). *Dissertation Abstracts*, 1968, *29*, 2290–2291. (University Microfilms No. 68-17, 359)

Boyle, J. D., & Radocy, R. E. Evaluation of instructional objectives in comprehensive musicianship. *Council for Research in Music Education*, 1973, *32*, 2–21.

Brand, M. Effectiveness of simulation techniques in teaching behavior management. *Journal of Research in Music Education*, 1977, *25*, 131–318.

Cobes, C. J. The conditioning of a pitch response using uncertain singers (Doctoral dissertation, Pennsylvania State University, 1969). *Dissertation Abstracts International*, 1970, *31*, 1829–1830A. (University Microfilms No. 70-19, 398)

Colwell, R. *Music Achievement Tests*. Chicago: Follett, 1968.

Cooksey, J. M. A facet-factorial approach to rating high school choral music performance. *Journal of Research in Music Education*, 1977, *25*, 100–114.

Croft, J. E. A related arts approach to the band: Aesthetic growth through performance (Doctoral dissertation, University of Oklahoma, 1970). *Dissertation Abstracts International*, 1971, *32*, 474A. (University Microfilms No. 71-17, 040)

Culbert, M. E. The effects of using a portion of the rehearsal time for developing skills in describing music on the performance level and musical achievement of high school band students (Doctoral dissertation, Temple University, 1974). *Dissertation Abstracts International*, 1974, *35*, 3486. (University Microfilms No. 74-28, 259)

Davies, A. D. M., & Roberts, E. Poor pitch singing: A survey of its incidence in school children. *Psychology of Music*, 1975, *6*(2), 24–36.

Davies, J. B., & Yelland, A. Effects of two training procedures on the production of melodic contour, in short-term memory for tonal sequences. *Psychology of Music*, 1977, *5*(2), 3–9.

Deihl, N. C., & Radocy, R. E. Computer-Assisted Instruction: Potential for instrumental music education. *Bulletin of the Council for Research in Music Education*, 1969, *15*, 1–7.

Deihl, N. C., & Zeigler, R. H. Evaluation of CAI program in articulation, phrasing, and rhythm for intermediate instrumentalists. *Bulletin of the Council for Research in Music Education*, 1973, *31*, 1–11.

Dodson, T. A. The effects of a creative-comprehensive approach and a performance approach on acquisition of music fundamentals by college students. *Journal of Research in Music Education*, 1980, *28*, 103–110.

Dorman, P. E. A review of research on observational systems in the analysis of music teaching. *Bulletin of the Council for Research in Music Education*, 1978, *57*, 35–44.

Dowling, W. J., & Fujitani, D. S. Contour, interval, and pitch recognition in memory for melodies. *Journal of the Acoustical Society of America*, 1971, *49*, 524–531.

Drake, R. M. *Drake Musical Aptitude Tests.* Chicago: Science Research Associates, 1957.

Duerksen, G. L. *Teaching Instrumental Music.* Washington, D.C.: Music Educators National Conference, 1972.

Elliott, C. A. Attacks and releases as factors in instrument identification. *Journal of Research in Music Education*, 1975, *23*, 35–40.

Erbes, R. L. The development of an observational system for the analysis of interaction in the research of musical organizations (Doctoral dissertation, University of Illinois, 1972). *Dissertation Abstracts International*, 1976, *34*, 806A. (University Microfilms No. 73-17, 197)

Farnsworth, P. R. *The Social Psychology of Music* (2nd ed.). Ames: Iowa State University Press, 1969.

Foley, E. A. Effects of training in conservation of tonal and rhythmic patterns on second-grade children. *Journal of Research in Music Education*, 1975, *23*, 240–248.

Forsythe, J. L. Elementary student attending behavior as a function of classroom activities. *Journal of Research in Music Education*, 1977, *25*, 228–239.

Friesen, J. M. Vocal mutation in the adolescent male: Its chronology and a comparison with fluctuations in musical interest (Doctoral dissertation, University of Oregon, 1972). *Dissertation Abstracts International*, 1973, *33*, 5429A. (University Microfilms No. 73-7891)

Froehlich, H. C. An investigation of the relationship of selected observational variables to the teaching of singing (Doctoral dissertation, University of Texas, 1976). *Dissertation Abstracts International*, 1977, *37*, 4947A. (University Microfilms No. 77-3898)

Funk, J. D. Some aspects of the development of music perception. (Doctoral dissertation, Clark University, 1977). *Dissertation Abstracts International*, 1977, *38*, 1919B. (University Microfilms No. 77-20, 301)

Gamble, S. G. A spiral curriculum utilizing the music of Java and Bali as a model for teaching ethnic music from kindergarten through grade eight (Doctoral dissertation, Pennsylvania State University, 1978). *Dissertation Abstracts International*, 1979, *39*, 9796–4797A. (University Microfilms No. 7902601)

Garafalo, R. J., & Whaley, G. Comparison of the unit study and traditional approaches for teaching music through school band performance. *Journal of Research in Music Education*, 1979, *27*, 137–142.

Gaston, E. T. *Test of Musicality.* Lawrence, Kan.: Odell's Instrumental Service, 1957.

Gipson, R. C. An observational analysis of wind instrument private lessons (Doctoral dissertation, Pennsylvania State University, 1978). *Dissertation Abstracts International*, 1978, *39*, 2118–2119A. (University Microfilms No. 7818757)

Glenn, N. E. A review of recent research in high school general music. *Bulletin of the Council for Research in Music Education*, 1972, *27*, 17–24.

Gonzo, C. Research in choral music: A perspective. *Bulletin of the Council for Research in Music Education*, 1973, *33*, 21–33.

Gonzo, C., & Forsythe, J. Developing and using videotapes to teach rehearsal techniques and principles. *Journal of Research in Music Education*, 1976, *24*, 32–41.

Gordon, E. *Musical Aptitude Profile.* Boston: Houghton Mifflin, 1965.

Gordon, E. *Iowa Tests of Music Literacy.* Iowa City: University of Iowa, Bureau of Educational Research and Service, 1971. (a)

Gordon, E. *The Psychology of Music Teaching.* Englewood Cliffs, N.J.: Prentice-Hall, 1971. (b)

Gordon, E. *Primary Measures of Music Audiation.* Chicago: GIA Publications, 1979.

Grashel, J. W. Strategies for using popular music to teach form to intermediate instrumentalists. *Journal of Research in Music Education*, 1979, *27*, 185–191.

Greenberg, M. Research in music in early childhood education: A survey with recommendations. *Bulletin of the Council for Research in Music Education*, 1976, *45*, 1–20.

Greer, R. D.; Randall, A.; & Timberlake, C. The discriminate use of music listening as a contingency for improvement in vocal pitch acuity and attending behavior. *Bulletin of the Council for Research in Music Education*, 1971, *26*, 10–18.

Gregory, T. B. The effects of rhythmic notation variables on sight-reading errors. *Journal of Research in Music Education*, 1972, *20*, 462–468.

Hagan, M. T. The structural method of teaching music listening, grades kindergarten through nine (Doctoral dissertation, Washington University, 1971). *Dissertation Abstracts International*, 1972, *32*, 5826A. (University Microfilms No. 72-9340)

Hall, B., & Thuernau, P. Formative research in the aesthetic education program. *Bulletin of the Council for Research in Music Education*, 1975, *43*, 50–64.

Hall, D. E. *Musical Acoustics: An Introduction.* Belmont, Calif.: Wadsworth, 1980.

Hanshumaker, J. The effects of arts education on intellectual and social development: A review of selected research. *Bulletin of the Council for Research in Music Education*, 1980, *61*, 10–28.

Hedden, S. K. Development of music listening skills. *Bulletin of the Council for Research in Music Education*, 1980, *64*, 12–22.

Hedden, S. K. Music listening skills and music listening preferences. *Bulletin of the Council for Research in Music Education*, 1981, *65*, 16–26.

Hedrick, G. L. The development of a verbal analysis system for self-evaluation of preservice music teachers (Doctoral dissertation, Florida State University, 1976). *Dissertation Abstracts International*, 1977, *37*, 6334A. (University Microfilms No. 77-8590)

Heller, J. J. Electronic graphs of musical performance: A pilot study in perception and learning. *Journal of Research in Music Education*, 1969, *17*, 202–216.

Hicks, C. E. The effect of training in interaction analysis on the verbal teaching behaviors and attitudes of prospective school instrumental music education students studying conducting (Doctoral dissertation, Michigan State University, 1976). *Dissertation Abstracts International*, 1977, *37*, 5671A. (University Microfilms No. 77-5718)

Higgins, W. R. *The Feasibility of Teaching Beginning Applied Clarinet with the Microcomputer.* Unpublished doctoral dissertation, Pennsylvania State University, 1981.

Hoffer, C. R. The development of a musicianship test for students in high school performing organizations. *Bulletin of the Council for Research in Music Education*, 1977, *50*, 37–43.

Hofstetter, F. T. Computer-based recognition of perceptual patterns in harmonic dictation exercises. *Journal of Research in Music Education*, 1978, *26*, 111–119.

Hofstetter, F. T. Evaluation of a competency-based approach to teaching aural interval identification. *Journal of Research in Music Education*, 1979, *27*, 201–213.

Hofstetter, F. T. Computer-based recognition of perceptual patterns in chord quality dictation exercises. *Journal of Research in Music Education*, 1980, *28*, 83–91.

Houpt, J. W. *The Status of Chamber Music in the Middle Schools of Pennsylvania*. Unpublished master's thesis, Pennsylvania State University, 1980.

Houtsma, A. J. M., & Goldstein, J. L. The central origin of the pitch of complex tones: Evidence from musical interval recognition. *Journal of the Acoustical Society of America*, 1972, *51*, 520–529.

Hufstader, R. A. Predicting success in beginning instrumental music through use of selected tests. *Journal of Research in Music Education*, 1974, *22*, 52–57.

Hufstader, R. A. An investigation of a learning sequence of music listening skills. *Journal of Research in Music Education*, 1977, *25*, 184–196.

Hylton, J. B. The meaning of high school choral experience and its relationship to selected variables (Doctoral dissertation, Pennsylvania State University, 1980). *Dissertation Abstracts International*, 1981, *41*, 2987A. (University Microfilms No. 8024457)

Jersild, A. T., & Bienstock, S. A study of the development of children's ability to sing. *Journal of Educational Psychology*, 1934, *25*, 481–503.

Jones, R. L. The development of the child's conception of meter in music. *Journal of Research in Music Education*, 1976, *24*, 142–154.

Joseph, W. Vocal growth in the human adolescent and the total growth process. *Journal of Research in Music Education*, 1966, *14*, 135–141.

Joyner, D. R. The monotone problem. *Journal of Research in Music Education*, 1969, *17*, 115–124.

Kidd, R. L. The construction and validation of a scale of trombone performance skills (Doctoral dissertation, University of Illinois, 1975). *Dissertation Abstracts International*, 1976, *36*, 5905A. (University Microfilms No. 76-6820)

Kirkpatrick, W. C., Jr. Relationships between the singing ability of pre-kindergarten children and their home musical environment (Doctoral dissertation, University of Southern California, 1962). *Dissertation Abstracts*, 1962, *23*, 886. (University Microfilms No. 62-3736)

Klemish, J. J. A comparative study of two methods of teaching music reading to first grade children by developing a vocabulary of tonal patterns (Doctoral dissertation, University of Wisconsin, 1968). *Dissertation Abstracts*, 1969, *30*, 355A. (University Microfilms No. 69-942)

Klemish, J. J. A review of recent research in elementary music education. *Bulletin of the Council for Research in Music Education*, 1973, *34*, 23–40.

Klemish, J. J. Treating the uncertain singer through the use of the tape recorder. *Bulletin of the Council for Research in Music Education*, 1974, *37*, 36–45.

Kramme, J. Research in choral music education: A synthesis. *Iowa Journal of Research in Music Education*, 1976, *1*, 34–43.

Kresteff, A. D. The growth of musical awareness in children. *Bulletin of the Council for Research in Music Education*, 1963, *1*, 4–10.

Lathrop, R. L., & Boyle, J. D. Interdisciplinary model program in the arts for children and teachers: An interim report on the Arts IMPACT Project. *Bulletin of the Council for Research in Music Education*, 1972, *29*, 1–8.

Lawrence, V. P. A comparison of three methods of instruction in junior high school general music (Doctoral dissertation, Case Western Reserve University, 1973). *Dissertation Abstracts International*, 1974, *34*, 7021–7022A. (University Microfilms No. 74-10, 803)

Lehman, P. R. *Tests and Measurements in Music*. Englewood Cliffs, N.J.: Prentice-Hall, 1968.

Leonhard, C. Toward a contemporary program of music education. *Bulletin of the Council for Research in Music Education*, 1980, *63*, 1–10.

Leonhard, C., & Colwell, R. J. Research in music education. *Bulletin of the Council for Research in Music Education*, 1976, *49*, 1–30.

Long, P. A. Pitch recognition in short melodies (Doctoral dissertation, Florida State University, 1975). *Dissertation Abstracts International*, 1976, *36*, 3840A–3841A. (University Microfilms No. 76-2264)

MacKnight, C. B. Music reading ability of beginning wind instrumentalists after melodic instruction. *Journal of Research in Music Education*, 1975, *23*, 23–34.

Maddox, R. L. The construction and validation of an instrument to measure relevance perception in band students (Doctoral dissertation, New York University, 1973). *Dissertation Abstracts International*, 1973, *34*, 810A. (University Microfilms No. 73-19, 435)

Madeja, S. A. *All the Arts for Every Child*. New York: John D. Rockefeller III Fund, 1969.

Madeja, S. S. The aesthetics of education: The CEMREL Aesthetic Education Program. *Bulletin of the Council for Research in Music Education*, 1975, *43*, 1–18.

Madsen, C. K. Modulated beat discrimination among musicians and non-musicians. *Journal of Research in Music Education*, 1979, *27*, 57–67.

Madsen, C.; Greer, R. D.; & Madsen, C. H., Jr. (Eds.). *Research in Music Behavior*. New York: Columbia University, Teachers College Press, 1975.

Marchand, D. J. A study of two approaches to developing expressive performance. *Journal of Research in Music Education*, 1975, *23*, 14–22.

Marciniak, F. M. Investigation of the relationships between music perception and music performance. *Journal of Research in Music Education*, 1974, *22*, 35–44.

May, W. V., & Elliott, C. A. Relationships among ensemble participation, private instruction, and aural skill development. *Journal of Research in Music Education*, 1980, *28*, 155–161.

McDaniel, M. A. A comparison of Music Achievement Test scores of fourth-grade students taught by two different methods: Kodaly (Threshold to Music) and traditional (Making Music Your Own) (Doctoral dissertation, Louisiana State University and Agricultural and Mechanical College, 1974). *Dissertation Abstracts International*, 1975, *35*, 4594A. (University Microfilms No. 75-1942)

McDonald, D. Environment: A factor in conceptual listening skills of elementary school children. *Journal of Research in Music Education*, 1974, *22*, 205–214.

McMullen, P. T. Influence of number of different pitches and melodic redundancy on preference responses. *Journal of Research in Music Education*, 1974, *22*, 198–204.

McNitt, H. H. A self-instructional program for uncertain singers (Doctoral dissertation, Pennsylvania State University, 1971). *Dissertation Abstracts International*, 1972, *32*, 6479A. (University Microfilms No. 72-13, 896)

Mitchell, J. R. The effectiveness of an original band composition and its accompanying instructional packet in developing competencies for identifying structural elements of music (Doctoral dissertation, Pennsylvania State University, 1974). *Dissertation Abstracts International*, 1975, *36*, 168A. (University Microfilms No. 75-15, 795)

Moog, H. The development of musical experience in children of pre-school age. *Psychology of Music*, 1976, *4*(2), 38–47.

Multer, W. Solmization and musical perception. *Theory and Practice*, 1978, *3*(1), 29–51.

Nyberg, R. The development, implementation, and evaluation of an introductory course in ethnic music for use in the secondary schools (Doctoral dissertation, University of Miami, 1975). *Dissertation Abstracts International*, 1975, *36*, 2693A. (University Microfilms No. 75-25, 425)

Olson, E. E. A comparison of the effectiveness of wind chamber music ensemble experience with large wind ensemble experience (Doctoral dissertation, University of Southern California, 1975). *Dissertation Abstracts International*, 1975, *36*, 18A. (University Microfilms No. 75-15, 560)

Palmer, M. Relative effectiveness of two approaches to rhythm reading for fourth-grade students. *Journal of Research in Music Education*, 1976, *24*, 110–118.

Parker, R. C. The effectiveness of the TAP System in instruction in sight singing: An experimental study (Doctoral dissertation, University of Miami, 1979). *Dissertation Abstracts International*, 1980, *41*, 151A. (University Microfilms No. 8014160)

Pennsylvania Department of Education. *The Arts Process in Basic Education*. Harrisburg: Pennsylvania Department of Education, 1974.

Perney, J. Musical tasks related to the development of the conservation of metric time. *Journal of Research in Music Education*, 1976, *24*, 159–168.

Peters, G. D. Feasibility of Computer-Assisted Instruction for instrumental music education (Doctoral dissertation, University of Illinois, 1974). *Dissertation Abstracts International*, 1974, *35*, 1478A. (University Microfilms No. 74-14, 598)

Piper, R.; Greer, W. D.; & Zwissler, R. N. *An Evaluation Study of Nine Project Sites*. Westminster: California Learning Designs, Inc., 1979.

Porter, S. Y. The effect of multiple discrimination training on pitch matching behaviors of uncertain singers. *Journal of Research in Music Education*, 1977, *25*, 68–82.

Prince, W. F. A paradigm for research on music listening. *Journal of Research in Music Education*, 1972, *20*, 445–454.

Prince, W. F. Effects of guided listening on musical enjoyment of junior high school students. *Journal of Research in Music Education*, 1974, *22*, 45–51.

Radocy, R. E. A naive minority of one and deliberate mismatches of tonal stimuli. *Psychology of Music*, 1975, *3*(1), 9–20.

Radocy, R. E., & Boyle, J. D. *Psychological Foundations of Musical Behavior*. Springfield, Ill.: Thomas, 1979.

Rainbow, E. L. A pilot study to investigate the constructs of musical aptitude. *Journal of Research in Music Education*, 1965, *13*, 3–14.

Rainbow, E. L. Instrumental music: Recent research and considerations for future investigations. *Bulletin of the Council for Research in Music Education*, 1973, *33*, 8–20.

Ramsey, D. S. What music education research says about the beginning band. *Iowa Journal of Research in Music Education*, 1976, *1*, 44–58.

Ramsey, J. H. Effectiveness of various approaches and techniques in the development of listening skills of elementary school children: A review of recent research. *Iowa Journal of Research in Music Education*, 1976, *1*, 18–33.

Reynolds, K. Modification of the observational system for instructional analysis focusing on appraisal behaviors of music teachers in small performance classes (Doctoral dissertation, Ohio State University, 1974). *Dissertation Abstracts International*, 1974, *35*, 3040–3041A. (University Microfilms No. 74-24, 390)

Richner, S. S. The effect of classroom and remedial methods of music instruction on the ability of inaccurate singers, in the third, fourth, and fifth grades, to reproduce pitches (Doctoral dissertation, University of Idaho, 1976). *Dissertation Abstracts International*, 1976, *37*, 1447A. (University Microfilms No. 76-19, 898)

Roberts, E., & Davies, A. D. M. Poor pitch singing: Response of monotone singers to a program of remedial training. *Journal of Research in Music Education*, 1975, *23*, 227–239.

Roberts, E., & Davies, A. D. M. A method of extending the vocal range of "monotone" school children. *Psychology of Music*, 1976, *4*(1), 29–43.

Roederer, J. G. *Introduction to the Physics and Psychophysics of Music* (2nd ed.). New York: Springer-Verlag, 1975.

Rouintree, J. P. A theoretical position for the development of musical learning experiences for bands (Doctoral dissertation, University of Illinois, 1975). *Dissertation Abstracts International*, 1976, *36*, 5906A. (University Microfilms No. 76-6937)

Schneider, E. Music education. In R. L. Ebel (Ed.), *Encyclopedia of Educational Research* (4th ed.). New York: Macmillan, 1969.

Seashore, C. E.; Lewis, L.; & Saetveit, J. B. *Seashore Measures of Musical Talents*. New York: Psychological Corporation, 1960.

Sergeant, D., & Roche, S. Perceptual shifts in the auditory information processing of young children. *Psychology of Music*, 1973, *1*(2), 39–48.

Shrader, D. L. An aural approach to rhythmic sight-reading, based upon principles of programmed learning, utilizing a stereo-tape teaching machine (Doctoral dissertation, University of Oregon, 1970). *Dissertation Abstracts International*, 1970, *31*, 2426A. (University Microfilm No. 70-21, 576)

Simons, G. M. *Simons Measurements of Music Listening Skills*. Chicago: Stoelting, 1974.

Simons, G. M. *Early Childhood Musical Development: A Bibliography of Research Abstracts*. Reston, Va.: Music Educators National Conference, 1978.

Skornicka, J. E. The function of time and rhythm in instrumental music reading competency (Doctoral dissertation, Oregon State University, 1958). *Dissertation Abstracts*, 1958, *19*, 1406–1407.

Sloboda, J. The psychology of music reading. *Psychology of Music*, 1978, *6*(2), 3–20.

Smith, A. Feasibility of tracking musical form as a cognitive listening objective. *Journal of Research in Music Education*, 1973, *21*, 200–213.

Smith, W. P. A study and analysis of selected junior high school programs in general music (Doctoral dissertation, University of Oregon, 1972). *Dissertation Abstracts International*, 1972, *33*, 353–354A. (University Microfilms No. 72-20, 931)

Stegall, J. R.; Blackburn, J. E.; & Coop, R. H. Administrators' ratings of competencies for an undergraduate music education curriculum. *Journal of Research in Music Education*, 1978, *26*, 3–15.

Stephens, R. E. A comparative study of two instructional methods in music reading at the grade five and six level (Doctoral dissertation, University of Oregon, 1974). *Dissertation Abstracts*

International, 35, 3801A. (University Microfilms, No. 74-26, 566)

Stevens, S. S. *Psychophysics.* New York: Wiley, 1975.

Stuart, M. The use of videotape recordings to increase teacher trainees' error-detection skills. *Journal of Research in Music Education,* 1979, *27,* 14–19.

Sturges, P. T., & Martin, J. G. Rhythmic structure in auditory temporal pattern perception and immediate memory. *Journal of Experimental Psychology,* 1974, *102,* 377–383.

Swope, R. L. Improvement of rhythm sight reading ability through use of the Tap System. *Pennsylvania Music Educators Association Bulletin of Research in Music Education,* 1977, *8*(1), 23–26.

Tan, N. Tonal organization in the perception of melodies. *Psychology of Music,* 1979, *7*(1), 3–11.

Taylor, J. A. Perception of tonality in short melodies. *Journal of Research in Music Education,* 1976, *24,* 197–208.

Taylor, S. Musical development of children aged seven to eleven. *Psychology of Music,* 1973, *1*(1), 44–49.

Thackray, R. *An Investigation into Rhythmic Abilities.* London: Novello, 1968.

Thackray, R. Tests of harmonic perception. *Psychology of Music,* 1973, *1,* 49–57.

Thompson, K. P. Relative effectiveness of aural perception of televised verbal descriptions and visual representations of selected music events. *Contributions to Music Education,* 1972, *1,* 68–84.

Utley, E. *The Effectiveness of the Shrader TAP System in Improving Music Reading and General Reading Comprehension.* Unpublished report, Norfolk (Virginia) Public School District, 1978.

Verrastro, R. E. Verbal behavior analysis as a supervisory technique with student teachers of music (Doctoral dissertation, Pennsylvania State University, 1970). *Dissertation Abstracts International,* 1970, *31,* 2781A. (University Microfilms No. 70-24, 201)

Wassum, S. Elementary school children's concept of tonality. *Journal of Research in Music Education,* 1980, *28,* 18–33.

Webber, G. H. The effectiveness of musical and non-musical measures as predictors of success in beginning instrumental music classes (Doctoral dissertation, University of Texas at Austin, 1974). *Dissertation Abstracts International,* 1975, *35,* 5457–5458A. (University Microfilms No. 75-4306)

Welch, G. F. Poor pitch singing: A review of the literature. *Psychology of Music,* 1979, *7*(1), 50–58. (a)

Welch, G. F. Vocal range and poor pitch singing. *Psychology of Music,* 1979, *1*(2), 13–31. (b)

Whitehill, C. D. The application of Flanders' system of classroom interaction analysis to general classroom music teaching (Doctoral dissertation, West Virginia University, 1970). *Dissertation Abstracts International,* 1970, *31,* 2428A. (University Microfilms No. 70-22, 623)

Whybrew, W. E. Research in evaluation in music education. *Bulletin of the Council for Research in Music Education,* 1974, *35,* 9–19.

Williams, D. B. Short-term retention of pitch sequence. *Journal of Research in Music Education,* 1975, *23,* 53–66.

Wing, H. D. *Standardised Tests of Musical Intelligence.* The Mere, England: National Foundation for Education Research, 1961.

Wolff, K. The non-musical outcomes of music education: A review of the literature. *Bulletin of the Council for Research in Music Education,* 1978, *55,* 1–27.

Woskowiak, L. F. Programmed music reading games for first grade utilizing certain principles of Dalcroze, Kodaly, and Orff (Doctoral dissertation, Pennsylvania State University, 1973). *Dissertation Abstracts International,* 1973, *34,* 1959–1960A. (University Microfilms No. 73-24, 051)

Yank, S. H. The effect of multiple discrimination training on pitch-matching behaviors of uncertain singers (Doctoral dissertation, Columbia University, 1975). *Dissertation Abstracts International,* 1975, *36,* 25A. (University Microfilms No. 75-15, 766)

Zorn, J. D. Effectiveness of chamber music ensemble experience. *Journal of Research in Music Education,* 1973, *21,* 3–19.

Zumbrunn, K. A guided listening program in twentieth-century music for junior high school students. *Journal of Research in Music Education,* 1972, *20,* 370–378.

NATIONAL DEVELOPMENT AND EDUCATION

"National development" is defined for the purposes of this article as economic development. This does not mean that concern is limited to economic growth in the conventional sense of a rising GNP, either aggregate or per capita. Difficult as they may be to measure, the nonmonetary components of economic development can be substantial and should not be ignored. National economic development is nevertheless inseparable from economic growth in a double sense: if the underlying processes that sustain national development are blocked, growth will cease; and economic stagnation in turn can inhibit the operation of those processes. A fundamental element in development is participation of increasing proportions of the population in both creating products and services and enjoying the rewards of those activities. Those who have seriously addressed problems of development, whatever their individual political or ideological leanings may be, increasingly realize that sustained development presupposes broadened participation.

Just as economic development is more than economic growth, so "education" is more than schooling. Especially important in the present context are learning and training at work, whether in formal or informal ways. As with economic development, the broader view of education may pose difficulties for empirical measurement, but this does not justify proceeding as if only schooling constituted investment in the formation of human resources.

Recently, two basic ideas concerning relationships between education and development have begun to receive the attention that they have long deserved. First is what Schultz (1975) called "the ability to deal with disequilibria" in a world of continual change. Second is the development of competencies and know-how by training and learning on the job—not so much substituting for school learning as supplementing and complementing such learning. Few

analytical models and few empirical investigations of development have focused on these themes or on the related broad theme that national development entails the involvement of rising proportions of the population in changing ways of producing and living. This bias in the literature is not surprising; change and successive disequilibria go hand in hand, and our equilibrium models are much simpler and more elegant than those dealing with the nature and dynamics of change. Unavoidably the pages that follow reflect in some degree this uneven state of our models. Discussion is organized under the following headings: (1) the importance of literacy and primary schooling; (2) assessing the education mix; (3) manpower, jobs, and postschool learning; (4) schooling and small enterprisers; (5) human resources in aggregate growth accounting; (6) a reconsideration of how education contributes to growth.

Literacy and Primary Schooling

The most fundamental contribution of schooling to economic development is the inculcation of basic, general cognitive skills and the spread of increasing mastery in their application. In this sphere schools can do better than other agencies, and for a large part of the population no adequate alternative for such instruction is available. Although historical and cross-societal comparisons underline the importance of literacy, they demonstrate also interdependence of the expansion of literacy and economic advance. Case studies reveal the different uses that individuals, families, and communities make of literacy as well as showing the circumstances under which literacy lapses. Perforce literacy is essential for activities that require reading and writing. More than that, literacy also changes individuals' perceptions of the alternatives open to them and offers clues to unconventional ways of doing things. On tracing out these effects it is sterile to try to decide whether literacy was required for a job. Both what is required for a job and the nature of the job will change as new human resources emerge and as the whole economic structure is transformed by educational and economic development. Even when literacy is not essential to an activity, it fosters adaptability to changes introduced by employers or innovative competitors. And old lines of work are altered when literacy and other components of the "three Rs" permit access to how-to-do-it handbooks.

Each small improvement in adaptations, for example, reading instructions for handling fertilizer or dried milk, makes people better off materially. The gain is not less important merely because the way in which we measure economic growth neglects the effects of education on productivity in the home (and for that matter, in all nonmarket production). At the same time, even meager schooling can affect the kind of life people seek and what they do. To be sure, change-fostering traits are displayed only weakly by most literate persons, just as most university graduates do little hard reading and display ingenuity only now and then, but it is in the multiplication of small changes that national development is diffused and sustained.

Assertions that widespread literacy provides the foundation for economic development have been challenged on one ground or another. Most skeptics doubt certain benefits from literacy but defend others, some of which the next critic may discount. The finding that rates of return for elementary schooling nearly everywhere are high (and university rates of return generally lower) may be waved aside with doubts about the empirical validity of the estimates, and indeed those estimates are unquestionably biased in many instances. Nevertheless no one seems to have found elementary rates anywhere to be low, despite fine tuning to correct for biases. Literate peasants are not always more productive than illiterate neighbors, but this fact is not inconsistent with a conclusion that schooling profoundly transforms a peasantry. It has been said (occasionally even with citations to my writings on this point) that cross-national correlations between literacy and per capita income reflect the fact that higher incomes permit a society to afford schools. But it is also true that without literacy among 40 to 50 percent of a population, there has seldom been economic development; this, indeed, is a serious problem that has been facing Saudi Arabia despite all its oil wealth. There is mounting evidence of the importance of widespread primary education for cumulative economic advance, given policies otherwise favorable to opportunities for people to use their literacy.

The foregoing arguments resemble the much older but always reviving dispute as to whether policies should focus on redistributing the gains from development or should concentrate on accelerating growth in national product. How, in fact, do we perceive economic growth—or better, economic development—as a goal? The movement to develop social indicators and debates over how they might be combined and whether they should be included in some new omnibus welfare measure, of which conventionally measured per capita GNP would be only a part, derives

from just such concerns. From that perspective, literacy would be entered as an explicit component of a summary national welfare indicator. By contrast literacy appears in conventional national income and wealth accounting only by the most indirect, circuitous, and partial routes, through factor inputs into primary schooling (which leave out entirely the inputs of time spent in acquiring literacy). So omnibus an aggregation as is sometimes contemplated would be more likely to blur than to illuminate understanding, however, and it is neither surprising nor unfortunate that even as papers and books on "basic needs" have proliferated, no one has succeeded in establishing an acceptable overall "national welfare index."

Meanwhile three related efforts have been made in this area: (1) health indicators have been introduced into longitudinal accounting studies of the determinants of national income, as quality adjustments on inputs of human capital; (2) attempts have been made to identify factors that may explain the levels that countries attain on variously specified "national needs"; and (3) indicators of a country's standing on selected "basic needs" have been incorporated with other variables in global models of the determinants of per capita income using cross-national data. Recently Wheeler (1980) introduced literacy rates both as a change variable and as a measure of base-year stock in a complex multistage global model of development. He then went on to simulation experiments projecting future relationships. He drew the following conclusions about literacy: "In extensive experiments with different schooling intensities over very long time periods . . . it became clear that the final results of a continuation of low schooling rates is an apparent failure of the society to reach the point of self-sustaining increase in per capita income growth. Unless the primary-school enrollment ratio is over 80 percent, the performance of the socio-economic system seems fundamentally constrained in the long run. All relevant curves become parabolic, and in the very long run the society seems to begin falling backward." (pp. 91–92). Although literacy had significant effects on birth rates, its main effect in his simulations was on productivity. It is of interest that even though Wheeler did not include advanced countries, his findings are consistent with the much simpler cross-national comparisons inclusive of advanced countries in the 1950s presented in Bowman and Anderson (1963).

Assessing the Education Mix

Writings and debates concerning the appropriate education mix are numerous, and such work often is cited in observations about the contributions of education to economic development. There can be considerable confusion here, however, if one fails to distinguish between decision criteria and the effects of various types and levels of education on aggregative growth. Though related, these are not the same. In particular, it must be remembered that rate-of-return analysis originated in microanalysis of decisions about private investments in human beings in a world of comparative certainty. Even when social or societal returns are distinguished from private returns, such analyses differ from an assessment of the part played by education in economic growth on two counts: they entail comparisons with costs, and they discount returns back to the decision point. Furthermore, variations in rates of return to different educational increments or types of education within a country reflect the existing education mix; the questions to which such an analysis is addressed, even when posed in a societal perspective, are concerned most directly with resource allocation and with income distribution, only indirectly with economic growth. It is important nonetheless that we look at just what these measures may and may not indicate concerning the place of various sorts and levels of education in economic development. I begin with the most familiar and the simplest sets of indicators: private and social rates of return to successive increments of schooling.

Private Rates of Return to Schooling. To understand what rates of return do and do not tell us, we need to know first just how private rates of return are normally estimated. For example, how would one estimate the private rate of return from investment in four years of college? The first step is to lay out the stream of earnings by age for those who enter the labor market at graduation from high school and to compare this with the stream of earnings (net of direct outlays on college) of those who complete four more years. During the years in college students spend most of their time in study, and their earnings are less than those of high school graduates. In addition college students may have substantial direct expenses (tuition, books, and so on) that may even bring their net income streams for that period to less than zero. However, at some point earnings of college graduates overtake those of high school graduates, and typically they continue higher from then on to retirement. The private internal rate of return to the investment in a college education is the discount rate that, applied to the high school earning stream and to the college stream, will equate their "present values" at the date of high school completion.

Two types of adjustments have frequently been made in these estimates of private rates of return. First, a somewhat arbitrary correction has been made to allow for bias in selectivity into college; it is assumed that those who attend college would have earned more than the high school graduates even if they had not continued with higher education. This article is not the place to join the debate about the correct magnitude of an "ability adjustment," which may differ substantially from one society to another, but I shall make a few comments later.

Second, in some cases adjustments have been made also to allow for effects of economic growth on real earnings. Such adjustments are not made when the data on earning streams come from longitudinal studies of cohort earning paths. They are introduced when the estimates for the high school and the college earning streams are taken from age-education-earnings data for a particular calendar date. This raises some pertinent issues to which I shall return shortly.

Rental values versus rates of return. The rental values attributable to an individual's study in college, for example, are the increments to earnings after entering the labor market that accrue from extra years of study. These are simply the differences in each successive year of what an individual with a college background earns over what he or she would have earned with only secondary education. No discounting is involved. If the differentials are in fact truly attributable to extra education, and if in addition they accurately reflect the individual's true increase in productivity, then these rental values will measure the contributions of the investment in college education to the national product. They will indicate the measured contribution of the investment to the national product even if the earnings misstate the individual's productivity.

It is just such rental values that form the basis of the aggregative assessments of contributions of education to growth in the national accounting models discussed later. Notice that no discounting is involved. Some investments may entail high costs, and not be justified even when they bring high rental values in the future; some investments may cost very little and even when the subsequent rental values look small the rates of return could be remarkably high, fully justifying the small outlays.

Social versus private rates. When seeking indicators for assessment of educational investments from a societal or social perspective as distinct from a private one, it is common practice to make two sorts of adjustments. First, when private rates are estimated, the extra income taxes paid by the college graduate are deducted from the difference between the college and high school earning streams. However, in most international comparisons (as Psacharopoulos, 1973) digging out the income-tax data is too big a job, and this adjustment is not made. Second, in estimating social rates of return, subsidies from government and foundations are added to the costs incurred by the individual. The result is of course to reduce the social rates thus estimated as compared with the private rates—unambiguously so when no income tax adjustment is introduced on the private side. Although these adjustments are appropriate for deciding whether the subsidy by the society to the costs of higher education was worthwhile, they bear no direct relevance for an analysis of relationships between education and economic growth. Obviously such costs would have to be considered if we were trying to estimate net contributions of education to growth, but to do this all around, for all measured inputs into the national product, would take us far afield, into problems that cannot be addressed in this article.

Growth adjustments and diminishing returns. In a relatively unchanging world in which "other things are equal," one might expect that the greater the number of people who continue through college (or through secondary school), the less would a college graduate earn relative to people who did not continue; the lower, accordingly, would be the rates of return to these increments of education. Actually there is some rough negative association between internal rates of return and the proportion of the labor force that has higher education or secondary education. As long as demands for the better-educated people do not keep rising and elasticities of substitution of more educated for less educated labor are less than infinite, increases in the proportion of more educated people will have this dampening effect on their earnings. Under such conditions, current rates of return (and rental values) associated with an increment of schooling understate the true contributions in the past, but tend to overstate prospective contributions in the future. What keeps this from happening is a continuing rise in demand for better-educated people. What, then, may either rates of return or rental-value estimates tell us of contributions of education to economic growth, and what in this context would be implied by upward adjustments in estimated rates of return to allow for growth?

With this question we confront one of the most elusive problems in the literature on the sources of economic growth. If there are indeed rising demands for better-educated people, what lies back of such demands? Are they in part at least a reflection of prior increases in supplies of human capital, as economic organization and technology adapt to rising levels of schooling in a population? If so, is this all a net gain economically, or has there been some partially offsetting loss (aside from the implied difficulties in efforts toward more equal distribution of income)? Or do the increases in demand for more-educated people arise primarily from forces that were essentially independent of prior gains in human capital but that maintained and even increased incentives to further education? The answers to these questions are important. If one accepts the position that growth requires development of human resources as well as other complementary factors, however, those answers may not matter for interpretation of growth adjustments in estimated rates of return and rental values. The fact that demand continues to rise means that the increments to education are contributing to growth, and the rental value measures of those contributions are in the same class with rental value measures of contributions of physical capital; both are needed and each would be worth less without the other.

The Screening Hypothesis. In recent years the "screening hypothesis" has been propounded as an attack on human capital theory when that theory is applied to evaluations of societal benefits as distinct from private benefits and costs of education. At the extreme of this line of reasoning, differentials in earnings associated with schooling tell us nothing about any contribution of the schooling to a person's productive potential. The schooling will still be a good investment from the point of view of the individual, but only because it can be used to certify competence, not because it has added anything to that competence. Few even of those who have joined in this attack have gone to such an extreme, but debates around related issues continue. "Certificitis" (Bowman, 1970) and what Dore (1976) has called "the diploma disease" pose more limited but related challenges. Gradually we are acquiring a more discriminating assessment of the balance between actual learning and mere selection in the schools. We are taking more discriminating looks also at the extent to which bureaucratic controls on both education and access to jobs may distort indicators of the sources of national income, with sometimes serious negative effects on economic development.

Roles of Vocational Schools. In principle the same logic is involved in assessing contributions of vocational schooling as in assessing those of more standard general education. It is more difficult to make initial estimates of rates of return because vocational schools are so diverse in curricula, in levels at which they are focused, in costs, and in selection of students. On the other hand, there can be no doubt about the pragmatic economic intent of those who establish and finance vocational training, whatever the perceptions of those schools may be among the youth who attend them (and especially among those who attend them only because they could not get places elsewhere). One may reason backwards, as it were, to what vocational schools contribute to growth by considering the rationale of their existence and their attributes in comparison with the general schools. Despite the emphasis in this article on the distinction between benefit-cost analysis and an examination of contributions of education to growth, it is useful here to consider prudent criteria in the public provision of vocational training in relation to the empirical manifestations of response to such considerations.

There are solid economic explanations of the fact that the teaching of basic language and mathematical skills has been everywhere assigned to agencies set up for this instruction (which we call "schools"), whereas specialized skills historically have more often been acquired through some form of apprenticeship. It is not surprising, furthermore, that "commerce" schools spring up quickly when economic development begins; this is a comparatively low-cost training that applies to a large proportion of enterprises, both public and private, and provides a broad road into modern sectors of the economy.

Almost universally, general or bookish schooling enjoys higher status than vocational instruction, except where there are highly technical mathematical-engineering sequences leading on up to higher education—and these are rarely regarded as vocational schools. Reasons for this attitude are complex, but in part they reflect the greater range of options opened up by general curricula, options both for further education and subsequent careers. Turning vocational schooling into terminal education has usually proved less than fully successful. When many individuals seek to transfer into general education, we have signals that something may be out of order. Labor market policies may be perverse, or the subsidies to the specialized vocational training may be ill-advised, or both. But it may also be that individuals perceive a need for more general skills with which to advance the development and deployment of their specialized skills. Of course, a dyseconomic cultural bias may also be present. Each of these situations can be illustrated from almost any part of the Third World, but correctly identifying the problem and making appropriate adjustments is not easy. Failures on this account impede the effective enlistment of education for economic development.

There is complementarity between general and trade schools, not merely substitution. Contrary to common belief, malallocation of educational resources is not indicated merely because many trade school students have previously attended an academic secondary school, even though planners had intended that the shorter vocational courses should follow elementary school. There are also many kinds of high-quality, full-term technical schools on the secondary level that incorporate in their programs strong elements of basic general education; this is one way of achieving complementarity in education, but by no means the only way. If one generalization can be made about contributions of formal vocational training to economic development, it is probably that there is a demonstrated value in diversity (in kinds and duration of curricula) and in readiness to adapt to continuously changing situations. Postschool training, learning at work, and vocational courses provided in other settings often overlap in function and even in organization. Before going on to postschool education, however, we might well discuss "manpower" approaches to education for growth.

Manpower, Jobs, and Postschool Learning

Rate-of-return analysis and related attempts at benefit-cost accounting in the assessment of investments in education start from the supply side of a human-resource assessment. Manpower planning starts from the demand side and focuses in the first instance on the jobs people perform and prospective job requirements. For the most part, no use is made of market prices (wages), in contrast to rate-of-return and benefit-cost analysis. Unemployment, like employment, is treated only in terms of numbers. Finally, postschool learning has received little attention in manpower planning theory and models. In this section these three interconnected topics are combined, nevertheless, because all of them relate more directly to labor markets than to education in schools.

Conventional Manpower Planning. Manpower planning and its associated rationale for the forecasting of manpower requirements have spread over the world during the epoch of development planning since the end of World War II. These activities always have the quality of "willing" more than of "planning" social change (Anderson & Bowman, 1965), although the estimates usually are linked to (derived from) general economic plans. It has taken some years for a general appreciation of the weak foundations

for manpower planning to emerge. The emphasis still is on skill packages, nevertheless. This orientation is not at all people-centered. The concept of "development men—and women" (Bowman, 1978) as creative and adaptive individuals prepared to grow in a world of change is rarely considered.

Most manpower planning is based on fixed-coefficient input-output models. Such models assume low (even zero) elasticities of substitution among designated categories of manpower, but implicitly they assume high to perfect elasticities of substitution within those categories. Changes in manpower and in associated educational requirements are attributed to changes (or projected changes) in technologies and in the mix of product and service outputs in the economy. Initially no account was taken of the effects of supplies of human resources on their allocation among activities, or on appropriate technologies and product mixes. Progressively more flexibility has been introduced into these models as experience in applying them has accumulated, but uses of wage data remain the exception.

With hindsight it can be said that attempts to apply manpower planning models over the world have provided tests of hypotheses about economic development and have revealed some unanticipated complexities in the ways in which human resources affect economic development. The Mediterranean Regional Project of the Organization for Economic Cooperation and Development (OECD) was an early landmark in this work; the technical evaluation of this project by Hollister (1966) mobilized economic theory to induce sharper thinking about manpower planning. The OECD published *Occupational and Educational Structures of the Labor Force and Levels of Economic Development* based on data from over fifty countries (Jallade, Croner, & Emmerij, 1970). The new outlook that emerged from that study was phrased as follows: "The findings 'strongly suggest that possibilities of partial substitution between types of labor exist at given levels of economic and technological development. As has already been indicated several times in the course of this analysis, other reasons besides substitution possibilities may exist to explain our findings, but the least one can say is that they cast serious doubt on the complementarity hypothesis usually adopted in manpower forecasting'" (p. 248). At no place in that study, except among outside scholars brought in to participate in the discussions, was there mention of the need to take account of relative wages. This is in striking contrast, for example, to studies at the National Bureau of Economic Research as long as twenty years ago of the intraoccupation or intrasector components of increases in productivity.

Filtering Down of People and Filtering Up of Jobs. "Filtering down" of educated people goes on everywhere, but its greater speed in many of the developing countries fixes our attention. When initially the base of human resources is small, even individuals with little schooling obtain much-desired jobs in the modern sector. The better-schooled have fine opportunities, and they find promotion to posts of high responsibility at an early age. But this situation does not last, and younger brothers cannot obtain jobs as good as those of older brothers with comparable schooling. Many of the later cohorts of graduates from each level of school "filter down" into jobs, or at least job titles, that are less attractive than the ones on which they had built high expectations of the payoff from schooling. If the observer views a job as a fixed sort of thing, irrespective of the capabilities of the person holding it, filtering down may seem to be wasteful. As long as years of schooling or qualifications for jobs are viewed in crude quantitative terms, better-educated people will be seen to be underemployed, and their education will be viewed as wasteful. Just such judgments have often confounded educational planning. But if one looks at performance and attends to actual changes in the nature of the job that accompany changes in the capabilities of those engaged in it, conclusions can be quite different.

Indeed it is only with such filtering down of people that one can have the filtering up of jobs that is needed for economic growth. Gradually the focus of attention may then shift to more sensitive indicators of excess or shortage of educational provision and educated people. At the same time, concern may be directed increasingly to the quality of education. Attention should be, but often is not, directed to how well or how poorly labor markets (and associated policies) are operating to make effective use of available human (and other) resources. Are incentives so structured as to attract individuals into those jobs or situations in which their skills will be most productive? How much scope is given for people to use their skills and their ingenuity in constructive ways? How much education can contribute to economic development depends on these among other factors.

Educated Unemployment. This oddly labeled problem (meaning unemployment of educated people) often is associated with filtering down of individuals, but it has received more widespread attention. How serious in fact is the problem of unemployment among better educated people, and what are its implications for assessments of the contributions of schooling to economic development? A common, but misleading, reaction to unemployment of better-educated individuals is to conclude offhand that this shows that their education has been a waste from a societal point of view. Such unconsidered assertions entail an implicit assumption that all individuals with the same schooling are alike and that the pool from which qualified people are drawn is of no importance once the required number of graduates are turned out. It assumes also that information networks are highly efficient. Even limiting analysis strictly to numbers unemployed, one should at the least consider the comparative rates of unemployment among variously schooled sets of people, and the timing of that unemployment over the life cycle. It is important to take into account the fact that job search to find a good match of abilities with entry jobs and career development prospects normally will have greater pay-offs for educated

individuals; this means also that in the end they will make greater contributions to national economic development. But this leads us into wage considerations.

The analysis for India by Blaug, Layard, and Woodhall (1969) is especially illuminating in two respects. It incorporates a dynamic component in the forward shifting demand for educated people that maintains their entry wages and salaries despite continuous increases in their numbers, and despite continuation of initial periods of unemployment before they find suitable work. At the same time, it incorporates an examination of social as compared with private rates of return to educational investments, finding that public subsidies to education substantially reduce the social returns as compared with the private returns. The estimates of both private and social rates of return take periods of unemployment of college graduates into account, along with the unemployment of the secondary-school graduates with whom they are compared. The conclusion is reached that there was indeed over-investment in higher education in India from a societal perspective, but this is attributed to the public subsidies and their effects on private incentives, not to the unemployment of educated people. This analysis has much in common with analyses of rural-urban migration and its relationship to urban unemployment wherever there is a protected modern sector in which both pay and future earning prospects are decidedly superior to those available elsewhere. As long as people see such possibilities as sufficiently attainable, they will queue up, even with some personal sacrifice. The economy loses what the migrants would have produced in the countryside during their period of waiting. Often both the migrants and the better-educated job searchers are at work off and on in the informal sector of the urban economy, but their production is overlooked.

Postschool Learning. Perhaps the single most important flaw in manpower economics has been its common disregard for postschool learning, other than to view it as a patching-up process to fill manpower gaps. Even where economic growth is sluggish, people learn both in school and after they leave school; no one comes out of school as a finished product, subject only to deterioration. The more impressive is the economic development and the associated expansion of schools, the more important is postschool learning. Learning by doing is not displaced by formal instruction, and on-the-job improvement in skills (whether through formal training or informally) tends to be more varied and larger in amount for those individuals who have received the most formal instruction. This postschool learning is needed if individuals are to take advantage of new opportunities over the course of their working lives.

Acquisition of many kinds of know-how is difficult except in association with postschool experience, but there is ample evidence also that general schooling lays down much of the capacity to learn and to adapt to new situations. Recent fashionable discussions about nonformal and recurrent education have been largely superficial, primarily because they have made little use of any analytical structure. The treatment by Becker (1962, 1975) of firm-specific training and the growing literature on "internal labor markets" as places for the formation and utilization of skills are relevant to this topic. These and related theories are central to the analysis of human resources in economic growth, but have rarely been used explicitly in the study of growth.

Some of the evidence as to how deficiencies of know-how have been circumvented was summarized more than fifteen years ago (Bowman, 1965). Even today, however, there seems to be considerable myopia on these matters in academic literature. Practical persons dealing with human-resource problems in less-developed countries bemoan the difficulties in developing competence in the labor force to handle problems that arise on the job when things for one reason or another go wrong, and some of these practical persons try to find new ways to foster the development of such know-how. At lower levels of skill considerable ingenuity is manifested by ordinary persons where conditions are reasonably favorable. Such ingenuity is displayed also in the search for and provision of learning opportunities outside of planned and formally recognized agencies, as King (1975) has shown for Kenya.

The problem of providing opportunities for learning in association with work, specifically for the kinds of learning rarely possible outside of work experience, will not quickly disappear in the less developed countries. Like the task of raising quality of instruction in the lower schools, this is inevitably a slow process. There is an asymmetry, however, in the possible relationships between national economic development and education in schools versus education at work. Those things traditionally taught in schools and most readily learned there do not depend on the economic environment nor on the opportunities it provides for participatory learning; schooling, therefore, can easily lead development if the motivations are there and the resources are available to support the schools. The acquisition of know-how, on the other hand, cannot proceed far ahead of the economic growth for which, nevertheless, it is needed.

Schooling and Small Enterprisers

In nearly every developing country, progress in agriculture is requisite for sustained growth. Small enterprisers in the nonfarm sphere are receiving more attention recently, although they have been neglected in manpower economics. In actual policies for development in many countries, they have been not only neglected but actively penalized. Yet for many decades in most societies, development of human resources in and for small-scale endeavors will remain important.

Agricultural Progress. It is for agriculture, paradoxically, that we have the best empirical research concerning how the human factor contributes to development. This is the sector for which one can most readily identify associations between schooling and innovative change. Research upholds the argument that schooling of farmers contributes to agricultural progress, provided circumstances and policies encourage new practices (see the review of this research by Lockheed, Jamison, & Lau, 1980). Farmers, including many peasants, are canny people who deal directly with most of the factors that affect the economic well-being of their activity. They will be innovative when they have access to relevant information, can decode this information, and have access to the needed inputs and to markets for their products.

Theoretical foundations for this research lie in the economic theory of decision making; schooling is presumed to affect the ability to allocate resources efficiently in situations in which opportunities are changing (see Chaudhri, 1968; Welch, 1970). This starting point has several implications for proper specification of the variables in the empirical research.

It is important to ask whether the populations studied actually make decisions in agriculture. If the data come from a household survey, for example, it will obviously be important to look into how responsibilities for various activities are shared and which individuals or combinations of individuals influence the decisions. If it is a study based on data by geographic area, can one distinguish between farm managers or proprietors and agricultural labor in measuring the distribution of school attainments? It was found that in India the education of women made much less difference, for example, than the education of male cultivators, and that variations in schooling of agricultural laborers had no effect on productivity (Ram, 1976).

It is essential that precisely those variables that would be altered by improvement in resource allocation on the farm not be entered as control variables in the analysis of effects of farmers' schooling (Welch, 1970).

Results of a study may vary according to whether at the time of a survey new methods of cultivation appropriate to the locality are potentially available, and the seeds, fertilizer, and so on needed in new methods also are available at reasonable cost. A study of Japanese farmers by Harker (1971) revealed that the less-educated farmers were just getting around to adopting new varieties of rice that had been adopted earlier by those with more schooling. The latter were moving into other ventures or adopting newer innovations. (In this particular case, the leaders and laggers could be sorted out because of the continuous appearance of new opportunities—a situation not so readily found in many places.) To the extent to which farmers quickly imitate successes of their neighbors, data on individuals will give misleading, and generally negative, results unless interviews happen to be well timed or to incorporate information about the nature and timing of past changes farmers have made in their practices.

It has been demonstrated repeatedly that effects of schooling on agricultural progress are consistently complementary with the extent of agricultural research activities relevant to an area. With respect to interactions between extension programs and farmers' schooling in their effects on productivity, findings have been mixed. This is not surprising. For one thing, the measures, the coverage, and the quality of extension services vary greatly from one study to another. Equally important, the general levels of farmers' schooling around which the variance in schooling is observed also differ. If the amount of farmers' schooling bears a nonlinear relationship to interactions between schooling and extension, it can easily turn out that one study will find that interaction to be substitutive, whereas another will find it to be complementary; there may, in other words, be a shift in these relationships from one range in farmers' schooling to another range.

The Small Nonfarm Enterpriser. If economic and social polarization is to be avoided in a society, the smaller enterprises must be kept central in policies to encourage development. The entrepreneurial experience in these small ventures offers the largest scope for wide participation in sustained growth in most of the Third World. Unfortunately we have much less information about what underlies success for nonfarm enterprisers than we do for peasants. Probably if an extension service for businessmen is to be successful, its clients need more formal schooling than is needed by an innovative peasant; with expansion of a business, systematic organization and control of records become increasingly essential.

A unique analysis of small enterprisers was completed by Koh (1977) for Japan. He built on many features of recent economic theory. He attempted to explain selection into entrepreneurship and into those activities that demand adaptive skills and the ability to make complex decisions in the face of uncertainty. Schooling was important in the various sorts of self-selection. The main thrust of his study, however, was the examination of relationships among innovative behavior, schooling, communication networks, and sources of information. Innovation was explored in three areas: techniques of production, marketing, and organizational matters (structure of firm, internal control systems, personnel policies and training). Within a context in which nearly all respondents had at least eight years of high-quality schooling, little association was found between schooling and technical innovations. Better-schooled enterprisers made more innovations in marketing, but especially, at the highest educational levels, in organizational features of the firm. Thus the three dimensions of innovation analyzed by Koh distinguished among three levels of sophistication in entrepreneurship.

Human Resources in Aggregative Growth Accounting

Rapid economic growth in much of the industrialized world in the late 1950s and on into the 1960s gave rise to a spate of aggregate production functions and of national accounting models that attempted to identify the sources of growth and to measure them more adequately.

Hunting "the Residual." The sources that had not been identified in earlier aggregate functions (most of which included only numbers of employed people and a crude measure of inputs of physical capital) came to be labeled "the residual." This was given various designations, among which were technical progress, the human factor, organization, advancement in knowledge, and the measure of our ignorance. These labels show where various economists were looking for answers.

The "residual" sources of growth were seen to find their way into production by different hypothesized routes, of which there have been three main variants. The first, which is closest to earlier views, specifies progress as capital-augmenting; the residual enters the production process through improvements in the quality of physical capital. Economists who worked with such models gave no credit to increases in the schooling attainments of the population. They did let learning-by-doing come into the analysis (Arrow, 1962), but they attributed that learning to technological progress embodied in new physical capital, and the emphasis was on learning by management.

In sharp contrast is the assumption that whatever the sources of change may be, they are labor-augmenting and are embodied in human beings. This does not mean that the entire residual was to be attributed to schooling. In theory, at least, even if not in empirical measurements, there could also be nonschool elements in the enrichment of the resources embodied in human beings. Although some scholars emphasized this orientation, it was not pushed as was the type of model that elaborated on physical capital.

Third is the neutral, essentially eclectic approach that underlies most aggregative growth accounting, exemplified by Denison (1962, 1964, 1967, 1976). This allows for embodiment of progress in both human and physical resources. Denison adds some nonembodied elements as well. Although he describes himself as a "standardizer," not "an aggregate production-function man," Denison's analysis incorporates an implicit Cobb-Douglas production function. The concepts of both capital and labor lose their abstract elegance (if they ever had it) in the heterogeneous world of national accounting, and Denison's first task was to construct indexes of the messy real-world components of capital and labor. This task goes beyond growth models that introduced heterogeneous capital, to incorporate differentiations within labor as well, and so allow human capital to get inside the implicit production function instead of leaving it in the residual, which he calls "advancement in knowledge." Whatever the residual may be, it remains totally unembodied, and deliberately so, in Denison's analysis. He adds a term for improvements in resource allocation in a world that is always in some degree out of equilibrium. However, he does not incorporate any theory about what processes may foster or inhibit improved allocation (nor does he introduce any specification of likely sources of advancement in knowledge). Finally, Denison introduces economies of scale as a simple proportionality to the level of national income attained. Differentiating a Cobb-Douglas function and extending it to incorporate Denison's elaborations would give us something like this:

$$\frac{dy}{y} = u \left[\beta \frac{dL}{L} + (1 - \beta) \frac{dK}{K} + \frac{dZ}{Z} + \frac{dA}{A} \right], \quad (1)$$

where u is a scale factor, L is a composite labor index, K is a composite capital index, β is the income share of labor, $(1 - \beta)$ is the share of capital, dZ/Z is the rate of improvement in resource allocation, and dA/A is the rate of "advancement in knowledge." Transposing, we get the definitional specification of dA/A as the residual:

$$\frac{dA}{A} = \frac{1}{u} \cdot \frac{dy}{y} - \left[\beta \frac{dL}{L} + (1 - \beta) \frac{dK}{K} + \frac{dZ}{Z} \right]. \quad (2)$$

Thus dA/A is just what could not be explained; if no estimate of dZ/Z is attempted, it can simply be added to dA/A in a somewhat larger residual. The econometric analysis of Jorgenson and Griliches (1967) resembles Denison's in that human and physical capital are treated symmetrically, but they differ from Denison in the significant fact (among others) that their aim was to account for all increases in "total factor productivity" by fully embodying advances in knowledge as quality adjustments in the labor and capital inputs.

One advantage in dealing with human capital as compared with physical capital in growth accounting is the fact that in the former case we can record the values of inputs as they occur. Physical capital usually is not valued in the market place after it is first put to work; it becomes difficult to estimate annual contributions from utilization of the stock of physical capital. Over the past decade efforts have been made to put both sorts of capital on the same base by measuring inputs of physical as well as human capital in terms of rental values. A major difficulty in dealing with human capital still remains, however; as in estimating internal rates of return, how can the differences in earnings attributable to contributions of schooling to productivity be separated from differences that reflect associations of schooling with other factors that affect the productivity of better-educated men and women? Denison's arbitrary correction on this account probably was exaggerated, both for the United States and in studies for other countries that have followed Denison's example. Moreover the size of a "correct" adjustment will differ from one society to another, among both economically advanced nations and Third World countries, depending on the extent and nature of selectivity in access to schooling and to the most lucrative careers.

Some economists have argued that the case for *not* making an "ability" or social background adjustment in growth accounting (in contrast to adjustments in rate-of-return analysis for any given cohort) is stronger than commonly is supposed. As education spreads through a society, suc-

cessive generations of young people have better-educated parents, and among the factors raising the quality of human resources over time are the intergeneration contributions that come from the environment of the home. This means that there is likely to be no deterioration and usually actual appreciation in the quality of entrants to postsecondary schools in later periods. Where this is the case, to make a static-model adjustment for ability is then inappropriate for measurement of changes in the quality of the labor force.

The Maintenance Component. Schultz (1975) never dealt with national-income or growth accounting. Although he did make some early estimates of contributions of education to economic growth, he began by looking at education as an investment, and his estimates of contributions of education to growth could be faulted because he used rate-of-return analysis in a round-about approach to the rental values used by Denison (Bowman, 1964). Schultz pursued a continuous search for "new sources of income streams." His investment approach led to another contrast with Denison that is more important for the present discussion than is his faulty application of rate-of-return estimates. A part of the investment in the education of new members of the labor force entails maintenance of the initial level of schooling per worker (see Bowman, 1964; Selowsky, 1969, 1971). By contrast, Denison and those who followed his methods in estimating contributions of education to growth count only that part of the schooling embodied in the labor force that *increases* per worker earnings (and hence, by their measures, contributions to the national income). As a "standardizer," this was a natural way for Denison to handle increases in the labor force; as long as there was no change in per capita human capital inputs into production, the standardizer credits only an increase in numbers. This seems logical enough at first sight, but the omission of the maintenance-of-standards component in the education of net additions to the labor force entails an asymmetry in Denison's treatment of human and physical capital. The downward bias in his estimates of the contributions of schooling relative to those of physical capital could be substantial. The greater the rate of population increase and the higher the mean level of schooling at the date taken as the starting point of the growth analysis, the greater will this understatement be.

Empirical Results. Following the early work by Schultz and Denison, there have been a number of studies by other economists, with several variants in the handling of education. Most, however, have been close imitators of Denison, with variations of detail that generally are of minor importance. Table 1 summarizes the findings of a number of these studies, some of which were assembled earlier by Nadiri (1972) in an excellent synthesis. In Table 1, countries are ranked by their estimated annual percentage-point growth rates. Two estimates are given in most cases under "education." The first column is without ability

TABLE 1. *Education in growth accounting, 1950–1962 (except as otherwise specified)*

Country	Rate of growth of income	Annual percentage point contributions						Education		Percentage of growth attributed to education	
		Total inputs	Output per unit of input	Physical capital	Employment	Health and nutrition	Labor reallocation[a]	(1)	(2)	(1)	(2)
Japan											
1955–68[b]	10.1	3.9	6.2	2.72	1.03	...*	...	0.23	0.14	2.3	1.4
1961–71[c]	9.3	6.8	2.5	2.57	1.09	...	0.62	0.53	0.35	5.7	3.8
1953–61[c]	8.1	3.5	4.6	1.62	1.14	...	0.67	0.50	0.33	6.2	4.1
Venezuela[d]	7.7	4.6	3.1	2.04	2.19	0.21	...	0.33	0.19	4.3	2.5
Germany[e]	7.3	3.3	4.0	1.41	1.49	0.28	0.77	0.18	0.11	2.5	1.5
Mexico[d]	6.0	5.7	0.7	2.82	1.43	0.93	...	0.11	0.05	1.8	0.8
1950–64[f]	6.0	4.4	1.6	2.81	1.46	...	...	0.41	...	6.6	...
Italy[e]	6.0	1.8	4.2	0.70	0.42	0.28	1.04	0.65	0.40	10.9	6.7
Greece											
1951–64[g]	5.7	2.8	2.9	1.55	0.65	...	...	0.55	...	9.7	...
1951–61[h]	5.3	3.1	2.2	2.44	0.45	...	...	0.24	0.15	4.6	2.8
Peru[d]	5.6	2.8	2.8	1.40	0.67	0.57	...	0.23	0.14	4.1	2.5
Brazil[d]	5.5	4.1	1.4	1.66	1.83	0.43	...	0.30	0.18	5.5	3.3
1950–69[i]	6.0	4.4	1.6	2.00	1.65	...	0.33	0.50	...	8.3	...
France[e]	4.9	1.3	3.6	0.79	0.07	0.15	0.65	0.47	0.29	9.6	5.9
Canada[j]	4.8	3.0	1.8	1.20	1.50	...	...	0.45	0.30	9.4	6.2
Colombia[d]	4.8	3.4	1.4	1.04	1.66	0.49	...	0.33	0.20	6.9	4.2
Netherlands[e]	4.7	2.1	2.6	1.04	0.78	0.04	0.21	0.39	0.24	8.2	5.1
Ecuador[d]	4.7	2.5	2.2	1.07	0.92	0.32	...	0.38	0.23	8.1	4.9
Honduras	4.3	2.9	1.4	0.95	1.06	0.82	...	0.48	0.29	11.1	6.7
Chile[d]	4.2	1.4	2.8	0.32	0.65	0.20	...	0.33	0.20	7.9	4.8
1950–64[f]	4.2	1.8	2.4	0.56	0.78	...	...	0.54	...	12.8	...
Denmark[e]	3.5	1.9	1.6	0.96	0.70	0.07	0.41	0.23	0.14	6.6	4.0
Norway[e]	3.5	1.4	2.1	0.89	0.13	0.14	0.54	0.39	0.24	11.3	7.0
United States[e]	3.3	2.2	1.1	0.83	0.90	0.02	0.25	0.78	0.49	23.5	14.8
Belgium[e]	3.2	1.3	1.9	0.41	0.40	0.09	0.20	0.70	0.43	21.9	13.4
Argentina[d]	3.2	3.0	0.2	1.43	0.93	0.12	...	0.88	0.53	27.6	16.6
United Kingdom[e]	2.3	1.3	1.0	0.51	0.50	−0.03	0.06	0.47	0.29	20.5	12.7
India											
1950–60[f]	2.2	1.8	0.4	0.76	0.91	...	...	0.13	...	5.9	...

* ...: No data.

SOURCES OF DATA. [a]Directly estimated by Langoni (1970) for Brazil. For Europe, Langoni's adjustment of Denison's estimates for "reallocation of resources." [b]Kanamori, 1972. [c]Denison and Chung, 1976, p. 38. [d]Correa, 1970. [e]Denison, 1967. [f]Selowsky, 1967. [g]Voloudakis, 1970; cited in Nadiri, 1972. [h]Bowles, 1971. [i]Langoni, 1970. [j]Walters, 1968, cited in Nadiri, 1972.

adjustments, the second is with those adjustments as made by the authors. One obvious feature of this table is the association between "output per unit of input" and the rate of growth: when growth is rapid, much of it remains unexplained by measured inputs. There are high contributions from physical capital in Japan and Mexico, toward the top of the list, but also in Greece and Brazil toward the middle. There is no systematic relation between percentage-point contributions of education and the pace of growth. Must the conclusion then be drawn that education contributes little to economic growth despite earlier opti-

mism on that score, or do the models conceal (or even distort) the picture of growth processes and of the part played by human development in them?

Reconsidering How Education Contributes to Growth

Several points deserve our attention here, some comparatively minor, some more fundamental. (1) Already mentioned is the omission of the educational maintenance component in the estimates of contributions of education.

(2) For long periods and where there has been substantial structural change, the share of labor in the GNP tends to rise; this means that constant-share weights (as used in the Denison models) will understate contributions of human resources to economic growth. (3) Either adjustments have been entirely to "correct" rental values downward, or there have been no adjustments in the rental-value measures used to assess contributions of education to economic growth. It is difficult to justify adjustments in the other direction within the framework of the accounting model, but this means that any spillover effects of having better-qualified people that are not reflected in their differential earnings escapes the accounting procedures. (4) The sources of innovation are not well identified in the accounting models, nor the factors that may impede innovative endeavor with any given measured inputs of human and physical capital. (5) Anticipated in part in the previous points and cross-cutting most of them is the problem of identifying the forms of interactions among various inputs into the national product. Denison's national accounting approach, which has led the field empirically, attempts to incorporate the main factors in growth in a balanced way, but it assumes a particular form of interactions among inputs. It is not easily adapted to deal with strong complementarities, for example. Other studies included in this overview have sought to pursue questions of substitution and complementarity among categories of human resources and between human and physical capital, but with still highly aggregated definitions of inputs. The greater the importance of complementarities, the more important it becomes to give more consideration to the mix of resources at the starting point. Most of the growth models have concentrated on measuring changes in inputs but have given little heed to how initial stocks may affect the results.

From the start of his involvement in the study of the economics of education, Schultz has asked what we could learn from the special experiments that history has provided. What, for example, can we learn from the success of the Marshall Plan in Europe, in contrast to the very different experiences with efforts to build physical capital in less-developed countries? Such a question immediately puts a spotlight on human resources, for whatever the losses of human capital during World War II, the populations of Europe had retained a large fund of human capital (skills acquired through schooling and experience). The imbalance, especially in Germany, was in the destruction of physical capital. The wealth of human resources made possible the efficient assimilation of large injections of new physical capital, incorporating major advances in technology. Similar conditions prevailed in Japan. But measuring the contributions of human and physical capital to economic growth under such circumstances will tip the scales heavily toward the importance of physical capital if a Denison approach is used. By contrast, at an early stage after the formation of the Soviet state, human capital was effectively destroyed by policies that penalized existing compe-

tence; the cultural revolution in China had similar effects. The effects in the Soviet Union showed up in national income accounting in an overexplanation of economic growth in the 1930s (DeWitt, 1962); output per unit of measured inputs left a negative residual. In this example the measures of inputs were unquestionably overstated because of economic perversities in the utilization of human resources. Attempts to break growth down into its parts and to measure their contributions separately will always give answers that are conditioned by starting situations as well as by investments of various sorts made over the period under examination. Those answers will be conditioned also by politically determined shifts and distortions in the allocation of resources that are not picked up in Denison's way of estimating "improvements (or deterioration) in the allocation of resources."

It is my considered judgment that only as we take account of initial stocks as well as flows of resources will we begin to identify the interplay between human and other resources in economic growth. By the same token, only as we give heed to disequilibria as a concomitant of growth processes, and to the associated importance of the ability to deal with those disequilibria and to take advantage of them, will we begin to get a better hold on the place of education and training in national development.

Mary Jean Bowman

See also Comparative Education; Culture and Education Policy; Economics and Education.

REFERENCES

Anderson, C. A., & Bowman, M. J. Theoretical considerations in educational planning. In D. Adams (Ed.), *Educational Planning*. Syracuse, N.Y.: Syracuse University Press, 1965.

Arrow, K. J. The economic implications of learning by doing, *Review of Economic Studies*, 1962, *29*, 155–173.

Becker, G. S. Investment in human capital: A theoretical analysis. In T. W. Schultz (Ed.), *Investment in Human Beings*, 1962, *70* (Supp. No. 5, Part 2), 9–49.

Becker, G. S. *Human Capital* (2nd ed.). New York: National Bureau of Economic Research, 1975.

Blaug, M.; Layard, R.; & Woodhall, M. *The Causes of Unemployment in India*. London: Penguin Books, 1969.

Bowles, S. Growth effects of changes in labor quality and quantity: 1951–61. In H. B. Chenery (Ed.), *Studies in Development Planning*. Cambridge, Mass.: Harvard University Press, 1971.

Bowman, M. J. Schultz, Denison, and the contribution of "eds" to national income growth. *Journal of Political Economy*, 1964, *72*, 450–465.

Bowman, M. J. Education and economic growth. In R. L. Johns (Ed.), *Economic Factors Affecting the Financing of Education in the Decade Ahead*. Gainesville, Fla.: National Educational Finance Project. 1970.

Bowman, M. J. Human resources and the contours of development. In A. B. Shah (Ed.), *The Social Context of Education: Essays in Honour of J. P. Naik*. New Delhi: Allied Publishers, 1978.

Bowman, M. J., & Anderson, C. A. Concerning the role of education in development. In C. Geertz (Ed.), *Old Societies and New States*. New York: Free Press, 1963.

Chaudhri, D. P. *Education and Agricultural Productivity in India*. Unpublished doctoral dissertation, University of Delhi, 1968.

Correa, H. Sources of economic growth in Latin America. *Southern Economic Journal*, 1970, *37*, 17–31.

Denison, E. F. *The Sources of Economic Growth in the United States and the Alternatives before Us*. New York: Committee for Economic Development, 1962.

Denison, E. F. Measuring the contribution of education to economic growth. In J. Vaizey (Ed.), *The Residual Factor and Economic Growth*. Paris: Organization for Economic Cooperation and Development, 1964.

Denison, E. F. *Why Growth Rates Differ: Postwar Experiences in Nine Western Countries*. Washington, D.C.: Brookings Institution, 1967.

Denison, E. F., & Chung, W. K. *How Japan's Economy Grew So Fast*. Washington, D.C.: Brookings Institution, 1976.

DeWitt, N. *Costs and Returns to Education in the U.S.S.R.* Unpublished doctoral dissertation, Harvard University, 1962.

Dore, R. *The Diploma Disease*. Berkeley: University of California, 1976.

Harker, B. R. *Education, Communication, and Agricultural Change: A Study of Japanese Farmers*. Unpublished doctoral dissertation, University of Chicago, 1971.

Hollister, R. G. *A Technical Evaluation of the First State of the Mediterranean Region Project*. Paris: Organization for Economic Cooperation and Development, 1966.

Jallade, J. P.; Croner, C.; & Emmerij, L. *Occupational and Educational Structures of the Labor Force and Levels of Economic Development*. Paris: Organization for Economic Cooperation and Development, 1970.

Jorgensen, D., & Griliches, Z. The explanation of productivity change. *Review of Economic Studies*, 1967, *34*, 249–283.

Kanamori, R. What accounts for Japan's high rate of growth? *Review of Income and Wealth*, 1972, *18*, 155–172.

King, K. Indo-African skill transfer in an East African economy. *African Affairs*, 1975, *74*, 65–71.

Koh, T. K. *Education, Entrepreneurial Formation, and Entrepreneurial Behavior in Japan*. Unpublished doctoral dissertation, University of Chicago, 1977.

Langoni, G. *A Study in Economic Growth: The Brazilian Case*. Unpublished doctoral dissertation, University of Chicago, 1970.

Lockheed, M. E.; Jamison, D. T.; & Lau, L. J. Farmer education and farm efficiency. In T. King (Ed.), *Education and Income*. Washington, D.C.: World Bank, 1980.

Nadiri, M. I. International studies of factor inputs and total factor productivity. *Review of Income and Wealth*, 1972, *18*, 129–154.

Psacharopoulos, G. *Returns to Education*. Amsterdam: Elsevier, 1973.

Ram, R. *Education As a Quasi-factor of Production: The Case of India's Agriculture*. Unpublished doctoral dissertation, University of Chicago, 1976.

Schultz, T. W. The value of the ability to deal with disequilibria. *Journal of Economic Literature*, 1975, *12*, 827–846.

Selowsky, M. *Education and Economic Growth: Some International Comparisons*. Unpublished doctoral dissertation, University of Chicago, 1967.

Selowsky, M. On the measurement of education's contribution to growth. *Quarterly Journal of Economics*, 1969, *83*, 449–463.

Selowsky, M. Labor input substitution in the study of the sources of growth and national planning. In H. B. Chenery (Ed.), *Studies in Development Planning*. Cambridge, Mass.: Harvard University Press, 1971.

Voloudakis, E. *Major Sources of the Postwar Growth of the Greek Economy*. Athens, 1970. (Mimeo)

Walters, D. Canadian growth revisited, 1953–1967 (Staff Study No. 28). In *Seventh Annual Review of the Economic Council of Canada* (table 15). Ottawa, 1968.

Welch, F. Education in production. *Journal of Political Economy*, 1970, *78*, 35–59.

Wheeler, D. *Human Resource Development and Economic Growth in LDCs*. Washington, D.C.: World Bank, 1980.

NATIVE AMERICAN EDUCATION

See American Indian Education.

NEUROSCIENCES

The neurosciences are a heterogeneous group of related disciplines, all with the goal of furthering the understanding of brain function. Disciplines in the neurosciences are, among others, neurochemistry, neuropharmacology, neuroanatomy, neurobiology, neurophysiology, neuropsychology, and certain parts of what has been termed "cognitive psychology." This last field is often termed "cognitive neuroscience" when methods and theories from cognitive psychology are applied to the study of brain-injured individuals. It is well beyond the scope of this article to review the field of the neurosciences in total. It is therefore limited to research in neurosciences and cognitive neuroscience that is relevant to human higher mental functions such as memory, reading, language, and hemispheric differences. Before summarizing research in these areas, it is necessary to describe the biological and physiological basis of the operation of the nervous system.

The Neuron. At a time when it had been firmly established that most organs of the body were made up of individual cells, the cellular nature of the nervous system was still in doubt. Argument on this issue raged from the 1890s, when the concept of the neuron was first proposed, through the 1950s, when the development of the electron microscope, and the ability to examine the ultrastructure of the nervous system, established that the nervous system was made up of individual cells, or neurons (Brodal, 1969).

The neuron is an excitable cell. That is, it can respond to stimulation. The neuron is an electrochemical system that transmits information. Within the neuron, information transmission is electrical. The transmission of information between neurons takes place chemically with few exceptions. The details of the intraneuronal and interneuronal transmission of information are becoming more and more important in the study of higher mental processes.

When the neuron is at rest, there is a slight electrical difference between the inside and the outside of the cell. The inside is electrically negative relative to the outside by about 70 millivolts (abbreviated "mv," a millivolt is one-thousandth of a volt). This difference in electrical potential across the nerve cell membrane is caused by different concentrations of various ions in the fluid inside and outside the cell.

In the resting state there is a greater concentration of positive sodium (Na^+) ions outside the cell than inside it. Similarly, there is a greater concentration of several negative ions inside the cell than outside. Combined, these different concentrations of positive and negative ions outside and inside the cell account for the negative resting potential of about -70 mv.

The cell membrane is not a solid sheet of tissue but a permeable membrane, and some types of ions can move across it. There are specific gaps or channels in the cell membrane that allow the smaller ions to pass back and forth between the inside and the outside of the cell. This being the case, one might expect that the concentrations of positive and negative ions would quickly equalize on the two sides of the membrane. This does not occur in the resting state, for two reasons. First, several of the negative ions found in greater concentrations inside the cell are too large to pass out through the membrane. Second, there is an active transport mechanism, or pump, that operates to keep sodium ions outside the cell. The pump extrudes sodium ions from the inside to the outside of the cell through specific sodium channels, keeping the concentration of sodium ions inside the cell lower than the concentration outside the cell.

When a neuron fires, or generates an action potential, several events occur in which the sodium pump and the sodium channels play important roles. At the start of an action potential, the sodium pump ceases to function. Thus, positively charged sodium ions flow into the cell in great enough numbers to cause one part of the inside of the cell to become, for a very brief moment (about 1 millisecond—one-thousandth of a second, abbreviated "msec"), electrically positive relative to the outside of the cell. An action potential does not render the sodium pump inactive at all locations within the neuron at the same time. Rather, the pump in a localized area of the neural membrane ceases to function, usually as a result of stimulation from another neuron. When this happens, as noted above, sodium ions flow into the cell across that section of membrane in which the sodium pump is no longer working. The interior of a localized portion of the cell thus becomes electrically positive. This local depolarization causes the sodium pump in adjacent areas of the cell to cease operation. Thus, the action potential is propagated down the nerve fiber.

Almost immediately following the breakdown of the sodium pump and the consequent influx of positive sodium ions, a second pump comes into operation. This is the potassium pump, which functions to pump positive potassium ions out of the cell, acting to restore the cell's internal negative charge. This pump functions for only a brief period following the breakdown of the sodium pump. Shortly after the potassium pump begins to operate, the sodium pump resumes operation and pumps out of the cell the excess sodium ions that entered during the millisecond or so that the sodium pump was inoperative. Thus, these two pumps act quickly to restore the internally negative resting potential following the passage of an action potential.

The action potential travels along the nerve fiber, or axon, until the fiber ends. There is a small gap, or synapse, between the end of the axon and the next neuron. Whereas the transmission of neural impulses down the axon is electrical, transmission between neurons is, with rare exceptions, chemical in nature. At the end of the axon is a specialized area of neural membrane, the presynaptic membrane, that contains small vesicles filled with specific chemicals called "neurotransmitters." It is these neurotransmitters that carry messages between nerve cells.

When an action potential arrives at the presynaptic membrane, it causes the vesicles to unite with the membrane and extrude their contents, a specific neurotransmitter, into the synapse. The neurotransmitter molecules quickly diffuse across the synapse and make contact with receptor sites on the postsynaptic membrane of the next neuron. The receptor sites are specialized molecules on the surface of the postsynaptic membrane to which a given neurotransmitter will bind, if it has the correct molecular structure and shape. Thus, the receptor site can be thought of as a keyhole and the neurotransmitter as the key. Only if the key is the appropriate shape will it operate the lock. That is, for a given receptor site, only the appropriate neurotransmitter will have an effect on the postsynaptic cell.

If binding of the neurotransmitter to the receptor site does occur, one of two events takes place. At an excitatory synapse, binding of the neurotransmitter to the receptor site causes the postsynaptic neuron to become more likely to fire—it is excited and an action potential is made more likely. The biochemical events that result in this heightened excitability are not totally clear, but basically the opening of the sodium channels in the area of neural membrane adjacent to the postsynaptic membrane is stimulated, resulting in an increase of the flow of sodium ions into the cell, making the interior more positive. If the interior becomes sufficiently positive (i.e., if it reaches threshold), an action potential is generated.

Whereas some synapses exert excitatory influences on the postsynaptic cell, others have inhibitory effects. That is, the postsynaptic cell is made less likely to fire when the neurotransmitter binds to the receptor site at an inhibitory synapse. Release of the neurotransmitter and binding at the receptor sites on the postsynaptic membrane operate in the same way at inhibitory as at excitatory synapses. The difference is that the effect of the former is to decrease the probability that the postsynaptic cell will generate an action potential.

A given neuron in the brain has on the order of 5,000 synaptic connections from other cells. At any given moment, the probability that a neuron will fire is a function of the sum of the multitude of excitatory and inhibitory influences from the thousands of other cells that influence it. Similarly, a single neuron will make synaptic contact with thousands of other cells, and thus it will be able to influence the activity of these many other cells. The brain is therefore an incredibly complex network of neurons with multitudinous interconnecting influences.

This description of neuronal function is, by necessity, brief. Several important concepts, such as slow electrical potentials that appear to play large roles in the modulation of neural transmission (Schmitt, Dev, & Smith, 1976), have not been described. Interested readers can find more detail on neural transmission in any of several excellent texts (Gazzaniga, Stein, & Volpe, 1979; Kalat, 1981; Kimble, 1977).

This seemingly esoteric neurochemistry and neurophysiology are much more relevant to issues of psychological processes in general and cognitive processes in particular than might appear to be the case. Conceptualizations about the workings of the nervous system have always had important influences on psychological theorizing.

Memory. The problem of the physiological representation of memory in the brain is one of the most difficult and challenging in neuroscience. It is far from solved, but interesting and clinically relevant findings have appeared in the last decade. The problem is deceptively easy to put: when something is stored in memory, some permanent change must take place in the brain. But where? And what sort of change—physical, biochemical, or both? Numerous attempts have been made to find physical changes (i.e., in number or size of neurons or synapses) and biochemical changes following learning in animals. Generally, such attempts have been unsuccessful (see Dunn, 1980). The changes that take place are probably so subtle as to elude currently available methods of investigation.

Approaches to the problem from different directions are possible. One attack has been to look at diseases in which memory is impaired and to attempt to correlate the memory impairment with the neurochemical or physiological disorders seen in the disease. A second approach has been to examine cases of amnesia due to brain damage in order to get a clearer idea of which areas of the brain are most important in the storage and retrieval of memories.

One disease in which memory loss is a major component is Alzheimer's disease, or senile dementia. In its early phase, the disease is characterized by memory loss. As the disease progresses, this memory loss becomes more and more severe and nonmemorial cognitive functions also become impaired until the patient is unable to perform even the most minimal intellectual tasks. The neuropatho-

logical basis of Alzheimer's disease has been elucidated in recent years. Especially in the later stages of the disease, there is a loss of neurons in the cerebral cortex. In terms of neurochemical disorders, there is a deficit in the synthesis of the neurotransmitter acetylcholine (Ach). The enzyme responsible for the manufacture of Ach from choline, choline acetyltransferase (CAT), is present in greatly reduced amounts in the brain of Alzheimer's disease patients (Davies & Maloney, 1976; Davies, 1978).

The specificity of the neurochemical deficit in this disease has led, quite naturally, to speculation that Ach plays an important role in normal memory function. Evidence from sources other than the study of Alzheimer's disease supports this belief. Drachman and Leavitt (1974) showed that administration of scopolamine, an anticholinergic drug that acts by blocking the receptor sites on postsynaptic neurons that bind with Ach, impairs memory performance in normal young subjects. Impairment is also seen on nonmemorial cognitive tasks. Interestingly, the pattern of impairment seen is similar to the pattern of memory impairment seen in normal elderly subjects who are not taking any drug (Drachman & Leavitt, 1974).

The mere finding that some substance impairs memory is, by itself, neither terribly interesting nor important. There are innumerable substances that will also impair memory (or any other type of performance, for that matter), but this fact alone gives little information about the biochemical basis of memory. More recent evidence has, in some cases, shown that drugs that increase the levels of Ach in the nervous system will improve memory performance. Drachman (1974) failed to find such an effect. At least three studies have now shown the memory-enhancing effects of cholinergic agonists and Ach precursors (Sitaram, Weingartner, & Gillin, 1978; Davies et al., 1978; Weingartner, Sitaram, & Gillin, 1979). This combination of findings of memory enhancement with increased brain Ach levels and memory impairment with decreased brain Ach levels gives one greater confidence that there is a real relationship between memory and Ach. It is important to note, however, that the demonstration of this relationship tells us little or nothing about the actual mechanics of how Ach functions in normal memory processing at the cellular or molecular level. Nonetheless, such behavioral findings give researchers working at the cellular and/or molecular levels important clues to guide their investigations.

The therapeutic possibilities of increasing Ach levels in patients with diseases that result in memory problems have not gone unnoticed. Many attempts have been made to treat Alzheimer's disease with drugs that increase Ach levels. Growdon and Corkin (1981) review several such studies. Generally, the results of these and similar studies have been unfavorable. This should not be greeted with undue pessimism, however. The studies done to date have all had some problem that weakens the negative conclusion. For example, many use very few patients or rather crude techniques to evaluate memory. Further, some studies include patients who are well along in the disease and hence are impaired in several areas. It may be that these patients are too far gone for any treatment to work, even one that might be effective with less seriously impaired patients. The definitive study would be one that uses an adequate number of patients along with sophisticated measures of memory function and is careful to exclude very impaired patients. Such a study has not yet been done.

Attempts have also been made to treat the memory problems and complaints of normal elderly persons with drugs that increase Ach levels and with other drugs that have been shown to improve memory function in younger subjects. Here, too, the results at first appear discouraging. However, some of the problems seen in the studies of the effects of increased Ach levels on memory in Alzheimer's disease patients noted above also appear in the studies using normal elderly persons with memory difficulties. (For details on these studies and their methodological problems, see Hines & Fozard, 1980; Reisberg, Ferris, & Gershon, 1981.)

McEntee and Mair (1978, 1980) have demonstrated an important relationship between one particular neurotransmitter and impaired memory function in a disease known as Korsakoff's syndrome. Seen most commonly in chronic alcoholics, it is due to a thiamine deficiency and includes memory disorders as a major symptom (Victor, Adams, & Collins, 1971). McEntee and Mair (1978) examined the cerebrospinal fluid (CSF) levels of the primary metabolites of the neurotransmitters dopamine, noradrenaline, and seratonin in nine patients with Korsakoff's syndrome. Only the noradrenaline metabolite 3-methoxy 4-hydroxyphenyl glycol (MHPG) was present in lower-than-normal levels in these patients. All patients were given tests of memory and general intellectual functioning. The correlation between the degree of memory impairment and CSF levels of MHPG was −.83, indicating that the higher the MHPG level in CSF was, the less memory was impaired. In their second paper, McEntee and Mair (1980) report that administration of a drug that increases noradrenaline levels improves memory performance in patients with Korsakoff's syndrome.

McEntee and Mair's results indicate the importance of noradrenaline in normal memory functioning. Work on the Ach system, mentioned earlier, indicates the importance of the neurotransmitter in memory function. This poses no logical difficulties. The neurochemical basis of memory will certainly turn out to be exceedingly complex, and it is quite reasonable to find that different neurotransmitters are involved.

Nor should the reader be puzzled by the fact that reduction in noradrenaline levels may be linked to endogenous depression. It is true that people with Korsakoff's syndrome are not depressed and that depressed persons do not show the profound memory deficits found in Korsakoff's syndrome, even though both disorders are related to deficits in noradrenaline. The solution to this puzzle is that the deficits in noradrenaline levels are located in different brain areas in the two disorders. In Korsakoff's syndrome, cells in the periventricular gray matter are most seriously affected, whereas other brain areas are relatively normal (Victor, Adams, & Collins, 1971). The anatomical location of the noradrenaline deficit in endogenous depression has yet to be located, but it is probably more diffuse and less severe than that seen in Korsakoff's syndrome. This demonstrates an important point: different brain areas can be involved in totally different functions, even though they use the same neurotransmitter.

Several other substances with unclear neurochemical actions have been reported to enhance memory in normal human subjects or animals. Among them are piracetam, adrenocorticotropic hormone (ACTH) and its fragments, vasopressin (Weingartner et al., 1981), and the enkephalins (for specific references, see Hines & Fozard, 1980; Reisberg, Ferris, & Gershon, 1981). These reports are most exciting and, if confirmed and expanded, may offer hope for something akin to the "memory pill" long dreamed of by science fiction writers and students the night before an exam.

A second approach to the study of the physiology of memory has been to examine the memory deficits, if any, associated with damage to different parts of human and animal brains. The hippocampus, a structure in the medial portion of the temporal lobe, has a history of providing data on the relationships between the brain and memory processes. When, in 1959, Penfield and his group at Montreal began performing unilateral lobectomies for the treatment of severe epilepsy, a large population of patients with hippocampi absent on one side was created. The studies of Milner and her group have provided extensive experimental evidence of the specific types of memory disturbances associated with right and left hippocampal destruction. Several reviews of this literature have appeared elsewhere (Milner, 1966; Iversen, 1977). The widely known conclusion of this work is that left and right hippocampal damage is associated with different types of memory impairments. Damage on the left causes difficulties in the processing of verbal materials; right hippocampal damage results in impairments of nonverbal, visual-spatial materials.

As with so much work attempting to define the differences between the two hemispheres of the brain, the characterizations of the nature of the processing deficits associated with left and right hippocampal removal leave much to be desired. The terms "verbal" and "visual-spatial" are at best vague descriptions. Recent work has provided a sharper definition of just what the right hemisphere appears to be best at. Using a split-brain patient, Gazzaniga and LeDoux (1978) repeated a previous study by Milner and Taylor (1972) and added some additional conditions. In the original study, subjects had to palpate unnamable wire figures, without seeing them, and then pick the palpated figure from several different such figures, again without looking. The results showed that the left hand–right hemisphere combination was considerably better on this task than the right hand–left hemisphere combination.

Gazzaniga and LeDoux (1978) replicated this finding and added a condition in which the task was modified to a purely visual one in which pictures of the stimuli were tachistoscopically lateralized to only one hemisphere. Responses were made by pointing to the correct figure in a set of visually presented figures. If the right-sided advantage lies in the nature of the stimuli and not in the nature of the response, this change should not have affected differences between left and right found by Milner and Taylor (1972). But it did—in the visual condition, both hemispheres performed at perfect levels. Gazzaniga and LeDoux argued that this finding showed that the right hemisphere is specialized, not so much for processing "visual-spatial" stimuli, but for "manipulospatial" activities, which they define as the "mechanisms by which spatial context is mapped onto perceptual and motor activity of the hand" (p. 55). The issues of hemispheric differences in general will be dealt with in detail later in this article. At this point it will suffice to point out that the conclusion that left and right hippocampal damage results in distinguishable memory disorders is substantially correct. However, the characterization, in terms of psychological processes, of these differences found in the original literature on this topic is probably inadequate.

If unilateral hippocampal damage resulted in fairly specific memory deficits, bilateral hippocampal damage caused deficits of a totally different character. The most famous case of bilateral hippocampal removal was HM, reported by Scoville and Milner (1957). HM underwent bilateral temporal lobectomy for the removal of epileptic foci in both temporal lobes. Following surgery HM apparently had normal short-term memory, normal recall from preoperative long-term memory, but a profound inability to transfer new information into long-term memory.

In 1968 Atkinson and Shiffrin presented their influential three-stage model of human memory. In this model the first stage is usually termed short-term sensory store (STSS). This is a very brief stage of memory, lasting about 250 msec for visually presented stimuli and about 1,000 msec for auditory presentation. The second stage, short-term memory (STM), lasts from 10 to 15 seconds. Information in STM is maintained by active rehearsal and is generally thought to be represented in an auditory form or code (Keele, 1973). The final stage of memory in this model is long-term memory (LTM), which contains the permanent store of memories of each individual. Information in LTM is generally stored in terms of meaning or semantics.

An important characteristic of Atkinson and Shiffrin's model was its serial nature. Before information could enter LTM, it had to pass through STSS and STM. Based on HM's apparently specific deficit in transferring information from STM to LTM, Atkinson and Shiffrin concluded that it was the hippocampus that performed, somehow, the transformation of short-term memory into long-term memory.

Research conducted since 1968 has forced a rejection of Atkinson and Shiffrin's model in many respects. Neither the belief that the stages of memory are organized in serial order nor the view that the hippocampus is responsible for the permanent storage of new information in LTM has held up.

Recent research on memory has focused on the multiple aspects of any item stored in memory. Consider memory for a given word. That word has at least one meaning, perhaps more. It also has a particular shape when printed in uppercase letters and a very different shape when printed in lowercase letters. It also has a sound. All these different aspects of the word are stored in memory. The important question is whether or not they are all stored in the same memory "location." That is, are the several aspects of a stimulus separable psychologically? Further, if there is such psychological separability of different aspects of a stimulus, do anatomically different brain areas underlie different aspects of the stimulus? Recent research shows that the answer to both questions is yes.

Corcoran and Besner (1975) have examined the question of the separability of different aspects or codes of memory for single letters. Each letter has a name and a shape in lowercase and a different shape in uppercase. Corcoran and Besner had their subjects make speeded same/different judgments of letter pairs based either on their names or on their physical shapes. Size and contrast of letters in the pairs were varied. The manipulations of the physical characteristics of the stimuli allowed decisions based on letter shape. That is, it took longer to decide that two letters were the same if they were of the same shape (e.g., A, A) but differed in size or contrast than if they did not. In the name match condition, using different-case "same" pairs (e.g., A, a), changes in size and contrast did not have any affect on reaction time. That only the reaction times for the matches based on letters' physical characteristics were slowed by manipulation of stimulus size and contrast points to the existence of psychologically separable representations of physical and name information in memory. In a similar study, Buggie (1970) showed that rotating letters slowed reaction time in physical match but not in name match conditions. Posner (1978) reviewed in detail further studies showing the psychological independence or separability of the codes of the physical and semantic aspects of words and letters.

Studies of brain-damaged patients have further demonstrated that the psychological separability of different aspects of words has anatomical reality. The neural systems subserving these different aspects of stimuli are located in distinct brain areas. Excellent examples in this regard are studies of phonetic or deep dyslexia (Marshall & Newcombe, 1973), a rare acquired dyslexia seen in adults following left-hemisphere damage. The most striking feature of this syndrome is the inability to read even common words combined with a high rate of semantically related errors when attempts to read words are made. For example, when asked to read "speak" a patient may respond "talk." "Hen" may be the response for "egg." Studies of these patients by Patterson and Marcel (1977) and Saffran and Marin (1977) have demonstrated that the basic inability in this disorder is one of accessing or deriving a phonetic code of a word from its printed form. These patients cannot pronounce pronounceable nonwords (e.g., *gorp*), but can repeat them if the examiner says them first. In a lexical decision task in which one has to decide whether a string of letters is or is not a real word, normal subjects are slower to reject strings that are pronounced like real words (e.g., *bote, flore, kote*) than strings that are not. Patterson and Marcel (1977) showed that deep dyslexics do not suffer from such interference in spite of their normal ability to distinguish words from nonwords. These results show that the phonetic coding system is impaired in these patients, while other code systems are intact. Meaning codes are preserved as shown by the close semantic associates frequently given for words that cannot be correctly read. The patients know what the word means, but they have lost the ability to produce its exact phonological representation. The existence of this type of dissociation indicates that the brain systems storing information about words' sounds and words' meanings are anatomically distinct.

An early paper by Lyman, Kwan, and Chao (1938) presents another excellent example of a specific loss of one code system. The patient was a 42-year-old Chinese businessman living in Peking. His native language was Chinese and he had a fluent command of English. A left parietal-occipital tumor was removed. Following surgery the patient was severely alexic in Chinese, his native tongue, but there was little disturbance of reading in English. This differential impact of the brain damage on reading in the two languages depended on the different ways in which meaning can be accessed from print in Chinese and English. In English, either the phonetic or orthographic codes of a word can be used to contact meaning. That is, given a printed English word, the word can be sounded out and this phonetic code used to contact or access meaning. This is in addition to the more direct route from orthography to meaning that is apparently used in normal reading (Baron, 1973). In Chinese, however, only the orthographic code is available to contact meaning. Although Chinese characters can be named, if a character is not known, or has been forgotten, there is no way to derive its name from its shape. Lyman, Kwan, and Chao's patient had lost the ability to use the orthographic code to access meaning. This was fatal to reading Chinese, where this is the only pathway available, but not terribly serious in reading English where the alternate pathway from phonology to meaning was still available.

Similar dissociations are seen in Japanese aphasics. Japanese script contains two types of characters. "Kana characters" function like syllables and can be pronounced. "Kanji characters," like the Chinese characters from which they are derived, can only be named. Thus, meaning of the kana characters can be accessed via either the orthographic or phonetic route. Kanji characters' meaning can

only be accessed via the direct orthographic route. Sasanuma (1973) has demonstrated that brain damage in different brain areas impairs processing of kana and kanji characters differently. This indicates once again that different brain areas are involved in the processing of the different memory codes.

The studies reviewed above show that the original concept of long-term memory as a nondifferentiated store is incorrect. Multiple features of stimuli are stored in LTM. These features are stored in memory locations that are both psychologically and anatomically separate. Further, the multiple features of a stimulus are activated in parallel upon stimulus presentation.

A second important postulate of the Atkinson and Shiffrin (1968) model is that the hippocampus is somehow involved in the transfer of information from short-term memory into long-term memory. This is not the case. Even in 1968 it was known that HM, the most famous case of bilateral hippocampal removal, could learn and retain new motor skills (Corkin, 1968), although he denied having any previous experience with the tasks involved. In an extensive series of studies on amnesiac patients, Weiskrantz (1977) and his colleagues have shown that, given appropriate retrieval cues, amnesiacs do show considerable long-term retention.

Although there is little disagreement that bilateral hippocampal damage is one important cause of amnesia, it is clear that damage to other limbic system structures can also produce amnesia (Horel, 1978; Whitty & Zangwill, 1979). Another extremely important issue in the study of amnesia, and one about which there has been much controversy, concerns the nature of the amnesiac's memory deficit. The issue is usually stated in terms of a dichotomy between a storage and a retrieval failure.

Most amnesiacs have both a retrograde and an anteriorgrade component in their amnesia (Whitty & .Zangwill, 1979). The retrograde component, covering a variable time period before the amnesiac event, must be due to a retrieval failure since storage was normal previous to the amnesiac event. Further, the period of retrograde amnesia (RA) usually shrinks in the months following the amnesic event. Only for a small period of time, measured in minutes, preceding the amnesic event, does the RA frequently fail to clear. This unresolved short period of RA is usually explained as a failure of consolidation.

The characterization of anteriorgrade amnesia as either a retrieval or a storage and consolidation problem has always been more problematical. Proponents of a retrieval failure theory could always contend that the failure of a given test to demonstrate memory was due simply to the insensitivity of the test used. If only the right test was used, significant storage of information could be demonstrated. Since it is impossible to prove that memory failure was not due to poor testing, the burden of proof has quite properly fallen on the retrieval failure theorists to come up with the "right" tests that will demonstrate presence of new information in amnesic memory. Several lines of evidence now suggest that, when the appropriate cues are used, a great deal of retention of new information by amnesiacs can be demonstrated.

In one particularly interesting study, Warrington and Weiskrantz (1968) attempted to teach lists of words to amnesiac patients. Although the patients showed almost no recall, the errors they made had a high probability of being intrusions from lists they had previously attempted, without success, to learn.

In a later study, Warrington and Weiskrantz (1970) used cuing by partial information to examine storage in amnesiac patients. Degraded versions of common words were presented, starting with the most degraded version and continuing through the intact version. The subjects' task was to name the word from the most degraded version possible. Later subjects were given three types of retention tests: a conventional recall test, a conventional recognition test, and a partial information task. The last involved the representation of the degraded words, subjects being asked to identify them. As originally, the most degraded version was presented first, and if the subject was unable to name it, the next most degraded version was presented until naming was correct. Amnesiacs did very poorly on the recall test; better, but still much more poorly than normal controls, on the recognition task; and best on the partial recognition task.

In a second study reported in the same paper, Warrington and Weiskrantz used a standard word learning paradigm to teach a list of words to the amnesiac and control patients. Following learning, memory was tested as before by means of recall, recognition, and partial information tests. However, another partial information condition was included in which the first three letters of the word were presented as a retrieval cue. As in the first experiment, amnesiac subjects were very poor on recall, better but far from normal on recognition, and equal to controls on tests involving presentation of partial information. The use of partial information as a retrieval cue is a technique that demonstrates that amnesiacs in fact retain a considerable amount of information. This information is not retrievable through the use of standard measures of memory.

As Warrington and Weiskrantz point out, the finding that the performance of amnesiacs on recognition tests is worse than on tests using partial information as a cue is a bit of a paradox. One might expect that if partial information is a good cue, complete information would be better. As Warrington and Weiskrantz further note, in conventional recognition tasks in which the subject sees a succession of words, half from a previously learned list and half new, proactive interference builds up rapidly (Wickelgren, 1977), thus depressing performance. This suggests that amnesiacs are more susceptible to the effects of proactive interference than normals. Additional evidence, such as the finding from Warrington and Weiskrantz (1968) of high levels of intrusion errors from previous lists in amnesiacs, suggests that although information is stored in amnesiac memory, the procedures used nor-

mally for correctly filing the information are not operating at all well in amnesiacs. This appears to be the source of the deficit in amnesiac memory—a terrible filing system, not a lack of filing altogether. The structures, damage to which results in amnesia, appear to be more important for the orderly filing of, and later recovery of, new information rather than its storage *per se*.

Language. The first observations on the relationships between human brain anatomy and higher mental processes were concerned with the effects of localized cerebral lesions on language. Thus Broca (1865) and Wernicke (1874) first noted that damage in specific areas of the left hemisphere resulted in language impairment while damage in analogous areas did not result in any such impairment. Since these early observations, a vast amount of clinical and experimental research on aphasia has converged on a conceptualization of the anatomical representation of language that divides language behavior into two broad categories. The expressive aspects of language are generally represented in the anterior portions of the left hemisphere, in what is called Broca's area of the left frontal lobe. The receptive aspects of language, language understanding, lie more posteriorly in Wernicke's area of the left temporal lobe. These two language areas, each with its own specific functions, are connected via the angular gyrus of the parietal-occipital lobe. Lesions in these different language areas result in different types of language impairment.

Lesions in Broca's area result in greater impairments in the ability to express oneself linguistically. Wernicke's area lesions cause greater impairments in the ability to understand language. A much more fine-grained analysis of the correlation between discrete lesions and the resultant disturbances of language behavior is possible. This area of research is reviewed in detail by Hecaen and Albert (1978) and Goodglass and Kaplan (1979).

One can characterize the approach of correlating damage to a particular area with a specific type of language disturbance as a list approach. Relatively little effort has been directed toward an explication of the mechanisms linking the specific lesion and the specific deficit. This is certainly not to say that attempts have never been made to explain the deficits associated with different lesions. The most systematic such attempt has been the work of Geschwind (1965) on what he terms "disconnection syndromes." Different brain areas subserve in different cognitive functions, and normal cognition consists of the sum of the operations of these different brain areas. In the intact brain the interactive function of numerous different anatomically distinct areas is required for normal cognitive function. Obviously, brain areas interact. Information from one area is required by other areas if they are to carry out their normal function. According to Geschwind, brain lesions affect behavior by destroying not only specific brain areas performing specific cognitive functions, but also by cutting connections between otherwise intact brain areas. This conceptualization of the effect of brain lesions has been most valuable in the understanding of the often bizarre results of localized cortical damage. A few examples will illustrate the important aspects of this approach.

The corpus callosum is the largest fiber tract in the brain and is constantly transferring information between the hemispheres. Section of the corpus callosum for the treatment of intractable epilepsy in humans produces a dramatic disconnection syndrome in which the left hemisphere and the right hemisphere are each unaware of the stimuli perceived by the other (Gazzaniga, 1970; Gazzaniga & LeDoux, 1978). The degree of this disconnection can be demonstrated by flashing visual stimuli to the left or right visual fields for durations of 150 msec or less. This lateralized presentation assures that stimuli are projected only to the hemisphere contralateral to the stimulated visual field since 150 msec is too short a time to permit eye movements to the stimuli.

Under the conditions described above, stimuli presented to the right visual field–left hemisphere can be named normally. Stimuli presented to the left visual field–right hemisphere cannot be named. Nonetheless, the right hemisphere is quite capable of indicating that it has perceived the stimuli if permitted to do so in some nonverbal fashion. Thus, the left hand, controlled by the right hemisphere, can pick the item presented visually from an array of items. The inability of the right hemisphere to name stimuli projected to it reflects a disconnection of the mechanisms in the right hemisphere that identify visual stimuli from the left hemisphere mechanisms that control vocal output.

Equally dramatic and puzzling symptomatology occurs with smaller lesions. Geschwind (1965) described a case originally reported by Dejerine in 1892. This patient suffered from alexia without agraphia. He was unable to read printed letters, words, or music. He could still write spontaneously and write material that was dictated to him. He was unable to read what he had just written. Importantly, he also suffered from a right hemianopsia. A few days before his death, agraphia, an inability to write, developed. Autopsy revealed two lesions of different ages. The older lesion had infarcted the left occipital cortex, destroying the primary visual area, and had also destroyed the posterior portion of the corpus callosum. The second lesion was very recent and had destroyed the angular gyrus on the left.

The destruction of the left visual cortex by the older lesion meant that all visual processing had to be done in the right hemisphere. The lesion had also destroyed that portion of the corpus callosum that transfers visual information from the right visual cortex to the language processing areas of the left hemisphere. Thus, visual information reaching the right hemisphere could go no farther—it was disconnected from the language areas on the left side. However, before the second lesion, the language areas of the left hemisphere were intact and could support all linguistic functions such as writing, speaking, and decoding spoken language. The second lesion destroyed the

angular gyrus, an area important for the intermodal integration of linguistic input and output, and thus abolished the ability to write.

The previous section presented evidence that argues that memory for different aspects of a particular stimulus are stored in anatomically and psychologically distinct brain areas. The syndrome of semantic dyslexia was presented in this framework. The alert reader will have realized that semantic dyslexia represents an instance of a disconnection syndrome in which the brain area subserving the phonetic coding of words is disconnected from the rest of the language area.

The similarity between the concepts of multistore memory presented in the last section and the view of language reflected by the existence of disconnection syndromes is striking. It is interesting that these two complementary theoretical viewpoints developed essentially independently, one from work in academic experimental psychology, the other from clinical neurology.

There has been much controversy over the issue of whether specific language areas in the brain are present at birth or develop during childhood. Lenneberg (1967) argued, on the basis of evidence that childhood damage to the language areas of the left hemisphere does not result in aphasia in the adult, that specific language areas are not present at birth but develop. Other authors (e.g., Kinsbourne, 1976) argue that specific language areas are present at birth. This is a false dichotomy, and it now appears that a combination of these two positions is closest to the true situation. Specific language areas do seem to be present at birth, but they develop during childhood and come to subserve more and more aspects of language function. This development is accompanied by a corresponding decrease in the ability of other brain areas to subserve language function if the primary areas are damaged. Dennis and Whitaker (1977), for example, have shown that although childhood damage to left-hemisphere language areas does not, in fact, result in aphasia, it does slow the acquisition of normal language. This suggests that although the right hemisphere is capable of subserving language function if damage to the left-hemisphere language areas occurs early enough, it does not possess the innate facility for language present in the left-hemisphere language areas.

Recent work in linguistics has emphasized the distinction between syntax and semantics (e.g., Fodor, Bever, & Garrett, 1974). "Syntax" refers to the rules of a language, its grammar, while "semantics" refers to the meaning conveyed in a language. Evidence suggests that these two aspects of language are differentially impaired by damage to different brain areas. Caramazza and Zurif (1976) examined the performance of several types of aphasics in a task that required them to pick from a pair of pictures the one that matched a sentence that had been read to them. Sentences varied in terms of whether the interpretation of the meaning was semantically constrained. For example, "The book that the girl is reading is yellow" is a sentence in which semantics constrains meaning since reversing the noun and verb phrases ("The girl that the book is reading is yellow") results in a meaningless sentence. Other sentences were not so constrained: "The cat that the dog is biting is black" makes sense when the noun and verb phrases are reversed ("The dog that the cat is biting is black"). These reversible sentences could only be correctly interpreted if the subject had an intact system for using syntactic information. Nonreversible sentences could be correctly interpreted without an intact syntactic system since, as pointed out, their semantics constrains their meaning.

Aphasics with relatively anterior lesions performed normally on the meaning-constrained sentences but were significantly impaired in the ability to understand the sentences that required syntactic knowledge for correct interpretation. Aphasics with more posterior lesions were impaired to some degree on all sentence types. The anterior aphasics, then, evidence a fairly specific disorder of syntactic processing, leaving the ability to interpret the semantic contents of a sentence largely intact.

The specific nature of the deficit in the anterior aphasics naturally brings to mind the question of the existence of the reverse disorder—impaired semantics with intact syntax. Whitaker (1976) has reported such a patient, a 59-year-old woman suffering from chronic alcoholism and presenile dementia. This patient's "general behavior, the neuropsychological tests, and the general language tests all indicate a severe loss of comprehension" (p. 27). In spite of this loss of comprehension, the most remarkable aspect of this patient's behavior was her profound echolalia. She would repeat almost anything said to her. In addition, when the sentence or phrase spoken to her was syntactically incorrect, her repetition corrected the error in more than half the cases. She would not correct semantically incorrect sentences. This case is a particularly compelling example of the preservation of an intact syntactic system in the face of an almost complete destruction of the semantic system. Unfortunately, the pathological changes in the brain, as would be expected in a case of presenile dementia and alcoholism, were widespread. Thus, no conclusion can be drawn regarding the anatomical localization of syntactic processing abilities.

Global aphasia is the most severe type of aphasia and includes a profound disorder of both the receptive and expressive aspects of language. Very little work has been done with patients suffering from global aphasia because of the obvious difficulties of communicating with subjects who, essentially, are languageless. Nonetheless, it is this very lack of a language system that makes these patients of such great potential interest. They are the best population in which to study questions regarding the nature of the human cognitive system in the absence of language.

In a rare study of global aphasics, Glass, Gazzaniga, and Premack (1973) examined the cognitive capacities remaining in seven patients who had suffered massive stroke. Of these seven, five were able to correctly sort CVC trigrams into word and not-word categories. They were unable, however, to distinguish between different classes of words (e.g., nouns and verbs) or between consonant-vowel-consonance (CVC) and consonant-consonant-consonant (CCC) nonwords. Thus, even in these severely impaired patients, some basic ability to distinguish between meaningful and meaningless stimuli was preserved. In a further test of these patients' cognitive abilities, four were presented with pictures of various objects and required to sort these into two groups as demonstrated by the experimenter, following some particular rule (e.g., animate versus inanimate, human versus animal, child versus adult). Two of the patients correctly performed all the sorting tasks given to them, while the other two failed only one out of five and two out of eight, respectively. Again, this points to a cognitive apparatus much more intact than might be predicted from the degree of language impairment evidenced by these patients. It is also of interest that the patients' general demeanor was good: "Despite their severe deficiencies in natural language, these globally aphasic patients appeared both responsive and aware of their surroundings. They seemed to notice incongruities and inappropriate use of objects; they responded appropriately to pictures of various stimuli by facial expressions and gestures" (p. 97).

Following testing of language and cognitive abilities, Glass, Gazzaniga, and Premack attempted to teach their patients an artificial language in which colored paper shapes took the place of words. The procedure was derived from earlier work by Premack (1971) teaching a similar symbol language to chimpanzees. This result indicated the impressive ability of most of the patients to master the new language at quite high levels of complexity. As the authors point out, "Even the most elementary constructions used, such as same-different, required the knowledge and application of the concept of identity-nonidentity. Additionally, successfully completed generalization tests argue against the notion that this relational statement between objects was made purely on a simple associative, S-R basis" (p. 101).

In another study, Reisse (1977) examined whether different types of aphasics reverted to more primitive cognitive stages, as defined in Piaget's stage theory of cognitive development in children. Overall, no evidence for such a regression was found. The two global aphasics tested performed the various tasks given them quite well.

Although additional work is obviously needed, the existing studies of global aphasics suggest that it is possible to have a cognitive system largely intact in spite of the loss of receptive and expressive language capacity. The studies reviewed earlier show that the opposite dissociation is also possible: one can have certain rather high-level language capabilities (e.g., the ability to make grammatical corrections) in the absence of any demonstrable cognitive system at all.

Language, then, appears to be only one, albeit an extremely important one, of the multiple brain systems involved in conscious experience. Gazzaniga and LeDoux (1978) have discussed the implications of the existence of such multiple, and potentially independent, brain systems for general issues of consciousness and memory.

Reading. Interest in reading, both from the practical standpoint of improving instructional and remedial methods and from the theoretical standpoint of better understanding the cognitive processes that take place during reading, has greatly expanded in the last several years. Henderson (1977) reviews much of the complicated research on the processes underlying word recognition, and several books dealing with the information-processing aspects of reading have appeared over the past few years (e.g., Reber & Scarborough, 1977; LaBerge & Samuels, 1977; Spiro, Bruce, & Brewer, 1981).

One issue that has attracted much attention in the literature is whether the reader must activate some phonetic representation of the printed word before the meaning of the word can be accessed or retrieved. For normal adult readers, it now appears, such phonetic code activation is not necessary when reading material that contains few new or unusual words. Baron (1973) demonstrated this point when he had subjects decide whether or not short word strings (e.g., "my new car") were meaningful. The nonmeaningful word strings either sounded meaningless when pronounced (e.g., "I am kill") or sounded meaningful when pronounced (e.g., "the rough sees" or "in the haul"). The subjects' task was to make the meaningfulness judgment as quickly as possible, and reaction time was recorded as the dependent measure. Baron reasoned that if the word strings had to be converted to a phonological representation before meaning could be retrieved, then subjects should be slowed on judgments of strings that were meaningless but *sounded* meaningful. No such effect was found, indicating that a phonological representation need not be activated in order to retrieve meaning. The research reviewed earlier on deep dyslexia also shows that phonetic recoding is at least sometimes unnecessary for an understanding of a word's meaning. It appears, then, that the meaning of a word can be activated in memory directly from some features of the word's shape. However, there are certainly situations in which phonetic recoding does take place, such as when new words are encountered and when children are learning to read (Gleitman & Rozin, 1977).

In languages like English, information about the sound or pronunciation of a word is coded in a peculiar way in the printed word. Contrary to much popular belief, for example, the sound of the word *bat* is not produced by simply saying the sound *b*, the sound *a*, and the sound *t* in fast temporal sequence. As an exercise, the reader should try saying, slowly at first, *buh, ah,* and *te,* the sounds associated with the letters *b, a,* and *t*. Now say these three sounds in order faster and faster. It can obviously be done, and the result bears almost no resemblence to the sound of the word *bat*. A further demonstration of the fact that the pronounciation of a word is not simply the sum of

the pronunciations of the individual letters is that it is not possible to take a tape recording of someone saying the word *bat,* cut it into three pieces, and get out the sounds *buh, ah,* and *te*.

As Gleitman and Rozin (1977) point out, the way a given letter is pronounced depends very much on the letters that precede and follow it. Thus, the *a* in *bad* is acoustically very different from the *a* in *dad*. Similarly, the *b* in *bad* is different, acoustically, from the *b* in *bed*. At any given point in the speech signal, information is usually being conveyed to the listener about more than one of the letters in the word. This is a basic characteristic of what Gleitman and Rozin term an "alphabetic" script. It is this lack of direct correspondence between the sound of a word and its printed instantiation that, they feel, poses a great difficulty for beginning readers. They state: "An even more fundamental barrier to reading is the problem of segmenting the speech wave into discrete terms: the reader of an alphabet must relate the continuously varying acoustic wave of speech to a writing system that represents it in terms of a linear array of discrete symbols" (p. 50). Imagine the difficulty of the reading teacher who ignores this characteristic of English and attempts to teach students to say *bad* by getting them to say the *b* sound, the *a* sound, and the *d* sound in rapid temporal order. The children may comply, and if they do they will not produce *bad*. The teacher, probably unaware of the real relationship between the sound of a word and its printed version, will become frustrated, urging the student on to greater and greater speeds. This, too, will not produce *bad,* and the children who fail to adopt spontaneously the correct strategy of "shingling" pronunciation may end up being labeled as "reading-disabled."

One solution to this problem has been to try to bypass the pronunciation aspect of reading by teaching children to associate a given sound with the shape of a given set of squiggles (the printed word). No mention is made of the rules used to derive the pronunciation from the squiggles. In essence, this converts English into a language like Chinese. In Chinese, each character has a name, but there are no rules for deriving the name from the shape of the character.

This approach has two advantages. First, disabled readers can learn to read Chinese characters as readily as nondisabled readers (Rozin, Ploritsky, & Sotsky, 1971). Second, there is a very low incidence of developmental reading disability among Chinese children (Rozin & Gleitman, 1977), suggesting that such a method does away with the problem of developmental dyslexia, at least to a great extent.

These seeming advantages, however, are undermined by severe disadvantages. As noted above, the cognitive processes that come into play in reading Chinese are vastly different from those used in reading English or any other alphabetic language. The "reader" of Chinese is performing what is essentially a memory task in which the meaning of each character must be separately memorized. This loads memory rather to the brim and limits the number of characters the average Chinese can read (i.e., recognize). The reader of an alphabetic language, if he or she has learned the principles of reading appropriately, faces a much less demanding memory task. Thus, relying on teaching children direct memorial associations between word shapes and their meanings may eliminate early problems in learning to "read" (because one is not really teaching reading, in the usual sense of that term when it is applied to reading English script), but it will also result in "readers" with very limited reading vocabularies.

Hemispheric Differences. That the two hemispheres of the human brain are functionally asymmetrical is well known. In the past few years, however, claims have been made that the two hemispheres operate with completely different cognitive styles or modes. Such claims have often been naively accepted in the educational community, and attempts have been made to tie the alleged differences between the hemispheres in cognitive style to educational practice, especially in the field of art. I feel that claims for vast differences in cognitive style between the hemispheres are unsupported by the research literature and that attempts to base educational practice on nonexistent differences are exercises in futility.

No one is denying that differences in function between the hemispheres exist. They do, and their exact nature is a continuing source of debate and research (for detailed reviews of this research, see Gazzaniga & LeDoux, 1978; Springer & Deutsch, 1981; Bradshaw & Nettleton, 1981). What we must take vigorous exception to are claims such as those found in Edwards's *Drawing on the Right Side of the Brain* (1979). Edwards tells us that "the right brain—the dreamer, the artificer, the artist—is lost in our school system and goes largely untaught" (p. 37). She sees art as "in" the right hemisphere, along with creativity, imagination, and the like. The left hemisphere, according to Edwards and other proponents of what Corballis (1980) has termed "hemisphere mythology," is the site of rationality, logic, science, and the like. This is a naive view of brain function. Even at the purely logical level, it makes no sense. If art is "in" the right hemisphere and science "in" the left, for example, then the proponents of hemisphere mythology would have to contend that Einstein could have developed the theory of relativity even if the right side of his brain had been cut out, and that Beethoven could have written his Ninth Symphony and Leonardo could have painted the Mona Lisa had their left hemispheres been removed. More than anything else, such simplistic hemispherizing is a throwback to the nineteenth-century days of phrenology, a pseudoscience in which every conceivable cognitive function was assigned, totally without factual basis, to a particular area of brain. Thus, "love of country" was supposedly in a particular brain area, "parental affection" in another, "modesty" in yet another, and so on.

The truth of the matter is that any higher mental function like art, science, or creativity must draw on the entire brain. As any working scientist will affirm, there is a large creative aspect to good science, to coming up with new and original ideas and ways to test them. Similarly, there is a certain amount of logic and structure involved in any artistic effort. The musician does not simply randomly jot down notes. In fact, there is evidence that in professional musicians it is the *left* hemisphere that is superior in tasks involving memory of melodies, whereas the opposite is the case in the nonprofessional musician (Bever & Chiarello, 1974). Thus, attempts to teach drawing or music by activating or "shifting attention" to the right hemisphere are badly misguided. Such teaching regimens may occasionally be successful, but their success will be due to various other aspects of the training program and will have nothing to do with the activation of one hemisphere over the other.

Rather than show great differences in undefined, and probably undefinable, "cognitive style," the two hemispheres appear to exhibit one major difference: the left hemisphere (in about 95 percent of right-handers and 70 percent of left-handers) can speak. The right hemisphere can't. By "speak" I mean control the vocal apparatus and associated musculature. This does *not* mean that the right hemisphere has no linguistic capabilities. One can distinguish between the production of language and its perception or understanding (Sussman & MacNeilage, 1975). The right hemisphere is surprisingly good at the latter and usually terrible at the former. Searlman (1977) reviews much evidence for this position, and Day (1977) and Marcel and Patterson (1978) provide specific experimental tests and examples.

The division of hemispheric labor into "speaking" and "nonspeaking" makes good evolutionary sense. It used to be thought that lateralization of function was uniquely human, owing to our use of words and symbols (Penfield & Roberts, 1959). In the early 1970s, Nottebohm (1971, 1972) discovered that the control of song in one species of song bird was lateralized to the left side of the bird's nervous system. Since then, song control has been shown to be under lateralized control in several other species of song birds (see Nottebohm, 1979, for a review). It may be that lateralization of function, at least in birds and humans, developed to allow one side of the nervous system unimpaired control over the complex, midline vocal apparatus. What differences do exist in cognitive capabilities between the human hemispheres are relatively slight, seen mostly with difficult tasks, and are secondary to differences in control of vocalization.

Terence M. Hines

See also Cognitive Development; Handicapped Individuals; Learning; Learning Disabilities; Physical Development; Psychology.

REFERENCES

Atkinson, R., & Shiffrin, R. Human memory: A proposed system and its control processes. In K. Spence & J. Spence (Eds.),

The Psychology of Learning and Motivation (Vol. 2). New York: Academic Press, 1968.

Baron, J. Phonemic stage not necessary for reading. *Quarterly Journal of Experimental Psychology*, 1973, *25*, 241–246.

Bever, T., & Chiarello, R. Cerebral dominance in musicians and non-musicians. *Science*, 1974, *185*, 137–139.

Bradshaw, J., & Nettleton, N. The nature of hemispheric specialization in man. *Behavioral and Brain Sciences*, 1981, *4*, 51–91.

Broca, P. Du siège de la faculté du langage articulé. *Bulletin de la Société d'Anthropologie*, 1865, *6*, 399–405.

Brodal, A. *Neurological Anatomy* (2nd ed.). New York: Oxford University Press, 1969.

Buggie, S. *Stimulus Preprocessing and Abstraction in the Recognition of Disoriented Forms*. Unpublished master's thesis, University of Oregon, 1970.

Caramazza, A., & Zurif, E. Dissociation of algorithmic and heuristic processes in language comprehension: Evidence from aphasia. *Brain and Language*, 1976, 3, 572–582.

Corballis, M. Laterality and myth. *American Psychologist*, 1980, *35*, 284–295.

Corcoran, D., & Besner, D. Application of the Posner technique to the study of size and brightness irrelevancies in letter pairs. In P. Rabbitt (Ed.), *Attention and Performance V*. New York: Academic Press, 1975.

Corkin, S. Acquisition of motor skill after bilateral temporal lobe excision. *Neuropsychologia*, 1968, *6*, 255–265.

Davies, P. Studies on the neurochemistry of central cholinergic systems in Alzheimer's disease. In R. Katzman, R. Terry, & K. Bick (Eds.), *Alzheimer's Disease: Senile Dementia and Related Disorder*. Vol. 7 of *Aging*. New York: Raven Press, 1978.

Davies, P., & Maloney, A. Selective loss of central cholinergic neurons in Alzheimer's disease. *Lancet*, 1976, *2*, 1403.

Davies, P.; Mohs, R.; Tinklenberg, J.; Pfefferbaum, A.; Hollister, L.; & Kopell, B. Physostigmine: Improvement of long-term memory processes in normal humans. *Science*, 1978, *201*, 272–274.

Day, J. Right-hemisphere language processing in normal right-handers. *Journal of Experimental Psychology: Human Perception and Performance*, 1977, *3*, 518–528.

Dennis, M., & Whitaker, H. Hemispheric equipotentiality and language acquisition. In S. Segalowitz & F. Gruber (Eds.), *Language Development and Neurological Theory*. New York: Academic Press, 1977.

Drachman, D., & Leavitt, J. Human memory and the cholinergic system. *Archives of Neurology*, 1974, *30*, 113–121.

Dunn, A. Neurochemistry of learning and memory: An evaluation of recent data. *Annual Review of Psychology*, 1980, *31*, 113–121.

Edwards, B. *Drawing on the Right Side of the Brain*. Los Angeles: Taracher, 1979.

Fodor, J.; Bever, T.; & Garrett, M. *Psychology of Language*. New York: McGraw-Hill, 1974.

Gazzaniga, M. *The Bisected Brain*. New York: Appleton-Century-Crofts, 1970.

Gazzaniga, M., & LeDoux, J. *The Integrated Mind*. New York: Plenum, 1978.

Gazzaniga, M.; Stein, D.; & Volpe, B. *Functional Neuroscience*. New York: Harper & Row, 1979.

Geschwind, N. Disconnection syndromes in animals and man. *Brain*, 1965, *88*, 237–294, 585–644.

Glass, A.; Gazzaniga, M.; & Premack, D. Artificial language training in global aphasics. *Neuropsychologia*, 1973, *11*, 95–103.

Gleitman, L., & Rozin, P. The structure and acquisition of reading: I. Relations between orthographies and the structure of language. In A. Reber & D. Scarborough (Eds.), *Toward a Psychology of Reading*. Hillsdale, N.J.: Lawrence Erlbaum Associates, 1977.

Goodglass, H., & Kaplan, E. Assessment of cognitive deficit in the brain-injured patient. In M. Gazzaniga (Ed.), *Neuropsychology*, Vol. 2 of *Handbook of Behavioral Neurobiology*. New York: Plenum, 1979.

Growdon, J., & Corkin, S. Neurochemical approaches to the treatment of senile dementia. In J. Cole & J. Barrett (Eds.), *Psychopathology in the Aged*. New York: Raven Press, 1981.

Hecaen, H., & Albert, M. *Human Neuropsychology*. New York: Wiley, 1978.

Henderson, L. Word recognition. In N. Sutherland (Ed.), *Tutorial Essays in Psychology* (Vol. 1). Hillsdale, N.J.: Lawrence Erlbaum Associates, 1977.

Hines, T., & Fozard, J. Memory and aging: Relevance of recent developments for research and application. In C. Eisdorfer (Ed.), *Annual Review of Gerontology and Geriatrics*, 1980, *1*, 97–120.

Horel, J. The neuroanatomy of amnesia. *Brain*, 1978, *101*, 403–445.

Iversen, S. Temporal lobe amnesia. In C. Whitty & O. Zangwill (Eds.), *Amnesia* (2nd ed.). London: Butterworths, 1977.

Kalat, J. *Biological Psychology*. Belmont, Calif.: Wadsworth, 1981.

Keele, S. *Attention and Human Performance*. Pacific Palisades, Calif.: Goodyear, 1973.

Kimble, D. *Psychology as a Biological Science* (2nd ed.). Santa Monica, Calif.: Goodyear, 1977.

Kinsbourne, M. Ontogeny of cerebral dominance. In R. Rieber (Ed.), *Neuropsychology of Language*. New York: Plenum, 1976.

LaBerge, D., & Samuels, S. (Eds.). *Basic Processes in Reading*. Hillsdale, N.J.: Lawrence Erlbaum Associates, 1977.

Lenneberg, E. *Biological Foundations of Language*. New York: Wiley, 1967.

Lyman, R.; Kwan, S.; & Chao, W. Left occipito-parietal brain tumor with observations on alexia and agraphia in Chinese and English. *Chinese Medical Journal*, 1938, *54*, 491–516.

Marcel, A., & Patterson, K. Word recognition and production: Reciprocity in clinical and normal studies. In J. Requin (Ed.), *Attention and Performance VII*. Hillsdale, N.J.: Lawrence Erlbaum Associates, 1978.

Marshall, J., & Newcombe, F. Patterns of paralexia. *Journal of Psycholinguistic Research*, 1973, *2*, 179–199.

McEntee, W., & Mair, R. Memory impairment in Korsakoff's psychosis: A correlation with brain noradrenergic activity. *Science*, 1978, *202*, 905–907.

McEntee, W., & Mair, R. Memory enhancement in Korsakoff's psychosis by clonidine: Further evidence for a noradrenergic deficit. *Annals of Neurology*, 1980, *7*, 466–470.

Milner, B. Amnesia following operation on the temporal lobes. In C. Whitty & O. Zangwill (Eds.), *Amnesia*. London: Butterworths, 1966.

Milner, B., & Taylor, L. Right-hemisphere superiority in tactile pattern recognition after cerebral commissurotomy: Evidence for non-verbal memory. *Neuropsychologia*, 1972, *10*, 1–15.

Nottebohm, F. Neural lateralization of vocal control in a passerine bird: I. Song. *Journal of Experimental Zoology*, 1971, *177*, 229–262.

Nottebohm, F. Neural lateralization of vocal control in a passerine bird: II. Subsong, calls, and a theory of vocal learning. *Journal of Experimental Zoology*, 1972, *179*, 35–49.

Nottebohm, F. Origins and mechanisms in the establishment of cerebral dominance. In M. Gazzaniga (Ed.), *Neuropsychology*, Vol. 2 of *Handbook of Behavioral Neurobiology*. New York: Plenum, 1979.

Patterson, K., & Marcel, A. Aphasia, dyslexia, and the phonological coding of written words. *Quarterly Journal of Experimental Psychology*, 1977, *29*, 307–318.

Penfield, W., & Roberts, L. *Speech and Brain Mechanisms*. Princeton, N.J.: Princeton University Press, 1959.

Posner, M. *Chronometric Explorations of Mind*. Hillsdale, N.J.: Lawrence Erlbaum Associates, 1978.

Premack, D. Language in chimpanzees? *Science*, 1971, *172*, 808–822.

Reber, A., & Scarborough, D. (Eds.). *Toward a Psychology of Reading*. Hillsdale, N.J.: Lawrence Erlbaum Associates, 1977.

Reisberg, B.; Ferris, S.; & Gershon, S. An overview of pharmacologic treatment of cognitive decline in the aged. *American Journal of Psychiatry*, 1981, *138*, 593–600.

Reisse, G. *Cognitive Structure in Aphasic Disorders*. Unpublished doctoral dissertation, State University of New York at Stony Brook, 1977.

Rozin, P., & Gleitman, L. The structure and acquisition of reading II: The reading process and the acquisition of the alphabetic principle. In A. Reber & D. Scarborough (Eds.), *Toward a Psychology of Reading*. Hillsdale, N.J.: Lawrence Erlbaum Associates, 1977.

Rozin, P.; Ploritsky, S.; & Sotsky, R. American children with reading problems can easily learn to read English represented by Chinese characters. *Science*, 1971, *171*, 1264–1267.

Saffran, E., & Marin, O. Reading without phonology: Evidence from aphasia. *Quarterly Journal of Experimental Psychology*, 1977, *29*, 515–525.

Sasanuma, S. Impairment of written language in Japanese aphasics: Kana versus kanji processing. *Journal of Chinese Linguistics*, 1973, *2*, 141–158.

Schmitt, F.; Dev, P.; & Smith, B. Electrotonic processing of information by brain cells. *Science*, 1976, *193*, 114–120.

Scoville, W., & Milner, B. Loss of recent memory after bilateral hippocampal lesions. *Journal of Neurology, Neurosurgery, and Psychiatry*, 1957, *20*, 11–21.

Searlman, A. A review of right-hemisphere linguistic capabilities. *Psychological Bulletin*, 1977, *84*, 503–528.

Sitaram, N.; Weingartner, H.; & Gillin, J. Human serial learning: Enhancement with arecholine and choline and impairment with scopolamine. *Science*, 1978, *201*, 274–276.

Spiro, R.; Bruce, B.; & Brewer, W. (Eds.). *Theoretical Issues in Reading Comprehension*. Hillsdale, N.J.: Lawrence Erlbaum Associates, 1981.

Springer, S., & Deutsch, G. *Left Brain, Right Brain*. San Francisco: Freeman, 1981.

Sussman, H., & MacNeilage, P. Hemispheric specialization for speech production in stutterers. *Neuropsychologia*, 1975, *13*, 19–26.

Victor, M.; Adams, R.; & Collins, G. *The Wernicke-Korsakoff Syndrome*. Philadelphia: Davis, 1971.

Warrington, E., & Weiskrantz, L. A study of learning and retention in amnesic patients. *Neuropsychologia*, 1968, *6*, 283–291.

Warrington, E., & Weiskrantz, L. Amnesic syndrome: Consolidation or retrieval? *Nature*, 1970, *228*, 628–630.

Weingartner, H.; Gold, P.; Ballenger, J.; Smallberg, S.; Summers, R.; Rubinow, D.; Post, R.; & Goodwin, F. Effects of vasopressin on human memory. *Science*, 1981, *211*, 601–603.

Weingartner, H.; Sitaram, N.; & Gillin, J. The role of the cholinergic nervous system in memory consolidation. *Bulletin of the Psychonomic Society*, 1979, *13*, 9–11.

Weiskrantz, L. Trying to bridge some neuropsychological gaps between monkey and man. *British Journal of Psychology*, 1977, *68*, 431–445.

Wernicke, C. *Der aphasische Symptomenkomplex*. Breslau: Cohn & Weigart, 1874.

Whitaker, H. A case of the isolation of the language function. In H. Whitaker & H. Whitaker (Eds.), *Studies in Neurolinguistics* (Vol. 2). New York: Academic Press, 1976.

Whitty, C., & Zangwill, O. (Eds.). *Amnesia* (2nd ed.). London: Butterworths, 1979.

Wickelgren, W. *Learning and Memory*. Englewood Cliffs, N.J.: Prentice-Hall, 1977.

NEW TECHNOLOGIES IN EDUCATION

Throughout most of the history of civilization, technology has been linked to learning. Generations of students have been taught using, first, clay tablets and papyrus, later paper, pen and ink, the hornbook, chalkboards, books and pictures, and more recently films, records, and transparency projectors. In today's world, many learners are receiving instruction by radio, television, electronic sound and visuals stored on tape, the telephone, computer, and communications satellite. Further, the present and growing availability of videodiscs, microcomputers, computer graphics, and electronic terminals with a high degree of "intelligence," fiber optics, lasers, communications satellites that operate into low-cost terminals, and a large number of devices that function with telephone lines is stimulating the creation of new approaches to learning and providing opportunities to implement applications that were unfeasible, either technically or economically, even in the recent past.

The telephone, for instance, is primarily thought of as a device for conducting conversations. Yet it can be used to transmit data and a wide variety of graphic and pictorial information, from freehand drawings to photographs and still pictures to paper facsimiles and computer-generated graphics. For instruction, this means that visuals can accompany the audio information that is transmitted or dialogue that takes place. In administrative applications, charts and diagrams can supplement teleconferences to facilitate decision making or the transfer of information. Full-motion video applications of telecommunications provide even greater promise, as new systems make it economically feasible to transmit television lectures or conduct "face-to-face" seminars among people dispersed over large distances.

For purposes of this review, existing technologies used in education will be categorized according to their accessibility, whether used locally or over distance, and their capability, whether primarily audio and audiographic, computer, or video. The technologies to be discussed, to-

TABLE 1. *Classification of various technologies used in education*

CAPABILITY	ACCESSIBILITY			
	Used locally		Used over distance	
	Hardware	Typical applications	Hardware	Typical applications
Audio and audiographic	Audiotapes	Stored lectures and discussions Instructions	Radio Telephone Dial access Electronic blackboard Slow-scan television (SSTV) Facsimile	Preproduced and edited programs Lectures, seminars, and discussions Retrieval of audio information Transmission of documents, still images, and handwritten information Audio conferencing
Computer	Minicomputers Personal computers	Computer-assisted instruction (CAI) Computer-managed instruction (CMI) Computer-aided testing Problem solving	Central computers Remote terminals Time-shared computing	Information retrieval Computer-assisted instruction (CAI) Computer-managed instruction (CMI) Computer-aided testing Problem solving Electronic message delivery Computer conferencing
Video	Videotape Videodisc	Stored lectures and presentations Interactive instructional programs	Instructional Television Fixed Service (ITFS) Cable Satellites Broadcast television	Preproduced and edited programs Lectures, seminars, and discussions Video conferencing

gether with typical applications of the hardware, are listed according to this classification in Table 1. This approach follows the developments in hardware and their uses in education, rather than taking the broader view of the entire learning environment as it interacts with the technology.

A complete study of the role of technology in education would cover numerous aspects of teaching, learning, and information delivery and would go well beyond the scope of a short article. It should treat the types of learning that are facilitated by technology, the roles of teachers and learners, the environment for learning necessitated by technology, procedures for materials development, and techniques for evaluating technology-mediated learning. It should give consideration to planning, implementing, and evaluating technology systems, the theories of learning that form the basis for many technology applications in education, the enormous body of research findings that have emerged from the study of media in education, and other aspects of the field referred to as "educational technology" or "instructional technology." Educational technology was defined by Grayson (1972) as "a systems approach to instruction, incorporating specific measurable

instructional objectives, diagnostic testing, criteria for student performance . . . and the repeated redesign of the curriculum materials until the criteria are achieved. . . . As defined, educational technology involves the application of scientifically tested principles of learning to an instructional environment in a consistent and coherent manner. It incorporates the media and may involve hardware materials, and methods of instruction" (p. 1216). This scope of the subject was adopted in the important reports by Tickton (1970, 1971), the Carnegie Commission on Higher Education (1972), and the National Academy of Engineering (1974), as well as for an extensive bibliography prepared for the Subcommittee on Science, Research, and Development of the U.S. House of Representatives (Congressional Research Service, 1971). This viewpoint of the subject is treated by Seibert (1982).

Audio and Audiographic

Speech has been a primary means for instruction throughout history, achieving some of its most effective use in the gardens of Akademos. In the past one hundred years, as increasing numbers of people were to be educated and teachers had to deal with larger numbers of students, technology advanced. Developments allowed a voice to be recorded—first on records, later on erasable tapes—for replay at the convenience of the listener, and to be transmitted over distances by radio for one person to address many people or by telephone so that two or a few people could carry on a conversation. There is no doubt that speech can be used effectively in education; the only question is how it can be used most effectively.

Radio and Audiotapes. Records and audiotapes have been used for self-study courses since World War II, largely in the teaching of languages but more recently in a growing number of other areas, particularly continuing education. The media were used to present models of speech, lectures, drill-and-practice routines, and instructions to engage in reading or other exercises. A significant use of audiotapes in altering traditional classroom approaches was made by Postlethwait in 1961 when he developed the audio-tutorial method for providing remedial instruction for the students in his introductory botany class at Purdue University. The approach has three major components: independent study sessions in which students learn from audiotapes and other media in self-instructional carrels; general assembly sessions that are held regularly and in which students hear guest lecturers, view films, or take major examinations; and weekly integrated quiz sessions in which an instructor deals on a more individualized basis with six to ten students (Postlethwait, Novak, & Murray, 1971). The approach was very successful and has been imitated and adapted in many other subject areas at numerous colleges and universities. A great deal of research has been conducted on the effectiveness of the audio-tutorial approach, with mixed results. Kulik, Kulik, and Cohen (1979) have summarized much of the research and conducted a meta-analysis of the results from forty-eight studies reported by others. Their major conclusions are that this approach has a significant but small overall effect on student achievement in college courses, and it has no significant effect on student course evaluations or course completions. Since this approach is no less effective than traditional methods, it can be used effectively in situations where traditional classroom methods are inappropriate, as when an instructor is not available or when small numbers of students are to be taught.

Speech is an effective medium of instruction even when it is transmitted over distance to learners who are not in the physical presence of the instructor. Almost fifty years of research (Cohen, 1937; Woelfel & Tyler, 1945) show that radio, a medium that was first applied to education in the 1920s and whose use continues today, can be effective in instruction. Lumley (1933) studied high school students who were taught foreign languages with the aid of radio and found that these students achieved better pronunciation than did students who did not hear the radio lessons. The University of Wisconsin Research Project in School Broadcasting (*Radio in the Classroom*, 1942) undertook an extensive two-year study of the use of radio broad-

casts at several grade levels in seven subject areas. In controlled comparisons, no significant differences were noted between students in the control and experimental groups, in most subjects. In music, however, the radio classes did significantly better in recognizing note values, sight reading, and recognizing rhythms, but showed no significant differences in taking musical dictation. The Japan Broadcasting Company (*Effects of Educational Radio*, 1957) used radio to teach English to students in the third, fifth, and seventh grades, and the radio classes experienced learning gains in every case at or above the level of conventionally taught classes. Constantine (1964) studied students who were taught science by radio in elementary schools and found that on the average they gained fourteen months in one school year on standardized tests of scientific information, and fifteen months on standardized tests of work study skills.

In many ways, radio has been a forgotten medium of instruction. Although there are many fine educational programs broadcast on radio today, the amount of time devoted to instruction in over-the-air broadcasting is very small. In an analysis of public radio programming, Katzman and Katzman (1978) found that of the 199 public radio stations that qualified for assistance from the Corporation for Public Broadcasting (CPB), 178 broadcast over 1.2 million hours of material during fiscal year 1978, for an average of 18 hours, 33 minutes per station per day. Instructional programming, however, constituted only 1.2 percent of the hours broadcast for grades K–12; 0.2 percent for college credit instruction; 1.2 percent for continuing education; and 0.6 percent for other categories of instruction. Since there are about 900 public radio stations in the United States, the majority of which are small or of limited operation and do not qualify for CPB support, it is possible that the figures for the amount of instruction provided by the CPB-supported stations may not be representative of the total group. More accurate figures, however, do not exist.

Telephone. The use of the telephone in instruction is more recent than that of radio, and few statistically significant studies of its effectiveness have been conducted. Conceptually, however, the telephone should be at least as effective, if not more so, since it is more versatile than radio and allows interactive as well as one-way communications. Several telephone-based educational delivery systems are presently in use, with the largest operated by the University of Wisconsin–Extension. In existence since 1965, this system reaches tens of thousands of students located at 200 sites around the state of Wisconsin each year. Telephone systems are most effective in tasks that stress an exchange of information, a generation of problem solutions, or straightforward administrative agendas. They are less appropriate for tasks that require interpersonal aspects, such as getting to know someone or appreciating nonverbal reactions to others.

The telephone, however, does not have to be used only for conversations or for audio presentations. It also is possible to transmit visual information from one location to another using voice-grade telephone lines or other narrow-band communications channels. Rapid and continuing technological development is going on in this area, referred to as "audiographics," so that by the end of the 1980s a large number of products with different capabilities should be available from many manufacturers for use in education. Audiographic equipment can be categorized into three divisions, which are not mutually exclusive: telewriter devices, compressed video or slow-scan television systems, and facsimile equipment.

Telewriters. Telewriter systems link two mechanical devices or a mechanical with an electronic device to transmit handwritten information. The material may be entered using electronic pens, tablets, blackboards, or video writers. Although telewriting devices differ in specifics, they are based on the common principle that visual information can be transformed into electronic signals by writing on a special conductive surface. Within a defined area, the location of a writing implement can be determined by sensing its horizontal and vertical positions as a point on a conductive grid. This information is used to generate an appropriate electrical signal, which is transmitted over a telephone line and used at the receiving end to position a mechanical pen or, more often, the electron beam of a television monitor. As someone draws or writes on the sending device, the points are transmitted to the receiver and a corresponding line or word is traced to reproduce the given information.

The "Electrowriter," a device using an electromechanical pen and first marketed in the early 1960s, was one of the earliest telewriters. Freehand graphics and script are written on a paper-covered paten with a special pen. The pen produces electronic signals that are processed and transmitted to any number of remote locations via telephone lines, where they direct a mechanical pen that reproduces the original information on paper or acetate film. The paper is usually roll-fed and can be advanced by the sender.

A more recent and more sophisticated device, and one better suited to the traditional classroom format, is the electronic blackboard. The primary component is a specially designed surface that in appearance is similar to an easel-mounted blackboard. The writing surface is used like an ordinary blackboard, the instructor writing on it with chalk and erasing either part or all of the drawings with an ordinary blackboard eraser. The chalk strokes are converted into electronic signals that can be transmitted to one or more remote locations, where they are reproduced on a television monitor. By means of a storage tube memory at the receiving site, the graphics are displayed on the monitor as white lines on a black background for easy viewing in ordinary indoor light, and they remain until erased. If more writing surface is required, two or three blackboards can be connected using the same phone lines. In addition, it is possible to connect a hard-copy printer to a receiving unit to obtain paper copies of the

graphics, use a stereo tape recorder to record the voice and graphics for later replay, and connect audio-conference devices for large group interaction. A one-year trial of the system was conducted by the University of Illinois at Urbana, using three blackboards to teach eight graduate-level engineering courses in each of two semesters. Reports are that the system was found acceptable by both the students and instructors and that there was no perceptible difference in grade-measured performance between students at the remote locations and students at the originating site. If anything, the quality was believed to have improved because the teachers were more deliberate in their presentations (Shah & Torok, 1979).

Slow-scan television. A second major class of telewriting devices is termed "slow-scan television" (SSTV). These devices appear to have great potential for educational and other telecommunications applications in which the full pictorial capability of ordinary television, other than full motion, is desired. The relationship between the transmission of full-motion video and SSTV is similar to that of sending water from one location to another through a pipe. In order to get a certain amount of water at the receiving location, either a large-diameter pipe can be used for a short period of time or a small-diameter one can be used for a longer period of time. The same amount of water can be sent, but the time to transmit it will vary inversely with the diameter of the pipe. In SSTV, telephone lines (which have about one three-thousandth the capacity of a conventional television channel) require 100 seconds or so to send a single picture, rather than being able to transmit thirty images per second as in the more familiar full-motion, broadcast television. A current large-scale application of SSTV is a twenty-four-hour-a-day news program initiated by United Press International (UPI) that uses a satellite and cable systems for delivery to homes. UPI employs a single-frame "newspaper" photo format to accompany the voice of a narrator, a format that could satisfy certain educational requirements.

Facsimile. Facsimile equipment allows documents to be transmitted over long distances and be reproduced on paper in a matter of minutes or seconds. The material may be printed, written, drawn, or in the form of computer printouts. A facsimile system consists of two machines (transceivers) connected through voice-grade telephone lines. Input documents are scanned by an optical device in a line-by-line fashion. The dark and light areas are sensed and converted into electrical signals that are transmitted to the receiver, which uses this information synchronized with the input scanner to reproduce the original image. Although newspapers were using facsimile devices in the 1920s, the business market for them did not materialize until the 1960s. Since then, major improvements have been made in facsimile systems, especially with the advent of microelectronics and digital signal processing.

Telephone networks. The University of Wisconsin has created several state-wide networks, using the telephone system, to provide a variety of educational services to diverse client groups. More than any other organization, the university has demonstrated with large-scale operating programs that the telephone can be an effective and affordable means for providing continuing, professional, and adult education.

An Educational Telephone Network (ETN) delivers credit, continuing education, and public service programs to learners in their home communities. It is a dedicated network that links about 200 study centers in the state with extension officers, campus centers, hospitals, libraries, and other sites as necessary. Learners at the sites hear the instructor through a speaker and use individual microphones to ask questions or make comments. ETN programs enroll about 32,000 learners a year in about 260 offerings.

The Statewide Extension Education Network (SEEN), also a two-way interactive audio system, delivers education to twenty-three Wisconsin communities. Its distinctive feature is the ability to transmit line-drawn graphic material in real time over telephone lines and display it at the receiving site on a television monitor. SEEN also is experimenting with the use of slow-scan television to augment the line graphics capability.

A Meet-Me Teleconference System, using the same two-way telephone links, connected twenty locations in 1980 for 256 sessions of faculty, staff, and committee meetings, planning sessions, student conferences, and other activities.

A dial-access system provides telephone access for anyone in the state of Wisconsin to a prerecorded library of more than 1,000 audiotapes on a broad range of topics of educational and consumer interests. In 1980, more than 90,000 requests were received. The system is semiautomated at present. The caller gives the answering operator the number of the tape he or she wishes to hear; the tape is accessed and played for the caller. Thw Wisconsin system is in the process of converting to an automated system in which the caller's voice activates a microprocessor unit, which asks the number of the tape being requested, recognizes the numbers given, and retrieves and plays the tape for the caller. Each module in the system (for health, agriculture, commerce, law, etc.) can store up to 1,040 tapes, which can be accessed simultaneously through twenty telephone lines. The university estimates that the amortized cost to purchase and record a tape is three to four cents per call.

Computers

The earliest work in applying computers to education began in the late 1950s, with activities at International Business Machines' (IBM) Thomas J. Watson Laboratory to develop the COURSEWRITER language and at the University of Illinois, where initial work began on the PLATO system. Since then there has been a great deal of effort in applying computers to education, although the intensity has varied over time. Although the use of a computer for direct instructional presentations has not yet fulfilled its total potential, computers have become important and essential elements in education.

Expenditures. In the area of higher education alone, the total expenditures for computing have been estimated to be $1.2 billion in 1980, which far surpasses the $51 million expended in 1963 and the $472 million in 1970 (Hamblen & Baird, 1979). It is estimated that currently 2,163 institutions of higher education, with a combined enrollment of almost 10 million, provide students access to computers, although it does not follow that all students attending those institutions are exposed to computers. In 1976/77, funds for administrative uses of computers were about 45 percent of the total expenditures, for research about 22 percent, and for instruction about 27 percent (Molnar, 1980).

A significant impetus for computing in education has come from the federal government, although that influence has declined significantly in recent years. In 1965, 36 percent of the funding for computers came from the federal government. By 1970, the federal share had declined to 17 percent, and today it is estimated to be much lower. The states and the institutions themselves provide the major sources of funding for computing in colleges and universities, whereas local sources provide the greatest portion of the costs at the elementary and secondary education levels (Molnar, 1977). In the area of instructional applications, the civilian agencies of the federal government expended about $7.5 million in 1966. The expense rose by 1969 to a high of $37.4 million and then declined in 1971 to $6.6 million, a level from which it has varied very little, reaching a low of $3.4 million in 1977 (*Computers and the Learning Society*, 1978).

Trends in Computer Hardware. Two trends have been observed in the development of computers. One is the development of larger and larger machines, often interconnected or accessed through telecommunications. The other is the development of smaller and smaller computers having greater and greater capacities at less and less cost. Both trends have affected education, the first primarily in research and administrative applications, the second in instructional applications. A major force affecting the widespread use of computers has been developments in semiconductor electronics that have allowed the production of semiconductor chips, each about two-tenths of an inch on a side, with processing capabilities that have doubled every fourteen to fifteen months, since the mid-1960s. The first chips each contained a single electronic element. Today, on a chip of the same size and at approximately the same cost, over 64,000 elements are packaged, and the growth in capability is continuing. These developments have made possible the personal computer and the widespread availability of hand-held calculators. Tens of millions of calculators have been sold, some of which are now available at under $10. Hand-held instructional devices that provide drill-and-practice exercises in arithmetic and spelling are available for $15 to $25, with units that simulate a human voice priced at about $60. Home computers containing a video display, keyboard, processor, and sizable memory are available for under $500. These have enough capability to do limited computer-assisted instructional activities, carry out computations, create small files of information, and play interactive games. In 1979, the annual personal computer sales, mainly to professionals, people in business, and hobbyists for personal use, was estimated to be about 350,000 units with a value of $500 million (LeBoss, 1980).

Availability of Computers. The Minnesota Educational Computing Consortium (MECC) recently purchased 700 microcomputers, 555 of which were installed in elementary and secondary schools and the remainder in institutions of higher education. Eighty villages in Alaska have purchased microcomputers in order to provide village children with a core curriculum at the ninth- and tenth-grade levels. This curriculum will shortly be made available to every school in the state that wishes to use it and purchase the necessary computers. In both states, a large number of subject areas are available for study by computer. The State University of New York at Stony Brook has established a National Coordinating Center for Curriculum Development, which is attempting to motivate students through the use of computers into pursuing engineering careers. Students have an opportunity to check out microcomputers overnight or to use them on weekends at youth centers. Papert (1979) has been working with elementary school children to teach computer-based problem solving in mathematics, physics, biology, and music, using a variety of innovative approaches, including a "slot machine" that allows students to select a program by choosing a card having functions pictorially displayed on it from a set of cards, and a computer-controlled motor-driven "turtle" that allows students to draw figures or explore concepts in science. Using more sophisticated computing devices, Bork (1975, 1977) has investigated the use of graphics in computer-based instruction and the use of visual information as an alternative to alphanumeric tools. Dwyer (1974, 1977) has developed a computer-based mathematics laboratory for secondary school students that creates a rich learning environment in which a student first works in a dual training mode with a teacher and then in a creative way in a solo phase.

Computers are also used extensively to provide certain types of training and education in several large corporations, in the military, and in federal government agencies. IBM, for example, provides over 800,000 student-hours a year or about 40 percent of the training of its 18,000 customer engineers and program support personnel through computer terminals at 160 branch offices located throughout the United States. United Airlines now is providing a significant amount of the training for the several hundred new pilots it hires each year by computer instructional methods, and expects to conduct its entire pilot transition training program for the Boeing 767 using a com-

puter-based system to manage the complete course from the acquisition of knowledge through exercises and practice in an airplane simulator. A Lowry Technical Training Center, the U.S. Air Force provides training and training management for up to 2,100 students per day in several courses. In addition, the Boeing Company, the Internal Revenue Service, the Civil Service Commission, the U.S. Army, the U.S. Navy, the Federal Aviation Administration, and others are expending large amounts to offer and investigate computer-based instructional methods.

Computer-based Instruction. Computer-based instruction includes a broad range of applications that can be divided into the two general categories of direct instruction and instructional management. The former is usually referred to as "computer-assisted instruction" (CAI), and includes such activities as drill and practice, tutoring, simulations and gaming, inquiry and dialogue, information retrieval, and problem solving. The second category, often termed "computer-managed instruction" (CMI), includes instructional support functions such as testing, prescribing, record keeping, scheduling, monitoring, and time and resource management. The hardware for both categories of applications is the same.

Perhaps the largest system combining both computer-assisted and computer-managed instruction is at the Lowry Technical Training Center. With fifty interactive student terminals and ten management terminals, supported by a high-level computer language called CAMIL, the system offers a rich variety of information to students, instructors, and training managers. For students, the system (1) scores tests; (2) lists objectives not mastered; (3) makes individualized assignments, including remediation by objective; (4) assigns and locates resources required to accomplish an assignment; (5) provides target completion times and rates of progress; and (6) selects and assigns alternative lesson treatments. A limited number of lessons are presented via CAI, with on-line testing imbedded within the module.

For instructors, the system (1) flags students with entry deficiencies and proficiencies; (2) scores tests by objective, critical "must pass" items and overall percentage correct; (3) ensures that lessons are taken in proper sequence; (4) tracks completed lessons; (5) tracks alternative modules and assigns students accordingly; (6) provides random assignment of lesson and block tests; (7) furnishes daily learning-center rosters that flag students with deficiencies in rate of progress and indicate absences; (8) maintains a resource inventory in real time; (9) provides reports on individual student performance; and (10) allows recall of student data profiles for use in counseling and student progress management.

In addition, training managers and course designers are furnished information that can be used to (1) standardize the course presentation; (2) balance utilization of training resources, such as student loads across shifts, learning centers, and curricula; (3) determine times to complete instructional segments; (4) provide test security through on-line testing and random assignment of tests; (5) describe characteristics of students in the course through preassessment test data; (6) report student attitudes toward the course; and (7) provide performance summaries of item analysis data for evaluating and reviewing course materials and tests (Yasutake & Stobie, 1979). Computer-assisted and computer-managed instructional systems, with a large variety of services, do not necessarily require large systems, however, and it is possible to implement these types of systems on microcomputers (Milner, 1980; Mitzel, 1974).

Course Materials. Computers used for instruction, however, are no better than the material they contain. While there have been great gains in computer hardware, with mass production driving down costs while maintaining high quality, similar gains have not occurred in the software (or courseware) aspects. A distributor of course material for microprocessors has stated that buyers should be careful and selective, for 95 percent of all the programs carried should never have been offered for sale (Purser, n.d.). In an effort to assist the educator, the Northwest Regional Educational Laboratory has established a national clearinghouse for microcomputer-based instructional materials designed for use in grades K–12 (*Micro-SIFT News*, 1980). The laboratory's approach is to collect and evaluate instructional programs and to disseminate information about them to educators. CONDUIT is a nonprofit, university consortium that disseminates computer-based educational programs, including microcomputer materials developed for use at the postsecondary level. These two efforts are important because of their quality-assurance aspects and because of the potential widespread use of these materials in the future, which can be stimulated by declining costs. One publishing firm had advertised a mathematics series on a microcomputer for grades 1–6 for ten cents per student-hour (*Mathematics Series*, 1979). The Dallas Independent School District plans to offer bilingual instruction for fifty cents per student hour (Dooley, 1978).

Evaluations of Computer-based Instruction. Evaluation studies of computer-based instruction can be categorized into two groups. First are the large-scale evaluations of the major projects, such as the development of PLATO, TICCIT, and the remedial drill-and-practice materials of the Computer Curriculum Corporation, each of which has received from $2 million to $20 million in research and development funding. Then there are the shorter, less extensive studies of other efforts.

PLATO utilizes a large computer to support 400 to 500 terminals distributed throughout the country and connected by telephone lines. Many programs are stored centrally and delivered to the remote sites that require them. Control Data Corporation, which now markets PLATO, has made it available from about 130 centers throughout the country to minimize communications costs. A large-scale evaluation of the PLATO system by Educational Testing Service has found that there was no significant difference in student achievement or in attrition rates be-

tween PLATO-taught and non–PLATO-taught classes, but that both students and teachers liked the idea of using PLATO (Murphy & Appel, 1977). Although the evaluations may not be so positive as one would like, the use of the PLATO system is increasing. The University of Delaware, for instance, installed a PLATO system in 1975, and by the spring of 1980 faculty members, students, and programmers were spending over 200,000 hours annually developing programs in over eighty subject areas, using the university's 132 on-campus terminals, and with support also given to another seventy terminals off campus (Hofstetter, 1980). Further, Control Data Corporation, which has made a sizable corporate investment in the PLATO hardware using central computers and in courses for it, has introduced a version that operates on microcomputers.

TICCIT uses stand-alone minicomputers to serve terminals that incorporate standard TV sets, with the courses developed by teams of instructional developers. After Educational Testing Service evaluated the effectiveness of three courses, developed at a cost of almost $1.9 million each, in three post-secondary institutions and found that TICCIT-taught students scored on the average 5 percent higher on final examinations, but had markedly lower completion rates and felt more often ignored as individuals than did students in teacher-led courses (Alderman, 1978).

Crandall (*Computers and the Learning Society*, 1978) reports that the students at grade levels 4–6 who used computer-based remedial drill-and-practice materials developed by the Computer Curriculum Corporation performed 30 percentile points higher in mathematics and 13 percentile points higher in reading than those who did not use the materials; the former also exhibited less truancy, tardiness, and vandalism.

Very few programs have been run as extensively or with as much support as these three. In evaluating the effectiveness of other efforts, Kulik, Kulik, and Cohen (1980) reviewed the results of fifty-nine studies of computer-based education using meta-analysis techniques and found that at the college level the computer made a small but significant contribution to the effectiveness of the teaching of students of all aptitude levels, raising student scores on examinations by about one-quarter of a standard deviation; moreover, it had a small but positive effect on the attitudes of students toward the instruction they received and toward the subject matter. At the elementary school level, the results were even more dramatically in favor of computer-based education used in a supplementary fashion, as the studies of Edwards et al. (1975) and Vinsonhaler and Bass (1972) have shown. A meta-analysis of evaluations of the effectiveness of computer-based teaching at the elementary level conducted by Hartley (1977) showed gains of at least one-half of a standard deviation in favor of computer-supplemented teaching of children.

In all of the evaluations of computer-based education, numerous effects can be introduced, and so the evaluators must be cautious. Anastasio (*Information Technology in Education*, 1980) states that the results of many of the evaluations that have been conducted could have been determined simply by reviewing the contents of the treatment curriculum, of the comparison curriculum, and of the test used. He further states that in the evaluation of the remedial mathematics programs discussed above, children may have learned test-taking skills more than mathematics since CAI-taught students continued to make the same frequency of errors as did non–CAI-taught students.

Computer-assisted Testing. Computers are also playing an increasing role in the administration of tests. Efforts to develop computer-assisted tests have followed three approaches: the construction of tests from computer-based item pools of varying complexity; the administration of tests; and the tailoring of tests to match the ability of the test taker. The National Association of Security Dealers, for example, currently offers twelve different qualifications tests for stockbrokers and managers, at times they request, by computer at sixty-nine sites around the country. In each of the twelve subject areas, the computer creates a test for the individual by selecting items from a group of 200 to 2,000 items stored in a data bank, presents and scores the tests, and then reports the results to appropriate officials in state agencies and security firms (Milner, 1979).

While the National Association of Security Dealers relies on large-scale computers to support remote terminals for testing, Educational Testing Service is carrying out a variety of research activities using hand-held calculators and microcomputers to enhance the testing situation. They are particularly investigating how computers can simultaneously be used to test a student's ability and as an instructional device, by providing the student with encouragement when a testing item is correctly answered or giving hints and allowing the student to try again when errors are made ("Technology and Education," 1980). These are new applications but appear to have the potential to grow significantly in the next decade.

In addition to the applications already described, terminals interconnected by telecommunications can also be used to create messages and deliver them electronically. Electronic mail is a computerized way of creating, editing, filing, storing, and distributing to one or more locations any information that can be entered into a computer. This can include course schedules, teaching tips, administrative announcements, requests for information, tabular material, and any other information necessary to conduct an effective educational enterprise. Electronic mail systems are easy to operate, using language that is similar to English commands. Sent via telecommunications to a central computer, the information can be made available to all or a selected number of persons. All messages are secure and will be displayed only to someone entering the correct code for his or her "mailbox."

In Alaska, an electronic mail system has been installed as part of an educational delivery system. It links together, via satellite and computer, all fifty-two school districts in the state, several regional centers, and the state Department of Education. Although telephone service exists in all of these locations, 350 teachers and administrators sent over 10,000 messages through electronic mail in 1980 (*Expanding Educational Opportunities*, 1980).

Computer Conferencing. An application that combines the characteristics of electronic mail with those of audio conferencing is computer conferencing. The participants in a computer conference, using a computer terminal, can ask questions of other participants, answer queries, make comments to a few or all participants, or ask for a recall and possibly an analysis of previously provided information. Similar to an audioteleconference, a computer conference can involve two or a large number of participants located at many sites, each of which is connected to the computer through a communications link. The participants all may be on line simultaneously or, since the messages are stored in a computer, they can participate at different times over an extended period to suit their schedules. This approach might be particularly useful for course managers, allowing them to conduct a conference with a large number of teacher-leaders who are at many locations in the field. In addition to providing flexibility in times to participate, the computer can accommodate responses from large numbers of conferees to a given question from the course manager and can even analyze the responses to determine common positions.

Video

The use of television in education has grown sharply in the United States in recent years. This has been stimulated by the development of public broadcasting, by the increasing availability of communications satellites and other communications media for educational applications, and by the interest of colleges and universities in exploring and developing new markets in a period when the traditional college age-group is declining in numbers.

Broadcast Television. Although television has been utilized in education for thirty years, it received a significant impetus in 1967 with the passage of the Public Broadcasting Act. This legislation and the subsequent 1975 Public Broadcasting Act and the 1978 Public Telecommunications Financing Act ensured federal support for public broadcasting through the Corporation for Public Broadcasting. Since the beginning of federal involvement, public broadcasting has grown substantially. The number of public television stations increased from 126 in 1967 to 290 in 1980, and they now provide coverage to 90 percent of the American households with television receivers. In March 1980, over 68 percent of the nation's television households tuned to at least one program on public television. The average annual broadcast hours per station was 4,894 hours in 1979, an increase of 26 percent over 1974, with more than 1,000 instructional series at the K–12 levels broadcast on one or more public television stations, and with 137 of these series carried by ten or more licensees.

Instructional television for use in the schools comprised 14.8 percent of the total hours broadcast, and broadcasts of "Sesame Street" and "The Electric Company" for home viewing totaled to another 14.5 percent (Lee, 1981).

Educational uses of broadcast television began a new phase in reaching mass audiences when "Sesame Street" was first put on the air in 1971. Developed by the Children's Television Workshop (CTW), with funding primarily from the U.S. Office of Education and the Corporation for Public Broadcasting, its purpose is to teach youngsters of ages 3 to 5 years basic skills such as recognition of letters and number concepts. The programs have been developed using a combination of sound pedagogical approaches and the techniques of entertainment television, together with formative research and evaluation. The program was an immediate success. The show, which consists of 130 one-hour programs that are partially revised each year, is viewed by about 8 to 9 million children annually. It currently is carried by 97 percent of the public television stations in the United States, as well as a number of commercial stations in areas where there is no public television, and reaches 85 percent of the 3- to 5-year-olds in inner cities. In addition, it is shown in modified versions in forty foreign countries.

Based on the success and approach of "Sesame Street," CTW introduced "The Electric Company" in 1973 to teach basic concepts and skills in reading. Today, about 6 million viewers, including some 2.5 million children in grades 1–6, watch the program in school. It is seen in about half of the nation's homes where there are children under 6, and by at least some children in about 30 percent of the country's elementary schools. In 1980, "3–2–1 Contact," a series designed to teach basic skills in science, was aired and in that first year was seen by 4 to 5 million children.

In the late 1970s, public television stations also broadcast a series of programs that included "The Ascent of Man," "The Adams Chronicles," "Classic Theatre: The Humanities in Drama," and others. While these programs were designed for general audience viewing, ancillary study materials were developed that allowed interested colleges to award credit for the successful completion of courses "wrapped around" these shows. It is estimated that more than 600 American colleges now provide credit for courses delivered to viewers by cable, satellite, commercial, and public television (Luskin, 1981). As part of its Adult Learning Service, the Public Broadcast Service (PBS) is televising college credit courses, informal learning series, and professional and career training programs for adult learners. Each of the approximately 500 colleges and universities that chose in 1980 to award grades and credit for these courses selected its offerings from nine available courses and then worked with its local public television station to develop a broadcast schedule that met local needs.

The University of Mid-America, a consortium of eleven state universities, produced and offered courses by television and other media for most of the 1970s and then began planning for a nationwide American Open University that would offer both graduate and undergraduate courses through television. The National University Consortium for Telecommunications has begun to offer courses for undergraduate degrees via television and other nontraditional delivery systems. The Central Education Network, composed of the public television stations in ten midwestern states, together with representatives from institutions of higher education, has formed a postsecondary council to determine the needs for telecommunications at the 821 colleges and universities in its area, and to obtain savings by group purchases of telecourses and equipment (Scully, 1980). Recognizing the role that television has played and can play in American education, Walter H. Annenberg, in early 1981, donated $150 million to be distributed over a fifteen-year period to the Corporation for Public Broadcasting to support the production of high-quality college-level courses for distribution through existing and developing telecommunications systems (Scully, 1981).

Instructional Television Fixed Service Systems. Broadcast television is used most effectively when it is necessary to reach large numbers of people dispersed over relatively broad areas, since it is a means for mass distribution. When small or localized audiences are to be reached, other means of delivery, such as Instructional Television Fixed Service (ITFS), are more appropriate. ITFS was established by the Federal Communications Commission in 1963 as a "point-to-points" distribution system for transmitting as many as four channels of black-and-white or color TV to predetermined receiving sites, such as schools, colleges, hospitals, or industrial plants, equipped with special receiving antennas.

Although the most extensive use of ITFS has been by parochial school systems for the delivery of classroom television for elementary and secondary classes, it is used regularly by institutions of higher education to provide graduate education to engineers and other professionals located at plant and office sites, as well as for meeting a wide variety of other educational needs. The Center for Excellence in Williamsburg, Virginia, has served the peninsular area with improved educational services for the handicapped and is expanding its system into a multichannel, multiservice, two-way public telecommunications network (Roth, 1980). The South Carolina Educational Television Commission is establishing a four-channel ITFS system to improve basic skills for schoolchildren, provide adult education, meet in-service needs of school staffs, and meet communications needs of the residents of a rural county. Stanford University and the University of Southern California are utilizing an ITFS system with interactive "talkback" to provide a variety of educational courses for engineers in many high-technology companies in the Palo Alto area. In the northeastern part of the state, California State University at Chico is extending its ITFS network to meet the higher-educational needs of a widely distributed rural population of about 511,000 persons spread over twelve counties. The development of several systems to serve a wide variety of local needs is significant because it occurred with little or no federal support. Funds to construct and operate these systems have come from administrators who chose ITFS over other competing demands.

Satellites and Cable Systems. The recent availability of high-powered satellites that operate into moderate- to low-cost receivers has stimulated an even greater interest in the use of television for education. All public television stations are now interconnected by satellite, through PBS, so that programs can be distributed rapidly and reliably. In addition, large numbers of cable systems have added satellite antennas to their systems to receive, from a variety of distribution services, programming that they make available to their subscribers. The number of such cable systems has increased from about 200 in 1978 to more than 3,000 in 1981; it is projected to rise to 7,500 in 1983. Several organizations have been created to take advantage of this new capability by operating satellite-based delivery systems for education. A good example is the Appalachian Community Service Network, which currently offers sixty-four hours per week of college courses, adult education programs, seminars, and community-interest programming to over $1\frac{1}{2}$ million homes throughout the nation. Originating in Lexington, Kentucky, the programs are transmitted via an orbiting satellite and received by a large number of cable systems, which in turn make them available to their subscribers in homes, schools, hospitals, and community centers. At current growth rates, the network should reach almost 3 million homes by the end of 1982. More than fifty colleges and universities offer graduate-level credit for courses taken through the Appalachian network.

The Association for Media-Based Continuing Education for Engineers (AMCEE) is investigating the use of satellites to distribute videotaped courses to engineers throughout the nation. AMCEE has already offered a course in engineering economics via the Appalachia network, for which graduate-level credit was granted to those persons who enrolled in one of the many participating colleges or universities and successfully completed the course. The American Educational Television Network, a public-service pay TV network broadcasting adult education via satellite through cable systems, has been designed to assist members of professional associations and employee organizations in meeting state licensing and college credit requirements. Formed in June 1979, the network is focusing its programming and marketing efforts to meet the needs of dentists, physicians, nurses, lawyers, engineers, accountants, social workers, pharmacists, and many other professional groups. These examples clearly show that satellites are becoming a more common means of distributing education via television to those who need it, regardless of their locations.

Satellites scheduled to be launched in the next several years will be even more powerful than present ones and will be capable of broadcasting materials directly to homes and schools. Satellite Television Corporation (STC), a subsidiary of Comsat, filed in 1980 an application with the Federal Communications Commission (FCC) to design and launch a 3-channel direct broadcast system consisting of separate satellites to serve the four time zones in the continental United States. STC proposes to lease the receiving antenna and associated hardware and make the programming available to home subscribers for a fee of $20 to $25 per month ("Comsat Sets DMS Proposal," 1981). In response to an FCC request, twelve other organizations submitted by the filing deadline of July 16, 1981, applications to create direct broadcast systems. Each of those that provided cost data estimated that its system would cost between $200 million and $800 million (Dassler, 1981). Although these systems are not designed for education, their ability to broadcast directly into homes and schools, as well as the fact that more than 100 television channels will be available by 1984 on satellites already launched or scheduled to be launched, provides opportunities for one or more organizations to serve education through this medium.

Video Recording Media. While television is a means for transmitting video program over large distances, other, less expensive, media have been used since the early part of this century to record and distribute full-motion visual information for education. Experiments with instructional films were conducted as early as 1918 (Hoban & Van-Ormer, 1950; Greenhill, 1967). As new technologies for prerecording materials developed, they also were incorporated into education. Added to film as a means for delivery were videotape and videocassettes, and, most recently, videodiscs.

Videotaped courses are used extensively in continuing engineering education. Twenty-one engineering colleges and universities have joined together as the Association for Media-Based Continuing Education for Engineers, a nonprofit corporation, to produce and distribute videotapes of courses, seminars, short courses, and symposia for off-campus use. The guides and/or textbooks are of two types. One type corresponds to regularly scheduled undergraduate and graduate courses given to on-campus students. The "candid classroom" is recorded, allowing the viewer to hear and see everything that the on-campus student does. The viewer also receives the same class handouts and may participate in tests and receive credit for successfully completing the course. The second type consists of courses that have been specially prepared in TV studios under broadcast quality conditions and that are not tied to a university's scheduled on-campus offerings (*AMCEE Videotape Courses*, n.d.).

The videodisc is the most recent of the media for storing and playing video materials. A disc, which is similar in appearance to a long-playing record, is about twelve inches in diameter and can store up to 54,000 individual frames or pictures, or thirty to sixty minutes of full-motion video on each side. It is viewed by using a player, which is about the size of a portable phonograph, connected to an ordinary TV set. A disc has two tracks that allow narration in two languages to accompany the visuals, separate narrative information for two levels of background knowledge of the students, or music in stereo. In addition, a disc can be used to store about 10 billion bits of information, which is about five times the amount of information necessary to encode the entire *Encyclopaedia Britannica,* or enough to store the contents of about 300 books on each side of the disc.

No single standard exists as yet for videodiscs, so several incompatible versions are being developed and marketed. Some are more suitable for educational purposes than others. A very popular type that is widely marketed for home entertainment is a capacitance disc. Although the player is lower in cost than the players for other types of discs, the capacitance disc can play only full-motion sequences. Optical or laser-read discs, in contrast, can have the frames individually coded and displayed so that a single side of the disc can store 54,000 slides, a half-hour of continuous motion pictures, or a combination of the two. It also is possible to use the disc in a dynamically programmed format for stand-alone use or in conjunction with an external computer in an interactive mode. The interactive videodisc system can be used in instruction in five nondiscrete approaches. It may be used as (1) an instructor-controlled support mechanism for interactive or passive group presentations. It can be used for individualized stand-alone presentations as (2) a nonprogrammed device; (3) a dynamically programmed device in which the program is entered from a remote keypad; or (4) a device in which the controlling program is stored on the disc. In addition, the disc can be used as (5) an ancillary device to a computer external to the one contained within the disc player (Long, 1981; Eastwood, 1978–1979).

A number of groups are designing and evaluating courses for presentation by videodiscs in combination with microcomputers. In these early stages of application, the purposes of the efforts are to determine the instructional strategies employed by teachers who use videodiscs, determine cost-efficient ways to develop quality materials, and assess the attitudes of teachers toward the equipment and the materials. Among the organizations doing this type of work are the videodisc design/production group at KUON-TV/University of Nebraska–Lincoln (Daynes, Brown, & Newman, 1981), WICAT Incorporated (Heuston, 1977), and the Minnesota Educational Computing Consortium.

In addition, several large corporations are using videodiscs for education and training purposes. One of the most extensive applications for customer education is by IBM, which has established over thirty-six Guided Learning Centers around the country to train customers of small business sytems about the equipment they purchase. Each center, which is equipped with three videodisc players, remote control units, TV monitors, audio cassette recorders, and surrogate computer terminals for completing student exercises, can accommodate sixteen students simultaneously. The company has about twenty training programs, which vary in length from one to five days, on videodiscs. In 1980, the first year of operation of the centers, 21,000 customers completed slightly over 40,000 student-days of instruction (Stegmann, 1980; "How IBM Uses Videodiscs," 1981).

Evaluation.   The use of television in education has been well researched, with studies ranging from the evaluation of groups in tightly controlled classroom situations to research on students learning at home and in normal class settings. Ball and Bogatz (1970) reported the results of learning measures from the first year of "Sesame Street" based on a large sample of children in four geographic areas of the United States. They found that the program benefitted children from ghetto communities, middle-class suburbs, and isolated rural areas by teaching them the functions of body parts and the meanings of matching and relational terms. They also found that among all groups the amount of learning that occurred was directly related to the amount of viewing by the children. In a follow-up study the next year, Bogatz and Ball (1971) showed some of the subtle differences that can occur in teaching by television. "Sesame Street" had a noticeable effect in teaching children to name letters but no effect on alphabet recitation, and it had an effect on teaching them to match by form but none in matching by position.

A similar series of evaluations of "The Electric Company" (Ball & Bogatz, 1972; Ball et al., 1974) found that in-school viewing by children in the first and second grades yielded significant gains across the full spectrum of the program's curriculum goals. At the first-grade level, parents of viewing children regarded their children as better readers than parents of nonviewing children, and there seemed to be a long-term gain, as children who watched the program for two years did no better than those who watched it for one year. Herriott and Liebert (1972) surveyed the teachers of the children who watched "The Electric Company" in school and found that about 80 percent of the teachers surveyed noted some gains in specific reading skills of the children who watched the series; about 24 percent noted a great increase in reading interest by the students; and 38 percent reported great improvements in the ability of students to decode words, to spell words (21 percent), and in basic sight vocabulary (33 percent).

Chu and Schramm (1968), in a major study on learning from television, state: "There can no longer be any doubt that children and adults learn a great amount from instructional television, just as they do from any other experience that can be made to seem relevant to them—experiences as different as watching someone rotate a hula hoop or reading the encyclopedia. The effectiveness of television has now been demonstrated in well over 100 experiments, and several hundred separate comparisons, performed in many parts of the world, in developing as well as industrialized countries, at every level from preschool through adult education, and with a great variety of subject matter and methods."

Technology developments are resulting in new hardware devices that are providing a plethora of opportunities for improved learning by people at all age levels, both in school and in nontraditional settings. The problems that confront educators are to use these technologies in ways that are effective and affordable, by focusing on the needs of the learner and using the full capabilities of the technology to meet those needs, and to assure that the technology is not misused, creating greater problems than it was meant to solve (Grayson, 1976a, 1976b, 1978).

Lawrence P. Grayson

See also Computer-Based Education; Distance Education; Libraries; Media Use in Education; Systems Design in Instruction.

REFERENCES

Alderman, D. L. *Evaluation of the TICCIT Computer-assisted Instructional System in the Community College* (PR-77-10). Princeton, N.J.: Educational Testing Service, 1978.

AMCEE Videotape Courses for Engineers, Scientists, and Technical Managers, 1980/1981 Catalog. Atlanta, Ga.: Georgia Institute of Technology, Association for Media-Based Continuing Education for Engineers, n.d.

Ball, S., & Bogatz, G. A. *The First Year of Sesame Street: An Evaluation* (PR-70-15). Princeton, N.J.: Educational Testing Service, October 1970.

Ball, S., & Bogatz, G. A. *Reading with Television: An Evaluation of The Electric Company* (PR-72-2; 2 vols.). Princeton, N.J.: Educational Testing Service, February 1972.

Ball, S.; Bogatz, G. A.; Kazarow, K. M.; & Rubin, D. B. *Reading with Television: A Follow-up Evaluation of The Electric Company* (PR-74-15). Princeton, N.J.: Educational Testing Service, June 1974.

Bogatz, G. A., & Ball, S. *The Second Year of Sesame Street: A Continuing Evaluation* (PR-71-21; 2 vols.). Princeton, N.J.: Educational Testing Service, November 1971.

Bork, A. *The Physics Computer Development Project.* Irvine: University of California at Irvine, Department of Physics, 1975. (ERIC Document Reproduction Service No. ED 123 098)

Bork, A. Learning through graphics. In R. J. Seidel (Ed.), *Computers and Communications: Implications for Education.* New York: Academic Press, 1977.

Carnegie Commission on Higher Education. *The Fourth Revolution: Instructional Technology in Higher Education.* New York: McGraw-Hill, 1972.

Catalog '81: Videocassettes and Films for Schools, Colleges, Libraries, and Business. Lincoln, Nebr.: University of Mid-America, n.d.

Chu, G. C., & Schramm, W. *Learning from Television: What the Research Says.* Washington, D.C.: National Association of Educational Broadcasters, 1968.

Cohen, I. D. *The Relative Value of Silent Reading and Radio Broadcasting.* Unpublished doctoral dissertation, New York University, 1937.

Computers and the Learning Society (Report of the Committee on Science and Technology, U.S. House of Representatives).

Washington, D.C.: U.S. Government Printing Office, June 1978.

Comsat sets DBS proposal. *Satellite Communications,* February 1981, pp. 32–33.

Congressional Research Service. *New Technology in Education: Selected References* (Prepared for the Subcommittee on Science, Research, and Development of the Committee on Science and Astronautics, U.S. House of Representatives). Washington, D.C.: U.S. Government Printing Office, 1971.

Constantine, M. Radio in the elementary school. *Science Education,* 1964, *48,* 121–132.

Curtis, J. A. *ITFS Survey Information* (Information Report No. 80-50). Williamsburg, Va.: National Instructional Telecommunications Council, Inc., August 27, 1980.

Dassler, A. F. What are they doing to direct broadcast satellite services? *Telecommunications,* November 1981, pp. 29–32.

Daynes, R.; Brown, R. D.; & Newman, D. L. Field test evaluation of teaching with videodiscs. *Educational and Industrial Television,* March 1981, pp. 54, 55–58.

Dooley, A. For bilingual instruction school shifting teaching aid to micros. *Computerworld,* November 6, 1978, p. 63.

Dwyer, T. A. Heuristic strategies for using computers to enrich education. *International Journal of Man-Machine Studies,* 1974, *6.*

Dwyer, T. A. An extensible model for using technology in education. In R. J. Seidel (Ed.), *Computers and Communications: Implications for Education.* New York: Academic Press, 1977.

Eastwood, L. F., Jr. Motivations and deterrents to educational use of "intelligent videodisc" systems. *Journal of Educational Technology Systems,* 1978–1979, *7*(2), 303–335.

Edwards, J.; Norton, S.; Taylor, S.; Weiss, M.; & Dusseldorp, R. How effective is CAI? A review of the research. *Educational Leadership,* 1975, *33,* 147–153.

The Effects of Educational Radio Musical Classroom (Report of the Radio-Television Cultural Research Institute). Tokyo: NHK, 1957.

Expanding Educational Opportunities through Telecommunications (Report of the Educational Telecommunications Project for Alaska). Juneau: Alaska State Department of Education, February 1980.

Grayson, L. P. Costs, benefits, effectiveness: Challenges for educational technology. *Science,* 1972, *175,* 1216–1222.

Grayson, L. P. Educational satellites: A goal or gaol? *Institute of Electrical & Electronics Engineers Transactions on Education,* 1976, *E-19*(2), 38–45. (a)

Grayson, L. P. Instructional technology: On diversity in education. *Communications Review,* 1976, *24*(2), 117–134. (b)

Grayson, L. P. Education, technology, and individual privacy. *Educational Communication and Technology,* 1978, *26*(3), 195–206.

Greenhill, L. P. Review of trends in research on instructional television and films. In *Research in Instructional Television and Film* (U.S. Office of Education Report OE-34041). Washington, D.C.: U.S. Government Printing Office, 1967, p. 1.

Hamblen, J. W., & Baird, T. B. *Fourth Inventory of Computers in Higher Education, 1976–1977.* Princeton, N.J.: EDUCOM, 1979.

Hartley, S. S. Meta-analysis of the effects of individually paced instruction in mathematics (Doctoral dissertation, University of Colorado, 1977). *Dissertation Abstracts International,* 1978, *38*(7-A), 4003. (University Microfilms No. 77-29, 926).

Herriott, R. E., & Liebert, R. J. *"The Electric Company," In-school*

Utilization: 1971–1972 School and Teacher Survey. New York: Children's Television Workshop, 1972.

Heuston, D. H. *The Promise and Inevitability of the Videodisc in Education.* Orem, Utah: WICAT, Inc., 1977. (ERIC Document Reproduction Service No. ED 153 636)

Hoban, C. F., & VanOrmer, E. B. *Instructional Film Research, 1918–1950* (SDC 269-7-19). Port Washington, N.Y.: U.S. Naval Training Devices Center, December 1950.

Hofstetter, F. T. *Synopsis of the University of Delaware's Office of Computer-based Instruction.* Unpublished paper, University of Delaware, July 21, 1980.

How IBM uses videodiscs for customer training. *Educational and Instructional Television*, March 1981, *13*(3), 31–34.

Information Technology in Education (Report of the joint hearings of the Committee on Science and Technology and the Committee on Education and Labor of the U.S. House of Representatives, April 2-3, 1980). Washington, D.C.: U.S. Government Printing Office, 1980, p. 163.

Katzman, S., Katzman, N. *Public Radio Programming: Content by Category, Fiscal Year 1978.* Washington, D.C.: Corporation for Public Broadcasting, 1978.

Kulik, J. A.; Kulik, C-L. C.; & Cohen, P. A. Research on audio-tutorial instruction: A meta-analysis of comparative studies. *Research in Higher Education*, 1979, *11*(4), 321–341.

Kulik, J. A.; Kulik, C-L. C.; & Cohen, P. A. Effectiveness of computer-based college teaching: A meta-analysis of findings. *Review of Educational Research*, Winter 1980, *50*(4), 525–544.

LeBoss, B. 1980 could be the year of the consumer. *Electronics*, January 31, 1980, pp. 70–71.

Lee, S. Y. *Status of Public Broadcasting, 1980.* Washington, D.C.: Corporation for Public Broadcasting, March 1981.

Long, H. A. The videodisc: A picture book in the round. *Technological Horizons in Education Journal*, May 1981, *8*(4), 39–42.

Lumley, F. J. Rates of speech in radio-speaking. *Quarterly Journal of Speech*, June 1933.

Luskin, B. J. Force or vision: The choice. *Technological Horizons in Education Journal*, January 1981, *8*(1), 60–61.

Mathematics Series. St. Louis: Milliken, 1979.

MicroSIFT News, October 1980, *1*(1). Portland, Oreg.: Northwest Regional Educational Laboratory.

Milner, S. D. *Determining the Feasibility of Computer-based Instruction.* Unpublished paper, U.S. Office of Personnel Management; Training Research and Evaluation Division; Workforce, Effectiveness, and Development Group, Washington, D.C., October 1979, pp. 40–41.

Milner, S. D. How to make the right decisions about microcomputers. *Instructional Innovator*, September 1980, *25*(6), 12–19.

Mitzel, H. E. (Ed.). *An Examination of the Short-range Potential of Computer-managed Instruction* (Conference Proceedings). University Park: Pennsylvania State University, 1974.

Molnar, A. R. *National Policy toward Technological Innovation and Academic Computing.* Unpublished paper, National Science Foundation, Education Directorate, Washington, D.C., 1977.

Molnar, A. R. Microcomputers and videodiscs: Innovations of the second kind. *Technical Horizons in Education Journal*, November 1980, *7*(6), 58.

Murphy, R. T., & Appel, L. R. *Evaluation of the PLATO IV Computer-based Education System in the Community College* (PR-77-10). Princeton, N.J.: Educational Testing Service, 1977.

National Academy of Engineering. *Issues and Public Policies in Educational Technology.* Lexington, Mass.: Lexington Books, 1974.

Papert, S.; Watt, D.; diSessa, A.; & Weir, S. *Final Report of the Brookline LOGO Project. Project Summary and Data Analysis.* Cambridge, Mass.: MIT, 1979.

Postlethwait, S. N.; Novak, J.; & Murray, H. T., Jr. *The Audio-tutorial Approach to Learning* (2nd ed.). Minneapolis: Burgess, 1971.

Purser, R. E. *Reference List of TRS 80, PET, and APPLE II.* El Dorado, Calif.: Author, n.d.

Radio in the Classroom (Report of the Wisconsin Research Project in School Broadcasting). Madison: University of Wisconsin Press, 1942.

Roth, E. B. Two-way television trains teachers. *American Education*, November 1980, *16*(9), 20–28.

Scully, M. G. Use of television gaining on campuses after years of promise, disappointment. *Chronicle of Higher Education*, September 2, 1980, pp. 1, 14.

Scully, M. G. Annenberg's $150-million gift to public television to be used to produce courses for existing colleges. *Chronicle of Higher Education*, March 9, 1981, pp. 1, 15.

Seibert, W. F., & Ullmer, E. J. Media use in education. In H. E. Mitzel (Ed.), *Encyclopedia of Educational Research* (5th ed.). New York: Macmillan, 1982.

Shah, P. H., & Torok, G. P. Have blackboard, needn't travel. *Bell Laboratories Record*, October 1979, *57*(9), 255–258.

Stegmann, C. Disco: New beat in do-it-yourself computer-assisted instruction. *Think*, November/December 1980, *46*(6), 30–34.

Technology and education: Here comes the future. In *1980 Annual Report*. Princeton, N.J.: Educational Testing Service, 1980, pp. 5–8.

Tickton, S. G. (Ed.). *To Improve Learning: An Evaluation of Instructional Technology, Part One—A Report by the Commission on Instructional Technology.* New York: Bowker, 1970.

Tickton, S. G. (Ed.). *To Improve Learning: An evaluation of Instructional Technology, Part Two—Instructional Technology, Selected Working Papers on the State of the Art.* New York: Bowker, 1971.

Vinsonhaler, J. F., & Bass, R. K. A summary of ten major studies on CAI drill and practice. *Educational Technology.* 1972, *12*, 29–32.

Woelfel, N., & Tyler, I. K. *Radio and the School* (A summary of a six-year research project begun in 1937). Yonkers-on-Hudson, N.Y.: World Book, 1945.

Yasutake, J. Y., & Stobie, W. H. *Issues Involved in AIS Implementation: Closing the Gap between Theory and Practice.* Paper presented at the annual meeting of the American Educational Research Association, 1979.

NONTRADITIONAL HIGHER EDUCATION PROGRAMS

Perhaps no term was used with a greater array of meanings in the 1970s than "nontraditional." This broad usage makes the term difficult to define, as the members of the Commission on Nontraditional Study (1973), among others, have pointed out. Other alternatives have been considered, such as "nonconventional," which was intended to convey the important point that what has passed for "tradition" in higher education has often been simply a set of conventions. Greek was required at Harvard for a bachelor of arts degree until 1897, Latin until 1905. A Harvard degree could be attained after 1905 without either Greek or Latin, but it was a B.S. degree, not a B.A. (Veysey, 1973). Such benchmarks as the establishment of the land grant colleges by the Morrill Act of 1862 and the introduction of the elective system at Harvard during President Eliot's tenure also had their effect. But between 1870 and 1910 a standard American college and university model emerged, the result of strategic compromises by strong presidents, thus accommodating both the British collegiate and German research orientations, the defenders of what was then termed "liberal culture" and the new utilitarians: general education for the traditionalists, subject majors for the vocationalists, and free electives for everyone. Consequently, "nontraditional" might be applied to those changes, reforms, or innovations that represented new or different ways of doing higher education. But when the fourth edition of the *Encyclopedia of Educational Research* (1969) appeared, the normal or standard American college was characterized by a population of students typically between 17 and 23 years of age, many in residence on or near a campus, who attended classes held at fixed times and in determined places, following a set curriculum of sequenced courses. It is against this traditional model that the nontraditional programs and institutions of the 1970s can be most conveniently described.

In its discussion of the difficulties of defining "nontraditional," the Commission on Non-Traditional Study (1973) reported that the consensus reached was that "nontraditional study is more an attitude than a system and thus can never be defined except tangentially" (p. xv). The commission report goes on to state that this attitude "puts the student first and the institution second, concentrates more on the former's need than the latter's convenience, encourages diversity of individual opportunity rather than uniform prescription, and deemphasizes time, space, and even course requirements in favor of competence and, where applicable, performance" (p. xv).

Two principal purposes appear to have motivated the creation of new and nontraditional programs in the 1970s. The first, a social purpose, sought ways to increase access to education for potential students who were not previously well served. For such students, opportunity for access was achieved by creating different arrangements in the place, time, and method of study. A second motivation for nontraditional programs, more directly educational in nature, aimed to improve teaching and student learning through new instructional approaches. Such modifications and reforms were especially important if the new student populations brought to the university by improved access were to be effectively educated rather than admitted to a revolving door system and quickly cast out. Nontraditional educational reforms included different approaches to curriculum content as well as different ways of meeting degree requirements.

Access for New Students. The new student population served by nontraditional programs is best described by stating who they are not: learners who fall within the traditional college age range of 17 to 22. There have long been students outside this normal range, of course. However, few colleges were designed primarily for part-time, older, nonresidential students, often with family and occupational responsibilities, or others unable or unwilling to attend classes on a college campus.

Many of these students were of minority ethnic background or those, such as women and older Americans, who had been unable to gain a college education at an earlier time. They are well described in *Beyond the Open Door* (Cross, 1971). Because serving these students met important social and political commitments of our nation, government and foundation dollars flowed generously to support the creation of programs for nontraditional access. The creation of the Department of Health, Education, and Welfare's Fund for the Improvement of Postsecondary Education in 1972 highlighted the national importance of new educational programs.

Programs in the 1970s that specifically addressed access for students included courses offered by newspapers (University Extension, University of California), on television (Coastline Community College, California), and on commuter trains (Adelphi University); the open admission experiment (City University of New York); adult degree programs through existing evening or extension divisions (University of Oklahoma); programs where much of the learning occurs at noncampus locations in communities, industry, or government agencies (University Without Walls); and degrees by examination or assessment (New York Regents External Degree).

Program classification. In Houle's useful work (1973) for the Commission on Non-Traditional Study, programs are classified as extension degrees, adult degrees, and assessment degrees. A somewhat different, but not dissimilar, classification is provided by Medsker et al. (1975). Houle's extension degree is termed the "extended-campus approach" by Medsker et al. (1975), who characterize the institutions they studied in terms of time and space arrangements and curricular requirements. Thus, programs such as the Evening College of Johns Hopkins University and the Bachelor of General Studies of Roosevelt University are on-campus programs with traditional curricular requirements, but with flexible scheduling, time, and residency requirements. These may be supplemented by off-campus classes and some use of media, such as radio and television.

The "liberal studies–adult degree approach" of Medsker et al. (1975) is the adult degree in Houle's classification. These programs accommodate the special needs and circumstances of adult students, with greater opportunities for independent study and less emphasis on classroom instruction. However, the curricular requirements are themselves fixed, not individually tailored, and some period of campus residency has been required. Typically, students are expected to complete a broad distribution of subjects in social sciences, humanities, and physical or natural sciences. Examples of such programs are the Bachelor of Liberal Arts Program at the University of Oklahoma; the Independent Study Degree Programs of Syracuse University; and the Bachelor of Arts in Liberal Studies Program at State University of New York, College at Brockport.

Degree-by-examination. Houle (1973) includes a variety of programs in his discussion of assessment degrees. One of these, the New York Regents External Degree Program, is categorized separately by Medsker et al. (1975) as an example in their research of the "degree-by-examination approach." The New York State Education Department established the College Proficiency Examination Program (CPEP) in 1963 with aid from the Ford Foundation to provide an enlargement of opportunities for students to gain advanced college placement by passing course equivalency examinations. More than 22,000 persons had taken these exams by 1971. The considerable success of CPEP was a major consideration in the establishment of the Regents External Degree Program, which came into being in 1971 under the aegis of the University of the State of New York and its Board of Regents.

The degree-by-examination approach represented the breaking of a long-standing tradition in American higher education. Unlike the University of London, which was established in 1836 to conduct examinations and confer degrees, colleges and universities in the United States have rarely separated examination from direct instruction. When the Regents External Degree Program came into being, a number of changes in society and the academy served to call the conventional mode into question. A postindustrial society (Bell, 1973) and changing job market placed greater emphasis on "competence" and fostered a competence-based movement in higher education (Grant et al., 1979). Business and industry were offering increasing numbers of in-service training programs, leading the Office on Noncollegiate Sponsored Instruction of the New York State Education Department, established in 1974, to make credit recommendations for such courses, as the Commission on Accreditation of Service Experiences of the American Council on Education had done since 1945 for courses taken on military bases. The increased availability of television and other off-campus teaching aids raised additional questions about the necessity of direct classroom instruction. Projected declines in numbers of students of traditional college age (e.g., Carnegie Council on Policy Studies in Higher Education, 1980) caused institutions to turn their attention to new sources of clients, for reasons of commitment (Carnegie Commission on Higher Education, 1971, 1972; Cross, 1971) and for expediency.

The Regents External Degree Program has no campus, no resident faculty, no age or residency requirements. Many of its enrollees—those who take their examinations or who meet the full requirements of their established degree programs—are not residents of New York State; a large contingent resides on military bases throughout the world. The degree is awarded by a university that is part of a state department of education, to students it has not directly taught, but who have passed its degree requirements through examination. Faculty, who are drawn from New York State colleges and universities, do not provide instruction. Rather, they define the content which the student is expected to master and prepare the examinations that test the student's achievement. The faculty also define degree requirements in the four associate degree and four bachelor degree areas in which programs are available. Over eleven thousand degrees were awarded in the Regents External Degree Program's first decade, and more than twenty thousand students are working toward degrees as this contribution is written. Thomas A. Edison College of New Jersey operates in much the same way.

Educational Reform and Improvement. Although these new programs have significantly increased the accessibility of higher education, many nontraditional programs have also sought to improve the quality of teaching and learning, especially for the new students. Of course there have long been colleges and universities that have sought curriculum reforms to improve the quality of teaching and learning. Alternative educational arrangements have been, in Grant and Riesman's term, "the perpetual dream." In their book of that title (1978), on reform and experiment in the American college, Grant and Riesman develop a typology of reform movements that places recent developments in sociological and historical perspective. In this context, they consider telic reforms, embodying conceptions of the goals of undergraduate education that are significantly different from or even opposed to those of both traditional colleges and universities and the nontraditional institutions already discussed, which Grant and Riesman view as simply variations of the standard college and university model. Their telic reforms include such ventures as Alexander Meiklejohn's experimental programs at Amherst and the University of Wisconsin (Meiklejohn, 1932), and the neoclassical St. John's College, with a curriculum based entirely on the Great Books.

Grant and Riesman's most extensive study of a telic reform of the 1970s is Kresge College, one of the cluster colleges at the University of California at Santa Cruz, the purest surviving institutional realization of what they term the "communal-expressive movement" of the 1960s and early seventies. Kresge College describes itself as a living-learning community concerned with the human as well as the intellectual needs of its members. It places considerable emphasis on the techniques of the encounter group and certain mystical and religious practices that once flourished on many campuses. Kresge is certainly nontraditional. To discuss it in detail requires consideration of other innovative institutions of the 1970s, such as Hampshire College, Evergreen State College, or the ever evolving

Antioch University, and exceeds the boundaries of those defining characteristics that are set for the present discussion of nontraditional higher education.

Individualized programs. Houle (1973) included a type of institution under his assessment degrees which Medsker et al. (1975) characterize more properly as the "individualized study approach," a term which describes the programs of such institutions as the State University of New York's Empire State College, Metropolitan State University of the Minnesota State system, the Community College of Vermont, and certain units of the University Without Walls, four of the most visible nontraditional programs founded in the 1970s. In addition to addressing the access issue, these colleges attempted responses to those students of the late 1960s who asked the question "Education for what?" and generally sought greater relevance in their study.

In Medsker et al. (1975), a capsule description of the individualized study approach includes "individualized, student-centered contracts developed between student and program staff which outline content and competencies to be mastered, the method by which goals are to be achieved, and the nature of the evaluation procedure," and refers to "special attention to alternative strategies for learning and development of various resources, including use of community resource persons . . . directed learning packages . . . community learning resources [such as] libraries, galleries, and museums" (p. 13).

Empire State College is representative of the individualized study approach. Those who designed a new university college (State University of New York, 1971) within the State University of New York (SUNY) (the postwar system of university centers, four-year, technical, and community colleges that was then approaching its silver anniversary) raised many basic questions: whether it mattered when, how, or where a student had learned, so long as the outcome of this learning could be assessed; whether conventional time and space constraints made sense for adult learners; whether greater educational benefits might sometimes be gained from opportunities available through one's occupational and avocational involvements rather than through formal, structured courses; whether traditionally trained faculty were necessarily the best teachers for all students; and, central to all of these, whether it should not be the student, rather than the institution, who is the focus of the educational process, and whose educational needs and life commitments should determine the form and substance of the academic experience.

The learning contract mentioned above by Medsker et al. (1975) is not the most distinctive characteristic of Empire State College. Many colleges have used more or less formalized agreements between faculty members and students, often under the rubric of independent study. But the contract mode of learning itself is less distinctive than two other characteristics of Empire State College: placing the student at the center of the curriculum through individually designed degree programs and the

acceptance for credit of demonstrable, nonclassroom, college-level learning. These are at the heart of what is nontraditional about many new colleges of the 1970s.

Working directly with a faculty mentor at one of the college's thirty-two locations in New York State, each student develops an individually tailored program leading to a bachelor degree. Each degree program includes a provision for assessment of learning already acquired, which may be applied in partial fulfillment of the degree program, and projects a series of detailed learning contracts that define the learning yet to be achieved. When these contracts are completed and evaluated by faculty, the degree is awarded. Most study is undertaken through independent reading and research, although some classroom instruction may be included. Some mentors do a substantial amount of tutoring, in addition to their central role of planning and advising students in the development of their programs. They may also communicate with students by telephone, mail, tape cassette, or through the college's Center for Distance Learning, which is modeled on Britain's Open University (Perry, 1977).

Credit for prior learning. Perhaps the most controversial characteristic of nontraditional programs has been the commitment to grant credit for prior learning—regardless of when or where the learning occurred, if it can be demonstrated and evaluated (e.g., by standardized tests or recognized authorities in a field), and if it is appropriate to the student's degree program. Much of this evaluation is of noncourse or noncollege and experiential learning. Although this kind of evaluation had been done by such organizations as the Commission on the Accreditation of Service Experiences and the College Level Examination Program (CLEP) at the College Board in the 1960s, it was a radical and controversial venture at the time the practice was initiated. Part of the explanation for the controversy lies in the loose usage of such terms as "experiential" to describe the types of learning that are considered appropriate for college credit. Although many institutions were careful to emphasize that credit is granted only for learning, not for experience and that experience must be evaluated in an academically acceptable way, some popular accounts of "credit for living" made the assessment of prior learning suspect in traditional academic institutions. Nor was the situation improved by some institutions that did, in effect, offer credit for living in their desperate efforts to attract students. But, with the support of the Commission on Non-Traditional Study (1973) and the formation of the consortium sponsoring the Cooperative Assessment of Experiential Learning (CAEL) in 1973 have come criteria, methods, and a wider acceptance of assessment of nonclassroom learning. The approach is widely used today, and some of the earlier nontraditional colleges find themselves in the role of traditional defenders of academic quality control in the assessment process. The best source for an overview of the rationale and methods of assessing nonclassroom learning is the volume by Keeton and Associates (1976).

The assessment of college-level learning taking place outside the classroom often requires the use of experts in fields that are not typically represented on college and university faculties. Such individuals might be in public administration, human services, business, law, and many other fields. Increasing use of such people led to a questioning of the qualities and credentials that made most sense for faculty in many nontraditional programs. In institutions such as Metropolitan State University in Minnesota, there is a very small core faculty. In addition, there are community faculty members, with whom students work in studies that demonstrate one or more of the competencies comprising a Metropolitan State University student's requirements. Students also enroll in "group learning opportunities," which are very much like classes, although they may be held in community centers, union halls, storefronts, or places of work. The Community College of Vermont and Empire State College also make use of part-time, adjunct faculty.

Interdisciplinary approaches. Although these approaches to individualized curriculum have had a major impact in the 1970s, other institutions have sought to improve teaching and learning through the design of new interdisciplinary curricula or core general-education courses. Such new colleges in the late 1960s as Ramapo College (New Jersey), Evergreen State College (Washington), and Old Westbury (New York) created new curricular formations designed to improve the educational program and make it more relevant and effective for particular student groups. In fact, as the 1970s were drawing to a close, probably no academic issue was on so many agendas as the long-standing question of an appropriate core curriculum. Both Veysey (1973) and Bell (1966) point out that there are only a few axes along which curricular variations can be found: the contrast between depth and breadth; the contrast between prescribed curricula and elective freedom; and the extent, or abundance, of course offerings.

The issues of increasing access to higher education and the improvement of teaching and student learning are intertwined, as any reading of the history of American higher education clearly indicates (Rudolph, 1962; 1977; Veysey, 1973). This is not always clear in recent discussions of a core curriculum (e.g., Change Magazine Press, 1979). American educators and other citizens have long agonized over the content question, in large part because of the broader range of postsecondary educational opportunities in the United States. When only a small proportion went "up to university," as had been the case in countries such as England, the curriculum issue was thought by many to have been long solved.

Distance learning: the British Open University. The question of curriculum surfaced with the postwar expansion of higher education in Britain and took on even greater prominence with the creation of the government-funded British Open University (BOU) in 1969 (Perry, 1977). From its inception, it was clear that the BOU was to be open to new people, methods, and ideas. Traditional

standards for matriculation were abolished; students had to be 21 or older (modified in 1974 to allow the annual admission of five hundred students, half of whom met standard university entrance requirements and half of whom did not); and efforts were made to attract a disproportionate number of working-class students. In 1980, the BOU enrolled about sixty-three thousand students.

Delivery of instruction includes correspondence materials, television and radio, and student centers. At the heart of all courses, however, are the high-quality distance-learning materials, including the correspondence texts which take the place of classroom lectures, assigned readings, written assignments graded by tutors and sometimes computers, and self-assessment tests. Television components, as well as radio broadcasts and audiotapes, prepared in collaboration with the British Broadcasting Company, are an integral part of most courses. The availability of counseling and tutorial assistance in the 280 study centers throughout the United Kingdom provides relatively easy access to assistance for all students. However, most of the BOU students study in their own homes.

In developing curricula, the BOU's designers were determined to remain open to nontraditional program components. Faculty are organized into six fields: arts, educational studies, mathematics, science, social sciences, and technology. The courses run for a full academic year, roughly equivalent to sixteen to eighteen semester hours in U.S. academic credit terms. The bachelor's degree is awarded for the completion of six such courses (some half courses also exist), an honors degree for eight. A full-time student takes only two courses concurrently. A great deal of innovation has gone into the design of courses. For example, the first-level course in the social sciences was designed by a course team working for over three years, representing such fields as psychology, social psychology, sociology, geography, economics, and political science. In addition, there are upper-level interdisciplinary courses, such as Science and Belief, Art and Environment, and Man's Religious Quest. These are highly integrated courses, often unified by a set of themes that make them more difficult to adapt than some users in this country had anticipated; but their high quality continues to make the courses attractive. Such courses are tangible evidence of the significance of the British Open University.

Issues for Nontraditional Education. A variety of significant issues for nontraditional programs must be addressed in the 1980s. A first issue for the future is the continued availability of fiscal support for nontraditional programs. The social agenda for the 1980s appears significantly changed from that of the 1970s, and programs created to increase access to higher education no longer receive the priority earlier accorded to them by government and foundations. Moreover, the inflationary strains of the late 1970s have sharply curtailed the funds within university budgets available for change and experimentation. Further, although new educational approaches have been shown to be less costly in certain respects than traditional residential programs, costs are nonetheless significant. Especially costly are developments in educational technology, such as video courses, computerized instruction, and other interactive systems. Consequently, nontraditional programs will be pressed even more strongly to demonstrate their effectiveness relative to cost.

A second issue, made even more urgent by campus cost cutting, is the possible exploitation of nontraditional approaches by institutions to attract students in order to boost sagging enrollments. Without sound academic controls and solid fiscal support, some academic entrepreneurs are tempted to offer attractive, but poor or fraudulent, programs that lack academic integrity (Riesman, 1980). Programs that reduce or eliminate faculty responsibility for the academic program in an effort to maintain low costs are particularly vulnerable to such abuse. Even colleges with solid reputations can experience difficulties as they begin to operate at numerous off-campus locations with part-time instructors who are not part of the regular faculty. Institutions with lesser reputations may be tempted to offer low-cost programs to enhance their profitability. Nontraditional programs can vastly improve both access to higher education and the quality of teaching and learning. But because such programs are especially liable to abuse and fraud, special attention is needed to ensure proper evaluation and monitoring of program quality.

Another issue for nontraditional programs is the problem of success. Regional accreditation associations had, by 1980, evaluated and certified most of the new institutions of the 1970s. The wide acceptance of many of the educational principles and strategies developed for nontraditional programs in the 1970s is changing the shape of all higher education (Hall, 1979; Hall & Kevles, 1982). The boundary between educational institutions and other organizations that provide educational opportunities is becoming more difficult to define and will probably become increasingly so. Nontraditional colleges, no less than others, will be forced to articulate clearly their reasons for staying in business. They will face greater competition. Not only have many institutions adopted the practices considered radical when the nontraditional colleges of the 1970s were begun but there is also increasing competition for the adult student, as demographic projections clearly indicate a smaller pool of traditional college-age students in the years ahead. For example, in New York State, a 27 percent decline in college and university enrollments of students 18 to 21 years old is forecast by the 1990s. The postwar "boom" babies are now in their 30s. As this age-group moves through the population, of course, it may take only a relatively small increase in the proportion of this cohort enrolling in postsecondary educational institutions to offset the decline of younger students. There is some evidence that the shift has already begun. In the autumn of 1980, the total enrollment of State University of New York was 357,803, and more than one-third were age 25 or older. Many of these are the new student groups, including women, minorities, professionals seeking occupational ad-

vancement, second-chance students who missed out earlier because of opportunity or capacity, the retired, and those with handicapping conditions. This diverse student population will require not only greater attention to the increasing body of theory and data on adult development (e.g., Carnegie Commission on Higher Education, 1973; Chickering, 1981; Knox, 1977; Levinson, 1978; Loevinger, 1976; Perry, 1970) but further modification of space, time, and curricular requirements.

In fact, the future of nontraditional higher education may be linked intimately with the emerging communications technologies that are becoming commercially available to many homes. For example, the technological capabilities of minicomputers in each home and the vastly expanded reception of educational broadcasts from communication satellites and community cable systems promise to make possible for the first time higher education programs entirely separate from the college or university as it has been known and understood in the past.

One likely development is the creation of some version of an American Open University. Such a system, with its sophisticated materials, media components, and support and delivery requirements would be an operation very difficult to fund on a national basis in a country as large as the United States, to say nothing of the political difficulties of its implementation. It is questionable, therefore, whether adequate fiscal support will be available on a national basis or whether state and institutional prerogatives can be successfully meshed into an American Open University, as the University of Mid-America is seeking to do, or into a National University Consortium, which the University of Maryland is undertaking. But it does seem likely that increased cooperation will occur, if on a more limited (e.g., statewide) basis. And almost certainly, more teaching-at-a-distance operations, such as Empire State College's Center for Distance Learning, will come into being. At this writing, the Public Broadcasting System is introducing educational broadcasts through its national network.

With these and other nontraditional approaches, the opportunities for both high access and learning quality will be significantly greater in the year 2000 than in 1980. The impetus and experimental basis for much that is then common will be found to have germinated in the nontraditional programs of the 1970s.

James W. Hall
Robert Hassenger

See also Curriculum and Instruction in Higher Education; Distance Education; Experiential Education; Higher Education; History and Philosophy of Higher Education.

REFERENCES

Bell, D. *The Reforming of General Education.* New York: Columbia University Press, 1966.
Bell, D. *The Coming of Post-industrial Society.* New York: Basic Books, 1973.

Carnegie Commission on Higher Education. *New Students and New Places: Policies for the Future Growth and Development of American Higher Education.* New York: McGraw-Hill, 1971.

Carnegie Commission on Higher Education. *Reform on Campus: Changing Students, Changing Academic Programs.* New York: McGraw-Hill, 1972.

Carnegie Commission on Higher Education. *Toward a Learning Society: Alternative Channels to Life, Work, and Service.* New York: McGraw-Hill, 1973.

Carnegie Council on Policy Studies in Higher Education. *Three Thousand Futures: The Next Twenty Years for Higher Education.* San Francisco: Jossey-Bass, 1980.

Change Magazine Press. *The Great Core Curriculum Debate: Education as a Mirror of Culture.* New Rochelle, N.Y.: The Press, 1979.

Chickering, A., & Associates (Eds.). *The Modern American College.* San Francisco: Jossey-Bass, 1981.

Commission on Non-Traditional Study. *Diversity by Design.* San Francisco: Jossey-Bass, 1973.

Cross, K. P. *Beyond the Open Door.* San Francisco: Jossey-Bass, 1971.

Gould, S., & Cross, K. P. (Eds.). *Explorations in Nontraditional Study.* San Francisco: Jossey-Bass, 1972.

Grant, G.; Elbow, P.; Ewens, T.; Gamson, Z.; Kohli, W.; Neumann, W.; Olesen, V.; & Riesman, D. *On Competence: A Critical Analysis of Competence-based Reforms in Higher Education.* San Francisco: Jossey-Bass, 1979.

Grant, G., & Riesman, D. *The Perpetual Dream.* Chicago: University of Chicago Press, 1978.

Hall, J. W. Regional accreditation and nontraditional colleges. *Journal of Higher Education,* 1979, *50*(2), 171–177.

Hall, J. W., & Kevles, B. L. *In Opposition to Core Curriculum: Alternatives for the Future.* Westport, Conn.: Greenwood, 1982.

Houle, C. *The External Degree.* San Francisco: Jossey-Bass, 1973.

Keeton, M. T., & Associates. *Experiential Learning: Rationale, Characteristics, and Assessment.* San Francisco: Jossey-Bass, 1976.

Knox, A. B. (Ed.). *Adult Development and Learning: A Handbook on Individual Growth and Competence in the Adult Years for Education and the Helping Professions.* San Francisco: Jossey-Bass, 1977.

Levinson, D. *The Seasons of a Man's Life.* New York: Knopf, 1978.

Loevinger, J. *Ego Development.* San Francisco: Jossey-Bass, 1976.

Medsker, L.; Edelstein, S.; Kreplin, H.; Ruyle, J.; & Shea, J. *Extending Opportunities for a College Degree: Practices, Problems, and Potentials.* Berkeley, Calif.: Center for Research and Development in Higher Education, 1975. (ERIC Document Reproduction Service No. ED 125 418)

Meiklejohn, A. *The Experimental College.* New York: Harper & Brothers, 1932.

Perry, W. *The Open University.* San Francisco: Jossey-Bass, 1977.

Perry, W. G. *Forms of Intellectual and Ethical Development in the College Years.* New York: Holt, Rinehart & Winston, 1970.

Riesman, D. *On Education: The Academic Enterprise in an Era of Rising Student Consumerism.* San Francisco: Jossey-Bass, 1980.

Rudolph, F. *The American College and University: A History.* New York: Knopf, 1962.

Rudolph, F. *Curriculum: The American Undergraduate Courses of Study since 1636.* San Francisco: Jossey-Bass, 1977.

State University of New York. *A Prospectus for a New University College, 1971.* Albany, N.Y.: The University, 1972.

Veysey, L. Stability and change in the undergraduate curriculum. In C. Kayson (Ed.), *Content and Context: Essays on College Education.* New York: McGraw-Hill, 1973, pp. 1–63.

NORMS AND SCALES

The process of standardizing an objective test involves one or more formal administrations of the test, precisely as it is intended to be given in practice, in order to provide supplementary information to aid in the use of the test scores. These administrations are designed to yield data that may form the basis for establishing a scale system for the test. They may be used to derive a set of norms or interpretive data, and, for tests that are made available in more than one form, to determine a set of equivalency tables that will serve to calibrate the scores on the different forms of the test and to convert them to a common scale. The present treatment will devote a section to each of these three aspects of the process of test standardization. A fourth section deals with the matter of comparable scores on tests of dissimilar psychological functions.

Scaling. Unlike the more common scales of physical measurement such as height, weight, and temperature, which have acquired meaning through continued use and familiarity, the raw score scales of educational and psychological tests have no interpretable meaning of their own. For this reason, among others, test scores are seldom reported in terms of the raw score scales. Rather, they are given in terms of derived scales, some of which have been defined and constructed to have special normative meaning, and, in that particular sense, to be self-interpreting. The intelligence quotient (IQ) and grade equivalent scales and McCall's *T*-Scale (McCall, 1939) are typical of those that have normative meaning. There are, however, additional reasons for using systems of derived score scales for standardized tests in preference to the original raw score scales (Angoff, 1962).

First, the raw score scale, representing as it does merely a count of the number of items answered correctly (frequently, minus a correction for haphazard guessing), is no more than an ordinal scale. As such, the raw score scale only ranks individuals with respect to their performance on the test. Unlike the fundamental physical scales of height and weight, it gives no assurance of equally spaced units (except in the purely arbitrary sense of equal increments of items answered correctly), nor does it yield a meaningful absolute zero. The characteristic of equal units, possessed by the interval scale, allows us to say that the difference in John's and Linda's heights (or weights) is (say) twice as great as the difference between Martha's and Jim's heights (or weights). The characteristic of the real zero, possessed by the ratio scale, allows us to say that Jean is twice as tall (or heavy) as Steven. An interval scale, at least, is essential if score differences in different regions of the score scale are to be compared meaningfully. To permit this kind of comparison, raw score scales are sometimes converted into derived scales in which the scale separations are equal in some defined sense. The Flanagan Scaled Score System (Flanagan, 1939, 1951) and Gardner's K-Scores (Gardner, 1947) are derived scales of this sort.

Second, derived score scales are employed when several forms of a test are in use and the forms are to be used interchangeably. In such instances the scores on the several forms are equated in order to adjust for form-to-form differences in raw score characteristics, and are expressed in terms of a single, specially derived scale, clearly different from the raw score scale of any of the forms. The College Board scale is one of a number of such scales (Angoff, 1971c, pp. 32–40). Finally, for the sake of simple convenience in handling score data, it is thought to be desirable to convert scores into scales with preassigned anchor points expressed in round numbers that are easy to use and remember. The Stanine Scale (Flanagan, 1948, 1951) is one of many such scales. Nearly all published tests have scales defined with this characteristic in mind.

One way to classify the scales that are currently in use is to say that there are distributive scales, whose numerical values have been derived on the basis of the test performance of a group of examinees, and nondistributive scales, or those defined independently of, and without reference to, any particular group. Examples of the latter are the scales developed by Tucker (1951, 1953), Rasch (1960), and others, which are invariant with respect to the group on which data were collected for its determination. Within the category of distributive scales are the normative scales, based on the performance of a group randomly selected from an explicitly defined population whose characteristics give interpretive meaning to the scores—for example, the IQ scale (Terman & Merrill, 1937) and McCall's T-Scale (McCall, 1939). There are also nonnormative distributive scales, based on the performance of groups that do not have normative or interpretive value. An example is the scale for the College Board Scholastic Aptitude Test (SAT) (Angoff, 1971c, pp. 32–40), which was based on a self-selected, available group of examinees. As illustrated later, it is possible, and frequently useful, to develop nondistributive scales that do not depend on any data for this definition, and therefore are free of normative interpretations and, often, normative confusions.

A number of different derived scales are in existence. One is the percentage mastery scale, on which the scores are taken to represent an absolute kind of judgment that the student has mastered some percentage of the subject matter under consideration. Thus a score of 83 percent, for example, is taken to imply that an examinee who has successfully answered 83 percent of the test has mastered 83 percent of the material on which the test is based.

An additional feature of the scale is that certain specified percentages are taken to indicate "passing" or "honors" performance. Although the percentage mastery scale is still widely used, especially in the classroom, it is generally considered one of the poorest ways to express test performance. It implies an "absolute" type of evaluation, which is not only illusory but untenable, and it disregards the difficulty of the test items, which naturally will vary from test to test.

In contrast to the percentage mastery scale, criterion-referenced measurement, in which such performance standards as "passing," "minimum acceptable," and "honors" are also set, calls for an explicit and rational procedure for setting standards, either by judgmental methods (Angoff, 1971a, pp. 514–515; Ebel, 1972, p. 492 ff.; Nedelsky, 1954) or by empirical methods (Zieky & Livingston, 1977).

A frequently used scale is the linear transformation, or standard score, scale (Hull, 1922), in which the obtained mean and standard deviation for a group of examinees (ω) are assigned arbitrary, convenient values. The formula for making the transformation is given in equation (1):

$$\frac{s - M_{s_\omega}}{\sigma_{s_\omega}} = \frac{x - M_{x_\omega}}{\sigma_{x_\omega}}, \qquad (1)$$

where x and s refer, respectively, to raw and scaled scores. Upon rearrangement the equation may be expressed in the form, $s = Ax + B$, a linear equation that permits the conversion of raw scores to scaled scores. In this equation, A is the slope of the conversion line,

$$A = \sigma_{s_\omega} / \sigma_{x_\omega},$$

and B is the intercept, that is, the value of s when $x = 0$,

$$B = M_{s_\omega} - A M_{x_\omega}.$$

M_{s_ω} and σ_{s_ω} are the arbitrarily assigned values for the mean and standard deviations of scaled scores. For example, for the deviation IQ scale these values are 100 and 15, respectively; for the College Board SAT scale they are 500 and 100, respectively. Because the conversion from raw to scaled scores is linear, utilizing only the first two moments for the distribution (i.e., the mean and standard deviation), it simply relocates the mean and changes the size of the units uniformly; it does not exert any effect on the shape of the distribution.

Another type of linear transformation is the percentile derived linear scale, which is defined by assigning a particular scaled score (say, 175 for "honors") to one percentile (say, the 95th percentile) and a second scaled score (say, 100 for "passing") to a second percentile (say, the 60th percentile). The raw scores corresponding to these percentiles (say, 73 and 39 respectively) are then transformed to the desired scaled scores as in equations (2) and (3):

$$s_h = Ax_h + B \qquad (2)$$

and

$$s_p = Ax_p + B, \qquad (3)$$

where s_h and s_p refer, respectively, to the scaled scores designating honors and pass, and x_h and x_p are the observed raw scores corresponding to the arbitrarily chosen percentile ranks. The values of A and B (the slope and intercept of the conversion equation), where

$$A = \frac{s_h - s_p}{x_h - x_p}$$

and

$$B = s_h - Ax_h (= s_p - Ax_p)$$

are found by solving the simultaneous equations (2) and (3), and the conversion line is extrapolated over the entire raw score range. In our example,

$$s_h = 175 = 73\,A + B$$

and

$$s_p = 100 = 39\,A + B.$$

Solution of these equations yields the conversion equation: $A = 2.2059$ and $B = 13.9696$. These conversion parameters indicate that if the test contains eighty-five items, the possible scaled scores will range from 14 to 201. (For convenience in score reporting, the highest scaled score possible might be limited to 200.)

Perhaps the most familiar scale in use for reporting test scores is the percentile rank scale, which gives the percentage of individuals in a particular group scoring below the midpoint of each score or score interval. The precise percentile rank is obtained by totaling the frequencies for all the scores below the score (or score interval) in question, adding half the frequencies at the score (or score interval), and dividing by the total number of cases. Percentile ranks are essentially self-interpreting scale values and are used for making normative evaluations of an individual's performance. Thus an individual scoring at a given percentile rank is said to exceed in performance that percentage (given by the percentile rank) of individuals in the group specified. Distributions of percentile ranks for the group on which the ranks are based are necessarily rectangular. The percentile rank scale itself is ordinal, and its units are generally considered unequal, since they represent equal proportions of a group, not equal intervals on a scale of ability.

In spite of its simplicity, the percentile rank can be a source of confusion. First, it is often defined imprecisely as the percentage falling below a score, as though the score were meant to be taken as a discrete value. However, the fact that the ability underlying the scores is assumed to be a continuous variable compels its consideration as an interval, extending from half a point below the score to half a point above. Thus a score of 23 is meant to imply the interval 22.5000 $\cdots$ to 23.4999 $\cdots$ .This being the case, the percentile rank of 23 is not to be calculated simply by summing all frequencies for score 22 and below and dividing by the total N, but by calculating that sum and adding to it half the frequencies at 23 and then dividing the entire sum by the total N in the distribution.

Second, it is useful to make a distinction between scores, which are measurements, and percentile ranks, which are not measurements, but evaluations of measurements, and which will vary depending on the nature of the group on which the percentile rank is based. The failure to make this distinction frequently causes confusion when it is observed that the same performance may carry with it more than one percentile rank designation.

Third, the inexperienced test user may confuse "percentile" with "percentile rank." The percentile rank is a percentage that designates the relative number in a specified group whose performance is exceeded by the score in question. The percentile is a score, corresponding to a specified percentage. Thus it may be found in a given distribution of scores that the percentile rank of the score of 157 is 75. The 75th percentile is the score of 157.

The normalized scale is a scale developed for the purpose of giving the scores specific meaning. Thus, like the percentile rank scale, it invests scores with special meaning. Part of the reasoning behind the normalized scale is that because the raw score scale, or a linear transformation of it, depends on the characteristics of the particular items chosen for the test, it is advisable to transform the scores to some other system of units that would be independent of these characteristics and, in the sense of a particular operational definition, equally spaced. The transformation to a normalized scale is based on the assumption that mental ability is basically normally distributed for an unselected population, and that equal segments on the baseline of the normal curve mark off equal units of ability. The procedure followed in deriving such a scale results in a systematic expansion and contraction of the units in different regions of the raw score scale in order to transform the distribution of raw scores to a normal shape. The steps in the process are as follows: The test is administered to a random sample of a defined population. A distribution of raw scores is formed and percentile ranks are calculated, plotted, and smoothed. Smoothed percentile ranks are read off the graph, converted to normal deviates (z), and then further converted to a scale (s) with a defined mean (M_{s_ω}) and standard deviation (σ_{s_ω}) by means of equation (4):

$$s = \sigma_{s_\omega} z + M_{s_\omega}. \qquad (4)$$

A well-known normalized scale is the Stanine Scale (Flanagan, 1948, 1951), used in the U.S. Army Air Force Aviation Psychology Program during World War II. This is a single-digit scale extending from 1 to 9, with preassigned percentages, derived from a table of the normal curve, as follows: 4, 7, 12, 17, 20, 17, 12, 7, and 4 percent, yielding a distribution with a mean of 5 and standard deviation of about 2.

Another system of scaled scores based on the normal curve is Flanagan's Scaled Score System (Flanagan, 1939, 1951), which attempts to normalize the distributions of several partially overlapping groups simultaneously. A variant of the Flanagan system is one provided by Gardner's K-Scores (1947). This scale follows the Flanagan model, but assumes the more general Pearson Type III curve instead of the normal curve (which is a Pearson Type III curve with zero skewness).

The IQ scale (Terman & Merrill, 1937), originally defined as the ratio (× 100) of mental age to chronological age, is used to convey the meaning of test performance in terms of normally expected performance for a child of a given age, and is used chiefly at those ages where the mental function increases rapidly with age. The procedure for producing the scale of age units is as follows: (1) Representative samples of children up to about age 15 are tested with the intelligence test. (2) The mean (or median) test score of children at each age interval (essentially the regression of score on age) is plotted against the midpoint of the age interval. (3) A smooth curve is drawn through the points. (4) The age corresponding to each level of performance is read off the curve and is thus defined as the mental age for that level of performance. The mental age therefore is the chronological age for which a given test performance is average.

The value of the IQ is its apparent simplicity and its built-in comparability from one age level to the next (IQ constancy), which holds if the sampling is adequate and comparable across ages, if the growth pattern is essentially the same for all children, and if the dispersion of scores is the same at every age.

The disadvantages of the IQ are quite serious, however, but not so apparent. For example: (1) Since age and test score correlate imperfectly, there are necessarily two quite different regressions—the regression of age on score and the regression of score on age—that yield two possible and very different definitions of mental age. As a result the definition of mental age is not a unique one (Thurstone, 1926). (2) The comparability of the mental age across different chronological ages depends on the constancy of the dispersion at different ages, and there is nothing in the ratio IQ that controls for the fact that these dispersions are not constant, but are systematically different from one age to the next. (3) A mental age is meaningful only if there is an age for which test performance is average. Therefore, mental ages, and IQs, are not meaningful for superior children in midadolescence, where performance on these abilities levels off, and beyond. (4) The mental age notion implies that a 6-year-old with a "mental age" of 9 years has the mental equipment of a 9-year-old. This may be true, but only in an extremely narrow sense. Obviously, even the extremely bright 6-year-old does not have the experiential background of the average 9-year-old, and so is highly unlikely to have the mental age of the average 9-year-old—at least in the broader sense of the term.

The popularity of the IQ has led to the development of other ratios, such as the educational quotient (EQ), the ratio of "educational age" to the chronological age, and the achievement quotient (AQ), or the ratio of the EQ to the IQ. The AQ is often regarded as the ratio of "actual achievement" to "potential ability" and so is used to represent overachievement and underachievement. In addition

to the fact that these conceptions rest on entirely undefinable constructs, it is also the case that whatever psychometric and educational inadequacies inhere in the IQ also inhere, and are more serious, in the AQ, because the AQ compounds the errors and inadequacies of both the EQ and the IQ. Flanagan (1951, p. 716) has reviewed the educational and psychometric inadequacies inherent in the AQ that severely limit its usefulness.

Because of the observed variation in the standard deviations of ratio IQs at different ages, an IQ for an individual could easily shift about from one age to the next, and not necessarily because of any change in the level of intelligence. To eliminate this type of variation, the IQs that are commonly developed today are "deviation IQs" rather than ratio IQs. Deviation IQs are essentially standard scores, in which the mean and standard deviation of IQs have been set at 100 and 16 (or, in some tests, 15), respectively, at each age level. In some tests the shape of the distribution of IQs at each level has also been altered in order to yield normalized scores.

Another scale, similar in its important developmental respects to the IQ scale, is the grade equivalent scale. Grade equivalents are derived much as mental ages are, differing chiefly in the fact that test performance is plotted against grade rather than age. In a manner parallel to that for mental age, the grade equivalent is defined as the grade for which a given performance is average. Unlike the mental age scale, which is more appropriate to tests of general intellectual ability, grade equivalent scales are typically developed for achievement tests in specific subject areas. The disadvantages of grade equivalent scales parallel most of the disadvantages of mental age scales, but are even more serious. First, the grade equivalent varies, depending on the nature of the particular subject tested and the manner in which the subject is introduced in the school and pursued through the grades. Second, the grade equivalent is dependent on the particular customs of promotion and retardation in the schools, which vary widely with locality and time. Third, the grade equivalent has little meaning in any subject area in which teaching is closely tied to the grade level and in which the student has no opportunity to learn the material prior to or beyond that grade level. There are even further difficulties with the interpretation of the grade equivalents (and mental ages). The reader is referred to Angoff (1971a, pp. 523–525, 537) and Flanagan (1951, pp. 706–713) for fuller discussions of grade equivalents.

Attempts have been made to modify the grade equivalent to avoid its more serious drawbacks. In its development of the grade level indicator (GLI) system, the replacement for the grade equivalent for its Circus C and D and STEP III basic assessment measures, the Educational Testing Service devised a plan in which (1) the range of grade levels for which a GLI is interpreted for a test is restricted to the specific grades and months for which the test is appropriate and at which the particular test was normed, so that no extrapolations are made to grades at which empirical data on the particular test are unavailable; (2) norming administrations were conducted at three points during the year—fall, winter, and spring—in order to limit interpolations between testings to a maximum of two months (where the actual interval between testings is four months); and (3) GLI determinations are restricted to the results of tests based on content appropriate to the student's own grade level (Educational Testing Service, 1980).

Some recognition has been given of late to the view that the normative type of scale is not the most useful (Angoff, 1962, 1971a, p. 528; Lindquist, 1953; Tucker, 1953). Although (the argument goes) the normative scale does give immediate normative meaning, the norms on which it is based can become obsolete and thereby cause the scale itself to become obsolete. Nonnormative scales, however, like the physical scales in common use, can be retained indefinitely because they do not depend on published norms for their interpretation. Moreover, the commitment of a scale to a particular norms group is unnecessarily restrictive since that norms group may not always be the relevant one. Finally, it is argued, the real meaning associated with a scale of measurement is not necessarily the one that is embodied in the scale, but one that develops over time with familiarity and use. This is achieved by the constancy of meaning of the scale values—by rigorous form-to-form equating, for example, when two or more forms are available—and by the provision of separate and supplementary interpretive data that are revised as conditions warrant.

That scales may be developed without any reference to normative, or even distributive, considerations is often overlooked. One type of nonnormative scale, which is useful when there are several forms of the test, or when there is an articulated set of tests extending from early age or grade levels upward, may be derived directly from the scores of the test itself simply by renaming any two raw score values with arbitrary scaled score designations. The relationship between the two raw-score-scaled pairs automatically defines the linear conversion from all possible raw scores to the derived scale. The details of the method are quite simple. One scaled score number, s_1, is arbitrarily assigned to some raw score value, say zero, and another scaled score, s_2, is assigned to another raw score value, say the maximum score on the test. These two relationships define a pair of simultaneous equations

$$s_1 = Ax_1 + B \qquad (5)$$

and

$$s_2 = Ax_2 + B, \qquad (6)$$

which, when solved, define the slope

$$A = \frac{s_1 - s_2}{x_1 - x_2},$$

and the intercept

$$B = s_1 - Ax_1 \; (= s_2 - Ax_2).$$

In the case of this scale, as with all others, later forms of the test perpetuate the scale simply as a result of having been equated to the initial reference form.

Another, better known, nondistributive scale is the Guttman Scale, originally developed for opinion and attitude measurement (Guttman, 1950). A perfect scale in the Guttman sense is one in which any individual who passes an item will necessarily pass all easier items, and any individual who fails an item will necessarily fail all harder items. Thus a score on such a test will define (or reproduce) a person's actual responses perfectly. In this sense the Guttman scale is completely deterministic. However, this property is not likely to be realized in practice for ability test data, because of their low interitem correlations. An alternative approach, referred to as item characteristic curve theory, or, more recently, as item response theory, has been suggested in the models of a number of investigators (Birnbaum, 1968; Lawley, 1943; Lazersfeld, 1950; Lord, 1952a, 1952b, 1980; Rasch, 1960; Tucker, 1951). In these the probability of a correct response to a given item is determined by (1) the examinee's ability, (2) the difficulty of the item, (3) its discriminating power, and (4) a "guessing" parameter. (This model is discussed more fully later.)

Norms: Interpretive Data

Types of Norms. Test norms are useful principally for interpreting the scores of individuals, in acquiring a familiarity with the test, and in developing an understanding of the characteristic differences among the subgroups of the general population. They are usually presented in the form of percentile rank distributions, based on the performance of well-defined groups of examinees whose characteristics are thought to be known to, and understood by, the test user. As indicated earlier, the percentile rank is properly regarded as an evaluation of performance in statistical terms—that is, by comparison with other individuals—as distinct from the score, which represents the measurement of performance (although, as pointed out previously, normative evaluations are not always kept distinct from the scores, but are sometimes incorporated directly in the score scales). Thus, while there may be as many evaluations, and percentile ranks, of an individual's score as there are relevant groups with which an individual with that score may be compared, there is obviously only one score. But such multiple evaluations are useful. Because an individual has membership in more than one group, it is frequently desirable to develop norms on a number of different populations, each of which may yield a different percentile rank for that same level of performance.

The most general, and possibly the most commonly used, norms group is the national norms, appropriate to each of the educational or age levels for which the test is intended. One of the difficulties in defining the national norms group arises from the large number, variety, and complexity of the characteristics of students, schools, curricula, and communities that are correlated with, or relevant to, test scores. Because of this vast heterogeneity the national norms group is not always considered ideally suited for making the kinds of evaluations and decisions for which test scores are often sought. For these reasons, when the categories are sufficiently distinct and meaningful, differentiated norms are prepared separately by category of the relevant variables—for example, age, sex, educational level, region, type of school, type of community, type of student body.

In many instances the most useful norms are local norms, collected by the test users themselves and based on students enrolled in their own institutions. Such norms have the advantage of representing a homogeneous group, familiar to the test user, and characterized by the effects of the particular local conditions and practices in the context of which the scores will be used. Since norms are useful to the extent that the reference group is known and meaningful to the user, a valid case can be made for norms that are *not* based on a random sample of some defined population, but on all the students of a special, hand-picked, well-known population segment. Examples would be all senior students at the Seven Sister colleges, all male freshmen enrolled in the Big Ten universities, or all ninth-grade students in cities with populations of more than a million. These "special study" norms capitalize on the familiarity of these groups to the test user, and are helpful in answering specific questions that the user may have in the formation of specific decisions. Conceivably, a college will want to compare the distribution of its students' scores with those of other colleges it regards as its competitors for the same applicant pool—for example, colleges that normally attract different types of students but are competitive because they are near each other. Such institutions may manage to exchange their data individually and directly. Sometimes the test publisher can make available to the test user a set of "user-selected" norms—a combined distribution for the students enrolled at certain institutions specified by the user. It would be expected that the publisher would specify some minimum number of institutions for such a norms group, and also the manner in which the students must be selected to represent each institution.

Differentiated norms are multiple sets of norms prepared separately by category on a second variable or set of variables in combination—for example, age, grade, socioeconomic status (ordered variables); and sex, geographical region, type of school support, type of community (unordered variables). Age or grade norms are a common type of differentiated norms. They make use of the relationship between test performance and age or grade, as is done with age and grade equivalents, but they avoid some of the hidden problems of interpreting the equivalents—such as the variation in dispersion from age to age and from grade to grade and from test to test for individuals at the same age or grade level. These problems are avoided

by recognizing the inherent dispersion among individuals and the lawful differences in dispersions among groups of individuals, and capitalizing on them in interpreting scores, as is typically done in the preparation of norms. Some of the difficulties with grade norms still remain, however, in interpreting the scores on achievement tests. These have to do with the fact that test performance is highly dependent on the curriculum's subject-matter emphases, which, expectedly, change with the times, as well as with the more subtle effects of policies and practices regarding promotion and retardation. These also change with the times, and have a fundamental effect on the distribution of ages for children in the same grade. To help standarize the distribution of age within grade for purposes of test score interpretation, some test constructors have suggested the development of modal age norms, which are grade norms for children of approximately the same age.

Differentiated test score norms may be regarded as bivariate norms, in which the second variable is the variable on which the differentiation has been made. Generally these norms are distributions of test scores for different categories on the second variable. Under some circumstances, however, it is preferable for the norms to be presented as distributions of scores on the second variable for different categories of test score. One of the best examples of this latter type of norm is the expectancy table, which gives percentile rank distributions on the criterion variable (for example, grade-point average in college) for each of a number of categories of test score. The expectancy table itself is worked out directly from the scatterplot of test score *versus* criterion. Its figures give the likelihood, for an individual who has earned a score of x on the test, of earning a criterion score of y or better. There are other bivariate norms. Ebel (1962) has suggested that a test score x be interpreted in terms of an individual's likelihood of earning a score of y or better on a short test of parallel content and difficulty that has been made available to the test user for examination and study. A test score can also be made more meaningful by describing the likelihood that an individual will perform satsifactorily tasks of familiar difficulty (for example, by saying, on the basis of data collected for this purpose, that a person who earns a score of x on a French test is highly likely to be able to read a French newspaper with comprehension); or by estimating the likelihood that the individual will later earn quality ratings such as "outstanding," "excellent," "good," "fair," and "poor," or "high honors," "honors," "pass," and "fail" on some criterion performance. In all these types of score interpretation the bivariate plot of scores versus rating is a necessary part of the process. The value of referring the test scores to these ratings lies in the assumption that the ratings are familiar and meaningful to the user, and reasonably reliable.

There are other methods of borrowing from one variable to give meaning to another. For example, the College Board Admission Testing Program presented, in its *Guide for High Schools and Colleges* (College Entrance Examination Board, 1976, pp. 8–10), a set of items at several levels of difficulty, and gave the proportions of students scoring at different levels on the SAT scale who answered each item correctly. Here, familiarity with the item, gained by examining it, was used to give meaning to the scale of scores.

Although test publishers customarily have issued norms based on the performance of individuals for use in the evaluation of individuals, they increasingly are making available distributions of school means for use in the evaluation of the mean performance of groups of individuals. This procedural change represents an improvement because distributions of means are much less dispersed than distributions of individual scores and thus are not useful for evaluating the performance of individuals.

Finally, emphasis should be given to an important recent development in the field of test development, interpretation, and use called criterion-referenced testing (CRT). First introduced in the early 1960s (Glaser, 1963), criterion-referenced measurement is seen as a necessary complement to the normative, or person-and-group referenced, measurement that has characterized so much of mental test theory in the past. Then, as now, tests were developed to provide discriminations along the entire scale of measurement in order to make possible interpretive statements regarding the standing of individuals scoring at any point along the scale in relation to other individuals and in relation to groups of individuals chosen to provide frames of reference.

The interest in criterion-referenced measurement arose in recognition of the fact that normative interpretations were not enough, and indeed often irrelevant, in some situations. What is often relevant is how well an individual is performing in relation to a predefined goal or standard of performance. Thus, what is at issue is not necessarily whether one student's skills are more advanced than another's, but how well the student has mastered those skills.

The applications of criterion-referenced testing appear to be twofold: (1) estimating how well a person would perform, if asked to do so, on the entire universe or domain of items in which the test is a sample; and (2) classifying an individual as either a "master" (competent, passing, acceptable, etc.) or "nonmaster" of the material being tested. As a consequence of these applications, interest has focused among CRT specialists on methods of assessing content validity and in defining criteria, goals, and standards of performance. As a necessary part of this effort, considerable attention has been given to developing reliable procedures for setting cutting scores—in order to distinguish those students who have achieved mastery (or competency, acceptability, etc.) in a particular domain from those who have failed to achieve mastery—and for assessing the reliability and validity of criterion-referenced tests in making such classifications (Livingston, 1972). Clearly, the adequacy of a criterion-referenced test in

making such classifications is reflected in the number of misclassifications that result from its use: the number of masters incorrectly classified as nonmasters, and the number of nonmasters incorrectly classified as masters. An extended review of the present status of CRT may be found in Berk (1980).

It is safe to say that the interest in CRT and its implications for test score interpretation and decision making go back well beyond Glaser's 1963 article. Indeed, that interest has been evident as long as tests have been used for decision making, although not as highly focused as at present. The distinction between criterion-referenced interpretation and norm-referenced interpretation, and in their complementary use, has long been recognized in other fields as well—in medicine, for example, when an individual's state of health is evaluated not only in comparison with that of others of the same sex, age, and history (differentiated-normative comparison), but also in comparison with some desired, or goal-defined, state of health (criterion-referenced comparison). Finally, it is clear that even criterion-referenced comparisons (performance as it should be) are necessarily normatively dependent, since *what should be* must perforce be defined with reference to *what actually is* in the normative world.

Sampling for Norms. One of the principal sources of error in norms arises from the methods of drawing the sample from the norms population. But even when the sample is drawn correctly, with appropriate attention to the principles of random selection, there is a characteristic of norms that is often overlooked and which deserves special mention. Like the error of measurement in a mean, for example, which tends to vanish as a function of the size of the sample tested, the error in norms tends to vanish as a function of the size of sample used for developing the norms. However, once the norms are determined, the error, which may be considered random at the time of sample selection (if the sampling has been done appropriately), now remains in the norms in the form of a bias and is transmitted to all evaluations of the score equally, whether it is an individual's score or the mean score for many individuals.

As indicated, the foregoing will occur even when the sampling from the population of interest is random and unbiased. Other errors of sampling, however, cannot be assessed, and these are likely to result in biased norms (Cornell, 1960). They include (1) a conveniently available sample; (2) a sample drawn to represent what are thought to be "typical" cases; (3) a sample selected on the basis of "expert" opinion; (4) a sample with a high proportion of nonparticipation (almost inevitable in norms development); (5) a sample based on an outdated or otherwise inadequate list of the members in the target population; (6) a "quota" sample, in which the choice of the particular school within the general framework of the sampling plan is not automatic, as random sampling should be, but deliberate and conscious.

There are several methods of selecting samples that

most often are used in combination. (See Lord, 1959, for an excellent treatment of sampling for norms.) The simplest is the unrestricted or simple random method, which essentially calls for casting all individuals into a common pool and selecting a sample of specified size from the pool, preferably with the aid of a table of random numbers. A modification of this procedure is the stratified-random process, in which the total population is first divided into homogeneous categories (or strata) on the basis of one or more variables (sometimes in weighted combination) that are correlated with test score (age, sex, socioeconomic status, etc.). The sample is formed by drawing individuals at random within each stratum, taking care to ensure that each stratum will be appropriately and proportionately represented in the sample. A third type is the systematic or spaced sample, in which the list of individuals in the population is divided into as many blocks as desired for the sample (the number of blocks equals the number of individuals in the sample), and every nth individual is selected (where n = number of individuals in each block), starting with a randomly selected individual in the initial block. A preferred method, especially if the population list has been prepared in some systematic order (e.g., alphabetically), is to draw an individual at random from each block.

The foregoing procedures may be used either in drawing samples of individuals from populations of individuals, or in drawing samples of schools from populations of schools. Very seldom, however, are norms samples chosen with the individual as the sampling unit. For reasons of economy, the school is usually selected as the primary unit of sampling for norms, and all the students, or a random sample of all students, in each school are selected for the norms. This kind of successive sampling is called two-stage sampling. The procedure can be extended, of course, to multistage sampling. It is important to recognize that the sampling error of norms in which "natural groups" or clusters of individuals have been selected is necessarily different from, and generally larger than, the sampling error associated with simple random sampling of individuals. This is true because such groupings—communities, schools, and classrooms, for example—generally represent homogeneous clusters whose means are more dispersed than the means of random samples of the same size in which the individual is the unit of sampling. Generally speaking, for a sample of a particular size, the more reliable norms are those based on a large number of clusters and a small number of individuals drawn at random from each cluster, rather than the reverse.

Equating

When two or more forms of a test are made available for interchangeable use, it is generally considered necessary to adjust the scores provided by the forms to account for differences among them with respect to level and range of difficulty. This adjustment involves a process of equating

the forms, that is, of converting the system of units on one form to the system of units on another form so that scores earned on the two forms will, after conversion, be directly equivalent. What is sought here is a conversion between two measures of the same function, in the sense of a conversion from inches to centimeters, pounds to kilograms, degrees Fahrenheit to Celsius, and so on. Given this sense in which the concept of equating is used, the conversion will be unique (Angoff, 1966), except for random error, and independent of the particular data used to derive the conversion. Similarly, the conversion will be general in the sense that it will be applicable to all individuals for whom the measures are appropriate. A generally accepted operational definition of equating is as follows: Two scores, one on Form x and the other on Form y (where x and y are parallel in function and equally reliable), are equivalent if their corresponding percentile ranks in any group are equal. The procedure following from this definition is one that adjusts the scale of scores of Form x (say) to yield the same distribution in all respects as exists for Form y. If the distributions are dissimilar in shape, then this general (equipercentile) definition will result in a curvilinear conversion from the raw score scale of one form to the scale of another form. The curvilinearity reflects a systematic expansion and contraction in different regions of the raw score scale of one form in order to cause its distribution to conform to the shape of the distribution of the other form. If, however, the two distributions already have the same shape, then the conversion will approximate a straight line. In such instances a linear definition of equating will be adequate, by which one explicitly asserts that the first two moments of the two distributions (the means and standard deviations), but none beyond the second, are respectively equal. That is to say, the mean and standard deviation of raw scores on one form are simply redefined as equivalent, respectively, to the mean and standard deviation on the other form. Paralleling the equipercentile definition of equating, the linear definition of equating specifies that two scores, one on Form x and the other on Form y, are equivalent if their corresponding standard-score deviates in any group are equal. In statistical notation this is to say that

$$z_y = z_x$$

or

$$\frac{y - M_y}{\sigma_y} = \frac{x - M_x}{\sigma_x}, \tag{7}$$

which is a linear equation, more conveniently expressed in the form $y = Ax + B$, where A (the slope of the line) = σ_y/σ_x and B (the intercept of the line) = $M_y - AM_x$.

A number of different equating methods are available, appropriate for different types of data and described in some detail by Angoff (1971a). In the present discussion three major types of methods are presented.

Design I. Design I involves random groups, with one form administered to each group (Lord, 1950).

A large, heterogeneous group of examinees is chosen

and divided into two random halves. One half (α) takes Form x and the other half (β) takes Form y.

A. *Linear.* Under the assumption that the two groups are strictly equivalent, the mean and standard deviation on Form x are redefined to be equal, respectively, to the mean and standard deviation on Form y. Specifically, with the means and standard deviations available—on Form x for Group α and on Form y for Group β—equation (7) is applied to the data, with the appropriate group-identifying subscripts for x and y, to yield the conversion equation, $y = Ax + B$.

B. *Curvilinear.* Again under the assumption that the two groups are strictly equivalent, the percentiles (i.e., the scores attaching to particular percentile ranks) on Form x are redefined as equivalent to the corresponding percentiles (i.e., the scores attaching to the same percentile ranks) on Form y. The details of the procedure may be described as follows: Two distributions are formed, one on Form x for Group α and another on Form y for Group β. Percentile ranks are computed on each distribution for each of about thirty score points and the ogives are plotted and smoothed. Corresponding percentiles for each of about thirty percentile ranks are read from the two smoothed ogives and plotted, one against the other. This plot is then smoothed and extrapolated to the end points on each form and used to record the conversion from Form x to Form y, and vice versa.

Design II. Random groups are used, with both forms administered to each group in counterbalanced order (Lord, 1950).

A large, heterogeneous group of examinees is chosen and divided into two random halves, one half (α) taking the forms in the order x–y, and the other half (β) taking the forms in the order y–x. The basic assumption in this method is that the practice effect, expressed in standard-score units, of Form y on Form x performance is the same as the practice effect of Form x on Form y performance, and independent of score level.

A. *Linear.* The average of the means and the average of the standard deviations (more precisely, the square root of the average of the variances) on Form x are redefined to be equal, respectively, to the averages of the means and standard deviations on Form y. Otherwise stated, we use the data from this administration to find a linear equation of the form $y = Ax + B$, where

$$A = \sqrt{\frac{\sigma_{y_\alpha}^2 + \sigma_{y_\beta}^2}{\sigma_{x_\alpha}^2 + \sigma_{x_\beta}^2}}, \tag{8}$$

and

$$B = \frac{1}{2}(M_{y_\alpha} + M_{y_\beta}) - \frac{A}{2}(M_{x_\alpha} + M_{x_\beta}). \tag{9}$$

B. *Curvilinear.* An approximate analog of this method calls for combining the data on Form x and also on Form y for the two half-groups, and applying the equipercentile (curvilinear) method described in Design I.

Design III. Two groups are used, with one form administered to each group, and a common equating test administered to both groups (Gulliksen, 1950; Lord, 1950, 1955).

If the method of Design I is used, then inevitably there will be differences in the mean levels and dispersions of the two groups, α and β, used for equating. To adjust for these differences, an additional (equating) test, Form v, equivalent in function and difficulty to Forms x and y (but perhaps shorter), is administered to both groups. The differences between Groups α and β, as observed in their performance on Form v, are then used as a basis for adjusting the observed statistics on Forms x and y. Form v may be a separately timed test distinct from x and y, or a set of common items interspersed throughout x and y. In any case it should be administered in precisely the same way to both groups. That is, the Form v items, in so far as possible, should be equally subject to contextual and ordinal effects for both groups, and equally subject to the effects of speed, motivation, practice, boredom, or fatigue. The assumption basic to this method is that the regression of Form x on Form v is the same for the combined group, $\alpha + \beta$, as for Group α; also that the regression of Form y on Form v is the same for the combined group as for Group β.

A. *Linear.* Using the data from this administration, estimates of mean and variance are made on both Forms x and y for the combined group of examinees, t, taking Form v ($t = \alpha + \beta$). As before, the (estimated) mean and standard deviation on Form x are redefined to be equal, respectively, to the (estimated) mean and standard deviation on Form y. These estimates are given in equations (10)–(13), followed by a brief description of the use of the estimated statistics in the formation of the conversion equation:

$$\hat{M}_{x_t} = M_{x_\alpha} + b_{xv_\alpha}(M_{v_t} - M_{v_\alpha}), \tag{10}$$

$$\hat{M}_{y_t} = M_{y_\beta} + b_{yv_\beta}(M_{v_t} - M_{v_\beta}), \tag{11}$$

$$\hat{\sigma}_{x_t}^2 = \sigma_{x_\alpha}^2 + b_{xv_\alpha}^2(\sigma_{v_t}^2 - \sigma_{v_\alpha}^2), \tag{12}$$

and

$$\hat{\sigma}_{y_t}^2 = \sigma_{y_\beta}^2 + b_{yv_\beta}^2(\sigma_{v_t}^2 - \sigma_{v_\beta}^2), \tag{13}$$

in which

$$b_{xv} = r_{xv}\frac{\sigma_x}{\sigma_v} \quad \text{and} \quad b_{yv} = r_{yv}\frac{\sigma_y}{\sigma_v}.$$

These estimates,

$$\hat{M}_{x_t}, \ \hat{M}_{y_t}, \ \hat{\sigma}_{x_t}^2, \ \hat{\sigma}_{y_t}^2,$$

are applied to form the conversion equation

$$y = Ax + B,$$

where

$$A = \hat{\sigma}_{y_t}/\hat{\sigma}_{x_t} \quad \text{and} \quad B = \hat{M}_{y_t} - A\hat{M}_{x_t}.$$

It should be noted here that this equating procedure may be derived by assuming, as Lord (1955) does, that the α

and β groups are randomly drawn from the same population.

B. *Curvilinear.* A curvilinear analog of this method, suggested by Lord, is one that estimates the frequencies in the distributions of scores on Forms x and y for the combined group, Group t. Using these estimated distributions, the Form x and Form y scores are equated by means of the equipercentile method described in Design I. The steps are as follows: (1) Combine the two distributions of Form v to form one distribution for Group t. (2) Working with the scatterplot of v versus x (v on the horizontal axis, x on the vertical axis), multiply, for each interval of score, i, on Form v, the ratio of frequencies, f_{i_t}/f_{i_α}, by each of the cell frequencies in the column for score v_i. When this is completed for the columns of all intervals, v_i, there will be a new scatterplot of v versus x, estimated for Group t. (3) Sum the new frequencies in the cells across the values of v for each value of x. These summed frequencies now represent the estimated distribution on Form x for Group t. The next steps in the process repeat the procedure described in steps (1), (2), and (3) for the scatterplot of v versus y for Group β. With these two estimated distributions, one for Group t on Form x and the other for Group t on Form y, the two forms, may be equated by the equipercentile method described in Design I.

The three designs presented here are all appropriate in different situations. Design II is the most demanding because it calls for the administration of both forms to all examinees. It is also the most reliable. Design III is next in order of the time demands it imposes on the student (depending on the length of Form v), but of the three procedures it offers the greatest degree of flexibility and variety, because Form v can be conceived and used in a number of ways. Design I is the simplest of the three procedures, but also the least precise. However, because of its simplicity it is probably the least susceptible to clerical and administrative errors. For the same reason, it may ease the task of attracting larger groups of examinees for the equating administration, and the use of larger groups will naturally tend to enhance the precision of the equating.

Other methods of equating are also available, some of them variations on Design III, some based on other conceptions of the use of an equating test, and still others that make use of item data rather than score data (Angoff, 1971a, pp. 584–586); see also the following section on item response theory.

In some tests and testing programs forms are available at a number of levels of difficulty. Such test forms are often equated, or "articulated," by means of one of the three methods described here, or by a variant of one of these methods. Although these articulated test forms are highly useful, especially for tracking individual and group progress, a principal concern is that the psychological function measured—especially when the function is highly dependent on the curriculum—may change from one level to the next, with the result that the notion of a single reference scale for all forms may tend to lose its meaning. Difficulties attendant on the use of conversion systems for tests that do not measure the same psychological function are discussed in the section of comparable scores.

Item Response Theory. As discussed previously, item response theory (IRT) uses a model of examinee performance in which the probability of an examinee giving a particular response to an item is completely determined by the examinee's ability and the characteristics of the item. The number of characteristics or parameters of an item used in this model is generally no more than three: (1) the item difficulty, (2) the discriminating power of the item, and (3) the "pseudo-guessing" parameter, that is, the probability that an examinee of very low ability will answer the item correctly. The two most common models are (1) the use of all three item characteristics, called the three-parameter model (Lord, 1952b, 1980), and (2) the use of only item difficulty (assuming all items are equally discriminating and there is no possibility of guessing), called the Rasch (1960) model.

Item response function. The mathematical function used to describe the probability of a correct response to an item is called an item response function (IRF); it assumes, as stated earlier, that this probability is determined only by the examinee's ability and the characteristics of the item. If we represent ability by the symbol θ, the IRF for item i may be summarized by $P_i(\theta)$, where $P_i(\theta)$ is defined as the probability of a correct response, given θ and the characteristics of the item. In practice, the two most common functional forms for the IRF are the logistic and the normal ogive.

Parameter estimation. Where a test is given to a group of examinees, methods exist for using the results to estimate an ability for each examinee, and the item parameters (difficulty, discrimination, and guessing) for each item. If, as in equating, we wish to make comparisons between scores on two different forms of a test, say Form x and Form y, we must first make sure that the item parameter and ability estimates made on the basis of data from those forms can be expressed on the same scale. This is possible if (1) Form x and Form y contain common items, (2) the group taking Form x and the group taking Form y are the same group or are representative samples drawn from the same population, and (3) the group taking Form x overlaps with the group taking Form y.

True score equating. Once the two test forms have been administered, and estimates of abilities and item characteristics have been calculated and expressed on the same scale, the two tests can be equated by using item response theory.

Consider an examinee's observed score on a test. If number-right scoring is used, the observed score is simply a count of the number of items an examinee answered correctly. If each item score, u_i, is coded as zero for an incorrect response ($u_i = 0$) and one for a correct response ($u_i = 1$), the observed number-right score for an m-item test may be expressed as the sum, over all the items in the test, of the u_i-values, or

$$x = \sum_{i=1}^{m} u_i.$$

An examinee's true score is defined as the expected value of the observed score. In IRT the expected value of an item score, u_i, is simply the IRF, $P_i(\theta)$. Therefore, the true number-right score, T_x, for Form x, which consists of m items, may be written:

$$T_x = \mathcal{E}\left(\sum_{i=1}^{m} u_i\right) = \sum_{i=1}^{m} P_i(\theta). \qquad (14)$$

Similarly, the true number-right score, T_y, for Form y, which consists (say) of n items, may be written:

$$T_y = \mathcal{E}\left(\sum_{j=1}^{n} u_i\right) = \sum_{j=1}^{n} P_j(\theta). \qquad (15)$$

Equations (14) and (15) mean that an individual's true score on a test is the sum of the IRFs for each item for that individual's particular level of ability. They also imply that for a given level of ability, θ, it is possible to calculate a true score on Form x and, correspondingly, a true score on Form y. These two true scores are said to be equated because they correspond to the same level of the ability, θ, that both Form x and Form y are designed to measure.

In practice estimated item parameters are substituted into these two equations, and equated pairs of true scores are calculated for successive values of θ. Although the result of this process equates true scores on Forms x and y, it is assumed that the same equating relationship holds for observed scores.

Further applications of item response theory. The application of IRT to mental test data has many other advantages. New and powerful tools become available for test analysis and design. It is possible to speak of the amount of information a test provides at *each level of ability,* as opposed to classical methods that only allow such analyses for the test as a whole. Tests can be designed to yield maximum information at specified levels of ability. This, of course, makes for more efficient test construction.

In addition, an entirely new type of testing becomes possible. A special set of items, designed to be most appropriate for each examinee, can be drawn from the pool of available items and used for testing that examinee. Thus examinees at each level of ability may be tested with their own individual tests, different from the tests administered to examinees at all other levels of ability. Yet, using IRT, the estimates of abilities for this kind of "tailored" or "adaptive" test will be comparable. The test administration becomes more complex, usually requiring a computer to select and administer items, but this type of testing, in general, will produce more precise ability estimates with many fewer items than is possible with conventional testing. As a consequence of the rapidly declining costs of computers, tailored or adaptive testing may well be the most common type of testing in the near future.

Comparable Scores

Unlike equivalent scores, which result from the equating of test forms that measure the same psychological function, comparable scores may be thought of simply as the result of "equating" tests of different psychological functions (Angoff, 1966). Although score equivalence for parallel forms, when defined on the basis of one group of examinees, will be equally applicable to any group of examinees, comparability across nonparallel tests can be depended on to hold only with other groups that are drawn from the same population as the group for whom the comparability was first established. Thus comparability between two tests is defined only with respect to a particular group, or population, of examinees. In addition, it is defined only with respect to a particular sense of comparability or a particular method of deriving it.

The logic of the distinction between equivalent and comparable scores may be illustrated when, for example, we ask if Person A is "larger" than Person B. If both persons are measured in the same way and with the same type of instrument, say an extended ruler, then the comparison can be made meaningful without qualification, even though one ruler is laid off in feet and inches and the other in centimeters. If, on the other hand, different dimensions are under consideration, say height for Person A and weight for Person B, then the comparison of size for these two persons is meaningful only in a particular sense, for example, with reference to a group or population designated for this purpose.

Although the notion of comparability has some serious restrictions, it is particularly useful, and indeed necessary, when, for example, we wish to compare and rank the general level of scholarship of students who have taken different combinations of courses in college. If the terms of the comparability have been appropriately defined, then such a ranking may be appropriate. However, all too often the comparability is not properly defined and so is open to serious question.

Although the logic of comparable scores is different from the logic of equivalent scores, the procedures for deriving these scores are similar, and often identical. Very likely the most defensible procedure for deriving comparable scores is that described under Design I, in which tests (note: *not* test forms) x and y are administered to random halves of a group that is drawn, also at random, from a defined population. However, with some reservations, the method of Design III is also appropriate. One example of the application of Design III, described by Angoff (Coffman, 1971, pp. 62–71), may be found in the achievement tests of the College Board. Their scales are adjusted to reflect the abilities, as measured by the College Board Scholastic Aptitude Test, of the students who choose to take them. The basic reference group for defining this comparability is the group on which the scale for the SAT is defined.

If the methods of equating parallel tests are adapted to the problem of comparable scores on nonparallel tests, then two sets of criteria must be applied for evaluating the appropriateness of the comparability—one relating to the equating of tests of the same function, and one relating to the "equating" of tests of different function. In the former instance there are at least three sources of error: (1) the reliability of the measuring instruments themselves; (2) the design of the equating experiment and the method of treating the data; and (3) the choice of samples used to establish the conversion. In the matter of comparability these same sources of error are applicable, as well as two other sources of error. These relate to (4) the degree to which the tests for which comparable scores are sought are similar in function; and (5) the degree to which the group on whom the table of comparable scores is based is appropriate, when one considers the type of individual for whom the table is to be used. With these criteria in mind it is then necessary to consider the purpose for which the table is to be used and the nature of the decisions that will be based on it, in order to evaluate the degree of error that might be tolerated in the course of its use.

William H. Angoff

See also Achievement Testing; Intelligence Measurement; Item Analysis; Measurement in Education; Reliability of Measurement.

REFERENCES

Angoff, W. H. Scales with nonmeaningful origins and units of measurement. *Educational and Psychological Measurement,* 1962, *22,* 27–34.

Angoff, W. H. Can useful general-purpose equivalency tables be prepared for different college admissions tests? In A. Anastasi (Ed.), *Testing Problems in Perspective.* Washington, D.C.: American Council on Education, 1966, pp. 251–264.

Angoff, W. H. Scales, norms, and equivalent scores. In R. L. Thorndike (Ed.), *Educational Measurement.* Washington, D.C.: American Council on Education, 1971, pp. 508–600. (a)

Angoff, W. H. Test scores and norms. In L. C. Deighton (Ed.), *Encyclopedia of Education.* New York: Macmillan, 1971, pp. 153–165. (b)

Angoff, W. H. (Ed.). *The College Board Admissions Testing Program: A Technical Report on Research and Development Activities Relating to the Scholastic Aptitude Test and Achievement Tests.* New York: College Entrance Examination Board, 1971. (c) (ERIC Document Reproduction Service No. ED 050 181)

Berk, R. A. (Ed.). *Criterion-referenced Measurement: The State of the Art.* Baltimore: Johns Hopkins University Press, 1980.

Birnbaum, A. In F. M. Lord & M. R. Novick, *Statistical Theories of Mental Test Scores.* Reading, Mass.: Addison-Wesley, 1968, pp. 397–479.

Coffman, W. E. The achievement tests. In W. H. Angoff (Ed.), *The College Board Admissions Testing Program: A Technical Report on Research and Development Activities Relating to the Scholastic Aptitude Test and Achievement Tests.* New York:

College Entrance Examination Board, 1971, pp. 49–78. (ERIC Document Reproduction Service No. ED 050 181)

College Entrance Examination Board. *Guide for High Schools and Colleges.* Princeton, N.J.: College Entrance Examination Board, 1976.

Cornell, F. G. Sampling methods. In C. W. Harris (Ed.), *Encyclopedia of Educational Research* (3rd ed.). New York: Macmillan, 1960, pp. 1181–1183.

Ebel, R. L. Content standard test scores. *Educational and Psychological Measurement,* 1962, *22,* 15–25.

Ebel, R. L. *Essentials of Educational Measurement.* Englewood Cliffs, N.J.: Prentice-Hall, 1972.

Educational Testing Service. *STEP Manual and Technical Report.* Menlo Park, Calif.: Addison-Wesley, 1980.

Flanagan, J. C. *The Cooperative Achievement Tests: A Bulletin Reporting the Basic Principles and Procedures Used in the Development of Their System of Scaled Scores.* New York: Cooperative Test Service of the American Council on Education, 1939.

Flanagan, J. C. Units, scores, and norms. In E. F. Lindquist (Ed.), *Educational Measurement.* Washington, D.C.: American Council on Education, 1951, pp. 695–763.

Flanagan, J. C. (Ed.). *The Aviation Psychology Program in the Army Air Forces* (Report No. 1). Washington, D.C.: U.S. Government Printing Office, 1948.

Gardner, E. F. *Determination of Units of Measurement Which Are Consistent with Inter- and Intra-grade Differences in Ability.* Unpublished doctoral dissertation, Harvard University, Graduate School of Education, 1947.

Glaser, R. Instructional technology and the measurement of learning outcomes: Some questions. *American Psychologist,* 1963, *18,* 519–521.

Gulliksen, H. *Theory of Mental Tests.* New York: Wiley, 1950.

Guttman, L. The basis for scalogram analysis. In S. A. Stouffer; L. Guttman; E. A. Suchman; P. F. Lazarsfeld; S. A. Star; & J. A. Clausen, *Studies in Social Psychology in World War II* (Vol. 4). *Measurement and Prediction.* Princeton, N.J.: Princeton University Press, 1950, pp. 60–90.

Hull, C. L. The conversion of test scores into series which shall have any assigned mean and degree of dispersion. *Journal of Applied Psychology,* 1922, *6,* 298–300.

Lawley, D. N. On problems connected with item selection and test construction. *Proceedings of the Royal Society of Edinburgh,* 1943, *61-A* (Part 3), 273–287.

Lazarsfeld, P. F. In S. A. Stouffer; L. Guttman; E. A. Suchman; P. F. Lazarsfeld; S. A. Star; & J. A. Clausen. *Studies in Social Psychology in World War II* (Vol. 4). *Measurement and Prediction.* Princeton, N.J.: Princeton University Press, 1950, pp. 362–472.

Lindquist, E. F. Selecting appropriate score scales for tests. *Proceedings of the 1952 Invitational Conference on Testing Problems.* Princeton, N.J.: Educational Testing Service, 1953, pp. 34–40.

Livingston, S. A. Criterion-referenced applications of classical test theory. *Journal of Educational Measurement,* 1972, *9,* 13–26.

Lord, F. M. *Notes on Comparable Scales for Test Scores* (Research Bulletin 50-48). Princeton, N.J.: Educational Testing Service, 1950.

Lord, F. M. *The Scale Proposed for the Academic Ability Test* (Research Memorandum 52-3). Princeton, N.J.: Educational Testing Service, 1952. (a)

Lord, F. M. *A Theory of Test Scores* (Psychometric Monograph No. 7). Richmond, Va.: William Byrd Press, 1952. (b)

Lord, F. M. Equating test scores: A maximum likelihood solution. *Psychometrika*, 1955, *20*, 193–200.

Lord, F. M. Test norms and sampling theory. *Journal of Experimental Education*, 1959, *27*, 247–263.

Lord, F. M. *Applications of Item Response Theory to Practical Testing Problems*. Hillsdale, N.J.: Lawrence Erlbaum Associates, 1980.

McCall, W. A. *Measurement*. New York: Macmillan, 1939.

Nedelsky, L. Absolute grading standards for objective tests. *Educational and Psychological Measurement*, 1954, *14*, 3–19.

Rasch, G. *Probabilistic Models for Some Intelligence and Educational Tests* (Studies in Mathematical Psychology, No. 1). Copenhagen: Danish Institute for Educational Research, 1960.

Terman, L. M., & Merrill, M. A. *Measuring Intelligence*. New York: Houghton Mifflin, 1937.

Thurstone, L. L. The mental age concept. *Psychological Review*, 1926, *33*, 268–278.

Tucker, L. R. *Academic Ability Test* (Research Memorandum 51–17). Princeton, N.J.: Educational Testing Service, 1951.

Tucker, L. R. Scales minimizing the importance of reference groups. *Proceedings of the 1952 Invitational Conference on Testing Problems*. Princeton, N.J.: Educational Testing Service, 1953, pp. 22–28.

Zieky, M. J., & Livingston, S. A. *Manual for Setting Standards on the Basic Skills Assessment Tests*. Princeton, N.J.: Educational Testing Service, 1977.

NURSERY SCHOOL EDUCATION

See Early Childhood Development; Early Childhood Education.

NURSING EDUCATION

This article surveys major issues and research related to nursing education. Except for some historical background, reviews of research are limited to the past ten years. Topics discussed include types of programs; studies of nursing education; credentialing; provision of nursing services; studies of teaching; prediction studies; and program evaluation.

Types of Programs. Because the different types of programs that prepare nurses are confusing to persons outside the field of nursing education, it is necessary to begin with a brief explanation. Historically, there have been three types of basic programs that enable one to become eligible to take the state board examination and become a registered nurse (R.N.): baccalaureate programs, associate degree programs, and diploma programs. The first two programs grant degrees and are affiliated with junior and senior colleges and universities. Diploma programs are affiliated with hospitals and grant diplomas rather than degrees. Recently a fourth type of program referred to as a "professional doctorate," has been initiated at Case Western Reserve University (Schlotfeldt, 1978). Although called a doctorate program, it offers basic and not advanced prep-

aration. It is comparable to programs offering doctorates in other professional disciplines such as medicine, law, dentistry, and pharmacy.

Nursing education began as apprenticeship training, accounting for the fact that nursing education programs were initially located in hospitals. The first program to be affiliated with a university was initiated at the University of Minnesota in 1909. By 1916, sixteen programs were located in colleges and universities. Associate degree programs were started by Montag in 1952 with the goal of preparing a technical nurse to assist professional nurses. Over the years, enrollment in diploma programs has gone down, whereas enrollment in associate degree and baccalaureate programs has steadily increased. In 1965, 77.3 percent of graduating nurses received their basic preparation in diploma programs, 7.2 percent in associate degree programs, and 15.5 percent in baccalaureate programs. In 1970, these figures were 52.4 percent, 26.8 percent, and 20.8 percent, respectively. In 1975 they were 29.1 percent, 43.8 percent, and 27 percent (American Nurses' Association, 1977). In 1979 they were 20.3 percent, 47.2 percent, and 32.5 percent (National League for Nursing, 1980).

Failure to clarify the differing roles and functions of graduates of different types of programs has resulted in considerable confusion in both practice and educational settings. Fagin, McClure, and Schlotfeldt (1976) made recommendations regarding the problems created by the various types of nursing preparation programs. Montag (1980) reemphasized the need to distinguish between technical and professional education for nursing and highlighted current issues pertaining to the failure to do so. *Nursing Outlook* (1977) published a series of articles considering contemporary issues in associate degree programs for nurses. Schlotfeldt (1977) clearly outlined the differences between technical and professional preparation for nursing as well as some implications of these differences.

Basic programs offer generalist preparation; that is, graduates are prepared to function in various health care settings. Nurses who wish specialty preparation for particular clinical roles or for roles as teachers or administrators may obtain a master's degree in nursing. Doctoral programs in nursing, of relatively recent origin, are also available. As in other disciplines, the doctorate emphasizes preparation for research. Downs (1978) and Cleland (1976) discuss various facets of doctoral programs in nursing.

Studies of Nursing Education. A major and recurring issue in nursing education for more than half a century has been the failure of the nursing profession to have the education of its members take place completely within educational institutions. Coupled with this issue is the related one of inadequate public financial support for nursing education. In the decade following the Flexner report (1910), medical education secured its ties with universities. No such rapid change occurred in nursing education, although the recommendation for such change has been made each time that the profession was seriously examined. Christy (1980), in a historical analysis, noted that the many studies of nursing and nursing education in the United States have "from the first to the last . . . recommended that the educational preparation for nursing take place in institutions of higher learning" (p. 487). Isabel Stewart (1921) of Teachers College, Columbia University, recommended that schools of nursing be removed from hospitals and become independent financially and administratively. The Goldmark Report (1923), which issued from the Committee for the Study of Nursing Education in 1919, exposed many problems affecting both nursing and nursing education. This report similarly recommended independent schools of nursing with an adequate financial base.

The Committee on the Grading of Nursing Schools issued two reports. *Nurses, Patients, and Pocketbooks* (Burgess, 1928) dealt with supply of and demand for nurses. *Nursing Schools Today and Tomorrow* (Committee on the Grading of Nursing Schools, 1934) examined weaknesses in nursing education and made recommendations for improvement. This report, like the prior ones, exposed the inadequate financial support that plagued nursing education. It also revealed deficits in preparation of faculty, use of students to staff hospitals, poor instruction, and an over-enrollment of nursing students resulting in an oversupply of graduate nurses. The committee recommended reducing the number of applicants to schools and improving their quality; employing graduate rather than student nurses to staff hospitals; helping hospitals secure funds to hire graduate nurses; and obtaining public funds to support nursing education. Nursing education, the committee emphasized, is a public and not a private responsibility.

In her 1948 report, *Nursing for the Future,* Esther Lucile Brown of the Russell Sage Foundation noted that many of the nursing profession's problems stemmed from its educational system. She recommended collegiate nursing education, a system of accreditation, the closing of weak schools, and public assumption of financial responsibility for nursing education. *Nursing Schools at the Mid-century* (West & Hawkins, 1950), published as an outgrowth of the Brown report, included a classification of the quality of nursing schools. In 1953 Bridgman reemphasized that nursing education should take place in a collegiate setting, and that it should compare with other college programs.

The Surgeon General's report, *Toward Quality in Nursing—Needs and Goals* (U.S. Public Health Service, 1963), issued from the Consultant Group on Nursing that was appointed to study nursing's needs and the federal government's role in relation to these needs. This report emphasized again that lack of financial resources was a basic problem in nursing and nursing education and that more collegiate schools of nursing were needed. The report made many recommendations regarding numbers and types of nurses required, the financing necessary to advance the education of nurses, provision of nursing services, and nursing research. Based on the recommendations of the Surgeon General's report, federal aid to

nursing was greatly expanded in the form of the Nurse Training Act of 1964. This act, which was extended to 1971, provided for loans and scholarships, graduate education, and improved educational programs and facilities. Kalisch and Kalisch (1978) summarized improvements in the education of nurses made possible by increased federal funding. They also noted the retrenchment during the Nixon administration. Nurses struggled with attempts at rescissions during the Carter administration, and it appears that they will also be required to do so during the current administration. The American Nurses' Association (ANA) has published recommendations (ANA, 1980) concerning priorities for funding in nursing education.

In 1966, the American Nurses' Association published its first position paper (ANA, 1966) stating that all education for nurses should take place within educational institutions. The association maintained that the minimum preparation for professional practice should be a baccalaureate degree; that the minimum preparation for technical practice should be an associate degree; and that nursing assistants should be prepared in vocational education programs and not through on-the-job training. This position of the ANA resulted in much dissension within the nursing profession. Although the ANA was attempting to improve the education of nurses and the provision of nursing services, diploma schools of nursing and the graduates of these schools felt threatened. The controversy over the continuation of diploma schools of nursing continues to the present day.

One outgrowth of the Surgeon General's report was the formation of the National Commission for the Study of Nursing and Nursing Education in the United States. The commission's report, *An Abstract for Action,* also called the Lysaught report (1970), recommended that nursing education take place in collegiate settings and that government at all levels increase its financial support. Background papers and follow-up reports have also been published by Lysaught (1973, 1974, 1981).

This review has highlighted major studies during the years of the organization and financing of nursing education. More detail about these studies and other historical aspects of nursing and nursing education may be found in Ashley (1976) and Kalisch and Kalisch (1978).

Credentialing. Following the Brown report (1948), the National Committee for the Improvement of Nursing Services appointed a subcommittee to study nursing schools. Schools were examined through use of a survey questionnaire and were classified in three groups according to level of excellence. From 1952 to 1957, the National League for Nursing Education (forerunner of the National League for Nursing) conducted a temporary accreditation program intended to improve educational programs. By the end of the five-year period, the number of accredited schools had increased by 72.4 percent. Nursing education programs are presently accredited by the National League for Nursing (NLN), which publishes the list of accredited schools in *Nursing Outlook.*

Although the NLN has been the official accrediting body for nursing education programs of all types since the 1950s, there has recently been some movement to change the accreditation mechanism. In 1976, the ANA appointed a committee to study all aspects of the credentialing process, including accreditation, certification, licensing, and degree designation. The committee's report, entitled *The Study of Credentialing in Nursing: A New Approach* (1979), examined each aspect of credentialing and, based upon defined principles, made recommendations regarding licensure, registration, certification, educational degrees, and accreditation. The committee recommended that states license professional nurses as the persons accountable for nursing care, and that registration for assisting personnel be national. Certification, as recognition of excellence in specialty practice, would be nongovernmental. Regarding educational degrees, the committee recommended that the nursing profession establish minimum degree requirements for entry into practice. The committee also recommended that the professional society (ANA) establish definitions and standards for accreditation of both nursing education programs and organized nursing services. To implement its recommendations, the committee proposed the establishment of a national nursing credentialing center. Such a center would provide cohesive governance to coordinate planning, policies, and action. In its report, the committee outlined the projected center's specific functions, characteristics, and structure.

Provision of Nursing Services. Because nursing is a national resource, assuring an adequate supply of nurses is a concern of the federal government. In 1975, the federal division of nursing contracted with the Western Interstate Commission for Higher Education (WICHE) to undertake the Analysis and Planning Project, the goal of which was "to strengthen the nursing community's ability to analyze and plan for the improved distribution of nursing personnel and services" (Elliott & Kearns, 1978, p. 2). To achieve this goal the project's objectives were directed toward "(1) developing new methodologies for projecting nursing requirements and resources at the national and state levels, (2) developing a planning capability among nursing leaders throughout the nation, and (3) providing insights into ways of improving the distribution of nursing personnel and services" (Elliott & Kearns, 1978, p. vii).

One of the activities of WICHE in the project was the development of what has been called the "state model," which was intended to be used by the state planners to project nursing personnel needs and requirements for the next five years. The major steps projected in the model reflect its complexity. They are (1) differentiating the client population, (2) assessing the health care needs of each population grouping, (3) formulating health care goals and priorities for each population grouping, (4) estimating health program and service requirements, and (5) estimating appropriate staffing patterns.

To obtain the input needed to facilitate the various steps

of the model and also to project national and state nursing requirements, a panel of expert consultants was convened. Based on its projection of nursing requirements through 1982, the panel determined that there is a shortage of nurses in every state, especially of nurses with baccalaureate and graduate preparation. The panel made a number of specific recommendations to strengthen the educational preparation of nurses. It also made recommendations regarding the distribution of nursing services, the delivery of health care, the improvement of nursing practice, and the improvement of planning. The panel's complete set of recommendations are well worth reading (Elliott & Kearns, 1978), and for the purpose of this article, may be summarized as follows: "The present problems in health care delivery and the requirements projections clearly point to the need for (1) more registered nurses to be prepared at baccalaureate and higher degree levels to ensure appropriate competencies for the provision of quality nursing services; (2) improved health care services for the elderly; and (3) increased emphasis on preventive care, including community health services" (p. 97).

Studies of Teaching. A number of studies have examined the outcomes in nursing students of various approaches to teaching or have examined correlates of various attitudes and behaviors. These studies will be reviewed briefly in chronological order. They are based upon experimental and quasi-experimental as well as descriptive and correlational research.

Experimental and quasi-experimental research. Kalisch (1971) compared twelve and a half hours of empathy training to a control treatment of lecture-discussions on human behavior in an attempt to increase empathy in associate degree students. Forty-nine students were randomly assigned to the two experimental and two control groups. Significant differences were noted on four of the seven "empathy" measures, one of which was a performance evaluation by clinical instructors. Some measures showed retention of behavior on follow-up after six weeks.

Walsh (1971) studied the effect of a course in psychiatric nursing on students in five baccalaureate nursing programs with respect to level of anxiety, direction of change in attitudes toward mental illness, and relationship between these two variables. There were 159 experimental subjects, with a control group of 11 students enrolled in public health nursing. Results showed anxiety to be decreased in two of the five groups as well as some change to a more positive attitude toward mental illness. Anxiety and attitude were not correlated.

McLaughlin, Davis, and Reed (1972) examined the effect of three types of group leadership on the self-perceptions of sixty-six baccalaureate students randomly assigned to one of three groups. The leaderless group using "encounter-tapes" showed significant gains when compared to groups in which a leader was present during all or alternate sessions.

Quiring (1972) studied the effect of immediate and delayed videotaped feedback upon seventy-two baccalaureate students' skills in giving injections. No differences were noted in feedback conditions, but feedback by videotape was more effective than teacher demonstration. Students high in critical thinking also did better than low critical thinkers.

Steele, Fuller, and Langhoff (1972) assigned sixty matched baccalaureate students to independent, self-paced, or traditional classroom instruction. There were no differences in examination scores, but high grade point average (GPA) extroverts showed higher achievement orientation, more anxiety, and increased self-concept.

Thompson (1972) compared traditional and autotutorial approaches in teaching medical-surgical nursing to forty diploma students. Fifty-five percent preferred the mediated instruction, and faculty were able to teach more students. Retention was the same in both groups on follow-up after one year.

Mealey and Peterson (1974), administering the Personal Orientation Inventory to thirty-nine diploma students before and after a course in psychiatric nursing, noted a significant improvement in inner-directedness and time competence.

Mims, Yeaworth, and Hornstein (1974) found a significant improvement in sexual knowledge and attitudes following a five-day interdisciplinary course on sexuality attended by 143 nursing and other students.

Dye (1974) studied the effect of human relations training on the self-concepts, anxiety level, and group awareness of fifty-six associate degree students randomly assigned to one of five groups (three treatment groups and two controls). The treatments applied were a leaderless structured group, sensitivity training, and communication experience. One control group kept individual journals of critical incidents; a second group with no treatment also served as a control for comparison purposes. Only the leaderless structured group showed a significant difference on some outcome measures after pretest and posttest comparisons and a one-month follow-up.

Woods and Mandetta (1975) found an increase in knowledge but no attitude change after a course in sexuality had been taught to eleven baccalaureate nursing students and twelve male undergraduates in other programs.

Godejohn et al. (1975) selected baccalaureate students who had scored high on authoritarianism and social restrictiveness to study the effect of simulation games. Seven students were randomly assigned to the simulation condition and eighteen to a control group. Significant differences were noted on posttesting.

Huckaby and Arndt (1976) compared the effect of mastery learning to lecture-discussion in sixty-nine graduate students, with the mastery group showing significantly greater knowledge gain than the control group.

Wilhite and Johnson (1976) attempted to decrease stereotypical attitudes toward the aged by means of an eight-week course on aging. Stereotypical attitudes decreased from pretest to posttest in eighty baccalaureate students. They also found significant correlations between attitudes of students and clinical instructors when students were randomly assigned to instructors.

Crosby (1977) used microteaching to improve the teaching skills of fifty-seven graduate nursing students and nurses. The subjects, whose performance was videotaped and rated prior to the course, mid-course, and after its completion, showed significant improvements at each rating.

Griggs (1977) randomly assigned 137 baccalaureate students to three treatment groups and one control group to evaluate the effect of a minicourse upon handling problems related to contaminated respiratory equipment. The treatment groups received programmed instruction, audiovisual instruction, and combined programmed and audiovisual instruction. All three treatment groups performed better on a written test than did the control group, with the programmed instruction group and the audiovisual and programmed combination scoring highest.

Waltz (1978) studied the convergence of students' preferences for nursing practice with those of their clinical faculty. Subjects were 170 baccalaureate students and 14 faculty. Results showed that preferences were not convergent during the course. Student preferences were associated with preferences attributed to the faculty, with perception of faculty reputation, and with students' clinical grades.

Huckaby (1978) examined the effect of formative evaluation on the cognitive learning and affective behavior of graduate students. The experimental group received mastery learning that made use of formative testing, and the control received lecture-discussions. Results indicated that experimental subjects had higher affective scores, that both groups' knowledge increased but that the experimental group was significantly higher in knowledge, that students preferred the mastery approach, and that cognitive and affective scores were significantly and positively correlated.

Brock (1978) evaluated the impact of a management course taught to eighty baccalaureate students. Using a Solomon four-group design with random selection and assignment, the researcher found significant differences in knowledge and clinical performance for experimental groups, but noted that values were not correlated with performance.

Layton (1979) used various combinations of videotaped modeling, labeling, and rehearsal to increase the empathy of fifty-six junior and senior baccalaureate students who were randomly assigned to four experimental groups and one control group. Subjects were posttested immediately after treatment and three weeks later. The treatment was effective for junior but not for senior students, with the group receiving the rehearsal condition performing significantly better. Construct validity of the three instruments was also investigated.

Robb (1979), whose primary purpose was instrument development, also examined the effect of a course on the elderly on the beliefs and behavioral intentions of 153 baccalaureate students at three levels. Short-term evaluation revealed changes in behavioral intentions but not in beliefs; and after follow-up measurement one and two years later, all values remained constant. Beliefs and behavioral intentions were not correlated.

Huckabay (1979) compared grading and nongrading of formative evaluation on cognitive learning and affective behavior of graduate students. The group that was not graded performed better on cognitive measures. There were no affective differences.

Harlow and Goby (1980) examined the effect of a three-week clinical experience in an alcoholism treatment program on diploma students' attitudes toward alcoholism. Significant differences were noted between pretest and posttest results.

Critique of research methodologies. After examining this group of experimental and quasi-experimental studies, some general observations and suggestions are in order concerning future research with respect to independent and dependent variables, measurement, design, and analysis.

Independent variables are usually well explained and are practical in terms of their usefulness in the education of nursing students. Dependent variables deal with outcomes of knowledge, attitudes, and performance, with performance evaluation done infrequently. Measurement of knowledge outcomes is important and should continue to be emphasized. Usually teacher-made tests are used, and content validity and reliability are discussed. Teacher-made tests are often preferable in studies of teaching since they can be designed specifically to assess course or content objectives. However, adequate test development procedures, including content validity, reliability, item analysis, and pilot testing should definitely be addressed.

The frequent practice of attitude measurement is of questionable value. First, the precise nature of what is being measured is often unclear; and second, the relationship of attitudes to knowledge or behavior has not been clearly established. At times, there appears to be an assumption that attitudes are related to performance. Such an assumption is unwarranted and needs to be empirically established.

Performance or clinical evaluation is carried out too infrequently. Although measurement of performance is difficult, it is very important because of the clinical nature of nursing. The main objectives for nursing courses are usually clinical and not cognitive in nature. An alternative to evaluation in the actual clinical setting is assessment of videotaped performance and/or assessment in simulated situations. These procedures allow for more control, while retaining considerable external validity. Whether actual or simulated clinical settings are used, establishing interrater agreement is a necessity when doing performance evaluation.

Follow-up measurement of dependent variables should be done whenever possible. Nursing educators are concerned with maintenance of behavior as well as with immediate outcomes. Follow-up measurement, together with evaluation of performance, will add greatly to the quality and generalizability of studies of the teaching of nursing.

A few of the studies reviewed are experimental, using random assignment of subjects and a control group. Most studies fall into the quasi-experimental category, with many employing comparison of pretest and posttest measurement of a single group. Experimental design is preferable whenever possible. It allows the greatest control of confounding variables. When quasi-experimental designs are used, possible confounding variables should be identified and discussed. Also a stronger design, such as time-series, is preferable and pretest and posttest measurement of a single group.

Finally, it should be mentioned that many studies confuse "unit of treatment" and "unit of analysis." When treatments are carried out in a group, in which members interact with and influence one another, the group and not the individual should be the unit of analysis. Only when subjects cannot influence one another's level of performance is the use of the individual as the unit of analysis appropriate.

Descriptive and correlational studies. A number of studies correlate various qualities or characteristics of nursing students, and a few studies are simply descriptive in nature. Characteristics of students, such as their creativity (Marriner, 1977), their conceptual systems (Watson, 1978), and their concerns upon graduation (Packard, Schwebel, & Ganey, 1979) have been studied. A number of researchers have examined self-actualization (Goldstein, 1980; Sobol, 1978) and values (Garvin, 1976; May & Ilardi, 1970; O'Neill, 1973). Some studies looked at students' feminism (Moore, Decker, & Dowd, 1978), their sex-role identity (Stromborg, 1976), and the characteristics of male students (Williams, 1973).

A large number of studies have examined various cognitive and/or psychosocial characteristics of nursing students (Adams & Klein, 1970; Frerichs, 1973; Johnson & Leonard, 1970; Krall, 1970; Lewis, Bentley, & Sawyer, 1980; Meleis & Farrell, 1974; Richards, 1972; Richek & Nichols, 1973; Wren, 1971). Some researchers have studied various professional characteristics of students, such as their images of nursing (Brown, Swift, & Oberman, 1974), their management profiles (Gilbert, 1975), and their professional attitudes (Tetreault, 1976).

Finally, students' attitudes toward, reactions to, and experiences with various clinical phenomena are the subjects of considerable research. The clinical phenomena include situations involving death (Denton & Wisenbaker, 1977; Yeaworth, Kapp, & Winget, 1974); contraception (Elder, 1976); alcoholism (Schmid & Schmid, 1973); mental illness (Swain, 1973); crying patients (Forster & Forster, 1971); and the aged (Kayser & Minnigerode, 1975).

Formulating general comments or observations about the correlational and descriptive studies reviewed here is somewhat difficult. Most of them are meaningful only when viewed within specific theoretical or educational frameworks. However, it is suggested that studies of attitudes and other characteristics of students be related to specific educational concerns, such as the admission or retention of students or the teaching of certain behaviors. Only a few of the studies reviewed were related to such concerns.

The meaning of the measurements performed is another general consideration. As with the experimental studies, the precise nature of what is being measured is often unclear, especially when standardized tests are used. It is important to know whether instruments used measure what the researcher intends to measure. Construct validation of instruments used could be included as a research objective with some additional effort.

Prediction Studies. Studies pertaining to admission of students, attrition, and prediction of success are important because attrition and failure are expensive to schools, students, and society. A number of studies using various predictor and criterion or outcome measures have examined the prediction of success. For purposes of this review, these studies are divided into three categories: studies of graduate programs, basic programs, and prediction of performance on the State Board Test Pool Examination.

Graduate programs. Studies carried out in graduate nursing programs are aimed at finding predictors of success. The predictor variables are usually the Graduate Record Examination (GRE), the undergraduate grade point average (GPA), and, sometimes, demographic variables. Stein and Grun (1970) found positive correlations of the quantitative GRE score and undergraduate GPA with master's degree GPA. They also noted some differences among different nursing majors (e.g., psychiatric nursing, medical-surgical nursing).

Thomas (1974) also found positive correlations of GRE scores and undergraduate GPA with master's GPA. When master's GPA was separated into four program components, significant correlations were found for the administration and research components, but not for the clinical or nursing perspectives components.

A study by Ainslie et al. (1976) found correlations of GRE and years since undergraduate education with master's GPA. No correlation was found with age. Thomas (1977) found both GRE and undergraduate GPA to be correlated with master's GPA. There were some differences among different nursing majors and in different years of this five-year study.

The above studies, although small in number, suggest that the GRE and the undergraduate GPA are positively correlated with master's GPA and could therefore serve as useful predictors of success. Some of these studies were done over a period of years in single schools. Studies carried out over time in several schools, perhaps on a regional basis, would be useful. Such an approach would provide large numbers of subjects, and differences between schools as well as between majors could be examined.

Basic programs. This group of studies examined success in associate degree, diploma, or baccalaureate programs. Most of the studies were carried out with the aim of identifying differences between students who complete or do not complete programs.

Owen and Feldhusen (1970) used three models of combining variables to predict success of students in five associate degree programs. Their general conclusion was that prior semester GPA is the best predictor of present GPA, a finding consistent with a number of other studies predicting grades. They suggest using high school grades and one or two ability measures for admission decisions and prior semester grades for predicting grades in subsequent semesters. Owen, Feldhusen, and Thurston (1970) also found that, when added to the cognitive predictors, divergent thinking tests increased predictability of success. Attitudinal measures also contributed to the predictors for some groups.

Michael et al. (1971) found that the comprehension subtest of the California Reading Test was the best predictor of success in a diploma nursing program, followed by high school GPA. Personality inventories were not correlated with success. Halpin, Halpin, and Hauf (1976) noted that both high school GPA and American College Test (ACT) scores correlated significantly with nursing GPA in a diploma program, and that predictive efficiency increased by over 100 percent when the ACT was used along with the GPA.

Baker (1975) examined noncognitive differences between dropouts and graduates in five associate degree programs. Graduates were more likely to be older; married; more achievement-oriented, responsible, and self-controlled; and more accepting and nonjudgmental toward others.

Studies of baccalaureate programs used either success or attrition as criterion variables, with most studies using attrition. Liddle et al. (1971), using the TAV selection system based upon Horney's model of adult behavior, found that two of the nine predictors were related to degree attainment in baccalaureate students. Burgess, Duffey, and Temple (1972) found the prenursing, college GPA to be the most significant predictor of success in baccalaureate programs. Lewis and Welch (1975) noted significant correlations with achievement for required and elective prenursing GPA and high school rank, but only required prenursing GPA was significant in the regression equation.

Wittmeyer, Camiscioni, and Purdy (1971), who examined both completion and performance, found the ACT mathematics score and two of sixteen measures on the Personality Factor Inventory differentiated those who completed the program from those who did not complete the program. Performance, as measured by score on the state board examination, however, was best predicted by the prenursing GPA. There was no overlap in the variables predicting completion and performance.

Raderman and Allen (1974), examining factors associated with completion of a baccalaureate program by registered nurses, found that the GPA, the Scholastic Aptitude Test (SAT) verbal score, and the medical-surgical NLN examination discriminated between those who finished and those who dropped out. Rezler and Moore (1978) found that the liberal arts GPA was the best predictor of exit GPA's for RN's enrolled in a baccalaureate program, regardless of when the GPA was obtained. They also noted that diploma graduates performed better in both theory and clinical courses than associate degree graduates and that age was not a factor in predicting success.

In a preliminary study, Hutcheson, Garland, and Prather (1973) found that clinical performance may indicate dropout risk. Hutcheson, Garland, and Lowe (1979) later examined attitudinal and noncognitive indicators of attrition in four classes of students. No correlations were found with attitudinal measures. Educational level of parents was correlated with attrition, with higher levels of education of fathers associated with attrition, whereas higher educational levels of mothers were associated with completion.

Knopke (1979), in a six-year study, developed a model to predict attrition. Significant predictors of continuing in the program were first-semester GPA, high school percentile rank, science score on the College Qualification Test, and Edwards Personal Preference Scale (EPPS) scores on order, dominance, and aggression. Using the model, 78 percent of dropouts and 76 percent of those continuing were predicted. The researcher notes that the results are specific to the program, but that any school can develop a similar prediction model.

Munro (1980) used "path analysis" on data from the National Longitudinal Study of the High School Class of 1972 to examine attrition in students who entered associate degree and baccalaureate nursing programs. Using a theoretical model that predicted the relationships among various background and individual attribute variables, the author studied those who persisted as well as those who dropped out. For associate degree students educational aspirations had the strongest effect on persistence, whereas academic ability was the best predictor for baccalaureate students. The reason most frequently cited for withdrawal was loss of interest. Financial difficulties were also common.

From examining studies of attrition and success in basic programs, GPA and standardized tests appear to be the best predictors, especially for students enrolled in baccalaureate programs. For associate degree students, some noncognitive measures also seem important. The Munro study (1980), which is worthy of special note because of national sampling, found educational aspiration most important in the success of associate degree students. The studies reviewed indicate that noncognitive measures, such as personality and attitude, are not significant predictors.

Performance on state board examinations. Reed and Feldhusen (1972) used preadmission and college predictors in five associate degree programs to determine who would take state boards and what would best predict state board scores. The SAT verbal score was the best predictor of who would take boards and of the scores.

Deardorff, Denner, and Miller (1976) and Bell and Martindill (1976) used National League for Nursing Achievement Tests to predict state board performance. Both studies showed certain sets of tests to be effective predictors. Bell and Martindill (1976) also noted that all five board examinations measure a common ability. Pascale and Port (1978) found significant correlations between each state board examination and its corresponding NLN achievement test. Haney, Michael, and Martois (1977), examining the performance of three ethnic samples, noted significant correlations with state board scores of preenrollment reading skills, program GPA, and NLN Achievement Tests.

Wolfle and Bryant (1978), noting that NLN tests predict state board performance, constructed a causal model to explain why. Their data, collected from six classes of associate degree students, indicate that some examinations depend upon mastery of subject matter, and others depend on ability acquired prior to entering nursing school.

The studies predicting success on state board examinations indicate that NLN achievement tests are good predictors. In the future, however, more studies will be needed, since the organization of the state board examinations will be changed in the summer of 1982 (Test Plan for the Registered Nurse State Board Test Pool Examinations, 1980).

Program Evaluation. Some understanding of curriculum patterns is necessary as background for examining evaluations of nursing education programs. Longway (1972) gives a historical perspective on the organization of nursing curricula over the years. Only recent patterns need be discussed here. For a number of years, most curricula were organized according to medical specialties or body systems, so that students took courses in medical-surgical nursing, maternity nursing, psychiatric-mental health nursing, and so on. This pattern is sometimes referred to as a "blocked" curriculum. More recently, curricula have begun to be organized around concepts. This pattern is referred to as an integrated curriculum, since medical specialties are often not identifiable. Styles (1976) reviewed some issues and problems related to developing and implementing an integrated curriculum. Curriculum evaluations comparing old and new curricula are usually comparing a blocked to an integrated curriculum.

Various studies might be classified as program evaluations. A number of these studies compare types of curricula or programs. Others examine specific outcomes or facets of a single curriculum. Stone and Green (1975) carried out an extensive five-year evaluation of a new curriculum.

They followed one class for four years, in addition to four groups in the old and new curricula and two groups from a new curriculum in a comparable program. They used a variety of measurement approaches and instruments to analyze students' perceptions as well as cognitive and non-cognitive characteristics. Their findings were too numerous to discuss here, but the authors considered their most significant findings to concern changes in personality, attitude, and leadership in the class that was studied intensively. The same class in the comparable program did not show such changes.

Richards (1977) compared students in a new integrated curriculum to those in the old curriculum. Students in the new curriculum were higher in leadership and lower in critical thinking. All students were low in empathy. Results on state board examinations and NLN tests were mixed. When rated by supervisors in their first jobs, graduates of the new curriculum were rated higher than average. Pardue (1979), comparing four blocked and four integrated curricula, found that type of curriculum did not make a difference in faculty satisfaction or critical thinking ability of students and that students in the blocked curricula performed significantly better on state board examinations. Thomas (1979) noted mixed results when comparing the creativity of students in a new integrated curriculum with those in the old curriculum. Seniors in the old curriculum and beginning students in the new curriculum performed better than advanced students in the new curriculum.

Gray et al. (1977) compared graduating seniors in the associate degree and baccalaureate programs of a single school, using a written test of students' essay responses to clinical situations. Baccalaureate students had more concerns for long-range problems, family issues, and leadership, indicating their greater breadth of knowledge and ability to see beyond the specific problem presented. Nelson (1978) polled the graduates of three types of programs—baccalaureate, diploma, and associate degree—regarding their perceptions of their competence in technical, communication, and administration skills. The graduates' supervisors, who were asked the same questions, rated the baccalaureate graduates highest. The graduates' ratings of themselves differed on the specific parameters, but, in general, diploma graduates rated themselves highest on overall competence, whereas, baccalaureate graduates rated themselves higher on administration and communication skills.

Williams, Bloch, and Blair (1978) examined the values of graduating students upon entry into the program and at the end of one year. They also looked at congruence with faculty values. Results were mixed, with some values changing and some not, and some becoming congruent and some not. Faculty rated the influence of specific educational factors higher than did students.

Behm and Warnock (1978), attempting to determine the appropriateness of state board examinations for program evaluation, correlated ratings of thirteen associate degree programs with graduates' state board scores. A positive but nonsignificant correlation ($r = .34$) led the authors to conclude that state board examinations should not be used as a measure of program effectiveness.

Based upon the studies reviewed, some general comments and recommendations can be made with respect to program evaluation in nursing education. There is a problem in interpreting the results of most studies, especially when the results are mixed. There is also difficulty in determining the origin of the changes noted. Since it is not feasible to use experimental design along with random assignment of students when curricula are compared, other means of making comparisons must be used. Measurements before and after implementation of a curriculum or comparisons of one class in the old curriculum and one or two classes in the new curriculum do not provide adequate control of alternative explanations for the changes noted. In fact, the interaction of many factors probably accounts for the mixed results noted in several studies. Time-series designs, with a series of measurements both before and after the implementation of change, would be better indicators of the effect of changes.

Other factors besides the change of curriculum, such as quality of teaching, should also be measured. Quality of teaching is likely to be at least as significant in explaining outcomes as curriculum change. Also, both the variables selected for measurement and the instruments chosen to measure them are crucial. The same recommendations with respect to measurement given in the discussion of research methodology also apply here and need not be repeated.

Faculty devote considerable time and effort attempting to improve curriculum. Unfortunately, planning for evaluation of change does not receive equal attention. Planning for evaluation needs to be started at the same time as planning for change. In fact, if ongoing program evaluation were carried out, it would provide data to help determine whether a change was needed. Only if evaluation is meaningful and well designed can faculty know the results of their curriculum efforts.

Summary. This article has discussed types of nursing programs and studies of nursing education, background information necessary to understand contemporary nursing education. Studies of credentialing and provision for nursing services were also reviewed. Major issues emerging from this group of studies include the insufficient number of nurses prepared at the baccalaureate and graduate levels, recurrent inadequate funding for nursing education, and confusion about the roles and functions of nurses with different educational preparation. In the latter portion of this article, studies of the nursing education process were reviewed. Specific recommendations were made with respect to research on the teaching of nursing, and conclusions were drawn on the bases of predictive studies. More effective planning for program evaluation was recommended to document the need for and effect of curriculum changes.

Janice M. Layton

See also Licensing and Certification; Medical Education; Professions Education.

REFERENCES

Adams, J., & Klein, L. R. Students in nursing school: Considerations in assessing personality characteristics. *Nursing Research*, 1970, *19*, 362–366.

Ainslie, B. S.; Andersen, L. E.; Colby, B. K.; Hoffman, M. A.; Meserve, K. P.; O'Connor, C.; & Ouimet, K. M. Predictive value of selected admission criteria for graduate nursing education. *Nursing Research*, 1976, *25*, 296–299.

American Nurses' Association. First position on education for nursing. *American Journal of Nursing*, 1966, *66*, 515.

American Nurses' Association. *Facts about Nursing, 1976–1977* (Publication No. D-60). The Association, 1977.

American Nurses' Association. *Funding Nursing Education* (Publication No. NE-7). The Association, 1980.

Ashley, J. *Hospitals, Paternalism, and the Role of the Nurse.* New York: Teachers College Press, 1976.

Baker, E. J. Associate degree nursing students: Nonintellective differences between dropouts and graduates. *Nursing Research*, 1975, *24*, 42–44.

Behm, R. J., & Warnock, F. N. State board examinations and associate degree program effectiveness. *Nursing Research*, 1978, *27*, 54–56.

Bell, J. A., & Martindill, C. F. A cross-validation study for predictors of scores on state board examinations. *Nursing Research*, 1976, *25*, 54.

Bridgman, M. *Collegiate Education for Nursing.* New York: Russell Sage Foundation, 1953.

Brock, A. M. Impact of a management-oriented course on knowledge and leadership skills exhibited by baccalaureate nursing students. *Nursing Research*, 1978, *27*, 217–221.

Brown, E. L. *Nursing for the Future.* New York: Russell Sage Foundation, 1948.

Brown, J. S.; Swift, Y. B.; & Oberman, M. L. Baccalaureate students' image of nursing: A replication. *Nursing Research*, 1974, *23*, 53–59.

Burgess, M. A. *Nurses, Patients, and Pocketbooks.* New York: Committee on the Grading of Nursing Schools, 1928.

Burgess, M. M.; Duffey, M.; & Temple, F. G. Two studies of prediction of success in a collegiate program of nursing. *Nursing Research*, 1972, *21*, 357.

Christy, T. E. Entry into practice: A recurring issue in nursing history. *American Journal of Nursing*, 1980, *80*, 485–488.

Cleland, V. Developing a doctoral program. *Nursing Outlook*, 1976, *24*, 631–635.

Committee on the Grading of Nursing Schools. *Nursing Schools: Today and Tomorrow.* New York: National League of Nursing Education, 1934.

Crosby, M. H. Teaching strategies: A microteaching project for nurses in Virginia. *Nursing Research*, 1977, *26*, 144–147.

Deardorff, M.; Denner, P.; Miller, C. Selected National League for Nursing Achievement Test scores as predictors of state board examination scores. *Nursing Research*, 1976, *25*, 35–38.

Denton, J. A., & Wisenbaker, V. B. Death experience and death anxiety among nurses and nursing students. *Nursing Research*, 1977, *26*, 61–64.

Downs, F. S. Doctoral education in nursing: Future directions. *Nursing Outlook*, 1978, *26*, 56–61.

Dye, C. A. Self-concept, anxiety, and group participation: As affected by human relations training. *Nursing Research*, 1974, *23*, 301–306.

Elder, R. G. Orientation of senior nursing students toward access to contraceptives. *Nursing Research*, 1976, *25*, 338.

Elliott, J. E., & Kearns, J. M. *Analysis and Planning for Improved Distribution of Nursing Personnel and Services: Final Report* (DHEW Publication No. HRA 79-16). Hyattsville, Md.: U.S. Department of Health, Education, and Welfare, December 1978. (ERIC Document Reproduction Service No. ED 176 065)

Fagin, C. M.; McClure, M.; & Schlotfeldt, R. M. Can we bring order out of the chaos of nursing education? *American Journal of Nursing*, 1976, *76*, 98–107.

Flexner, A. *Medical Education in the United States and Canada.* New York: Carnegie Foundation for the Advancement of Teaching, 1910.

Forster, B., & Forster, F. Nursing students' reaction to the crying patient. *Nursing Research*, 1971, *20*, 265–268.

Frerichs, M. Relationship of self-esteem and internal-external control to selected characteristics of associate degree nursing students. *Nursing Research*, 1973, *22*, 350.

Garvin, B. J. Values of male nursing students. *Nursing Research*, 1976, *25*, 352.

Gilbert, M. A. Personality profiles and leadership potential of medical-surgical and psychiatric nursing graduate students. *Nursing Research*, 1975, *24*, 125.

Godejohn, C. J.; Taylor, J.; Muhlenkamp, A. F.; & Blaesser, W. Effect of simulation gaming on attitudes toward mental illness. *Nursing Research*, 1975, *24*, 367–370.

Goldmark, J. C. *Nursing and Nursing Education in the United States: Report of the Committee for the Study of Nursing Education and Report of a Survey by Josephine Goldmark.* New York: Macmillan, 1923.

Goldstein, J. O. Comparison of graduating A.D. and baccalaureate nursing student's characteristics. *Nursing Research*, 1980, *29*, 46–49.

Gray, J. E.; Murray, B. L. S.; Roy, J. F.; & Sawyer, J. R. Do graduates of technical and professional nursing programs differ in practice? *Nursing Research*, 1977, *26*, 368–373.

Griggs, B. M. A systems approach to the development and evaluation of a minicourse for nurses. *Nursing Research*, 1977, *26*, 34–41.

Halpin, G.; Halpin, G.; & Hauf, B. Incremental validity of the ACT test battery for predicting success in a school of nursing over a ten-year period. *Educational and Psychological Measurement*, 1976, *36*, 433–437.

Haney, R.; Michael, W. B.; & Martois, J. The prediction of success of three ethnic samples on a state board certification examination for nurses from performance on academic course variables and on standardized achievement and study skills measures. *Educational and Psychological Measurement*, 1977, *37*, 949–964.

Harlow, P. E., & Goby, M. J. Changing nursing students' attitudes toward alcoholic patients: Examining effects of a clinical practicum. *Nursing Research*, 1980, *29*, 59–60.

Huckabay, L. M. Cognitive and affective consequences of formative evaluation in graduate nursing students. *Nursing Research*, 1978, *27*, 190–194.

Huckabay, L. M. Cognitive-affective consequences of grading versus nongrading of formative evaluations. *Nursing Research*, 1979, *28*, 173–178.

Huckabay, L. M., & Arndt, C. Effect of acquisition of knowledge on self-evaluation and the relationship of self-evaluation to perception of real and ideal self-concept. *Nursing Research*, 1976, *25*, 244–251.

Hutcheson, J. D., Jr.; Garland, L. M.; & Lowe, L. S. Antecedents of nursing school attrition: Attitudinal dimensions. *Nursing Research*, 1979, *28*, 57–62.

Hutcheson, J. D., Jr.; Garland, L. M.; & Prather, J. E. Toward reducing attrition in baccalaureate-degree nursing programs: An exploratory study. *Nursing Research*, 1973, *22*, 530–533.

Johnson, R. W., & Leonard, L. C. Psychological test characteristics and performance of nursing students. *Nursing Research*, 1970, *19*, 147–150.

Kalisch, B. J. An experiment in the development of empathy in nursing students. *Nursing Research*, 1971, *20*, 202–209.

Kalisch, P. A., & Kalisch, B. J. *The Advance of American Nursing.* Boston: Little, Brown, 1978.

Kayser, J. S., & Minnigerode, F. A. Increasing nursing students' interest in working with aged patients. *Nursing Research*, 1975, *24*, 23.

Knopke, H. J. Predicting student attrition in a baccalaureate curriculum. *Nursing Research*, 1979, *28*, 224–227.

Krall, V. Personality factors in nursing school success and failure. *Nursing Research*, 1970, *19*, 265–268.

Layton, J. M. The use of modeling to teach empathy to nursing students. *Research in Nursing and Health*, 1979, *2*, 163–176.

Lewis, J.; Bentley, C.; & Sawyer, A. The relationship between selected personality traits and self-esteem among female nursing students. *Educational and Psychological Measurement*, 1980, *40*, 259–260.

Lewis, J., & Welch, M. Predicting achievement in an upper-division bachelor's degree nursing major. *Educational and Psychological Measurement*, 1975, *35*, 467–469.

Liddle, L. R.; Heywood, H. L.; Hankey, R. O.; & Morman, R. R. Predicting baccalaureate degree attainment for nursing students: A theoretical study using the TAV selection system. *Nursing Research*, 1971, *20*, 258–261.

Longway, I. M. Curriculum concepts: An historical analysis. *Nursing Outlook*, 20, 1972, 116–120.

Lysaught, J. P. *An Abstract for Action.* New York: McGraw-Hill, 1970.

Lysaught, J. P. *From Abstract into Action.* New York: McGraw-Hill, 1973.

Lysaught, J. P. *Action in Affirmation: Toward an Unambiguous Profession of Nursing.* New York: McGraw-Hill, 1981.

Lysaught, J. P. (Ed.). *Action in Nursing: Progress in Professional Purpose.* New York: McGraw-Hill, 1974.

Marriner, A. The student's perception of his creativity. *Nursing Research*, 1977, *26*, 57–60.

May, N. T., & Ilardi, R. L. Change and stability of values in collegiate nursing students. *Nursing Research*, 1970, *19*, 359–362.

McLaughlin, F. E.; Davis, M. L.; & Reed, J. L. Effects of three types of group leadership structure on the self-perceptions of undergraduate nursing students. *Nursing Research*, 1972, *21*, 244.

Mealey, A. R., & Peterson, T. L. Self-actualization of nursing students resulting from a course in psychiatric nursing. *Nursing Research*, 1974, *23*, 138.

Meleis, A. I., & Farrell, K. M. Operation concern: A study of senior nursing students in three nursing programs. *Nursing Research*, 1974, *23*, 461–468.

Michael, W. B.; Haney, R.; Lee, Y. B.; & Michael, J. J. The criterion-related validities of cognitive and noncognitive predictors in a training program for nursing candidates. *Educational and Psychological Measurement*, 1971, *31*, 983–987.

Mims, F.; Yeaworth, R.; & Hornstein, S. Effectiveness of an interdisciplinary course in human sexuality. *Nursing Research*, 1974, *23*, 248.

Montag, M. L. Looking back: Associate degree education in perspective. *Nursing Outlook*, 1980, *28*, 248–250.

Moore, D. S.; Decker, S. D.; & Dowd, M. W. Baccalaureate nursing students' identification with the women's movement. *Nursing Research*, 1978, *27*, 291–295.

Munro, B. H. Dropouts from nursing education: Path analysis of a national sample. *Nursing Research*, 1980, *29*, 371–377.

National League for Nursing. *State-approved Schools of Nursing-RN* (Publication No. 19-1823). The League, 1980.

Nelson, L. F. Competence of nursing graduates in technical, communicative, and administrative skills. *Nursing Research*, 1978, *27*, 121–125.

Nursing Outlook, 1977, *25*, 496–518.

O'Neill, M. F. A study of baccalaureate nursing student values. *Nursing Research*, 1973, *22*, 437–443.

Owen, S. V., & Feldhusen, J. F. Effectiveness of three models of multivariate prediction of academic success in nursing education. *Nursing Research*, 1970, *19*, 517–525.

Owen, S. V.; Feldhusen, J. F.; & Thurston, J. R. Achievement prediction in nursing education with cognitive, attitudinal, and divergent thinking variables. *Psychological Reports*, 1970, *26*, 867–870.

Packard, K. L.; Schwebel, A. I.; & Ganey, J. S. Concerns of final semester baccalaureate nursing students. *Nursing Research*, 1979, *28*, 302–304.

Pardue, S. F. Blocked and integrated content baccalaureate nursing programs: A comparative study. *Nursing Research*, 1979, *28*, 305–311.

Pascale, P. J., & Port, P. The relationship between subtest scores of the National League for Nursing Achievement Tests and subtest scores of the Ohio State Board Examinations for nursing certification. *Educational and Psychological Measurement*, 1978, *38*, 1049–1052.

Quiring, J. The autotutorial approach: Effect of timing of videotape feedback on sophomore nursing students' achievement of skill in giving subcutaneous injections. *Nursing Research*, 1972, *21*, 332.

Raderman, R., & Allen, D. V. Registered nurse students in a baccalaureate program: Factors associated with completion. *Nursing Research*, 1974, *23*, 71–73.

Reed, C. L., & Feldhusen, J. F. State board examination score prediction for associate degree nursing program graduates. *Nursing Research*, 1972, *21*, 149–153.

Rezler, A. G., & Moore, J. S. Correlates of success in the baccalaureate education of registered nurses. *Research in Nursing and Health*, 1978, *1*, 159–164.

Richards, M. A. A study of differences in psychological characteristics of students graduating from three types of basic nursing programs. *Nursing Research*, 1972, *21*, 258.

Richards, M. A. One integrated curriculum: An empirical evaluation. *Nursing Research*, 1977, *26*, 90–95.

Richek, H. G., & Nichols, T. Personality and cognitive characteristics of prenursing majors. *Nursing Research*, 1973, *22*, 443–448.

Robb, S. S. Attitudes and intentions of baccalaureate nursing students toward the elderly. *Nursing Research*, 1979, *28*, 43–50.

Schlotfeldt, R. M. *Entrance into Registered Nursing: Issues and*

Problems (Publication No. 23-1685). National League for Nursing, 1977.

Schlotfeldt, R. M. The professional doctorate: Rationale and characteristics. *Nursing Outlook,* 1978, *26,* 302–311.

Schmid, N. J., & Schmid, D. T. Nursing students' attitudes toward alcoholics. *Nursing Research,* 1973, *22,* 246.

Sobol, E. G. Self-actualization and the baccalaureate nursing students' response to stress. *Nursing Research,* 1978, *27,* 238–244.

Steele, L.; Fuller, M.; & Langhoff, H. F. A multimedia independent approach: For improving the teaching-learning process in nursing. *Nursing Research,* 1972, *21,* 436–447.

Stein, R. F., & Grun, E. J. The Graduate Record Examination as a predictive potential in the nursing major. *Nursing Research,* 1970, *19,* 42–47.

Stewart, I. M. Developments in nursing education since 1918. *U.S. Bureau of Education Bulletin,* 1921, *20,* p. 1.

Stone, J. C., & Green, J. L. The impact of a professional baccalaureate degree program. *Nursing Research,* 1975, *24,* 287–291.

Stromborg, M. F. Relationship of sex-role identity to occupational image of female nursing students. *Nursing Research,* 1976, *25,* 363.

Study of Credentialing in Nursing: A New Approach (Vol. 1, Publication No. G-136 5M 3/79). American Nurses' Association, 1979.

Styles, M. M. In the name of integration. *Nursing Outlook,* 1976, *24,* 738–744.

Swain, H. L. Nursing students' attitudes toward mental illness. *Nursing Research,* 1973, *22,* 59.

Test Plan for the Registered Nurse State Board Test Pool Examination. Chicago: National Council of State Boards of Nursing, Inc., 1980. (Suite 2010, 303 East Ohio St., Chicago, Illinois, 60611, 1980.)

Tetreault, A. I. Selected factors associated with professional attitude of baccalaureate nursing students. *Nursing Research,* 1976, *25,* 49–53.

Thomas, B. Prediction of success in a graduate nursing service administration program. *Nursing Research,* 1974, *23,* 156–159.

Thomas, B. Differential utility of predictors in graduate nursing education. *Nursing Research,* 1977, *26,* 100–102.

Thomas, B. Promoting creativity in nursing education. *Nursing Research,* 1979, *28,* 115–119.

Thompson, M. Learning: A comparison of traditional and autotutorial methods. *Nursing Research,* 1972, *21,* 453.

U.S. Public Health Service. *Toward Quality in Nursing—Needs and Goals: Report of the Surgeon General's Consultant Group on Nursing.* Washington, D.C.: U.S. Government Printing Office, 1963. (ERIC Document Reproduction Service No. ED 021 994)

Walsh, J. E. Instruction in psychiatric nursing, level of anxiety, and direction of attitude change toward the mentally ill. *Nursing Research,* 1971, *20,* 522–529.

Waltz, C. F. Faculty influence on nursing students' preferences for practice. *Nursing Research,* 1978, *27,* 89–97.

Watson, J. Conceptual systems of undergraduate nursing students as compared with university students at large and practicing nurses. *Nursing Research,* 1978, *27,* 151–155.

West, M., & Hawkins, C. *Nursing Schools at the Mid-century.* New York: National Committee for the Improvement of Nursing Services, 1950.

Wilhite, M. J., & Johnson, D. M. Changes in nursing students' stereotypic attitudes toward old people. *Nursing Research,* 1976, *25,* 430–432.

Williams, M. A.; Bloch, D. W.; & Blair, E. M. Values and value changes of graduate nursing students: Their relationship to faculty values and to selected educational factors. *Nursing Research,* 1978, *27,* 181.

Williams, R. A. Characteristics of male baccalaureate students who selected nursing as a career. *Nursing Research,* 1973, *22,* 520–521.

Wittmeyer, A. L.; Camiscioni, J. S.; & Purdy, P. A. A longitudinal study of attrition and academic performance in a collegiate nursing program. *Nursing Research,* 1971, *20,* 339–347.

Wolfle, L. M., & Bryant, L. W. A causal model of nursing education and state board examination scores. *Nursing Research,* 1978, *27,* 311–315.

Woods, N. F., & Mandetta, A. Changes in students' knowledge and attitudes following a course in human sexuality: Report of a pilot study. *Nursing Research,* 1975, *24,* 10.

Wren, G. R. Some characteristics of freshmen students in baccalaureate, diploma, and associate-degree nursing programs. *Nursing Research,* 1971, *20,* 167–172.

Yeaworth, R. C.; Kapp, F. F.; & Winget, C. Attitudes of nursing students toward the dying patient. *Nursing Research,* 1974, *23,* 20–24.

NUTRITION EDUCATION

Nutrition education was initiated in the United States at the turn of the century. According to Martin (1980), the earliest nutrition teaching occurred in health classes for under-par children in medical clinics in 1908. The classes were usually conducted by physicians, and the focus was on health habits, including food habits. Soon after the discoveries of vitamins, beginning about 1913, and the creation of the War Food Administration during World War I, advice was given to housewives on planning meals containing more fruits, vegetables, milk, and eggs. Early vitamin discoveries were based on animal-feeding experiments. The techniques of these experiments were adapted for demonstration to intermediate-grade children of health differences among animals that were fed good and poor diets. Classroom demonstration of experiments was thought to be an excellent teaching technique. Indeed, animal experiments are still used in classrooms today.

History. Historically, nutrition education has been tied to health improvement education programs and school feeding programs. Mary Schwarz Rose, of Teachers College, Columbia University, in New York City, and Lydia Roberts, of the University of Chicago, were pioneers of nutrition education in the 1920s. The target of their programs often was the attainment of desirable body weight by undernourished children. Rose focused on nutrition information and animal experiments as teaching tools. Roberts conducted a Child Health School that admitted school-age children; health lessons emphasized eating wholesome foods and improving health habits. Martin (1980) also reported that during the 1920s and 30s there were some demonstrations on the use of the lunchroom as a place to teach good habits of food selection.

The Food and Nutrition Board (FNB) of the National Research Council established the first version of the recommended dietary allowances (RDA) in 1941. The RDAs were the first standards available for teaching human nutrition needs. The Food and Nutrition Board (1980a) has revised these standards about every five years. Mead (1964) recalled that in 1941 the Food Habits Committee of the Department of Anthropology and Psychology, National Research Council, gave serious thought to analyzing the factors that influence the formation of food habits. These findings are reflected in approaches to teaching used extensively throughout the 1960s.

The RDAs provided standards for identifying and targeting programs for specific needs and certain age-groups and populations. Food guides to be used as teaching tools based on the RDAs were developed by a federal agency. In 1943, the government produced a poster, *Eat the Basic Seven Every Day*. In 1958, it was decided that seven groups were too difficult for people to remember, and the food groupings were reduced to four. This grouping is still used as a basic teaching tool today, and many of the most widely used curricula are based upon it. However, Contento (1980) suggested that in our much expanded food marketplace, characterized by sophisticated processing, prepackaging of food, and environmental concerns, it is an inadequate tool.

The National School Lunch Program established by the National School Lunch Act of 1946 was designed to improve the nutrition of children and, in some instances, has been used as a learning laboratory. In the early 1960s, the School Health Education Study (1967) developed a set of ten health education concepts, one of which focused on food selection and nutrient needs. Since then, many of the comprehensive health education curricula that were developed have incorporated nutrition education into the curriculum, according to reports of the Curriculum Framework Criteria Committee on Health (1978).

The White House Conference on Food, Nutrition, and Health, in 1969, brought the social issues and educational needs relating to nutrition and health to the attention of policy makers. It served as a major impetus for providing food for those in need and heightened awareness of nutrition needs in the population. The Panel on Nutrition Education in Elementary and Secondary Schools (Ullrich & Briggs, 1973) recommended a conceptual framework for nutrition education in schools that included generalizations such as (1) "nutrition is the process by which food and other substances later become you;" (2) "food is made up of certain chemical substances that work together and interact with body chemicals to serve the needs of the body;" (3) "the way a food is handled influences the amount of nutrients in the food, its safety, appearance, taste, and cost" (p. 185). Since 1969, most nutrition education curricula have been based on versions of this conceptual framework. A decade later, Contento et al. (1980) reviewed these concepts, along with the set developed in a research project at Pennsylvania State University. They recommended

an additional eight concepts in light of current knowledge about nutrition and current food supply conditions.

Sponsored Research and Development. In 1977, Congress enacted Public Law 95-166—the National School Lunch Act and Child Nutrition Amendments—which provided grants to state education agencies for nutrition education and training. The Nutrition Education and Training Program was to include programs for students, school foodservice personnel, and teachers, as well as for the development, demonstration, testing, and evaluation of classroom materials and curricula (Ullrich, 1977).

The Society for Nutrition Education (SNE) was founded in 1968 and published its first issue of the *Journal of Nutrition Education* some months before the White House conference. Its strong peer review policy has led to an effective increase in the level of sophistication and validity of research in nutrition education. Ten years later, a position paper was published regarding the functions and qualifications of nutrition education specialists in school grades K–12. This paper represented the consensus of a representative group of nutritionists on the functions and qualifications of nutrition specialists ("Nutrition Education Specialists," 1978).

Recognizing the growing need for additional guidance in food selection beyond the basic four food groups, the U.S. Senate Select Committee on Nutrition and Human Needs, in 1977, recommended dietary goals for the United States. These goals were based on testimony presented before the committee in the course of its investigation of nutrition issues. The committee found that the relationships between contemporary American diets and patterns of disease indicated a need to alter diets in the direction of consumption of fewer calories; less fat, especially animal fat; less cholesterol; less refined sugar; increased complex carbohydrates; and limited salt. McNutt (1978) analyzed the process of further refining and reviewing dietary goals. The publication *Nutrition and Your Health: Dietary Guidelines for Americans,* released jointly by the United States Department of Agriculture and the Department of Health and Human Services in 1980, provides seven dietary guidelines: "eat a variety of foods; maintain ideal weight; avoid too much fat, saturated fat, and cholesterol; eat foods with adequate starch and fiber; avoid too much sugar; avoid too much sodium; if you drink alcoholic beverages, do so in moderation" (p. 1). A committee of the Food and Nutrition Board (1980b) reviewed the current literature and came up with somewhat different recommendations. These caused considerable discussion in the professional nutrition community.

Nutrition education may be defined as the process enabling individuals to gain understanding and skills needed to promote and protect their nutritional well-being through food choices. Methods and techniques from the behavioral sciences may naturally facilitate that process. Olson and Gillespie (1981) have indicated that nutrition educators recognize the need for the integration of principles from the behavioral sciences into planning, implementation, and evaluation programs—a need that has not been met in the past. As a result, Olson and Gillespie coordinated a workshop on nutrition education research at Cornell University, in April 1980, that focused upon identifying theories, research perspectives, and methods from behavioral sciences applicable to research efforts. The workshop groups identified the need to understand better the factors that influence dietary behavior and the problems of measuring knowledge, attitudes, and behavior in nutrition education research. The four behavioral disciplines discussed in the workshop were anthropology, communications, psychology, and social psychology. These theoretical perspectives can be used to examine different aspects of nutrition education intervention.

Several reports have indicated the need for research in nutrition education (Dwyer, 1980). The task force concerned with "Pregnant Women, Children, and Adolescents" made recommendations relating to general and school education. It stated that the nutrition education curricula for preschool through secondary schools must be evaluated, and if necessary, designed and reinforced to the target group's level of understanding. Citing the need for expansion of research in nutrition, the task force suggested such research topics as the development of validation techniques for evaluating curricula and reinforcement materials, and the study of the developmental levels of young children as they relate to the children's perception of the relationships between food, nutrition, and health.

Earlier, the Office of Technology Assessment (1978) published the results of a series of study-advisory panels on human nutrition research. Nutrition education was indicated as one of the focal points in a recommended seven-point nutrition education research strategy. One research strategy concerned the identification and teaching of the factors affecting lifetime eating habits and times in our life cycle when educational approaches would be more effective.

The National Dairy Council held a conference on nutrition education research in December 1978 (Brun, 1980). The need for increased research was related to the desire to improve goals and content, educational strategies, and information about the effectiveness of nutrition education programs, and to increase the number of audiences to be reached. The need for improvement of interdisciplinary efforts, including application of research techniques from disciplines such as education, sociology, and anthropology, was also recognized.

Although a number of definitive recommendations have been made, very little funding is currently available for nutrition education research. The majority of funds come from federal government sources most notably from the Department of Agriculture. Some university programs have been funded by the Nutrition Foundation, which is supported by a group of food companies. Under the School Lunch Act, the Nutrition Education and Training Program provides some funds to the states for curriculum development, especially for classroom teaching and school food-

service personnel training. However, with major federal budget cuts, no more funds may be available. The health promotion programs under the U.S. Department of Education offer opportunities for curriculum development in nutrition as a component of health education. Funds for special consumer education pilot projects have been provided by the Department of Education, which views nutrition education of consumers as an appropriate topic for projects.

Recent Research Trends. Although nutrition education has been promoted in a limited way as part of the school curriculum for many years, it has only been recognized as a specialized field since the White House Conference on Food, Nutrition and Health was held in 1969, and the continuous publication of the *Journal of Nutrition Education* that was then initiated.

Some studies have provided insights about methods of integrating nutrition teaching into the school program. Cook, Eiler, and Kaminaka (1977) surveyed the extent of nutrition education in grades K-6 in New York and New Jersey. They found that about nine clock hours per year were spent teaching nutrition. About one-half of the teachers felt that it could be effectively taught in grades other than their own. At the high school level, Levine, McChesney, and Brush (1979) found that the home economics program contained the highest level of nutrition education. Very little time in health and sciences courses was given to the subject. These authors indicated a need for coordination of efforts by teachers of appropriate subjects. Marr, Shannon, and Spanier (1980) found that teachers and administrators in Pennsylvania favored integrating nutrition into existing courses in grades 7 through 12. Support was given for "mini courses," with a preference for integration into health and home economics courses and, to a lesser extent, for biology and physical education. Gould-Gillis and Sabry (1980) found a positive view of the importance of nutrition in day care settings, but the nutrition knowledge of day care teachers was low. They recommended evaluation of preservice training and encouragement of in-service programs. Since the mid-1970s, several research projects have resulted in the development of new curricula. Cooper and Go (1976) reviewed twenty-two curriculum guides and indicated concern about the potential effectiveness of many of them.

A major nutrition education project carried out at Pennsylvania State University has resulted in a number of curriculum and support materials. Sherman, Lewis, and Guthrie (1978) described forty project learning objectives, developed as one step in the identification of appropriate nutrition content for nutrition education curricula. These objectives, defined for the high school graduate, were developed by an interdisciplinary team and surveyed by a group of professional nutritionists. Using a factor analysis of survey responses, Barnette and Branca (1978) arranged eight identified factors in order of priority. Shannon et al. (1981) reported the evaluation of instruction and teacher preparation for the K–12 curriculum developed in this program. They examined three levels of teacher preparation according to student outcomes and found that guidance material prepared the teacher sufficiently without supplementary preparation.

Brown, Wyse, and Hansen (1979) reported on the development of a nutrient density concept in the elementary curriculum. They found that children in grades K–6 possess sufficient academic skills to work with the nutrient density concept.

Talmage, Hughes, and Eash (1978) discussed the role of evaluation research in nutrition education and reviewed the definitions, dimensions, models, and applications for evaluation research procedures. The model was applied to the National Dairy Council curriculum entitled "Food . . . Your Choice." Talmage, Haertel, and Brun (1981) further reported the use of learning environment data to evaluate the effects of a new curriculum at the formative stages of its development.

Several educational approaches have been reported in the literature. Lovett, Baker, and Marcus (1970) and Head (1974) reported the first studies on the effectiveness of nutrition education at various grade levels. Smith and Justice's studies (1979) found that a parent education–student education combination during third grade significantly increased participation in a school lunch program. MacKenzie and Arbor (1979) found that cross-age teaching involving high school students as tutors significantly increased their knowledge. Smith and James (1980) showed that school lunch experiences serve to reinforce classroom learning.

A number of alternatives to traditional methods of teaching nutrition have been tried and reported in the literature. These include the use of comic books for teaching teenagers (Mapes, 1977) and public service announcements for ninth-grade students (Axelson and DelCampo, 1978). The use of a graphic robot figure as opposed to the traditional numerical method of transmitting nutrient-calorie information was tested with 4-year-olds to 10-year-olds by Deitch-Feshback et al. (1978); the use of teams, games, and tournaments was tested by Wodarski et al. (1980); and the comparison of games and audiovisual aids for preadolescents at the sixth-grade level was tested by Cuffaro and Shymko (1980). This last study showed no learning advantage of active games over passive audiovisuals. Spitze (1976) demonstrated a positive reaction to the use of games and other "discovery learning" techniques.

Carver and Lewis (1979) report the development of a knowledge test, which is a useful tool in diagnosing the need for preservice and in-service training of elementary school teachers. Grogan (1978) found, through teacher in-service training, that instructional units can be developed and incorporated into existing curricula to maximize materials and existing resources and minimize effects of scheduling changes.

Various approaches to nutrition education have been explored. Contento (1980) points out problems with various concepts used in curriculum guides, such as the four food groups or a nutrient-density scoring procedure. For example, the values and assumptions expressed by each food group and the kinds of foods contained within these groups can be misleading. The author describes additional issues involved in choice of either the nutrient approach or foods approach. Both the content and underlying values or assumptions implicit in these approaches contribute to national health and optimal use of the current food supply. The literature also provides information about cultural impact and home-based learning, as well as parental influence on children, especially those in the preschool and early school years.

Nutrition educators have had difficulty in developing research with a strong theoretical base. Few of the research efforts have drawn from appropriate theories or methodologies developed by the behavioral sciences. However, there are some reports of studies concerning changes in knowledge. There appears to be very little work reported on attitude and behavioral change resulting from nutrition education. The impact of the Nutrition Education and Training Program has led to attempts to develop some methodologies for evaluating programs; these should emerge in the literature in the near future. Maretzki (1979) defines the problem in the following way: "Teaching nutrition cannot be equated with practicing 'good food habits' any more than teaching reading can be equated with reading 'good books.' Making the distinction between teaching children nutrition facts and enabling them to think about food can help to clarify the hazy relationships which have existed among nutritionists, classroom teachers, and parents in the area of nutrition education" (p. 177).

Policy Concerns.   As concerns about the conservation of energy resources, the world food supply, the population explosion, and the costs of health care maintenance increase, the social implications of nutrition education become more significant. Throughout the 1970s, nutrition education concerns have been involved in policy discussions and developments. Nutrition education should affect all grade levels of children and all school personnel, as well as parents and the community. It should be an integral part of teaching students how to cope with the environment, whether in the form of food costs, information on food labels, or effects of food selection on dental health. If nutrition education is to be nurtured and to grow in the schools, those involved must meet the challenge of bringing ideas and concepts about food and nutrition to bear on the whole range of social, economic, and political problems involved in decision making about food.

Helen D. Ullrich

See also Consumer Economics Education; Health Education; Home Economics Education.

REFERENCES

Axelson, J. M., & DelCampo, D. S. Improving teenagers' nutrition knowledge through the mass media. *Journal of Nutrition Education,* 1978, *10,* 30–33.

Barnette, J. J., & Branca, M. Learner objectives for a nutrition education curriculum—Part two: Factor analysis. *Journal of Nutrition Education*, 1978, *10*, 65–68.

Brown, G.; Wyse, B. W.; & Hansen, R. G. A nutrient density–nutrition education program for elementary schools. *Journal of Nutrition Education*, 1979, *11*, 31–36.

Brun, J. K. (Ed.). *Nutrition Education Research Directions for the Future*. Rosemont, Ill.: National Dairy Council, 1980.

Carver, L. R., & Lewis, K. J. A nutrition knowledge test for elementary school teachers. *Journal of Nutrition Education*, 1979, *11*, 68–71.

Contento, I. Thinking about nutrition education: What to teach, how to teach it, and what to measure. *Teachers College Record*, 1980, *81*, 142–147.

Contento, I.; Olson, C.; Tuckwell, M. H.; Weaver, M.; & Weiss, E. Resolution 8 committee report. *Journal of Nutrition Education*, 1980, *12*, 180.

Cook, C. B.; Eiler, D. A.; & Kaminaka, E. C. How much nutrition education in grades K–6? *Journal of Nutrition Education*, 1977, *9*, 131–135.

Cooper, K. A., & Go, C. E. Analysis of nutrition curriculum guides at the K–12 level. *Journal of Nutrition Education*, 1976, *8*, 62–66.

Cuffaro, C., & Shymko, D. L. Games and audiovisual aids in preadolescent nutrition education. *Journal of Nutrition Education*, 1980, *12*, 162–164.

Curriculum Framework Criteria Committee on Health. *Health Instruction Framework for California Public Schools, Preschool through Young Adult Years*. Sacramento: California State Department of Education, 1978. (ERIC Document Reproduction Service No. ED 152 710)

Deitch-Feshbach, N.; Jordan, T.; Dillman, A.; & Choate, R. A demonstration of the use of graphics in teaching children nutrition. *Journal of Nutrition Education*, 1978, *10*, 124–126.

Dwyer, J. (Ed.). National conference on nutrition education: Directions for the 1980s. *Journal of Nutrition Education*, 1980, *12* (Suppl. 1), 79–137.

Food and Nutrition Board, National Research Council. *Recommended Dietary Allowances* (9th ed.). Washington, D.C.: National Academy of Sciences, 1980. (a)

Food and Nutrition Board, National Research Council. *Toward Healthful Diets*. Washington, D.C.: National Academy of Sciences, 1980. (b)

Gould-Gillis, D. E., & Sabry, J. H. Daycare teachers: Nutrition knowledge, opinions, and use of food. *Journal of Nutrition Education*, 1980, *12*, 200–204.

Grogan, J. Teacher inservice for nutrition education: An interdisciplinary approach in the school system. *Journal of Nutrition Education*, 1978, *10*, 119–120.

Head, M. K. A nutrition education program at three grade levels. *Journal of Nutrition Education*, 1974, *6*, 56–59.

Levine, R. R.; McChesney, A. S.; & Brush, M. K. An assessment of high school nutrition education. *Journal of Nutrition Education*, 1979, *11*, 124–126.

Lovett, R.; Barker, E.; & Marcus, B. The effect of a nutrition education program at the second-grade level. *Journal of Nutrition Education*, 1970, *2*(1), 77–95.

MacKenzie, L., & Arbor, E. Cross-age teaching: An important concept for nutrition education. *Journal of Nutrition Education*, 1979, *11*, 138–140.

Mapes, M. C. "GULP": An alternate method for reaching teens. *Journal of Nutrition Education*, 1977, *9*, 12–16.

Maretzki, A. N. A perspective on nutrition education and training. *Journal of Nutrition Education*, 1979, *11*, 176–180.

Marr, T.; Shannon, B.; & Spanier, G. B. Nutrition education for grades 7–12: The perspective of Pennsylvania teachers and administrators. *Journal of Nutrition Education*, 1980, *12*, 148–152.

Martin, E. A. Historical foundations for nutrition education research. In J. K. Brun (Ed.), *Nutrition Education Research Directions for the Future*. Rosemont, Ill.: National Dairy Council, 1980, pp. 3–16.

McNutt, K. An analysis of dietary goals for the United States (2nd ed.). *Journal of Nutrition Education*, 1978, *10*, 61–62.

Mead, M. *Food Habits Research* (Publ. No. 1225). Washington, D.C.: National Academy of Sciences, National Research Council, 1964.

Nutrition and Your Health, Dietary Guidelines for Americans (Home and Garden Bulletin No. 232). Washington, D.C.: U.S. Department of Agriculture, 1980.

Nutrition education specialists in school systems, K–12: A position paper on functions and qualifications. *Journal of Nutrition Education*, 1978, *10*, 6.

Office of Technology Assessment. *Nutrition Research Alternatives*. Washington, D.C.: U.S. Government Printing Office, 1978.

Olson, C. M., & Gillespie, A. H. (Eds.). Workshop on nutrition education research. *Journal of Nutrition Education*, 1981, *13* (Suppl. 1).

School Health Education Study. *Health Education: A Conceptual Approach to Curriculum Design, Grades Kindergarten through Twelve*. Minneapolis: 3M Educational Press, 1967.

Shannon, B.; Bell, P.; Marbach, E.; O'Connell, L. H.; Graves, K. L.; & Nicely, R. F., Jr. A K–6 nutrition curriculum evaluation: Instruction and teacher preparation. *Journal of Nutrition Education*, 1981, *13*, 9–13.

Sherman, A. R.; Lewis, K. J.; & Guthrie, H. A. Learner objectives for a nutrition education curriculum—Part 1: Identification and priority ranking. *Journal of Nutrition Education*, 1978, *10*, 63–65.

Smith, S. F., & James, M. A. School lunch as a nutrition education resource for fourth-graders. *Journal of Nutrition Education*, 1980, *12*, 46–49.

Smith, H. M., & Justice, C. L. Effects of a nutrition program on third-grade students. *Journal of Nutrition Education*, 1979, *11*, 92.

Spitze, H. T. Curriculum materials and nutrition learning at the high school level. *Journal of Nutrition Education*, 1976, *8*, 59–61.

Talmage, H.; Haertel, G. D.; & Brun, J. K. Using learning environment data in formative curriculum evaluation. *Journal of Nutrition Education*, 1981, *13*, 14–16.

Talmadge, H.; Hughes, M.; & Eash, M. J. The role of evaluation research in nutrition education. *Journal of Nutrition Education*, 1978, *10*, 169–172.

Ullrich, H. D. Congress passes nutrition education bill. *Journal of Nutrition Education*, 1977, *9*, 168A–168D.

Ullrich, H. D., & Briggs, G. M. The general public. In J. Mayer (Ed.), *U.S. Nutrition Policies in the Seventies*. San Francisco: Freeman, 1973, p. 185.

Wodarski, L. A.; Adelson, C. L.; Todd, M. T.; & Wodarski, J. S. Teaching nutrition by teams, games, tournaments. *Journal of Nutrition Education*, 1980, *12*, 61–65.

OPEN LEARNING

See Distance Education.

ORGANIZATION AND ADMINISTRATION OF HIGHER EDUCATION

This article provides an overview of the organization and administration of higher education in the United States and a list of references of pertinent research and commentary on the subject. The article is divided into two major sections. The first section reviews the structural elements of higher education and discusses significant actors and important issues. The second section discusses the administration as a process, links it to the discussion of open systems, and illustrates the interaction of colleges and universities and their environments by referring to three issue areas: autonomy versus accountability, efficiency and effectiveness, and collective bargaining.

The Structure of American Higher Education

Higher education in the United States dates from 1636, the year of the incorporation of Harvard College. After a tenuous beginning, nine students were finally graduated in 1642. All nine pursued the same course of instruction over a three-year period from the same man in the same building. The instructor, who was also the president, provided room and board for the students as well. Today, nearly three and a half centuries later, over 11 million students are enrolled in over 3,100 different institutions of higher education. Each year, more than 1.5 million degrees are awarded in over 300 different fields of study. Over 2 million people are employed in institutions of higher education, and in fiscal year 1977 alone, over $43

billion was expended by these institutions. The property value and assets of the approximately 3,100 institutions totaled more than $84 billion in 1977 (National Center for Education Statistics, 1980).

Five Types of Higher-education Institutions. Even more important than the scope of the enterprise as a whole is the great variety represented in these 3,100 institutions. In size, they range from less than 50 to more than 50,000 students. Various typologies have been used to group similar institutions on a variety of measures (Pace & Stern, 1958; Astin & Holland, 1961; Astin, 1962; Bowen & Minter, 1976). The most recent and well-known typology uses measures of degrees granted, federal support, enrollment, curriculum, and student ability to classify institutions into five broad types.

One hundred eighty-four institutions are classified as doctorate granting. These represent only 6 percent of the total number of institutions, but these universities enroll 27.4 percent of all students, just over 3 million. The doctorate-granting institutions represent a strong commitment to graduate education and research. A second group of institutions are called comprehensive colleges and universities. These may have small graduate programs leading to master's degrees, and they usually have one or more professional programs, such as education or engineering. Nineteen percent (594 institutions) are classified in this major category. However, they enroll about the same number of students as doctorate-granting institutions: 3.2 million students, or 28.4 percent of all students. Another 19 percent of all schools are classified as liberal arts colleges (583 institutions). These schools maintain a strong emphasis on the traditional liberal arts curriculum with its intellectual roots in the trivium (grammar, logic, and rhetoric) and quadrivium (arithmetic, geometry, astronomy, and music). These institutions enroll only about 4.8 percent of all students, or about 531,000. The largest group of institutions are the two-year colleges, offering the first two years of undergraduate education. There are 1,147 institutions classified in this category, representing 37.3 percent of all institutions. Two-year colleges' commitment to teaching and public service is shown in their enrollments: nearly 4 million students are enrolled in two-year-colleges, or 35.6 percent of all students. The fifth group of institutions, specialized institutions, include theological seminaries; business, medical, and law schools; teachers colleges; and technological institutes. They number about 560, or 18.2 percent of all schools. They enroll just over 415,000 students, or only 3.7 percent of all students (Carnegie Council, 1976).

Holistic Framework of Organization and Administration. To many observers, the organization and administration of such a vast and diverse enterprise seem chaotic. Some of the apparent confusion, however, stems from a conception of organization as something static, and of administration as something very routine or merely the implementation of predetermined policies and procedures. A more useful conception views the organization and administration of higher education as dynamic processes, each continually modifying the other in a context of changing issues and multiple constituencies at several societal levels. To even begin to understand such a dynamic system requires a holistic framework of at least four dimensions. A crucial dimension in a holistic framework is time. Ironically, although many good institutional histories have been written, few longitudinal research studies have been conducted on the organization and administration of colleges and universities. The other three dimensions in the holistic framework are the level at which a decision is being made, the participants in the decision-making process, and the issue that is being decided (Mortimer & McConnell, 1978). The following discussion demonstrates how the many actors (e.g., faculty, administrators, governments) interact on different issues at various levels of the higher-education enterprise.

The department. Most colleges and universities are organized along disciplinary lines into departments or divisions. The academic department is the fundamental unit in the institution, because it is the focus of the basic functions of the institution: teaching, research, and service. The department is responsible for providing instruction, offering courses, and establishing degree requirements. In most institutions, instructional faculty also engage in scholarly research. Upon evidence of scholarly achievement in teaching and/or research, faculty are awarded tenure in a department. Faculty also are expected to advise students and participate in faculty and institutional committees. Dressel, Johnson, and Marcus (1970) have reported that functions performed at the departmental level have proliferated in recent years to the detriment of the core functions of teaching and research.

The department head or chair has the responsibility of managing or leading a department and usually consults with the faculty, especially the senior faculty. Decision making within the department usually takes place in committees, where the faculty, department head, and sometimes student representatives participate. Student representation in departmental governance is one of the results of the protest movements of the 1960s. McHenry (1977) has focused on the subject of leadership at the departmental level, while Bragg (1980) has explored the variety of roles different department heads play. Smart and Elton (1976) also focus on the administrative roles of department chairmen. They were able to discern four distinct roles among the department heads they surveyed: "faculty member," "coordinator," "researcher," and "instructor." In some departments, the headship rotates among tenured professors; in others, a department head is appointed for an indefinite period. Various other perspectives on departmental functioning can be found in a volume edited by Smart (1976).

After World War II, some institutions, especially the research-oriented universities, began parallel structures devoted to research on the social and technical problems of the nation (Ikenberry & Friedman, 1972). By 1975, over 5,000 such organized research units (ORUs), as they have come to be called, were counted (Friedman, 1977). These parallel structures differ from departments in a number of ways. They tend not to be disciplinary in scope; they emphasize research much more heavily than teaching or service; and they are much more dependent on outside monies (i.e., grants, contracts, foundation support) than departments. Many ORUs are staffed with professionals who hold similar credentials to faculty, but who do not occupy tenure-track positions (Kruytbosch, 1970).

Colleges and/or schools. At the next level, individual departments collect to form colleges, the leadership of which is entrusted to a dean. The liberal arts college is perhaps the most familiar and oldest, with its intellectual roots in the trivium and quadrivium. Other colleges are more professional in orientation, such as business administration and engineering. Like the functioning of departments, much of the decision making in colleges takes place in committees, with faculty and student representatives from the various constituent departments included. There is a dearth of systematic research on the college as an organizational subunit and on the role of the dean.

Campus: The college president, board of trustees, and campus senate. The college or collection of colleges forms the academic subsystem of the individual campus. In addition to this academic subsystem, a variety of support functions, such as maintenance, auxiliary enterprises, and administrative services, join to define a campus. Coordinating and managing these various subsystems are cadres of administrative personnel ranging from directors of public relations to senior vice-presidents for fiscal affairs to directors of security operations (Knowles, 1970). The proliferation of administrative roles in the past twenty years underscores the increasing complexity of the organization and administration of higher education. The 1977–1978 edition of the National Center for Education Statistics's *Education Directory, Colleges and Universities* listed over 38,000 administrators occupying seventy-five different administrative roles for the approximately 3,100 different campuses. As in the case of deans, there is little research on these administrative roles and their occupants, with the exception of the role of college president (Scott, 1978).

Reflecting its central and highly visible role, the college presidency is perhaps one of the most studied positions in higher education. Almost every account of administration and governance includes a section on the president, and numerous books have been devoted to the subject. In an early book, Dodds (1962) portrays the presidency in a period of transition from an older world of relative simplicity, when the president truly was *primus inter pares*, to a newer, more complicated world of conflicting pressures. He argues the president must recognize and assume the mantle of leadership. The theme of role conflict and ambiguity is again sounded in Cohen and March's study (1974) of the college presidency (see also Kerr, 1972). Kauffman (1980) provides a cogent description of the numerous facets of the role of president and argues it should be conceived in terms of public service. The title of Kauffman's book *At the Pleasure of the Board* emphasizes the special relationship between the college president and the board of trustees: the president is the administrative officer of the board of trustees and serves at its pleasure.

The lay board of trustees is unique to American higher education and dates back to the founding of Harvard (Ingram, 1980). In addition to hiring and firing the president, the board also serves as the ultimate repository of formal authority on campus. Although, in practice, the board delegates much decision-making authority to the president, other administrative offices, and sometimes the faculty itself, that authority may be rescinded, in theory and in the eyes of the appropriate court. A third general function of the board is to maintain the fiscal integrity of the institution. In the eyes of the law, the board holds in trust the charter granting the institution corporate status. (See Nason, 1980, for a detailed description of board responsibilities.)

Two persistent questions about a governing board are "Who are its members?" and "How are they selected?" Both answers depend on whether the institution is public or independent. Although the distinction between the two sectors has blurred a little recently, the composition of governing boards varies most between the two kinds of institutions. Boards of public institutions are more likely to have elected officials sitting *ex officio* than are independent institutions. On the other hand, boards of independent institutions average twenty-six members, whereas boards of public colleges have about nine members (Gomberg & Atelsek, 1977). Principal reasons for larger independent boards are the close relationship board members have with fund raising and the greater fund-raising efforts of independent schools.

Lay governing boards have been critized for their lack of representativeness—they tend to be dominated by relatively wealthy white males over 50 years of age—and for the way in which they are chosen. Boards of independent institutions tend to be self-perpetuating, and boards of public institutions tend either to be appointed by the prevailing political authority or to be chosen in partisan elections. In 1980, a national commission issued fourteen recommendations for improving trustee selection in independent colleges and universities and eighteen recommendations for public instituions (National Commission on College and University Trustee Selection, 1980a, 1980b). Both sets of recommendations encourage more thorough review and broader participation in trustee selection.

Another important governance structure is the campus senate or academic assembly. The existence of a separate decision-making structure, parallel to the administrative subsystem, emphasizes the traditional importance of the faculty and is unique among professional organizations. Millett (1978) reviews thirty case studies of campuswide governance structures in light of four models drawn from the literature. Mortimer and McConnell (1978) outline the roles of academic senates and distinguish three degrees of senate authority: legislative, advisory, and forensic. Mason (1972) has written a handbook that details the variety of senate or council structural arrangements in use around the country. Both Chambers (1973) and Mortimer and McConnell (1978) emphasize the point that senates, like presidents, derive their formal authority from the board of trustees.

Multicampus systems. Most institutions consist of a single campus. However, one of the greatest structural changes in higher education over the past century has been the growth of multicampus systems. According to Lee and Bowen (1971), over 40 percent of all students attend schools that are part of multicampus systems. In effect, the multicampus system adds another administrative layer between the campus and the board. An individual campus may be headed by a president or chancellor who reports to a systemwide administration headed by a system president or chancellor. In their 1975 book, Lee and Bowen discuss some of the advantages and disadvantages of a multicampus system structure in times of scarce resources. They identify as advantages that (1) younger campuses can borrow prestige and stability from older ones; (2) financially pressed campuses can rely on those more abundantly endowed; (3) retrenchment is less likely to affect as many people; and (4) a single, larger university may have more influence in state legislatures. Some of the disadvantages stem from the same elements promoting advantages: (1) intercampus rivalries; (2) unwillingness of more prestigious campuses to underwrite less prestigious campuses; (3) distrust of central administration; and (4) a larger target for legislatures and state agencies with coordinating, budgeting, and control mandates. Lee and Bowen maintain that the advantages can be capitalized on only if the system administration maintains flexibility.

State Government and Higher Education. The separate states invest heavily in their own systems of public higher education, which coexist with the older, more established independent sector. In 1977/1978, publicly controlled institutions in the United States received over $16 billion in revenue from their state governments. This represented just over 50 percent of the total current fund revenue. Of course, there was great variation, ranging from a high of 75.6 percent in the District of Columbia to a low of 23.7 percent in Vermont. By contrast, the independent institutions across the United States received only 2.7 percent of their total current fund revenue from state governments (National Center for Education Statistics, 1980). Between 1949 and 1975, enrollments in the public sector increased 609 percent, while enrollments in the private sector increased only 96 percent (Petersen & Smith, 1975). This explosion in the public sector has resulted in greater efforts at the state level, especially by the executive and legislative branches, to coordinate and control educational resources.

A popular structure at the state level to coordinate and control educational resources is the statewide coordinating board. The responsibility for planning, coordinating, and regulating public higher education is entrusted to such a single state agency in thirty-five states (*Challenge*, 1980). In the remaining fifteen states, several agencies divide the responsibilities.

A recent report by the Education Commission of the States (1980), *Challenge: Coordination and Governance in the 80's*, identifies three major types of boards: consolidated governing boards for all or most types of institutions (twenty-two states), coordinating boards with program-approval authority (eighteen states), and coordinating boards with program-review and recommendation authority only (eight states). The remaining two states have executive-appointed agencies. The report goes on to discuss statewide coordination, control, evaluation, and review in light of the expected limits in the decade of the 1980s. The Carnegie Commission's report (1971) on statewide planning and coordination remains a good introduction to the topic. Halstead (1974) emphasizes the major planning problems facing administrations involved in state coordination systems. Berdahl (1971, 1975) provides an in-depth analysis of the structure, functions, and relationships of various types of state higher-education coordinating agencies.

The independent sector has not been immune to the attempts by such external agencies to assume control. The 1972 education amendments to the Higher Education Act of 1965 emphasized the states' responsibility for statewide planning by authorizing states to designate or create State Postsecondary Commissions for planning in all sectors. As of the end of 1980, all but one state, North Carolina, had designated such a 1202 Commission, as it has come to be called. The lack of promised federal funding to assist the planning process has shifted the emphasis slightly to state-planning agreements, in which states specify agencies responsible for comprehensive planning. According to Millard (1980), the major impact of the 1202 legislation has been to extend the scope of statewide planning beyond the public sector to other segments of postsecondary education in the state.

The Federal Government and Higher Education. Although no mention is made of education in the Constitution, the federal government has not been absent from the scene. Beginning with the 1787 Northwest Ordinance, which supplied funds for educational institutions, the federal government has influenced higher education in a variety of ways. (See Frances, 1980, pp. 22–25, for a list of significant events.)

An exponential increase in federal involvement in higher education has taken place since World War II. The Servicemen's Readjustment Act of 1944, more commonly referred to as the GI Bill, and the establishment of the National Science Foundation in 1950 symbolize the two biggest areas of interest for the postwar government: support for students and scientific research. By 1977, the federal government was spending over $8 billion on student assistance and nearly $5 billion on research and development in colleges and universities. Most of the activity in these two areas emanated from the legislative branch of the federal government.

The influence of the executive branch on higher education has been equally powerful. During the early 1960s, the civil rights movement gained momentum in this country, and it did not take long for its ramifications to reach higher education. Various titles of the 1964 Civil Rights Act, the 1973 education amendments, and executive orders 11245 and 11375 prohibit discrimination against employees and students on the basis of race, color, religion, national origin, or sex. The crucial part of the executive orders is a section calling for a written plan of "affirmative action," designed to overcome deficiencies in the utilization of minority groups and women (Carnegie Council, 1975).

An attempt on the part of one university to give preference to minorities in admission to medical school led to one of the most celebrated Supreme Court cases in recent times and is a good example of the judicial branch of the federal government's involvement in higher education. In 1974, a student, Alan Bakke, was denied admission to the medical school of the University of California at Davis, despite the fact that he scored higher on standardized tests than did sixteen minority applicants who had been accepted as part of the program to admit disadvantaged students. Bakke brought suit against the university, alleging violation of the equal-protection clause of the Fourteenth Amendment to the United States Constitution, a similar provision in the California Constitution, and Title VI of the Civil Rights Act of 1964. The trial court and the State Supreme Court of California ruled in Bakke's favor, and the university appealed to the Supreme Court. More than fifty *amicus curiae* briefs were filed by June 1977, including one by the government in qualified support of the university. In June of 1978, the U.S. Supreme Court ruled against the university, declaring its minority admissions program unconstitutional and ordering Bakke admitted. The decision, however, did not rule that all minority admission programs are unconstitutional, just the program at the University of California at Davis (*Bakke and Beyond,* 1978).

The Supreme Court's involvement in higher education has not been limited to affirmative action and preferential admissions cases. A more recent case has raised basic questions about the role of faculty in institutional governance. Since 1970, the National Labor Relations Board (NLRB) has held that faculty members at private institutions are employees entitled to collective bargaining rights under the National Labor Relations Act. In 1974, the Yeshiva University Faculty Association filed a representation petition with the NLRB. The petition was approved in 1975, and, in the subsequent election, the Faculty Association won the right to represent the faculty in collective negotiations. The university refused to negotiate, however, claiming, as it had all along, that faculty were, in fact, managerial. Eventually, the Court of Appeals for the Second Circuit ruled that the Yeshiva faculty members are, in effect, substantially and pervasively operating the enterprise. The NLRB appealed to the Supreme Court, which refused to overturn the lower court's ruling.

The significance of both of these cases is beyond the scope of this article, except to illustrate the increased role of external constituencies on internal campus governance. To a great extent, the important issues today in higher education arise out of conflict between the various structural levels discussed earlier. In effect, they are issues over the legitimate basis and distribution of authority among levels. More and more, the process of administration is devoted to the resolution of these kinds of conflicts (Balderston, 1974; Corsen, 1975; Epstein, 1974; Mortimer & McConnell, 1978; Richardson, Blocker, & Bender, 1972; Riley & Baldridge, 1977).

The Administration of Higher Education

The elements of the holistic approach to the organization and administration of colleges and universities—time, issue, level, and participants—have to be matched with a process orientation. Administration is a process with several functions, all of which have been a part of the vocabulary of those who study organizations. The more common functions of the administrative process are planning, organizing, directing, staffing, coordinating, reviewing, and budgeting. In this regard, college and university administration is like that of other organizations.

The literature on academic administration has tended to concentrate on colleges and universities as closed rather than open systems (Keeton, 1971). Pfeffer and Salancik (1978) argue that there has not been enough emphasis on the ecology or organizational environments. Under the open systems approach, the basic question becomes how much of the variance in organizational activities can be associated with the environment (external factors) and how much with the organization itself (internal factors).

Katz and Kahn (1966) identify nine characteristics of open systems. The important point to note is the stress put on the environment as a determinant of organizational behavior. The popularity of the open systems approach has arisen in direct reaction to a major failure on the part of organizations like colleges and universities to recognize fully that an organization is continually dependent on inputs from the environment and that the interaction of the organization and its environment is an important consideration in internal decision-making processes.

Models and Metaphors of the Administrative Environment.   The literature on college and university administration as a process stresses a great degree of ambiguity in decision making, in contrast to the literature on efficiency-oriented criteria that tends to characterize discussion of internal decisions. There is a tendency to treat the environment as an uncontrollable force and one that constrains the freedom of the college and university to operate in a predictable fashion. The prevailing administrative environment is one of ambiguity rather than certainty (March & Olsen, 1976).

The bureaucratic model.   One of the basic ambiguities that emerge from the literature of the 1960s and 1970s is the question of the extent to which colleges and universities are similar to or different from other organizations (Perkins, 1973; Baldridge, 1971a, 1971c). Some argue that colleges and universities have many of the basic characteristics of bureaucracies (Stroup, 1966). Their regulation is based on a principle of legal, rational decision making. Their structure is hierarchical and tied together by formal chains of command and systems of communication. Personnel are appointed to office and are paid salaries as a rational form of compensation for their services, and competency is the basis of promotion. Others put a great deal more emphasis on the collegial authority of the faculty, who tend to operate through quasi-autonomous clusters (Anderson, 1963; Clark, 1961; & Millett, 1962).

The political model.   Perhaps the richest of the models is the political model, which, according to Baldridge et al. (1978), is characterized by six assumptions. First, inactivity prevails in decision making: most people most of the time do not participate in decision making. Second, participation in policy making is fluid: people move in and out of the process. Third, colleges and universities, like most other social organizations, are fragmented into separate interest groups with different goals and values. Fourth, conflict is normal. Fifth, authority is limited, and the formal authority system prescribed in the bureaucratic model is severely limited by the political pressure that groups can exert. Sixth, external interest groups are important to understanding the decision-making process. These groups exert a great deal of influence over the policy-making process. In other words, colleges and universities are open rather than closed systems.

Assorted other models.   These models tend to have an influence on the approach that a given author takes to the study of college and university administration. For example, Cohen and March (1974) argue that presidents and other participants within the university are confronted with an assortment of metaphors. The competitive market metaphor describes universities and the services and opportunities they provide simply as a bundle of goods in a free market. Therefore, effective internal governance takes place through the operation of markets, and quality, price, and quantity are determined as in the usual competitive market. The administrative metaphor assumes that the university has well-defined objectives specified by some formal group—ideally the board of trustees. The collective bargaining metaphor assumes that there are fundamentally conflicting interests within the university, and they are resolved by bargaining among representatives of the major parties. The democratic metaphor pictures the university as a community consisting of students, faculty, alumni, citizens, and so forth, and the distribution of formal participation in the electorate is the underlying power question. This metaphor tends to underlie a great many of the suggestions for university reform that dominated the late 1960s and is directly related to another metaphor, the consensus metaphor, describing the situation in which demands are expressed, alternatives considered, and an effort to achieve consensus is made. The anarchy or garbage-can metaphor stresses that each individual in the organization makes autonomous decisions. The faculty decide if, when, and what to teach; students decide if, when, and what to learn; and so forth. In other words, the organization is a loosely connected world, and leaders have relatively modest status in that world. In the anarchy model, there is a constituency without explicit leadership; in the independent judiciary model, there is leadership without an explicit constituency. In the plebiscitary autocracy metaphor, the ruler is chosen by some arbitrary process, and the constituents and the autocrat make all decisions on behalf of the university as long as the electorate considers him or her acceptable.

Organizational Characteristics. Although there is probably no final answer to these fundamental debates, Baldridge and his colleagues offer a useful summary device (1978). Colleges and universities are complex organizations: they have goals, hierarchical systems and structures, officials that carry out specified duties, and all the other characteristics of complex organizations.

There are, however, some critical differences. Goal ambiguity is common in academic organizations. As long as goals are expressed in relatively abstract terms, there is a consensus about the prevailing values of colleges and universities (Gross & Grambsh, 1968, 1974). As soon as they are specified, however, they become highly contested and a source of basic disagreement about fundamental choices within the university (Richman & Farmer, 1974). Second, academic organizations are client-serving institutions. As such, they may be compared fruitfully to public school systems, hospitals, welfare agencies, and other people-processing institutions. Third, colleges and universities have problematic technologies. Serving clients is a difficult task to define, to accomplish, and to evaluate. Fourth, high

professionalism dominates the academic task. Problematic technology demands a highly professional staff, and there are a number of important facts about such employees. Professionals tend to demand work autonomy and freedom from supervision; they tend to have divided loyalties between their professions and the organization that employs them; they experience strong tensions between the professional's values and the bureaucratic expectations of those who manage the organization; and they demand and will accept only peer evaluation of their work. Fifth, professional staff tend to be fragmented in their organization. Faculty expertise is a disunifying, rather than unifying influence on the organization.

These organizational characteristics are tied in fundamental ways to the prevailing value structure that dominates discussions about internal governance in colleges and universities. The value structure emphasizes shared authority between inescapably interdependent parties and the importance of expertise in decisions about curriculum and personnel.

Authority Shared by Faculty and Administration. The widespread acceptance of shared authority as an ideal towards which college and university governance should strive derives largely from the influence of two policy statements on academic government issued in the 1960s, one by the American Association of University Professors in 1966 and the other by the American Association for Higher Education in 1967 (Mortimer & McConnell, 1978; American Association for Higher Education, 1967). Under a system of shared authority, the faculty and the administration (and occasionally the students) have effective influence on a variety of different issues. Faculty influence tends to be heavy on such issues as grading, curriculum matters, academic and faculty personnel policies, faculty economic matters, and tenure and promotion. The administrative influence is more effective on business management and other such matters. Some of the basic conflict that occurs in college and university administration is over the appropriate spheres of influence of administration and faculty, but there appears to be little disagreement in the literature and in the prevailing value structure of academic governance that authority *should* be shared between parties to the enterprise and that the faculty should have a major role in academic governance.

This fundamental consensus about the predominant values of academic administration has been characterized as the prevailing academic ideology (Lunsford, 1970). According to this view, administrators seek to legitimate their authority by building networks of wholly rational decision making. It is through the consultative process, which tends to characterize decision making in colleges and universities, that the administrator legitimates the decisions that one has to make. By referring to myths or metaphors of consensus and shared interests and authority, often combined in a broad reference to the "institutional interests," an administratively dominated situation is sustained. Whether such terms as "shared authority," "consensus," "consistent values," and so forth are accurate descriptions or merely references to a vague ideology is an empirical question that future researchers will need to examine. It is clear, however, that these terms tend to sustain one of the fundamental ingredients of the academic milieu, the link between academic freedom and tenure.

Tenure and academic freedom. According to Metzger (1973), "An academic who traces the history of academic tenure recapitulates the evolution of his species and comes into more knowing terms with himself" (p. 94). In the academic environment, tenure is not merely job security but is intimately tied with academic freedom—the faculty's right to teach and research those areas deemed within the realm of their expertise. An attack on tenure is often, then, equated with an attack on intellectual freedom and the faculty's right to control the use of their expertise. Furthermore, the standards and quality judgments that determine whether a faculty member is granted tenure or is promoted from one rank to the next should be under the control of the faculty (Seldin, 1980; Kirschling, 1978; Commission on Academic Tenure in Higher Education, 1973).

The previous discussion establishes the point that the process of administration in American colleges and universities takes place in a peculiar culture. One of the fundamental characteristics of the open systems approach to academic administration is the interaction of the academic culture with its environment. The resultant conflict is illustrated in the issue-oriented discussion that follows.

Autonomy versus accountability. Colleges and universities are in a continuous debate over the balance between public accountability and institutional autonomy. Although the issue is finding new meaning in the current spate of federal regulations, it is in the context of state coordination of higher education that the debate has been most vigorous and well developed.

In 1971, the Carnegie Commission on Higher Education stated that

under no circumstances can institutional independence be considered absolute. Not even its strongest advocates can seriously question the legitimacy of requiring some degree of public accountability from educational institutions receiving public support. . . . The techniques used to achieve public accountability of educational institutions must be balanced against the need of educational institutions for that degree of institutional independence which is essential for their continued vitality. (p. 104)

The case for institutional independence relies on assumptions about the value of universities and colleges in American society. The commission argued that a viable society requires institutions of higher education to have sufficient independence so that their members feel free to comment upon, criticize, and advise on a variety of policy and practices. Furthermore, the commission believed that creative research and effective teaching require some independence from external control and that this freedom facilitates intelligent planning and management.

Although there is disagreement about the details of ap-

propriate mechanisms and specific decisions over which the state coordinating boards should exercise control and those which should be under the independent control of institutions, there are some general guidelines. For example, it is generally agreed that the number of places available in state institutions, the number and location of new campuses, general admissions policies, general level of budgets, salaries, and even accounting practices are appropriate spheres of influence for the states. On the other hand, a number of people, including the Carnegie Council (1971), have argued that external budget control should be limited to the total amount of the budget but that salary schedules for individual classification should be set by the institution, as well as the mix of faculty and staff at various levels. External authorities, according to the 1971 report, should not be involved in the development of admissions policies or in the decisions on individual admissions or applicants. The hiring, firing, and assignment of faculty and staff are institutional matters, as are building, equipment, and design. Furthermore, the colleges and universities should be assured the essential elements of academic freedom if they are to exist and function as educational institutions. These elements include, but are not limited to, the appointment and promotion of faculty and administrators, the content and termination of courses of instruction, the selection of individual students and awarding of degrees, the selection and conduct of individual research projects, and the freedom to publish or otherwise disseminate research results.

Another context for the discussion of autonomy and accountability is the relationship of faculty to the institution that employs them. Baldridge et al. (1978) and Blau (1973) are fundamentally concerned about the relationship between bureaucracy and professional autonomy in academic work. Baldridge made three findings. (1) The degree of formal control over an institution does not necessarily predict the levels of bureaucratization of professional autonomy within it: "The variations in bureaucratic roles and professional autonomy seem to have to do more with institutional quality than with whether they are state or private. Among the public institutions are some of the very best, and among the private institutions are some of the very worst. And the higher quality public institutions have far more professional autonomy than the lower quality private ones" (p. 120). (2) The more wealthy the institution, the less bureaucratization and the more professional autonomy there is. In short, rich institutions hire better faculty, who in turn receive more autonomy. And (3) when faculty perceive external interference to be high, bureaucratization is high, and faculty autonomy is low. Here one seems to have an empirical link and a positive association between outside influence and feelings of faculty autonomy. The greater the bureaucratization, the lower the faculty's professional autonomy.

Efficiency and Effectiveness. Another of the fundamental conceptual debates in American higher education concerns efficiency and effectiveness (Cameron, 1978). The open systems model concentrates more attention on effectiveness as a measure of external importance and efficiency as a matter of internal control.

According to Bowen (1980), the underlying concepts are two: the use of resources involves an opportunity cost and results in an outcome, and efficiency is measured or judged as a ratio between the outcome and the costs. The discussions about efficiency in higher education frequently make two errors. The first is to judge efficiency only in relation to cost, without a concomitant attention to outcomes. That is, it is assumed, without any attention given to the results and/or outcome, that an institution that can educate a student for $2,000 a year is somehow more efficient than one that spends $3,000 a year. The second error is to judge efficiency only in relation to outcomes. It is assumed that improved outcomes are desirable regardless of cost.

Bowen (1980) and others (Mortimer & McConnell, 1978) argue that assessing institutional outcomes is directly related to the concept of educational effectiveness, or what some refer to as "accountability for student learning": "At present, institutions know very little about their results and next to nothing about the effects of changes in their procedures and methods on the results. There have been sporadic one-time studies of outcomes in particular institutions and also a number of one-time studies of small samples of institutions, but few systematic ongoing efforts to assess outcomes and certainly few cases where the study of outcomes has been linked with either accountability or management" (Bowen, 1980, p. 169).

Mortimer and McConnell (1978) describe the difficulties of measuring effectiveness, that is, the amount of value absorbed by a college student from the college experience: (1) few institutions have determined their goals and can formulate measures of their impact on students; (2) the personal characteristics of some students make them more educable, or ready or eager to learn, than others, and it would be necessary to have better measures of student inputs if one is to concentrate on outputs; (3) students of varying background skills and interests and educability will require multiple measures of impact, a technical task of no small significance; and (4) students often undergo changes that are not attributable to the college experience, and isolation of these makes the task more difficult (see also Cameron, 1978). The difficulties in assessing education outcomes make it easier for administrators and others concerned with colleges and universities to accept measures of educational efficiency that tend to be easy to determine.

Collective Bargaining. Another example of the interaction between internal and external forces is revealed in the move to faculty collective bargaining that occurred in the 1970s. At the beginning of the decade, few faculty were unionized, but, in 1980, faculty were represented by unions at almost 700 campuses. About 60 percent of these 700 campuses were public community colleges, and about 80 percent of them were public institutions.

The rise of faculty bargaining is directly related to a change in the attitude of public agencies about colleges and universities (Garbarino, 1975; Kemerer & Baldridge, 1975). In 1970, the National Labor Relations Board reversed its previous position and brought all private institutions with gross revenues of over $1 million under the jurisdiction of the National Labor Relations Act. Public institutions were affected by changed public and legislative attitudes about the appropriateness of collective bargaining for employees of state and local governments. Public employees received collective bargaining rights in approximately twenty-five states, and college and university faculty were included in that legislation, normally without consultation with university officials.

Collective bargaining as a process requires that an outside agency examine the extent to which an appropriate bargaining unit has been identified. This process involves determining the answers to some uncomfortable question, such as "What are the distinctions between managers and faculty?" "Which professional employees share a community of interest?" "Are department heads or chairs really management or are they basically faculty?" Where the administration and faculty unions are unable to agree about such matters, public-employee relations boards or the National Labor Relations Board decides the issue.

Once these matters have been decided, an election is held under the direction of the appropriate labor board. Once a faculty union has been determined, negotiations take place within a legal structure determined by precedents set in the industrial sector since the 1930s. The question of the applicability of such standards to academic practice is a major point of dispute in such negotiations, and the answer may require litigation. The *Yeshiva* decision, discussed earlier, is a classic example of such litigation. The Supreme Court eventually ruled that, in a mature university, the faculty wield authority that, in any other context, would unquestionably be managerial.

It is clear that the process of negotiation requires that the parties assume that there is a fundamental conflict of interest between managers and employees that the parties behave accordingly. In negotiation, this fundamental conflict often results in impasses. In the administration of contracts, it may lead to grievance settlements through binding arbitration. Since about 75 percent of the contracts negotiated in higher education end in binding arbitration, the appropriate role of external parties in looking at internal decisions again becomes an issue (Angell et al., 1977; Begin, Settle, & Alexander, 1975).

The Context of the 1980s

Since the context and culture of college and university administration give it its uniqueness, a word about the changing conditions of the 1980s is appropriate (Mortimer & Tierney, 1979; Carnegie Council on Policy Studies in Higher Education, 1980). It is fairly clear that the country is undergoing some fundamental demographic changes that are likely to have substantial impact on institutions of higher learning. It is likely that the nation will encounter at least a 19 or 20 percent decline in the number of 18-year-olds between 1980 and 1990. This will mean a concomitant decline in the potential pool of college students of traditional age. The second part of this demographic shift appears to be a change in student preference patterns away from the traditional liberal arts towards more professional or career-related choices. The extent to which institutions will have to be involved in reallocating existing resources in a time of declining environment will occupy substantial attention in the 1980s. Finally, it is not yet clear whether the impact of the inflation or the "cost-income" squeeze will continue. It is clear that creative talent will have to manage a growing gap between institutional revenues and institutional expenditures. Researchers currently do not have the longitudinal capacities necessary to assess the impact of declining environments on internal college and university administration.

Kenneth P. Mortimer
Stephen M. Bragg

See also Accreditation; Admission to Colleges and Universities; Curriculum and Instruction in Higher Education; Financing Colleges and Universities; Graduate Education; Higher Education; History and Philosophy of Higher Education.

REFERENCES

American Association for Higher Education. *Faculty Participation in Academic Governance*. Washington, D.C.: National Education Association, 1967. (ERIC Document Reproduction Service No. ED 018 850)

American Association of University Professors. Statement on government of colleges and universities. *AAUP Bulletin*, 1966, *52*(4), 375–379.

Anderson, G. L. The organizational character of American colleges and universities. In T. F. Lunsford (Ed.), *The Study of Academic Administration*. Boulder, Colo.: Western Interstate Commission for Higher Education, 1963.

Angell, G. W.; Kelley, E. P., Jr.; & Associates. *Handbook of Faculty Bargaining*. San Francisco: Jossey-Bass, 1977.

Astin, A. W. An empirical characterization of higher education. *Journal of Educational Psychology*, 1962, *53*(5), 224–235.

Astin, A. W., & Holland, J. L. The environmental assessment technique: A way to measure college environments. *Journal of Educational Psychology*, 1961, *52*, 308–316.

Bakke and Beyond. Denver, Colo.: Education Commission of the States, 1978.

Balderston, F. E. *Managing Today's University*. San Francisco: Jossey-Bass, 1974.

Baldridge, J. V. (Ed.). *Academic Governance: Research on Institutional Politics and Decision Making*. Berkeley, Calif.: McCutchan, 1971. (a)

Baldridge, J. V. Images of the future and organizational change: The case of New York University. In *Academic Governance*. Berkeley, Calif.: McCutchan, 1971. (b)

Baldridge, J. V. *Power and Conflict in the University*. New York: Wiley, 1971. (c)

Baldridge, J. V.; Curtis, D. V.; Ecker, G.; & Riley, G. L. *Policy Making and Effective Leadership*. San Francisco: Jossey-Bass, 1978.

Begin, J. P.; Settle, T.; & Alexander, P. *Academics on Strike*. New Brunswick: Institute of Management and Labor Relations, 1975.

Berdahl, R. O. *Statewide Coordination of Higher Education*. Washington, D.C.: American Council on Education, 1971.

Berdahl, R. O. (Ed.). *Evaluating Statewide Boards*. San Francisco: Jossey-Bass, 1975.

Blau, P. M. *The Organization of Academic Work*. New York: Wiley, 1973.

Bowen, H. R. *The Costs of Higher Education*. San Francisco: Jossey-Bass, 1980.

Bowen, H. R., & Minter, W. J. *Private Higher Education: Second Annual Report on Financial and Educational Trends in the Private Sector of American Higher Education*. Washington, D.C.: Association of American Colleges, 1976.

Bragg, A. K. *Relationship between the Role Definition and Socialization of Academic Department Heads*. Unpublished doctoral dissertation, Pennsylvania State University, 1980.

Cameron, K. Measuring organizational effectiveness in institutions of higher education. *Administrative Science Quarterly*, December 1978, *23*(4), 604–632.

Carnegie Commission on Higher Education. *Capitol and Campus: State Responsibility for Postsecondary Education*. New York: McGraw-Hill, 1971.

Carnegie Commission on Higher Education. *Higher Education: Who Pays? Who Benefits? Who Should Pay?* New York: McGraw-Hill, 1973.

Carnegie Council on Policy Studies in Higher Education. *Making Affirmative Action Work in Higher Education*. San Francisco: Jossey-Bass, 1975.

Carnegie Council on Policy Studies in Higher Education. *A Classification of Institutions of Higher Education*. Berkeley, Calif.: Carnegie Foundation for the Advancement of Teaching, 1976.

Carnegie Council on Policy Studies in Higher Education. *Three Thousand Futures*. San Francisco: Jossey-Bass, 1980.

Carr, R., & Van Eyck, D. *Collective Bargaining Comes to the Campus*. Washington, D.C.: American Council on Education, 1973.

Challenge: Coordination and Governance in the Eighties. Denver, Colo.: Education Commission of the States, 1980.

Chambers, M. M. *The Colleges and the Courts: Faculty and Staff before the Bench*. Danville, Ill.: Interstate, 1973.

Clark, B. R. Faculty authority. *American Association of University Professors Bulletin*, 1961, *47*(4), 471.

Clark, B. R. *The Distinctive College: Antioch, Reed, and Swarthmore*. Chicago: Aldine, 1970.

Cohen, M. D., & March, J. G. *Leadership and Ambiguity: The American College President*. New York: McGraw-Hill, 1974.

Commission on Academic Tenure in Higher Education. *Faculty Tenure*. San Francisco: Jossey-Bass, 1973.

Corsen, J. J. *The Governance of Colleges and Universities*. New York: McGraw-Hill, 1975.

Dodds, H. W. *The Academic President: Educator or Caretaker?* New York: McGraw-Hill, 1962.

Dressel, P. L.; Johnson, F. C.; & Marcus, P. M. *The Confidence Crisis*. San Francisco: Jossey-Bass, 1970.

Epstein, L. B. *Governing the University*. San Francisco: Jossey-Bass, 1974.

Frances, C. Influence of federal programs. In P. Jedamus & M. W. Peterson (Eds.), *Improving Academic Management*. San Francisco: Jossey-Bass, 1980.

Friedman, R. C. *The Continuing Saga of Institutes and Centers*. University Park: Pennsylvania State University, 1977.

Garbarino, J. W., & Aussieker, B. *Faculty Bargaining: Change and Conflict*. New York: McGraw-Hill, 1975.

Gomberg, I. L., & Atelsek, F. J. *Composition of College and University Governing Boards* (Higher Education Panel Report No. 35). Washington, D.C.: American Council on Education, 1977.

Gross, E., & Grambsh, P. V. *University Goals and Academic Power*. Washington, D.C.: American Council on Education, 1968.

Gross, E., & Grambsh, P. V. *Changes in University Organization, 1964–1971*. New York: McGraw-Hill, 1974.

Halstead, D. K. *Statewide Planning in Higher Education*. Washington, D.C.: U.S. Government Printing Office, 1974.

Ikenberry, S. O., & Friedman, R. C. *Beyond Academic Departments: The Story of Institutes and Centers*. San Francisco: Jossey-Bass, 1972.

Ingram, R. T., & Associates. *Handbook on College and University Trusteeship*. San Francisco: Jossey-Bass, 1980.

Katz, D., & Kahn, R. L. *The Social Psychology of Organizations*. New York: Wiley, 1966.

Kauffman, J. *At the Pleasure of the Board*. Washington, D.C.: American Council on Education, 1980.

Keeton, M. *Shared Authority on Campus*. Washington, D.C.: American Association for Higher Education, 1971.

Kemerer, F. R., & Baldridge, J. W. *Unions on Campus*. San Francisco: Jossey-Bass, 1975.

Kerr, C. *The Uses of the University*. Cambridge, Mass.: Harvard University Press, 1972.

Kirschling, W. R. (Ed.). *Evaluating Performances and Vitality: New Directions for Institutional Research*. San Francisco: Jossey-Bass, 1978.

Knowles, A. *Handbook of College and University Administration*. New York: McGraw-Hill, 1970.

Kruytbosch, C. E. Unequal peers: The situation of researchers at Berkeley. In C. E. Kruytbosch & S. L. Messinger (Eds.), *The State of the University*. Beverly Hills, Calif.: Sage, 1970.

Kruytbosch, C. E., & Messinger, S. L. (Eds.). *The State of the University: Authority and Change*. Beverly Hills, Calif.: Sage, 1970.

Ladd, E. D., Jr., & Lipset, S. M. *Professors, Unions, and American Higher Education*. Berkeley, Calif.: Carnegie Commission on Higher Education, 1973.

Lee, E. C., & Bowen, F. M. *The Multicampus University*. New York: McGraw-Hill, 1971.

Lee, E. C., & Bowen, F. M. *Managing Multicampus Systems*. San Francisco: Jossey-Bass, 1975.

Lunsford, T. F. Authority and ideology in the administered university. In C. E. Kruytbosch & S. L. Messinger (Eds.), *The State of the University*. Beverly Hills, Calif.: Sage, 1970.

March, J. G., & Olsen, J. P. *Ambiguity and Choice in Organization*. Bergen, Sweden: Universitebsforlaget, 1976.

Mason, H. L. *College and University Government: A Handbook of Principle and Practice*. New Orleans: Tulane University, 1972.

McHenry, D. E., & Associates. *Academic Departments*. San Francisco: Jossey-Bass, 1977.

Metzger, W. P. Academic tenure in America: A historical essay. In *Faculty Tenure*. San Francisco: Jossey-Bass, 1973.

Millard, R. M. Power of state coordinating agencies. In P. Jedamus & M. W. Peterson (Eds.), *Improving Academic Management*. San Francisco: Jossey-Bass, 1980.

Millett, J. D. *The Academic Community: An Essay on Organization*. New York: McGraw-Hill, 1962.

Millett, J. D. *New Structures of Campus Power*. San Francisco: Jossey-Bass, 1978.

Mortimer, K. P., & McConnell, T. R. *Sharing Authority Effectively*. San Francisco: Jossey-Bass, 1978.

Mortimer, K. P., & Tierney, M. L. *The Three "R's" of the Eighties: Reduction, Reallocation, and Retrenchment*. Washington, D.C.: American Association for Higher Education, 1979.

Nason, J. W. Responsibilities of the governing board. In R. T. Ingram & Associates (Eds.), *Handbook of College and University Trusteeship*. San Francisco: Jossey-Bass, 1980.

National Center for Education Statistics. *Education Directory: Colleges and Universities, 1977–1978*. Washington, D.C.: U.S. Government Printing Office, 1978.

National Center for Education Statistics. *Digest of Educational Statistics, 1979*. Washington, D.C.: U.S. Government Printing Office, 1980.

National Commission on College and University Trustee Selection. *Recommendations for Improving Trustee Selection in Private Colleges and Universities*. Washington, D.C.: Association for Governing Boards, 1980. (a)

National Commission on College and University Trustee Selection. *Recommendations for Improving Trustee Selection in Public Colleges and Universities*. Washington, D.C.: Association for Governing Boards, 1980. (b)

Pace, C. R., & Stern, G. G. An approach to the measurement of psychological characteristics of college environments. *Journal of Educational Psychology*, 1958, *49*, 269–277.

Perkins, J. A. (Ed.). *The University as an Organization*. New York: McGraw-Hill, 1973.

Petersen, R. J., & Smith, C. R. *Migration of College Students: Preliminary Analysis of Trends in College Student Migration*. Washington, D.C.: National Center for Education Statistics, 1975.

Pfeffer, J., & Salancik, G. R. *The External Control of Organizations: A Resource Dependence Perspective*. New York: Harper & Row, 1978.

Richardson, R. C., Jr.; Blocker, C. E.; & Bender, L. W. *Governance for the Two-year College*. Englewood Cliffs, N.J.: Prentice-Hall, 1972.

Richman, B. M., & Farmer, R. M. *Leadership, Goals, and Power in Higher Education*. San Francisco: Jossey-Bass, 1974.

Riley, G. L., & Baldridge, J. V. *Governing Academic Organizations*. Berkeley, Calif.: McCutchan, 1977.

Scott, R. A. *Lords, Squires, and Yeomen: Collegiate Middle Managers and Their Organizations*. Washington, D.C.: American Association for Higher Education, 1978.

Seldin, P. *Successful Faculty Evaluation Programs: A Practical Guide to Improve Faculty Performance and Promotion-Tenure Decisions*. New York: Coventry Press, 1980.

Smart, J. C. Examining departmental management. In *New Directions for Institutional Research*. San Francisco: Jossey-Bass, 1976.

Smart, J. C., & Elton, C. F. Administrative roles of department chairmen. In J. C. Smart & J. R. Montgomery, *Examining Departmental Management: New Directions for Institutional Research*. San Francisco: Jossey-Bass, 1976.

Stroup, H. *Bureaucracy in Higher Education*. New York: Free Press, 1966.

OUTDOOR EDUCATION

See Environmental Education; Recreation.

P

PARAPROFESSIONALS

See Teacher Aides.

PARENT EDUCATION

The development of programs concerned with educating or reeducating parents has become a significant educational thrust, particularly in early childhood education. A number of factors are responsible for the renewed interest in parent education programs, which have a history dating back to the 1800s; as a consequence, a variety of forms and emphases have emerged. Although the overall effectiveness of several types of parent education efforts has been supported, there has been relatively little systematic examination of the significance of the various specific facets of the programs. Therefore, although guidelines and suggestions for program development are available, many implementation issues and questions remain.

A wide range of activities have occurred and contine to occur under the term "parent education." In the broadest sense, the generalized familial and cultural transmission of child-rearing values, skills, and techniques can be considered parent education. Strictly speaking, however, the term "parent education" is used to denote organized activities that have been developed in order to further parents' abilities to raise their children successfully. Because of the variability in philosophical convictions and theoretical positions regarding what constitutes successful parenting, as well as what parents need to be able to know and do in order to achieve that end, organized parent education programs have reflected these differences.

In recounting the history of education for child rearing, Brim (1965) reports that the early group meetings of parents (those occurring in the 1800s) were concerned with the moral and religious improvement of their children. The wisdom and strength needed to fulfill this aim were provided by group discussion of problems, prayer, and reference to biblical texts.

The 1880s marked the beginning of formal organizations for parent education, which expanded both the extent and variety of parent education programs. By 1935, "the U.S. Office of Education catalogued the agencies, public and private which had programs in this field, with the list covering 53 pages. Noteworthy expansion occurred in the public schools and in nursery school and preschool settings" (Brim, 1965, p. 333). Programs during this time were concerned with a multitude of topics, including child welfare, child study, child development, child behavior, child care, nutrition and health, mental hygiene, and home management and family living. The major emphasis was on parent's role in dealing with the physical, social, and emotional needs and problems of the child in the context of the home and family.

During the 1940s and 1950s, parent education programming began to place major emphasis on mental health as a means of preventing mental illness. The shift in emphasis began because the mental health screening procedures employed during World War II revealed a high prevalence of mental illness. In addition, the passage of the National Mental Health Act in 1946, which provided federal funds for community mental health programs including parent education, furthered this direction. In working with parents, attention was directed towards influencing child-rearing practices in order to promote the mental health of children, and thus to prevent mental illness. The availability of substantial funds in the area of mental health during the 1950s stimulated the growth and expansion of these parent education activities. For example, at the national level, the Department of Agriculture developed materials and provided direct-contact extension programs for families; in the Department of Health, Education, and Welfare, the Division of State and Local Systems developed programs to train teachers for more effective counseling of parents; the Social Security Administration's Division of Health Services' Nursing Section emphasized the professional training of nurses for leadership in parent education; and the National Institute of Mental Health funded research to assess the effects of parent education. In addition, various national organizations and corporations, state departments and agencies, colleges and universities, community groups, and individuals provided extensive and varied parent education publications, activities, and services.

A number of social, political, economic, and educational events which changed, developed, or converged during the 1960s and 1970s resulted in a refocusing of attention on a variety of problems affecting children and families. Among the more important of these events and problems were (1) the civil rights movement, which brought attention to the economic and educational deprivation of minorities; (2) increased occupational mobility, which drastically reduced the opportunities for intergenerational and neighborhood provisioning of child-rearing information, modeling, and support; (3) the increasing number of single-parent families, reconstituted families, and blended families, together with the expanding career opportunities for women, which brought about significant changes in family structures, patterns, problems, and relationships for which little experiential guidance was available; (4) increasing educational costs, declining achievement scores, growing distrust of bureaucratic institutions, feelings of alienation, and a renewed interest in the basic American concept of participatory democracy, all of which caused renewed emphasis to be placed on the rights, responsibilities, and influence of parents to effect significant changes. Again, as in the past, parent education programs emerged in response to these difficult social and educational problems and the changing cultural and societal norms.

Parent education programs have been developed (1) to help parents of children with special needs (mentally, physically, and learning disabled; socially, emotionally, and behaviorally disturbed) deal with family adjustment problems and with the behavior, development, and educational needs of the children (e.g., Forehand & King, 1977; Gardner, 1976; Levitt & Cohen, 1976; Miller & Sloan, 1976); (2) to further parents' general knowledge about family life and basic child-rearing practices and the development of positive parent-child relationships (e.g., Cantoni, 1975; Cox & Matthews, 1977; Koegel, 1978; Sutherland, 1980); (3) to aid prospective parents in preparing for parenthood (e.g., Fuchs, 1979; Radeloff, 1978; Rickett & Towns, 1980); (4) to assist families in adjusting to, caring for, and stimulating their infants (e.g., Charnley & Myre, 1977; Kleinman, 1977); (5) to teach parents techniques for changing their children's attitudes and behaviors (e.g., Donofrio, 1976; Forehand & King, 1977; Gardner, 1976; Horne, 1974); (6) to help parents change their own negative behaviors toward their children and lessen the chance for child abuse and neglect (e.g., Daniel & Hyde, 1975; Davoren, 1975);

(7) to assist teenage, school-age parents in adjusting to their role as parents (e.g., Carta, 1976; Malony, 1978; Robertson, 1978); (8) to aid adoptive parents and foster parents in carrying out their special parenting role (e.g., Paget & Thierry, 1976); (9) to provide parents with health, nutrition, and sex education information (e.g., Murrah, 1967; Scales & Everly, 1977); (10) to help parents deal with adolescents (e.g., Dougherty & Dyal, 1976); (11) to provide information about gifted and talented children (e.g., Colangelo & Pfleger, 1977); (12) to help parents become aware of their rights (e.g., Markel, 1976); (13) to educate parents about education and to teach parents to become involved in the schools and to assume leadership roles regarding educational decision making (e.g., Lichtman, 1974; Roehm, 1977); and (14) to teach parents how to assist in the education process and to further the cognitive development and achievement level of their children—the area of probably the greatest interest to educators (e.g., Andrews et al., 1975; Goldman, 1973; Gordon, 1973; Grantham-McGregor & Desai, 1975; Gray & Klaus, 1970; Henderson & Garcia, 1973; Johnson et al., 1974; Karnes, 1968; Karnes et al., 1970; Kogan & Gordon, 1975; Lasater et al., 1975; Levenstein, 1970, 1974; Radin, 1969, 1972; Sandler et al., 1973; Weikart, 1973; Wittes & Radin, 1971).

From a review of the literature on parent education, it becomes clear that although there is an abundance of enthusiastic testimony regarding the effectiveness of various programs in reaching their goals, only a relatively small number of programs have collected empirical data to substantiate their claims. Furthermore there have been even fewer attempts to systematically relate specific characteristics of effective programs to their outcomes. Therefore in order to establish some conclusions about the nature and conditions of effective parent education programs, specific results are examined in this article only in terms of the area for which the most extensive research has been conducted. Thus, the rest of this article concerns research results from parent education programs designed to train parents—particularly low-income parents—how to teach their children in order to prevent or remediate basic cognitive and school achievement deficiencies.

There is considerable evidence that parent education programs are effective in improving the intellectual functioning of children as measured primarily on standardized intelligence tests (Andrews et al., 1975; Gordon, 1973; Grantham-McGregor & Desai, 1975; Gray & Klaus, 1970; Johnson et al., 1974; Karnes, 1968; Karnes et al., 1970; Lasater et al., 1975; Levenstein, 1970; Radin, 1969, 1972; Weikart, 1973; Wittes & Radin, 1971). There is also evidence that the gains achieved have been sustained for at least one year—and in several cases for three, four, and five years—after completion of the program (Gordon, 1973; Gray & Klaus, 1970; Levenstein, 1974; Radin, 1972). Evidence also indicates significant improvements in children's language performance (Andrews et al., 1975; Henderson & Garcia, 1973; Lasater et al., 1975); in their performance on standardized achievement tests (Gray & Klaus, 1970; Weikart, 1973); and in their general school behavior (Levenstein, 1974; Weikart, 1973).

Moreover, significant positive changes have been shown in parents' teaching styles, in their interactions with their children, and in the provisioning of more stimulating home learning environments (Andrews et al., 1975; Gray & Klaus, 1970; Kogan & Gordon, 1975; Lasater et al., 1975; Sandler et al., 1973; Weikart, 1973). These areas of parental behaviors are considered of critical importance in influencing the intellectual development and school achievement orientations of children.

There is less direct evidence regarding the relationships of specific program characteristics and program effectiveness. Some indications can be drawn, however, from the program analysis works of Goodson and Hess (1975, 1976) and Stevens (1978). These analyses, which were supported by this review of research, cautiously suggest that (1) programs that use home visits by either professional or paraprofessionals, either alone or in combination with preschool classes for children, are apparently more effective in bringing about cognitive gains in children than programs utilizing parent classes also alone or in combination with preschool classes; (2) programs that place a high emphasis on the parent-teaching component produce more stable, long-term gains in children, although both the high- and medium-emphasis programs produce positive long-term effects; (3) no one type of program content (language development, sensorimotor development, cognitive development, child development principles, etc.) appears more effective than another; (4) a one-to-one parent-teacher relationship produces greater effects than a group instructional relationship; (5) highly structured, prescriptive, concrete tasks for parents produce more stable gains than less structured programs; (6) there is no difference in the effectiveness of programs that teach parents specific teaching techniques versus programs that encourage a general style of interaction; (7) programs that are most effective in producing considerable changes in both children and parents involve long-term consultation for a minimum of 18 to 24 months; and (8) effective programs are both prescriptive (attempting quality control through clearly specified goals, objectives, activities, and careful monitoring) and personalized (emphasizing the modification of content to achieve a proper fit for each parent-child dyad).

In conclusion, although a great deal more remains to be learned about which aspects of parent education programs contribute to their effectiveness, it can be said with confidence that parent education programs are effective in teaching parents, particularly low-income parents, how to help their children avoid or remediate basic cognitive and school achievement deficiencies.

Rhoda McShane Becher

See also Adult Education; Home-School Relationships; Women's Education.

REFERENCES

Andrews, S. R.; Blumenthal, J. M.; Bache, W. L.; & Wiener, G. The New Orleans Model: Parents as Early Childhood Educators. Paper presented at the biennial meeting of the Society for Research in Child Development, Denver, April 1975.

Brim, O. G. Education for Child Rearing. New York: Russell Sage, 1965.

Cantoni, L. Family life education: A treatment modality. Child Welfare, 1975, 54(9), 658–665.

Carta, E. Education for School-age Parenting: Final Report. Norwalk, Conn.: Norwalk Board of Education, 1976. (ERIC Document Reproduction Service No. ED 138 716)

Charnley, L., & Myre, G. Parent-infant education. Children Today, 1977, 6(2), 18–21.

Colangelo, N., & Pfleger, L. R. A model counseling laboratory for the gifted at Wisconsin. Gifted Child Quarterly, 1977, 21(3), 321–325.

Cox, W. D., & Matthews, C. D. Parent group education: What does it do for the children? Journal of School Psychology, 1977, 15(4), 349–356.

Daniel, J. H., & Hyde, J. N. Working with high-risk families. Children Today, 1975, 4(6), 23–25, 36.

Davoren, E. Working with abusive parents. Children Today, 1975, 4(3), 2–6.

Donofrio, A. F. Parent education as child psychotherapy. Psychology in the Schools, 1976, 13(2), 176–180.

Dougherty, A. M., & Dyal, M. Community involvement: Training parents as tutors in a junior high. School Counselor, 1976, 23(5), 353–356.

Forehand, R., & King, H. E. Noncompliant children: Effects of parent training behavior and attitude change. Behavior Modification, 1977, 1(1), 93–108.

Fuchs, K. D. The relationship between childbirth education and mother and infant characteristics during feeding. 1979. (ERIC Document Reproduction Service No. ED 172 957)

Gardner, H. L. Time-out with children: Effects of an explanation and brief parent-training on child and parent behaviors. Journal of Abnormal Child Psychology, 1976, 4(3), 277–288.

Goldman, R. Cross-cultural adaptation of a program to involve parents in their children's learning. Child Welfare, 1973, 52(8), 521–532.

Goodson, B. D., & Hess, R. D. Parents as Teachers of Young Children: An Evaluative Review of Some Contemporary Concepts and Programs. Washington, D.C.: Bureau of Educational Development (DHEW/OE), 1975. (ERIC Document Reproduction Service No. ED 136 967)

Goodson, B. D., & Hess, R. D. The Effects of Parent Training Programs on Child Performance and Parent Behaviors. 1976. (ERIC Document Reproduction Service No. ED 136 912)

Gordon, I. J. The Florida Parent-education Early Intervention Projects: A Longitudinal Look. Gainesville: Institute for Development of Human Resources, College of Education, University of Florida, 1973.

Grantham-McGregor, S. M., & Desai, P. A home visiting intervention programme with Jamaican mothers and children. Developmental Medicine and Child Neurology, 1975, 17, 605–613.

Gray, S., & Klaus, R. The early training project: A seventh-year report. Child Development, 1970, 41 909–924.

Henderson, R. W., & Garcia, A. B. The effects of a parent-training program on question-asking behavior of Mexican-American children. American Educational Research Journal, 1973, 10, 193–201.

Horne, A. Teaching parents a reinforcement program. *Elementary School Guidance and Counseling*, 1974, *9*(2), 102–107.

Johnson, D.; Leler, H.; Rios, L.; Brandt, L.; Kahn, A. J.; Mazeika, E.; Frede, M.; & Bissett, B. The Houston parent-child development center: A parent education program for Mexican-American families. *American Journal of Ortho-Psychiatry*. 1974, *44*(1), 121–128.

Karnes, M. B. An approach for working with mothers of disadvantaged preschool children. *Merrill-Palmer Quarterly*, 1968, *14*(2), 1974–184.

Karnes, M. B.; Teska, J. A.; Hodgins, A. S.; & Badger, E. D. Educational intervention at home by mothers of disadvantaged infants. *Child Development*, 1970, *41*, 925–935.

Kleinman, H. M. Effects of a mother-infant program on positive feelings of new mothers: A pilot investigation, 1977. (ERIC Document Reproduction Service No. ED 140 949)

Koegel, R. L. Generalization of parent-training results. *Journal of Applied Behavior and Analysis*, 1978, *11*(1), 95–109.

Kogan, K. L., & Gordon, B. N. A mother-instruction program documenting change in mother-child interactions. *Child Psychiatry and Human Development*, 1975, *5*, 189–200.

Lasater, T. M.; Briggs, J.; Malone, P.; Gilliom, C. F.; & Weisberg, P. *The Birmingham Model for Parent Education*. Paper presented at the biennial meeting of the Society for Research in Child Development, Denver, April 1975.

Levenstein, P. Cognitive growth in preschoolers through verbal interaction with mothers. *American Journal of Orthopsychiatry*, 1970, *40*(3), 426–432.

Levenstein, P. A message from home: A home-based intervention method for low income preschoolers, 1974. (ERIC Document Reproduction Service No. ED 095 992)

Levitt, E., & Cohen, S. Educating parents of children with special needs: Approaches and issues. *Young Children*, 1976, *31*(4), 263–272.

Lichtman, E. *Educating Parents about Education: A Review of Some Issues, Methods, and Sources of Information*. Palo Alto, Calif.: Standford Center for Research and Development in Teaching, 1974. (ERIC Document Reproduction Service No. ED 129 710)

Malony, H. N. Can adolescents be taught to parent? *Adolescence*, 1978, *13*(49), 121–128.

Markel, G. *Assertive Training for Parents of Exceptional Children*. Paper presented at the Annual International Convention of the Council for Exceptional Children, Chicago, April 4–9, 1976. (ERIC Document Reproduction Service No. ED 122 569)

Miller, S. J., & Sloan, H. N., Jr. The generalization effects of parent-training across stimulus settings. *Journal of Applied Behavior Analysis*, 1976, *9*(3), 355–370.

Murrah, P. *Leader's Handbook for a Nutrition and Food Course: Parent Education in Nutrition and Food—A Series of Ten Lessons for Parents*. Washington, D.C.: Child Development Services Bureaus (DHEW/OCD), Project Head Start, 1967. (ERIC Document Reproduction Service No. ED 121 460)

Paget, N. W., & Thierry, P. A. Adoptive parent education: An agency service. *Children Today*, 1976, *5*(2), 13–15, 35.

Radeloff, D. J. Education for parenthood. *Illinois Teacher of Home Economics*, 1978, *21*(4), 189–196.

Radin, N. The impact of a kindergarten home-counseling program. *Exceptional Children*, 1969, *36*(4), 251–256.

Radin, N. Three degrees of maternal involvement in a preschool program: Impact on mothers and children. *Child Development*, 1972, *43*, 1355–1364.

Rickett, D., & Towns, K. Education for parenthood: Eighth grad-

ers change child-rearing attitudes, 1980. (ERIC Document Reproduction Service No. ED 184 705)

Robertson, E. E. *Effects of Parent Training on Teenage Mothers*. Unpublished doctoral dissertation, Walden University, 1978. (ERIC Document Reproduction Service No. ED 170 671)

Roehm, J. Leadership training for policy advisory committees: Conducting business meetings effectively, 1977. (ERIC Document Reproduction Service No. ED 141 359)

Sandler, H. M.; Dokecki, D. R.; Stewart, L. T.; Britton, V.; & Horton, D. M. The evaluation of a home-based educational intervention for preschoolers and their mothers. *Journal of Community Psychology*, 1973, *1*, 372–374.

Scales, P., & Everly, K. A community sex education program for parents. *Family Coordinator*, 1977, *26*(1), 37–43.

Stevens, J. H., Jr. Parent education programs: What determines effectiveness. *Young Children*, 1978, *33*(4), 59–65.

Sutherland, K. *Qualitative Evaluation of Parent-education Workshops and the Use of Parenting Models*. Austin, Tex.: Southwest Educational Development Laboratory, 1980. (ERIC Document Reproduction Service No. ED 183 285)

Weikart, D. *Development of Effective Preschool Programs: A Report on the Results of the High/Scope-Ypsilanti Preschool Projects*. Ypsilanti, Mich.: High/Scope Research Foundation, 1973.

Wittes, G., & Radin, N. Two approaches to group work with parents in a compensatory preschool program. *Social Work*, 1971, *16*(1), 42–50.

PARENT-TEACHER RELATIONSHIPS

See Home-School Relationships.

PAROCHIAL SCHOOLS

See Catholic Schools; Private Schools; Religion and Education.

PATH ANALYSIS

Broadly defined, "path analysis" is a strategy for understanding causal processes through the analysis of correlational data. First developed by the geneticist Sewall Wright (1921) as a quantitative aid for biological research, path analysis was introduced to the social sciences by Simon (1954, 1957), and later by Blalock (1961, 1962, 1964), who extended and popularized Simon's work. Through additional contributions by Boudon (1965) and Duncan (1966), path analysis became a viable method for rationally inferring causal relationships from correlations, provided certain highly restrictive assumptions are met.

Starting with a causal model that has been specified by the researcher after a careful consideration of relevant theoretical and substantive issues, the path analytic strategy provides a method for estimating the magnitude of the causal relationships that are assumed to operate among the variables in the model. Moreover, the plausibility of the causal model can thus be evaluated in light of the empirical results obtained. Results that are deemed inconsistent with the causal model would call for a reformulation of the model, and perhaps a "reconstruction of the substantive theory that generated the causal model at the outset" (Land, 1969, p. 4). Results judged consistent with the model would support the model's plausibility.

Beginning with a section on basic concepts and definitions, an attempt will be made to clarify the path analytic strategy outlined previously. Several of the major problems associated with the method are discussed.

Basic Concepts and Definitions. Consider, for illustration, a causal model specified by three measured variables X_1, X_2, and X_3, which are assumed to be interrelated linearly. Suppose that X_1 and X_2 are causally prior to X_3, and that X_1 and X_2 are not dependent on X_3. Suppose also that X_1 and X_2 do not completely determine X_3, and that a residual variable e is introduced to account for the combined effect on X_3 of all variables not explicitly considered. As opposed to X_1, X_2, and X_3, the variable e is not actually measured. Moreover, e is assumed to be uncorrelated with X_1 and X_2; that is, no variables included in e are causes of X_1 or X_2.

A diagram for the causal model described is shown in Figure 1. Such a diagram, called a *path diagram*, was introduced by Wright (1921) as a convenient way to represent the causal relationships specified by a causal model. In a path diagram unidirectional straight arrows represent the flow of causal influences from one variable to another and curved double-headed arrows represent correlations or covariances between variables whose causal relationships are not specified. In Figure 1 unidirectional arrows are drawn between X_1 and X_3 and X_2 and X_3 to represent the causal relationships postulated between these variables. Variables X_1 and X_2 are connected by a curved, double-headed arrow to represent the observed correlation or covariance between them. Since variables X_1 and X_2 are outside the control of the other variables in the model, they are labeled *exogenous* variables. Variable X_3, on the other hand, being dependent on both X_1 and X_2 (variables that are explicitly included in the model), is an *endogenous* variable in this system. Consistent with the assumptions made with respect to the residual variable e (that it accounts for the effect on X_3 of all variables other than X_1 and X_2 and that it is uncorrelated with X_1 and X_2), a unidirectional arrow pointed only at the endogenous variable X_3 is used to represent it. Finally, the symbols p_{31} and p_{32} on the unidirectional arrows reflect the magnitude of the *direct effect* of variables X_1 and X_2, respectively, on variable X_3.

A path diagram may be translated directly into a system of equations. In particular, one equation may be defined for each endogenous variable specified in the causal model (Asher, 1976). In the example under discussion, there is one endogenous variable, and hence one equation. If the variables are in standardized form, the equation for the diagram shown in Figure 1 is $X_3 = p_{31}X_1 + p_{32}X_2 + e$. If the variables' means were not zero, an intercept term

FIGURE 1. *Path diagram of a three-variable causal model*

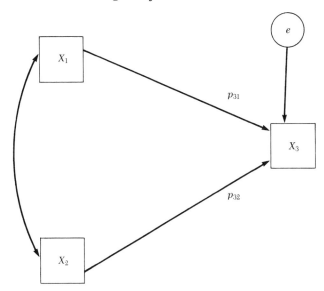

would be added to the equation. This equation is a linear regression equation. The weights (regression weights) may be estimated from sample data using ordinary least squares methods. If the variables are in standardized form, the weights will be standardized partial regression weights; if not, they will be unstandardized ("raw score") regression weights. Once the weights have been estimated, the variable e may be calculated as the residual $(X_3 - p_{31}X_1 - p_{32}X_2)$.

Within the context of a causal model, the linear regression equation is called a *structural equation* because it "represents a causal link rather than a mere empirical association" (Goldberger, 1972, p. 979). In this context the regression coefficients are called *path coefficients* or *structural parameters*.

Path Coefficients in Model Modification. Returning to the model shown in Figure 1, the values of p_{31} and p_{32}, estimated from ordinary least squares analysis, may be used to assess the magnitude of the direct effects of X_1 on X_3 and of X_2 on X_3 respectively. For example, if the path coefficients are standardized regression coefficients with values $p_{31} = .20$ and $p_{32} = .75$, one may conclude that variable X_2 has a greater direct effect on X_3 than does variable X_1. Moreover, one may conclude that X_3 will increase .20 standard deviations for each standard deviation increase in X_1 when X_2 is held constant. Similarly, one may conclude that X_3 will increase .75 standard deviations for each standard deviation increase in X_2 when X_1 is held constant.

Once path coefficients have been estimated, one may be interested in evaluating whether the model as specified by the researcher is plausible or needs to be modified. One approach might be to test hypotheses about specific parameters of the model. For example, one may test whether or not there is a direct causal link between X_1

FIGURE 2. *Causal model with indirect effects*

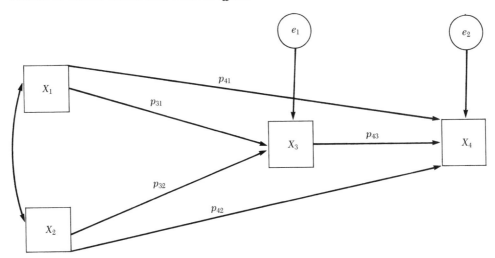

and X_3. This is equivalent to testing the null hypothesis, H_0: $p_{31} = 0$. If the result of the test is not to reject the null hypothesis, then the causal model may have to be modified by the removal of the path connecting X_1 to X_3 (assuming an adequate level of statistical power). The absence of an arrow connecting X_1 to X_3 would suggest that X_1 and X_3 are not directly causally related in the modified causal model.

Although path analysis may be used to assess the plausibility of a particular causal model because there will always be alternative causal models that fit the same data equally well (Blalock, 1964), it cannot be used to establish a particular causal model as the "true" one. Thus, consistent with the method of scientific inquiry, the method of path analysis helps to eliminate inadequate models, thereby reducing an investigator's choice among plausible alternatives.

Indirect Effects. One of the advantages of path analysis is that it allows for the estimation of *indirect* as well as direct effects. In the model shown in Figure 1 only direct causal effects are postulated (those between X_1 and X_3, and X_2 and X_3); hence only direct causal effects are estimated. By introducing another variable, X_4, into the model described by Figure 1, a new causal model is specified—one that postulates indirect effects. This model is shown in Figure 2, and, for concreteness, is illustrated in substantive terms in Figure 3 by a model hypothesized by Stayrook, Corno, and Winne (1978) in their research on teacher education. Variables X_1, X_2, X_3, and X_4 are measured variables; e_1 and e_2 are unmeasured residual variables. According to Figure 2, direct causal links between X_1 and X_3, X_1 and X_4, X_2 and X_3, X_2 and X_4, and X_3 and X_4 are postulated. In addition, indirect causal effects are postulated between X_1 and X_4 and X_2 and X_4, with X_3 as the intervening or mediator variable in both cases.

To assess indirect effects, one may employ a method originally suggested by Wright (1921) for decomposing measures of total association between variables. That

method, described by Duncan (1966), and later by Wolfle (1980), may be expressed in terms of the following formula defined for standardized variables:

$$r_{ij} = \sum_q p_{iq} r_{jq}, \qquad (1)$$

where i and j denote two variables in the model, r_{ij} is the correlation coefficient between X_i and X_j; and q is an index that refers to those variables having a direct causal link to X_i.

Applied to r_{41}, the measure of total association between variables X_1 and X_4 in Figure 2, equation (1) yields by iteration the following decomposition:

$$r_{41} = p_{41} + p_{31}p_{43} + (p_{42} + p_{43}p_{32})r_{12}. \qquad (2)$$

From this decomposition it may be noted that the total association between X_4 and X_1 may be partitioned into three effects: the direct effects of X_1 on X_4 expressed as p_{41}, the indirect effects of X_1 on X_4 via X_3 expressed as $p_{31}p_{43}$ (called a *compound path coefficient*), and effects expressed as $(p_{42} + p_{43}p_{32})r_{12}$, which cannot be interpreted causally because they rely on the association between X_1 and X_2 (variables that are exogenous to the system) (Kenny, 1979).

It is worth noting that with respect to the causal model shown in Figure 2, X_3 is not simply causally dependent on X_1 and X_2, but X_3 causally influences X_4 as well. Thus, in more complex models, the same variable may be both causally dependent as well as causally prior to other variables. Since one equation may be defined for each endogenous variable, it follows that more complex models are characterized by having more than one structural equation (Bentler, 1980).

Assumptions. Although path analysis makes use of ordinary least squares methods to infer causal relationships from correlational ones, it does not contradict a basic tenet of statistics: causal relationships may not be deduced from

FIGURE 3. *Causal model of Figure 2 in substantive terms*

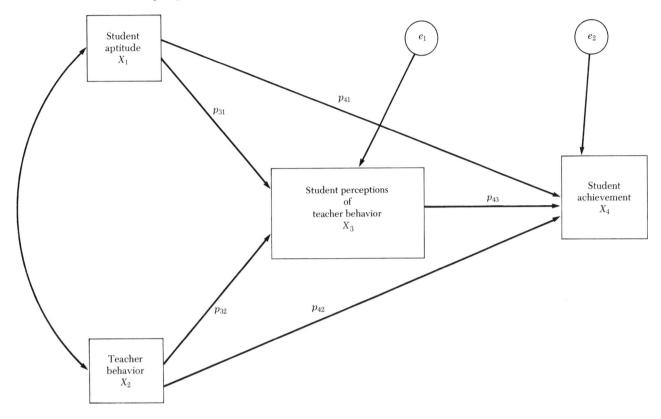

correlational data. As the existence of a nonzero correlation coefficient between two variables may be due to an important third variable (a confounding variable), one is not justified in making causal inference from correlational coefficients *per se*. In path analysis, because certain highly restrictive assumptions concerning the influence of such confounding variables must be met, the path analytic technique does not violate this basic tenet of statistics.

In the ideal experiment conditions are satisfied that provide for the complete determination of the form and parameters of a causal model. The effects of confounding variables are controlled through randomization, and the causal effects of carefully manipulated experimental variables on dependent variables may be assessed (Heise, 1969). In the not-so-ideal experiment, randomization helps to control for the effects of confounding variables, but one can never be certain that control has been effected completely. In the case where randomization is not possible (e.g., in cross-sectional studies), the kind of simplifying assumptions one must make concerning the effects of confounding variables may be highly implausible and unrealistic. Yet where they are satisfied, a path analytic approach can serve to help close the gap between empirical research and related theory.

The assumptions in question were mentioned briefly earlier and are considered here in greater detail. A list of these assumptions follows (Heise, 1969).

Assumption 1: The structure of the causal model is linear and additive in terms of the path coefficients, p_{ij}.

The causal model satisfies the form of the general linear model (e.g., $X_i = \Sigma_j \ p_{ij}X_j + e$).

Assumption 2: The causal flow between variables in the model is unidirectional; *simultaneous* or *reciprocal causation* cannot be accommodated.

That is, if X_1 causes X_3, X_3 cannot affect X_1 either directly or indirectly through a series of intervening variables. In terms of the path coefficients, this means that if $p_{31} \neq 0$, then logically p_{13} must be zero. Figures 1–3 are examples of causal systems in which the causal flow is unidirectional. Such systems are *recursive*. Figure 4 is an example of a causal system in which simultaneous or reciprocal causation is present. Such systems are called *nonrecursive*. The importance of this assumption should become clear in the following discussion.

Assumption 3: All variables that might affect the dependent variable in a structural equation are either included in the equation or are not causes of any of the variables which are included; that is, there are no common causes, or confounding variables (Kenny, 1979, p. 51).

Because causal laws are really only applicable to systems that are completely isolated and free from outside influences (Russell, 1929, as cited in Blalock, 1964), "the only

FIGURE 4. *Causal model with reciprocal causation*

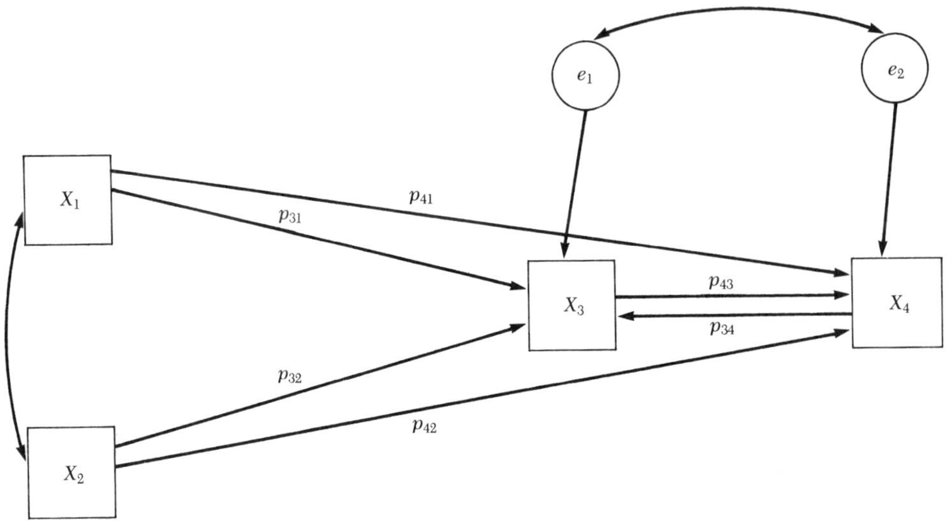

way we can make causal inferences at all is to make simplifying assumptions about such disturbing influences" (Blalock, 1964, p. 13). Assumption 3 is concerned with the effects of these disturbing influences that are reflected in the error terms of a set of structural equations. Restating assumption 3 explicitly in terms of error or residual terms, we have the following:

All residual variables are uncorrelated with each other and with the independent variables in the same structural equation.

When assumption 3 is met (as well as assumptions 1 and 2), the path coefficients in a recursive system will be "identifiable" in the sense that they will have unique values (Duncan, 1975). Moreover, when assumption 3 is met, ordinary least squares methods may be used to provide unbiased estimates of the path coefficients.

When assumption 3 is not met (although assumptions 1 and 2 are met), in some cases the estimates of the path coefficients using ordinary least squares methods may be seriously biased (Duncan, 1975). When assumption 3 fails because causal systems are nonrecursive—that is, the error terms can no longer be assumed to be uncorrelated with the independent variables in each equation—ordinary least squares methods break down. The use of more complicated methods of analysis, such as two-stage least squares or maximum likelihood methods (Jöreskog, 1973), are required but are beyond our scope here. The issue of "identifiability" and two-stage least squares estimation in nonrecursive models are discussed in the literature (Duncan, 1975; Heise, 1975; James & Singh, 1978; Kenny, 1979).

Unfortunately, an investigator can seldom, if ever, be sure that assumption 3 is met, and that variables have not been left out that should have been included, or conversely. The "correctness" of a specified causal model depends upon how well relevant theories have been developed, and how carefully the investigator has considered them in delineating the model. Models that are not delineated correctly are said to have *specification error*. Procedures for assisting in the analysis of specification error are found in such works as Duncan (1975), Heise (1975), and Kenny (1979).

Assumption 4: The usual assumptions of multiple regression analysis are met.

A discussion of these assumptions and the effects of their violations on results may be found in Cohen and Cohen (1975).

Assumption 5: All of the independent variables in a structural equation have been measured without error.

It is difficult to imagine a situation in educational research wherein all independent variables under investigation are measured without error. Where the presence of random measurement error is considered negligible, the consequent effects of violating assumption 5 will be negligible. Where the presence of random measurement error is considered nonnegligible, however, the use of ordinary least squares methods to estimate the population path coefficients will be both biased and inconsistent (James & Singh, 1978).

Approaches have been proposed and discussed in the psychometric and econometric literature for dealing with random measurement error, especially if the variables actually measured are considered merely as indicators of an underlying (or latent) theoretical construct that is inherently unobservable (Bentler, 1980; Hauser & Goldberger, 1971; Jöreskog & Goldberger, 1975; Werts, Jöreskog, & Linn, 1973; Werts & Linn, 1970; and Werts, Linn & Jöreskog, 1971).

Conclusions. Where causal hypotheses can be delineated in a manner compatible with the set of statistical and substantive assumptions it requires, path analysis provides a rational basis for making causal inferences from correlations. In addition, the requirement of path analysis to think causally about a problem, and emphasize the theoretical and substantive issues involved, may help a researcher to understand better the nature of the problem at hand and to delineate more clearly the hypotheses in question. Indeed, the heuristic value of path analysis ranks high on its list of potentials for increasing the interaction between theory and empirical research.

Sharon L. Weinberg

See also Causal Modeling; Regression Analysis; Statistical Methods.

REFERENCES

Asher, H. B. *Causal Modeling.* Beverly Hills, Calif.: Sage, 1976.

Bentler, P. M. Multivariate analysis with latent variables: Causal modeling. In M. R. Rosenzweig & L. W. Porter (Eds.), *Annual Review of Psychology* (Vol. 31). Palo Alto, Calif.: Annual Reviews, 1980, pp. 419–456.

Blalock, H. M. Correlation and causality: The multivariate case. *Social Forces,* 1961, *39,* 246–251.

Blalock, H. M. Four-variable causal models and partial correlations. *American Journal of Sociology,* 1962, *68,* 182–194.

Blalock, H. M. *Causal Inferences in Nonexperimental Research.* Chapel Hill: University of North Carolina, 1964.

Boudon, R. A method of linear causal analysis: Dependence analysis. *American Sociological Review,* 1965, *30,* 365–374.

Cohen, J., & Cohen, P. *Applied Multiple Regression–Correlation Analysis for the Behavioral Sciences.* Hillsdale, N.J.: Lawrence Erlbaum Associates, 1975.

Duncan, O. D. Path analysis: Sociological examples. *American Journal of Sociology,* 1966, *72,* 1–16.

Duncan, O. D. *Introduction to Structural Equation Models.* New York: Academic Press, 1975.

Goldberger, A. S. Structural equation methods in the social sciences. *Econometrica,* 1972, *40,* 979–1001.

Hauser, R. M., & Goldberger, A. S. The treatment of unobservable variables in path analysis. In H. L. Costner (Ed.), *Sociological Methodology.* San Francisco: Jossey-Bass, 1971, pp. 81–117.

Heise, D. R. Problems in path analysis and causal inference. In E. F. Borgatta (Ed.), *Sociological Methodology.* San Francisco: Jossey-Bass, 1969, pp. 38–73.

Heise, D. R. *Causal Analysis.* New York: Wiley, 1975.

James, L. R., & Singh, B. K. An introduction to the logic, assumptions, and basic analytic procedures of two-stage least squares. *Psychological Bulletin,* 1978, *85,* 1104–1122.

Jöreskog, K. G. A general method for estimating a linear structural equation system. In A. S. Goldberger & O. D. Duncan (Eds.), *Structural Equation Models in the Social Sciences.* New York: Academic Press, 1973, pp. 85–112.

Jöreskog, K. G., & Goldberger, A. S. Estimation of a model with multiple indicators and multiple causes of a single latent variable. *Journal of the American Statistical Association,* 1975, *70,* 631–639.

Kenny, D. A. *Correlation and Causality.* New York: Wiley, 1979.

Land, K. C. Principles of path analysis. In E. F. Borgatta (Ed.), *Sociological Methodology.* San Francisco: Jossey-Bass, 1969, pp. 3–37.

Russell, B. *Mysticism and Logic and Other Essays.* New York: Norton, 1929.

Simon, H. A. Spurious correlation: A causal interpretation. *Journal of the American Statistical Association,* 1954, *49,* 467–479.

Simon, H. A. *Models of Man.* New York: Wiley, 1957.

Stayrook, N. G.; Corno, L. C.; & Winne, P. H. Path analysis relating student perceptions of teacher behavior to student achievement. *Journal of Teacher Education,* 1978, *29,* 51–56.

Werts, C. E.; Jöreskog, K. G.; & Linn, R. L. Identification and estimation in path analysis with unmeasured variables. *American Journal of Sociology,* 1973, *78,* 1469–1484.

Werts, C. E., & Linn, R. L. Path analysis: Psychological examples. *Psychological Bulletin,* 1970, *74,* 193–212.

Werts, C. E.; Linn, R. L.; & Jöreskog, K. G. Estimating the parameters of path models involving unmeasured variables. In H. M. Blalock, Jr. (Ed.), *Causal Models in the Social Sciences.* Chicago: Aldine-Atherton, 1971.

Wolfle, L. M. Strategies of path analysis. *American Educational Research Journal,* 1980, *17,* 183–209.

Wright, S. Correlation and causation. *Journal of Agricultural Research,* 1921, *20,* 557–585.

PERCEPTION

This article on perception (1) defines perception; (2) discusses the experimental study of perception; (3) describes the coordination of several sense modalities in perceptual systems; (4) gives examples of the development of perception in the child; (5) contrasts abilities of young blind and sighted subjects; and (6) describes perception under very special conditions, such as sensory deprivation.

Definition. People in general are familiar with "perception" as a word. They hear it, they use it, and they see it in print. Like many other words, it has a diversity of meanings, rather than a single definition. Sixty years ago one classroom teaching was that perception is "sensation plus meaning" (Bartley, 1980). This definition implied that sensation is the elemental experience. From the long failure to isolate sensation as an elemental experience, we now see that perception is the immediate response at the personalistic level to energistic inputs to sense organs. The receptors of sense organs translate the environmental input into a neural discharge going to the central nervous system. The brain uses the input with its own organization, which, of course, varies from time to time. On this account, not only the input to the receptors but also the state and activity of the central nervous system must be taken into account in explaining perception.

"Perception" is not a synonym of "understanding," "knowledge," or "judgment"; it is the immediate result of the environmental input and the state of the brain. The terms "knowledge" and "understanding" do not have the temporal boundaries nor the other restricted characteristics that pertain to perception. "Sensation" is the experience of certain qualities, like color, loudness, coldness, whereas perception is more inclusive and pertains to reacting for example, to objects.

Variations. There are three general states of the individual: the appreciative, the active-motor, and the meditative. Perception varies accordingly. For example, in a football game, the players respond to sensory input largely by muscular movement. In a meditative state, the individual doesn't hear or otherwise consciously respond to much of the sensory input; that is, one's perception is greatly reduced, and whatever perception there may be, will likely be unconscious. In the individual's appreciative state, perception differs still from the other two states. In specific instances, not all "stimuli" stimulate; therefore, they should not be called stimuli. In general, the energy that reaches receptors can be called impingements. Impingements that result in response are the actual stimuli. Thus, all impingements impinge, but those that are effective in eliciting a response are the stimuli. This distinction is only slowly becoming recognized but is logically necessary.

Studying Perception. Our knowledge of perception has come from two sources: the experimental psychology laboratory and the observation of children in other contexts. Because perception is a product of both the impingement (stimulus) input and the processes within the perceiver, studies of learning and information processing are important. Studies that interest the educator are of this global kind. They compare the child's responses to specific test encounters over a period of years and determine the rates and features of perceptual development during that time. Such studies are aimed at determining not only the response outcome to a test condition but also the nature of the child's cognitive resources that are brought to bear on the child's development.

The study of perception is one of experimental psychology's major endeavors. The state of the subject, or "observer," is intentionally controlled both by instructions about what to attend to and by selection of impingements and other physical conditions. This control allows the experimenter to obtain quantitative assessment of the response of the subject (dependent variable) to a given condition (independent variable).

Perceptual systems and the senses. There are ten or more senses, and the perceptual response of the organism is the result of a combination of two or more classes acting at a time. For example, when a room is at a low temperature, certain bed covers may seem inadequate and light; but the same covers will seem warm and heavy when the room temperature is higher. Thus, the weight of the bed cover is a function of the action of the thermal receptors as well as of the action of the pressure receptors.

Gibson (1966) was the first to deal systematically with perceptual systems. He described five: (1) the basic orientation system, (2) the haptic system, (3) the taste-smell, or savor, system, (4) the auditory system, and (5) the visual system. What psychologists and laymen alike were earlier calling the five senses are made up of contributions of several sense departments. We now see that the five are

actually five perceptual systems. The sense departments, or "senses," are (1) the vestibular sense (reacting to gravity), (2) the muscle sense (kinesthesis), (3) the temperature sense, (4) the tactual sense, (5) the taste sense (gustatory sense), (6) the sense of smell (olfactory sense), (7) the hearing sense, (8) the visual sense, (9) the sense of pain and (10) the common chemical sense. These mechanisms in systematic combinations give us the five perceptual systems. There are also receptors dealing with pressure and temperature within the body. They constitute the sixth perceptual system, the homeostatic perceptual system, as yet not widely recognized (Bartley, 1980).

Research on visual perception. The research on visual perception falls into a number of fairly general categories: (1) findings regarding the vision of individuals blind until the removal of cataracts (Senden, 1960); (2) studies of animals reared in totally unilluminated environments (no clear conclusions were drawn) (Riesen, 1950); (3) studies of the blind to note the consequences of the absence of vision (Revesz, 1950); (4) theories regarding the early growth and nature of perception (e.g., Hebb, 1949; Gibson, 1950; Werner, & Wapner, 1952; Allport, 1955) (5) studies by Birch and Lefford (1963) and Birch and Belmont (1964) on the interplay of the sense modalities in children's performances, including those of the brain-damaged, and studies of comparison between blind and sighted subjects (Witkin et al., 1971); (6) studies by Gibson and Walk (1960), Walk and Dodge (1962), Walk and Trychin (1964), and Walk (1978) of the "visual cliff"; (7) the work on young infants to show the initial emergence of certain features of perception (Fantz, 1961, 1964; Bower, 1965, 1971); (8) studies showing the role of the muscles and the muscle sense in visual achievement (Held & Schlank, 1959; Held & Freedman, 1963; Held & Mikaelian, 1964; Held, 1965); and (9) studies of split-brain animal and human subjects (Sperry, 1964a, 1964b; Gazzaniga, Bogen, & Sperry, 1965; Sperry & Gazzaniga, 1966).

Some stimulation is imposed on the body, forced on a passive organism; other stimulation is obtained by the organism's own activity (Gibson, 1966).

Development of Perception. Several significant changes in perception develop as a child grows. Increasing knowledge about the environment allows the child to exercise more obtained perception. The child makes more specific searches. Between the ages of 5 and 7, there is a great improvement in solving problems that require focused and sustained attention (Mussen, Conger, & Kagan, 1979). As the child becomes older, it is able to focus attention in a more organized way and for longer stretches of time; it is also able to shift attention more rapidly.

Perceptual systems of infants. The sequence of maturation of the sensory modalities in the embryo is as follows: tactual, vestibular, auditory, visual (Gottlieb, 1971). Although the basic neural mechanisms begin to emerge in the early weeks of prenatal life, the neuromuscular mechanism for vision is still not complete at birth. The infant, however, is able to see light, dark, and color at birth (Pratt,

1934, 1954). After a few days, the infant is able to follow moving lights, but it is not able to accommodate until at least 1 month old. As early as the age of 16 weeks, it can focus on near and far targets (Haynes, White, & Held, 1965). Fantz (1964) and Bower (1965, 1971) have performed some of the most significant visual experiments, some of which show the cooperation of hearing and vision in the interpretation of object movement.

When 13-week-old infants are shown pairs of patterns—some having curved lines, others having straight ones—they prefer to look at curved-line patterns and to look at concentric patterns longer than nonconcentric ones (Ruff & Birch, 1974). Infants do not always look longest at targets with the greatest amount of contour. With paired targets of equal amount of contour, those with the greatest number of discrete elements tend to be viewed longer than those with fewer. What the limit to this is has not been determined (Fantz & Fagan, 1975). Infants use relational information to recognize shape and appear to be innately predisposed to the perception of shapes (Swartz & Day, 1979).

Held and associates (1959, 1961, 1963, 1964, 1965), in a series of experiments, confirmed the assumption that a single basic mechanism underlies both the *original acquisition* of visually guided skill and its *adaptation* to changes in visual situations later on into adulthood.

Newborns can hear at birth and are sensitive to location of acoustic sources. They also can detect the difference between acoustic frequencies of 200 and 250 cps. (Bridger, 1961). They are able to perceive the difference between sweetness and saltiness (Crook & Lipsitt, 1976). They are soon able to distinguish between various olfactory substances, present, for example, in the clothing of the mother and other women (Lipsitt, 1977). Pain does not seem to have as simple and discrete a sensory mechanism as the other senses; hence, responses taken to signify pain do not show up as early as others.

Meltzoff and Moore (1977) showed that infants between 12 and 17 days old could imitate adult facial and manual gestures. Piaget, Feller, and McNear (1958) earlier thought that imitation began at the age of 8 to 12 months.

Blind and Sighted Subjects. Blind and sighted subjects have been experimentally compared in various ways. The attentional component in perception shows up more strongly in the congenitally blind than in the the sighted as tested by the ability of the two groups to identify simple auditory patterns within complex ones (Witkin et al., 1971). The same blind subjects performed less well than the sighted on a tactile abstraction test.

When Ayres (1966) compared the performances of early blind and sighted adolescents in identifying familiar objects by tactually gained information, the sighted subjects performed much better. In other studies of comparing the blind and sighted, mixed results were obtained.

According to Warren (1978), discriminative abilities of blind subjects appear to be comparable to those of sighted subjects. There is evidence that blind subjects have better habits of attention and therefore may make more effective functional use of auditory and tactual input.

Colon (1960) showed that the blind reacted to lifted objects of various sizes in a manner that manifests the size-weight illusion. Later, Bartley and Colon (unpublished paper) found that the sighted-not-blindfolded and the congenitally blind performed about equally well. The sighted when blindfolded performed much less well than with their eyes open; they performed less well than the congenitally blind when the latter used either the pincer, the palmer, or the grasp method for their observations.

White et al. (1970), using a vision substitution system, found that the third dimension of objects presented to the blind subjects could be perceived by tactile perception. Apkarian-Stielau and Loomis (1975) did further work, using the same visual substitution system, and tested hypotheses concerning the degree of tactile resolution as compared to the degree of visual resolution. Two types of comparisons supported the supposition that limited tactile resolution of the blind was responsible for its being inferior to the resolution of sighted subjects. A third type of comparison did not support the supposition, and possible reasons for this were given.

Special Stimulus Conditions. Perception is modified by special conditions. One of these is sensory deprivation, brought about by (1) transcendental meditation and allied practices, (2) relaxation methods, (3) experimental deprivation, and (4) isolation. Another set of special conditions is brought about by use of drugs and alcohol. Some studies of perception in alcoholics are beginning to suggest that one basis for alcoholism is genetic (Nelson, Sinha, & Olson, 1977).

The foregoing topics, although dealt with briefly, contain experimental material meant to aid school teachers in assessing childhood abilities and in forming their expectations about children.

S. Howard Bartley
Cynthia Daniel

See also Cognition and Memory; Learning; Listening; Neurosciences; Psychology.

REFERENCES

Allport, F. *Theories of Perception and the Concept of Structure.* New York: Wiley, 1955.

Apkarian-Stielau, P., & Loomis, J. M. A comparison of tactile and blurred visual form perception. *Perception and Psychophysics,* 1975, *18*(5), 362–368.

Ayres, A. F. *A Comparison of Selected Perception among Early Blind and Sighted Adolescents.* Unpublished doctoral dissertation, Rutgers University, 1966.

Bartley, S. H. *Introduction to Perception.* New York: Harper & Row, 1980.

Bartley S. H., & Colon, F. *A Story of the Blind's Response to Size-Weight Combinations.* Unpublished paper.

Birch, H. G., & Belmont, L. Auditory-visual integration in normal and retarded readers. *American Journal of Orthopsychiatry*, 1964, *34*, 853–861.

Birch, H. G., & Lefford, A. Intersensory development in children. *Monographs of the Society for Research in Child Development*, 1963, *28*, 1–28.

Bower, T. G. R. Stimulus variables determining space perception in infants. *Science*, 1965, *149*, 88–89.

Bower, T. G. R. The object world of the infant. *Scientific American*, 1971, *225*, 30–38.

Bridger, W. H. Sensory habituation and discrimination in the human neonate. *American Journal of Psychiatry*, 1961, *117*, 991–996.

Colon, F. *The Size-Weight Illusion in Blind Persons*. Unpublished master's thesis, Michigan State University, Department of Psychology, 1960.

Crook, L. K., & Lipsitt, L. P. Neonative nutritive sucking. *Child Development*, 1976, *47*, 518.

Fantz, R. L. The origin of form perception. *Scientific American*, 1961, *204*, 66–72.

Fantz, R. L. Visual experiments in infants: Decreased attention to familiar patterns relative to novel ones. *Science*, 1964, *145*, 668–670.

Fantz, R. L., & Fagan, J. F. Visual attention to size and number of pattern details during the first six months. *Child Development*, 1975, *46*, 3–18.

Gazzaniga, M. S.; Bogen, J. E.; & Sperry, R. W. Observations on visual perception after disconnection of the cerebral hemispheres in man. *Brain*, 1965, *88*, 221–236.

Gibson, E. J., & Walk, R. D. The visual cliff. *Scientific American*, 1960, *202*, 62–71.

Gibson, J. J. *The Perception of the Visual World*. Boston: Houghton Mifflin, 1950.

Gibson, J. J. *The Senses Considered as Perceptual Systems*. Boston: Houghton Mifflin, 1966.

Gottlieb, G. Ontogenesis of sensory function in bird and mammals. In E. Tobach, L. R. Aronson, & E. Shaw (Eds.), *The Biopsychology of Development*. New York: Academic Press, 1971.

Haith, M. M. The response of the human newborn to visual movement. *Journal of Experimental Child Psychology*, 1966, *3*, 235–243.

Haynes, H.; White, B. L.; & Held, R. Visual accommodation in human infants. *Science*, 1965, *148*, 528–530.

Hebb, D. O. *The Organization of Behavior: A Neurological Theory*. New York: Wiley, 1949.

Held, R. Plasticity in sensory-motor systems. *Scientific American*, 1965, *213*, 84–95.

Held, R., & Bossom, J. Neonatal deprivation and rearrangement. *Journal of Comparative Physiology*, 1961, *51*, 33–37.

Held, R., & Freedman, S. J. Plasticity in human sensory-motor control. *Science*, 1963, *142*, 455–462.

Held, R., & Mikaelian, H. Motor sensory feedback versus need in adaptation to rearrangement. *Perceptual and Motor Skills*, 1964, *18*, 685–688.

Held, R., & Schlank, M. Adaptation to disarranged eye-hand coordination in the distance dimension. *American Journal of Psychology*, 1959, *72*, 603–605.

Lipsitt, L. P. The study of sensory and learning processes of the newborn. *Symposium on Neonatal Neurology, Clinics in Perinatology*, 1977, *4*(1), 163–186.

Meltzoff, A. N., & Moore, M. K. Imitation of facial and manual gestures by human neonates. *Science*, 1977, *198*, 75–78.

Mussen, P. H.; Conger, J. J.; & Kagan, J. *Child Development and Personality*. New York: Harper & Row, 1979.

Nelson, T. M.; Sinha, B. K.; & Olson, W. M. Short-term memory for hue in chronic alcoholics. *British Journal of Addiction*, 1977, *72*, 301–307.

Piaget, J.; Feller, Y.; & McNear, E. Essai sur la perception des vitesses chez l'enfant et chez l'adulte. *Archives de Psychologie* (Geneva), 1958, *36*, 253–327.

Pratt, K. C. The effects of repeated visual stimulation on the activity of newborn infants. *Journal of Genetic Psychology*, 1934, *44*, 117–126.

Pratt, K. C. The neonate. In L. Carmichael (Ed.), *Manual of Child Psychology*. New York: Wiley, 1954.

Revesz, G. *Psychology and Art of the Blind*. New York: McKay, 1950.

Riesen, A. H. Arrested vision. *Scientific American*, 1950, *183*, 16–19.

Ruff, H. A., & Birch, H. G. Infant visual fixation. *Journal of Experimental Child Psychology*, 1974, *17*, 460–473.

Senden, M. von. *Space and Sight* (P. Heath, Trans.). New York: Free Press, 1960.

Sperry, R. W. The great cerebral commissure. *Scientific American*, 1964, *210*, 45–52. (a)

Sperry, R. W. *Problems Outstanding in the Evolution of Brain Function*. New York: American Museum of Natural History, 1964. (b)

Sperry, R. W., & Gazzaniga, M. S. Simultaneous double discrimination response following brain bisection. *Psychonomic Science*, 1966, *4*, 261–262.

Swartz, M., & Day, R. H. Visual shape perception in early infancy. *Monographs of the Society for Research in Child Development*, 1979, *44*(7, Serial No. 182).

Walk, R. D. Perceptual learning. In E. C. Carterette & M. P. Friedman (Eds.), *Handbook of Perception* (Vol. 9). New York: Academic Press, 1978.

Walk, R. D., & Dodge, S. H. Visual depth perception of a ten-month-old monocular human infant. *Science*, 1962, *137*, 529–530.

Walk, R. D., & Trychin, S., Jr. A study of the depth perception of monocular hooded rats on the visual cliff. *Psychonomic Science*, 1964, *1*, 53–54.

Warren, D. H. Perception by the blind. In E. C. Carterette & M. P. Friedman (Eds.), *Handbook of Perception* (Vol. 9). New York: Academic Press, 1978.

Werner, H., & Wapner, S. Toward a general theory of perception. *Psychological Review*, 1952, *59*, 324–338.

White, B. W.; Saunders, F. A.; Scadden, L.; Bach-y-Rita, P.; & Collins, C. C. Seeing with the skin. *Perception and Psychophysics*, 1970, *7*(1), 23–27.

Witkin, H. A.; Altman, P. K.; Chase, J. B.; & Friedman, F. Cognitive patterning in the blind. In J. Helmuth (Ed.), *Cognitive Studies*. New York: Brunner/Mazel, 1971.

PERSONALITY ASSESSMENT

Personality assessment is focused on describing and understanding the characteristics of people as revealed in particular situations, at specific points in time. Of course, almost everyone forms informal judgments about the self and others. For example, a student might decide that he or she is too shy to appear in a dramatic production, or a teacher might perceive in a student a lack of respect for authority. Informal methods of personality assessment have been with us since prebiblical times. Historians since the ancient Greeks have written biographies; educators have traditionally been called upon to provide letters of recommendation for their students. But such informal methods are inadequate for most educational research purposes for three important reasons: (1) the number and nature of personality terms used by different people vary widely, so there are few bases for comparing descriptions of different people; (2) there is no universal consensual frame of reference for definitions of personality terms; what, for example, is seen as a lack of respect for authority by one judge of personality may be perceived as a spirit of independence and autonomy by another; and (3) informal descriptions do not lend themselves readily to quantification, resulting in severe limitations upon the application of statistical procedures. For these reasons, most educational and psychological studies investigating the role of personality employ formal methods for delineating and measuring the personality dimensions of interest.

In educational settings, personality assessment procedures are employed for four major purposes: diagnosis, counseling, personnel selection, and educational research. A teacher might refer an adolescent showing disordered behavior to a school psychologist for personality appraisal and educational recommendations. Measures yielding profiles of personality needs might be routinely employed together with test of vocational interests and abilities in a vocational counseling setting. Personality tests of psychopathology might be employed together with a psychiatric interview to screen teachers who are prospective candidates for tenure against the possibility of subsequent psychotic breakdown. Another application of personality as-sessment in personnel selection is the practice of many medical and other professional school selection committees to require an interview of candidates for admission. There are many possible examples of the use of personality assessments in educational research, ranging from the study of the personality characteristics of more popular and less popular university teachers (Rushton, Murray, & Paunonen, 1980), to the study of the interaction of learning environments and personal characteristics (Messick, 1979).

Methods for Measuring Personality. Methods for studying personality may be divided, following Wiggins (1973), into (1) observational procedures, (2) behavioral analysis, and (3) structured tests. Observational procedures may be considered to have a number of facets or sources of variation, including: (1) settings, (2) observers, (3) instruments, (4) occasions, and (5) attributes.

Settings may be "naturalistic-immediate," as when a day's activities in the life of a single boy are recorded (Barker & Wright, 1951), or "naturalistic-retrospective," as when people are asked to record their earliest memories. Settings may also be "controlled," as in the well-known laboratory studies of Witkin (1974) and his co-workers on field articulation and its relation to personality and learning styles, or "contrived," as when an experimenter places a confederate on a highway shoulder next to an automobile with a flat tire to study helping behavior.

Observers may be "participant" or "nonparticipant," with or without the prior knowledge of the persons being observed. To advise people that they are being observed may cause reactive effects, such as the elicitation of censoring, whereas to fail to advise them may raise important ethical questions. Table 1, adapted from Wiggins (1973, p. 303), illustrates further combinations of settings and observers.

TABLE 1. *Classification of observational procedures*

	Observers	
Settings	Participant	Nonparticipant
Naturalistic:		
Immediate	Anthropologist working as kitchen helper in order to observe workers in restaurant industry	Psychologist observing drivers' compliance with vehicle code in large city
Retrospective	Peer rankings Sociometric ratings	Accretion indices, such as number of beer bottles returned, as an indication of consumption; quantitative analysis of voice recordings
Controlled	Formal interview; reaction to stress induced by experimenter present in room	Reaction to stressful experiment observed through one-way mirror
Contrived	"Lady in distress" experiment, in which experimenter poses as a person experiencing automobile trouble	"Lost letter" technique in which stamped letters bearing various addresses are dropped in city

SOURCE: Adapted from Wiggins, 1973, p. 303.

Instruments may be "mechanical," such as a tape recorder or a psychogalvinometer to measure skin conductance under stressful conditions, or "encoding devices," providing rules and a framework for recording observational data. Encoding devices may be categorical, in which behavior is classified into a number of classes thought to be diagnostic, as in Withall's study of teacher behavior (Withall, 1949). Withall assessed social-emotional climate using seven categories into which teacher statements were classified by an inferential process. These categories were learner-supportive, acceptant and clarifying, problem-structuring, neutral, directive, reproving, and teacher self-supporting. Although categorical, these were taken together as a continuum. Encoding devices include a variety of types of rating scales, including numerical, graphic, forced-choice, and cumulated-points (Guilford, 1954, pp. 263–301; Wiggins, 1973, pp. 310–313).

Rating scales, although widely used, are subject to certain well-known sources of error and distortion. The "leniency error," the tendency to attribute desirable traits to ratees, may be alleviated by asking judges to rank ratees on traits, or to choose between one of two equally desirable traits to describe the ratee. The "halo error" is the tendency to rate persons in the direction of a general evaluative impression, rather than in terms of specific traits. This may be reduced by using descriptive terms that contain a minimum of evaluation and by asking raters to rate a number of people in terms of a single attribute before going on to the next attribute. The "central tendency error" is the tendency to use middle rather than extreme categories. To reduce the effects of this source of distortion, each judge's ratings may be standardized by adjusting statistically the range of ratings made by the judge before combining them, or, alternatively, forced-choice rankings or ratings may be employed. The "logical error" is the tendency to rate people similarly on attributes thought logically to be related, although in fact they are not. To avoid this, maximally distinct trait terms should be used with clear definitions. The "contrast error" is the tendency to exaggerate the differences between ratees' and judges' location on the trait dimension. This occurs less frequently than the other sources of distortion but may be reduced by averaging the ratings of judges with diverse standings on attributes. The "proximity error," the tendency to rate traits close together on a rating schedule in a similar way, may be avoided by varying the order of attribute ratings for different judges.

The two remaining important facets of observation, "occasions" and "attributes," refer respectively to the time span over which the behavior is to be sampled and the dimensions that are to be evaluated. Occasions may be divided arbitrarily into time units, as when an observer selects random samples of three-minute periods to observe nursery school children or when inferences about personality are made on the basis of a half-hour interview. Alternatives to time sampling are event sampling (the number of affiliative interactions are counted), or episodes, as when behavior is observed in a recurring naturalistic situation (e.g., when a child experiences frustration in problem solving in the classroom). The choice of occasions for observation will rest in part with the kind of behavior being observed, its frequency, and, importantly, on the reliability reasonably to be expected using different methods. Altruistic behavior may occur infrequently and only when the situation warrants it. Sampling three-minute intervals might be quite inappropriate for studying altruism, but quite appropriate for studying sociability. The reliability of observation will be a function, among other things, of the extent of sampling of behavior relevant to the attribute and to the number of judges (Jackson, in press; Spearman, 1910).

The choice of attributes for study is of fundamental importance and depends largely on the theoretical or pragmatic aims of the educational research worker. The particular hypotheses, their relation to underlying theory, and the opportunities to observe and record reliably the relevant behavior are some of the controlling factors in their choice. Of particular concern is the degree to which judges can grasp the behavioral implications of a trait definition and, if so, whether or not behavior relevant to the trait will appear in the time span and under the conditions of observation. Table 2 contains a set of trait terms used by judges in a study by Jackson and Guthrie (1968) in which university students made peer ratings of the personality of roommates. Also contained in Table 2 are the corresponding more technical terms comprising scale names for the Personality Research Form (Jackson, 1974; cf. Murray, 1938) with which peer ratings were correlated, and the trait definitions given raters. Note that trait names were chosen so as to be familiar to raters and that definitions were written to be as distinct as possible.

The interview. The interview is a type of observational setting deserving special consideration because of its almost universal use in practical and research contexts.

Interviews vary widely in the settings in which they take place as well in their purposes. Table 3 identifies a range of interview types and purposes. Of these, the employment interview has been most thoroughly investigated. There is a paradoxical quality to the application of findings to this kind of interview: whereas research findings have apparently been quite negative concerning its reliability, validity, and utility (Mayfield, 1964; Ulrich & Trumbo, 1965), practical decision makers continue to employ it widely. Interviewers have been observed to form an impression shortly after the interview begins and to search for data supporting their impression (Webster, 1964). But few studies have explicitly examined the process of forming impressions of personality from interview material and how these are linked to the personality-relevant behavior required on a particular job. Rather, studies have focused upon the overall favorability of candidates (e.g., Hakel & Schuh, 1971). An exception to this approach is reflected in a series of studies (Jackson, Peacock, & Smith, 1980; Rothstein & Jackson, 1980) conducted at the

TABLE 2. *Personality traits and descriptions*

Trait	Psychological name	Description
Sociable	Affiliation	friendly, outgoing, enjoys being with friends and people in general; makes an effort to win friendships and maintain associations with people
Supporting	Nurturance	gives sympathy and comfort; helpful, maternal/paternal indulgent; assists others whenever possible
Dominant	Dominance	attempts to control the environment; attempts to influence or direct other people; forceful, decisive, authoritative
Thrill-seeking	Opposite of "harmavoiding"	enjoys all exciting activities even if, perhaps especially if, danger is involved; in contrast to someone who avoids danger, is fearful, cautious, vigilant
Fun-loving	Playful	playful, easy-going, light-hearted; spends most of spare time partying, enjoying sports, games, going out; does many things just for fun
Attention-seeking	Exhibitionism	enjoys being conspicuous, dramatic, colorful; wants to be the center of attention
Ambitious	Achievement	aspires to accomplish difficult tasks; maintains high standards and is willing to work toward distant goals; desires to excel; competitive, hardworking
Aesthetic, sensual	Sentience	sensitive to sounds, sights, tastes, smells, and the way things feel; remembers these sensations and thinks that they are an important part of life; aware
Independent	Autonomy	tries to avoid or break away from restraints, confinements or restrictions of any kind; enjoys being unattached, free, not tied to people, places or obligations
Meek	Abasement	mild mannered; accepts blame or criticism frequently, even when not deserved; admits inferiority; exposes self to situations where he or she is in an inferior position
Impulsive	Impulsivity	tends to act or speak on the spur of the moment and without deliberation or hesitation; spontaneous, hasty, impetuous and uninhibited
Approval-seeking	Need for social recognition	desires to be held in high esteem, to have a good reputation; concerned about what people think about one; works for approval and recognition of others rather than for one's own satisfaction
Changeable	Changeable	flexible, restless; likes new and different experiences; dislikes routine and avoids it; adapts self readily to changes in environment and circumstances

Continued on following page

TABLE 2. *Personality traits and descriptions (cont.)*

Trait	Psychological name	Description
Intellectually curious	Understanding	seeks understanding in many areas of knowledge; reflective, rational, intellectual; likes logical thought, synthesis of ideas, verifiable generalizations
Seeks help and advice	Succorance	desires and needs support, protection, love, advice; feels insecure without this, seeks sympathy and reassurance; confides difficulties to a receptive person
Orderly	Order	concerned with keeping personal effects and surroundings neat and organized; dislikes clutter, confusion, lack of organization
Aggressive	Aggressive	gets angry easily; quarrelsome, revengeful, destructive; swears; willing to hurt others to get own way; throws or breaks things
Seeks definiteness	Need for cognitive structure	does not like ambiguity or uncertainty in information; wants all questions answered completely; desires to make decisions based upon definite knowledge rather than upon guesses or probabilities
Defensive	Defensive	suspicious, guarded, touchy; readily suspects that people mean harm or are against one; ready to defend self at all times; takes offense easily
Persistent	Endurance	willing to work long hours; doesn't give up quickly on a problem; persevering, steadfast, patient, unrelenting

SOURCE: Adapted from Jackson & Guthrie, 1968, and from the *Personality Research Form Manual* (Jackson, 1974) with the permission of Research Psychologists Press, Inc.

University of Western Ontario. Judges formed impressions of job candidates on the basis of statements the candidates made about themselves in the job interview. Interview judges consistently rated candidates' job suitability and probable satisfaction as higher for the candidates showing personality congruence with the job. For example, applicants for an accounting job were rated higher when their self-references indicated high orderliness and cognitive structure and low impulsivity, autonomy, and need for change, whereas applicants for the job of advertising copywriter were rated higher if they showed the opposite pattern. These effects were stronger than the effects of prior job experience or general favorability of self-characterizations. One can argue that almost the sole purpose of an employment interview is to elicit job-relevant personality information, because other information can usually be obtained more efficiently by simpler methods. The fact that judges can link interview-revealed personality variables to differential job performance is cause for some encouragement, but more research is needed regarding (1) the

conditions under which interviewers can elicit relevant personality information; probably a structured interview would prove most effective; (2) the selection of effective judges of personality, since interviewers vary widely in their skill; and (3) the personality variables affecting successful job performance. Some important findings relating personality traits to school and work have been uncovered (Edwards, 1977; Landy, 1976), including student performance (Harper, 1975), but most job families have not been mapped.

Behavioral analysis. The personality concept of traits, upon which most of traditional personality assessment rests, has not been universally acknowledged as useful, particularly by those theorists who, in the tradition of Skinner (1959), assert that behavioral consistencies are a function of the environmental conditions eliciting the behavior. For those who focus on behavior modification, the task is to identify antecedent conditions relating to the response classes where change is sought. Unfortunately, although a good many practical prescriptions for

TABLE 3. *Types of interviews and their settings, purposes, and problems*

Type of interview	Setting	Purpose	Problem
Personnel	Industry	To assess candidate's qualifications	Interviewer's dual role
Troubleshooting	Industry	To determine cause of interpersonal difficulties	Interviewer's dual role
Poll	Door-to-door	Assess attitudes, opinions, beliefs	Rigid structure and leading questions
Stress	Military or training programs	Assess reactions to unusual circumstances	Generalizability
Medical diagnostic	Clinic or hospital	Diagnosis	Accuracy of reporting
Psychiatric intake	Mental hygiene clinic or hospital	Gather preliminary information about patient and establish relationships	Patient's anxiety
Mental status	Mental hygiene clinic or hospital	Ascertain patient's mental state	Overprobing and pathological bias
Case history	Clinic, hospital, or home	Background information	Selectivity of information
Pretest and posttest	Psychiatric	Before-and-after test decision making	Amount of test information to impart
Termination	Psychiatric	Set patient free	Premature timing

SOURCE: Adapted from Kleinmuntz, 1982, with the permission of the author.

bringing about behavior change have been published, assessment procedures for identifying and linking antecedent conditions and behavioral classes have been informal and judgmental rather than empirical (Wiggins, 1973), so that measurement procedures have been slow in developing.

Projective procedures. Projective tests, such as the Rorschach Inkblot Test and the Thematic Apperception Test (TAT) are not as popular in the 1980s as they were 30 years ago. While they still have their adherents in clinical and cross-cultural settings, they are rarely used in educational contexts because they are expensive to administer, do not permit simple quantification, require specialized training, and frequently have not yielded sufficiently high levels of reliability and validity in educational research to justify their use. Like the interview, they perhaps might best be considered as semistructured procedures, as settings for observing behavior in more-or-less controlled conditions. They are "broad bandwidth," "low fidelity" (Cronbach & Gleser, 1965) procedures in the sense that they yield information about a broad range of behavior, but not necessarily with high reliability. There is even evidence that the high levels of training usually considered essential for the accurate use of these techniques may not be essential. For example, one study demonstrated that psychology graduate students who had completed coursework in TAT interpretation were no more accurate in their interpretations than those who had not. A second

study indicated that experienced Rorschach examiners' judgments of intelligence correlated .82 with scores from a standardized intelligence test. But this value was almost equaled by undergraduate students having no Rorschach training, whose correlation was .78. Although there are well-developed scoring systems for both the TAT and Rorschach, these in general have serious psychometric limitations, restricting their usefulness for research. Particularly troublesome is the high correlation usually found between record length or response total and scores. Thus, the person who responds with four human movement percepts of a total of 10 responses on the Rorschach is not easily compared with the person who gives 20 human movement responses out of a total of 100. Holtzman et al. (1961) has sought to remedy this problem by permitting only one response to each of a new longer series of inkblots contained in the Holtzman Inkblot Technique. This psychometrically sound instrument is a considerable improvement over the Rorschach, but the scores it provides are not yet completely understood. For many problems, educational research workers will be well advised to seek more specific measures than those contained in global, semistructured projective personality tests. Such measures reflecting specific hypothesized processes will usually provide greater measurement fidelity than will more general measures.

Structured personality assessment. A great deal has been learned about developing structured personality tests since Woodworth's first application to screen World War I soldiers for psychoneurosis. This approach has several advantages, including the standardization implicit in the use of discrete items and objective scoring. This approach allows the analysis and selection of better items, high reliability, and replicability. Pragmatically it has proved to be more valid than other approaches.

The three major approaches to personality scale construction are the (1) rational, (2) empirical, and (3) construct methods. The "rational method" assumes a correspondence between the individual's self-report and actual behavior, as when an individual reports behavior relevant to particular neurotic acts. It also assumes that the respondent is truthful and has sufficient self-insight to recognize the behavior, and that the psychologist constructing the scale has been clever enough to phrase the items so that they accurately elicit responses relevant to the behavior in question. Because these responses are often difficult to verify, psychologists are very skeptical of personality tests employing this approach, particularly when evidence of validity is missing or weak. The "empirical approach," perhaps best exemplified by the Minnesota Multiphasic Personality Inventory (MMPI) or the California Psychological Inventory (CPI), seeks to identify items bearing some stable relationship to a criterion behavior or state. Thus the MMPI consists of a number of clinical scales, each developed from items showing a different proportion of critical responses for psychiatric patients and persons not so classified. The CPI was developed in a similar manner, but employed nonpsychiatric criteria, such as the number of organizations and activities in which a student participated, or status as a delinquent. Developing scales in this way avoids the tenuous assumptions of the rational method, but is not without difficulties. Criteria change, and items may not cross-validate. It may be hazardous to attribute a single underlying process or construct to the empirical scale score because these scales may be heterogeneous and therefore of relatively low reliability, and may contain variance other than that which was intended, because of uncontrolled differences between criterion and control groups (age or social class). Empirical scales are also particularly susceptible to response biases. Two studies (Ashton & Goldberg, 1973: Jackson, 1975) found that carefully developed empirical scales from the CPI were inferior in validity to scales developed by undergraduate students working for a couple of hours, using a definition of an underlying construct.

"Construct validity" (Cronbach & Meehl, 1955), the idea that psychological tests should be faithful to an underlying theoretically derived concept, implies a particular method of test construction (Jackson, 1971; Loevinger, 1957). The latter author has suggested that there are three components of validity—the substantive, structural, and external—all of which are necessary and none in itself is sufficient. The substantive component refers to the degree to which the underlying definition or theory is adequately incorporated in the item pool; the structural component represents the degree to which the items adhere to the measurement model implied by the theory; and the external component includes evidence that scores derived from item responses are consistent with scores derived from nontest behavior. Thus, one would expect that an expert judge, knowledgeable about the underlying theory or definition, would be able to decide reliably whether or not items belonged in a pool to measure, for example, achievement. One would also expect that the structure of item responses would be such that items designed to measure a particular dimension would hang together, and that irrelevant content and response bias could be identified and suppressed by choosing appropriate items. One important aspect of external validation is the demonstration of convergent and discriminant validity (Campbell & Fiske, 1959), involving evidence that questionnaire measures correlate higher with same-trait measures based on different methods than they do with different traits. Jackson (1971) suggested that this property must be explicitly included in a program of test development if it is to be demonstrated later at the stage of external validity.

Examples of Personality Questionnaires. Among the most popular personality inventories are the MMPI, the CPI, the 16 PF, the Edwards Personality Inventory, the Personality Research Form, the Jackson Personality Inventory, the State-Trait Anxiety Inventory, and the Test Anxiety Inventory. The description of each of these in the following paragraphs is necessarily brief. For more complete details and for descriptions of a wide variety of other structured personality tests, the reader is referred to test manuals and the Buros (1978) Mental Measurement Yearbooks.

Although there are almost 300 scales based on MMPI items, as well as more than 3,000 published studies, most users score the 10 clinical scales, Hypochondriasis, Depression, Hysteria, Psychopathic Deviate, Masculinity-Femininity, Paranoia, Psychasthenia, Schizophrenia, Hypomania, and Social Introversion, and three clinical scales, F (Infrequency), K (Correction for defensiveness), and L (Lie). Interpretation is often made in terms of profile shape (Guthrie, 1950) and the presence of one or more scales elevated above a critical level, usually two standard deviations above the mean of the normative sample. Although the MMPI is one of the most widely used psychological tests, it has problems associated with response biases. These biases are troublesome especially because the tendency to endorse undesirable personality items is of necessity associated with the tendency to endorse psychopathologically related item content, and each in turn is related to psychopathology. The difficulty is that these general tendencies cause scales to be much more correlated than they should be, and that affects their construct validity.

The California Psychological Inventory (CPI) (Gough, 1968) shares with the MMPI a largely empirical rationale and a large number of items in common. Rather than employing psychiatric diagnosis criteria for selecting items, Gough employed normal, largely positive characteristics to define criterion groups, such as academic achievement, social class, or dominance, the latter based on ratings. The 18 scales include Dominance (Do), Capacity for Status (Cs), Socioability (Sy), Social Presence (Sp), Self-acceptance (Sa), Sense of Well-being (Wb), Responsibility (Re), Socialization (So), Self-control (Sc), Tolerance (To), Good Impression (Gi), Communality (Cm), Achievement via Conformance (Ac), Achievement via Independence (Ai), Intellectual Efficiency (Ie), Psychological Mindedness (Py), Flexibility (Fx), and Femininity (Fe).

The Sixteen Personality Factor questionnaire (16 PF) is based on the factor analytic studies of personality by Raymond B. Cattell (Cattell & Eber, 1964). Although the manual is not entirely explicit on this point, the items were apparently selected intuitively rather than by factor analytic means. The 16 PF is published in a variety of forms, including a form for persons with limited vocabularies. The scales are as follows: Reserved versus Outgoing (A), Less Intelligent versus More Intelligent (B), Affected by Feelings versus Emotionally Stable (C), Humble versus Assertive (E), Sober versus Happy-go-lucky (F), Expedient versus Conscientious (G), Shy versus Venturesome (H), Tough-minded versus Tender-minded (I), Trusting versus Suspicious (L), Practical versus Imaginative (M), Forthright versus Shrewd (N), Placid versus Apprehensive (O), Conservative versus Experimenting (Q1), Group-dependent versus Self-sufficient (Q2), Undisciplined versus Controlled (Q3), and Relaxed versus Tense (Q4). Some scales are substantially correlated, and some show very modest reliability.

The Edwards Personality Inventory consists of 53 scales organized into five booklets. Items were chosen by factor analytic means, so that items clustering on a factor defined that particular factor. Unlike some personality inventories, scale names are direct and simple, drawn from everyday language. Scales include Plans and Organizes Things, Conforms, Likes to Be Alone, Self-centered, Is a Hard Worker, Neat in Dress, Likes a Set Routine, and Shy. The Edwards Personality Inventory may achieve wider use when data become available about scale validities.

The Personality Research Form (PRF) (Jackson, 1974) was developed using a sequential strategy of scale construction (Jackson, 1970) in which large item pools were prepared on the basis of definitions of constructs of personality drawn largely from the work of Murray (1938). Items were selected on the basis of item analyses designed to minimize correlations with desirability response bias, while maximizing an item's association with its own scale and reducing interscale correlations. The PRF is available in a number of forms. Form E contains 352 items arranged in 22 scales of 16 items each. Scales include Abasement (Ab), Achievement (Ac), Affiliation (Af), Aggression (Ag), Autonomy (Au), Change (Ch), Cognitive Structure (Cs), Defendence (De), Dominance (Do), Endurance (En), Exhibition (Ex), Harmavoidance (Ha), Impulsivity (Im), Nurturance (Nu), Order (Or), Play (Pl), Sentience (Se), Social Recognition (Sr), Succorance (Su), Understanding (Un), In-

frequency (In), and Desirability (Dy). The PRF manual contains norms for students from seventh grade through university.

The Jackson Personality Inventory (JPI) (Jackson, 1976), like the PRF, was developed from a large item pool using a construct approach and an algorithm designed to suppress scale intercorrelations and correlations with desirability. There are 320 items divided into 16 scales. Scale names are Anxiety (Anx), Breadth of Interest (Bdi), Complexity (Cpx), Conformity (Cny), Energy Level (Enl), Innovation (Inv), Interpersonal Affect (Iaf), Organization (Org), Responsibility (Rsy), Risk Taking (Rkt), Self-esteem (Ses), Social Adroitness (Sca), Social Participation (Spt), Tolerance (Tol), Value Orthodoxy (Vlo), and Infrequency (Inf). The last scale was included to detect careless or random responding or errors in scoring.

The State-Trait Anxiety Inventory (STAI) (Spielberger, Gorsuch, & Lushene, 1970) is designed to distinguish between trait anxiety, a long-term disposition to manifest anxiety symptoms, and state anxiety, the presence of anxiety symptoms at a particular point in time, such as just before giving a speech. The STAI has been used widely in anxiety research, particularly when a measure sensitive to the arousal of anxiety is needed.

The Test Anxiety Inventory (TAI) (Spielberger, 1980) is designed to evaluate the effectiveness of various behavior therapies in the treatment of college students suffering from text anxiety, and may be employed more generally in the appraisal of test anxiety. It contains 20 items asking respondents how frequently they experience symptoms of anxiety before, during, and after examinations. Worry and Emotionality are separately scored subscales and are also components of the total anxiety score. Results with the TAI indicate that it is sensitive to reduced levels of text anxiety expected from the effects of behavior therapies in combination with study-skills training.

Douglas N. Jackson

See also Attitude Measurement; Individual Differences; Interests Measurement; Measurement in Education; Personality Theory.

REFERENCES

Ashton, S. G., & Goldberg, L. R. In response to Jackson's challenge: The comparative validity of personality scales constructed by the external (empirical) strategy and scales developed intuitively by the experts, novices, and laymen. *Journal of Research in Personality,* 1973, *7,* 1–20.

Barker, R. G., & Wright, H. F. *One Boy's Day.* New York: Harper & Brothers, 1951.

Buros, O. K. (Ed.). *The Eighth Mental Measurements Yearbook.* Highland Park, N.J.: Gryphon Press, 1978.

Campbell, D. T., & Fiske, D. W. Convergent and discriminant validation by the multitrait-multimethod matrix. *Psychological Bulletin,* 1959, *56,* 81–105.

Cattell, R. B., & Eber, H. W. *Handbook for the Sixteen Personality Factor Questionnaire.* Champaign, Ill.: Institute for Personality and Ability Testing, 1964.

Cronbach, L. J., & Gleser, G. L. *Psychological Tests and Personnel Decisions* (2nd ed.). Urbana: University of Illinois Press, 1965.

Cronbach, L. J., & Meehl, P. E. Construct validity in psychological tests. *Psychological Bulletin*, 1955, *52*, 281–302.

Edwards, R. C. Personal traits and "success" in schooling and work. *Educational and Psychological Measurement*, 1977, *37*, 125–138.

Gough, H. G. An interpreter's syllabus for the California Psychological Inventory. In P. McReynolds (Ed.), *Advances in Psychological Assessment* (Vol. 1). Palo Alto, Calif.: Science and Behavior Books, 1968.

Guilford, J. P. *Psychometric Methods* (2nd ed.). New York: McGraw-Hill, 1954.

Guthrie, G. M. Six MMPI diagnostic profile patterns. *Journal of Clinical Psychology*, 1950, *30*, 317–323.

Hakel, M. D., & Schuh, A. J. Job applicant attributes judged important across seven diverse occupations. *Personnel Psychology*, 1971, *24*, 45–52.

Harper, F. B. W. The validity of some alternative measures of achievement motivation. *Educational and Psychological Measurement*, 1975, *35*, 905–909.

Holtzman, W. H.; Thorpe, J. S.; Swartz, J. D.; & Herron, E. W. *Inkblot Perception and Personality: Holtzman Inkblot Technique.* Austin: University of Texas Press, 1961.

Jackson, D. N. A sequential system for personality scale development. In C. D. Spielberger (Ed.), *Current Topics in Clinical and Community Psychology* (Vol. 2). New York: Academic Press, 1970, pp. 61–96.

Jackson, D. N. The dynamics of structured personality tests. *Psychological Review*, 1971, *78*, 229–248.

Jackson, D. N. *Personality Research Form Manual.* Port Huron, Mich.: Research Psychologists Press, 1974.

Jackson, D. N. The relative validity of scales prepared by naive item writers and those based on empirical methods of scale construction. *Educational and Psychological Measurement*, 1975, *35*, 361–370.

Jackson, D. N. *Jackson Personality Inventory Manual.* Port Huron, Mich.: Research Psychologists Press, 1976.

Jackson, D. N. Some preconditions for valid person perception. In M. P. Zanna, E. T. Higgins, & C. P. Herman (Eds.), *Consistency in Social Behavior: The Ontario Symposium* (Vol. 2). Hillsdale, N.J.: Lawrence Erlbaum Associates, in press.

Jackson, D. N., & Guthrie, G. M. Multitrait-multimethod evaluation of the Personality Research Form. In *Proceedings of the Seventy-sixth Annual Convention of the American Psychological Association, 1968*, pp. 177–178.

Jackson, D. N.; Peacock, A. C.; & Smith, J. P. Impressions of personality in the employment interview. *Journal of Personality and Social Psychology*, 1980, *39*, 294–307.

Kleinmuntz, B. *Personality and Psychological Assessment.* New York, N.Y.: St. Martin's Press, 1982.

Landy, F. J. The validity of the interview in police-officer selection. *Journal of Applied Psychology*, 1976, *61*, 193–198.

Loevinger, J. Objective tests as instruments of psychological theory. *Psychological Reports*, 1957, *3*, 635–694.

Mayfield, C. C. The selection interview: A re-evaluation of published research. *Personnel Psychology*, 1964, *17*, 239–260.

Messick, S. Potential uses of noncognitive measurement in education. *Journal of Educational Psychology*, 1979, *71*, 281–292.

Murray, H. A. *Explorations in Personality.* Cambridge, Mass.: Harvard University Press, 1938.

Rothstein, M., & Jackson, D. N. Decision making in the employ- ment interview: An experimental approach. *Journal of Applied Psychology*, 1980, *65*, 271–283.

Rushton, J. P.; Murray, H. G.; & Paunonen, S. V. *Personality Characteristics of University Professors.* Paper presented at the twenty-second International Congress of Psychology, Leipzig, German Democratic Republic, July 1980.

Skinner, B. F. *Cumulative Record.* New York: Appleton-Century-Crofts, 1959.

Spearman, C. Correlation calculated from faulty data. *British Journal of Psychology*, 1910, *3*, 271–295.

Spielberger, C. D. *Preliminary Manual for the Test Anxiety Inventory.* Palo Alto, Calif.: Consulting Psychologists Press, 1980.

Spielberger, C. D.; Gorsuch, R. L.; & Lushene, R. E. *Test Manual for the State-Trait Anxiety Inventory.* Palo Alto, Calif.: Consulting Psychologists Press, 1970.

Ulrich, L., & Trumbo, D. The selection interview since 1949. *Psychological Bulletin*, 1965, *63*, 100–116.

Webster, E. C. *Decision Making in the Employment Interview.* Montreal: McGill University, Industrial Relations Center, 1964.

Wiggins, J. S. *Personality and Prediction: Principles of Personality Assessment.* Reading, Mass.: Addison-Wesley, 1973.

Withall, J. Development of a technique for the measurement of socioemotional climate in classrooms. *Journal of Experimental Education*, 1949, *17*, 347–361.

Witkin, H. A.; Dyk, R. B.; Faterson, H. F.; Goodenough, D. R.; & Karp, S. A. *Psychological Differentiation: Studies of Development.* Hillsdale, N.J.: Lawrence Erlbaum Associates, 1974.

PERSONALITY THEORY

The concept of personality is easier to use than it is to define. Numerous attempts at providing definitions of personality are extant (Allport, 1937). Their number and variety bear testimony to the fact that no single definition is completely satisfactory. Allport (1961) provided a statement that perhaps comes closest to encompassing the scope of the various uses of the term and concept: "Personality is the dynamic organization within the individual of those psychophysical systems that determine his characteristic behavior and thought" (p. 28).

This concise definition is focused upon three aspects of personality: individuality, consistency, and organization. In reference to individuality, personality consists of those behaviors that are distinctive of a particular person. Murray and Kluckhohn (1953) have stated that "every person is in certain respects (1) like all other people, (2) like some other people, (3) like no other person" (p. 53). The first of these three topics falls within the domain of general psychology, with its search for universal laws of human behavior. Psychology of personality concerns itself with the second part of the definition and attempts to determine how a person resembles some people and differs from others. It also aspires to the third: how to capture individual uniqueness by the procedures of scientific investigation. In reference to consistency, the study of personality has been traditionally focused upon these characteristics that are stable across situations and across time. The student of personality is little interested in momentary, fleeting responses; his or her attention is concentrated upon those behaviors that, within the response repertoire of an individual, tend to recur and are predictable and characteristic. Along these lines, personality can be construed as consisting of behaviors that endure over time and are consistent across situations. Personality can also be conceived as a "brake" that slows down the pace of behavioral change and reduces the impact of environmental influences. Finally, the third task of personality investigation concerns the organization, pattern, or hierarchy of behaviors within an individual. It is widely assumed that all the responses within a person's behavioral repertoire are not equally important; some are more potent than others and more likely to occur. Therefore, personality investigators and theorists attempt to account for the interrelationship of responses and response tendencies within the person. How responses are organized, how they are dominant or subordinate in relation to other responses, and how actual or potential conflict among competing response tendencies is handled—these are important topics within the study of personality.

Investigation and specification of personality are further complicated by the fact that personality, as the German psychologist Herrmann (1976) points out, is a hypothetical construct several steps removed from observable behavior. Personality cannot, then, be observed or measured directly; rather, particular bits of behavior are recorded, tallied, and interpreted in terms of specific personality variables—for example, introversion-extraversion, external versus internal locus of control, repression versus sensitization, orality or anality. The composite of these observations and inferences pertaining to several personality variables and dimensions constitutes an approximation of an individual's personality, that which is characteristic of him or her in a stable and organized fashion.

How personality develops, what the important influences are upon its formation, what the basic units of personality are, how personality influences behavior, and how a person's needs and potentialities are channeled and expressed are some of the questions addressed by personality theories. As in other fields, theory of personality aspires to two objectives: explanation and prediction. In the ideal case, explanation and prediction merge or at least complement each other; that which is fully explained is most effectively predicted and vice versa. In actuality, these two goals of theoretical activity often exercise a pull in opposite directions. Explanation is often, although not inevitably, retrospective; the present is explained on the basis of the past. Prediction is directed to the future; behavior that has not yet occurred is foretold on the basis of the individual's past and present experiences and characteristics. Psychoanalytic theory of personality by Freud and others, and the various psychodynamic theories derived from it, are principally concerned with explanation and are little oriented toward prediction. By contrast,

some of the current behavioristic formulations of personality—for instance, social learning theory (Bandura, 1977b; Krasner & Ullmann, 1973)—emphasize prediction of behavior over its explanation. In the case of Skinner's radical behavioristic view, which was not designed as a theory of personality but has been applied to the domain of personality by others (see Hall & Lindzey, 1978; Lundin, 1974; Pervin, 1980), prediction is the principal conceptual activity and overshadows all others, including explanation.

The field of personality psychology in the late twentieth century is characterized by a multiplicity of personality theories, many of which go back to the first three decades of this century. In the view of some observers (Fiske, 1978; Sechrest, 1976), both the age and the number of theories extant constitute problems. In terms of age, a great many of the theories reflect the thinking of an earlier era, which defies integration with more current and modern psychological findings and concepts. The large number of theories—a prominent current text (Hall & Lindzey, 1978) deals with twenty-one of them—augments difficulties in differentially designing crucial experiments and comparatively assessing the respective merits of the various theories.

In the space available it is impossible to do justice to the number and variety of personality theories. Instead, an attempt will be made to provide a few reference points on a number of prominent and representative theoretical positions. In the process, particular attention will be paid to the historical and empirical bases of these selected theories, their current status in relation to data accumulated on personality, and their heuristic value—that is, their potential for generating new data.

Representative Theories. The oldest current personality theory is Freud's psychoanalysis (1963 [1917]; 1964a [1933]; 1964b [1940]). It represents its author's attempt to imbue with meaning the phenomena he encountered in developing and applying a number of methods designed to get at the root of a variety of psychological symptoms. The orientation of the theory was clinical; the data base from which Freud proceeded was the observation of his patients' subjective experience by naturalistic means. The conceptual operation in which Freud engaged was that of providing a comprehensive explanation of the phenomena observed. In the process, Freud linked behavior in the present with experience in the past, with particular emphasis upon the formative events of infancy and early and middle childhood. He also traced present symptoms and other behaviors to the operation of unconscious motives, active and effective in impelling particular acts, yet operating outside of the person's range of awareness. "Why is the unconscious so important?" Freud asked. The answer at which he arrived was that it is the repository of unacceptable sexual and aggressive impulses, repressed or banished from consciousness because they create intrapsychic conflict and generate anxiety. A distinctive feature of Freud's explanation of the mainsprings of our behavior is the emphasis upon the lifelong nature of sexual drives, which, as Freud maintained, are present at birth and undergo a series of qualitative transformations in the course of early childhood, in the form of oral, anal, and phallic stages of psychosexual development. The last of these stages culminates in the Oedipal conflict, characterized by intense erotic attraction of the child toward the parent of the opposite sex and accompanied by equally intense hostility toward the parent of the same sex. An individual's personality is to a large measure dependent upon how these crucial psychosexual experiences are handled and resolved.

Although Freud's observations pertained to neurotic patients in Vienna in the period between 1895 and 1938, he felt that the principles he uncovered held true for all people, regardless of their psychiatric diagnosis or lack thereof, across space and across time. What he discovered—the operation of the unconscious and the influence of the experiences of early childhood—was indeed timeless and universal. The trappings of visible surface behavior might differ, but the nature of the biological impulses that crave expression—sexuality and aggression—does not. Neurotics and normal people might act very differently, but the sources of their behavior in the unconscious are more similar than different. Freud was also convinced that the clinical method that he espoused and practiced was adequate for both generating hypotheses and conclusively testing them. Indeed, he revised several of his formulations on the basis of clinical evidence. He saw little value, however, in demonstrating the validity of his theoretical tenets by experimental laboratory studies or by statistical evidence.

While differing greatly in their specific content, the personality theories of Adler (1927), Jung (1968), Horney (1937), Sullivan (1953), Fromm (1947), and others share a number of basic resemblances with Freud's theoretical contribution. All of them rest upon a clinical base, and all of them attach great importance to unconscious determinants of behavior and to childhood experience. They differ on the nature and content of the unconscious and on the kind of childhood experience they deem crucial. Collectively, these theories, together with Freud's, are known as psychodynamic, because they capitalize on the operation of complex motivational forces that are thought to impel all or most of human social behavior.

In contrast to these theories stand the conceptualizations that are based on the general theoretical position of behaviorism. Behaviorism, originated by Watson (1919) and articulately represented in contemporary psychology by Skinner (1974), stresses objective observation of behavior, control of responses by external reinforcement, and avoidance of explanation on the basis of mentalistic constructs. The evidential base of behaviorism has historically rested on animal experiments, typically concerned with learning. In the process, two basic models of learning, applicable over a wide range of animal and human behavior, have been identified: the classical conditioning of Pavlov (1927) and the operant conditioning of Skinner (1953). By

means of the former, connections are established between a previously effective (or unconditioned) stimulus and a new and hitherto neutral (or conditioned) stimulus, both of which come to elicit the same response. In the original experimental demonstration, dogs that without special training salivated at the sight of meat powder came to salivate at the sound of the bell that preceded the presentation of meat powder. In the case of the latter model of learning, the animal learns to emit a response that is followed by reinforcement. In the well-known Skinner box, the rat comes to press the lever that releases a pellet of food that is dropped into the chute. In operant conditioning, then, a response is acquired that has an effect upon the environment. The organism learns from the consequences of its responses.

Traditional extensions of behaviorism to personality are based upon these models of learning and their operation in complex human behavior. They differ among themselves in postulating one model of learning (Dollard & Miller, 1950) to which all learning is reduced or in drawing a sharp line between the respective roles of the two kinds of conditioning (Mowrer, 1950). In Mowrer's view, for example, classical Pavlovian conditioning is responsible for the experience of feelings and emotions and results in a lot of originally neutral stimuli acquiring the power of eliciting affective responses. Skinnerian operant conditioning has the role of providing us with motor and other skills. According to Mowrer, by means of classical conditioning we learn signs, by means of operant conditioning we acquire solutions. Dollard and Miller (1950), on the other hand, rigorously trace all human experiences and acts to the sequence of cue, drive, response, and reward and maintain that this series of events equally obtains in the case of operant and classical conditioned responses, between which, in any case, no qualitative distinction exists.

More modern and contemporary extensions of behaviorism to personality theory are skeptical of the ability of the two traditional models of learning to account for all human behavior. Modern social learning theory (Bandura, 1977b) postulates a more characteristically human model of learning based on observation and imitation. By means of this type of learning, complex patterns of acts are rapidly acquired, in contrast to the plodding pace of the trial-and-error learning of the classical or operant variety. Moreover, observational learning and imitation involve the distinction between acquiring the ability to perform a pattern of acts and actually performing it. The former activity is cognitive, the latter observable and motoric. Reinforcement is indispensable for the performance, but not for the acquisition, of imitated acts (Bandura, Ross, & Ross, 1963). More recently, social learning theorists have turned their attention to other cognitive variables, such as self-reinforcement, problem-solving strategies, and self-dialogues. In contrast to the traditional version of the behaviorist view, in which the person is seen as being under the control of external environment, modern social learning theorists emphasize the extent to which the person is capable of controlling and reinforcing his or her behavior (Bandura, 1977a, 1978; Mahoney, 1974). Moreover, in traditional behaviorism, the person is considered to be the recipient of environmental influences. Modern social learning theorists (e.g., Bandura, 1978) emphasize the reciprocal and multilateral nature of influences involving the person, the environment, and behavior. According to this view, the person is both affected by, and acts upon, the environment; behavior is the function of the person and the environment and yet influences both of them in the process. An important concept in contemporary social learning theory is self-efficacy, the extent to which the person feels capable of controlling the situation (Bandura, 1977a).

Whereas social learning theory has made important strides in the cognitive direction, certain other theories have started with cognition as their point of departure. George Kelly's personal construct theory (1955) exemplifies this position. Kelly rejects the traditional view that our behavior is impelled by a variety of motives. Instead, in Kelly's words, "[a] person's processes are psychologically channelized by the ways in which he anticipates events" (p. 46). Thus, attention is focused on the future and on the person's hypothesis-testing activity. Kelly explicitly proceeds from the metaphor of man as a scientist, engaged in predicting the future and working hard to make these predictions come true. The basic tool of this heuristic activity is the construct that Kelly (1955) likened to transparent patterns, or templates, created in order to fit the perceived realities of an individual's personal world. A person's personality is the system of his or her constructs that are developed, elaborated, revised, discarded, and replaced in the continuous interplay between the person and the environment. It is difficult to know, influence, or change the behavior of another person without, implicitly or explicitly, knowing that person's constructs. Special methods have been devised, by Kelly and others, to ascertain a person's constructs (Bannister & Fransella, 1977) and to bring about their change in psychotherapy (Kelly, 1955).

Kelly's emphasis on subjective reality, future-oriented activity, and the processes of personality change is paralleled and extended by a number of humanistic and existentialist personality theorists. The gist of their views is perhaps best introduced by contrast. Whereas behaviorists proceed from that which human beings and animals have in common, humanists and existentialists focus upon the distinctively and uniquely human. These theories are perhaps best exemplified by the contribution of Carl Rogers (1959). The central concept in his theory is the self, and the fundamental objectives of the person are to maintain and enhance his or her self-concept. Tension is created by discrepancies between the actual and the ideal self-concepts, that which the person believes himself or herself to be and that which he or she would like to be. Self-concept is developmentally enhanced by the experience of unconditional positive regard, love with no strings at-

tached. This experience is contrasted with having to meet conditions of worth, or being loved only if certain conditions are fulfilled and certain requirements are met. Experiencing conditions of worth is injurious to healthy personality development and may well result in personality problems later in life. Experience is not automatically incorporated into self-concept; experiences that threaten one's self-concept are distorted and denied. Incongruence between experience and self-concept results in anxiety. A fully functioning person is characterized by openness to experience, by experiencing his or her life fully at all times, by trusting his or her intentions and decisions, by feeling free to choose, and by being creative and innovative.

Finally, there are personality theories based on the empirical determination of basic units of personality. Whereas the origins of psychodynamic, humanistic, and cognitive theories are for the most part clinical and those of behavioristic theories experimental, the empirical foundations of the theories about to be discussed rest on large-scale, complex statistical manipulation of personality data. By means of multivariate techniques of data analysis, notably factor analysis, the number of independently varying dimensions, or factors, is ascertained. Such theorists as Cattell (1965), Eysenck (1970), and Guilford (1959) have relied upon this procedure in order to establish the nature of basic or source personality traits. To this end, they have carefully included in their data collection a comprehensive and systematic sample of different methods and instruments. With these precautions, they believe that they are justified in equating the factors empirically derived with conceptually fundamental units of personality. Since the details of their methods differ, they come up with different resulting dimensions. Eysenck's scheme is the simplest and consists of three irreducible personality dimensions: introversion-extraversion, neuroticism, and psychoticism. The first of these encompasses a major share of variation of behavior and refers to the surface ease with which a person interacts with his or her social milieu. On the more fundamental plane, Eysenck has traced individual differences in introversion-extraversion to ease of conditionability and to the reactivity of the central nervous system. In his formulation, introverts are overreactive and are easily conditioned; as a result, they carry a disproportionate load of social learning and are oversocialized. Extraverts tend to be undersocialized, condition sluggishly, extinguish conditioned responses quickly, and are underreactive to stimulation in their central nervous system. Neuroticism is equated by Eysenck with proneness to disruption to stressful stimuli and psychoticism, with a tendency to withdraw into a world of fantasy. Both of the above characteristics are conceived of as continua rather than categories; everybody possesses some degree of neuroticism and psychoticism; neurotics and psychotics, as a rule, possess higher degrees of their respective traits than do normal people.

Cattell's and Guilford's formulations are considerably

more complicated. Cattell, for example, has identified six-teen personality factors that defy being described in the available space. Although Eysenck's tripartite scheme appears to have the advantage of parsimony, Cattell would probably argue that his more complicated system represents a closer approximation of the units that go into the construction of human personality.

Theories and Research. The several theoretical positions presented above serve as both explanations of the available evidence and guides to future data gathering. Ideally, personality research should stand in an organic relationship to personality theory. In fact, it is a matter of broad agreement that it does not (Fiske, 1978; Helson & Mitchell, 1978; Sechrest, 1976). This lack of interrelatedness is variously blamed on the vagueness and complexity of personality theories or on the triviality of many personality research studies. As Carlson (1971) has pointed out, a typical research project in personality is concerned with the collection of limited data on a large number of subjects. As a consequence, one might well ask, with Carlson, "Where is the person in personality research?" Fiske (1978) has decried the gap in personality psychology between "cosmopolitan constructs" and "provincial observations," the latter subject to limitations due to observers, cognitions, and places, three variables insufficiently controlled in personality research. Moreover, because of the complexity of validating tenets of various personality theories, the results of personality research remain ambiguous. In the case of psychoanalysis, two recent reviews (Fischer & Greenberg, 1977; Silverman, 1976) of research were moderately positive, one middle-of-the-road (Kline, 1972), and one overwhelmingly and outspokenly negative (Eysenck & Wilson, 1973). While difficulties of drawing conclusions from empirical studies are compounded in the case of psychoanalysis, room for disagreement remains in the case of other personality theories as well.

Given this state of affairs, a number of personality investigators have turned to topics and problem areas that are extraneous, or at best tangential, to the traditional global theories of personality. Thus, a great deal of research has been done on internal versus external locus of control (Lefcourt, 1977; Phares, 1976) and on the antecedents, correlates, and consequences of prosocial behavior (Staub, 1980), to mention just two topics that are outside the scope of major personality theories. Eventually, the accumulation of work on these and other active research areas will be brought to bear upon the existing personality theories by way of confirming, revising, expanding, or refuting them. Alternatively, these topics may constitute building blocks for the construction of new comprehensive theories. It should be added, however, that recent decades have not been propitious for the development of new personality theories; most of the current personality theories are twenty or more years old.

Current Issues. A major issue dividing the field of theoretical personality psychology concerns the scope of personality psychology and the role of personality variables in predicting behavior. Mischel (1968) raised this question on the basis of the low intercorrelations of various personality measures and their low relationships with a variety of criteria, rarely exceeding Pearson product moment correlations of .30. Mischel (1968) concluded that the role of the person as a determinant of behavior has been overestimated and the role of the situation underestimated. In his more recent writings, Mischel (1973, 1977, 1979) has expanded and elaborated this argument. What consistencies there are within personality are cognitively mediated. Moreover, they are not identical across people. Therefore, it becomes essential to find out from the individual what his or her lines of consistency and equivalence are. To this end, the person must be engaged as an expert on his or her own behavior in a collaborative enterprise with the investigator. The idea that a person has valuable and unique information to impart to the investigator is novel in personality psychology and clashes with deeply engrained distrust of the human informant in both the behavioristic and the psychoanalytic camps. The behaviorists object to the unreliability of self-report, the psychoanalytic theorists are impressed with the limitations and distortions of conscious self-knowledge (see Draguns, 1975). Furthermore, Mischel feels that the scope of most personality variables is rather narrow and that personality characteristics are best revealed in interaction with specific situations. Along these lines, Mischel (1979) suggests that there is more stability of behavior across time than across situations.

Mischel's formulations (1968, 1973, 1977, 1979) have engendered a storm of controversy and provoked a number of critiques of his views (Bowers, 1973; Hogan, DeSoto, & Solano, 1977; Olweus, 1978). Most authorities in the field of personality are in agreement that behavior is a function of person and situation, but room for disagreement remains as to what the relative weights of the two components to this equation are and, more fundamentally, what the nature of this relationship is (see London, 1978; Magnusson & Endler, 1977). As a result of this controversy, the focus of personality theorizing shifted in the seventies to the interaction between the person and the situation. Mischel's outspoken pronouncements have also moved a number of empirical investigators to demonstrate that his view of the situational specificity of behavior is exaggerated. Block (1971) studied consistencies in personality traits longitudinally and was able to demonstrate impressively high correlation coefficients (.75 to .77) over short spans of time, such as from junior to senior year of college, and substantial ones over longer periods, such as from senior high school to adulthood, in the range from .54 to .56. But the picture is more complicated than that; Block identified subgroups of "changers" and "nonchangers" within her total pool of subjects and found that these characteristics were associated with different personality traits. Changers, for example, were found to be less self-confident than nonchangers. More recently, Epstein (1979, 1980) sought to demonstrate personal consistency of behavior through another route. He found that single ratings and observations at a point in time did indeed have a high degree of situational specificity. By aggregating and pooling a multitude of these observations, he was able to come up with ratings that were both more stable and more predictive. Thus, if a specific act is to be predicted, knowledge of personality would appear to be of little value. If the probability of a behavior across times and situations is to be ascertained, having information on personality is useful.

Another trend that is detectable at this time is the revival of interest in the cultural determinants of personality. At the interface of anthropology and psychoanalysis, culture and personality as a topic and movement occupied a prominent place from the 1930s through the 1950s. With the decline of psychoanalytic influence and the disenchantment with the empirical yield this effort had produced, culture and personality were eclipsed as a topic of conceptualization and research (see Draguns, 1979). Recent signs are detectable that the topic, although not necessarily the theoretical orientation to it, is demonstrating a degree of recrudescence. This revival of interest is sparked by the recognition that our personality theories as well as the data on which they are based are almost exclusively Western in origin. Thus, these formulations encompass less than the totality of human experience. Moreover, they neglect as part of their potential data base valuable laboratories of nature in the form of socialization experiences, habitats, values, and norms that influence personality formation and functioning differentially in a variety of cultural settings. On the conceptual plane, certain attempts have been made to transform statements drawn from the philosophical and theological traditions of the Far East into the form resembling tenets of modern and scientific personality theory (Hall & Lindzey, 1978; Pedersen, 1977); articles have also been contributed on implicit personality theory within the Far East. On the empirical plane, much of the scattered and fragmented work on personality and culture has been surveyed (Draguns, 1979; Triandis, 1977). The concept of subjective culture and methods for ascertaining it have been introduced by Triandis and collaboraters. While the concept is not synonymous with personality, it refers to "a cultural group's characteristic ways of perceiving the man-made part of the environment" (Triandis et al., 1972, p. 4). Thus, it represents a vital link between the physical and external attributes of a culture and its personal effects, on the plane of personality formation. According to Triandis (1977), subjective culture encompasses approximately 50 percent of the variance in social behavior. The question is open as to how much, if at all, this share of variance could be increased if personality variables were taken into account.

Juris G. Draguns

See also Affective Education; Individual Differences; Motivation; Personality Assessment; Psychology.

REFERENCES

Adler, A. *Practice and Theory of Individual Psychology.* New York: Harcourt, Brace, 1927.

Allport, G. W. *Personality: A Psychological Interpretation.* New York: Henry Holt, 1937.

Allport, G. W. *Pattern and Growth in Personality.* New York: Holt, Rinehart, 1961.

Bandura, A. Self-efficacy: Toward a unified theory of behavioral change. *Psychological Review,* 1977, *84,* 191–215. (a)

Bandura, A. *Social Learning Theory.* Englewood Cliffs, N.J.: Prentice-Hall, 1977. (b)

Bandura, A. The self system in reciprocal determinism. *American Psychologist,* 1978, *33,* 344–358.

Bandura, A.; Ross, D.; & Ross, S. Vicarious reinforcement and imitative learning. *Journal of Abnormal and Social Psychology,* 1963, *67,* 601–607.

Bannister, D., & Fransella, F. *A Manual for the Repertory Grid Technique.* New York: Academic Press, 1977.

Block, J. *Lives through Time.* Berkeley, Calif.: Bancroft, 1971.

Bowers, K. S. Situationism in psychology: An analysis and a critique. *Psychological Review,* 1973, *80,* 307–336.

Carlson, R. Where is the person in personality research? *Psychological Bulletin,* 1971, *75,* 203–209.

Cattell, R. B. *The Scientific Analysis of Personality.* Baltimore: Penguin Books, 1965.

Dollard, J., & Miller, N. E. *Personality and Psychotherapy.* New York: McGraw-Hill, 1950.

Draguns, J. G. *Assessment of Personality.* Homewood, Ill.: Learning Systems Company, 1975.

Draguns, J. G. Culture and personality. In A. J. Marsella, R. G. Tharp, & T. J. Ciborowski (Eds.), *Perspectives on Cross-cultural Psychology.* New York: Academic Press, 1979.

Epstein, S. The stability of behavior: I. On predicting most of the people much of the time. *Journal of Personality and Social Psychology,* 1979, *37,* 1097–1126.

Epstein, S. The stability of behavior: II. Implications for psychological research. *American Psychologist,* 1980, *35,* 790–806.

Eysenck, H. J. *The Structure of Human Personality.* London: Methuen, 1970.

Eysenck, H. J., & Wilson, G. D. *The Experimental Study of Freudian Theory.* London: Methuen, 1973.

Fischer, S., & Greenberg, R. P. *The Scientific Credibility of Freud's Theories and Therapy.* New York: Basic Books, 1977.

Fiske, D. W. *Strategies for Personality Research.* San Francisco: Jossey-Bass, 1978.

Freud, S. Introductory lectures on psychoanalysis. In J. Strachey (Ed.), *Standard Edition of the Complete Psychological Works of S. Freud* (Vols. 15 and 16). London: Hogarth Press, 1963. (Originally published, 1917)

Freud, S. New introductory lectures on psychoanalysis. In J. Strachey (Ed.), *The Standard Edition of the Complete Psychological Works of S. Freud* (Vol. 22). London: Hogarth Press, 1964. (a) (Originally published, 1933)

Freud, S. An outline of psychoanalysis. In J. Strachey (Ed.), *The Standard Edition of the Complete Psychological Works of S. Freud* (Vol. 23). London: Hogarth Press, 1964. (b) (Originally published, 1940)

Fromm, E. *Man for Himself: An Inquiry into the Psychology of Ethics.* New York: Rinehart, 1947.

Guilford, J. P. *Personality.* New York: McGraw-Hill, 1959.

Hall, C. S., & Lindzey, G. *Theories of Personality* (3rd ed.). New York: Wiley, 1978.

Helson, R., & Mitchell, V. Personality. *Annual Review of Psychology*, 1978, *29*, 555–585.

Herrmann, T. *Lehrbuch der empirischen Persönlichkeitsforschung* (3rd ed.). Göttingen, West Germany: Verlag für Psychologie Hogrefe, 1976.

Hogan, R.; DeSoto, C. B.; & Solano, C. Traits, tests, and personality research. *American Psychologist*, 1977, *32*, 255–264.

Horney, K. *The Neurotic Personality of Our Time*. New York: Norton, 1937.

Jung, C. G. *Analytical Psychology: Its Theory and Practice*. New York: Random House, Vintage Books, 1968.

Kelly, G. A. *The Psychology of Personal Constructs*. New York: Norton, 1955.

Kline, P. *Fact and Fantasy in Freudian Theory*. London: Methuen, 1972.

Krasner, L., & Ullmann, L. P. *Behavior Influence and Personality*. New York: Holt, Rinehart & Winston, 1973.

Lefcourt, H. M. *Locus of Control: Current Trends in Theory and Research*. Hillsdale, N.J.: Lawrence Erlbaum Associates, 1977.

London, H. (Ed.), *Personality: A New Look at Metatheories*. Washington: Hemisphere, 1978.

Lundin, R. W. *Personality: A Behavioral Analysis* (2nd ed.). New York: Macmillan, 1974.

Magnusson, D., & Endler, N. S. (Eds.), *Personality at the Crossroads: Current Issues in Interactional Psychology*. Hillsdale, N.J.: Lawrence Erlbaum Associates, 1977.

Mahoney, M. J. *Cognitive Behavior Modification*. Cambridge, Mass.: Ballinger, 1974.

Mischel, W. *Personality and Assessment*. New York: Wiley, 1968.

Mischel, W. Toward a cognitive social learning reconceptualization of personality. *Psychological Review*, 1973, *80*, 252–283.

Mischel, W. On the future of personality measurement. *American Psychologist*, 1977, *32*, 246–254.

Mischel, W. On the interface of cognition and personality: Beyond the person-situation debate. *American Psychologist*, 1979, *34*, 740–754.

Mowrer, O. H. *Learning Theory and Personality Dynamics*. New York: Ronald Press, 1950.

Murray, H. A., & Kluckhohn, C. Outline of a conception of personality. In C. Kluckhohn, H. A. Murray, & D. Schneider (Eds.), *Personality in Nature, Society, and Culture* (2nd ed.). New York: Knopf, 1953.

Olweus, D. Stability of aggressive patterns in males: A review. *Psychological Bulletin*, 1978, *69*, 56–68.

Pavlov, I. P. *Conditioned Reflexes*. New York: Oxford University Press, 1927.

Pedersen, P. Asian personality theories. In R. Corsini (Ed.), *Current Personality Theories*. Itaska, Ill.: F. E. Peacock, 1977.

Pervin, L. A. *Personality: Theory, Assessment, and Research* (3rd ed.). New York: Wiley, 1980.

Phares, E. J. *Locus of Control in Personality*. Morristown, N.J.: General Learning Press, 1976.

Rogers, C. R. A theory of therapy, personality, and interpersonal relationships as developed in the client-centered framework. In S. Koch (Ed.), *Psychology: A Study of a Science* (Vol. 3). New York: McGraw-Hill, 1959.

Sechrest, L. Personality. *Annual Review of Psychology*, 1976, *27*, 1–28.

Silverman, L. H. Psychoanalytic theory: The reports of its death are greatly exaggerated. *American Psychologist*, 1976, *31*, 621–637.

Skinner, B. F. *Science and Human Behavior*. New York: Macmillan, 1953.

Skinner, B. F. *About Behaviorism*. New York: Knopf, 1974.

Staub, E. Social and prosocial behavior: Personal and situational influences and their interaction. In E. Staub (Ed.), *Personality: Basic Aspects and Current Research*. Englewood Cliffs, N.J.: Prentice-Hall, 1980.

Sullivan, H. S. *The Interpersonal Theory of Psychiatry*. New York: Norton, 1953.

Triandis, H. C. Cross-cultural social and personality psychology. *Personality and Social Psychology Bulletin*, 1977, *3*, 143–158.

Triandis, H. C.; Vassiliou, V.; Vassiliou, G.; Tanaka, Y.; & Shanmugam, A. V. *The Analysis of Subjective Culture*. New York: Wiley, 1972.

Watson, J. B. *Psychology from the Standpoint of a Behaviorist*. Philadelphia: Lippincott, 1919.

PHILANTHROPIC FOUNDATIONS

The importance of philanthropic foundations to the field of education cannot be overestimated. Education was one of the earliest and largest recipients of foundation support, and it has retained its prominence. As the field of education has grown and matured, the range of educational activities supported by foundations has broadened.

American philanthropic foundations share the following characteristics: they are nongovernmental; they have a principal fund and function as a nonprofit organization; they are managed by their own trustees and directors; and they are established to maintain or aid social, educational, charitable, religious, or other activities serving the common welfare.

This article describes the rise of foundations and concentrates on how these foundations have contributed to the field of education. Information about foundations is collected and analyzed by the Foundation Center in New York City, which has an excellent library.

Foundations: Beginnings and Assets. Prior to 1900, there were only 18 American foundations. By 1920, this number had increased by almost 100, and in the next thirty years more than 2,000 additional foundations were created. The largest growth period was 1950 to 1959, when 2,839 foundations were established. These numbers represent only those foundations with assets over $100,000. There are also approximately 9,000 smaller foundations with assets under $100,000. These smaller foundations often have a relatively short life and tend to limit their attention to a local community. In 1979, 50 leading foundations provided grant payments of $703 million. The market value of these foundations' assets totaled $13 billion.

Education: A Foundation Recipient. The field of education has been a principal recipient of foundation grants from the beginning of the century to the present time. From 1921 to 1930, 43 percent of foundation funds were granted to education, with health receiving the second largest amount, 33 percent (Lindemann, 1936). By 1974, only 28 percent of total dollars granted went to education.

Nevertheless, education remained the largest recipient (Lewis, 1975).

Types of Support. There is a distinction between foundation grants for the endowment and support of existing educational institutions and grants aimed at supporting educational change and improvement. Funds of the first type are typically used to augment established programs. This type is generally considered a constructive activity, allied with the educational establishment or mainstream. The second type of support, however, is used to fund new programs, which are often a dramatic departure from those in existence. This initiative occasionally creates controversy. One historical example of controversy was the creation of the Lincoln School in 1917, made possible by a $6 million grant from the Rockefeller General Educational Board in collaboration with Teachers College of Columbia University. The public announcement of the award stated that the Lincoln School would "frankly discard the theory of education known as 'formal discipline' and will undertake to secure training through careful study of subjects which are in themselves valuable." Some educational leaders reacted negatively, especially teachers of Latin.

A more benign type of foundation support is to individuals, directly or indirectly, in the form of fellowships, scholarships, and training programs. Roughly 10 percent of the money granted for educational programs and projects by the nine foundations studied by Havighurst et al. (1976) was devoted to fellowships and scholarships. Some foundations find it desirable to give money for fellowships and scholarships to agencies or organizations, which in turn select the recipients. Other foundations such as Ford, Carnegie, and Rockefeller have officers located in various parts of the world who discover and advise individuals—U.S. citizens as well as foreigners—and award fellowships or travel grants directly to them.

This form of support is viewed as a long-term investment in the future. According to John H. Knowles, former president of the Rockefeller Foundation, "More than 10,000 fellowships and scholarships have been awarded since 1913, when the Foundation was established. If one had to name the most important single contribution of the Foundation, it would certainly have to be that of supporting the development of promising young men and women" (1974).

Program Emphases. It is easiest to understand the influence of philanthropic foundations on American education by looking at the program emphases of the major foundations from 1900 to 1980.

1900–1920. The General Education Board (GEB), founded by John D. Rockefeller, and the Carnegie Foundation for the Advancement of Teaching, founded by Andrew Carnegie, were the principal sources of support for improvement of education during the first two decades.

Aid to eduction in the South was the main interest of the GEB. Efforts focused on the development of public high schools in rural areas. The Carnegie Foundation granted money to state and private colleges for the salaries of professors of secondary education, whose job was to train high school teachers and to promote the creation of publicly supported secondary schools.

The GEB also promoted the education of black children. In an effort to increase the number of students who stayed in school, the GEB provided the salaries of state agents for negro schools, employees of the state departments of education, who worked to expand schools for black pupils and to promote the training of black teachers. In 1920, 85 percent of the black school children in the southern states were in the first four grades of elementary schools. The dropout rate for blacks beyond the elementary grades was extremely high.

Another major activity of foundations during this period was the reform of medical education. Abraham Flexner, an educator, was employed by the Carnegie Foundation for the Advancement of Teaching to study medical schools in the United States and Canada. The study concluded that 124 of 155 schools were so poor that they should be abolished, and that the faculty members should be full-time employees of universities and should not have private patients (1909). The report caused a tumult. The GEB, acting upon the report's advice, made a first grant to Johns Hopkins Medical School in 1913 of $1.5 million to place the departments of medicine, surgery, and pediatrics on a full-time faculty basis. This was followed by similar grants to Vanderbilt, Yale, the University of Chicago, and Washington University in St. Louis. Mr. Rockefeller contributed $45 million to approximately 25 medical schools between 1919 and 1921 for this purpose.

1920–1940. The purchasing power of the dollar was cut in half between 1914 and 1920, and salaries of college teachers were relatively low. In 1919/20, three-fourths of full-time college teachers earned less than $2,500 per year. At this time, Mr. Rockefeller gave the GEB $50 million to raise the salaries of college teachers in private colleges and universities. By 1924, more than 170 private institutions had received permanent endowment grants from the GEB, and they in turn had raised $66 million to match the board's conditional grants. It should be noted that from 1925 to 1930 one dollar had three times the purchasing power of a dollar in 1975.

The Carnegie Foundation for the Advancement of Teaching undertook to help colleges and universities establish an adequate pension system. This program resulted in the creation of the Teachers Insurance and Annuity Association, today a major institution for retirement benefits to educators.

The decade of the 1930s saw a need for innovation in secondary and higher education. There were very few jobs for youth during the Depression. Consequently, young adults remained in school. The proportions of 14–17-year-olds in school increased from 32 percent in 1920 to 51 percent in 1930 to 73 percent in 1940. The most pressing educational problem became finding ways to serve adolescent youth who would neither need nor want a college education.

In response, the GEB made a grant to the American Council on Education to support the American Youth Commission, which consisted of leading educators and businessmen. The American Youth Commission became a kind of public conscience, surveying in-school and out-of-school youth. The commission explored the problem of black youth through a task force of sociologists, psychologists, anthropologists, and educators.

Seven studies were published by the commission, the most widely read was *Children of Bondage,* by Davis and Dollard (1940). A survey of youth in the state of Maryland, *Youth Tell Their Story* (Bell, 1938), helped to convince the public that the government had a responsibility for the care as well as the education of youth in the economic depression. In a final report, entitled *Youth and the Future* (1942), the American Youth Commission concluded that every young person who did not desire to continue in school after 16, and who could not get a job in private enterprise, should be provided under public auspices with employment in some form of service.

1940–1960. National organizations of educators were keenly aware of the need to assess educational policy and to undertake basic changes in public schools, and college and university programs. The National Education Association was the largest organization of educators in the country, consisting of classroom teachers, school principals, and superintendents of school systems. This organization joined with the American Association of School Administrators to create the Educational Policies Commission in 1935, for which the GEB provided $355,000 to support its work over the next seven years.

Among the members of the Educational Policies Commission in those years were President James B. Conant of Harvard; historian Charles A. Beard; and Professor George S. Counts of Columbia University, a leader among educators who were pressing for changes in school curriculum and educational policy. The commission produced several reports that were widely read and discussed by educators and that set the character of educational practice at the elementary and secondary school levels, and at the early college levels. Under the commission's auspices, Charles Beard published a major book on the subject entitled *The Unique Function of Education in American Democracy* (1937).

Foundation activity was relatively quiescent during the World War II period, but expanded greatly after 1950. The Ford Foundation was established and provided grants of more than $500 million for general support of colleges and universities and for faculty salary increases. This foundation also granted more than $100 million to medical schools.

Other foundations moved vigorously into the field of education. The Carnegie Corporation supported the influential studies of James B. Conant, which focused on the American high school and on teacher education. The Kellogg Foundation supported the expansion of adult education. The Mott Foundation built a solid base for the community school movement. The Grant Foundation supported child study programs for the training of teachers. The Danforth Foundation commenced its major Graduate Education Fellowship Program in 1952.

Several foundations began to support production of educational television programs. The Kellogg Foundation in 1951 provided $300,000 to establish the National Association of Educational Broadcasters. These funds were supplemented by the Ford Foundation, the Carnegie Corporation, and the Sloan Foundation (Havighurst, 1981, pp. 208–209).

1960–1980. After 1960, the federal government joined the foundations in providing funds for educational innovations and experimentation. Congress provided funds to the U.S. Office of Education to establish a program of research grants. These funds were vastly increased by the Elementary and Secondary Education Act of 1965, which supplied grants to individual researchers and to regional research and development centers.

In 1973, the National Institute of Education became a major source of support for educational research and has continued to surpass the private foundations in this area of activity. Other federal agencies have also supported research and development in the educational field, including the National Science Foundation, the National Endowment for the Humanities, the National Institute of Mental Health, and the National Institute of Child Health and Human Development. The total of federal funds given for educational research and development was approximately $225 million in 1970.

This level of support has been continued during the decade of the 1970s. It has been estimated that for the year 1980, the federal government paid about 70 percent of the cost of educational innovation, experimentation, and training. The foundations paid about 20 percent of this cost, and the remainder was paid by universities and school systems through their research budgets and their support of staff time devoted to research and writing.

Conclusions. As this brief overview indicates, private foundations have made an enormous contribution to the field of education. This support includes the endowment of institutions, grants for experimental and innovative educational programs, fellowships to individuals, and much more. It is interesting to note that government has taken over some of these activities that previously might have been the domain of private foundations, and it is even more interesting to speculate on how government and private foundations together might contribute to the field of education in the near future.

Robert J. Havighurst

See also History and Philosophy of Higher Education; U.S. Department of Education.

REFERENCES

American Council on Education, & American Youth Commission. *Youth and the Future*. Washington, D.C.: American Council on Education, 1942.

American Youth Commission. *Youth and the Future*. Washington, D.C.: The Commission, 1942.

Beard, C. A. *The Unique Function of Education in American Democracy*. Washington, D.C.: Educational Policies Commission, National Education Association, and Department of Superintendence, 1937.

Bell, H. M. *Youth Tell Their Story*. Washington, D.C.: American Council on Education, 1938.

Davis, A., & Dollard, J. *Children of Bondage* (Prepared for the American Youth Commission). Washington, D.C.: American Council on Education, 1940.

Flexner, A. *Medical Education in the United States and Canada: A Report to the Carnegie Foundation for the Advancement of Teaching*. New York: Carnegie Foundation, 1910.

Grants of fifty leading foundations. *Chronicle of Higher Education*, June 9, 1980, 10.

Havighurst, R. J. Philanthropic foundations as interest groups. In *Education and Urban Society* (Special issue on interest groups in education), February 1981.

Havighurst, R. J.; Holsinger, D. B.; & Lunde, S. E. *Education and Major Philanthropic Foundations*. Washington, D.C.: National Academy of Education, 1976.

Lewis, M. O. (Ed.). *The Foundation Directory* (5th ed.). New York: Columbia University Press, 1975.

Lindemann, E. C. *Wealth and Culture*. New York: Harcourt, Brace, 1936.

Rockefeller Foundation. *The President's Review and Annual Report*. New York: The Foundation, 1974.

PHILOSOPHY OF EDUCATION

There are three perspectives from which to view philosophy of education: the personal, the public, and the professional (Soltis, 1981a, 1981b, 1981c). Every practicing educator operates with some personal beliefs about what are the sensible, right, and good things to do in promoting human learning. A set of such beliefs constitutes one's personal philosophy of education and is developed and refined over a lifetime of commitment to educating. The first part of this article discusses this way of being philosophical about educating.

But there are also public views of educating. Sometimes these are compatible with a personal position and sometimes not. Sometimes they are formulated in technical, philosophical terminology and sometimes in the language of the political, the ideological, or the practical. Sometimes they are highly critical or impossibly utopian, and sometimes they are doable and desirable. Public philosophy of education is everybody's business, and everybody seems to feel that way; but philosophers are expected to have some special role in developing and appraising public

views on educating. The second part of this article sketches aspects of philosophy of education viewed from its public perspective.

The third part treats the professional dimension of the philosophy of education. In this century, for the first time, philosophers have been trained specifically as philosophers of education. They are professional philosophers concerned with anything that is philosophically relevant to the context, design, and activities of educating. A rich literature written by contemporary philosophers of education has become available to professional educators. Some of this literature is personal and public in scope, but much of it also speaks professionally to the special interests of discrete subgroups of educational specialists and to other philosophers. A survey and sampling of this literature are provided.

In addition, each part addresses three questions. What is the point of being philosophical about education in this way? How are the claims of each of the philosophical perspectives critically assessed? What is the relationship between philosophy of education and practice? The answers to these questions will differ when looked at from personal, public, and professional perspectives, but the differences should be seen as complementary and compatible and not as mutually exclusive. Professional philosophers of education can and do operate from each perspective and often blend them together.

Personal Perspectives. Having a personal philosophy of education is much like having a philosophy of life. It is adopting and acting on a personally meaningful view of what education should be about. It can range in structure from being an unexamined general point of view to being a thoughtful, systematic development of a justified and highly articulated position. The point of being philosophical about education in this way lies in its motivating and meaningful force for the individual. It is both the engine that drives a person's commitment to educating and the rails that guide the way.

When Silberman (1970) complained about the "mindlessness" he found in American classrooms, he was pointing to educators whom he saw as acting without clear purpose or personal commitment. For him, they were like inert mechanical parts functioning in an insensitive bureaucratic machine rather than autonomous actors whose activities were directed by intelligence and compassion. Having a personal view of educating is to have some basic beliefs about educational purposes, which in turn give meaning to the activities one designs and engages in to achieve those aims. If, for instance, one is committed to helping children achieve a sense of personal worth as well as a mastery of basic skills, then one teaches reading and writing in a manner that fosters both and avoids whatever might thwart one, even if it is the most efficient means for producing the other.

Personal philosophies of education can be articulated in many ways: in discussions, in interviews, in job applications, in meetings, in articles, in the quiet of one's mind, and in the deliberateness of one's actions. One of the classic philosophical statements of a personal point of view was *My Pedagogic Creed* (Dewey [1897], 1973). In it, Dewey made clear his commitment to democracy and the role of the school in fostering social and personal growth. It became the cornerstone of his more formal "public" system of progressive education definitively presented in *Democracy and Education* (Dewey, 1916). In a way, Maria Montessori's work with disadvantaged children in Italy at the turn of the century and A. S. Neill's school without compulsion, Summerhill (Neill, 1960), were the practical and systematic workings out of personal philosophies of education, just as Skinner's *Walden Two* (1948) was a fictional yet personal view of the educational potential of radical behaviorism.

Even professional philosophers, while making public statements, have used the occasion to present their highly personal views of educating. William Heard Kilpatrick, near the end of his life, in *Philosophy of Education* (1951), wrote what was at once the last major book of his career and the first comprehensive treatment of his own personal philosophy; and Bertrand Russell in *Education and the Good Life* (1970), provided a less systematic but nonetheless intensely personal view of the proper ways of parenting and educating.

In more recent years, whether emphasizing personal growth (Mann, 1972), liberal humanism (Wales, 1979), intelligence (Skemp, 1979), or absolute principles (Adler, 1977), there seems to be no dearth of published works that either express personal positions on educating or advise and help teachers develop their own ideologies (Bernier & Williams, 1973)—ideologies and aims that can then be translated into appropriate methods of instruction (Moore, 1974). To enhance the educator's ability to develop a sophisticated personal philosophy of education has been a responsibility taken on by various professional philosophers of education. For example, Harry S. Broudy (1977) has provided generations of teachers with a systematic way to work at building a philosophy of education, and Maxine Greene's existential approach entreats teachers to do the same by facing and making personally meaningful choices (Greene, 1973).

Thus there seems to be good reason to believe that philosophers, educators, and people in general are correct when they assert either implicitly or explicitly that the relation between a personal philosophy of education and one's practice is direct and crucial to meaningful educating. By definition, having a personal philosophy of education is being committed to doing certain things in certain ways. This fact also is reflected in the highly influential "Tyler rationale" found in curriculum development theory, which gives high priority to the use of one's philosophy of education as a filter through which to strain curriculum proposals and teaching strategies.

How is a personal philosophy of education critically assessed? Clearly the center of gravity is within the individ-

ual, but while assessment is personal, it need not lack objectivity or rationality. It can be tested in the world and discussed with others. Face-to-face discussion and debate force better articulation and sounder justification of one's personal position. Often reading and paying attention to public proposals and vocal critics will bring about modification and sometimes even rejection of one's ideas or values. The process is a continuing one of reflecting upon, testing, extending, adding to, and modifying one's views in the crucible of daily educational practice.

Public Perspectives. The basic difference between personal and public conceptions of the philosophy of education is that while both can serve to guide individual practice, the latter seek to alter, create, or justify practices of the many. Public expressions of philosophy of education can be found in federal policies (e.g., Head Start, bilingual education, and desegregation); in state mandates and requirements (e.g., minimum competency testing, sex education, and citizenship education); and in local board policies (e.g., "that each may learn," alternative schools, and open classrooms). These are governmental expressions of what the people through their representatives take to be good and right to do in education. The people expect educators to adopt the philosophical positions that stand behind these policies and to implement them meaningfully.

Individual critics. But public philosophy of education is not only manifested in political and institutional forms. It is also found in the reflective writings of the public critics of education (e.g., Goodman, 1964; Holt, 1964; Kozol, 1967). Such critics force the public to reflect on the faults of education and urge a philosophically based redirection of practice. Some go so far as to recommend "deschooling society" (Illich, 1971) in order to make learning meaningful by removing it from bureaucratic institutionalization. Others force us to look closely at the institutional forms education takes to see how they might carry within them invidious capitalist-industrialist modes of social control (Apple, 1979; Bowles & Gintis, 1976). Not only philosophers and educators but politicians, clerics, historians, journalists, and intellectuals of all sorts engage in public philosophy of education. The point of this enterprise is to get people to reflect philosophically on education as it is and as it might be and then to act accordingly.

Philosophical schools. Public philosophy of education is also found in more systematic forms. The progressive education movement during the first half of this century was perhaps the quintessence of a public philosophy of education put into practice, even though practitioners often misunderstood the philosophy and political forces behind it (Cremin, 1961). Basically, progressive education was a liberal philosophy directed at educating members of a democratic community who could think, solve problems, and make intelligent adjustments to a world where change is bound to happen. Conservatives opposed progressives insofar as progressive educators neglected traditional subject matter. The conservative "essentialist" believed that the central purpose of education is to acquire the organized knowledge of one's tradition, that such acquisition defines a civilized and educated person. But the essentialists in turn were criticized by the reactionary "perennialists," who argued that traditions and knowledge change; therefore, it is necessary to pass on to future generations not traditional views but knowledge of unchanging first principles, of what in all times and places constitutes truth, beauty, and goodness.

The philosopher of education Theodore Brameld (1971) used these conflicts in the public philosophy of education at mid-century to provide a platform for advocating his own politically radical alternative, which he called "reconstructionism." By means of an intelligently directed educational system, he claimed that society and culture can be reconstructed and a new world built on our best vision of its possibilities, if only we actively work at it and school for it. Needless to say, not all public philosophies of education are put into practice. The relation between a publicly advocated theory and public practice is complex.

Philosophers also adopt metaphysical systems of philosophy that underwrite fundamental world views, which in turn provide a context for thinking about public forms of education compatible with those views (Morris & Pai, 1976). For example, Marxism has been treated both formally as a philosophical system with relevance to understanding education (Sarup, 1978), and programmatically (Freire, 1970, 1974, 1976) as a means of using education to lift the perceived oppressiveness of alienation from the shoulders of the people. Existentialism and phenomenology have been used as methods for approaching and thinking about education as a means of choosing oneself and achieving understanding through the richness of phenomenal experience (Chamberlin, 1969; Denton, 1974; Greene, 1978; Morris, 1966; Vandenberg, 1971). Other philosophical schools, such as pragmatism (Bayles, 1966), realism (Martin, 1969), and idealism (Butler, 1966) have provided general views of education from each of their particular perspectives. This schools-of-philosophy approach dominated professional philosophy of education around mid-century (Brubacher, 1942, 1955). Although it still provides a useful public way of classifying and understanding positions and proposals, it is no longer the way most professionals conceive of and act in the field (Soltis, 1981a, 1981b).

Contemporary criticism. Philosophers of education also view taking a critical stance toward contemporary critics and fads as part of their public responsibility. They have systematically examined the works of public figures with views on education such as Conant, Brameld, Barzun, Skinner, and Goodman (McClellan, 1968), as well as A. S. Neill, Ivan Illich, Everett Reimer, Neil Postman, and Charles Weingartner (Barrow, 1978). Some have critically dealt with such "innovations" in education as competency-based teacher education, mainstreaming, career education, accountability, and teaching machines (Broudy, 1972; Rich, 1975).

Other philosophers have continued the tradition of for-mulating their own public views on educating. In the 1970s, for example, Itzkoff (1976) promised a new public education based on the idea of creating a variety of learning communities in a pluralistic society, which would be possible, he argued, only if a voucher system, with free choice among schooling practices, were developed. Tesconi and Morris (1972) blamed "bureautechnology" for the loss of personal identity and free choice, urging that the schools turn back to a basic consideration of the moral sphere and the problem of how to live well. And Crittenden (1973) argued that all human beings have a right to a liberal education, because it is crucial to the attainment of the capacity to live the full moral life.

Assessment and practice. Of course, philosophers are critical of each other too, but most critical assessment of public philosophy of education is public, political, ideological, and practical rather than technically philosophical. Whether criticism occurs in the press, on television, at legislative hearings, in journals, magazines, or books, at professional or citizens' meetings, public proposals and criticisms get heard, debated, and tested in the marketplace of conflicting pressure groups, differing personal philosophies, and existing social conditions. In such situations, professional educators provide expert testimony when the facts of the matter are called into question, and they respond with their best-reasoned justification for practices they have made both personal and public in their lives as educators. Philosophers of education also offer analyses and clarifications of arguments and positions and try to keep the public debate rational in the best sense of that term.

Obviously, there is no single or simple relationship between public philosophy of education and practice. If a proposal is not adopted, then there is no relationship at all. If it is adopted as policy, there is no guarantee that those who carry it out understand it or are committed to it. If it fails, it is difficult to determine how much of the cause of failure is attributable to the philosophy itself and how much to the adverse conditions in which it was tried. If it succeeds, we have the hardworking and skillful educators to applaud as well as the policy creators and all who stand in between.

Still, public philosophy of education is needed in a democratic society because it articulates public aspirations and values, gives sense and purpose to the public enterprise of education, and provides the opportunity for thoughtful participation in the direction of education by all who care seriously about it.

Professional Perspectives. I have already indicated that some philosophers articulate their own personal philosophy of education and some try to help educators develop a philosophy of their own. Professional philosophers of education also participate in the arena of public philosophy of education as critics, as critics of critics, and as proposers and evaluators of educational programs and policies. To this extent, professional philosophy of education includes both the personal and public dimensions. But it also goes beyond these predominantly programmatic and valuational ways of philosophically treating education to make special use of the technical tools of the professional philosopher in dealing with conceptual issues relevant to educating. When philosophers perform this function, there is less proposing and more analyzing, examining, reflecting, and seeking a clearer understanding of educational matters. There is more emphasis on ascertaining the logical soundness of arguments, explicating the meaning of ideas, and providing proposals for ways to think about educational phenomena and related tasks and problems, than on proposing ways to do or solve them. When engaged in this sort of philosophizing, a philosopher of education is more intent on providing illumination, understanding, and perspective for educators to think with than on providing programs and policies for educators to act on.

The point of being philosophical about education in this way is to make the educational enterprise as rationally self-reflective as possible by providing philosophically rigorous examinations, critiques, analyses, and syntheses of aspects of the educator's conceptual domain. The ability of professional philosophers of education to do this well is directly dependent upon their rigorous training in and mastery of philosophical skills and literature. They are philosophical scholar-teachers who do technical philosophical work demanding rigor, precision, and adherence to their own professional canons of scholarship, just as sociologists, biologists, historians, psychologists, and other academics do in their research and teaching. As college and university professors, they are also keepers of the philosophical tradition that Ulich (1954) considered three thousand years of educational wisdom. They mine this wisdom to shed light on current educational concerns, to keep educators from continually reinventing the wheel, and sometimes just for its own sake, as scholars in every field are inclined to do. With some regularity, new studies of the educational thought of such philosophers as Plato, Aristotle, Rousseau, Locke, Whitehead, and Dewey appear in professional journals and stimulate scholarly thought and debate.

Topics of inquiry. But this is not where the major research effort in contemporary professional philosophy of education is exerted. Philosophical knowledge and skill in the main are brought to bear on a multiplicity of topics, issues, and problems, which are all relevant in some way to education. Some topics come from the forms and features of the daily practices of education itself: justification of special admission standards for minorities (Weinberg, 1979), open education (Goldstone, 1979; Nyberg, 1975), student rights (Bandman, 1977; Kerr, 1978; Sutton, 1978; Worsfold, 1979), ethics of unionism in education (Hetenyi, 1978), per pupil expenditure and equality of educational opportunity (LaBrecque, 1978). Topics of concern and interest to other researchers in the field of educational inquiry are also explored, for example, philosophical examination of the usefulness and potential of information-pro-

cessing theory in educational research (Dejonghe, 1979), the relation between psychological theories and educational theories (Egan, 1979), or the limits of ATI (aptitude-treatment-interaction) research (Phillips, 1979).

Not infrequently in much of the contemporary literature of professional philosophy of education, philosophers argue with each other in order to get the logic of their own research straight and their claims clear. Sometimes they also draw on the literature of general philosophy if that helps to illuminate topics relevant to educational ideas they are working on. For example, in the 1970s, journals and proceedings in philosophy of education were full of references, explications, and debates about the educational relevance of such influential works in general philosophy as *The Structure of Scientific Revolutions* (Kuhn, 1962) and *A Theory of Justice* (Rawls, 1971).

One recent attempt to provide a conceptual framework for viewing the diverse array of contemporary scholarship in professional philosophy of education was made in *Philosophy and Education* (Soltis, 1981b), a yearbook of the National Society for the Study of Education (NSSE). There, various subareas of philosophy (aesthetics, epistemology, logic, social philosophy, ethics, and philosophy of science) were used as general contexts within which philosophers of education located, defined, and discussed such specific topics of educational interest as aesthetic literacy (Greene, 1981), teaching practical reasoning (Ennis, 1981), values education (Beck, 1981), and school desegregation (Strike, 1981). The contexts of curriculum and theory of teaching were also singled out as special subareas indigenous to educational philosophy itself. The major advantage claimed for this organization was to focus the expectations of educational specialists on some narrower area of their philosophical concern, while still representing the wide range of work done by philosophers of education in a systematic way.

Survey of contemporary scholarship. Borrowing the framework of the NSSE yearbook, it is possible to give a sample of contemporary scholarship in professional philosophy of education.

Aesthetics. Using a concept of mind drawn from the Dewey tradition, Arnstine (1967) has stressed the importance of aesthetic quality in all experience and especially in learning and schooling. Ralph Smith in his own work (1970) and in his editing of the *Journal of Aesthetic Education* has provided a forum for philosophers to connect topics in aesthetics to problems and ideas in aesthetic education.

Epistemology. Contemporary views of mind and learning with special emphases on the theories of the psychologists Skinner and Piaget have been philosophically examined in schooling contexts (Pai, 1973) and in the broader tradition of philosophical theories of knowledge (Hamlyn, 1979). Other significant treatments of the concept of knowledge have come from Hirst (1975), arguing that there are several distinct forms of knowledge (scientific, religious, mathematical, artistic), and from Scheffler's classic treatment of Ryle's distinction between "knowing how" and "knowing that" (Scheffler, 1965).

Logic. Logic and thinking in the educational context have been treated by Ennis (1969), with his description of logical moves made by teachers in classrooms, and by Belth (1977), who argues that all effective thinking in all subjects is based on the power of the human imagination to create symbolic worlds in the form of models, analogies, and metaphors.

Social Philosophy. Viewing institutionalized education as a vast social system, Green (1980) provides a philosophical model for predicting the system's behavior, and Pratte (1977) analyzes the concept of ideology to show how it operates in marshaling thought and actions around the agenda of schooling and cultural diversity.

Ethics. There have been a number of works on moral education (Chazan & Soltis, 1973; Cochrane, Hamm, & Kazepides, 1979; Wilson, 1972), and philosophers have also treated ethical problems regarding the neutrality of universities, the nature of student academic freedom, the legal rights of children, the justice of compulsory education, and equality in education (Strike & Egan, 1978). Peters's classic work in analytic philosophy *Ethics and Education,* (1966) examines the related concepts of education, justification, equality, worthwhile activities, interests, freedom, respect, authority, punishment, and democracy.

Philosophy of science. The relation of thought in philosophy of science to issues in contemporary educational research has included consideration of such topics as observation, inference, hypothesis testing, causation, behaviorism, and the nature of educational research itself (Broudy, Ennis, & Krimerman, 1973; Millman & Gowin, 1974; Thomas, 1972).

Professional philosophers of education have also devoted considerable attention to illuminating such central areas of educational concern as the aims of education (Brown, 1970; Dearden, Hirst, & Peters, 1972; Hare, 1979), curriculum (Dearden, 1968; Levit, 1971; Martin, 1970; White, 1973), teaching (Green, 1971; Komisar, 1976; MacMillan & Nelson, 1968; Passmore, 1980), and educational policy (Kerr, 1976).

Assessment and practice. How are claims, arguments, explications, and ideas critically assessed in professional philosophy of education? Most frequently they are assessed by fellow philosophers using the standards and canons of the discipline of philosophy. Being reflectively critical of the ideas of others is part of what it means to be a practicing professional philosopher. Unlike empirical claims backed by data as evidence, philosophical descriptions and arguments are tested by their ability to withstand critical examination in terms of their reasonableness, logical consistency, theoretical adequacy, meaningfulness, and illuminative value.

What is the relation of the scholarship of professional philosophy of education to practice? It is seldom direct, but that does not mean it has no effect or is irrelevant. Sound and deep thinking about what one does before,

after, and even while doing it can very directly affect one's practice. Philosophers work to make the thinking of educators about a multitude of topics clearer and more rational. They seek to give educators and researchers as much philosophical perspective on their practice as is possible. But perspective, clarity, critical insight, logic, and meaningfulness are only of value if they are used. Ultimately it is the practicing educator who must make good use of philosophy in all its senses: personal, public, and professional.

Jonas F. Soltis

See also Aesthetic Education; Curriculum History; History of Education; History and Philosophy of Higher Education; Philosophy of Science in Education.

REFERENCES

Adler, M. J. *Reforming Education.* Boulder, Colo.: Westview Press, 1977.

Apple, M. *Ideology and Curriculum.* Boston: Routledge & Kegan Paul, 1979.

Arnstine, D. *Philosophy of Education: Learning and Schooling.* New York: Harper & Row, 1967.

Bandman, B. Some legal, moral, and intellectual rights of children. *Educational Theory,* 1977, *27,* 169–178.

Barrow, R. *Radical Education.* New York: Wiley, 1978.

Bayles, E. E. *Pragmatism in Education.* New York: Harper & Row, 1966.

Beck, C. M. The reflective approach to values education. In J. F. Soltis (Ed.), *Philosophy and Education: Eightieth Yearbook of the National Society for the Study of Education* (Part 1). Chicago: University of Chicago Press, 1981.

Belth, M. *The Process of Thinking.* New York: McKay, 1977.

Bernier, N. R., & Williams, J. E. (Eds.). *Beyond Beliefs: Ideological Foundations of American Education.* Englewood Cliffs, N.J.: Prentice-Hall, 1973.

Bowles, S., & Gintis, H. *Schooling in Capitalist America.* New York: Basic Books, 1976.

Brameld, T. *Patterns of Educational Philosophy.* New York: Holt, Rinehart & Winston, 1971.

Broudy, H. S. *The Real World of Public Schools.* New York: Harcourt Brace Jovanovich, 1972. (ERIC Document Reproduction Service No. ED 075 984)

Broudy, H. S. *Building a Philosophy of Education* (2nd ed.). Huntington, N.Y.: Krieger, 1977.

Broudy, H. S.; Ennis, R. H.; & Krimerman; L. J. (Eds.). *Philosophy of Educational Research.* New York: Wiley, 1973.

Brown, L. M. (Ed.). *Aims of Education.* New York: Teachers College Press, 1970.

Brubacher, J. S. (Ed.). *Philosophies of Education: Forty-first Yearbook of the National Society for the Study of Education* (Part 1). Chicago: University of Chicago Press, 1942.

Brubacher, J. S. (Ed.). *Modern Philosophies of Education: Fifty-fourth Yearbook of the National Society for the Study of Education.* Chicago: University of Chicago Press, 1955.

Butler, J. D. *Idealism in Education.* New York: Harper & Row, 1966.

Chamberlin, J. G. *Toward a Phenomenology of Education.* Philadelphia: Westminster Press, 1969.

Chazan, B. I., & Soltis, J. F. (Eds.). *Moral Education.* New York: Teachers College Press, 1973.

Cochrane, D. B.; Hamm, C. M.; & Kazepides, A. C. (Eds.). *The Domain of Moral Education*. New York: Paulist Press, 1979.

Cremin, L. *The Transformation of the School*. New York: Knopf, 1961.

Crittenden, B. S. *Education and Social Ideals*. Ontario: Longman Canada, 1973.

Dearden, R. F. *The Philosophy of Primary Education*. New York: Humanities Press, 1968.

Dearden, R. F.; Hirst, P. H.; & Peters, R. S. (Eds.). *A Critique of Current Educational Aims*. Boston: Routledge & Kegan Paul, 1972.

Dejonghe, L. S. Information-processing approaches to cognitive structure: New look of educational research or degenerating paradigm? *Proceedings of the Philosophy of Education Society*, 1979, 236–248.

Denton, D. E. (Ed.). *Existentialism and Phenomenology in Education*. New York: Teachers College Press, 1974.

Dewey, J. *Democracy and Education*. New York: Macmillan, 1916.

Dewey, J. My pedagogic creed. In J. J. McDermott (Ed.), *The Philosophy of John Dewey* (Vol. 2). New York: Putnam, 1973. (Originally published, 1897)

Egan, K. Some differences between educational and psychological theories of educational development. *Proceedings of the Philosophy of Education Society*, 1979, 304–312.

Ennis, R. H. *Logic in Teaching*. Englewood Cliffs, N.J.: Prentice-Hall, 1969.

Ennis, R. H. Rational thinking and educational practice. In J. F. Soltis (Ed.), *Philosophy and Education: Eightieth Yearbook of the National Society for the Study of Education* (Part 1). Chicago: University of Chicago Press, 1981.

Freire, P. *Pedagogy of the Oppressed*. New York: Herder & Herder, 1970. (ERIC Document Reproduction Service No. ED 045 793)

Freire, P. *Education for Critical Consciousness*. New York: Seabury Press, 1974.

Freire, P. *Education: The Practice of Freedom*. London: Writers & Readers, 1976.

Goldstone, P. Open education and open marriage. *Proceedings of the Philosophy of Education Society*, 1979, 87–99.

Goodman, P. *Compulsory Mis-education*. New York: Horizon Press, 1964.

Green, T. F. *The Activities of Teaching*. New York: McGraw-Hill, 1971.

Green, T. F. *Predicting the Behavior of the Educational System*. Syracuse, N.Y.: Syracuse University Press, 1980.

Greene, M. *Teacher as Stranger*. Belmont, Calif.: Wadsworth, 1973.

Greene, M. *Landscapes of Learning*. New York: Teachers College Press, 1978. (ERIC Document Reproduction Service No. ED 156 568)

Greene, M. Aesthetic literacy in general education. In J. F. Soltis (Ed.), *Philosophy and Education: Eightieth Yearbook of the National Society for the Study of Education* (Part 1). Chicago: University of Chicago Press, 1981.

Hamlyn, D. W. *Experience and the Growth of Understanding*. Boston: Routledge & Kegan Paul, 1979.

Hare, W. *Open-mindedness and Education*. Montreal: McGill-Queens University Press, 1979.

Hetenyi, L. Unionism in education: The ethics of it. *Educational Theory*, 1978, 28, 90–95.

Hirst, P. H. *Knowledge and the Curriculum*. Boston: Routledge & Kegan Paul, 1975.

Holt, J. *How Children Fail*. New York: Pitman, 1964.

Illich, I. *Deschooling Society*. New York: Harper & Row, 1971. (ERIC Document Reproduction Service No. ED 057 615)

Itzkoff, S. W. *A New Public Education*. New York: McKay, 1976.

Kerr, D. H. *Educational Policy: Analysis, Structure, and Justification*. New York: McKay, 1976.

Kerr, D. H. Thinking about education with a strict typology of rights. *Educational Theory*, 1978, 28, 165–174.

Kilpatrick, W. H. *Philosophy of Education*. New York: Macmillan, 1951.

Komisar, B. P., et al. *Natural Teaching Encounters*. Philadelphia: KDC Enterprises, 1976.

Kozol, J. *Death at an Early Age*. Boston: Houghton Mifflin, 1967. (ERIC Document Reproduction Service No. ED 023 766)

Kuhn, T. S. *The Structure of Scientific Revolutions*. Chicago: University of Chicago Press, 1962.

LaBrecque, R. The shibboleth of equal per-student expenditures. *Proceedings of the Philosophy of Education Society*, 1978, 192–203.

Levit, M. *Curriculum: Readings in the Philosophy of Education*. Urbana: University of Illinois Press, 1971.

Macmillan, C. J. B., & Nelson, T. W. (Eds.). *Concepts of Teaching: Philosophical Essays*. Chicago: Rand McNally, 1968.

Mann, J. H. *Learning to Be: The Education of Human Potential*. New York: Free Press, 1972.

Martin, J. R. (Ed.). *Readings in the Philosophy of Education: A Study of Curriculum*. Boston: Allyn & Bacon, 1970.

Martin, W. O. *Realism in Education*. New York: Harper & Row, 1969.

McClellan, J. E. *Toward an Effective Critique of American Education*. Philadelphia: Lippincott, 1968.

Millman, J., & Gowin, D. B. *Appraising Educational Research*. Englewood Cliffs, N.J.: Prentice-Hall, 1974.

Moore, T. W. *Educational Theory: An Introduction*. Boston: Routledge & Kegan Paul, 1974.

Morris, V. *Existentialism in Education*. New York: Harper & Row, 1966.

Morris, V., & Pai, Y. *Philosophy and the American School* (2nd ed.). Boston: Houghton Mifflin, 1976.

Neill, A. S. *Summerhill: A Radical Approach to Childrearing*. New York: Hart, 1960.

Nyberg, D. (Ed.). *The Philosophy of Open Education*. Boston: Routledge & Kegan Paul, 1975.

Pai, Y. *Teaching, Learning, and the Mind*. Boston: Houghton Mifflin, 1973.

Passmore, J. A. *The Philosophy of Teaching*. Cambridge: Harvard University Press, 1980.

Peters, R. S. *Ethics and Education*. London: Allen & Unwin, 1966.

Phillips, D. C. The interactive universe and the limits of educational research. *Proceedings of the Philosophy of Education Society*, 1979, 135–145.

Pratte, R. *Ideology and Education*. New York: McKay, 1977.

Rawls, J. *A Theory of Justice*. Cambridge: Harvard University Press, 1971.

Rich, J. M. *Innovations in Education*. Boston: Allyn & Bacon, 1975. (ERIC Document Reproduction Service No. ED 103 559)

Russell, B. *Education and the Good Life*. New York: Liveright, 1970.

Sarup, M. *Marxism and Education*. Boston: Routledge & Kegan Paul, 1978.

Scheffler, I. *The Conditions of Knowledge*. Glenview, Ill.: Scott, Foresman, 1965.

Silberman, C. E. *Crisis in the Classroom*. New York: Random House, 1970.

Skemp, R. R. *Intelligence, Learning, and Action: Foundations for Theory and Practice in Education.* New York: Wiley, 1979.

Skinner, B. F. *Walden Two.* New York: Macmillan, 1948.

Smith, R. A. (Ed.). *Aesthetic Concepts and Education.* Urbana: University of Illinois Press, 1970.

Soltis, J. F. Philosophy of education for teachers. *Journal of Education* (Nova Scotia), 1981, 7(2), 9–11. (a)

Soltis, J. F. (Ed.). *Philosophy and Education: Eightieth Yearbook of the National Society for the Study of Education* (Part 1). Chicago: University of Chicago Press, 1981. (b)

Soltis, J. F. (Ed.). *Philosophy of Education since Mid-century.* New York: Teachers College Press, 1981. (c)

Strike, K. A. Toward a moral theory of desegregation. In J. F. Soltis (Ed.), *Philosophy and Education: Eightieth Yearbook of the National Society for the Study of Education* (Part 1). Chicago: University of Chicago Press, 1981.

Strike, K. A., & Egan, K. (Eds.). *Ethics and Educational Policy.* Boston: Routledge & Kegan Paul, 1978.

Sutton, T. L. Human rights and children. *Educational Theory,* 1978, *28*, 102–110.

Tesconi, C. A., & Morris, V. *The Anti-man Culture: Bureautechnocracy and the Schools.* Urbana: University of Illinois Press, 1972.

Thomas, L. G. (Ed.). *Philosophical Redirection of Educational Research.* Chicago: University of Chicago Press, 1972.

Ulich, R. *Three Thousand Years of Educational Wisdom* (2nd ed.). Cambridge: Harvard University Press, 1954.

Vandenberg, D. *Being and Education: An Essay in Existential Phenomenology.* Englewood Cliffs, N.J.: Prentice-Hall, 1971.

Wales, J. N. *Prologue to Education: An Inquiry into Ends and Means.* Boston: Routledge & Kegan Paul, 1979.

Weinberg, L. T. An answer to the "liberal" objection to special admissions. *Educational Theory,* 1979, *29*, 21–30.

White, J. P. *Towards a Compulsory Curriculum.* Boston: Routledge & Kegan Paul, 1973.

Wilson, J. *Practical Methods of Moral Education.* London: Heinemann Educational Group, 1972.

Worsfold, V. L. Justifying students' rights: John Rawls and competing conceptions. *Proceedings of the Philosophy of Education Society,* 1979, 323–333.

PHILOSOPHY OF SCIENCE IN EDUCATION

The role of philosophy of science in educational research requires four distinctions. We must distinguish between two major views of philosophy of science, the traditional and the modern, and two competing views of educational research, the conventional and the enlightened. By "traditional philosophy," I refer to rationalism (Descartes, Kant) and empiricism (Bacon, Locke). By "modern," I refer to a formulation by Rorty (1980) of the views of Heidegger, Dewey, and Wittgenstein. The distinction between "conventional" and "enlightened" educational research turns on whether problems of research are considered more important than problems of educating. We can look at a piece of research and ask whether it is educational *research* or *educational* research. Enlightened educational research is guided by a full conception of education and educating (Fenstermacher, 1977). Conventional educational research is guided by the view of science taken by the researchers; often this view of scientific knowledge is grounded in traditional formulations of rationalism or empiricism that modern philosophers have discredited.

Knowledge and Inquiry. "Inquiry" is a term we can use to include science, philosophy, and common sense. Inquiry is a matter of asking interesting questions, generating answers and deciding upon which answers are significant. When we complete a deliberately undertaken inquiry, we produce a meaningful piece of knowledge. Philosophers have long been interested in how we pose our questions and with what certainty we judge our answers. The rationalism of Descartes found the most certain and doubt-free knowledge to be a function of conscious thought ("I think, therefore I am"). The inner mind can make conceptions (e.g., a perfect circle) that the external world does not exhibit. Rationalism assumes that a gap exists between inner, conscious space and the external world. Bacon, Locke, and other empiricists make the same assumption, but start with the external world and somehow find the mind; knowledge is certain because as an object is presented to the senses we cannot doubt its existence ("Nothing is in the mind that does not come through the senses"). Modern philosophy cuts the ground from under both these views by rejecting the initial assumption that a knower exists antecedently to and independently of any object of knowledge. Further, the quest for certainty of knowledge is rejected (Dewey, 1929). What seems to rationalists to be certain knowledge may be nothing more than just another vocabulary, of which there are scores, through which the world is described (Wittgenstein, 1953). What seems to empiricists to provide certainty of knowledge is at best only an explanation of how we perceive, not a justification that what we claim about it is true. The general question "How can we know with certainty what is universally true (true without doubt)?" is rejected by modern philosophy. In the modern view, certainty is less important than our uses of knowledge. The character of what it is to be a knower or an object of knowledge is a function of the interactions between experience and nature. Both knowers and knowledge come to take on their special qualities as a consequence of actual attempts to think about and to know things in particular cases. There is no certain knowledge in general. The status of knowledge is relative to the context of inquiry in which knowledge claims are produced. Philosophy of science then becomes critical, reflective scrutiny of what we do when we come to know deliberately. We pay special attention to our best and worst cases, seeking criteria to distinguish them so as to improve our next efforts. This bootstrapping procedure—from analysis of clear cases to criteria for judging cases to the use of criteria for creating and judging new cases—is progressive, not circular. Such analyses are the source of our theory of inquiry (Dewey, 1938).

A simple—not simplistic—discussion of science, then, consists of asking telling questions about events and objects, following a method to get evidence to back significant answers. This viewpoint helps to bring into relation most of the elements of the scientific enterprise: questions, and the concepts used to formulate telling questions; the phenomena of interest, whether events or objects; techniques used to make records of events (facts), methods of inquiry, and assertions, in the form of answers typically judged significant because of their meaningfulness and their truth value. Telling questions are usually generated through theories, metaphors, and philosophic world views, but sometimes questions come from sheer invention, from the persistence and perversity of the questioner, and from the puzzling and problematic quality of some events and objects that come under scrutiny. Reliable techniques and procedural commitments (methods) are used to generate answers. Answers to questions, like solutions to problems, depend for acceptability on criteria of excellence, that is, the criteria of what counts as the best answer among a range of answers. These criteria include ideas of meaning, truth, explanation, prediction, and description. Answers to the questions of science often fruitfully produce further related questions, and a program of research may be initiated that exhibits continuity and validity over a widening set of events and objects (Schwab, 1978). But some veins of research are exhausted when no further interesting questions can be asked, and some lines of inquiry cease because no significant answers can be produced. Science, like all human activities, has its areas of growth and progress, as well as its areas of decay and decline (Lakatos, 1970).

Meaning and Scientific Claims. Scientific claims are never well understood as a literal description of the way things are as perceived by a naive observer. Inference, the taking of one thing *(A)* to stand for another *(B)*, is necessary to create meaning (Hospers, 1967). The visible is an index to the invisible, as, in genetics, phenotypes (wrinkled peas) are taken to stand for genotypes (recessive genes). When we take *A* to stand for another thing, *B*, we say that "*A* means *B*." The wrinkled peas "mean" recessive genes. If we take clouds to be a sign of rain, we say the clouds "mean" rain. The notion of meaning is central to modern thought. It helps us to connect experience with knowledge (Kaplan, 1964). Science can be seen as the search for valid construction of meaning. Scientific claims must first be meaningful before appropriate tests of truth or falsity can be rendered. Where the events of nature and human experience are so rich and the aptitude of scientists so inventive, the construction of valid meaning must have many levels.

Meaning depends upon a context of inquiry. The meaning of any given term, such as "root," depends upon its use within a particular context of inquiry, such as botany. Change the context and the meaning changes, because the use of the term changes ("root" has a different meaning in mathematics). Just as in grammar and syntax, where

the meaning of words depends upon their place in the linguistic structure, so, too, claims of science derive their meaning from the structure of inquiry in which they appear. On an imaginary scale of vastness, experience and nature would be the most inclusive, and the notion of experience divides into that with and without meaning. Direct, unmediated, preanalytic experience exists side by side with indirect, mediated, and analyzed experience. Meaning develops out of experience and returns to experience to make it intelligible, as in common sense and ordinary language (Dewey, 1958).

Can we trust experience as the testing ground for scientific claims? Is experience only a concatenation of events, some long-lasting, some brief, all in process, changeable? Or is experience of stable objects of nature, of things that do not change and that, therefore, make it possible to trust experience as if a set of uniform rails were underlying it? Are claims of knowledge about mutable experience, therefore, necessarily fallible, full of error, as well as of truth (Peirce, 1935)? Or does the invariance of reality permit permanent truths about it? We can bring these issues together by suggesting that philosophy of science links the theories and concepts pointing to regularities in the events and objects of experience that the science selects; and that it also links the techniques and methods that make records of events to produce the facts of science and its major claims of knowledge and value.

After such meanings develop, further refinement takes place in the inquiries of science to convert claims of meaning into knowledge claims, and these into truth claims. The spatial figure shows the vastness of experience and nature populated by millions of meaning claims, thousands of knowledge claims, and a much smaller number of truth claims. Science, in general, deals with a restricted range of meanings, and each of the scientific disciplines considers even less of the whole domain of experience and nature.

Some sciences deal with claims about nature (e.g., physics) that exclude human nature; other sciences include the interaction of the two (e.g., biology); and a few sciences concern primarily human interactions (e.g., sociology). Within each of the sciences, there are multiple sets of knowledge claims (i.e., no discipline is one "pure" subject matter, physics, e.g., being divided into theoretical physics and experimental physics and few physicists specializing in research in both areas). Furthermore, to each of these multiple sets of knowledge claims, different tests of truth are applied. We use an analytic test for the meaning of claims, a coherence test and a consensus test for theoretical claims, a correspondence test for experimental claims, and a pragmatic test of consequences of actions following the use of claims. These varied procedures for the refinement of meaning and assessment of truth in the context of different inquiries make it extremely difficult to generalize with precision about science, scientific knowledge, and scientific truths. Modern philosophy of science recognizes the facts of diversity, plurality, and fallibility within the overall scientific enterprise. Given these caveats and considerations, there are no unqualified prescriptions for educational research flowing from philosophy of science. Educational research itself is highly diverse, plural, and fallible. Indeed, one can wonder if there is any single reality to be referred to by the terms "educational research." A set of loosely related members of a community of educational researchers exists, but their activities have no central defining characteristics (Gowin, 1972).

The Human Sciences. The view of science as pluralistic is disturbing to those who believe in the unity of science (Brown, 1977). One view of the unity of all sciences claims that any proper notion of scientific knowledge does not rule out—in principle and prior to testing—the possibility that science can be applied to the study of any phenomena (such is the prestigious success of the past three hundred years of scientific knowledge making). If every event has a cause, then science ought to be able to find out what it is. Yet human beings invent meanings, create intentions, feel free to make choices, and generate purposes that give them power to cause events to happen in ways that defeat precise prediction and control. Moreover, when prediction and control of human beings themselves are at stake, many refuse on moral and humane grounds to treat people mechanistically. It is not a nice thing to do to people. It is socially acceptable to predict and therefore control material things, but people are not things; and if science is to help us understand people, then the human sciences have to be constructed toward that end. Further, if science is to govern people, then at least prior consent of the governed must be obtained; human subjects have rights that scientific procedures cannot override. This view puts a strain on the criterion that empirical science test claims through successful prediction and instrumental control of the external world, "external world" meaning a world where the claims of science are not altered by our personal or social interest in having the claims be favorable to ourselves. This independence from favored human purposes protects the truth of science from the inroads of authoritarian religion, vested political interests, commercial exploitation, and mere whimsy. Although modern philosophers generally agree that logical positivism is dead, many often forget that the early thinkers in the Vienna Circle were disturbed by social conditions of authoritarianism and hoped to set the authority of science on its own independent grounds (Cohen, 1967; Hesse, 1980).

Do human beings cause their own behavior? Although there are levels of cause—genetic, instinctual, social—the most personal cause is how a person explains the meaning of his or her actions. The reason a person gives to explain why he or she chose X over Y is also a cause of that person's behavior: I choose to do things that I think are reasonable and desirable for me. To understand the cause of an individual's actions, we must deal with "reasons." But reasons are the product of thinking and feeling and are not easily observable events. Only as people choose to reveal themselves can the scientist get to such events. The scientist of human action seeks to understand the world in the way the person understands it (Magoon, 1977). Actors' descriptions of the meaning of their actions are crucial information to the scientist. The task of science is to construct meaning congruent with that of the actor (Stake & Easley, 1978). Regularities are found by scientists when they chart the patterns of meanings that control the actions of people. Control mechanisms that govern behavior sometimes work as social control devices governing behavior by controlling meaning (Geertz, 1974).

Views of Educational Policy and Research. Because educational research is funded by local, state, and federal agencies, the issues of policy and research are important. Two views emerge. One has it that philosophy of science contributes nothing, in principle, to issues of policy. Questions of what exists and how such reality is described are questions of fact and truth; they are not questions of what the facts ought to be to suit human purposes. The task of science, in this traditional philosophical view, is to give an account of the world as it is independent of the meanings it might have for human subjects or of how it figures in their experience. Scientific claims ought to be "objective" absolutely to exclude the "bias" of human experience, especially the desire of human beings to want knowledge favorable to them. Succinctly stated, this view makes the claim that it is a point of logic that from statements only involving the use of "is," a conclusion involving "ought" cannot validly be deduced (Hudson, 1969). The language and terminology used in asking questions should be consistent with the language and terminology used in answers. Consistency in linguistic formulation is required to ensure meaningfulness for the claims of science.

The second view of the relation between policy and research begins with the observation that science is an activity of scientists and that, as persons, scientists have purposes, human desires, and criteria of what is desirable that influence the knowledge claims they produce. Thus, in principle, facts and values ride in the same boat. One cannot exclude "ought" judgments or value claims from the "correct" operation of science. If science is not for the uses of human beings, what justification is there in its pursuit? The justification of scientific utility is as important an issue as the verification of scientific claims. Truth is important because humankind makes it important. We human beings make it a supreme value of human life, and as a result, the absolute objectivity of science independent of human purposes makes no sense.

From this general view, two other possibilities emerge. One has it that policy issues are determined by policy makers and that these human beings can and do hold different views about the role of science. Such different views about science then become determinants in policy matters (Berger & Luckman, 1966). Find out what view of science the policy people have, and you will find out what kind of research may be funded. For example, if the policy maker believes that science finds absolute truths independent of particular contexts (the traditional position), then such a person will likely support science research that seeks basic laws and fundamental regularities. Page (1980) states that "broad research is inherently Federal" (p. 4). That is, the search for broad causal relations surpasses state and local boundaries; the increase of scientific knowledge in education, it is argued, depends on federal sponsorship as does any other science. Unfortunately, such an argument is easily extended to the claim that basic research goes beyond *any* political boundaries (local, state, national, international), since research claims are independent of the sources of funding. Governments and private agencies may have secrets, but nature, as described in broad causal laws, keeps none. If the policy maker believes that scientific truths are relative to the context of inquiry that produces the claims (a modern position), then such a person can support "local" research, using the power of money and politics to solve social issues at the point of their emergence in society. Thus, for example, research on youth and their problems with drugs, abortions, or unemployment, is justified because scientific claims are relative to human purposes and instrumental in the betterment of social conditions.

Another view on policy and research begins with a different view of philosophy. It ought to be social philosophy, rather than philosophy of science, that we call on because social philosophies directly concern policy, human issues, and the desirability of one form of society over others (Bernstein, 1976). From social philosophy we formulate a telling question: "How do we secure cooperation among people so that common purposes can be shared?" This question sets the task of governments, and different political orders (e.g., democratic, socialistic, fascistic) have different basic proposals for securing cooperation and achieving shared purposes (survival, safety, health, education). These proposals can, of course, provide the basis of research efforts. Only a philosophy of science that includes the terms and distinctions of everyday human problems is useful. If such terms (or their surrogates) as "cooperation," "shared experience," or "human purposes," cannot be tolerated in scientific discourse, then such science has no relevance to policy issues.

Educational research, if it is to be enlightened, probably needs to pay closer attention to philosophy of education. It helps us understand the concepts and criteria of what it means to be an educated individual (Green, 1971). Such claims lead to decisions about what is good and right to do to people to educate them, and such decisions determine the regularities of educational practice (Gowin, 1981). Empirical researchers who know these ideas will find apt directions for their inquiries.

D. Bob Gowin

See also History and Philosophy of Higher Education; Philosophy of Education.

REFERENCES

Berger, P., & Luckman, T. *The Social Construction of Reality.* London: Beacon Press, 1966.

Bernstein, Richard J. *The Restructuring of Social and Political Theory.* New York: Harcourt Brace Jovanovich, 1976.

Brown, H. *Perception, Theory, and Commitment.* Chicago: University of Chicago Press, 1977.

Cohen, R. Otto Neurath. In P. Edwards (Ed.), *The Encyclopedia of Philosophy.* New York: Macmillan and Free Press, 1967.

Dewey, J. *Quest for Certainty.* New York: Minton, Balch, 1929.

Dewey, J. *Logic.* New York: Henry Holt, 1938.

Dewey, J. *Experience and Nature,* New York: Dover, 1958.

Fenstermacher, G. A philosophical consideration of recent research on teacher effectiveness. *Review of Research of Education.* Itaska, Ill.: F. E. Peacock, 1977.

Geertz, C. The impact of the concept of culture on the concept of man. In Y. Cohen (Ed.), *Man in Adaptation: The Cultural Present.* Chicago: Aldine, 1974.

Gowin, D. B. Is educational research distinctive? *Philosophical Redirection of Educational Research.* Chicago: University of Chicago Press, 1972.

Gowin, D. B. *Educating.* Ithaca, N.Y.: Cornell University Press, 1981.

Green, T. F. *The Activities of Teaching.* New York: McGraw-Hill, 1971.

Hesse, M. *Revolutions and Reconstructions in the Philosophy of Science.* Bloomington: Indiana University Press, 1980.

Hospers, J. *An Introduction to Philosophical Analysis.* Englewood Cliffs, N.J.: Prentice-Hall, 1967.

Hudson, W. *The Is/Ought Question.* London: Macmillan, 1969.

Kaplan, A. *Conduct of Inquiry.* San Francisco: Chandler, Intext, 1964.

Lakatos, I. Falsification and the methodology of scientific research programmes. *Criticism and the Growth of Knowledge.* London: Cambridge University Press, 1970.

Magoon, J. A. Constructivist approaches in educational research. *Review of Educational Research,* 1977, *47*(4), 651–693.

Page, E. A conservative case for educational research. *Educational Researcher,* 1980, *9*(11), 4.

Peirce, C. *Collected Papers* (Vols. 2 & 4). Cambridge, Mass.: Harvard University Press, 1935.

Rorty, R. *Philosophy and the Mirror of Nature.* Princeton, N.J.: Princeton University Press, 1980.

Schwab, J. *Science, Curriculum, and Liberal Education.* Chicago: University of Chicago Press, 1978.

Stake, R., & Easley, J. *Case Studies in Science Education* (Vols. 1 & 2). Washington, D.C.: U.S. Government Printing Office, 1978. (ERIC Document Reproduction Service No. ED 166 058 and No. ED 166 059)

Wittgenstein, L. *Philosophical Investigations.* New York: Macmillan, 1953.

PHYSICAL DEVELOPMENT

Physical development occurs with the onset of certain physical and behavioral phenomena at certain stages of life. In order to establish a structural base, we have first introduced the roles of tissues, organs, and systems. Their functions are then related to their maturation potential in infancy, childhood, adolescence, and young adulthood. This succinct presentation should encourage interested persons to seek greater understanding of the complex relations between physical development and other structural and behavioral components of the human learner.

Body Tissue Functions and Coordination. All structures of the body are formed by combinations of the derivatives of the three primary germ layers of the human embryo: ectoderm, mesoderm, and endoderm (Copenhaver, Kelly, & Wood, 1978). The derived tissues consist of four groups: nerve (conductive), epithelial (lining), connective (supporting), and muscular (motor).

Nerve tissue. All protoplasm possesses the properties of being irritable and conductive. These two properties attain maximum development in the highly differentiated nerve cells. Nerve tissue forms the functional system of the brain, spinal cord, and the peripheral nerves. Nerve cells receive stimuli, transmit these irritations, interpret and select responses, and transmit the responses to motor end organs—muscles, glands, other cells, and tissues. Nerve tissue is concerned with the integration and coordination of internal behavior and its adaptation to external environmental variations.

Lining tissue. Lining tissue (epithelium) covers all surfaces of the body: the outer layer of the skin (epidermis); cavities or organs opening to the outside of the body (mucous membranes); and all nonaccess cavities (serous membranes). Secreting cells of both endocrine and exocrine glands are derived from epithelium. Surfaces subject to erosion and to dehydration are protected by the epithelium, which retains a lifelong ability to regenerate.

Connective tissue. Supporting connective tissues are roughly divided into two groups: loose and compact. Loose tissues (fatty, areolar, elastic) support the internal structure of organs. Compact tissues (tendons, ligaments, cartilage, and bone) join and give support to systems and to the body as a whole. Elastic fibers are prevalent in the blood-vessel walls and in the dermis of the skin. The skin and arterioles tend to lose their elasticity in adult and advanced years. Compact fibrous, inelastic connective tissue continues to regenerate, to form scar tissue, and to regenerate bone.

Muscle tissue. Muscle tissue is primarily of mesodermal origin and is fundamentally of two kinds: smooth and striated. Smooth muscle, innervated by the autonomic nervous system, contracts by slow rhythmic movement; striated muscle is capable of rapid, sustained, coordinated action. Smooth muscle is regenerative throughout life. Skeletal muscle retains a slight regenerative capability in the early years. Destroyed skeletal and cardiac, striated muscle has no regenerative ability and is replaced only by scar tissue. Muscle mass development results from an increase in the size of muscle fibers, not from an increase in the number of fibers.

Growth and Development of Body Systems. Growth is the increase in physical size of the whole body or any of its parts, whereas development indicates the emergence and expansion of skill and complexity of functions; these terms are inherently integrated. At birth the basic components for a human's internal and external environmental interactions are operational; further organic increase and functional development (maturation) parallel age in humans and are enhanced by experiential learning. Physical development, while uniquely individualistic, follows a generalized biochemical format in normal human aging. The stages described here are infancy (birth to 2 years); childhood (2 to 10 years); adolescence (10 to 20 years); young adulthood (20 to 35 years); mature adulthood (35 to 65 years); and old adulthood (65 years and over). These stages correlate roughly with physical growth, development, and decline. The last two life periods, representing maintenance and then slow decline of previously achieved physical maturation and performance, are not discussed. The body systems directly related to physical development considered here are the nervous, skeletal, muscular, cardiovascular, and respiratory systems. Supportive systems referred to indirectly are the digestive, endocrine, excretory, reproductive, and reticulo-endothelial systems. Motoric developmental characteristics are also summarized.

Infancy (Birth to 2 Years). At birth the infant is physically dependent upon other humans to meet its survival needs. Through continued maturation of body systems and exploratory learning, control over such body functions as locomotion, object identification, and manipulation is learned along with other basic modes of human interaction.

Nervous system. At the time of birth the central nervous system, ganglia, and peripheral nerves are completely functional, and the brain growth is 90 percent complete. Increase in the size of the brain after the first year is due to the formation of myelin (sheathing) and the development of neuroglia (supportive) tissue (Miller, Drakontides, & Leavell, 1977). Nerve-cell formation ceases by the end of the first year (Arey, 1974). The number of nerve cells for each individual is remarkably constant regardless of size. Reflexes (to position, movement, and sound, vision, blinking, rooting, sucking, swallowing, excretion, and spontaneous stepping) which appear at birth up to the age of 7 months gradually become conditioned (Johnson, Moore, & Jefferies, 1978). During this period communication occurs by vocalization such as crying; facial expressions of anger, fear, or joy; and body movements such as grasping and kicking. As the higher brain centers that house sense perceptions and intelligence assume more of the functions of the midbrain and spinal cord, voluntary control of behavior is increasingly effective. The eye at birth is capable of sight; but as this visual acuity of 20/150 (farsightedness) gradually moves toward the 4-year-old's normal acuity of 20/20, close objects are more clearly discriminated.

Skeletal system. The most useful parameters of the infant's physical growth are height and weight. The average height (length) at birth is approximately twenty inches, and weight is about seven and one-half pounds. Females are slightly smaller than males. Birth weight triples by age 1, quadruples by the age of 2, and is twentyfold at

FIGURE 1. *Development for the first year of life*[1]

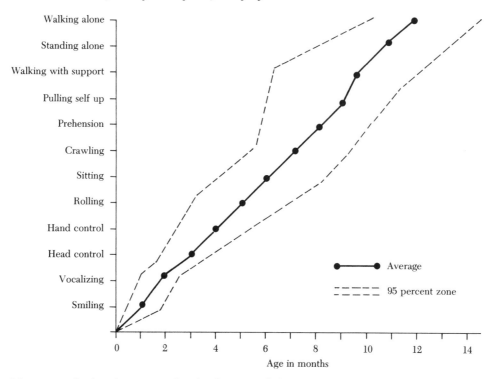

[1] Average age for the achievements selected and zone in which 95 percent of observations fell in a group of 215 normal infants.

SOURCE: Johnson, Moore, & Jefferies, 1978, p. 33; reprinted by courtesy of Ross Laboratories, Columbus, Ohio.

maturity. The newborn's height increases one-fourth by the age of 2, and about three and one-half times by maturity (Smith, Bierman, & Robinson, 1978). At that time, it correlates reasonably well with parents' average height. Stature is determined by bone development, which in turn is the major responsibility of the anterior pituitary and the parathyroid (endocrine) glands. Calcium, phosphorus, and vitamin D are vital to bone formation; so nutritional adequacy is essential.

Muscular system. The articulation of bone, tendons, ligaments, and muscles permits human movement through applied leverage. At birth muscles represent one-fourth to one-fifth of body weight in contrast to one-third at early adolescence and two-fifths at maturity (Watson & Lowrey, 1967). The cerebellum is concerned with equilibrium, posture, and muscle tonus and coordinates muscular movements so that they are smooth and efficient. Voluntary muscular reaction is initiated by the cerebral cortex response to sensory experiences. Through progressive differentiation, specialization, and integration, perceptual motor skills are developed (Cratty, 1970); however, maturation is the primary factor in the appearance of various motor skills (Evans & McCandless, 1978). Coordination of different maturing systems is vital for purposeful behavior, such as the coordination of visual, auditory, and motor

systems with cognitive processes required for picking up a pencil, catching a ball, or playing marbles (Evans & McCandless, 1978). The infant expresses intentions and feelings by the way the body is used; postural sequences can offer insight into psychological as well as physiological conditions. Sensory stimulation in infancy and childhood provides bases for future sensory development (Bruce, 1978). Five senses commonly considered are sight, sound, smell, taste, and touch. Additional skin senses of pressure, pain, temperature perception, along with kinesthesis (proprioceptive sensation), also furnish important information for body responses. The infant's communication and motor skills as they develop are charted in Figure 1.

Cardiovascular and respiratory systems. Independent cardiovascular and respiratory systems begin functioning at birth with the closing of the fetal cardiovascular shunts at the first breaths, thus replacing fluid in the lungs with air and raising arterial blood pressure. At rest the heartbeat of a newborn is 100 to 150 beats per minute, which gradually reduces to the young adult rate of about 60 to 76 beats per minute. The newborn's breathing of 34 respirations per minute gradually decreases to 12 respirations per minute of adults. Until about age 6, respiration is largely maintained by the diaphragm; later the thorax shares this function equally (Lowrey, 1978).

Motoric development. Prenatal physical movement, which can be identified by the tenth week, is slow, assymmetrical, diffuse, and uncoordinated. The total pattern response, developing by the twelfth week, involves increased reflex action. By the thirteenth week, every joint has mobility, and reflex complexity increases (Espenschade & Eckert, 1967). Motor development is cephalocaudal (from head to tail) and proximodistal (from center toward extremities). In infancy postural stability develops with crawls and squats, and upright locomotion is achieved (Stallings, 1973). Hearing response activities as well as verbal experimentation are practiced.

Childhood (2 to 10 Years). During this period the individual experiences rapid physical, mental, and emotional growth and development.

Nervous system. The central nervous system permits increasingly coordinated gross and fine motor control, such as buttoning coats by 4 four years of age, cutting with scissors by 5, riding a bike by 7, and sewing or building models by 9 years. The eye becomes anatomically mature by the third year. In the young child the eye is normally hypermetropic (farsighted), but compensated by excellent power of accommodation. Normally, as the eye length increases, the previously less distinct, near objects become more sharply focused. Astigmatism (variation of eye growth) should be corrected if it occurs. Hearing should be tested before school entrance because auditory development is essential to language development.

Skeletal system. The longitudinal development of a child is measured by several physical and mental attributes translated into age units: height, weight, number of erupted teeth, grip strength, carpal age, mental age, educational age, and social age. Examples of such scales are found in Bayley (1956), Marshall (1977), Lowrey (1978), and Tanner (1972). Skeletal proportions reflect differential growth rates; during the first half of childhood, extremities increase in size more quickly than does the trunk. As postural alignment adjusts to gravity, the temporary abdominal protrusion accompanying lumbar lordosis (lower spinal curvature) gradually diminishes, but it is followed by an increased thoracic (upper spinal) convex curve. After adolescent muscular growth, the final adult posture is completed. Generally heredity is reflected in linear growth. Deviations may indicate chronic problems such as brain-endocrine abnormalities in later childhood and early adolescence. By this time bone maturation, as measured by the degree of ossification of bone cartilage, nears completion. This process is correlated with increase of androgen hormones in the male and estrogen hormones in the female. Sometimes carpal ossification rates are used to determine physiological maturity of children, especially in competitive athletics. Abnormality of weight is an indicator of an acute problem, such as temporary illness, stress, or malnutrition. Height and weight growth patterns as general screening devices furnish excellent health status information about the child.

Muscular system. Movements of the body are produced through muscular action by virtue of their structure, attachments to bones, and innervation. Muscular patterns are evidenced by gross and fine motor movements. Gross movement skills using all or large segments or the body include axial or stationary movements, such as bending, stretching, or twisting; locomotor skills, such as walking, running, or leaping; and skills to challenge inertia or manipulate external objects, such as holding, pushing, throwing, catching, kicking, or striking (Espenschade & Eckert, 1967; Flinchum, 1975; Latchaw & Egstrom, 1969; Wickstrom, 1970). In early childhood fine motor movements appear incompletely organized and uncoordinated, such as eating, writing, or reading. Increasingly, competent skill acquisition occurs for both fine and gross motor skills in middle and later childhood; however, there is a comparatively low relationship between the two (Evans & McCandless, 1978).

Cardiovascular and respiratory systems. The expectancy and intensity of physical activity usually correlate with the limited size of the cardiovascular and respiratory systems. In up to 50 percent of children, a heart murmur may be heard; but this incidence is usually of little medical significance. Because of the small diameter of the upper respiratory tract, a child may suffer serious obstruction caused by inflammation from infection or inhalation of foreign bodies.

Motoric development. In early childhood such basic locomotor skills as walking, jumping, throwing, kicking, or running are perfected. This is a critical period for acquiring motor skills; ample opportunity, space, and equipment are needed. Later proficiencies increase the basic abilities and skills, although performance varies greatly and sex differences overlap. Interest in games and sports activities increases; the extent of participation is primarily a function of family interest (Stallings, 1973). Gesell and Ilg (1946) outline activities engaged in by age-groups of children: motoric play, reading, listening to music, listening to radio, and viewing cinema.

Adolescence (10 to 20 Years). Adolescence is highlighted by sexual maturation and secondary physical growth.

Nervous system. Neurophysiological maturation, which continues at a rapid pace throughout childhood, moves at a greatly reduced pace throughout adolescence and the years of young adulthood.

Skeletal system. The human growth velocity curve shows significant gains from birth through childhood, then decelerates until puberty. The growth spurt in height and weight is reflected in pelvic and shoulder diameters, hand and foot length, and head circumference. The average boy begins his growth spurt at about 12 years of age, reaching the maximum velocity in height at about 14 years of age; girls begin puberty approximately two years earlier and reach maximum velocity in height at about 12 years of age. Furthermore, the increase in weight from skeletal growth and augmented muscle mass is relatively lower for the female than for the male; thus maximum growth for girls is less than for boys.

Reproductive system. The rapid development of reproductive organs and the appearance of secondary sexual characteristics result from suddenly accelerated sex hormone secretion. In the male there is the appearance of facial, axillary, and pubic hair, increased development of testes and penis, nocturnal emissions, increasing activity of sweat glands, and voice change. In the female there is the appearance of menarche (menstruation), axillary and pubic hair, development of breasts, and increased activity of sweat glands (Smith, Bierman, & Robinson, 1978).

Muscular system. An increase in muscle mass during adolescence continues beyond the relative diminishing of height and weight growth. Under the effects of androgens, the adolescent male doubles the number of nuclei in the multinucleate muscle cells, and his muscle cells also hypertrophy. As a consequence, strength almost doubles, and coordination usually improves (Smith, Bierman, & Robinson, 1978). As in childhood, athletic prowess in teenagers is attributable more to bone age than to chronological age.

Cardiovascular and respiratory systems. Cardiovascular changes are reflected in the increase in systolic blood pressure (rhythmic heart contraction) in both sexes, with girls beginning earlier but with boys having a greater rise. There is little change in diastolic pressure (rhythmic heart dilation). The heart size increases in most girls at menarche, and in addition, the boys from 12 years on have larger valves proportionate to transverse cardiac diameters (Smith, Bierman, & Robinson, 1978). The vital capacity of the lungs increases rapidly in adolescence, but it is greater in boys than in girls. The respiratory rate continues to decrease to the adult level of twelve per minute.

Motoric development. Three factors combine to affect performance. Growth spurt may lead to temporary decrements; hormonal changes lead to changes in body shape; and cultural expectations influence type and intensity of activity (Stallings, 1973). This age-group is physically adventurous.

Young Adulthood (20 to 35 Years). The life stage of the young adult is the intersection of the descending curve of physical development and the ascending curve of aging. Psychosocially the young adult has the potential for peak performance in life situations. Maximum competence is usually reached by age 35.

Nervous system. At this time proprioceptive abilities, such as coordination and reaction time, have reached their maximum.

Skeletal system. Increase in height ceases with the complete ossification of bones at about the age of 26; however, face bones, nose cartilage, and the external ear may continue growth into old age and noticeably change an individual's appearance.

Muscular system. Muscle mass increases without important changes in height and weight. The average male has 50 percent more muscle mass than the female. If a moderate physical exercise program is continued during adulthood, the muscle mass level can be maintained and body-fat increase prevented.

Cardiovascular and respiratory systems. Beyond young adulthood through old age, most physical abilities, such as cardiovascular endurance, motor skill performance, strength, reaction time, and recall, gradually decrease; however, geriatric research indicates decline in abilities can be greatly minimized. Appropriate exercise and appropriate diet can postpone and somewhat alleviate the disabilities of middle and old age (Jayson & Dixon, 1974).

Motoric development. Peak proficiency in the young adult depends on the nature of the skill; however, proficiency can remain relatively high with experience. As years increase, the adult is less inclined to take up new activities (Stallings, 1973). Age slows perceptual and muscular capacity, but movement efficiency counters such deterioration.

Educational Planning. Refinement and maintenance of basic and advanced psychomotor skills are imperative for effective learning. The more educators understand human maturation and development, the better they are able to employ programs and techniques to realize the highest potential of each individual. The golden periods for learning many physical skills are closely tied to the maturation sequence, which is a primary factor in the appearance of various motor skills. When forced before they are ready, children simply do not learn, are unskillful, may require a longer time to learn the behavior, or may show undue strain (Breckenridge & Murphy, 1969). Premature demands waste educational and learner resources. Because maximum learning periods also have their upper age limits, optimum timing is essential to achieve the highest potential of skill performance. How effectively society implements human potential weighs heavily on educators' hands.

Alyce Taylor Cheska
Richard R. Marsh

See also Adolescent Development; Early Childhood Development; Health Education; Infant Development; Life-Span Development; Motor Skills Development; Nutrition Education; Preadolescent Development; Sex Differences.

REFERENCES

Arey, L. B. *Developmental Anatomy: A Textbook and Laboratory Manual of Embryology.* Philadelphia: Saunders, 1974.
Bayley, N. Growth curves of height and weight by age for boys and girls, scaled according to physical maturity. *Journal of Pediatrics,* 1956, *48,* 187–194.
Breckenridge, M. E., & Murphy, M. N. *Growth and Development of the Young Child.* Philadelphia: Saunders, 1969.
Bruce, R. L. *Fundamentals of Physiological Psychology.* New York: Holt, Rinehart & Winston, 1978.
Copenhaver, W. M.; Kelly, D. E.; & Wood, R. L. *Bailey's Textbook of Histology.* Baltimore: Williams & Wilkins, 1978.

Cratty, B. J. *Perceptual and Motor Development in Infants and Children*. New York: Macmillan, 1970.

Espenschade, A. S., & Eckert, H. M. *Motor Development*. Columbus, Ohio: Merrill, 1967.

Evans, E. D., & McCandless, B. R. *Children and Youth: Psychosocial Development* (2nd ed.). New York: Holt, Rinehart & Winston, 1978.

Flinchum, B. M. *Motor Development in Early Childhood*. St. Louis: Mosby, 1975.

Gesell, A., & Ilg, F. L. *The Child from Five to Ten*. New York: Harper, 1946.

Jayson, M. I. V., & Dixon, A. S. *Arthritis and Rheumatism*. New York: Pantheon Books, 1974.

Johnson, T. R.; Moore, W. M.; & Jefferies, J. E. (Eds.). *Children Are Different: Developmental Physiology*. Columbus, Ohio: Ross Laboratories, 1978.

Latchaw, M., & Egstrom, G. *Human Movement*. Englewood Cliffs, N.J.: Prentice-Hall, 1969.

Lowrey, G. H. *Growth and Development of Children*. Chicago: Year Book Medical Publishers, 1978.

Marshall, W. A. *Human Growth and Its Disorders*. London: Academic Press, 1977.

Miller, M. A.; Drakontides, A. B.; & Leavell, L. C. *Kimber-Gray-Stackpole's Anatomy and Physiology*. New York: Macmillan, 1977.

Moore, K. L. *The Developing Human: Clinically Oriented Embryology*. Philadelphia: Saunders, 1974.

Smith, D. W.; Bierman, E. L.; & Robinson, N. M. *The Biological Ages of Man*. Philadelphia: Saunders, 1978.

Stallings, L. M. *Motor Skills Development and Learning*. Dubuque, Iowa: Brown, 1973.

Tanner, J. M. *Education and Physical Growth*. London: University of London, 1972.

Watson, E. H., & Lowrey, G. H. *Growth and Development of Children*. Chicago: Year Book Medical Publishers, 1967.

Wickstrom, R. L. *Fundamental Motor Patterns*. Philadelphia: Lea & Febiger, 1970.

PHYSICAL EDUCATION

See Health Education; Motor Skills Development; Physical Development; Recreation.

POLITICAL SCIENCE

Concern about the political implications of education has existed as long as there has been systematic thought about politics. A major theme in Plato's *Republic* is the attempt to answer two questions: How can the state create a political elite based on merit? How can the state influence people to accept their appropriate functions in society? Aristotle, Locke, Rousseau, Marx, and others have treated educational policy as an important part of their political philosophy.

Every political community must make at least seven fundamental decisions about education. (1) To what extent should education be a public responsibility? (2) Should the state permit any educational competitors or delegate any of its educational responsibilities? (3) To what extent should education be used as a sorting device to allocate jobs and status? (4) Should education play a primarily affirmative or analytical role regarding the principal values of the community? (5) Which skills should the education system try to develop? (6) Who should pay for education? (7) Where and by whom in the community should these decisions be made?

As the scientific study of politics emerged in the twentieth century, the application of this approach to educational policy lagged behind psychology, sociology, and economics, partly because of conceptual and methodological problems in the discipline itself and partly because political scientists had accepted a myth promoted by American public school educators. As public schools developed, there was continuous struggle between politicians and professional educators for control of the school system. Sometimes the issues were genuine differences on the appropriate class or vocational orientation of the schools. Often the conflict was over the use of school employment for political patronage. In most places, the professional educators won. Through the creation of lay school boards to act as a buffer between the schools and political officials and establishment of academic tenure to protect jobs, the schools were "taken out of politics." Of course it was an illusion to think that any public institution dependent on public tax support and extensively regulated by state governments was not involved in politics, but the myth caused political scientists to lose interest in education policy.

Then, in 1959, in an influential essay in the *American Political Science Review*, Thomas H. Eliot placed education back on the political science research agenda. The schools, he noted, were the single largest budget item and employed the largest number of public employees in most local and state governments. Issues of funding, school location, district size, school board composition, curriculum objectives, teacher quality, and level of government control were important political issues, and they were researchable.

Once it became clear that political scientists could profitably study education, what was the proper approach? Some have focused on the values, particularly the civic values, transmitted in schools. Others have examined internal school politics. Three other alternatives are considered here.

The first is to seek some comprehensive theory that would integrate all the diverse elements of education. The most prominent of these attempts has been by Easton and his followers. According to Easton (1953), politics may be viewed as a system that authoritatively allocates values or benefits. The system is mobilized by inputs of both demands and supports, which are aggregated and articulated by gatekeepers (usually pressure groups or political parties). The gatekeepers channel these messages to the converter (government), which uses them to shape outputs (public policy). The outputs, of course, are fed back into the system, altering public opinion and thus affecting new demands and supports.

If the whole political system can be viewed from this perspective, then certainly so can the educational subsystem. Two of the most comprehensive treatments of educational politics (Massialas, 1969; Wirt & Kirst, 1972) use a systems framework. But if the systems approach provides a valuable framework for organizing information and formulating questions, it has significant limitations as a theory. It is neither predictive nor prescriptive and thus cannot satisfy the two major sources of demand for knowledge about educational politics.

The other serious attempt to apply a comprehensive theory to educational politics has been by scholars using Marxist perspectives (Bowles & Gintis, 1976; Carnoy, 1977). Overall, however, while concern for egalitarian ideals has been central in the political science literature on education, more attention has been paid to racial, sexual, religious, and geographic inequalities than to class.

Most of the recent work of political scientists on education can be classified into two broad categories: research focusing on the institutions that make education policy and studies of particular policies themselves. While most studies of educational politics contain information about and even analysis of both institutions and policies, it is convenient to divide research into two categories. Institutional studies place their greatest emphasis on the organizational contexts and relationships that define power and authority. From this perspective, policies come and go but institutions remain. Contemporary policy analysis includes examination of the origin, legitimization, consequences, and future of a policy, as well as prescriptive statement. Policy studies often involve many different types and levels of institutions but often treat them as background.

To be fair, it should be pointed out that political scientists have no monopoly on examining the political dimensions of education. Important studies have been done by sociologists, economists, lawyers, and journalists, among others. Indeed much of the writing on educational politics in recent years has been interdisciplinary, in the mode Lerner and Lasswell (1951) called policy sciences, combining the methods and perspectives of several different fields. This entry, however, focuses on the important work done by political scientists or done from a political science perspective.

Institutional Studies. The political scientist who wishes to examine educational politics from an institutional perspective has a wide variety of institutions from which to choose. Traditionally, one of the most characteristic features of American educational politics has been its decentralized nature. Although the United States gave education a seat in the president's cabinet in 1979, the Department of Education has been more concerned about survival than about exercising the kind of power wielded by European ministries of education. Not only are American educational decisions made by each of the three traditional

branches of government in each of three levels (federal, state, and local), but other agencies and organizations that lie in the interstices and on the peripheries of the three-by-three grid also influence and even establish educational policy. Regulatory commissions, accrediting and testing agencies, unions, and religious groups, among others, have *de facto*, if not *de jure*, made educational policy in recent years. The next sections discuss some of the major institutional studies.

Local government. The initial institutional focus of political scientists was on local school governance. In 1940 there were 110,000 school districts in the nation, almost always with a separate board and administrative structure. To most Americans, educational policy appeared to be made locally.

Political scientists have examined local school politics from a number of perspectives. Important overviews have been done by Gittell and Hollander (1968) and Zeigler and Jennings (1974). There have been excellent studies of particular cities: Chicago (Peterson, 1976), New York (Gittell, 1967; Rogers, 1968), and Boston (Schrag, 1967). The theory of the role (Mann, 1976) as well as the tumultuous careers (Cuban, 1976) of school administrators has been examined. The impossible task and declining power of school boards has been analyzed (Goldhammer, 1964; Pois, 1964; Cistone, 1975). Nunnery and Kimbrough (1971) have explored school board elections. Suburban schools have been given special attention by Martin (1962) and Massotti (1967).

In examining local school politics, political scientists have exploded some of the myths about politics and education. While school board politics may often be nonpartisan, representation is often by class, race, or religion. Despite attempts to make school administration a scientific profession, survival for administrators often depends on allegiance to the values of the dominant faction. Research attempts to produce a more general theory about elections, curriculum, or other local school issues have generally not been successful. Most of this research was completed in the sixties or by the mid-seventies. As the number of school districts has declined to less than 15,000 and other levels of government have increased their power in educational decision making, there has been a tendency for political scientists to shift the focus of their research to the state and federal governments.

State government. If one were to believe constitutions, education is strictly a state function. The federal constitution makes no mention of education, and legally local governments exercise only those powers that the states delegate to them. In fact, states do make at least five critical educational decisions: creating school district boundaries, certifying administrative and teaching personnel, determining the curriculum, structuring fiscal support of schools, and setting and maintaining minimum academic standards for public and private schools.

Traditionally, these state regulatory powers directly affected public elementary and secondary schools, whereas public colleges and universities had considerable autonomy. In an attempt to control costs, manage conflicts among campuses, and mitigate the effects of declining enrollment, many states have dramatically increased the power of coordinating boards of higher education. Some state universities have achieved levels of excellence of international importance, while other public institutions can do little more than provide remedial work for previously undereducated students. Given this diversity, attaining an appropriate balance of accountability and autonomy through state politics is very complex.

In addition to their concern with policy questions, political scientists have been interested in state government, because the fifty states form a manageable universe for testing various theories. Among the major studies are Zeigler and Johnson (1972), Wirt (1976), and Campbell and Mazzoni (1976).

Educational policy is generally made in three arenas at the state level: the legislature, the governor's office, and special educational agencies that have some political or legal autonomy. Historically, legislatures decided the major issues of school funding, certification, and curriculum. Consequently, in some states educational professionals created powerful lobbies to bargain with the legislature. More recently, governors have become the visible policy makers in some states. Since schools consume such a large percentage of the state's budget, education is often perceived as a "no win" issue. Real change involves raising taxes or interfering with local autonomy over structural issues. Further, gubernatorial leadership is often limited by the fact that in thirty-five states there is a specific administrator, often separately elected, who is charged with making and implementing education policy. In sixteen states the chief state school officer works with a separately elected state board of education, and together they have the authority for education decisions.

Political scientists have also studied the effects of partisanship, political culture, and economic resources on school issues (Dye, 1966). Statistically significant relationships can be found, but the enormous variety of state politics makes generalizations of policy consequences elusive. The construction of a general theory of state politics and education has hardly begun.

Federal government. Since the legislative and executive branches of the federal government were inactive historically as educational policy makers, political scientists interested in education ignored them until the federal aid controversies of the 1960s. Those political struggles were magnets for educational policy researchers. Important philosophical questions about the federal role in American society were at stake, as well as knotty legal issues over race and religion and traditional regional pork-barrel considerations. The political figures involved were colorful and their conflicts well publicized. Price (1962) and Munger and Fenno (1962) wrote about the federal aid issues, and Meranto (1967) and Eidenberg and Morey (1969) compiled comprehensive case studies about the principal legis-

lative outcome: the Elementary and Secondary Education Act of 1965 (ESEA).

Other legislation received book-length treatment as well: college aid (Gladieux & Wolanin, 1976), library support (Molz, 1976), and environmental education (Brezina & Overmyer, 1974). Presidential involvement in educational policy was traced by Sundquist (1968) and Finn (1977).

While the first focus was on policy development and legislation (the politics of subsidy), the more recent concern has been with the administrative process (the politics of implementation and regulation). Bailey and Mosher (1962) began this trend with their massive study of the impact of ESEA on the organization and function of the U.S. Office of Education. The National Institute of Education has received a critical review from Sproull, Weiner, and Wolf (1977). Kirst (1972) and many others have explored the implementation of Title I of ESEA, and Orfield (1969) has examined the impact of Title VI of the Civil Rights Act in desegregating public schools. These political science studies, along with overall treatments such as Thomas (1975) and Summerfield (1974), have effectively illuminated the rich tapestry of federal involvement with education.

The judiciary. Of all educational policy makers in recent years, the federal and state judiciaries have most often flexed their muscles. "The least dangerous branch," to quote Alexander Hamilton's pious prophecy and Alexander Bickel's mocking book title (1962), has exercised the dominant power in all school matters concerning race, religion, academic freedom, student rights, and—increasingly—sex and school finance.

Political scientists have, of course, been concerned about all these policy issues but have also examined the role and process of the courts in modern education decisions. Hogan (1974), Levin (1977), and Brubacher (1971) have all written overviews of the development. Perhaps the most sensitive critique of the expanded judicial role is by Horowitz (1977), whose chapter on *Hobson* v. *Hanson* explored the unintended consequences of judicial activism. Part of the judicial difficulty in making educational policy is the necessary dependence on social science evidence, which judges are not always able to comprehend, even when the adversary process permits that evidence to be fully and accurately given. The other area of political science concern has been with the process of compliance with judicial decisions. Wirt (1971) has explored compliance with school desegregation orders in the South, and several authors—Muir (1967) and Dolbeare and Hammond (1976)—have examined compliance with the school prayers decision.

There are several prominent themes in the writings of political scientists about the courts and education. There is a recognition of the important role the judiciary has played in advancing social justice in areas where other institutions have been slow to act. But there is awareness of the fragile membrane of public support that gives the branch without purse or sword its power. Although its educational decisions have always been influential, they have frequently been resisted, and compliance has been slow and erratic. Finally political scientists have reemphasized the old question about the role of the judicial review in a democratic society and articulated new questions about the practical capacity of the courts to make so many educational decisions the consequences of which they can neither fully understand nor manage.

Policy Issues. Political scientists who have approached education from a policy perspective have had two broad concerns: educational equity and educational governance.

In the last two decades, Americans have become increasingly aware of education's role in determining status, income—indeed, almost all the rewards of a modern society. Schools at every level are under intense pressure to provide not only equitable opportunities but also excellent results for each student. Under this compression all the inadequacies in the huge, diverse American school system stand out. Political scientists have been the principal policy analysts for many issues.

One of the most publicized issues has been school finance. American public schools receive their revenues from a variety of governments and taxes, but in many states the local property tax is the critical source. Consequently, these school districts are dependent on the vagaries of personal and commercial income for their funds. This inequitable fiscal arrangement has been attacked in both legislatures and courts. The reformers have not always been able to agree on the desired formula, and their success rate has been mixed. These issues have been chronicled by Wise (1968) and Berke, Campbell, and Goettel (1972), and the political battles have been described by Lehne (1978).

The paramount equity issue in educational policy, of course, concerns race. Political scientists have written about almost every aspect of the issue. Some of the major work on public school desegregation has been done by Crain (1968), Wirt (1971), and Orfield (1978). Judicial consideration of discrimination against whites was described by Sindler (1978). There has been less writing about other minority groups and women, but van Geel (1975) and Foster (1976) have described the bilingual education controversy, and Fishel and Pottker (1977) have discussed the political implications of sex discrimination in education.

The other major educational policy area of concern to political scientists is governance. If there is a single valid generalization about educational governance in the last two decades, it is that power has flowed away from consumers (parents and students) and lay boards (public school or college trustees) to agency bureaucrats and judges. Even college and school administrators have lost discretion on a number of issues. Not only power has shifted but also its location. Power seems to be flowing upward. States have increased their power over local schools by implementing accountability and other control mechanisms. The federal government has increased its control over the states by maximizing the leverage of federal dollars. The result has probably been an increase in educational equality but a growing feeling of powerlessness among those most directly affected by education (consumers and practitioners). Even higher education professionals who generally were ardent advocates of federal aid have grown restless and fearful over the growth of federal regulations of employment and research.

There have been several attempts to reverse this trend by changing educational governance. Teachers have sought to use collective bargaining to gain control not only over their working conditions but over educational policy as well (Rosenthal, 1969; Blum, 1969; Cresswell & Murphy, 1977). Where unions have been successful, parents and minority groups have often felt left out and have demanded school decentralization (Levin, 1970; LaNoue & Smith, 1973) and other forms of accountability (Wynne, 1972). As blacks have taken control of the majority of urban school systems, interest in school decentralization has waned. But white and minority middle-class parents have increasingly turned to private schools, spawning a renewed interest in tax credits and vouchers (LaNoue, 1972; Coons & Sugarman, 1978). If more students move to the private sector, the question of the public responsibility of these schools and how they are to be held accountable becomes more acute (Erickson, 1969).

Given the late start, the results of the last two decades of political science research on education are impressive, if incomplete. No new grand theory has emerged to tie together all elements. Yet most of the major institutional decision makers have been studied, though there are still uncharted areas, principally in the politics of higher education and educational interest groups. The most significant policy issues have also been researched, though the policy agenda keeps evolving. Certainly important questions such as the tradeoff between equality and excellence in education, the consequence of private versus public organization of schools, and the appropriate balance of power among consumers, practitioners, bureaucrats, politicians, and judges remain to be studied. Increasingly, this work will be interdisciplinary, but political science will have an important role to play.

George R. LaNoue

See also Economics and Education; Federal Influence on Education; Judicial Decisions; Legislation; Local Influences on Education; State Influences on Education.

REFERENCES

Bailey, S. K., & Mosher, E. *ESEA: The Office of Education Administers a Law.* Syracuse: Syracuse University Press, 1962.

Berke, J. S.; Campbell, A.; & Goettel, R. J. *Financing Equal Educational Opportunity: Alternatives for State Finance.* Berkeley, Calif.: McCutchan, 1972.

Bickel, A. *The Least Dangerous Branch*. Indianapolis: Bobbs-Merrill, 1962.

Blum, A. A. *Teachers' Unions and Associations*. Champaign: University of Illinois Press, 1969.

Bowles, S., & Gintis, H. *Schooling in Capitalist America*. New York: Basic Books, 1976.

Brezina, D. W., & Overmyer, A. *Congress in Action: The Environmental Education Act*. New York: Free Press, 1974.

Brubacher, J. S. *The Courts and Higher Education*. San Francisco: Jossey-Bass, 1971.

Campbell, R., & Mazzoni, T., Jr. *Policy Making in the States*. Berkeley, Calif.: McCutchan, 1976.

Carnoy, M. *Schooling in a Corporate Society*. New York: McKay, 1977.

Cistone, P. J. *Understanding School Boards*. Lexington, Mass.: Lexington Books, 1975.

Coons, J. E., & Sugarman, S. D. *Education by Choice: The Case for Family Control*. Berkeley: University of California Press, 1978.

Crain, R. *The Politics of School Desegregation*. Hawthorne, N.Y.: Aldine, 1968.

Cresswell, A. M., & Murphy, M. J. *Education and Collective Bargaining*. Berkeley, Calif.: McCutchan, 1977.

Cuban, L. *Urban School Chiefs under Fire*. Chicago: University of Chicago Press, 1976.

Dolbeare, K., & Hammond, P. E. *The School Prayer Decision*. Chicago: University of Chicago Press, 1976.

Dye, T. R. *Politics, Economics, and the Public: Policy Outcomes in the American States*. Chicago: Rand McNally, 1966.

Easton, D. *The Political System*. New York: Knopf, 1953.

Eidenberg, E., & Morey, R. D. *An Act of Congress*. New York: Norton, 1969.

Eliot, T. H. Toward an understanding of public school politics. *American Political Science Review*, December 1959, *53*, 1032–1051.

Erickson, D. *Public Control for Non-public Schools*. Chicago: University of Chicago Press, 1969.

Finn, C. E., Jr. *Education and the Presidency*. Lexington, Mass.: Heath, 1977.

Fishel, A., & Pottker, J. *National Politics and Sex Discrimination in Education*. Lexington, Mass.: Lexington Books, 1977.

Foster, W. P. Bilingual education: An educational and legal survey. *Journal of Law and Education*, April 1976, *5*, 149–171.

Gittell, M. *Participants and Participation: A Study of School Policy in New York City*. New York: Center for Urban Education, 1967.

Gittell, M., & Hollander, T. E. *Six Urban School Districts*. New York: Praeger, 1968.

Gladieux, L. W., & Wolanin, T. R. *Congress and the Colleges: The National Politics of Higher Education*. Lexington, Mass.: Lexington Books, 1976.

Goldhammer, K. *The School Board*. New York: Center for Applied Research, 1964.

Hogan, J. C. *The Schools, The Courts, and the Public Interest*. Lexington, Mass.: Heath, 1974.

Horowitz, D. L. *The Courts and Sound Social Policy*. Washington, D.C.: Brookings Institution, 1977.

Kirst, M. *Delivery Systems for Federal Aid to Disadvantaged Children: Problems and Prospects*. Stanford, Calif.: Stanford University Press, 1972.

LaNoue, G. R. *Educational Vouchers: Concepts and Controversies*. New York: Teachers College Press, 1972.

LaNoue, G. R., & Smith, B. L. R. *The Politics of School Decentralization*. Lexington, Mass.: Lexington Books, 1973.

Lehne, R. *The Quest for Justice: The Politics of School Finance Reform*. New York: Longman, 1978.

Lerner, D., & Lasswell, H. D. *The Policy Sciences*. Stanford, Calif.: Stanford University Press, 1951.

Levin, B. *The Courts as Educational Policy-makers and Their Impact on Federal Programs* (R-2224). Santa Monica, Calif.: Rand Corporation, 1977.

Levin, H. M. (Ed.). *Community Control of Schools*. Washington, D.C.: Brookings Institution, 1970.

Mann, D. *The Politics of Administrative Representation*. Lexington, Mass.: Lexington Books, 1976.

Martin, R. C. *Government and the Suburban School*. Syracuse, N.Y.: Syracuse University Press, 1962.

Massialas, B. G. *Education and the Political System*. Reading, Mass.: Addison-Wesley, 1969.

Massotti, L. *Education and Politics in Suburbia*. Cleveland, Ohio: Western Reserve, 1967.

Meranto, P. *The Politics of Federal Aid to Education in 1965*. Syracuse, N.Y.: Syracuse University Press, 1967.

Molz, K. R. *Federal Policy and Library Support*. Cambridge, Mass.: MIT Press, 1976.

Muir, W. K. *Prayer and the Public Schools: Law and Attitudes Change*. Chicago: University of Chicago Press, 1967.

Munger, F. J., & Fenno, R., Jr. *National Politics and Federal Aid to Education*. Syracuse, N.Y.: Syracuse University Press, 1962.

Nunnery, M. Y., & Kimbrough, R. *Politics, Power Polls, and School Election*. Berkeley, Calif.: McCutchan, 1971.

Orfield, G. *The Reconstruction of Southern Education: The Schools and the 1964 Civil Rights Act*. New York: Wiley Interscience, 1969.

Orfield, G. *Must We Bus? Segregated Schools and National Policy*. Washington, D.C.: Brookings Institution, 1978.

Peterson, P. *School Politics, Chicago Style*. Chicago: University of Chicago Press, 1976.

Pois, J. *The School Board Crisis*. Chicago: Educational Methods, 1964.

Price, H. D. Race, religion and the rules committee. In Alan Westin, *The Uses of Power*. New York: Harcourt, 1962.

Rogers, D. *110 Livingston Street*. New York: Random House, 1968.

Rosenthal, A. *Pedagogues and Power*. Syracuse, N.Y.: Syracuse University Press, 1969.

Schrag, P. *Village School Downtown*. Boston: Beacon, 1967.

Sindler, A. P. *Bakke, DeFunis, and Minority Admissions*. New York: Longman, 1978.

Sproull, L.; Weiner, S.; & Wolf, D. *Organizing and Anarchy: Belief, Bureaucracy, and Politics in the National Institute of Education*. Chicago: University of Chicago Press, 1977.

Summerfield, H. *Power and Process: The Formulation and Limits of Federal Education Policy*. Berkeley, Calif.: McCutchan, 1974.

Sundquist, J. L. *Politics and Policy: The Eisenhower, Kennedy, and Johnson Years*. Washington, D.C.: Brookings Institution, 1968.

Thomas, N. C. *Education in the National Politics*. New York: McKay, 1975.

van Geel, T. Law, politics, and the right to be taught English. *School Review*, February 1975, *83*, 245–272.

Wirt, F. *The Politics of Southern Equality*. Hawthorne, N.Y.: Aldine, 1971.

Wirt, F. Education politics and policies. In H. Jacobs & K. Vines (Eds.), *Politics in the American States*. Boston: Little, Brown, 1976.

Wirt, F. M., & Kirst, M. W. *The Political Web of American Schools*. Boston: Little, Brown, 1972.

Wise, A. *Rich Schools, Poor Schools*. Chicago: University of Chicago Press, 1968.

Wise, A. *Legislated Learning*. Berkeley: University of California Press, 1979.

Wynne, E. *The Politics of Public School Accountability*. Berkeley, Calif.: McCutchan, 1972.

Zeigler, H. L., & Jennings, M. K. *Governing American Schools*. Belmont, Calif.: Duxbury, 1974.

Zeigler, H. L., & Johnson, K. F. *The Politics of Education in the States*. Indianapolis: Bobbs-Merrill, 1972.

POLLING

The genesis of public opinion polls in the United States may well date back to "straw polls" conducted at town meetings in colonial New England. Owing to this heritage, public opinion polls often are associated with political concerns. Frequently they have been used for projecting election results, establishing indexes of presidential confidence, and examining public opinions on controversial, politically oriented topics. Today almost all candidates for major political offices retain private pollsters to supply the information needed to evaluate and guide their campaigns.

Wide-ranging developments in the area of computer technology during the past thirty years have done much to encourage public opinion polls to increase their frequency, and to promote the evolution of more sophisticated techniques. Current levels of sophistication virtually negate the possibility that the *Chicago Tribune*'s headline *faux pas* the day after the 1948 presidential election—"Dewey Defeats Truman"—will ever be repeated.

At the other extreme, political forecasting based on public opinion polls perhaps reached its zenith in the 1980 presidential election. According to Jordan (1981), the incumbent, President Carter, began preparing for defeat early on election day, after his private pollster predicted that what earlier had been believed to be a close race would result in a ten-point victory for Reagan. The final margin was just that, 51 percent for Reagan and 41 percent for Carter (Church, 1980). Similarly, based on postvoting interviews at selected polling places, NBC News projected Reagan the winner as early as 8:15 P.M. EST on election night, when less than 1 percent of the vote was in and hours before polls closed in other time zones. The latter announcement did little to endear public opinion polls to the hearts of the nation's citizenry—especially voters in western states—but it did promote begrudging respect for the capabilities and accuracy of well-designed polls.

Educationally Oriented Polls. Similarities between government and public education in the United States, largely because both depend upon public direction and support, have served to promote a quasi-political interest in public opinion polls related to educational endeavors. As with politically oriented public opinion polls, the increased use of educationally oriented polls has been promoted by advancements in computer technology.

The Gallup polls. Undoubtedly the most renowned of the educational polls is the annual Gallup poll of lay attitudes toward public education. The first of these was conducted in 1969. According to Stanley Elam, former direct of publications for Phi Delta Kappa: "The poll has profoundly influenced education policy in the U.S. since 1970 as state and federal law makers, boards of education . . . , and educators with policy-making and implementation responsibilities have used the results to study the public reaction to basic questions about public schools" (Elam, 1978, p. iv). These influences were particularly evident during the late 1970s in the promotion of the "back to basics" movement and the development of magnet schools founded on educational approaches and disciplinary standards more characteristic of earlier eras.

According to Elam (1978), the concept of a Gallup poll pertaining to education originated with CFK, Ltd., the foundation sponsored by Charles F. Kettering, which financed the polls during the first five years of their existence (through 1973). The Ford Foundation assumed temporary sponsorship of the poll in 1974 before I/D/E/A, the educational arm of the Kettering Foundation, took it over from 1975 to 1980. Subsequently the Lily Endowment of Indianapolis agreed to sponsor the poll for a minimum of three years in 1981. Regardless of sponsorship, throughout its existence the poll's results have been released in fall issues of the *Phi Delta Kappan*.

Each year the poll's results have been based on interviews with approximately 1,500 to 1,600 randomly selected adults (18 or over) in all parts of the country. Their selection has been based on randomly drawn sample clusters stratified according to locale and community population.

Although the Gallup poll's items have varied from year to year, consistent features have been the identification of major school problems, overall ratings of schools (A, B, C, D, and F), and improvements needed by public schools.

In summarizing the results of the first ten polls (1969–1978), Gallup (1978) indicated that lack of discipline topped problem lists in nine of the ten years (all but 1971). Ranked second overall were problems related to integration/segregation (largely busing). In third place was financial concerns. However, he cited the fact that student drug usage supplanted fiscal concerns as the third-ranking problem in 1978 as evidence of a possible future trend.

The pollster also drew attention to the steady decline observed in the public's attitudes toward its schools. He concluded that "unless measures are taken to alter present trends, a rocky and troubled future can be predicted for the public schools" (Gallup, 1978, p. 3). High on his list of needed corrective measures were the provision of greater financial support, improved public understanding of school operations, and expanded participation by citizens.

Generally the findings of the 1979 and 1980 Gallup polls (Gallup, 1979; 1980) were consistent with those of previous polls and the pollster's own earlier predictions. Discipline continued as the number one problem, and only minor changes were observed in the ranking of other problems.

However, in commenting on his twelfth poll, Gallup (1980) expressed cautious optimism about the first rise observed in the public's opinions of the schools since 1974: "The [rise] in the ratings may be due to changes in the emphasis upon basics in many school districts, or to a better understanding among the general public of just what the schools are achieving. In any event, the downward trend has ended, at least for the present" (p. 34).

Other educational polls. During the first eleven years of its existence, the Gallup poll went virtually unchallenged. Its findings received considerable attention in a variety of media, and many persons came to accept them as the "truth" about what is wrong with public education in America. Few, if any, opportunities existed for educators to make their collective opinions similarly known.

However, this changed in 1980 with the advent of the Phi Delta Kappa (PDK) and PROBE polls, which sought to collect and analyze opinions of professional educators. The PDK poll (Elam & Gough, 1980) included the reports of 202 of 400 randomly selected PDK members. The poll conducted by PROBE, an independent research agency based at the University of Northern Iowa (Duea & Bishop, 1980), focused on the opinions of nearly 1,300 public school superintendents in two slightly overlapping samples: 1,154 randomly selected and 133 representing the nation's 200 most populous districts.

In contrast to the Gallup poll, where discipline was the top-ranked problem in eleven of twelve years, educators in both the PDK and PROBE polls gave top billing to financial concerns. Other of the top five problems identified by PDK members were discipline, parental cooperation/support, student motivation, and declining enrollments/school closings.

In the PROBE survey, both random sample and large district superintendents agreed upon the top four problem areas: financial concerns, declining enrollment, governmental restrictions, and requirements for education of the handicapped. Discipline ranked thirteenth with both groups.

Professional educators rated schools considerably higher than lay respondents did; giving grades of either A or B to their schools were 61 percent of the PDK respondents and 84 percent of the district superintendents, compared to only 35 percent of the Gallup poll respondents.

Polling Considerations. Generally, education-oriented public opinion polls are designed to serve one or more objectives, which are frequently interrelated: (1) the examination of existing educational opinions and beliefs; (2) evaluation of the status of selected educational practices; (3) the compilation of demographic data (for identifying samples, for status studies, or for the establishing comparison groups); (4) needs assessment; (5) program evaluation; (6) the evaluation or promotion (or both) of public relations; and (7) the examination of shifting data trends on a longitudinal basis. Coupled with any or all of these major objectives may be the goal of fulfilling research requirements for advanced professional training and degree programs (i.e., research papers, theses, and dissertations).

Three objective areas—needs assessment, program evaluation, and public relations research—merit further discussion.

Needs assessment. Ralph Tyler (1949) has long been noted in the field of curriculum development for his advocacy of three major sources of input for objective formulation: studies of contemporary life, studies of learners, and suggestions from subject matter specialists (Short & Marconnit, 1968). The decade of the 1970s saw a great deal of attention focused on the first two of these sources, not only for curriculum development but for the justification of applications for government-sponsored grants. Some states went so far as to mandate needs assessment requirements for all school districts and, if the early part of the decade is any indication, there is little reason to expect needs assessment concerns to lessen appreciably in the 1980s.

Although empirical approaches often are favored for identifying societal needs and learners' needs, public (and professional) opinion polls can provide a means of guiding or complementing such approaches. They are especially effective for securing citizen participation in educational planning efforts, establishing guidelines for accountability programs, and meeting the community involvement requirements of regional accrediting associations.

However, needs assessment findings demand careful scrutiny and evaluation. Monette (1979) exposes the paradox that occurs when the learner "who does not know" or "has not learned" is expected to specify what should be learned. By implication, the same would appear to hold true for other, comparatively uninformed sources of such information.

Therefore, it is seldom practical to accept needs assessment results at face value. At the very least, they require knowledgeable, professional interpretation if they are to be translated into meaningful educational objectives.

Program evaluation. Rather closely allied with needs assessment is program evaluation. Whereas needs assessment is intended for the purpose of determining "what should be," program evaluation is intended as a determination of "what is." But unfavorable evaluation findings and the deficiencies exposed also serve as need indicators.

Public relations efforts. As related by Elam and Gough (1980), "George Gallup has often remarked that the closer the public gets to its schools and the more it gets to know them from first-hand experience, the more favorable are its attitudes" (p. 47). If one accepts this premise, it stands to reason that one cannot separate efforts directed toward evaluating public relations activities and efforts directed toward promoting them.

Data Collection Modes. Typically, public opinion polls are conducted in one of three modes: direct personal interviews, telephone interviews, or mailed questionnaires. Each has its advantages and disadvantages, many of which have been identified by Borg and Gall (1971).

Personal interviews. The four main advantages of the personal interview technique are a comparatively high rate of subject cooperation, immediacy of response, greater depth of response, and opportunity to explain nuances of potentially confusing questions. The latter two advantages also pose potential disadvantages in the form of recording and interpretation difficulties, excessive subjectivity, and interviewer bias based on leading questioning and other subtle influences. Other disadvantages include inefficiency in terms of time and travel considerations, interviewer training requirements, and the intrusion of interinterviewer biases when more than one interviewer is employed. Following up on missed contacts also can prove difficult.

Telephone surveys. This mode, except for somewhat lower rates of response, retains most of the advantages of direct personal interviews. It also retains most of the disadvantages, but it is considerably more efficient because of the absence of travel requirements. An additional disadvantage is that the lack of direct personal contact limits the development of rapport. Long-distance calls involving large numbers of subjects also may prove expensive.

Mail surveys. Far and away the most efficient mode, both in terms of researcher time and the cost of long-distance contacts, is the mail survey, which is readily applicable to large numbers of widely dispersed subjects. Tempering these advantages, however, are the more superficial questioning techniques this mode requires, the absence of opportunities to clarify confusing items, the propensity of subjects to give less complete responses and to omit certain items, time lags in the receipt of responses, and often lower response rates.

Sampling. A critical factor in determining applicability of a poll's findings to its target group is the use of appropriate sampling procedures. When numbers are manageable and adequate resources are available, entire populations may be polled but, more often than not, selective sampling procedures must be employed. For reasons of statistical inference, some form of randomization is desirable. Descriptions of common methods follow (Borg & Gall, 1971).

Simple random sampling. This sampling technique ensures that every individual in a defined population has an equal and independent chance of being selected. In small populations, it may be accomplished by simply drawing names or numbers but, more frequently, it involves selections based on random number tables or computerized randomization.

Stratified sampling. This technique is an extension of simple random sampling that may be used to ensure equitable representation among sample subgroups when comparisons between divergent-sized subgroups are to be made. It involves proportional random selections from predetermined subgroups based on the proportion of the population each subgroup represents.

Systematic sampling. Systematic sampling is exemplified by selecting every tenth name (or any consistent number) from a population listing. It does not meet the criterion of independence because once the first name is selected all others are thus determined. However, if the population list has been compiled in a random fashion, it will meet the criterion of randomization. But this does not apply to alphabetical and other uniformly compiled lists (telephone directories, etc.). The absence of independent selection in this method serves to restrict the statistical inferences that can be made from the results obtained.

Cluster sampling. Instead of the individual, the random selection unit utilized in cluster sampling is a naturally occurring group of individuals (a school, a classroom, a city block, etc.). A disadvantage of cluster sampling is the fact that the cluster rather than the individual must be used in determining degrees of freedom for statistical inferences because it represents the smallest, independently determined sample unit (Guilford, 1965). As a result, fewer degrees of freedom result and wider differences are required to achieve significance.

The PACE (Polling Attitudes of Community on Education) materials available from Phi Delta Kappa (Bugher, 1980) provide an excellent treatment of cluster sampling as well as other polling procedures, including instructions for its application in the selection of interview subjects in both urban and rural settings.

Sample size. Another important consideration is the matter of sample size. Among influential factors in this decision are the time and resources available to the researcher and the degree of precision desired in reporting findings.

As Bugher (1980) puts it: "If a sample is carefully chosen—that is, if it is selected according to the rules of probability sampling—it can be remarkably accurate as a representation of the larger population" (p. 3). Therefore, a large sample is not a requisite for the generation of meaningful findings. Let us then focus on the reliability of findings where sample size does make a difference.

The following formula may be used to establish the 95 percent confidence interval—the margin for error that will be exceeded only 5 percent of the time—whenever response percentages based on data obtained from randomly selected subjects are reported (adapted from Guilford, 1965, p. 161):

$$CI_{95} = \pm 1.96 \, (100\sqrt{pq/N}).$$

In the formula, CI_{95} is the 95 percent confidence interval; p is the proportion (decimal fraction) reported; $q = 1 - p$; and N is the number of subjects on which the proportion is based (the multiplier 100 simply converts p to a percentage).

It should be noted that both sample size *(N)* and the proportion reported *(p)* influence the size of the confidence interval. The larger N is, the smaller the confidence interval (potential error) will be; the error potential is greatest for percentages near 50, and it grows smaller as one progresses toward either extreme. For example, with a sample of 500, CI_{95} at 50 percent would be ±4.4 percent; at both 10 and 90 percent, it would be ±2.6 percent. Consequently, a sample of 500 will give reporting accuracy within a range of 4.4 percent at the 95 percent confidence level. Increasing sample size to 1,000 would reduce error potential to ±3.1 percent at 50 percent.

The error potential for stratified samples is somewhat lower because of the more restricted variability characteristic of such samples. Guilford (1965, p. 162) also provides a means for shrinking the standard error appropriately for stratified samples, but its explanation is too involved for presentation here.

In each report of the Gallup poll in the *Phi Delta Kappan* (and in the PACE materials), Gallup provides tables that show error estimates at the 95 percent confidence level for selected sample sizes and percentages. They are intended for use in the interpretation of findings based on cluster samples (see Gallup, 1979, 1980; Bugher, 1980). Also included are tables showing sampling errors for difference scores that may be used in comparing like results for independent subgroups. In both instances, the error rates reported for cluster samples are substantially higher than those that would be obtained with simple random and stratified samples.

Regarding difference scores, Guilford (1965) advocates using variations of Fisher's z statistic for purposes of evaluating differences between both correlated and uncorrelated percentages (proportions). By definition, correlated proportions are those involved in within-group comparisons (comparisons between two different proportions reported by the same group); uncorrelated proportions are those involved in comparisons between figures reported by two different sample subgroups (see pp. 185–189).

Data Collecting and Recording. Regardless of the data collection mode employed—personal interview, telephone survey, or mail survey—a standardized form of presenting questions and recording answers must be developed to promote data consistency and to facilitate its compilation and analysis. Major considerations should be efficiency and effectiveness: items should be presented in a manner that promotes consistent understandings, and the data recording format should readily accommodate desired statistical operations and computer input procedures. Whenever computer analysis is to be employed,

data processing personnel should be consulted about instrument design.

The first step in developing such instruments is settling on poll objectives. Second, one should generate as many potential items as possible. And then, because subject cooperation and response are usually inversely related to survey length, the item pool should be culled to eliminate inappropriate and repetitive items. Only those items necessary for meeting the poll's objectives should be retained: those needed for sample identification, subgroup definition, and the investigation of phenomena critical to the study. *If you don't need it or don't know what to do with it, don't ask it!*

The Delphi technique offers an alternate means of item generation, especially for mail surveys, but it requires considerable time and effort. The aim of the Delphi technique is to promote consensus of agreement among subjects; essentially it involves a series of up to four questionnaires. The first of these includes only a very few open-ended questions. The responses received are then used to generate closed-end items (multiple-choice, etc.) for a second questionnaire that is circulated two or three times. Agreement is encouraged by informing subjects of the response group's choices for each item on the previous administration of the questionnaire before they respond to the next round.

An adaptation of the Delphi approach utilizing only the initial, open-ended questionnaire can be an effective aid to researchers in developing items appropriate for the investigation of topics with which they have had little previous experience. Those who wish for a more complete explanation of this technique should see Dalkey (1970) and Rasp (1973).

In mail surveys, subjects generally are more favorably disposed to closed-end items (multiple choice, rating scales, etc.) than to open-ended items that require written responses. Questionnaire length is another important factor, since each additional page tends to reduce the rate of response. Whenever possible, single-page questionnaires (on one or both sides) should be used. By careful planning and effective use of typesetting and photo-reduction techniques, considerable information can be included on a single page.

Attractive, professional-looking questionnaire designs, brightly colored, attention-getting paper stock, and effective cover letters also can promote improved response rates. According to Borg and Gall (1971) better response rates are obtained if cover letters have technical merit and are neat, and if they include subtle flattery of subjects or their positions; emphasis on the importance of the study and persuasive reasons why the subject should participate; indications of publication plans and, when appropriate, opportunities to secure copies of the study's results; identification with prestigious institutions, organizations, or individuals (perhaps even noteworthy cosigners for the letter); specified, realistic return deadlines (usually within a week or ten days of receipt); and signatures that have been individually signed or reproduced in a different color of ink.

Interviewers and Their Training. Two important considerations in preparing for public opinion polls based on personal (and telephone) interviews are the selection and training of interviewers. According to Bugher (1980), among the desirable qualities that interviewers should possess are a strong commitment to task completion; the ability to converse easily with persons from varied backgrounds; a willingness to follow directions precisely; a sensitive, pleasing, and empathetic personality; aggressiveness but not in overabundance; the ability to ask questions without revealing personal biases; the patience to listen carefully; and the ability to comprehend and record information objectively.

Besides exercising the preceding qualities, programs for training interviews generally emphasize the processes involved in selecting subjects, establishing rapport, handling commonly encountered problems, developing a thorough, working familiarity with interview guides and data-recording techniques, and provide ample opportunities for supervised and critiqued practice. However, training does not stop there; it carries over into effective field supervision and the examination of early returns for evidence of needed refinements in technique.

One of the more detailed examples of interviewer training requisites is the *Handbook for Interviewers* that accompanies the PACE materials (Bugher, 1980). They are virtually a must for persons—especially neophytes—seriously considering public opinion research. Those intending to conduct telephone polls also would do well to examine Banach and Caudill's recommendations (1979).

Economy Measures. Polling efforts are seldom free from financial constraints and attendant demands for economies. Potential cost reduction measures in the area of research involving personal interviews and telephone surveys may include, when feasible, recruiting volunteer interviewers; utilizing college or university classes and other existing, intact groups to expedite recruitment and interviewer training efforts; and gaining access to WATS lines or other reduced service options for purposes of conducting telephone surveys.

In the realm of mail surveys, similar cost reductions may be achieved by utilizing bulk mail service and return postage permits. (Bulk rates—for 200 pieces or more—generally run about 75 percent lower than first-class rates; and even though a two-cent postage premium is involved, eliminating postage payments on unreturned questionnaires through the use of return postage permits works to the researcher's advantage when return rates fall below 80 percent.) Additional savings may be achieved by eliminating the need for return envelopes by printing self-mailing questionnaires on heavy paper stock and by reducing questionnaire printing costs through the use of photo-reduction techniques with typed copy instead of more expensive typesetting processes. Finally, the purchase of prepared mailing labels may prove more economical than compiling lists and typing envelopes when large samples are involved.

For purchasing prepared mailing labels, several firms, such as Market Data Retrieval (a firm based in Westport, Connecticut) offer a broad range of custom sample selection and mailing label services based on extensive, up-to-date computer listings of a wide variety of groups, both in and out of the field of education. Anyone considering moderate to large-scale survey research would do well to investigate the services of such firms.

Although some of the economy measures suggested may appear to be prerogatives limited to rather substantial enterprises, access to those services that normally are not readily available to individuals (bulk mailing, return postage permits, and WATS lines) sometimes can be arranged through educational institutions, business establishments, and civic or professional organizations. This is especially true during off hours and vacation periods when service demands are lessened. If the research is closely related to their interests, such agencies may even be persuaded to underwrite some of the costs.

Summary. Recurrent themes in this article have reflected the growth of interest in public opinion data, which is largely based on the nation's reliance on representative forms of civic and educational governance, and the examination of appropriate procedures intended for the accommodation of this interest. Because of wide-ranging developments in computer technology during the past thirty to forty years, large-scale public opinion research, once the exclusive domain of the federal government and a few well-endowed polling agencies, is now widely conducted and reported by increasing numbers of individuals, organizations, and news media. Undoubtedly improved access to such technology, facilitated by recent progress in microcomputer development, will continue to augment the nation's appetite for public opinion data and the capacity to feed it.

A by-product of these developments could well be the evolution of improved quality controls in the area of public opinion research. Whereas financial and other resource limitations once discouraged efforts to challenge the findings and methodology of major polls, recent technological advances have placed the capacity to do so well within the grasp of more modestly endowed organizations and individuals. The quality of public opinion research almost certainly will be enhanced by the system of checks and balances that has resulted and continues to grow.

Jerry Duea

See also Statistical Methods; Survey Research Methods.

REFERENCES

Banach, W. J., & Caudill, J. Survey starter: Now more than ever, what you don't know can hurt you! *National Association of Secondary School Principals Bulletin*, 1979, *63*, 29–38.

Borg, W. R., & Gall, M. D. *Educational Research: An Introduction* (2nd ed.). New York: McKay, 1971.

Bugher, W. *Polling Attitudes of Community on Education Manual*. Bloomington, Ind.: Phi Delta Kappa, 1980.

Church, G. J. Reagan coast to coast. *Time*, 1980, *116*(20), 22–24.

Dalkey, N. Use of the Delphi Technique in educational planning. *Educational Resources Agency Herald*, 1970, *4*(2), 1–6.

Duea, J., & Bishop, W. L. The PROBE results: Important differences in public and professional perceptions of the schools. *Phi Delta Kappan*, 1970, *62*, 50–52.

Elam, S. M. (Ed.). *A Decade of Gallup Polls of Attitudes toward Education, 1969–1978*. Bloomington, Ind.: Phi Delta Kappa, 1978.

Elam, S. M., & Gough, P. B. Comparing lay and professional opinion on Gallup poll questions. *Phi Delta Kappan*, 1980, *62*, 47–48.

Gallup, G. H. The first ten years: Trends and observations. In S. M. Elam (Ed.), *A Decade of Gallup Polls of Attitudes toward Education, 1969–1978*. Bloomington, Ind.: Phi Delta Kappa, 1978.

Gallup, G. H. The eleventh annual Gallup poll of the public's attitudes toward the public schools. *Phi Delta Kappan*, 1979, *61*, 33–45.

Gallup, G. H. The twelfth annual Gallup poll of the public's attitudes toward the public schools. *Phi Delta Kappan*, 1980, *62*, 33–46.

Guilford, J. P. *Fundamental Statistics in Psychology and Education* (4th ed.). New York: McGraw-Hill, 1965.

Jordan, H. The campaign Carter couldn't win. *Life*, 1981, *4*(1), 91–100.

Monette, M. L. Need assessment: A critique of philosophical assumptions. *Adult Education*, 1979, *29*(2), 83–95.

Rasp, A., Jr. Delphi: A decision maker's dream. *Nation's Schools*, 1973, *92*, 29–32.

Short, E. C., & Marconnit, G. *Contemporary Thought on Public School Curriculum*. Dubuque, Iowa: Brown, 1968.

Tyler, R. W. *Basic Principles of Curriculum and Instruction*. Chicago: University of Chicago Press, 1949.

PREADOLESCENT DEVELOPMENT

During the transition from childhood to adolescence, individuals undergo biological, cognitive, and social-emotional changes generally considered critical to "healthy and productive functioning" (Lipsitz, 1977, p. xi) throughout the rest of their lives. Although the uniqueness of this period of development was recognized from the beginning of American child psychology (Hall, 1904), as yet there is no consensus on how to conceptualize it or what to name it. Terms most frequently used to characterize the period ("late childhood," "preadolescence," and "early adolescence") are not always defined the same way; depending upon the context, they may refer to identical, different, or overlapping developmental periods. For example, Blair and Burton (1951), Cohen and Frank (1975) Kaluger and Kaluger (1979), Kohen-Raz (1971), Loomis (1959), Redl (1943–1944), and Thornburg (1974) place the period of preadolescence in the late childhood years—ages 9 to 11,

12, or 13—prior to the onset of pubescence. Where these authors consider preadolescence to end, others (Hurlock, 1978; Rogers, 1977) consider it to begin and from there continue for about two years, until sexual maturity is reached. Still other authors—Hurd (1978), Kagan and Coles (1972), Kaluger and Kaluger (1979), Lipsitz (1977), Mitchell (1974), and Sommer (1978)—demarcate the period of early adolescence with different age spans within the range beginning at 10 to 12 years and ending at 14 to 16 years.

This ambiguity in defining the period of transition from childhood to adolescence stems from several sources, including (1) use of the concepts "pubescence" and/or "puberty" as benchmark's to establish boundaries of the period while defining these concepts in varying ways; (2) variations in the criteria of sexual maturity, especially for boys; (3) difficulty of employing strictly comparable criteria of sexual maturity for girls and boys; (4) marked continuity in development, which tends to blur distinctions between middle and late childhood (or preadolsecence) and between preadolescence and early adolescence; (5) increments in rate of development over the last century resulting in pubescence beginning earlier in each generation and (6) paucity of research on development during this period.

As defined here, the period of "preadolescence" embraces the definitions of preadolescence referred to earlier as well as the age span that is sometimes assigned to early adolescence. Specifically, preadolescence, that period of the life span between childhood and adolescence, begins in the late childhood years just prior to the onset of pubescence, when children's intellectual and social-emotional behaviors permit distinctions between them and younger children, and ends with the production of sex cells and the appearance, but not complete development, of the secondary sex characteristics (physical features that differentiate males and females but are not directly related to reproduction as the primary sex characteristics are). For girls, this period roughly corresponds to ages 9 to 13 and grades 4 through 8; for boys, the age range is roughly 10 to 14, and the grade range is 5 through 9.

"Pubescence" refers to a more or less sequential pattern of physiological and physical changes initiated by hormonal activity, which results in the attainment of full reproductive capacity and the complete development of all the secondary sex characteristics. Thus pubescence is not coextensive with preadolescence as defined above; the preadolescent period begins before pubescence starts and ends while it is in progress. Nevertheless, the wide variability in time of onset and in rate of pubescent development increases the imprecision of age-span designations of the period. If one estimates the time of onset of pubescence on the basis of its earliest manifestations—"the budding of the female breast" and "accelerated growth of the testes and scrotum with reddening and wrinkling of the scrotal skin" (Tanner, 1971, p. 917)—the age range for girls is 8 to 13 years, and for boys 9.5 to 13.5 years. Likewise, variability in the duration of pubescence is indicated by the fact that "in girls the interval from the first signs of puberty to complete maturity varies from one and a half to six years [and] in boys a similar variability occurs" (Tanner, 1971, p. 919).

Finally, the intellectual and social-emotional behaviors that distinguish children entering preadolescence from younger children include rejection of adult standards; cleavage of the sexes accompanied by apparent antagonism toward members of the opposite sex; strong attachments to same-sex peers; reality seeking with respect to the physical world and relationships with others; use of causal relations in thinking; and more effective use of intellectual skills, especially reading (Blair & Burton, 1951). A vivid portrayal of the behavior of the child at the dawn of preadolescence has been given by Redl (1943–1944, 1969).

Physical Development. During preadolescence physical development proceeds through a prepubescent phase of slow, steady growth and a pubescent phase of rapid and drastic changes. From ages 9 to 11 boys and girls average a yearly gain in height of one to two inches and a yearly gain in weight of four to five pounds. Boys tend to be slightly taller than girls until age 11, when girls have a growth spurt that makes them temporarily taller. In the meantime, boys will have about two more years of growth before starting their own spurt, which on the average results in greater gains than in girls. Thus, by age 15, boys will be taller on the average than girls, and the difference will be relatively greater than before pubescence began. As long as pubescence starts within the normal age limits, prepubescent and postpubescent height are positively correlated (Ausubel, Montemayor, & Svajian, 1977).

Furthermore, during the prepubescent years manual dexterity, muscular strength, and resistance to fatigue increase, thereby accounting for greater muscular agility, accuracy, vigor, and endurance (Blair & Burton, 1951). Typically, these years are one's healthiest. The lymphoid masses that help fight infectious diseases peak in quantity, producing maximum resistance to illness (Kaluger & Kaluger, 1979).

Pubescence not only initiates sexual maturation and accelerates body growth but also increases muscular strength, alters body proportions, and fosters changes in various nonsexual functions involving the endocrine, cardiovascular, and respiratory systems. In addition, pubescence is associated with a number of preadolescent concerns. For example, interindividual asynchrony in the onset of pubescence even if only slight, may be troubling to preadolescents because of the premium they place on conformity. Early maturing girls and late maturing boys tend to have special social disadvantages and corresponding adjustment difficulties. Then, too, interindividual variation in rate and outcome of pubescent changes can cause anxiety, particularly unfavorable status in respect to penis growth and female breast development. Similarly, acne, body odor, and unwanted fat arouse concern because of

their centrality to heterosexual development (Ausubel, Montemayor, & Svajian, 1977; Sommers, 1978).

Cognitive Development.   Cognitive development during preadolescence can be characterized in terms of two of Piaget's stages: the second of two substages of concrete operations, which spans ages 9 to 11 (Inhelder & Piaget, 1958), and the first of two substages for formal operations, a transitional stage extending from age 11 or 12 to age 14 to 15 that Piaget labels "preadolescence" (Piaget & Inhelder, 1969). During the second concrete-operational substage, the "development, differentiation, and perfection of concrete operational thought" seem to reach their peak (Kohen-Raz, 1971, pp. 54–55). During the first of the formal-operational substages, "nascent formal thought restructures the concrete operations by subordinating them to new structures whose development will continue throughout adolescence and all of later life" (Piaget & Inhelder, 1969, p. 152).

The transition from the preoperational to the concrete-operational stage occurs at approximately age 6 or 7, when children's egocentric, perceptual-dominated, intuitive ways of representing and acting on the environment increasingly give way to an evolving integrated system of logical thought processes or operations (the logic of classes, relations, and number), which they can use in solving problems directly related to real objects and events. Compared with their younger counterparts, preadolescents approaching the end of the stage of concrete operations are considerably more advanced in cognitive functioning (Flavell, 1970; Inhelder & Piaget, 1958; Kohen-Raz, 1971): they employ concrete operations more widely within and across areas of experience; understand relations between abstract concepts, though dependence upon concrete examples subverts what Flavell calls "interpropositional" reasoning (1977, p. 105); think logically with less distraction from egocentric or fanciful intrusions, thus facilitating the construction of an objective and rational view of the world; integrate "emotional-bound fantasy . . . with realistically adapted thought" (Kohen-Raz, 1971, p. 60); and process information more efficiently, thereby improving their ability to abstract, generalize, and recall (Kohen-Raz, 1971; Mackworth, 1976; Ornstein, Naus, & Liberty, 1975).

During the first substage of formal operations, counting, classifying, and relating are liberated from objects and concrete events; hence, thought is no longer hobbled by content and intellectual powers are greatly expanded. Preadolescents become capable of reasoning from a proposition to its conclusions, no matter how theoretical or untenable; of approaching a problem with an awareness of all the possibilities that inhere in its solution and systematically exhausting these; of thinking logically about relations among a set of propositions; of understanding the concept of proportion in several areas; and of understanding combinatorial probabilities (Piaget & Inhelder, 1969). However, preadolescents are not yet able to articulate the "relevant laws of logic" (Piaget & Inhelder, 1969, pp. 135–136) or to write down a correct mathematical formula to support their thinking. Further, they can be expected to differ in respect to time of onset of formal thinking and kinds of tasks to which they may be able to apply it (Elkind, 1980; Kohlberg & Gilligan, 1971; Neimark, 1975, 1979; Piaget, 1972; Ross, 1974).

Social-Emotional Development. Major trends in social-emotional development are (1) increasing social understanding, (2) increasing assertion of autonomy in efforts to detach one's self and identity from the family; (3) increasing reliance upon peers as socializing agents; (4) increasing sexuality, changing same-sex attachments to heterosexual relations; and (5) increasing evaluation of previously accepted beliefs and values. The confluence of these trends results in an emerging new identity.

Preadolescents evidence significant developments in interpersonal understanding and in knowledge of the social world in general. They realize that the overt behavior of others does not always reflect their own subjective experience; show greater sensitivity to nonverbal cues in communication; become capable of simultaneously coordinating their perspective with that of another (Flavell et al., 1968; Selman, 1980); assume a more objective stance in describing others (Hill & Palmquist, 1978); and interpret friendship in terms of personhood, mutual dependence, and cooperation (Selman, 1980; Youniss, 1980). Additionally, preadolescents acquire increased understanding of such concepts as positive and distributive justice (Enright, Franklin, & Manheim, 1980; Piaget, 1932), equality (Streater & Chertkoff, 1976), and social conventions and rules (Damon, 1977; Turiel, 1980).

In spite of their rejection of parental control and strong allegiance to peer standards, preadolescents consider the family to be an important influence on their development. Although peers seem to be preferred as associates and as models for dress, speech habits, and other features of preadolescent life-styles, parents are sought for advice on matters of major significance and serve as models for future adult roles (Bowerman & Kinch, 1959; Douvan & Adelson, 1966).

The peer groups of younger preadolescents comprise same-sex members who exact conformity and loyalty to the group, which in turn serves as a refuge from adult surveillance and domination and as a needed source of emotional support. Within the safety of the group's confines preadolescents practice social skills, exchange intimacies and information, express sexual curiosity, acquire sexual knowledge, and develop sex roles. Strong attachments to same-sex peers (chums, pals, etc.), which may be critical in acquiring the capacity to love (Sullivan, 1953), as well as subsequent crushes on same-sex or opposite-sex adults (idols, heroes, etc.) are substitutive outlets for preadolescents' growing heterosexual interest. These attachments help preadolescents further to learn sex roles and make the transition to heterosexuality (Ausubel, Montemayor, & Svajian, 1977; Sommer, 1978). With the onset of pubescence, same-sex peer groups increasingly give way to groups in which both sexes enjoy common activities.

Pubescence intensifies sexuality and gives rise to a new sex drive that comes to involve impulses and feelings dependent upon both gonadal stimulation and new definitions of the self (Ausubel, Montemayor, & Svajian, 1977). Sexuality may be expressed in the form of "smutty" or "dirty" jokes, erotic fantasies, masturbation, and homosexual and heterosexual activity. For example, it is estimated that one-fifth of all young people aged 13 and 14 have had sexual intercourse and that approximately thirty thousand girls under age 15 become pregnant every year (Bromberg, Commins, & Friedman, 1980).

Conflicts typically arise out of inconsistencies between peer-group standards and those of the home or school, between parental or adult demands and reality, between preadolescents' new physical capacities and social restraints, and between mainstream and ethnic-group demands for loyalty and conformity. Additional sources of frustration are rejection by peers and dissatisfaction or uncertainly about one's physical adequacy. These conflicts and frustrations engender tension and anxiety, which lower thresholds for emotion-provoking stimuli, promote moodiness, and find expression in regressive, defensive, and compensatory behavior. With new "cognitive competence" (Kagan, 1971, p. 999) and greater autonomy, preadolescents are increasingly predisposed to examine cognitive conflicts such as those posed by inconsistent teachings about sexuality, drugs, authority, and honesty, and to arrive at conclusions that contribute to a personally constructed moral sense (Hoffman, 1980).

According to Ausubel, Montemayor, and Svajian (1977), preadolescence "precipitates a crisis in ego development" (p. 157) that demands reorganization of the personality. This process, continuous throughout adolescence, involves "desatellization" from parents, followed by "resatellization" with peers and ultimately by the acquisition of volitional independence and the establishment of earned status based on society's recognition and approval of one's achievement and morality.

Blos's reinterpretation and elaboration (1962, 1979) of the classical psychoanalytic view of adolescence involves five phases, among which preadolescence critically affects the course of the others. He sees preadolescence as initiating a process of "psychic restructuring" (1979, p. 142), which over the course of adolescence involves the individual's gradual relinquishment of family dependencies and emergence into the society at large, where "new identifications, loyalties, and intimacies" (1979, p. 118) are established.

Erikson (1950) maintains that the rapid body changes and new sexuality of pubescence prompt a sense of discontinuity with earlier development and generate an identity crisis. In order to resolve this crisis, the individual must accept the new physical body and sexuality as part of the self and integrate with it both past experiences and future goals and plans. Failure to resolve the crisis results in identity diffusion, which undermines personality development.

Policy Implications. Policy concerns and issues emanating from knowledge about development during the period of transition from childhood to adolescence are emphasized in several recent studies (Baumrind, 1978; Hurd, 1978; Johnson, 1980; Lipsitz, 1977, 1980; Stauber, 1977). Additionally, recent reports on secondary education (Brown, 1973; Coleman, 1974; Martin, 1974) and related critiques (Heyneman, 1976a, 1976b; *School Review*, 1974; Timpane et al., 1976) address policies that focus on the role of the high school in facilitating the transition from adolescence to adulthood. These policies are geared to reform of the secondary school, and therefore their relevance to preadolescence is limited.

Three conclusions commonly accepted by researchers on the period of transition from childhood to adolescence constitute major premises on which policy issues and recommendations pertaining to the period rest: (1) during preadolescence, developmental changes occur that strongly influence personality across the life span; (2) far too little is known about preadolescents to furnish information needed to assist them maximally with their developmental tasks; and (3) research on preadolescents is needed to fill gaps in current knowledge. From these conclusions certain general recommendations follow: (1) foundations, government agencies, and other institutions that support research on human development should give priority to the period of transition from childhood to adolescence; and (2) schools and other institutions and agencies committed to serving preadolescents should bring their programs more in line with what research and theory have revealed about preadolescent development.

Among specific policy matters that derive from knowledge of preadolescent development are problems of equity in the schooling of racial or ethnic minorities and mentally retarded, physically handicapped, and learning-disabled populations. Preadolescence brings special problems for minority youth. For them the normative process of finding an identity in the larger society is complicated by an additional process: finding an identity in their racial or ethnic group. This twofold identity struggle may pose contradictory expectations and demands that heighten inner and interpersonal conflicts (Gay, 1978; Lipsitz, 1977). Further, at the same time these young people become more conscious of the social realities of their minority status they begin to assess for themselves the value of schooling, and for the first time may seriously entertain the possibility of dropping out.

Although the failure of the schools to serve minority children and youth effectively is well known, little factual information exists on how the curriculum and social context in schools affect the dual identity crisis of minority preadolescents (Lipsitz, 1977; Paul & Fischer, 1980; Rosenberg, 1975) and there is equally little information on how this crisis affects their school achievement and adjustment (Lipsitz, 1977). Hence there is need for more research-based information. There is also need for educators to "become more knowledgeable of and responsive to the ethnic identification process as they design and implement instructional programs in the middle and junior high schools" (Gay, 1978, p. 655).

Schools attended by preadolescents typically do not have programs specifically designed for physically handicapped, mentally retarded, or learning-disabled students. Such programs are imperative if schools are to provide equity for all students. However, more knowledge is needed about these special groups. How, for example, does being handicapped affect the search for identity? How does the cumulative experience of failure affect the school achievement of mentally retarded preadolescents? How can these young people be helped to cope with their sexual vulnerability (Lipsitz, 1977)?

The influence of the structural organization of the educational system on the transition into adolescence is another area in which research is needed to guide policy decisions. For example, do the 6-3-3 and 6-6 educational systems differentially affect the social and psychological development of preadolescents (Blyth, Simmons, & Bush, 1978)? Some other sources of policy concerns pertain to the need for more research-based information as well as more effective prevention-and-treatment programs to deal with pregnancy, venereal disease, drug abuse, mental illness, suicide, and anorexia nervosa among preadolescents (Lipsitz, 1977; Hurd, 1978).

Wiley Bolden

See also Adolescent Development; Junior High and Middle School Education; Life-Span Development; Physical Development.

REFERENCES

Ausubel, D. P.; Montemayor, R.; & Svajian, P. *Theory and Problems of Adolescent Development* (2nd ed.). New York: Grune & Stratton, 1977.

Baumrind, D. Perspectives and recommendations for the Science Education Directorate. In P. D. Hurd (Ed.), *Early Adolescence: Perspectives and Recommendations to the National Science Foundation.* Washington, D.C.: U.S. Government Printing Office, 1978, pp. 32–45.

Blair, A. W., & Burton, W. H. *Growth and Development of the Preadolescent.* New York: Appleton-Century-Crofts, 1951.

Blos, P. *On Adolescence: A Psychoanalytic Interpretation.* New York: Free Press, 1962.

Blos, P. *The Adolescent Passage: Developmental Issues.* New York: International Universities Press, 1979.

Blyth, D. A., Simmons, R. G. & Bush, D. The transition into early adolescent: A longitudinal comparison in two educational contexts. *Sociology of Education,* 1978, 51, 149–162.

Bowerman, C. E., & Kinch, J. W. Changes in family and peer orientation of children between the fourth and tenth grades. *Social Forces,* 1959, 37, 206–211.

Bromberg, D.; Commins, S.; & Friedman, S. B. Protecting physical and mental health. In M. Johnson (Ed.), *Toward Adolescence: The Middle School Years* (Seventy-ninth Yearbook of the National Society for the Study of Education, Part 1). Chicago: University of Chicago Press, 1980.

Brown, B. F. (Ed.). *The Reform of Secondary Education: A Report* to the *Public and the Profession* (National Commission on the Reform of Secondary Education). New York: McGraw-Hill, 1973.

Cohen, D., & Frank, R. Preadolescence: A critical phase in biological and psychological development. In D. V. S. Sankar (Ed.), *Mental Health in Children* (Vol. 1). Westbury, N.J.: PJD Publications, 1975.

Coleman, J. S. *Youth: Transition to Adulthood* (Report of the Panel on Youth of the President's Science Advisory Committee). Chicago: University of Chicago Press, 1974.

Damon, W. *The Social World of the Child.* San Francisco: Jossey-Bass, 1977.

Douvan, E., & Adelson, J. *The Adolescent Experience.* New York: Wiley, 1966.

Elkind, D. Investigating intelligence in early adolescence. In M. Johnson (Ed.), *Toward Adolescence: The Middle School Years* (Seventy-ninth Yearbook of the National Society for the Study of Education, Part 1). Chicago: University of Chicago Press, 1980.

Enright, R. D.; Franklin, C.; & Manheim, L. Children's distributive justice reasoning: A standardized and objective scale. *Developmental Psychology,* 1980, *16,* 193–202.

Erikson, E. H. *Childhood and Society.* New York: Norton, 1950.

Flavell, J. H. Concept development. In P. M. Mussen (Ed.), *Carmichael's Manual of Child Psychology* (3rd ed., Vol. 1). New York: Wiley, 1970.

Flavell, J. H. *Cognitive Development.* Englewood Cliffs, N.J.: Prentice-Hall, 1977.

Flavell, J. H.; Fry, C.; Wright, J.; & Jarvis, P. *The Development of Role-taking and Communication Skills in Children.* New York: Wiley, 1968.

Gay, G. Ethnic identity in early adolescence: Some implications for instructional reform. *Educational Leadership,* 1978, *35,* 649–655.

Hall, G. S. *Adolescence* (Vols. I & II) New York: Appleton, 1904.

Heyneman, S. P. *Adolescence Research Opinion and National Youth Policy: What We Know and What We Don't Know.* Washington, D.C.: Social Research Group, George Washington University, 1976. (a) (ERIC Document Reproduction Service No. ED 140 151)

Heyneman, S. P. Continuing issues in adolescence: A summary of current transition to adulthood debates. *Journal of Youth and Adolescence,* 1976, *5,* 309–323. (b)

Hill, J. P., & Palmquist, W. J. Social cognition and social relations in early adolescence. *International Journal of Behavioral Development,* 1978, *1,* 1–36.

Hoffman, M. Fostering moral development. In M. Johnson (Ed.), *Toward Adolescence: The Middle School Years* (Seventy-ninth Yearbook of the National Society for the Study of Education, Part 1). Chicago: University of Chicago Press, 1980.

Hurd, P. D. *Early Adolescence: Perspectives and Recommendations* (Report prepared for the National Science Foundation Directorate for Science Education). Washington, D.C.: U.S. Government Printing Office, 1978.

Hurlock, E. B. *Child Development* (6th ed.). New York: McGraw-Hill, 1978.

Inhelder, B., & Piaget, J. *The Growth of Logical Thinking from Childhood to Adolescence.* New York: Basic Books, 1958.

Johnson, M. (Ed.). *Toward Adolescence: The Middle School Years* (Seventy-ninth Yearbook of the National Society for the Study of Education, Part 1). Chicago: University of Chicago Press, 1980.

Kagan, J. A conception of early adolescence. *Daedalus,* 1971, *100,* 997–1012.

Kagan, J., & Coles, R. (Eds.). *Twelve to Sixteen: Early Adolescence.* New York: Norton, 1972.

Kaluger, G., & Kaluger, M. F. *Human Development: The Life Span* (2nd ed.). St. Louis: Mosby, 1979.

Kohen-Raz, R. *The Child from Nine to Thirteen: The Psychology of Preadolescence and Early Puberty.* Chicago: Aldine, 1971.

Kohlberg, L., & Gilligan, C. The adolescent as a philosopher: The discovery of the self in a postconventional world. *Daedalus,* 1971, *100,* 1051–1086.

Lipsitz, J. *Growing Up Forgotten: A Review of Research and Programs Concerning Early Adolescence.* Lexington, Mass.: Heath, 1977.

Lipsitz, J. Public policy and early adolescent research. *High School Journal,* 1980, *63*(6), 250–256.

Loomis, M. J. *The Preadolescent: Three Major Concerns.* New York: Appleton-Century-Crofts, 1959.

Mackworth, J. F. Development of attention. In V. Hamilton & M. D. Vernon (Eds.), *The Development of Cognitive Processes.* New York: Academic Press, 1976.

Martin, J. H. *The Education of Adolescents* (National Panel on High Schools and Adolescent Education). Washington, D.C.: U.S. Office of Education, 1974.

Mitchell, J. J. *Human Life: The Early Adolescent Years.* Toronto: Holt, Rinehart & Winston of Canada, 1974.

Neimark, E. D. Intellectual development during adolescence. In F. D. Horowitz (Ed.), *Review of Child Development Research* (Vol. 4). Chicago: University of Chicago Press, 1975.

Neimark, E. D. Current status of formal operations research. *Human Development,* 1979, *22,* 60–67.

Ornstein, P. A.; Naus, M. J.; & Liberty, C. Rehearsal and organizational processes in children's memory. *Child Development,* 1975, *46,* 818–830.

Paul, M. J., & Fischer, J. L. Correlates of self-concept among black early adolescents. *Journal of Youth and Adolescence,* 1980, *9,* 163–173.

Piaget, J. *The Moral Judgment of the Child.* London: Kegan Paul, 1932.

Piaget, J. Intellectual evolution from adolescence to adulthood. *Human Development,* 1972, *15,* 1–12.

Piaget, J., & Inhelder, B. *The Psychology of the Child.* New York: Basic Books, 1969.

Redl, F. Preadolescents: What makes them tick? *Child Study,* 1943–1944, *21,* 44–48.

Redl, F. Adolescents: Just how do they react? In G. Caplan & S. Lebovici (Eds.), *Adolescence: Psychosocial Perspectives.* New York: Basic Books, 1969.

Rogers, D. *The Psychology of Adolescence* (3rd ed.). Englewood Cliffs, N.J.: Prentice-Hall, 1977.

Rosenberg, M. The dissonant context and the adolescent self-concept. In S. E. Dragastin & G. H. Elder, Jr. (Eds.), *Adolescence in the Life Cycle: Psychological Change and Social Context.* New York: Wiley, 1975.

Ross, R. J. The empirical status of formal operations. *Adolescence,* 1974, *9,* 413–420.

School Review, November 1974, *82*(1), special issue on responses to the Symposium on Youth: Transition to Adulthood.

Selman, R. L. *The Growth of Interpersonal Understanding: Developmental and Clinical Analyses.* New York: Academic Press, 1980.

Sommer, B. K. *Puberty and Adolescence.* New York: Oxford University Press, 1978.

Stauber, K. N. Early adolescents: Neglected, misunderstood, miseducated. *Foundation News*, 1977, *18*, 33–35.

Streater, A., & Chertkoff, J. Distribution of rewards in a triad: A developmental test of equity theory. *Child Development*, 1976, *17*, 800–805.

Sullivan, H. S. *Conceptions of Modern Psychiatry.* New York: Norton, 1953.

Tanner, J. M. Sequence, tempo, and individual variation in the growth and development of boys and girls aged twelve to sixteen. *Daedalus*, 1971, *100*, 907–930.

Thornburg, H. D. (Ed.). *Preadolescent Development.* Tucson: University of Arizona Press, 1974.

Timpane, M.; Abramowitz, S.; Bobrow, S.; & Pascal, A. *Youth Policy in Transition.* Santa Monica, Calif.: Rand Corporation, 1976.

Turiel, E. The development of social conventions and moral concepts. In M. Windmiller, N. Lambert, & E. Turiel (Eds.), *Moral Development and Socialization.* Boston: Allyn & Bacon, 1980.

Youniss, J. *Parents and Peers in Social Development: A Sullivan-Piaget Perspective.* Chicago: University of Chicago Press, 1980.

PREDICTION METHODS

Since the entry in the *Encyclopedia of Educational Research* concerned with prediction last appeared (Michael, 1969), the use of newly developed statistical procedures in the context of prediction has greatly increased because of the ever-growing storage capabilities of electronic computers. It is hoped that, within another ten or fifteen years, a considered judgment can be made as to whether, from a practical standpoint, the accuracy of predictions in the behavioral sciences has been enhanced significantly.

Prediction constitutes an effort to ascertain what will occur concerning an outcome or event not yet observed on the basis of information or data judged to be relevant to this unobserved event. For example, parents and registrars are interested in using test scores to forecast the level of achievement that a prospective student might display in an academic program; counselors in career education would like to prognosticate from ability and interest measures the probability of success of their advisees in various job categories; and coaches would like to be able to determine on the basis of a battery of psychomotor tests and motivational indicators which members of a freshman class are likely to be the most valuable competitors on the football field or in track events.

Some Definitions

Several standard terms are used in the prediction process. The observed event that provides information for forecasting the subsequent unobserved event is often called the antecedent, independent variable, or predictor variable. The outcome that has not yet been observed is typically the consequent or dependent variable. When a relatively objective indicator is available to reveal the degree of attainment or success in the outcome, such as grade-point average (GPA) earned, amount of time required to complete a task, or number of products sold, the term criterion measure or criterion variable is often employed.

A variable, which is often designated by a letter X or Y, represents a symbol for an event to which two or more numerical values can be assigned by the process of measurement. In the instance of the continuous variable, individuals are arranged in rank order along a continuum or scale relative to scores obtained from an instrument such as a test or rating form that is judged to reflect accurately the characteristic under study. For a qualitative or discrete variable such as girl/boy or veteran/nonveteran, values of 0 and 1 can be assigned—for example, 1 for girls and 0 for boys. In addition to such dichotomous variables, others may exist that require several steps or categories, such as gifted, normal, or mentally retarded children or dean/professor/teaching assistant. Several variables, such as those relating to marital or resident status, are truly dichotomous; others, such as owning three or more cars versus owning two or fewer cars, or failing versus passing a training course, are artificially dichotomous. Sometimes certain arbitrary cutting points are taken along a continuum of many values to afford a convenient scheme of classification or categorization.

Bivariate Prediction

The simplest form of prediction involves one dependent variable and one independent variable. Typically, for a group of individuals a two-dimensional diagram consisting of two perpendicular axes—the vertical one standing for the dependent (Y) and the horizontal for the independent (X) variable—is formed. Points are placed to designate the simultaneous standing of individuals on measures representing these two variables. The resulting scatter plot provides a basis for inspecting the trend of the relationship and for visually estimating the likely correlation index. Often a prediction (regression) line is drawn through the scattering of points (roughly through the means of several columns if the data are grouped) on the basis of an equation that has been derived to express mathematically the relationship observed. This line indicates that for each unit of change in the X variable a certain fixed amount of change will occur in the Y variable. If the relationship is curvilinear, then the amount of change in Y varies for each unit of change in X.

A correlation coefficient ranging from 1 (perfect positive relationship) to −1 (perfect negative relationship) can be found to reveal the degree to which individuals standing relatively high or low on one variable tend to place relatively high or low on the other. Information regarding the interpretation of correlation coefficients is available in a number of sources—for example, Guilford and Fruchter (1978) and Isaac and Michael (1981).

For either linear or nonlinear relationships, it is possible to devise expectancy tables that, given an X score, will indicate the probability of falling at or above a certain Y score. Such tables can be extended beyond one predictor variable (Schrader, 1965).

Multivariate Prediction: Overview

Within the past fifteen years the rapidly increasing application of multivariate analyses to investigations in the behavioral sciences, including education, has occurred largely because of the availability of giant computers to handle the immense complexities of data treatment. This ever-growing emphasis on multivariate analysis has been evidenced by several comprehensive volumes (Bishop et al., 1975; Bock, 1975; Finn, 1974; Harris, 1975; Lindeman, Merenda, & Gold, 1980; Tatsuoka, 1971; Timm, 1975; Van de Geer, 1971) and by contributions to the necessary computer programming (Cooley & Lohnes, 1971; Jöreskog & Sörbom, 1978; Nie et al., 1975). An important segment of multivariate analysis is that of multivariate prediction that involves one or more criterion variables (continuous or categorical) and two or more predictor variables (also continuous or categorical). In addition to the works just cited, a number of volumes dealing with correlation methods and multiple regression analysis have been particularly helpful to the educational researcher of limited mathematical maturity or statistical sophistication who is concerned with prediction problems (Cohen & Cohen, 1975; Kerlinger & Pedhazur, 1973; Thorndike, 1978).

Two separate chapters in different handbooks that employed charts to organize multivariate prediction in terms of the numbers and properties of variables present were those by Tatsuoka and Tiedeman (1963) and Weiss (1976). In classifying statistical techniques in multivariate prediction, Weiss has examined (1) the presence of linear or nonlinear relationships between dependent (criterion) and independent (predictor) variables; (2) the existence of a single or multiple criterion measure that in turn may be continuous or categorical; and (3) the occurrence of continuous predictor variables (including dichotomous ones with scores of zero or unity) in the linear case or of categorical predictors with three or more attributes in the nonlinear case. His framework lent considerable direction to the organization of this section.

Multivariate Prediction: Linear Case

In multivariate prediction a linear relationship is assumed not only between a criterion variable and each of two or more predictors but also among the predictors themselves. This assumption is made in an overwhelming number of prediction studies in the behavioral sciences, especially in the instance of cognitive variables (although numerous circumstances do arise in which such an assumption is not justified). The following are four common statistical techniques employed in linear prediction studies involving three or more variables.

1. *Multiple regression analysis* involves one criterion measure that is continuous, such as GPA, and two or more predictor variables that are continuous, such as scholastic aptitude tests or high school GPA (although one or more of the predictor variables could be a true dichotomy, such as sex or veteran status). Multiple regression analysis is by far the most frequently used method of multivariate prediction in educational research.

2. *Simple discriminant function* involves a single criterion variable with two categories, such as retainees versus dropouts, science majors versus humanities majors, or successful versus unsuccessful administrators, and two or more continuous predictor variables as in multiple regression analysis.

3. *Canonical correlation* requires two or more criterion measures that are continuous (e.g., GPAs earned in required humanities, social science, physical science, fine arts, and physical education classes) and two or more continuous predictor variables (e.g., scores earned in a battery of tests reflecting reading and language abilities, quantitative thinking, creativity, critical thinking, attitudes, achievement motivation, and psychomotor skills).

4. *Multiple discriminant function* utilizes three or more categorical criterion variables (e.g., classification as a business manager, architect–engineer, lawyer, or medical doctor) and two or more continuous predictor variables (as illustrated in the preceding method).

Multiple Regression Analysis. An involved mathematical technique that has been described and illustrated in a number of statistics texts (Cohen & Cohen, 1975; Guilford & Fruchter, 1978; Kerlinger & Pedhazur, 1973; Lindeman, Merenda, & Gold, 1980; McNemar, 1969), linear multiple regression analysis is a least squares procedure that requires the determination of a particular set of weights for a linear combination of predictor variables (weighted linear composite) so that the resulting multiple regression equation will provide the most nearly accurate possible prediction of scores on the criterion variable for all individuals in a group. Accuracy is thus defined in terms of obtaining a predicted score for all members in the sample such that the sum of the squares of the discrepancies (known as errors or residuals) between the scores actually earned (observed) and those predicted from the equation will be the smallest possible number. In essence, the method is a compensatory one in that a required predicted score can be obtained if one stands sufficiently high on a large enough number of predictors to offset a relatively low standing on other predictors. No absolute minimum score is required on any variable. Although most predictors carry positive weights, instances do occur in which a given predictor may show a substantial negative weight if it registers a high correlation with another predictor variable, but a zero or nearly zero correlation with a criterion variable. This negatively weighted predictor is called a suppressor variable (Lubin, 1957; McNemar, 1969).

Geometrically, the multiple regression equation is a plane of best fit (in contrast to a line of best fit for a simple regression equation with one dependent and one independent variable) in a space of obtained score points within which the axis representing the criterion variable is perpendicular to each of the axes portraying a predictor variable. Each predicted score lies on the plane and each observed score is a point usually above or below the plane, except in the virtually never attained circumstance of perfectly accurate prediction.

For the researcher to interpret the relative importance of each independent variable to the prediction of the dependent variable from an inspection of the magnitudes of the weights associated with the predictors all variables must be scaled in the same way. As a common standard scale score is used for all variables (a scale with a mean of zero and a standard deviation of unity for any variable), these coefficients, which are termed beta weights or standard score regression weights, form a standard score multiple regression equation. (If the original or raw score units corresponding to the variables are employed, then a new regression equation emerges for which the b weights are called partial regression coefficients—not readily interpretable—and for which a separate term a represents the intercept or distance above the origin on the axis of the dependent variable crossed by the plane of best fit.)

Associated with this equation is the multiple correlation coefficient (R) that expresses (1) the degree of relationship between the criterion score and the weighted sum of predictor scores across individuals or, equivalently, (2) the degree of association between observed criterion variable scores and the corresponding predicted scores. The squared value of this quantity R^2 is known as the coefficient of determination, which describes what proportion of the variance in the criterion measure (variance being the square of the standard deviation) is held in common with the weighted composite of predictors.

When standard scores are used, a simple expression is available that provides an indication of the margin of error in prediction; namely, $\sqrt{1 - R^2}$, known as the multiple standard error of estimate. This quantity reveals for every one hundred individuals with the same predicted score the distance above or below which approximately 68 percent of the observed scores would fall. Geometrically, 68 percent of the score points in space would fall between two planes parallel to the plane represented by the equation—the upper plane being one standard error above and the lower plane one standard error below the plane in which all predicted score points fall. It is apparent from the expression for the standard error that the higher the value for R or R^2, the lower the error of prediction. (Obviously, when $R = 1$, no error is present; when $R = 0$, errors are maximal.) All obtained statistics can be tested for significance.

Illustrative example. A simple illustrative example may serve to clarify the explanation just given. If variable 1 is a criterion measure (GPA) and variables 2 and 3 are predictors representing respectively scores on a scholastic aptitude test (SAT) and on a motivation measure (M), a reasonable set of zero-order correlation coefficients between pairs of variables for a hypothesized sample of 200 cases might be as follows: $r_{12} = .60$, $r_{13} = .40$, $r_{23} = .30$. The standard score multiple regression equation expressed in general symbolic terms is as follows:

$$z^{\prime}_{1.23} = \beta_{12.3}z_2 + \beta_{13.2}z_3, \qquad (1)$$

where $z^{\prime}_{1.23}$ = predicted standard score in variable 1 (GPA) from a weighted combination of standard scores in variable 2 (SAT) and variable 3 (M);

z_2 = earned standard score in variable 2 (SAT);

z_3 = observed standard score in variable 3 (M);

$\beta_{12.3}$ = beta weight associated with variable 2 (SAT) indicating its importance with the influence of variable 3 (M) removed or held constant; and

$\beta_{13.2}$ = beta weight corresponding to variable 3 (M) revealing its importance with the impact of variable 2 (SAT) eliminated.

It can be shown that the multiple regression equation becomes

$$z^1_{1.23} = .52747z_2 + .24176z_3,$$

and that

$$R^2 = .41318, \ R = .643, \ \sqrt{1 - R^2} = .766.$$

If John Smith places two standard deviations above the mean on SAT ($z_2 = 2$) and one standard deviation below the mean on M ($z_3 = -1$), the predicted score on the criterion measure is

$$z^1_{1.23} = .52747 \ (2) + .24176 \ (-1) = .81318.$$

The statistical information presented indicates that (1) the SAT measure is about twice as important as the M scale; (2) John's most likely GPA would be slightly more than .81 standard score units above the mean GPA earned; (3) the chances are about two out of three that his obtained GPA would fall within the interval $.813 \pm .766$ (i.e., between .047 and 1.579); (4) the proportion of variance in GPA accounted for by the two tests was about .413 in comparison with an amount of .360 relative to the SAT alone ($r^2_{12} = .360$)—an increment of .053 in the proportion of predicted variance that for a sample of 200 cases could be shown to be statistically very significant (not due to chance); and (5) for units of gain in z_2 and z_3 the corresponding increments in predicted scores would be .52747 and .24176. Had the coefficient r_{23} between SAT and M scores been 0 instead of .30, the resulting R^2 would have been $(.60)^2 + (.40)^2$, or .520, instead of the obtained .413.

Cross-validation. Sampling errors can contribute to bias or inaccuracies in the information provided by multiple regression analysis, especially if attempts are made to generalize outcomes to the population from which the sample studied was selected. Customarily, predictor variables chosen for the multiple regression equation are those showing the highest correlations with a criterion measure and lowest correlations among themselves. In a large correlation matrix the highest and lowest coefficients associated with the predictor selected could be the result of so-called lucky accidents of sampling. Thus, in a new sample from the same population—particularly for a sample of small size—the entire pattern of coefficients could change substantially with the not atypical finding of a marked reduction or shrinkage in the size of R and with a noticeable change in the magnitudes of beta weights.

A standard cross-validation procedure followed to overcome shrinkage problems associated with R's is the application of the multiple regression equation derived from one sample to the data present for a second sample. The correlation between observed criterion scores of the second members with their predicted scores obtained from the regression equation for the first sample is found and evaluated. An alternative procedure is one of double cross-validation (Mosier, 1951), in which a total sample is randomly split into two halves (subsamples). The regression equation developed from the first subsample is applied to the second subsample, and that from the second subsample to the first subsample. The results are compared. If the shrinkage is judged to be modest, one regression equation derived from the two subsamples combined may be used.

Stepwise multiple regression procedures. When a large number of predictor variables is potentially available, the researcher may be wise to select a relatively small number (perhaps three, four, or five) that will yield almost as high a multiple correlation coefficient as would the entire composite of ten or fifteen or more predictors, as in the development of an efficient test battery for selection of personnel. The task is usually accomplished in a stepwise manner (Cooley & Lohnes, 1971; Kerlinger & Pedhazur, 1973; Nie et al., 1975).

Thus one approach starts with a single predictor variable that yields the highest correlation coefficient with a criterion measure and then adds successive predictors until a statistical point is reached beyond which a remaining predictor does not add a statistically significant increment to the amount of variance accounted for in the criterion variable. This incremental or accretion method is sometimes called the forward solution. A second approach begins with the total composite of potential predictors and successively drops from it predictor variables the omission of which, in the investigator's judgment, does not reduce the size of R substantially, or decrease it to a statistically significant degree. This method is the decremental or deletion method that is sometimes labeled the backward solution. Customarily, the two methods lead to somewhat different results, although the practical difference in outcomes can be trivial.

Sometimes the procedures are mixed or applied alternatively if addition or removal of a predictor variable creates a dramatic change in R, if theoretical considerations suggest introduction or removal of a predictor, or if practical considerations (such as time or cost of administering a particular test) are either very unfavorable or very favorable. In any event, stepwise procedures tend to capitalize upon sampling errors and to yield regression equations affording substantially lower correlation coefficients for new samples. Thus cross-validation is almost a necessity.

Improving accuracy of prediction. To overcome distortions in the size of R and to minimize errors of prediction in composites of variables, efforts should be made (1) to employ large samples (perhaps thirty to fifty times as many individuals as there are predictor variables); (2) to check on the linearity of observations within the data set, as the computation of R in the presence of curvilinearity may lead to a gross underestimate of the amount of association present; (3) to use as highly reliable predictor and criterion measures as is possible; (4) to identify predictors that register low intercorrelations (in order to avoid redundancy arising from high intercorrelations as well as difficulties in interpreting the contributions of individual predictor variables to the criterion measure); and (5) to maximize construct validity and the relevance of both criterion and predictor measures. Techniques for improving the reliability and validity of measures can be found in most introductory measurement and evaluation texts (e.g., Sax, 1980) and in the *Standards for Educational and Psychological Tests* (American Psychological Association, 1974). In the previous edition of *Encyclopedia of Educational Research*, Michael (1969) discussed at length ways of carrying out criterion analyses to aid in the selection and development of predictors and in the improvement of validity. One contemporary review of test theory and methodology by Weiss and Davison (1981) updates contributions to validity.

Simple Discriminant Function. Whereas simple and multiple regression analyses are often concerned with the problem of selection, discriminant analysis is directed toward that of classification of individuals into two or more groups (categories). On the basis of scores earned on a linear composite of optimally weighted continuous predictor variables, the objectives of simple discriminant analysis are to ascertain (1) whether two groups differ significantly relative to mean score on the composite, and (2) if so, into which of two groups an individual is to be placed (as a function of the standard score distance of that individual's predicted score from the mean score of each group in the composite). In such an analysis a determination is made of the frequencies of correct and incorrect placements in relation to the actual placements of the sample members.

In the context of a simple discriminant function, a multiple regression analysis also can be carried out with the criterion variable of two categories being assigned a value of unity or zero. As the weights in the simple discriminant function are proportional to those in the multiple regression equation, the resulting classification decisions are the same. In any event, however, cross-validation procedures are recommended just as strongly for the simple (or multiple) discriminant analysis as for linear multiple regression analysis. A better understanding of both the simple discriminant function and the multiple discriminant function (to be described) can be acquired from a study of presentations by Cooley and Lohnes (1971), Kerlinger and Pedhazur (1973), Klecka (1980), Lindeman, Merenda, and Gold (1980), Rulon et al. (1967), Tatsuoka (1971, 1973), Thorndike (1978), and Weiss (1976).

Canonical Correlation. Developed almost fifty years ago by Hotelling (1936), canonical correlation analysis is basically an extension of multiple regression analysis. Customarily involving a set of several continuous criterion measures and a set of many continuous predictor variables, the essentially stepwise method affords (1) a selection of an initial pair of dimensions (linear composite of variables)—one from the set of criterion variables and the other from the set of predictor variables—that yields the highest possible degree of correlation; and (2) the successive selection of remaining pairs of dimensions until reliable score variance has been virtually exhausted, but of never more dimensions than the number of variables in the smaller set.

Each linear combination of variables within a set is called a canonical variate, and the product-moment correlation coefficient between scores arising from pairs of canonical variates (one from the criterion composite and the other from the predictor composite) is termed canonical correlation. The successive canonical correlations obtained may not necessarily be of descending magnitude. As indicated earlier, each canonical coefficient represents the maximum possible amount of correlation between two canonical variates within a given pair. In other words, the standard score weights assigned to a predictor composite (a canonical variate for a group of independent variables) provides the most nearly accurate possible prediction of the optimally but differently weighted criterion composite (a canonical variate for a set of dependent variables).

Within a given pair of canonical variates, the squared value of the canonical correlation coefficient reveals the proportion of variance shared by the two variates. The standard score weights in the predictor composite (first canonical variate within a pair) yields information regarding the relative importance of each of the predictor variables in forecasting the standing of individuals in the criterion composite (second canonical variate within a pair). Thus, for a group of required lower division general education courses in the humanities and social sciences, mathematics and physical and natural sciences, and the fine arts and performing arts (the grades in which serve as criterion measures), and for a battery of scholastic aptitude and ability tests and of interest and values measures (the scores in which serve as predictor variables), one might hypothesize three pairs of canonical variates cutting across the criterion and predictor variables. One pair might contain GPAs earned in humanities and social science courses (criterion canonical variate) and test measures reflecting verbal comprehension abilities (predictor canonical variate);

a second pair, GPAs received in the sciences (criterion canonical variate) and test scales portraying quantitative reasoning abilities (predictor canonical variate); and a third pair, GPAs obtained in the arts (criterion canonical variate) and scores in affective indicators revealing aesthetic interests and values (predictor canonical variate).

In any such study of canonical correlation, cross-validation efforts would be highly advisable. For the interested reader, introductory presentations regarding canonical analysis have been prepared by Cooley and Lohnes (1971), Kerlinger and Pedhazur (1973), Levine (1977), Lindeman, Merenda, and Gold (1980), Thorndike (1978), and Weiss (1976).

Multiple Discriminant Function. Involving the placement of individuals into one of three or more categories (e.g., one of five vocational classifications, one of six university majors, one of four personality types) relative to predicted scores arising from the use of a linear composite of independent variables, the multiple discriminant function is merely an extension of the simple discriminant function with analogous objectives. It maximizes, in essence, the ratio of the variance between the means of the several groups derived from their respective discriminant equations to the variance within the groups, and provides a predicted score for each individual, the distance of which from a mean composite score for each of the groups is evaluated. In relation to a mathematical function reflecting the distance of a predicted score of an individual from the centroid (mean) of scores of each of the groups in turn, a probability value can be found regarding the likelihood that a person belongs to a certain group or resembles that group most closely.

Frequencies of correct and incorrect placements of members of the sample within each of the categories or groups are determined to ascertain the percentages of "hits" or "misses." In other words, the numbers of correct and incorrect placements are compared with the actual placements of sample members. Upon cross-validation, a substantial reduction in the proportion of correct identifications is likely to occur.

Multivariate Prediction: Curvilinear Case

Because of space limitations, the discussion of nonlinearity in multivariate prediction is necessarily brief. Those readers seeking a comprehensive but not too technical treatment are referred to Weiss (1976, pp. 337–348), who examines alternative approaches for the single criterion variable when it is either continuous or categorical in form and for multiple criterion variables when they are categorical. Weiss declares that no appropriate methods apparently are available to deal with multiple continuous criterion measures that simultaneously show curvilinear regression with continuous or categorical independent variables.

Nonlinear Multiple Regression. Curvilinear multiple regression is associated with different rates of change in the magnitude of the criterion variable for each unit of change in one or more of the predictor variables. A predictor variable may be present (as in a linear multiple regression equation) with an exponent of unity or may occur in a polynomial function as a squared or cubed term. In still other functions, there may be product terms or reciprocals or square roots of the independent variables. Geometrically, the function is a surface that would give the appearance, at least in three dimensions, of a once-flat plane that had been distorted, bent, twisted, or warped. On the basis of a rationale derived from logical considerations and past experience, the investigator (1) selects the kind of mathematical function that seems most promising, (2) employs procedures of empirical curve fitting that are available in programs for large-size computers, and/or (3) makes use of coefficients of orthogonal polynomials.

Once the nature of the relationship between the criterion variable and each of the predictor variables (as well as among the predictors) is specified, a single, multiple nonlinear regression equation results. Procedures for carrying out the highly complex computations have been detailed by Ezekiel and Fox (1965), and by Cooley and Lohnes (1971, pp. 76–91) in the instance of polynomial functions. In nonlinear multiple regression, a holdout sample for cross-validation is necessary. More often than not, many higher-order terms (especially product terms) no longer show predictive promise in a new group.

Other Topics. Interactive models have been employed to predict a criterion variable from test score patterns (Maxwell, 1957; Saunders, 1956) involving product terms (moderator variables), and to forecast standing on a criterion measure from various configurations of scored responses to items instead of from a linear addition of scored responses to single items (Horst, 1954, 1957; Lubin & Osburn, 1957, 1960). As the results usually have been quite disappointing upon cross-validation, the methods are not generally recommended.

In some instances of personnel selection, one or more predictor variables may show a curvilinear relationship to a criterion measure. It may be advantageous to set multiple cutoff scores indicating the minimum levels of competence in several tests (predictors) judged essential for success on the job. Known as the multiple cutoff method, or one of successive hurdles, this approach may result in the selection of somewhat different personnel from those chosen through use of the compensatory multiple regression method. Additional details may be found in Weiss (1976).

Explanation in Multivariate Prediction

Renewed interest in establishing a basis for making statements of causal links between independent and dependent variables has sparked considerable controversy, as evidenced by the writings of those identified with philosophy of science (Braithwaite, 1953; Brodbeck, 1963; Feigl & Brodbeck, 1953; Kaplan, 1964; Nagel, 1965) and with sociology (Blalock, 1964, 1971; Duncan, 1966, 1970;

Stinchcombe, 1968). To examine causal inference in non-experimental studies, researchers in education and psychology have explored "cross-lagged panel correlation" techniques (Campbell & Stanley, 1963; Humphreys & Parsons, 1979; Pelz & Andrews, 1964; Rozelle & Campbell, 1969); however, the cross-lagged correlation has been rather severely criticized by Rogosa (1980) as not a defensible basis for causal inference in the analysis of longitudinal panel data.

Whenever a statistically significant degree of correlation is observed between an antecedent and consequent variable, one is likely to speculate as to whether there might be a causal connection. Causal inference probably can be justified with a high degree of confidence only in carefully controlled experiments involving the use of randomization procedures. Yet, even in correlational data suggesting a predicted direction, explanatory efforts to account for ways in which the independent variable might have contributed to the predicted variance in a dependent variable have been receiving increasing attention as revealed by the moderate use of commonality analysis and by substantial numbers of publications during the past fifteen years in which causal modeling has been applied.

Commonality Analysis. Developed by Mood (1969, 1971) and applied by Mayeske et al. (1969) of the United States Office of Education in reanalyzing data from the Coleman Report (Coleman et al., 1966), commonality analysis provides a technique for breaking down the variance in the dependent variable into those components that in a multiple regression analysis are contributed in a unique way by each independent variable and in a shared (common) manner by various combinations of independent variables. Thus, in a multiple regression analysis involving one dependent variable and three independent variables, the predicted variance in the criterion measure could be partitioned to include three unique components associated with the three independent variables, three shared or common portions comprising two predictor variables at a time, and a final common component jointly furnished by all three independent variables. To facilitate the calculation of commonality analyses, Kerlinger and Pedhazur (1973) and Pedhazur (1975) have furnished helpful formulas as well as illustrative examples. (In the instance of the illustrative problem in multiple regression analysis previously presented, the first and second predictor variables, yielded unique contributions of .2532 and .0532 respectively, and a shared contribution of .1068 to the total predicted variance of approximately .4132 within the criterion measure.)

These same researchers, however, have expressed serious reservations regarding the explanatory usefulness of the method and have emphasized instead its utility in selecting predictors in multiple regression analyses. With three or more predictor variables that are moderately interrelated, the resulting relatively high proportions of variance associated with each shared component, to say nothing of the rapidly increasing number of shared and unique components, poses difficulties in interpretation—a circumstance greatly magnified when the size of intercorrelations among predictors is high (the multicollinearity problem). Thus meaningful explicit or implicit causal statements concerning the influences of either individual predictors or combinations of them upon the dependent variable are indeed hard to formulate.

Causal Modeling. An alternative and generally somewhat more satisfactory analytic method than that of commonality analysis for the explanation of patterns of causal relations within a system of several independent (antecedent) variables and one or more dependent (outcome) variables has been one of causal modeling (Asher, 1976; Bentler, 1980; Blalock, 1971; Heise, 1975; Jöreskog & Sörbom, 1978; Kenny, 1979). Briefly, in its central goal to test a theory (not to devise one) the method involves (1) testing hypotheses of direct and indirect influences of several variables upon others (some variables serving as intermediate dependent ones upon which antecedent variables exert an effect and other variables being the final dependent ones in a temporal sequence) within a complex system for which a series of regression (structural) equations is used, and (2) eventually developing by logically based trial and error a model parsimonious enough to provide a meaningful explanation of complex patterns of apparent causal influence within a correlational data set.

Particularly suitable for nonexperimental or quasi-experimental studies intended to assess educational effects in school programs, causal (or structural) models often utilize a method of path analysis first introduced by Wright (1921, 1934) but recently elaborated upon, applied, and illustrated by several researchers (Bentler, 1980; Heise, 1975; Kenny, 1979; Kerlinger & Pedhazur, 1973; Li, 1975; Pedhazur, 1975; Werts & Linn, 1970). Typically, a path diagram furnishes a preliminary graphic display of the hypothesized causal relationships in terms of either a direct influence of one independent variable upon the final outcome (dependent) variable through use of one arrow from one box or circle (designating an initial variable) to another box or circle (representing an outcome variable), or an indirect effect of one independent variable upon the terminal dependent variable in terms of its influence being mediated by a chain of one or more independent variables (each one serving as an intermediate dependent variable) as portrayed by a series of arrows from one box or circle to another box or circle in the sequence. (Customarily, a box represents a directly observable or measured variable, and a circle designates a latent or nonobservable one— i.e., a hypothesized construct.) Thus a basis is afforded for guiding the investigator in setting up simultaneous regression equations for determining path coefficients (beta weights) indicating the relative strength of the influence of one variable upon another as revealed by assigning a number to the arrow (path) designating the strength and direction of the effect of an antecedent variable upon the consequent.

The occurrence of negligible weights that lack either statistical or judged practical significance can result in the elimination of certain variables from the model and can lead to the development of a simplified one to explain the causal patterns. Moreover, as the original correlation matrix can be reproduced from the path diagram including all variables in the initial data set, it is possible through the use of a chi-square goodness-of-fit test to ascertain how closely a simplified model can reproduce the initial correlation matrix. Hence a statistical means exists to permit the evaluation of the appropriateness of alternative parsimonious models that can be used in combination with the investigator's best judgment in selecting a revised model as adequate for explanatory purposes. Obviously, cross-validation procedures are also highly advisable to check on the stability of the weights and on the accompanying conclusions of directional influences in hypothesized causal linkages.

Although path diagrams have been used predominantly in the study of recursive models in which the causal flow has been unidirectional, nonrecursive models do exist that permit a consideration of feedback and reciprocal causation in a system (Kerlinger & Pedhazur, 1973; Pedhazur, 1975). A practical example of the application of a nonrecursive model would occur in an extended longitudinal study with many time points permitting the collection of data on the strength of academic self-concept and level of achievement in several school subjects. Although most theorists would probably take the position that the enhancement of self-concept and the realization of improvement in academic attainments are likely to be mutually reinforcing events, one could ask whether the directional influence is greater from a perception of improved self-concept to augmented achievement or from the attainment of higher proficiency in academic skills to a perception of a markedly noticeable growth in self-concept. A nonrecursive model involving use of path diagrams could be a useful approach to the acquisition of evidence indicating the probable predominant direction of causal influence.

William B. Michael

See also Aptitude Measurement; Measurement in Education; Regression Analysis; Statistical Methods.

REFERENCES

American Psychological Association. *Standards for Educational and Psychological Tests.* Washington, D.C.: The Association, 1974.

Asher, H. B. *Causal Modeling* (Sage University Papers Series on Quantitative Applications in the Social Sciences No. 3). Beverly Hills, Calif.: Sage, 1976.

Bentler, P. M. Multivariate analysis with latent variables: Causal modeling. In M. R. Rosenzweig & L. W. Porter (Eds.), *Annual Review of Psychology* (Vol. 31). Palo Alto, Calif.: Annual Reviews, 1980.

Bishop, Y. M. M.; Feinberg, S. E.; Holland, P. W.; Light, R. J.; & Mosteller, F. *Discrete Multivariate Analysis: Theory and Practice.* Cambridge, Mass.: MIT Press, 1975.

Blalock, H. M. *Causal Inferences in Nonexperimental Research.* Chapel Hill: University of North Carolina Press, 1964.

Blalock, H. M. (Ed.). *Causal Models in the Social Sciences.* Chicago: Aldine-Atherton, 1971.

Bock, R. D. *Multivariate Statistical Methods in Behavioral Research.* New York: McGraw-Hill, 1975.

Braithwaite, R. B. *Scientific Explanation.* Cambridge, England: Cambridge University Press, 1953.

Brodbeck, M. Logic and scientific method in research on teaching. In N. L. Gage (Ed.), *Handbook of Research on Teaching.* Chicago: Rand McNally, 1963.

Campbell, D. T., & Stanley, J. C. Experimental and quasi-experimental designs for research on teaching. In N. L. Gage (Ed.), *Handbook of Research on Teaching.* Chicago: Rand McNally, 1963.

Cohen, J., & Cohen, P. *Applied Multiple Regression–Correlation Analysis for the Behavioral Sciences.* Hillsdale, N.J.: Lawrence Erlbaum Associates, 1975.

Coleman, J. S.; Campbell, E. Q.; Hobson, C. J.; McPartland, J.; Mood, A. M.; Weinfeld, F. D.; & York, R. L. *Equality of Educational Opportunity* (United States Department of Health, Education, and Welfare, Office of Education). Washington, D.C.: U.S. Government Printing Office, 1966. (ERIC Document Reproduction Service No. ED 012 275)

Cooley, W. W., & Lohnes, P. R. *Multivariate Data Analysis.* New York: Wiley, 1971.

Duncan, O. D. Path analysis: Sociological examples. *American Journal of Sociology,* 1966, *72,* 1–16.

Duncan, O. D. Partials, partitions, and paths. In E. F. Borgatta & G. W. Bohrnstedt (Eds.) *Sociological Methodology.* San Francisco: Jossey-Bass, 1970.

Ezekiel, M., & Fox, K. A. *Methods of Correlation and Regression Analysis: Linear and Curvilinear.* New York: Wiley, 1965.

Feigl, H., & Brodbeck, M. *Readings in the Philosophy of Science.* New York: Appleton-Century-Crofts, 1953.

Finn, J. D. *A General Model for Multivariate Analysis.* New York: Holt, Rinehart & Winston, 1974.

Guilford, J. P., & Fruchter, B. *Fundamental Statistics in Psychology and Education* (6th ed.). New York: McGraw-Hill, 1978.

Harris, R. J. *A Primer of Multivariate Statistics.* New York: Academic Press, 1975.

Heise, D. R. *Causal Analysis.* New York: Wiley, 1975.

Horst, P. Pattern analysis and configural scoring. *Journal of Clinical Psychology,* 1954, *10,* 3–11.

Horst, P. The uniqueness of configural test item scores. *Journal of Clinical Psychology, 1957, 13,* 107–114.

Hotelling, H. Relations between two sets of variates. *Biometrika,* 1936, *28,* 321–377.

Humphreys, L. G., & Parsons, C. K. A simplex process model for describing differences between cross-lagged correlations. *Psychological Bulletin,* 1979, *86,* 325–334.

Isaac, S., & Michael, W. B. *Handbook in Research and Evaluation* (2nd ed.) San Diego, Calif.: EdITS Publishers, 1981.

Jöreskog, K. G., & Sörbom, D. *LISREL IV: Analysis of Linear Structural Relationships by the Method of Maximum Likelihood* (User's Guide). Chicago: National Educational Resources, 1978.

Kaplan, A. *The Conduct of Inquiry.* San Francisco: Chandler Intext, 1964.

Kerlinger, F. N., & Pedhazur, E. J. *Multiple Regression in Behavioral Research.* New York: Holt, Rinehart & Winston, 1973.

Kenny, D. A. *Correlation and Causality.* New York: Wiley, 1979.

Klecka, W. R. *Discriminant Analysis.* (Sage University Papers Series on Quantitative Applications in the Social Sciences No. 19). Beverly Hills, Calif.: Sage, 1980.

Levine, M. S. *Canonical Analysis and Factor Comparison.* (Sage University Papers Series on Quantitative Applications in the Social Sciences No. 6). Beverly Hills, Calif.: Sage, 1977.

Li, C. C. *Path Analysis: A Primer.* Pacific Grove, Calif.: Boxwood, 1975.

Lindeman, R. H.; Merenda, P. F.; & Gold, R. Z. *Introduction to Bivariate and Multivariate Analysis.* Glenview, Ill.: Scott, Foresman, 1980.

Lubin, A. Some formulae for use with suppressor variables. *Educational and Psychological Measurement,* 1957, *17,* 286–296.

Lubin, A., & Osburn, H. G. A theory of pattern analysis for the prediction of a quantitative criterion. *Psychometrika,* 1957, *22,* 63–73.

Lubin, A., & Osburn, H. G. The use of configural analysis for the prediction of a qualitative criterion. *Educational and Psychological Measurement,* 1960, *20,* 275–282.

Maxwell, A. E. Contour analysis. *Educational and Psychological Measurement,* 1957, *17,* 347–360.

Mayeske, G. W.; Wisler, C. E.; Beaton, A. E.; Weinfeld, F. D.; Cohen, W. M.; Okada, T.; Proshek, J. M.; & Tabler, K. A. *A Study of Our Nation's Schools* (U.S. Department of Health, Education, and Welfare, Office of Education). Washington, D.C.: U.S. Government Printing Office, 1969. (ERIC Document Reproduction No. ED 036 477)

McNemar, Q. *Psychological Statistics* (4th ed.). New York: Wiley, 1969.

Michael, W. B. Prediction. In R. L. Ebel (Ed.), *Encyclopedia of Educational Research* (4th ed.). New York: Macmillan, 1969.

Mood, A. M. Macro-analysis of the American educational system. *Operations Research,* 1969, *17,* 770–784.

Mood, A. M. Partitioning variance in multiple regression analyses as a tool for developing learning models. *American Educational Research Journal,* 1971, *8,* 191–202.

Mosier, C. I. Problems and designs of cross-validation. *Educational and Psychological Measurement,* 1951, *11,* 5–11.

Nagel, E. Types of causal explanation in science. In D. Lerner (Ed.), *Cause and Effect.* New York: Free Press, 1965.

Nie, N. H.; Hull, C. H.; Jenkins, J. G.; Steinbrenner, K.; & Bent, D. H. *SPSS: Statistical Package for the Social Sciences* (2nd ed.). New York: McGraw-Hill, 1975.

Pedhazur, E. J. Analytic methods in studies of educational effects. In F. N. Kerlinger (Ed.), *Review of Research in Education* (Vol. 3). Itasca, Ill.: F. E. Peacock, 1975.

Pelz, D. C., & Andrews, F. M. Detecting causal priorities in panel study data. *American Sociological Review,* 1964, *29,* 836–848.

Rogosa, D. A critique of cross-lagged correlation. *Psychological Bulletin,* 1980, *88,* 245–258.

Rozelle, R. M., & Campbell, D. T. More plausible rival hypotheses in the cross-lagged panel correlation technique. *Psychological Bulletin,* 1969, *71,* 74–80.

Rulon, P. J.; Tiedeman, D. V.; Tatsuoka, M. M.; & Langmuir, C. R. *Multivariate Statistics for Personnel Classification.* New York: Wiley, 1967.

Saunders, D. R. Moderator variables in prediction. *Educational and Psychological Measurement,* 1956, *16,* 209–222.

Sax, G. *Principles of Educational and Psychological Measurement and Evaluation* (2nd ed.). Belmont, Calif.: Wadsworth, 1980.

Schrader, W. B. A taxonomy of expectancy tables. *Journal of Educational Measurement,* 1965, *2,* 29–35.

Stinchcombe, A. L. *Constructing Social Theories.* New York: Harcourt, Brace & World, 1968.

Tatsuoka, M. M. *Multivariate Analysis: Techniques for Educational and Psychological Research.* New York: Wiley, 1971.

Tatsuoka, M. M. Multivariate analysis in educational research. In F. N. Kerlinger (Ed.), *Review of Research in Education* (Vol. 1). Itasca, Ill.: F. E. Peacock, 1973.

Tatsuoka, M. M., & Tiedeman, D. V. Statistics as an aspect of scientific method in research on teaching. In N. L. Gage (Ed.), *Handbook of Research on Teaching.* Chicago: Rand McNally, 1963.

Thorndike, R. M. *Correlational Procedures for Research.* New York: Gardner Press, 1978.

Timm, N. H. *Multivariate Analysis with Applications in Education and Psychology.* Monterey, Calif.: Brooks/Cole, 1975.

Van de Geer, J. P. *Introduction to Multivariate Analysis for the Social Sciences.* San Francisco: Freeman, 1971.

Weiss, D. J. Multivariate procedures. In M. D. Dunnette (Ed.), *Handbook of Industrial and Organizational Psychology.* Chicago: Rand McNally, 1976.

Weiss, D. J., & Davison, M. L. Test theory and methods. In M. R. Rosenzweig & L. W. Porter (Eds.), *Annual Review of Psychology* (Vol. 32). Palo Alto, Calif.: Annual Reviews, 1981.

Werts, C. E., & Linn, R. L. Path analysis: Psychological examples. *Psychological Bulletin*, 1970, 74, 193–212.

Wright, S. Correlation and causation. *Journal of Agricultural Research*, 1921, 20, 557–585.

Wright, S. The method of path coefficients. *Annals of Mathematical Statistics*, 1934, 5, 161–215.

PRESCHOOL EDUCATION FOR THE HANDICAPPED

Early childhood education for the handicapped (ECEH) has been an area of interest for many years. Yet, specific attention to the education and treatment of this population of young children has been slow in reaching fruition. Only recently, beginning in the 1970s, did ECEH become established as a field of study in its own right. The events that collectively provided the foundation from which ECEH could emerge came from three separate movements. The early kindergarten and nursery school movements, which began in the 1900s and continued into contemporary times, established preschool and nursery programs for normal children. These programs promoted the notion that early stimulation and educational enrichment can enhance development in young children. They also helped dispel the old belief that early education was injurious to children because it separated them from their mothers and imposed structure upon them too early (Weber, 1969). As a result of this movement, both professionals and lay citizens now accept preschool and nursery schools as a part of today's child care practices. The compensatory education movement brought the notion of educational intervention to the forefront. A number of research-oriented, early intervention experiments with disadvantaged youngsters and other compensatory education programs, such as Head Start and Follow Through, focused attention upon the importance of early education for children from deprived home environments. From this movement came research,

albeit controversial, that showed that early intervention programs are beneficial to children whose socioeconomic backgrounds place them at risk for developmental retardation and school failure. Children who participated in such programs showed developmental gains. Continued intervention was necessary, however, if gains were to be maintained into the elementary school years (Zigler, 1979; Bronfenbrenner, 1974). The special education movement gave rise to the growth of special support services and special education classes for school-aged handicapped students in public schools. From this movement came major changes in old attitudes that handicapped children were destined by their disabilities to be dependent, possibly uneducable, nonproductive members of society. A more positive attitude emerged: that handicapped persons can learn, that they can be educated to live productive lives, and that special education programs can increase their chances for more successful school careers. The special education movement also resulted in the affirmation, through Public Law 94-142, that handicapped persons are entitled to the same educational rights as their nonhandicapped peers. This includes any additional special services required to assure such children an equal opportunity to benefit from their educational training.

Several specific events gave ECEH a foothold within the field of education and established it as a separate field of study.

1. Enactment of the Handicapped Children's Early Education Assistance Act (Public Law 90-538) in 1968 launched the new movement. Because of the dearth of services for young handicapped children, and the absence of exemplary models, the act authorized funds for demonstration programs. Research has indicated that many programs continue to operate through state and local funds after their initial federal funding ends (Swan, 1980). By 1980, approximately 376 projects had been initiated, some of which are well recognized today (e.g., Portage Project in Portage, Wisconsin; PEECH Project in Champaign, Illinois; Rutland Center Program for Emotionally Disturbed in Athens, Georgia; and the Model Preschool Center for Handicapped Children at the University of Washington, Seattle).

2. The Bureau of Education for the Handicapped (BEH) began in the early 1970s to award special grants to universities for training personnel to work with young handicapped children. Around 1974, early childhood education was identified as one of BEH's top funding priorities to encourage universities to create formal training programs in this area. Prior to this time, special education training focused almost totally upon preparation of professionals to work with school-aged handicapped students.

3. A 1972 Head Start mandate, requiring centers to reserve no less than 10 percent of their enrollments for handicapped preschoolers, provided considerable help to the ECEH movement. To aid staff in serving these children, training programs and technical assistance-information centers (i.e., resource access projects) were created.

These projects brought considerable visibility to the needs of young handicapped children, as well as involvement from the professional community, parents, and the lay public.

4. The funding of state implementation grants, also authorized under Public Law 90-538, initiated systematic state and local program planning on behalf of young handicapped children. Beginning in 1974, these projects helped state departments of education and other agencies identify local needs, deal with state legislative and teacher certification issues, create formal state ECEH plans, create multiagency involvement, and build new service programs.

5. The Division for Early Childhood was organized within the National Council for Exceptional Children in 1973 to create the first formal organization for individuals working in this area. In 1977, the organization began publication of its *Journal of the Division for Early Childhood,* the first to devote exclusive attention to research and issues relating to ECEH.

6. The passage of Public Law 94-142 in 1975, the Education for All Handicapped Children Act, provided formal endorsement for the education of handicapped children under school age. Incentive moneys were provided to encourage local education agencies to serve children from ages 3 to 5. It should be noted that the law only endorsed, but did not actually mandate, programs for preschool handicapped children. Under the law, states are not required to make a free, appropriate education available to 3-, 4-, or 5-year-old children if state law prohibits or does not authorize the expenditure of public funds for the education of this age group (Cohen, Semmes, & Guralnick, 1979).

7. A national research effort to improve programs for handicapped children from birth to age 5 was launched with the funding of four early childhood research institutes in 1977 by what is now called the U.S. Office of Special Education. Each institute began longitudinal research on issues such as early intervention strategies and outcomes, assessment, and child characteristics. Institutes include the Carolina Institute for Research on Early Education for the Handicapped, University of North Carolina at Chapel Hill; the Kansas Early Childhood Research Institute, University of Kansas at Lawrence; the Institute for the Study of Exceptional Children, Educational Testing Service; and the UCLA Research Institute on Early Abilities of Children with Handicaps, University of California at Los Angeles.

8. Several states have passed legislation requiring local education agencies to provide early childhood education programs for handicapped children below age 5. As of 1978, thirteen states had passed such mandates, thus reflecting a slow but growing trend for state and local education agencies to assume responsibility for serving this population.

The Rationale for Early Intervention. Because ECEH programs are relatively new, research on their efficacy is only beginning to accumulate. Preliminary findings suggest that early education can generate and maintain more normal rates of development in Down's syndrome children (Hayden & Dmitriev, 1975; Clunies-Ross, 1979), and alter lowered performance expectancies in children whose mothers have borderline IQs and who come from low socioeconomic, disadvantaged homes (Garber & Heber, 1977; Ramey et al., 1976). Early intervention programs have also increased performance in mildly retarded children in ways that enhance later school achievement, reduce the need for placement in special education classes, and reduce school dropout rates (Weikart, Bond, & McNeil, 1978; Lazar & Darlington, 1979). A follow-up study by the Battelle Institute (Stock et al., 1976) on 688 randomly selected graduates of the Handicapped Children's Early Education Program (HCEEP) indicated that children showed positive outcomes after participating in these projects. Many children showed $1\frac{1}{2}$ to 2 times the expected developmental gains from pretesting to posttesting in language, motor, cognitive, adaptive, and social domains. Other evidence cited in the literature to build a rationale for intervention programs is gleaned inferentially from (1) theoretical frameworks on early development and learning, such as Piaget's theory; (2) research on the effects of early environment and stimulation on learning, including the impact of depriving and enriching environments; (3) research on the outcomes of early education programs with at-risk and disadvantaged children; and (4) expert opinion concerning the special needs of young children with developmental disabilities, such as cerebral palsy, auditory and visual impairments, health disorders, and brain injury. Using these sources, numerous publications present rationales attesting to the importance of early education for the handicapped (Caldwell, 1970; Stone, 1975; Hayden & McGinness, 1977; Bricker & Iacino, 1977; Hayden & Pious, 1979; Richmond & Janis, 1980; Peterson, forthcoming). In general, the arguments presented center around the following points:

1. Intelligence and other human capabilities are not fixed but are malleable as a result of learning and environmental influences.
2. The early years represent a time of unprecedented growth and development, when skills are acquired that provide the foundation for all subsequent learning. This is a time when educators can have the greatest impact upon a child and can reduce the potential effects of handicapping or adverse environmental conditions upon a child.
3. Handicapping conditions can interfere with a young child's ability to engage in important early experiences that foster skill acquisition. As a result, disabilities can become more severe and secondary handicapping conditions may appear. Early education programs can reduce these difficulties by bringing experiences to children that otherwise might be missed, and by providing the special training to help children progress through normal developmental processes.

4. Early intervention programs do make a difference in the developmental status of young children and can reduce the need for later, more intensive special education services.

5. Early intervention programs have economic benefits in that expenditures for preventative measures with young children can reduce the need for more costly, remedial programs for the handicapped during their school and adult years.

Unique Features of ECEH. Although early intervention programs reflect a blend of educational practices from the parent fields of special education and regular early childhood education, some unique features set it apart (Peterson, forthcoming). The primary purpose of these programs is intervention, that is, to minimize the impact of handicapping conditions upon early learning, to prevent developmental delays if possible, and to reduce the occurrence of secondary handicaps. In contrast, the purpose of traditional special education for school-aged students has been primarily that of remediation of existing learning or behavior problems. Treatment has typically begun after a student has experienced a history of abnormal development to the extent that the problem has become handicapping (Dunn, 1973). Programs for young children under school age are designed to intervene before this unchecked development occurs. Regular early childhood programs, on the other hand, have not shared the "treatment" orientation of special education, nor has it been necessary to do so. Because their clientele has been primarily normal youngsters, the purpose of these programs has been one of enrichment. Developmental processes are augmented through exposure to stimulating social and cognitive experiences.

Service delivery approaches employed with young handicapped children are somewhat unique, yet reflect a blend of practices from both special education and regular early childhood education. Services for school-aged handicapped students usually occur within public schools where special support services are provided. Service options for this population have been set in hierarchical models according to which options are most or least restrictive (Deno, 1970; Dunn, 1973). Yet what is a most restrictive educational environment for an elementary or secondary student may be a least restrictive one for a handicapped preschooler or toddler. Three types of service delivery models have evolved in programs for the very young: home-based programs involving the parent and the child, center-based programs, and combination home-center-based programs (Karnes & Zehrbach, 1977). Considerable emphasis has been placed across these models upon parental involvement, because the success of early intervention programs seems greatest when parents are a part of the treatment team (Bronfenbrenner, 1974).

Special programs for handicapped preschoolers, toddlers, and infants are operated by many different agencies across the country because of variations in funding sources and state laws. Center-based services also are found in an array of settings such as private centers, university laboratory schools or research centers, hospitals, community centers, and public schools. The mainstreaming of preschool handicapped children has been emphasized (Wynne, Ulfelder, & Dakof, 1975). However, the lack of a standardized system of regular preschools or nursery schools within states has made successful applications of mainstreaming difficult to achieve on a broad scale. Regular early childhood programs vary greatly. Many lack the specially trained staff, interdisciplinary services, and other resources necessary for appropriate educational-treatment programs for handicapped children. This problem has been especially true in programs for children with moderate to severe disabilities. Head Start represents the major large-scale effort attempted to mainstream handicapped preschoolers thus far. Some 41,339 children were mainstreamed in Head Start centers in 1979 (*Status of Handicapped Children*, 1980). The major vehicle through which handicapped children under age 5 have been served is in separate, special programs created through funds earmarked specifically for this population. Segregated programs, however, have not been viewed within special education as a best alternative, at least for school-aged students. Hence, there are questions concerning the desirability of such practices for the preschooler. Restrictions on the use of public funds for nonhandicapped preschoolers, however, have made other alternatives more difficult.

An emerging trend to counteract the absence of normal peer models in these segregated programs is a form of reverse mainstreaming. Nonhandicapped preschoolers are integrated into special preschools to serve as peer models. They usually constitute a minority, approximately $\frac{1}{3}$ to $\frac{1}{2}$ of the classroom enrollment. Several issues are raised by such practices in regard to the effects of integration upon the nonhandicapped minority, and the degree to which both groups of children actually integrate instructionally and socially in the same classroom. Early research suggests that successful integration is not necessarily a spontaneous outcome of mixed classes. It depends upon the skills of teachers to create opportunities for social and instructional integration between groups while simultaneously arranging activities in ways that meet the individual learning needs of both handicapped and nonhandicapped children (Peterson & Haralick, 1977; Guralnick, 1976, 1978, 1980).

Considerable attention by state legislatures, educators, and parents alike is needed to create early intervention programs for both handicapped preschoolers and infants. In many states these children continue to be an inadequately served population, despite the endorsement given in Public Law 94-142 for programs serving 3-to-5-year-olds. Estimates in 1976 suggested that as many as 74 percent of the population of preschool handicapped children were not receiving services (Ackerman & Moore, 1976). Special programs are increasing nonetheless and give promise for significant expansion in the present decade.

As ECEH programs continue to proliferate, a number of issues must be addressed both programmatically and empirically. These issues evolve out of discrepancies between the needs and unique characteristics of handicapped preschoolers and infants, and the established practices of special education and regular early childhood education. There is a tendency to view ECEH as a simple downward extension of special education as it currently exists for school-aged students, or of traditional early childhood education as it evolved for normal children. Operational regulations, instructional practices, and philosophies that have dominated each field are easily imposed on new ECEH programs. Yet their direct applicability and appropriateness to young handicapped children may be questioned. A few of the emerging issues and questions are What constitutes the least restrictive environment for a handicapped preschooler or infant? If the purpose of preschool or infant programs is one of intervention, what diagnostic criteria should be used to identify children before disabilities produce significant deviations in behavior? What eligibility criteria should be used to identify children who need to be enrolled in intervention programs? Since most definitions of handicapping conditions are based upon performance deficits as described for older children and are contingent upon a significant developmental deficit that usually emerges over time, what definitions should be applied with young children who are only 2, 3, or 4 years old? (This question applies particularly to definitions of learning disabilities, mental retardation, and emotional disturbance.) Although academic achievement tests and intelligence tests are major diagnostic tools used to identify school-aged students with special problems, what system of assessment is most valid and reliable with very young children, who are only beginning to acquire testable developmental skills? Research on these and other issues, as well as policy clarification, will be an important priority as ECEH continues to grow.

Nancy L. Peterson

See also Behavioral Treatment Methods; Early Childhood Education; Handicapped Individuals; Special Education.

REFERENCES

Ackerman, P. R., & Moore, G. Delivery of educational services to preschool handicapped children. In T. D. Tjossem (Ed.), *Intervention Strategies for High-risk Infants and Young Children.* Baltimore: University Park Press, 1976.

Bricker, D. D., & Iacino, R. Early intervention with severely/profoundly handicapped children. In E. Sontag (Ed.), *Educational Programming for the Severely and Profoundly Handicapped.* Reston, Va.: Council for Exceptional Children, 1977.

Bronfenbrenner, U. *Is Early Intervention Effective?* Vol. 2 of *A Report on Longitudinal Evaluations of Preschool Programs* (DHEW Publication No. (OHD) 76-30025). Washington, D.C.: Department of Health, Education, and Welfare, 1974. (ERIC Document Reproduction Service No. ED 093 501)

Caldwell, B. M. The rationale for early intervention. *Exceptional Children,* 1970, *36,* 717–726.

Clunies-Ross, G. G. Accelerating the development of Down's syndrome infants and young children. *Journal of Special Education,* 1979, *13*(2), 160–177.

Cohen, S.; Semmes, M.; & Guralnick, M. J. Public Law 94-142 and the education of preschool handicapped children. *Exceptional Children,* 1979, *45,* 279–285.

Deno, E. Special education as developmental capital. *Exceptional Children,* 1970, *37*(3), 229–237.

Dunn, L. M. *Exceptional Children in the Schools: Special Education in Transition* (2nd ed.). New York: Holt, Rinehart & Winston, 1973.

Garber, H., & Heber, F. R. The Milwaukee Project: Indications of the effectiveness of early intervention in preventing mental retardation. In P. Mittler (Ed.), *Research to Practice in Mental Retardation: Care and Intervention* (Vol. 1). Baltimore: University Park Press, 1977.

Guralnick, M. J. The value of integrating handicapped and nonhandicapped preschool children. *American Journal of Orthopsychiatry,* 1976, *42,* 236–245.

Guralnick, M. J. Integrated preschools as educational and therapeutic environments: Concepts, design, and analysis. In M. J. Guralnick (Ed.), *Early Intervention and the Integration of Handicapped and Nonhandicapped Children.* Baltimore: University Park Press, 1978, pp. 115–145.

Guralnick, M. J. Social interactions among preschool children. *Exceptional Children,* 1980, *46*(4), 248–253.

Hayden, A. H., & Dmitriev, V. The multidisciplinary preschool programs for Down's syndrome children at the University of Washington Model Preschool Center. In B. A. Friedlander, G. M. Sterritt, & G. E. Kirk (Eds.), *Exceptional Infant: Assessment and Intervention* (Vol. 3). New York: Brunner/Mazel, 1975.

Hayden, A. H., & McGinness, G. D. Bases for early intervention. In E. Sontag (Ed.), *Educational Programming for the Severely and Profoundly Handicapped.* Reston, Va.: Council for Exceptional Children, 1977.

Hayden, A. H., & Pious, C. G. The case for early intervention. In R. L. York & E. Edgar (Eds.), *Teaching the Severely Handicapped* (Vol. 4). Seattle: American Association for the Education of the Severely/Profoundly Handicapped, 1979.

Karnes, M. B., & Zehrback, R. R. Alternative models for delivering services to young handicapped children. In J. B. Jordan, A. H. Hayden, M. B. Karnes, & M. M. Wood (Eds.), *Early Childhood Education for Exceptional Children: A Handbook of Ideas and Exemplary Practices.* Reston, Va.: Council for Exceptional Children, 1977. (ERIC Document Reproduction Service No. ED 132 788)

Lazar, I., & Darlington, R. *Summary Report: Lasting Effects after Preschool* (DHEW Publication No. OHDS 79–30179). Washington, D.C.: Department of Health, Education, and Welfare, 1979. (ERIC Document Reproduction Service No. ED 175 523)

Peterson, N. L. *Early Childhood Education for the Handicapped.* Boston: Little, Brown, forthcoming.

Peterson, N. L., & Haralick, J. G. Integration of handicapped and nonhandicapped preschoolers: An analysis of play behavior and social interaction. *Education and Training of the Mentally Retarded,* 1977, *12,* 235–245.

Ramey, C. T.; Collier, A. M.; Sparling, J. J.; Loda, F. A.; Campbell, F. A.; Ingram, D. L.; & Finkelstein, N. W. The Carolina Abecedarian Project: A longitudinal and multidisciplinary approach to the prevention of developmental retardation. In T. D. Tjossem (Ed.), *Intervention Strategies for High-risk Infants and Young Children.* Baltimore: University Park Press, 1976.

Richmond, J. B., & Janis, J. A perspective on primary prevention in the earliest years. *Children Today,* May-June 1980, pp. 2–6.

Status of Handicapped Children in Head Start Programs (DHEW Publication No. 0-620-232-4273). Washington, D.C.: Department of Health, Education, and Welfare, 1980. (ERIC Document Reproduction Service No. ED 189 807)

Stock, J. R.; Wnek, L. L.; Newborg, J. A.; Schenck, E. A.; Gabel, J. R.; Spurgeon, M. S.; & Ray, H. W. *Evaluation of Handicapped Children's Early Education Programs (HCEEP)* (Final Report from the Battelle Institute). Columbus, Ohio: Battelle Institute, 1976. (ERIC Document Reproduction Service No. ED 125 165).

Stone, J. W. A plea for early intervention. *Mental Retardation,* 1975, *13*(5), 16–18.

Swan, W. W. The handicapped children's early education program. *Exceptional Children,* 1980, *47*(1), 12–16.

Weber, E. *The Kindergarten: Its Encounter with Educational Thought in America.* New York: Teachers College Press, 1969.

Weikart, D. P.; Bond, J. T.; & McNeil, J. T. The Ypsilanti Perry Preschool Project: Preschool years and longitudinal results through fourth grade. *Monographs of the High/Scope Educational Research Foundation,* 1978, No. 3. (ERIC Document Reproduction Service No. ED 156 755)

Wynne, S.; Ulfelder, L. S.; & Dakof, G. *Mainstreaming and Early Childhood Education for Handicapped Children: Review and Implications of Research* (HEW Final Report, Contract No. 0EC-74-9056). Washington, D.C.: Wynne Associates, 1975. (ERIC Document Reproduction Service No. ED 108 426)

Zigler, E., & Valentine, J. *Project Head Start: A Legacy of the War on Poverty.* New York: Free Press, 1979.

PRIMARY EDUCATION

See Elementary Education.

PRIVATE SCHOOLS

The term "private schools" is used here to identify schools that are not operated by government, that function in lieu of government-operated (public) schools for compulsory school-attendance purposes, and that offer some or all of the elementary and secondary levels of instruction. "Private" is used increasingly in the United States to identify such schools, though they are sometimes called "nonpublic" or "independent." "Independent" is the most common label in Canada. To confuse matters more, schools of the same type are dubbed "nongovernment" in Australia, and some elitist schools in the group are known as "public" in Australia and Great Britain. Additional terms crop up elsewhere in the world. In the United States, there is further confusion as to what various groups *within* the private school sector should be called. Sometimes all religiously affiliated schools are loosely designated as "paro-

chial," although the term strictly means "associated with or run by the local parish" and thus would not apply to a school run by a diocese, a religious order, a denomination, a collection of cooperating churches, or a society of parents. Similarly, Catholics often use the term "private" to refer exclusively to schools run by exempt religious orders, such as the Jesuits. A more consistent terminology would facilitate discussion considerably. In keeping with our definition, a school may be "private" even if some of its support is derived from taxation, so long as it is not administered by an agency of government. Although fascinating comparisons can be made among private schools in various nations, space dictates that the present article focus on private schools in the United States.

Magnitude. Private schools appear to constitute about 18 percent of the total number of elementary and secondary schools in the United States, enroll about 10 percent of all students at the elementary and secondary levels, produce about 10 percent of all high school graduates, and employ 11 percent of all teachers in the elementary and secondary grades (Eldridge, 1980; McLaughlin & Wise, 1980).

In 1976/77, the quality of data concerning private schools was considerably enhanced by the introduction of periodic national surveys by the National Center for Education Statistics (NCES). NCES estimates of the number of private elementary and secondary schools in the United States were 20,083 in 1976/77, 20,073 in 1977/78, and 19,666 in 1978/79 (Eldridge, 1980). Total enrollment in private schools was estimated at 5,167,000 in 1976/77, 5,140,000 in 1977/78, and 5,086,000 in 1978/79. This enrollment was 10.4 percent of the national total (for public and private schools combined) in 1976/77, 10.5 percent in 1977/78, and 10.7 percent in 1978/79 (Eldridge, 1980). The private school enrollment decline—1.6 percent—during the three years was considerably less than the public school enrollment decline—3.9 percent—during the same period. Private schools have been increasing their share of the school-age population, in contrast to a decrease of that share between 1965/66 and 1975/76 (Erickson, Nault, & Cooper, 1978).

Enrollment Trends. These figures obscure important differences among private schools of different types. A closer look at the NCES data and data for the preceding decade shows that the enrollment decline was largely limited to Catholic schools (Erickson, Nault, & Cooper, 1978; McLaughlin & Wise, 1980). Between 1965/66 and 1975/76, enrollment did not fluctuate dramatically in Lutheran schools and in schools not religiously affiliated, but recently enrollment has increased significantly in them (Senske, 1980; Stockdale, 1981). Most other private schools suffered modest enrollment losses.

The NCES data, however, may have entirely missed the most dramatic growth recently occurring in private schools. It appears that as many as 1,200 to 3,000 fundamentalist schools, enrolling as many as 1 to 1.5 million students, may have failed to participate in the NCES surveys, either because they were not listed in the "universe list" that identified the sample, because they declined to cooperate when asked, or because NCES (unfortunately) eliminated all schools not offering grades above the first (Billings, 1981; Carper, 1980). In the late 1950s and early 1960s, the number of fundamentalist schools was apparently negligible. No one knows how many there are today, and estimates vary wildly, although it is obvious that explosive expansion has occurred.

A parenthetical word on the reasons for the inadequate data is important. Most states require by law that private schools report their enrollment annually; however, the requirement is unevenly enforced. Many unconventional private schools, preferring to remain unnoticed (partly to ward off government interference), simply ignore the requirement. The major private school agencies can usually provide reasonably reliable data on their member schools. But many private schools do not belong to such agencies, and other private schools are reported twice or more because they belong to more than one agency. Partly because they have been widely misunderstood and criticized, many fundamentalist schools (and other private schools as well, particularly the more radical varieties) are loathe to release data about themselves, fearing that data will be used against them or that the act of providing data will compromise the principle—to which many of them strongly adhere—that they are responsible to no one except their patrons, their churches, and God.

The reasons why fundamentalist schools expanded explosively and Catholic schools dramatically declined, during a period when most private schools maintained relatively stable enrollments, have never been explained conclusively. One can, however, discern plausible reasons for both departures from the norm of private school enrollment. Both relate basically to ideological shifts.

Prior to the Supreme Court's decisions to outlaw official prayer and Bible reading in public schools, most fundamentalist churches were officially opposed to the Christian day-school movement, insisting that public schools were sufficiently neutral religiously and morally to be used by fundamentalists and that fundamentalists had an obligation to witness to their faith in those schools. The Court's decisions apparently did much to reverse that position. In addition, drug use, sexual promiscuity, and other behavior repugnant to fundamentalists appeared to increase dramatically in many public schools. Many public school leaders began to insist on sex education—generally anathema to fundamentalists—and other controversial materials. More and more public school systems were refusing to discuss creationism, as an alternative theory to evolution, in classrooms. For whatever reasons, it is now a fact that fundamentalist schools are actively promoted by church leaders, including Jerry Falwell and other nationally visible Moral Majority spokesmen (McQuilkin, 1977). No other group of private schools appears to have benefited from such a dramatic reversal of official ideology in recent decades. Fundamentalists now seem to be rushing into their own schools about as fast as the schools can be founded. Founding has been given strong impetus by a firm known as Accelerate Christian Education (ACE). With programmed-learning materials and other extensive assistance from ACE, almost any concerned group can set up an instant school, much like a franchise. Some academic risk is obviously involved, but parents, though not unconcerned about student achievement, seem to be reacting primarily to their perception that public schools are hostile to their religious and moral views.

The opposite, downward, trend in Catholic schools also seems primarily attributable, in major measure, to a shift in official ideology. In the minds of many Catholics, the Second Vatican Council (ending in 1965), and several associated developments in the church, raised serious new questions about the religious value of Catholic schools (Ryan, 1963). The same shift in church teachings gave nuns and priests new freedom to choose their areas of service and placed new emphasis upon service to the poor. In apparent response, and because the religious orders were rapidly diminishing in size, "sisters" (nuns) and brothers disappeared from Catholic schools in enormous numbers, forcing the schools to replace them with far more costly lay teachers. Sensing that religious motivations for enrollment in the schools were weakening, many Catholic school leaders sought increased academic respectability in expensive ways, such as reducing class size and increasing teacher salaries. At the same time, many Catholic schools were losing enrollment because of the birthrate decline, changing values, and other factors; so many closed because decreasing economies of scale compounded the spiraling costs. Partly because they were as yet unaware of the impact of the declining birthrate, most bishops thought the loss of clients signified widespread disenchantment with Catholic schools, and for this reason and others, forbade further construction of schools in the suburbs to which many upwardly mobile Catholics were then moving (Donovan, Erickson, & Madaus, 1971; Erickson, Nault, & Cooper, 1978; Greeley, McCready, & McCourt, 1976).

Major Patron Motives. The strength of the current demand for private schools seems attributable to many more factors than can be discussed here. Disenchantment with public schools is probably one of the most important reasons, especially in areas where public schools are in ill repute or affected by particularly controversial policies (Ballweg, 1980; Becker, 1978; Carper, 1980; Cunningham, 1980; Cunningham & Husk, 1979; Donovan & Madaus, 1969; Erickson, Nault, & Cooper, 1978; Gratiot, 1979; Nordin & Turner, 1980; Schaller, 1979; Skerry, 1980). The evidence, though still somewhat sketchy, suggests that the disenchantment primarily concerns moral climate and is felt especially by lower-socioeconomic parents, except those in the inner city, where increasing numbers of low-income families appear to be choosing church-related schools not primarily for religious or moral reasons, but because they view their children's upward mobility as blocked in nearby public schools (Cibulka, 1981; Fay,

1973). As one considers families higher in socioeconomic status, parental rejection of public schools seems more and more predominantly due to academic quality, although rarely exclusively so (Baird, 1977; Kamin & Erickson, 1981). Within the largely nonsectarian high-tuition private schools, accordingly, academic motivations loom very large, and the facilities and programs reflect that emphasis. Within the religiously affiliated schools, which generally cater to less wealthy parents, religious and moral motivations are strong, although they are probably stronger in schools associated with churches leaning toward the fundamentalist pole than in schools run by the more liberal denominations (Kamin & Erickson, 1981).

Major Types. There are numerous indications that private schools function in a manner that is somewhat predictable on the basis of patron motivations. Schools patronized by people who voice primarily academic concerns *look* as though they are catering to those concerns. Schools patronized by people concerned about morality and religion generally permeate their activities with that emphasis. Scholars may often find it essential, then, to categorize private schools rather than trying to understand them all together. The high-tuition schools are in many ways different from the lower-tuition schools. Catholic schools are in many ways different from schools operated by fundamentalists, with schools associated by conservative but not strongly fundamentalist churches somewhere in between. Difficulties are posed, in this regard, by the fact that broad denominational affiliations often mask a wide variety of doctrine postures and social class attributes. Most Friends' churches in the East are resoundingly liberal, for example, but some Friends' churches in the West are quite fundamentalist. High church Episcopals in the Northeast would hardly recognize some of their hard-line conservative Episcopal *confrères* in the South. Lutherans and Mennonites range from staunchly fundamentalist to avowedly ecumenical.

For some purposes, even finer breakdowns will be essential for scholars seeking to understand private schools, for these schools are tremendously variegated. Within the high-tuition group, it is easy to find campuses and endowments that many colleges and universities would envy, some of the nation's most impressive educational facilities, elaborate recreational activities, many advanced-placement courses, experimental programs of many kinds, teachers with extensive academic backgrounds, exceptionally small classes, student bodies destined for major colleges and universities in large proportions, and graduates in the highest levels of business, government, and academe. But some high-tuition schools are surprisingly modest. In the same private sector are one-room Amish schoolhouses, with neither plumbing or electricity, with primitive materials and curricula, and with teachers who have never attended a college. The mainline religiously affiliated schools (Catholic, Lutheran, Calvinist, and Seventh-Day Adventist) run the gamut from traditional to experimental, generally leaning toward the former pole.

Fortunately, descriptions of the major groups are available (Erickson, Nault, & Cooper, 1978; Kraushaar, 1972).

As Table 1 indicates, private schools are affiliated with many different religious denominations. The few fundamentalist or Evangelical schools and enrollments reflected in this table (most are probably omitted) appear under the categories "Baptist" and "Other," although not all "Other" schools are fundamentalist. Most high-tuition schools, though far from all, are found in the "Nonaffiliated" category; many others are categorized here as "Episcopal" and "Friends"; and a few, no doubt, as "Catholic," "Presbyterian," "Methodist," and "Other." Catholic schools, though a diminishing proportion of the private school sector, still account for 64.3 percent of the student body, according to these estimates. Private school enrollment is unevenly distributed geographically, and schools affiliated with different groups are concentrated in different areas.

Common Characteristics. Despite the notable variety among private schools, these schools share fiscal and affiliational arrangements that seem likely to have a profound influence, and thus may exhibit some similar attributes. Virtually all private schools in the United States are privately supported and voluntarily patronized. They may select their students as rigorously as the market permits. They may expel those who prove troublesome, though this apparently is done less frequently than is widely assumed. Authority is concentrated in the individual school. Private schools are generally much smaller than public schools.

Since most private schools exact fees, and many involve parents in other burdens, they seem likely to be patronized primarily by parents with unusual concern for their children's education. They seem likely to attract clients only by offering something that allegedly cannot be obtained "free" in public schools. Confronted with costs and burdens, their clients appear unlikely to choose schools with whose emphases they disagree, so the constituencies of these schools may be unusually like-minded. The cost and effort involved in patronizing a private school may also, like other investments, elicit further commitment and concern. The jeopardy generally associated with privately supported schools may induce people to band together to make the enterprise succeed. It does not seem unreasonable to hypothesize, then, that private schools will generally be distinguished from public schools by the extent of parent commitment and involvement, social cohesion, and sense of doing something special. These phenomena could easily elicit cooperative attitudes and behavior from teachers and students as well. And since it is known that many, if not most, private school patrons have unusually high academic aspirations for their children, one would expect private schools to manifest more down-to-business, orderly conditions, a strong stress on learning, and, at least partly because of conducive home environments, above-average levels of academic achievement (Erickson, 1979; Erickson, MacDonald, & Manley-Casimir, 1979).

TABLE 1. *Distribution of private schools and students by church affiliation, 1978/79*

Affiliation	Number of schools	Percentage	Number of students	Percentage
Baptist	858	4.4%	204,144	4.0%
Calvinist	166	0.8	47,269	0.9
Catholic	9,849	50.1	3,269,761	64.3
Eastern Orthodox	14	0.1	2,682	0.1
Episcopal	314	1.6	76,452	1.5
Friends	50	0.3	14,611	0.3
Jewish	406	2.1	101,758	2.0
Lutheran	1,485	7.6	217,406	4.3
Methodist	60	0.3	11,187	0.2
Presbyterian	60	0.3	12,823	0.3
Seventh-Day Adventist	1,106	5.6	148,157	2.9
Other	1,351	6.7	231,317	4.5
Nonaffiliated	3,944	20.1	746,730	14.7

SOURCE OF DATA: National Center for Education Statistics surveys.

These predictions appear to be supported by all recent studies with relevant evidence, although many private schools are exceptions to the general pattern. In 1977, Morton et al. reported a study designed to determine why Catholic schools in Rhode Island were consistently superior in levels of student academic achievement to the state's public schools. Although the researchers compared many aspects of public and Catholic schools, the most consistent differences appeared in the area of social climate. Catholic schools as a whole were distinguished from public schools by greater attention to the central academic subjects (as reflected in more instructional time), fewer student absences, more effective discipline, more supportive parents (in the matter of insisting that homework be done, for example), and teachers who found their work more rewarding in several ways (partly, perhaps, because of the other characteristics mentioned). Erickson's comparison of British Columbian public and private schools in the spring of 1978 indicated that the latter were generally superior in such respects as commitment by teachers, students, and parents; social cohesion; responsiveness to parents; parent involvement; teacher work rewards; the perception by parents and teachers that the schools were superior academically; student enthusiasm for work; attractiveness to students of teachers and classes; and the extent to which students felt they were treated fairly (Erickson, MacDonald, & Manley-Casimir, 1979). The same general pattern has been found in a comparison of public and private schools in Merced, California (Williamson, 1981). More recently, in his analysis of the first wave of data from the "High School and Beyond" longitudinal study, Coleman found that, in private schools compared with public schools, teachers seem more committed to ensuring that students learn, more time is spent in instruction in the central academic subjects, every type of problematic student behavior considered is less frequent, discipline is rather strict (although students feel treated more fairly), students are less frequently absent, they skip classes less often, more homework is assigned and done, parents are more supportive, and students spend less time watching television (Coleman, Hoffer, & Kilgore, 1981). In the high-tuition schools, according to one scholar, teachers and parents are such close allies that students complain (Coles, 1977). In her ethnographic study, seeking reasons for the apparent marked success of a Catholic school in Alaska, Kleinfeld (1979) identified essentially the same social climate characteristics discussed in the studies just mentioned.

If an evaluative tone is attached to these comparisons, in some respects the comparisons are unfair, since private schools enjoy many advantages generally denied to public schools (such as the freedom to select their own clients and to expel students who do not cooperate). But if differences between public and private schools are adequately studied and understood, we may become aware of advantages in private schools that should be introduced into public schools (Erickson, 1978; Clinchy & Cody, 1978).

Finance. If reliable enrollment figures are difficult to obtain for private schools, it does not take much imagination to predict that finances will be particularly hard to investigate. There are problems even apart from the reluctance of many private schools to release data. Accounting procedures are often incompatible, and definitions of "current" or "operating" expenditures are diverse. Adequate estimates of costs in private schools should include contributed services of many kinds, but the value of these services is difficult to estimate and is therefore generally ignored. Despite these problems, some documented fiscal differences are illuminating. According to the NCES survey (1978/79), average tuitions in that year were $561 in Catholic schools, $651 in Lutheran schools, $1,822 in religiously unaffiliated schools, and $981 in other private schools (Eldridge, 1980). The differences reflect the fact that religiously affiliated schools often provide numerous forms of direct or indirect subsidy, thus holding costs within the reach of many families unable to afford more costly private schools. It is not surprising that Catholic schools, which have the lowest average costs, are the private schools with the highest proportion of parents with modest incomes (Coleman, Hoffer, & Kilgore, 1981).

Major Issues. The most serious controversies over private schools in recent years seem to center on four questions. (1) Are private schools divisive along religious, ethnic, racial, socioeconomic, or other lines, thus posing a threat to national unity? (2) Do private schools compromise equality of educational opportunity? (3) Need private schools be regulated to ensure that their students will not be deprived of educational or social experiences needed in order to reach their full potential? (4) Should private schools or their patrons be given some form of direct or indirect fiscal assistance or relief?

Divisiveness. The most comprehensive data relating to the possible divisiveness of private schools are found in the current longitudinal study, "High School and Beyond." In his analysis of the first wave of those data, Coleman found that when Catholic blacks were compared with Catholic whites, and when non-Catholic blacks were compared with non-Catholic whites, blacks at the high and low income levels attended Catholic schools to a disproportionate extent. In general, the proportion of students who were black was far lower in Catholic schools as a whole than in public schools as a whole, but the blacks who were in Catholic schools were far less likely than blacks in public schools to have predominantly black classmates. Coleman found that private schools did contribute significantly to religious segregation of the school-age population. He thought the extent of socioeconomic segregation was considerably less pronounced than was generally believed (Coleman, Hoffer, & Kilgore, 1981).

More serious than the question of physical segregation, perhaps, is the matter of how schools influence the attitudes of students. Here the evidence is sparse, but apparently consistent. Greeley and Rossi (1966) found that Catholics educated exclusively in Catholic schools are just as likely as Catholics educated exclusively in public schools to associate with non-Catholics in later years, and they produced some evidence that Catholic schools may contribute to reducing prejudice. Johnstone's study (1966) of Lutheran schools also led to the conclusion that church schooling may diminish prejudice. It has recently been found that, in British Columbia, prejudice is less evident in private than in public schools (Erickson, MacDonald, & Manley-Casimir, 1979). Greeley and Rossi (1966) offered a tentative explanation for these surprising findings: being reared in a situation in which one belongs to the majority may produce a better sense of identity than being reared as a minority member, and thus may contribute to the ability to open up to others and take psychological risks. At the same time, private schools seem incapable of gener-

ating greater social concern than public schools generate (Coleman, Hoffer, & Kilgore, 1981; Brekke, 1974).

A related concern has to do with the extent to which white parents patronize private schools in an effort to escape contact with blacks and other minorities in public schools, thus helping defeat efforts to achieve racial integration. Fundamentalist schools have been criticized particularly in this regard, especially when located in the South or in cities where public school busing has been mandated by the courts as an instrument of racial integration. Though no comprehensive study has been done in this regard, the numerous small studies all reach the conclusion that allegations of racial motives have been overstated, since the motivations of patrons of fundamentalist schools, as evidenced both in their own statements and in the policies of their schools, are substantially those indicated earlier in this article (Ballweg, 1980; Carper, 1980; Cunningham, 1980; Nevin & Bills, 1976; Nordin & Turner, 1980; Palmer, 1974; Schaller, 1979; Skerry, 1980). Several scholars point out that fundamentalist schools are often confused in the minds of the public with the "segregation academies" that sprang up in the South in earlier years, usually in connection with covert government efforts to subvert court orders to integrate public schools; those academies, like the fundamentalist schools, were often called "Christian schools."

Equal opportunity. The question of whether private schools compromise national efforts to achieve equality of opportunity is difficult to answer. Not much clear evidence is yet available. Data from British Columbia suggest, however, that patrons of private schools are unusually concerned about their children's schooling, virtually all the notably unconcerned (and apparently alienated) parents having children in public schools (Kamin & Erickson, 1981). It is not difficult to argue that, if children of most concerned parents leave public schools for private ones, the social climate in the public schools will hardly be conducive to effective learning, especially in disadvantaged areas. Since that concern has often been expressed in the context of recent enrollment shifts from public to private schools (e.g., Gratiot, 1979), there is room for careful research in this regard.

Academic quality. As for the possibility that private schools may deprive some students of the experiences they need to realize their full potential, the most direct evidence is Coleman's (Coleman, Hoffer, & Kilgore, 1981). Exercising a variety of impressive controls for home background and other factors, Coleman concluded that the private schools in his national sample made an independent contribution to the superior academic performance of their students. His evidence, however, was inadequate to support that conclusion. Even if private school and public school students are equated on a wide variety of factors, one inevitable inequality remains: the parents in the one group have gone to the extra effort and expense of sending their children to private schools, whereas the other parents have not. This one inequality may be associated with parental attitudes and behavior that are uncontrolled yet exert a powerful influence on students. In Levine's comparison of a Catholic school of high achievers and a nearby public school, for example, he found the parents highly similar in socioeconomic background, but the home environments of the Catholic school students were more educationally supportive (Levine et al., 1972). Greeley and Rossi (1966) reported evidence suggesting that Catholic schools had contributed to the upward mobility of Catholics in earlier decades, but for the same reasons of self-selection, their data, like Coleman's, are not conclusive.

Even if there were conclusive evidence that private schools as a whole are superior to public schools, the possibility would remain that some private schools were depriving their students of essential aspects of an adequate preparation for adulthood in our complex society. Two serious complications arise in this regard. First, what is adequate for one adult life-style may be totally inadequate for another, yet in democratic societies government has no right to dictate life-styles, and thus the state is in a questionable position to dictate which form of preparation must be adopted. Second, even if there were agreement on the objectives of education, educational research has not yet identified criteria that can be used to differentiate dependably between good and bad schools (Erickson, 1969). Nevertheless, allegations that some private schools are inferior, or will be inferior unless the state regulates them, lead to regulatory efforts in an increasing number of states and, on increasingly frequent occasions, to court battles over the constitutional limits of the state's regulatory authority. In recent years, these cases have involved fundamentalist schools primarily. The schools have been victorious on more occasions than not, but enough cases have gone the other way to put the eventual outcome in doubt (Ball, 1980a, 1980b).

Many private schools would never find themselves involved in this type of litigation, for many that consider state regulation an impediment to good educational practice have sufficient influence to ward off political attack. Many others (Catholic schools, especially) have often declared publicly (usually in the context of efforts to obtain public aid) that they see no problem in state regulation or even welcome it.

State regulation of private schools runs the gamut from utter laissez-faire to "standards" that, if enforced, would be extremely demanding (Jellison, 1975; O'Malley, 1980). The attitude of private school leaders toward regional accrediting associations is similarly varied; the gamut runs from ignoring the associations to providing considerable leadership within them. In three states (Pennsylvania, Oklahoma, and New Mexico), private school associations are permitted to decide which schools of a particular type will be approved for official purposes.

Tax support or tax relief. Key representatives of private schools would like to secure some diminution of the handicap imposed by the fact that patrons must be willing to shoulder private school costs while simultaneously paying their share of public school costs through taxation. Earlier efforts to secure direct public subvention ran afoul of the Supreme Court's current interpretation of the First Amendment's establishment clause, because most private schools are religiously affiliated (Moynihan, 1979). Since there is some chance that the Supreme Court will not outlaw broadly written tax credit or education voucher schemes, efforts are being made to propose legislation along those lines. Much debate is predicted on this subject (Catterall, 1981).

Research Resources. Scholars interested in this area of research will find that the best sources of basic statistics are the National Center for Education Statistics, the Council for American Private Education, the National Catholic Education Association, and the other private school groups these three can identify. Assistance may be obtained from Associates for Research on Private Education (ARPE), a special-interest group within the American Education Research Association, and from ARPE's quarterly bibliographic journal, *Private School Monitor.*

Donald A. Erickson

See also Catholic Schools; Jewish Education; Laboratory Schools; Protestant Education.

REFERENCES

Baird, L. L. *The Elite Schools.* Lexington, Mass.: Heath, 1977.

Ball, W. B. Family freedom in education. *Human Life Review,* 1980, *6,* 60–69. (a)

Ball, W. B. How to be a loyal citizen when government is subversive. *Administrator,* 1980, *1,* 1–7. (b)

Ballweg, G. R. *Growth in the Number and Population of Christian Schools since 1966: A Profile of Parental Views Concerning Factors Which Led Them to Enroll Their Children in a Christian School.* Unpublished doctoral dissertation, Boston University, 1980.

Becker, J. B. *The Impact of Racial Composition and Public School Desegregation on Changes in Non-public School Enrollment by White Pupils* (Report No. 252). Baltimore: Center for Social Organization of Schools, Johns Hopkins University, 1978.

Billings, B. (Special Assistant to the Secretary of Education, U.S. Department of Education). Personal communication, May 1981.

Brekke, M. L. *How Different Are People Who Attended Lutheran Schools?* St. Louis: Concordia, 1974.

Carper, J. C. In the way he should go: An overview of the Christian day-school movement. *Review Journal of Philosophy and Social Science,* 1980, *4,* 119–131.

Catterall, J. Tuition tax credits for schools: A federal priority for the 1980s? *IFG Policy Perspectives.* Stanford, Calif.: Institute for Research on Educational Finance and Governance, Stanford University, 1981.

Cibulka, J. G. *Public Policy Options for Inner-city Private Schools.* Paper presented at the annual meeting of the American Educational Research Association, Los Angeles, April 13, 1981.

Clinchy, E., & Cody, E. A. If not public choice, then private escape. *Phi Delta Kappan,* 1978, *60,* 270–273.

Coleman, J.; Hoffer, T.; & Kilgore, S. *Public and Private Schools.* (Report to the National Center for Education Statistics). Chicago: National Opinion Research Center, University of Chicago, 1981.

Coles, R. Privileged ones. In *Children of Crisis* (Vol. 5). Boston: Little, Brown, 1977.

Cunningham, G. K. *Parents Who Avoid Bussing: Attitudes and Characteristics.* Paper presented at the annual meeting of the American Educational Research Association, Boston, April 1980.

Cunningham, G. K., & Husk, W. L. *The Impact of Court-ordered Desegregation on Student Enrollment and Residential Patterns in the Jefferson County Kentucky Public School District.* Louisville, Ky.: Jefferson County Education Consortium, 1979.

Donovan, J. D.; Erickson, D. A.; & Madaus, G. F. The social and religious sources of the crisis in Catholic schools. In *Issues of Aid to Nonpublic Schools.* Vol. 2 of *Report to the President's Commission on School Finance.* Chestnut Hill, Mass.: Boston College, 1971.

Donovan, J. D., & Madaus, G. F. *Catholic Education in the Archdiocese of Boston: The Voices of the People.* Chestnut Hill, Mass.: New England Catholic Education Center, 1969.

Eldridge, M. D. America's nonpublic schools: A quantification of their contribution to American education. *Private School Quarterly,* Fall 1980, pp. 4–7.

Erickson, D. A. *An Agenda for Research on Private Education: An Analysis of a National Institute of Education Conference.* Washington, D.C.: National Institute of Education, February 23, 1978.

Erickson, D. A. Should *all* the nation's schools compete for clients and support? *Phi Delta Kappan,* 1979, *61,* 14–17, 77.

Erickson, D. A. (Ed.). *Public Controls for Nonpublic Schools.* Chicago: University of Chicago Press, 1969.

Erickson, D. A.; MacDonald, L.; & Manley-Casimir, M. E. *Characteristics and Relationships in Public and Independent Schools.* San Francisco: Center for Research on Private Education, University of San Francisco, 1979.

Erickson, D. A.; Nault, R. L.; & Cooper, B. S. Recent enrollment trends in U.S. non-public schools. In S. Abramowitz & S. Rosenfeld (Eds.), *Declining Enrollment: The Challenge of the Coming Decade.* Washington, D.C.: National Institute of Education, 1978, pp. 81–127.

Fay, L. F. Catholics, parochial schools, and social stratification. *Social Science Quarterly,* 1973, *43,* 520–527.

Gratiot, M. *Why Parents Choose Non-public Schools: Comparative Attitudes and Characteristics of Public and Private School Consumers.* Paper presented at the annual meeting of the American Educational Research Association, San Francisco, April 1979.

Greeley, A. M., & Rossi, P. H. *The Education of Catholic Americans.* Chicago: Aldine, 1966.

Greeley, A.; McCready, W.; & McCourt, K. *Catholic Schools in a Declining Church.* Kansas City, Mo.: Sheed & Ward, 1976.

Jellison, H. M. (Ed.). *State and Federal Laws Relating to Nonpublic Schools.* Washington, D.C.: U.S. Office of Education, 1975.

Johnstone, R. L. *The Effectiveness of Lutheran Elementary and Secondary Schools as Agencies of Christian Education.* St. Louis: Concordia, 1966.

Kamin, J., & Erickson, D. A. *Parent Choice of Schooling in British Columbia: Preliminary Findings.* Paper presented at the annual meeting of the American Educational Research Association, Los Angeles, April 16, 1981.

Kleinfeld, J. S. *Eskimo School on the Andreafsky.* New York: Praeger, 1979.

Kraushaar, O. F. *American Nonpublic Schools: Patterns of Diversity.* Baltimore: Johns Hopkins University Press, 1972.

Levine, D. U.; Lachowicz, H.; Oxman, K.; & Tangeman, A. The home environment of students in a high achieving inner-city parochial school and a nearby public high school. *Sociology of Education,* 1972, *45,* 435–445.

McLaughlin, D. H., & Wise, L. L. *Nonpublic Education of the Nation's Children.* Palo Alto, Calif.: American Institutes for Research, 1980.

McQuilkin, J. R. Public schools: Equal time for Evangelicals. *Christianity Today,* 1977, *22,* 404–407.

Morton, D. S.; Bassis, M.; Brittingham, B. E.; Ewing, P.; Horwitz, S.; Hunter, W. J.; Long, J. V.; Maguire, J.; & Pezzullo, T. R. *A Comprehensive Analysis of Differences in Public and Parochial School Student Performance on Standardized Tests of Achievement.* Paper presented at the annual meeting of the American Educational Research Association, New York, April 1977.

Moynihan, D. P. Private schools and the first amendment. *National Review,* August, 3, 1979, pp. 962–66, 987, 999.

Nevin, D., & Bills, R. E. *The Schools That Fear Built: Segregationist Academies in the South.* Washington, D.C.: Acropolis Books, 1976.

Nordin, V. D., & Turner, W. L. More than segregation academies: The growing Protestant fundamentalist schools. *Phi Delta Kappan,* 1980, *61,* 391–394.

O'Malley, C. *Unofficial Study of Governance of Private Schools.* Tallahassee: Florida Department of Education, 1980.

Palmer, J. M. *The Impact of Private Education on the Rural South.* Austin: National Educational Laboratory Publishers, 1974.

Ryan, M. P. *Are Parochial Schools the Answer? Catholic Education in the Light of the Council.* New York: Holt, Rinehart, 1963.

Schaller, L. E. Public versus private schools: A divisive issue for the 1980s. *Christian Century,* September 1979, pp. 1086–1090.

Senske, A. *Early Childhood and Elementary Schools of the Lutheran Church—Missouri Synod* (Statistical Report, Information Bulletin No. 33980). St. Louis: Lutheran Church—Missouri Synod, Board of Parish Education, 1980.

Skerry, P. Christian schools versus the IRS. *Public Interest,* 1980, *61,* 18–24.

Stockdale, J. *Enrollment Trends in NAIS Schools, 1969–70 through 1979–80: Some Implications for the Eighties.* Paper presented at the National Association of Independent Schools Annual Convention, Boston, February 23, 1981.

Williamson, B. L. *A Study of the Characteristics and Relationships in Public and Private Elementary and Junior High Schools in Merced, California.* Unpublished doctoral dissertation, University of San Francisco, 1981.

PROFESSIONAL ORGANIZATIONS

The United States is frequently described as a nation of organizations, and U.S. education has its full share. An estimated 3 million persons are employed in lower- and higher-education institutions (U.S. Department of Education, 1980), and these individuals constitute most of the membership of an estimated 30,000 local, state, and national professional educational organizations.

The range among such groups is remarkable. The National Education Association (NEA) has approximately 1.5 million members. By contrast, the teacher or administrator association in a small rural school district may have but a few members. Between such extremes, are hundreds of general associations of professors, researchers, budget officers, language specialists, driver-education teachers, and other groups. These thousands of professional educational associations frequently are nested hierarchically into local, state, and national tiers.

In addition, another 10,000 organizations exist composed of lay persons connected with education. Some of these are employees, such as school bus drivers, custodians, and clerks. Others may hold a contractual relationship with educational institutions, for example, evaluation consultants or school attorneys. Organizations exist for members of boards of trustees of universities, local school districts, counties, and states. Still more organizations exist to link professional and lay groups connected with education. For example, the National Parent-Teacher Association (PTA) estimates its total membership at 9 million. Thus, both diversity and numbers are awesome. This article defines, classifies, and describes these education-related professional organizations and analyzes their functions.

Definition, Classification, and Description. Professional educational organizations are those chartered associations composed of individuals whose training, experience, and employment are directed primarily at the systematic generation and transmission of knowledge. The overwhelming majority of the approximately 3 million persons in the United States employed in education belong to one or more professional organizations. Also, an estimated 1 million lay persons are employed by education institutions, and they, as well as the clients of educational institutions, contribute membership to 10,000 additional formal organizations related to professional education.

Professional educational associations can be divided into three major categories: (1) associations encompassing generic occupational functions, for example, teachers, administrators, counselors, researchers, and trustees; (2) organizations oriented toward subject matter or narrow functional specialties, for example, teachers of English or physics, or professors of educational administration; and (3) associations of education-related institutions.

These divisions themselves frequently divide along lines of higher and lower education. For example, the American Association of University Professors (AAUP) serves some of the same purposes for higher-education faculty as the NEA serves for elementary and secondary teachers. For higher-education professionals, identification with subject specialization is typically more intense than is the case with lower-education employees. Conversely, higher-education professionals tend to pay less allegiance as individuals to their institutional or occupational associations than do lower-education professionals. Perhaps as a conse-

quence of this tendency, higher-education organizations generally consist of institutions. There even exists an almost all-encompassing higher-education umbrella organization, the American Council on Education (ACE), which has many members that are themselves associations of institutions.

Some organizations cut across divisional boundaries. For example, the American Federation of Teachers (AFT) has both lower- and higher-education affiliates. Similarly, the American Association of School Administrators (AASA), made up of principals and superintendents, has a higher-education membership subunit for professors of educational administration. Also, these organizational levels need not be mutually exclusive. Individuals frequently hold membership in associations located in two or more of the sectors pictured in Figure 1.

The sixfold classification—lower-education generic occupational, subject matter–oriented, and institutional organizations and higher-education generic occupational, subject matter–oriented, and institutional organizations—is joined on the periphery by a substantial number of organizations, the membership of which consists of lay persons connected with educational institutions. For example, in this category are found the organizations of so-called classified employees, such as school clerks and custodians. ("Classified" in this instance denotes the absence of a state license or credential for the performance of the task involved.) These employees are frequently governed and protected by civil service regulations. Also, abutting the general classification of professional educational employees are associations of school district and higher-education trustees, such as the National School Boards Association (NSBA) and the National Association of State Boards of Education (NASBE).

The largest professional educational organizations are dominated by individual members. A typical member of the NEA is a classroom teacher. The relatively few organizations consisting of institutional affiliates tend to be smaller as measured by number of members. In this category are the American Association of Community and Junior Colleges (AACJC), the American Council on Education (ACE), and the National Association of Independent Colleges and Schools (NAICS). "Small," in this sense, should not be interpreted as lacking influence.

As might be imagined, nonpublic institutions, both nonsectarian and church-related, have their share of professional organizations. On some dimensions, these nonpublic professional educational organizations share a community of interests with public-sector occupational and institutional levels. The desire to protect academic freedom is a good example. On other issues, such as tuition tax credits or federal or state financial aid to nonpublic schools, nonpublic institutions may differ with those public-sector levels and be engaged in opposing political activities. This is much less the case for subject matter–oriented groups that tend more easily to encompass both public and nonpublic interests.

FIGURE 1. *Taxonomy of educational associations*

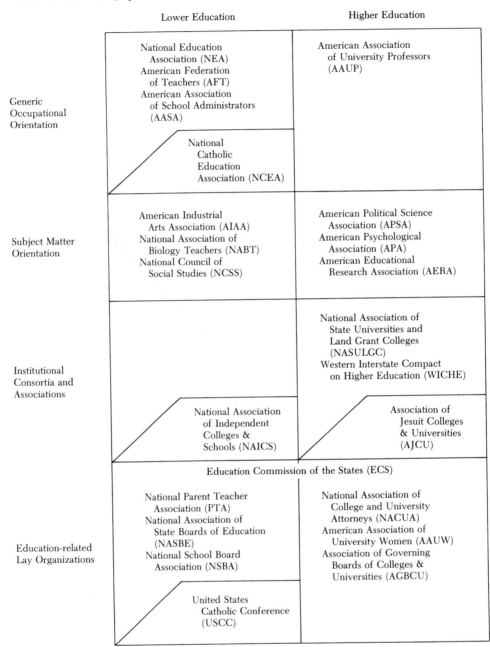

Lower Education | Higher Education

Generic Occupational Orientation

National Education Association (NEA)
American Federation of Teachers (AFT)
American Association of School Administrators (AASA)

National Catholic Education Association (NCEA)

American Association of University Professors (AAUP)

Subject Matter Orientation

American Industrial Arts Association (AIAA)
National Association of Biology Teachers (NABT)
National Council of Social Studies (NCSS)

American Political Science Association (APSA)
American Psychological Association (APA)
American Educational Research Association (AERA)

Institutional Consortia and Associations

National Association of Independent Colleges & Schools (NAICS)

National Association of State Universities and Land Grant Colleges (NASULGC)
Western Interstate Compact on Higher Education (WICHE)

Association of Jesuit Colleges & Universities (AJCU)

Education Commission of the States (ECS)

Education-related Lay Organizations

National Parent Teacher Association (PTA)
National Association of State Boards of Education (NASBE)
National School Board Association (NSBA)

United States Catholic Conference (USCC)

National Association of College and University Attorneys (NACUA)
American Association of University Women (AAUW)
Association of Governing Boards of Colleges & Universities (AGBCU)

No simple classification scheme can capture the diversity of so many organizations. Figure 1 is meant only to convey the general range of professional educational associations. The names of organizations listed in each compartment are intended only for illustrative purposes. The omission of any organization bears no relationship to its significance. Also, many organizations do not fit neatly in a single compartment. The Education Commission of the States (ECS), with its headquarters in Denver, falls into almost every classification, except that it does not have individual members. Each organization is listed in terms of the major constituency it serves, not in terms of its exclusive function. Organizations listed below the diagonal lines are oriented primarily to nonpublic education institutions.

Functions. Professional educational organizations encompass an agenda of purposes equal to their remarkable numbers and diversity.

General. In general, professional educational organizations exist to enhance the flow of information among members and to represent the interest of members with other organizations, particularly governmental agencies. In order to facilitate these functions, many professional organizations are organized in local and state units, which telescope into an overall umbrella organization with a national headquarters and staff. Such professional societies generally have newsletters or other regular publications, hold annual conventions, select national officers, and make awards for outstanding professional achievement and service. Those with a subject matter orientation may sponsor the publication of a specialized and refereed journal devoted to the dissemination of research findings and technical knowledge.

Political activity. The most dramatic characteristic of professional educational organizations in the last quarter of the twentieth century is the newly developed intensity of their political activity and the resultant fragmentation and conflict that have occurred in their ranks. Gilb (1966) describes the formative stages through which many of the largest professional organizations evolved and analyzes their conventional concern for enhancement of professional standards and improvement of instruction. These earlier activities were consistent with the social and government reforms influencing American education in the nineteenth and early twentieth centuries (Tyack, 1974). During this period, education was enshrouded in what has come to be labeled the "apolitical myth." The public was encouraged to view education and politics as necessarily being separate undertakings. The contention was widespread that educational improvements could best be generated by the application of private-sector industrial management techniques to the operation of schools (Callahan, 1962). Consistent with such views, professional educational organizations concentrated primarily on curriculum issues and professional training and paid relatively little attention to political matters.

After World War II, elementary and secondary teachers began to organize intensely, initially in large eastern and midwestern cities and subsequently in suburban areas throughout the nation. By the mid-1970s, the National Education Association and American Federation of Teachers had organized an overwhelming majority of the nation's classroom instructors into two huge unions. Initial efforts to combine the two proved unsuccessful. Nevertheless, from time to time, consolidation efforts occurred (Harlacher, 1973). These unions began to engage in collective bargaining with management representatives. The adversary process in bargaining, the intense interest of union representatives in teacher-welfare issues, and the willingness of union militants to strike provoked substantial conflict among many of the formerly united professional organizations in lower education. Administrators initially, and then other groups as well, broke from their teacher colleagues to form more clearly identified separate organiza-

tions, for example, the American Association of School Administrators (AASA), the National Association of Elementary School Principals (NAESP), and the National School Boards Association (NSBA).

In addition to the advent of collective bargaining and the proliferation of separate organizations, the mid-1960s were characterized by the onset of intensified political activities on the part of professional educational organizations. This activity was true for both higher- and lower-education associations, public and private. Many of them began to endorse and provide financial support for candidates for public office at the local, state, and national levels. Their professional staffs expanded, particularly in state capitals and in Washington, D.C. Organizations began to become active in Republican and, particularly, in Democratic political conventions (Brodey, 1975). For example, several hundred NEA teachers constituted the largest single bloc of delegates to the 1980 Democratic presidential nominating convention. Another measure of the expansion of political activities on the part of professional educational organizations is the proliferation of offices in Washington, D.C. Bailey (1975) lists in excess of 200 in an index meant only to be illustrative. Bloland (1969) and Bloland and Bloland (1974) list more than 200 in higher education alone.

Such political activity has exacerbated the conflict among organizations. Teacher and administrator associations frequently find themselves on opposite sides of political issues. Similarly, on occasion, higher- and lower-education organizations engage in conflict. For example, the formation of a federal-level Department of Education was strongly supported by the NEA and opposed by the National Association of State Universities and Land Grant Colleges (NASULGC).

Generally, however, the level of political conflict among various segments of the higher-education community itself is not as intense as the level among lower-education associations. This fact is perhaps a function of the previously mentioned tendency of higher-education employees to identify more closely with their field of knowledge or professional training than with the institutions in which they are employed.

One of the unintended consequences of fragmentation, interorganizational conflict, and politicization has been the relative inability of professional educational leaders to present a united front either to the public or to public officials. This condition may account, in part, for the ebbing of support of education, beginning in 1975. On those rare, recent occasions when professional educational organizations have closed ranks for a common purpose, they have been remarkably successful. The Committee for Full Funding, formed in the 1970s to increase congressional education appropriations, is an example. Hence, the admonition from several quarters that association leaders should attempt to regain a measure of the cohesion and cooperation that characterized educational organizations in the first and second quarters of the twentieth century.

James W. Guthrie

See also Academic Freedom and Tenure; Collective Negotiations; Educational Research Associations; Governance of Schools; Teacher Centers.

REFERENCES

Bailey, S. K. *Education Interest Groups in the Nation's Capital.* Washington, D. C.: American Council on Education, 1975.

Bloland, H. G. *Higher Education Associations in a Decentralized Education system.* Berkeley: University of California, Center for Research and Development in Higher Education, 1969.

Bloland, H. G., & Bloland, S. M. *America's Learned Societies in Transition.* New York: McGraw-Hill, 1974. (ERIC Document Reproduction Service No. ED 029 619)

Brodey, J. Teachers spend millions to elect new congress: Now what's to be their payoff? *American School Board Journal,* 1975, *162*(1), 42–43.

Callahan, R. E. *Education and the Cult of Efficiency.* Chicago: University of Chicago Press, 1962.

Gilb, C. L. *Hidden Hierarchies.* New York: Harper & Row, 1966.

Harlacher, F. There's one giant national teacher union in your future. *American School Board Journal,* 1973, *160*(9), 36–37.

Tyack, D. *The One Best System.* Cambridge, Mass.: Harvard University Press, 1974.

U.S. Department of Education, National Center for Educational Statistics. *The Conditions of American Education, 1980.* Washington, D.C.: U.S. Government Printing Office, 1980.

PROFESSIONS EDUCATION

It is extremely difficult to discuss professional education in general, because the disparate components make it virtually impossible to set forth propositions that hold for all or most professional fields. Clearly, what is true for engineering need not be true for social work. Hence, in this article we try to indentify issues that cut across the various professional fields and to mention noteworthy developments in particular fields, but we do not claim to cover each field exhaustively.

The 1970s, unlike the previous decade, were not years of intellectual ferment in professional education. However, some of the major issues of the seventies were legacies of earlier times (for example, equity of access, the interest in "clinical" work as part of students' training, and shifts in student interests and the job market). Thus dramatic change and experimentation probably will not characterize professional education in the 1980s, although continuing concern is likely to be expressed about equity in admissions policies, new types of delivery systems, the integration of theory and practice, and the integration, cooperation, and collaboration between the professions, professional schools, and government agencies (Nyre & Reilly, 1979).

In recent years there has not been an emergence of major new professional fields, although there was a significant development in the field of public administration: the rise of a small group of schools of public policy analysis at several leading universities. These are independent of traditional schools of public administration. A parallel development was the growth of specialized programs in public managment and health management within the thriving business schools. These often were (and remain) substantially independent of traditional schools of public administration and public health located on the same campus. In contrast to many of the arts and science fields, whose curricula have remained relatively unresponsive to changing labor markets (quite properly so, some would argue), the professional fields have demonstrated a continuing willingness to develop new programs to reflect new societal needs and priorities.

The Student Demand. Perhaps the major issue facing professional education in most fields is how to respond to the continuing surge in student demands for admission to both undergraduate and graduate-level programs. Medicine and dentistry are almost exclusively postbaccalaureate programs that award a "first professional" degree to those already holding the bachelor's. Law is also overwhelmingly a postbachelor's program, although bachelor's, master's, and doctor's degrees are all awarded. Most of the other professional fields (business, education, social work, theology, etc.) award degrees at several levels.

We can see from Table 1 that with the exception of the field of education, almost all professional fields have demonstrated dramatic growth in degrees awarded between 1965 and 1978 (the most recent year for which data are available). This growth contrasts with that in the arts and science fields (see the bottom three rows of Table 1), where growth in doctorates awarded occurred generally until the early 1970s but has either slowed down or been reversed since then. At the bachelor's and master's levels, the number of arts and science degrees has also peaked, while the share of these degrees that are in professional fields has risen dramatically. Numbers of "first professional" degrees awarded—these include the M.D., D.D.S., L.L.B., J.D., and other degrees awarded only by professional schools—have climbed steadily.

Professional schools in many fields, especially those in medicine, veterinary medicine, law, and business and management, and especially those at the leading universities, have substantial surpluses of qualified applicants. In medicine, for example, fewer than half of all applicants to U.S. schools are admitted to any school, and thousands each year seek training abroad (Hook, 1980). In the leading busiiness schools, applicants, most of whom would have been considered fully qualified a few years ago, exceed places by a factor approaching ten to one. Admission to the leading law schools is also very competitive.

The popularity of the professional fields is in sharp contrast to the situation in the 1960s, when studies in the liberal arts and sciences attracted a much larger share

TABLE 1. *U.S. bachelor's, master's, first professional,[1] and doctor's degrees conferred by institutions of higher education, by field and year[2]*

Degree and year

Field of study	1965/66				1970/71				1974/75				1977/78			
	Bachelor's	Master's	First professional	Doctor's	Bachelor's	Master's	First professional	Doctor's	Bachelor's	Master's	First professional	Doctor's	Bachelor's	Master's	First professional	Doctor's
Architecture	2,401	381		9	3,459	625		6	4,908	990		14	5,405	1,386		14
Business and management	13,500	12,988		387	115,527	26,544		810	133,822	36,364		1,011	161,271	48,484		867
Journalism	3,131	523		15	5,144	853		15	7,092	973		28	8,299	797		32
Education	118,399	50,478		3,063	176,571	88,716		6,398	166,969	119,778		7,443	136,079	118,562		7,586
Engineering	35,815	13,678		2,304	50,046	16,443		3,638	46,852	15,348		3,108	55,654	16,398		2,440
Health professions	3,912	1,817		383	25,226	5,749		466	49,090	10,692		618	59,434	14,325		654
Nursing	7,831	863		1	12,199	1,530		7	23,713	2,204		16	30,003	3,779		56
Optometry					351	12	531	2	320	8	792		385	7	1,014	7
Pharmacy	3,311	187	452	78	4,549	194		94	6,336	285		206	7,296	320	547	96
Law	245	780	13,442	29	545	955	17,421	20	436	1,245	29,296	21	653	1,786	34,402	39
Public administration					425	1,406		36	1,471	4,128		84	2,034	6,833		153
Social work	1,664	3,912		64	4,608	6,019		126	10,351	8,763		135	12,423	9,737		138
Theology	4,036	1,946	4,443	333	3,744	2,710	5,055	312	4,809	3,228	5,095	872	6,319	3,329	6,367	1,160
Medicine			7,720				8,919				12,447				14,279	
Dentistry			3,264				3,745				4,773				5,189	
Social science/psychology	110,691	18,990		3,204	193,206	20,932		5,441	186,662	23,990		6,651	157,778	22,794		6,170
Physical and natural sciences	70,015	15,362		6,461	97,016	21,331		10,448	113,261	22,050		9,189	116,908	22,801		8,414
Arts and humanities	34,196	8,650		988	125,953	25,147		3,962	119,000	25,164		4,169	100,870	22,698		3,517

[1] First professional degrees require at least six years of study.
[2] For 1965/66, numbers include degrees conferred in outlying areas in addition to the United States.

SOURCES OF DATA: U.S. Department of Health, Education, and Welfare, 1968, 1973, 1977, 1980.

1459

of students at both the undergraduate and graduate levels. Clearly, a less expansive economy has made students more concerned about ensuring that their years spent in school pay off in the job market. Indeed the liberal arts have lost students both to professional education and to noncollegiate (or to community college) vocational training. Demographics and more restricted federal support for research have also played an important role as students correctly perceive more limited career opportunities in college and university teaching and in research. In the past, merely having any college degree made graduates special, and hence qualified for any number of professional-level jobs. Now, because such a high proportion of new entrants to the labor force hold college degrees, employers look to the type of training acquired, and that obtained in professional schools or programs is often deemed most desirable.

But societal attitudes and values have also played a part. The student and community demands of the 1960s for relevance in academe have very probably had something to do with the current interest in professional education. After all, among the defining characteristics of a profession are that it applies advanced knowledge to the problems of men and their affairs—to paraphrase Professor Everett Hughes (Glazer, 1974)—and that it embodies an ethic of service to society. Professional education then is one way of making one's years of study relevant to the problems of people and society. Of course, it also fits nicely with current societal concerns about getting one's (or society's) money's worth out of investments in education.

Enrollment Trends. Some have argued that the growth in many of the professional fields will continue through the 1980s (Anderson, 1974; Nyre & Reilly, 1979), despite the widely predicted decline in aggregate higher education enrollments. It should be mentioned at the outset that the general growth in professional field enrollments has not been shared by all fields and probably will not be in the future.

Changing student and societal demands on professional education have led to responses by the academic institutions and to problems for them. The largest professional field, education, is the most notable exception to the general growth trend. Of course, the primary reason for the enrollment decline in education is the same demographic reality that has dried up the market for higher education faculty: there are fewer students to teach. Data provided by the National Center for Education Statistics show that enrollment in kindergarten through grade 12 was 49,239,000 in fall 1966 and rose to only 49,335,000 by fall 1976. And the projected enrollment for these grades in fall 1986 drops to 45,277,000 (National Center for Education Statistics, 1978). However, a small increase in the birthrate could cause an increasing demand for elementary school teachers only four or five years later. Since it takes four years to train a teacher, the potential volatility of education school enrollments is obvious.

Education schools adapted to the sharp decline in new

demand for those who train teachers in part by emphasizing continuing education, both in and out of graduate degree programs, for already employed teachers and for school administrators and other nonteaching specialists. In 1977/78 more than 7,500 doctoral degrees in education were awarded (nearly one-fourth of all doctoral degrees awarded in the United States) and some 118,500 master's degrees (U.S. Department of Health, Education, and Welfare, 1978). Most of these went to people already employed as educators who studied for their degrees part-time. The sharp decline in enrollments in teacher preparation programs (Table 1 shows that bachelor's degrees in education fell from 176,571 in 1970/71 to 136,079 in 1977/78) and recent increases in births in the United States (Langway, 1981) have already begun to improve the job market outlook for teachers, and education school enrollments should soon begin to revive somewhat (Watkins, 1981).

But in some other professional fields the long period of growth in student demand seems to have peaked. Applications to and enrollments in the nation's law schools have declined slightly over the last several years as the market for lawyers has softened (Jacobson, 1981a). Even in medicine there are reports of surpluses of practitioners, especially in the major cities, with more general surpluses impending (Hook, 1980). Still, physician income data do not yet show evidence of surplus, perhaps partly because physicians have substantial control over the demand for their services. The leveling off of applications to and enrollments in medical schools are more likely the result of, in the former case, the large surpluses of applicants, which probably discourages some prospective applicants, and in the latter, the difficulty in securing funds to expand very expensive medical school capacity. Similar considerations limit enrollments in such other costly health professions fields as dentistry and veterinary medicine, though in the latter case, in particular, market demand is very strong.

In public administration and public policy there are signs of a leveling off or decline in enrollments as governments attempt to reduce their size and hence their hiring. Similar forces may affect schools of urban planning, social work, public health, and education, where many graduates seek employment in government or in agencies supported by government funds. But of course, government policies change frequently, and the fortunes of professional schools and their graduates in these fields can change as suddenly as policies change.

The real growth area among the major professional fields, indeed in all of higher education, in the 1980s (at least in the early part of the decade) seems to be in business and management education. As seen in Table 1, between 1965/66 and 1977/78, bachelor's degrees in business and management grew from 13,500 to over 161,000. Over the same period, master's degrees in business grew from 12,988 to 48,484.

The growth in demand for business school education shows no signs of abating in the short term. Both undergraduate and master's degree winners in business and management generally have a variety of desirable job opportunities to choose from upon graduation and receive high and rapidly growing starting salaries (Jacobson, 1981b). This circumstance, combined with the relatively soft job market for graduates in many other fields, has led to student demand growth that has substantially outstripped the institutions' ability (or, in some cases, willingness) to respond. Business schools have thus had the opportunity to be selective in student admissions to a degree they would have thought inconceivable ten years ago. This should bode well for the future management of our business and other enterprises. (The same could also be said about our future doctors and lawyers.)

How long the remarkable growth in business school enrollments can continue is an open question. In the short run the prospects for continued growth look good as long as the economy grows. But the question of how many highly trained managers the economy can usefully absorb is little understood and clearly in need of research. Moreover, quite aside from labor market demand considerations, recent developments (such as limited growth of business doctorate production) have shown that other factors will very probably constrain sharply the rate of growth of business and other professional schools with pools of surplus qualified applicants seeking admission.

Limits to Growth. Rapid growth and changing student and societal demands on professional education have led to some problems and conflicts as well as to the benefits of growth.

Qualified faculty. A persistent, if little appreciated, constraint on the growth of professional schools is a general, shortage of qualified faculty. Academe is widely believed to suffer from a large surplus of Ph.D. holders qualified for faculty positions, but in many of the professional fields it does not. Medical and other health professions schools have great difficulty luring trained people away from much more lucrative clinical practice. Law schools sometimes have similar problems, and the problem has become quite serious in the business and engineering schools (Jacobson, 1981b). In these fields new graduates can often command salaries comparable to those of their professors, whose academic salaries are usually limited by rigid salary scales and norms of cross-campus equity. One result is that professional schools must allow faculty substantial time to consult or work as private practitioners. At some point, this must have consequences for the attention students and their educational programs receive.

The result is not only a serious constraint on the expansion of programs but also problems between professional schools and the rest of the campus and within the professional schools themselves. Professional schools have always employed some practitioners of the profession as faculty (for sound reasons), but many now have quite high proportions of such people. When practioners are hired as full-time faculty, they often have difficulty meeting academic standards for promotion (i.e., doctoral degrees and research accomplishment). Thus, many are employed on a part-time basis while they continue to practice their professions. For example, Chambers (1977) notes that in 1976, 55 percent of the nearly 11,500 American dental educators held part-time appointments. In many professions, there may well be a different status ordering of professors, administrators, consultants, and practitioners than the one that exists in the universities. The status of a faculty member in a professional field may be lower than that of his or her practicing colleague. A program's academic status may depend upon the proportion of full-time publishing faculty rather than upon the number of successful practitioners of high professional status who teach. Yet the question of the relative impact on students of those faculty with "hands-on" experience and those committed to full-time teaching is unresolved empirically.

The use of practicing professionals as teachers would seem to have real benefit for students; however, the presence of too many part-time faculty makes it difficult to maintain program continuity and coherence and places substantial "overhead" work load burdens on the regular faculty. It also tends to reduce the research output of the school and limits the exposure of students to those who are concerned with research and criticism designed to improve the performance of the profession. At the extreme, students may learn little more in school than the ways of the current generation of practitioners.

There are few signs that the faculty shortage problem will improve anytime soon. In many of the professional fields, especially business and engineering, the numbers of Ph.D.'s awarded each year is roughly level or is actually declining (National Research Council, 1976, 1979), and in the clinical health fields most holders of professional doctorate degrees lack appropriate research training for faculty careers (National Research Council, 1978).

The problem appears, once again, to be related to economics. Students who can instead pursue lucrative professional careers are hard to attract to lengthy research training programs and lower-paying academic careers. Of great importance is the question of the relative abilities of those who opt for academic versus professional careers. Will those who train the next generation of practitioners be at least as capable as their practitioner colleagues and also capable of serious research? Here research is badly needed, for there are no systematic data to answer these questions (Klitgaard, 1979).

The only solution to the faculty shortage on the horizon is a very partial one. For some faculty positions in most professional schools, Ph.D. holders in one of the traditional disciplines may be candidates, and these people are generally in plentiful supply. Health professions schools have long used Ph.D.'s in the sciences to teach basic science courses to their professional students, business schools hire Ph.D.'s in economics and psychology, even law schools now have a few nonlawyers on their faculties. But there are real limits to how much further this sort of staffing pattern can go in most schools, since, for example, biochemists cannot teach clinical medicine.

Cost constraints. A second serious constraint on professional school expansion is related to costs. All higher education is costly, and many professional programs are especially so because they are typically graduate programs and, in the case of the health professions, require expensive facilities and equipment. Expansion of any programs, and particularly costly ones, will be hard to accomplish in light of the financial circumstances facing higher education now and probably throughout the eighties.

One possible way to raise revenue for socially desirable expansion plans is to increase tuition for professional programs. This option merits serious consideration. Indeed, it has been considered and adopted by some institutions, both provate and public, with George Washington University's (private) medical school now charging students $15,000 a year (Derbarics, 1981).

The rationales for differential tuition charges in different programs are that (1) costs for different programs vary widely, and (2) the excess of qualified applicants, where it exists, suggests that enough students could be attracted at reduced subsidy levels to meet society's needs. The latter is likely to be true because the benefit of a professional degree in terms of career success and particularly lifetime earnings make high cost investments in professional education worthwhile. Thus, considerations of economic efficiency would argue for tuition charges closer to the true incremental cost of educating additional students. Such a policy would also generate some revenue to finance desirable program expansion and would reallocate educational costs much more equitably to those who benefit from the education by receiving high incomes after graduation.

The trend toward differential tuition for professional programs with high costs and/or large excess applicant pools will, however, probably not gather momentum very quickly, at least not in public institutions. Relatively low, non–field-differentiated tuition rates in public universities have a long tradition and apparently considerable political support. Moreover, public universities are loath to raise the issue of differential tuition because of the internal conflict it would cause and because it could open the door to government pressure to raise tuition across the board. Thus the cost constraint on professional school expansion remains a serious one.

Internal campus conflict. The changing fortunes of the professional fields vis-à-vis many of the arts and science disciplines have created some conflict. Thus, another obstacle to expansion of professional programs arises entirely from within the campuses. There is genuine concern on the part of many institutional administrators, beleaguered arts and science faculties, and even some professional school faculty that the traditional liberal arts and disciplinary studies traditions of the university are in danger of being swamped by the growing "professionalization" of the campus. There are several concerns in this area, some of which will be touched upon subsequently, but the major point here is that there is some fundamental resistance on many campuses to further substantial growth in professional schools (and hence their power and influence on campus) while the rest of the campus is not growing. At the University of California these concerns have been recognized to the extent that a major academic planning criterion is the vaguely defined notion of campus "academic balance" (*University of California*, 1974; *University of California*, 1975).

Accreditation. In most professional fields there exist bodies, usually outside the academic world (often they are professional associations), that accredit academic programs in the field. The procedures are generally sanctioned in some way or other by governments occasionally even run by governments (Harcleroad, 1980). Their ostensible purpose is to protect students and the ultimate consumers of professional services from inferior treatment that might be provided by graduates of inadequate educational programs.

The rapid growth of professional education has contributed to a climate of controversy surrounding accreditation and its consequences and effectiveness (Jacobson, 1980; Orlans, 1975). Since it is difficult to measure the qualitative results of educational processes, accreditation standards typically focus on inputs (Green, 1981; Lawrence & Green, 1980), which are believed to be related to quality of results (Lawrence & Green, 1980). The standards and the people who apply them also tend to use widely respected programs as models in their evaluations (Green, 1981; Harcleroad, 1980). This is particularly troublesome in those fields where no standardized curriculum has been generally accepted (e.g., education). Thus, new approaches tend to be downgraded, not because they have been shown to be ineffective but because they differ from approaches adopted by "flagship" programs, even though the accepted standards have not been shown to be the only route to success. For example, use of part-time faculty, extensive emphasis on practice rather than theory, and attempts to reduce educational costs by shortening and streamlining programs tend to be looked upon with disfavor by accrediting groups. Some say that the inevitable rigidities in the accreditation process have also made it difficult for some quality programs to expand (Jacobson, 1979).

Other issues of some concern may include the infringement of accreditation on academic autonomy by forcing schools to use resources in ways that may not make the most sense academically, and the use of accreditation by school officials to pressure campus administrators to allocate money to them that they would not otherwise get.

Finally, government agencies and others are increasingly expressing doubts that accrediting agencies are fully independent of the institutions they accredit and sufficiently willing to render discriminating and critical judgments (Jacobson, 1980; Watkins, 1980b).

Perhaps the most controversial issue in regard to accreditation is directly related to the rapid growth of demand for professional education. The sudden surge of student demand and the limited response of many of the established institutions has led to a proliferation of new programs of, some would say, questionable quality in certain professional fields. Many institutions have established branch locations, distant from the main campus, that cater to employed people seeking to upgrade their credentials. Some independent professional schools have been established offering degree programs in one area only, usually law or clinical psychology, without benefit of any university affiliation. In many cases such "nontraditional" programs are staffed largely by part-time faculty.

Some established institutions and traditional educators, including some in government agencies, have questioned the quality of the training provided by such programs, and there is considerable controversy about how to evaluate them for accreditation purposes. Their defenders claim that at least many of the programs are innovative and responsive to genuine student needs. They point to the market test that the programs must pass to survive, and they claim that much of the opposition is grounded in the established programs' fear of competition. Many supporters of the nontraditional programs feel that the traditionalists have an unfair dominance over the accreditation process itself. Hanging over all this wrangling is an apparently growing impatience with it on the part of the federal and some state governments. There are some signs that the historic degree of government-sanctioned self-regulation professional education has enjoyed in the United States may be in jeopardy (Harcleroad & Dickey, 1975). This potential threat to the autonomy of professional education is no doubt related to a broader suspicion of the effectiveness and "public interestedness" of self-regulation of the professions themselves. Among other criticisms of them, many of the professions in recent years have been accused of limiting their own numbers in order to protect their incomes (First, 1979; Freeman, 1976). Presumably this is accomplished in part by influence over the accreditation process.

Selectivity. An area of great current concern in many professional schools today—particularly in the leading universities' schools of law, business, and the several health professions—is the set of issues related to selectivity. The pools of excess qualified applicants enjoyed by many professional schools give them the opportunity, and the burden, of deciding whom to educate for privileged roles in society.

Most colleges and universities have, to a greater or lesser extent, sought to diversify their student bodies by including more women and members of minority groups. Responding to a political mandate dating back to the 1960s, the federal government has encouraged and monitored these "affirmative action" efforts. Some progress has undeniably been made, particularly in regard to women. According to a new report by the National Center for Education Statistics, the number of first professional degrees awarded to women in 1979 was ten times the number awarded in 1969. For example, "fields such as medicine,

law, and dentistry showed a rise in the number of degrees awarded to women from 1,612 in 1968 to 16,313 at the end of 1979" (Project on the Status and Education of Women, 1981, p. 10). Data from the Association of American Law Schools and the Association of American Medical Colleges show increased trends in enrollments by blacks, Chicanos, Puerto Ricans, and American Indians in law and medical schools to the mid-1970s with little change since. For example, 2.7 percent of the total first-year enrollments in medical schools were black in 1968/69 as compared with 7.5 percent in 1973/74 and 5.7 percent in 1980/81 (Table 2). Six-tenths of 1 percent of the total law school enrollment in 1969/70 were Chicano, increasing to 1.2 percent in 1973/74 and remaining relatively stable since then (Table 3).

In any case, government policies in this area have inevitably been controversial, with some arguing that the government has not pushed the institutions hard enough and others, including many educators, saying that government pressures on universities are too severe and have serious side effects (Bennett & Eastland, 1978; Glazer, 1978). The professional schools have been at the center of these controversies in recent years, because they are seen as offering the most desirable educational opportunities for previously disadvantaged groups.

An important turning point was reached in 1978 with regard to the affirmative action issue when the United States Supreme Court ruled in the now-famous *Bakke* decision that institutions could not reserve a specific number of places for students solely on the basis of their race or ethnic status (Astin, Fuller, & Green, 1978). To date the decision has generally been interpreted to permit "race-conscious" admissions procedures that take minority status positively into account, as long as no ethnic quotas are used (Van Alstyne, 1978; McCormack, 1978). However, litigation over the admissions policies of particular schools continues (e.g., over the weighting of the ethnic factor) and will no doubt continue for years to come.

The debate over how scarce, coveted places in professional schools will be rationed will be a major issue for the schools as long as the opportunities they offer are in great demand. Some schools are experimenting with procedures that seek to take into account factors, other than test scores and grades, that are presumed to be related to future professional effectiveness (Fuller, McNamara, & Green, 1978; Furniss, 1979). For example, admission requirements may be expanded to include evidence of past and potential personal development and of interpersonal skills considered essential for the successful delivery of services to clients. But these other factors tend to be hard to measure reliably and their relationship to future effectiveness difficult to establish. Moreover, they do not necessarily increase the intake of minorities (Furniss, 1979).

Many professional schools are finding the effort to recruit qualified minority students increasingly expensive and frustrating. The very limited stock of such students is sought by many schools, with the result that their "price"

TABLE 2. *Trends in first-year medical school enrollments, 1968–1981*

Year	Total first-year enrollment	Percentage of total first-year enrollment accounted for by			
		Blacks	Chicanos	Puerto Ricans	American Indians
1968/69	9,863	2.7	.2	.03	.03
1969/70	10,401	4.3	.4	.1	.05
1970/71	11,348	6.2	.6	.2	.1
1971/72	12,361	7.2	1.0	.3	.2
1972/73	13,726	6.4	1.1	.3	.2
1973/74	14,185	7.5	1.2	.4	.3
1974/75	14,963	6.5	1.4	.4	.5
1975/76	15,351	5.9	1.4	.5	.4
1976/77	15,667	6.0	1.5	.5	.3
1977/78	16,134	6.0	1.3	1.4[a]	.3
1978/79	16,620	5.8	1.5	1.6	.3
1979/80	17,014	5.7	1.5	1.9	.3
1980/81	17,204	5.7	1.4	1.8	.4

[a] For this year and beyond, the Puerto Rican group includes mainland and island Puerto Ricans.

SOURCES OF DATA: American Medical Association, 1971–1981; Odegard, 1977, p. 30.

(the financial aid offers they receive) is bid up to quite high relative levels (Furniss, 1979). Unfortunately, this expensive competition does nothing to increase the pool of qualified minority candidates, which is the only way in the end to increase the number of minority professionals. This latter problem is partly a function of the widely heralded decline in educational standards and proficiency throughout the education system, and to that extent is particularly difficult to combat. Indeed, one of the major challenges to professional and other graduate schools in the eighties will be to maintain the quality of their product in the face of poorer-quality "inputs." Most professional schools should have, for some time at least, the advantage of being able to choose their students from a large pool of applicants.

Educational Issues. In general, professional education in the 1970s continued to move, as it has for decades, in the direction of increased scientific content (Glazer, 1974). The university base of most professional schools strongly encourages this trend, because the academic culture val-

TABLE 3. *Trends in total law school enrollments, 1969–1980*

Year	Total enrollment	Percentage of total enrollment accounted for by			
		Blacks	Chicanos	Puerto Ricans[1]	American Indians
1969/70	68,386	3.1	.6	.1	.1
1970/71	82,041	—	—	—	—
1971/72	93,118	4.0	.9	.1	.2
1972/73	101,664	4.4	1.0	.1	.2
1973/74	106,102	4.5	1.2	.2	.2
1974/75	110,713	4.5	1.2	.2	.2
1975/76	116,991	4.4	1.1	.3	.2
1976/77	117,451	4.7	1.3	.3	.2
1977/78	118,557	4.5	1.2	.3	.3
1978/79	121,606	4.4	1.2	.4	.3
1979/80	122,860	4.3	1.3	.4	.3

[1] Puerto Rican students enrolled in ABA approved schools located in Puerto Rico are not included in these statistics.

SOURCE OF DATA: American Bar Association, 1979, pp. 60, 61, and 63.

ues scientific knowledge most highly and rewards faculty for achieving advanced research degrees and publishing scientifically oriented research.

Most of the health professions schools, except perhaps nursing, had gone a long way in this direction before 1970. During the seventies, however, there were clear movements (in general, continuing long-term trends in the same direction) toward a more science-based curriculum and body of knowledge in nursing (Fields, 1980), management, and public administration. Even in law schools there has been a noticeable growth in interest in scientific knowledge and research in fields related to the law, such as criminology, psychology, sociology, and economics.

Probably the influence of practically minded students and practitioners and their associations would in any case prevent any complete "academization" of professional education (Glazer, 1974). But the shortage of academic (as opposed to practitioner) faculty to staff many professional schools, and unusual student and community pressures that began in the 1960s, have no doubt slowed the trend. Indeed, one of the more significant developments in professional education over the last ten to fifteen years—a development that would seem to run counter to the trend toward increased academization—has been the new emphasis on "clinical work" for students in professional schools outside the health professions. The best example is probably found in the law schools, most of which have now set up fairly extensive legal practice clinics and trial work courses for advanced students. But analogous attempts to provide both relevant experiences for students and service to the community have taken root in schools of business and the new public policy schools. Many business schools now offer courses that are essentially management consulting practicums, where students' clients are sometimes nonprofit or government organizations (UCLA Graduate School of Management, 1980). The public policy schools often require similar field work projects of students, and also typically include a summer "apprenticeship" period as part of the professional degree program (Sloan Foundation, 1976). Of course, in schools of education and social work a supervised practicum has long been part of the professional degree program (Morehead, 1973).

Although such supervised apprenticeship experiences no doubt represent a creative response to the inevitable tension between the academic and the practice-oriented sides of professional education, there remains the danger that these programs will lose status and thus attention within the schools (Glazer, 1974). The challenge for the schools is to ensure that the full-time faculty take an interest in these activities and attempt to integrate them seriously into their teaching and research.

Another long-standing but now perhaps more salient educational issue is the role of the liberal arts and sciences vis-à-vis professional education. The friction on many campuses over the relative size and influence of professional schools has been mentioned. There is also concern among many faculty and administrators, including many in the professional schools, about the content of the education of professional students. It is a widely shared view that the goals of professional education are best served if students take broad programs and liberal arts majors as undergraduates, pursuing professionally oriented programs only at the graduate level (Lieb, 1980). But there is also powerful student (and parental) pressure to "professionalize" early in order, they think, to get a jump on the competition. If a campus does not offer an undergraduate business major, for example, students demand undergraduate courses in the field, fill up their programs with courses and majors they believe to be related (e.g., economics), and participate in "pre-M.B.A." clubs.

Many professional school faculty believe that such premature specialization does not serve the students' or society's ultimate interests well. In addition, there has been growing concern in recent years that professional degree programs, whether at the undergraduate or the graduate level, are too narrowly focused. As a result there have been some efforts to broaden professional school curricula to give more attention to topics that have generally been within the province of the humanities or social sciences. For example, medical schools over the last ten years have developed courses in such areas as medical ethics and health economics. Business schools have developed courses and programs in business-government relations and broader business and society interactions. Indeed, many business schools have broadened their purview considerably and now call themselves schools of generic "management" or "administration." Thus, to some degree at least, they have recognized a need to broaden their curricula to cover topics quite different from the traditional business skill and technique courses. Schools of public administration and policy often offer courses that deal with ethical concerns in public policy. Many law schools also offer professional ethics courses. In the past few years many professional schools, like other parts of the educational system, have become aware of the communication difficulties of many of their students and are moving to offer courses in writing and communication skills.

So far the moves in this direction have been modest in most professional schools, and it seems likely that more can be expected in the future. Here perhaps may lie a partial remedy for the friction between the liberal arts faculty, who are threatened by declining enrollments, and the professional faculties, who are often swamped by student numbers and concerned about the the breadth of the education their students are getting. A promising area for future development that deserves administrative and professional faculty support is the building of bridges to the arts and sciences departments. This might be healthful for scholarship in both areas as well as for the economies of the arts and sciences departments and the education of professional students.

Continuing Education. Continuing education for professionals has always been encouraged in our society both by professional schools, which have provided it, and by employers of professionals, who have often rewarded it with promotions or salary increases. Indeed in some fields (business, engineering, education, and formerly law) there has not traditionally been a requirement that an individual hold a professional degree in order to practice the profession. Thus continuing education represented a certification that knowledge was possessed and/or had been updated.

Interest in continuing professional education has increased substantially in recent years. There are many reasons for this surge of interest. The increasing rate of change in the knowledge base of the professions has required that professionals be constantly aware of the most up-to-date information in their fields; the consumerism and broader antiauthority movements in society have affected people's attitudes toward the professions and have increased the demand for assurance that professionals are competent; and university interest in continuing education has increased in the face of impending enrollment declines. The last is true even though much of the continuing education for the professions still takes place outside the university setting (Maxwell, 1980). The interests of university-based professional schools in this area will almost certainly grow substantially in the 1980s. The combination of these developments has led to government-mandated continuing education in many professions and in many states (Watkins, 1980a).

Although the theory behind continuing education for professionals seems plausible, more research is needed to determine the effectiveness of such programs and to identify circumstances in which benefits of continuing professional education exceed the costs of its provision. Some say the quality of the education received is not worth the time and the money required (Watkins, 1979). It is a reasonable hypothesis that a substantial portion of continuing education for professionals is a waste of resources or at least is inappropriately targeted. It has not been clearly shown that continuing education for professionals protects the public from incompetent practitioners, which is ostensibly one of its primary purposes. But it has been and continues to be the most convenient method of seeking to satisfy the public interest in having qualified practicing professionals.

Conclusions. In the 1980s many professional education programs, unlike most academic departments in American universities, find themselves in generally prosperous times and dealing with surplus demand. In that context, future enrollment trends will have to be considered in light of the limits to growth: faculty shortages, increasing costs, limited budgets, and internal campus conflicts. Accreditation is bound to get increasing attention, as will access issues for minorities and women. Long-standing curricular issues will also be of continuing concern: the conflict between practical and academic emphases and particularly the role of part-time faculty. The direction of continuing education for professionals will also require careful attention. Yet those involved in professions education have a luxury available to few of their university colleagues: they can make their decisions without the pressing need to cope with retrenchment.

William Zumeta
Lewis C. Solmon

See also Accreditation; Adult Education; Equity Issues in Education; Graduate Education; Licensing and Certification.

REFERENCES

American Bar Association. *A Review of Legal Education in the United States, Fall 1979.* Chicago: The Association, 1979.

American Medical Association. Medical education in the United States (Annual Report). *Journal of the American Medical Association,* 1971–1981.

Anderson, G. L. *Trends in Education for the Professions* (AAHE/ERIC/Higher Education Research Report No. 7) Washington, D.C.: American Association for Higher Education, 1974. (ERIC Document Reproduction Service No. ED 096 889)

Astin, A. W.; Fuller, B.; & Green, K. C. *Admitting and Assisting Students after "Bakke."* San Francisco: Jossey-Bass, 1978.

Bennett, W. J., & Eastland T. Why *Bakke* won't end reverse discrimination: 1. *Commentary,* September 1978, pp. 29–35.

Chambers, D. W. Faculty evaluation: Review of the literature most pertinent to dental education. *Journal of Dental Education,* June 1977, *41,* 290–299.

Derbarics, C. Ford passes sweeping tuition hike: Undergrad increases $700: Med school jumps $2,200. *G. W. Hatchet,* January 19, 1981, *77.*

Fields, C. M. Nurses' Association backs flexible B.A. programs. *Chronicle of Higher Education,* June 23, 1980, *20.*

First, H. Competition in the legal education industry (11): An antitrust analysis. *New York University Law Review,* December 1979, *54.*

Freeman, R. B. *The Overeducated American.* New York: Academic Press, 1976.

Fuller, B.; McNamara, P. P.; & Green, K. C. Alternative admissions procedures. In A. W. Astin, B. Fuller, & K. C. Green, *Admitting and Assisting Students after "Bakke."* San Francisco: Jossey-Bass, 1978.

Furniss, W. T. Professional education after *Bakke. Educational Record,* Spring 1979, *60.*

Glazer, N. The schools of the minor professions. *Minerva,* 1974, *12,* 346–364.

Glazer, N. Why *Bakke* won't end reverse discrimination: 2. *Commentary,* September 1978, pp. 36–41.

Green, K. C. *Accreditation and Quality: Distinguishing Characteristics versus Minimum Requirements.* Los Angeles: Higher Education Research Institute, 1981.

Harcleroad, F. F. *Accreditation: History, Process, and Problems* (AAHE-ERIC/Higher Education Research Report No. 6). Washington, D.C.: American Association for Higher Education, 1980.

Harcleroad, F. F., & Dickey, F. G. *Educational Auditing and Voluntary Institutional Accreditation* (ERIC/Higher Education Research Report No. 1). Washington, D.C.: American Association for Higher Education, 1975. (ERIC Document Reproduction Service No. ED 102 919)

Hook, J. Congress passes $48 billion bill extending college-aid programs. *Chronicle of Higher Education,* October 6, 1980, *21.*

Jacobson, R. L. Business-School accrediting unit reverses itself on accounting, will permit separate standards. *Chronicle of Higher Education*, June 25, 1979, *28*.

Jacobson, R. L. States dissatisfied with voluntary efforts, weigh bigger role. *Chronicle of Higher Education*, June 16, 1980, *20*.

Jacobson, R. L. Notes on . . . law schools. *Chronicle of Higher Education*, February 17, 1981, *21*. (a)

Jacobson, R. L. Salaries for new teachers alarm business schools. *Chronicle of Higher Education*, January 19, 1981, *21*. (b)

Klitgaard, R. E. *The Decline of the Best? An Analysis of the Relationships between Declining Enrollments, Ph.D. Production, and Research* (No. 65D). Cambridge, Mass.: Harvard University, John Fitzgerald Kennedy School of Government, May 1979.

Langway, L., with Weathers, D.; Walters, S.; & Hager, M. At long last motherhood. *Newsweek*, March 16, 1981, pp. 86–86d.

Lawrence, J. K., & Green, K. C. *A Question of Quality: The Higher Education Rating Game* (AAHE-ERIC/Higher Education Research Report No. 5). Washington, D.C.: American Association of Higher Education, 1980.

Lieb, I. C. Professional education: Who's in charge? *Chronicle of Higher Education*, July 7, 1980, *20*.

Maxwell, J. F. Who will provide continuing education for professionals? *American Association for Higher Education Bulletin*, December 1980, *33*.

McCormack, W. (Ed.). *The "Bakke" Decision: Implications for Higher Education Admissions*. Washington, D.C.: American Council on Education, Association of American Law Schools, 1978.

Morehead, J. Professional education: The theory-practice issue reconsidered. *College Student Journal*, 1973, *7*.

National Center for Education Statistics. *Projections of Education Statistics to 1986–87*. Washington, D.C.: U.S. Government Printing Office, 1978.

National Research Council. *Summary Report 1975: Doctorate Recipients from United States Universities*. Washington, D.C.: National Academy of Sciences, 1976.

National Research Council. *Personnel Needs and Training for Biomedical and Behavioral Research*. Washington, D.C.: National Academy of Sciences, 1978.

National Research Council. *Summary Report 1978: Doctorate Recipients from United States Universities*. Washington, D.C.: National Academy of Sciences, 1979.

Nyre, G. F., & Reilly, K. C. *Professional Education in the Eighties: Challenges and Responses* (AAHE-ERIC/Higher Education Research Report No. 8). Washington, D.C.: American Association for Higher Education, 1979 (ERIC Document Reproduction Service No. ED 179 187)

Odegard, C. E. *Minorities in Medicine: From Receptive Passivity to Positive Action, 1966–76*. New York: Josiah Macy, Jr. Foundation, 1977.

Orlans, H., with Levin, N. J.; Bauer, E.; & Arnstein, G. E. *Private Accreditation and Public Eligibility* (National Academy of Public Administration Foundation). Lexington, Mass.: Lexington Books, Heath, 1975.

Project on the Status and Education of Women. On campus with women. *Newsletter of Association of American Colleges*, No. 29, Winter 1981, p. 10.

Sloan Foundation. *Education for the Public Service: Amelia Island Seminar*. Unpublished report of conference held at Amelia Island, Fla., June 1976.

University of California, Los Angeles, Graduate School of Management. *Management Field Studies*. Los Angeles: UCLA Graduate School of Management, 1980.

University of California Academic Plan, 1974–1978. Berkeley: University of California Systemwide Administration, 1974.

University of California Academic Plan, Phase II: Campus Academic Plans. Vol. 1. *The University-wide Perspective*. Berkeley: University of California Systemwide Administration, 1975.

U.S. Department of Health, Education, and Welfare, Office of Education. *Earned Degrees Conferred: 1965/66*. Washington, D.C.: U.S. Government Printing Office, 1968.

U.S. Department of Health, Education, and Welfare, U.S. National Center for Education Statistics. *Earned Degrees Conferred: 1970/71*. Washington, D.C.: U.S. Government Printing Office, 1973.

U.S. Department of Health, Education, and Welfare, U.S. National Center for Education Statistics. *Earned Degrees Conferred: 1974/75*. Washington, D.C.: U.S. Government Printing Office, 1977.

U.S. Department of Health, Education, and Welfare, U.S. National Center for Education Statistics. *Earned Degrees Conferred: 1977/78*. Washington, D.C.: U.S. Department of Education, 1980.

Van Alstyne W. A preliminary report on the Bakke case. *American Association of University Professors Bulletin*, December 1978, *64*.

Watkins, B. T. Continuing education for professionals. *Chronicle of Higher Education*, September 4, 1979, *19*.

Watkins, B. T. Move to require continuing education for professionals appears to be stalling. *Chronicle of Higher Education*, November 17, 1980, *21*. (a)

Watkins, B. T. Report criticizes teacher-education accreditation. *Chronicle of Higher Education*, November 24, 1980, *21*. (b)

Watkins, B. T. A "critical" shortage of schoolteachers likely by 1985, education deans warn. *Chronicle of Higher Education*, March 23, 1981, *22*.

PROGRAMMED INSTRUCTION

See Computer-Based Education; Individualized Systems of Instruction; Instruction Processes; Systems Design in Instruction.

PROMOTION POLICY

If one could have questioned a nineteenth-century rural school student about his or her grade in school, the answer might well have been "I'm in the three syllables," or "I'm in *McGuffey's Fifth Reader*," or "I sit in the third row." It was not unusual, in the nineteenth century, for students of greatly varying ages to be seated together and instructed in the common content they were to master. For these students the concept of grade was an unusual one. Yet if one could have questioned early-twentieth-century students in the same fashion, their answer would have been "I'm in the first grade," or "I'm in grade 7," or "I'm in 1-B." By this time, the United States was no longer an agrarian society, but had become an urbanized, industrialized nation, and as the society changed so did the schools. As one historian of the period points out, the schools had become bureaucratized; they had become graded (Katz, 1971). Among a number of alternatives, educational reformers of the progressive era settled upon the graded school with students grouped by age, starting at age 5 in kindergarten and progressing annually until they finished grade 12. And further, unlike the common school of the nineteenth century, the twentieth-century school is compulsory. This graded, compulsory school has become the predominant model for school organization today.

The question of promotion policy, however, should not be seen as necessarily universal in nature; that is, the question of student promotion is bound by the history and current organization of our schools. Promotion policy must not consider only the question of who should be promoted and when, although it surely deals with this central issue; it must also deal with the question of the very purposes of public education. Over seventy years ago, a pioneering work on retention in school raised this issue of purposes: "What is the function of our common schools?" The writer elaborated: "If it is to sort out the best of the pupils and prepare them for further education in higher schools, then the most rigorous system, with the severest course of study and the lowest percentage of promotions and the highest percentage of nonpromotions is the best system. But if the function of the common school is, as this author believes, to furnish an elementary education to the maximum number of children, then *other things being equal* that school is best which regularly promotes and finally graduates the largest percentage of its pupils" (Ayres, 1909, p. 199).

This statement was published half a century ago, but the issue of promotion, including concern about the policy called "social promotion," is still current. Indeed, it may well stand as a proxy for many other social concerns. For example, a large segment of the public today seems to believe that too many children are promoted, regardless of academic achievement, simply on the basis of their age and for social reasons. Those who hold this consensus view social promotion negatively and appear to long for an earlier era when higher standards were in effect. There is currently a national movement for a return to promotion based exclusively upon achievement. This movement is motivated by a drop in standardized test scores, by a conservative national mood, and by a belief that there is a rising tide of social promotions.

An analysis of Ayres's data (1909) as well as of more contemporary data suggests that American education has typically practiced both promotion and nonpromotion. Failure rates of 10 to 15 percent, which were regularly reported early in the century, have been dropping over the intervening years. Contemporary analyses by the National Center for Educational Statistics (Grant & Eiten, 1980) show a steady increase in the number of fifth-graders who are graduated by elementary schools and, in turn,

graduate from high school. Whereas 30 percent of fifth-graders in 1924 completed high school, almost 75 percent of fifth-grade students entering in 1969 were graduated by 1977. Although this is a remarkable increase in the number of fifth-graders who finish high school, the point here is that more than 25 percent, even today, do not graduate. This 25 percent cannot be considered a population that has been nonpromoted in the sense of being held in grade. They have, indeed, dropped out. In the heat of the promotion versus nonpromotion debate, the dropout rate is often not considered. Nevertheless, the issue of whether these increasing rates of promotion are good or bad or whether a 25 percent dropout rate is desirable will not be decided by the numbers themselves. One report indicates that public schools currently do not promote more than 1 million young people; and the National Center for Educational Statistics bases its retention figures on fifth-grade enrollment, because the number of children who spend more than one year in the same grade in the early elementary grades inflate enrollment figures for those grades.

The history of promotion in this century has indeed been one of increasing number: more children are being promoted. But the question of what the figures mean remains, and the answer depends on one's vision of the purpose of schooling. At its root, the promotion versus nonpromotion debate is an ethical one. Policies relating to social promotion and its effects can be informed by studies and statistics, but not made by them. Policy makers are responsible for evaluating not only the policies themselves but also the effects of these policies.

Student Promotion Policies. It is useful to consider some general policies relating to student promotion. Thirty years ago, in the *Encyclopedia of Educational Research,* Sumption and Phillips (1950) identified three policies governing promotion. Although they did not cover all possibilities, they were helpful in framing the research findings on the subject. The first, identified as the "grade standards" policy, may be considered the most traditional. It interprets the curriculum as a series of graded activities, with promotion based exclusively upon successful achievement of each successive grade's standards. Students progress or do not progress according to their achievement. A second policy, identified as "continuous promotion," moves students forward exclusively upon the basis of chronological age. Students entering kindergarten at age 5 can be expected to be found in grades 1, 2, and 3 at ages 6, 7, and 8. Although there is controversy relating to all policies of student promotion, this policy has most recently drawn the public's attention when identified as "social promotion." Public outcry over declining Scholastic Aptitude Test (SAT) scores and a general concern over lax standards in many areas of public life have resulted in considerable pressure on school personnel to replace this policy with one closer to the grade standards policy. One contemporary response to this demand has been the competency-based curriculum movement. A third policy for student promotion is "continuous progress." Factors of academic, social, psychological, and physical development are considered, and promotion becomes a decision about each individual student. Organizational and curriculum responses to this policy include individualized instruction, individually guided instruction, individually prescribed instruction, and nongraded schools.

The studies of promotion that follow parallel these three policies, asking questions relating to student social development and academic achievement. The research review is presented in some detail, because policy makers, in order to develop informed judgments, must have more than a mere summary of research findings with which to work. They need to know not only what was found but also how it was found and with what degree of confidence they can generalize from these findings to policy. As Jackson (1975) noted, an extensive body of literature on promotion and retention is available; however, much of it is problematic. Recognition of this latter point is of critical importance to policy makers. If research studies have neither asked the same questions as policy makers nor answered them with cogency, then care must be taken in using the studies in rational planning activities. Specifically, when presented with numerous options, policy makers need information that includes more than separate descriptions of students who have been retained or promoted. Policy makers need data on the *differential effects* of promotion and nonpromotion.

When considering separate descriptive studies, i.e., studies relating student academic achievement or social adjustment to promotion or nonpromotion, one needs to know the direction of the influence. For example, Did the poor behavior lead to nonpromotion, or was the behavior itself a consequence of the student being retained? Was the student's poor academic development the reason for grade repetition, or did the repetition itself influence the student's academic achievement? Without answers to these questions, it is impossible to determine whether the studies analyzed the effects of nonpromotion or simply described nonpromoted pupils. For policy making, the former is needed and the latter is insufficient. And, in studies that directly compare promoted and nonpromoted students, that is, studies that search for differential effects, one needs to know if the students were similar enough to assume that only the treatment—promotion or nonpromotion—varied.

Self-concept Correlates of Promotion and Nonpromotion. For more than fifty years, researchers have attempted to identify the influence of promotion or nonpromotion on the social or emotional characteristics of students. Most of the studies have considered the influence of the grade standards policy. That is, given a graded school, what are the consequences of promotion or nonpromotion? Critical summaries of a number of these studies follow.

An early study by McElwee (1932) sought to compare the degree to which desirable and undesirable character traits were possessed by groups of New York City second-graders, third-graders, and fourth-graders who had been retained in grade, had been regularly promoted, or had advanced in grade ahead of their peers. The children's teachers evaluated the students on a scale of seven positive and seven negative characteristics, ranging from "gets along well with others" to "listless." McElwee found that all groups possessed more desirable than undesirable traits and that accelerated students were judged as having more desirable traits than their regularly promoted peers, who in turn received higher scores than the nonpromoted students. The inverse was found to be true for undesirable traits, with the nonpromoted judged as most disobedient. Although the study found that some negative traits were associated with nonpromotion, it did not match the students in any characteristic except grade placement. It is therefore impossible to determine whether the negative traits led teachers to retain the students or whether retained students developed undesirable traits in response to their position.

In 1933 Farley, Frey, and Garland also reported an attempt to identify the personal qualities associated with promotion and retention. Their search was similar to McElwee's, but all pupils were matched for age. Twelve-year-olds in grades 4 through 8 in Newark, New Jersey, were selected for the study. Information was gathered on their mental ability, academic achievement, health, social status, attendance, and character traits. The data were then divided in terms of the grade placement of the 12-year-olds, and correlations between the ratings and grades were developed. High positive correlations were found between achievement, ability, and grade placement. This is not surprising, since the brighter and more capable students, in a rational system of grade standards, should be found in the advanced grades. Interestingly, the study also revealed that boys are more likely to be improperly placed below their achievement-indicated grade level than are girls. As with the McElwee study, the direction of the influence between grade placement and personal qualities was impossible to determine.

In these two studies, then, researchers found a correlation between nonpromotion and what might be called "poor character," but they were unable to determine whether negative character ratings led to nonpromotion or vice versa. The studies could not make this determination partly because of limitations in the research design; that is, students who were matched for such characteristics as age, sex, years in school, and social class were not randomly passed or failed. Although legitimate ethical constraints have kept studies that randomly assign students to promotion or nonpromotion from being undertaken, one such experimental study was reported by Cook and Kearney (1940).

In the winter of 1938, principals in St. Paul, Minnesota, identified pupils in grades 1B through 8A who were expected to fail at half-year. Pairs of students were matched in each grade for age, intelligence, achievement, and personality traits. One member of each pair was promoted and one was not. The researchers hypothesized that students who are retained have more time to make satisfactory personality adjustments than those promoted. The findings were statistically insignificant, and the hypothesis was rejected; nonpromotion did not seem to lead to improved personality measures. Achievement comparisons were also made between the groups in reading, arithmetic, and English, with sixteen differences favoring the promoted group and sixteen favoring the nonpromoted. None of these differences was found to be significant. "The crucial issue," the authors concluded, "appears to be not whether the slow learning pupil is passed or failed, but how adequately his needs are being met" (Cook & Kearney, p. 49).

Anfinson (1941) presented a study of junior high school students that attempted to determine whether nonpromoted students are less well adjusted than their peers. Pairs of students were matched for attendance, chronological age, intelligence, and socioeconomic status, and were given two personality inventories. One member of each pair had failed a grade, or portion of a grade, and the other member had not. The author found that although promoted students seemed better adjusted than repeaters to the school's curriculum, the two groups did not differ appreciably in other ways. Retention, the study concluded, does not lead to student maladjustment. It should be noted that this study was methodologically different from that of Cook and Kearney, in which students were chosen, matched, *and then* promoted or nonpromoted. In this study, students were matched and effects were sought *after* the promotion of nonpromotion had taken place. A limitation of this type of study is that one does not know the qualities of the students before they are promoted or retained. It is a study of characteristics of promoted and retained pupils, not of promotion policy.

A study directed by Sandin (1944) also dealt with the issue of adjustment and came to conclusions different from those of Anfinson. Sandin compared children who had failed at least once in the first eight grades with their peers who had been promoted. Except for first-graders, the study found that nonpromoted students were not perceived as appropriate seatmates by their peers, and the former often chose companions from higher grades. Repeaters were also given significantly more ratings by their classmates as being unfriendly, cruel, or bullying, and teachers, too, gave them lower ratings on social and personal characteristics. By the time the nonpromoted pupils had been in school for a number of years, they eagerly anticipated the age at which they could leave.

In light of these findings, it is important to recognize that Sandin did not match individual promoted and nonpromoted students; rather, they were groups of students who had or had not failed a grade. There is no evidence that if a matched population of failing pupils had been promoted, they would have done significantly better by comparison. Some might propose that these students, even if promoted, would have been as unhappy in school as their nonpromoted peers, that the factor of importance was not promotion at all. Indeed, Sandin himself suggested that a study identifying matched groups of promoted and nonpromoted pupils was needed, and Goodlad (1954) reported on such an investigation.

Goodlad (1954) selected two groups of fifty boys and girls, matched for mental age, chronological age, and achievement. The first group was composed of nonpromoted first-graders, and the second of their promoted peers. At the end of the second year of schooling, the groups were compared in terms of social and personal development. Students' self-perception of adjustment was determined by scores on a self-rating instrument; peer ratings were determined by responses to sociometric questions; and teacher ratings were determined by responses on a pupil behavior rating scale. Neither the pupils' self-ratings nor the teachers' behavior ratings showed significant differences between the groups. The sociometric data did, however, reveal significant differences; the general effect of nonpromotion on the group was negative. Goodlad concluded, "The whole picture of sociometric change over the school year was one of decline in desirable adjustment for the nonpromoted children and improvement for the promoted children" (p. 321). Policy makers should pay particular attention to the level of analysis in this study: it is at the group level. The findings of this research should be seen as relevant to policy questions concerning not individuals but groups of students to be promoted or retained in grade. The findings relate nonpromotion to group effects, not to individuals. Further, one must note, as with other studies, that although the retained pupils were similar to those promoted, they were different in one major characteristic: they were judged as failures and were not promoted.

Morrison and Perry (1956) supported Goodlad's findings that pupils above the typical age in classes were perceived as less popular than their regularly promoted peers. In their studies, fourth-graders through eighth-graders were asked to complete sociometric questionnaires. In one study, students were asked to choose three friends each: for play, for committee work, and for a party at home. In the second study, students were asked to identify one student with whom they would like to sit. Ranked lists of students based on the number of times they were chosen were created for each study. The lists were divided into quarters, by class, with the highest quarter designated as first and the lowest as fourth. The authors were able to determine the sociometric status of the older students in each class as indicated by the quarter in which they were found. In Morrison's study, 86 percent of the students above the typical age were found below the sociometric median for their class; Perry reported that 90 percent of the older pupils were below this median. The authors concluded that students above the normal age in grade had, as a group, little chance for social acceptance and that nonpromotion had negative social consequences for them.

Findings such as these should be viewed with the understanding that "above normal age in grade" may be a proxy for other factors. Boys, for example, are less likely to be promoted than girls. That is, nonpromotion may not be the cause of social stigma; the school itself may be causing behavior in boys that initially leads to nonpromotion. A sensitive promotion policy has to consider not only promotion effects but also differential treatment by sex of pupils in the primary grades.

A number of more recent studies have continued to evaluate the relationship between nonpromotion and student self-concept. White and Howard (1973) administered a 100-item self-concept inventory to sixth-grade boys and girls from six school systems in North Carolina. The students were classified into groups based upon their having been promoted or held back. Forty-three boys and thirty girls had failed to be promoted at least once. The authors correlated nine subscales of the self-concept inventory with promotion and nonpromotion. A positive correlation was found between promotion on eight of the nine subscales. Conversely, as the number of grades the students failed increased, their self-concept measures declined; the authors found a high correlation between poor self-concept and grade failure. As with the studies of Morrison and Perry (1956), the data were collected after students had been either promoted or kept back, making it difficult to determine whether poor self-concepts influenced nonpromotion or vice versa. Similarly, the substantially larger number of nonpromoted boys may indicate the need for further analyses of the school environment rather than of the promotion policy alone.

Finlayson (1977) attempted to deal with some of the methodological questions raised above. He pointed out that a limitation of most studies attempting to identify the effect of nonpromotion on self-concept was that they were *post hoc* studies. That is, self-concept inventories were administered to pupils after they had moved through the repeated or nonrepeated grades and therefore the studies did not measure self-concept change over time. Finlayson sought to avoid this problem by studying groups of primary school children for a two-year period during which a self-concept inventory was administered on four occasions. Groups of promoted, borderline, and nonpromoted pupils were identified from a total sample of first-graders who had never previously failed a grade. Each group contained twenty-five students. It was anticipated that the self-concepts of the borderline and promoted pupils would remain constant, whereas the self-concepts of the nonpromoted pupils would decline. No attempt was made to match characteristics of promoted pupils with nonpromoted pupils; the promoted students were randomly sampled from the promoted first-graders. This lack of comparability between groups is a significant limitation, since it leaves the reader with essentially parallel pretest and posttest analyses of nonpromoted and promoted pupils. Further, the nonpromoted population is described only in terms of number. Policy makers need to consider other factors when attempting to determine *why* these students were not promoted. It is possible that they were less socially mature than their promoted peers or that they had learning difficulties, and these possibilities would make them a very different population than the promoted students. Although the study found that nonpromotion did not negatively influence self-concept, it could not present conclusions on the comparative influences of promotion and nonpromotion.

Achievement Correlates of Promotion and Nonpromotion. Research studies have also considered the relationship between promotion and achievement. As with the above adjustment studies, they have methodological limitations that must be recognized.

Keyes (1911) studied the achievement of approximately five thousand repeaters by comparing their performance before and after nonpromotion. He reported that 21 percent of the pupils did better after repeating, that 39 percent did worse, and that for 50 percent nonpromotion had no effect. The study did not compare these nonpromoted pupils with a matched population of their promoted peers and therefore does little to assist those needing information on the differential effects of promotion versus nonpromotion.

Klene and Branson (1929) reported the findings of an experimental study that did compare promotion and nonpromotion. The authors matched the mental age, chronological age, IQ, and grade placement of elementary school pupils who were expected to repeat a grade. The students were randomly assigned to nonpromotion or trial promotion. Neither the pupils nor their parents knew of the experiment, and it is very doubtful that such a methodology would be used today in the context of the ethical concerns manifested in human-subjects legislation. The experiment lasted for one semester, and the students were tested at the beginning and end of that semester. Although the study concluded that the promoted group showed greater academic progress than the repeaters, the findings were not statistically significant.

Arthur (1936) also attempted to study the effects of promotion and nonpromotion on academic achievement. At the end of a two-year period, 60 nonpromoted first graders were compared to 418 of their peers who had been promoted. The students were matched for mental age on tests administered at the beginning of first grade, and their reading scores were compared after they completed two years in school. Since there are no pretest reading data on these groups of students, the finding that the nonpromoted pupils learned no more in two years than did the promoted in one tells little about the differential effects of promotion and nonpromotion. Current statistical techniques would also call into question the report's claim that the nonpromoted pupils achieved 99.3 percent as much as did their promoted peers.

A study that compared pupil achievement before and after promotion and nonpromotion was reported by Coffield and Bloomers (1956). The research compared seventh-graders who had failed a grade with a matched sample who had been regularly promoted. However, the students were only matched on four subscales of the Iowa Test of Basic Skills, administered before and after the failed grade; they were not matched, for example, for age, socioeconomic status, or behavior. The differences between the groups, the fact that some were recommended for promotion and others were failed, make them so unlike that one can learn very little about the differential effects of promotion on achievement from this study. This limitation also calls into question the report's conclusion that the rigidity or leniency of the promotion policy did not appear to have any effect upon the general level of achievement of the seventh-graders.

A study that did search for the effects of strict and lenient promotion policies on *both* promoted and nonpromoted students was reported by Kowitz and Armstrong (1961). They compared student data from two schools in New York State that had divergent promotion policies. Longitudinal achievement data on individual students in each school were developed; the study then attempted to determine the relationship between the type of policy in effect in the school and achievement growth over time. The findings of the study—that strict promotion policy is positively related to increased achievement growth—are called into question by limitations in the research design. For example, an indicator of differential policy was identified as the percentage of retained pupils in each school. Although the percentage was higher in the supposedly "strict" school, there is no indication that its retained students were descriptively or statistically different than their counterparts in the "lenient" school. The study reported greater achievement increases in the strict school, but there was no theoretical basis offered for the relationship between rigidity of policies and achievement. The study compared achievement *increases* rather than *levels,* and since achievement levels of the students in the two schools were not compared the policy maker cannot conclude that the strict policy improved achievement. The evidence could be seen as supporting an alternative hypothesis, namely, that the strict standards initially depressed scores and that their measured increase was an indication of their eventual return to "normal" in spite of the stringent policy.

A study that also considered the influence of a rigid promotion policy was reported by Gaite (1969). The study attempted to determine if nonpromotion improves high school pupils' grades. Student grades were analyzed in all subject-matter areas, prior to nonpromotion and at the end of the repeated year, since students failing one subject area had to repeat all subjects. Although Gaite found statistically significant differences in some areas, he concluded that the amount of growth was not justified by the extra time spent in the grade. Policy makers should note that use of teachers' grades as the criterion in this study makes even these findings questionable; teachers may have considered other factors besides academic performance when

they submitted grades at the end of the repeated year. They probably knew that a second failure would increase either the dropout rate or the number of pupils who were significantly above typical age in the following year's classes, and neither of these is a desirable situation. For these reasons alone, the students' grades may have improved. The study was essentially a version of Keyes's research (1911). As a description solely of the effects of nonpromotion, it could not report on differential effects, and as indicated earlier, it is research of this type that policy makers need.

Conclusions. In summary, research findings on the differential social and academic effects of promotion and nonpromotion—when available—are at best equivocal. Educators advocating either the continuous promotion policy or the grade standards policy will *not* find significant support for their positions in the research literature. Yet current educational debate reflects a national dissatisfaction with the *presumed* ineffectiveness of the social promotion policy and an acceptance of the *presumed* effectiveness of a rigid grade standards policy. As a result of the scanty empirical evidence, promotion policy debates in the 1980s will be held not between competing data-based positions but between competing value positions. Supporters of continuous promotion will probably emphasize students' emotional and social needs, and supporters of grade standards will probably emphasize the value of academic achievement. And the values of the grade standards policy are currently on the ascent.

The emphasis upon grade standards was strengthened in the 1970s as a result of increased concern for accountability. By the early 1980s demand for educational accountability had developed into the "minimum competency" or "competency-based education" movement, and a majority of the states had mandated some form of minimum competency testing for promotion or graduation. In brief, the minimum competency movement assumes a publicly agreed-upon set of minimums for the public schools, with student achievement assessed through criterion-referenced rather than norm-referenced tests (Haney & Madaus, 1978). Students are passed or failed depending upon success or failure in acquisition of the set of minimums. Although this proposal seems reasonable and is supported by many, the movement has generated considerable controversy. One reviewer notes, "Minimal competency testing for high school graduation and grade-to-grade promotion continues to be one of the most explosive issues on the educational scene today" (Pilpho, 1977, p. i). The controversy focuses upon at least three issues: the definition of what is a competency; how one might specify what is a minimum; and whether competencies can be evaluated on a paper-and-pencil exam. As the movement reaches its maturity in the 1980s, the questions of how to deal with students who fail competency exams will have to be confronted along with the potential problem of a disproportionately high rate of failure among economically disadvantaged and culturally different students. It appears that each policy carries with it its own inherent contradictions, contradictions that eventually lead to its replacement. The social promotion policy, for example, paid too little attention to achievement and was replaced by the grade standards policy.

As the strengths and weaknesses of the competency-based education movement become clearer in the decade ahead, so, too, may the need for a new promotion policy. If public demand for grade standards results in an increased number of failing pupils, then the issue of what to do with these students, pedagogically, will have to be answered. To the extent that both the continuous promotion and grade standards policies are concerned primarily with exit gates, for example, promotion based upon age or achievement alone, they will not suffice in dealing with these new demands. It may be that a continuous progress policy that considers both grade standards *and* individual learning experiences will be required of educational planners. Ellinger (1965) suggested that such a policy is less interested in arbitrary standards, grade lines, or failure and promotion than in the optimum growth of each child and the continuity of learning. The policy permits very slow students to progress without being subjected to repetition or failure, and more able students to realize their potential instead of being held to unrealistically low standards. The academic and social adjustment effects of schooling will be dealt with by focusing upon the curricular experiences of the student. Factors that will influence these experiences include evaluation, teaching, and school organization. A recent report suggested that educational policy makers support the following positions: "(1) that student evaluation should be an integral part of instruction rather than an external reward or punishment for low achievement; (2) that evaluation and reporting systems should furnish feedback to help teachers improve learning and should be compatible with new approaches to the learning process; and (3) that school organization should be sufficiently flexible to promote continuous progress and to provide special resources and alternative programs for students who are not achieving rather than recycling them through the same grade" (Horacek, 1979, p. 34).

These three points can serve as a tentative set of general guidelines for action—as the beginning of a promotion policy. They will be little informed by research, since research to date has been found to be inconclusive. Policy will therefore be strongly influenced by values, but that is not to say *merely* by values. These values will be presented in the public forum, where their consequences will be discussed. They will have to be values that meet the current demand for academic achievement and the burgeoning demand for the provision of quality educational experiences for young people. And, embedded in this promotion policy, whatever form it may take, will be the response to Ayres's seventy-year-old question, "What is the function of our common schools?"

Steven Selden

See also Achievement Testing; Attendance Policy; Marking Systems; Truants and Dropouts.

REFERENCES

Anfinson, R. D. School progress and pupil adjustment. *Elementary School Journal*, 1941, *41*(6), 504–514.

Arthur, G. A study of the achievement of sixty grade one repeaters as compared with that of non-repeaters of the same age. *Journal of Experimental Education*, 1936, *5*, 203–205.

Ayres, L. P. *Laggards in Our Schools*. New York: Russell Sage Foundation, 1909.

Coffield, W. H., & Bloomers, P. Effects of non-promotion on educational achievement in elementary school. *Journal of Educational Psychology*, April 1956, *47*, 235–250.

Cook, W. W. *Grouping in the Elementary School*. Minneapolis: University of Minnesota Press, 1941.

Cook, W. W., & Kearney, N. E. *Effects of Nonpromotion on Achievement and Personality Traits*. Unpublished manuscript, University of Minnesota, Bureau of Educational Research, 1940. (Cited in Cook, 1941, pp. 44–49)

Ellinger, B. Nonpromotion: A review essay. *Theory into Practice*, 1965, *4*, 122–128.

Farley, E. S.; Frey, A. J.; & Garland, G. Factors related to the grade progress of pupils. *Elementary School Journal*, 1933, *34*(3), 186–193.

Finlayson, H. J. Nonpromotion and self-concept development. *Phi Delta Kappan*, November 1977, pp. 205–206.

Gaite, A. J. H. *On the Validity of Non-promotion as an Educational Procedure* (Report to U.S. Office of Education). Madison: University of Wisconsin, 1969. (ERIC Document Reproduction Service No. ED 046 043)

Goodlad, J. I. Some effects of promotion upon social and emotional adjustment of children. *Journal of Experimental Education*, 1954, *22*(4), 301–328.

Grant, W. V., & Eiden, L. J. (Eds). *Digest of Educational Statistics: 1980*. Washington, D.C.: U.S. Government Printing Office, 1980.

Haney, W., & Madaus, G. Making sense of the competency testing movement. *Harvard Educational Review*, November 1978, *48*(4).

Horacek, T. *Grading and Grade Placement*. Washington, D.C.: National Education Association, 1979.

Jackson, G. The research evidence on the effects of grade retention. *Review of Educational Research*, 1975, *45*(4), 613–635.

Katz, M. B. *Class, Bureaucracy, and Schools: The Illusion of Educational Change in America*. New York: Praeger, 1971.

Keyes, C. H. *Progress through Grades of City Schools* (Contributions to Education, No. 4). New York: Columbia University, Teachers College, Bureau of Publications, 1911.

Kowitz, G. T., & Armstrong, C. M. The effect of promotion policy on academic achievement. *Elementary School Journal*, 1961, *61*, 435–443.

Klene, V., & Branson, E. P. Trial promotion versus failure. *Education Research Bulletin*, 1929, *8*, 6–11.

McElwee, E. W. A comparison of personality traits of accelerated, normal, and retarded children. *Journal of Educational Research*, 1932, *26*, 31–34.

Morrison, I. E., & Perry, I. F. Acceptance of overage children by their classmates. *Elementary School Journal*, 1956, *56*, 217–220.

Pilpho, C. *Update VII: Minimal Competency Testing*. Denver: Educational Commission of the States, 1977.

Sandin, A. A. *Social and Emotional Adjustment of Regularly Promoted and Non-promoted Pupils* (Development Monographs, No. 32). New York: Columbia University, Teachers College, 1944.

Sumption, M. R., & Phillips, T. A. School progress. In W. S. Monroe (Ed.), *Encyclopedia of Educational Research* (2nd ed.). New York: Macmillan, 1950, pp. 1121–1126.

White, K., & Howard, J. L. Failure to be promoted and self-concept among elementary school children. *Elementary School Guidance and Counseling*, 1973, 7, 182–187.

PROPRIETARY SCHOOLS

Proprietary institutions are privately owned postsecondary schools that offer development programs leading to diplomas and college-level degrees. They are part of the American free enterprise system and the history of the United States (Knowles, 1962).

A full fifty years before any organized form of vocational business education was offered by colleges or secondary schools, the first independent business school was established in America in 1835. The independent business school, which antedates all other educational institutions in the nation offering specialized training for business, was born to fill a specific need not supplied by any other educational agency (Miller, 1964). Although business education was subsequently introduced into the senior colleges, into the junior and community colleges, and into the high schools, the independent business schools have survived and prospered, and they continue to make significant contributions to business education in the United States.

As the word "independent" implies, these schools are able to act in educational matters with a minimum of restraint and a maximum of direct action, both of which contribute to their effectiveness in satisfying an education need. Independent business schools are indeed independent in many respects, but there are a number of restraints under which they operate, none of which is viewed as undesirable by the majority of these schools. For example, the schools are obliged to accept a reasonable amount of state supervision; they are subject to indirect pressures exerted by their own professional associations, such as the Association of Independent Colleges and Schools (AICS), and through the enforcement of ethical standards established by the Accrediting Commission of AICS, a commission recognized by the U.S. Office of Education. Probably the most immediate, though subtle, restraint on these schools is competition, a factor often overlooked by those who favor legislation as a means of control, forgetting that our national economy and our business school are based on the free enterprise system. From 1835 to the present, the proprietary school has been the principal source of job-oriented education in America (Clark & Sloan, 1966).

Purpose. Times have changed little: today's proprietary schools exist with the same purposes in mind; the preparation of students with skills and abilities that will satisfy an employment need in the shortest possible time, with the greatest amount of in-depth instruction in the skills desired and necessary for employment, with the latest of teaching aids, with real-life materials, and with highly qualified teachers who recognize employment for their graduates as being the primary goal of the institution.

The establishment of this type of educational enterprise with this singular objective has been echoed in the public sector, perhaps most clearly in the community colleges that have expanded to include continuing education and personal enhancement education. As a result, students may now choose from a variety of educational presentations when deciding to pursue a vocational objective.

In the early days the training programs were short, with completion anticipated in a matter of weeks or months at the most. As the world has grown more complicated and the need for more basic knowledge has increased, these programs have been expanded in many cases to take from a matter of months to four years to complete. There are now many institutions that provide programs of instruction that culminate in associate and baccalaureate degrees, whereas they formerly were recognized by the awarding of a certificate or diploma.

Financing. The eductional administrators of proprietary institutions take pride in the contribution they make to their communities by giving meaningful skills to people who seek employment. Many administrators view their schools and colleges as "independent" as well as proprietary, emphasizing their tax-paying status and uniqueness and noting the lack of any direct governmental financial support. The students who attend these schools can utilize most of the federal and state scholarship and loan funds to support their educational costs.

The fact that these schools do not receive funds directly from the government as public institutions does result in seemingly higher tuition costs. When state and federal subsidies are taken into consideration, the costs of proprietary education are significantly less. For example, it is estimated that for a typical state-supported college the student pays only 9.4 percent of the actual expenses of his or her education, while the state pays for 42.9 percent and federal funds pay for 16.1 percent. The remaining funds needed are derived from various other sources, including research grants, scholarship foundations, and endowments. The community colleges, like state-supported four-year institutions, also receive a portion of their operating capital from the taxpayer. Thus, in most instances, the cost cited to the student is not the full cost incurred to educate the student (Talley, 1977). Community colleges are finding it necessary to raise costs at a faster rate than others. Tuition and fees are on the rise at a rate of 29 percent at public two-year colleges, according to an article in the *Chronicle of Higher Education* ("Tuition Increases," 1981).

Some tax-paying proprietary schools have become tax-exempt by organizing into nonprofit corporations. Although nonprofit, they maintain their proprietary attitude and dedication to vocational instruction for the employment opportunities of the students. One of the largest in this category is Johnson and Wales College in Providence, which has over 8,000 students currently enrolled and a broad vocational curriculum that includes programs in marketing, managing, secretarial science, fashion merchandising, data processing, hospitality and hotel management, and culinary arts.

Student Characteristics. Students entering proprietary schools come from a wide variety of socioeconomic backgrounds, covering the complete spectrum of the American population. Nearly all such schools require a high school diploma or the completion of a General Education Development (GED) certificate for admittance. It is not unusual for students possessing associate or baccalaureate degrees to apply for the specialized training in the broad variety of educational presentations. This has been particularly true in recent years, when students have graduated with degrees in subject areas in which employment opportunities were slim to nonexistent.

A primary frustration of the proprietary school educators is the lack of skills in the three R's of entering students. This lack is detrimental to their ability to succeed in the accelerated programs of instruction often used by these institutions. The institutions have thus had to develop specialized remedial education programs to enable these students to achieve the basic skills needed to pass the course. Proprietary institutions report a sharp decrease in student ability over the past several years, indicating a decline in the quality of public school preparation, a problem that has been noted and documented by numerous postsecondary institutions as unfortunately universal (Wilms, 1973).

When students attend proprietary schools, they expect the institution to actively seek employment opportunities for them. This is a natural assumption, since the schools report that approximately 85 percent of their graduates gain employment immediately or shortly after graduation (AICS, 1979/80). The chairman of the board of directors of the Association of Independent Colleges and Schools, Jan V. Eisenhour, who is also the director of the Executive Secretarial School in Dallas, sums this up by saying, "We have to have as our primary concern the students' ability to function effectively on the job. If they can't, we simply won't get more students—we'll go out of business. Ours is a very market-oriented business."

Accreditation and Regulation. Accreditation as a process is approximately 100 years old and is unique to the United States. When the first accrediting associations were formed, they restricted their membership and service to private nonprofit institutions. This action denied access to specialized schools and colleges such as those in the proprietary sector. As a consequence, specialized institutional accrediting associations were created to respond to the interest and need of those schools that could not come under the umbrella of a regional association. In recent years, as more and more schools closed their doors because of financial troubles, there developed an atmosphere that encouraged the regional accrediting associations to reconsider their restrictive membership policies. This practice has resulted in a modification in almost all of the six regional associations, making regional accreditation available to proprietary schools. As a result, many schools and colleges have dual institutional accreditation, with recognition from a regional association as well as from the Association of Independent Colleges and Schools or the National Association of Trade and Technical Schools.

There are four national associations that represent proprietary institutions and also function as accrediting agencies recognized by the United States Department of Education. These are Association of Independent Colleges and Schools (AICS), Cosmetology Accrediting Commission (CAC), National Association of Trade and Technical Schools (NATTS), and National Home Study Council (NHSC). The number of institutions accredited by each is as follows: AICS, 524; CAC, 1,220; NATTS, 581; NHSC, 82.

Cosmetology schools also are represented by an educational trade association, the National Association of Cosmetology Schools. Plans are under way to merge the two cosmetology organizations by creating the American Council on Cosmetology Education.

The Association of Independent Colleges and Schools accredits institutions that prepare students primarily in the area of business careers, such as secretarial, accounting, marketing, medical administrative assisting, drafting, data processing, court reporting, and fashion merchandising. The National Association of Trade and Technical Schools generally accredits institutions that present programs in various technical and trade areas. Institutions accredited by the Cosmetology Accrediting Commission are limited to cosmetology subjects by and large. The National Home Study Council limits its accreditation to correspondence course institutions.

AICS (1980) reports that the number of institutions it has accredited for the past five years has remained rather level, with about as many new institutions seeking accredited status as those resigning membership or having their accreditation withdrawn. The Cosmetology Accrediting Commission, on the other hand, reports an overall growth of about 100 schools per year (unpublished survey, 1981); NATTS has gained approximately 10 to 20 percent per year for the past five years (unpublished survey, 1980); and NHSC membership has declined about 10 percent (unpublished survey, 1979). With the exception of the Cosmetology Commission, each of the organizations is a charter member of the Council on Postsecondary Accreditation (COPA), which represents the accrediting community through membership from the regional accrediting associations, institutional associations of higher education, and other institutional and specialized accrediting bodies. COPA serves the accrediting community through its efforts to coordinate the development of standards, the promotion of a clearer understanding of the appropriate role of accreditation, and the encouragement of a consolidation rather than a proliferation of accrediting agencies. COPA serves also as a source of information about accreditation to parents, counselors, legislators, and others who look to accreditation as a symbol of quality in education.

In 1973 the Federal Trade Commission (FTC) began an in-depth study of trade and correspondence schools to determine if some trade regulation should be proposed to correct the causes of complaints of students and parents who were dissatisfied with proprietary institutions. The FTC collected two years of hearing testimony from all parts of the country and issued a proposed trade regulation that would have prevented the schools from operating in a competitive manner with the public vocational institutions (FTC, 1978). Several individual schools and colleges, as well as the above-mentioned four national associations, challenged the FTC in federal court, arguing that the proposal was unfair—an ineffective response to the perceived problems in the presentation of proprietary educational programs.

The FTC is limited in its rule-making authority to jurisdiction over tax-paying institutions only, although there are sometimes identical programs in private, nonprofit institutions and public institutions. Is it appropriate to make certain demands or restrictions on some schools and not others? Should the rights of students be assured in all types of educational institutions or only those that are organized as tax-paying institutions? These and other questions convinced the federal courts that much rethinking must be given to the concerns of students as consumers before any trade regulation could go into effect. This view was further upheld by the appellate court when the FTC took the case on appeal (*Katharine Gibbs School et al.* v. *Federal Trade Commission*, No. 78-4204, 2d Cir., 1978).

The question of the need for a trade regulation, based on data now eight years old, that does not take into account the vast number of changes that have come about by new and demanding criteria of accrediting agencies and sterner laws and regulations remains in the hands of the FTC for consideration and revision. No announced intentions of the commission about a new rule have been made public.

Program Completion. One of the important and significant characteristics of proprietary schools is their ability to hold their students through to graduation. In a report prepared by the Association of Independent Colleges and Schools, based on data supplied by their accredited institutions, it was estimated that 75 to 80 percent of all proprietary school students complete their programs. This compares with the 25 percent that complete public vocational education programs and the 25 to 35 percent that complete community college degrees.

A specific comparison was made by Wilms (1980), of the Center for Research and Development in Higher Education at the University of California, who has studied vocational training for several years. He notes that his survey "showed that although the proprietary and public postsec-

ondary schools started with about the same number of secretarial, data processing enrollees, the proprietary schools graduated four to six times as many as the public community colleges" (Wilms, 1974).

In a more recent study Wilms makes some further comparisons that are favorable to the proprietary sector. He was examining the effectiveness of the educational process in preparing students for the labor market. His study points out that the high dropout rate experienced in public vocational training institutions, coupled with their tendency to be less responsive to the ever-changing needs of the marketplace, makes them less effective than the proprietary schools. He reported that although there has been a decrease of 40 percent between the two studies in the number who drop out of community colleges, the proprietary schools still hold a better record, at a 28 percent dropout rate. "Put another way," says the report, "proprietary school students' chances of graduating within $2\frac{1}{3}$ years are $1\frac{1}{2}$ times greater than their public school counterparts" (Wilms, 1980).

Future Challenges. Proprietary schools are enjoying a prosperous period as a result of the nation's economic condition. It has been traditional that as the economy worsens, resulting in an increase in unemployment, proprietary educational programs have become more popular because of their direct link between education and employment. Proprietary schools and colleges report enrollments running 10 to 20 percent higher in 1980 than in previous years. They also report that the average age of the student body is on the increase. It has risen to twenty-three years, indicating that students are entering the proprietary programs later in life.

As public secondary schools are pressed for difficult educational decisions, because of a declining economy and inflationary expenses, many are discontinuing traditional programs. A push to make the public schools more "basic-oriented," coming at a time when few new tax dollars are available, may result in a continuing decline in vocationally oriented program offerings. This decline will in turn place a heavier responsibility on postsecondary proprietary institutions and community colleges to make their programs more accessible.

A significant negative result of this decline in programs may be a scarcity of qualified teachers in the future. Although many programs of instruction in the business area are being eliminated from secondary school curricula, and although the few colleges preparing business education teachers are eliminating those programs of instruction that prepare business teachers for high schools and postsecondary institutions, the greatest employment opportunity in the United States is in the business area, which is forecasting a growing need for secretaries, accountants, and data processing specialists (Brower, 1980).

Teachers employed in proprietary schools must have appropriate credentials to qualify for the classroom. These standards coincide with the requirements of each state for public school teachers as well as specific criteria of the accrediting agencies that mandate teaching credentials. However, the faculty in proprietary schools exhibit certain differences from their counterparts in public education. First, because the primary motivation of a proprietary school is the ultimate employment of the graduate, teachers must play a vital role in the plans of the school for student retention. They must give students individualized attention to whatever degree possible so that the entire class, which is usually smaller than in the public schools, completes the program and individuals achieve their employment objectives (Wine, 1977).

Second, teachers have only one responsibility, to teach. They do not have to monitor lunchrooms or study halls or perform other duties unrelated to teaching. This leads to the utilization of an evaluation system that rewards teachers who are truly outstanding. Teachers do not generally work under contract, and there are almost no unions and no tenure policies. Because of the different, more favorable teaching atmosphere, teaching vacancies are usually easy to fill.

The decline in the number of students graduating from high school is also having its impact on the proprietary sector of education. Such schools, which have been known for aggressive recruitment programs utilizing all forms of media to attract the attention of prospective students, are now finding their public and nonprofit counterpart institutions competing head to head for the shrinking student pool.

The future of the proprietary school, existing in a marketplace where the public institution benefits from tax support and greater access to scholarship and foundation grants, is a challenging one, as it has always been. This status, however, has never prevented the proprietary institution from meeting the challenges with innovative educational offerings geared to the ambitions of students and the needs of business and industry. Being one step ahead, more alert to changes and interests, has always given proprietary institutions an upper hand, which they are unlikely to lose given the cumbersome governance structure imposed on most other types of institutions.

The independent business schools will continue to make major contributions to business education in America in the future as they have throughout their long history. They will do so because of their concern for curriculum review and because of their concern for providing quality instruction that not only prepares students for initial employment but seeks to make them promotable as well. The independent business school will also continue to provide leadership to business education at all levels.

                                                           Stephen B. Friedheim

See also Adult Education; Business Education; Higher Education; Private Schools.

REFERENCES

Association of Independent Colleges and Schools. *Annual Reports*. Washington, D.C.: The Association, 1979–1980.

Association of Independent Colleges and Schools. Unpublished survey, 1980.

Brower, W. A. *Our Future Grows Out of Our Present: We Must Light the Path*. Address before Phi Delta Kappa, April 23, 1980. Rider College, School of Education, Lawrenceville, N.J.

Clark, H. F., & Sloan, H. S. *Classrooms on Mainstreet*. New York: Columbia University Press, 1966.

Cosmetology Accrediting Commission. Unpublished survey, 1981.

Federal Trade Commission. Proprietary vocational and home study schools: Trade regulation rules. *Federal Register*, December 28, 1978, pp. 60797–60827.

Knowles, M. S. *The Adult Education Movement in the United States*. New York: Holt, Rinehart, 1962.

Miller, J. W., & Hamilton, W. J. *The Independent Business School in America*. New York: McGraw-Hill, Gregg Division, 1964.

National Association of Trade and Technical Schools. Unpublished survey, 1980.

National Home Study Council. Unpublished survey, 1979.

Tuition increases. *Chronicle of Higher Education*, February 1981.

Talley, M. G. *Reassessing Values in Postsecondary Education*. Washington, D.C.: Association of Independent Colleges and Schools, 1977. (ERIC Document Reproduction Service No. ED 148 224)

Wilms, W. W. *Proprietary versus Public Vocational Training*. Berkeley, Calif.: Center for Research and Development in Higher Education, 1973.

Wilms, W. W. *Effectiveness of Public and Proprietary Occupational Training*. Berkeley, Calif.: Center for Research and Development in Higher Education, 1974.

Wilms, W. W. *Vocational Training and Social Mobility: A Study of Public and Proprietary School Dropouts*. Los Angeles: University of California, 1980.

Wine, M. B. Proprietary schools. In *International Encyclopedia of Higher Education*. San Francisco: Jossey-Bass, 1977.

PROTESTANT EDUCATION

Describing his impressions of Colonial America, St. John de Crèvecoeur wrote, "The easiest way of becoming acquainted with the modes of thinking, the rules of conduct, and the prevailing manners of any people, is to examine what sort of education they give their children; how they treat them at home, and what they are taught in their places of public worship" (Crèvecoeur, 1957, p. 108). This article sets out to trace the history of and current problems pertaining to those "modes of thinking, rules of conduct, and prevailing manners" found in Protestant education, both formal and nonacademic, with particular emphasis upon Protestant education in the United States (Gaebelein, 1951). Because of the diversity of denominations and sects popularly classified as Protestant, no definitive statement about any single group is possible here; only a sketch of the broad outline of principles and practices common among those groups historically identified as mainline Protestants (Gaustad, 1968) or evangelicals (Henry, 1968) will be attempted.

Although the bulk of this article will be devoted to formal education in institutions sponsored by Protestant sects, some space must also be given to endeavors outside schooling. Brief reference will be made to efforts such as church schools (Sunday school, vacation school, and other church-related programs), parachurch activities (youth groups, student groups in schools and colleges), foreign missions (literacy, translation, and schooling at all levels), religious broadcasting, and religious publishing.

The term "Protestant" derives from the *Protestation* of 1529, a manifesto issued by German princes supporting Martin Luther's attempt to reform the Roman Catholic church. Responding to the second Diet of Speyer (Cross, 1958), which attempted to curtail the rights of each territorial ruler in determining the religion of his region, this document declared that "in matters which concern God's honor and salvation and the eternal life of our souls, everyone must stand and give an account before God for himself" (p. 1280). Thus at the heart of Protestantism lies the fundamental concept of an individual's relationship with God, made possible only through grace. From this relationship spring both personal communication with God and personal responsibility to God (Lewis, 1954). But as historians have also noted, Protestant doctrine of individual respect and responsibility is a corollary to the contemporaneously growing idea of the independent nation-state (White, 1967).

Thereafter, "Protestant" became a designation by which to identify Christians who had broken with the Roman Catholic church, establishing their own ecclesiastical authority and often, thereby, altering the nature of political and social conventions as well. Hence the double term "Protestant Reformation" refers to ecclesiastical changes initiated by and resulting from the actions of Martin Luther, Philip Melanchthon, Huldreich Zwingli, John Calvin, John Knox, and others (Douglass, 1960) and to political and social changes marked by a modern spirit of private judgment and personal accountability, as proclaimed by Luther in his defense at Worms (Henry, 1957). Notable among these events was the establishing of loosely similar educational systems characterized by the same spirit of reform that marked the new ecclesiastical structures (Boyd, 1969).

Whereas under Rome, education had been regarded as the particular function of the church and state, as a result of the Protestant Reformation parents in each local community and reformed church obtained a heightened sense of personal responsibility to provide education for their children (Boyd, 1969). Borrowing from the Jewish tradition as dictated by Mosaic law (e.g., Deuteronomy 6), Protestants have always contended that first among each parent's primary duties is the instruction of every child in the family. Some critics, however, would contend that, historically, this principle has been more honored in the breach than in the observance by Protestants, with parents entrusting the schooling of their children to others, including nonbelievers teaching in secular schools (Kienel, 1976). In spite of a burgeoning of church-related and inde-

pendent "Christian schools," by far the majority of Protestant families in North America and Europe still send their children to state-controlled, tax-supported schools (Lockerbie, 1980). Nonetheless, schools, colleges, Bible institutes, and seminaries sponsored by a constituency of Protestant supporters seem to be thriving at the beginning of the 1980s, especially those of conservative, evangelical, or fundamentalist persuasion (Briggs, 1980).

Roots of Academic Education.

In purely technical terms, Protestant education as such cannot be said to have existed before 1517, when Luther promulgated his Ninety-five Theses. Still, Protestants generally claim to share with Roman Catholics in the same broad educational tradition of Western civilization, originating in the pagan, pre-Christian centuries (Wolterstorff, 1970). Christianity's earliest educated believers (e.g, Paul of Tarsus, Timothy of Lystra) benefited from both rabbinical and Greco-Roman studies, principally the classical liberal arts. By the second century after Christ, converts included philosophers and teachers such as Justin Martyr, who taught in a school for Christians in Rome (Clasper, 1980). Thereafter, most of the leading church fathers of the pre-Nicene and post-Nicene period were advocates of formal education, including the rigorous study of rhetoric and pagan literature. Augustine, for example, argued that truth is universal and of divine origin and therefore not to be shunned, since "every good and true Christian should understand that wherever he may find truth, it is his Lord's" (Augustine, 1958, p. 54).

Christian Humanists. Throughout the Middle Ages, universities and schools founded by various religious societies turned inward, largely ignoring the educational needs of the illiterate masses. Even when Vittorino da Feltre founded his school in Mantua, in 1423, establishing the precedent of removing younger students from the immediate influence of their parents and asserting the authority of the teacher to act *in loco parentis*, he was not opening the doors to popular education (Woodward, 1964a). Nor did the later Christian humanists of the Renaissance choose to offer education for the common man; instead, they remained for the most part within the very institutions and system whose "scholasticism" they deplored (Wolterstorff, 1970). Only gradually did these bastions of rarefied intellectualism yield to acknowledge common concerns. Yet the Christian humanists did revive the church fathers' understanding that all truth finds its source in God and that, as Desiderius Erasmus said, "all studies, philosophy, rhetoric are followed for this one object, that we may know Christ and honor him" (Bush, 1939, p. 64; Woodward, 1964b). This pious learning, however, was carried on in a language exclusive to clerics and scholars, the Latin of the Roman church, although in the preface to his Greek New Testament, Erasmus looked foward to a time when the Scriptures would be available in the national language of every person.

Thus the Protestant Reformation and its corollary upheavals derive from the Renaissance and from Christian humanism. Indeed, the origins of a specifically Protestant education may be rooted as much in social revolution as in theological controversy (White, 1967). For while the principal argument over salvation by grace alone raged at a theological level, a more mundane dispute—national identity—was being settled in favor of teaching and learning in the native languages rather than in traditional Latin. Hence two important developments go hand in hand: the translation of Scripture into indigenous languages and the instruction of all youth for the purpose of making them competent to read and understand the Bible in their own tongues. The local church and the local schoolhouse thus were partners in creating a Protestant culture (Brubacher, 1966).

Martin Luther himself led the way in this transformation of a purely classical and theological Latin schooling into a modern education in the vernacular language. In so doing, Luther built upon the earlier work of Jacob Wimpheling, whose *Isodoneus Germanicus,* published before 1500, had called for devout and learned teachers of the German language (Boyd, 1969). Early in the Reformation period, Luther's friend Johann Bugenhagen founded the first common schools for children of all social classes and offering instruction in German. Luther supported such ventures. As early as 1530, he preached a sermon entitled "On the Duty of Sending Children to School," insisting that children be educated in the arts and history, as well as in languages. To this end he produced a children's catechism to accompany his German translation of the Bible, published in 1534.

Considerable emphasis in early Protestant education rested upon the creating of a literate populace capable of reading and interpreting the Holy Scriptures for themselves. Yet many of the reformers were also men of broad learning who participated in the thought and ideals of Christian humanism, with its emphasis upon classical studies (Bush, 1939). At the same time, these reformers also offered a new spiritual certainty and its accompanying freedom to experience what Calvin called "the lawful enjoyment of God's blessings" (Lewis, 1954, p. 35). While that tradition may be suspect among today's neofundamentalists in the "Christian school movement," it remains an orthodox position among Protestants that "all study, all thought, all education, are for caring, for the care of some particular aspect of the structures of the earth, finally for the true care of people in their pilgrimage in the earth" (Dixon, 1979, p. 305).

Luther's Legacy. Foremost among these enlightened reformers was Luther's younger colleague, the precocious Philip Melanchthon, who carried out in a more directly personal way what Luther spoke in theory. A scholar and translator by age 16, Melanchthon was respected among Christian humanists like Erasmus, and his reputation extended throughout northern Europe and England. Arriving at Wittenberg a year after Luther's Ninety-five Theses,

Melanchthon became strongly attached to Luther and his cause. In 1528 he proposed a new plan for German education, thereby establishing what became the German school system in some fifty-six cities. He conducted a school in his own house in Wittenberg, wrote textbooks in German, and was also responsible for organizing the first Protestant universities at Marburg, Königsberg, Jena, and Helmstedt, with high schools at Eisleben and Nuremberg. Under his influence the older universities at Wittenberg, Tübingen, Leipzig, Frankfurt, and Rostock joined the reformed camp. For all this, Melanchthon is justifiably known as *Praeceptor Germaniae,* "the Teacher of Germany" (Manschreck, 1958).

The magnetism of Luther's revolt spread quickly to Switzerland, France, and Scotland. In Zurich, Huldreich Zwingli led the Swiss Reformation of 1522, one of the earliest results of which was the publication of the first book to be written concerning education from the Protestant point of view, *The Christian Education of Boys,* in 1523 (Boyd, 1969). In Paris a young scholar named Jean Cauvin (John Calvin) came first under the influence of Christian humanism and subsequently of Lutheranism; by 1534, he had written a preface to a French translation of the Bible and was a declared evangelical. Exiled to Geneva, he helped to found an elementary school in 1537. In the prospectus that Calvin wrote for this school, he showed his continuing concern for balancing an evangelical regard for the Bible with the new humanist curriculum: "The Word of God is indeed the foundation of all learning, but the liberal arts are aids to the full knowledge of the Word and not to be despised" (Boyd, 1969, p. 198). Through Calvin's auspices, Heidelberg became a reformed university, and new Protestant institutions of learning were begun at Edinburgh, Leiden, Amsterdam, Utrecht, and Cambridge, where Emmanuel College was founded by Calvinists in 1584 (Wolterstorff, 1970). At St. Andrews, John Knox became the spokesman of the Scottish reformers. Persecuted, imprisoned in French galleys, exiled by the coming to power of Mary Tudor, Knox fled to Geneva to learn from Calvin. When Elizabeth I's accession restored her father's anti–Roman Catholicism, Knox returned home, where, in 1560, he published *The First Book of Discipline* for Scottish Presbyterians. In this treatise he laid out the details for a compulsory and free education for all, with special provisions to ensure that children of the poor would also receive an education (Ridley, 1968).

Meanwhile in England, the revolt from Rome received its impetus from the notorious and personal grievances of Henry VIII with the pope; however, a decade before 1529, when Parliament recognized the king as head of the Church of England, there had been evidences of continental reform throughout England. Publication in 1526 of William Tyndale's English translation of the New Testament added fuel to the movement. Eventually, an anti–Roman Catholic spirit showed itself in the suppression of the monasteries and the call for wider learning in a book published in 1546, *The Necessary Doctrine and Erudition of Any Christian Man.* Archbishop of Canterbury Thomas Cranmer's eloquent litany and prayers, in the Book of Common Prayer, raised the English language almost to the level of the sublime Latin mass. But also with the prayer book came the Act of Uniformity, compelling its use; every schoolchild in England learned to read the language heard each Sunday at Morning Prayer. So the young Will Shakespeare, for instance, knew both the English Bible and the Anglican Prayer Book (Alexander, 1961).

But while English Protestants flourished under the reign of Elizabeth I, she was not a supporter of the more radical reformers, especially those who both opposed the rule of women and cited their own interpretation of Scripture. To squelch this opposition, Parliament passed laws requiring kneeling and a robed clergy, both offensive to reformers. Out of their distress grew the Puritan movement, with its wish to "purify" the Church of England and restore it to a primitive simplicity derived from New Testament models. Thwarted by the queen from officially instituting their demands, some Puritans reorganized themselves as Separatists and, in 1608, fled royal persecution to Holland. From there, in 1620, a group of English men and women, including some, such as Captain Myles Standish, who had no religious connection with Separatism, sailed for the New World (Bailey, 1956).

Developments in America. It is an American axiom that the pilgrim fathers came to America in search of religious liberty. The established church had grown increasingly uneasy with the Puritan sect's demands and had forbidden the Separatists to meet as household congregations. In their new circumstances, however, the English settlers found themselves not only able but also forced to do what had previously been forbidden. Home became both church and school (Axtell, 1974).

But soon a more systematic education became desirable. In 1635, the Boston Latin School was begun to prepare boys for university, presumably a return to Cambridge, from which most of New England's scholars had been graduated. The following year, however, the General Court of Massachusetts appropriated money for the founding of a college in a location named for the English university town; two years later, a dying clergyman named John Harvard bequeathed half of his estate for the purpose of supporting the fledgling college. Its mission, as inscribed in 1643, was to preclude "an illiterate Ministry to the Churches, when our present Ministers shall lie in the Dust" (Sweet, 1950, p. 54). A similar declaration of purpose also marks the founding of America's second college, William and Mary, whose Virginia founders enacted a law providing land for a college and free schools "for the advance of learning, education of youth, supply of the ministry and promotion of piety" (Smylie, 1978). So reads the charter of almost every college in America until well into the early nineteenth century (Kelly, 1940); in fact, before the Civil War, the vast majority of colleges founded in America were church-related and intended for the continuing supply of educated ministers (Tewksbury, 1932).

So too with the founding of preparatory schools in America. The charters of the earliest such schools are explicit in identifying their common purpose, to preserve and promote the Christian faith. The earliest legislation—a 1647 Massachusetts law establishing a school in every town of fifty or more families, a Latin school in larger communities—held even those parents in remote settlements responsible for teaching their children well enough "to read and understand the principles of religion and the capital laws of the country" (Lockerbie, 1972, p. 12). Aids to teaching included *The Bay Psalm Book, The New England Primer* ("In Adam's fall/We sinned all"), the shorter catechism of the 1648 Westminster confession, and the previous Sunday's sermon, which schoolchildren were expected to be able to recall point for point (Axtell, 1974; Brubacher, 1966). Thus the earliest common schools in this country were, in fact, extensions of the Protestant homes and churches with which they were aligned, and schooling remained so until long after Horace Mann inaugurated the public school system in 1837 (McLachlan, 1970).

During the same period in Europe, the dominant figure in education was John Amos Comenius, a bishop in the Moravian church (Sadler, 1966; Spinka, 1967). Like other Christian leaders before him, Comenius called for a literate society to ensure that there would be literate Christian believers. But in his most famous work, *The Great Didactic* (1627–1632), Comenius went beyond his predecessors in calling for universal compulsory education for all, without regard for religion, girls as well as boys. Furthermore, while his educational reforms offered what can only be considered as commonplace wisdom today (e.g., "Nothing to be memorized unless it is understood," p. 15), his ideas were entirely revolutionary in their time (Comenius, 1896). He saw and warned against the coming trend for parents to abdicate their responsibilities for the moral instruction of their children, passing it on to teachers instead. Exiled for much of his life because of religious persecution and the Thirty Years' War, Comenius left his mark upon schooling in various European countries; his influence led to the founding of England's Royal Society, and in 1642 he was thought to be a candidate for the presidency of Harvard College. According to some observers, to Comenius belongs the title Father of Modern Education (Silberman, 1970).

Pluralism. Crèvecoeur's observations of life in America, first published in 1782, comment on a growing religious indifference complementing the mixture of races and nations that became the American norm (Crèvecoeur, 1957). Today we call this mixture pluralism (Rainey, 1965; McLoughlin & Bellah, 1968). Its development grows out of at least three sources: first, the language of the First Amendment to the Constitution, explicitly forbidding the establishing of any state religion while at the same time permitting the free exercise of all religion; second, the vast influx into American life of people from every conceivable non-Protestant background; third, the determination of individual states to undertake what Comenius had dreamed but no people had ever attempted—the free education of an entire nation's youth. Before the American Civil War, 90 percent of the children in school attended private academies, with only 10 percent in public schools. By 1930, just 100 years after the appearance of public schools, the population statistics had reversed (Boyd, 1969).

Obviously, these three factors mitigated against perpetuating a singularly Protestant theology in schools provided by tax support as public institutions, although there were—and still are—many Protestants in America who supposed that the public schools were intended to function as centers for religious, specifically Protestant, instruction (Harvey, 1976). Behind this spirit lay a combination of fears: xenophobia in the face of expanding immigration, territorial protection, and isolationism from what was still perceived as the corruption and decadence of Europe, a theme promoted in nineteenth-century fiction (Parkes, 1959). In addition, the old reformationist antipathy for the Roman Catholic church led advocates of a Protestant-controlled public school system to insist upon religious practices in school that offended the Roman Catholic minority (Lockerbie, 1972). Other Protestants were dissatisfied with Horace Mann's including Bible reading in his curriculum (Rushdoony, 1968) or Henry Barnard's poetic description of "every schoolhouse" as "a temple consecrated in prayer to the physical, intellectual, and moral culture of every child in the community" (Lockerbie, 1980, p. 76). These opponents to secular public schooling feared a diluting of the pure gospel, as they understood it, by teachers whose orthodoxy might be questionable.

McGuffey's Readers.   Perhaps the most sustaining influence for the Protestant ethic in nineteenth-century American public schools was William Holmes McGuffey, educator and textbook compiler (Westerhoff, 1978). A self-trained schoolteacher at age 13, McGuffey attained professorships and college presidencies while helping to found the Ohio public school system. But his primary contribution to education was his set of six readers, published from 1836 to 1857. *McGuffey's Eclectic Readers,* says Henry Steele Commager, "helped to shape that elusive thing we call the American character" (Westerhoff, 1978, p. 16). Highly moralistic and didactic without being explicitly denominational or sectarian, McGuffey's books nonetheless assumed and took for granted the universal acceptance of orthodox Protestant morality, particularly the Calvinist emphasis upon the rewards inherent in hard work (Bailey, 1956). More than 120 million copies of McGuffey's books were sold.

Religion in Public Schools.   McGuffey's contemporary, Horace Bushnell, represents a different strain in American Protestant thinking. This liberal intellectual pastor and theologian championed the case for public schooling in spite of the public school's inability to inculcate Christian doctrine, a responsibility he laid at the door of parents and the church, as the title of his book *Christian Nurture* indicates (Bushnell, 1906). Today the same arguments may

be heard between those who prefer, if necessary, a religious vacuum to develop in the public schools (Postman, 1979), rather than risk religious indoctrination, and those who accuse the public schools of having extirpated all religion and religious sensibility (Gaebelein, 1967). The contemporary ramifications of this controversy, beginning in 1948 *(McCollum* v. *Board of Education)* and stimulated in the Supreme Court decisions of 1962 and 1963 *(Engel* v. *Vitale; Abington School District* v. *Schempp),* have received new fuel from efforts in the Congress and various state legislatures, where politicians appear determined to write laws or, if possible, amend the Constitution to restore devotional prayer and Bible reading to the public classroom or require equal time for the teaching of biblical creationism along with evolutionary explanations in public school science courses (Lammers, 1980; Lockerbie, 1980). Other more cautiously reasoned approaches, however, are also possible within the law (Panoch & Barr, 1968).

The roots of such dissension over the public school's reluctance over teaching Protestant dogma go back to the beginning of this century. Pressed by German radical theologians and by naturalistic scientific theory, Protestants in most mainline denominations revised their theology (Henry, 1968). To them "modernism" meant diminishing the strict view of sin and the need for personal salvation, and adopting as a new tenet social salvation, through John Dewey's "progressive education" (Dewey, 1938; Dworkin, 1959). Experience became the ethical criterion, eliminating the possibility of living by moral absolutes (Childs, 1931). With their own schools, colleges, and seminaries no longer committed to a historic Reformational theology, many conservative Protestants, who considered "modernism" a defection from the faith and "progressive education" an unacceptable development, began to separate themselves from their denominations. These supporters of so-called fundamentalism generally started their own schools, colleges, and seminaries—for example, Westminster Theological Seminary, founded by J. Gresham Machen and others in 1929, as a protest against the alleged liberalism of Princeton Theological Seminary (Machen, 1925).

Alternatives in Education.   During this same period, a new form of American education made its appearance, the nondenominational Bible institute, patterned after Nyack Missionary College (1882) and Moody Bible Institute, founded by the evangelist Dwight L. Moody (1886). Pietistic and evangelistic in purpose, these training centers and the nearly 200 that followed in the next century specialized in preparing young converts for Christian service by steeping them in the study of the Scriptures. As a result of the bloodletting between modernism and fundamentalism in the 1920s and 1930s, conservative Protestants tended to regard all theological seminaries with suspicion; instead, they turned with favor toward the simple curriculum of the Bible institute, with its primary focus upon studying the Bible itself (Witmer, 1962).

By no means were all liberal Protestants happy with these schismatic effects of modernism upon the American church, especially as they pertained to education. Many who had supported the public schools, for instance, were chagrined to discover that public education now asserted an official position of nonsectarian neutrality inimical even to the most tolerant Protestantism (Kraushaar, 1972). Other liberal theologians also argued that stripping the public schools of any Protestant bias ought not to be construed as an invitation for the state to promote atheism as a substitute religion (Weigle, 1929). Clearly, a return to a balance of intellectual integrity with religious orthodoxy was needed. Thus, for example, the accord granted the founders of the Stony Brook School, in 1922, came equally from both conservative and liberal branches of American Protestantism (Lockerbie, 1972).

Advocates of Dewey's philosophy, however, attempted to counter the movement toward a resurgence of Protestant schooling by arguing that private education, especially religious-based education, is narrow, provincial, and antidemocratic (Bode, 1943; Kilpatrick, 1951). Yet in the 1925 test case, *Pierce* v. *Society of Sisters,* the Supreme Court had already ruled that the state of Oregon had no authority to force pupils "to accept instruction from public teachers only." From that time schools as well as colleges of all religious persuasions have been free to assert their educational and philosophical distinctiveness from the public system's necessary pluralism. Foremost among these distinctions is "the integration of faith and learning" (Gaebelein, 1954; Kraushaar, 1972; Postman, 1979). Teachers in such schools and colleges are expected to be more than academicians; the content of their courses is more than mere information. Teachers must be models of Christian behavior whose lives exemplify a wholeness of scholarship and belief, whose teaching finds the source of truth in God (Haroutunian, 1957). Evangelical Protestants in particular insist that the *sine qua non* for Christian schooling is a unitedly believing Christian faculty (Gaebelein, 1951). Other Protestants reject the need for a common faith among faculty, preferring their church-related institutions to reflect more accurately the fact that faith exists in tension with unbelief (Johnson, 1978); yet the call continues for church-related colleges to retain their religious identification and differences from secular institutions (Arrowsmith, 1970; Coughlin, 1979).

Leading the Protestant movement since the end of World War II have been evangelical schools and colleges in the Christian Reformed, Lutheran—Missouri Synod, and independent Baptist denominations. School federations include Christian Schools International, merging two older groups, National Union of Christian Schools and National Association of Christian Schools (Swets, 1979); Association of Christian Schools International; and American Association of Christian Schools (Petersen, 1980). More than sixty colleges representing two dozen Protestant denominations and enrolling 75,000 students belong to the Christian College Coalition (Briggs, 1980; Novotney, 1981). Academic respectability, measured by graduate and professional school admissions, has been achieved by many of these institutions, although some remain ultraconserva-

tive in their social ethics and parochial in their denominationalism (Rian, 1949; Malik, 1980).

Christian School Movement. Just when private schooling seemed moribund in America, an astonishing surge of parental concern swept through the 1970s. Two major issues provided impetus: dismay over court-enforced busing to achieve racial balance and the belief that conditions in public schools were deteriorating to their children's jeopardy. Parents turned to private schooling in a wave that shocked the public education establishment (Press, 1981). New fundamentalist "Christian schools," in particular, have been springing up at a rate of three per day. Most of these are parent-controlled, church-related operations, dependent upon programmed instruction, lacking either conventional school facilities or professionally qualified personnel (Daly, 1981). As part of their fundamentalist subculture in Protestantism, these schools, often reactionary, see themselves as the providers of refuge from a hostile, secularist public education system (Lockerbie, 1980). In some respects, the fears that drive supporters of these "Christian schools" are shared by Roman Catholic and Jewish parents, as well as by some of no religious persuasion (Gallup, 1981): lack of discipline, presence of drugs, absence of moral teaching in the public schools. These concerns are not necessarily unique to fundamentalist families. Politically, these schools can call upon a constituency strong enough to cause a state legislature to reverse its course, as in the North Carolina 1979 exemption of "Christian schools" from meeting that state's minimal standards (North Carolina, General Assembly, 1979). Lurking always in the background, however, are also the efforts of racists to use the guise of private schooling to avoid compliance with laws forbidding racial segregation (Williams, 1981). In certain settings, the phrase "Christian school" may be tacitly understood as a signal that black or other minority students need not apply (Lockerbie, 1971; Petersen, 1980).

The future for "Christian schools" depends upon several external factors. Academically, the overwhelming majority of these new schools must prove that their graduates can rank with graduates of conventional public or other private schools and can compete with them in postsecondary studies, as well as eventually in business and the professions. Politically, such schools may be increasingly under attack by supporters of public education who see "Christian schools" as responsible for a sudden and catastrophic collapse in public school support and student population. Religiously, it remains to be seen if indifference will arise when "Christian schools" achieve such power as their enthusiasts predict. Perhaps the greatest strength possessed by "Christian schools" is their degree of parental support, manifest in voluntarism and financial commitment (Wolterstorff, 1979). As Theodore Sizer, headmaster of Phillips Andover Academy, says of this spate of new schools, "The one thing that really works for these schools is that the parents have opted in" (Williams, 1981, pp. 68–69).

Nonacademic Education. Since 1520, when Luther published a primer of reformed doctrine, Protestants have encouraged religious education, particularly through the study of a catechism or confession leading to confirmation or other rites of belief (Haughwout, 1975). Not until the 1780s, however, when Robert Raikes experimented with a Sunday school in Gloucester, England, was there any systematic method of instructing children and adults in Christian dogma. Raikes's original concept called for five hours of lessons each Sunday, including instruction in reading and writing for those poor children not enrolled in regular schools (Gaebelein, 1951). So well received was Raikes's program, it soon spread throughout England and was carried to Philadelphia by 1790, where Sunday school became less academic and more rigorously religious. By 1824 the American Sunday School Union had been organized, largely by laymen, for the purposes of promoting the establishment of Sunday schools and preparing for publication suitable books and manuals for Sunday school use (Sweet, 1950). Thus, in America, the Sunday school provided a model for Horace Mann and Henry Barnard in their common schools, thereby helping to forge traditional Protestant values into a stereotypical American character (Kennedy, 1966).

Every Protestant denomination continues to place great weight upon the importance of its Sunday school program, with qualified personnel possessing academic credentials through the doctoral degree in religious education, and curriculum experts creating and publishing study guides and aids to instruction (Cully, 1965). Independent, nondenominational publishers, such as David C. Cook (founded in 1875), also provide materials for the rapidly expanding evangelical market. The Religious Education Association, founded in 1903, and the International Council of Religious Education (1922) have offered forums for leadership and scholarship in the vast Sunday school enterprise (Wyckoff, 1959).

Other elements of a Protestant church's religious education program may include vacation school with daily meetings for intensive instruction during some part of the summer months; youth fellowships, some of which may hold membership in external parachurch organizations (see below); age or interest groups; candidate classes for confirmation, baptism, or church membership; teacher-training courses; marriage-counseling courses; weekend retreats; summer camps and resorts offering recreation along with Bible instruction, growing out of the Chautauqua assembly begun in 1874; mission-emphasis conferences; and local, regional, or national denominational and ecumenical conventions (Wyckoff, 1959; Sweet, 1950). Nursery schools and day care centers, along with vacation school, may also function as social services to a community in which an increasing number of families require child supervision while both parents are at work. Theological distinctions among Protestant denominations—such as the difference between those who practice infant baptism and those who withhold baptism for confessing believers only—may alter the emphasis in any phase of religious instruction (Richards, 1975; Miller, 1980).

Parachurch Organizations. Adjunct to the Protestant church's own religious education structure are various parachurch organizations, some with long histories of their own. Inter-Varsity Christian Fellowship, for instance, traces its origins to the late eigtheenth century, when Charles Simeon, vicar of Holy Trinity Church in Cambridge, England, began a Bible study for Cambridge students (Moule, 1948). From this developed the Cambridge Inter-Collegiate Christian Union, with its counterpart at Oxford. Joint meetings between universities gave the organization its name (Johnson, 1964). The first American chapter met in 1937 at the University of Wisconsin. Forty years later, chapters convened in 900 secular institutions, including the University of North Carolina at Chapel Hill, where more than 600 students attend a weekly Bible study (Hammond, 1978).

The Young Men's Christian Association, founded in London in 1844, established as its purpose "the improvement of the spiritual condition of young men" in the manual trades (Sweet, 1950, p. 335). By 1851, an American YMCA had opened in Boston; by 1855, an international headquarters in Geneva, Switzerland, the same year that saw the founding of the Young Women's Christian Association. Two of the most famous American evangelists, Dwight L. Moody and Billy Sunday, were YMCA religious workers in Chicago early in their careers. Today's YMCA concentrates upon physical and social programs, although in some American universities religious activities are still coordinated through the campus "Y" (Johnson, 1978).

Among agencies working with children and youth, Christian Service Brigade in North America resembles, but has no direct connection with, Britain's Boys' Brigade, founded in 1883 to train leaders among boys attending Sunday schools. Its American counterpart, begun in 1937, offers uniforms, a merit badge system, and an emphasis upon camping skills (Christian Service Brigade Staff, 1968); it differs, however, from the Boy Scouts of America by its pointedly Christian theological and devotional elements. In 1981 some 2,200 Christian Service Brigade troops met throughout the United States and Canada, in churches representing some forty Protestant denominations, each troop led by volunteer adults connected with each sponsoring church.

In a culture in which sports personalities are idolized, some parachurch groups concentrate their efforts upon converting and disciplining college and professional athletes, then using these already famous personalities as evangelists. Campus Crusade for Christ sponsors basketball and track teams called Athletes in Action; the Fellowship of Christian Athletes holds high school and college meetings; Pro Athlete Outreach conducts Bible studies and pregame chapel services for professionals in several sports (Vecsey, 1981). While such organizations risk exposing their constituents' religious practices to undue publicity, athletes themselves appreciate and benefit from sharing interests in their faith and work.

Protestant Missions. The history of Protestant missionary endeavor combines evangelism with education at every turn. From 1701 until the Revolutionary War, England's Society for the Propagation of the Gospel in Foreign

Parts sent more than 300 missionaries to the American colonies. In addition to starting churches, they also attempted to educate native Americans and blacks (Sweet, 1950). The same is true of Isaac McCoy at Fort Wayne and members of the "Illinois Band," graduates of Yale Divinity School who committed themselves as missionary teachers to the Illinois wilderness (Kelly, 1940). Translation and literacy programs led to the founding of schools and colleges, a pattern that continues in modern missions, with their emphasis on the educated convert who can appreciate all that is best in his or her own culture (Clasper, 1980). As a result, a new awareness of the universality of the Christian gospel, without regard for one nation's cultural superiority over another, now marks much of Protestant missiology.

Religious instruction sometimes verges on indoctrination when the medium of radio and television broadcasting becomes the message (Armstrong, 1979). Almost 1,500 radio stations and 50 television stations are operated by religious broadcasters; another 700 programs are distributed to secular stations (Lammers, 1980). Some of these programs can claim audiences larger than any regularly scheduled commercial show. From certain politically active airwave preachers, their audiences learn which politician and party will support their special interest. Other more traditional broadcasters confine their ministry to a systematic survey of the Bible, program by program. Closely related to religious broadcasting's rise in popularity is the commercial success of religious publishing, much of which depends upon publicity obtained by authors' appearances on radio and television interviews (McDowell, 1981). With 5,500 bookstores specializing in religious literature, a vast audience is now consuming more than a billion dollars' worth of published material each year. What these listeners hear and what these readers read, in the privacy of their own homes, may influence what they know about the Christian faith far more than all the formal instruction in Protestant schools and colleges over the past five centuries.

D. Bruce Lockerbie

See also Private Schools; Religion and Education.

REFERENCES

Alexander, P. *Shakespeare's Life and Art.* New York: New York University Press, 1961.

Armstrong, B. L. *The Electric Church.* Nashville: Nelson, 1979.

Arrowsmith, W. Idea of a new university. *Center Magazine,* 1970, *2,* 47.

Augustine. *On Christian Doctrine.* Indianapolis: Bobbs-Merrill, 1958.

Axtell, J. L. *The School upon a Hill: Education and Society in Colonial New England.* New Haven., Conn.: Yale University Press, 1974.

Bailey, T. A. *The American Pageant: A History of the Republic.* Boston: Heath, 1956.

Bode, B. H. *Democracy as a Way of Life.* New York: Macmillan, 1943.

Boyd, W. *The History of Western Education.* New York: Barnes & Noble, 1969.

Briggs, K. Evangelical colleges reborn. *New York Times Magazine,* December 14, 1980, pp. 140–154.

Brubacher, J. S. *A History of the Problems of Education.* New York: McGraw-Hill, 1966.

Bush, D. *The Renaissance and English Humanism.* Toronto: University of Toronto Press, 1939.

Bushnell, H. *Christian Nurture.* New York: Scribner, 1906.

Childs, J. L. *Education and the Philosophy of Experimentalism.* New York: Century, 1931.

Christian Service Brigade Staff. *Boys for Christ: A Manual for Leaders of Boys.* Wheaton, Ill.: Christian Service Brigade, 1968.

Clasper, P. *Eastern Paths and the Christian Way.* Maryknoll, N.Y.: Orbis, 1980.

Comenius, J. A. *The Great Didactic* (W. S. Monroe, Ed.) Boston: Heath, 1896.

Coughlin, E. K. Church-related colleges urged to resist secularization. *Chronicle of Higher Education,* 1979, *18,* 1+.

Crèvecoeur, J. H. St. J. de. *Letters from an American Farmer.* New York: Dutton, 1957.

Cross, F. L. (Ed.). *The Oxford Dictionary of the Christian Church.* London: Oxford University Press, 1958.

Cully, K. B. *The Search for a Christian Education since 1940.* Philadelphia: Westminster, 1965.

Daly, N. The genesis of a program built on creation. *New York Times,* April 26, 1981, Section 12, pp. 18–19.

Dewey, J. *Experience and Education.* New York: Macmillan, 1938.

Dixon, J. W., Jr. *The Physiology of Faith: A Theory of Theological Relativity.* New York: Harper & Row, 1979.

Douglass, T. B. Protestantism. In M. Halverson & A. A. Cohen (Eds.), *A Handbook of Christian Theology.* New York: Meridian Books, 1960.

Dworkin, M. S. (Ed.). *Dewey on Education.* New York: Teachers College, Bureau of Publications, 1959.

Gaebelein, F. E. *Christian Education in a Democracy.* New York: Oxford University Press, 1951.

Gaebelein, F. E. *The Pattern of God's Truth: Problems of Integration in Christian Education.* New York: Oxford University Press, 1954.

Gaebelein, F. E. Education and the evangelical minority. In *A Varied Harvest.* Grand Rapids, Mich.: Eerdmans, 1967.

Gallup, G. How Americans grade their schools. *Newsweek,* April 20, 1981, p. 64.

Gaustad, E. S. America's institutions of faith: A statistical postscript. In W. G. McLoughlin & R. N. Bellah (Eds.), *Religion in America.* Boston: Houghton Mifflin, 1968.

Hammond, P. A response. In J. H. Westerhoff (Ed.), *The Church's Ministry in Higher Education.* New York: United Ministries in Higher Education Communication Office, 1978.

Haroutunian, J. A Protestant theory of education. In J. P. von Grueningen (Ed.), *Toward a Christian Philosophy of Higher Education.* Philadelphia: Westminster, 1957.

Harvey, P. Introduction. In P. A. Kienel, *The Christian School: Why It Is Right for Your Child.* Wheaton, Ill.: Victor Books, 1976.

Haughwout, L. M. A. *The Ways and Teachings of the Church: A Course of Instruction.* New York: Morehouse-Barlow, 1975.

Henry, C. F. H. *Christian Personal Ethics.* Grand Rapids, Mich.: Eerdmans, 1957.

Henry, C. F. H. (Ed.). *Contemporary Evangelical Thought: A Survey.* Grand Rapids, Mich.: Baker, 1968.

Johnson, D. (Ed.). *A Brief History of the International Fellowship of Evangelical Students.* Lausanne: International Fellowship of Evangelical Students, 1964.

Johnson, R. L. Ministry in secular colleges and universities. In J. H. Westerhoff (Ed.), *The Church's Ministry in Higher Education.* New York: United Ministries in Higher Education Communication Office, 1978.

Kelly, R. L. *The American Colleges and the Social Order.* New York: Macmillan, 1940.

Kennedy, W. B. *The Shaping of Protestant Education.* New York: Association Press, 1966.

Kienel, P. A. *The Christian School: Why It Is Right for Your Child.* Wheaton, Ill.: Victor Books, 1976.

Kilpatrick, W. H. *Philosophy of Education.* New York: Macmillan, 1951.

Kraushaar, O. F. *America's Nonpublic Schools: Patterns of Diversity.* Baltimore: Johns Hopkins University Press, 1972.

Lammers, N. (Ed.). *Congressional Quarterly Guide to Current American Government.* Washington: Congressional Quarterly, Inc., 1980.

Lewis, C. S. *English Literature in the Sixteenth Century.* London: Oxford University Press, 1954.

Lockerbie, D. B. *The Way They Should Go.* New York: Oxford University Press, 1972.

Lockerbie, D. B. *Who Educates Your Child? A Book for Parents.* Garden City, N.Y.: Doubleday, 1980.

Machen, J. G. *Christianity and Liberalism.* New York: Macmillan, 1925.

Malik, C. *The Two Tasks.* Westchester, Ill.: Cornerstone Books, 1980.

Manschreck, C. L. *Melanchthon: The Quiet Reformer.* New York: Oxford University Press, 1958.

McDowell, E. Religious publishing: Going skyward. *New York Times,* May 12, 1981, p. C10.

McLachlan, J. *American Boarding Schools.* New York: Scribner, 1970.

McLoughlin, W. G., & Bellah, R. N. (Eds.). *Religion in America.* Boston: Houghton Mifflin, 1968.

Miller, R. C. *The Theory of Christian Education Practice: How Theology Affects Christian Education.* Birmingham, Ala.: Religious Education Press, 1980.

Moule, H. C. G. *Charles Simeon.* London: Inter-Varsity Fellowship, 1948.

North Carolina, General Assembly. Chapter 505. Senate Bill 383. A bill to create an article to deal specifically with private church schools and schools of religious character. May 2, 1979.

Novotney, J. (Ed.). *Christian College News,* April 24, 1981.

Panoch, J. V., & Barr, D. L. (Eds.). *Religion Goes to School: A Practical Handbook for Teachers.* New York: Harper & Row, 1968.

Parkes, H. B. *The American Experience.* New York: Random House, Vintage Books, 1959.

Petersen, W. J. (Ed.). How wise is the spectrum in Christian schools? *Eternity,* 1980, *9,* 24–31.

Postman, N. *Teaching as a Conserving Activity.* New York: Dell, Delacorte Press, 1979.

Press, A., & Wassner, R. Teaching from God's point of view. *Newsweek,* April 20, 1981, p. 71.

Rainey, H. P. Introduction. In D. W. Beggs & R. B. McQuigg (Eds.), *America's Schools and Churches: Partners in Conflict.* Bloomington: Indiana University Press, 1965.

Rian, E. H. *Christianity and American Education.* San Antonio, Calif.: Naylor, 1949.

Richards, L. O. *A Theology of Christian Education.* Grand Rapids, Mich.: Zondervan, 1975.

Ridley, J. *John Knox.* New York: Oxford University Press, 1968.

Rushdoony, R. J. *The Messianic Character of American Education.* Nutley, N. J.: Craig Press, 1968.

Sadler, J. E. *J. A. Comenius and the Concept of Universal Education.* New York: Barnes & Noble, 1966.

Silberman, C. E. *Crisis in the Classroom.* New York: Random House, 1970.

Smylie, J. H. Hope, history, and higher education in the South. In J. H. Westerhoff (Ed.), *The Church's Ministry in Higher Education.* New York: United Ministries in Higher Education Communication Office, 1978. (ERIC Document Reproduction Service No. ED 158 690)

Spinka, M. *John Amos Comenius: That Incomparable Moravian.* New York: Russell & Russell, 1967.

Sweet, W. W. *The Story of Religion in America.* New York: Harper & Brothers, 1950.

Swets, K. Christian schools international: Today and tomorrow. *Banner,* 1979, *10,* 18–19.

Tewksbury, D. G. *The Founding of American Colleges and Universities before the Civil War.* New York: Teachers College, 1932.

Vecsey, G. Religion becomes an important part of the baseball scene. *New York Times,* May 10, 1981.

Weigle, L. B. Religious and secular education. In W. M. Howlett (Ed.), *Religion, the Dynamic of Education: A Symposium on Religious Education.* New York: Harper & Brothers, 1929.

Westerhoff, J. H. *McGuffey and His Readers: Piety, Morality, and Education in Nineteenth-century America.* Nashville, Tenn.: Abingdon, 1978.

White, R. J. *A Short History of England.* Cambridge, England: Cambridge University Press, 1967.

Williams, D. The bright flight. *Newsweek,* April 20, 1981, pp. 66–73.

Witmer, S. A. *The Bible College Story: Education with Dimension.* Manhasset, N.Y.: Channel Press, 1962.

Wolterstorff, N. P. (Ed.). *Christian Liberal Arts Education: Report of the Calvin College Curriculum Study Committee.* Grand Rapids, Mich.: Calvin College, and Eerdmans, 1970.

Wolterstorff, N. P. Is it worth it? *Christian Home and School,* 1979, *7,* 6–7.

Woodward, W. H. *Vittorino da Feltre and Other Humanist Educators.* New York: Teachers College, 1964. (a)

Woodward, W. H. (Trans.). Desiderius Erasmus, *Concerning the Aim and Method of Education.* New York: Teachers College, 1964. (b)

Wyckoff, D. C. *The Gospel and Christian Education: A Theory of Christian Education for Our Times.* Philadelphia: Westminster, 1959.

PSYCHOLOGICAL SERVICES

Although nearly all professional educators have some background in psychology, school psychologists are the principal representatives of the discipline of psychology in educational settings. Formal definitions of school psychology have varied over the years in terms of the amount of emphasis placed on psychology or education. A representative definition recognizes roots in both education and psychology, with emphasis on the application of psychological theory, research, and intervention methods to the learning and adjustment problems of school-age children.

School psychologists differ from other related services personnel in education in that they (1) have more training in psychology; (2) typically work on an itinerant basis, meaning that they serve two or more pupil attendance centers; (3) generally work on a referral basis, meaning that the principal focus of their efforts involves students who are referred for learning or adjustment problems; (4) are deeply involved with exceptional children, particularly the handicapped; and (5) principally work at the elementary-grade level rather than the secondary-grade level.

The graduate training and the roles of school psychologists do overlap to some degree with those of other specialists, such as counselors, social workers, and special educators. The actual services provided by a school psychologist in a specific setting often vary, depending on the availability of other specialists and the kinds of services they provide. This article considers typical roles of school psychologists as they have developed over the past twenty years, influences on these roles, various professional issues, and suggestions concerning future trends in school psychology.

Knowledge Base. Most of the information concerning the profession of school psychology is based upon periodic surveys of school psychologists, university faculty, or state departments of education. Results from surveys of school psychologists may not be entirely representative, since not all school psychologists are members of the national professional organizations and the return rate of the surveys is generally in the range of 40 percent to 60 percent (Farling & Hoedt, 1971; Meacham & Peckham, 1978; Ramage, 1979). Surveys of graduate programs or state departments of education are generally more accurate, since their return rate is usually higher, often 80 percent or more, or the information sought may be available in public records.

Graduate education. Graduate programs in school psychology have expanded rapidly over the past twenty years (Bardon & Wenger, 1974; Brown, 1979; Goh, 1977). In 1960, there were approximately 40 such graduate programs in the United States, in 1970 about 110, and currently there are about 200. Approximately two-thirds of these are located in either departments of psychology or departments of educational psychology. Approximately one-third either are interdepartmental or are located in other departments in colleges of education, such as special education or counselor education. The general trend is toward the location of school psychology programs in departments of educational psychology in major universities where doctoral degrees are offered, and in departments of psychology in institutions that do not offer doctoral programs. Many of the nondoctrinal programs are located in departments of psychology in colleges of education. Thus the educational emphasis in school psychology training is well established by department or college affiliation.

Through the efforts of professional organizations, the general course content and organization of programs in school psychology has become more standardized over the past twenty years. The typical program is organized around four areas: (1) psychological foundations (basic courses in human learning, motivation, development, abnormal or exceptional patterns of behavior, research design, measurement, and statistics); (2) psychological methods and techniques (didactic and practical courses in psychoeducational assessment, counseling, consultation, etc.); (3) educational foundations (curriculum, remedial methods, and special education); and (4) professional school psychology (seminars on roles, professional issues, ethics, and internship experiences). Considerable variation exists among programs in theoretical orientation (e.g., behavioral versus psychodynamic). The typical distribution of content across the four areas is about 30 percent to psychological foundations, about 30 percent to psychological methods and techniques, and about 20 percent each to educational foundations and professional school psychology.

The most common level of graduate education in school psychology is the specialist degree, requiring sixty semester hours and two years of full-time graduate study (Brown, 1979; Brown & Lindstrom, 1977). A few programs are at the traditional master's level (thirty to thirty-five semester hours), but these programs are increasingly rare because of accreditation requirements and state department of education certification standards. There are approximately seventy doctoral degree programs, but most of these programs provide training at both the specialist and doctoral levels.

The undergraduate majors and previous employment experiences of persons enrolled in school psychology programs appear to have changed during the 1970s. Before 1970, most students had other career experiences, usually in education, typically as teachers or as counselors. Since 1970, school psychology graduate students have more often entered programs without teaching or other professional education experiences. Contemporary students usually have completed undergraduate majors in the behavioral sciences, most often psychology. Teaching experience is usually not a prerequisite for entry into a graduate program or for state department of education certification in school psychology. Opinions have been frequently expressed in the literature emphasizing the value of teaching experience, but studies do *not* indicate that school psychologists with teaching experience are more effective (Gerken & Landau, 1979).

Certification. State department of education certification requirements have been upgraded and more widely adopted in recent years (Brown, Horn, & Lindstrom, 1980). The number of states certifying school psychologists has grown from ten in 1950, to twenty-five in 1960, to forty in 1970; and now, all states have established certification requirements. State department of education certification provides a person with authority to practice school psychology in the public school setting. Most states maintain separate agencies and requirements governing licensure for private practice. The licensure requirements vary considerably, but many do not allow private practice of psychology by nondoctoral professionals. State department of education certification standards in school psychology also vary considerably (see Brown, Horn, & Lindstrom, 1980, for a review). The trend is toward requiring sixty semester hours in an approved or accredited graduate program in school psychology.

Employment characteristics. Brown (1979) estimated the number of school psychologists employed in the United States at 15,000. Of this number, approximately 8,000 are members either of the National Association of School Psychologists (NASP) or of the Division for School Psychologists in the American Psychological Association (Division 16). Most of the information on employment characteristics of school psychologists is based upon surveys of NASP or Division 16 members. It is important to note that these surveys may not be entirely representative of the current situation in school psychology.

Individual school districts or consortiums of school districts are far and away the most common employers of school psychologists (Ramage, 1979). The second most common employer is university-training programs. Some school psychologists work in medical settings or in private schools; others open up private practices. However, it is likely that 90 percent or more of all school psychologists in the United States are employed by public schools. Their employment with public schools typically involves a ten-month contract requiring from 190 to 210 days of service.

The distribution of school psychologists across the United States is quite uneven. Ratios of psychologists to students vary from as low as 1 to 1,000 students to as high as 1 to 60,000 students (Kicklighter, 1976). Some states have virtually no school psychologists. The median ratio across the United States according to Kicklighter's survey conducted in the mid-1970s was approximately 1 school psychologist per 4,800 students. However, because of the uneven distribution of school psychologists across districts and across states, this ratio may not be typical. Ramage's survey (1979), conducted later in the 1970s, suggested that two-thirds of the respondents worked in districts where the ratio of psychologists to students was less than 1 to 3,000. With the rapid expansion of school psychology that apparently has continued in recent years, the overall ratio of school psychologists to students has probably improved, and in many instances, is now near the recommended level of 1 to 2,000 students.

In localities that have both elementary and secondary school districts, school psychologists are more often employed in elementary school settings. Overall, school psychologists spend more of their time with elementary school children than with secondary school children.

Professional organizations. There are two national organizations in school psychology. Division 16 of the American Psychological Association (APA) was formed in the late 1940s to represent school psychology within the broader community of academic and professional psychology (Tindall, 1979). Persons without doctorates (that is, most school psychologists) are excluded from full membership in APA. For this reason and others, the National Association of School Psychologists (NASP) was organized in 1969 to provide better representation for all school psychologists, strongly emphasizing the interests and needs of nondoctoral school psychologists (Farling & Agner, 1979). There are now approximately 6,200 members of NASP and approximately 2,600 members of Division 16. Approximately 20 percent of the members of Division 16 are also members of NASP. Out of the 15,000 school psychologists nationally, slightly more than one-half are members of one or the other national organization.

In recent years there has been a high level of cooperation between Division 16 and NASP. Their major disagreements concern standards for accreditation of training programs and standards for certification. Division 16, following overall APA policy, advocates the doctoral level as the minimum for full certification and licensure as a school psychologist. In contrast, NASP advocates the specialist level. Current negotiations among representatives of the two organizations may lead to resolution of these disputes. Both organizations provide a full array of services to the profession, including publications, conventions, and in-service education.

State associations of school psychologists now exist in nearly every state. Some of the state associations have several hundred members and provide an active program of in-service training, publications, and other services within the profession.

Service Roles. School psychological services are generally initiated by teacher referral of a child because of learning and/or adjustment problems in the classroom. The vast majority of the professional activities of school psychologists are devoted to these individual cases. Individual casework sometimes leads to involvement with larger units within the educational system or broader community, for example, classrooms, district policies or programs, or community mental health agencies.

About 60 percent of referrals to school psychologists involve learning or achievement problems in the classroom, and about 30 percent, behavior problems exhibited in the classroom (Monroe, 1979). Other referral problems involve concerns about personal adjustment, for example, excessive shyness or intellectual giftedness. The population of students referred to school psychologists is somewhat uneven, with considerably more boys than girls referred and more minority students referred (Tomlinson et al., 1977). School psychological services are more likely to be provided at the elementary level, grades K–6, than at the secondary level, grades 7–12. Surveys suggest that approximately two-thirds to three-quarters of school psychologists' time is spent with elementary school children. There is also evidence to suggest that the types of services provided by school psychologists may differ, with a greater number of counseling and consultation services provided at the secondary level and more individual psychoeducational assessment at the elementary level (Carroll, Harris, & Bretzing, 1979; Monroe, 1979).

The roles of school psychologists are difficult to characterize because of the diversity of student populations, variations in state policies, and differences among school districts. Certainly, one of the major influences on the role of school psychologists is the ratio of psychologists to students. Broader roles involving more consultation, in-service training, and counseling are fostered by favorable ratios, for example, 1 to 1,000. A narrow role, sometimes restricted almost exclusively to individual testing, is associated with less favorable ratios, for example, above 1 to 3,000.

The major roles of school psychologists—counseling, psychoeducational assessment, consultation, in-service training, and research—can be organized along a continuum of the direct or indirect nature of the relationship with students. The counseling role, involving direct contact with students, is the most direct. The research role, involving communication of research results or evaluation of district programs, is seen as the least direct (Monroe, 1979).

Counseling and therapy.   The issue of whether school psychologists should provide individual psychotherapy to students has been debated over the past thirty years (Bernstein, 1976; Cutts, 1955; Gray, 1963; Jackson & Bernauer, 1975; Magary, 1967; White & Harris, 1961). Although there has been a great deal of discussion of the potential to provide long-term individual psychotherapy, surveys of school psychologists suggest that, for a variety of reasons, long-term individual therapy is not customarily provided. Provision of this kind of service in schools is limited chiefly by available resources, amount of time that can be devoted to a specific child, and the nature of school psychologists' training. Most school psychologists are not trained to provide long-term in-depth psychotherapy. Finally, serious questions have been raised about the effectiveness of long-term in-depth psychotherapy with children (Clarizio, 1979).

School psychologists are generally trained in counseling techniques, and most surveys suggest that school psychologists spend at least some of their time in counseling with children or parents. Data are not available to provide a precise generalization concerning the amount of time spent in counseling activities, but based on the other information, it appears that this has been an important but subsidiary role, accounting for perhaps 20 percent of the typical school psychologist's time. The counseling role overlaps that of other pupil personnel professionals. Some of this overlap may be more apparent than real, since school psychologists spend more of their time at the elementary level and counselors are more often employed at the secondary level.

Psychoeducational assessment.   All major surveys suggest that the school psychologist's principal role, account-

ing for as much as 80 percent of work time, is individual psychoeducational assessment (for reviews, see Monroe, 1979; Trachtman, 1981). The psychoeducational assessment provided by school psychologists is usually devoted to one of two purposes, either classification-placement or program planning–intervention. The classification-placement purpose generally involves determining whether or not referred children are eligible for various special education programs, such as learning disability, mild mental retardation, or emotional disturbance–behavior disorders. Involvement of school psychologists with these classification decisions is mandated by many states. The psychoeducational assessment role typically involves extensive individual contact with a child on a one-to-one basis, teacher interview and classroom observations, written reports, and conferences with parents and other school personnel. Administration of norm-referenced and criterion-referenced tests is nearly always part of this process. The information gathered through formal tests, observation, and interview is used to arrive at a classification decision and to design remedial educational programs. The amount of follow-up and type of involvement with students after the classification-placement decisions are made vary as a result of a number of factors. Direct involvement with instruction is extremely rare. Follow-up activities such as counseling, consultation, and monitoring effects of special programs are crucial to the overall success of psychoeducational assessment services.

Consultation.   Consultation as a role for school psychologists has been emphasized in the literature for at least the past thirty years. Recent evidence suggests that school psychologists are spending more time in consultation activities. The meaning of the term "consultation" often is ambiguous, with practically any kind of professional service sometimes referred to as "consultation." The more precise meaning of consultation within school psychology was suggested by Reschly (1976). Consultation is in the center of the continuum of directness of influence on children, since it typically refers to services provided by a professional to some other person who is in direct contact with a child. Most often, that is, a school psychologist serves as a consultant to a consultee who is a teacher or parent. The focus of the activity is on the behavior of a child who may be referred to as "the client." Activities that do not have this indirect characteristic should not be classified as consultation.

There are three major theoretical approaches to school psychology consultation: organization development consultation, mental health consultation, and behavioral consultation (Reschly, 1976). Consultation in school psychology settings generally involves either the mental health or the behavioral approach. Mental health consultation (Caplan, 1970) generally involves helping the consultee gain more insight into normal and abnormal emotional development and personality dynamics. The increased affective understanding pursued through mental health consultation is assumed to lead to better emotional adjustment on the part of consultees and, in turn, to a healthier climate for children. In contrast, the behavioral consultation approach provides a more direct focus on specific learning and/or adjustment problems of children (Bergan, 1977). Behavioral consultation involves a four-step problem-solving strategy in which (1) learning or adjustment problems are first described in behavioral terms through a Problem Identification Interview; (2) an intervention is designed to change the behavior using a Problem Analysis Interview; (3) the intervention or plan is put into effect; and (4) the intervention or plan is evaluated in a Plan Evaluation Interview.

The increased emphasis on consultation in school psychology arises from a variety of influences, including dissatisfaction with individual psychoeducational assessment, efforts to provide more effective services, efforts to exercise positive influence over greater numbers of children, and concern to improve the skills of consultees.

In-service training. The in-service role of school psychologists involves training teachers, parents, or others who deal with children. The purpose of this training is to increase knowledge, change attitudes, or develop skills that presumably would make these people more effective in dealing with children. Much of the impetus for the in-service role comes from concerns about social problems that schools are expected to address. Some of the social problems that are addressed through in-service activities are drug abuse, family disruption, and teenage pregnancy. In-service training of teachers and parents is potentially an important service, but is unlikely ever to constitute a major portion of the time or activity of school psychologists. Surveys suggest that school psychologists are involved with some in-service training and that this kind of activity has moderate support among teachers and administrators.

Research. The school psychologist's research role is the least direct of the five major roles. Through the research role, school psychologists exert influence on children by systematically gathering data to aid in making decisions about school programs, by systematic efforts to communicate the results of research to school personnel, and by efforts to implement the results of research. The kind of research envisioned for school psychologists tends to be applied rather than basic, and is often oriented toward evaluation of specific programs in the local setting rather than production of knowledge generalizable to other settings.

School psychologists have been seen as having high potential for, and solid training in, research activities (Bennett, 1976; Guttentag, 1968; Reger, 1964). However, other responsibilities have usually prevented school psychologists from accomplishing very much in this area. Kratochwill's description of research methods applicable to single cases or sample sizes of one subject or one child or $N = 1$ provides a promising approach to combining traditional case study and research activities (Kratochwill, 1977). The single-case methods can be used to evaluate consultation

interventions, individual counseling, or the effects of special education placement. These techniques have potential both for generating knowledge and for improving services provided to individuals.

Effectiveness. Research on the effectiveness of school psychological services has been largely restricted to examination of the psychoeducational assessment and consultation roles. Little or no research has appeared on the other three roles within the school psychology literature.

Psychoeducational assessment. The traditional psychoeducational assessment role has been repeatedly maligned in the school psychology literature. Some of the criticism has limited value because a very narrow, and probably atypical type of assessment is assumed to exist. Despite the criticism, there is firm support for the existence and importance of this role as part of special services in the schools (Ford & Migles, 1979; Kaplan, Clancy, & Chrin, 1977; Roberts, 1970). Surveys of teachers and school administrators generally reveal a strong expectation that school psychologists will provide individual psychoeducational assessment and that this service is highly valued. Perhaps the more important questions have to do with the amount of time devoted to individual psychoeducational assessment, the kinds of assessment conducted, and the outcomes of assessment.

School psychologists' dissatisfaction with the amount of time devoted to individual psychoeducational assessment has been pronounced in the school psychology literature. Several studies have compared school psychologists' perceptions of actual role versus ideal role (Farling & Hoedt, 1971; Ramage, 1979; Roberts, 1970). All such comparisons suggest that school psychologists believe that too much time is spent in individual psychoeducational assessment and too little time in preventive mental health, early detection of problems, and direct intervention with children, teachers, and families.

Actual teacher satisfaction with individual psychoeducational assessment has, surprisingly, not been thoroughly studied. Two studies suggest that teachers express a good bit of dissatisfaction with a narrow psychoeducational assessment role that involves simply determining whether or not children are eligible for special classes (Gilmore & Chandy, 1973; Grubb, Petty, & Flynn, 1976). Both studies indicate, however, that teachers value the psychoeducational assessment role. This role is viewed as potentially useful if follow-up is provided and if the information gathered was translated into specific changes in the classroom environment. Clearly, the need for more research on the psychoeducational assessment role exists. Information is needed on the specific kinds of assessment and the specific services that lead to positive outcomes in the classroom.

The quality and relevance of specific tests commonly used in psychoeducational assessment have been questioned in recent years (Bersoff, 1973; Keogh 1972; Keogh et al., 1975; Ysseldyke, 1979). Some studies indicate that the kinds of instruments used by school psychologists were excessively narrow, and lacking desirable characteristics in terms of reliability and validity. Much recent school psychology literature has emphasized developing a broader variety of information, more relevant information, and linking assessment with classroom interventions (Reschly, 1980a; Tucker, 1977).

Another disadvantage of the amount of time devoted to psychoeducational assessment is that other roles that might be more useful do not receive enough time and attention. Tindall (1964) pointed out the potential of school psychologists to provide a broad variety of mental health services to the public schools. These services would involve more emphasis upon systematic screening of primary school children, interviews with parents to further assist in early detection, consultation with teachers and others in efforts to develop solutions to learning and adjustment problems in the regular classroom, and, finally, the supervision of nonprofessional change agents to carry out interventions (Cowen & Lorion, 1976). Although psychoeducational assessment has been criticized a great deal in the literature, it continues to be the principal role of the school psychologist. This service can be very useful to children who are having learning and adjustment problems. In the absence of these services, many problems would go unrecognized and untreated and, conversely, many other students would be improperly classified. Current trends in assessment in school psychology suggest that this role will continue to be important, but that it will be modified to place more emphasis upon gathering information that translates directly into interventions that can be carried out in the regular classroom and to place more emphasis upon observation and data gathering in the natural setting rather than in a one-to-one situation outside of the classroom (Reschly, 1980a).

Consultation. Systematic research on the effects of consultation services provided by school psychologists has become increasingly prominent in the literature since the early 1970s. This research involves comparisons of consultation with other kinds of services by soliciting perceptions of significant consumers, examination of the effects of consultation on students, and comparisons of different forms of consultation, such as mental health versus behavioral consultation. Reviews of this literature indicate that both mental health and behavioral consultation are highly valued by various respondents, but behavioral consultation appears to be more effective, at least in terms of direct effects on students (Medway, 1979; Medway & Foreman, 1980).

Much of the research on behavioral consultation has been guided by the general model of behavioral consultation developed by Bergan (1977). Tombari and Davis (1979) describe this approach as representing a combination of nondirective counseling techniques and behavioral methods. Behavioral consultation stresses the importance of the verbal cues provided by the consultant during the interview. The problem-solving process is guided by skillful use of questions and summary statements. Through these techniques, the consultee defines the problem, sug-

gests a method for gathering data, designs the intervention, and evaluates the outcome. Consultant skills in conducting the interviews and teacher involvement with designing the interventions are related to successful outcome (Bergan & Neuman, 1980; Bergan & Tombari, 1976). The approach is successful with academic problems and classroom behavior problems (Bergan, Byrnes, & Kratochwill, 1979; Tombari & Davis, 1979). Consultation services are strongly supported by recent research. Consultation techniques that lead to specific changes in the classroom environment, e.g., behavior consultation, are particularly promising.

Influences on School Psychology. Throughout the history of school psychology, various external forces, such as special education, legal requirements, and the testing movement have exerted a strong influence on the daily activities of school psychologists (Tindall, 1979; Trachtman, 1981; Wallin & Ferguson, 1967). The external influences generally set broad parameters within which a particular professional can operate.

Special education. Special education funding patterns have been a kind of two-edged sword in school psychology. One one hand, special education funding provides a solid basis of support for the existence of school psychological services in most states. A strong correlation has always existed between the level of special education funding in a particular state and the number of school psychologists employed in that state. On the other hand, however, special education funding patterns have been blamed for leading to an excessively narrow role for school psychologists (Gutkin & Tieger, 1979). State and federal special education funds are usually provided to districts according to the number of students classified and placed in special education programs. Classification and placement often generate moneys for school psychological services as well as for special programs. These funding mechanisms lead to strong pressures on school psychologists to conduct psychoeducational assessments for the purpose of classifying and placing students (Meyers, Sundstrom, & Yoshida, 1974). If this works is not done, the special programs and the psychological services might well cease to exist.

Recent changes in special education have led to less emphasis on simple classification and more emphasis on providing services in the regular classroom. A further trend is possible revision of the classification system from diagnostic categories, for example, learning disability and educable mental retardation, to simple descriptions of the needed services, for example, part-time remedial mathematics and work-study experiences (Hobbs, 1975). These changes in special education will influence school psychology (and children) in a positive direction. The development of school psychology has been and, in all likelihood, will continue to be deeply affected by special education.

Legal requirements. All areas of public education, especially school psychology, have been increasingly influenced by litigation (court cases) and legislation (Cardon, Kuriloff, & Phillips, 1975; Kirp & Kirp, 1976). The general progression of events in the 1970s was litigation first, followed by legislation (Turnbull, 1978). During the 1970s nearly every state passed mandatory special education legislation that requires school districts to provide educational services to handicapped students. This legislation was particularly important in guaranteeing the rights of the more severely handicapped to public education services. Many severely handicapped students had previously been excluded from participation in public school programs. The trends from the courts and state legislatures were further enhanced by the enactment of Public Law 94-142, the Education for All Handicapped Children Act of 1975 (*Federal Register*, 1977).

Three general trends can be identified in the litigation and legislation. First, ensuring the rights of all handicapped children to educational services paid for out of public moneys and provided in as normal a situation as possible became important. Second, emphasis was placed on protection of the rights of parents and children through procedures such as informed consent, due process, multifactored assessment, parental access to records, three-year reevaluations of handicapped students, nonbiased assessment, and classification and placement decisions made by a multidisciplinary team. These protections were designed to ensure that children are not misclassified and that parents and children have the right to participate in and, if desired, to appeal classification and placement decisions. Third, an effort was made to ensure, to the greatest extent possible, that the educational programs provided as a result of classification are effective. The individualized educational program, the multidisciplinary team, the three-year reevaluations, and the requirement of least-restrictive environment are all related to ensuring that special education programming is indeed beneficial for the individual.

The legal requirements established in the 1970s had vast implications for the training and the practice of school psychology (Mowder, 1979; Prasse, 1978). Multifactored assessment became a legal requirement. New areas of assessment, such as adaptive behavior, primary language, and sociocultural background, were added to traditional areas (Reschly, 1981). The classification and placement decisions had to be made in conjunction with a multidisciplinary team, and with the participation of parents and other professionals. This is in contrast to traditional practices that, in many instances, involved classification and placement decisions made principally, or sometimes even solely, by the school psychologist. Assessment procedures and placement decisions were required to be nondiscriminatory with respect to cultural and racial status (*Federal Register*, 1977). Finally, school psychologists were required to develop skills in dealing with populations of children that previously were not included in public school programs (e.g., preschool handicapped children and children with low-incidence handicaps, such as hearing or visual impairments). Gerken (1979) noted that most school psychology graduate programs, past and present, provide generalist skills with little specific training in working with

these new populations of students. Considerable activity within the profession has been apparent over the past five years with respect to providing in-service training in the areas of multifactored assessment, nonbiased assessment, and services for low-incidence handicapped and preschool populations.

Although the legal requirements may appear to provide very specific guidelines for practice, in fact, they are highly ambiguous. Legal requirements, whether based on court cases or legislation, provide general guidelines, often in the form of strongly worded statements. However, a considerable amount of ambiguity usually exists in putting the guidelines into practice. Contrasts between the spirit and intent of federal legislation and simple compliance with the letter of the law were demonstrated well by Bersoff (1978), with respect to the due process provisions, and by Yoshida (1980), with respect to the multidisciplinary team requirements.

Perhaps the area that presents the greatest challenge to school psychologists is the legal requirement to provide nonbiased assessment and placement services to all children. This requirement is based upon a concern with overrepresentation of minority students in special education programs, particularly overrepresentation in programs for the mildly retarded. The federal rules and regulations (*Federal Register*, 1977) provide a strong mandate to eliminate all vestiges of discrimination in assessment and placement procedures. However, there is no definition of discrimination in the rules and regulations, nor are criteria provided to determine whether or not particular assessment procedures or placement practices are discriminatory, either in intent or effect (Reschly, 1979). A focal point in the discussions on nonbiased assessment has been the fairness of traditional tests of intelligence when used with minority students. An example of how legal requirements continue to change and evolve is provided by federal district court decisions in 1979 and 1980. In the *Larry P.* v. *Riles* case (1979) and the *PASE* v. *Hannon* case (1980), different federal district courts reached contradictory decisions on the issue of whether intelligence tests are fair when used with black students. Bersoff (forthcoming) provided a detailed commentary on the reasoning used in these cases. The basic problem is that many issues with which the courts have been asked to deal are ambiguous. Research related to these issues is not definitive. The federal courts, by their nature, are required to come up with unequivocal decisions. However, unequivocal decisions with respect to bias and IQ tests are impossible (Reschly, 1979).

The overall influence of legal requirements on the practice of school psychology has been enormous. In recent years, school psychologists have modified their practices in order to achieve highly desirable objectives established through litigation and legislation. The net effect of these changes has been greater protection of the rights of parents and children, greater sensitivity concerning appropriate assessment of minority students, and concerted efforts to ensure that classification results in effective educational programming. The continued challenge to school psychology is to avoid simple, rigid compliance with rules and regulations and to develop creative means to achieve the spirit and intent of the legal requirements.

Economic and social issues. The development of school psychology and the continued existence of the profession are intimately related to public support for special services for school-age children. Trachtman (1979) noted the developing problems with respect to continued state and federal support for school psychology and other human services. Deep concern now exists about continued state and federal support for school psychology and other human services professions.

School psychology, perhaps like other human services professions, has been called upon to address current social problems and to expand roles and services to meet ever increasing perceptions of needs. Some recent examples are advocacy of school psychology roles with respect to child abuse and neglect (Kline, Cole, & Fox, 1981), disruption of the family unit (Drake & Shellenberger, 1981; Lombard, 1979), and substance abuse (Friedman & Meyers, 1975). Furthermore, school psychologists have frequently been asked to provide services of a different nature (e.g., psychoneurological assessment) or to different populations (e.g., adults) (Hohenshil, 1979; Hynd, Quackenbush, & Obrzut, 1980). A further trend has been the emphasis on the potential of school psychology for delivering useful services in other settings, including higher education (Sandoval & Love, 1977), medicine (Givens & Hartlage, 1979), and secondary education as instructors in psychology courses (Medway & Elkin, 1975).

As Gerken (1979) pointed out, it is impossible for any individual to possess all the competencies and skills that have been advocated for persons in the profession. The trend today, almost by necessity, is toward specialization. Specialization should exist within the framework of a basic set of skills and competencies possessed by all school psychologists. The specialization represents training, competence, and experience with unique populations of children (e.g., preschool handicapped) or specific kinds of services (e.g., neuropsychological assessment). Continuing education for school psychologists to ensure the basic set of competencies as well as to develop needed specializations represents one of the most important challenges in the field. Both national professional organizations, APA and NASP, have placed increasing emphasis on continuing education in recent years.

Summary. School psychology has developed rapidly over the past fifteen years. Perhaps we have witnessed its most rapid period of development. During this period much of the literature in school psychology reflected a rather self-critical stance. There have been and continue to be concerted efforts to expand and to change the role and the services provided by school psychologists. The self-critical nature of the school psychology literature had an extremely positive aspect in that it provided a basis

for stimulating improvements in the field, many of which are under way or have taken place. However, the self-critical nature can lead to a loss of perspective on what has transpired in the field over the past fifteen years or so (Reschly, 1980b). School psychology has changed and has improved dramatically during this period. There have been great changes in the level of graduate education of the typical school psychologist. There have been significant improvements in ratios of school psychologists to students. Most important, however, are the improvements in the quality of psychoeducational assessment and the enormous changes in the knowledge base and the technology related to providing interventions within regular and special education settings. Some of the changes concerning interventions include the development and widespread use of short-term counseling techniques, group counseling procedures, more specific and more effective special education programs, and the development of effective consultation techniques, especially the behavioral consultation approach. We can anticipate further developments along these lines in the future that will have the effect of improving school psychological services for children.

School psychology continues to be strongly influenced by various external forces. However, Grimes (1981) notes a variety of techniques that can be used by the school psychologist to improve roles and services. These techniques are designed to be used within the context of external forces and provide the basis for the school psychologist to develop a broad, flexible, and effective role. Although external forces have shaped school psychology, wide latitude continues to exist for the school psychologist to exercise a positive influence over the lives of children.

                                                    Daniel J. Reschly

See also Behavioral Treatment Methods; Counseling; Special Education; Mental Health; Rehabilitation Services; Speech-Language Services; Student Personnel Work.

REFERENCES

Bardon, J., & Wenger, R. Institutions offering graduate training in school psychology. *Journal of School Psychology,* 1974, *12,* 70–83.

Bennet, V. "Applied" research can be useful: An example. *Journal of School Psychology,* 1976, *14,* 67–73.

Bergan, J. *Behavioral Consultation.* Columbus, Ohio: Merrill, 1977.

Bergan, J.; Byrnes, I.; & Kratochwill, T. Effects of behavioral and medical models of consultation on teacher expectancies and instruction of a hypothetical child. *Journal of School Psychology,* 1979, 307–316.

Bergan, J., & Neuman, A. The identification of resources and constraints influencing plan design in consultation. *Journal of School Psychology,* 1980, *18,* 317–323.

Bergan, J., & Tombari, M. Consultant skill and efficiency and the implementation and outcomes of consultation. *Journal of School Psychology,* 1976, *14,* 3–14.

Bernstein, M. Psychotherapy in the schools: Promise and perplexity. *Journal of School Psychology,* 1976, *14,* 314–321.

Bersoff, D. Silk purses into sow's ears: The decline of psychological testing and a suggestion for its redemption. *American Psychologist*, 1973, *28*, 892–899.

Bersoff, D. Procedural safeguards. In L. Morra (Ed.), *Due Process: Developing Criteria for the Evaluation of Due Process Procedural Safeguards Provisions*. Washington, D.C.: United States Office of Education, Bureau of Education for the Handicapped, 1978.

Bersoff, D. *Larry P.* and *PASE:* Judicial report cards on the validity of individual intelligence tests. In T. Kratochwill (Ed.), *Advances in School Psychology* (Vol. 2). Hillsdale, N.J.: Lawrence Erlbaum Associates, forthcoming.

Brown, D. Issues in accreditation, certification, and licensure. In G. Phye & D. Reschly (Eds.), *School Psychology: Perspectives and Issues*. New York: Academic Press, 1979.

Brown, D.; Horn, A.; & Lindstrom, J. *The Handbook of Certification/Licensure Requirements for School Psychologists*. Washington, D.C.: National Association of School Psychologists, 1980.

Brown, D., & Lindstrom, J. *Directory of School Psychology Training Programs in the United States and Canada*. Washington, D.C.: National Association of School Psychologists, 1977.

Caplan, G. *The Theory and Practice of Mental Health Consultation*. New York: Basic Books, 1970.

Cardon, B.; Kuriloff, P.; & Phillips, B. *Law and the School Psychologist: Challenge and Opportunity*. New York: Human Science Press, 1975. (Also appeared as a special issue of the *Journal of School Psychology*, 1975, *13*(4).)

Carroll, J.; Harris, J.; & Bretzing, B. A survey of psychologists serving secondary schools. *Professional Psychology*, 1979, *10*, 766–770.

Clarizio, H. School psychologists and the mental health needs of students. In G. Phye & D. Reschly (Eds.), *School Psychology: Perspectives and Issues*. New York: Academic Press, 1979.

Cowen, E., & Lorion, R. Changing roles for the school mental health professional. *Journal of School Psychology*, 1976, *14*, 131–138.

Cutts, N. (Ed.). *School Psychologists at Mid-century*. Washington, D.C.: American Psychological Association, 1955.

Drake, E., & Shellenberger, S. Children of separation and divorce: A review of school programs and implications for the psychologist. *School Psychology Review*, 1981, *10*, 54–61.

Farling, W., & Agner, J. History of the National Association of School Psychologists: The first decade. *School Psychology Digest*, 1979, *8*, 140–152.

Farling, W., & Hoedt, K. *National Survey of School Psychologists*. Washington, D.C.: National Association of School Psychologists, 1971. (ERIC Document Reproduction Service No. ED 061 553)

Federal Register, August 23, 1977, pp. 42474–42518. (Public Law 94-142)

Ford, J., & Migles, M. The role of the school psychologist: Teachers' preferences as a function of personal and professional characteristics. *Journal of School Psychology*, 1979, *17*, 372–378.

Friedman, M., & Meyers, J. A workshop for training the school psychologist in drug intervention techniques. *Journal of School Psychology*, 1975, *13*, 63–67.

Gerken, K. Assessment of high risk preschoolers and children and adolescents with low-incident handicapping conditions. In G. Phye & D. Reschly (Eds.), *School Psychology: Perspectives and Issues*. New York: Academic Press, 1979.

Gerken, K., & Landau, S. Perceived effectiveness of school psychological services: A comparative study. *Journal of School Psychology*, 1979, *17*, 347–354.

Gilmore, G., & Chandy, J. Educators describe the school psychologist. *Psychology in the Schools*, 1973, *10*, 397–404.

Givens, T., & Hartlage, L. *School Psychology Applies to Medical College*. Paper presented at the annual convention of the American Psychological Association, New York, 1979. (ERIC Document Reproduction Service No. ED 181 686)

Goh, D. Graduate training in school psychology. *Journal of School Psychology*, 1977, *15*, 207–218.

Gray, S. *The Psychologist in the Schools*. New York: Holt, 1963.

Grimes, J. Shaping the future of school psychology. In J. Ysseldyke & R. Weinberg (Eds.), *The Future of Psychology in the Schools: Proceedings of the Spring Hill Symposium*, special issue of *School Psychology Review*, 1981, *10*, 206–231.

Grubb, R.; Petty, S.; & Flynn, D. A strategy for the delivery of accountable school psychological services. *Psychology in the Schools*, 1976, *13*, 39–44.

Gutkin, T., & Tieger, A. Funding patterns for exceptional children: Current approaches and suggested alternatives. *Professional Psychology*, 1979, *10*, 670–680.

Guttentag, M. Research is possible: New answers to old objections. *Journal of School Psychology*, 1968, *6*, 254–260.

Hobbs, N. *The Futures of Children*. San Francisco: Jossey-Bass, 1975.

Hohenshil, T. Adulthood: New frontier for vocational school psychology. *School Psychology Digest*, 1979, *8*, 193–198.

Hynd, G.; Quackenbush, R.; & Obrzut, J. Training school psychologists in neuropsychological assessment: Current practices and trends. *Journal of School Psychology*, 1980, *18*, 148–153.

Jackson, J., & Bernauer, M. A responsibility model for the practice of professional school psychology: Psychoeducational therapy. *Journal of School Psychology*, 1975, *13*, 76–81.

Kaplan, M.; Clancy, B.; & Chrin, M. Priority roles for school psychologists as seen by superintendents. *Journal of School Psychology*, 1977, *15*, 75–80.

Keogh, B. Evaluation of exceptional children: Old hangups and new directions. *Journal of School Psychology*, 1972, *10*, 141–145.

Keogh, B.; Kukic, S.; Becker, L.; McLaughlin, R.; & Kukic, M. School psychologists' services in special education programs. *Journal of School Psychology*, 1975, *13*, 142–148.

Kicklighter, R. School psychology in the U.S.: A quantitative survey. *Journal of School Psychology*, 1976, *14*, 151–156.

Kirp, D., & Kirp, L. The legalization of the school psychologist's world. *Journal of School Psychology*, 1976, *14*, 83–89.

Kline, D.; Cole, P.; & Fox, P. Child abuse and neglect: The school psychologist's role. *School Psychology Review*, 1981, *10*, 65–71.

Kratochwill, T. $N = 1$: An alternative research strategy for school psychologists. *Journal of School Psychology*, 1977, *15*, 239–249.

Larry P. et al. v. *Wilson Riles et al.* U.S. District Court, Northern District of California, Case No. C-71-2270 RFP (1972, 1974, 1979).

Lombard, T. Family-oriented emphasis for school psychologists: A needed orientation for training and professional practice. *Professional Psychology*, 1979, *10*, 687–696.

Magary, J. (Ed.). *School Psychological Services in Theory and Practice: A Handbook*. Englewood Cliffs, N.J.: Prentice-Hall, 1967.

Meacham, M., & Peckham, P. School psychologists at three-quarters century: Congruence between training, practice, preferred role, and competence. *Journal of School Psychology*, 1978, *16*, 195–206.

Medway, F. How effective is school consultation? A review of recent research. *Journal of School Psychology*, 1979, *17*, 275–282.

Medway, F., & Elkin, V. Psychologist-teacher collaboration in developing and team-teaching high school psychology courses. *Psychology in the Schools*, 1975, *12*, 107–111.

Medway, F., & Foreman, S. Psychologists' and teachers' reactions to mental health and behavioral school consultation. *Journal of School Psychology*, 1980, *18*, 338–348.

Meyers, C.; Sundstrom, P.; & Yoshida, R. The school psychologist and assessment in special education: A report of the Ad Hoc Committee of APA Division 16. *Monographs of Division 16 of the American Psychological Association*, 1974, *2*(1), 3–57.

Monroe, V. Roles and status of school psychology. In G. Phye & D. Reschly (Eds.), *School Psychology: Perspectives and Issues*. New York: Academic Press, 1979.

Mowder, B. Legislative mandates: Implications for changes in school psychology training programs. *Professional Psychology*, 1979, *10*, 681–686.

(PASE) Parents in Action on Special Education v. *Joseph P. Hannon*. U.S. District Court, Northern District of Illinois, Eastern Division, No. 74(3586) (July 1980).

Prasse, D. Federal legislation and school psychology: Impact and implication. *Professional Psychology*, 1978, *9*, 592–601.

Ramage, J. National survey of school psychologists: Update. *School Psychology Digest*, 1979, *8*, 153–161.

Reger, R. The school psychologist and research for the future. *Psychology in the Schools*, 1964, *1*, 415–419.

Reschly, D. School psychology consultation: "Frenzied, faddish, or fundamental?" *Journal of School Psychology*, 1976, *14*, 105–113.

Reschly, D. Nonbiased assessment. In G. Phye & D. Reschly (Eds.), *School Psychology: Perspectives and Issues*. New York: Academic Press, 1979.

Reschly, D. School psychologists and assessment in the future. *Professional Psychology*, 1980, *11*, 841–848. (a)

Reschly, D. *What's Good about School Psychology*. Unpublished manuscript, Iowa State University, 1980. (b)

Reschly, D. Assessing mild mental retardation: The influence of adaptive behavior, sociocultural status, and prospects for nonbiased assessment. In C. Reynolds & T. Gutkin (Eds.), *A Handbook for School Psychology*. New York: Wiley, 1981.

Roberts, R. Perceptions of actual and desired role functions of school psychologists by psychologists and teachers. *Psychology in the Schools*, 1970, *7*, 175–178.

Sandoval, J., & Love, J. School psychology in higher education: The college psychologist. *Professional Psychology*, 1977, *8*, 328–339.

Tindall, R. Trends in the development of psychological services in the schools. *Journal of School Psychology*, 1964, *1*, 1–12.

Tindall, R. School psychology: The development of a profession. In G. Phye & D. Reschly (Eds.), *School Psychology: Perspectives and Issues*. New York: Academic Press, 1979.

Tombari, M., & Davis, R. Behavioral consultation. In G. Phye & D. Reschly (Eds.), *School Psychology: Perspectives and Issues*. New York: Academic Press, 1979.

Tomlinson, J.; Acker, N.; Canter, A.; & Lindborg, S. Minority status, sex, and school psychological services. *Psychology in the Schools*, 1977, *14*, 456–460.

Trachtman, G. The clouded crystal ball: Is there a school psychology in our future? *Psychology in the Schools*, 1979, *16*, 378–387.

Trachtman, G. On such a full sea. In J. Ysseldyke & R. Weinberg (Eds.), *The Future of Psychology in the Schools: Proceedings of the Spring Hill Symposium*, a special issue of *School Psychology Review*, 1981, *10*, 138–181.

Tucker, J. Operationalizing the diagnostic-intervention process. In T. Oakland (Ed.), *Psychological and Educational Assessment of Minority Children*. New York: Brunner/Mazel, 1977.

Turnbull, H. The past and future impact of court decisions in special education. *Kappan*, 1978, *60*, 523–527.

Wallin, J., & Ferguson, D. The development of school psychological services. In J. Magary (Ed.), *School Psychological Services in Theory and Practice: A Handbook*. Englewood Cliffs, N.J.: Prentice-Hall, 1967.

White, M., & Harris, M. *The School Psychologist*. New York: Harper & Brothers, 1961.

Yoshida, R. Multidisciplinary decision making in special education: A review of issues. *School Psychology Review*, 1980, *9*, 221–227.

Ysseldyke, J. Issues in psychoeducational assessment. In G. Phye & D. Reschly (Eds.), *School Psychology: Perspectives and Issues*. New York: Academic Press, 1979.

PSYCHOLOGY

Psychology is often defined as the science of mind and of behavior. It is, therefore, a very broad discipline. Every kind of human thought and every kind of action by human beings and other animals is an appropriate phenomenon to study. Most areas of psychological inquiry—thinking, learning, memory, attitude formation, development, and so on—have easily recognized links to education. But even such areas of psychology as animal learning, or physiological psychology, provide important concepts for education. For example, from studies of pigeons, rats, and chimpanzees have come theories and principles of learning that apply to human beings. Physiological psychologists have contributed to educational knowledge by studying sensation, perception, and the way the brain functions. These are the ways we receive, interpret, and come to act upon information from our environment, issues of obvious concern to educators. Thus, virtually every area of psychology may have relevance for those who work in education. In fact, a branch of psychology, educational psychology, has developed in order to make the links between psychological inquiry and education explicit. Educational psychologists apply psychological knowledge to educational issues and develop generalizable knowledge about human beings that is of interest to all social scientists.

Educational psychology is the application of scientific method to the study of the behavior of people in instructional settings. The scientific methods used by educational psychologists are those of the behavioral scientist. They include observational techniques, such as those used in anthropology; methods of interviewing, such as those used in political science; methods of data analysis, such as those used in economics or sociology; and true experimental designs, such as those used in general psychology and other areas of science. The scientific methods of educational psychology have been used for inquiry into a broad range of educational phenomena, but these methods stand in contrast to another educational tradition. Educators have commonly held romantic, artistic, and philosophic visions of the teaching-learning process and have not always regarded science as very useful.

The people whose behavior is of most interest to the educational psychologist are teachers and students. But the educational psychologist may also be interested in studying the behavior of teacher aides, principals, parents, infants, migrants, or the aged. It is the behavior of people in relation to certain variables, such as the organization of texts, competitiveness, test anxiety, or the physical arrangement of classrooms, that is of most interest. The impact of these variables on behavior is scientifically studied by an educational psychologist in order to understand or improve the way teaching and learning occur.

The instructional settings of interest to an educational psychologist vary widely. They include a child's crib, a jet aircraft cockpit, a skating rink on a Saturday night, an automobile shop, and, of course, the classroom. Of primary interest to the educational psychologist is how information, attitudes and beliefs, and psychomotor skills are taught and learned in such settings.

The broad range of areas covered by educational psychology makes overlap with other domains of psychology inevitable. Close ties, therefore, exist to the researchers in child and adolescent development, social psychology, psychological testing, and the psychology of counseling and adjustment.

Origins and Development. The earliest records of philosophy show concern about educational and psychological issues, such as how we come to know things (learning) and what it is that knows (mind). Thus, although it would be centuries until it became a distinct field, educational psychology had its roots in the earliest philosophic discourses about human beings (Boring, 1950).

Philosophy, rather than science, was the primary method for inquiry about learning and the mind until the late nineteenth century. In 1879, at Leipzig, Germany, Wilhelm Wundt founded the first university-affiliated laboratory devoted to the *scientific* study of psychology. Although Wundt's work brought psychology to the attention of the academic world, it was another German scholar of the same time, Hermann Ebbinghaus, whose studies were to show how the new scientific psychology was useful in education. Ebbinghaus developed techniques for the experimental study of memory and forgetting. These had been topics of philosophic interest for centuries, but until the late nineteenth century these higher mental processes had never been scientifically studied. Psychologists and educators immediately recognized the importance of this scientific work for the practical world of schooling.

Meanwhile, in the late 1870s at Harvard University, the distinguished American philosopher and psychologist William James had also started a laboratory for the scientific study of psychology. His classic *Principles of Psychol-*

ogy, published in 1890, arrived on the scene only six years after the first English-language text of the new scientific psychology. James's text adopted a Darwinian approach to the study of behavior. He was interested in how one's mental life and other behavior adapted to different environments. This "functional" approach to the study of behavior led James and his students to study practical areas of human endeavor such as schooling. Thus, in 1899, James published his *Talks to Teachers*. In that volume he discussed the relations between the science of psychology and the art of teaching.

But the title of "first" educational psychologist is not usually awarded to James. Rather, it is James's student E. L. Thorndike who usually receives this honor. In 1903 Thorndike published the first text of renown with the explicit title *Educational Psychology*. In that volume he managed to alienate most educators whose scholarly traditions were different from his own. He said: "This book attempts to apply to a number of educational problems the methods of exact science. I have therefore paid no attention to speculative opinions and very little attention to the conclusions of students who present data in so rough and incomplete a form that accurate quantitative treatment is impossible" (p. v). In 1910, in response to the growth in empirical research, the *Journal of Educational Psychology* was founded. The first article in the first issue was by Thorndike (1910). He promised great contributions to education from the science of educational psychology. In 1913 and 1914 he published a three-volume educational psychology containing reports of virtually all scientific study in psychology that had relevance to education (Thorndike, 1913–1914). With his colleagues and students at Teachers College, Columbia University, Thorndike made major contributions to the study of intelligence and ability testing, arithmetic and algebra instruction, vocabulary and reading instruction, and the way learning transfers from one situation to another. In addition, he developed an important theory of learning, describing how environments affect the way stimuli and responses are connected. This theory evolved into instrumental or operant learning theory and is recognized as having great practical utility for teachers.

Most educational psychologists were optimistic about their future. They flourished within the progressive and scientific movements in education that had begun around the turn of the century. But when the great depression of the 1930s swept America, a distrust of science and technology became evident, and the scientific movement in education faltered.

Educational psychology then adopted a more modest position about its achievements and its potential for improving education. From approximately the early 1930s until the end of World War II, empirical research in educational psychology was conducted by only a small number of people. Four things changed that: World War II, the postwar baby boom, the curriculum-reform movement, and concern for the disadvantaged.

Many psychologists were in the armed forces during World War II. They were required to solve practical educational problems. They learned how to predict who would be a good pilot and who would be a good radio repairman. They learned how to teach aircraft gunnery or cooking in eight weeks to students who sometimes were neither especially intelligent nor motivated. Since so many of these psychologists studied and learned how to validly test and efficiently instruct, many of them turned their attention to testing and instruction in education when the war ended. A second factor in the growth of the field was the postwar baby boom. As the school population grew, educational psychologists with knowledge of testing and instruction were needed to design and evaluate instructional materials, training programs, and educational tests. Furthermore, the growth in the school population after World War II included a slow but steady growth in populations that formerly did not always demand special services from schools. These groups included minorities, poor people, and retarded and handicapped students. As the schools learned to serve more and more people of greater diversity, they had more need for the services of psychologists. At about the same time there was a concern that the curriculum of the schools needed major revision. When *Sputnik* was launched by the Soviet Union, in 1957, America's modest efforts to update the school curriculum were increased. Educational psychologists worked with leaders in science and mathematics to develop and evaluate new curricula and design new teacher education programs to accompany these new curricula. The heavy commitment of federal money to this effort resulted in a large increase in people doing psychological research. Finally, with the national concern for the disadvantaged, millions of dollars of federal money became available to improve the academic performance of students in the lower social class. Psychologists of many different persuasions were deeply involved in the design and evaluation of programs to accomplish this goal.

These societal forces led to rapid growth in the number of people who entered the field of educational psychology, particularly from 1960 to 1980. Today, more than 3,000 members of the American Psychological Association identify themselves as educational psychologists. The division of learning and instruction of the American Educational Research Association has almost 5,500 members, who study problems that are usually in the domain of educational psychology. The major journals of the association— the *American Educational Research Journal* and *Review of Educational Research*—are dominated by psychological investigations. At annual meetings of the American Psychological Association and the American Educational Research Association, hundreds of psychologists disseminate their recent research through oral presentations of research papers. The 1981 meetings featured papers and symposia on such topics as how the mind organizes information; how we learn from texts and lectures; how we learn information and attitudes from television; nutrition and learning; how instructional time and effort relate to

school achievement; the use of interactive microcomputers for instruction; how to solve complex problems; and the development of the concept of space in males and females.

The sheer number of empirical and theoretical psychological research studies reported at these meetings provides evidence of the breadth and vigor of educational psychology in the early 1980s. New journals to publish the thousands of reports issued each year have recently been initiated. Scientific research by and for educational psychologists is reported in over a dozen journals. The research is generated by scientists working in four different institutional settings. The primary contributors to the research literature are professors of educational psychology and their students from universities and colleges. The next largest group are the personnel from the dozens of federally funded educational research-and-development laboratories and centers. The third group who contribute to the field are the state and local school district personnel who engage in psychological research. Finally, psychological research is conducted by personnel of the hundreds of private research companies that were organized or expanded over the last two decades. A few of these companies have hundreds of people engaged in psychological research in education, but most have only a few employees who work on only a small number of projects at one time.

Today, educational psychology is not as optimistic a field as it was in Thorndike's time. Contemporary psychologists in education are not so naive as to think that science will solve all the problems of education. But the field is every bit as vigorous as it was when Thorndike was at his zenith, and it is likely to continue to be a dynamic and productive discipline.

Teaching Psychology in Education. Educational psychology is taught at almost all universities and colleges that have a teacher education program. The courses are usually taught through a department of educational psychology. Most states require a prospective teacher to have passed at least one course in educational psychology. Thus, a "basic" course in educational psychology is taken by thousands of students each year. It has been estimated that 350,000 students a year were enrolled in these "basic" courses during the 1960s. In 1981, with a reduction in the numbers of people preparing to teach, that number is estimated at about 150,000 per year.

The textbooks in any science are usually examined periodically because textbooks often help in defining the boundaries of a field. The first such review in educational psychology, by Hall-Quest (1915), reported that there simply was no agreement either on terminology or on the structure of courses in educational psychology. Remmers and Knight (1922) also analyzed textbooks and found no agreement on content, organization, or viewpoint. Worcester (1927) analyzed the five leading textbooks in educational psychology in the mid-1920s and reported that one could hardly find five books on the same subject that varied more! Blair (1949), Hendrickson and Blair (1950),

Nunney (1964), and others all reached the same conclusion: educational psychology is an incredibly diverse field. yet, within that diversity is some modicum of agreement.

Englander (1976), searching for "fundamental" concepts, had educational psychology teachers rate seventy-five concepts. Behavior modification was chosen by *all* respondents as a fundamental concept. Close behind in the ratings were a set of developmental concepts such as readiness, the stages in Piaget's developmental theory, intrinsic and extrinsic motivation, self-concept, and level of aspiration. The concepts with high agreement in the teaching and learning area included operant conditioning and discovery learning. In the area of measurement there was relatively high agreement that performance objectives and mastery learning were fundamental concepts. Feldhusen (1977) asked thirty-two teachers of educational psychology to rate twenty topical areas on their importance in a basic educational psychology course. They rated as unnecessary or unimportant such topics as research methods; educational psychology as a discipline; special groups such as the gifted, the disadvantaged, the handicapped, and so on; and character, values, and morals. They rated as important, and necessary to teach, instruction and teaching, motivation, learning outcomes, and measurement and testing. In these two samples, then, *practical* issues of teaching, learning, motivation, behavioral management, and testing seem to have the attention of teachers of the basic course in educational psychology. Perhaps, since that is a course for future teachers, it is appropriate for professors of educational psychology and textbook writers to focus on these central concerns. As long as some central core concerned with teaching, learning, motivation, management, and testing is taught, the diversity in the field is probably quite tolerable. In fact, it may be inevitable in a field that has loose boundaries, such as educational psychology.

Of the dozens of textbooks in educational psychology now on the market, a few have managed to accrue substantial sales through more than one edition. These may properly be called the popular texts of 1981. They include *Psychology Applied to Education,* 3rd edition, by Biehler (1978); *Psychology for Teaching,* 3rd edition, by LeFrançois (1979); *Educational Psychology,* 2nd edition, by Gage and Berliner (1979); *Educational Psychology,* 2nd edition, by Good and Brophy (1980); and *Educational Psychology: A Developmental Approach,* 3rd edition, by Sprinthall and Sprinthall (1981).

At the graduate level, diversity also reigns (DeCecco & Richards, 1977). There are no common texts or common sets of courses given throughout the country. Graduate programs in educational psychology may lead to expertise in knowledge about statistics and experimental design, testing and measurement, behavioral and cognitive learning, development, teaching, evaluation, counseling, or school psychology. A well-rounded educational psychologist would have some knowledge of each of these areas

of psychology and be expected to have special expertise in at least one of the areas.

Enrollment in graduate programs of educational psychology has decreased recently. From 1974/75 to 1979/80, first-year doctoral enrollments were down 33 percent (Stapp, 1980). Two trends seem to account for this decline. First, declining birthrates have resulted in a major reduction in enrollment at schools of education across the country. Thus, almost all fields in education show decline. Second, just a few years ago 50 percent of all doctorates in educational psychology were employed as professors of educational psychology in colleges and universities (DeCecco & Richards, 1977). The growth in all academic jobs has slowed. This, too, has resulted in a decline in enrollment for graduate work in educational psychology.

Psychologists in the public schools, however, are actually on the increase. Many psychology departments offer advanced degrees in school psychology, a field of psychology that provides direct clinical and testing services for students and consultation services for teachers and parents. Doctoral enrollment in school psychology has increased 45 percent from 1974/75 to 1979/80 (Stapp, 1980). Job opportunities for school psychologists now seem to be plentiful. Many of these people are trained in a similar manner to educational psychologists, though they have considerably more clinical experience. Furthermore, because school districts have had to comply with federal and state requirements that educational programs be evaluated, they have come to employ large numbers of educational psychologists to perform the evaluations. The field of social and educational program evaluation has grown enormously in the last twenty years. Many of the leaders in this new field were originally trained as psychologists.

Psychological Theory in Education. Once it was believed that a single learning theory would be discovered and that it would be applicable to a wide range of instructional settings, for persons of all ages and aptitudes. Most educational psychologists no longer believe such parsimony is probable, because of the wide diversity in human beings, instructional settings, and the kinds of things to be learned. Instead, psychologists work on developing small theories within areas of special interest such as learning, motivation, development, teaching, and instruction.

Learning. Dozens of theories of learning are useful to the understanding of different kinds of phenomena. Psychologists have developed mathematical models of learning that make use of the number of correct and incorrect responses a person makes to the same stimuli. This mathematical theory of learning is used to design instruction in mathematics, reading, and foreign language vocabulary learning. For understanding a child's emotional aversion to school, the respondent (or classical) conditioning theory of Ivan Pavlov (Bower & Hilgard, 1981) may be used. That theory describes how stimuli that occur together may come to evoke similar responses. To inquire about the origins of a child's disruptive classroom behavior, the operant (or instrumental) conditioning theory of E. L. Thorndike and B. F. Skinner may be applicable (Bower & Hilgard, 1981). This theory describes how rewards shape and maintain behavior. School violence and vandalism may be partially understood by reliance on the social learning theory of Albert Bandura (1977). This theory describes the conditions under which people learn to imitate the behavior of models. To understand how people solve problems by analogy, information-processing theory is used. This theoretical position uses computer simulations and the reaction time of people to posit the mental processes that are used to solve particular kinds of problems. Many different theories of learning help educational psychologists understand, predict, and control human behavior. The theories differ in the breadth of phenomena to which they apply.

Motivation. The refinement of theories about achievement motivation has produced attribution theory (Fyans, 1980; Weiner, 1976). This theory describes the role of the cognitive attributions that a person makes about what caused success or failure in school situations. For example, success on a classroom test could be attributed to luck rather than hard work. Attribution theory is intended to predict characteristics of learners who respond in one way or the other.

Development. Educational psychologists have been busy verifying and refining the developmental theories of the Swiss psychologist Jean Piaget (Flavell, 1963). His theory of how intellectual functioning is qualitatively different at different ages and how the child needs interaction with the environment to gain intellectual competence has changed educational and psychological thought. The design of environments for young children, the design of mathematics and science programs, and conceptions of intelligence have been strongly influenced by this theory.

Developmental theory has also begun to describe the physical, social, and intellectual needs of those beyond the age of youth. Educational psychology relies on such theory to help understand the teaching and learning process for mature adults, who are entering instructional settings in increasing numbers.

Teaching. The scientific study of teaching, based on systematic classroom observation, is a relatively new development. Until the 1950s there was very little classroom observation and experimentation. Thus, theory development in research on teaching is in a primitive stage. The research, however, is consistent in its implications for academic achievement. The variables that educational psychologists have found to be important in classroom teaching include the time teachers allocate to instruction, the amount of content they cover, the engagement of students with the material, the relationship between what is taught and what is tested, and the ability of the teacher to be clear in directions, provide feedback, hold students accountable for their behavior, and create a warm, democratic atmosphere for learning (Berliner & Rosenshine, 1977).

Instruction. The development by Gagné (1977) of a hierarchical theory of how some kinds of learning are prerequisite to other kinds of learning has had many implications for the sequencing of instruction. Theories of how teaching and learning can take place with algorithms and heuristics are also influencing the design of instructional materials and methods. The theory of hierarchical, algorithmic, and heuristic learning, along with the development of a technology of instruction that makes use of behavioral objectives and criterion-referenced tests, has made the development of a science of instruction possible (Merrill, Kowallis, & Wilson, 1981).

Applications. Educational psychologists apply their knowledge and skill about teaching and learning to a diverse set of problems, including design of instructional tours of breweries, evaluation of corporate management training programs, and development of instructions to fill out federal income tax forms. A sampling of recent applications in school settings provides some sense of the usefulness of the field.

In hundreds of schools educational psychology has recently been applied in the creation of mastery learning. Mastery learning is a system of instruction based on the belief that 90 percent of the students can achieve the equivalent of A or B grade if (1) the curriculum is broken down into logically sequenced small units of about two weeks in duration; (2) the student is required to pass a test at the end of each unit before proceeding to the next unit; (3) alternative forms of instruction and alternative tests are available so that students can do remedial work if they fail the test the first time; (4) the students determine for themselves the amount of time they need to complete a unit. This form of instruction, or a related method called the personalized system of instruction (PSI), has been thoroughly evaluated from elementary to college level. It has been found remarkably successful in courses in which basic acquisition of knowledge and skills is required (Block & Burns, 1976).

Educational psychologists frequently engage in curriculum development and evaluation. Objectives for an instructional program must be specified and test items must be matched to those objectives. Instructional treatments to accomplish the goals must be designed. The treatments must be pilot-tested and redesigned on the basis of empirical findings. Field testing of the materials, including testing of student comprehension, must also be accomplished. Educational psychologists have become specialists at this kind of research and development. These techniques have been used to design training materials for computer-assisted instruction, curriculum material for biology classes, and sequences of instruction for "Sesame Street" and other instructional television programs; they have also been used in the development of films on the skills of teaching for use in teacher education programs. Using empirical data, the educational psychologist tries to improve materials and evaluate their success in meeting instructional goals.

In programs to train parents and teachers, educational

psychologists apply behavior modification principles of reward and punishment to a wide set of problems: shaping cooperative behavior in a child who plays alone, reducing the noise level of disorderly classrooms, increasing the engaged time of students who daydream, and reducing the number of aggressive acts initiated by frustrated students.

It has been psychologists, too, from the clinical fields, who have provided much of the leadership in the training of parents and teachers to communicate openly with children and provide environments for the growth of mentally healthy youngsters. These kinds of concerns for the affective life of students in schools became more prevalent in the 1960s. The writings of the Freudian educator A. S. Neill (1960) and the eminent therapist Carl Rogers (1969) provided persuasive arguments for more open and more humanistic educational programs. Their concerns for self-directed and self-initiated learning, emotional and affective learning, and the learning of communication skills between adults and students in schools were directed toward promoting the psychological well-being of students. The recommendations from them and their many coworkers about how teachers and students should interact have resulted in dramatic changes in school practices at many locations.

Educational psychologists have devised in-service teacher-training programs to improve reading and mathematics instruction in accordance with the findings of recent empirical research. These studies have demonstrated that research on teaching can be used to train teachers in ways that increase student achievement. Even some very low-achieving classrooms have been shown to improve when there was systematic application of the findings from research on teaching.

Educational Practice and Psychological Theory. Because educational psychology has often been conceived of as the application of psychological concepts and methods to educational problems, it is important to point out that the study of instructional processes has impacted on psychological theory (Calfee, 1981). Dozens of recent research programs are leading to improved understanding of learning, cognition, problem solving, and memory in human beings. Among these are studies of procedural misunderstandings in the learning of mathematics (Brown & Burton, 1978); metacognition, or self-awareness of one's own learning processes (Brown, Campione, & Day, 1981); memory for school subjects in cross-cultural perspective (Cole & Scribner, 1977); reading and comprehension (Kintsch, 1974); and problem solving in physics (Larkin, 1979). Greeno (1980) has said it best: "A pleasant prospect . . . now emerging is the revival of strong connections between the psychology of learning and the practice of instruction in schools. . . . Instructional tasks constitute a domain of study and analysis that is potentially productive for psychological theory. Learning tasks in the school curriculum are complex enough to raise nontrivial theoretical questions. . . . A deep theoretical understanding of the psychological processes involved in school learn-

ing could become the keystone of a significant new theory of learning" (p. 726). Thus, it is very apparent that the flow of ideas between psychology and education goes both ways (Farley & Gordon, 1981; Resnick, 1981).

Research Trends. By far the most important trend in any science occurs when there is a shift in the paradigm within which research is conducted. With the growth of the cognitive sciences in general, and cognitive psychology in particular, there has been a profound change in the nature of the research being conducted (Mayer, 1981). From a few key papers in the late 1950s, a fertile field of cognitive studies has now emerged as an alternative to behaviorism, which had been the previously dominant paradigm within which much of psychology had worked.

In educational psychology the changes are occurring both in the problems that are addressed and in the methods for investigating those problems. New means of research that are of considerable importance to education include research on differences in the knowledge and strategies for problem solving by experts and novices in an area such as physics; the assessment and comparison of the structure of the cognitive knowledge held by a person and the structure of the knowledge that was taught by teachers or learned from prose; and analyses of the cognitive information-processing systems needed in tasks requiring reasoning. The methods now used to study these phenomena did not exist twenty years ago. The trend to develop a psychology of cognition is expected to grow among psychologists, and this new psychology is expected to have a great impact on education (Scandura et al., 1978).

A second trend in psychological research has to do with the development of more respect for qualitative data and small samples. Thorndike (1903) dismissed any research that was not quantitative. Most psychologists now regard such a view as too narrow. Today, the methodology of psychology includes descriptive field methods, such as the ethnographic techniques of anthropology, descriptive case studies such as those used by ethologists, and research designs involving careful study of a single subject. This broadening of the methodology of psychology has, at times, blurred the distinctions between educational psychologists, sociologists, anthropologists, clinical psychologists, and social psychologists.

Other trends in psychological research in education have roots in the natural changes in society and in the changes required of society by law. The political and economic pressure for "cradle to grave" education (Samuels & Terry, 1977) has provided the support for continued interest in early childhood education and the impetus for growth in adult psychology and the psychology of the aging. In recent years many adults have needed retraining because of discontinuities in their careers, and many retired older persons have requested the services of the schools. To accommodate this new population of adult and older persons in educational settings requires some changes in teaching practices. Psychologists are working in this area in increasing numbers.

In the 1970s the United States Congress, through Public Law 94-142, decreed that handicapped, retarded, and other special students must be educated in regular classes for as much of the time as possible. This resulted in the placement of children with special needs in classrooms that usually are filled with twenty-five to thirty heterogeneous children. The special educational needs of these students and the special training required for teachers is receiving the attention of many psychologists in education.

For psychologists in the last decade, there has also been an increase in evaluation work, in research and development in medical education, and in the scientific design of instructional materials and programs for industry, publishing, and the military. These fields are providing new areas of research and new employment opportunities for educational psychologists.

It has often been noted that if other areas of education such as elementary education, curriculum and instruction in social studies, reading, and so on were to adopt the methods of the social sciences, there would be very little need for psychologists in education. But somehow the discipline of psychology gives to psychologists working in education a peculiar point of view that seems to have a special usefulness. Since the turn of the century psychologists have believed that they should play a leading role in the study of educational processes (Travers, 1969). They have done so, and now others in the field of education have come to expect psychologists to provide leadership in the scientific study of education. Thus, a field such as educational psychology is likely to remain vigorous as it attempts to understand, predict, and control educational phenomena.

David C. Berliner

See also Cognition and Memory; Creativity; Individual Differences; Intelligence; Learning; Motivation; Perception; Personality Theory; Readiness; Transfer of Learning.

REFERENCES

Bandura, A. *Social Learning Theory*. Englewood Cliffs, N.J.: Prentice-Hall, 1977.

Berliner, D. C., & Rosenshine, B. The acquisition of knowledge in the classroom. In R. C. Anderson, R. J. Spiro, & W. E. Montague (Eds.), *Schooling and the Acquisition of Knowledge*. Hillsdale, N.J.: Lawrence Erlbaum Associates, 1977.

Biehler, R. *Psychology Applied to Education* (3rd ed.). Boston: Houghton Mifflin, 1978.

Blair, G. M. The content of educational psychology. *Journal of Educational Psychology*, 1949, *40*, 267–273.

Block, J. H., & Burns, R. B. Mastery learning. In L. S. Shulman (Ed.), *Review of Research in Education* (Vol. 4). Itasca, Ill.: F. E. Peacock, 1976.

Boring, E. G. *A History of Experimental Psychology* (2nd ed.). New York: Appleton-Century-Crofts, 1950.

Bower, G. H., & Hilgard, E. J. *Theories of Learning* (2nd ed.), Englewood Cliffs, N.J.: Prentice-Hall, 1981.

Brown, A.; Campione, J. C.; & Day, J. D. Learning to learn: On training students to learn from texts. *Educational Researcher*, 1981, *10*(2), 14–21.

Brown, J. S., & Burton, R. R. Diagnostic models for procedural bugs in basic mathematical skills. *Cognitive Science*, 1978, *2*, 155–192.

Calfee, R. Cognitive psychology and educational practice. In D. C. Berliner (Ed.), *Review of Research in Education* (Vol. 9). Washington, D.C.: American Educational Research Association, 1981.

Cole, M., & Scribner, S. Cross-cultural studies of memory and cognition. In R. V. Kail, Jr., & J. W. Hagen (Eds.), *Perspective on the development of Memory and Cognition*. Hillsdale, N.J.: Lawrence Erlbaum Associates, 1977.

De Cecco, J. P., & Richards, A. K. Graduate training in educational psychology. In D. J. Treffinger, J. K. Davis, & R. E. Ripple (Eds.), *Handbook on Teaching Educational Psychology*. New York: Academic Press, 1977.

Englander, M. E. Educational psychology and teacher education. *Phi Delta Kappan*, 1976, *57*, 440–442.

Farley, F. H., & Gordon, N. J. (Eds.). *Psychology and Education*. Berkeley, Calif.; McCutchan, 1981.

Feldhusen, J. Issues in teaching undergraduate educational psychology courses. In D. J. Traffinger, J. K. Davis, & R. E. Ripple (Eds.), *Handbook on Teaching Educational Psychology*. New York: Academic Press, 1977.

Flavell, J. H. *The Developmental Psychology of Jean Piaget*. New York: Van Nostrand, 1963.

Fyans, L. (Ed.). *Achievement Motivation*. New York: Plenum, 1980.

Gage, N. L., & Berliner, D. C. *Educational Psychology* (2nd ed.). Boston: Houghton Mifflin, 1979.

Gagné, R. M. *The Conditions of Learning* (3rd ed.). New York: Holt, Rinehart & Winston, 1977.

Good, T. L., & Brophy, J. E. *Educational Psychology* (2nd ed.). New York: Holt, Rinehart & Winston, 1980.

Greeno, J. G. Psychology of learning, 1960–1980: One participant's observations. *American Psychologist*, 1980, *35*, 713–728.

Hall-Quest, A. L. Present tendencies in educational psychology. *Journal of Educational Psychology*, 1915, *6*, 601–614.

Hendrickson, G., & Blair, G. M. Educational psychology. In W. S. Monroe (Ed.), *Encyclopedia of Educational Research* (2nd ed.). New York: Macmillan, 1950.

James W. *Principles of Psychology*. New York: Henry Holt, 1890.

James, W. *Talks to Teachers*. New York: Henry Holt, 1899.

Kintsch, W. *The Representation of Memory in Memory*. Hillsdale, N.J.: Lawrence Erlbaum Associates, 1974.

Larkin, J. H. *Models of Strategy for Solving Physics Problems*. Paper presented at the annual meeting of the American Educational Research Association, 1979. (ERIC Document Reproduction Service No. ED 178 264)

LeFrançois, G. *Psychology for Teaching*. Belmont, Calif.: Wadsworth, 1979.

Mayer, R. E. *The Promise of Cognitive Psychology*. San Francisco, Calif.: Freeman, 1981.

Merrill, M. D.; Kowalis, T.: & Wilson, B. G. Instructional design in transition. In F. H. Farley & M. J. Gordon (Eds.). *Psychology and Education*. Berkeley, Calif.: McCutchan, 1981

Neill, A. S. *Summerhill: A Radical Approach to Child-rearing*. New York: Hart, 1960.

Nunney, D. H. Trends in the content of educational psychology. *Journal of Teacher Education*, 1964, *15*, 372–377.

Remmers, H. H., & Knight, F. B. The teaching of educational psychology in the United States. *Journal of Educational Psychology*, 1922, *13*, 399–407.

Resnick, L. B. Instructional psychology. In M. R. Rosenzweig & L. W. Porter (Eds.), *Annual Review of Psychology*. Palo Alto, Calif.: Annual Reviews, 1981.

Rogers, C. *Freedom to Learn*. Columbus, Ohio: Merrill, 1969.

Samuels, S. J., & Terry, P. Future trends and issues in educational psychology. In D. J. Treffinger, J. Kent Davis, & R. E. Ripple (Eds.), *Handbook on Teaching Educational Psychology*. New York: Academic Press, 1977.

Scandura, J. M.; Frase, L. T.; Gagné, R. M.; Stolurow, K. A.; Stolurow, L. M.; & Groen, G. J. Current status and future directions of educational psychology as a discipline. *Educational Psychologist*, 1978, *13*, 43–56.

Sprinthall, R. C., & Sprinthall, N. A. *Educational Psychology* (3rd ed.). Reading, Mass.: Addison-Wesley, 1981.

Stapp, J. *Summary Report of 1979–1980 Survey of Graduate Departments of Psychology*. Washington, D.C.: American Psychological Association, July 1980.

Thorndike, E. L. *Educational Psychology*. New York: Lemcke & Bruchner, 1903.

Thorndike, E. L. The contributions of psychology to education. *Journal of Educational Psychology*, 1910 *1*, 5–12.

Thorndike, E. L. *Educational Psychology* (Vols. 1–3). New York: Teachers College, Columbia University, 1913–1914.

Travers, R. M. W. *Educational Psychology*. In R. L. Ebel (Ed.), *Encyclopedia of Educational Research* (4th ed.). New York: Macmillan, 1969.

Weiner, B. An attributional approach for educational psychology. In L. S. Shulman (Ed.), *Review of Research in Education* (Vol. 4). Itasca, Ill.: F. E. Peacock, 1976.

Worcester, D. A. The wide diversity of practice in first courses in educational psychology. *Journal of Educational Psychology*, 1927, *18*, 11–17.

PUBERTY

See Adolescent Development; Junior High and Middle School Education; Preadolescent Development; Sex Differences.

PUBLIC SUPPORT FOR EDUCATION

See Local Influences on Education; Polling; School Boards; State Influences on Education.

QUALITATIVE CURRICULUM EVALUATION

In the past decade, several qualitative approaches to curriculum evaluation have been developed. Such qualitative evaluations disclose the character, nature, essence, or qualities of a curriculum in use or of curriculum materials. This article discusses eight forms of qualitative curriculum evaluation, their theoretical orientations and methods, and their similarities and differences.

Definition and Objectives. Qualitative approaches to curriculum evaluation have been developed primarily in response to several critics' observations that evaluators have been preoccupied with whether student outcomes match prespecified objectives. These critics have argued that students acquire other than solely intended learnings that must also be evaluated, and that an examination of the entire process of education, not only its outcomes, is necessary in order to improve curricula. These approaches to qualitative evaluation address a number of concerns. Qualitative evaluators usually study the character of curriculum use, although some qualitative evaluators examine the nature of curriculum documents such as workbooks, audiovisual materials, textbooks, and teachers' guides (e.g., Anyon, 1979; Vallance, 1977). Both the overt and hidden curriculum can be evaluated by means of qualitative curriculum evaluation; ways in which users follow a curriculum explicitly as well as the quality and causes of deviating from it can be considered. Either the entire curriculum or one program or course can be evaluated. Moreover, examination of curriculum use in one setting or comparative studies of several settings can be carried out.

The main reason for using a qualitative approach to curriculum evaluation is to provide a deep, complex understanding of the curriculum in use. Such an understanding can then be used to improve implementation of the curriculum and its materials, and to make possible informed decisions about matters such as adoption, funding, and dissemination.

Qualitative curriculum evaluations can be helpful to people who are outsiders as well as to its participants. Since outsiders, such as policy makers, administrators, and teachers elsewhere, are unable to experience the curriculum directly, a deep understanding of it may be impossible without such an evaluation. Qualitative evaluations enable outsiders to envision the curriculum in action; as a result, they may be able to weigh its intrinsic merit and its suitability for their own settings, teaching styles, and aims. Without such an evaluation, participants may be unable to perceive the curriculum as a whole. Furthermore, understanding by outsiders of their own contributions to the entire curriculum may improve it in several respects. The sequence, continuity, integration, and scope may be improved; and teachers who understand the general nature of the program may change features such as classroom climate, what they choose to emphasize, or particular instructional strategies. In addition, qualitative curriculum evaluations may imply or raise issues not considered previously by participants, such as a curriculum's appropriateness for all students, its relevance to current learning theories, its accordance with current understanding of subject matter, and the value of the hidden curriculum. Evaluators using an autobiographical approach may perceive the benefit of self-study for the individual autobiographer, who comes to understand various factors about his or her setting, practice, curriculum, and the like. Outsiders, then, may be able to make grounded decisions about the curriculum as a result of a qualitative curriculum evaluation, and participants may be better able to implement the program and to make other decisions about its improvement.

Eight of the most commonly used forms of qualitative curriculum evaluation are discussed in this article and listed in Table 1. It should be noted, however, that these approaches overlap greatly and that other approaches also exist.

TABLE 1. *Frequently used qualitative approaches to curriculum evalation*

Form	Aims	Major proponents
Autobiography/ biography	To depict the impact of curricular activities upon the individual.	L. Berk (1980) M. Grumet (1980)
Case study	To document and reveal how a curriculum is reinterpreted in its use in varied settings.	B. MacDonald & R. Walker (1977)
Educational criticism	To gather evidence about a curriculum and present the nature of a curriculum in use through description, interpretation, and appraisal.	E. Eisner (1979) G. McCutcheon (1979) E. Vallance (1977) G. Willis (1978)
Ethnographic approach	To document and reveal the nature of a program in use and its fit or lack of fit with the wider culture.	L. Smith & P. Keith (1971)
Illuminative evaluation	To document and reveal the process of curriculum implementation.	D. Hamilton & M. Parlett (1977)
Critical science evaluation	To interpret curricular phenomena through a Marxist perspective. To point out needs for change in practice and theory.	J. Anyon (1979) M. Apple (1979)
Portrayal evaluation	To create a vicarious experience so that the audience can be informed and make judgments. To tell the story of the curriculum by revealing its nature in use.	B. J. Fraser (1980) S. Kemmis (1977)
Responsive evaluation	To characterize program activities with respect to the audience's requests for information and varied value perspectives.	R. Stake (1975)

Case study and ethnographic and illuminative evaluations bear striking resemblance to one another, as do educational criticism and portrayal evaluation.

Theory and Methods. All eight forms of qualitative curriculum evaluation draw upon other disciplines and philosophical orientations for theory and methods. A source of theory for the autobiography/biography approach is psychoanalysis. The orientation of aesthetic criticism is adopted most heavily by educational criticism and portrayal evaluation, in which the implementation of a curriculum is viewed as a performing art and curriculum materials are viewed as aesthetic objects (Fraser, 1980; Kemmis, 1977; McCutcheon, 1979). In this view, the critic is a connoisseur (Eisner, 1979), who makes public his or her thinking about the curriculum in use and its materials. Cultural anthropology is drawn upon to some extent by many qualitative evaluators when discussing theoretical matters such as objectivity-subjectivity, generalizability, intersubjectivity, universality, validity, and reliability. Phenomenological assumptions appear in all forms of qualitative evaluation in different degrees, with the possible exception of the critical science approach. For example, the primary aim of the autobiography/biography approach is to convey the impact of curricular activities upon an individual as well as the meaning ascribed to those activities (Grumet, 1980). Portrayal and responsive and illuminative evaluation, enterprises generally considered to be phenomenological, attempt to reveal what it is like to be a teacher or student using the curriculum; the felt meaning of the curriculum, along with the values and feelings of participants, is revealed. These enterprises are generally considered to be phenomenological. Critical science forms the basis of one approach in which Marxist, neo-Marxist, and psychoanalytic theories are employed to interpret and appraise what was observed in order to suggest changes in practice or in theories. Many such evaluations focus upon the hidden curriculum (e.g., Anyon, 1979; Apple, 1979).

Methods of qualitative curriculum evaluation have been borrowed from the social sciences (particularly ethnography), investigative journalism, psychoanalysis, and the arts. A qualitative curriculum evaluator might observe a curriculum in use, maintain field notes, analyze students' work, follow one student for a week, solicit responses to questionnaires, and interview users of the curriculum. The evaluator might discuss with teachers their planning for activities, reasons for innovative deviations from a guide, as well as satisfaction or dissatisfaction with the curriculum. The autobiographical approach entails maintaining a journal, depicting events, and reflecting upon them. The choice of methods depends upon the evaluator's beliefs about the worth of each form of evaluation, the purpose of the evaluation, the opportunity to use methods, the evaluator's expertise, and a method's apparent applicability for gathering relevant evidence.

The evaluator collects and categorizes evidence, indexes the materials, then describes and interprets the use of the curriculum. In the process of description, the evaluator answers the questions "What was the curriculum like in action? What happened when it was being used?" In the process of interpretation, the evaluator wonders about the meaning of events for the participants or the evaluator. Educational critics and critical scientists add a third process—appraisal. Critical scientists interpret and appraise events from a neo-Marxist perspective, whereas educational critics relate what was described in research and theory in the social sciences, history of education, and various current trends or practices. Description, interpretations, and criticisms can be written up separately in a qualitative curriculum evaluation, but they are frequently interwoven.

Similarities. Similarities among the eight forms of qualitative curriculum evaluation include the following: investigating the quality, character, or nature of the curriculum in use or curriculum materials; providing an audience with an understanding of the nature of curriculum use or materials; drawing upon varied methods from the humanities and social sciences for collecting documentary evidence; applying these methods as the occasion arises or because of their applicability to a particular issue or problem. Similarities can also be thought of in terms of what qualitative curriculum evaluation is *not*. Qualitative curriculum evaluators generally are not concerned primarily with objectives and student outcomes or with measuring quantities of phenomena, although some evaluators may collect information about student outcomes or objectives. Although qualitative evaluations could be carried out with respect to the nature of student learnings, they usually are not. Autobiographers and biographers frequently focus upon the impact of a curriculum on students—not in terms of intended outcomes, however, but rather in terms of the meanings students make of what has happened in school.

Clearly, there is a quantitative dimension to many qualitative evaluations. Comparisons are made about the extent of various matters, and frequently some data are collected—how often students have turns or how many groups are working on certain activities. However, these evaluators are not primarily interested in student outcomes and collecting numbers but, rather, in the use of the curriculum and the character, or quality, of that use.

Differences. Whereas these forms of qualitative curriculum evaluation exhibit strong similarities, several issues distinguish them from one another. One such issue considers whether a problem or question should guide evaluators from the beginning or whether they should enter the setting without such guidance, formulating questions while engaged in the evaluation. All approaches appear to vary regarding this issue of posing questions or problems prior to or during the evaluation; some qualitative curriculum evaluations may include questions posed beforehand and those that emerge in the course of the evaluation. Related to this concern is the issue of the origin of such questions. Should they emanate from the evaluator, from participants, or from the audience of the evaluation? Responsive

evaluators rely upon the audience, which may include the participants, for such questions. Educational critics and critical scientists select the problems to be addressed themselves. Others may or may not consult with the participants or audience for guidance in this regard.

Another difference among the eight forms of qualitative curriculum evaluation revolves around the issue of whether evaluators should themselves make judgments or appraisals of the curriculum and recommend courses of action or whether they should merely provide information to enable others to make these judgments or recommendations. Educational critics and critical scientists appraise curriculum use and materials, whereas most others merely depict the program in order to enable others to make decisions. Clearly the choice of information to be provided can affect decisions, one reason why responsive evaluators have the audience of the evaluation choose the questions to be addressed. Evaluators who appraise a curriculum generally attempt to make their own theoretical and value perspectives apparent within the evaluation.

A third difference concerns methods of reporting the evaluation. Portrayal evaluators, educational critics, and many who use an autobiographical or biographical approach rely upon a literary style to facilitate understanding through vicarious experience, imagery, and metaphor as well as through analytic interpretations. Case study and ethnographic evaluations are usually reported in straightforward prose in the hope of enhancing objectivity. This issue, in part, concerns communication. Those relying on literary styles hope to communicate the nature of a curriculum in use and the attitudes and feelings of participants by enhancing the audience's ability to envision the curriculum's use; they attempt to develop intersubjective, empathic communication. Evaluators relying upon straightforward prose hope to communicate objectively by discussing the curriculum in use in commonly used and understood language. Styles of responsive evaluations vary with respect to their audiences' requests for information.

These issues of difference indicate the difficulty of comparison among evaluations. If several curricula are being evaluated in different settings by different teams of evaluators, the evidence they collect, styles of reporting, and issues they address may vary. However, this does not imply that studies cannot be done in a parallel fashion; meetings of teams before and during the evaluation may be necessary to bring about an understanding of different styles and values and to clarify the questions being addressed in different settings.

Qualitative curriculum evaluation characterizes the nature of the curriculum in use and its materials, providing the understanding necessary for decision making and enhanced curriculum use.

Gail McCutcheon

See also Curriculum Development and Organization; Curriculum Research; Evaluation of Programs.

REFERENCES

Anyon, J. Ideology and United States history textbooks. *Harvard Educational Review*, 1979, *49*, 361–386.

Apple, M. *Ideology and Curriculum*. London: Routledge & Kegan Paul, 1979.

Berk, L. Education in lives: Biographic narrative in the study of educational outcomes. *Journal of Curriculum Theorizing*, 1980, *2*(2), 88–154.

Eisner, E. W. *The Educational Imagination*. New York: Macmillan, 1979.

Fraser, B. J. Portrayal approach to curriculum evaluation. *Journal of Curriculum Studies*, 1980, *12*, 364–367.

Grumet, M. Autobiography and reconceptualization. *Journal of Curriculum Theorizing*, 1980, *2*(2), 155–158.

Kemmis, S. Telling it like it is. In L. Rubin (Ed.), *Handbook of Curriculum*. Boston: Allyn & Bacon, 1977.

MacDonald, B., & Walker, R. Case study and the social philosophy of educational research. In D. Hamilton & M. Parlett (Eds.), *Beyond the Numbers Game*. Berkeley, Calif.: McCutchan, 1977.

McCutcheon, G. Educational criticism: Methods and application. *Journal of Curriculum Theorizing*, 1979, *1*(2), 5–25.

Parlett, M., & Hamilton, D. Evaluation as illumination: A new approach to the study of innovatory programmes. In D. Hamilton & M. Parlett (Eds.), *Beyond the Numbers Game*. Berkeley, Calif.: McCutchan, 1977.

Smith, L., & Keith, P. *Anatomy of Educational Innovation*. New York: Wiley, 1971.

Stake, R. *Evaluating the Arts in Education: A Responsive Approach*. Columbus, Ohio: Merrill, 1975.

Vallance, E. The landscape of the Great Plains experience. *Curriculum Inquiry*, 1977, *7*, 87–105.

Willis, G. *Qualitative Evaluation*. Berkeley, Calif.: McCutchan, 1978.

R

RACIAL INTEGRATION

See Equity Issues in Education; Federal Influence on Education; Judicial Decisions; Multicultural and Minority Education; Transportation of Students; Urban Education.

RACISM AND SEXISM IN CHILDREN'S LITERATURE

In the field of children's literature, the recognition of racial and sexual bias is a relatively new concept. What started more than 200 years ago, as Blacks began their fight against slavery and discrimination in the United States, and more than 100 years ago, as women began their pursuit of the right to vote, has now broadened into a quest for equal treatment and respect for all groups. No social, political, or educational institution has been spared scrutiny by racial minority groups and women in the attempt to overcome racial and sexual bias. In particular, children's literature, recognized as an integral part of social and educational institutions, has been subjected to this scrutiny.

"Racism" and "sexism" in children's literature can be defined as attitudes, actions, or words that subordinate a person by assigning him or her a role or characteristic on the basis of race or sex. Although occasional articles on racism and sexism in children's literature have appeared in such specialized periodicals as the *Journal of Negro Education* and *College English*, it was not until the latter half of the 1960s and the decade of the 1970s that documentation of racial and sexual bias in children's literature was noticeable. This entry on racism and sexism bias in children's literature deals with this topic both separately and collectively, whenever appropriate. Five major areas of concern are discussed: (1) the characteristics of bias, (2) the documentation of bias, (3) the effects of bias, (4) the ways of correcting bias, and (5) the implications of these four areas for educational policy.

Characteristics of Bias in Children's Literature

Racial and sexual bias in children's literature have similar characteristics. Bias, which is an inclination toward partiality, appears in both text and illustrations. It is revealed in many forms.

Language. Bias can be expressed by language, that is, certain words or phrases are used to describe one race or gender as opposed to another race or gender. Rollins (1967) draws attention to the use of dialect, false idiom, and racially potent words in children's literature, especially the literature portraying blacks. For example, she discusses the author-created dialect (as opposed to the authentic dialect of regional and social groups) that is so often found in children's books. Research on racially potent words pertaining to Black Americans is also presented. Rollins believes that the caricature of language should be replaced by the accurate, understandable use of the vernacular in books for children.

An analysis of language, as it pertains to individual minority groups, can be readily found in studies that document racism in general terms in children's books. There is a paucity of studies in children's literature, however, devoted entirely to language as it pertains to an individual minority group. Noteworthy as an exception is an extensive study on Native American (American Indian) verbal images in children's literature (Wickersham, 1979). *Racism in the English Language* (Moore, 1976) is a booklet that helps to identify racist language about racial minority groups.

Sexism and Language (Nilsen et al., 1977) is an in-depth analysis of so-called gender vocabulary in children's books. English language gender-associated components in other media, such as dictionaries, texts of various kinds, legal documents, and elementary teaching materials, are also discussed in detail. Among the sexist patterns in children's literature noted by Madsen (1979) is a listing of gender-associated verbs and nomenclature. Madsen discusses the sexist implications of the use of such gender-associated words. The word "need," for example, is associated mostly with the female in children's books, implying incapability, whereas "can," so often associated with males, implies ability and capability.

Language, in any form, written or spoken, is communication. It plays a central role in the socialization of children's lives. As language helps children to conceptualize their ideas about their world, it also teaches them about the roles and behavior that are expected of them. Language, therefore, can be a form of bias in children's literature that has serious developmental implications.

Illustrations. Illustrations are an integral part of children's books. Because they are a form of communication, they are a vehicle for transmitting bias in children's literature. The bias in illustrations is depicted in a number of different ways.

Racial bias against a minority group is evident in the depiction of poor postures, featureless faces, abnormally unkempt hair, and unrealistic body parts (such as grotesque hands and feet), abnormally thin legs, and protruding eyes. Members of any group illustrated generally in a derogatory and/or demeaning manner are not depicted as individuals; authentic characteristics of members of racial minority groups are not observable. Byler, an Eastern Cherokee Native American, in her introduction to *American Indian Authors for Young Readers* (1973), comments extensively on such negative illustrations of Native Americans in children's literature. What appears to be an ongoing issue about the illustrations in *The Five Chinese Brothers* (Bishop, 1938) clearly demonstrates the importance of illustrations relative to bias in children's books. Although Schwartz (1977) and the Asian American Cultural Heritage Program and the Asian American Education Association (1975) find the illustrations in this book very demeaning and negative, Lanes (1977) and Weston Woods (1980), a commerical publisher of audiovisual materials based on children's literature, apparently find them an appropriate depiction of the Chinese people. *The Story of Little Black Sambo* (Bannerman, 1900) is another demonstration of just how important bias in illustrations of minority groups has become; important points about the illustrations in this book have been made by Rollins (1967) and Yuill (1976).

Sexual bias in children's books often illustrates the female as being afraid, crying, or giggling. She is often depicted wearing an apron out of context, is seldom seen outside of a domestic situation, and is in a supportive or passive role, rather than an assertive or active role in associations with males. She is shown with small animals, such as "bunnies," "kittens," and "ponies" instead of "rabbits," "cats," and "horses."

Through illustrations, children can vicariously experi-

ence the world around them and learn how it came to be. It is said that during an average person's lifetime, some 50,000 words, and even more pictures, are among the billions of items that are stored in the human memory (Edson et al., 1975). If these facts are true, then biased illustrations in children's books become a significant factor in the formation of children's attitudes.

Messages. The "messages" of both racial and sexual bias in children's literature are similar. They come in the form of omissions and/or distortions, which, in turn, leave the reader with a stereotyped image. Taken collectively or individually, biased messages mean that racial minority groups and females are either omitted entirely from a story or are only given token (superficial recognition) roles. When the language and illustrations of groups are biased, images about those in question become distorted, and continual misrepresentation forms a stereotype in an individual's mind, a "standardized mental picture" of what one is supposed to be like or look like, based on bias rather than fact.

The messages of bias in children's literature are detailed in Zimet's book, *Print and Prejudice* (1976). Zimet presents a composite review of the research in this area, arriving at the conclusion that biased messages in children's literature affect children in different ways. Most of the research on biased messages in children's literature deals with fiction. Haskins (1976) writes on racism and sexism in nonfictional children's literature. He presents some alternative views to be considered.

Documentation of Bias

There are numerous studies on bias in children's literature. One has only to scan the indexes of periodicals, such as *The Reading Teacher, School Library Journal,* and *Language Arts* (formerly *Elementary English*), to note the studies on racial and sexual bias in children's literature conducted during the last decade. Notable compilations of such studies are found in *Print and Prejudice* (Zimet, 1976), *Children's Literature: An Issues Approach* (Rudman, 1976), *Interracial Digest 1* (Council on Interracial Books for Children, 1976) and *Interracial Digest 2* (Council on Interracial Books for Children, 1978). In an annotated bibliography titled *Research in Children's Literature* (Monson & Peltola, 1976), the compilers cite 21 out of 39 studies on race that document racial bias in children's books. Out of the 16 studies related to sexism in children's literature, 12 document sexual bias. The 332 studies reported by Monson and Peltola were completed between 1960 and 1974.

Currently, *Children's Literature Abstracts,* published quarterly by the Children's Libraries Section of the International Federation of Library Associations, documents studies on racial and sexual bias in children's literature under the section Psychological, Educational, and Social Criteria. It is an international publication, documenting children's literature studies conducted worldwide. *Phae-*

drus, an international journal of children's literature research, likewise publishes noteworthy research on racial and sexual bias. This journal reviews the research in greater detail than *Children's Literature Abstracts,* but is not as active in its reports on racial and sexual bias. The *Bulletin,* published by the Council on Interracial Books for Children, which was founded in 1965 for the purpose of bringing to the public's attention bias in children's literature, is well known for reporting studies on the documentation of racial and sexual bias in children's books.

Racial Bias. Most of the documentation of racial bias in children's literature deals with the portrayal of blacks. This is not to say that major studies of other racial minority groups have not been reported, but by comparison they are few. The studies on racial bias that follow are representative of those that have made a significant contribution to the research literature.

Black Americans. In the same year that the Council on Interracial Books for Children was founded, Larrick produced her report, "The All-White World of Children's Books" (1965). In this survey of children's books published during the years of 1962 to 1964 by sixty-three publishers, only four-fifths of 1 percent of all books dealt with black people. Of these books, over 25 percent featured blacks only in the illustrations. Chall et al. (1979) replicated the Larrick study, using it as a comparative base for the years 1973–1975, and examining trade books published by the fifty-one publisher members of the Children's Book Council. Findings indicated that children's books with black characters had more than doubled since the Larrick study, but the authors questioned the quality of many of the books.

A study of racial bias conducted on the *Doctor Dolittle* series (Suhl, 1969) stimulated many people to reexamine those classics of children's literature, as well as other so-called classics, for their possible racist content. Schwartz (1970) seriously criticized *Sounder,* the 1970 Newbery Award book by Armstrong (1969), because of the stereotypes it supports. Schwartz's article *"The Cay:* Racism Rewarded" (1971) was instrumental in aiding pressure groups to cause the chairperson of the Jane Addams Children's Book Award Committee in 1974 publicly to regret giving the "brotherhood award" to Taylor's *The Cay* (1969). Taylor was strongly criticized for his portrayal of a black sailor and his relationship with a white boy.

Image of the Black in Children's Fiction (Broderick, 1973) gives the historical, literary, and critical analysis of blacks who appear in children's books published between 1827 and 1967. The writer concludes that the black image revealed in those books is directly related to the values of the society in which the books were produced. Although some of the books were "outright racist," most of them fell into the category of "condescendingly racist books" and "traditionally do-gooder books" (Broderick, 1973, p. 177). Mathis, in her "True/False Messages for the Black Child" (1974), criticizes a number of children's books pub-

lished since 1967 that demean blacks by the use of stereotypes and language.

Native Americans. Noteworthy in-depth studies on bias concerning the image of the Native American (American Indian) in children's books have been conducted by Native American associations. The preliminary research on *American Indian Authors for Young Readers* (Byler, 1973) first appeared in the *Bulletin* (Newman, 1969). In this preliminary study, more than 200 books were read, out of which 63 were selected for realistic and unbiased presentations of Native Americans. One will find a sharp contrast in Byler's comments on the bias in this 200-book sample to Stoodt and Ignizio's comments on the bias in another sample of books (some of which are the same) (Stoodt & Ignizio, 1976). On the other hand, Fisher's analysis (1974) of clichés, distortions, and stereotypes in children's books on Native Americans is more compatible with the point of view of the Association on American Indian Affairs (Byler, 1973).

Although textbooks are not considered children's literature, studies on bias in textbooks depict some of the same kinds of bias that have been found in children's trade books. One such study that reviewed all children's textbooks with Native American characters was published by the Indian Historian Press (1970). This volume reviews in detail the omissions, distortions, and ultimate stereotypes about Native Americans not only in popular textbooks but also in other curriculum materials.

Asian Americans. In contrast to in-depth studies that have ferreted out bias in children's books about Black Americans and Native Americans, significant studies of bias in the literature on other racial minority groups are few. As in the case of identifying Native American bias in textbooks, one must draw upon the intensive study of how Asians are depicted in American school textbooks to help understand how Asian children are treated in children's trade books (Asia Society, 1976). The study analyzed 306 social studies texts in use in the fifty states as of 1975. The findings of that study supported the earlier pleas for authenticity documented by Scott (1974). The Asia Society's findings were subsequently supported in an extensive review of Asian Americans in children's books published by the Council on Interracial Books for Children (1976a).

Puerto Ricans and Mexican Americans. By far, the most definitive study on bias against Puerto Ricans in children's books was conducted by the Council on Interracial Books for Children (1972). It revealed the traditional stereotypes stemming from racism, sexism, and colonialism. Bias against Mexican Americans in children's literature was also given attention by the Council on Interracial Books for Children (1975). Traditional stereotypes and cultural misrepresentations were similarly identified in approximately 200 books about the Chicano culture. One of the earliest studies to appear about Mexican American literature was published by Blatt (1968). This analysis appears to contrast sharply with the analysis of the Council on Interracial Books for Children (1975) and Schon's publication eight years later on Mexican American children's literature (1976). A more recent publication by Schon (1981) presents a study on new books about Mexico, Mexicans, and Mexican Americans.

One can certainly conclude from this review of studies in children's literature that racial bias does exist. Although some of the outstanding studies were conducted by nonminority persons, all of those studies that were compatible with minority viewpoints were either conducted by minority persons or were endorsed by them.

Sexual Bias. Although studies of the image of women in children's literature began to appear in the 1960s, the most significant study to identify sexual bias in children's trade books did not appear until 1971 (Feminists on Children's Media). Subsequently, a booklet entitled *Little Miss Muffet Fights Back* provided an extensive annotated bibliography of recommended nonsexist books about girls for young readers (Feminists on Children's Media, 1974).

The early 1970s produced a number of other noteworthy studies on sexual bias in children's literature. Nilsen (1971) analyzed the Caldecott Award books and their runners-up from 1951 to 1970 for sexism. Weitzman et al. (1972) analyzed the Caldecott Award books from their inception in 1939, concentrating on the award books and their runners-up between 1967 and 1971, with reference to relevant data on sex-role socialization. In addition, Newbery Medal books and Little Golden Books were also analyzed for sexual bias. Subsequently, studies on sexual bias in children's textbooks, as opposed to trade books, appeared in the literature. Women on Words and Images (1972) published an extensive report on sexual bias in children's developmental reading textbooks. Weitzman and Rizzo (1974), among others, also published an impressive study on sex-biased textbooks. The findings of all of these studies, and others like them, deal with books published before 1970. They reflect findings similar to sexual bias noted in trade books.

In the studies that followed, questions were raised about progress that might have been made since the early data on sexism in children's trade books and textbooks became available. Collectively, the later reports about sex-role stereotyping in children's books suggest that to date no real significant progress has been made in removing the frequent criticism of sex discrimination in books for children (Madsen & Wickersham, 1980; Stewig & Knipfel, 1975; Tibbetts, 1975).

Effects of Bias

The opinions and data about the effects of bias in children's literature are supported by theories of thinking and learning. A brief discussion of these underlying theories will aid in better understanding of the research data that follow.

Although Piaget (1963) is widely respected and quoted, not all theorists agree with his principles of cognitive development. Bruner (1960) and Gagné (1970), for example,

depart from Piaget's stages of learning at different points. They all agree, however, that each child is unique and perceives situations differently and that attitudes are learned, not innate. Kohlberg (1973) believes that everyone passes through six stages of moral development relevant to debatable interpretations of what is right and wrong, such as different views of authority and law. Because most of Kohlberg's subjects were male, his classification of moral stages is questioned (Simpson, 1974). In spite of doubts, Glazer and Williams (1979) explain how Kohlberg's theories do help us to understand children's reactions to books.

Support for Glazer and and Williams's opinion is supplied by evidence that children learn more through pictorial than through verbal presentations (Pressley, 1977). If racial bias and sexual bias are present in illustrations in children's books, then children will probably develop biased attitudes.

Zimet suggests in her investigation of the effects of books on attitudes towards minority groups that "the process of attitude change through reading may be related to the process of identification with the story characters in the reading material" (1976, p. 19). One notable study that supports this hypothesis suggests that there is a significant difference in the way different races respond to literary fare, in particular, poetry (Menchise, 1972). In this study, black and white students, respectively, ranked poems written by authors of their own race higher than those written by authors of the other race. A much earlier, but relevant, study (Williams & Edwards, 1959) reports that by using selected school and literary experiences, black children's attitudes toward themselves and whites have been positively modified.

A recent impressive report on research showing how books influence children upholds the hypothesis that bias in children's literature is a significant factor in attitude formation (Campbell & Wirtenberg, 1980). The authors conclude from the research that both children's attitudes and achievement are affected by racial and sexual bias in the materials they read. In another recent publication (Scott, 1980), five extensive research studies on the impact of sexist and nonsexist children's reading materials further support the premise that children's books do influence children's attitudes toward themselves and others.

Another body of research deals with the use of unbiased reading material, including children's literature, to change the attitudes of majority group children from negative to positive toward minority groups (Lichter & Johnson, 1969; Singh & Yancey, 1974; Yawkey, 1973). In these studies, children's biased attitudes have been assessed prior to their exposure to unbiased reading material.

It has long been the opinion of members of such organizations as the American Library Association (ALA), the National Education Association (NEA), the National Association for the Advancement of Colored People (NAACP), the National Indian Education Association (NIEA), and the National Organization for Women (NOW) that children's books do have an effect on children, even though for many years the views of these organizations were polarized and remain so to some degree even today. Review of the research to date shows some evidence for the hypothesis that biased and unbiased reading materials do have an effect on children's attitude formation toward themselves and/or others. It must be remembered, however, that this research is only relative, not definitive or absolute by any means; definitions and degrees of bias are debatable and change as the values of society change.

Correcting Bias

Suggestions, guidelines, and materials of all kinds to help combat racism and sexism in general do not appear to be scarce. As the documentation of racial and sexual bias in children's literature in particular has become more pronounced, concerned groups have offered workable solutions and resource information to help correct it. The following organizations are representative of those that offer such information:

- American Library Association, 50 East Huron Street, Chicago, Ill. 60611
- Council on Interracial Books for Children, Racism and Sexism Resource Center for Educators, 1841 Broadway, New York, N.Y. 10023
- Far West Laboratory, 1855 Folsom Street, San Francisco, Calif. 94103
- International Reading Association, 800 Barksdale Road, P.O. Box 8139, Newark, Del. 19711
- National Council of Teachers of English, 111 Kenyon Road, Urbana, Ill. 60611

Among the materials developed for distribution by the Racism and Sexism Resource Center for Educators, for example, are at least six practical aids to understand and combat the "isms" in children's literature. Also the Council on Interracial Books for Children's *Human (and Anti-Human) Values in Children's Books* (1976b) contains an easy-to-use content rating device with specific examples of children's book evaluations.

In addition, most state departments of education have made efforts to correct racial and sexual bias in instructional programs and materials. For example, the state of Washington offers a publication entitled *State of Washington: Models for the Evaluation of Bias Content in Instructional Materials* (1975). The Wisconsin Department of Public Instruction (1972) has produced *Starting Out Right: Choosing Books about Black People for Young Children*. The Pennsylvania Department of Education makes available *New Perspectives, A Bibliography of Racial, Ethnic, and Feminist Resources* (1977) and the *Pennsylvania Department of Education Guidelines for Creating Positive Sexual and Racial Images in Educational Materials* (1975), which were adapted from Macmillan's *Guidelines for Creating Positive Sexual and Racial Images in Educational Materials* (1975). Information about what each state has

developed in the area of correcting racial and sexual bias in children's literature can be obtained by asking the individual state department of education located in the state's capital.

Methods. A closer look at the sharp contrasts in the documentation of racial bias frequently reveals the difference in a minority researcher's and a nonminority researcher's perception. This difference has been a critical issue in the evaluation of children's literature ever since the topic of racial bias in children's books first appeared. It must be remembered that it was not the majority group who first raised this concern, but a minority group, Black Americans, during the Black Revolt of the 1960s (Banks, 1979). Subsequently, studies of children's literature from a minority's point of view became available. The Council on Interracial Books for Children and the Far West Laboratory each has developed guidelines for evaluating children's books from specific racial minority group perspectives.

Guidelines can be modified into a rating scale with the potential for a more critical assessment of children's books than so-called descriptive studies. Pratt developed what he calls Evaluation Coefficient Analysis (ECO Analysis), "designed specifically as a relatively simple instrument which can provide valid and reliable quantitative measurement of value judgments about minority groups in textbooks" (1972, p. 13). The ECO Analysis can be used with both children's nonfictional trade books and textbooks and can be modified to analyze children's fiction as well. Studies in children's literature, as opposed to textbooks (McDiarmid & Pratt, 1971), have thus far lacked this kind of quantitative analysis.

Supported by the descriptive data on both racial and sexual bias in children's literature, the research route for correcting the bias reflects search-and-compile characteristics. Racial minority and feminist groups conduct searches and compile bibliographies and source lists of nonbiased children's books, which, in their view, authentically represent their respective groups. By their publications, these groups hope to educate the public about the characteristics of a nonbiased book. Representative sources that review and recommend such children's books are listed in Table 1.

It should be noted that some of the larger book publishing companies have published their own sets of guidelines. For example, McGraw-Hill Book Company (1974) has developed a set of guidelines on equal treatment of the sexes for writers of the company's nonfiction. McGraw-Hill's guidelines are often used for ferreting out sexual bias in children's literature. The *School Library Journal* (1975) has reprinted them in full. In addition, Macmillan Publishing Co., Inc. (1975) has developed *Guidelines for Creating Positive Sexual and Racial Images in Educational Materials*. To date, no in-depth studies of children's books published since the appearance of the 1974 and 1975 guidelines have been reported to see if these companies are indeed following their own advice. Such studies would

TABLE 1. *Specialized review sources for children's books*

Group	Organization or periodical	Address
Asian American	*Bridge, An Asian-American Perspective*	P.O. Box 477 Canal Street Station New York, N.Y. 10013
Asian American	*Focus on Asian Studies*	Association for Asian Studies Ohio State University 29 W. Woodruff Ave. Columbus, Ohio 43210
Black American	*Black Books Bulletin*	Institute of Positive Education 7524 S. Cottage Grove Ave. Chicago, Ill. 60619
Black American	Johnson Publishing Co.	820 South Michigan Ave. Chicago, Ill. 60605
Mexican American	The Chicano Education Project	1444 Stuart St. Denver, Colo. 80204
Native American	The American Indian Historical Society	1451 Masonic Ave. San Francisco, Calif. 94117
Native American	The Association on American Indian Affairs	432 Park Avenue South New York, N.Y. 10016
Native American	The National Indian Education Association	3036 University Ave., SE Suite 3 Minneapolis, Minn. 55414
Puerto Rican American	The Puerto Rican Research and Resource Center	1519 Connecticut Ave., NW Washington, D.C. 20036
Female	The Feminists on Children's Media	P.O. Box 4315 Grand Central Station New York, N.Y. 10017
Female	The Feminist Press	Box 334 Old Westbury, N.Y. 11561
Female	*Ms.* (Free Stories for Free Children)	123 Garden Street Marion, Ohio 43302
Female	The Non-Sexist Curriculum Development Program	Dr. Barbara Hutchinson Northwest Educational Lab. 701 West Second Ave. Portland, Oreg. 92204
Female	The Non-Sexist Teacher Education Project	Drs. David & Myra Sadker The American University Washington, D.C. 20016
Female	The Women's Action Alliance	370 Lexington Ave. Room 603 New York, N.Y. 10017

help to determine whether or not bias is actually being corrected in children's literature.

Implications for Educational Policy

The documentation of racial and sexual bias in children's literature and its suspected effects on children has had an impact on educational policy. A case in point of exacerbated tension between old and new values as it relates to children's literature *per se* and policy change is the "1976 American Library Association Council Document No. 83: Resolution on Racism and Sexism Awareness" (Council on Interracial Books for Children, 1976d). This particular resolution, to take aggressive steps to combat racism and sexism within the library profession and services, was a direct result of pressure exerted by the Council on Interracial Books for Children. Based on the documentation of racial and sexual bias in children's books, the American Library Association (ALA) made a major policy shift in its recognition of the pervasiveness of racism and sexism in literature.

The ALA resolution escalated the censorship issue within the organization. In itself, censorship has always been an issue shaded by different interpretations. As recently as October 7, 1980, the *Los Angeles Times* charged that the San Francisco Public Library had banned *Mary Poppins* by Travers (1962), a charge denied by the library (Council on Interracial Books for Children, 1980a). In this case, the ALA Office for Intellectual Freedom did not support the San Francisco Public Library's views on the interpretation of "ban" and "censorship," and so, the issue of "What is censorship?" continues.

Massie (1980) identifies the censors of children's educational materials as school boards, school administrators, teachers, librarians, state education agencies, textbook publishers, and potentially the U.S. Congress, by its introduction of S. 1808, the Family Protection Act, of which educational issues are a major part. The underlying censor in many of the censorship incidents cited, however, such as the much publicized book protest in Kanawha County, West Virginia, is parents. Often it is parents who set educational policy at the local level and exert extensive unofficial pressure—especially when children's books are involved. Peterson, Rossmiller, and Volz report that the ALA estimates that "virtually every literary work of any importance [for children] has been banned somewhere in the United States" (1978, p. 333). The recent censorship incidents of both children's trade books and textbooks cited by Massie (1980) support the premise that racial and sexual bias in children's literature does have a direct impact on educational policy making.

The documentation of racial and sexual bias in children's literature has played a supporting role in the politics of educational policy making. Boyd (1978) documents and underscores the politics of educational policy making, as do Drummond and Andrews (1980), Kirst and Mosher (1969), and Tomlinson (1981).

Politics in educational policy making is observed especially at the federal level. Farrar, DeSanctis, and Cohen describe federal policy as "only a set of broad and often diverse intentions or dispositions which changes and develops as the federal program is harnessed to local needs and priorities" (1980, p. 167). The Civil Rights Act of 1964, undergirding the desegregation of public education, is clearly an example of the role of politics in educational policy making. The complex relationships between federal guidelines and local interpretations are explored by Kirp and Yudof (1974). It is enough to say here that under Public Law 88-352, Title IV, §401, technical assistance was authorized and supported by federal funds for school districts that made application for the "preparation, adoption, and implementations of plans for the desegregation of public schools." Under Title IV, such publications as *Starting Out Right: Choosing Books about Black People for Young Children* (Wisconsin Department of Public Instruction, 1972) are published. In such publications, children's books with noted racial bias are discussed, criteria for evaluation are given, and annotations with commentaries on available books are written. Thus, children's literature became a very real part of the educational policies set by the Civil Rights Act of 1964.

It was not until 1972 that Public Law 92-318, Title IX, Article 1681, the first comprehensive federal law to prohibit sex discrimination in programs, policies, and administration of educational programs and activities, was made into law. Similar to the Civil Rights Act in philosophy, it provided moneys for aiding the elimination of sexual bias at all levels. Sexism in children's books has often been a part of awareness workshops for educators, especially at the local levels. Under the heading of Instructional Materials, Formal and Informal, children's books became a bona fide component of the Title IX regulations.

Perhaps not as political in the same sense as Title IV or Title IX, but "political" nevertheless, was the earlier legislation of the National Defense Education Act (NDEA) of 1958 in response to *Sputnik*. This act actually set aside moneys that could be used to buy books "other than textbooks" and other instructional materials in the areas of mathematics, science, and modern foreign languages. Thus, the school library gained in importance and acquired holdings that had not been enjoyed previously. The school library, however, was to become the target for studies of racism and sexism in literature for children. The racial and sexual bias characteristics of omissions, distortions, and stereotypes in children's books were found to be blatant, as the data show.

The statutes of a number of states have sought to interpret federal legislation. For example, §51500 and §51501 of California's Education Code deal pointedly with prohibiting discrimination on the basis of race or sex in reference to instruction, activities, and means of instruction, as does a New Jersey statute, N.J.S.A. 18A:36-20, dealing with equality in educational programs. Unless specifically stated to the contrary in any such statutes, children's books are subsumed under Instructional Materials or Supplementary Materials within the school's jurisdiction. And it is here, at the local level, that finally the bias in children's literature is most carefully scrutinized based on the research studies that document it, by, for the most part, the unofficial pressure of parents concerned about the impact that racial and sexual bias in children's books can have on their children.

It is clear from the foregoing discussion of racial and sexual bias in children's literature that there is a great deal of research needed. If respect for cultural pluralism in the United States is to survive, the gap between what is accepted as authentic and what is authentic still needs to be explored. If respect for cultural pluralism is to thrive in the United States, this gap needs to be closed. The politics in educational policy making, therefore, must continue to recognize that literary fare for children is a strong influential source for nurturing both the cognitive and affective domains of children's minds as long as children's books are a part of the instructional program in schools.

Jane M. Madsen

See also Equity Issues in Education; Literature; Multicultural and Minority Education; Textbooks.

REFERENCES

Armstrong, W. H. *Sounder.* New York: Harper & Row, 1969.

Asia Society. *Asia in American Textbooks.* New York: The Society, 1976. (ERIC Document Reproduction Service No. ED 127 232)

Asian American Cultural Heritage Program & Asian American Education Association. *A Bibliography of Asian and Asian American Books for Elementary School Youngsters.* Olympia, Wash.: Department of Public Instruction, 1975. (ERIC Document Reproduction Service No. ED 117 286)

Banks, J. A. *Teaching Strategies for Ethnic Studies* (2nd ed.). Boston: Allyn & Bacon, 1979.

Bannerman, H. *The Story of Little Black Sambo.* Philadelphia: Lippincott, 1900.

Bishop, C. H. *The Five Chinese Brothers.* Illustrated by Kurt Weise. New York: Coward-McCann, 1938.

Blatt, G. T. The Mexican-American in children's literature. *Elementary English,* April 1968, *45,* 446–451.

Boyd, W. L. The changing politics of curriculum policy-making for American schools. *Review of Educational Research,* Fall 1978, *48,* 577–628.

Broderick, D. M. *Image of the Black in Children's Fiction.* New York: Bowker, 1973.

Bruner, J. S. *The Process of Education.* Cambridge, Mass.: Harvard University Press, 1960.

Byler, M. G. (Comp.). *American Indian Authors for Young Readers.* New York: Association on American Indian Affairs, 1973.

Campbell, P. B., & Wirtenberg, J. How books influence children: What the research shows. Council on Interracial Books for Children, *Bulletin,* 1980, *11,* 6.

Chall, J. S.; Radwin, E.; French, V. W.; & Hall, C. R. Blacks in the world of children's books. *Reading Teacher,* February 1979, *32,* 527–533.

Council on Interracial Books for Children. Special issue on Puerto Rican materials. *Bulletin,* Spring 1972, *4,* 1–16.

Council on Interracial Books for Children. Special issue on Chicano materials. *Bulletin,* 1975, *5,* 1–20.

Council on Interracial Books for Children. Asian Americans in children's books: Special double issue. *Bulletin,* 1976, *7,* 1–38. (a)

Council on Interracial Books for Children. *Human (and Antihuman) Values in Children's Books.* New York: The Council & the Resource Center, 1976. (b)

Council on Interracial Books for Children. *Interracial Digest,* Number 1, 1976. (c)

Council on Interracial Books for Children. 1976 American Library Association council document No. 83: Resolution on racism and sexism awareness. *Bulletin,* 1976, *7,* 75. (d)

Council on Interracial Books for Children. *Interracial Digest,* Number 2, 1978.

Council on Interracial Books for Children. Editorial on censorship. *Bulletin,* 1980, *11,* 3–4. (a)

Council on Interracial Books for Children. *1980–1981 Catalog: Racism and Sexism—Resource Center for Educators.* New York: The Council & the Resource Center, 1980. (b)

Drummond, W. H., & Andrews, T. E. The influence of federal and state government on teacher education. *Phi Delta Kappan,* October 1980, *62,* 97–99.

Edson, L., & the Editors of Time-Life Books. *How We Learn.* New York: Time-Life Books, 1975.

Farrar, E.; DeSanctis, J. E.; & Cohen, D. K. The lawn party: The evaluation of federal programs in local settings. *Phi Delta Kappan,* November 1980, *62,* 167–171.

Feminists on Children's Media. A feminist look at children's books. *School Library Journal,* January 1971, *18,* 19–24.

Feminists on Children's Media. *Little Miss Muffet Fights Back.* New York: Author, 1974.

Fisher, L. All chiefs, no Indians: What children's books say about American Indians. *Elementary English,* February 1974, *51,* 185–189.

Gagné, R. N. *The Conditions of Learning* (2nd ed.). New York: Holt, Rinehart & Winston, 1970.

Glazer, J. I., & Williams, G. III. *Introduction to Children's Literature.* New York: McGraw-Hill, 1979.

Haskins, J. *Racism and Sexism in Children's Nonfiction.* Vol. 5 of *Children's Literature.* Philadelphia: Temple University Press, 1976.

Indian Historian Press. *Textbooks and the American Indian.* San Francisco: Indian Historian Press, 1970.

Kirp, D. L., & Yudof, M. G. *Educational Policy and the Law.* Berkeley, Calif., McCutchan, 1974.

Kirst, M. W., & Mosher, E. K. Politics of education. *Review of Educational Research,* December 1969, *39,* 623–640.

Kohlberg, L. Moral development and the new social studies. *Social Education,* May 1973, *37,* 369–375.

Lanes, S. G. A case for *The Five Chinese Brothers. School Library Journal,* October 1977, *24,* 80–81.

Larrick, Nancy. The all-White world of children's books. *Saturday Review,* September 1965, *48,* 63–85.

Lichter, J., & Johnson, D. W. Changes in attitudes toward Negroes of White elementary school students after use of multiethnic readers. *Journal of Educational Psychology,* April 1969, *60,* 148–152.

Macmillan Publishing Co., Inc. *Guidelines for Creating Positive Sexual and Racial Images in Educational Materials.* New York: Macmillan, 1975.

Madsen, J. M. Women and children's literature. In E. C. Snyder (Ed.), *The Study of Women: Enlarging Perspectives of Social Reality.* New York: Harper & Row, 1979.

Madsen, J. M., & Wickersham, E. B. A look at young children's realistic fiction. *Reading Teacher,* December 1980, *34,* 273–279.

Massie, D. C. Censorship in the schools: Something old and something new. *Today's Education,* November-December 1980, *69,* 22E–26E.

Mathis, S. B. True/false messages for the black child. *Black Books Bulletin,* Winter 1974, *2,* 12–19.

McDiarmid, G., & Pratt, D. *Teaching Prejudice.* Toronto, Canada: Ontario Institute for Studies in Education, 1971.

McGraw-Hill Book Company. *Guidelines for Equal Treatment of the Sexes in McGraw-Hill Book Company Publications.* New York: McGraw-Hill, 1974.

Menchise, D. N. *Racial Bias as a Determinant of Literary Preference and the Relationship of Selected Variables to Patterns of Preference and Reflection of Literary Works Whose Author's Race Is Known.* University of Connecticut, 1972. (University of Connecticut Microfilm No. 32-236)

Monson, D. L., & Peltola, B. J. *Research in Children's Literature.* Newark, Del.: International Reading Association, 1976. (ERIC Document Reproduction Service No. ED 126 489)

Moore, R. E. *Racism in the English Language.* New York: Council on Interracial Books for Children, Racism and Sexism Resource Center for Educators, 1976. (ERIC Document Reproduction Service No. ED 144 080)

Newman, J. Indian Association attacks lies in children's literature. Council on Interracial Books for Children, *Bulletin,* Summer 1969, *2,* 3.

Nilsen, A. P. Women in children's literature. *College English,* May 1971, *32,* 918–926.

Nilsen, A. P.; Bosmajian, H.; Gershuny, H. L.; & Stanley, J. P. *Sexism and Language.* Urbana, Ill.: National Council of Teachers of English, 1977. (ERIC Document Reproduction Service No. ED 136 260)

Pennsylvania Department of Education. *Guidelines for Creating Positive Sexual and Racial Images in Educational Materials.* Harrisburg, Pa.: The Department, 1975. (ERIC Document Reproduction Service No. ED 117 687)

Pennsylvania Department of Education. *New Perspectives: A Bibliography of Racial, Ethnic, and Feminist Resources.* Harrisburg, Pa.: The Department, 1977. (ERIC Document Reproduction Service No. ED 146 284)

Peterson, L. J.; Rossmiller, R. A.; & Volz, M. M. *The Law and Public School Operation* (2nd ed.). New York: Harper & Row, 1978.

Piaget, J. *The Origins of Intelligence in Children* (M. Cook, Trans.). New York: Norton, 1963.

Pratt, D. *How to Find and Measure Bias in Textbooks.* Englewood Cliffs, N.J.: Educational Technology Publications, 1972.

Pressley, M. Imagery and children's learning: Putting the picture in developmental perspective. *Review of Educational Research,* Fall 1977, *47,* 585–622.

Rollins, C. (Ed.). *We Build Together.* Champaign, Ill.: National Council of Teachers of English, 1967. (ERIC Document Reproduction Service No. ED 076 998)

Rudman, M. K. *Children's Literature: An Issues Approach.* Lexington, Mass.: Heath, 1976.

Schon, I. Looking at books about Latin Americans. *Language Arts,* March 1976, *53,* 265–271.

Schon, I. Recent notorious and noteworthy books about Mexico, Mexicans, and Mexican Americans. *Journal of Reading,* January 1981, *24,* 293–299.

School Library Journal. McGraw-Hill guidelines for equal treatment. *School Library Journal,* January 1975, *21,* 23–27.

Schwartz, A. V. *Sounder:* A black or a white tale? Council on Interracial Books for Children, *Bulletin,* 1970, *3,* 1.

Schwartz, A. V. *The Cay:* Racism rewarded. Council on Interracial Books for Children, *Bulletin,* 1971, *3,* 4.

Schwartz, A. V. *The Five Chinese Brothers:* Time to retire. Council on Interracial Books for Children, *Bulletin,* 1977, *8,* 3.

Scott, D. Chinese stories: A plea for authenticity. *School Library Journal,* April 1974, *20,* 21–25.

Scott, K. P. Sexist and nonsexist materials: What impact do they have? *Elementary School Journal,* September 1980, *81,* 48–52.

Simpson, E. L. Moral development research: A case study of scientific cultural bias. *Human Development,* 1974, *17,* 81–106.

Singh, J. M., & Yancey, A. V. Racial attitudes in white first-grade children. *Journal of Educational Research,* April 1974, *67,* 370–372.

State of Washington: Models for the Evaluation of Bias Content in Instructional Materials. Olympia, Wash.: Department of Public Instruction, 1975.

Stewig, J. W., & Knipfel, M. L. Sexism in picture books: What progress? *Elementary School Journal,* December 1975, *76,* 151–155.

Stoodt, B. D., & Ignizio, S. The American Indian in children's literature. *Language Arts,* January 1976, *53,* 17–19.

Suhl, I. Doctor Dolittle—The great white father. Council on Interracial Books for Children, *Bulletin,* 1969, *2,* 1–2.

Taylor, T. *The Cay.* New York: Doubleday, 1969.

Tibbetts, S-L. Children's literature: A feminist viewpoint. *California Journal of Educational Research,* January 1975, *26,* 1–5.

Tomlinson, T. M. The troubled years: An interpretive analysis of public schooling since 1950. *Phi Delta Kappan,* January 1981, *62,* 373–376.

Travers, P. L. *Mary Poppins.* New York: Harcourt Brace, 1962.

Weitzman, L. J.; Eifler, D.; Hokada, E.; & Ross, C. Sex role socialization in picture books for preschool children. *American Journal of Sociology,* May 1972, *77,* 1125–1150.

Weitzman, L. J.; & Rizzo, D. *Biased Textbooks: A Research Perspective.* Washington, D.C.: Resource Center on Sex Role in Education, National Foundation for the Improvement of Education, 1974.

Weston Woods Company. *Audio-Visual Catalog, Twenty-fifth Anniversary Edition.* Weston, Conn.: Author, 1980.

Wickersham, E. B. An analysis of Native American verbal images as they are related to children's literature (Doctoral dissertation, Pennsylvania State University, 1979). *Dissertation Abstracts International,* 1979, *39,* 6371A-7024A. (University Microfilms No. 7909149, 6520)

Williams, J., & Edwards, C. An exploratory study of the modification of color and racial attitudes in preschool children. *Child Development,* December 1959, *30,* 737–750.

Wisconsin Department of Public Instruction. *Starting Out Right: Choosing Books about Black People for Young Children* (B. I. Latimer, Ed.). Madison, Wis.: The Department, 1972. (ERIC Document Reproduction Service No. ED 065 656)

Women on Words and Images. *Dick and Jane as Victims: Sex Stereotyping in Children's Readers.* Princeton, N.J.: Carolingian Press, 1972.

Yawkey, T. Attitudes toward Black Americans held by rural and urban white early childhood subjects based upon multiethnic school studies materials. *Journal of Negro Education,* Spring 1973, *42,* 164–169.

Yuill, P. *Little Black Sambo:* The continuing controversy. *School Library Journal,* March 1976, *22,* 71–76.

Zimet, S. G. *Print and Prejudice.* London: Hodder & Stoughton, 1976. (Available through the International Reading Association, P.O. Box 8139, 800 Barksdale Road, Newark, Del. 19711)

RACISM AND SEXISM IN RESEARCH

In the past twenty-five years, there have been a number of efforts to eliminate prejudice and discrimination in American society. Although these efforts have met with some success, an unbiased society is still a dream for the future. The biases that still exist in society affect both researchers and the research that they do. The purpose of this entry is to examine some of the ways that social biases, specifically racism and sexism, negatively affect research topic selection, sampling, measurement, and the generation of conclusions. It will also cover ways that the negative effects of these biases can be minimized.

Topic Selection. "The things a social scientist selects for study are determined by his [sic] concept of what are socially important values. The student of human affairs deals only with materials to which he [sic] attributes 'cultural significance'" (Nagel, 1961, p. 485). Traditionally, the "cultural significance" of minorities and women, other than in a pathological sense, has been minimal, as has the amount of research that has been done *for* them. Much research has been done *on* minorities; however, most of it has come from a "blame the victim" perspective and focuses on the pathological aspects of minority life. As a result "seen narrowly as a 'victim,' the black man appears in the learned journals as a patient, a petitioner for aid, rarely as a rounded human being" (Thomas & Sillen, 1972, p. 47).

As distorted and ethnocentric as the images of black men are, they do at least exist. Images of black women or indeed of any minority women are found rarely, if at all, in much of the research literature. Researchers from education (Shakeshaft, 1979), sociology (Tresemer, 1975), and psychology (Kearney, 1979) have all commented on how sexism in society and the resultant devaluing of women and areas associated with women have limited the selection of research topics focusing on minority and majority women.

"The bulk of work in the social sciences has focused on phenomena and areas in which men dominate: territoriality, aggression, politics, and economics" (Shakeshaft, 1979, p. 214). Work on patterns of research in early childhood education has found that the majority of male researchers (who are themselves the majority of researchers) tend to study control of persons and institutions, philosophy, and methodology; while women tend to study the family, the role of women, and the development of young children (McDonald, 1976).

Bias influences *how* research questions are asked as well as *what* research questions are asked. Researchers have asked, "Why can't Johnny read?" (not "Why can't Janey add?") or "Are women feminizing our schools?" (not "Are men polarizing our schools and causing them to become violent places?") (Shakeshaft, 1979, p. 217). In the area of race, "What are the effects of racism on blacks?" has been asked, not "What are the effects of racism on whites?" Students of prejudice frequently ask, as did Bettelheim and Janowitz (1964), "Are Negroes as intelligent as white people?" (not "Are Caucasians as intelligent as black people?" or even "How biased are our intelligence tests?").

These are only some indications of the significant gaps in the knowledge generated from research. Information about behaviors and characteristics of minorities and women is frequently unavailable. Neither is there much research-based information about social and educational inequity or ways to allieviate it. Because of the gaps, decisions are being made, programs are being developed, and services are being offered without an adequate research base.

Design. The sources of bias in design include four areas: knowledge of appropriate literature, selection of independent variables, control of sources of invalidity, and techniques used in data analysis. Race and sex bias can affect our knowledge of appropriate literature in a number of ways. First, as indicated previously, one of the results of bias in topic selection is the existence of gaps in research areas in which information pertinent to the research topic

just does not exist. The devaluing of research on minorities and women also frequently means that the research that is done is published out of the mainstream, in places that may be difficult to find, and is not read by a majority of the researchers who could benefit from it. Even if the work is available, researchers may not see how work on, for example, sex roles or racial bias in testing could affect their work on achievement motivation or self-concept.

The selection of independent variables is a second source of bias in design. Socioeconomic status (SES) is often used as an independent variable on samples of women and men, even though the common methods of assessing people's socioeconomic status use the husband's or father's status as the determinant of the women's status (Edelsky, 1978). Race is another independent variable influenced by bias. Often two nonidentical concepts, social race and biological or genetic race, are combined, and a common racial label is used for individuals from markedly different backgrounds. For example, the children of a black parent and a white parent are identified and studied as black (Proshansky & Newton, 1968).

A third source of bias can be found in the controlling of potential sources of invalidity. If one is not aware of or sensitive to possible threats to validity, it is impossible to control for them. For example, in many of the early studies of racial differences, the effects of socioeconomic status were not controlled, and the SES of the majority group sample was higher than that of the minority group being compared (Pettigrew, 1964). Other variables related to SES, such as educational level, are frequently not controlled in cross-race studies. And even when differences in educational levels are controlled, differences in the quality of schooling, particularly important because of the existence of dual school systems for minorities and majorities, are not.

Finally, the techniques used in the analysis of the data can themselves be a source of bias. Data that do not fit the expected pattern can be ignored or not used, as was the case in Yerkes' research on sex roles in chimps, often used as evidence of the genetic basis of sex roles. Yerkes (1943) omitted data on a number of animals when the results were "statistically disappointing" and, in particular, dropped the data for two females because they were highly dominant. Techniques that allow for the analysis of sex and race differences as well as for the interaction of sex and race are available, but they are frequently not used (Etaugh & Spandikow, 1979).

A major effect of bias on design has been the failure to use existing information about minorities and women in the design in order to increase the validity of the study. For example, Caplan (1975) found that the presence of an adult investigator caused boys to become more antisocial, whereas the absence of an adult was more conducive to finding no sex differences in antisocial behavior. A study of antisocial behavior designed without knowledge of this information and without the necessary controls could then lead to an inaccurate conclusion about sex differences and a reinforcing of stereotypes about boys' antisocial behavior. Researchers have found a number of race, sex, and class differences that, like Caplan's, can invalidate studies unless they are controlled in the design (Maccoby & Jacklin, 1974; Graves & Glick, 1978).

As a result of bias in design, inaccurate information is generated and incorrect conclusions are drawn from that information. Particularly in areas involving race and sex roles and differences, bias in design has influenced research toward stereotypic explanations and away from examinations of complex realities—a dangerous direction for both research and researchers.

Sampling. Bias can affect sampling in terms of the composition of samples and the generalizations that are made from them. Except in traditionally feminine areas dealing with care of children and home, men and boys have been the population studied in research. And except in the case of research specifically on minorities and on pathological areas such as cultural deprivation, delinquency, and the effects of discrimination, the men and boys who have been studied have been white.

Analyses of journal articles have shown that a number of single-sex studies have been done and that prior to 1974 these samples were disproportionately male. More recent research indicates that while single-sex research is still being done, it is being done with female samples as well as male (Reardon & Prescott, 1977). Regardless of the sex of the subjects, there is a strong tendency for researchers to generalize the results of their single-sex samples. Research has found that over 90 percent of the male sample studies were generalized to both males and females and anywhere from 61 to 97 percent of the female samples were overgeneralized (Schwabacker, 1972; Reardon & Prescott, 1977).

Finding comparable data on minorities is difficult, because while researchers frequently indicate the sex of their samples, they rarely give the racial composition. The exception is in studies that deal with issues such as desegregation or with other specific ethnic or racial issues. In these cases, the racial composition of the samples is given, and the samples are likely to be disproportionately minority.

A major result of bias in sample composition and generalization is that minorities and women have been viewed as the "deviant," that which confounds the results. Social science "takes for granted that the human we seek to understand is a White male" (Long Laws, 1978, p. 6). Thus if white males are the norm, then research on general areas of interest can be done with white male samples. Then either the results can be generalized to other groups, or the other groups can be studied in terms of the ways that they deviate from the norm. Minorities and women thus become a topic, something to be studied, as opposed to a sample to be used to study some general phenomena.

Another effect of bias on sampling is the inaccurate attribution of characteristics to one sex based solely on the study of the other sex. Discussions from studies of one sex frequently conclude, without data, that the other sex is either equivalent or opposite (Parlee, 1975).

Nowhere is the effect of bias on sampling more evident than in the newly popular and growing field of the life cycles or stages. Beginning with Erikson's work on the "Eight Stages of Man" (1959) through Levinson's *Seasons of a Man's Life* (1978), the study of life cycles has focused on male subjects. When women are examined, it is in terms of how they fit or don't fit the male model. Without empirical verification, women are said to go through the same cycles as men (Stewart, 1977) or are said to go through cycles that are antithetical to men's (Sheehy, 1977). The samples are overwhelmingly white as well as male, with racial differences rarely ever being theorized.

Sanguiliano (1978, p. 44) concluded after a survey of the literature on life cycles that "mostly we [researchers] persist in seeing her [woman] in the reflected light of men." Her conclusion seems to hold for women and for minority men in a number of other social science areas as well.

Measurement. Although many researchers are not aware of the effects of race and sex bias in such areas as design and sampling, the controversy and debate about race and ability testing has made a number of educators and researchers sensitive to the existence of race bias in testing. The development of tests by white, middle-class authors, which are standardized and normed on white middle-class students and then used to make decisions about minority and poor children, is a problem that has been recognized by many test publishers and users. Fewer people are aware of the effects that sexism can also have on ability testing and the negative influences that both race and sex bias can have in other areas of measurement, such as personality testing and observations. Since tests and measures are the basis of data collection for research, bias in measurement can have a large effect on research in general.

Test format (multiple choice, fill-in-the-blank, essay) and the context in which test items are set can affect the test performance of females and males (Donlon, 1971; Murphy, 1977). Females have a tendency to score better on essay items and on test items written in a context that includes stereotypically feminine activities. Thus "sex differences" can be created or eliminated through the selection of items to be included in a test (Dwyer, 1976.). Race differences, too, can be expanded or contracted according to the items selected. Items with a high cultural loading (those that would be more familiar to people from one culture than from another) or that use language and syntax unfamiliar to some of those taking the test can cause a test to favor or not favor a specific group (Campbell & Scott, 1980).

Personality tests normed and developed on majority populations may also be biased. Cowan, Watkins, and Davis (1975), for example, found that the Minnesota Multiphasic Personality Inventory (MMPI) classified nine of a group of twenty nonschizophrenic blacks as schizophrenic.

Unawareness of different perceptions of reality, caused

by living in a biased society, can affect personality test development and particularly interpretation. For example, studies of Locus of Control often find sex differences that indicate that males are more internal and females are more external (Feather, 1969; Brannigan & Tolor, 1971). These differences are frequently interpreted as sex differences in personality. Rather than tapping a subtle, pervasive, and dynamic dimension on which females and males differ, this test and others may be eliciting a realistic appraisal by minorities and women of the extent to which their own efforts determine whether they succeed or fail (Parlee, 1975). This measuring of reality rather than a personality trait may also be the case in the use of black and white dolls to measure children's racial attitudes and self-concept (Pettigrew, 1964). Giving black dolls the lesser choices in areas such as jobs or housing may be a reflection of reality rather than low black self-concept or individual white racism.

Sex and race bias may influence observations as well. Several studies have found that observers rate young children differently according to their perceived sex of the child and suggest that a "healthy caution" should be exercised in interpreting sex differences obtained by observers who know the sex of the child (or adult) being studied (Meyer & Sobieszik, 1972).

Just as the sex and race of the subject may influence the observer, the sex and race of the observer may influence the subject. While the effects of the experimenter's race and sex on research are complex and inconsistent, they do exist, and systematic use of testers of one race or sex may have a long-range effect on research (Sattler, 1970; Samuel, 1977).

Almost any measure can be influenced by bias and, as a result of that influence, cause inaccurate results to be generated. These results can be influenced by obvious factors like the language of a question, such as "Should Jews be forced to leave the country?" (Bettelheim & Janowitz, 1964). Inaccurate results can also be attributed to more subtle factors. In one instance the Scholastic Aptitude Test (SAT) was used to track sex differences in mathematics without accounting for the potential effect of a change in test content. This change involved removing items dealing with data insufficiency, an item type on which women scored well (Dwyer, 1976). Women, in fact, do better than men on data-insufficiency items. Thus when the authors of the SAT removed its data-insufficiency items, they may have created a test on which women do not score as well. On a longitudinal study of sex differences, based on the SAT, changes in sex differences may thus be an artifact of the test (Dwyer, 1976).

Generation of Conclusions. The expectations of the researcher, colored by stereotypes and biases, can, and frequently do, have more effect on the generation of conclusions than do the data. Herschberger humorously, yet effectively, summarized this problem in her analysis of the conclusions of Yerkes's studies of sex roles in chimpanzees. Writing from the perspective of Josie, a female chimp

in Yerkes's sample, Herschberger (1970) commented: "When Jack takes over the food chute, the report calls it his "natural dominance." While I'm up there lording it over the food chute, the investigator writes down "the male temporarily defers to her and allows her to act as if dominant over him." Can't I get any satisfaction out of life that isn't allowed me by some male chimp, damn it?" (p. 10).

A similar phenomenon occurs when the data indicate differences in the behaviors of groups of subjects. Data are reported, but the explanations for the differences are based on stereotypes and rarely are other, equally plausible, but nonstereotyped explanations considered or presented. For example, based on their study of the behavior of infants when confronted with a barrier keeping them from a desired object, Goldberg and Lewis (1969) concluded that boys attack and girls give up. An equally plausible, nonstereotyped explanation that the more verbal girls were crying not because they gave up but to attract the attention of those who could remove the barrier was not, however, reported. Thus the reader was left with the impression that one sex sought to solve problems while the other did not.

The preceding have been examples of researchers trying to fit the stereotyped conclusions to the reality of the data, but there are also examples of researchers denying the reality of the data. As Nobles (1973, p. 18) asserts, "Oftentimes researchers have demonstrated only one insignificant finding and, regardless of their own results, concluded their studies with assertions which were contrary to their own evidence." For example, one study concluded that black students were more apt than white students to think that teachers perceived them negatively in terms of characteristics such as clothes and intelligence. This conclusion was made even though no significant differences were actually found between black and white students' perceptions of their teachers' feelings about them (Nobles, 1973).

Bias can also affect the generation of conclusions through the selective reporting of research results. For example, Moynihan (1965, p. 30) concluded in support of his theory of black matriarchy that "it is clear that Negro females have established a strong position for themselves in white collar and professional employment." He based his conclusion on data indicating that black males represented 1.2 percent of all males in white-collar occupations, whereas black females represented 3.1 percent of all females in white-collar occupations. He did not report that, at the time, employed black men earned on the average 1.5 times as much as employed black women or that the smaller number of women in white-collar occupations and the location of most white-collar women in clerical occupations made the comparison at best misleading (Wallace, 1978). The major effect of bias on the generation of conclusions is that inaccurate conclusions are drawn and incorrect myths, stereotypes, and theories are perpetuated.

Minimizing Bias. Bias in research is not an infrequent phenomenon, and the examples cited are not isolated examples of "bad research." Schwabacker's (1972) and Reardon and Prescott's (1977) work indicating that 90 percent of studies using male samples were generalized to both women and men is an indication of how widespread bias is. Another indicator is Maccoby and Jacklin's (1974, p. 7) conclusion that "stereotypes about what kind of behavior is to be expected from the two sexes run very deep and even when sex differences are incidental to the main focus of a study, the observers must almost inevitably be biased to some extent," which may also hold for race.

While the effects bias has on research may be widespread, researchers are frequently unaware of it. The researcher who, for example, uses white, male samples is generally not consciously excluding minorities and women, yet this is the result. Social biases in research are more a result of a lack of awareness and an acceptance of the status quo than a result of intentional efforts. Those who deliberately bias their research are few and are far outnumbered by the majority of researchers, whose awareness of the effects of bias is followed by attempts to eliminate or minimize them.

The negative effects of racism and sexism on research can be minimized, and efforts are being made in that direction. Most of the efforts are being centered on the development of guidelines to reduce bias for researchers and evaluators of research and research proposals. Sample guidelines should include areas such as the following:

Research questions on minorities and women should include investigations of causes as well as effects. For example, work on the relative intelligence of minority and majority group members should also include the potential for examining the effects of biased tests. (Campbell, 1981, p. 50.)

Researchers should determine the validity of independent variables dealing with race and sex. For example, social, or nongenetic, definitions of race should not be used in studies of possible genetic differences in intelligence of different racial groups. (Campbell, 1981, p. 50.)

Results from studies should not be generalized to members of racial and gender groups not represented in the sample. (Campbell, 1981, p. 51.)

Instruments used in research studies should be examined to ensure that they do not favor one racial or gender group. For example, instruments whose item contexts deal primarily with scientific, mathematical, or mechanical areas to the exclusion of contexts in areas such as human relations should not be used to assess general achievement. (Campbell, 1981, p. 52.)

Researchers should refer their conclusions directly to the results of the study. For example, if nonsignificant differences are found, then these should not be reported simply as differences. (Campbell, 1981, p. 52.)

Guidelines similar to those above are being developed by the American Education Research Association. Other social science groups, such as the American Psychological Association and the American Sociological Association (Committee on the Status of Women in Sociology, 1980), either have developed guidelines or are working on them.

Use of these guidelines by researchers, journal editors, and those who make research grants can do much to make research both more complete and more accurate. Use of the guidelines by consumers in their assessments of research may help to reduce the perpetuation of incorrect myths, stereotypes, and theories.

Patricia B. Campbell

See also Experimental Methods; Experimental Validity; Standards for Tests and Ethical Test Use; Survey Research Methods.

REFERENCES

Bettelheim, B., & Janowitz, M. *Social Change and Prejudice.* New York: Free Press, 1964.

Brannigan, G. G., & Tolon, A. Sex differences in adaptive styles. *Journal of Genetic Psychology,* 1971, *119,* 143–149.

Campbell, P. B. *The Impact of Societal Biases on Research Methods.* Washington, D.C.: National Institute of Education, 1981.

Campbell, P. B., & Scott, E. Non-biased tests can change the score. *Inter-racial Books for Children Bulletin,* 1980, *11*(6), 7–9.

Caplan, P. J. Sex differences in anti-social behavior: Does research methodology produce or abolish them? *Human Development,* 1975, *18*(6), 444–460.

Committee on the Status of Women in Sociology. Sexist biases in sociological research: Problems and issues. *American Sociological Association Footnotes,* 1980, *1,* 8–9.

Cowan, M. A.; Watkins, B. A.; & Davis, W. E. Level of education, diagnosis, and race-related differences in MMPI performance. *Journal of Clinical Psychology,* 1975, *31*(3), 442–444.

Donlon, T. F. *Content Factors in Sex Differences on Test Questions.* Paper presented to the annual meeting of the American Educational Research Association, Boston, April 1971.

Dwyer, C. A. Test content and sex differences in reading. *Reading Teacher,* 1976, *29,* 753–759.

Edelsky, C. *Genderlects: A Brief Review of the Literature.* Paper presented at the annual meeting of the National Council of Teachers of English, Kansas City, Mo., November 1978. (ERIC Document Reproduction Service No. ED 165 187)

Erikson, E. Growth and crises of the healthy personality. *Psychological Issues,* 1959, *1,* 1–171.

Etaugh, C., & Spandikow, D. B. Attention to sex in psychological research as related to journal policy and author sex. *Psychology of Women Quarterly,* 1979, *4*(2), 175–184.

Feather, N. T. Level of aspiration and performance variability. *Journal of Personality and Social Psychology,* 1967, *6,* 37–46.

Goldberg, S., & Lewis, M. Play behavior in the year-old infant: Early sex differences. *Child Development,* 1969, *40,* 21–31.

Graves, Z. R., & Glick, J. The effect of context on mother-child interaction: A progress report. In W. S. Hall & M. Cole (Eds.), *Quarterly Newsletter of the Institute for Comparative Human Development.* New York: Rockefeller University Press, 1978, pp. 41–46.

Herschberger, R. *Adam's Rib.* New York: Harper & Row, 1970.

Kearney, H. R. Feminist challenges to the social structure and sex roles. *Psychology of Women Quarterly,* 1979, *4*(1), 16–31.

Levinson, D. J. *The Seasons of a Man's Life.* New York: Knopf, 1978.

Long Laws, J. *Feminism and Patriarchy: Competing Ways of Doing Social Science.* Paper presented at the annual meeting of the American Sociological Association, San Francisco, September 1978. (ERIC Document Reproduction Service No. ED 166 081)

Maccoby, E., & Jacklin, C. N. *The Psychology of Sex Differences.* Stanford, Calif.: Stanford University Press, 1974.

McDonald, G. *Two Windows on Research.* Paper presented at the meeting at the Auckland Institute for Educational Research, Auckland, New Zealand, October 1976. (ERIC Document Reproduction Service No. ED 133 053)

Meyer, J. W., & Sobieszik, B. J. The effect of a child's sex on adult interpretations of its behavior. *Development Psychology,* 1972, *6,* 42–48.

Moynihan, D. P. *The Negro Family: The Case for National Action.* Washington, D.C.: U.S. Department of Labor, 1965.

Murphy, R. C. *Sex Differences in Examination Performance.* Paper presented to the International Conference on Sex Role Stereotyping, Cardiff, Wales, 1977. (ERIC Document Reproduction Service No. ED 154 265)

Nagel, T. *The Structure of Science.* New York: Harcourt Brace and World, 1961.

Nobles, W. W. Psychological research and the black self-concept: A critical review. *Journal of Social Issues,* 1973, *33*(4), 11–31.

Parlee, M. B. Psychology. *SIGNS: A Journal of Women in Culture and Society,* 1975, *1*(1), 119–138.

Pettigrew, T. Negro-American personality: Why isn't more known? *Journal of Social Issues,* 1964, *20*(2), 4–23.

Proshansky, H., & Newton, P. The nature and meaning of Negro self-identity. In M. Deutsch, I. Katz, & A. R. Jensen (Eds.), *Social Class, Race, and Psychological Development.* New York: Holt, Rinehart & Winston, 1968.

Reardon, P., & Prescott, S. Sex as reported in a recent sample of psychological research. *Psychology of Women Quarterly,* 1977, *2*(2), 57–61.

Samuel, W. Observed IQ as a function of test atmosphere, tester expectation, and race of tester: A replication for female subjects. *Journal of Experimental Psychology,* 1977, *69*(5), 593–604.

Sanguiliano, I. *In Her Time.* New York: Morrow, 1978.

Sattler, J. Racial experimenter effects in experimentation, testing, interviewing, and psychotherapy. *Psychological Bulletin,* 1970, *73,* 137–160.

Schwabacker, S. Male versus female representation in psychological research: An examination of the *Journal of Personality and Social Psychology,* 1970, 1971. *Journal Supplement Abstracts,* 1972, *2,* 20–21.

Shakeshaft, C. *Dissertation Research on Women in Academic Administration: A Synthesis of Findings and Paradigm for Future Research.* Unpublished doctoral dissertation, Texas A & M University, 1979.

Sheehy, G. *Passages.* New York: Bantam Books, 1977.

Stewart, W. A. *A Psychosocial Study of the Formation of Early Adult Life Structure in Women.* Unpublished doctoral dissertation, Columbia University, 1977.

Thomas, A., & Sillen, S. *Racism and Psychiatry.* New York: Brunner/Mazel, 1972.

Tresemer, D. Assumptions made about gender roles. In M. Millman & R. Kanter (Eds.), *Another Voice.* New York: Doubleday, Anchor Books, 1975, pp. 308–339.

Wallace, M. *Black Macho and the Myth of Superwoman.* New York: Dial Press, 1978.

Yerkes, R. M. *Chimpanzees.* New Haven, Conn.: Yale University Press, 1943.

RADIO EDUCATION

See Distance Education; Mass Media: Media Use in Education.

READABILITY

The study of readability is an active research area, with well over a thousand publications from the 1920s to the present. From the first, "readable" has meant "understandable," and the emphasis on this meaning (as opposed to "legible" or "interesting") has grown with the research.

Formal efforts to determine levels of readability grew out of the problem of assigning appropriate materials to readers in various school grades. Interest in determining degree of difficulty of reading matter has since spread rather widely to the areas of mass communication, military training, and public forms and documents. This growth recognizes the concern of teachers, librarians, and writers about whether potential readers' skills are likely to be adequate to their reading task.

The major methods of determining readability fall into three classes: judgments, measures, and readability formulas (predictors). Each of these is discussed in turn, with the emphasis upon recent research. Following this, controversial aspects of readability are related to the critical distinction between predicting readable writing and producing readable writing (a far more complex and difficult problem). Special attention is then given to controversial aspects of readability formulas in education, and to some suggestions for their reliable application.

Judging Readability. Recent studies indicate that judgments of readability may or may not be reliable. Fortunately enough work has been done to indicate something about conditions that affect the accuracy of judgments.

Readability estimates are generally made in one of two ways; experts may read material and estimate how well it can be understood, or the reader's understanding of material may be tested directly. Individuals, according to this research, are unreliable judges because their judgments on the same materials vary so widely, either from each other or from tested criteria of difficulty. Subjects in such studies have been

- School and public librarians, who rated one Newbery-Award-winning book from third-grade to twelfth-grade in difficulty (Jongsma, 1972);
- Professional writers, who assigned each of five passages to five possible levels of difficulty (Klare, 1976a);
- Teachers, in both the United States and Great Britain, who assigned varying grade level difficulty ratings to passages from a basal reader of known grade placement (Jorgenson, 1975; Miller & Marshall, 1978); judgments of this type are often six to nine age-levels apart (Harrison, 1977, 1979, 1980a).

Furthermore the judges' experience in teaching or reading coursework made little difference (Miller & Marshall, 1978). Irwin and Davis (1979) suggest that teachers use a checklist to improve their judgments. But whether they *will* use a lengthy checklist and whether they *can* use it reliably remain uncertain. Considering the number of judgments teachers must make, these findings have disturbing implications for the matching of text difficulty to student ability. And since such matches can affect achievement (see Chall & Feldman, 1966; Jorgenson, 1975), the concern grows.

Under certain conditions reliable judgments of readability can be obtained:

- Individuals can be good judges of the relative difficulty of simple versus complex sentences (Schwartz, Sparkman, & Deese, 1970; Wang, 1970).
- Small groups of two or three individuals can provide accurate judgments for books (Porter & Popp, 1973) and passages (Carver, 1974; Singer, 1975) *if* the judges are experts or are trained to evaluate tests.
- Groups of about twenty or more can provide reliable pooled judgments of passages even though their individual judgments vary widely (Klare, 1976a; Harrison, 1977, 1979, 1980a).

These studies provide encouraging evidence that human judges can indeed be accurate, and at the same time provide discouraging evidence of why this procedure has never really caught on. Reliable text rating procedures that are appropriate for use in evaluating shorter pieces of reading material cannot be adapted easily to the longer pieces of reading material most teachers want to evaluate. Furthermore ratings obtained under different judge selection procedures provide contradictory results (Froese, 1980).

Measuring Readability. Performance of readers on comprehension tests is often used as an index of readability, with multiple-choice or short-answer tests the typical measuring instruments. Development by Taylor (1953) of "cloze procedure" appeared to improve comprehension testing because it tests understanding as a text is being read rather than after it has been read (when memory capabilities may play too large a role in test results).

Cloze procedure, as a measure of comprehension, typically involves a passage in which standard-length blanks replace every *n*th word. This is most commonly every fifth word and is called a deletion ratio of 1:5 or an every-fifth deletion ratio. Subjects attempt to fill in the blanks with the words the author used at those points. Comprehension scores consist of the percentage of blanks where readers were able to supply these same words (except for minor misspellings); this "exact" scoring method lends the procedure its objectivity. Developing this kind of test offers advantages in time and effort over developing and refining a comparable multiple-choice test, plus another major advantage: the test consists of the text. The old criticism that one may unintentionally end up writing easy

questions on hard text, and vice versa, can be handled in a much more straightforward fashion than with a multiple-choice test.

Strictly speaking, however, the cloze test consists of the text only when a blank replaces every single word. Since that cannot be done with one form, *n* forms are needed where every *n*th word has been deleted. If, in other words, an every-fifth deletion ratio is used, there must be five forms, one beginning with word 1, another beginning with word 2, and so on, up to word 5. Otherwise, cloze developers may fall victim to the same kind of criticism as the multiple-choice test developer, since percentages correct on five cloze forms may vary significantly from each other, with differences as great as 15 percent. Some cloze test users apparently have not realized this, or perhaps have been deterred by the requirements of five groups and five forms, since many single-form cloze studies have been published. For some purposes two forms appear to be a desirable minimum. Another possibility is a random, rather than an every-fifth, deletion pattern on one form (Meredith & Vaughan, 1978).

As the foregoing discussion suggests, cloze procedure may have certain advantages over multiple-choice measures, but it can still take considerable time and effort to administer. One might hope to increase efficiency by deleting every third word rather than every fifth, for example. This change would yield more responses per student over a passage, an important consideration for reliability and readability, and make only three forms necessary to test the entire passage. MacGinitie (1960) and Fillenbaum, Jones, and Rapoport (1963) have shown, however, that four or more words are needed between blanks in order to obtain the most reliable and valid measures. In fact, one may sometimes want to increase the number of words between deletions even beyond four, as with readers of limited ability, since this may improve acceptance of cloze tests (Klare, Sinaiko, & Stolurow, 1972).

In most applications, the every-fifth deletion ratio has become the standard. It has proved to be sufficiently reliable (Vaughan & Meredith, 1978) and adaptable for many diverse applications and populations. The literature on cloze contains well over a thousand references, too many to summarize briefly here. Bormuth (1968a); Klare, Sinaiko, and Stolurow (1972); Rankin (1965); and Weaver (1965) have, however, published reviews of the research. Jongsma (1971, 1980), Rankin (1977), and Streiff (forthcoming) cover classroom use for teaching and testing. A bibliography on the cloze procedure appears in Buros (1978), and McKenna and Robinson (1980) have provided an annotated bibliography. Several cloze-based reading comprehension tests have been published; see, for example, McLeod (1970), McLeod & Anderson (1973), NFER (1977), and College Entrance Examination Board (1980). Bormuth (1967, 1968b) and Rankin and Culhane (1969) have published comparisons and equivalence values for cloze and multiple-choice scores. Bormuth (1969) has also related cloze scores to information gain, and Rankin (1971) to grade levels. Considering the widespread use of cloze procedure in education and some puzzling disagreements in evaluating comprehension levels, this area deserves further research.

Cloze procedure, for all its widespread usefulness, has not been free of criticisms. Among those raised are that (1) it cannot measure all the different kinds of comprehension skills that multiple-choice or similar objective test items can; (2) it may depend on general knowledge of the language more than on special knowledge of the material being read; and (3) it may depend too much on "short-range constraints," notably the four or five words on each side of a blank. These criticisms are themselves controversial, and proponents of cloze feel each can be answered. Kintsch, a comprehension theorist, has raised a more serious question. The cloze procedure, he argues, is probably actually misleading (Kintsch & Vipond, 1979). He considers it to be a measure of the statistical redundancy of a text, with which many cloze proponents would readily agree. But this, he says, is a far cry from text comprehensibility. He considers such measures as reading time, amount recalled, number of inferences answered correctly, the effort required to type or translate a text, and various eye movement data all to be more adequate indicators of comprehension difficulty. Similar basic disagreements exist in the definitions of comprehension, from 1697 (John Locke's) to the present (Klare, forthcoming).

These considerations suggest that the field of reading comprehension needs, to use the words of Simons (1971), a new perspective. Recent work in text analysis promises a new point of view for understanding the process of comprehension, and the work of Kintsch (1979) and Kintsch and van Dijk (1978) appears especially promising. Better understanding can make the measurement of readability with comprehension tests more appealing. But there are other drawbacks with testing. The time, effort, and expertise needed to develop good comprehension tests rule out their use on a day-to-day basis as a measure of readability. Tests, like other evaluations, tend to be used more often for research than for practice. An easier method is needed.

Readability Formulas. Two research tools came together in the 1920s and led to a new method of assessing readability. The two were Thorndike's *The Teacher's Word Book* (1921) and statistical techniques of increased sophistication. The new method was the so-called readability formula. To date, well over 200 formulas have been published, the exact number depending upon how one defines "formula" (see Klare, 1963 and 1974–1975, for the period up to 1974). A general definition is "a predictive device that uses counts of word and sentence variables in a piece of writing to provide a quantitative, objective index of style difficulty."

The device is predictive because typically it uses the counts themselves to predict how well readers will understand the writing. No readers and no testing are needed to get the index value. Comprehension tests, whether cloze or multiple-choice, involve readers; they are, in that sense, measures rather than predictors. In fact, a comprehension test usually provides the criterion data on which to base a formula. Formulas are typically predictive in another sense: they are employed with text samples to predict overall scores for an entire work (story, textbook, article). Most often formulas involve 100-word samples, and developers usually advocate spacing them throughout a text in some random or numerically patterned fashion in order to predict the readability level of a complete work.

This predictive device typically uses word and sentence counts to provide a quantitative, objective index of difficulty. No case is made that particular word and sentence characteristics *cause* difficulty, only that they *index* difficulty. They are analogous to a thermometer, and like a thermometer, can be misleading if used improperly. It is not enough, for example, to tinker with the word and sentence variables in the hope of changing difficulty proportionately, just as it does relatively little good to hold a match under a thermometer in the hope of warming a room. It would be desirable to use counts of something besides words and sentences in the formulas, since many other variables in writing (to say nothing of those in readers) influence comprehension. Gray and Leary (1935) hoped to use format, organization, and content in their formula, but they found no way of counting or incorporating them into an index that is quantitative and objective. Furthermore, other language variables, such as counts of prepositional phrases or embedded clauses, add relatively little to the predictiveness of the formula, especially compared to the effort required to include them.

After application, formulas typically provide a quantitative, objective index of style difficulty, but say nothing about content. Ideally, therefore, a formula is content-free and should apply equally well to all prose contents except such atypical writing as that of Gertrude Stein or James Joyce, or hopelessly scrambled texts. Specialized formulas are of course needed, and have been developed, for such specialized contents as mathematical text and tests and questionnaires.

To achieve a quantitative, objective index of style difficulty, the typical formula uses a regression equation, with scores for word counts and sentence counts weighted to predict a comprehension score. This score, in turn, typically falls along a scale that corresponds roughly to a tested reading-grade level (in the United States) or a reading-age level (in Great Britain).

Readability formulas are of two types: one relies on word lists for scores which estimate semantic difficulty; another relies on counts of syllables for this purpose. A typical readability formula of the first type is that of Dale and Chall (1948). This formula became one of the most used in the field of education shortly after its appearance, and remains widely known and used:

$$X_{c_{50}} = .1579x_1 + .0496x_2 + 3.6365,$$

where $X_{c_{50}}$ = reading grade score of a pupil who could answer one-half the test questions on a passage correctly;

x_1 = Dale score, or percentage of words outside the Dale list of 3,000;

x_2 = average sentence length in words.

To apply this formula, the user must have the list of 3,000 words and also the many specific instructions for how to count special cases (e.g., proper names, abbreviations, present and past participial forms). In addition, a special table corrects the raw score obtained to a grade at which the piece of writing can be read with understanding.

The best-known example of the second type of measure is Flesch's Reading Ease formula (Flesch, 1948):

$$R.E. = 206.835 - .846wl - 1.015sl,$$

where $R.E.$ = reading ease, a score on a scale from 0 (hard to read) to 100 (easy to read);

wl = number of syllables per 100 words;

sl = average number of words per sentence.

The user of this formula must consult the reference for the special instructions needed to apply it. Another publication (Flesch, 1949) provides tables for converting the raw score to an approximate grade level.

The most frequently used formula in education currently is not a formula at all, but a graph (Fry, 1968; 1977). The reason for its popularity is that the graph was developed as "a formula that saves time" (Fry, 1968). The attempt to save time and effort has been prevalent in readability research, and application aids have appeared for most of the well-known formulas in the guise of tables (or charts) and computer programs (see Klare, 1974–1975, pp. 87–91). Yet one formula (designed for computer use) has twenty variables (Bormuth, 1969), and another is said to be so complex it can be applied only by computer (Jacobson, 1974). Most formulas were developed for use with the English language, but formulas also exist for Chinese, Dutch, Finnish, French, German, Hebrew, Russian, Spanish, Swedish, and Vietnamese languages (see Klare, 1974–1975, pp. 91–95, for references to many of these). The history of readability research is too extensive for more than the brief summary of major trends below.

Early emphasis on word frequency as an indicator of word difficulty supplied the basis for many of the earliest formulas, with the first usually conceded to be that of Lively and Pressey (1923). Readability formulas quickly evolved into statistical regression equation form, the first example being the Vogel and Washburne method (1928).

Well over a hundred language variables have been examined for possible use in formulas; Bormuth (1966, 1969) and Coleman (1965 or 1971) have made the most extensive investigations. Most of these can be subsumed under semantic (word) or syntactic (sentence) factors, as Entin and Klare (1978a) have shown in a recent factor analysis. Attempts to involve variables other than semantic or syntactic (e.g., format, organization, content) in formulas failed almost entirely, as illustrated in the early study of Gray and Leary (1935). Recently, however, Harris and Jacobson (1979) have again argued for trying to involve them.

Because their early use was largely in selecting school reading texts, developers began to use grade-level scales so that mismatches between readers' ability and text readability could be minimized. Vogel and Washburne used a closely related "reading score" scale for their early formula (1928) and were the first to adopt an actual grade-placement scale for their later formula (Washburne & Morphett, 1938). Various writers have criticized both this notion and the scales themselves, as is noted later.

Early criticism of the criteria for formula development led first to the use of the objective (largely multiple-choice) McCall-Crabbs *Standard Test Lessons in Reading* (1925, 1950, 1961). This test served as a convenient criterion for formula development because it contained an extensive set of reading passages with grade-equivalent scoring, Lorge (1939) was the first among many to use it. Various writers have criticized this criterion, among them Harris and Jacobson (1976), Fitzgerald (1980), and Stevens (1980). Harris and Jacobson have, however, readministered the McCall-Crabbs passages to large groups of new students and have continued to use these new data for the development of their formulas. Others have moved in two new directions, use of cloze procedure—first by Coleman (1965) and since by many others—and of specialized criteria for specialized formulas.

Users found early formulas tedious to apply; efficiency grew in importance as formulas became more widely used (and led, in turn, to still wider usage). One direction this trend took was toward reduction in the number of formula variables without a significant loss in predictiveness; the three-variable formula of Lorge (1939) was a landmark. Most modern formulas have two variables, but some have only one, usually a semantic index variable. This index proves consistently more predictive than a syntactic index, but eliminating the latter altogether typically lowers predictiveness somewhat. Another direction this trend took was toward use of manual aids and computer programs. Fry's Readability Graph (1968, 1977) has achieved wide usage owing to its convenience and ease of application, and the more recent Readability Estimate of Raygor (1977) has been found even quicker to use by Baldwin and Kaufman (1979). The reason presumably lies in Raygor's use of a count of words of six or more letters versus Fry's use of a count of syllables, since both formulas involve a sentence-length count and use a graph to get grade-level scores. And both authors have recommended still another (and recently criticized) direction for increasing efficiency: reducing to three the number of 100-word samples for getting overall scores for a body of text such as a book. (Earlier formulas advocated as many as twenty-five to thirty samples for this purpose.)

Formula usage has continued to grow over the years, both within and outside the field of education. At least five reasons can readily be found:

1. *Convenience.* Formulas take the place of collecting judgments or developing tests to evaluate a piece of writing or larger body of text.
2. *Efficiency.* For small amounts of written material, use of samples and application aids speeds the process of evaluation (with one sample typically taking less than five minutes). For large amounts of text, computer programs are becoming more and more widespread (at least four companies provide such analyses on a commercial basis).
3. *Scaling.* Formulas provide a metric for comparing different bodies of writing and—even more crucially—evaluating one body of writing. In other words, they provide their own benchmark, typically a grade level. Use of judges does not provide such a convenient evaluative scale.
4. *Predictiveness.* Modern formulas typically correlate in the .80s or low .90s with the comprehension criterion on which they were based, and often even maintain this level in cross-validation. This is especially the case for formulas using a cloze criterion (see, for example, Szalay, 1965, or Bormuth, 1969), although formulas based on the recently readministered McCall-Crabbs passages (see Harris & Jacobson, 1976) have yielded similar high values. And modern formulas, in general, yield satisfactory standard errors of estimate of one grade or less (in some cases considerably less).
5. *Publicity.* The number of publications on readability formulas has grown enormously over the years, and the topic now appears in the prospectus for many college reading courses as well as many textbooks on reading, and also in the requirements for accepting certain written materials.

On the basis of such advantages, and compared to other kinds of psychoeducational prediction such as school grades or sales, readability formulas stand up very well indeed (Chall, 1979; Klare, 1979). Furthermore, research has shown that writing with more readable versus less readable formula scores *can* produce increases in comprehension (Klare, 1976b), reading rate (Coke, 1976), readership (Kern, Sticht, & Fox, 1970), and perseverance (Klare & Smart, 1973). Yet these effects cannot always be found, as the research—and the critics—have also pointed out.

Controversy. There has been controversy over the use of formulas almost from the beginning of readability research. In an early published example, Moore (1935) predicted that readers would "recoil from reading" the rewritten classics then being introduced. Literary scholars have been particularly concerned with the role of formulas; Fitzgerald (1953), for one, deplored "literature by slide rule." But some of the severest critics have been professional educators themselves. Manzo (1970), for example, has pictured readability research as a "construct without a point of reference." Recent writers have voiced the most serious criticisms of all. Maxwell (1978) has wondered if we have "gone too far" with readability and has suggested

that an obsession with it may even be an important factor in the decline of inferential reading skills of teenagers in the period of 1970–1974. Chall (1979) has, in fact, reported that a study in her laboratory at Harvard found the current decline in SAT scores to be associated with a decline in the difficulty of textbooks over a thirty-year period. This must seem the unkindest self-inflicted wound of all, since she is a highly respected research worker and also the codeveloper of one of the most widely used formulas.

But there is another side to this coin of controversy. As Chall (1979) also points out, adopting more difficult texts in primary schools has recently led to an increase in reading scores; and readability formulas can be used for that choice as well as its opposite. Shepherd and Dickerson (1977) make the same points for writing, suggesting that the Fry Graph can be used to show up the low level of some student writers. Tibbetts (1973) argues that critics of formulas expect things that were never intended, largely because they lack other convenient ways—or any way, in many cases—to do things they feel ought to be done to help readers.

What should we make of it all? Or better yet, how should we proceed from here? We need answers, since readability testing is now truly extensive and formulas have become more controversial than ever; recent issues of three journals, *IEEE Transactions on Professional Communications* (1981), the *Journal of Business Communication* (1981), and *Information Design Journal* (forthcoming) attest to this. One procedure is to divide the issue into manageable chunks according to the two basic questions users ask of readability research:

1. How can I tell if readers will find this piece of writing readable?
2. How can I change this piece of writing to make it more readable?

These can be called, respectively, the "prediction" question and the "production" question (Klare, 1976b). Though they appear similar and though formulas have been used in attempts to answer both, they are quite different. For prediction, only index variables need be found, since they need only show a correlational relationship with the criterion of comprehension. For production, causal variables must be found, since they must show an experimental relationship with the criterion of comprehension. Prediction research has yielded impressive-looking results, in terms of the high correlations noted earlier. Production research, by contrast, has yielded inconsistent results, in terms of significant differences between experimental versions (Klare, 1976b, pp. 129–136). Problems with both have, however, contributed to the controversy over formulas and readability applications.

Prediction of Readable Writing. A good first question concerns why the correlation studies have yielded such impressively high values. The answer lies at least partly in the nature of the correlation statistic itself. The magnitude of coefficients depends partly upon the range of difficulty in the materials being studied and the range of talent in the readers. Where readability prediction studies have yielded high coefficients, one or both ranges have typically been large. However, Rodriguez and Hansen (1975) have demonstrated what can happen when they are not present, in a study of seventh-graders using reading materials such as textbooks, newspapers, and leisure reading passages generally appropriate for that level. They found that the correlation coefficients between readability estimates and comprehension scores dropped from around the value of .90 reported in the original norming study of the formulas (Bormuth, 1969) to around .45. In many such instances, the standard error of estimate would be the preferable statistic for evaluation purposes.

The specific nature of the criterion of reading comprehension used in developing formulas also affects the size of the correlation coefficient. Miller (1972), for example, has shown a cloze criterion easier to predict than a much-used multiple-choice criterion, the McCall-Crabbs passages. Using the same index variables, he found correlation coefficients to be around .15 to .25 points higher for the former than the latter. The understandable desire to achieve high correlation coefficients has also taken another direction, use of the so-called 50 percent criterion. Where it can be applied, this means developing formulas by using the reading grade-level score at which 50 percent of the questions on a passage can be answered correctly, since the range tends to be greatest at that point. Because most educators would consider this level of comprehension inadequate, however, some readability grade scores have been adjusted upward to the 75 percent level (sometimes called the "instructional" level). And at least one formula developer, McLaughlin (1969), has insisted upon the 100 percent level (whatever that may actually mean).

This confusing state has created problems for formula users. Most obviously, as several critics have pointed out, formulas do not agree with each other in assigning grade levels, though they may show high intercorrelations. A related problem concerns the grade-level scale itself. In our system of education, numbered grades make sense through high school and perhaps even through college, if they connote levels of schooling where such material might be typical. But after that, they become meaningless, and particularly so if interpreted to mean number of years of schooling needed to comprehend a particular passage. And in computer programs, the temptation to relate grade numbers to indices of difficulty in a linear fashion can lead to ludicrous outputs from analyses of highly difficult passages. The military scale for the Flesch-Kincaid readability program, in an extreme case, characterized a passage from the California probate code as requiring 122 years of schooling for comprehension!

The more obvious problem for users, however, is formula disagreement. How might users deal with it? How might corrections be made? There are several possibilities:

- Adjust formula scores on the basis of comparative applications. Pauk (1969) and Vaughan (1976) have found that Dale-Chall (1948) and Fry (1968) agree rather consistently, but that SMOG scores (McLaughlin, 1969) tend to run about two grade levels higher.
- Modify formulas to account for differences. Smith (n.d.) has suggested a way to adapt the SMOG formula so that it will yield primary grade levels comparable to those from the Fry (1968) and Spache (1974) formulas. In another example, Kincaid and Fishburne (1977; see also Kincaid et al., 1975) renormed and adapted the Flesch Reading Ease formula for use with Navy enlisted personnel. The U.S. military services have recently adopted this formula (usually referred to as the Flesch-Kincaid) as the basis for deciding whether technical manuals from suppliers meet newly established readability requirements (Kniffin, 1979).
- Regress formulas on each other. No regression equations of this sort have been published, apparently because of the magnitude of the task. Analysis could, however, be limited to the more popular formulas and to typical materials, where usage is heaviest and value to users would be greatest.
- Compare formula scores with a consensus of teacher judgments. Harrison (1980b, pp. 58–62) compared the scores from several formulas with the pooled judgments of teachers on twenty-four first-year secondary texts and sixteen fourth-year secondary texts used in British schools. The teachers' judgments yielded average reading-age scores of 11.30 and 13.14 respectively. The two most predictive formulas, those of Dale-Chall (1948) and Mugford (1970), differed by half a year or less, up or down, from these values. The Flesch Reading Ease formula (1948) differed by one year; the FORCAST (Caylor et al., 1973) and SMOG (McLaughlin, 1969) by about two years; and the Fog Index (Gunning, 1952) differed by almost three years. The less predictive formulas in all cases, incidentally, yielded higher (more difficult) average ratings than the teachers. This kind of comparison of predictive accuracy might well be tried with American texts and teachers.

Dolch (1930) was apparently the first to call attention to the related issue of sampling problems, noting that a formula must be applied to the entire contents of a book to get the most accurate evidence of its true readability. On the other hand, many of the later studies have reassuringly indicated that a relatively small number of samples will yield much the same mean value as a larger number. When entire books have been analyzed, however, the degree of intrabook variation in readability has often proved surprisingly high.

Bradley and Ames have reported making several such studies (see Luiten, Ames, & Bradley, 1979), and even more crucially, have reported that such variation does affect reader performance (Bradley & Ames, 1976). McCuaig and Hutchings (1975) had pointed out that mean values for a book based on only the three 100-word samples suggested by Fry when using his graph could mask such variation. They had suggested taking six samples, using the standard deviation of the sentences and syllables to create an interval on the graph that would contain 68 percent of all 100-word samples in a book. Luiten, Ames, and Bradley (1979), however, found that this method underestimates consistently the observed readability variation in whole-book samplings, covering 46 percent rather than 68 percent. They suggest more research to determine needed sample size.

Fitzgerald (1980) computed both confidence intervals and power functions and also found Fry's suggested number of three 100-word samples to be inadequate. She frequently found high standard errors among samples, confidence intervals so broad as to be almost useless, and probability of Type II errors unacceptably high. The suggestion of a need for further research on adequate sample sizes should be heeded since the trend has been to cut the recommended number of samples; Raygor (1977) has joined Fry in suggesting three samples.

Little doubt remains that the selection of appropriate levels of difficulty deserves closer study. The off-hand presumption appears generally to be that reading materials should be "matched" in difficulty to readers' skill levels. But this is too simple; reading purpose must also be considered. If the purpose is to improve the skills of readers, a higher level appears desirable. Chall (1979), as noted, has reported an association between a recent increase in difficulty in primary texts and rising reading scores. Yet publishers claim, she says, that teachers of the elementary grades request science and social studies texts two years below the grade placement of the children, and studies by Jorgenson (1977) and Duffy and Sachar (1977) suggest why: in general, classroom behavior improves as reading materials become easier. Choosing materials below, or even at, children's tested reading levels may thus be a mismatch if the goal is to improve reading skills, but not if it is to maintain classroom order or to reduce the frustration of the poorer readers. But even with the goal of improving skills, what should be the preferred method of presenting more difficult materials? Should the average level of difficulty be raised, or can the high degree of variation typically found in textbooks accomplish the same purpose? Should a text begin with relatively easy material, as generally assumed, or with relatively difficult material? Klare, Mabry, and Gustafson (1955) found a tendency for readers to get higher comprehension scores on an experimental passage when preceded by a difficult than when preceded by an easy passage. Rothkopf and Coatney (1974) found the same effect for reading rate.

Mismatch problems appear easier to resolve when the goal is to entertain adult readers. Studies of the "literacy gap," or difference between the tested reading skills of readers and the readability of their reading materials, highlight the difficulties that occur when the purpose is to inform rather than entertain. Johnson, Relova, and Stafford (1972) found that discrepancies by military personnel in following written procedures increased as the gap increased; Kulp (1974) has shown that errors by clerical workers follow the same pattern. Kern, Sticht, and Fox (1970) have shown that military personnel will turn from manuals to colleagues for help as the gap grows; the general public may well avoid altogether materials they find difficult (*Focus: Learning to Read,* 1978).

Furthermore at least two other major reader variables can either contribute to or compensate for a mismatch: level of motivation and degree of prior knowledge. Both Fry (1975) and Klare (1976b) have stressed the role of motivation, and Denbow (1973) and Fass and Schumacher (1978) have shown experimentally that it may interact with readability to affect comprehension. The greater comprehension of a more readable passage over a less readable can be weakened or washed out by the addition of a content preference or a monetary incentive, (Kniffin et al., 1980). But, as Entin has shown (1980), the motivational value of more interesting material may not overcome the effects of poorer readability if both easier and harder versions of passages are at and clearly above the readers' tested skill levels.

The readers' degree of prior knowledge about a topic may also play a part in whether a formula score correctly signals a mismatch, as Klare has pointed out (1976). Entin and Klare (1978b) found essentially no correlation between readability levels and average multiple-choice comprehension scores on the passages in a published reading test. However, when readers' comprehension was corrected for prior knowledge (by removing average scores on test questions taken prior to reading the passages) they found moderately high correlation coefficients. This study used college students as subjects, which illustrates another problem: the meaning of formula scores at the level of college or above (as opposed to below). Readability scores can be too glibly equated with comprehensibility scores. It is clear that comprehension of material on advanced topics depends increasingly upon knowledge of content rather than upon difficulty of style alone. It is not so clear, on the other hand, that readers will be offended by writing much below their level of education. Sometimes they show this reaction (especially for "primerized" material), but tax instructions registering sixth-grade level have been welcomed. Once again, though, formula scores expressed as grade levels beyond 16 or 17 certainly have little justification.

Production of Readable Writing. Almost from the beginning of readability research, formula developers have warned against "writing to formula." That alone would seem to make a section called "production" unnecessary in this discussion of criticisms. Yet formulas have become involved in controversy in this area also.

How did this happen? In brief, the scenario seems to have run somewhat as follows. Research workers and reading specialists began to apply readability formulas to available textbooks and library books, and much of the early literature included scores suggesting that material was too difficult for intended readers. Teachers, school boards, and even state education commissions began requesting or even requiring graded difficulty scores before selecting textbooks. Publishers responded to these pressures by producing graded materials, and the controversy began to take shape.

The picture outside education appears similar, at least if the military services can be taken as an example. Early work with formulas led to research on the difficulty of training materials. Suggestions that the materials were often too difficult for trainees led finally to imposing readability requirements as a prerequisite for acceptance of training materials and eventually for manuals from outside suppliers.

Suspicion naturally grew that writers must be writing to formula, whatever they said or even whatever they intended. The temptations, presumably, were too great. But does this really happen? If so, how often? No one really knows. Research is clearly needed, and several relevant studies have now been published.

In one approach, formulas and readability data have been examined as guides for adapting materials to student levels. Sometimes this has been recommended (Coleman, 1979) and sometimes deplored (Campbell, 1979). Davison et al. (1980) have published by far the most extensive critical linguistic study to date. They compared four texts in original versions with adaptations for younger readers. Editorial changes appeared to be interdependent and influenced by such factors as assumed knowledge of readers' background, definition of the topic, logical ordering of ideas, and syntactic structure, as well as limits imposed on passage length, sentence length, and vocabulary choice. A large number of these kinds of changes, they felt, illustrated that trying to make a text fit the specifications of a readability formula might make it harder to understand instead of easier. This seemed especially likely when length was also closely limited for the writers. Actual tests of these assumptions would be desirable additions at this point.

In another approach, many writers have developed experimental versions of material at different levels of readability (according to formula scores) and tested their relative comprehensibility. The author (Klare, 1976b) located thirty-six studies through 1974, with nineteen yielding significant differences favoring the version with the more readable score, eleven yielding nonsignificant differences, and six producing mixed results. A comparison of the thirty-six studies on twenty-eight characteristics indicated that the factors affecting comprehension fell into five categories: (1) reader competence (prior knowledge and ability); (2) content of material (in relation to reader knowledge and motivation); (3) readability level of material (how far apart the versions were); (4) reader motivation (incentives and interests); and (5) the test situation (motivating conditions *plus* conditions which allowed the motivation to have an effect).

These latter observations deserve special emphasis. First, significant effects on comprehension did not occur automatically, even when the formula scores of the experimental versions were rather widely separated (four or more grades). Second, the level of motivation of readers combined with the opportunity for it to have an effect (e.g., through liberal amounts of time for reading and/or testing, or provision for rereadings) appeared to be critical. Given highly motivated readers with adequate time, readability played a much diminished role in comprehension. Third, the ways the writers created the more comprehensible versions could not be easily specified; whatever they were, both formula scores and comprehension scores reflected them.

What *should* writers be doing to create more readable versions? Research in this area has been growing, but the task is enormous, involving as it does both developing readers and mature ones. Furthermore changing one language variable without affecting others or without creating clumsy, dull, or stilted writing can be a major problem. Using sentence-length material makes the job easier, but practical concerns dictate longer bodies of material.

The number of candidate variables is itself an obstacle to research. A survey of fifteen books on clear writing (Klare, unpublished) turned up 156 suggestions for text simplification. The study of Davison et al. (1980) also suggests that there are many things writers can do linguistically to make writing harder rather than easier to understand.

There is no way, of course, that writers can hope to keep such a large number of desirable features in mind while writing. However, as often happens in modern society, computers are being recruited to help writers see potential trouble spots. Frase (1980) chaired a symposium discussing ongoing work by Bell Laboratories personnel on several kinds of computer aids for writing. His own "Writer's Workbench" programs provide information on the following aspects of text segments: (1) readability formula score (grade level); (2) variability in sentence types (including length); (3) sentence structure (such as passives and nominalizations); (4) statistics (on various aspects of style); and (5) organization (headings and divisions). Kincaid, Aagard, and O'Hara (1980; see also Kincaid et al., 1981) have also developed a computer readability editing system for writers in the U.S. Navy. Applied to text, it provides a readability formula score (grade level), flags and lists uncommon words, and offers the writer more common options in the text itself alongside the uncommon words and the awkward words and phrases. Both systems cover special groups of writers for mature readers, but the approach could well be tried with writers of children's material. If, that is, enough becomes known about what to look for and what to build into the writing.

Using Readability Formulas. Readability formulas can beguile proponents and critics alike into expecting them to do more than they were intended to do. They provide convenient numbers for research, and they lend an objective appearance to the process of evaluating writing. Since comprehension, reading efficiency, and readership might be predicted through using them, more readable writing might also be produced through using them. But—they do not take into account such features as format, illustrations, and content. They do not even do a thorough job of evaluating all aspects of writing style, since they have only word and sentence factors; using them could therefore lead to text that is harder rather than easier to understand. What should we then expect of readability formulas? Here are some suggestions for users:

- Remember that different formulas may give different grade-level scores on the same piece of writing. Though they resemble thermometers in giving index values, they differ in that (like most educational and psychological tests) they do not have a common zero-point.
- Look over existing formulas and pick a good one for your intended use; but consider all formulas as screening devices and all scores as probability statements, as Monteith (1976) expresses it.
- Choose a formula with two index variables, one semantic and one syntactic, for most uses; having only one variable decreases predictiveness, but having more than two usually increases effort more than predictive power.
- Increase the value of your analysis by taking a rather large random (or numerically spread) sampling. For most uses, three samples *may* give a fairly good average score but say little if anything useful about variations in difficulty.
- Bear in mind that formula scores derive from counts of style difficulty. Therefore, they become poorer predictors at higher grade levels, where content weighs more heavily.
- Consider the purpose of the reading. Training readers calls for more challenging material than merely informing or, especially, entertaining them.
- Take into account other recognized contributors to comprehension, especially levels of motivation and of prior knowledge; otherwise, formula scores may overestimate or underestimate difficulty. For example, using special interests or incentives to get above-average motivation can help to keep challenging material from being frustrating.
- Do not rely on formulas alone in selecting reading materials when you can avoid this; seek judges for characteristics that formulas cannot predict and to be sure formulas have not been misused in preparing materials. But not just any judges: select experts or get reliable consensus opinions.
- Keep formulas out of the writing process itself, but let feedback from formulas in. Use something like the writing-rewriting cycle, as Macdonald-Ross (1979) describes it: "write → apply formula → revise → apply formula."

Where to draw the line between reading material that frustrates readers or that challenges them cannot be specified easily, so be prepared when you can be to shift reading material after tentative placement. This question cries out for more research, and the need continues to grow as determinants of readability continue to grow in use and influence.

George R. Klare

See also Reading; Textbooks.

REFERENCES

Baldwin, R. S., & Kaufman, R. K. A concurrent validity study of the Raygor Readability Estimate. *Journal of Reading*, 1979, 22, 148–153.

Bormuth, J. R. Readability: A new approach. *Reading Research Quarterly*, 1966, 1, 79–132. (ERIC Document Reproduction Service No. ED 011 480)

Bormuth, J. R. Comparable cloze and multiple-choice comprehension test scores. *Journal of Reading*, 1967, 10, 291–299.

Bormuth, J. R. The cloze readability procedure. *Elementary English*, 1968, 45, 429–436. (a) (ERIC Document Reproduction Service No. ED 010 983)

Bormuth, J. R. Cloze test readability: Criterion scores. *Journal of Educational Measurement*, 1968, 5, 189–196. (b)

Bormuth, J. R. *Development of Readability Analyses* (Final report, Project No. 7-0052, Contract No. OEC-3-7-070052-0326). U.S. Office of Education, Bureau of Research, 1969. (ERIC Document Reproduction Service No. ED 029 166)

Bradley, J. M., & Ames, W. S. The influence of intrabook variability on oral reading performance. *Journal of Educational Research*, 1976, 70, 101–105.

Buros, O. K. (Ed.). Cloze procedure (Ebbinghaus Completion Method) as applied to reading. In *Eighth Mental Measurements Yearbook* (vol. 2). Highland Park, N.J.: Gryphon Press, 1978, pp. 1163–1178.

Campbell, A. How readability formulae fall short in matching student to text in the content areas. *Journal of Reading*, 1979, 22, 683–689.

Carver, R. P. *Improving Reading Comprehension: Measuring Readability* (Final Report, Contract No. N00014-72-C-0240, Office of Naval Research). Silver Spring, Md.: American Institutes for Research, 1974. (ERIC Document Reproduction Service No. ED 092 920)

Caylor, J. S., Sticht, T. G.; Fox, L. C.; & Ford, J. P. *Methodologies for Determining Reading Requirements of Military Occupational Specialties* (Technical Report No. 73-5). Presidio of Monterey, Calif.: Human Resources Research Organization, March 1973. (ERIC Document Reproduction Service No. ED 074 343)

Chall, J. S. Readability: In search of improvement. *Publisher's Weekly*, October 29, 1979, pp. 40–41.

Chall, J. S., & Feldman, S. First-grade reading: An analysis of the interactions of professed methods, teacher implementation, and child background. *Reading Teacher*, 1966, 19, 569–575.

Coke, E. U. Reading rate, readability, and variations in task-induced processing. *Journal of Educational Psychology*, 1976, 68, 167–173. (ERIC Document Reproduction Service No. ED 092 902)

Coleman, E. B. *On Understanding Prose: Some Determiners of Its Complexity* (NSF Final Report GB-2604). Washington, D.C.: National Science Foundation, 1965.

Coleman, E. B. Developing a technology of written instruction: Some determiners of the complexity of prose. In E. Z. Rothkopf & P. E. Johnson (Eds.), *Verbal Learning Research and the Tech-*

nology of Written Instruction. New York: Teachers College Press, Columbia University, 1971. (ERIC Document Reproduction Service No. ED 062 340)

Coleman, L. J. Using readability data for adapting curriculum materials. *Education and Training of the Mentally Retarded,* 1979, *14,* 163–169.

College Entrance Examination Board. *Degrees of Reading Power.* Readability Report. New York: The College Board, 1980.

Dale, E., & Chall, J. S. A formula for predicting readability. *Educational Research Bulletin,* 1948, *27,* 11–20, 37–54. (January 21 and February 17 issues.)

Davison, A.; Kantor, R. N.; Hannah, J.; Herman, G.; Lutz, R.; & Salzillo, R. *Limitations of Readability Formulas in Guiding Adaptations of Texts* (Technical Report No. 162). Cambridge, Mass.: Bolt, Beranek & Newman; and Urbana: University of Illinois, Center for the Study of Reading, 1980. (ERIC Document Reproduction Service No. ED 184 090)

Denbow, C. J. *An Experimental Study of the Effects of a Repetition Factor on the Relationship between Readability and Listenability.* Unpublished doctoral dissertation, Ohio University, 1973.

Dolch, E. W. Sampling of reading matter. *Journal of Educational Research,* 1930, *22,* 213–215.

Duffy, T. M., & Sachar, J. *Reading Skill and Military Effectiveness.* Paper presented at the annual meeting of the American Educational Research Association, 1977. (ERIC Document Reproduction Service No. ED 151 745)

Entin, E. B. *Relationships of Measures of Interest, Prior Knowledge, and Readability to Comprehension of Expository Passages.* Unpublished doctoral dissertation, Ohio University, 1980.

Entin, E. B., & Klare, G. R. Factor analyses of three correlation matrices of readability variables. *Journal of Reading Behavior,* 1978, *10,* 279–290. (a)

Entin, E. B., & Klare, G. R. Some interrelationships of readability, cloze, and multiple-choice scores on a reading comprehension test. *Journal of Reading Behavior,* 1978, *10,* 417–436. (b)

Fass, W., & Schumacher, G. M. Effects of motivation, subject activity, and readability on the retention of prose materials. *Journal of Educational Psychology,* 1978, *70,* 803–808.

Fillenbaum, S.; Jones, L.; & Rapoport, A. Predictability of words and their grammatical classes as a function of rate of deletion from speech transcript. *Journal of Verbal Learning and Verbal Behavior,* 1963, *2,* 186–194.

Fitzgerald, G. G. Reliability of the Fry sampling procedure. *Reading Research Quarterly,* 1980, *15,* 489–503.

Fitzgerald, S. E. Literature by slide rule. *Saturday Review,* February 14, 1953, *36,* 15–16, 53–54.

Flesch, R. F. A new readability yardstick. *Journal of Applied Psychology,* 1948, *32,* 221–233.

Flesch, R. F. *The Art of Readable Writing.* New York: Harper and Brothers, 1949.

Focus: Learning to Read (Focus No. 4). Princeton, N.J.: Educational Testing Service, 1978.

Frase, L. T. *Computer Aids for Writing and Text Design.* Symposium presentations at the annual meeting of the American Educational Research Association, 1980.

Froese, V. Rauding and SEERing: Judging global readability. *Perspectives on Reading Research and Instruction: Twenty-ninth Yearbook of the National Reading Conference.* Washington, D.C.: National Reading Conference, 1980, pp. 309–312. (ERIC Document Reproduction Service No. ED 178 886)

Fry, E. B. A readability formula that saves time. *Journal of Reading,* 1968, *11,* 513–516, 575–578. (ERIC Document Reproduction Service No. ED 079 702)

Fry, E. B. The readability principle. *Language Arts,* 1975, *52,* 847–851.

Fry, E. B. Fry's Readability Graph: Clarifications, validity, and extension to level 17. *Journal of Reading,* 1977, *20,* 242–252.

Gray, W. S., & Leary, B. E. *What Makes a Book Readable: An Initial Study.* Chicago: University of Chicago Press, 1935.

Gunning, R. *The Technique of Clear Writing.* New York: McGraw-Hill, 1952.

Harris, A. J., & Jacobson, M. D. Predicting twelfth-graders' comprehension scores. *Journal of Reading,* 1976, *20,* 43–46.

Harris, A. J., & Jacobson, M. D. A framework for readability research: Moving beyond Herbert Spencer. *Journal of Reading,* 1979, *22,* 390–398. (ERIC Document Reproduction Service No. ED 159 610)

Harrison, C. Assessing the readability of school texts. In J. Gilliland (Ed.), *Reading: Research and Classroom Practice.* London: Ward Lock Educational, 1977.

Harrison, C. Assessing the readability of school texts. In E. A. Lunzer & W. K. Gardner (Eds.), *The Effective Use of Reading.* London: Heinemann, 1979.

Harrison, C. *Readability and Pupil Response in Relation to Samples of Eleven- and Fourteen-year-olds' Reading Material in Four Subject Areas.* Unpublished doctoral dissertation, University of Nottingham, 1980. (a)

Harrison, C. *Readability in the Classroom.* Cambridge, England: Cambridge University Press, 1980. (b)

IEEE Transactions on Professional Communication. Special issue, Making Information Usable. 1981, PC-24 (1)

Information Design Journal. Special issue, Document Design. Forthcoming.

Irwin, J. W., & Davis, C. A. *Assessing Readability: The Checklist Approach.* Unpublished paper, Purdue University, 1979.

Jacobson, M. D. Predicting reading difficulty from spelling. *Spelling Progress Bulletin,* 1974, *14,* 8–10.

Johnson, K. H.; Relova, R. P., Jr.; & Stafford, J. P. *An Analysis of the Relationship between Readability of Air Force Procedural Manuals and Discrepancies Involving Non-compliance with the Procedures* (Document AD 750 917, National Technical Information Service). Unpublished master's thesis, Air Force Institute of Technology, Air University, 1972. (ERIC Document Reproduction Service No. ED 070 941)

Jongsma, E. A. *The Cloze Procedure as a Teaching Technique.* Newark, Del.: International Reading Association, 1971. (ERIC Document Reproduction Service No. ED 055 253)

Jongsma, E. A. The difficulty of children's books: Librarians' judgments versus formula estimates. *Elementary English,* 1972, *49,* 20–26.

Jongsma, E. A. *Cloze Instruction Research: A Second Look.* Newark, Del.: International Reading Association, 1980. (ERIC Document Reproduction Service No. ED 194 881)

Jorgenson, G. W. An analysis of teacher judgments of reading level. *American Educational Research Journal,* 1975, *12,* 67–75.

Jorgenson, G. W. Relationship of classroom behavior to the accuracy of the match between material difficulty and student ability. *Journal of Educational Psychology,* 1977, *69,* 24–32.

Journal of Business Communication. Special issue, Readability. 1981, *18.*

Kern, R. P.; Sticht, T. G.; & Fox, L. C. *Readability, Reading Ability, and Readership* (Professional Paper 17-70). Alexandria, Va.:

Human Resources Research Organization, 1970. (ERIC Document Reproduction Service No. ED 043 834)

Kincaid, J. P.; Aagard, J. A.; & O'Hara, J. W. *Development and Test of a Computer Readability Editing System (CRES)* (TAEG Report No. 83). Orlando, Fla.: U.S. Navy Training Analysis and Evaluation Group, 1980. (ERIC Document Reproduction Service No. ED 190 064)

Kincaid, J. P.; Aagard, J. A.; O'Hara, H. W.; & Cottrell, L. K. Computer readability editing system. *IEEE Transactions on Professional Communications*, March 1981.

Kincaid, J. P., & Fishburne, R. P. Readability formulas for military training materials. *Human Factors Society Bulletin*, July 1977, *20*. (ERIC Document Reproduction Service No. ED 108 134)

Kincaid, J. P.; Fishburne, R.; Rogers, R. L.; & Chissom, B. S. *Derivation of New Readability Formulas for Navy Enlisted Personnel* (Branch Report 8-75). Millington, Tenn.: Chief of Naval Personnel, 1975. (ERIC Document Reproduction Service No. ED 108 134)

Kintsch, W. On modeling comprehension. *Educational Psychologist*, 1979, *14*, 3–14

Kintsch, W., & Vipond, D. Reading comprehension and readability in educational practice and psychological theory. In L. G. Nilsson (Ed.), *Perspectives on Memory Research*. Hillsdale, N.J.: Lawrence Erlbaum Associates, 1979.

Kintsch, W., & van Dijk, T. A. Toward a model of text comprehension and production. *Psychological Review*, 1978, *85*, 363–394.

Klare, G. R. *The Measurement of Readability*. Ames: Iowa State University Press, 1963.

Klare, G. R. Assessing readability. *Reading Research Quarterly*, 1974–1975, *10*, 62–102.

Klare, G. R. A second look at the validity of readability formulas. *Journal of Reading Behavior*, 1976, *8*, 129–152. (b)

Klare, G. R. Judging readability. *Instructional Science*, 1976, *5*, 55–61. (a)

Klare, G. R. *Readability Standards for Army-wide Publications* (Evaluation Report 79-1). Fort Benjamin Harrison, Ind.: U.S. Army Administration Center, Directorate of Evaluation, 1979.

Klare, G. R. Readability and comprehension. In R. S. Easterby & H. Zwaga (Eds.), *Visual Presentation of Information*. New York: Wiley, forthcoming.

Klare, G. R. *Some Suggestions for Clear Writing Found in Fifteen Source Books*. Unpublished and undated paper, Ohio University Department of Psychology.

Klare, G. R.; Mabry, J. E.; & Gustafson, L. M. The relationship of style difficulty to immediate retention and to acceptability of technical material. *Journal of Educational Psychology*, 1955, *46*, 287–295.

Klare, G. R.; Sinaiko, H. W.; & Stolurow, L. M. The cloze procedure: A convenient readability test for training materials and translations. *International Review of Applied Psychology*, 1972, *21*, 77–106.

Klare, G. R., & Smart, K. Analysis of the readability level of selected USAFI instructional materials. *Journal of Educational Research*, 1973, *67*, 1976.

Kniffin, J. D. The new readability requirements for military technical manuals. *Technical Communication*, 1979, *26*(3), 16–19.

Kniffin, J. D.; Klare, G. R.; Stevenson, C. R.; Entin, E. B.; Slaughter, S. L.; & Hooke, L. *Operational Consequences of Literacy Gap* (AFHRL-TR-79-22). Brooks Air Force Base, Texas: Air Force System Command, 1980. (ERIC Document Reproduction Service No. ED 179 942)

Kulp, M. J. *The Effects of Position Practice Readability Level on Performance*. Unpublished master's thesis, San Jose State University, 1974.

Lively, B. A., & Pressey, S. L. A method for measuring the "vocabulary burden" of textbooks. *Educational Administration and Supervision*, 1923, *9*, 389–398.

Lorge, I. Predicting reading difficulty of selections for children. *Elementary English Review*, 1939, *16*, 229–233.

Luiten, J.; Ames, W. S.; & Bradley, J. M. Using Fry's Graph to describe the variation of readability: A corrected procedure. *Reading World*, 1979, *18*, 361–367. (ERIC Document Reproduction Service No. ED 159 602)

Macdonald-Ross, M. Language in texts. In L. S. Shulman (Ed.), *Review of Research in Education* (No. 6, 1978). Itasca, Ill.: F. E. Peacock, 1979.

MacGinitie, W. H. *Contextual Constraint in English Prose*. Unpublished doctoral dissertation, Teachers College, Columbia University, 1960.

Making the grade. *New York Times*, November 6, 1977.

Manzo, A. Readability: A postscript. *Elementary English*, 1970, *47*, 962–965.

Maxwell, M. Readability: Have we gone too far? *Journal of Reading*, 1978, *21*, 225–530.

McCall, W. A., & Crabbs, L. M. *Standard Test Lessons in Reading*. New York: Teachers College, Columbia University, Bureau of Publications, 1925: later editions, 1950, 1961.

McCuaig, S. M., & Hutchings, B. Using Fry's Graph to describe the variation of readability. *Journal of Reading*, 1975, *18*, 298–300.

McKenna, M. C., & Robinson, R. D. *An Introduction to the Cloze Procedure: An Annotated Bibliography*. Newark, Del.: International Reading Association, 1980. (ERIC Document Reproduction Service No. ED 184 087)

McLaughlin, G. SMOG grading: A new readability formula. *Journal of Reading*, 1969, *22*, 639–646.

McLeod, J. *Manual: Gap Reading Comprehension Test*. London: Heinemann, 1970.

McLeod, J., & Anderson, J. *Manual: Gapadol Reading Comprehension Test*. London: Heinemann, 1973.

Meredith, K. E., & Vaughn, J. L. Stability of cloze scores across varying deletion patterns. In P. D. Pearson & J. Hansen (Eds.), *Reading—Disciplined Inquiry in Process and Practice: Twenty-seventh Yearbook of the National Reading Conference*, pp. 181–184. Clemson, S.C.: National Reading Conference, 1978.

Miller, J. W., & Marshall, F. W. *Teachers' Abilities to Judge the Difficulty of Reading Materials*. Paper presented at the annual meeting of the International Reading Association, Houston, Texas, May 1978. (ERIC Document Reproduction Service No. ED 159 627)

Miller, L. R. *A Comparative Analysis of the Predictive Validities of Four Readability Formulas*. Unpublished doctoral dissertation, Ohio University, 1972.

Monteith, M. K. Readability formulas. *Journal of Reading*, 1976, *19*, 604–607.

Moore, A. C. Recoiling from reading: A consideration of the Thorndike Library. *Library Journal*, 1935, *60*, 419–422.

Mugford, L. A new way of predicting readability. *Reading*, 1970, *4*, 31–35.

NFER. *Reading Level Tests*. Windsor, England: NFER Publishing Company, 1977.

No final answer yet on questions about test score decline. *ACTivity*, May 1979, *17*, 4–5.

Pauk, W. A practical note on readability formulas. *Journal of Reading*, 1969, *13*, 207–210.

Porter, D., & Popp, H. M. *An Alternative to Readability Measures: Judging the Difficulty of Children's Trade Books*. Paper presented at the annual meeting of the American Educational Research Association, February 1973.

Rankin, E. F. The cloze procedure: A survey of research. In E. L. Thurston & L. E. Hafner (Eds.), *The Philosophical and Sociological Bases of Reading: Fourteenth Yearbook of the National Reading Conference*. Milwaukee: National Reading Conference, 1965, pp. 133–150.

Rankin, E. F. Grade level interpretation of cloze readability scores. In F. P. Greene (Ed.), *Reading—The Right to Participate: Twentieth Yearbook of the National Reading Conference*. Milwaukee, Wis.: National Reading Conference, 1971, pp. 30–37. (ERIC Document Reproduction Service No. ED 046 657)

Rankin, E. F. Sequence strategies for teaching reading comprehension with the cloze procedure. In P. D. Pearson & J. Hansen (Eds.), *Reading—Theory, Research, and Practice: Twenty-sixth Yearbook of the National Reading Conference*. Clemson, S.C.: National Reading Conference, 1977, pp. 92–98.

Rankin, E. F., & Culhane, J. W. Comparable cloze and multiple-choice comprehension test scores. *Journal of Reading*, 1969, *13*, 193–198.

Raygor, A. L. The Raygor Readability Estimate: A quick and easy way to determine difficulty. In P. D. Pearson & J. Hansen (Eds.), *Reading—Theory, Research, and Practice: Twenty-sixth Yearbook of the National Reading Conference*. Clemson, S.C.: National Reading Conference, 1977, pp. 259–263.

Rodriquez, N., & Hansen, L. H. Performance of readability formulas under conditions of restricted ability level and restricted difficulty of materials. *Journal of Experimental Education*, 1975, *44*, 8–14.

Rothkopf, E. Z., & Coatney, R. Effects of readability of contest passages on subsequent inspection rate. *Journal of Applied Psychology*, 1974, *59*, 679–682.

Schwartz, D.; Sparkman, J. P.; & Deese, J. The process of understanding and judgments of comprehensibility. *Journal of Verbal Learning and Verbal Behavior*, 1970, *9*, 87–93.

Shepherd, J. W., & Dickerson, F. E. The Fry Graph wakes up student writers. *Journal of Reading*, 1977, *20*, 292–294.

Simons, H. D. Reading comprehension: The need for a new perspective. *Reading Research Quarterly*, 1971, *6*, 338–363.

Singer, H. The SEER technique: A non-computational procedure for quickly estimating readability level. *Journal of Reading Behavior*, 1975, *7*, 255–267.

Smith, L. L. *Modifying the SMOG*. Unpublished paper, University of Florida, n.d.

Spache, G. D. *Good Reading for Poor Readers* (Rev. ed.). Champaign, Ill.: Garrard, 1974. (ERIC Document Reproduction Service No. ED 037 326)

Stevens, K. C. Readability formulae and the McCall-Crabbs *Standard Test Lessons in Reading*. *The Reading Teacher*, 1980, *33*, 413–415.

Streiff, V. *Cloze in the Classroom*. Rowley, Mass.: Newbury House, forthcoming.

Szalay, T. G. Validation of the Coleman readability formulas. *Psychological Reports*, 1965, *17*, 965–966.

Taylor, W. L. Cloze procedure: A new tool for measuring readability. *Journalism Quarterly*, 1953, *30*, 415–433.

Thorndike, E. L. *The Teacher's Word Book*. New York: Teachers College, Columbia University, 1921.

Tibbetts, S-L. How much should we expect readability formulas to do? *Elementary English*, 1973, *50*, 75–76.

Vaughan, J. L. Interpreting readability assessments. *Journal of Reading*, 1976, *19*, 635–639.

Vaughan, J. L., & Meredith, K. E. Reliability of the cloze procedure as assessment of various language elements. In P. D. Pearson & J. Hansen (Eds.), *Reading—Disciplined Inquiry in Process and Practice: Twenty-seventh Yearbook of the National Reading Conference*. Clemson, S.C.: National Reading Conference, 1978, pp. 175–180.

Vogel, M., & Washburne, C. An objective method of determining grade placement of children's reading material. *Elementary School Journal*, 1928, *28*, 373–381.

Wang, M. D. The role of syntactic complexity as a determiner of comprehensibility. *Journal of Verbal Learning and Verbal Behavior*, 1970, *9*, 398–404.

Washburne, C., & Morphett, M. V. Grade placement of children's books. *Elementary School Journal*, 1938, *38*, 355–364.

Weaver, W. W. Theoretical aspects of the cloze procedure. In E. L. Thurston & L. E. Hafner (Eds.), *The Philosophical and Sociological Bases of Reading: Fourteenth Yearbook of the National Reading Conference*. Milwaukee, Wis.: National Reading Conference, 1965, pp. 115–132.

READINESS

"Readiness" is one of the few technical terms that has a direct counterpart in the nontechnical language of ordinary conversation. The concept is associated with maturational issues, development, and environmental stimulation. This article reviews some of the recent literature investigating readiness, addresses the question whether readiness can be stimulated, and discusses the issue whether it is appropriate to take a concept with relevance principally to motor development and apply it to cognitive development.

People are "ready" when their preparation is completed and it is necessary for them to meet expectations for performance. Educators are, of course, concerned with readiness. They want to know when students are ready for school and when it is best to introduce various curriculum tasks. It is generally assumed that learning occurs best when people are ready to learn and that without being ready little learning will occur (Sawyer, 1975). It also is assumed that a major component of readiness is maturation, based on biological growth.

Readiness, Maturation, and Development. Developmental psychologists have taken one of three perspectives on the question of maturation (Kohlberg & Mayer, 1972). From the nativists' perspective, development toward maturation is principally biological (genetic). Advocates of this perspective include Neill (1960) and Gesell (1954).

A second perspective—advocated by social learning theorists, behavior modifiers, reinforcement theorists, and learning theorists—assumes that development toward maturation is largely environmental (Langer, 1969). Depending upon environmental design, one can affect varying outcomes of the developmental process. Advocates of this perspective believe that one can take any child and have that child develop in ways that the modifiers choose. They also assume that the younger the child, the greater the range of possible outcomes. Older children are more difficult to work with for they have had more environmental influences "written into" their developmental histories. Advocates of this perspective include Hull (1943), Guthrie (1952), Skinner (1953), and Bereiter and Englemann (1966).

The third perspective may be viewed as a compromise, for its advocates assume that development is the result of both genetic inheritance and environmental effects. In addition, advocates of this perspective assume that development results from the organism's own actions. In short, according to this perspective, development occurs from the interaction of biological, environmental, and organism-generated features. Representatives of this perspective are variously referred to as cognitive-developmentalists, cognitive-discovery theorists, interactionalists, or structuralists. They include Piaget (1970), Bruner (1960), and Kohlberg (1969).

As a result of these assumptions, each orientation has its own perspective on readiness. The nativists assume that readiness is principally a biological function and one must wait for the appropriate chronological period before the organism is ready for any given activity. The environmentalists assume that readiness is largely a result of matching reinforcement contingencies with the needs of the organism, although they also realize that one cannot expect individuals to perform certain physical acts if they are insufficiently prepared biologically. The cognitive-developmentalists assume that if the genetic and environmental conditions are appropriate, children will be ready to perform provided the children also perceive the situation appropriately. In this perspective people are assumed to seek naturally the resolution of problematic situations by adapting to the situation and organizing their thinking so as to resolve previously existing uncertainties and confusions. In fact, in this perspective development is viewed as movement toward increasing differentiations and hierarchical integration of conceptualizations regarding phenomena (Werner, 1948).

Policy implications associated with the concept will be discussed in a subsequent section of this article, yet it is clear that advocates of each theoretical orientation take varying viewpoints on readiness recommendations. The nativists advocate waiting until the child is biologically ready before introducing curriculum innovations. The behaviorists work to design environments that maximize the child's skill and thereby attempt to promote readiness. Advocates of the cognitive-developmental perspective believe that the child's maturation cannot be accelerated, but that development is best promoted in environments that provide cognitive challenges to active children.

For any policy implications, however, it is first essential

to assess readiness, discover what is known about it, and empirically test hypotheses about its promotion. We now turn to these matters.

Recent Empirical Research.   Nearly all of the research on readiness is based on kindergarten or first-graders, although there have been some exceptions where the intent was to assess the predictive ability of readiness measures (Perry, Guidubaldi, & Kehle, 1979; Pikulski, 1973). Various populations have been investigated, including groups with upper-middle socioeconomic status (SES) (Becher & Wolfgang, 1977) and lower SES (Scott & Kobes, 1975), inner-city (Richek, 1977) and rural (Knox & Glover, 1978) children, Latinos (Vincent, Bright, & Dickason, 1976), and Orientals, Puerto Ricans, and Eskimos (Mitchell, 1967).

Various measures of readiness have been employed in an effort to find the most useful instrument. The Metropolitan Reading Readiness Test (Becher & Wolfgang, 1977; Hayes, Mason, & Covert, 1975; Mitchell, 1967; Pikulski, 1973; Rude, 1973; Vincent, Bright, & Dickason, 1976), the Gates-MacGinite Reading Test (Brekke, Williams, & Harlow, 1973; Glazzard, 1979; and Shapiro, 1976), and the Gesell School Readiness Test (Kaufman, 1971) have been employed. In addition, various self-concept measures (Flynn, 1975), Piagetian measures (Becher & Wolfgang, 1977; Kaufman, 1971), and criterion-referenced measures (Gacka, 1978) have been assessed. Intelligence measures have also been investigated as correlates or indicators of readiness (Feshbach, Adelman, & Fuller, 1974; Huberty & Swan, 1974; Knox & Glover, 1978; Kulberg & Gershman, 1973; and Telegdy, 1976).

Obviously some standardized measures of readiness are better predictors than others (Kapelis, 1975). An expedient and useful measure of readiness is based on teachers' ratings (Flook & Velicer, 1977; Glazzard, 1977, 1979). Yet one of the simplest measures of reading readiness is letter recognition. Simply seeing if children can recognize and recite the letters of the alphabet serves as a reliable indicator of readiness to read.

Unfortunately there is little evidence that increased teaching of reading readiness skills insures success in learning to read (Rude, 1973). In fact, there is no simple way to identify children who are likely to encounter reading difficulty (Pikulski, 1974), although it is likely that family size (Scott & Kobes, 1975), and socioeconomic status (Telegdy, 1974) affect readiness in predictable fashions: low SES children score less well and children from smaller families score better.

On the other hand, it appears that the Western Institute for Science and Technology (WIST) Program can produce readiness skills in disadvantaged preschoolers (Vincent, Bright, & Dickason, 1976). It also is clear that preschool educational experiences can benefit children's readiness to learn (Knox & Glover, 1978). This is especially so if early diagnosis of oral language deficits occurs (Newcomer & Magee, 1977). Attention to self-concept, delay of gratification, and self-control are also recommended (Flynn, 1975). Even so, if a single prescription were offered to increase reading readiness, it would be to encourage children to recognize the letters of the alphabet (Hoskisson, 1977; Richek, 1977–78; Telegdy, 1975).

The Problem of Readiness.   Despite the large number of investigations relating to readiness, many questions about the concept remain. (a) Can readiness be stimulated by experience? (b) For students who are not ready to learn, what (if anything) can be done to stimulate readiness? (c) How appropriate is it to generalize about cognitive processes with a concept having relevance to motor development?

There have been several notable attempts to stimulate readiness (Bronfenbrenner, 1974; Wargo et al., 1972; Zigler, 1970). Some of the most significant attempts were incorporated in Project Head Start and in Follow Through (Maccoby & Zellner, 1970). The people connected with the Children's Television Workshop (Lesser, 1974) have also sought to assist children to become ready for school through watching "Sesame Street" or for doing well in reading by watching "The Electric Company." Title I federally appropriated funds were used to help poor children of school age. A thorough review of these Title I or compensatory education programs (White, 1973) concludes that some programs are effective and others are not. Characteristics of successful programs include: specifying objectives, careful planning, training teachers in the methods employed, small group or individualized instruction, high-intensity instruction; and active parental involvement. The results of carefully planned programs such as "Sesame Street" also indicate that children can be prepared for school and assisted to do better if attention is given to making them ready (Lesser, 1974).

Turiel (1966) suggested that children are best assisted toward development when instruction is slightly ahead of the child's current level. If the content is too advanced, children may appreciate it but be unable to assimilate it into their current thinking. Consequently it is recommended that teachers carefully assess the child's reasoning abilities and provide questions and problems that are likely to puzzle the child at first but are sufficiently matched to the child's abilities that children can handle them.

Bloom (1976) assumes that children can learn anything if they are allowed to proceed at their own pace with carefully designed instruction. He advocates learning for mastery, especially in the learning of content that has a single correct response (e.g., what do the letters d-o-g spell?). Children are given units of material to master at their own pace; when they are ready, they request a test for mastery. If they are successful, they move on to additional units; if they are not successful, they repeat the until until they master it.

The results of these efforts in compensatory and preparatory education have been mixed. They generally indicate that experience can affect readiness in beneficial ways when the experience is carefully planned, administered, and assessed. The issue is not so much when to teach as how to do so. Events carry varying meanings at different phases of the life span. It is unreasonable to expect that an elementary school student understands mathematical formulations in the same way as a high school student, but it is still reasonable to develop instructional strategies that give mathematics meaning for both students.

This leads to the question of what can be done to stimulate readiness for students who are not ready to learn. To begin, it is advisable to realize that readiness refers to a type of learning experience, not to a given subject. Children are always ready to learn from some type of experience. If they are not ready to learn differential calculus, they may be ready to learn fractions. The teacher's task is to identify how best to assess the relation between the child's current developmental level and the directions the teacher would like the student to take. Usually the better the match between the child and the educational environment, the higher the possibility that readiness will be enhanced. Small group work is preferred to large; individual reaction is preferred to group interaction.

In addition the educator is advised to avoid classifying children under any label (Hobbs, 1975a, 1975b). Development of profiles identifying the child's specific strengths and limitations are preferred. Readiness is thus viewed as part of a total life perspective, rather than one limited exclusively to schooling. Children encouraged in both home and school are far more likely to meet readiness demands than those encouraged in only one of those environments.

The results of controlled, short-term experiments on problem-solving have reported both successes and failures (Brainerd, 1978). Frequent repetition of reasoning strategies leads to retention, especially with children who are most ready to develop. Development of cognitive problem-solving strategies occurs more expeditiously, however, if the child is encouraged to be active by playing with puzzles, toys, clay, or beads and encouraged to think about how best to resolve problems.

Finally, advocates of all three theoretical orientations previously discussed are willing to extrapolate the concept of readiness from motor to cognitive development. Each orientation recognizes the inextricable influence of maturation on development, but each also recognizes that cognitive functioning is also influenced by environmental influences. Consequently each is willing to examine when a child is best suited biologically for further growth, so that the most appropriate environmental situation may be arranged. The readiness concept is particularly appropriate for all those interested in providing the best educational experience, one that matches biological competence with the demands of the environment.

Policy.   In thinking about policy implications relating to readiness, we should focus on programs designed to encourage a positive attitude toward school while also teaching letter recognition. The work of the Children's Television Workshop is particularly noteworthy, for the program "Sesame Street" is enormously successful in both of these areas. Since kindergarten education has become a nationwide phenomenon, it is likely that readiness assessments will continue. Considerably more research must be done on how to encourage readiness. There continues to be a need to develop programs that teach children in ways that maintain their curiosity, interest, and desire to learn. The fact of the matter is that children of all ages can and do learn. Parents are best advised to teach rather than to wait to teach. If the material is beyond the child's ability, the child will not learn it as the parent wishes, even though the child will learn something from the exposure. Exposing children to interesting environments is preferable to waiting until children are ready. If the consequences for failing to learn information that is beyond the child's ability are nonpunitive, then the child will most likely come to realize that the world is filled with interesting opportunities for those ready to meet the challenges.

                                                                    Neal J. Gordon

See also Aptitude Measurement; Early Childhood Education; Learning; Learning Disabilities; Motivation; Reading.

REFERENCES

Becher, R. M., & Wolfgang, C. An exploration of the relationship between symbolic representation in dramatic play and art and the cognitive and reading readiness levels of kindergarten children. *Psychology in the Schools*, 1977, *14*, 377–381.

Bereiter, C., & Engelmann, S. *Teaching Disadvantaged Children in the Preschool.* Englewood Cliffs, N.J.: Prentice-Hall, 1966.

Bloom, B. *Human Characteristics and School Learning.* New York: McGraw-Hill, 1976.

Brainerd, C. J. *Piaget's Theory of Intelligence.* Englewood Cliffs, N.J.: Prentice-Hall, 1978.

Brekke, B. W.; Williams, J. D.; & Harlow, S. D. Conservation and reading readiness. *Journal of Genetic Psychology*, 1973, *123*, 133–138.

Bronfenbrenner, U. *Is Early Education Effective?* Washington, D.C.: Office of Human Development, 1974.

Bruner, J. F. *The Process of Education.* Cambridge, Mass.: Harvard University Press, 1960.

Feshbach, S.; Adelman, H.; & Fuller, W. W. Early identification of children with high risk of reading failure. *Journal of Learning Disabilities*, 1974, *7*, 639–644.

Flook, W. M., & Velicer, W. F. School readiness and teachers' ratings: A validation study. *Psychology in the Schools*, 1977, *14*, 140–146.

Flynn, T. M. Behavioral components of school readiness. *Journal of Experimental Education*, 1975, *44*, 40–45.

Gacka, R. C. The Basic School Skills Inventory as a preschool screening instrument. *Journal of Learning Disabilities*, 1978, *11*, 593–595.

Gesell, A. The ontogenesis of infant behavior. In L. Carmichael (Ed.), *Manual of Child Psychology* (2nd ed.). New York: Wiley, 1954.

Glazzard, P. The effectiveness of three kindergarten predictors for first-grade achievement. *Journal of Learning Disabilities*, 1977, *10*, 95–99.

Glazzard, P. Kindergarten predictors of school achievement. *Journal of Learning Disabilities*, 1979, *12*, 689–694.

Guthrie, E. R. *The Psychology of Learning.* New York: Harper & Brothers, 1952.

Hayes, M.; Mason, E.; & Covert, R. Validity and reliability of simple device for readiness screening. *Educational and Psychological Measurement*, 1975, *35*, 495–498.

Hobbs, N. *The Futures of Children.* San Francisco: Jossey-Bass, 1975. (a)

Hobbs, N. (Ed.). *Issues in the Classification of Children* (2 vols.). San Francisco: Jossey-Bass, 1975. (b)

Hoskisson, K. Reading readiness: Three viewpoints. *Elementary School Journal*, 1977, *78*, 44–52.

Huberty, C. J., & Swan, W. W. Preschool classroom experience and first-grade achievement. *Journal of Educational Research*, 1974, *67*, 311–316.

Hull, C. *Principles of Behavior.* New York: Appleton-Century-Crofts, 1943.

Kapelis, L. Early identification of reading failure: A comparison of two screening tests and teacher forecasts. *Journal of Learning Disabilities*, 1975, *8*, 638–641.

Kaufman, A. F. Piaget and Gesell: A psychometric analysis of tests built from their tasks. *Child Development*, 1971, *42*, 1341–1360.

Knox, B. J., & Glover, J. A. A note on preschool experience effects on achievement, readiness, and creativity. *Journal of Genetic Psychology*, 1978, *132*, 151–152.

Kohlberg, L. The cognitive-developmental approach to socialization. In D. Goslin (Ed.), *Handbook of Socialization Theory and Research.* Chicago: Rand McNally, 1969.

Kohlberg, L., & Mayer, R. Development as the aim of education. *Harvard Educational Review*, 1972, *42*, 449–496.

Kulberg, J. M., & Gershman, E. S. School readiness: Studies of assessment procedures and comparison of three types of programming for immature five-year-olds. *Psychology in the Schools*, 1973, *10*, 410–420.

Langer, J. *Theories of Development.* New York: Holt, Rinehart & Winston, 1969.

Lesser, G. S. *Children and Television: Lessons from "Sesame Street."* New York: Random House, 1974.

Maccoby, E. E., & Zellner, M. *Experiments in Primary Education: Aspects of Project Follow-Through.* New York: Harcourt Brace Jovanovich, 1970.

Mitchell, B. C. Predictive validity of the Metropolitan Readiness Tests and the Murphy-Durrell Reading Readiness Tests for white and Negro students. *Educational and Psychological Measurement*, 1967, *27*, 1047–1054.

Neill, A. S. *Summerhill.* New York: Hart, 1960.

Newcomer, P. L., & Magee, P. Predictive indices of reading failure in learning for disabled children. *Educational Research Quarterly*, 1977, *2*, 17–23.

Perry, J.; Guidubaldi, J.; & Kehle, T. J. Kindergarten competencies as predictors of third-grade classroom behavior and achievement. *Journal of Educational Psychology*, 1979, *71*, 443–450.

Piaget, J. Piaget's theory. In P. Mussen (Ed.), *Carmichael's Manual of Child Psychology* (Vol. 1). New York: Wiley, 1970.

Pikulski, J. J. Predicting sixth-grade achievement by first-grade scores. *Reading Teacher*, 1973, *27*, 284–287.

Pikulski, J. J. Assessment of pre-reading skills: A review of frequently employed measures. *Reading World*, 1974, *13*, 171–197.

Richek, M. A. Readiness skills that predict initial word-learning using two different methods of instruction. *Reading Research Quarterly*, 1977–78, *13*, 200–222.

Rude, R. T. Readiness tests: Implications for early childhood education. *Reading Teacher,* 1973, *26,* 572–580.

Sawyer, D. J. Readiness factors for reading: A different view. *Reading Teacher,* 1975, *28,* 620–624.

Scott, R., & Kobes, D. A. The influence of family size on learning readiness patterns of socioeconomically disadvantaged preschool blacks. *Journal of Clinical Psychology,* 1975, *31,* 85–88.

Shapiro, J. E. The effect of visual discrimination training on reading readiness test performance of impulsive first-grade boys. *Journal of Educational Research,* 1976, *69,* 338–340.

Skinner, B. F. *Science and Human Behavior.* New York: Macmillan, 1953.

Telegdy, G. A. The relationship between socioeconomic status and school readiness. *Psychology in the Schools,* 1974, *11,* 351–356.

Telegdy, G. A. The effectiveness of four readiness tests as predictors of first-grade academic achievement. *Psychology in the Schools,* 1975, *12,* 4–11.

Telegdy, G. A. The validity of IQ scores derived from readiness screening tests. *Psychology in the Schools,* 1976, *13,* 394–396.

Turiel, E. An experimental test of the sequentiality of developmental stages in the child's moral judgments. *Journal of Personality and Social Psychology,* 1966, *3,* 611–618.

Vincent, J.; Bright, R. L.; & Dickason, J. B. Effects of the WIST Reading Readiness Program on first-grade readiness and later academic achievement. *Journal of Educational Research,* 1976, *69,* 250–253.

Wargo, M. J.; Tallmadge, G. G. K.; Michael, S. D.; Lipe, D.; & Morris, S. J. *ESSA Title I: A Reanalysis and Synthesis of Evaluation Data from Fiscal Year 1965 through 1970.* Palo Alto, Calif.: American Institutes for Research, 1972. (ERIC Document Reproduction Service No. ED 059 415)

Werner, H. *Comparative Psychology of Mental Development.* Chicago: Follett, 1948.

White, S. H.; Bay, M. C.; & Freeman, P. K. *Federal Programs for Young Children: Review and Recommendations.* Washington, D.C.: Department of Health, Education, and Welfare, 1973. (ERIC Document Reproduction Service No. ED 092 230 233)

Zigler, E. Social class and the socialization process. *Review of Educational Research,* 1970, *40,* 87–110.

READING

This article covers the period of the 1970s and includes some of the trends at the beginning of the 1980s. Reference is occasionally made to some of the research trends of the late 1960s.

A vast amount of research in reading was published during this period. One measure of this growth is found in the *Annual Summaries of Investigations Relating to Reading* since 1965. By 1978/79, the reviews included about 5,800 articles, books, monographs, and other publications. This constituted about half of all the research reviewed since 1925. The following year's reviews, 1979/80, covered about 1,100 items, double that of 1978–1979.

Part of this growth can be attributed to the increasing contributions of scholars from the basic disciplines of linguistics, psycholinguistics, literature and the humanities, neurosciences, sociology, anthropology, and economics. About twenty-five or more new journals containing reading-related research began publication in the past decade, including *Cognitive Science, Journal of Reading Behavior, Journal of Research in Reading, Literacy Work, Journal of Learning Disabilities,* and *Discourse Processes.*

Increased interest in reading is evident also from the growth of professional associations directly or indirectly concerned with reading, greater interest of the home and community in reading achievement, growth of federally funded programs for the study and improvement of reading, and the increasing concern about the possible decline in reading achievement nationally (*Basic Skills,* 1979; Chall, 1977; National Assessment of Educational Progress, 1981; Wirtz, 1977).

Further evidence of growth in the study of reading can be found in the number of collections and reviews of reading research, on a wide range of reading topics (Pflaum-Connor, 1978; Weaver, 1978; Williams, 1979); on beginning reading (Bond & Dykstra, 1967; Calfee & Drum, 1978; Chall, 1967, 1978; Guthrie, 1976, Resnick & Weaver, 1979); on comprehension (Anderson, Spiro, & Montague, 1977; Carroll & Freedle, 1972; Guthrie, 1977; Just & Carpenter, 1977; LaBerge & Samuels, 1977; Spiro, Bruce, & Brewer, 1980); on the psychology of reading (Gibson & Levin, 1975; Kavanaugh & Mattingly, 1972; Reber & Scarborough, 1977); and on reading and learning disabilities (Benton & Pearl, 1978; Chall & Mirsky, 1978; Knights & Bakker, 1976).

Some of the big trends of the 1970s were the shift in focus from beginning reading to reading at the upper levels, including adult literacy and reading in the content areas. The greater interest in the higher levels of reading is seen also in the growing emphasis on the study of reading comprehension, as compared with word recognition and phonics at the beginning of the 1970s.

The decade was also characterized by a growing concern with reading achievement and how best to test it. The beginning of the era saw a negative reaction to norm-referenced tests with proposals for using criterion-referenced or mastery tests. The latter half of the decade also saw a greater use of minimum competency tests as a means of assuring sufficient literacy of high school graduates and as a means of selecting students requiring extra help (Jaeger & Tittle, 1980).

Probably the most dramatic phenomenon of testing during the decade was the start of the National Assessment of Educational Progress. As of 1980, three reading testings were completed of students at ages 9, 13, and 17; with national estimates as well as groupings by geography, urban-rural-suburban dwelling, ethnicity, and so on.

Another trend was a shift from socioeconomic factors in reading achievement to a renewed interest in school, classroom, teacher, and other "alterable" factors in reading success and failure. Still another trend was the shift in the study of reading and learning disabilities from dysfunctions in perceptual factors to the dysfunctions of language, and an increased interest in writing and in the relationship between reading and writing.

Disciplines Basic to 1970s Research.   The 1970s were characterized by the strong influence of two disciplines on the research and theories of the reading process: linguistics and cognitive psychology.

The earlier influence came from linguistics, and it took many forms. Generally, the linguistics influence of the early 1960s had its roots in linguistics that predated the Chomsky revolution (e.g., Bloomfield & Barnhart, 1961; Fries, 1962). The later influence, beginning in the later 1960s, was based on transformational grammar and phonology. There was a concern for language acquisition, which influenced the works of Bormuth (1969), C. Chomsky (1970), Goodman (1967, 1976), Read (1971), and Smith (1971, 1975). More recently, studies of the structure of texts (Halliday & Hasan, 1976; van Dijk, 1977) have been applied increasingly in reading research. A comprehensive view of psycholinguistics and reading is provided by Carroll (1978).

During the 1970s, the influence of cognitive psychology became stronger, especially in the research in comprehension, memory, and knowledge integration. Toward the end of the decade, the influence of educational psychology seems to be resuming its former importance in studies of school and classroom factors that influence reading success. Another research group that is concerned with reading difficulties and failure has also grown during the past decade, aided by advances in the neurosciences (Chall & Mirsky, 1978).

The diversity of scholars concerned with the study of reading has enriched the field, but it has also brought difficulties. Some confusion may be expected when people with such diverse backgrounds attempt to study the same or similar problems. Perhaps of greater consequence is the difficulty in communication that often results when researchers from different disciplines work in the same area and produce so many diverse research reports. There is some evidence of discontinuity between subfields, as in the fields of reading and learning disabilities, which have used different terminology and techniques to describe and treat the same children. The same is true of the fields of prose comprehension and readability. Overall, this diversity has tended to advance the field, as will be shown in the sections below.

Models of Reading.   One of the characteristics of the decade is the profusion of reading models: conceptualizations of the reading process for the purpose of deepening the understanding of the process and for developing greater insight into improving practice (see Singer & Ruddell, 1976). Essentially these models may be classified into two main types: developmental models, which attempt to explain and conceptualize the development of the reading process in individuals (and societies) from prereading to mature reading, and models of proficient reading, which

are concerned with explaining the reading act among proficient readers.

Developmental models.   Carroll (1976) described the reading process in terms of the tasks necessary to reach the most advanced level of reading, critical understanding of the message. These tasks include knowledge of language, learning that words consist of sounds, learning letter-sound correspondences, learning spelling patterns, using a variety of cues to recognize words, comprehending the meaning of what is read, and using reasoning skills. No order was prescribed for learning these skills; instead, Carroll suggests that different models of the reading process would suggest different orders of instruction.

More recently, Carroll (1977) proposed another developmental conceptualization of the reading process. He proposed that reading comprehension was dependent on three major components—language, cognition, and decoding—and that deficiencies in comprehension may stem from deficiencies in any of these areas.

Chall (1979a) has proposed a reading development scheme ranging from the elementary, primitive abilities in reading to the most advanced and skillful, in terms of six stages—from the "make believe" reading of the preschool child to the creative and recreative reading of the advanced college student and scholar. Although it is not a strict hierarchical model (it employs many "top-down" processes as well as "bottom-up" processes, described below), it tends to view the development of reading in the individual and in societies in terms of broad qualitative changes in ability and in the uses of reading. Thus, the early stages are mainly concerned with acquiring the skill to read texts already largely within the reader's knowledge and linguistic capabilities, while at later stages (beginning at about grade 4), reading becomes more skillful and can be used for learning new knowledge, ideas, values, feelings in more linguistically, cognitively, and experientially complex forms.

Models of proficient reading.   These models are concerned with explaining the reading act in terms of the cognitive, linguistic, and other processes used by proficient readers. The processes can be characterized as "bottom-up," in which lower-level or perceptual processes precede higher-level processes during the reading act; "top-down," which emphasize the importance of higher cognitive processes, with lower-level processes utilized only when needed; and "interactive" models, which propose that "bottom-up" and "top-down" processes interact with each other in the understanding of a text.

In his "bottom-up" models, Gough (1972) postulated that the reader perceives individual letters and words and then transforms these into a phonemic code. From this code, meanings of individual words are ascertained; then syntactic and semantic rules are applied, until the text ends up in the "Place Where Sentences Go When They Are Understood." Gough's model is a serial one, with the completion of lower processes necessarily preceding the higher processes. Gough and Cosky (1977) have recently published an updated statement of this model. As in his earlier statement, in this one he conceptualizes the decoding process as being first and essential, which is then followed by comprehension of the meaning.

LaBerge and Samuels (1976; see also LaBerge, 1979; Samuels & Eisenberg, 1981) postulate a similar "bottom-up" model, except that they emphasize the roles of attention and automaticity. They also give greater importance to prior knowledge, which permits the reader to bypass some of the lower processes. LaBerge and Samuels (1976) emphasize that for a reader to be proficient, the lower processes, such as letter and word recognition, must be "automatized" or be done quickly without conscious attention (Schneider & Schiffrin, 1977).

Other models that might be considered essentially bottom-up include those of Mackworth (1972); Rubenstein, Lewis, and Rubenstein (1971); Massaro (1975); Perfetti and Lesgold (1979).

"Top-down" models emphasize the importance of higher processes—such as the reader's prior knowledge in controlling the reading process, with lower-level processing utilized only when needed. Goodman (1967, 1976) and Smith (1971, 1973, 1978) view the reader not as a perceiver of text but as a questioner of text, making hypotheses about the meaning of the text based on the reader's prior knowledge, making predictions about meaning and word form, and sampling the text to confirm these hypotheses and predictions. In their view, comprehension of meaning precedes perception of individual words, which may not be encoded fully if not needed for comprehension. In contrast to bottom-up theorists, the Goodman and Smith theories view the reader as going directly from the visual input to the meaning of a text without necessarily using an intermediate phonemic code (see Baron, 1973; Rubenstein, Lewis, & Rubenstein, 1971). They rely not as much on psychological or educational research to support their theories, as on linguistic and psycholinguistic insights and on analyses of children's oral reading errors or "miscues" (Goodman, 1967; Goodman & Goodman, 1977). For different views of the Smith and Goodman positions, see Carroll (1978), Chall (1979a), and Samuels and Schachter (1978).

Interactive models such as that of Rumelhart (1977a), conceptualize reading not as a linear progression from sensory impressions to meaning, nor as a progression from the reader's previous knowledge to understanding of the text, but as an interaction of both ways operating in parallel. In Rumelhart's conceptualization, perceptual information, orthographic knowledge, word knowledge, syntactic and semantic knowledge, and so on interact in a given reader to create a probable interpretation of the text. Other interactive models are Adams and Collins' (1979) and in reports of the conference "Interactive Processing in Reading" (Lesgold & Perfetti, 1981).

Just and Carpenter (1980) proposed another interactive model, based on their work with eye movements in reading. Assuming that the reader tries to interpret each con-

tent word as it is encountered, and that the eye remains fixated on a word as long as it is being processed, Just and Carpenter found that a regression model containing factors relating to encoding and lexical access (semantic level), case role assignment (syntactic level), and interclause integration (text level) accounted for 87 percent of the variance in length of fixation on content words for college students reading scientific passages. Greater processing loads at any of these levels generally meant longer fixation durations. See Carpenter and Just (1977), McConkie and Rayner (1976), and Rayner (1978, 1981) for other research on eye movements. For other reviews of reading models, see Calfee and Drum (1978), deBeaugrande (1981), and Gibson and Levin (1975).

Readiness. The last decade has seen a number of changes in the concept of reading readiness. The largest change appears to be in a questioning of the concept of readiness itself, with a movement away from a global notion of readiness to an attempt to find specific underlying abilities related to specific beginning reading programs.

Group-administered readiness tests, usually given to kindergartners and beginning first-graders, are still widely used; however, their use has been criticized (Dykstra, 1967; Farr & Anastosiow, 1969; MacGinitie, 1969; Nurss, 1979). These researchers point out that although children who score high on these tests usually become good readers in grade 1, the tests are poor predictors of first-grade reading for children who score low on them. In addition, the individual subtests, usually tests of visual and auditory perceptual skills, language, and fine motor abilities, do not have satisfactory reliability to be used for diagnostic purposes. Often the prediction of kindergarten teachers has been found to predict first-grade reading achievement as well as or better than readiness tests (Downing & Thackray, 1975).

In the past decade, the use of early prediction tests has become more widespread. While readiness tests are group-administered and show the student's relative performance in relation to other students of the same age, early prediction tests are individually administered for the purpose of determining whether a child is "at risk" for reading failure. In spite of these differences, early prediction and readiness tests predict reading achievement to about the same extent: multiple correlations of between .6 and .7 (Chall, 1977). The early prediction test developed by Jansky and deHirsch (1972), based also on their earlier work in prediction of reading failure (deHirsch, Jansky, & Langford, 1966), correctly identified 79 percent of the children who would fail reading at the end of second grade. However, they also falsely labeled as "at risk" 22 percent of the children who would eventually succeed.

On both readiness tests and early prediction tests, the subtest with the highest predictive value for beginning reading is a letter-naming test (Chall, 1967; Downing & Thackray, 1975; Gibson & Levin, 1975; Wanat, 1976). Recent studies, however, have found that training in letter names appears to have no direct facilitative effect on learning to read (Jenkins, Bausell, & Jenkins, 1972; Samuels, 1972; Venezky, 1975). Venezky has suggested that knowledge of letter names is not directly related to reading but instead is reflective of other factors, such as interest in literacy and exposure to written materials. With widespread exposure to "Sesame Street" (Gibbon, Palmer, & Fowles, 1975), most children enter kindergarten knowing the names of letters; thus, letter-name knowledge may not be as good a predictor of beginning reading achievement as it has been in the past (Chall, 1979a).

Factor analysis of readiness tests (Calfee & Venezky, 1968) found that the individual subtests did not appear to measure discrete abilities. Jansky and deHirsch's (1972) multiple correlations of their screening tests with reading achievement also revealed some degree of overlap between the tests. Calfee, Chapman, and Venezky (1972) developed twelve tests in four areas to determine the level of visual skills, acoustic-phonetic skills, learning skills, and vocabulary. Calfee (1977) reports high correlations of the segmentation test (see below) and the letter-naming test with first-grade reading achievement.

Some authors have suggested that specific readiness skills are necessary for specific reading programs. Goodman and Goodman (1979) have suggested certain language experience activities as a prerequisite for their meaning-based program (see also Torrey, 1979). Popp (1978) analyzed four major approaches to beginning reading and suggested that different readiness skills probably underlie success in the different programs. These suggestions are more sophisticated than earlier suggestions with regard to aptitude-treatment interactions, which looked only at strengths in auditory and visual modalities. Robinson (1972) evaluated this kind of aptitude-treatment interaction and found that both auditory and visual learners learned better with a phonics program (see also Bateman, 1979).

Haddock (1976, 1978) found that sound blending training had a significant effect on the ability of children taught letter-sound correspondences to decode single words. Marsh and Sherman (1970) found transfer from learning "sounded out" words to learning whole words but little direct transfer between learning letter sounds and words (see also Gibson & Levin, 1975, pp. 291–292). In addition, Pflaum et al. (1980), in their meta-analysis, found that programs with a sound-blending component were generally more effective than beginning reading programs without such a component.

The relation of metalinguistic awareness to beginning reading success has also been one of the more active "newer" areas of research. Metalinguistic awareness refers to the child's conscious awareness of word boundaries in spoken sentences, of phonemic composition of words, of syntactic rules, and so on.

Downing, Ollila, and Oliver (1977); Downing & Oliver, 1973–1974; see also Holden & MacGinitie, 1972, 1973; MacGinitie, 1978) have found individual differences in ability to segment sentences into words, and Johns (1977),

Kelly (1977), and McNinch (1974) have found significant correlations between awareness of word boundaries and first-grade reading achievement (see Ehri, 1979).

Children's ability to segment a spoken word into its constituent phonemes has also been found to be related to beginning reading—specifically, to the learning of phonics. Liberman and her associates (Liberman, 1971, 1973; Liberman et al., 1974; Liberman et al., 1977; Liberman & Shankweiler, 1979) have found that words are more easily segmented into syllables than into phonemes and that both abilities appear to develop between the ages of 4 and 6. Fox and Routh (1976) found that a sound-blending training program was effective only with children who had been previously identified as being able to segment words into phonemes. Liberman (1973) and Calfee (1977) found a segmentation task to be an effective predictor of first-grade reading success (see Chall, Roswell, & Blumenthal, 1963, for correlations of sound blending with reading achievement in elementary grades). Others who have studied the relation between phonemic segmentation and reading are Helfgott (1976), Marsh and Mineo (1977), and Tompkins (1975).

The relation between measures of metalinguistic awareness and reading achievement has been explained two ways. Liberman and Shankweiler propose that metalinguistic awareness is a necessary precursor to learning to read. Ehri (1979) suggests that metalinguistic awareness comes as a result of learning to read, or from exposure to reading tasks. Vernon (1977) suggests the possibility of both explanations: that tasks now considered "metalinguistic" require both "growth" and teaching.

Metalinguistic awareness has been incorporated into formal measures to predict reading success. Evanechko et al. (1973) have developed a test of the child's concept of the reading task, including awareness of word boundaries, which has been used to assess readiness. Rosner and Simon (1971) report that their Auditory Analysis Test might be useful in predicting reading success. As discussed above, the segmentation task of Calfee, Chapman, and Venezky (1972; Calfee, 1977) has been shown to correlate highly with first-grade reading achievement.

Some authors have suggested that phonemic segmentation can be trained and that this training should be incorporated into beginning reading instruction. Rosner (1971, 1974) has developed a program to do this, as have Wallach and Wallach (1976, 1979). Liberman and Shankweiler (1979) suggest several different methods of training. These programs all posit an instructional sequence of segmentation training, letter-sound correspondence training, and sound blending as an effective beginning reading program. A similar program has been used to teach children in the Soviet Union for many years with apparent success (Elkonin, 1973).

Since words can be segmented into syllables more easily than into phonemes, Gleitman and Rozin (1973, 1977) have suggested beginning reading instruction with a syllabary. For further support, they noted that Japanese is written with a syllabary, and educators in Japan report few cases of reading failure (Mikita, 1970). The Rozin and Gleitman (1977) syllabary program has gone through some experimentation but its effectiveness is yet to be demonstrated.

Metalinguistic awareness has been proposed as a factor in advanced reading development as well. Thus while phonemic awareness is posited to be an important factor in beginning reading achievement, semantic and syntactic awareness become more important in reading achievement at the intermediate and upper grades (Chomsky et al., 1981).

Early Reading and Writing. During the past decade, many authors have questioned a later start in reading (Coltheart, 1979; MacGinitie, 1976; Singer, 1978). Fowler (1971) reports the success of a systematic phonics program in teaching reading to three- and four-year-olds. Durkin (1966, 1974) studied children who learned to read before the traditional first-grade start and found that their early superiority held until the sixth grade. See reviews of the effects of early reading by Smethurst (1975) and Coltheart (1979).

Chomsky (1971, 1979) and Read (1971) studied children who learned to read through early writing by their invented spelling and found that these childrens' spelling reflected their ability to isolate phonological features in their speech. Torrey (1979) studied other readers who had learned to read through a meaning approach. Bissex (1980) and Clay (1966) provide in-depth studies of the development of reading and writing of individual children, the problem-solving processes they go through, and the concepts of literacy held by these early readers.

Researchers who have studied the relation between Piagetian tasks and beginning reading add a cautionary note to the issue of early reading. Elkind (1976), Elkind, Larsen, and van Doorninck (1976), Murray (1978), and Waller (1977) argue that a child should reach the concrete operational stage (usually achieved between the ages of 6 and 7) before reading instruction can be successful. They present correlations between performance on Piagetian tasks involving field independence, perceptual decentration, and other conservation tasks and reading achievement. Elkind (1976) also reports that children who learned to read early were superior to matched nonreaders on conservation tasks.

Beginning Reading. During the late 1960s and 1970s, several large research projects were undertaken in beginning reading, including the USOE first- and second-grade studies (Bond & Dykstra, 1966–1967; Dykstra, 1968), the research review of Chall (1967), Project Literacy (Levin & Williams, 1970), and the Follow Through evaluation (Abt Associates, 1977; House et al., 1978; Stallings, 1975). Although some were concerned with basic research, most were concerned with the effectiveness of different methods and materials. Chall (1967) reviewed nearly a half century's research into beginning reading and found that "code emphasis" approaches (emphasis on sound-letter re-

lations at the beginning) produced better achievement both in word recognition *and* comprehension than "meaning emphasis" approaches (emphasis on meaning from the beginning) through the third grade, beyond which there was no research evidence. The research also indicated that earlier, more systematic phonics produced better word recognition and reading comprehension than did later, less systematic instruction.

This finding was essentially confirmed by the twenty-seven USOE first-grade studies (Bond & Dykstra, 1966–1967; Dykstra, 1968), although there have been some differences in the interpretation of these findings. Some reviewers concluded that the method made no difference; only the teacher did. Yet only one study was directly concerned with the influence of the teacher (Chall & Feldmann, 1966). This lack of agreement on the meaning of the findings was found also in a later, independent review by Corder (1971), which concluded that it was impossible to draw any clear-cut conclusions from the studies. See the review of Diederich (1973) for another opinion on the Corder conclusion.

In spite of this lack of agreement, Popp (1975) reports that most of the widely used basal reading series published after 1967 included more phonics instruction and introduced more phonic elements earlier than was common in the 1950s and early 1960s.

Later methods studies also found results favoring an early emphasis on phonics, including Kean et al. (1979), the Follow Through evaluations (Abt Associates, 1977; Becker, 1978; see House et al., 1978, for critique), the meta-analysis of Pflaum et al. (1980), and the analysis of teacher's manuals by Beck and Block (1979) and Beck and McCaslin (1977).

Support for early directed instruction in phonics can also be found in laboratory studies—Carnine (1977), Fox and Routh (1976), Haddock (1978), Jeffrey and Samuels (1967), Jenkins, Bausell, and Jenkins (1972), and Muller (1972–73)—which found that when students were merely taught regularly spelled pseudowords, they were less able to read novel pseudowords containing the same letter-sound correspondences than were those students who were given practice in sounding and blending each of the letters.

Criticism of early emphasis on systematic phonics has come from Goodman (1976) and Smith (1971, 1978). As noted in the discussion of models of reading, both Goodman and Smith propose that the main purpose of reading, right from the start, is meaning and that emphasis on decoding distracts children from this task, creating "word callers." Beck (1977) has argued that decoding instruction and comprehension are not mutually exclusive and that reading programs can teach both decoding and reading for meaning simultaneously. (See Samuels & Schachter, 1978, for additional discussion.)

Word Recognition. A great deal of basic research on word recognition of both adults and children was published during the 1960s and early 1970s. For reviews, see

Calfee and Drum (1978), Gibson and Levin (1975), Kavanaugh and Mattingly (1972), Massaro (1975), and Venezky and Massaro (1979). Much of this work stems from Cattell's classic experiments (cited in Gibson & Levin, 1975), which found that words were recognized tachistoscopically as quickly as individual letters. This "word superiority" effect had been used early in this century to justify the practice of teaching words as wholes (see Chall, 1967; Singer, 1978). Recent reinterpretations have cast doubt on this application (see Venezky & Massaro, 1979).

Some authors (Smith, 1971; Smith & Holmes, 1973) argue, as did Cattell, that words are identified as wholes by their own distinctive features, such as shape, and not by identifying their component letters. Smith, Lott, and Cronnell (1969) found that alternating upper- and lower-case letters did not affect word recognition if the shape of the word was maintained. McConkie and Rayner (1976) report from their studies of eye movements that proficient readers do use word shape and length information both to guide eye movements and to aid in identification of words.

Some studies, based on reaction time of tachistoscopic presentations, found that pronounceability, or orthographic regularity, are the prime cues used in word recognition. Gibson et al. (1962) and Gibson and Levin (1975) have shown that college students could read pronounceable words more quickly than nonpronounceable letter strings. A similar effect was found for third-graders by Biemiller and Levin (1968). Rubenstein, Lewis, and Rubenstein (1971) confirmed this effect and proposed that written words are translated into a phonemic code, which is comprehended by the language system (see also Conrad, 1972; Gough, 1972; LaBerge & Samuels, 1976; Levy, 1978). Hardyck and Petrinovitch (1970) found that even proficient readers might engage in observable subvocalization when reading difficult text.

Use of orthographic redundancy, rather than explicit phonemic recoding, has been proposed as a word recognition cue by Baron (1973) and Venezky and Massaro (1979). Baron (1973), using homophones, found that meaning in reading can be derived without using an intermediate phonemic code, contrary to the theory of Rubenstein, Lewis, and Rubenstein (1971). Gibson, Shurcliff, and Yonas (1970) found a superiority for pronounceable over nonpronounceable nonwords with congenitally deaf subjects, concluding that orthographic structure and not pronounceability leads to the word superiority effect. Venezky and Massaro (1979), using Massaro's (1975) model of the reading process, present a review of the literature that supports the role of orthographic regularity in reading.

Related to the question of orthographic regularity is the question of phonic generalizations. Smith (1978) has argued that phonic rules have too many exceptions for efficient use by students. Chomsky and Halle (1968) showed that English orthography is indeed rule-governed, even when spelling appears unrelated to pronunciation. Venezky (1970, 1976) has delineated a rule system for

English orthography based on intraword relations, and Venezky and Massaro (1979) propose that phonics instruction calls attention to the regularity of English orthography, thus leading to efficient word recognition. (See also Gough & Hillinger, 1980.)

Most of the basic research on word recognition cited above was on mature, skilled readers. There is some evidence, however, that word recognition strategies develop from components (letters, clusters) to holistic patterns (whole words or orthographic patterns) as the child develops proficiency in reading (Rosinski & Wheeler, 1972; Samuels, LaBerge, & Bremer, 1978; Santa, 1976–1977).

Studies have demonstrated that words are recognized quicker in an appropriate semantic context, even at second grade (Schvaneveldt, Ackerman, & Semlear, 1977). Both top-down theorists (e.g., Smith, 1971) and interaction theorists (Rumelhart, 1977a) propose that the linguistic context of a word is used to identify the word (see also Mosenthal, Walmsley, & Allington, 1978). Stanovich (1980) proposes that both automatized word recognition processes and top-down predictive processes are used in normal reading. He further proposes that good readers rely more on efficient automatized word recognition during reading, whereas poor readers rely more heavily on context to recognize words. Stanovich suggests that prediction is less efficient and requires cognitive processing resources that would otherwise be used for comprehension accounting for the difficulties of poor readers.

From "Errors" to "Miscues." During the 1970s a number of researchers used children's oral reading errors as a "window onto the reading process at work" (Goodman & Goodman, 1977). There was a tendency to refer to these errors as "miscues" and to look with disfavor at the teacher's corrections of these "miscues," since theoretically they were representative of the readers' attempts to make meaning of what they read. Goodman (1967) found that most substitution errors were syntactically and semantically constrained, as did Weber (1970). Biemiller (1970) found three stages in his study of first-grade readers' oral reading errors. In the first stage, children tended to substitute a word that would make sense for an unknown word, even if the substitution was not graphically similar to the text word. The second was characterized by an increase in "no responses." In the third, children substituted a word that made sense in the context as they did in stage 1, but these substitutions were graphically similar to the text word.

Barr (1972, 1974–1975) found that beginning readers taught with a phonics method made more "no response" errors than children taught with a sight method. Children taught with a sight method tended to substitute words that had been taught at about the same time. Those who learned by a phonic method also tended to substitute words that were graphically similar although not semantically correct.

Goodman (1967) proposes that the number of semantically and syntactically constrained errors indicates that some children can have problems reading individual words but still can grasp the meaning of passages. Shankweiler and Liberman (1972) found a moderate to high correlation between their single-word test and the Gray Oral Reading Test, leading them to conclude that the most common locus of difficulty in early reading lies not at the passage level but at the single-word level. They also found that vowels were more often misread than consonants, which they attributed to the more complex encoding of vowels in speech and the greater difficulty of isolating vowels.

Dialect Differences and Reading. Some authors (see review in Shuy, 1979) have speculated that the difficulties in learning to read among children who speak a nonstandard dialect stem from the mismatch between the child's spoken language and the language used in the materials of instruction. Most of the research in this area has dealt with black dialects (see Lucas & Singer, 1976, for a study of Mexican American dialects). Reviews by Harber and Bryan (1976), Pflaum-Connor (1978), Shuy (1979), Simons (1979), and Somervill (1975) have found that phonological, syntactic, and semantic interference may affect oral reading but not silent reading comprehension. Pflaum-Connor (1978) cites four studies that found no advantages for black-dialect speakers reading passages written in black dialect. Melmed (1971) reports that dialect speakers show some confusion in isolated word reading with words that are homophones in black dialect (e.g., seed-see, row-road) but no confusion when the words were set in context.

Karger (1973) suggests that dialect differences may be most important when children are learning to decode, but because ability to decode may slow up the comprehension process (Perfetti & Lesgold, 1979) there may in fact be some interference in reading achievement over time. A study of the reading of black children on word recognition and reading comprehension over the elementary school years seems to confirm Karger's hypothesis (Hall, 1982).

Some authors have begun to turn away from direct interference of dialect as an explanation for reading difficulties. Simons (1979) suggests that a child speaking a black dialect interacts with the teacher in a manner different from that of a white child (see also MacDermott, 1976). He cites the work of Piestrup (1973), who observed black children in a variety of classes and found that some teachers spent a disproportionate amount of time correcting features of their children's speech. The children's achievement was generally higher in the classes with the least amount of correction. Simons suggests that correction time not only takes away from instruction time (see Guthrie, Martuza, & Seifert, 1979) but also may convey disapproval by the teacher. Rist (1970) observed a class of black children from kindergarten to second grade and found that standard English speakers were put into the top group in kindergarten, whereas dialect speakers predominated in the middle and low groups. This pattern continued through the second grade. MacDermott (1976) argues that such grouping may create a situation in which the children

"learn not to learn," thus confirming their teacher's low expectations.

Some suggestions for minimizing the hypothesized interference of black dialect for beginning reading have been to use materials written in dialect (Leaverton, 1973), to use a language experience approach (Serwer, 1969), to use beginning reading materials written to avoid dialect features (see Pflaum-Connor, 1978), or to use regular materials but with the teachers alerted to accept dialect pronunciations and syntactic patterns (Goodman & Burke, 1973).

Reading Comprehension. If the 1960s were the time of large-scale studies of beginning reading, the 1970s were the time of large-scale studies of reading comprehension. These were set off by a series of conferences sponsored by the National Institute of Education and the establishment in 1976 of the Center for the Study of Reading at the University of Illinois. The center's researchers—representing a variety of disciplines—have put primary emphasis on reading beyond the beginning stage and on basic research into the cognitive aspects of reading comprehension. Numerous reports are available from the center, and several volumes present the theoretical and research concerns of the researchers (Anderson, Spiro, & Montague, 1977; Spiro, Bruce, & Brewer, 1980).

Much of this research in reading comprehension, both at the center and elsewhere, has been concerned with the reader's prior knowledge and with text characteristics. Other topics studied during the decade are whether reading comprehension is a single skill or a cluster of subskills, and how reading comprehension can be taught effectively.

Prior knowledge. The prior knowledge research of the center draws its basic theory from Bartlett (1932), who found that British subjects when asked to read and recall a North American folk tale tended to recast it into a more English-appearing tale. He proposed that his subjects used a mental framework, or schema, into which they incorporated the facts and ideas from the tale. After their memory for the actual tale faded, they tended to use this schema to reconstruct the tale. (See also Kintsch & Greene, 1978, and Steffenson, Joag-Dev, & Anderson, 1979, for other cross-cultural studies.) This notion of story schema has been developed into story grammars or specifications of the types of information that might be contained in a story schema (Mandler & Johnson, 1977; Rumelhart, 1975, 1977b; Stein & Glenn, 1979; Thorndyke, 1977). These initial grammars had limited power, being able to explain only stories with one major character and one major setting (Graesser, Robertson, & Anderson, 1981). In addition, Black and Wilensky (1979) have questioned their empirical and formal validity as grammars, and P. A. Weaver and Dickinson (in press) have questioned their usefulness for studying individual differences. DeBeaugrande and Colby (1979) and Graesser, Robertson, and Anderson (1981) have proposed more involved techniques for describing story structures.

Story schemata are one form of the reader's knowledge

that influences the comprehension of a text. Anderson, Spiro, and Anderson (1978; see also Anderson, 1977) found that the topic of a passage influenced which specific details were remembered. Anderson and Pichert (1977) found that after subjects read a story from one perspective, a shift to a different perspective helped them recall details they could not previously recall. Bower (1978) found that taking a particular point of view influenced how readers interpreted neutral stories. Chiesi, Spillich, and Voss (1979) found that readers with a great deal of prior knowledge about a subject recalled more from a passage than readers with little such knowledge.

Schema theorists (e.g., Adams & Collins, 1979; Anderson, 1977; Rumelhart & Ortony, 1977; Spiro, 1977; for a related approach see Schank and Abelson, 1977) propose that during reading or during recall, the reader activates schemata relevant to the topic of the passage. These schemata have slots for information, which are filled, or instantiated (Anderson et al., 1976), with information from the text. If the information is not explicitly given in the text, the reader fills in information from the schema (Anderson & Pichert, 1977). If the reader does not have a ready schema to fit the content of the story, comprehension may suffer (Chiesi, Spillich, & Voss, 1979).

Schema theory might be used to explain the effects of advance organizers or information given to readers prior to their reading (Ausabel, 1968; see reviews by Barnes & Clawson, 1974; Luiten, Ames, & Ackerman, 1980; Mayer, 1979; Slobody, 1981); prequestions (Gagné, 1978; Rothkopf & Bisbicos, 1967; or instructional objectives presented to students before learning (Rothkopf & Kaplan, 1972). Ausabel (1968) states that advance organizers provide the "ideational scaffolding" for the retention of the material that follows, or in schema theory terms, they either activate relevant schemata for the reader or help the reader develop a schema relevant to the text. Bransford and Johnson (1973) and Bransford and McCarrell (1975) have constructed ambiguous passages and sentences and found that when readers were given a topic in advance that would allow them to interpret the passages, it greatly increased retention. The effect was not as great if the topic was provided after the passage was read (see also Dooling & Lachman, 1971; Dooling & Mullet, 1973; Schallert, 1976).

Reder (1980) argues that to explain an activity that uses long-term memory, such as comprehension, one must postulate both a structure and the processes that act on that structure. She reviews much of the literature cited above and concludes that schema theorists do not adequately describe the processes acting on schemata, such as how relevant schemata are chosen and how two or more schemata needed to understand a text work together. She proposes that schemata may allow the reader to form elaborations using the text material and that these elaborations are more memorable than less elaborate memory traces. (See also Anderson & Reder, 1979; Schallert, 1976; Schwartz, 1980.)

Prior knowledge has also been proposed as an important factor in achievement testing. In an early study, W. W. Weaver (1967, reprinted in W. W. Weaver, 1977) found that college sophomores could answer 67 percent of the questions sampled from standardized reading-comprehension tests without having read the passages. Tuinman (1973–1974), comparing students answering questions with and without reading the passage, found that between 54 and 75 percent of the correct responses might be attributed to prior knowledge. Hanna and Oaster (1978–1979) developed a formula for measuring the passage dependency of individual test items, and Entin and Klare (1980) have applied this formula to the Nelson-Denny Reading Test.

Text-related variables. Recent research in text factors has been concerned with text organization, aided by propositional systems, such as those of Kintsch (1974, 1976, 1977; Kintsch & van Dijk, 1978; Kintsch & Vipond, 1979) and Meyer (1975, 1977a, 1977b). These propositional schemes break text down into hierarchically ordered series of idea units. Using this form of text analysis, Kintsch and Keenan (in Kintsch, 1974) found that reading time varied with the number of underlying propositions or idea units in a text and also with the number of propositions recalled in a free-recall task, rather than with the number of running words. Kintsch (1976) further reports that the complexity of the encoding of propositions (syntax, etc.) also affected reading time (see also Kintsch & Vipond, 1979), as did the number of different arguments in the text, and that the level of the propositions in the text (how central the idea units were to the total meaning of the passage) directly affected the idea unit's probability of being recalled.

Meyer (1975, 1977a, 1977b) also found a relation between the importance of an idea in the text and its probability of being recalled. She found that information in a target paragraph was recalled significantly better when the paragraph was high in the passage structure, or more central to the total meaning, than when the paragraph was lower in the structure. This was found using passages from about three different topics and with both immediate and delayed recall. (See also Clements, 1979.)

Meyer and Freedle (cited in Meyer, 1977a) found that the type of overall organization of a passage can affect recall. They found that passages organized in terms of an antecedent and its consequences were recalled better than other types of organizations they studied.

Kintsch and van Dijk (1978) and van Dijk (1977) have developed Kintsch's work with propositional structure and van Dijk's work with text grammars into a general theory of discourse. This theory has been used to explain the consistency of readers' recalls and summaries by postulating sets of processes used by readers to construct summaries from a given text. These processes include making inferences based on information implied in the text or on information in the reader's knowledge base (see also Fredericksen, 1977, 1979). This theory has also been applied to readability theory (Kintsch & Vipond, 1979). Other reviews of this work are presented by Gagné (1978), Lachman, Lachman, and Butterfield (1979), and Reder (1980).

Readability. A traditional way of viewing the relation of text variables to comprehension is the study of readability. Readability research relates the comprehensibility of texts to various factors related to semantics (e.g., word frequency, difficulty, length, abstractness) to syntax (e.g., sentence length), and less frequently to the phonemic aspects. During the decade several reviews of research and applications of readability appeared by Bormuth (1975), Chall (1979b, 1981a, b), Clifford (1978), and Klare (1974). Several new readability formulas were developed (Bormuth, 1969; Fry, 1977; Harris & Jacobson, 1974, 1980; Sticht, 1975), and widely used formulas were revised (Dale & Chall, forthcoming; Spache, 1974). In addition, Botel, Dawkins, and Granowsky (1973) published a procedure for measuring syntactic complexity, and scaled passages for estimating readability were developed by Carver (1975–1976); Chall et al. (forthcoming); and Singer (1975).

Practical uses of readability formulas increased greatly, with applications not only in textbook selection and development (Chall, 1981) but in adult literacy, in training programs for the armed forces (Sticht, 1975), in the testing and writing of government forms and manuals, and in consumer information (Chall, 1979b). There has also been a considerable increase in the use of computers in obtaining readability scores. Computer programs have been developed for the most widely used formulas.

A recent use of readability has been as a measure, among others, of the challenge or difficulty of text materials. Chall, Conrad, and Harris (1977) used readability formulas in this way in a study of the declining Scholastic Aptitude Test (SAT) scores. From a study of elementary and secondary textbooks over a thirty-year period, they found an association between the challenge level of the textbooks and the SAT scores of students who had used the textbooks. On the whole, the textbooks declined in difficulty over the thirty years—with the exception of basal readers, which stopped declining in difficulty in the late 1960s—and the more difficult the texts, the higher the SAT scores.

Concern with the misuse of formulas was voiced by Davison et al. (1980) in the writing of textbooks, and by Huggins and Adams (1980) for the inadequate attention to text organization. Kintsch and Vipond (1979) discuss text organization factors in relation to readability. A partial test of their readability model was performed by Miller and Kintsch (1980) (see review by Chall, 1981a).

Comprehension abilities. Carroll (1977) has proposed that reading comprehension be viewed in terms of language, cognition, and reading skills. He proposes that a child's cognitive ability might provide an upper limit for the comprehension of oral language, which might in turn provide an upper limit for the child's comprehension of text.

Sticht et al. (1974) reviewed the literature comparing listening comprehension (auding) and reading comprehension and found support for four hypotheses: (1) auding surpasses reading in the early years of schooling, but the gap closes as the child acquires reading ability; (2) ability to comprehend language by auding is predictive of reading comprehension, when the child is past the decoding stage (Chall, 1979a); (3) the most efficient rates of auding and reading are similar when the child is past the decoding stage; and (4) training in critical listening transfers to critical reading past the decoding stage. Other analyses of the relation between spoken and written language have been provided (Kavanaugh & Mattingly, 1972; Rubin, 1980; Schallert, Kleiman, & Rubin, 1977; Spearitt, 1980).

Pearson (1978) proposes that both reading and language can be analyzed in terms of three levels of understanding: graphemic-phonetic, semantic, and syntactic. The graphemic-phonetic level has been reviewed in the discussion of word recognition, and the semantic level will be reviewed in the vocabulary discussion below. Several different research methods have been used to show the effects of syntax on reading (see Huggins & Adams, 1980 for review). Using the eye-voice span or the distance that the eyes are ahead of the voice in oral reading, Levin and Turner (1968) found significantly longer eye-voice spans for grammatically structured sentences than for unstructured word lists. They also found that all tested groups except second-graders tended to extend the span to the end of phrases. Gibson and Levin (1975) and Levin (1979) provide reviews of eye-voice span research. Franks and Bransford (1976) and Pearson (1974–1975) have also found that different syntactic structures affect comprehension differently. Weaver (1979) found that a sentence structure training program appeared to improve the reading comprehension ability of poor readers.

Attempts to analyze the cognitive components of reading have been made by Otto (1977) and Otto and Askov (1972) for the Wisconsin Design for Reading Skill Development. The reading process was broken down into six skills areas, each of which was further broken down into subskills. Different objectives for each subskill were provided at different reading levels, in order to develop a curriculum that allows for continuous progress through the elementary reading levels. Mason, Osbourne, and Rosenshine (1977); Smith (1975); and Tuinman (1978) have raised some questions about the value of teaching subskills, and Vacca (1980) found no difference in reading achievement between junior high students using a subskill approach and those using sustained silent reading.

Some reading-comprehension subskills have also been studied developmentally. Otto, Barrett, and Koenke (1969) and Otto and Koenke (1970) found an increase from grades 2 to 5 in the ability of children to state the main idea of a passage. Brown and Smiley (1977) found that second-graders were unable to label the relative importance of ideas in a text. However, in free recall these second-graders recalled more main ideas than details, as did fifth- and seventh-graders and adults. Smiley et al. (1977) similarly found that the recall of good seventh-grade readers was related to the structural importance of ideas in the text, while the recall of poor seventh-grade readers was not. However, Tierney, Bridge, and Cera (1978–1979) did not find a relationship between the importance of the ideas in the passage they studied and third-graders' recall of those ideas.

Another approach to the question of reading comprehension subskills comes from factor-analytic studies of comprehension tests. Davis (1968) found that reading-comprehension ability was composed of distinguishable factors. R. L. Thorndike (1973–1974), reanalyzing Davis's correlations using different factor-analytic techniques, found that one factor—verbal reasoning—could account for nearly all the variance in reading comprehension. Spearitt (1972) in a further reanalysis of Davis's data (1968), using another technique, found four distinguishable factors—word meaning, inferences, author's purpose, and passage structure—but that the last three were highly intercorrelated and could be measuring a single factor. More recently, Carroll (1981) performed a factor analysis on different test data and concluded that reading comprehension had distinguishable subskills.

Samuels (1976) faults these factor-analytic studies for not separating good and poor readers. In good readers, the subskills have been mastered, and the result is a single process called reading. In poor readers, the subskills have not been mastered and might be distinguishable. He cites the work of Guthrie (1973), who found such a pattern in the decoding skills of poor readers.

Research on the teaching of reading comprehension by Durkin (1978–1979), based on observations of third- to sixth-grade classrooms during reading and social studies periods, found that very little time was spent on comprehension instruction. Instead, noninstructional activities and transitions between activities occupied a sizable amount of time. Of the time spent on comprehension, most of it was devoted to assessment, not instruction. Hodges (1980) argued that assessment should be considered an instructional activity and that with the inclusion of assessment, over 30 percent of classroom time was devoted to comprehension.

It has been quite common to note that relatively little is known about how to teach reading comprehension (Durkin, 1978–1979). Yet many areas related to reading-comprehension instruction have been researched—for example, the effects of pre- and postquestions (Rothkopf, 1972; Rothkopf & Bisbicos, 1967; see reviews by Faw & Waller, 1976; Gibson & Levin, 1975; Reder, 1980), having students generate their own questions during comprehension (André & Anderson, 1978–1979), the use of advance organizers (Ausubel, 1968; Bransford et al., 1979; Dooling & Mullet, 1973). In addition, Frase (1975) reports that asking higher-level inferential questions aids reading comprehension, and Watts and Anderson (1971) found that posttest questions that required the reader to integrate the material were more effective than low-level questions.

Meyer, Brandt, and Bluth (1980) found that signaling, or underlining cues to the structure of a passage, aided the comprehension of low achievers but not high achievers, presumably since the high achievers did not need any outside aid to use the passage structure.

Brown, Campione, and Day (1981) reviewed several studies involving the teaching of active strategies for learning from text and suggest that explicit instruction in such skills as summarization rules, self-testing and monitoring, sensitivity to text structure, and activation of background knowledge can facilitate learning from text.

Vocabulary. Along with the increased research interest in comprehension, there are signs of an increased interest in meaning vocabulary acquisition. This section reviews three areas of recent concern with vocabulary: the relationship of vocabulary and reading comprehension, the development of children's word knowledge, and the effects of vocabulary instructional programs.

Vocabulary and comprehension. The strong association of vocabulary to reading comprehension is taken into account both in subskill theories of comprehension (Davis, 1968; Spearitt, 1972) and in global theories (Thorndike, 1973). Studies of readability have also consistently found that the most important correlate and predictor of a passage's difficulty is a vocabulary factor (Chall, 1958; Klare, 1974–1975). Anderson and Freebody (1979) discuss three possible explanations for this relationship: the instrumentalist position, which holds that vocabulary knowledge directly facilitates reading comprehension (Becker, 1978; Yap, 1979; see also Jenkins, Pany, & Schreck, 1978; Pany & Jenkins, 1977; Tuinman & Brady, 1974); the general-aptitude position, which holds that vocabulary knowledge is reflective of general aptitude, which in turn is related to comprehension ability; and the general-knowledge position, which holds that vocabulary knowledge reflects general knowledge, which in turn affects comprehension.

Quantitative studies. The question of how many words children and adults know has been of considerable interest to educational researchers for many decades (Lorge & Chall, 1963), but interest declined during the 1960s. However, there seems to be a current renewal of interest in this aspect of vocabulary research (Anderson & Freebody, 1979). As in the past, the literature cites widely varying estimates of word knowledge, from 7,000 "basic" words for high school seniors (Becker, 1978) to 200,000 total words for college sophomores (Anderson & Freebody, 1979). Lorge and Chall (1963) presented a historical overview of the different estimates, together with an analysis of the reasons for the different estimates based on such methodological issues as dictionary size, methods of sampling, and methods used to test words.

The 1970s produced several new word lists: the Carroll, Davies, and Richman (1971) list, based on the frequency of appearance of words in textbooks; the Dale and O'Rourke (1981) list, based on knowledge of words by students in grades 4–12; and the Harris-Jacobson (1972) list, based on the words most commonly used in basal reading textbooks. Less extensive and more specialized word lists were also published by Johnson (1976).

Acquisition of word meaning. A review of studies on the nature of representation of word meanings in adult long-term memory (Stahl, 1980) found two aspects in mature word knowledge: definitional knowledge, or knowledge of how a word relates to other words in a semantic network (Collins & Loftus, 1975; Rumelhart, Lindsay, & Norman, 1972), and contextual knowledge, or knowledge of how the meaning of a word is affected by its context (Anderson et al., 1976; Labov, 1978; Miller, 1978). Studies of school-aged children's word associations (see Nelson, 1977, for review; and Petrey, 1977), children's definitions of words (Al-Issa, 1969; Feifel & Lorge, 1950; Maguire, Patsula, and Evanechko, 1975; Russell & Saadeh, 1962), children's ability to use context (Bransford & Nitsch, 1978; Werner & Kaplan, 1950, 1952), and children's classifications (Anglin, 1970; Miller, 1969) found a general trend from concrete, context-bound concepts to more abstract, context-free knowledge of words (Nelson & Nelson, 1978). However, other researchers have found that children as young as six organize their mental lexicons in associational groupings or networks (Mansfield, 1977; Nelson & Kosslyn, 1975; Schvaneveldt, Ackerman, & Semlear, 1977; Steinberg & Anderson, 1975). One interpretation of this literature is that children and adults go through a similar process of decontextualization while learning new words, but once the word is known, both retain definitional and contextual knowledge of the word (Bransford & Nitsch, 1978; Nelson, 1978).

Vocabulary teaching. In a natural setting, children learn most words from context. However, there is evidence that this process can be accelerated through the direct teaching of vocabulary in schools (Carroll, 1964; Petty, Herold, & Stoll, 1968). Studies have found that methods providing the student with both definitional information (definitions, synonyms, etc.) and contextual information (use in sentences, etc.) were more effective than methods providing only one type of information (Anderson & Kulhavy, 1972; Crist & Petrone, 1977; Gipe, 1979; Johnson & Stratton, 1966). Others have found greater success for methods involving more directed instruction (Jenkins, Pany, & Schreck, 1978; Pany & Jenkins, 1977).

O'Rourke (1974) proposed teaching vocabulary by an analysis of word parts in known words and extending these word parts to unknown words, by using context clues (see also Humes, 1978; Quealy, 1969) and by learning words in broad classifications through synonyms and antonyms. His proposal, based on his reading of the psychological, structural linguistic, and physiological literature, provides a systematic order for vocabulary instruction (see Stotsky, 1976). Instructional procedures based on these theoretic rationales have been provided by Dale and O'Rourke (1973). Suggestions for vocabulary development are also found in Johnson and Pearson (1978).

Schooling and Related Characteristics. Widely influential large-scale studies during the late 1960s and early 1970s (Coleman et al., 1966; Jencks et al., 1972; Thorndike, 1973) tended to find that school and classroom characteristics had less effect on reading achievement than student characteristics such as socioeconomic status (SES), education of parents, and ethnicity. At the same time, however, Chall and Feldmann (1966) found in an observational study of inner city first-grade classes that teacher and method factors distinguished high-achieving from low-achieving children. Jansky and deHirsch (1972) compared first- and second-grade teachers rated by principals as "adequate" or "inadequate" and found that teachers rated as adequate had half as many reading failures as inadequate teachers. Other studies of teaching excellence are reviewed by Bloom (1976), Brophy (1979), Good (1979), and Rosenshine (1976, 1979).

The study of school factors that probably had the greatest impact on later research was that of Weber (1971). He found that grade-three children in inner-city schools achieved at the national norms if the principal was a strong leader, had high expectations, provided reading specialists to help teachers with reading assessment, provided extensive reading materials, and used a strong phonics program. Thus, administrative and other school conditions were judged to be primary in reading achievement.

The Weber study has been replicated in more extensive form with essentially the same results (Edmonds, 1977; Fredrickson, 1980; Guthrie, Martuza, & Seifert, 1979; Popp & Lieberman, 1977; Venezky, 1978). Related to them is the study of Rutter et al. (1979) in England, which also concluded that the nature of the school and its instruction had a significant effect on academic achievement, including reading.

Evidence for the importance of classroom and teacher factors comes also from the "mastery learning" research of Bloom (1976). It shows that when proper provision is made for students' entering abilities, the time needed to learn, and help for faltering students, the low achiever can learn as well as the good achiever. Several mastery learning programs have been published and are being used by large school systems. These systems are based on Bloom's principle that, given the appropriate conditions, nearly all students can learn to mastery.

Direct instruction. The amount of direct instruction a student receives and the amount of academically focused time spent in class have been found to be significantly related to reading achievement. Rosenshine (1976, 1979) reviewed a number of elementary classroom observation studies and found that classrooms providing more direct instruction, both in teacher-centered lessons and in appropriate seatwork, had higher achievement than classrooms with less direct instruction time. Direct-instruction classes covered more content during the school year, a fact that also was positively related to reading achievement. Guthrie, Martuza, and Seifert (1979) also found that students who had high amounts of instructional time outperformed students with low amounts.

Rosenshine (1976, 1979) also found from his reviews

of related studies that students in direct instruction classes had more time-on-task behaviors than those in classes with less direct instruction. The amount of on-task behavior was also positively related to reading achievement (Stallings, 1975).

Cazden (1979, 1981) reviews studies of time-on-task and ethnographic research such as that of MacDermott (1976) and Piestrup (1974) and concludes that different student-teacher interactional patterns might produce differences in on-task behaviors. She also discusses the role of classroom "rituals" in focusing attention on relevant portions of a lesson and proposes more use of ethnographic techniques to study classroom behaviors.

Most of the research reported above studied classrooms with predominantly low SES students. Guthrie, Martuza, and Seifert (1979) found that effects of instructional time were different for children of different social classes. Although all children appeared to benefit from more instructional time, lower-SES children appeared to benefit the most on achievement measures. Peterson (1979) points out that classes with a less structured, "discovery" approach might have desirable effects in other areas, such as creativity and problem solving (Stallings, 1975).

Most of the studies reviewed above were done with primary-grade classrooms. MacDonald (1976) found that fifth-grade classrooms in which the teacher spent more time discussing, explaining, questioning, and stimulating cognitive processes had higher reading achievement.

Pacing. Barr (1973–1974) examined the effects of different rates of instruction on word learning and mastery in first-grade classrooms and found that a faster pace was generally associated with better word learning and mastery for average- and high-ability students. All low-ability students in her study were paced slowly; their word-learning and mastery scores were lower than those of average- and high-ability students.

Some other classroom characteristics found positively related to achievement are a variety of instructional materials (MacDonald, 1976), positive feedback (Bloom, 1976; MacDonald, 1976), a less competitive atmosphere (Talmadge & Walberg, 1978), more attention to individual differences (MacDonald, 1976; Rosenshine, 1979), an appropriate level of difficulty (Chall, Conard, & Harris, 1977; Chall & Feldmann, 1966), thinking approach to learning (Chall & Feldmann, 1966), and excellence in teaching (Chall & Feldmann, 1966).

Reading and Learning Disabilities. During the early 1970s, it was common practice to diagnose reading and learning disabilities with tests of visual perception or perceptual motor skills, auditory discrimination, or "psycholinguistic" abilities (Kirk, McCarthy, & Kirk, 1968) and to prescribe remediation programs based on the results of these tests. By the end of the decade, the usefulness of these categories was being questioned (Balow, 1971; Coles, 1978) and many researchers and clinicians were returning to more traditional, reading-centered approaches to diagnosis and remediation (Bateman, 1979; Chall, 1978).

Research of the late 1960s and early 1970s had failed to establish a relation between poor performance on tests of visual perception and perceptual motor skills and reading (Balow, 1971; Coles, 1978), except for beginning readers (Fletcher, 1981), or between instructional programs based on these tests and progress in reading (Bateman, 1979; Hallahan & Cruikshank, 1973; Hammill, Goodman, & Wiederholt, 1974). More recently some researchers have concluded that observed difficulties in visual perception (e.g., reversals) are artifacts of deficiences in verbal processing (Shankweiler & Liberman, 1972; Vellutino, 1977, 1979) or of selective attention (Hallahan & Cruikshank, 1973; Ross, 1976). Others have proposed that visual perceptual deficits represent a small percentage of reading disabilities (Gross & Rothenberg, 1979; Mattis, 1981; Mattis, French, & Rapin, 1975) or occur primarily in younger children (Fletcher, 1981; Fletcher & Satz, 1979).

As with visual perception, tests of auditory discrimination and diagnostic-remedial programs based on them have not proved positive. Dykstra (1966) found that the range of correlations between auditory discrimination tests and reading was large but none of the correlations was of a high magnitude. Liberman (1973) and Shankweiler and Liberman (1972) found that poor readers who made many errors on the same/different auditory discrimination tasks had little problem pronouncing the words in isolation. Kamil and Rudegair (1972) and Karger (1973) found that scores on the Wepman test improved with repeated administrations and with instruction, indicating that the poor reader's difficulties might be due at least in part to a lack of understanding of the task itself. Hallahan and Cruikshank (1973) and Ross (1976) suggest that problems in auditory discrimination may be symptomatic of a general problem in selective attention (for additional reviews see Hammill & Larsen, 1974; Robinson, 1972; Vellutino, 1979).

Other kinds of auditory factors, however, are significantly correlated with reading. See earlier section on metalinguistic awareness, particularly word segmentation and auditory blending.

Another view of learning disabilities is represented by the model used in the development of the Illinois Test of Psycholinguistic Abilities (ITPA) (Kirk & Kirk, 1971; Kirk, McCarthy, & Kirk, 1968). Studies of learning disabilities using the ITPA were numerous during the 1960s and early 1970s. Soon its validity for diagnosing reading and learning disabilities began to be questioned (Coles, 1978; Hammill & Larsen, 1974; Richardson et al., 1980), as have the programs for improving reading skills based on the test (Bateman, 1979; Newcomer & Hammill, 1975). Kirk and Kirk (1978) have responded to some of the criticisms leveled at the ITPA, citing methodological deficiencies in the studies reviewed by Newcomer and Hammill (1975), and cite other studies in which the ITPA was found to have value for diagnosing reading and other academic disabilities. They state that the ITPA was intended as a diagnostic test of language abilities and never claimed to have predictive value for reading.

Newer approaches. More recent research has concentrated on linguistic factors and found that learning-disabled readers differ from normal readers in phonological segmentation abilities (Johnson & Hook, 1978; Liberman, 1973), comprehension of certain syntactic structures (Denner, 1970; Fry, Johnson, & Muehl, 1970; Roit, 1980; Vogel, 1974, 1975; Wiig & Fleischmann, 1980; Wiig, Lapointe, & Semel, 1977; Wiig & Semel, 1976; see also Guthrie & Tyler, 1976), and speed of naming pictures, colors, and words (Denckla & Rudel, 1976a, 1976b; Farnham-Diggory, 1978; Perfetti & Lesgold, 1979; Spring & Capps, 1974; Wolf, 1979). Vellutino (1979) reviews these studies and proposes a theory of language-based reading disabilities.

Other researchers (Hagen & Kail, 1975; Hallahan & Cruikshank, 1973; Ross, 1976) have proposed that children with learning disabilities have difficulty selecting which aspect of a perceptual array to attend to and that their difficulty in reading is due to problems in maintaining attention on relevant stimuli. Ross (1976) has provided a detailed account of how this theory applies to reading and proposes that the success of such remedial programs as the Orton-Gillingham (Gillingham & Stillman, 1960) and Fernald (1943) is due to their focusing of attention onto letter shapes and sounds (see also Bateman, 1979).

Others have proposed that children with learning disabilities can perform the same perceptual and cognitive operations as normally achieving children but perform them slower. Children with learning disabilities have been found to be slower than their normal counterparts at naming letters and numbers (Denckla & Rudel, 1976a, 1976b; Mattis, French, & Rapin, 1975; Spring & Capps, 1974; Wolf, 1979) and in decoding single words (Perfetti & Hogaboam, 1975; Perfetti & Lesgold, 1979). Perfetti and Lesgold propose that this lack of automaticity (LaBerge & Samuels, 1976) in decoding creates a "bottleneck" in working memory, which impairs comprehension (see also Gollinkoff, 1975–1976). Fleisher, Jenkins, and Pany (1979) tested a strong form of this hypothesis, training poor readers to decode as rapidly as good readers. In spite of the training, the poor readers were still significantly poorer in comprehension.

Other clinicians have proposed that children with reading and learning disabilities can be divided into several groups, each with a different etiology. Boder (1971) found three subgroups of reading disabled children, a group with visual perceptual deficits, a group with auditory and language deficits, and a mixed group. Mattis, French, and Rapin (1975; see also Mattis, 1981; Roit, 1977) found three subtypes: a group with articulatory and other phonological problems, a group with naming and syntax difficulties, and a group with visual perceptual difficulties. Denckla (1977)

found the three subgroups of Mattis, French, & Rapin (1975) in her clinical sample, with the addition of a fourth group exhibiting phonemic sequencing difficulties (see Satz & Morris, 1981 for review).

Neurological perspectives. A strong current of influence on theories of etiology and diagnosis stems from the neurosciences (Benton & Pearl, 1978; Chall & Mirsky, 1978; Denckla, 1977; Geschwind, 1979). Many neuroscientists have examined acquired alexia in adults (e.g., Benson, 1981) and the implications that these syndromes have for children's reading problems. A recent study (Galaburda & Kemper, 1979) found abnormalities in the left hemisphere of a young man who had a known history of severe disability (dyslexia), providing a strong confirmation of a neurophysiological basis for severe reading disability in some children. Other contributions from the neurosciences are electronic assessment procedures for measuring various aspects of brain functioning (Duffy et al., 1980), including the use of the new brain scanners.

Treatment of disabled readers. In her review, Chall (1978) found a trend toward the task analysis of reading, especially basic reading skills such as decoding, and away from attempts to remediate through perceptual training programs (see also Artley & Hardin, 1976). Bateman (1979) reviewed several reading programs that have proved effective in teaching reading to disabled readers. These programs all appear to break down the reading process into small steps, with each step or subskill being given a great deal of repetition.

Adult Literacy. Surveys have indicated a considerable extent of adult illiteracy in the United States and in other countries, both total and functional illiteracy. Various government programs have been developed to solve the problem: Right to Read Effort, Adult Basic Education (Kavale & Lindsey, 1977), and special literacy training programs in the armed forces (Ryan & Furlong, 1975; Sticht, 1975) in the United States, and literacy campaigns in Cuba (Kozol, 1978; Morales, 1981), Nicaragua (Cardenal & Miller, 1981), and Brazil (Freire, 1970).

Literacy has been defined in terms of school grade reached or by a score on a norm-referenced test. Both of these means have been criticized as lacking validity for an adult population. The use of highest grade completed in school as an estimate of reading level has been criticized, because not all who complete high school can be said to possess equal skills (Bormuth, 1975; Peck & Kling, 1977). Similarly, a score on a test normed on grade school children will not necessarily be valid for an adult population (Bormuth, 1975; Harmon, 1970). In addition, it is difficult to state that a given performance on a norm-referenced test constitutes adequate literacy. For example, some definitions of functional literacy use fifth-grade reading level as a cutoff, because it is believed that it represents the ability to use everyday reading materials. Yet reading materials that are increasingly required in everyday situations (tax forms, instructional manuals, etc.) have significantly higher readabilities, closer to twelfth-grade level (Carroll & Chall, 1975).

Sticht (1975, 1979) and his associates in Project REALISTIC and Project 100,000 used an approach to literacy that compares the literacy skills people possess with the skills they need to function in their employment. They analyzed the readability of instruction manuals used by army trainees and compared it with the reading skills of trainees who successfully used the materials and with those who did not. They concluded that a ninth- to twelfth-grade reading level was necessary to learn successfully from these manuals. They proposed three possible solutions to the problem of training recruits with low reading skills: presenting the materials orally through compressed speech tapes (see Sticht, 1979), lowering the readability of the materials, or raising the reading level of enlistees through special training programs. Sticht cites problems with all three approaches. Since auding (oral comprehension) levels were found to be comparable with reading levels for students past the decoding stage (Sticht et al., 1974), using tapes may not solve the problems for all trainees. There is also the practical problem of lowering the readability of complex materials while maintaining the depth of information needed to perform the tasks described. And third, literacy training programs previously undertaken by the army had not been totally successful.

Other researchers, using "real-life" reading tasks (Kirsch & Guthrie, 1977–1978; Peck & Kling, 1977), found different estimates of illiteracy and have proposed different standards of adult functional illiteracy.

A historical perspective on literacy was taken by Resnick and Resnick (1977), who concluded that literacy demands are likely to increase with the increasing demands for technical skills in our society. They found historically that schools have generally been expected to provide either a low level of literacy for the masses or a high level of literacy for an elite. The current demand for a high level of literacy for the masses is unprecedented, they argue, and the current gap between the reading abilities of adults and the needs of society may be caused by increasing demands, rather than by changes in the student population (Carroll & Chall, 1975).

For adults in the work force, Adult Basic Education courses have been developed and grew with the enactment of the Adult Basic Education Act of 1966 (P.L. 89–750, Title III), which terminated in June 1973. Although this program has recorded some success with adults who attended the courses, it has not been so successful in attracting adults to take the courses or to complete them once enrolled (Hunter & Harmon, 1979; Weber, 1975). Kavale and Lindsey (1977) review some of the obstacles adults returning to school must face; including economic problems, home-related problems, and social and psychological problems. These outside pressures are accompanied by the same problems with reading that the adults faced when they were in school. They call for, as do Hunter and Harmon (1979) and Weber (1975), renewed attention to the nature of the adult literacy process, with attention to devising appropriate strategies to meet the special needs of illiterate and marginally literate adults.

More successful literacy programs, at least in terms of participation, have been undertaken in several revolutionary Third World nations. Many of these programs have been based on the philosophy of Freire (1970, 1981), who proposed combining literacy training with acculturation and political consciousness raising. Reports of such programs in Cuba (Kozol, 1978; Morales, 1981), Nicaragua (Cardenal & Miller, 1981), and São Tomé and Príncipe (Freire, 1981) note success, but these programs have not been evaluated by noninvolved analysts.

The literacy requirements of society have increased, yet the verbal scores on the Scholastic Aptitude Test have declined throughout the past decade (Wirtz, 1977). A similar decline has been observed on the American College Test program (Cramer, 1978). The panel on the decline of the SAT scores reported that many factors were involved, including such school factors as a loosening of curriculum and a lowering of the difficulty (readability) of textbooks (Chall et al., 1977).

As a result of declining reading skills of entering freshmen and the opening of admission to more marginally equipped high school graduates, many colleges have begun or expanded their remedial skills programs in reading and writing for incoming freshmen (Cross, 1981; Dempsey, 1978; Smith, Enright, & Devirian, 1975).

Conclusions. We have, in this article, reported what we consider to be the important basic and applied research on reading of the past decade. Our emphasis has been on reading research, with reference, where possible, to the influence of that research on educational practice. This could not be done for all of the research—particularly on reading comprehension—since it is too recent. Indeed, most of the papers in the volume published in 1980 by the Center for the Study of Reading (Spiro, Bruce, & Brewer, 1980) conclude that the educational applications of the new comprehension research have yet to be worked out.

Other reading research, particularly that on beginning reading methods, early reading, and word recognition, has had visible and significant influence on practice. The major influences have been on teaching reading earlier in grade 1 and kindergarten, and on earlier and heavier phonics in the primary grades. Other, almost direct uses of research, are found in readability measurement, and in criterion-reference and mastery tests in reading.

The rhetoric of reading research and practice has changed during these ten years. Such widely used concepts as automaticity, metalinguistic awareness, miscue analysis, story grammar, text base, discourse analysis, criterion-referenced tests, direct instruction, metacognition, ethnographic observations, national assessment, and minimum competency tests were virtually unknown ten years ago. And yet, on closer examination, the basic ideas behind these new reading terms were known and practiced by reading teachers for many decades, but under different labels. Thus, it would seem that the flow of ideas in reading may not be in one direction only—the traditional one of research to practice. Indeed, the flow may often be in the reverse direction, with research serving to give confirmation to the long-established practices of experienced teachers. For example, the new concept of automaticity seems to confirm the old practice of using flashcards of words and phrases to speed up word recognition; the concept of metalinguistic awareness confirms the teaching of letter sounds, word segmentation, and sound blending; miscue analysis extends the long practice of analytic testing of oral reading. One can continue with examples for each of the other new concepts.

Essentially, it would seem that the relationship between reading research and practice has not been unidirectional, with practice influencing research, which in turn has influenced practice.

Jeanne S. Chall
Steven A. Stahl

See also Elementary Education; English Language Education; Language Development; Literature; Racism and Sexism in Children's Literature; Readability; Textbooks.

REFERENCES

Abt Associates. *Effects of Follow Through Models.* Vol. 4B of *Education as Experimentation: A Planned Variation Model.* Cambridge, Mass.: Abt, 1977.

Adams, M. J., & Collins, A. M. A schema theoretic view of reading. In R. O. Freedle (Ed.), *New Directions in Discourse Processing* (Vol. 2). Norwood, N.J.: Ablex, 1979.

Al-Issa, I. The development of word definition in children. *Journal of Genetic Psychology,* 1969, *114,* 25–28.

Anderson, J. R., & Reder, L. M. An elaboration processing explanation of depth of processing. In L. S. Cermak & F. I. M. Craik (Eds.), *Levels of Processing in Human Memory.* Hillsdale, N.J.: Lawrence Erlbaum Associates, 1979.

Anderson, R. C. *Schema-directed Processes in Language Comprehension* (Tech. Rep. No. 50). Urbana: University of Illinois at Urbana-Champaign, Center for the Study of Reading, 1977.

Anderson, R. C., & Freebody, P. *Vocabulary Knowledge* (Tech. Rep. No. 136). Urbana: University of Illinois, Center for the Study of Reading, 1979.

Anderson, R. C., & Kulhavy, R. W. Learning concepts from definitions. *American Educational Research Journal,* 1972, *9,* 385–390.

Anderson, R. C., & Pichert, J. W. *Recall of Previously Unrecallable Information following a Shift in Perspective* (Tech. Rep. No. 41). Urbana: University of Illinois, Center for the Study of Reading, 1977. (ERIC Document Reproduction Service No. ED 142 974)

Anderson, R. C.; Pichert, J. W.; Goetz, E. T.; Schallert, D. L.; Stevens, K. V.; & Trollip, S. Instantiation of general terms. *Journal of Verbal Learning and Verbal Behavior,* 1976, *15,* 667–679.

Anderson, R. C.; Spiro, R. J.; & Anderson, M. C. Schemata as scaffolding for the representation of information in connected discourse. *American Educational Research Journal,* 1978, *15,* 433–440.

Anderson, R. C.; Spiro, R. J.; & Montague, W. (Eds.). *Schooling and the Acquisition of Knowledge.* Hillsdale, N.J.: Lawrence Erlbaum Associates, 1977.

André, M. E. D., & Anderson, T. H. The development and evaluation of a self-questioning study technique. *Reading Research Quarterly,* 1978–1979, *14,* 605–623.

Anglin, J. *The Growth of Word Meaning,* Cambridge, Mass.: MIT Press, 1970.

Artley, A., & Hardin, V. A current dilemma: Reading disability or learning disability. *Reading Teacher,* 1976, *29,* 361–366.

Ausabel, D. P. *Educational Psychology: A Cognitive View.* New York: Holt, Rinehart & Winston, 1968.

Balow, B. Perceptual activities in the treatment of severe reading disability. *Reading Teacher,* 1971, *24,* 513–525.

Barnes, B. R., & Clawson, E. V. Do advance organizers facilitate learning? Recommendations for further research based on an analysis of thirty-two studies. *Review of Educational Research,* 1974, *45,* 637–659.

Baron, J. Phonemic stage not necessary for reading. *Quarterly Journal of Experimental Psychology,* 1973, *25,* 241–246.

Barr, R. C. The influence of instructional conditions on word recognition scores. *Reading Research Quarterly,* 1972, *7,* 509–529.

Barr, R. C. Instructional pace differences and their effect on reading acquisition. *Reading Research Quarterly,* 1973–1974, *9,* 527–549.

Barr, R. C. The effect of instruction on pupil reading strategies. *Reading Research Quarterly,* 1974–1975, *10,* 555–582.

Bartlett, F. C. *Remembering.* Cambridge, England: Cambridge University Press, 1932.

Basic Skills, 1979: Hearings before the Subcommittee on Education, Arts, and Humanities of the Committee on Labor and Human Resources, United States Senate. Washington, D.C.: U.S. Government Printing Office, 1979.

Bateman, B. Teaching reading to learning disabled and other hard-to-teach children. In L. B. Resnick & P. A. Weaver (Eds.), *Theory and Practice of Early Reading* (Vol. 1). Hillsdale, N.J.: Lawrence Erlbaum Associates, 1979.

Beck, I. L. Comprehension during the acquisition of decoding skills. In J. T. Guthrie (Ed.), *Cognition, Curriculum, and Comprehension.* Newark, Del.: International Reading Association, 1977.

Beck, I. L., & Block, K. An analysis of two beginning reading programs: Some facts and some opinions. In L. B. Resnick & P. A. Weaver (Eds.), *Theory and Practice of Early Reading* (Vol. 1). Hillsdale, N.J.: Lawrence Erlbaum Associates, 1979.

Beck, I. L., & McCaslin, E. S. *An Analysis of Dimensions That Affect the Development of Code-breaking Ability in Eight Beginning Reading Programs.* Pittsburgh: University of Pittsburgh, Learning Research and Development Center, 1977.

Becker, W. Teaching reading and language to the disadvantaged. *Harvard Educational Review,* 1978, *47,* 518–543.

Benson, D. F. Alexia and the neuroanatomical basis of reading. In F. J. Pirozzolo & M. C. Wittrock (Eds.), *Neuropsychological and Cognitive Processes in Reading.* New York: Academic Press, 1981.

Benton, A. L., & Pearl, D. (Eds.). *Dyslexia: An Appraisal of Current Knowledge.* New York: Oxford University Press, 1978.

Biemiller, A. The development of the use of graphic and contextual information as children learn to read. *Reading Research Quarterly,* 1970, *6,* 75–96.

Biemiller, A., & Levin, H. Studies of oral reading: II. Pronounceability. In *The Analysis of Reading Skill: A Program of Basic and Applied Research* (Final Report, Project No. 5-1213). Ithaca: Cornell University and U.S. Office of Education, 1968.

Bissex, G. *Gnys at wrk.* Cambridge, Mass.: Harvard University Press, 1980.

Black, J. B., & Wilensky, R. An evaluation of story grammars. *Cognitive Science,* 1979, *3,* 213–230.

Bloom, B. S. *Human Characteristics and School Learning.* New York: McGraw-Hill, 1976.

Bloomfield, L., & Barnhart, C. *Let's Read: A Linguistic Approach.* Detroit: Wayne State University Press, 1961.

Boder, E. Developmental dyslexia: A diagnostic screening procedure based on three characteristic patterns of reading and spelling. In B. Bateman (Ed.), *Learning Disorder.* Seattle: Special Child Publications, 1971.

Bond, G., & Dykstra, R. The cooperative research program in first-grade reading instruction. *Reading Research Quarterly,* 1966–1967, *2,* 5–142.

Bormuth, J. *Development of Readability Analysis* (Bureau No. BR-7-0052). Chicago: University of Chicago, Office of Education, Bureau of Research, 1969. (ERIC Document Reproduction Service No. ED 209 166)

Bormuth, J. Reading literacy: Its definition and assessment. In J. B. Carroll & J. S. Chall (Eds.), *Toward a Literate Society.* New York: McGraw-Hill, 1975.

Botel, M.; Dawkins, J.; & Granowsky, A. A syntactic complexity formula. In W. MacGinitie (Ed.), *Assessment Problems in Reading.* Newark, Del.: International Reading Association, 1973.

Bower, G. H. Experiments on story comprehension and recall. *Discourse Processes,* 1979, *1,* 211–231.

Bransford, J. D.; Franks, J. J.; Morris, C. D.; & Stein, B. S. Some general constraints on learning and memory research. In L. S. Cermak & F. I. M. Craik (Eds.), *Levels of Processing in Human Memory.* Hillsdale, N.J.: Lawrence Erlbaum Associates, 1979.

Bransford, J. D., & Johnson, N. K. Consideration of some problems in comprehension. In W. Chase (Ed.), *Visual Information Processing.* New York: Academic Press, 1973.

Bransford, J. D., & McCarrell, N. W. A sketch of a cognitive approach to comprehension: Some thoughts about understanding what it means to comprehend. In W. Weiner & D. Palermo (Eds.), *Cognition and the Symbolic Processes.* Hillsdale, N.J.: Lawrence Erlbaum Associates, 1975.

Bransford, J. D., & Nitsch, K. E. Coming to understand things we could not previously understand. In J. Kavanaugh & W. Strange (Eds.), *Speech and Language in the Laboratory, School, and Clinic.* Cambridge, Mass.: MIT Press, 1978.

Brophy, J. E. Teacher behavior and its effects. *Journal of Educational Psychology,* 1979, *71,* 733–750.

Brown, A. L.; Campione, J. C.; & Day, J. D. Learning to learn: On training students to learn from texts. *Educational Researcher,* 1981, *10*(2), 14–21.

Brown, A. L., & Smiley, S. S. Rating the importance of structural units of prose passages: A problem of metacognitive development. *Child Development,* 1977, *48,* 1–8.

Calfee, R. C. Assessment of independent reading skills: Basic research and practical applications. In A. S. Reber & D. L. Scarborough (Eds.), *Toward a Psychology of Reading.* Hillsdale, N.J.: Lawrence Erlbaum Associates, 1977.

Calfee, R. C.; Chapman, R.; & Venezky, R. L. How a child needs to think to read. In L. Gregg (Ed.), *Cognition in Learning and Memory.* New York: Wiley, 1972.

Calfee, R. C., & Drum, P. A. Learning to read: Theory, research, and practice. *Curriculum Inquiry,* 1979, *8,* 183–249.

Calfee, R. C., & Venezky, R. L. Component skills in beginning reading. In K. S. Goodman & J. T. Fleming (Eds.), *Psycholinguistics and the Teaching of Reading.* Newark, Del.: International Reading Association, 1968.

Cardenal, F., & Miller, V. Nicaragua 1980: The battle of the ABC's. *Harvard Educational Review,* 1981, *51,* 1–26.

Carpenter, P. A., & Just, M. A. Reading comprehension as the eyes see it. In M. Just & P. Carpenter (Eds.), *Cognitive Processes in Comprehension.* Hillsdale, N.J.: Lawrence Erlbaum Associates, 1977.

Carnine, D. W. Phonics versus look-say: Transfer to new words. *Reading Teacher,* 1977, *30,* 636–640.

Carroll, J. B. Words, meanings, and concepts. *Harvard Educational Review,* 1964, *34,* 178–202.

Carroll, J. B. The nature of the reading process. In H. Singer & R. Ruddell (Eds.), *Theoretical Models and Processes of Reading* (2nd ed.). Newark, Del.: International Reading Association, 1976.

Carroll, J. B. Developmental parameters of reading comprehension. In J. T. Guthrie (Ed.), *Cognition, Curriculum, and Comprehension.* Newark, Del.: International Reading Association, 1977.

Carroll, J. B. Psycholinguistics and the study and teaching of reading. In S. Pflaum-Connor (Ed.), *Aspects of Reading Education.* Berkeley, Calif.: McCutchan, 1978.

Carroll, J. B. *New Analyses of Reading Skills.* Research address at the International Reading Association Conference, New Orleans, 1981.

Carroll, J. B., & Chall, J. S. (Eds.). *Toward a Literate Society.* New York: McGraw-Hill, 1975.

Carroll, J. B.; Davies, P.; & Richman, B. *The American Heritage Word Frequency Book.* Boston: Houghton Mifflin, 1971.

Carroll, J. B., & Freedle, R. O. (Eds.). *Language Comprehension and the Acquisition of Knowledge.* Washington, D.C.: Winston, 1972.

Carver, R. Measuring prose difficulty using the rauding scale. *Reading Research Quarterly,* 1975–1976, *11,* 660–685.

Cazden, C. B. Learning to read in classroom interaction. In L. B. Resnick & P. A. Weaver (Eds.), *Theory and Practice of Early Reading* (Vol. 3). Hillsdale, N.J.: Lawrence Erlbaum Associates, 1979. (A longer version of this article appeared in J. T. Guthrie (Ed.), *Comprehension and Teaching Research Reviews,* Newark, Del.: International Reading Association, 1981.)

Chall, J. S. *Readability: An Appraisal of Research and Application.* Columbus: Ohio University Press, 1958.

Chall, J. S. *Learning to Read: The Great Debate.* New York: McGraw-Hill, 1967.

Chall, J. S. *Reading 1967–1977: A Decade of Change and Promise.* Bloomington, Ind.: Phi Delta Kappa Foundation, 1977.

Chall, J. S. A decade of research on reading and learning disabilities. In S. J. Samuels (Ed.), *What Research Has to Say about Reading Instruction.* Newark, Del.: International Reading Association, 1978.

Chall, J. S. The great debate: Ten years later, with a modest proposal for reading stages. In L. B. Resnick & P. A. Weaver (Eds.), *Theory and Practice of Early Reading* (Vol. 1). Hillsdale, N.J.: Lawrence Erlbaum Associates, 1979. (a)

Chall, J. S. Readability: In search of improvement. *Publisher's Weekly,* 1979, *216,* 18. (b)

Chall, J. S. Readability and prose comprehension: Continuities and discontinuities. In J. Flood (Ed.), *Understanding Reading Comprehension*. Newark, Del.: International Reading Association, 1981. (a)

Chall, J. S. Middle and secondary school textbooks. In T. G. Sticht & J. Y. Cole (Eds.), *The Textbook in American Education*. New York: Academic Press, 1981. (b)

Chall, J. S. *Stages of Reading Development*. New York: McGraw-Hill, 1982.

Chall, J. S.; Bissex, G.; Conard, S. S.; & Harris-Sharples, S. *Readability Assessment Scales for Literature, Science, and Social Studies*. New York: McGraw-Hill, forthcoming.

Chall, J. S.; Conard, S. S.; & Harris, S. *An Analysis of Textbooks in Relation to Declining SAT Scores*. New York: College Entrance Examination Board, 1977.

Chall, J. S., & Feldmann, S. First-grade reading: An analysis of the interactions of professed methods, teacher implementation, and child background. *Reading Teacher*, 1966, *19*, 569–575.

Chall, J. S., & Mirsky, A. Education and the brain. In *The Seventy-seventh Yearbook of the National Society for the Study of Education* (Part II). Chicago: National Society for the Study of Education, 1978.

Chall, J. S.; Roswell, F.; & Blumenthal, S. H. Auditory blending ability: A factor in success in beginning reading. *Reading Teacher*, 1963, *17*, 113–118.

Chiesi, H. L.; Spillich, G. J.; & Voss, J. F. Acquisition of domain-related information in relation to high and low domain knowledge. *Journal of Verbal Learning and Verbal Behavior*, 1979, *18*, 257–273.

Chomsky, C. Reading, writing, and phonology. *Harvard Educational Review*, 1970, *40*, 287–309.

Chomsky, C. Write first, read later. *Childhood Education*, 1971, *47*, 296–299.

Chomsky, C. Approaching reading through invented spelling. In L. B. Resnick & P. A. Weaver (Eds.), *Theory and Practice of Early Reading* (Vol. 2.). Hillsdale, N.J.: Lawrence Erlbaum Associates, 1979.

Chomsky, C.; Hirshberg, J.; Cadogan, P.; & Cohen, S. *Metalinguistic Awareness: Preschool through Adolescence*. Symposium presented at the International Reading Association National Convention, New Orleans, April 29, 1981.

Chomsky, N., & Halle, M. *Sound Patterns of English*. New York: Harper & Row, 1968.

Clay, M. M. The reading behavior of five-year-old children: A research report. *New Zealand Journal of Educational Studies*, 1966, *2*, 11–31.

Clements, P. The effects of staging on recall from prose. In R. O. Freedle (Ed.), *Discourse Processes: A Multidisciplinary Approach*, Norwood, N.J.: Ablex, 1979.

Clifford, G. J. Words for schools: The applications in education of the vocabulary researches of Edward L. Thorndike. In P. Suppes (Ed.), *Impact of Research on Education*. Washington, D.C.: National Academy of Education, 1978.

Coleman, J. S.; Campbell, E.; Hobson, C.; McPartland, J.; Mood, A.; Weinfeld, F.; & York, R. *Equality of Educational Opportunity*. Washington, D.C.: U.S. Government Printing Office, 1966.

Coles, G. S. The learning-disabilities test battery: Empirical and social issues. *Harvard Educational Review*, 1978, *48*, 313–340.

Collins, A. M., & Loftus, E. A spreading activation theory of semantic processing. *Psychological Review*, 1975, *82*, 407–428.

Coltheart, M. When can children learn to read: And when should they be taught? In T. G. Waller & G. E. MacKinnon (Eds.),

Reading Research: Advances in Theory and Practice (Vol. 1). New York: Academic Press, 1979.

Conrad, R. Speech and reading. In J. Kavanaugh & I. Mattingly (Eds.), *Language by Ear and by Eye*. Cambridge, Mass.: MIT Press, 1972.

Corder, R. *An Information Base for Reading: A Critical Review of the Information Base for Current Assumptions Regarding the Status of Instruction and Achievement in Reading in the United States* (Project 0-903). ETS Berkeley Office, U.S. Office of Education, 1971. (ERIC Document Reproduction Service No. ED 054 922)

Cramer, E. H. Current issues in secondary school reading instruction. In S. Pflaum-Connor (Ed.), *Aspects of Reading Instruction*. Berkeley, Calif.: McCutchan, 1978.

Crist, R., & Petrone, J. Learning concepts from contexts and definitions. *Journal of Reading Behavior*, 1977, *9*, 301–303.

Cross, K. P. *Adults as Learners*. San Francisco: Jossey-Bass, 1981.

Dale, E., & Chall, J. S. *The Dale-Chall Readability Formula* (Rev. ed.). New York: McGraw-Hill, forthcoming.

Dale, E., & O'Rourke, J. *Techniques of Teaching Vocabulary*. Chicago: Field Enterprises, 1971.

Dale, E., & O'Rourke, J. *The Living Word Vocabulary*. Chicago: World Book-Childcraft International, 1981.

Davis, F. B. Research in comprehension in reading. *Reading Research Quarterly*, 1968, *3*, 499–545.

Davison, A.; Kantor, R.; Honnan, J.; Hermon, G.; Lutz, R.; & Salzillo, R. *Limitations of Readability Formulas in Guiding Adaptations of Text* (Tech. Rep. No. 162) Urbana: University of Illinois, Center for the Study of Reading, 1980.

deBeaugrande, R. Design criteria for process models of reading. *Reading Research Quarterly*, 1981, *16*, 261–315.

deBeaugrande, R., & Colby, B. N. Narrative models of action and interaction. *Cognitive Science*, 1979, *3*, 43–66.

deHirsch, K.; Jansky, J.; & Langford, W. S. *Predicting Reading Failure*. New York: Harper & Row, 1966.

Dempsey, J. Learning assistance: Charting our course within reach. In G. Enright (Ed.), *Learning Assistance: Charting Our Course—Proceedings of the Eleventh Annual Western College Reading Association Conference*, San Diego, 1978, *11*, 1–11.

Denckla, M. B. Minimal brain damage and dyslexia: Beyond diagnosis by exclusion. In M. E. Blaw, I. Rapin, & M. Kinsbourne (Eds.), *Topics in Child Neurology*. New York: Spectrum, 1977.

Denckla, M. B., & Rudel, R. Naming of pictured objects by dyslexic and other learning disabled children. *Brain and Language*, 1976, *3*, 1–15. (a)

Denckla, M. B., & Rudel, R. Rapid "automatized" naming (RAN): Dyslexia differentiated from other learning disabilities. *Neuropsychologia*, 1976, *14*, 471–479. (b)

Denner, B. Representational and syntactic competence of problem readers. *Child Development*, 1970, *41*, 881–887.

Diederich, P. *Research 1960–1970 on Methods and Materials in Reading* (ERIC TM Report No. 22). Princeton, N.J.: Educational Testing Service, 1973. (ERIC Document Reproduction Service No. ED 072 115)

Dooling, D. J., & Lachman, R. Effects of comprehension on retention of prose. *Journal of Experimental Psychology*, 1971, *88*, 216–222.

Dooling, D. J., & Mullet, R. L. Locus of thematic effects in retention of prose. *Journal of Experimental Psychology*, 1973, *97*, 404–406.

Downing, J., & Oliver, P. The child's concept of a "word." *Reading Research Quarterly*, 1973–1974, *9*, 568–582.

Downing, J.; Ollila, L.; & Oliver, P. Concepts of language in children from differing socio-economic backgrounds. *Journal of Educational Research*, 1977, *70*, 277–281.

Downing, J., & Thackray, D. *Reading Readiness* (2nd ed.). London: Hodder & Stoughton, 1975.

Duffy, F.; Dencklar, M.; Bartels, P.; & Sardini, G. Dyslexia: Regional differences in brain electrical activity by topographic mapping. *Annals of Neurology*, 1980, *7*, 412–420.

Durkin, D. The achievement of pre-school readers: Two longitudinal studies. *Reading Research Quarterly*, 1966, *1*(4), 5–36.

Durkin, D. A six-year study of children who learned to read in school at the age of four. *Reading Research Quarterly*, 1974–1975, *10*, 9–61.

Durkin, D. What classroom observations reveal about reading instruction. *Reading Research Quarterly*, 1978–1979, *14*, 481–533.

Dykstra, R. Auditory discrimination abilities and beginning reading achievement. *Reading Research Quarterly*, 1966, *1*(3), 5–34.

Dykstra, R. The use of reading readiness tests for prediction and diagnosis: A critique. In T. Barrett (Ed.), *The Evaluation of Children's Reading Achievement*. Newark, Del.: International Reading Association, 1967.

Dykstra, R. The effectiveness of code- and meaning-emphasis beginning reading programs. *Reading Teacher*, 1968, *22*, 17–23.

Edmonds, R. Effective schools for the urban poor. *Educational Leadership*, 1977, *37*(1), 15–24.

Ehri, L. C. Linguistic insight: Threshold of reading acquisition. In T. G. Waller & G. E. MacKinnon (Eds.), *Reading Research: Advances in Theory and Practice* (Vol. 1). New York: Academic Press, 1979.

Elkind, D. Cognitive development and reading. In H. Singer & R. Ruddell (Eds.), *Theoretical Models and Processes of Reading* (2nd ed.). Newark, Del.: International Reading Association, 1976.

Elkind, D.; Larsen, M.; & van Doorninck, W. Perceptual decentration learning and performance in slow and average readers. In H. Singer & R. Ruddell (Eds.), *Theoretical Models and Processes of Reading*. Newark, Del.: International Reading Association, 1976.

Elkonin, D. B. U.S.S.R. In J. Downing (Ed.), *Comparative Reading*. New York: Macmillan, 1973.

Entin, E. B., & Klare, G. B. Components of answers to multiple-choice questions on a published reading comprehension test: An application of the Hanna-Oaster approach. *Reading Research Quarterly*, 1980, *15*, 228–236.

Evanechko, P.; Ollila, L.; Downing, J.; & Braun, C. An investigation of the reading readiness domain. *Research in the Teaching of English*, 1973, *7*, 61–78.

Farnham-Diggory, S. *Learning Disabilities*. Cambridge, Mass.: Harvard University Press, 1978.

Farr, R., & Anastosiow, N. *Tests of Reading Readiness and Achievement: A Review and Evaluation*. Newark, Del.: International Reading Association, 1969.

Faw, H. W., & Waller, T. G. Mathemagenic behaviors and efficiency in learning from prose: Review, critique, and recommendations. *Review of Educational Research*, 1976, *46*, 691–720.

Feifel, H., & Lorge, I. Qualitative differences in the vocabulary responses of children. *Journal of Educational Psychology*, 1950, *41*, 1–18.

Fernald, G. M. *Remedial Techniques in Basic School Subjects*. New York: McGraw-Hill, 1943.

Fleisher, L. S.; Jenkins, J. R.; & Pany, D. Effects on poor readers'

comprehension of training in rapid decoding. *Reading Research Quarterly*, 1979, *15*, 30–48.

Fletcher, J. M. Linguistic factors in reading acquisition: Evidence for developmental changes. In F. J. Pirozzolo & M. C. Wittrock (Eds.), *Neuropsychological and Cognitive Processes in Reading*. New York: Academic Press, 1981.

Fletcher, J. M., & Satz, P. Unitary hypotheses of reading disabilities: Has Vellutino led us astray? *Journal of Learning Disabilities*, 1979, *12*, 155–159.

Fowler, W. A developmental learning strategy for early reading in a laboratory nursery school. *Interchange*, 1971, *2*, 106–125.

Fox, B., & Routh, D. Phonemic analysis and synthesis as word-attack skills. *Journal of Educational Psychology*, 1976, *68*, 70–74.

Franks, J. J., & Bransford, J. D. Memory for syntactic form as a function of semantic context. In H. Singer & R. Ruddell (Eds.), *Theoretical Models and Processes of Reading*. Newark, Del.: International Reading Association, 1976.

Frase, L. T. Prose processing. In G. Bower (Ed.), *Psychology of Learning and Motivation* (Vol. 9). New York: Academic Press, 1975.

Fredricksen, C. H. Semantic processing units in understanding text. In R. O. Freedle (Ed.), *Discourse Production and Comprehension* (Vol. 1). Norwood, N.J.: Ablex, 1977.

Fredricksen, C. H. Discourse comprehension and early reading. In L. B. Resnick & P. A. Weaver (Eds.), *Theory and Practice of Early Reading* (Vol. 1). Hillsdale, N.J.: Lawrence Erlbaum Associates, 1979.

Fredricksen, J. *Models for Determining School Effectiveness*. Paper presented at the annual meeting of the American Educational Research Association, Boston, April 1980. (ERIC Document Reproduction Service No. ED 189 149)

Freire, P. Cultural action for freedom. *Harvard Educational Review*, 1970, *40*, 205–225.

Freire, P. The people speak their word: Learning to read and write in São Tomé and Príncipe. *Harvard Educational Review*, 1981, *51*, 27–30.

Fries, C. *Linguistics and Reading*. New York: Holt, Rinehart, 1962.

Fry, E. Fry's readability graph: Clarifications, validity, and extension to level seventeen. *Journal of Reading*, 1977, *21*, 242–252.

Fry, M. A.; Johnson, C. S.; & Muehl, S. Oral language production in relation to reading achievement among selected second graders. In D. J. Bakker & P. Satz (Eds.), *Specific Reading Disability: Advances in Theory and Method*. Rotterdam: Rotterdam University Press, 1970.

Gagné, E. D. Long-term retention of information following learning from prose. *Review of Educational Research*, 1978, *48*, 629–665.

Galaburda, A. M., & Kemper, T. L. Cytoarchitectonic abnormalities in developmental dyslexia: A case study. *Annals of Neurology*, 1979, *6*, 94–100.

Geschwind, N. Assymetries of the brain: New developments. *Bulletin of the Orton Society*, 1979, *29*, 67–73.

Gibbon, S. Y.; Palmer, E. L.; & Fowles, B. R. "Sesame Street," "The Electric Company," and reading. In J. B. Carroll & J. S. Chall (Eds.), *Toward a Literate Society*. New York: McGraw-Hill, 1975.

Gibson, E. J., & Levin, H. *The Psychology of Reading*. Cambridge, Mass.: MIT Press, 1975.

Gibson, E. J.; Pick, A.; Osser, H.; & Hammond, M. The role of grapheme-phoneme correspondences in the perception of words. *American Journal of Psychology*, 1962, *75*, 554–570.

Gibson, E. J.; Shurcliff, A.; & Yonas, A. Utilization of spelling patterns by deaf and hearing subjects. In H. Levin & J. Williams (Eds.), *Basic Studies in Reading*. New York: Basic Books, 1970.

Gillingham, A., & Stillman, B. W. *Remedial Training for Children with Specific Disability in Reading, Spelling, and Penmanship*. Cambridge, Mass.: Educators Publishing Service, 1960.

Gipe, J. Investigating techniques for teaching work meanings. *Reading Research Quarterly*, 1979, *14*, 624–645.

Gleitman, L., & Rozin, P. Teaching reading by use of a syllabary. *Reading Research Quarterly*, 1973, *8*, 447–483.

Gleitman, L., & Rozin, P. The structure and acquisition of reading: I. Relations between orthographies and the structure of language. In A. S. Reber & D. L. Scarborough (Eds.), *Toward a Psychology of Reading*. Hillsdale, N.J.: Lawrence Erlbaum Associates, 1977.

Gollinkoff, R. M. A comparison of reading comprehension processes in good and poor readers. *Reading Research Quarterly*, 1975–1976, *11*, 623–259.

Good, T. L. Teacher effectiveness in the elementary school: What we know about it now. *Journal of Teacher Education*, 1979, *30*, 52–64.

Goodman, K. S. Reading: A psycholinguistic guessing game. *Journal of the Reading Specialist*, 1967, *6*, 126–135.

Goodman, K. S. Behind the eye: What happens in reading. In H. Singer & R. Ruddell (Eds.), *Theoretical Models and Processes in Reading*. Newark, Del.: International Reading Association, 1976.

Goodman, K. S., & Burke, C. Dialect barriers to reading comprehension revisited. *Reading Teacher*, 1973, *27*, 6–12.

Goodman, K. S., & Goodman, Y. Learning about psycholinguistic processes by analyzing oral reading. *Harvard Educational Review*, 1977, *43*, 217–333.

Goodman, K. S., & Goodman, Y. Learning to read is natural. In L. B. Resnick & P. A. Weaver (Eds.), *Theory and Practice of Early Reading* (Vol. 1). Hillsdale, N.J.: Lawrence Erlbaum Associates, 1979.

Gough, P. B. One second of reading. In J. Kavanaugh & I. Mattingly (Eds.), *Language by Ear and by Eye*. Cambridge, Mass.: MIT Press, 1972.

Gough, P. B., & Cosky, M. J. One second of reading again. In N. J. Castellan, Jr., D. B. Pisoni, & G. R. Potts (Eds.), *Cognitive Theory* (Vol 2). Hillsdale, N.J.: Lawrence Erlbaum Associates, 1977.

Gough, P. B., & Hillinger, M. L. Learning to read: An unnatural act. *Bulletin of the Orton Society*, 1980, *30*, 179–196.

Graesser, A. C.; Robertson, S. P.; & Anderson, P. A. Incorporating inferences in narrative representations: A study of how and why. *Cognitive Psychology*, 1981, *13*, 1–26.

Gross, K., & Rothenberg, S. An examination of the methods used to test the visual perceptual deficit hypothesis of dyslexia. *Journal of Learning Disabilities*, 1979, *12*, 670–677.

Guthrie, J. T. Models of reading and reading disability. *Journal of Educational Psychology*, 1973, *65*, 9–18.

Guthrie, J. T. (Ed.), *Aspects of Reading Acquisition*. Baltimore: Johns Hopkins University Press, 1976.

Guthrie, J. T. (Ed.). *Cognition, Curriculum, and Comprehension*. Newark, Del.: International Reading Association, 1977.

Guthrie, J. T.; Martuza, U.; & Seifert, M. Impacts of instructional time in reading. In L. B. Resnick & P. A. Weaver (Eds.), *Theory and Practice of Early Reading* (Vol. 3). Hillsdale, N.J.: Lawrence Erlbaum Associates, 1979.

Guthrie, J. T., & Tyler, S. J. Psycholinguistic processing in reading and listening among good and poor readers. *Journal of Reading Behavior*, 1976, *8*, 415–425.

Haddock, M. The effects of an auditory and auditory-visual method of blending instruction on the ability of prereaders to decode synthetic words. *Journal of Educational Psychology*, 1976, *68*, 825–831.

Haddock, M. Teaching blending in beginning reading instruction is important. *Reading Teacher*, 1978, *31*, 654–658.

Hagen, J. W., & Kail, R. V., Jr. The role of attention in perceptual and cognitive development. In W. M. Cruikshank & D. P. Hallahan (Eds.), *Perceptual and Learning Disabilities in Children: Research and Theory* (Vol. 2). Syracuse, N.Y.: Syracuse University Press, 1975.

Hall, S. *Reading and the Black Child: The Relationship of Some Components of Reading and Language*. Unpublished doctoral dissertation, Harvard University, 1982.

Hallahan, D. P., & Cruikshank, W. M. *Psychoeducational Foundations of Learning Disabilities*. Englewood Cliffs, N.J.: Prentice-Hall, 1973.

Halliday, M. A. K., & Hasan, R. *Cohesion in English*. London: Longman, 1976.

Hammill, D.; Goodman, L.; & Wiederholt, J. L. Visual-motor processes: Can we train them? *Reading Teacher*, 1974, *27*, 469–478.

Hammill, D., & Larsen, S. The relationship of selected auditory perceptual skills and reading ability. *Journal of Learning Disabilities*, 1974, *7*, 429–435.

Hanna, G. S., & Oaster, T. R. Toward a unified theory of context dependence. *Reading Research Quarterly*, 1978–1979, *14*, 226–243.

Harber, J. R., & Bryan, D. N. Black English and the task of reading. *Review of Educational Research*, 1976, *46*, 387–405.

Hardyck, C. D., & Petrinovitch, L. F. Subvocal speech and comprehension level as a function of the difficulty level of reading material. *Journal of Verbal Learning and Verbal Behavior*, 1970, *9*, 647–652.

Harmon, D. Illiteracy: An overview. *Harvard Educational Review*, 1970, *40*, 226–243.

Harris, A. J., & Jacobson, M. D. *Basic Elementary Reading Vocabularies*. New York: Macmillan, 1972.

Harris, A. J., & Jacobson, M. D. *Revised Harris-Jacobson Readability Formulas*. Paper presented at the annual convention of the College Reading Association, Bethesda, Md., October 31, 1974.

Harris, A. J., & Jacobson, M. D. A comparison of the Fry, Spache, and Harris-Jacobson readability formulas for primary grades. *Reading Teacher*, 1980, *33*, 920–924.

Helfgott, J. Phonemic segmentation and blending skills of kindergarten children: Implications for beginning reading. *Contemporary Educational Psychology*, 1976, *1*, 157–169.

Hodges, C. A. Commentary: Toward a broader definition of comprehension instruction. *Reading Research Quarterly*, 1980, *15*, 299–306.

Holden, M., & MacGinitie, W. Children's conceptions of word boundaries in speech and print. *Journal of Educational Psychology*, 1972, *63*, 551–557.

Holden, M., & MacGinitie, W. *Metalinguistic Ability and Cognitive Performance in Children from Five to Seven*. Paper presented at annual meeting of the American Educational Research Association, New Orleans, February 26 to March 1, 1973. (ERIC Document Reproduction Service No. ED 078 436)

House, E.; Glass, G. V.; McLean, L.; & Walker, D. F. No simple answer: Critique of the Follow Through evaluation. *Harvard Educational Review*, 1978, *48*, 129–160.

Huggins, A. W. F., & Adams, A. J. Syntactic aspects of reading comprehension. In R. Spiro, B. Bruce, & W. Brewer (Eds.), *Theoretical Issues in Reading Comprehension*. Hillsdale, N.J.: Lawrence Erlbaum Associates, 1980.

Humes, A. Structures, signals, and cognitive processes in context clues. *Research in the Teaching of English*, 1978, *12*, 321–334.

Hunter, C. St. J., & Harmon, D. *Adult Illiteracy in the United States*. New York: McGraw-Hill, 1979.

Jaeger, R. M., & Tittle, C. K. Minimum competency testing: Motives, models, measures, and consequences. Berkeley, Calif.: McCutchan, 1980.

Jansky, J., & deHirsch, K. *Preventing Reading Failure*. New York: Harper & Row, 1972.

Jeffrey, W. S., & Samuels, S. J. Effect of method of reading training on initial learning and transfer. *Journal of Verbal Learning and Verbal Behavior*, 1967, *6*, 354–358.

Jencks, C.; Smith, M.; Acland, H.; Bane, M.; Cohen, D.; Gintis, H.; Heyns, B.; & Michelson, F. *Inequality*. New York: Basic Books, 1972.

Jenkins, J. R.; Bausell, R. B.; & Jenkins, L. M. Comparison of letter name and letter sound training as transfer variables. *American Educational Research Journal*, 1972, *9*, 75–86.

Jenkins, J. R.; Pany, D.; & Schreck, J. *Vocabulary and Reading Comprehension: Instructional Effects* (Tech. Rep. No. 100). Urbana-Champaign: University of Illinois, Center for the Study of Reading, 1978.

Johns, J. *Relationships between Metalinguistic Awareness and Reading Achievement*. 1977. (ERIC Document Reproduction Service No. ED 136 225)

Johnson, D. D. *Johnson Basic Sight Vocabulary Test Manual*. Lexington, Mass.: Ginn, 1976.

Johnson, D. D., & Pearson, P. D. *Teaching Reading Vocabulary*. New York: Holt, Rinehart, & Winston, 1978.

Johnson, D., & Stratton, P. Evaluation of five methods of teaching concepts. *Journal of Educational Psychology*, 1966, *57*, 48–53.

Johnson, D. J., & Hook, P. E. Reading disabilities: Problems of rule acquisition and linguistic awareness. In H. Myklebust (Ed.), *Progress in Learning Disabilities* (Vol. 4). New York: Grune & Stratton, 1978.

Just, M. A., & Carpenter, P. A. A theory of reading: From eye fixations to comprehension. *Psychological Review*, 1980, *87*, 329–354.

Just, M. A., & Carpenter, P. A. (Eds.). *Cognitive Processes in Comprehension*. Hillsdale, N.J.: Lawrence Erlbaum Associates, 1977.

Kamil, M. L., & Rudegair, R. E. Methodological improvements in the assessment of phonological discrimination in children. *Child Development*, 1972, *43*, 1087–1089.

Karger, G. W. *The Performance of Lower Class Black and Lower Class White Children on the Wepman Auditory Discrimination Test: The Effects of Dialect and Training, and the Relationship to Reading Achievement*. Unpublished doctoral dissertation, Harvard University, 1973.

Kavale, K. A., & Lindsey, J. D. Adult basic education: Has it worked? *Journal of Reading*, 1977, *21*, 368–376.

Kavanaugh, J., & Mattingly, I. (Eds.). *Language by Ear and by Eye*. Cambridge, Mass.: MIT Press, 1972.

Kean, M. H.; Summers, A. A.; Raivitz, M.; & Farber, I. *What Works in Reading? Summary and Results of a Joint School District/Federal Reserve Bank Empirical Study in Philadelphia*. Philadelphia: School District Office of Research and Evaluation, May 1979. (ERIC Document Reproduction Service No. ED 176 216)

Kelly, A. M. *Children's Ability to Segment Oral Language*. 1977. (ERIC Document Reproduction Service No. ED 145 402)

Kintsch, W. *The Representation of Meaning in Memory*. Hillsdale, N.J.: Lawrence Erlbaum Associates, 1974.

Kintsch, W. Memory for prose. In C. N. Cofer (Ed.), *The Structure of Human Memory*. San Francisco: Freeman, 1976.

Kintsch, W. Reading comprehension as a function of text structure. In A. S. Reber & D. L. Scarborough (Eds.), *Toward a Psychology of Reading*. Hillsdale, N.J.: Lawrence Erlbaum Associates, 1977.

Kintsch, W., & Greene, E. The role of culture-specific schemata in the comprehension and recall of stories. *Discourse Processes*, 1978, *1*, 1–13.

Kintsch, W., & van Dijk, T. A. Toward a model of text comprehension and production. *Psychological Review*, 1978, *85*, 363–394.

Kintsch, W., & Vipond, D. Reading comprehension and readability in educational practice and psychological theory. In L. Nilsson (Ed.), *Proceedings of the Conference on Memory, University of Uppsala*. Hillsdale, N.J.: Lawrence Erlbaum Associates, 1979.

Kirk, S. A., & Kirk, W. D. *Psycholinguistic Learning Disabilities: Diagnosis and Treatment*. Urbana: University of Illinois Press, 1971.

Kirk, S. A., & Kirk, W. D. Uses and abuses of the ITPA. *Journal of Speech and Hearing Disorders*, 1978, *43*, 58–75.

Kirk, S. A.; McCarthy, J. J.; & Kirk, W. D. *Illinois Test of Psycholinguistic Abilities* (Rev. ed.). Urbana: University of Illinois Press, 1968.

Kirsch, I., & Guthrie, J. The concept and measurement of functional literacy. *Reading Research Quarterly*, 1977–1978, *13*, 304–345.

Klare, G. R. Assessing readability. *Reading Research Quarterly*, 1974–1975, *10*, 62–102.

Knights, R. M., & Bakker, D. J. (Eds.). *Neuropsychology of Learning Disorders*. Baltimore: University Park Press, 1976.

Kozol, J. A new look at the literacy campaign in Cuba. *Harvard Educational Review*, 1978, *48*, 341–377.

LaBerge, D. The perception of units in beginning reading. In L. B. Resnick & P. A. Weaver (Eds.), *Theory and Practice of Early Reading* (Vol. 3). Hillsdale, N.J.: Lawrence Erlbaum Associates, 1979.

LaBerge, D., & Samuels, S. J. Toward a theory of automatic information processing in reading. In H. Singer & R. Ruddell (Eds.), *Theoretical Models and Processes of Reading* (2nd ed.). Newark, Del.: International Reading Association, 1976.

LaBerge, D., & Samuels, S. J. (Eds.). *Basic Processes in Reading: Perception and Comprehension*. Hillsdale, N.J.: Lawrence Erlbaum Associates, 1977.

Labov, W. Gaining access to the dictionary. In J. Kavanaugh & W. Strange (Eds.), *Speech and Language in the Laboratory, School, and Clinic*. Cambridge, Mass.: MIT Press, 1978.

Lachman, R.; Lachman, J. L.; & Butterfield, E. C. *Cognitive Psychology and Information Processing*. Hillsdale, N.J.: Lawrence Erlbaum Associates, 1979.

Leaverton, L. Dialectal readers: Rationale, use, and value. In J. Laffey & R. Shuy (Eds.), *Language Differences: Do They Interfere?* Newark, Del.: International Reading Association, 1973.

Lesgold, A. M., & Perfetti, C. *Interactive Processes in Reading.* Hillsdale, N.J.: Lawrence Erlbaum Associates, 1981.

Levin, H. *The Eye-Voice Span.* Cambridge, Mass.: MIT Press, 1979.

Levin, H., & Turner, A. Sentence structure and the eye-voice span. In H. Levin, E. J. Gibson, & J. J. Gibson (Eds.), *The Analysis of Reading Skill* (Final Report Project No. 5-1213). Ithaca, N.Y.: Cornell University, U.S. Office of Education, 1968.

Levin, H., & Williams, J. *Basic Studies in Reading.* New York: Basic Books, 1970.

Levy, B. A. Speech analysis during sentence processing: Reading and listening. *Visible Language,* 1978, *12,* 81–101.

Liberman, I. Y. Basic research in speech and laterality: Some implications for reading disability. *Bulletin of the Orton Society,* 1971, *41,* 71–87.

Liberman, I. Y. Segmentation of the spoken word and reading acquisition. *Bulletin of the Orton Society,* 1973, *23,* 65–77.

Liberman, I. Y., & Shankweiler, D. Speech, the alphabet, and learning to read. In L. B. Resnick & P. A. Weaver (Eds.), *Theory and Practice of Early Reading* (Vol. 2). Hillsdale, N.J.: Lawrence Erlbaum Associates, 1979.

Liberman, I. Y.; Shankweiler, D.; Fischer, F. W.; & Carter, B. Explicit syllable and phoneme segmentation in the young child. *Journal of Experimental Child Psychology,* 1974, *18,* 201–212.

Liberman, I. Y.; Shankweiler, D.; Liberman, A. M.; Fowler, C.; & Fischer, F. W. Phonetic segmentation and recoding in the beginning reader. In A. S. Reber & D. L. Scarborough (Eds.), *Toward a Psychology of Reading.* Hillsdale, N.J.: Lawrence Erlbaum Associates, 1977.

Lorge, I., & Chall, J. S. Estimating the size of vocabularies of children and adults: An analysis of methodological issues. *Journal of Experimental Education,* 1963, *32,* 147–157.

Lucas, M. S., & Singer, H. Dialect in relation to oral reading achievement: Recoding, encoding, or merely a code? In H. Singer & R. Ruddell (Eds.), *Theoretical Models and Processes of Reading.* Newark, Del.: International Reading Association, 1976.

Luiten, J.; Ames, W.; & Ackerman, G. A meta-analysis of the effects of advance organizers on learning and retention. *American Educational Research Journal,* 1980, *17,* 211–218.

MacDermott, R. P. Achieving school failure: An anthropological approach to literacy and social stratification. In H. Singer & R. Ruddell (Eds.), *Theoretical Models and Processes of Reading* (2nd ed.). Newark, Del.: International Reading Association, 1976.

MacDonald, F. J. Report on phase II of the beginning teacher evaluation study. *Journal of Teacher Education,* 1976, *27,* 39–42.

MacGinitie, W. H. Evaluating readiness for learning to read: A critical review and evaluation of research. *Reading Research Quarterly,* 1969, *4,* 396–410.

MacGinitie, W. H. When should we begin to teach reading? *Language Arts,* 1976, *53,* 878–882.

MacGinitie, W. H. Children's understanding of linguistic units. In S. J. Samuels (Ed.), *What Research Has to Say about Reading Instruction.* Newark, Del.: International Reading Association, 1978.

Mackworth, J. F. Some models of the reading process: Learners and skilled readers. *Reading Research Quarterly,* 1972, *7,* 701–733.

Maguire, T. O.; Patsula, R. B.; & Evanechko, P. O. The develop-

ments of word meaning discrimination in children. *Alberta Journal of Educational Research,* 1975, *21,* 154–165.

Mandler, J. S., & Johnson, N. S. Remembrance of things parsed: Story structure and recall. *Cognitive Psychology,* 1977, *9,* 111–151.

Mansfield, A. Semantic organization in the young child: Evidence for the development of semantic feature systems. *Journal of Experimental Child Psychology,* 1977, *23,* 57–77.

Marsh, G., & Mineo, J. Training preschool children to recognize phonemes in words. *Journal of Educational Psychology,* 1977, *69,* 748–753.

Marsh, G., & Sherman, M. *Transfer from Word Components to Words and Vice Versa in Beginning Reading* (Tech. Rep. No. 23). Englewood, Calif.: Southwest Regional Educational Laboratory, 1970. (ERIC Document Reproduction Service No. ED 042 587)

Mason, J.; Osbourne, J.; & Rosenshine, B. *A Consideration of Skill Hierarchy Approaches to the Teaching of Reading* (Tech. Rep. No. 42). Urbana-Champaign: University of Illinois, Center for the Study of Reading, 1977.

Massaro, D. (Ed.). *Understanding Language: An Information-processing Analysis of Speech Perception, Reading, and Psycholinguistics.* New York: Academic Press, 1975.

Mattis, S. Dyslexia syndromes in children: Toward the development of syndrome-specific treatment programs. In F. J. Pirozzolo & M. C. Wittrock (Eds.), *Neuropsychological and Cognitive Processes in Reading.* New York: Academic Press, 1981.

Mattis, S.; French, J. H.; & Rapin, I. Dyslexia in children and young adults: Three independent neuropsychological syndromes. *Developmental Medicine and Child Neurology,* 1975, *17,* 150–163.

Mayer, R. E. Can advance organizers influence meaningful learning? *Review of Educational Research,* 1979, *49,* 371–383.

McConkie, G. W., & Rayner, K. Identifying the span of the effective stimulus in reading: Literature review and theories of reading. In H. Singer & R. Ruddell (Eds.), *Theoretical Models and Processes of Reading* (2nd ed.). Newark, Del.: International Reading Association, 1976.

McNinch, G. Awareness of aural and visual word boundaries within a sample of first graders. *Perceptual and Motor Skills,* 1974, *38,* 1127–1134.

Melmed, P. J. Black English phonology: The question of reading interference. *Monographs of the Language Behavior Research Laboratory* (University of California at Berkeley), 1971, *1.*

Meyer, B. J. F. *The Organization of Prose and Its Effect on Recall.* Amsterdam: North Holland, 1975.

Meyer, B. J. F. What is remembered from prose: A function of passage structure. In R. O. Freedle (Ed.), *Discourse Production and Comprehension* (Vol. 1). Norwood, N.J.: Ablex, 1977. (a)

Meyer, B. J. F. The structure of prose: Effects on learning and memory and implications for educational practice. In R. C. Anderson, R. J. Spiro, & W. Montague (Eds.), *Schooling and the Acquisition of Knowledge.* Hillsdale, N.J.: Lawrence Erlbaum Associates, 1977. (b)

Meyer, B. J. F.; Brandt, D. M.; & Bluth, G. J. Use of top-level structure in text: Key for reading comprehension of ninth-grade students. *Reading Research Quarterly,* 1980, *16,* 72–103.

Mikita, K. The rarity of reading disability in Japanese children. In D. Gunderson (Ed.), *Language and Reading.* Washington, D.C.: Center for Applied Linguistics, 1970.

Miller, G. A. A psychological method to investigate verbal concepts. *Journal of Mathematical Psychology,* 1969, *6,* 169–191.

Miller, G. A. Lexical meaning. In J. Kavanaugh & W. Strange

(Eds.), *Speech and Language in the Laboratory, School, and Clinic.* Cambridge, Mass.: MIT Press, 1978.

Miller, J. R., & Kintsch, W. Readability and recall of short prose passages: A theoretical analysis. *Journal of Experimental Psychology: Human Learning and Memory,* 1980, *6,* 335–354.

Morales, A. P. The literacy campaign in Cuba. *Harvard Educational Review,* 1981, *51,* 31–39.

Mosenthal, P.; Walmsley, S.; & Allington, R. Word recognition reconsidered: Toward a multi-context model. *Visible Language,* 1978, *12,* 450–467.

Muller, D. Phonic blending and transfer of letter-training to word-reading in children. *Journal of Reading Behavior,* 1972–1973, *5,* 212–217.

Murray, F. Implications of Piaget's theory for reading instruction. In S. J. Samuels (Ed.), *What Research Has to Say about Reading Instruction.* Newark, Del.: International Reading Association, 1978.

National Assessment of Educational Progress. *NAEP Newsletter,* 1981, *14*(1), 1–2.

Nelson, K. The syntagmatic-paradigmatic shift revisited. *Psychological Bulletin,* 1977, *84,* 93–119.

Nelson, K. Semantic development and the development of semantic memory. In K. E. Nelson (Ed.), *Children's Language* (Vol. 1). New York: Gardner Press, 1978.

Nelson, K., & Nelson, K. E. Cognitive pendulums and their linguistic realization. In K. E. Nelson (Ed.), *Children's Language* (Vol. 1). New York: Gardner Press, 1978.

Nelson, K. E., & Kosslyn, S. Semantic retrieval in children and adults. *Developmental Psychology,* 1975, *11,* 807–813.

Newcomer, P., & Hammill, D. D. ITPA and academic achievement: A survey. *Reading Teacher,* 1975, *28,* 731–741.

Nurss, J. R. Assessment of readiness. In T. G. Waller & G. E. MacKinnon (Eds.), *Reading Research: Advances in Theory and Practice* (Vol. 1). New York: Academic Press, 1979.

O'Rourke, J. P. *Toward a Science of Vocabulary Development.* The Hague: Mouton, 1974.

Otto, W. Design for developing comprehension skills. In J. T. Guthrie (Ed.), *Cognition, Curriculum, and Comprehension.* Newark, Del.: International Reading Association, 1977.

Otto, W., & Askov, E. Wisconsin design for reading skill development. In H. A. Klein (Ed.), *The Quest for Competency in Teaching Reading.* Newark, Del.: International Reading Association, 1972.

Otto, W.; Barrett, T. C.; & Koenke, K. Assessment of children's statements of the main idea in reading. In J. A. Figuerel (Ed.), *Reading and Realism.* Newark, Del.: International Reading Association, 1969.

Otto, W., & Koenke, K. *Scaling Children's Statements of Main Idea in Reading* (Working Paper No. 31). Madison: University of Wisconsin, Wisconsin Research and Development Center for Cognitive Learning, 1970.

Pany, D., & Jenkins, J. R. *Learning Word Meanings: A Comparison of Instructional Procedures and Effects on Measures of Reading Comprehension with Learning Disabled Students* (Tech. Rep. No. 25). Urbana-Champaign: University of Illinois Center for the Study of Reading, 1977. (ERIC Document Reproduction Service No. ED 136 237)

Pearson, P. D. The effects of grammatical complexity on children's comprehension, recall, and conception of certain semantic relations. *Reading Research Quarterly,* 1974–1975, *10,* 155–192.

Pearson, P. D. Some practical applications of a psycholinguistic model of reading. In S. J. Samuels (Ed.), *What Research Has*

to Say about Reading Instruction. Newark, Del.: International Reading Association, 1978.

Peck, C. V. N., & Kling, M. Adult literacy in the seventies: Its definition and measurement. *Journal of Reading,* 1977, *21,* 677–682.

Perfetti, C., & Hogaboam, T. The relationship between single-word decoding and comprehension skill. *Journal of Educational Psychology,* 1975, *67,* 461–469.

Perfetti, C., & Lesgold, A. M. Coding and comprehension in skilled reading and implications for reading instruction. In L. Resnick & P. Weaver (Eds.), *Theory and Practice of Early Reading* (Vol. 1). Hillsdale, N.J.: Lawrence Erlbaum Associates, 1979.

Peterson, P. Direct instruction reconsidered. In P. Peterson & H. Walberg (Eds.), *Research on Teaching: Concepts, Findings, and Implications.* Berkeley, Calif.: McCutchan, 1979.

Petrey, S. Word associations and the development of lexical memory. *Cognition,* 1977, *5,* 57–71.

Petty, W.; Herold, C.; & Stoll, E. *The State of the Knowledge about the Teaching of Vocabulary* (Cooperative Research Project No. 3128). Champaign, Ill.: National Council of Teachers of English, 1968.

Pflaum, S.; Walberg, H.; Karegianes, M. L.; & Rasher, S. P. Reading instruction: A quantitative analysis. *Educational Researcher,* 1980, *9,* 12–18.

Pflaum-Connor, S. (Ed.). *Aspects of Reading Education.* Berkeley, Calif.: McCutchan, 1978.

Piestrup, A. M. Black dialect interference and accommodation of reading instruction in first grade. *Monographs of the Language Behavior Research Laboratory* (University of California at Berkeley), 1974, *4.*

Popp, H. M. Current practices in the teaching of beginning reading. In J. B. Carroll & J. S. Chall (Eds.), *Toward a Literate Society.* New York: McGraw-Hill, 1975.

Popp, H. M. Selecting reading instruction for high-risk children: A theoretical approach. *Bulletin of the Orton Society,* 1978, *28,* 15–42.

Popp, H. M., & Lieberman, M. *A Study of the Relationship of Student Achievement to Components of Reading Programs and Environmental Characteristics* (Final Report), Contract No. 400-75-0064. Cambridge, Mass.: Harvard Graduate School of Education, May 1977.

Quealy, R. J. Senior high school students' use of contextual cues in reading. *Reading Research Quarterly,* 1969, *4,* 513–533.

Rayner, K. Eye movements in reading and information processing. *Psychological Bulletin,* 1978, *85,* 618–660.

Rayner, K. Eye movement and the perceptual span in reading. In F. J. Pirozzolo & M. C. Wittrock (Eds.), *Neuropsychological and Cognitive Processes in Reading.* New York: Academic Press, 1981.

Read, C. Preschool children's knowledge of English phonology. *Harvard Educational Review,* 1971, *41,* 1–34.

Reber, A. S., & Scarborough, D. L. *Toward a Psychology of Reading.* Hillsdale, N.J.: Lawrence Erlbaum Associates, 1977.

Reder, L. M. The role of elaboration in the comprehension and retention of prose: A critical review. *Review of Educational Research,* 1980, *50,* 5–53.

Resnick, D. P., & Resnick, L. B. The nature of literacy: An historical exploration. *Harvard Educational Review,* 1977, *47,* 370–385.

Resnick, L. B., & Weaver, P. A. (Eds.). *Theory and Practice of Early Reading* (Vols. 1–3). Hillsdale, N.J.: Lawrence Erlbaum Associates, 1979.

Richardson, E.; Benedetto, B.; Christ, A.; & Press, M. Relationship of auditory and visual skills to reading retardation. *Journal of Learning Disabilities*, 1980, *13*, 77–82.

Rist, R. Student social class and teacher expectation. *Harvard Educational Review*, 1970, *40*, 411–451.

Robinson, H. M. Perceptual training: Does it result in reading improvement? In R. C. Aukerman (Ed.), *Some Persistent Questions about Beginning Reading*. Newark, Del.: International Reading Association, 1972.

Roit, M. L. *A Re-evaluation of a Multiple-syndrome Theory of Dyslexia*. Unpublished qualifying paper, Harvard University, 1977.

Roit, M. L. *Syntactic Development in Normals and Dyslexics: An Empirical Examination of Two Theoretical Explanations of Dyslexia*. Unpublished doctoral dissertation, Harvard University, 1980.

Rosenshine, B. Recent research on teaching behaviors and student achievement. *Journal of Teacher Education*, 1976, *27*, 61–64.

Rosenshine, B. Content, time, and direct instruction. In P. Peterson & H. Walberg (Eds.), *Research on Teaching: Concepts, Findings, and Implications*. Berkeley, Calif.: McCutchan, 1979.

Rosinski, R., & Wheeler, K. Children's use of orthographic structure in word discrimination. *Psychonomic Science*, 1972, *26*, 97–98.

Rosner, J. *Phonic Analysis Training and Beginning Reading Skills*. Pittsburgh: University of Pittsburgh, Learning Research and Development Center, 1971.

Rosner, J. Auditory analysis training with preschoolers. *Reading Teacher*, 1974, *24*, 379–384.

Rosner, J., & Simon, D. The auditory analysis test: An initial report. *Journal of Learning Disabilities*, 1971, *4*, 384–392.

Ross, A. O. *Psychological Aspects of Learning Disabilities and Reading Disorders*. New York: McGraw-Hill, 1976.

Rothkopf, E. Z. Structural text features and the control of processes in learning from text. In J. B. Carroll & R. O. Freedle (Eds.), *Language Comprehension and the Acquisition of Knowledge*. Washington, D.C.: Winston, 1972.

Rothkopf, E. Z., & Bisbicos, E. Selective facilitative effects of interspersed questions on learning from written material. *Journal of Educational Psychology*, 1967, *58*, 56–61.

Rothkopf, E. Z., & Kaplan, R. Exploration of the effect of density of instructional objectives on learning from text. *Journal of Educational Psychology*, 1972, *63*, 309–313.

Rozin, P., & Gleitman, L. The structure and acquisition of reading, II. In A. S. Reber & D. L. Scarborough (Eds.), *Toward a Psychology of Reading*. Hillsdale, N.J.: Lawrence Erlbaum Associates, 1977, pp. 55–141.

Rubenstein, H.; Lewis, S. S.; & Rubenstein, M. A. Evidence for phonemic recoding in visual word recognition. *Journal of Verbal Learning and Verbal Behavior*, 1971, *10*, 645–657.

Rubin, A. D. A theoretical taxonomy of the differences between oral and written language. In R. J. Spiro, B. C. Bruce, & W. F. Brewer (Eds.), *Theoretical Issues in Reading Comprehension*. Hillsdale, N.J.: Lawrence Erlbaum Associates, 1980.

Rumelhart, D. E. Notes on a schema for stories. In D. G. Bobrow & A. M. Collins (Eds.), *Representation and Understanding: Studies in Cognitive Science*. New York: Academic Press, 1975.

Rumelhart, D. E. Toward an interactive model of reading. In S. Dornic (Ed.), *Attention and Performance VI*. Hillsdale, N.J.: Lawrence Erlbaum Associates, 1977. (a)

Rumelhart, D. E. Understanding and summarizing brief stories.

In D. LaBerge & S. J. Samuels (Eds.), *Basic Processes in Reading: Perception and Comprehension*. Hillsdale, N.J.: Lawrence Erlbaum Associates, 1977. (b)

Rumelhart, D. E.; Lindsay, P.; & Norman, D. A process model for long-term memory. In E. Tulving & W. Donaldson (Eds.), *Organization of Memory*. New York: Academic Press, 1972.

Rumelhart, D. E., & Ortony, A. The representation of knowledge in memory. In R. C. Anderson, R. J. Spiro, & W. Montague (Eds.), *Schooling and the Acquisition of Knowledge*. Hillsdale, N.J.: Lawrence Erlbaum Associates, 1977.

Russell, D. H., & Saadeh, I. Q. Qualitative levels in children's vocabularies. *Journal of Educational Psychology*, 1962, *53*, 170–174.

Rutter, M.; Maughan, B.; Mortimore, P.; Ouston, J.; & Smith, A. *Fifteen Thousand Hours: Secondary Schools and Their Effects on Children*. Cambridge, Mass.: Harvard University Press, 1979.

Ryan, T. A., & Furlong, W. Literacy programs in industry, the armed forces, and penal institutions. In J. B. Carroll & J. S. Chall (Eds.), *Toward a Literate Society*. New York: McGraw-Hill, 1975.

Samuels, S. J. The effect of letter name knowledge on learning to read. *American Educational Research Journal*, 1972, *9*, 65–74.

Samuels, S. J. Hierarchical subskills in the reading acquisition process. In J. T. Guthrie (Ed.), *Aspects of Reading Acquisition*. Baltimore: Johns Hopkins University Press, 1976.

Samuels, S. J., & Eisenberg, P. A framework for understanding the reading process. In F. J. Pirozzolo & M. C. Wittrock (Eds.), *Neuropsychological and Cognitive Processes in Reading*. New York: Academic Press, 1981.

Samuels, S. J.; LaBerge, D.; & Bremer, C. D. Units of word recognition: Evidence for developmental changes. *Journal of Verbal Learning and Verbal Behavior*, 1978, *17*, 715–720.

Samuels, S. J., & Schacter, S. W. Controversial issues in beginning reading instruction: Meaning versus subskill emphasis. In S. Pflaum-Connor (Ed.), *Aspects of Reading Education*. Berkeley, Calif.: McCutchan, 1978.

Santa, C. M. Spelling patterns and the development of flexible word recognition strategies. *Reading Research Quarterly*, 1976–1977, *12*, 125–144.

Satz, P., & Morris, R. Learning disabilities subtypes: A review. In F. J. Pirozzolo & M. C. Wittrock (Eds.), *Neuropsychological and Cognitive Processes in Reading*. New York: Academic Press, 1981.

Schallert, D. L. Improving memory for prose: The relationship between depth of processing and context. *Journal of Verbal Learning and Verbal Behavior*, 1976, *15*, 621–632.

Schallert, D. L.; Kleiman, G. M.; & Rubin, A. D. *Analysis of Differences between Oral and Written Language* (Tech. Rep. No. 29). Urbana-Champaign: University of Illinois Center for the Study of Reading, 1977. (ERIC Document Reproduction Service No. ED 144 035)

Schank, R. C., & Abelson, R. *Scripts, Plans, Goals, and Understanding*. Hillsdale, N.J.: Lawrence Erlbaum Associates, 1977.

Schneider, W., & Shiffrin, R. Automatic and controlled information processing in vision. In D. LaBerge & S. J. Samuels (Eds.), *Basic Processes in Reading: Perception and Comprehension*. Hillsdale, N.J.: Lawrence Erlbaum Associates, 1977.

Schvaneveldt, R.; Ackerman, B. P.; & Semlear, T. The effect of semantic context on children's word recognition. *Child Development*, 1977, *48*, 612–616.

Schwartz, R. M. Levels of processing: The strategic demands of reading comprehension. *Reading Research Quarterly*, 1980, *15*, 433–450.

Serwer, B. Linguistic support for a method of teaching beginning reading to black children. *Reading Research Quarterly*, 1969, *5*, 449–467.

Shankweiler, D., & Liberman, I. Y. Misreading: A search for cause. In J. Kavanaugh & I. Mattingly (Eds.), *Language by Ear and by Eye*. Cambridge, Mass.: MIT Press, 1972.

Shuy, R. The mismatch of child language and school language: Implications for beginning reading instruction. In L. B. Resnick & P. A. Weaver (Eds.), *Theory and Practice of Early Reading* (Vol. 1). Hillsdale, N.J.: Lawrence Erlbaum Associates, 1979.

Simons, H. D. Black dialect, reading interference, and classroom interaction. In L. B. Lesnick & P. A. Weaver (Eds.), *Theory and Practice of Early Reading* (Vol. 3). Hillsdale, N.J.: Lawrence Erlbaum Associates, 1979.

Singer, H. The SEER technique: A noncomputational procedure for quickly estimating readability levels. *Journal of Reading Behavior*, 1975, *7*, 255–267.

Singer, H. Research in reading that should make a difference in classroom instruction. In S. J. Samuels (Ed.), *What Research Has to Say about Reading Instruction*. Newark, Del.: International Reading Association, 1978.

Singer, H., & Ruddell, R. (Eds.). *Theoretical Models and Processes of Reading*. Newark, Del.: International Reading Association, 1976.

Slobody, L. *The Directed Reading Activity: A Theory and Research-based Foundation and Design*. Unpublished qualifying paper, Harvard University Graduate School of Education, 1981.

Smethurst, W. *A Review of the Literature on the Non-professional Teaching of Reading to Young Children outside Schools*. Unpublished qualifying paper, Harvard University Graduate School of Education, 1975.

Smiley, S. S.; Oakley, D. D.; Worthen, D.; Campione, J. C.; & Brown, A. L. Recall of thematically relevant material by adolescent good and poor readers as a function of written versus oral presentation. *Journal of Educational Psychology*, 1977, *69*, 381–387.

Smith, F. *Understanding Reading*. New York: Holt, Rinehart & Winston, 1971.

Smith, F. *Comprehension and Learning*. New York: Holt, Rinehart & Winston, 1975.

Smith, F. *Reading and Nonsense*, New York: Teachers College Press, 1978.

Smith, F. (Ed.). *Psycholinguistics and Reading*. New York: Holt, Rinehart & Winston, 1973.

Smith, F., & Holmes, D. L. The independence of letter, word, and meaning identification in reading. In F. Smith (Ed.), *Psycholinguistics and Reading*. New York: Holt, Rinehart & Winston, 1973.

Smith, F.; Lott, D.; & Cronnell, B. The effect of type size and case alternation on word identification. *American Journal of Psychology*, 1969, *82*, 248–253.

Smith, G. D.; Enright, G.; & Devirian, M. A national survey of learning and study skills programs. In G. H. McNinch & W. D. Miller (Eds.), *Reading: Convention and Inquiry: Twenty-fourth Yearbook of the National Reading Conference*, Clemson, S.C.: N.R.C., 1975.

Somervill, M. A. Dialect and reading: A review of alternative solutions. *Review of Educational Research*, 1975, *45*, 247–262.

Spache, G. D. The Spache readability formula. In G. D. Spache (Ed.), *Good Reading for Poor Readers*. Champaign, Ill.: Garrard, 1974.

Spearitt, D. Identification of subskills of reading comprehension by maximum likelihood factor analysis. *Reading Research Quarterly*, 1972, *8*, 93–111.

Spearitt, D. Relationships among four communications skills during the school years. In W. J. Crocker (Ed.), *Developing Oral Communication Competence*. Armidale, N.H.: University of New England, 1980.

Spiro, R. J. Remembering information from text: Theoretical and empirical issues concerning the "State of Schema" reconstruction hypothesis. In R. Anderson, R. Spiro, & W. Montague (Eds.), *Schooling and the Acquisition of Knowledge*. Hillsdale, N.J.: Lawrence Erlbaum Associates, 1977.

Spiro, R. J.; Bruce, B.; & Brewer, W. *Theoretical Issues in Reading Comprehension*. Hillsdale, N.J.: Lawrence Erlbaum Associates, 1980.

Spring, C., & Capps, C. Encoding speed, rehearsal, and probed recall of learning disabled boys. *Journal of Educational Psychology*, 1974, *66*, 780–786.

Stahl, S. A. *Words, Words, Words: A Psychosemantic Framework for Evaluating Vocabulary Instruction*. Unpublished qualifying paper, Harvard University Graduate School of Education, 1980.

Stallings, J. Implementation and child effects of teaching practices in Follow Through classrooms. *Monographs of the Society for Research in Child Development*, 1975, *40*(163 No. 7–8).

Stanovich, K. E. Toward an interactive-compensatory model of individual differences in the development of reading fluency. *Reading Research Quarterly*, 1980, *16*, 32–71.

Steffensen, M. S.; Joag-Dev, C.; & Anderson, R. C. A cross-cultural perspective on reading comprehension. *Reading Research Quarterly*, 1979, *15*, 10–29.

Stein, N., & Glenn, C. An analysis of story comprehension in elementary school children. In R. O. Freedle (Ed.), *New Directions in Discourse Processing* (Vol. 2). Norwood, N.J.: Ablex, 1979.

Steinberg, E., & Anderson, R. C. Hierarchical semantic organization in six-year-olds. *Journal of Experimental Child Psychology*, 1975, *19*, 544–553.

Sticht, T. G. Applications of the audread model to reading evaluation and instruction. In L. B. Resnick & P. A. Weaver (Eds.), *Theory and Practice of Early Reading* (Vol. 1). Hillsdale, N.J.: Lawrence Erlbaum Associates, 1979.

Sticht, T. G. (Ed.). *Reading for Working*. Alexandria, Va.: Human Resources Research Organization, 1975.

Sticht, T. G.; Beck, L. T.; Hauke, R. N.; Kleiman, G. M.; & James, J. H. *Auding and Reading: A Developmental Model*. Alexandria, Va.: Human Resources Research Organization, 1974.

Stotsky, S. L. *Toward a More Systematic Development of Children's Reading Vocabulary in Developmental Reading Programs in the Middle to Upper Elementary Grades*. Unpublished Ed.D. thesis, Harvard University Graduate School of Education, 1976.

Talmadge, H., & Walberg, H. J. Naturalistic, decision-oriented evaluation of a district reading program. *Journal of Reading Behavior*, 1978, *10*, 185–195.

Thorndike, R. L. *Reading Comprehension Education in Fifteen Countries: International Studies in Evaluation III*. Stockholm: Almqvist & Wiksell, 1973.

Thorndike, R. L. Reading as reasoning. *Reading Research Quarterly*, 1973–1974, *9*, 137–147.

Thorndyke, P. W. Cognitive structures in comprehension and

memory of narrative discourse. *Cognitive Psychology*, 1977, *9*, 77–110.

Tierney, R. J.; Bridge, C.; & Cera, M. J. The discourse processing operations of children. *Reading Research Quarterly*, 1978–1979, *14*, 539–573.

Tompkins, C. *Young Children's Awareness of Sound Segments in Spoken Language as a Factor in Learning to Read*. Unpublished qualifying paper, Harvard University Graduate School of Education, 1975.

Torrey, J. W. Reading that comes naturally: The early reader. In T. G. Waller & G. E. MacKinnon (Eds.), *Reading Research: Advances in Theory and Practice* (Vol. 1). New York: Academic Press, 1979.

Tuinman, J. J. Determining the passage dependency of comprehension questions in five major tests. *Reading Research Quarterly*, 1973–1974, *9*, 207–224.

Tuinman, J. J. Criterion-referenced measurement in a norm-referenced context. In S. J. Samuels (Ed.), *What Research Has to Say about Reading Instruction*. Newark, Del.: International Reading Association, 1978.

Tuinman, J. J., & Brady, M. E. How does vocabulary account for variance on reading comprehension tests? A preliminary instructional analysis. In P. Nacke (Ed.), *Twenty-third National Reading Conference Yearbook*, 1974.

Vacca, R. T. A study of holistic and subskill instructional approaches to reading comprehension. *Journal of Reading*, 1980, *23*, 512–518.

van Dijk, T. A. Macro-structures and cognition. In M. Just & P. Carpenter (Eds.), *Cognitive Processes in Comprehension*. Hillsdale, N.J.: Lawrence Erlbaum Associates, 1977.

Vellutino, F. R. Alternative conceptualizations of dyslexia: Evidence in support of a verbal deficit hypothesis. *Harvard Educational Review*, 1977, *47*, 334–354.

Vellutino, F. R. *Dyslexia: Theory and Research*. Cambridge, Mass.: MIT Press, 1979.

Venezky, R. L. *The Structure of English Orthography*. The Hague: Mouton, 1970.

Venezky, R. L. The curious role of letter names in reading instruction. *Visible Language*, 1975, *9*, 7–23.

Venezky, R. L. *Theoretical and Experimental Bases for Teaching Reading*. The Hague: Mouton, 1976.

Venezky, R. L. Two approaches to reading assessment: A comparison of apples and oranges. In S. Pflaum-Connor (Ed.), *Aspects of Reading Education*. Berkeley, Calif.: McCutchan, 1978.

Venezky, R. L., & Massaro, D. W. The role of orthographic regularity in word recognition. In L. B. Resnick & P. A. Weaver (Eds.), *Theory and Practice of Early Reading* (Vol. 1). Hillsdale, N.J.: Lawrence Erlbaum Associates, 1979.

Vernon, M. D. Varieties of deficiency in the reading processes. *Harvard Educational Review*, 1977, *47*, 396–410.

Vogel, S. A. Syntactic abilities in normal and dyslexic children. *Journal of Learning Disabilities*, 1974, *7*, 103–108.

Vogel, S. A. *Syntactic Abilities in Normal and Dyslexic Children*. Baltimore: University Park Press, 1975.

Wallach, M. A., & Wallach, L. *Teaching All Children to Read*. Chicago: University of Chicago Press, 1976.

Wallach, M. A., & Wallach, L. Helping disadvantaged children learn to read by teaching them phoneme identification skills. In L. B. Resnick & P. A. Weaver (Eds.), *Theory and Practice of Early Reading* (Vol. 3). Hillsdale, N.J.: Lawrence Erlbaum Associates, 1979.

Waller, T. G. *Think First, Read Later!* Newark, Del.: International Reading Association, 1977.

Wanat, S. F. Reading readiness. *Visible Language*, 1976, *10*, 101–127.

Watts, G. H., & Anderson, R. C. Effects of three types of inserted questions on learning from prose. *Journal of Educational Psychology*, 1971, *62*, 387–394.

Weaver, P. A. *Research within Reach*. St. Louis: CEMREL, 1978.

Weaver, P. A. Improving reading comprehension: Effects of sentence organization instruction. *Reading Research Quarterly*, 1979, *15*, 129–146.

Weaver, P. A., & Dickinson, D. Scratching below the surface structure: Exploring the usefulness of story grammars. *Discourse Processes*, in press.

Weaver, W. W. *Toward a Psychology of Reading and Language*. Athens: University of Georgia Press, 1977.

Weber, G. *Inner City Children Can Be Taught to Read*. Washington, D.C.: Council for Basic Education, 1971.

Weber, R. M. First graders' use of grammatical context in reading. In H. Levin & J. Williams (Eds.), *Basic Studies in Reading*. New York: Basic Books, 1970.

Weber, R. M. Adult illiteracy in the United States. In J. B. Carroll & J. S. Chall (Eds.), *Toward a Literate Society*. New York: McGraw-Hill, 1975.

Werner, H., & Kaplan, E. Development of word meaning through verbal context: An experimental study. *Journal of Psychology*, 1950, *29*, 251–257.

Werner, H., & Kaplan, E. The acquisition of word meanings: A developmental study. *Monographs for the Society for Research in Child Development*, 1952, *15*(Serial No. 1).

Wiig, E. H., & Fleischmann, N. Prepositional phrases, pronominalization, reflexivization, and relativization in the language of learning disabled college students. *Journal of Learning Disabilities*, 1980, *13*, 571–579.

Wiig, E. H.; Lapointe, C.; & Semel, E. M. Relationships among language-processing and production abilities of learning disabled students. *Journal of Learning Disabilities*, 1977, *10*, 38–45.

Wiig, E. H., & Semel, E. M. *Language Disabilities in Children and Adolescents*. Columbus, Ohio: Merrill, 1976.

Williams, J. Reading instruction today. *American Psychologist*, 1979, *34*, 917–922.

Wirtz, W. *On Further Examination: Report of the Advisory Panel on the Scholastic Aptitude Test Score Decline*. Princeton, N.J.: College Board Publications, 1977.

Wolf, M. *The Relationship of Disorder of Word-finding and Reading in Children and Aphasics*. Unpublished doctoral dissertation, Harvard University, 1979.

Yap, K. O. Vocabulary: Building blocks of comprehension. *Journal of Reading Behavior*, 1979, *11*, 49–59.

RECREATION

Until recently research in recreation has been fragmentary and superficial. During the past two decades, however, with the establishment in the United States and Canada of over 350 college and university curricula in recreation, parks, and leisure studies (Stein & Henkel, 1979), a substantial body of both theoretical and applied research in recreation and leisure has emerged.

Theoretical research studies have examined the historical background of recreation and leisure, the psychological and anthropological aspects of play, the sociology of leisure, and the economic outcomes of recreational programs and participation. Applied research has analyzed the role of public, voluntary, commercial, and other types of leisure-service agencies, as well as more specialized aspects of recreation management, such as fiscal planning, facilities development, programming, and leadership. Other concerns, including the needs of the physically or mentally disabled, travel and tourism, or education for leisure, have also received considerable attention.

Historical Development. Dulles (1965) carried out a detailed historical analysis of recreation participation in the United States, describing various forms of play from the early Colonial period through World War II. Rainwater (1922), Doell and Fitzgerald (1954), and Knapp and Hartsoe (1980) documented the growth of the public recreation and park movement and the evolution of the National Recreation Association, later to become the National Recreation and Park Association, the leading professional and service organization in this field. Highlights of this development were also provided in a chronology of major events in recreation and parks prepared by Van Doren and Hodges (1975).

Several authors have studied the history of recreation in earlier centuries and on the international scene, including Weir (1937), Kraus (1978), Chubb and Chubb (1981), and Shivers (1981). Analyzing the influence of government, religion, economic development, and other social factors on leisure, they depict recreation as far more than children's play or light-hearted amusement. Instead it is seen as an important aspect of social life, involving significant community goals and values.

Conceptual Analysis. In addition to examining recreation as a form of social institution or government responsibility, a number of authors have reviewed it as a form of human experience. Sapora and Mitchell (1961) and Ellis (1973) have critically analyzed the traditional theories of play formulated by others. During the initial stages of development of the recreation movement in the United States, Lee (1915), Gulick (1920), and Nash (1953) formulated significant philosophies of play as an important social concern and form of community service. Recreation was generally defined by such authors as active, socially desirable, and voluntarily chosen leisure activity or experience.

More recently such authors as Gray and Greben (1974), Godbey (1981), and Murphy (1981) have conceptualized recreation as a form of human experience, with emphasis on its emotional or psychological outcomes for participants, rather than as the act of engaging in recreation itself. Recent writings depict recreation and leisure as a humanistic and holistic sphere of involvement, with important potential for self-actualization.

Behaviorial Sciences. A number of leading psychologists, including Menninger (1948), Sutton-Smith & Roberts (1962), Millar (1968), and Bruner (1975), have studied play.

They depict it primarily as a form of developmental experience and social acculturation for children and youth, but also regard it as closely linked to creativity, effective learning, and mental health and social adjustment. Ellis (1973) in particular has critically reviewed the traditional theories of play and identified two newer psychological theories of play as "competence-effectance" (the need to demonstrate personal mastery) and "stimulus-arousal" (seeking challenge, excitement, or sensation through play).

Norbeck (1971), an anthropologist, concluded that play was both a biological and sociocultural phenomenon and a form of universal human behavior with significant personal and social functions that have not been sufficiently recognized in Western society. Keesing (see Kraus, 1978, pp. 25–26) presented an analysis of the functions of play in primitive cultures, including the following: pleasurable or hedonistic, relaxing or energy-restorative, integrative or socially cohesive, therapeutic or sublimative, creative or self-expressive, communicative, and educative.

Caillois (1961) extensively analyzed play and games in various primitive societies and defined several widely found categories. Elements such as gambling, competition, make-believe, or seeking physical sensations comparable to vertigo appear to be cultural universals. Huizinga (1960), a social historian, has documented the thesis that play is a significant element underlying many important aspects of human culture, such as religion, business, law, or even the practice of warfare. Recent collections of anthropological studies of play, games, sports, and other pastimes have been edited by Lancy and Tindall (1976) and Salter (1977).

Sociological Research. Several major sociologists both in western Europe and in the Soviet bloc have carried out large-scale studies of leisure. Among these, Szalai (1966) and Dumazedier (1975) have been preeminent in conceptualizing the meaning of leisure in industrial society and in carrying out time-use studies in a broad sampling of European countries. An American sociologist, Kaplan (1975), has developed a number of significant models of leisure, placing it within a holistic framework of human existence.

Several American sociologists, such as Lynd and Lynd (1929), Warner and Lunt (1941), and Hollingshead (1961), saw recreation and leisure as a significant component in their studies of American communities and usually devoted separate chapters to it in their reports. A number of other investigators carried out more sharply focused studies of leisure participation in relation to such socioeconomic variables as occupation, age, status, or prestige levels. These included White (1955), Clarke (1956), Dubin (1956), Lundberg, Komarovsky, and McInerney (1958), and Gerstl (1963). Larrabee and Meyersohn (1958) edited a major work summing up such studies in the late 1950s.

In the 1960s, sociological research in recreation and leisure moved away from the correlation of leisure pursuits with work-related or other demographic variables into such areas as attitudes and motivations for participation or more complex kinds of social interactions among participants. Sutton-Smith and Roberts (1962) and Lamme and Lamme (1979) examined patterns of children's play behavior, and Magill and Ash (1979) studied the academic, psychosocial, and motor characteristics of participants and nonparticipants in children's sports. Yoesting and Burkhead (1973) reported on the relationship between childhood recreation experience and later adult leisure involvements. Neulinger and Breit (1969) studied the full spectrum of adult attitude dimensions of leisure. Kelly (1974) analyzed leisure socialization and developed a typology of leisure in relation to work and other social constraints and expectations (1978).

A number of research studies by sociologists and recreation and sports analysts examined the influence of racial or ethnic identity on leisure attitudes and involvements. Several studies, including those by Frazier (1962), Myrdal (1962), Short and Strodtbeck (1965), and Kraus (1968) analyzed participation by American blacks in community recreation activities. Studies by Edwards (1969) and Loy (1975) dealt with participation by blacks in amateur and professional sports. Although primary emphasis has been on blacks, other minorities have been studied as well; Jackson (1973) compared the leisure-related attitudes of Mexican Americans and Anglos on two occupational levels.

Sexual identification has also been an important focus of many recent studies, because of the influence of the feminist movement and the drive for sex equality in many areas of daily life. Theobald (1976) carried out an exhaustive study of the historical and present-day involvement of women as participants and professional workers in recreation, an issue also studied by Dunn (1977). The question of sex-role orientation and choice of leisure involvements was explored by Gentry and Doering (1979), who examined participation in activities that were perceived as masculine, feminine, or androgynous, in relation to the degree of masculinity or femininity of participants. Similarly Sage and Loudermilk (1979) studied the effects of role conflicts and social stigmas on female athletes who engaged in activities perceived as either traditional and acceptable for women or as nontraditional and disapproved.

In a related area, researchers have examined patterns of leisure involvement in relation to family life. Bell and Healey (1973) studied family leisure patterns within a framework of traditional and nontraditional family structures. Orthner (1976) examined a large sample of married couples to determine the relationship among leisure choices, communication, task-sharing, and other aspects of married life. West and Merriam (1970) studied the relationship between shared family outdoor recreation interests and family cohesiveness in general.

Still other sociological studies have examined motivations or social grouping within specific forms of leisure activity. Lentnek, Van Doren, and Trail (1969) and Field and O'Leary (1973) studied spatial behavior and social grouping patterns in varied forms of water-based recreation. Knopp and Tyger (1973) examined two popula-

tions—snowmobilers and cross-country skiers—with respect to their attitudes toward environmental issues and policies. Roberts, Koenig, and Stark (1969) analyzed craft shows as a form of competition.

As motivations, values, and the psychological antecedents and outcomes of participation have become more important subjects for research, a number of investigators have focused on what has been termed the social psychology of leisure. Crandall (1980), Iso-Ahola (1980), Kelly (1978), and Neulinger (1981) have contributed significantly to this approach.

Economic Research. A growing body of research has examined outdoor recreation in particular, as an important element in the economic structure of modern society. Several writers, including Wilensky (1963), have described the impact of economic growth on free time, with implications for leisure involvement. Clawson and Knetsch (1960) were among the first to study the economics of outdoor recreation systematically.

Numerous other studies have dealt with specific aspects of recreation that have economic significance. The Rockefeller Panel Report (1965), Baumol and Bowen (1966), and Kando (1980) examined the economic status of the performing arts and related cultural programs in America. Crompton and Van Doren (1976) studied recent trends in amusement parks and theme parks, as a major aspect of recreational travel. Research studies by Shafer (1975), Van Doren (1975), Stottlemeyer (1975), and Andresen (1975) have focused on the impact of recreation on the natural environment, and on measuring the carrying capacity of outdoor recreation resources, which are both critical issues for government or commercial recreation planners and developers. Still other research studies—by Cheung (1972), James, Sanford, and Searcy (1972), Knopp (1974), Gamble (1975), and McAllister and Klett (1976)—deal with the origins of recreation visitors, environmental factors that influence recreation behavior, park visit models, and market segmentation, all important concerns for recreation planners and managers. Epperson (1977) has analyzed the field of commercial recreational enterprise in terms of its employment potential and economic impact.

Research in Management Practices. A considerable body of literature concerns the administration and supervision of recreation and park agencies or departments. Textbooks by Hjelte and Shivers (1972), Sessoms, Meyer, and Brightbill (1975), Reynolds and Hormachea (1976), Edginton and Williams (1978), Kraus and Curtis (1977), Farrell and Lundegren (1978), Godbey (1978), Jubenville (1978), Graham and Klar (1979), Howard and Crompton (1980), Lutzen (1980), and Rodney and Toalson (1981) focus on practical aspects of recreation and park management but also draw heavily on past research in this field.

City and county recreation departments or other municipal agencies or departments may also commission studies dealing with recreation and park issues or needs. For example, most major cities or county governments periodically sponsor planning studies in which recreation and parks are examined either as a major concern or as part of overall planning. In some cases such research studies are in direct response to social unrest or community demands; for example, both Los Angeles (Staley, 1966) and New York City (Community Council of Greater New York, 1963) carried out detailed studies of their recreation and park facilities and programs during the 1960s in response to demand by inner-city, minority-group populations for improved leisure opportunities. In other cases local organizations or professional societies carry out studies related to facilities management, vandalism, barrier-free design, fees and charges, and similar problems.

Professional Development. In the United States more than in any other country, recreation service has emerged as a career field, staffed by professionals with a background of specialized training. Sessoms, Meyer, and Brightbill (1975), Kraus (1978), and Carlson et al. (1979) have examined the recreation profession and evaluated its current level of development.

Over a period of years, Stein and later Stein and Henkel (1979) carried out surveys of the growing number of specialized college and university curricula in recreation and parks. A number of studies have been made of specific aspects of recreation and park education. In 1973 the American Association for Health, Physical Education and Recreation and the U.S. Bureau of Education for the Handicapped (J. Stein, 1973) developed and published recommendations for preparing individuals to work with the handicapped in physical education and recreation programs. Later Anderson and Stewart (1980) extensively studied such curricula throughout the United States. Other researchers have examined the background of professional employees in public recreation and park departments (Henkel & Godbey, 1977) and the career opportunities for women in leisure service agencies (Dunn, 1977). Other reports of career trends in such areas as commercial and voluntary agency recreation, industrial concerns, campus recreation, and residential settings (Dunn, 1979) have appeared in special issues of *Leisure Today,* published by the American Association for Leisure and Recreation.

Therapeutic Recreation Service. The provision of special recreation programs for the physically or mentally handicapped or those with other forms of disability, known today as therapeutic recreation service, has been the subject of considerable research. An early national study in this field by Silson, Cohen, and Hill (1959) examined various types of hospital recreation programs and the personnel who conducted them. Later studies of recreation programs for disabled children in both institutional and community settings were carried out by Williams (1970) and Berryman, Logan, and Lander (1971). Other studies of therapeutic recreation service on state or regional levels, sometimes in such special settings as psychiatric hospitals, nursing homes, or summer camps, have been done by Hayes (1969), Peters and Verhoven (1970), Kraus (1973), Kelley (1974), Buchan (1975), and Austin, Peterson, and Peccarelli (1978).

Numerous investigators have focused on the needs and interests of special populations, including Menninger (1948), Sessoms and Oakley (1969), Babow and Simkin (1971), Bigelow (1971), Nigro (1973), Morgan and Godbey (1978), McAvoy (1979), and Lewko and Crandall (1980). Others have done research on the nature of special programs for the disabled and their outcomes, including Avedon and Arje (1966), Endres (1971), Mitchell (1971), Lundegren (1974, 1975), Leanse (1975), Salter and Salter (1975), Sheridan (1976), Gibson (1979), and Kaplan (1979).

Education for Leisure. A continuing concern for many educators has been the need to provide education for leisure in American schools and colleges. This was first expressed as an important priority of American education in the *Cardinal Principles of Secondary Education* (U.S. Department of Interior, 1918). Later reports of the Educational Policies Commission (1946) confirmed leisure education as an important objective of schools and colleges. A historical review of this movement by Kraus (1964) included a national survey of the role of public school systems in sponsoring or cosponsoring community recreation programs in the early 1960s.

More recently Staley and Miller (1972), Mundy and Odum (1979), and Godbey (1981) have written on education for leisure, analyzing various philosophical approaches to this task. Supported by the Lilly Foundation, the National Recreation and Park Association sponsored a major curriculum development project in leisure education, coordinated by Odum and Lancaster (1977).

New Directions in Recreation Research. As indicated earlier, research efforts in recreation and leisure studies have expanded steadily over the past two decades, in both theoretical and applied areas of concern (van der Smissen, 1966). With the growing number of graduate recreation curricula in colleges and universities, thousands of theses and dissertations in recreation, leisure, camping, and outdoor education have been written. Van der Smissen and Joyce (1970) and van der Smissen (1979) have compiled extensive bibliographies of such studies. Other bibliographers of research in recreation and leisure have included Meyersohn (1969) and Crandall and Lewko (1976). Dunn (1980) has compiled abstracts of research papers presented at National Recreation and Park Congresses. Studies related to sport and physical education have been published by the Research Council of the American Alliance for Health, Physical Education, and Dance.

In general the highest level of support has been given to research on outdoor recreation, with substantial federal funding given to support such investigations. The report of the Outdoor Recreation Resources Review Commission (1962) and other national planning studies have emphasized the need for sound outdoor recreation research, and the National Academy of Sciences (1969) has made recommendations for new research directions in this area. Hundreds of outdoor recreation research studies dealing with resource planning, land and water management, and economic outcomes of tourism and travel have been reported in annual compilations by the Bureau of Outdoor Recreation.

Various authors, including Ver Lee (1966) and McCool and Schreyor (1977), have discussed the value of research in the management of recreation agencies and programs. McLellan (1980) analyzed the current status of recreation research as shown by articles appearing in the *Journal of Leisure Research,* showing the subjects most frequently studied and the academic affiliations of active researchers. Finally, Mobley (1980) identified an important concern of scholars in this field: to bridge the gap between researchers and practitioners, to help make research both more significant and a more effective means of improving management practices and guiding government policies, and also to help practitioners become more aware of the value of theoretical and applied research studies.

Richard G. Kraus

See also Environmental Education; Motor Skills Development; Physical Development; School Plant and Facilities.

REFERENCES

Adams, S. W. Segmentation of a recreational fishing market: A canonical analysis of fishing attributes and party composition. *Journal of Leisure Research,* 1979, *11*(2), 82–91.

Anderson, S., & Stewart, M. Therapeutic recreation education: 1979 survey. *Therapeutic Recreation Journal,* 1980, *14*(3), 4–10.

Andresen, J. W. Urban vegetation management research: Responses to intensifying human relations demands. In B. van der Smissen (Ed.), *Indicators of Change in the Recreation Environment: A National Research Symposium.* University Park: Pennsylvania State University, 1975.

Austin, D. R.; Peterson, J. A.; & Peccarelli, L. M. Status of services for special populations in park and recreation departments in the state of Indiana. *Therapeutic Recreation Journal,* 1978, *12*(1), 50–56.

Avedon, E. M. *Therapeutic Recreation Service: An Applied Behavioral Science Approach.* Englewood Cliffs, N.J.: Prentice-Hall, 1974.

Avedon, E. M., & Arje, F. *Socio-recreative Planning for the Retarded: A Handbook for Sponsoring Groups.* New York: Teachers College Press, 1966.

Babow, I., & Simkin, S. The leisure activities and social participation of mental patients prior to hospitalization. *Therapeutic Recreation Journal,* 1971, *5*(4), 161–167.

Baumol, W. J., and Bowen, W. G. *Performing Arts: The Economic Dilemma.* New York: The Twentieth Century Fund, 1966.

Bell, C., & Healey, C. The family and leisure. In M. A. Smith, S. Parker, & C. S. Smith (Eds.), *Leisure and Society in Britain.* London: Allen Lane, 1973.

Berryman, D. L., & Lefebvre, C. B. A computer-based system for comprehensive activity analysis and prescriptive recreation programming for disabled children and youth. In B. van der Smissen (Ed.), *Indicators of Change in the Recreation Environment: A National Research Symposium.* University Park: Pennsylvania State University, 1975.

Berryman, D. L.; Logan, A.; & Lander, D. *Enhancement of Recreation Service to Disabled Children.* New York: New York University, and U.S. Children's Bureau, 1971.

Bigelow, G. W. A comparison of active and passive recreational activities for psychotic patients. *Therapeutic Recreation Journal,* 1971, *5*(4), 145–151.

Bruner, J. Child development: Play is serious business. *Psychology Today,* January 1975, p. 83.

Buchan, S. C. Camping for the handicapped in selected camps in California. *Therapeutic Recreation Journal,* 1975, *9*(1), 38–41.

Caillois, R. *Man, Play, and Games.* London: Thames & Hudson, 1961.

Carlson, R. E.; MacLean, J. R.; Deppe, T. R.; & Peterson, J. A. *Recreation and Leisure: The Changing Scene.* Belmont, Calif.: Wadsworth, 1979.

Cheung, H. K. A day-use park visitations model. *Journal of Leisure Research,* 1972, *4*(2), 139–156.

Chubb, M., & Chubb, H. R. *One Third of Our Time: An Introduction to Recreation Behavior and Resources.* New York: Wiley, 1981.

Clarke, A. C. Leisure and levels of occupational prestige. *American Sociological Review,* 1956, *21,* 301–307.

Clawson, M., & Knetsch, J. *Economics of Outdoor Recreation.* Baltimore: Johns Hopkins University Press, 1960.

Community Council of Greater New York. *Comparative Recreation Needs and Services in New York Neighborhoods.* New York: The Council, 1963.

Compton, D. M., & Price, D. Individualizing your treatment program: A case study using LMIT. *Therapeutic Recreation Journal,* 1975, *9*(4), 127–134.

Crandall, R. Motivations for leisure. *Journal of Leisure Research,* 1980, *12*(1), 45–53.

Crandall, R., & Lewko, J. Leisure research, present and future: Who, what, where. *Journal of Leisure Research,* 1976, *8*(3), 150–159.

Crompton, J. L., & Van Doren, C. Amusement parks, theme parks, and municipal leisure services: Contrasts in adaptation in cultural change. *Journal of Physical Education and Recreation (Leisure Today),* October 1976, *47,* 18–22.

Doell, C. E., & Fitzgerald, G. B. *A Brief History of Parks and Recreation in the United States.* Chicago: Athletic Institute, 1954.

Dubin, R. Industrial workers' worlds. *Social Problems,* 1956, *3,* 131–140.

Dulles, F. R. *A History of Recreation: America Learns to Play.* New York: Appleton-Century-Crofts, 1965.

Dumazedier, J. *Sociology of Leisure.* Amsterdam: Elsevier, 1975.

Dunn, D. R. Women in recreation. *Parks and Recreation,* July 1977, *12,* 24–29.

Dunn, D. R. Leisure careers in an era of limits. *Journal of Physical Education,* April 1979, *50*(3), 35–38.

Dunn, D. R. *Abstracts of the 1980 Symposium on Leisure Research.* Washington, D.C.: National Recreation and Park Association, and University of Arizona, 1980.

Edginton, C. R., & Williams J. G. *Productive Management of Leisure Service Organizations: A Behavioral Approach.* New York: Wiley, 1978.

Educational Policies Commission. *Policies for Education in American Democracy.* Washington, D.C.: National Education Association, 1946.

Edwards, H. *The Revolt of the Black Athlete.* New York: Free Press, 1969.

Ellis, M. J. *Why People Play.* Englewood Cliffs, N.J.: Prentice-Hall, 1973.

Endres, R. Northern Minnesota therapeutic camp. *Journal of Health, Physical Education, and Recreation,* May 1971, *42*(5), 75–76.

Epperson, A. F. *Private and Commercial Recreation: A Text and Reference.* New York: Wiley, 1977.

Farrell, P., & Lundegren, H. M. *The Process of Recreation Programming.* New York: Wiley, 1978.

Field, D. R., & O'Leary, J. T. Social groups as a basis for assessing participation in selected water activities. *Journal of Leisure Research,* 1973, *5*(2), 16–25.

Frazier, E. F. *Black Bourgeoisie.* New York: Collier, 1962.

Gamble, H. B. Regional economic impacts from outdoor recreation. In B. van der Smissen (Ed.), *Indicators of Change in the Recreation Environment: A National Research Symposium.* University Park: Pennsylvania State University, 1975.

Gentry, J. W., & Doering, M. Sex roles orientation and leisure. *Journal of Leisure Research,* 1979, *11*(2), 102–111.

Gerstl, J. E. Leisure, taste, and occupational milieu. In E. O. Smigel (Ed.), *Work and Leisure: A Contemporary Social Problem.* New Haven, Conn.: College and University Press, 1963.

Gibson, P. M. Therapeutic aspects of wilderness programs: A comprehensive literature review. *Therapeutic Recreation Journal,* 1979, *13*(2), 21–33.

Godbey, G. *Recreation, Park, and Leisure Services: Foundations, Organization, Administration.* Philadelphia: Saunders, 1978.

Godbey, G. *Leisure in Your Life: An Exploration.* Philadelphia: Saunders, 1981.

Graham, P. J., & Klar, L. R., Jr. *Planning and Delivering Leisure Services.* Dubuque, Iowa: Brown, 1979.

Gray, D. E., & Greben, S. Future perspectives. *Parks and Recreation,* July 1974, *9*(7), 49.

Gulick, L. H. *A Philosophy of Play.* New York: Scribner, 1920.

Gunn, S. L., & Peterson, C. A. *Therapeutic Recreation Program Design: Principles and Procedures.* Englewood Cliffs, N.J.: Prentice-Hall, 1978.

Hayes, G. A. Recreation services for the mentally retarded in the state of Kansas. *Therapeutic Recreation Journal,* 1969, *3*(3), 13–19.

Henkel, D., & Godbey, G. *Parks, Recreation, and Leisure Services Employment in the Public Sector: Status.* Arlington, Va.: National Recreation and Park Association, 1977.

Hjelte, G., & Shivers, J. S. *Public Administration of Recreational Services.* Philadelphia: Lea & Febiger, 1972.

Hollingshead, A. B. *Elmtown's Youth: The Impact of Social Class for Adolescents.* New York: Wiley, 1961.

Howard, D. R., & Crompton, J. L. *Financing, Managing, and Marketing Recreation and Park Resources.* Dubuque, Iowa: Brown, 1980.

Huizinga, J. *Homo Ludens: A Study of the Play Element in Culture.* Boston: Beacon Press, 1960.

Iso-Ahola, S. *The Social Psychology of Leisure and Recreation.* Dubuque, Iowa: Brown, 1980.

Jackson, R. G. A preliminary bicultural study of value orientations and leisure attitudes. *Journal of Leisure Research,* 1973, *5*(4), 10–22.

James, G. A.; Sanford, G. R.; & Searcy, A., Jr. Origin of visitors to developed recreational sites on national forests. *Journal of Leisure Research,* 1972, *4*(2), 90–118.

Jubenville, A. *Outdoor Recreation Management.* Philadelphia: Saunders, 1978.

Kando, T. M. *Leisure and Popular Culture in Transition.* St. Louis: Mosby, 1980.

Kaplan, M. *Leisure: Theory and Policy.* New York: Wiley, 1975.

Kaplan, M. *Leisure: Lifestyle and Lifespan, Perspectives for Gerontology.* Philadelphia: Saunders, 1979.

Kelley, J. D. A status report on therapeutic recreation in the state of Illinois. In J. D. Kelley (Ed.), *Expanding Horizons in Therapeutic Recreation II.* Champaign: University of Illinois, Office of Recreation and Park Resources, 1974.

Kelly, J. R. Socialization toward leisure: A developmental approach. *Journal of Leisure Research,* 1974, *6*(3), 181–193.

Kelly, J. R. Leisure styles and choices in three environments. *Pacific Sociological Review,* April 1978, *21*(2), 187–207.

Knapp, R. F., & Hartsoe, C. E. *Play for America, 1906–1965.* Arlington, Va.: National Recreation and Park Association, 1980.

Knopp, T. B. Environmental determinants of recreation behavior. *Journal of Leisure Research,* 1974, *4*(2), 129–138.

Knopp, T. B., & Tyger, J. D. A study of conflict in recreational land use: Snowmobiling versus ski-touring. *Journal of Leisure Research,* 1973, *5*(3), 6–17.

Kraus, R. G. *Recreation and the Schools.* New York: Macmillan, 1964.

Kraus, R. G. *Public Recreation and the Negro.* New York: Center for Urban Education, 1968.

Kraus, R. G. Recreation and related therapies in psychiatric rehabilitation. *Therapeutic Recreation Journal,* 1973, *7*(3), 12–18.

Kraus, R. G. *Recreation and Leisure in Modern Society.* Santa Monica, Calif.: Goodyear, 1978.

Kraus, R. G., & Curtis, J. E. *Creative Administration in Recreation and Parks.* St. Louis: Mosby, 1977.

Lamme, L. L., & Lamme, A. J., III. Patterns of children's play. *Journal of Leisure Research,* 1979, *11*(4), 253–270.

Lancy, D. F., & Tindall, B. A. (Eds). *The Anthropological Study of Play: Problems and Perspectives—Proceedings of the Association for the Anthropological Study of Play.* Cornwall, N.J.: Leisure Press, 1976.

Larrabee, E., & Meyersohn, R. (Eds.). *Mass Leisure.* New York: Free Press, 1958.

Leanse, J. (Project Director). *Senior Centers: Report of Senior Group Programs in America, 1975.* Washington, D.C.: National Institute of Senior Centers, 1975.

Lee, J. *Play in Education.* New York: Macmillan, 1915.

Lentnek, B.; Van Doren, C. S.; & Trail, J. R. Spatial behavior in recreational boating. *Journal of Leisure Research,* 1969, *1*(2), 69–79.

Lewko, J., & Crandall, R. Research trends in leisure and special populations. *Journal of Leisure Research,* 1980, *12*(1), 69–70.

Loy, J. W., Jr. A case for the sociology of sport. In Neal, L. (Ed.), *Leisure Today: Selected Readings.* Washington, D.C.: American Association for Leisure and Recreation, 1975.

Lundberg, G. A.; Komarovsky, M.; & McInerny, M. A. The amounts and uses of leisure. In E. Larrabee & R. Meyersohn (Eds.), *Mass Leisure.* New York: Free Press, 1958.

Lundegren, H. (Ed.). *Pennsylvania State Studies on Recreation and the Aging.* University Park: Pennsylvania State University, 1974.

Lundegren, H. (Ed.). *Physical Education and Recreation for the Mentally Retarded.* University Park: Pennsylvania State University, 1975.

Lutzin, S. G. (Ed.). *Managing Municipal Leisure Services.* Washington, D.C.: International City Management Association, 1980.

Lynd, R. S., & Lynd, H. M. *Middletown*. New York: Harcourt Brace, 1929.

Magill, R. A., & Ash, M. J. Academic, psycho-social, and motor characteristics of participants and nonparticipants in children's sport. *Research Quarterly*, 1979, *50*(2), 230–240.

McAllister, D. M., & Klett, F. R. A modified gravity model of regional recreation activity with an application to ski trips. *Journal of Leisure Research*, 1976, *8*(2), 21–34.

McAvoy, L. H. The leisure preferences, problems, and needs of the elderly. *Journal of Leisure Research*, 1979, *11(1)*, 40–47.

McCool, S. F., & Schreyer, R. M. Research utilization in wildland recreation management. *Journal of Leisure Research*, 1977, *9*(2), 98–109.

McLellan, R. Research. *Parks and Recreation*. July 1980, *15*(7), 62–67.

Menninger, W. C. Recreation and mental health. *Recreation*, November 1948, *40*(6), 340.

Meyersohn, R. The sociology of leisure in the United States: Introduction and bibliography, 1945–1965. *Journal of Leisure Research*, 1969, *1*(1) 53–67.

Millar, S. *The Psychology of Play*. Baltimore: Penguin Books, 1968.

Mitchell, H. J. A community recreation program for the mentally retarded. *Therapeutic Recreation Journal*, 1971, *5*(1), 3–8.

Mobley, T. A. Practitioner/researcher: A team? *Parks and Recreation*, 1980, *72*, 40–41.

Morgan, A., & Godbey, G. The effect of entering an age-segregated environment upon the leisure activity patterns of older adults. *Journal of Leisure Research*, 1978, *10*(3), 177–189.

Mundy, J., & Odum, L. *Leisure Education: Theory and Practice*. New York: Wiley, 1979.

Murphy, J. F. *Concepts of Leisure*. Englewood Cliffs, N.J.: Prentice-Hall, 1981.

Myrdal, G. *The American Dilemma*. New York: Harper & Row, 1962.

Nash, J. B. *Philosophy of Recreation and Leisure*. Dubuque, Iowa: Brown, 1953.

National Academy of Sciences. *A Program for Outdoor Recreation Research* (Conference report). U.S. Department of Interior, Bureau of Outdoor Recreation, 1969.

National Recreation Association. *Recreation and Park Yearbook, 1960*. New York: The Association, 1961.

Neulinger, J. *To Leisure: An Introduction*. Boston: Allyn & Bacon, 1981.

Neulinger, J., & Breit, M. Attitude dimensions of leisure. *Journal of Leisure Research*, 1969, *1*(3), 255–261.

Nigro, G. *Sexuality in the Handicapped*. Lecture at New York Institute of Rehabilitation Medicine, November 1973.

Norbeck, E. Man at play. *Natural History* (Special Magazine Supplement), December 1971.

Odum, L. L., & Lancaster, R. A. *Leisure Education Curriculum for Kindergarten—Grade Twelve* (Vols. 1 and 2). Washington, D.C.: National Recreation and Park Association, Leisure Education Advancement Project, 1977.

O'Morrow, G. S. *Therapeutic Recreation: A Helping Profession*. Reston, Va.: Reston, 1976.

Orthner, D. K. Patterns of leisure and marital interaction. *Journal of Leisure Research*, 1976, *8*(2), 98–111.

Outdoor Recreation Resources Review Commission. *Outdoor Recreation for America: A Report to the President and to the Congress* (27 vols.). Washington, D.C.: U.S. Government Printing Office, 1962.

Peters, M., & Verhoven, P. J. A study of therapeutic recreation services in Kentucky nursing homes. *Therapeutic Recreation Journal*, 1970, *4*(4), 19–22.

Peterson, C. A. Applications of systems analysis procedures to program planning in therapeutic recreation service. In E. M. Avedon (Ed.), *Therapeutic Recreation Service: An Applied Behavioral Science Approach*. Englewood Cliffs, N.J.: Prentice-Hall, 1974.

Rainwater, C. E. *The Play Movement in the United States*. Chicago: University of Chicago Press, 1922.

Reynolds, J. A., & Hormachea, M. N. *Public Recreation Administration*. Reston, Va.: Reston, 1976.

Roberts, J. M.; Koenig, F.; & Stark, R. B. Judged display: A consideration of a craft show. *Journal of Leisure Research*, 1969, *1*(2), 163–180.

Rockefeller Panel Report. *The Performing Arts: Problems and Prospects*. New York: McGraw-Hill, 1965.

Rodney, L. S., & Toalson, R. F. *Administration of Recreation, Parks, and Leisure Services*. New York: Wiley, 1981.

Sage, G. H., & Loudermilk, S. The female athlete and role conflict. *Research Quarterly*, 1979, *50*(1), 88–96.

Salter, C. de L., & Salter, C. A. Effects of an individualized activity program on elderly patients. *Gerontologist*, October 1975.

Salter, M. A. (Ed.). *Play: Anthropological Perspectives*. Cornwall, N.Y.: Association for Anthropological Study of Play, and Leisure Press, 1977.

Sapora, A. V., & Mitchell, E. D. *The Theory of Play and Recreation*. New York: Ronald Press, 1961.

Sessoms, H. D.; Meyer, H. D.; & Brightbill, C. K. *Leisure Services: The Organized Recreation and Park System*. Englewood Cliffs, N.J.: Prentice-Hall, 1975.

Sessoms, H. D., & Oakley, S. R. Recreation, leisure, and the alcoholic. *Journal of Leisure Research*. 1969, *1*(1), 21–31.

Shafer, E. L. The impact of human needs on the natural environments for recreation. In B. van der Smissen (Ed.), *Indicators of Change in the Recreation Environment: A National Research Symposium*. University Park: Pennsylvania State University, 1975.

Sheridan, P. M. Therapeutic recreation and the alcoholic. *Therapeutic Recreation Journal*, 1976, *8*(1), 14–17.

Shivers, J. S. *Leisure and Recreation Concepts: A Critical Analysis*. Boston: Allyn & Bacon, 1981.

Shivers, J. S., & Fait, H. *Therapeutic and Adapted Recreational Services*. Philadelphia: Lea & Febiger, 1975.

Short, J. F., & Strodtbeck, F. L. *Group Process and Gang Delinquency*. Chicago: University of Chicago Press, 1965.

Silson, J. E.; Cohen, E. M.; & Hill, B. H. *Recreation in Hospitals: Report of a Study of Organized Recreation Programs in Hospitals and the Personnel Conducting Them*. New York: National Recreation Association, 1959.

Staley, E. J. *Study of Recreation Needs and Services: South Central Los Angeles*. Los Angeles: Recreation and Youth Services Planning Council, August 1966.

Staley, E. J., & Miller, N. P. (Eds.). *Leisure and the Quality of Life: A New Ethic for the Seventies and Beyond*. Washington, D.C.: American Association for Health, Physical Education, and Recreation, 1972. (ERIC Document Reproduction Service No. ED 073 382)

Stein, J. (Project Director). *Guidelines for Professional Preparation Programs for Personnel Involved in Physical Education and Recreation for the Handicapped*. Washington, D.C.: U.S. Bureau of Education for the Handicapped, and American Association for Health, Physical Education, and Recreation, 1973.

Stein, T. A., & Henkel, D. Recreation and park education in the United States and Canada, 1978. *Parks and Recreation,* January 1979, *14*(1), 29–36.

Stein, T. A., & Sessoms, H. D. *Recreation and Special Populations.* Boston: Holbrook, 1977.

Stottlemyer, R. Estimated carrying capacity for the national parks. In B. van der Smissen (Ed.), *Indicators of Change in the Recreation Environment: A National Research Symposium.* University Park: Pennsylvania State University, 1975.

Sutton-Smith, B., & Roberts, J. M. Child-training and game involvement. *Ethnology,* 1962, *1*, 166–185.

Szalai, A. Trends in comparative time-budget research. *American Behavioral Scientist,* May 1966, *9*(9), 3–8.

Theobald, W. F. *The Female in Public Recreation: A Study of Participation and Administrative Attitudes.* Toronto: Ontario Ministry of Culture and Recreation, 1976.

U.S. Department of Interior. *Cardinal Principles of Secondary Education: Report of the Commission on the Reorganization of Secondary Education of the National Education Association.* Washington, D.C.: Bureau of Education, 1918.

van der Smissen, B. (Ed.). *Recreation Research: Collected Papers from the National Conference on Recreation Research.* Washington, D.C.: American Association for Health, Physical Education, and Recreation, and National Recreation and Park Association, 1966.

van der Smissen, B. (Ed.). *Bibliography of Theses and Dissertations in Recreation and Parks.* University Park: Pennsylvania State University, 1979.

van der Smissen, B., & Joyce, D. V. (Eds.). *Bibliography of Theses and Dissertations in Recreation, Parks, Camping, and Outdoor Education.* Washington, D.C.: National Recreation and Park Association, 1970.

Van Doren, C. S. Spatiality and planning for recreation. In B. van der Smissen (Ed.), *Indicators of Change in the Recreation Environment: A National Research Symposium.* University Park: Pennsylvania State University, 1975.

Van Doren, C. S., & Hodges, L. *America's Park and Recreation Heritage: A Chronology.* Washington, D.C.: Bureau of Outdoor Recreation, 1975.

Ver Lee, J. M. The role of research in the recreation services in the urban complex. In B. van der Smissen (Ed.), *Recreation Research: Collected Papers from the National Conference on Recreation Research.* Washington, D.C.: American Association for Health, Physical Education, and Recreation, and National Recreation and Park Association, 1966, pp. 11–17.

Warner, W. L., & Lunt, P. S. *The Social Life of a Modern Community.* New Haven, Conn.: Yale University Press, 1941.

Weir, L. H. *Europe at Play: A Study of Recreation and Leisure Time Activity.* San Diego: Barnes, 1937.

West, P. C., & Merriam, L. C., Jr. Outdoor recreation and family cohesiveness. *Journal of Leisure Research,* 1970, *2*(2), 251–259.

White, R. C. Social class differences in the uses of leisure. *American Journal of Sociology,* September 1955, *6*(2), 145–150.

Wilensky, H. L. The impact of economic growth on free time. In E. O. Smigel (Ed.), *Work and Leisure: A Contemporary Social Problem.* New Haven, Conn.: College and University Press, 1963.

Williams, L. W. An analysis of the recreational pursuits of selected parolees from a state correctional institution in Pennsylvania. *Therapeutic Recreation Journal,* 1972, *6*(3), 134–140.

Williams, Y. B. Therapeutic play services in children's general hospitals in the United States. *Therapeutic Recreation Journal,* 1970, *4*(2), 17–21.

Yoesting, D. R., & Burkhead, D. L. Significance of childhood recreation experience on adult leisure behavior: An exploratory analysis. *Research Quarterly,* 1973, *44*(1), 25–35.

REFLECTIVE TEACHING

See Games and Simulations; Laboratory Experiences in Teacher Education; Teacher Education Programs; Teaching Styles.

REGRESSION ANALYSIS

Because of its versatility, regression analysis is one of the most popular methods used in educational research. It is adaptable not only to various research goals (e.g., explanation, prediction), but also to diverse designs (e.g., experimental, nonexperimental) and to different types of variables (e.g., continuous, categorical). It is *not* the purpose of this presentation to discuss the mechanics of regression analysis. Such discussions may be found in various statistics and research design books. In addition, books devoted entirely to regression analysis are available. Of these, probably the most useful to educational researchers are Cohen and Cohen (1975), Draper and Smith (1981), Ezekiel and Fox (1959), Kerlinger and Pedhazur (1973), McNeil, Kelly, and McNeil (1975), Ward and Jennings (1973), and Williams (1959).

The present statement is designed to serve as a conceptual and intuitive overview of the role of regression analysis in the overall research endeavor. Accordingly, major applications of the method are emphasized, and attention is drawn to important limitations in the hope of warning against misuses and abuses. In line with these aims, attempts have been made to minimize the use of formal statistical formulations and complex symbolism lest they confuse rather than enlighten readers not conversant with statistics. For the same reasons only major statistical assumptions whose violation is particularly deleterious to the valid application and interpretation of regression analysis are discussed. Finally, issues concerning tests of significance are not included.

Basic ideas of regression analysis are presented first, followed by a brief discussion of its uses for prediction or explanation of phenomena. The remainder of the presentation, which is addressed to regression analysis in explanatory research, is divided into two major sections: variance partitioning and analysis of effects.

Basic Ideas of Regression Analysis. Broadly speaking, regression analysis is a method for analyzing the variability of a dependent variable, or a criterion, Y, by using information contained in one or more independent variables, or predictors, X_i.

Simple linear regression. When only one independent variable is used, and it is assumed that the regression is linear (for each unit change in X there is constant change in Y), a score on the dependent variable can be expressed as follows:

$$Y = a + bX + e, \qquad (1)$$

where Y = a person's score on the dependent variable;
$\quad a$ = Y intercept, or constant;
$\quad b$ = regression coefficient;
$\quad X$ = a person's score on the independent variable; and
$\quad e$ = an error term, or residual.

Essentially, the aim of regression analysis is to find a solution for the regression coefficient *(b)* so that when it is applied to subjects' scores on X, explanation or prediction of Y is maximized. Stated differently, a solution for b is sought so that the sum of the squared errors (Σe^2) for all subjects is minimized, hence the name "least squares" given to this approach.

The least squares solution leads to the following regression equation:

$$Y' = a + bX, \qquad (2)$$

where Y' is a predicted score of Y on the basis of a given X. Note that $Y - Y' = e$. That is, the deviation of the observed score Y from the predicted score Y' is the error or the residual. As discussed later, under e are subsumed all factors, other than X, that affect Y.

The regression coefficient *(b)* is interpreted as the expected change in Y that is associated with a unit change in X. Assume, for example, that Y is a measure of academic achievement, X is a measure of mental ability, and the regression equation calculated in a given sample is $Y' = 15 + 3X$. On the basis of this equation it is concluded that for each unit change in mental ability *(X)* a change of three units in achievement *(Y)* is expected (see discussion of this point under "Analysis of Effects").

It was said above that the aim of regression analysis is to explain the variability of Y on the basis of information contained in X. Instead of working with the variance of Y, it is convenient to work with its deviation sum of squares, Σy^2. (Note that $\Sigma y^2/N$ is the variance of Y.) Now, a very important aspect of regression analysis is that it leads to the partitioning of the total sum of squares (Σy^2) into two additive components: (1) sum of squares attributable to regression (ss_{reg}), and (2) sum of squares attributable to residuals (ss_{res}). That is,

$$\Sigma y^2 = ss_{reg} + ss_{res}. \qquad (3)$$

Consequently, it is possible to calculate the proportion of Σy^2 due to regression and the proportion due to residuals.

It can be shown that the proportion of the sum of squares (or the variance) that is due to the regression of Y on X is equal to the squared correlation between them. That is,

$$r_{yx}^2 = \frac{ss_{reg}}{\Sigma y^2} = 1 - \frac{ss_{res}}{\Sigma y^2}. \qquad (4)$$

From the preceding it follows that the proportion of the sum of squares (or the variance) attributable to residuals is equal to $1 - r_{yx}^2$.

The r_{yx}^2, then, indicates how useful or meaningful X is in predicting or explaining Y. A relatively small r^2 may be a consequence of several factors, among which are that (1) X is largely irrelevant to the explanation or the prediction of Y; (2) there is a good deal of error in the measurement of X and/or Y; and (3) there is little variability in the sample being studied.

Because phenomena studied in educational research are generally complex and affected by many variables, it is not uncommon to find that one independent variable accounts for a rather small proportion of the variability of the dependent variable. This is why researchers most often resort to multiple regression analysis.

Multiple regression analysis. When more than one independent variable is used in regression analysis, the method is referred to as multiple regression (MR) analysis. The regression equation with k independent variables is

$$Y' = a + b_1 X_1 + b_2 X_2 + \cdots + b_k X_k, \qquad (5)$$

where Y' = predicted score, a = intercept or constant, and b's = regression coefficients. Each b is interpreted as indicating the expected change in Y associated with a unit change in a given variable while partialing, controlling for, or holding "constant" the effects of the remaining independent variables. This is why the b's are referred to as partial regression coefficients.

As in simple regression, a solution is sought for the b's in MR so that the sum of the squared residuals is minimized. Stated differently, a set of weights (b's) is sought to be applied to the X's so that the resulting linear combination will be maximally correlated with Y. Analogous to r_{yx}^2, a squared multiple correlation ($R_{y \cdot 12 \ldots k}^2$) is calculated, indicating the proportion of the variance of Y that is explainable or predictable on the basis of the X's.

The magnitude of R^2 is affected by, among other things, the intercorrelations among the independent variables. Ideally, the independent variables should not be intercorrelated at all. Under such circumstances each variable provides unique information, and R^2 is equal to the sum of the squared correlations of each independent variable with the dependent variable:

$$R_{y \cdot 12 \ldots k}^2 = r_{y1}^2 + r_{y2}^2 + \cdots + r_{yk}^2. \qquad (6)$$

Note carefully that equation (6) obtains only when the k independent variables are not correlated among themselves. Such a situation can be easily created in experimental research, but in nonexperimental research the independent variables are almost always intercorrelated. The higher the intercorrelations among them, the more redundant the information they provide, and therefore the less useful each of them is in the presence of the others. The types of variables used in educational research tend to be moderately to highly intercorrelated—which explains why the educational research literature is replete with instances of diminishing returns as additional variables are introduced into a regression analysis. In most instances increments in R^2 that result from the addition of variables after three or four have already been taken into account are so small as to render them both theoretically and practically meaningless.

An obvious question therefore arises: How does one select from the large pool of variables potentially available in educational research the subset that will prove to be the most useful or meaningful? Much of what follows may be viewed as variations on the answer to this question, given from different perspectives and focusing on different aspects of MR.

The first perspective concerns the goal of the research—explanation or prediction. These have been subjects of controversy among philosophers of science. Some view them as synonymous, whereas others treat them as logically and epistemologically distinct operations (see Brodbeck, 1968, pt. 5; Hempel, 1965; Kaplan, 1964; Scheffler, 1957; Scriven, 1959). It is neither possible nor necessary to deal with this controversy here. Suffice it to point out that, regardless of one's philosophical stance on this issue, it is often easy and useful to distinguish between studies whose purpose is either prediction or explanation. Examples of studies whose sole purpose is prediction are frequently encountered in such areas as personnel selection, college admissions, and vocational guidance. Studies in areas such as the effect of schooling, the learning process, and moral development are primarily concerned with attempts to explain these phenomena.

Multiple regression can play an important role in both predictive and explanatory studies. But, as will be shown, specific applications and interpretations of results from MR depend on such factors as the purpose of the study in which it is used.

Prediction. A notable feature of the use of MR in predictive research is the great latitude the researcher has in the selection of predictors. Various elements play a role in this process, including economy, availability, and ease of data collection, but the ultimate decision about the inclusion of a specific predictor is made in the light of its contribution to the prediction of the criterion. However, the decision is not always simple and obvious, because what appears to be a poor predictor by itself may prove very useful in combination with other predictors. Or several relatively poor but inexpensive predictors when combined may do as good a job as a single powerful but expensive predictor. Also, different combinations of predictors may be equally effective in predicting the same criterion. The selection of a specific combination from among them

would depend on various considerations, such as cost and ready availability.

When the number of predictors is relatively large, the task of studying the potential usefulness of each of them separately and in combination with various other predictors may become onerous. Diverse procedures for variable selection—stepwise selection, for example—have therefore been developed. For discussions of such procedures see Draper and Smith (1981), Kerlinger and Pedhazur (1973), Pedhazur (1982), and Lewis-Beck (1978).

Whatever the considerations and the procedures used in the selection of predictors, the process is essentially an empirical search for the "best" combination. Of course, the meaning of "best" may vary depending on, among other things, the concerns of a given researcher and the specific variable-selection procedure used.

Be that as it may, it is very important to remember that when the goal of optimizing the prediction of a criterion governs the selection of predictors, the results *should not* be used for explanatory purposes. Perhaps this can be understood best when it is realized that from an analytic frame of reference any one of a set of variables may be designated as the criterion, and a search for a best combination from the other variables to predict it may be undertaken. Thus one may use age, sex, mental ability, and motivation to predict achievement. But there is nothing to stop a researcher from designating age as the criterion and noting how well achievement, sex, mental ability, and motivation serve to predict it. It would be ludicrous, of course, to conclude that the aforementioned variables can serve to explain the phenomenon of age, even if it turned out that R^2 is close to 1.00. Although this is grossly obvious, more subtle but equally wrong examples are encountered in educational research because of the lack of clear distinctions between predictive and explanatory studies.

Finally, the use of proxies or surrogates of variables may often be efficacious in predictive research but highly misleading in explanatory research. For example, in a reanalysis of the Coleman Report data (Armor, 1972) it was found that an index of nine particular household items (such as a television set, a telephone, or a dictionary) had the highest correlation with verbal achievement (.80 for black and .72 for white sixth-grade students). While it is valid to conclude that this index is very useful for predictive purposes, even a naive researcher should not be tempted to use it to explain verbal achievement.

Explanation

The distinctive characteristic of an explanatory study is that it is designed on the basis of a theoretical formulation. Not only does theory dictate the choice of the variables, but from it are also derived hypotheses about the manner in which the explanatory, or independent, variables affect the phenomenon that is to be explained—the dependent variable. Obviously, theories vary in different ways, including their comprehensiveness and the degree to which they elaborate the patterns of the relations among the variables under study. As shown in the following, this elaboration largely determines the specific applications and interpretations of MR.

This section is divided into two major parts. In the first, approaches to the partitioning of the variance of the dependent variable are discussed. The second part focuses on the use and interpretation of regression coefficients as indices of the effects of the variables with which they are associated. In connection with this topic, some crucial assumptions of MR are discussed and some specific applications presented.

Variance Partitioning.   It was noted earlier that R^2 indicates the proportion of the variance of the dependent variable that is attributable to the independent variables. Researchers have developed different approaches to partitioning R^2 into components attributable to different independent variables, in the hope of ascertaining the relative importance of each. Two of these approaches are discussed here: (1) incremental partitioning of variance and (2) commonality analysis.

First, however, some general remarks about variance partitioning are in order. It will be recalled [see equation (6)] that when the independent variables are not correlated among themselves, the square of the correlation of each of them with the dependent variable indicates the proportion of variance it accounts for. Under such circumstances, variance partitioning is straightforward and unambiguous. One of the advantages of experimental research is that it affords the researcher the capability of ensuring that there are no correlations among the independent variables. In nonexperimental research, on the other hand, the independent variables are almost always intercorrelated. It is the presence of intercorrelations among the independent variables that poses problems of whether and how one can attribute different portions of the variance of the dependent variable to each of them.

Because of the inherent ambiguity of the situation, various authors (e.g., Darlington, 1968; Goldberger, 1964; Johnston, 1972; Tukey, 1954; Ward, 1969) have suggested that variance partitioning be abandoned when the independent variables are intercorrelated. Moreover, as is pointed out by some authors—see, in particular, Tukey (1954)—because R^2 is sample specific not much is lost by not partitioning it. It is possible for R^2 to vary greatly in samples from different populations, and yet indices of the effects of the independent variables (i.e., the regression coefficients) may be very similar in all samples.

Variance partitioning is, however, used frequently in educational research, and in fact was the major analytic approach employed in some of the most influential studies, such as the Coleman Report and the International Association for the Evaluation of Educational Achievement (IEA) studies. It is therefore important to outline, albeit briefly, the conditions under which variance partitioning may be validly applied, and the nature of the information that it yields.

Incremental partitioning of variance. Issues concerning partitioning of the variance of the dependent variable can be understood best in the context of a miniature, though admittedly unrealistic, example from educational research. Suppose that the dependent variable is academic achievement *(A)*, and that only two independent variables are used: student background *(B)* and type of school *(S)*. *B* and *S* may be single variables or, as is more commonly the case, they may represent blocks of variables. Thus *B* may include parents' socioeconomic status, attitudes, and expectations. Similarly, *S* may include types of teachers, programs, and support services. For the purpose of the present discussion it makes no difference whether *B* and *S* each represents a single variable or a block of variables.

Now, as is well known, *B* and *S* are generally correlated; that is, certain types of parents gravitate to certain types of schools, and/or they affect the nature and policies of the school their children attend. Whatever the reason for the correlation between *B* and *S,* the R^2 of *A* with *B* and *S* can be expressed in one of the following forms:

$$R^2_{A \cdot BS} = r^2_{AB} + r^2_{A(S \cdot B)} = R^2_{A \cdot B} + (R^2_{A \cdot BS} - R^2_{A \cdot B}) \qquad (7)$$

or

$$R^2_{A \cdot BS} = r^2_{AS} + r^2_{A(B \cdot S)} = R^2_{A \cdot S} + (R^2_{A \cdot BS} - R^2_{A \cdot S}). \qquad (8)$$

In equation (7) R^2 is partitioned into two components. One component is the proportion of variance due to *B*: r^2_{AB}. When *B* represents a block of variables, the proportion of variance it accounts for is $R^2_{A \cdot B}$. The other component is the proportion of variance due to *S* over and above what *B* accounts for. Note that $r^2_{A(S \cdot B)}$ is the squared semipartial correlation of *A* with *S*, after partialing out from *S* the variance that it shares with *B*. Equivalently, the squared semipartial correlation is the difference between R^2 for both *B* and *S* and the one for *B* only; see the right-hand term of equation (7). The main thing to be noted about this form of partitioning is that the proportion of variance attributed to *B* also includes variance that may be attributable to *S* because of the correlation between *B* and *S*. If, instead, the partitioning is done by beginning with *S*, as in equation (8), then part of the proportion of variance that may be attributable to *B* is attributed to *S*.

The answer to the obvious question as to which of the two approaches is correct depends on the theory advanced about the operation of the variables. It will now be shown that for certain theoretical formulations either equation (7) or (8) is valid, and that for others neither is valid. This will be done with the aid of four possible models, depicted in Figure 1.

It will be noted that in Model (a) the correlation between *B* and *S* is left unexplained. That is, the researcher is either unwilling or unable to state the causes for the correlation between *B* and *S*. In the terminology of econometrics and path analysis, *B* and *S* are exogenous variables and *A* is an endogenous variable. There is no meaningful approach to the partitioning of the variance in this model. Clearly, the analytic method cannot do what the re-

FIGURE 1. *Four possible models of the correlations between A, B, and S*

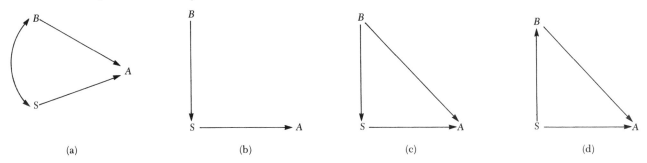

(a)   (b)   (c)   (d)

searcher is unable to do. All that can be done is determine the proportion of the variance accounted for by *both B and S* (i.e., R^2). Much of educational research, though involving more variables, is as in Model (a) and therefore not susceptible to variance partitioning.

Models (b) and (c) of Figure 1 are similar to each other, except that according to the former *B* does not affect *A* directly. In both models one may validly do an incremental partitioning of the variance, beginning with the more remote cause *(B)* and moving forward, as indicated in equation (7). It is important, however, to note what each component thus obtained signifies. Briefly, r^2_{AB} indicates the squared total effect of *B* on *A*, that is, its direct and indirect effect in (c), or its indirect effect in (b). On the other hand, $r^2_{A(S\cdot B)}$ does not indicate the squared total effect of *S* on *A*, but only the square of that part of its effect that is independent of *B*. In other words, this component does not include that part of the effect of *B* that *S* transmits.

Because the two indices reflect different types of effects, they are not comparable. That is, it is not meaningful to compare the magnitudes of the two components in order to answer the question about the relative importance of the variables with which they are associated, which is why the partitioning of the variance presumably is undertaken in the first place. (For discussions of this and related issues, see Coleman, 1975, 1976; MacDonald, 1979; and Pedhazur, 1982.)

The reasoning advanced regarding Models (b) and (c) applies also to Model (d), except that for this model the partitioning has to begin with *S*. In this case r^2_{AS} indicates the squared total effect of *S* on *A*—its direct effect and its indirect effect, via *B*; $r^2_{A(B\cdot S)}$ indicates the squared effect of *B* that is independent of *S*.

In general, the proportion of variance that is attributed to a given variable reflects its squared effect that is independent of the variables that precede it in the causal model. It is obvious that, depending on its position in the causal model, the same variable may be said to account for different proportions of the variance of the dependent variable.

What should be noted here is that the indices obtained from an incremental partitioning of the variance are asymmetric and therefore cannot be compared with each other

to determine the relative importance of the variables with which they are associated. Yet one frequently encounters such interpretations of variance partitioning in educational research, even when the researchers admit to being unable to posit a causal model concerning the operation of the variables they are studying, or when the model used is, at best, tentative and ambiguous. This state of affairs is particularly worrisome because it applies also to studies that have had, and will probably continue to have, strong impacts on legislative and judicial bodies, on boards of education and school personnel, and on the public at large. Prime examples of such studies are the Coleman Report (Coleman et al., 1966) and studies conducted under the auspices of the IEA (Carroll, 1975; Comber & Keeves, 1973; Peaker, 1975; Purves, 1973).

Grant (1973), among others, has provided a detailed review of the impact of the Coleman Report on the shaping of social policies. Methodological critiques of the Coleman Report will be found in Bowles and Levin (1968a, 1968b), Cain and Watts (1968, 1970), Mosteller and Moynihan (1972), and Pedhazur (1982). For a general review of the IEA studies, see Inkeles (1977). Methodological critiques of these studies are presented by Coleman (1975, 1976), and Pedhazur (1982).

Research applications. Because of space limitations it is not possible to discuss the aforementioned studies in the detail that they deserve. Instead, a few brief remarks will have to suffice. These studies have relied almost exclusively on incremental partitioning of variance for the purpose of determining the relative importance of variables (e.g., student background, type of school). Essentially, the justification for the order in which the variables were entered into the analysis was based on their presumed temporal sequence. Purves (1973) has stated this most succinctly: "Time provided the rationale for the ordering of the blocks to be entered in the regression equation" (p. 118). First, it will be noted that although temporal priority is a necessary condition for one variable to be the cause of another, it is by no means a sufficient condition. Second, while authors of the aforementioned studies were able to indicate temporal priority only regarding some student background variables, they themselves express doubts about the temporal and causal status of the other variables (see Coleman et al., 1966, p. 320; Purves, 1973, p. 118; Torney, Oppenheim, & Farnen, 1975, p. 127). In fact, the reasons given for the ordering of some of the variables in the IEA studies are patently wrong from a theoretical viewpoint. This is particularly true regarding the order of entry of what are essentially students' abilities. These variables were entered last because the authors of the IEA studies wanted to show that other variables account for meaningful proportions of variance. Thus, for example, Purves (1973) argues that to enter student abilities first "would deny any of the other predictors a chance to show their contributions . . ." (p. 156). And Carroll (1975) justifies entering student abilities last "in order to allow other types of variables to 'show their colors' *independently even if they happened also to be correlated with verbal ability*" (p. 207, italics added).

The ambivalence of the different authors about the questionable ordering of the variables is expressed in various places in the IEA reports. It becomes particularly evident when the authors of the studies show how different orderings of the variables lead to different conclusions about their relative importance. Indeed, when student abilities are entered early in the analysis virtually nothing, or very little, of the variance is attributed to the remaining variables (Purves, 1973, pp. 160–163).

In sum, incremental partitioning of variance, even when it is carried out in accordance with a tenable causal model, cannot be used to determine the relative importance of variables. When, as is often the case in educational research, no causal model is advanced, there is no valid way of deciding how to partition the variance, even if one wishes to use the partitioning for purposes other than assessing the variables' relative importance.

Commonality analysis. In commonality analysis the variance of the dependent variable is partitioned into unique components attributable to each of the independent variables and into commonalities, components common to combinations of independent variables. This will be illustrated for the three variables used in the preceding section:

$$U(B) = R^2_{A \cdot BS} - R^2_{A \cdot S}, \qquad (9)$$

$$U(S) = R^2_{A \cdot BS} - R^2_{A \cdot B}, \qquad (10)$$

and

$$C(BS) = R^2_{A \cdot BS} - U(B) - U(S) = R^2_{A \cdot B} + R^2_{A \cdot S} - R^2_{A \cdot BS}, \qquad (11)$$

where $U(B)$ = unique contribution of student background, $U(S)$ = unique contribution of school, and $C(BS)$ = commonality of B and S. From the foregoing it can be seen that the uniqueness of a variable is defined as its contribution when it is entered last into the analysis, and the commonality is defined as the proportion of R^2 that is left unaccounted for by $U(B)$ and $U(S)$. Clearly, the higher the correlation between B and S, the smaller the uniqueness of each, and the larger the commonality.

$C(BS)$ is referred to as a second-order commonality.

With more than two independent variables, commonalities are calculated for all possible combinations of the independent variables: pairs, triads, and so forth. The number of components for k independent variables is equal to $2^k - 1$. Thus, for example, with six independent variables sixty-three components are calculated: six unique and fifty-seven commonalities (fifteen second-order, twenty third-order, fifteen fourth-order, six fifth-order, and one sixth-order). Methods for calculating commonality analysis are given in Kerlinger and Pedhazur (1973), Mayeske, Wisler, et al. (1969), Mood (1969, 1971), and Newton and Spurrell (1967a, 1967b).

The most important point to note about commonality analysis is that while it may be useful as a variable-selection procedure in predictive research—e.g., as an alternative to stepwise regression analysis; see Newton and Spurrell (1967a, 1967b)—it is not useful at all in explanatory research. The reason is that for a given set of variables commonality analysis is applied in exactly the same manner, regardless of whether or not the researcher advances a theory about the patterns of the relations among them, and, if one is offered, no matter how crude or elaborate that theory is. In short, commonality analysis is neutral, so to speak, to different theoretical formulations and therefore cannot be used to test them.

While the meaning of the uniqueness of a variable is clear in a predictive framework, it is not at all clear what it signifies in an explanatory framework. The ambiguity is even greater concerning the commonality elements, as is evidenced by the following statement by one of the leading exponents of commonality analysis: "In the strictest sense this common portion represents an intermediate situation. That is to say, we cannot tell to which of the two sets . . . all or some of this common portion should be attributed" (Mayeske, 1970, p. 105). The preceding refers to a second-order commonality; the situation is more complex and ambiguous regarding the interpretation of higher-order commonalities. Thus it is not surprising that some researchers (e.g., Cooley & Lohnes, 1976; Purves, 1973) lump all the commonalities together instead of reporting them separately. This, of course, does not enhance the interpretation of the results, but rather underscores the ambiguous status of the commonalities.

Despite the foregoing, "enthusiasm for commonality partitioning of variance is running high" (Cooley & Lohnes, 1976, p. 220). In fact, Cooley and Lohnes "strongly recommend" it as "an informative, conservatively safe method for most situations likely to arise in evaluations" (p. 219). There is no denying that commonality analysis is safe. But its safety lies in its failure to address questions regarding the process by which a set of variables operates, and therefore it is *not* informative in this regard.

Research applications. Regardless of one's stand concerning the meaningfulness of commonality analysis, it is necessary to recognize that because the variables in nonexperimental educational research tend to be correlated most of the variance is attributed to commonalities. This is amply demonstrated in various studies. For example, in extensive reanalyses of the Coleman Report data (e.g., (Mayeske & Beaton, 1975; Mayeske, Cohen, et al., 1972; Mayeske, Okada, & Beaton, 1973; Mayeske, Okada, et al., 1973; Mayeska, Wisler, et al., 1969) the not unexpected principal findings were that "On the whole, the influence of the school cannot be separated from that of student's social background—and vice versa. Moreover, the common influence [?] of the school and the student's social background [far] exceeds either of their distinguishable influences [?]" (Mayeske, Cohen, et al., 1972, p. ix).

Large proportions of variance attributable to commonalities were also found in some of the IEA studies in which commonality analysis was used (Purves, 1973). The dubious value of variance partitioning for the purpose of assessing the relative importance of variables is highlighted in Purves's study. Using six blocks of variables, incremental partitioning of variance was done in which home background was entered first. In this analysis, home background appropriated the major share of the variance accounted for. But when commonality analysis was applied to the same data, the sum of the unique proportions of variance for the six blocks (i.e., including home background) was very small, whereas the sum of the commonalities was very large. Is home background, then, an important variable? On the basis of the incremental partitioning of variance, the answer is yes. But on the basis of the commonality analysis, the answer is no. As was argued in this section, neither approach is valid for the purpose of answering such questions.

Analysis of Effects. By analysis of effects is meant here the interpretation of regression coefficients as indices of the effects of the variables with which they are associated. It is the purpose of this section to discuss the conditions under which such an interpretation is generally valid and straightforward, and when it is questionable or ambiguous. This is done in the context of several topics: (1) experimental versus nonexperimental research; (2) the role of theory; (3) specification errors; (4) measurement errors; (5) multicollinearity; and (6) standardized and unstandardized coefficients.

Experimental versus nonexperimental research. Distinctions between these two types of research settings cannot be dealt with here in detail (see Campbell & Stanley, 1963; Kerlinger, 1973). Suffice it to note that in experimental research subjects are randomly assigned to treatments or treatment combinations in order to study the effect of each and their interactions on the dependent variable of interest. In nonexperimental research, on the other hand, an observed variable that is designated as the dependent variable is regressed on other variables that presumably affect it.

The interpretation of regression coefficients as indices of the effects of the variables with which they are associated is relatively unambiguous and straightforward in experimental research. Barring subject attrition, and assuming that the experiment was validly executed, the

researcher can create the condition that the independent variables are not intercorrelated. Moreover, measurement and specification errors can be effectively minimized. Under such circumstances, there is a relatively strong assurance that the regression coefficients in fact indicate the effects of the treatments.

The interpretation of regression coefficients as indices of effects in nonexperimental research is much more ambiguous (some would argue that it is entirely inappropriate) because, strictly speaking, the regression equation does not reflect the effects of what are presumably independent variables on what is presumably a dependent variable, but rather average relations between the former and the latter (for detailed discussions, see Cook and Campbell, 1979; Luecke & McGinn, 1975; Michelson, 1970; Snedecor & Cochran, 1967).

Box's dictum that "to find out what happens to a system when you interfere with it you have to interfere with it (not just observe it)" (1966, p. 629) is incontestable. Yet situations in which the conduct of experiments is not possible or feasible (because of ethical considerations, administrative constraints, infeasibility of manipulations, complexity of phenomena, etc.) come readily to mind. Therefore, to rule out the use of regression equations for the purpose of studying the effects of variables in nonexperimental research would exclude much of human behavior from the realm of scientific inquiry. Guided by sound theoretical formulations and clear thinking, and used with care and constant vigilance against the many pitfalls, regression analysis can be a most powerful tool in nonexperimental research. Much of the remainder of this section may be viewed as an elaboration of the preceding statement.

The role of theory. The most important point to bear in mind when interpreting the regression equation as indicating the effects of the independent variables on the dependent variable is that regression analysis is not a theory-generating but a theory-testing process. Therefore the valid interpretation of the regression coefficients is predicated, first and foremost, on the assumption that the regression equation is a valid depiction of the process by which the variables under study operate. To the extent that this assumption is not tenable, misinterpretations may run the gamut from exercises in futility to flights of fantasy and delusion.

One never knows whether the regression equation is indeed a valid depiction of the process by which the variables operate, particularly in nonexperimental research. All one can do is advance a theoretical formulation about the nature of the relations among the variables under study. Regression equations are then constructed in accordance with the specific theoretical formulation. The purpose of the analysis is to determine whether or not the theoretical formulation is consistent with the data.

The role of theory in the application of regression analysis can be best illustrated in reference to the three alternative miniature models of the process of achievement that are depicted in Figure 2. It cannot be overemphasized

FIGURE 2. *Three alternative models of the process of achievement*

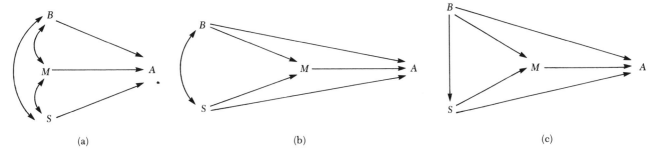

(a)   (b)   (c)

that these models are used for illustrative purposes only, and that no validity claims are made for any of them.

In Model (a) student background *(B)*, student motivation *(M)*, and type of school *(S)* are treated as exogenous variables. That is, according to this model no statement is being made about the causes of the correlations among the three independent variables. Consequently, all one can do is determine the direct effect of each on achievement *(A)*. This can be accomplished by regressing *A* on *B*, *M*, and *S*, and studying, for example, the standardized coefficients. Incidentally, most analyses in educational research use models such as (a) either by design or by default. That is, when a dependent variable is regressed on all the independent variables, and the regression coefficients are used to study the effects of each of the independent variables, a model such as (a) is being used, whether wittingly or unwittingly.

In Model (b) of Figure 2, *B* and *S* are treated as exogenous variables. According to this model *B* and *S* affect *A* directly as well as indirectly, via *M*. Assuming that the residuals of *M* are not correlated with *B* and *S*, and the residuals of *A* are not correlated with *B*, *S*, and *M*, two regression equations would be calculated for Model (b): (1) regressing *M* on *B* and *S*; and (2) regressing *A* on *M*, *B*, and *S*.

In Model (c) only *B* is treated as an exogenous variable. For this model one can calculate the direct effect of *B* on *A*, as well as its indirect effects, via *S* and *M*. For *S*, too, a direct as well as an indirect effect on *A*, via *M*, can be calculated. For *M*, only a direct effect on *A* is indicated. The preceding terms would be obtained by doing three regression analyses: (1) *S* on *B*; (2) *M* on *B* and *S*; and (3) *A* on *B*, *S*, and *M*.

It is important to note that the direct effects of *B*, *S*, and *M* on *A* would be identical regardless of which of the three models is used. The models differ in their hypotheses regarding indirect effects of the independent variables on the dependent variables. The implications of the differences among the three models will be illustrated in connection with the effect of *B* on *A*. Assume, for example, that the direct effect of *B* on *A* is very small and deemed not meaningful. If Model (a) were used, the inescapable conclusion would be that *B* is not an important determiner of *A*. But if Model (b) or (c) is used, it may turn out that

B has a sizable indirect effect on *A*, thereby leading to the opposite conclusion—namely, that it is an important variable, although most of its effect is indirect. Depending on the pattern of relations among the variables, it may also turn out that the indirect effect of *B* on *A* in Model (c) far exceeds its indirect effect on *A* in Model (b), thereby leading to different conclusions about the effect of this variable in the two models. To repeat: It is theory that dictates the analytic approach, not the other way around.

Specification errors. Specification errors refer to the use of a wrong or inappropriate model. Such errors include the omission of relevant variables, the inclusion of irrelevant variables, or the use of a linear additive model when a nonlinear or a nonadditive one is more appropriate (for discussions, see Bohrnstedt & Carter, 1971; Deegan, 1974; Graybill, 1961; Johnston, 1972; Pedhazur, 1982; Theil, 1957; Wold, 1956).

Probably the most crucial and detrimental of the specification errors is the omission of variables that are correlated with the ones being used. It will be recalled that omitted variables are subsumed under the residuals [see *e* in equation (1)]. In regression analysis it is assumed that the residuals are not correlated with the variables in the equation. Violation of this assumption may result in serious biases in the estimation of regression coefficients, thereby leading to erroneous conclusions about the effects of the variables with which they are associated.

Much, if not most, nonexperimental educational research suffers from specification errors. In most of this research little perspicacity is required to come up with a host of variables that have not been used in a study and that are correlated with the ones used. Unfortunately, researchers often introduce such specification errors when they attempt to cope with problems posed in the analysis. The assumption that variables not included in the model are not correlated with those in the model is particularly questionable when, as often happens in educational research, R^2 is relatively low.

In view of the foregoing one cannot but question the validity of the interpretation of regression coefficients as indices of effects in much of what is currently done in educational research. It is not possible to deal here with the details of detection and treatment of specification errors. It will be noted, however, that sound theory is the most important safeguard against the commission of such errors.

Measurement errors. In regression analysis it is assumed that the independent variables are measured without error. The presence of measurement errors in simple regression analysis leads to an underestimation of the regression coefficient. In MR, on the other hand, measurement errors may lead to either overestimation or underestimation of regression coefficients. Even estimates of coefficients associated with variables that are measured without error may be biased when such variables are correlated with others that contain errors.

Because many of the measures used in educational research have moderate reliabilities, the danger of arriving at erroneous conclusions about the effects of variables on the basis of the magnitudes of their regression coefficients is very real. Unfortunately, not enough attention has been paid by educational researchers to the deleterious effects of measurement errors. When the reliabilities are high, and it is assumed that the errors are random, one may resort to conventional corrections for attenuation (Lord & Novick, 1968; Nunnally, 1978). The situation is far more complex when it cannot be assumed that the errors are random (Bohrnstedt & Carter, 1971; Cochran, 1968).

Among recent promising approaches to the treatment of measurement errors is the use of multiple indicators of variables in the context of linear structural equation models (Bentler, 1980; Bielby & Hauser, 1977; Blalock, 1969, 1970; Costner & Schoenberg, 1973; Hauser & Goldberger, 1971; Jöreskog & Sörbom, 1979; Long, 1976; Rock et al., 1977; Werts et al., 1976). Important as these and other attempts to deal with measurement errors are, they cannot undo their damage. The greatest promise lies in more concerted efforts by educational researchers to develop and use highly reliable measures.

Multicollinearity. Problems that arise because of intercorrelations among the independent variables are generally discussed under the heading of multicollinearity. There is, however, no consensus about the definition of this term (see Farrar & Glauber, 1967). While some authors use it to refer to the existence of any correlations among the independent variables, others reserve its use for situations in which the correlations are high. Whatever the specific definition of multicollinearity, it is important to recognize that when more than two independent variables are used, it does not refer to the zero-order correlations among the independent variables, but rather to correlations of each independent variable with all the remaining ones.

Essentially, multicollinearity refers to redundancy of information provided by the independent variables. The ambiguities that this leads to when one attempts to partition the variance of the dependent variable have already been discussed. The regression coefficients, too, are adversely affected by multicollinearity. Recall that when each regression coefficient is calculated the remaining independent variables are partialed out. Therefore, the higher the correlation between a given independent variable and the remaining ones, the greater the effect of the partialing process on the calculation of the regression coefficient. In general, when multicollinearity is high the regression coefficients are very unstable, and their magnitudes may be substantially affected by even slight changes in the patterns of the intercorrelations among the variables (for instance, slight fluctuations resulting from, for example, sampling or measurement errors).

Consider the case of two highly correlated independent variables. Assume, first, that they have identical correlations with the dependent variable, and that partial standardized coefficients, or β's (betas), are calculated. Under such circumstances, the β that would have been obtained if only one of the variables had been used would be split between the two variables. Assuming that the β's are used as indices of the effects of the variables with which they are associated, it may turn out that when both variables are used it will be concluded that their effects are small or not meaningful.

Assume now that one of the independent variables has a slightly higher correlation with the dependent variable. In this situation the scales will be tipped in favor of this variable, leading to its having a disproportionately larger β than the one associated with the second variable. Depending on the specific magnitudes of the two β's, one may be led to the conclusion that one of the variables has a much stronger effect than the other, or that one of them has a meaningful effect whereas the other does not. What was said about two independent variables also holds for more than two, except that the situation is aggravated by greater splintering and wider fluctuations of the β's, depending on the pattern of the intercorrelations among the variables (for a very good discussion and illuminating illustrations, see Gordon, 1968).

In addition to the foregoing problems, high multicollinearity poses logical and substantive problems in the interpretation of regression coefficients as indices of effects. While it is possible to use a process of partialing to "hold constant" other variables when studying the effect of a given variable, this may lead to substantively strange results or interpretations that often have an air of fantasy about them. Thus, for example, it is possible to partial motivation, anxiety, locus of control, and the like, from mental ability when its effect on achievement is being studied. But it does not follow that it makes sense on theoretical and conceptual grounds to speak of varying mental ability while holding the other variables constant, particularly when the causes of the patterns of the correlations among what are presumably the independent variables are unknown or not clear. Assuming there is high multicollinearity among the variables in the preceding example, it is even possible to find that the sign of the regression coefficient for mental ability, for example, is negative, thereby leading to the strange conclusion that it has a negative effect on achievement (examples of some strange results are given under "Research Applications").

In view of the serious problems caused by high multicollinearity, two questions arise. (1) How does one detect it? (2) What can be done about it? With regard to detection, it will be noted that the determinant of the correlation matrix of the independent variables may serve as a rough indication of whether or not it contains high multicollinearity (Farrar & Glauber, 1967; Pedhazur, 1975). But what is more important is to pinpoint the sources of multicollinearity. This can be accomplished by calculating the squared multiple correlation (R^2) of each independent variable with the remaining ones. The higher the R^2 for a given independent variable, the greater the potential problems in the estimation and the interpretation of the regression coefficient associated with it. It is not necessary actually to go through the calculations of such R^2's because, as is shown in various statistics books, this information may be obtained from the diagonal elements of the inverse of the correlation matrix of the independent variables. For those not conversant with matrix algebra, Lemieux (1978) provides a simple formula for calculating all the R^2's from standard computer output for the regression of the dependent variable on all the independent variables. Other approaches to the detection of multicollinearity are discussed by Chatterjee and Price (1977) and Gunst and Mason (1977).

There is no simple or agreed-upon solution to the problem of multicollinearity. Researchers are often tempted to solve the problem by deleting variables that have been identified as sources of high multicollinearity. Such an approach is wrong because when attempts are made to detect multicollinearity it is assumed that the regression equation is correctly specified. Consequently, deletion of variables may reduce multicollinearity but at the same time introduce specification errors, thereby leading to bias in the estimation of the coefficients for the variables that are retained.

A solution that is often of use is to group highly correlated variables in blocks, on the basis of a priori judgment, principal components, or factor analysis (Chatterjee & Price, 1977). This may be particularly useful when multiple indicators of variables are used. It will be noted, however, that when variables are grouped in blocks it is not possible to obtain a regression coefficient for a block of variables, unless one first forms a linear combination of the variables that comprise the block (see Coleman, 1975, 1976; Igra, 1979). Unfortunately, even when such linear combinations are formed, the regression coefficients associated with them may prove of little use when it is desired to interpret them as indices of effects, or when one wishes to utilize the results for policy decisions. Although blocking multiple indicators of variables is not wrong, it is preferable not to do so, but instead to employ them in linear structural equation models.

Some researchers recommend that, when high multicollinearity is present in a set of data, ordinary least squares not be used at all. Of the various alternatives that have been suggested, ridge regression has been gaining in popularity (see Chatterjee & Price, 1977; Draper & Smith, 1981; Horel & Kennard, 1970a, 1970b; Marquardt & Snee, 1975; Mason & Brown, 1975; Schmidt & Muller, 1978; for a critique of ridge regression, see Rozeboom, 1979).

In sum, there is no instant or simple cure for high multicollinearity. As with other problems, the best safeguard against misinterpretations of results in the presence of multicollinearity and the best hope for arriving at a reasonable solution lie in an understanding of its causes in a given study.

Standardized and unstandardized coefficients. Regression coefficients may be calculated for use with either raw scores or standard (z) scores. The coefficients to be used with raw scores are referred to as unstandardized regression coefficients (b's), and those with standard scores as standardized regression coefficients (β's). The interpretation of b's was discussed earlier. β's are similarly interpreted, except that each β is said to indicate the expected change in the dependent variable associated with one standard deviation change in a given independent variable, while partialing the remaining ones.

The β's, then, are scale-free. That is, they are interpreted without reference to the specific units of the scales used to measure the variables with which they are associated. This property of the β's renders them comparable across different variables measured with different units. Accordingly, many researchers use the relative magnitudes of the β's as indices of the relative effects or importance of the variables in a given equation. However, the β's suffer from a serious drawback in that their magnitudes are affected by such considerations as the variances and the covariances of the variables in the model, and the variances of the variables subsumed under the residuals. Consequently, the β's are sample specific, and may vary widely from sample to sample not because of differences in the effects of the variables in the different samples, but because of the aforementioned factors (for detailed discussions and numerical illustrations of this point, see Blalock, 1964; Ezekiel & Fox, 1959; Fox, 1968; Pedhazur, 1982).

The b's, on the other hand, tend to be fairly stable across samples, even when the variances and the covariances of the variables differ in the samples. Moreover, the b's more closely reflect scientific laws, and are more directly interpretable for the purpose of policy decisions. It is because of these properties that most authors (e.g., Blalock, 1968; Kim & Mueller, 1976; Tukey, 1954; Wright, 1976) recommend that b's be used instead of β's. For a dissenting view see Hargens (1976).

The meaningful interpretation of the b's, however, is predicated on the use of scales that have meaningful units. Unfortunately, many of the measures used in educational research do not lend themselves to an unambiguous or substantively meaningful interpretation of a unit change. This is one of the reasons why researchers are often forced to use β's. But doing so does not solve the problem of the meaning of the units of measurement, it only evades it.

Because of the differences in the properties of the b's and the β's one may arrive at contradictory conclusions about the relative importance of variables in a given study, depending on which of the two indices is used (examples of such occurrences are given in the reanalysis by Smith, 1972, of the Coleman Report data).

Are there, then, any guides to choosing between b and β? When the units of measurement are meaningful, b's are preferable. When it is desired to compare coefficients across variables within a given sample, β's have to be used, unless the variables whose coefficients are to be compared are measured in the same units. When it is desired to compare the effects of variables across samples, b's should be used. Examples of such comparisons, using data from the Coleman Report, will be found in Michelson (1970) and Smith (1972). Methods for comparing regression equations across samples are discussed in Chow (1960), Johnson and Jackson (1959), Kerlinger and Pedhazur (1973), Schoenberg (1972), Specht and Warren (1975), Walker and Lev (1953), and Williams (1959). It will be noted that the same methods are used in aptitude-treatment-interaction studies (Cronbach & Snow, 1977), and in some models of test bias (Cleary, 1968).

Research applications. One often encounters educational research studies in which regression coefficients are interpreted as indices of effects, despite the absence of a theoretical rationale for the regression equations used, or in the presence of questionable theoretical formulations. Moreover, one frequently encounters interpretations of regression coefficients associated with what are clearly proxy variables as indices of their effects on the dependent variable. It is therefore not surprising that readers of such reports, particularly those not conversant with regression analysis, are baffled by results that seem to make no sense.

Following are a few examples that illustrate some problems and pitfalls discussed in this section. No attempt is made here either to summarize or to evaluate the studies from which the examples have been taken. It is worth noting, however, that results and policy recommendations based on these studies have been widely publicized in the mass media as well as in the professional literature.

The first set of examples is taken from two studies conducted in the Philadelphia School District under the auspices of the Federal Reserve Bank of Philadelphia. In a technical report of the first study (referred to here as Study I), Summers and Wolfe (1977) describe the analysis, saying: "In winnowing down the original list of variables to get the equation of 'best fit,' *many* regressions have been run. The data have been *mined* of course. Variables which had coefficients whose significance were very sensitive to the introduction and discarding of other variables were not retained" (p. 642, italics added). The preceding should suf-

fice to cast doubts on the validity of the final equation as a reflection of the process of achievement.

It is not possible to list here all the questionable and strange "findings," nor to attempt to explain why they have emerged. The following are but a few of the findings. (1) Number of library books per pupil has a *negative* effect on learning. (2) Presence of disruptive incidents in the classroom has a *positive* effect on learning. (3) Students whose teachers were graduated from highly rated colleges achieve more than those whose teachers were graduated from colleges that received low ratings. (4) Teachers' advanced degrees or advanced studies have no effects on students' achievement.

The authors accept their findings at face value, and do not hesitate to make sweeping recommendations for policy changes on that basis. For example, on the basis of items (3) and (4) they call for changes in the hiring of and salary scales for teachers. Even the finding concerning disruptive incidents in the classroom is taken seriously by the authors, though mercifully they stop short of recommending that such incidents be encouraged, because "it would seem a bit premature" (p. 647) to do so. The recommendations of this study were summarized in the *New York Times* (February 12, 1975, p. 27B) and elsewhere. Readers were also informed of the availability of a free booklet from the Federal Reserve Bank of Philadelphia describing the report in nontechnical language. The potential damage of such wide dissemination of highly questionable "findings" cannot be overestimated.

In a follow-up study conducted under the same auspices (Study II), the authors (Kean et al., 1979) report: "Over 500 multiple regression equations were run" (p. 7). *"The final equation was regarded as the theory"* (p. 37, italics added). In view of the preceding, it comes as no surprise that some of the findings in Study II are contradictory to, or inconsistent with, those of Study I. Thus, for example, in Study I it was found that class size has a *negative* effect on student achievement, whereas in Study II class size was found to have *positive* effect.

Contrary to the findings in Study I, the type of college from which teachers were graduated has no effect according to Study II. No mention of this inconsistency is made in the report of Study II, nor do the authors allude to their policy recommendations, which were based on the presumed findings regarding this variable in Study I.

While it is unfortunate that authors advance questionable findings and policy recommendations based on them, the situation is aggravated when such reports receive wide publicity, and what may appear to be implicit endorsement from prestigious organizations. For example, "findings" from Study II were presented in a front-page feature story entitled: "Philadelphia Study Pinpoints Factors in Improving Reading Achievement," in a publication of Division H of AERA (*Pre Post Press*, September 1979, vol. 1, p. 1). Among factors said to make *no* difference in improvement in reading are: "The number of graduate courses in reading taken by the teacher and the teacher's experience. The time spent on reading instruction . . ." (p. 1). The story does not even suggest that the study may be deficient. On the contrary, it reports that the Philadelphia school's research director (who, incidentally, is the senior author of the report of Study II) is "convinced that the findings are solid" (p. 1). Moreover, it is reported that the Philadelphia school superintendent "praised the study which he said would result in 'specific recommendations' to the Board for major changes in reading instruction" (p. 1).

The second set of examples is taken from the IEA studies. In general, it will be noted that extensive use of stepwise regression analysis in these studies casts doubts as to the validity of interpreting the regression coefficients of the surviving variables as indices of their effects. The following examples result, at least in part, from the questionable analytic approaches taken in the IEA studies. (1) In four countries, time spent on science homework had a *positive* effect on achievement in science, whereas in three countries it had a *negative* effect (Comber & Keeves, 1973, p. 231). (2) In a study of the teaching of French as a foreign language (Carroll, 1975, pp. 217–218), it was found that teachers' training in French had a *positive* effect in some samples, a *negative* effect in others, and *no* effect in still others. A similar pattern of findings emerged regarding the time spent by teachers in marking student papers.

Finally, an example from Carroll's study (1975) will be used to illustrate the hazards of interpreting regression coefficients as indices of effects in the presence of high multicollinearity. In an analysis of a listening test and a reading test in French, each of the preceding was regressed separately on seven variables. For present purposes, the interest is solely in two of these: (1) students' aspirations to be able to read French and (2) students' aspirations to understand spoken French. The correlation between these two indices of the same variable (i.e., aspirations regarding knowledge of French) is .762, and the correlations of each of them with the other "independent variables" are about the same. But aspirations to be able to read French had a slightly higher correlation with the reading test than did aspirations to be able to understand spoken French (.385 and .344 respectively). Because of the high correlation between the two indices, aspiration to be able to read French had a considerably higher β than the aspiration to be able to understand spoken French (.18 and .03, respectively).

The results concerning the listening test are in the opposite direction. Because aspirations to be able to understand spoken French had a slightly higher correlation with listening than did aspirations to be able to read French (.337 and .322, respectively), the β for the former was .12 and that for the latter was .06.

Yet Carroll (1975) offers the following interpretation of the above noted results: "Of interest is the fact that aspiration to learn to understand spoken French makes *much more contribution* to Listening scores than to Read-

ing, and conversely, aspiration to learn to read French makes *much more contribution* to Reading scores than to Listening scores" (p. 274, italics added).

Note that Carroll draws his conclusions on the basis of comparisons of β's across equations and variables—a potentially hazardous approach. But even if the comparisons were to be made within a single equation (e.g., the β's for the two indices for the reading scores), one would have to question their validity as indices of effects. Finally, because of slight fluctuations in the correlations, opposite results could have been obtained.

Because of space limitations it was not possible to deal with several important aspects of MR, notably curvilinear relations, interactions, the use of categorical variables by themselves and in combination with continuous variables, and the analysis of residuals. Discussions of these topics will be found in the books cited previously.

It is hoped, however, that it has been demonstrated that MR is a versatile analytic technique that may be used to answer different questions in which educational researchers are interested. But, as has been stressed throughout this presentation, the very generality of MR renders it susceptible to misapplication and misinterpretation. As is true of any analytic technique, valid application and interpretation of MR are predicated on such factors as the research goal, the theoretical framework, the research design, the type and properties of the variables, and the degree to which the assumptions on which it is based are met.

Elazar J. Pedhazur

See also Multivariate Analysis; Path Analysis; Prediction Methods; Statistical Methods; Validity of Tests.

REFERENCES

Armor, D. J. School and family effects on black and white achievement: A reexamination of the USOE data. In F. Mosteller & D. P. Moynihan (Eds.), *On Equality of Educational Opportunity.* New York: Random House, Vintage Books, 1972.

Bentler, P. M. Multivariate analysis with latent variables: Causal modeling. In M. R. Rosenzweig & L. W. Porter (Eds.), *Annual Review of Psychology* (Vol. 31). Palo Alto, Calif.: Annual Reviews, 1980.

Bielby, W. T., & Hauser, R. M. Structural equation models. In A. Inkeles, J. Coleman, & N. Smelser (Eds.), *Annual Review of Sociology* (Vol. 3). Palo Alto, Calif.: Annual Reviews, 1977.

Blalock, H. M. *Causal Inferences in Nonexperimental Research.* Chapel Hill: University of North Carolina Press, 1964.

Blalock, H. M. Theory building and causal inferences. In H. M. Blalock & A. B. Blalock (Eds.), *Methodology in Social Research.* New York: McGraw-Hill, 1968.

Blalock, H. M. Multiple indicators and the causal approach to measurement error. *American Journal of Sociology,* 1969, 75, 264–272.

Blalock, H. M. Estimating measurement error using multiple indicators and several points in time. *American Sociological Review,* 1970, 35, 101–111.

Bohrnstedt, G. W., & Carter, T. M. Robustness in regression analysis. In H. L. Costner (Ed.), *Sociological Methodology 1971*. San Francisco: Jossey-Bass, 1971.

Bowles, S., & Levin, H. M. The determinants of scholastic achievement: An appraisal of some recent evidence. *Journal of Human Resources*, 1968, *3*, 3–24. (a)

Bowles, S., & Levin, H. M. More on multicollinearity and the effectiveness of schools. *Journal of Human Resources*, 1968, *3*, 393–400. (b)

Box, G. E. P. Use and abuse of regression. *Technometrics*, 1966, *8*, 625–629.

Brodbeck, M. (Ed.). *Readings in the Philosophy of the Social Sciences*. New York: Macmillan, 1968.

Cain, G. G., & Watts, H. W. The controversy about the Coleman Report: Comment. *Journal of Human Resources*, 1968, *3*, 389–392.

Cain, G. G., & Watts, H. W. Problems in making policy inferences from the Coleman Report. *American Sociological Review*, 1970, *35*, 228–242.

Campbell, D. T., & Stanley, J. C. Experimental and quasi-experimental designs for research on teaching. In N. L. Gage (Ed.), *Handbook of Research on Teaching*. Chicago: Rand McNally, 1963.

Carroll, J. B. *The Teaching of French as a Foreign Language in Eight Countries*. New York: Wiley, 1975.

Chatterjee, S., & Price, B. *Regression Analysis by Example*. New York: Wiley, 1977.

Chow, G. C. Tests of equality between sets of coefficients in two linear regressions. *Econometrica*, 1960, *28*, 591–605.

Cleary, T. A. Test bias: Prediction of grades of Negro and white students in integrated colleges. *Journal of Educational Measurement*, 1968, *5*, 115–124.

Cochran, W. G. Errors of measurement in statistics. *Technometrics*, 1968, *10*, 637–666.

Cohen, J., & Cohen, P. *Applied Multiple Regression/Correlation Analysis for the Behavioral Sciences*. Hillsdale, N.J.: Lawrence Erlbaum Associates, 1975.

Coleman, J. S. Methods and results in the IEA studies of effects of school on learning. *Review of Educational Research*, 1975, *45*, 335–386.

Coleman, J. S. Regression analysis for the comparison of school and home effects. *Social Science Research*, 1976, *5*, 1–20.

Coleman, J. S.; Campbell, E. Q.; Hobson, C. J.; McPartland, J.; Mood, A. M.; Weinfeld, F. D.; & York, R. L. *Equality of Educational Opportunity*. Washington, D.C.: U.S. Government Printing Office, 1966. (ERIC Document Reproduction Service No. ED 012 275)

Comber, L. C., & Keeves, J. P. *Science Education in Nineteen Countries*. New York: Wiley, 1973.

Cook, T. D., & Campbell, D. T. *Quasi-experimentation: Design and Analysis Issues for Field Settings*. Chicago: Rand McNally, 1979.

Cooley, W. W., & Lohnes, P. R. *Evaluation Research in Education*. New York: Wiley, 1976.

Costner, H. L., & Schoenberg, R. Diagnosing indicator ills in multiple indicator models. In A. S. Goldberger & O. D. Duncan (Eds.), *Structural Equation Models in the Social Sciences*. New York: Seminar Press, 1973.

Cronbach, L. J., & Snow, R. E. *Aptitudes and Instructional Methods*. New York: Irvington, 1977.

Darlington, R. B. Multiple regression in psychological research and practice. *Psychological Bulletin*, 1968, *69*, 161–182.

Deegan, J. Specification error in causal models. *Social Science Research*, 1974, *3*, 235–259.

Draper, N., & Smith, H. *Applied Regression Analysis* (2nd ed.). New York: Wiley, 1981.

Ezekiel, M., & Fox, K. A. *Methods of Correlation and Regression Analysis* (3rd ed.). New York: Wiley, 1959.

Farrar, D. E., & Glauber, R. R. Multicollinearity in regression analysis: The problem revisited. *Review of Economics and Statistics*, 1967, *49*, 92–107.

Fox, K. A. *Intermediate Economic Statistics*. New York: Wiley, 1968.

Goldberger, A. S. *Econometric Theory*. New York: Wiley, 1964.

Gordon, R. A. Issues in multiple regression. *American Journal of Sociology*, 1968, *73*, 592–616.

Grant, G. Shaping social policy: The politics of the Coleman Report. *Teachers College Record*, 1973, *75*, 17–54.

Graybill, F. A. *An Introduction to Linear Statistical Models* (Vol. 1). New York: McGraw-Hill, 1961.

Gunst, R. F., & Mason, R. L. Advantages of examining multicollinearities in regression analysis. *Biometrics*, 1977, *33*, 249–260.

Hargens, L. L. A note on standardized coefficients as structural parameters. *Sociological Methods and Research*, 1976, *5*, 247–256.

Hauser, R. M., & Goldberger, A. S. The treatment of unobservable variables in path analysis. In H. L. Costner (Ed.), *Sociological Methodology, 1971*. San Francisco: Jossey-Bass, 1971.

Hempel, C. G. *Aspects of Scientific Explanation*. New York: Free Press, 1965.

Horel, A. E., & Kennard, R. W. Ridge regression: Biased estimation for nonorthogonal problems. *Technometrics*, 1970, *12*, 55–67. (a)

Horel, A. E., & Kennard, R. W. Ridge regression: Applications to nonorthogonal problems. *Technometrics*, 1970, *12*, 69–82. (b)

Igra, A. On forming variable set composites to summarize a block recursive model. *Social Science Research*, 1979, *8*, 253–264.

Inkeles, A. The international evaluation of educational achievement. *Proceedings of the National Academy of Education*, 1977, *4*, 139–200.

Johnson, P. O., & Jackson, R. W. B. *Modern Statistical Methods: Descriptive and Inductive*. Chicago: Rand McNally, 1959.

Johnston, J. *Econometric Methods* (2nd ed.). New York: McGraw-Hill, 1972.

Jöreskog, K. G., & Sörbom, B. *Advances in Factor Analysis and Structural Equation Models*. Cambridge, Mass.: Abt Books, 1979.

Kaplan, A. *The Conduct of Inquiry*. San Francisco: Chandler, Intext, 1964.

Kean, M. H.; Summers, A. A.; Raivetz, M. J.; & Farber, I. J. *What Works in Reading?* Philadelphia: School District of Philadelphia, Office of Research and Evaluation, 1979. (ERIC Document Reproduction Service No. ED 176 216)

Kerlinger, F. N. *Foundations of Behavioral Research* (2nd ed.). New York: Holt, Rinehart & Winston, 1973.

Kerlinger, F. N., & Pedhazur, E. J. *Multiple Regression in Behavioral Research*. New York: Holt, Rinehart & Winston, 1973.

Kim, J. O., & Mueller, C. W. Standardized and unstandardized coefficients in causal analysis. *Sociological Methods and Research*, 1976, *4*, 423–438.

Lemieux, P. H. A note on the detection of multicollinearity. *American Journal of Political Science*, 1978, *22*, 183–186.

Lewis-Beck, M. S. Stepwise regression: A caution. *Political Methodology*, 1978, *5*, 213–240.

Long, J. S. Estimation and hypothesis testing in linear models containing measurement error. *Sociological Methods and Research*, 1976, *5*, 157–206.

Lord, F. M., & Novick, M. R. *Statistical Theories of Mental Test Scores*. Reading, Mass.: Addison-Wesley, 1968.

Luecke, D. F., & McGinn, N. F. Regression analyses and education production functions: Can they be trusted? *Harvard Educational Review*, 1975, *45*, 325–350.

MacDonald, K. I. Interpretation of residual paths and decomposition of variance. *Sociological Methods and Research*, 1979, *7*, 289–304.

Marquardt, D. W., & Snee, R. D. Ridge regression in practice. *American Statistician*, 1975, *29*, 3–20.

Mason, R., & Brown, W. G. Multicollinearity problems and ridge regression in sociological models. *Social Science Research*, 1975, *4*, 135–149.

Mayeske, G. W. Teacher attributes and school achievement. In *Do Teachers Make a Difference?* Washington, D.C.: U.S. Office of Education, 1970. (ERIC Document Reproduction Service No. ED 040 253)

Mayeske, G. W., & Beaton, A. E. *Special Studies of Our Nation's Students*. Washington, D.C.: U.S. Government Printing Office, 1975. (ERIC Document Reproduction Service No. ED 118 701)

Mayeske, G. W.; Cohen, W. M.; Wisler, C. E.; Okada, T.; Beaton, A. E.; Proshek, J. M.; Weinfeld, F. D.; & Tabler, K. A. *A Study of Our Nation's Schools*. Washington, D.C.: U.S. Government Printing Office, 1972. (ERIC Document Reproduction Service No. ED 036 477)

Mayeske, G. W.; Okada, T.; & Beaton, A. E. *A Study of the Attitude toward Life of Our Nation's Students*. Washington, D.C.: U.S. Government Printing Office, 1973. (ERIC Document Reproduction Service No. ED 086 928)

Mayeske, G. W.; Okada, T.; Beaton, A. E.; Cohen, W. M.; & Wisler, C. E. *A Study of the Achievement of Our Nation's Students*. Washington, D.C.: U.S. Government Printing Office, 1973. (ERIC Document Reproduction Service No. ED 085 626)

Mayeske, G. W.; Wisler, C. E.; Beaton, A. E.; Weinfeld, F. D.; Cohen, W. M.; Okada, T.; Proshek, J. M.; & Tabler, K. A. *A Study of Our Nation's Schools*. Washington, D.C.: U.S. Department of Health, Education, and Welfare, Office of Education, 1969. (ERIC Document Reproduction Service No. ED 082 312)

McNeil, K. A.; Kelly, F. J.; & McNeil, J. T. *Testing Research Hypotheses Using Multiple Linear Regression*. Carbondale: Southern Illinois University Press, 1975.

Michelson, S. The association of teacher resourceness with children's characteristics. In *Do Teachers Make a Difference?* Washington, D.C.: U.S. Office of Education, 1970. (ERIC Document Reproduction Service No. ED 040 253)

Mood, A. M. Macro-analysis of the American educational system. *Operations Research*, 1969, *17*, 770–784.

Mood, A. M. Partitioning variance in multiple regression analyses as a tool for developing learning models. *American Educational Research Journal*, 1971, *8*, 191–202.

Mosteller, F., & Moynihan, D. P. (Eds.). *On Equality of Educational Opportunity*. New York: Random House, Vintage Books, 1972.

Newton, R. G., & Spurrell, D. J. A development of multiple regression for the analysis of routine data. *Applied Statistics*, 1967, *16*, 51–64. (a)

Newton, R. G., & Spurrell, D. J. Examples of the use of elements for clarifying regression analyses. *Applied Statistics*, 1967, *16*, 165–172. (b)

Nunnally, J. C. *Psychometric Theory* (2nd ed.). New York: McGraw-Hill, 1978.

Peaker, G. F. *An Empirical Study of Education in Twenty-one Countries: A Technical Report*. New York: Wiley, 1975.

Pedhazur, E. J. Analytic methods in studies of educational effects. In F. N. Kerlinger (Ed.), *Review of Research in Education 3*. Itasca, Ill.: F. E. Peacock, 1975.

Pedhazur, E. J. *Multiple Regression in Behavioral Research: Explanation and Prediction* (2nd ed.). New York: Holt, Rinehart & Winston, 1982.

Purves, A. C. *Literature Education in Ten Countries: An Empirical Study*. New York: Wiley, 1973.

Rock, D. A.; Werts, C. E.; Linn, R. L.; & Jöreskog, K. G. A maximum likelihood solution to the errors in variables and errors in equations model. *Multivariate Behavioral Research*, 1977, *12*, 187–198.

Rozeboom, W. W. Ridge regression: Bonanza or beguilement? *Psychological Bulletin*, 1979, *86*, 242–249.

Scheffler, I. Explanation, prediction, and abstraction. *British Journal for the Philosophy of Science*, 1957, *7*, 293–309.

Schmidt, P., & Muller, E. N. The problem of multicollinearity in a multistage causal alienation model: A comparison of ordinary least squares, maximum-likelihood and ridge regression estimators. *Quality and Quantity*, 1978, *12*, 267–297.

Schoenberg, R. Strategies for meaningful comparison. In H. L. Costner (Ed.), *Sociological Methodology, 1972*. San Francisco: Jossey-Bass, 1972.

Scriven, M. Explanation and prediction in evolutionary theory. *Science*, 1959, *130*, 477–482.

Smith, M. S. Equality of educational opportunity: The basic findings reconsidered. In F. Mosteller & D. P. Moynihan (Eds.), *On Equality of Educational Opportunity*. New York: Random House, Vintage Books, 1972.

Snedecor, G. W., & Cochran, W. G. *Statistical Methods* (6th ed.). Ames: Iowa State University Press, 1967.

Specht, D. A., & Warren, R. D. Comparing causal models. In D. R. Heise (Ed.), *Sociological Methodology, 1976*. San Francisco: Jossey-Bass, 1975.

Summers, A. A., & Wolfe, B. L. Do schools make a difference? *American Economic Review*, 1977, *67*, 639–652.

Theil, H. Specification errors and the estimation of economic relationships. *Review of the International Statistical Institute*, 1957, *25*, 41–51.

Torney, J. V.; Oppenheim, A. N.; & Farnen, R. F. *Civic Education in Ten Countries: An Empirical Study*. New York: Wiley, 1975.

Tukey, J. W. Causation, regression, and path analysis. In O. Kempthorne, T. A. Bancroft, J. W. Gowen, & J. D. Lush (Eds.), *Statistics and Mathematics in Biology*. Ames: Iowa State College Press, 1954.

Walker, H. M., & Lev. J. *Statistical Inference*. New York: Henry Holt, 1953.

Ward, J. H. Partitioning variance and contribution or importance of a variable: A visit to a graduate seminar. *American Educational Research Journal*, 1969, *6*, 467–474.

Ward, J. H., & Jennings, E. *Introduction to Linear Models*. Englewood Cliffs, N.J.: Prentice-Hall, 1973.

Werts, C. E.; Rock, D. A.; Linn, R. L.; & Jöreskog, K. G. Comparison of correlations, variances, covariances, and regression weights with or without measurement error. *Psychological Bulletin*, 1976, *83*, 1007–1013.

Williams, E. J. *Regression Analysis*. New York: Wiley, 1959.

Wold, H. Causal inference from observational data: A review of ends and means. *Journal of the Royal Statistical Society* (Series A), 1956, *119*, 28–61.

Wright, G. C. Linear models for evaluating conditional relationships. *American Journal of Political Science*, 1976, *20*, 349–373.

REHABILITATION SERVICES

Rehabilitation services are typically viewed as a broad array of medical, psychological, social, educational, and vocational services designed to assist handicapped persons to achieve physical, psychological, social, educational, and/or vocational adjustment. This definition reflects in general terms the types of available services and the objectives of a broader and more significant social concept: rehabilitation. In fact, the foundation upon which a personal understanding of rehabilitation services rests is the conceptualization of rehabilitation, whether seen as a philosophy, objective, and method (Allen, 1958); philosophy, area of practice, and area of research (Lofquist, 1969); social movement and process (Jaques, 1970); or process, service system, and discipline (Wright, 1980).

Although rehabilitation services typically focus upon rehabilitation as a method, process, or area of practice, a more inclusive understanding necessitates attention to the need for and objectives of the services; to the historical and legislative bases on which they rest; and to the research that gives rise to rehabilitation as an emerging science. These topics are presented in this article.

The need for a comprehensive approach does not reflect rehabilitation services as they were provided in the 1940s and 1950s. During that period rehabilitation clients were almost invariably handicapped physically rather than psychologically or socially. Nearly total focus was upon vocational rehabilitation rather than upon rehabilitation for improved independent or social living.

Because aiding clients to make vocational adjustments excludes those most severely vocationally disabled from rehabilitation services, concerns have arisen as to whether or not rehabilitation should be so narrowly defined. Rusalem (1976) has presented arguments both for and against broadening concepts of rehabilitation to include services that improve social and personal development without requiring a vocational goal. A major concern centers around whether rehabilitation as a concept and service system will be enhanced or weakened as a result of broadening goals.

History and Legislation. Rehabilitation services emphasizing the role of education and training have been provided in the United States since the early nineteenth century, with the development of schools for deaf, blind, mentally retarded, and physically disabled children. However, social movements, particularly the development of charity organizations at the turn of the century, were the chief contributors to the development of modern rehabilitation services (Judge, 1976). These service-providing agencies, which were often rooted in organized religious bodies, typically demonstrated a rehabilitation as opposed to a maintenance orientation. In addition, the casework methods used by their workers provided a model for the casework practices employed by early rehabilitation counselors, particularly those employed in agency settings (Rubin & Roessler, 1978).

The first nationwide publicly supported rehabilitation program began with the passage by Congress of the Smith-Sears Soldier Rehabilitation Act in 1917. During the same year the Smith-Hughes Vocational Education Act was passed. The passage of both of these bills provided a number of important requisites that eventually led to the initiation of the state-federal partnership in civilian vocational rehabilitation in 1920 with the Smith-Fess Civilian Vocational Rehabilitation Act. The Soldier Rehabilitation Act set a precedent for the provision of vocational rehabilitation services to citizens under the auspices of the federal government. Equally precedent-setting, the Vocational Education Act provided funds for the education of the citizenry under the auspices of the government (Lassiter, 1972). In addition, this legislation provided a model for cooperation between state and federal government in programs by requiring joint funding, a state plan for implementing service programs, and a state board for overseeing the service programs (McGowan & Porter, 1967). These provisions were all incorporated within the Civilian Vocational Rehabilitation Act and continue to be operational components of the state-federal rehabilitation programs.

The Civilian Vocational Rehabilitation Act itself construed rehabilitation to mean the employment of the disabled person either in industry or at home. This vocational goal continues to the present, although amendments passed in 1978 broadened the legislation to provide independent-living rehabilitation programs for those to whom the vocational programs do not apply. Although the legislation was initially concerned with persons whose disabilities occurred as a result of industrial accidents, persons with congenital disabilities were later included (Obermann, 1965). Amendments to the legislation passed in 1943 (P.L. 78-113) allowed services to be provided to the mentally retarded and mentally ill. In reality, however, these groups were significantly underserved until the 1960s (Marinelli, 1976). Services provided by the initial legislation were limited to vocational guidance, training, occupational adjustment, and placement services. Stimulated by the manpower needs of World War II and the restrictions imposed by limited medical services on the numbers of clients rehabilitated, a wide range of medical services became part of the state-federal rehabilitation program in the 1943 amendments. These services were broadened to include (1) corrective surgery or therapeutic treatment; (2) up to ninety days of hospitalization; (3) prosthetics; and (4) maintenance during training (McGowan & Porter, 1967).

The increased numbers of clients served, and limited tools, skills, facilities, professionals, and money to serve them, led to the passage of legislation in 1954 (P.L. 83-565) that allowed federal money to be used for the development of rehabilitation research centers, facility development, and rehabilitation training, particularly for rehabilitation counselors. Work evaluation and work adjustment services designed to evaluate work potential and adjust persons to work also developed from this legislation (Thomas, 1970). In addition, the funding base for client services dramatically increased.

The 1960s brought continued broadening of rehabilitation services. Stimulated by a tenfold increase in federal spending (Hunt, 1969), public and private rehabilitation centers, workshops, and related facilities proliferated. Provisions of the 1965 amendments (P.L. 89-333) allowing extended evaluation periods when it was difficult to determine whether or not a client could benefit from vocational rehabilitation services served more severely disabled clients. These clients were also served as a result of a cooperative relationship with the Social Security Administration that set up trust funds from which vocational rehabilitation services could be provided to disability insurance beneficiaries (P.L. 89-97).

The 1970s saw the rise of consumer activism among disabled persons as they became an organized and potent political force. This activism contributed to a basic change in the types of rehabilitation legislation initiated during this decade. Practical issues affecting the civil rights of disabled persons, such as discrimination in housing, transportation, education, and employment, became the focus of legislative change (DeLoach & Greer, 1981; Graves, 1979).

The Rehabilitation Act of 1973 (P.L. 93-112) mandated that disabled persons with the most severe disabilities be served first when using public funds. Section 502 of the act expanded the removal of architectural and transportation barriers. Affirmative action and nondiscrimination in employment and education in organizations receiving federal contracts or grants were mandated by sections 503 and 504. An individualized written plan developed and approved by both the counselor and client was also required.

The Comprehensive Rehabilitation Services Amendments of 1978 (P.L. 95-602), in recognition of the needs of severely handicapped persons for whom employment was not a realistic goal, included a provision for comprehensive independent-living rehabilitation services for those who could benefit from such services. The direction that rehabilitation services have taken is significantly affected by legislative mandates. Thus, it is likely that independent-living rehabilitation will not fare as well as vocational rehabilitation in an administration emphasizing cost-effectiveness and program accountability. Expansion of services to disabled persons will be dependent on a growing unity between consumers and professionals as well as on public support.

Impact of Disability. In estimating the impact of disability, a number of difficulties arise, including such problems of definition as the determination of what is meant by disability, impact, and so on. Perhaps the most significant difficulty relates to the definition of disability.

Although confusing and contradictory, particularly since medicine and rehabilitation use different terms to mean the same thing (Wright, 1980), there are some standardized definitions that help us with the definitional problem. Three interrelated terms are central: disability, functional limitation, and handicap. Although these terms are described differently by different authors, Wright (1980, p. 68) provides us with the clearest concept of their meaning in rehabilitation usage. He defines "disability" as "a long-term or chronic condition medically defined as a physiological, anatomical, mental, or emotional impairment, resulting from disease or illness, inherited or congenital defect, trauma or other insult (including environmental) to mind or body."

"Functional limitation" is described as "the hindrance or negative effect in the performance of tasks or activities, and other adverse and overt manifestations of a mental, emotional, or physical disability." He defines handicap as "A disadvantage, interference or barrier to performance, opportunity, or fulfillment in any desired role in life (e.g. vocational, social, educational, familial), imposed upon the individual by limitations in function or by other problems associated with disability."

As Wright (1980) points out, the conceptualization of disability, functional limitations, and handicaps in this hierarchy has important implications for the delivery of rehabilitation services. Because the differences in definition allow these concepts to be understood as specific, though related, phenomena, they have implications for both assessment and treatment. For example, if as a result of limited ability to cope with stress, a person was diagnosed by a psychiatrist as having an "anxiety neurosis, moderate," this diagnosis is the person's disability. The lack of ability to cope with stress is a functional limitation as a result of the disability. If through psychotherapy and medication the individual can substantially improve his or her ability to cope with stress, there is no longer a functional impairment. If this disability was no longer a relevant issue in the person's life he or she would not be considered disabled, functionally limited, or handicapped. If, however, an employer on the basis of the diagnosis and/or treatment should remove this person without consent from his or her position of employment, a vocational handicap would reoccur. Assuming no change in the client's disability, nonmedical interventions would probably be used to reduce the vocational handicap. Based on client preferences, these could include strategies such as filing a complaint of employment discrimination against the employer under Sections 503 of the Rehabilitation Act of 1973, consideration of vocational counseling training, and/or placement in another position.

Typically, estimates of the numbers of disabled persons consider those individuals whose functional limitations are severe enough to hamper them in one or more of their primary life roles. The Urban Institute (1975), by extrapolating the results of four surveys completed between 1966 and 1972, estimated that in 1975, 18.7 percent of the noninstitutionalized United States population aged 18–64 was handicapped either partially or totally from working. Of this group, 6.7 percent were severely handicapped from working in that they were either permanently or intermittently limited from working on a regular basis. Major disabling conditions are arthritis, rheumatism, and other musculoskeletal disorders (30.9 percent of the disabled population), cardiovascular disorders (24.8 percent), respiratory-related disorders (11.2 percent), digestive disorders (7.2 percent), mental disorders (6.3 percent), nervous system disorders (5.2 percent), diabetes (2.7 percent), urogenital conditions (2.5 percent), visual impairments (2.4 percent), neoplasms (1.7 percent), and other conditions (4.9 percent) (Allan & Cinsky, 1972).

The Urban Institute (1975) has estimated that another 500,000 persons of working age are receiving institutional care. Although those estimates of disablement constitute a considerable proportion of our population, they do not include children or senior citizens who are not of employment age (18–64). Considering persons of all ages, it has been estimated that 31 million persons were disabled in the United States during 1973 (Disability and Health Economics Research Section, 1975).

The economic impact of disability typically includes estimates of expenditures for disability-related income maintenance and medical and rehabilitation services from the more than eighty-five separate programs serving disabled persons. For 1973, these expenditures were estimated to be $83.1 billion, an increase of approximately 100 percent from 1967 to 1973 (Berkowitz, Johnson, & Murphy, 1976). The Disability and Health Economics Research Section at Rutgers University (1974) estimated that the percentage of increase from 1973 to 1980 will be greater than 100 percent; if this estimate is correct, the economic impact of disability exceeded $160 billion in 1980.

The manner in which persons are psychologically and socially affected by disability is more difficult to evaluate, since less tangible data are involved. The impact, however, is felt in many areas of human existence, including the personal meaning of disability to the disabled person, the attitudes and interpersonal behavior of able-bodied persons toward disabled persons and vice versa, the effects of disability on the family and on sexuality, and numerous other areas (Marinelli & Dell Orto, 1977). Although the understanding of this psychosocial impact is impaired by the limited quantity of research that is naturalistic and experimental in nature (Shontz, 1970), there are issues about which researchers, theoreticians, and practitioners tend to agree. (1) There is virtually no evidence that supports the notion that specific types of disabilities are associated with specific types of personality, for example, a deaf personality (McDaniel, 1976; Roessler & Bolton, 1978; Shontz, 1970, 1975). (2) There is no research support for the idea that severity of disability is directly related to

severity of personality disturbance or maladjustment (Roessler & Bolton, 1978; Shontz, 1970, 1975); the personal meaning of disability to each client appears central in his or her adjustment to disability (DeLoach & Greer, 1981; Shontz, 1970, 1975; Wright, 1960). (3) Disability, in addition to burdening persons with negative consequences, frequently generates gratification for life and living, and opportunity for continued participation in meaningful activities. (DeLoach & Greer, 1981; Wright, 1960; Wright & Shontz, 1968). (4) Following the occurrence of a disability, a person usually moves through stages similar to the stages that others who have suffered serious loss pass through (Fink, 1967); there is some question about the universality of these stages (DeLoach & Greer, 1981; Hohmann, 1975). (5) Many of the psychological and social handicaps that disabled persons face are inflicted by a society that shows limited concern for them by imposing architectural, transportation, employment, and other barriers that often lead to social isolation (DeLoach & Greer, 1981; English, 1971; Park, 1975). (6) Interactions between disabled persons and able-bodied persons are often strained with feelings of uncertainty, discomfort, and anxiety (Comer & Piliavin, 1972; Goffman, 1963; Kleck, 1966, 1968; Kleck, Ono & Hastorf, 1966; Marinelli, 1974; Marinelli & Kelz, 1973). (7) Although publicly expressed opinions about disabled persons are generally positive (Comer & Piliavin, 1975), recent research suggests that there may be significant underlying negative opinions (Siller, 1976).

Rehabilitation Procedures. Rehabilitation clients, in an attempt to reduce the effects of their disabilities, move through a process of exploration, understanding, and action that Carkhuff (1969), Egan (1975), and others find common to all helping processes. The purposes of each of the phases of this process can be identified.

The exploration phase is intended to clarify clients' knowledge of the rehabilitation process—and the services that are part of that process—and the role of rehabilitation counselors and other therapeutic agents (rehabilitationists) who are involved in the process. This phase also improves clients' and their helpers' awareness of the functional limitations and handicaps arising as a result of disability. Medical, psychological, social, and vocational evaluations assist in improving this awareness and making the eligibility decision. The development of therapeutic relationships between clients and their rehabilitationists is another important goal.

The understanding phase of rehabilitation is oriented primarily toward the development of rehabilitation plans to reduce the disability-related functional limitations and handicaps and to further strengthen developing facilitative relationships. Using the evaluation data obtained in the exploration phase, the client and counselor develop a step-by-step program and, typically, an increased commitment to work together to achieve rehabilitation goals.

The action phase involves the direct application of services—medical, educational, vocational, psychological, social, and/or legal—designed to attain the vocational or independent-living rehabilitation goals specified in the rehabilitation plan. Most frequently these services are health-related services designed for physical and/or mental restoration; educational and vocational training services aimed to improve academic and vocational knowledge and skills; personal-social and work adjustment training intended to enhance adaptation to home, community, and work environments; and job placement services. This section focuses on those services unique to rehabilitation—rehabilitation counseling, vocational evaluation, and work adjustment. Many of the above diagnostic and treatment services are obtained by contracting with individual practitioners, but are increasingly obtained from rehabilitation centers and workshops.

Rehabilitation counseling. Rehabilitation counseling is the central component in the delivery of rehabilitation services. This central role is a result of numerous factors, including historical and legislative ones. Rehabilitation counselors make up the largest single occupational group involved in rehabilitation, with over 19,000 practitioners in 1979 (U.S. Department of Labor, 1980).

By virtue of the Civilian Rehabilitation Act of 1920, a rehabilitation agent was required to direct the delivery of rehabilitation services. Federal legislation guiding state-federal programs continues to require this agent, who by the 1950s was called a rehabilitation counselor. Frequently, this agent was trained in school teaching, vocational education, school counseling, or social work because university training programs in rehabilitation counseling were not developed on a large scale until the middle 1950s (Obermann, 1965).

This legislation, as well as current legislation, mandates the involvement of rehabilitation counselors in all phases of the rehabilitation process. For example, rehabilitation counselors typically develop community resources to gain referrals, and study client medical, psychological, and other data to evaluate client eligibility for services. They refer clients for medical treatment and other services as necessary. They administer and interpret psychological tests and evaluate medical, psychological, and other data to plan appropriate rehabilitation service. The activities of different service providers are coordinated to maximize client benefits. Affective and vocational counseling and interventions with client families are provided as needed. The counselors assist with job placement. Both individual and group procedures are used throughout this process (Emener & Rubin, 1980; Muthard & Salomone, 1969; Rubin & Emener, 1978).

Although most rehabilitation counselors typically perform all these functions to some degree, emphasis may differ from setting to setting. The most recent large-scale study of counselor functions that compared counselors working in state vocational rehabilitation agencies, in private facilities, and in private practice or human service programs reported the following results: (1) all three groups reported case service coordination, affective counseling, and vocational counseling tasks as a substantial part

of their jobs; (2) private practice and private facility rehabilitation counselors place more emphasis on group procedures than state vocational rehabilitation counselors, although all counselors use individual procedures more than group ones; (3) state vocational rehabilitation counselors place more emphasis on medical referral, eligibility and case finding, and test interpretation than private practice and facility counselors; and (4) all three groups reported that test administration and intervention with client families are less substantial parts of their jobs (Emener & Rubin, 1980).

Since this study grouped the settings in which rehabilitation counselors work into three categories, it obviously limits the reader's understanding of the scope of employment in which rehabilitation counselors are involved. Most rehabilitation counselors work for governmental agencies, particularly the state divisions of vocational rehabilitation. Large numbers, however, are also employed within manpower programs, the Veterans Administration, state employment services, hospitals and medical centers, correctional facilities, welfare agencies, the Social Security Administration, and workmen's compensation insurance. Significant numbers are also employed in voluntary nonprofit facilities, such as rehabilitation workshops, centers, and independent-living centers; and voluntary nonprofit agencies, such as organizations working in behalf of blind, cerebral-palsied, and mentally retarded persons, as well as veterans and other disabled persons. Colleges, universities, and other special schools hire rehabilitation counselors to work with handicapped students.

The number of counselors working in the private-for-profit sector of the economy has greatly increased over the last five years. In this setting, counselors, working either privately or for corporations, provide evaluation, counseling, coordination, and/or vocational placement services for a fee. Some counselors also provide testimony as expert witnesses in legal action relating to civil suits, workmen's compensation insurance, or social security decisions (Sales, 1979).

The educational backgrounds of rehabilitation counselors are also quite diverse, in courses of study pursued and levels of education achieved. With the advent of rehabilitation-counselor training program accreditation through the Council on Rehabilitation Education (Berven & Wright, 1978; McAlees & Schumaker, 1975; Wright & Reagles, 1973) and the certification of practitioners through the Commission on Rehabilitation Counselor Certification (Carnes, 1972; Feinberg, 1977; Hansen, 1977; Livingstone & Engelkes, 1977; McAlees & Schumaker, 1975), more standardized training has evolved.

Discussions of training frequently focus on whether or not rehabilitation counseling is theory-based, that is, has a systematically organized body of knowledge. It is generally conceded that the field is "only now beginning to weave its components into a fabric of theory" (Brubaker, 1981, p. 47). There is also general agreement that the knowledge base primarily rests on older systems (psychology, medicine, sociology, etc.) (Brubaker, 1977, 1981). Accreditation and certification mechanisms have contributed to delineating the parameters of knowledge by providing a consensus of support for areas in which practitioners should be knowledgeable. For example, all persons who qualify for certification are required to show competence in the following areas through a certification examination: (1) rehabilitation philosophy, history, and structure; (2) medical aspects of disability; (3) psychosocial aspects of disability; (4) occupational information and the world of work; (5) counseling theory and techniques; (6) community organization and resources; (7) placement processes and job development; (8) the psychology of personal and vocational development; (9) evaluation and assessment; and (10) the ability to use research findings and professional publications (Commission on Rehabilitation Counselor Certification, 1978). Accreditation of training programs is largely based on whether or not the programs effectively transmit this knowledge. Because of the recency of accreditation and certification, the educational backgrounds of current practitioners is diverse. However, as greater numbers of certified practitioners from accredited programs enter the field, this should gradually change.

The differences in education, work setting, and clients served result in a diversity of opinion regarding what counselors should do and how they should do it. In fact, the issue of the appropriate roles, functions, and competencies of a rehabilitation counselor is a major concern in rehabilitation dialogue (Angell, DeSau, & Havrilla, 1969; Bourdon, 1970; Griffith, 1972; Hylbert & Kelz, 1970; Pankowski & Pankowski, 1974; Patterson, 1957, 1966, 1968, 1970; Porter, Rubin, & Sink, 1979; Rubin & Porter, 1979; Sales, 1979; Sussman, Haug, & Joynes, 1970; Stone, 1971; Wilkinson, 1977) and inquiry (Emener & Rubin, 1980; Fraser & Clowers, 1978; Muthard & Salomone, 1969; Parham & Harris, 1978; Rubin & Emener, 1978; Van Kuster et al., 1976; Zadny & James, 1977).

Early arguments about appropriate functions focused on whether all rehabilitation counselors should carry out the myriad tasks of counseling or whether some counselors should be specially trained to carry out those tasks that do not require face-to-face counseling (Angell, DeSau, & Havrilla, 1969; Hylbert & Kelz, 1970; Patterson, 1957, 1966, 1967, 1968, 1970; Sussman, Haug, & Joynes, 1970). A usual solution for this division of labor was to supplement "professional" counselor-consultants having master's degrees with coordinator–case managers having bachelor's degrees and lesser-trained aides for performing functions such as paperwork and monitoring client progress (Hylbert & Kelz, 1970).

In general, this type of specialization has not become prevalent in the practice of rehabilitation counseling. Instead, specialization has occurred on the basis of counselors working with specific disabilities (e.g., mental illness) or being involved in specialized occupations that encompass the professional functions traditionally performed by general rehabilitation counselors (Wright, 1980). Vocational

evaluation and work adjustment are two such specialities that are briefly described in the remainder of this section.

Vocational evaluation. A widely accepted definition of vocational evaluation is "a comprehensive process that systematically utilizes work, real or simulated, as the focal point for assessment and vocational exploration, the purpose of which is to assist individuals in vocational development" (Tenth Institute on Rehabilitation Services, 1972, p. 2).

These services developed out of a need for information about handicapped clients that could not be determined from medical, psychometric, or similar data. Observations of clients in work activities frequently contributed information, such as the understanding of mechanical processes and ability to work with other people, that could not be as accurately predicted from other data sources. These work observations became more sophisticated and ultimately evolved into three major work evaluation methods: (1) work samples; (2) situational assessment; and (3) on-the-job assessments (Nadolsky, 1973). Whereas on-the-job assessments are frequently used by agency rehabilitation counselors to determine client success within occupations consistent with client characteristics, work sample and situational assessment methodologies were primarily developed within rehabilitation centers and workshops. Vocational evaluators use work samples and situational assessments as primary tools. Typically, data from these processes are integrated with client background information and psychometric, medical, and related data to develop a vocational evaluation plan.

A work sample is "a well defined work activity involving tasks, materials, and tools which are identical or similar to those in an actual job or cluster of jobs. It is used to assess an individual's vocational aptitudes, worker characteristics, and vocational interests" (Task Force No. 2, 1975, p. 55). Although many work samples are "homemade," a number of commercially available work sample systems are available. For a review of seven major systems, see Botterbusch and Sax (1976).

Situational assessment typically refers to the systematic observation of clients in rehabilitation centers and workshops where clients are involved in jobs that attempt to simulate actual employment (Neff, 1976). In general, the purpose of these evaluations is to assess general employability factors, such as the manner in which clients respond to social situations on the job, tolerate frustration, and physically sustain a work day (Nadolsky, 1973). A number of assessment guides have been developed in an attempt to standardize the observations taken during situational assessment. See Esser (1975a) for a review of these methods.

Work adjustment. The major goal of the typical "sheltered workshop" is the maintenance of handicapped persons in noncompetitive employment. This contrasts with the primary goal of the "rehabilitation workshop," which is "to bring about fundamental changes in the person's work capabilities (Neff, 1970, p. 21). The process designed to bring about these fundamental changes in work capabilities is known as "work adjustment."

A widely accepted definition of work adjustment resulted from the Tenth Institute on Rehabilitation Services. "Work adjustment is a treatment/training process utilizing individual and group work, or work related activities, to assist individuals in understanding the meaning, value and demands of work; to modify or develop attitudes, personal characteristics and work behavior; and to develop functional capabilities, as required, in order to assist individuals towards their optimum level of vocational development" (Tenth Institute on Rehabilitation Services, 1972, p. 4).

Work adjustment training, although usually carried out in the rehabilitation workshop, can occur in a variety of settings, including comprehensive rehabilitation centers or on-the-job placements. Principles involved are typically a combination of behavior modification and teaching-counseling (Weiss, 1975). One important consideration is that the work adjustment setting resemble a future real-work setting. Wainwright and Couch (1978) label this principle the "generalization of behavior principle." A number of other behavioral principles have evolved. Ayers (1971) emphasizes role modeling by supervisors and more experienced workers, and videotaping to provide appropriate models and audiovisual feedback to clients. Campbell (1971) and Esser (1975b) suggest using verbal reinforcement, problem identification, extinction, time-outs, token economies, and other primarily operant techniques in work adjustment.

Teaching interventions typically employ individualized instruction in independent-living and social-living skills, job interviewing, and so on (Esser, 1975b; Ross & Brandon, 1971). This instruction is provided in a classroom and/or directly to the individual.

Counseling involves orientation of clients to work adjustment, assessment of client behaviors, development of an overall work adjustment plan, provision of feedback regarding work behavior, assistance in the resolution of problems among clients and supervisors, and modeling appropriate behavior (Ayers, 1971; Campbell & O'Toole, 1970). Although milieu and other group-counseling approaches are most typical, individual counseling is frequently used to augment these approaches.

Research. Although most federally supported rehabilitation research has focused on medical and engineering research, substantial support has been given to nonmedical research, particularly in vocational and related areas. The objective of this research is to carry out systematic inquiry in selected programmatic areas and to transmit the knowledge gained to practitioners, administrators, and other research consumers.

A number of key nonmedical rehabilitation research and training centers (RRTC) and regional rehabilitation research institutes (RRRI) are currently in operation.

The establishment of research centers in collaboration with universities has resulted in universities being the primary institutional source of literature in the field of reha-

bilitation (Perosa & Frantz, 1981; Rasch & Thomas, 1975; Thomas, 1972). These studies of the institutional affiliation of authors usually reveal a very high correlation between universities with research centers and scholarly productivity of their faculty.

The quality of rehabilitation research has been criticized for lack of experimental vigor and applicability to rehabilitation practices. Criticism of the infrequent use of single-subject designs has also been expressed. The only published large-scale evaluation of rehabilitation research (Berkowitz et al., 1975) resulted in considerable controversy because it was commissioned by the National Science Foundation and evaluated primarily federally funded research projects and because the results reflected negatively on the rehabilitation system both as a granter and grantee of research funds. Four hundred seventy-seven research projects completed between 1955 and 1973 were evaluated for overall methodological competence and policy utility. The findings were that 44 percent of the studies were methodologically poor, and 17 percent were excellent. Overall, 33 percent were considered to have poor policy utility, and 26 percent were rated high on this dimension. The research recommended closer ties between researchers and practitioners in project design and that "grantors [sic] need clearly stated goals for their funded research, and researchers and evaluators must make correct use of the appropriate means of project design and evaluation" (Berkowitz et al., 1976, p. 44).

There was considerable reaction to this study, although most reactions acknowledged a need for improvement in rehabilitation research. Miller (1976) expressed concern regarding the manner in which the sample was selected and the evaluation process itself. Moriarty (1976) questioned the validity of evaluating rehabilitation research using the methodological standards of the "hard" sciences. Wright (1976) questioned the evaluators' knowledge of vocational rehabilitation and, therefore, their competence to evaluate its research and the current generalizability and utility of their findings from studies up to ten years old. Noble (1976), who was more supportive of the evaluators, suggested that the findings were consistent with evaluations of similar research sponsored by federal agencies in such related fields as mental health and education.

                                        Robert P. Marinelli

See also Counseling; Deinstitutionalization of the Handicapped; Handicapped Individuals; Motor Skills Development; Psychological Services.

REFERENCES

Allan, K. H., & Cinsky, C. E. Social security survey of the disabled: 1966. In *General Characteristics of the Disabled Population* (Report No. 19). Washington, D.C.: Department of Health, Education, and Welfare, 1972.

Allen, W. S. *Rehabilitation: A Community Challenge.* New York: Wiley, 1958.

Angell, D. L.; DeSau, G. T.; & Havrilla, A. A. Rehabilitation counselor versus coordinator: One of rehabilitation's great straw men. *NRCA Professional Bulletin*, 1969, *9*, 1.

Ayers, G. Counseling in work adjustment programs. *Journal of Rehabilitation*, 1971, *37*, 31–33.

Berkowitz, M.; Englander, V.; Rubin, J.; & Worrall, J. D. *An Evaluation of Policy-related Rehabilitation Research.* New York: Praeger, 1975.

Berkowitz, M.; Englander, V.; Rubin, J.; & Worrall, J. D. A summary of "An evaluation of policy-related rehabilitation research." *Rehabilitation Counseling Bulletin*, 1976, *20*, 39–45.

Berkowitz, M.; Johnson, W. G.; & Murphy, E. H. *Public Policy toward Disability.* New York: Praeger, 1976.

Berven, N. L., & Wright, G. N. An evaluation model for accreditation. *Counselor Education and Supervision*, 1978, *17*, 188–194.

Botterbusch, K. F., & Sax, K. B. *A Comparison of Seven Vocational Evaluation Systems.* Menomonie: University of Wisconsin-Stout, Vocational Rehabilitation Institute, 1976.

Bourdon, R. D. The expanding role of the counselor as behavioral engineer. *Journal of Applied Rehabilitation Counseling*, 1970, *1*, 27–36.

Brubaker, D. Professionalization and rehabilitation counseling. *Journal of Applied Rehabilitation Counseling*, 1977, *8*, 208–218.

Brubaker, D. Professional status of rehabilitation counseling. In R. M. Parker & C. E. Hansen (Eds.), *Rehabilitation Counseling: Foundations, Consumers, Service Delivery.* Boston: Allyn & Bacon, 1981.

Campbell, J., & O'Toole, R. A situational approach. *Journal of Rehabilitation*, 1970, *37*, 11–13.

Campbell, N. Techniques of behavior modification. *Journal of Rehabilitation*, 1971, *37*, 28–31.

Carkhuff, R. R. *Selection and Training.* Vol. 1 of *Helping and Human Relationships.* New York: Holt, Rinehart & Winston, 1969.

Carnes, G. D. The certification of rehabilitation counselors. *Journal of Applied Rehabilitation Counseling*, 1972, *3*, 19–26.

Comer, R. J., & Piliavin, J. A. The effects of physical deviance upon face-to-face interaction: The other side. *Journal of Personality and Social Psychology*, 1972, *23*, 33–39.

Comer, R. C., & Piliavin, J. A. As others see: Attitudes of physically handicapped and normals toward own and other groups. *Rehabilitation Literature*, 1975, *36*, 206–221, 225.

Commission on Rehabilitation Certification. *Some Commonly Asked Questions about Rehabilitation Counselor Certification.* Chicago: Commission on Rehabilitation Counselor Certification, 1978.

Deloach, C., & Greer, B. G. *Adjustment to Severe Physical Disability: A Metamorphosis.* New York: McGraw-Hill, 1981.

Disability and Health Economics Research Section, Bureau of Economic Research. *Cost Burden of Disability Programs.* New Brunswick, N.J.: Rutgers University, 1974.

Disability and Health Economics Research Section, Bureau of Economic Research. *An Evaluation of the Structure and Function of Disability Programs: Year One Summary Report.* New Brunswick, N.J.: Rutgers University, 1975.

Egan, G. *The Skilled Helper.* Monterey, Calif.: Brooks/Cole, 1975.

Emener, W. G., & Rubin, S. E. Rehabilitation counselor roles and functions and sources of role strain. *Journal of Applied Rehabilitation Counseling*, 1980, *11*, 57–69.

English, R. W. Correlates of stigma toward physically disabled persons. *Rehabilitation Research and Practice Review*, 1971, *2*, 1–17.

Esser, T. J. *Client Rating Instruments for Use in Vocational Reha-*

bilitation Agencies. Menomonie: University of Wisconsin-Stout, Materials Development Center, 1975. (a)

Esser, T. J. The workshop environment: Some essential considerations. *Vocational Evaluation and Work Adjustment Bulletin*, 1975, *8*, 31–35. (b)

Feinberg, L. B. Employment of the certified rehabilitation counselor. *Journal of Rehabilitation*, 1977, *43*, 42–44.

Fink, S. L. Crisis and motivation: A theoretical model. *Archives of Physical Medicine and Rehabilitation*, 1967, *48*, 592–597.

Fraser, T. R., & Clowers, M. R. Rehabilitation counselor functions: Perceptions of time spent and complexity. *Journal of Applied Rehabilitation Counseling*, 1978, *9*, 31–35.

Goffman, E. *Stigma: Notes on the Management of Spoiled Identity.* Englewood Cliffs, N.J.: Prentice-Hall, 1963.

Graves, W. The impact of federal legislation for handicapped people on the rehabilitation counselor. *Journal of Applied Rehabilitation Counseling*, 1979, *10*, 67–71.

Griffith, W. S. The professional as a social change agent. *Journal of Applied Rehabilitation Counseling*, 1972, *3*, 3–9.

Hamilton, K. W. *Counseling the Handicapped.* New York: Ronald Press, 1950.

Hansen, C. E. The question of rehabilitation counselor certification. *Journal of Rehabilitation*, 1977, *43*, 2.

Hohmann, G. W. Psychological intervention in the spinal cord injury center: Some cautions. *Rehabilitation Psychology*, 1975, *22*, 194–196.

Hunt, J. A. A decade of progress. *Journal of Rehabilitation*, 1969, *35*, 9–12.

Hylbert, K. W., & Kelz, J. W. Combating rehabilitation counselor shortages in public agencies. *Journal of Applied Rehabilitation Counseling*, 1970, *1*, 13–26.

Jaques, M. *Rehabilitation Counseling: Scope and Services.* Boston: Houghton Mifflin, 1970.

Judge, M. A brief history of social services (Part 1). *Social and Rehabilitation Services Record*, 1976, *3*, 2–8.

Kleck, R. Emotional arousal in interactions with stigmatized persons. *Psychological Reports*, 1966, *19*, 1226.

Kleck, R. Physical stigma and nonverbal cues emitted in face-to-face interactions. *Human Relations*, 1968, *21*, 19–28.

Kleck, R; Ono, H.; & Hastorf, A. H. Effects of physical deviancy upon face-to-face interactions. *Human Relations*, 1966, *19*, 425–436.

Lassiter, R. A. History of the rehabilitation movement in America. In J. G. Cull & R. E. Hardy (Eds.), *Vocational Rehabilitation: Profession and Process.* Springfield, Ill.: Thomas, 1972.

Livingstone, R. H., & Engelkes, J. R. Certified rehabilitation counselors: A new era. *Journal of Applied Rehabilitation Counseling*, 1977, *8*, 228–234.

Lofquist, L. H. Rehabilitation. In R. L. Ebel (Ed.), *Encyclopedia of Educational Research* (4th ed.). New York: Macmillan, 1969.

Marinelli, R. P. Anxiety in interactions with visibly disabled persons. *Rehabilitation Counseling Bulletin*, 1974, *18*, 72–77.

Marinelli, R. P. Rehabilitation counseling. *Hospital and Community Psychiatry*, 1976, *27*, 502.

Marinelli, R. P., & Dell Orto, A. E. (Eds.). *Psychological and Social Impact of Physical Disability.* New York: Springer-Verlag, 1977.

Marinelli, R. P., & Kelz, J. W. Anxiety and attitudes toward visibly disabled persons. *Rehabilitation Counseling Bulletin*, 1973, *16*, 198–205.

McAlees, D. C., & Schumaker, B. Toward a new professionalism: Certification and accreditation. *Rehabilitation Counseling Bulletin*, 1975, *18*, 160–165.

McDaniel, J. W. *Physical Disability and Human Behavior* (2nd ed.). New York: Pergamon Press, 1976.

McGowan, J. F., & Porter, T. L. *An Introduction to the Vocational Rehabilitation Process.* Washington, D.C.: U.S. Government Printing Office, 1967. (ERIC Document Reproduction Service No. ED 042 011)

Miller, L. A. Reviewed by Leonard A. Miller. *Rehabilitation Counseling Bulletin,* 1976, *20,* 46–49.

Moriarty, J. B. Reviewed by Joseph B. Moriarty. *Rehabilitation Counseling Bulletin,* 1976, *20,* 49–52.

Muthard, J. E., & Salomone, P. R. Roles and functions of the rehabilitation counselor. *Rehabilitation Counseling Bulletin,* 1969, *13.*

Nadolsky, J. M. A model for vocational evaluation of the disadvantaged. In R. E. Hardy & J. G. Cull (Eds.), *Vocational Evaluation and Rehabilitation Services.* Springfield, Ill.: Thomas, 1973.

Neff, W. S. Work and rehabilitation. *Journal of Rehabilitation,* 1970, *36,* 16–22.

Neff, W. S. Assessing vocational potential. In H. Rusalem & D. Malikin (Eds.), *Contemporary Vocational Rehabilitation.* New York: New York University Press, 1976.

Noble, J. H. Reviewed by John H. Noble, Jr. *Rehabilitation Counseling Bulletin,* 1976, *20,* 52–54.

Obermann, C. E. *A History of Vocational Rehabilitation in America.* Minneapolis: T. S. Denison, 1965.

Pankowski, M. L., & Pankowski, J. M. Why a master's degree in rehabilitation counseling? *Journal of Applied Rehabilitation Counseling,* 1974, *5,* 147–152.

Parham, J. D., & Harris, W. M. *State Agency Rehabilitation Counselor Functions and the Mentally Retarded.* Lubbock: Texas Tech University, Research and Training Center in Mental Retardation, 1978.

Park, L. D. Barriers to normality for the handicapped adult in the United States. *Rehabilitation Literature,* 1975, *36,* 108–111.

Patterson, C. H. Counselor or coordinator. *Journal of Rehabilitation,* 1957, *23,* 13–15.

Patterson, C. H. The rehabilitation counselor: A projection. *Journal of Rehabilitation,* 1966, *32,* 31, 49.

Patterson, C. H. Specialization in rehabilitation counseling. *Rehabilitation Counseling Bulletin,* 1967, *10,* 147–154.

Patterson, C. H. Rehabilitation counseling: A profession or a trade? *Personnel and Guidance Journal,* 1968, *46,* 567–571.

Patterson, C. H. Powers, prestige, and the rehabilitation counselor. *Rehabilitation Research and Practice Review,* 1970, *1,* 1–7.

Perosa, L. M., & Frantz, T. T. Publishing in refereed journals: A ten-year survey in rehabilitation counseling. *Rehabilitation Counseling Bulletin,* 1981, *24,* 219–222.

Porter, T. L.; Rubin, S. E.; & Sink, J. M. Essential rehabilitation counselor diagnostic, counseling, and placement competencies. *Journal of Applied Rehabilitation Counseling,* 1979, *10,* 158–162.

Rasch, J. D., & Thomas, K. R. Institutional sources of articles in the *Journal of Applied Rehabilitation Counseling:* 1970–1974. *Journal of Applied Rehabilitation Counseling,* 1975, *6,* 195–199.

Roessler, R., & Bolton, B. *Psychosocial Adjustment to Disability.* Baltimore: University Park Press, 1978.

Ross, D., & Brandon, T. In pursuit of work adjustment. *Journal of Rehabilitation,* 1971, *37,* 6–8.

Rubin, S. E., & Emener, W. G. Recent rehabilitation counselor role changes and role strain: A pilot investigation. *Journal of Applied Rehabilitation Counseling,* 1978, *9,* 83–85.

Rubin, S. E., & Porter, T. L. Rehabilitation counselor and vocational evaluator competencies. *Journal of Rehabilitation,* 1979, *45,* 42–45.

Rubin, S. E., & Roessler, R. T. *Foundations of the Vocational Rehabilitation Process.* Baltimore: University Park Press, 1978.

Rusalem, H. Issues in rehabilitation. In H. Rusalem & D. Malikin (Eds.), *Contemporary Vocational Rehabilitation.* New York: New York University Press, 1976.

Sales, A. Rehabilitation counseling in the private sector. *Journal of Rehabilitation,* 1979, *45,* 59–61, 72.

Shontz, F. Physical disability and personality: Theory and recent research. *Psychological Aspects of Disability,* 1970, *17,* 51–70.

Shontz, F. *The Psychological Aspects of Physical Illness and Disability.* New York: Macmillan, 1975.

Siller, J. Attitudes toward disability. In H. Rusalem & D. Malikin (Eds.), *Contemporary Vocational Rehabilitation.* New York: New York University Press, 1976.

Stone, J. B. The rehabilitation counselor as a client advocate. *Journal of Applied Rehabilitation Counseling,* 1971, *2,* 46–54.

Sussman, M. B.; Haug, M. R.; & Joynes, V. A. The modern model of rehabilitation counselor roles. *Journal of Applied Rehabilitation Counseling,* 1970, *1,* 6–14.

Task Force No. 2. The tools of vocational evaluation. *Vocational Evaluation and Work Adjustment Bulletin,* 1975, *8,* 49–64.

Tenth Institute on Rehabilitation Services. *Vocational Evaluation and Work Adjustment Services in Vocational Rehabilitation.* Washington, D.C.: Department of Health, Education and Welfare, Rehabilitation Services Administration, 1972. (ERIC Document Reproduction Service No. ED 102 306)

Thomas, K. R. Institutional sources of articles in the *Rehabilitation Counseling Bulletin:* 1962–1971. *Rehabilitation Counseling Bulletin,* 1972, *15,* 172–175.

Thomas, R. E. The expanding scope of services. *Journal of Rehabilitation,* 1970, *36,* 37–40.

Urban Institute. *Report of the Comprehensive Service Needs Study.* Washington, D.C.: The Institute, 1975. (ERIC Document Reproduction Service No. ED 117 930)

U.S. Department of Labor. *Occupational Outlook Handbook* (1980–1981 ed.). Washington, D.C.: U.S. Government Printing Office, 1980.

Van Kuster, T. W.; Appel, G. W.; O'Connel, T.; & Sippel, C. L. *Manpower in Rehabilitation: A Survey of Training Programs and Service Facilities.* Minneapolis: Inter-study, 1976.

Wainwright, C. O., & Couch, R. Work adjustment: Potential and practice. *Journal of Rehabilitation,* 1978, *44,* 39–42.

Weiss, H. Work adjustment. In R. Hardy & J. Cull (Eds.), *Services of the Rehabilitation Facility.* Springfield, Ill.: Thomas, 1975.

Wilkinson, M. W. Rehabilitation counseling: In critical condition. *Journal of Applied Rehabilitation Counseling,* 1977, *8,* 15–21.

Wright, B. A. *Physical Disability: A Psychological Approach.* New York: Harper & Brothers, 1960.

Wright, B. A., & Shontz, F. C. Process and tasks in hoping. *Rehabilitation Literature,* 1968, *29,* 322–331.

Wright, G. N. Reviewed by George Wright. *Rehabilitation Counseling Bulletin,* 1976, *20,* 55–59.

Wright, G. N. *Total Rehabilitation.* Boston: Little, Brown, 1980.

Wright, G. N., & Reagles, K. W. RCE: Duly accredited? *Journal of Rehabilitation,* 1973, *39,* 33–35.

Zadny, J. J., & James, L. F. Time spent on placement. *Rehabilitation Counseling Bulletin,* 1977, *21,* 31–35.